DATE DUE

Reference

BREWER'S
CINEMA

A PHRASE AND FABLE
DICTIONARY

CASSELL

Compiled and typeset by:

Market House Books Ltd

Edited by:	Contributors:
Jonathan Law	John Wright
	Kyren Burns
Rosalind Fergusson	David Parkinson
Amanda Isaacs	Mark Salad
Martin Smith	John Morton
Alan Isaacs	Paul Cornell
	David Pickering
	Martin Day
	Adam Jezard
	Lynn Thomson
	Adam G. Smith

First published 1995 by Cassell
Wellington House, 125 Strand, London WC2R OBB
© Market House Books Limited 1995

Brewer's Trademark registered in Great Britain, British Patent Application No. 1137780
Distributed in the United States by Sterling Co. Inc., 387 Park Avenue South, New York, NY 10016-8810
Distributed in Australia by Capricorn Link (Australia) Pty Ltd, 2/13 Carrington Road, Castle Hill, NSW 2154

British Library Cataloguing-in-Publication Data
A catalogue record for this book is available from the British Library
ISBN 0-304-34235-1
Compiled and typeset by Market House Books Limited, Aylesbury
Printed and bound in Great Britain by Mackays of Chatham PLC, Chatham, Kent

Foreword

Those who know me are all too well aware that I cannot pass a book-shop. My house positively bulges with books – books that I absolutely have to possess even though every available shelf and coffee table is already overflowing and, in some rooms, they are stacked against the walls.

Above all, I simply adore and can rarely resist reference books about the movies. I must own close on a hundred. So the idea that there might be a single work that contains between its covers almost everything a serious movie aficionado might wish to know is one I embrace with the utmost difficulty.

Yet such a book is *Brewer's Cinema*. Foolishly perhaps, I had assumed that it would be simply a dictionary, a handy way to look up the meaning of such arcane professional terms as *brute* and *bloop*. It is, however, that and much much more.

In addition to sensible definitions of all the colourful idiom that has evolved over the years, *Brewer's Cinema* contains numerous assessments of individual films. These are no mere dry critiques of the good, the bad, and the truly awful but fully fleshed-out appraisals of movies that have earned a significant place in the history of world cinema. And each is crammed with the kind of inside knowledge that I, for one, find endlessly fascinating. For example, just delving into the earliest of the book's 3000 entries, I learned that Katharine Hepburn's character in *The African Queen* was based on Eleanor Roosevelt, that the classic *All Quiet on the Western Front* was a financial failure, that Satyajit Ray had to pawn his wife's jewellery to make *The Apu Trilogy*, and that Cary Grant wanted to play the lead in *Bicycle Thieves* but Vittorio de Sica turned him down.

Biographies of the industry's major international figures are also included. Again, these are not merely lists of movie titles and dates but considered and illuminating essays, setting each person and their body of work in the context of a particular life and time. I was, for instance, intrigued to find myself summarized as "a Brutus of the British Establishment, loyal and loving, but not averse to sticking the knife in when it takes a step too far in the direction of authoritarianism." Not bad. I'll buy that.

For the uninitiated, *Brewer's* provides a wealth of helpful information about what is surely the most complex industry in the world. Distribution practices such as *block booking* and *blind bidding* are clearly and concisely explained. So too is the all-important phraseology of budgeting, the various techniques used in special-effects shots, the terminology of editing... I could go on and on. Every one of the industry's major companies and trade organizations is listed and described. So too is every piece of equipment.

In short, *Brewer's* is a both a passport and a guide to the magic world of movie-making. This is a book for everyone – whether they are in the industry or simply love cinema. I recommend it wholeheartedly.

Richard Attenborough

March 1995

Preface

This dictionary is one of several that owe their origin to Dr Ebenezer Cobham Brewer's *Dictionary of Phrase and Fable*, first published by Cassell in 1870. Enormously successful in its own day and kept in print ever since, Brewer's *Dictionary* is a cornucopia of useful and curious information, combining etymology, folklore, and literary allusion with a wealth of anecdotal and historical material. Dr Brewer's stated aim was to provide "an almsbasket of words...giving the Derivation, source, or Origin of...Phrases, Allusions, and Words that have a tale to tell."

As its title suggests, *Brewer's Cinema* applies the Brewer's formula to the world of the movies. In doing so it provides not only authoritative guidance to a wide range of cinematic topics but also a treasury of fascinating and out-of-the-way information not usually included in conventional reference books. The approach is deliberately eclectic, with an emphasis on the humorous and quirky.

The book aims to cover all aspects of cinema life, language, and legend. It gives a clear account of the various stages in making a film, from *preproduction* to *editing*, while explaining the roles of the key personnel and the equipment they use. Special care has been taken to demystify the language of technicians and theorists; the book provides a glossary of words and phrases ranging from technical and critical terms (*aspect ratio, mise-en-scène*) to slang, jargon, and nicknames (*bug eye, fishpole, quonking*). Cinema history is approached in the same spirit. The role of the early pioneers, the introduction of *sound* and *colour*, and the rise and fall of the powerful *studio system* are all clearly explained, as are the various movements and genres, from *swashbucklers* to *slasher movies*. Biographies of all the cinema's legendary figures (and many of the lesser-known ones) appear, liberally garnished with anecdote and quotation. There are also detailed articles about important or representative films, giving plot summaries, production histories, and a wealth of intriguing background information. Finally, there are numerous miscellaneous entries ranging from articles on *gimmicks* and *in-jokes* to lists of notable *anachronisms, debuts,* and *directors' cameos*.

A word should perhaps be said about the arrangement of this material. Like other books in this series, *Brewer's Cinema* follows Dr Brewer's original system of grouping linguistically related but conceptually unconnected terms under a common headword; the main heading *black*, for instance, is followed by *black-and-white, Black Maria,* and *blaxploitation film*, amongst other miscellaneous subheadings. The curious juxtapositions thrown up by this system provide one of the chief pleasures of the original *Dictionary*.

Titles of foreign-language films are given in the form best known in this country (i.e. *Battleship Potemkin* but *La Dolce Vita*); where the British or US title differs significantly from the original, alternatives are supplied in parenthesis. Dates given are those of general release in the country of origin. Cross-references are indicated by the use of SMALL CAPITALS.

J. L.
1995

A

A A former category of film classification used by the British Board of Film Censors (*see* RATINGS). When classification was introduced in Britain in 1913 A (standing for *adult*) denoted that children over the age of 14 should only be admitted if accompanied by an adult. In 1970 a new system was introduced in which A (now standing for *advisory*) meant that, in the opinion of the censors, the film contained scenes that parents might not wish their children to see: unaccompanied children under 14 could, however, now be admitted to A films. The category was abolished in 1982; allowing for changing standards, the current rating PG is roughly equivalent to the former A certificate. *Compare* AA.

AA A former category of film classification used by the British Board of Film Censors. Introduced in 1970, the AA RATING meant that, in the opinion of the Board, the film was not suitable for children under 14 years of age, who should not be admitted even if accompanied by their parents. Contrary to popular belief, AA did *not* stand for Accompanied by Adult. The category was abolished in 1982; allowing for changing standards, the current rating 15 corresponds roughly to the former AA certificate.

A and B editing A method of editing in which action shot on two or more rolls of film is combined by overprinting rather than by cutting and splicing. In this way various special effects can be achieved, such as DISSOLVES, FADES, and MULTIPLE EXPOSURES.

A-movie or **-picture** A well-made feature film or an expensive and highly publicized one. In DOUBLE FEATURES the A-movie was shown before the less prestigious B-MOVIE.

AADA American Academy of Dramatic Arts. A drama school in New York. The oldest English-language acting academy in the world, it was established in 1884 (as the Lyceum Theatre School for Acting) by Steele MacKaye and others; it took its present name in 1888. The school is now affiliated with the State University of New York

(SUNY); another campus opened in 1974 in Pasadena, California. Courses in stage, film, and television are offered as part of the two-year curriculum.

Hollywood stars who were AADA students include William POWELL, Edward G. ROBINSON, Lauren BACALL, Rosalind RUSSELL, Spencer TRACY, Kirk DOUGLAS, Grace KELLY, Anne BANCROFT, John CASSAVETES, and Robert REDFORD.

Abbott and Costello The US comedy team of Bud Abbott (1895–1974) and Lou Costello (Lou Cristillo; 1906–59). Abbott was the generally bland but sometimes vicious straight man and Costello the chubby pathetic comedian with the catchphrases of "Heeeeeeey, Abbott!" and "I'm a baaaad boy". A former vaudeville team, they enjoyed great popularity as film stars during World War II, being Universal's top stars from 1940 to 1945 and the leading US box-office draw in 1942. At the height of their fame they attracted publicity by taking out a $100,000 insurance policy from Lloyds of London in case anyone died of laughter watching one of their films. Although their humour lacked the inventiveness and subtlety of LAUREL AND HARDY's, its rapid-fire repartee influenced many later double acts.

Abbott and Costello made their screen debuts in supporting roles in *One Night in the Tropics* (1940), a near disaster, but were a huge success the following year in their first starring vehicle *Buck Privates* (British title *Rookies*). The duo played bumbling army draftees, while THE ANDREWS SISTERS provided the music, including 'The Boogie Woogie Bugle Boy'.

Other successes included *Hold that Ghost* (1941), *Lost in a Harem* (1944), and *The Naughty Nineties* (1945), which featured their famous 'Who's on First' routine, in which Abbott baffles Costello by describing baseball players named Who, What, When, and I Don't Know. Subsequently their film careers went into a prolonged decline. The desperation of their later vehicles may be judged from such titles as *Abbott and Costello*

Meet Frankenstein (1948), *Abbott and Costello in the Foreign Legion* (1950), *Abbott and Costello Meet the Invisible Man* (1951), and *Abbott and Costello Meet Dr Jekyll and Mr Hyde* (1953).

In 1978 the film *Bud and Lou*, starring Harvey Korman and Buddy Hackett, explored the duo's often antagonistic personal relationship.

A Bout de souffle (*Breathless*; 1959) The influential debut feature by Jean-Luc GODARD. Set in Paris, the plot concerns a Bogart-obsessed petty criminal Michel Poiccard, alias Laszlo Kovacs (Jean-Paul BELMONDO), who takes refuge with a US girl (Jean Seberg) after murdering a traffic cop on a whim. Following lengthy discussions on art and philosophy, she betrays him to the police.

Like TRUFFAUT's THE 400 BLOWS and RESNAIS's HIROSHIMA, MON AMOUR, *A Bout de souffle* was one of the key films that launched the French NEW WAVE in 1959. The plot was inspired by a news story that Truffaut originally intended to film as a sequel to *The 400 Blows*. However, when Godard had trouble agreeing with producer Georges de Beauregard on a subject for his first film, Truffaut donated his treatment. Similarly Claude CHABROL, who had already established himself as a director, offered to act as production supervisor to appease the financiers. With its scenario written on a daily basis, the picture was completed in less than a month for just $90,000. Influenced both by US gangster movies and by such classics of French POETIC REALISM as *Pépé le Moko* (1936) and *Quai des brumes* (1938), it is packed with *hommages* to such crime directors as Samuel FULLER and Jean-Pierre MELVILLE. The latter actually makes a brief appearance in the film (as does Godard, in the role of an informer).

Technically, the film made innovative use of SEQUENCE SHOTS and JUMP CUTS to disrupt the conventions of linear narrative and classic continuity editing. Shooting on location in available light, Godard and cinematographer Raoul Coutard spurned sophisticated equipment and opted to move the hand-held camera around on such everyday items as a wheelchair, a pram, and a mail cart. In the tradition of NEOREALISM, the film was shot silently and the dialogue dubbed in postproduction. Godard later wrote:

> What I wanted was to take a conventional story and remake, but differently, everything the cinema had done. I also wanted to give the feeling that the technique of film-making had been discovered or experienced for the first time.

In 1983 Jim McBride remade the film in English as *Breathless*, with Richard GERE and Valerie Kaprisky.

above the line In a film budget, expenses incurred before shooting begins. Normally the major expenditures, they include the purchase of rights to a novel or play and fees negotiated by the producer, director, and stars. **Below-the-line** expenditures include payments to other actors and the production crew as well as spending on props and costumes, studio facilities, insurance, and travel, etc.

ABPC *See* ASSOCIATED BRITISH.

abstract film A film in which the separate shots have a formal relationship but no obvious narrative or content relationship. Abstract films may be created by the manipulation of live-action footage, by the use of animation, or by working directly onto film. An **absolute film** is one that is entirely non-representational, using shapes, colours, sounds, and movement to make its effect.

Abstract film was a development of the French AVANT-GARDE of the 1920s, the first notable work in the genre being Fernand Léger's *Le Ballet mécanique* (1924). At much the same time the German Oscar Fishinger (1900–67) experimented with choreographing abstract patterns to music; his work was the inspiration for the Bach sequence in DISNEY's FANTASIA (1940). The interplay of light was another concern of 'pure' cinema as, for example, in Man Ray's *Emak Batia* (1926).

Animation has offered virtually unlimited possibilities for abstract film-making; *30 Years of Experiment* (1951) is an important anthology of the best work from America and Germany. Len Lye (1901–80) has been almost the sole exponent of abstract cinema in Britain. A pioneer of working directly on film, he later developed new ideas in animation for the National Film Board of Canada. More recently, video and computer technology have greatly extended the possibilities of abstract film-making.

academy. **Academy Awards** The world's most prestigious film awards, presented each March in Los Angeles by the ACADEMY OF MOTION PICTURE ARTS AND SCIENCES. An award can mean an extra $30 million in box-office receipts and a corresponding boost in a star's future fee. The 1995 ceremony, hosted by David Letterman, was broadcast to an estimated one and a half billion viewers worldwide.

To qualify, a film must have been screened in the Los Angeles area for at least one week in the previous calendar year. Nominations in each category are chosen in January by the more than 5000 Academy members voting in their professional branches, while winners are selected by a general poll of members.

The Academy did not envision the giving of awards when it was founded in 1927. Its first president, Douglas FAIRBANKS, introduced them some two years later, the winners being nominated by members and chosen by committee. On 16 May 1929 Fairbanks handed out the first awards (for 1927–1928) at a black-tie banquet in the Hollywood Roosevelt Hotel, with 270 guests enjoying lobster and squab. The presentations, in seven major categories, took about ten minutes. *Wings* (1927) was chosen as the first Best Picture.

Categories have changed over the years: additions have included short subjects (1931), editing (1934), supporting roles (1936), foreign-language films (1956), and make-up (1981). Walt DISNEY is the top Oscar winner of all time, with 26 regular and six special awards to his credit. BEN-HUR (1959) is the most successful movie with 11 awards, John FORD is top director with four, and Katharine HEPBURN leads actors of both sexes with four Oscars (and a further eight nominations).

The giving of special awards has been a regular feature of the Oscars since the beginning; at the first ceremony they were bestowed on WARNER BROTHERS for THE JAZZ SINGER and on Charlie CHAPLIN. In 1972 Chaplin returned to accept an emotional special award for his "incalculable effect" on movies. In 1995 Clint EASTWOOD was presented with the Irving G. Thalberg Award for producers, Quincy Jones received the Jean Hersholt Humanitarian Award, and Michelangelo ANTONIONI was honoured for his lifetime achievement.

The name OSCAR, which has been explained in various ways, was adapted as a humorous, slightly derogatory, term for the statuette in the early 1930s. By this time members were already complaining of blatant lobbying and fraudulent tabulating. In 1935 the Academy hired accountants Price Waterhouse to conduct the balloting (as they still do).

Only winners attended the ceremony until 1940, when all the nominees were invited as a means of increasing tension and therefore public interest. Television broadcasting began in 1951, with the first live telecast going out two years later. Today, some 800 limousines are used to convey celebrities the ten miles from Beverly Hills to the Dorothy Chandler Pavilion.

Oscars have been refused and abused. George C. SCOTT rejected his Best Actor Award for *Patton* (1970), after calling the ceremonies "a meat parade", while two years later Marlon BRANDO, Best Actor for THE GODFATHER (1972), deputed a supposed American Indian (who turned out to be an unemployed actress) to make a speech denouncing Hollywood's image of her people. In 1977 Vanessa REDGRAVE made a vehement anti-Zionist speech while accepting her award for *Julia*.

Major talents have gone unrecognized. Richard BURTON and Peter O'TOOLE each received seven nominations without a win; Steven SPIELBERG suffered a long series of rejections before winning as Best Director with SCHINDLER'S LIST (1994). Directors never to have won a regular Oscar include Alfred HITCHCOCK, Stanley KUBRICK, and Martin SCORSESE. Superb films that failed to collect the Best Picture award include THE THIRD MAN (1949), HIGH NOON (1952), SINGIN' IN THE RAIN (1952), and PSYCHO (1960).

In 1938 Alice Brady, the winner of the Best Supporting Actress award for *In Old Chicago*, was stuck at home with a broken ankle on the night of the ceremony. A 'representative' accepted on her behalf and was never seen again.

In 1984 an Oscar nomination for screenwriting went to a dog. Robert TOWNE was so upset with changes in his script for *Greystoke: The Legend of Tarzan, Lord of the Apes* that he substituted the name of his sheepdog, P. H. Vazak, on the credits.

Academy Frame The standard film frame, having a ratio of width to height (ASPECT RATIO) of 4:3, which is usually expressed as 1.33:1. This was established in the silent era and remained dominant until the introduction of WIDESCREEN processes in the 1950s. The standard design for television screens observes the same ratio. Although it is sometimes explained in terms of the 'golden section' (a mathematically governed compositional technique much favoured by Renaissance painters), the ratio is in fact quite arbitrary.

Academy Mask A device introduced in 1932 by the ACADEMY OF MOTION PICTURE ARTS AND SCIENCES to maintain an ASPECT RATIO of 1.33:1 (width to height). With the advent of talkies, room had to be found on the edge of the film for the SOUNDTRACK; as a result filmmakers abandoned the established ACADEMY FRAME in favour of a square-shaped picture. The Academy Mask re-established the 1.33:1 ratio by masking off part of the camera's aperture.

Academy of Motion Pictures Arts and Sciences The US organization of film producers, directors, actors, and technicians that was founded in 1927 by Louis B. MAYER, mainly in an attempt to prevent actors and technicians from joining unions. The Academy is now mainly known for presenting the ACADEMY AWARDS or Oscars, which were introduced in 1929. It has also established technical **Academy Standards** to govern such matters as camera APERTURES, film LEADERS, and projectors.

accelerated. accelerated montage A film sequence in which progressively briefer shots of two or more different subjects are alternated; its effect is to heighten the dramatic tension. Accelerated montage is particularly popular at the climax of a CHASE scene, in which shots of e.g. a car and a train racing towards the same railway crossing will be intercut with increasing speed. A famous use of the device occurs in HIGH NOON, in which a sequence of 28 brief shots is used to build up to Gary COOPER's confrontation with the gang who have come to kill him.

accelerated motion Film action that appears in a speeded-up form when projected. The effect is achieved by passing the film through the taking camera at a speed slower than the standard 24 frames per second and then projecting normally. It is frequently used in chase scenes and comedy routines. Most silent films were shot at 18–20 frames per second and so appear in a speeded-up form when projected at standard sound speed. Accelerated motion has also been used in SPAGHETTI WESTERNS to make gunfighters appear quicker on the

draw and – allegedly – in many MARTIAL-ARTS MOVIES (although this is strongly denied by exponents of the genre). *See also* SLOW MOTION.

ACE American Cinema Editors. The US organization representing professional film and television editors. It presents the annual **Eddie Awards** for best film editing.

acetate Short for cellulose acetate, a non-flammable material used in the manufacture of film stocks. The first **safety film** using an acetate base was produced in 1908 by Eastman Kodak. *See also* CELLULOID.

acoustics The characteristics of a sound-recording stage, set, room, auditorium, or other enclosure as they affect the audibility or fidelity of sound.

act. acting "I became an actor because I couldn't stand myself", George C. SCOTT once said; "Acting is the only job that gives you a chance to be somebody else most of the days of the year. And you get paid for it."

The first professional actors appeared in films in 1896: in America John Rice and May Irwin kissed in Thomas EDISON's KINETOSCOPE loop *The Widow Jones*, while in Britain R. W. Paul appeared in the comedy *The Soldier's Courtship*. Early film actors were recruited from the stage and had to relearn much of their technique. Some, inevitably, proved more adaptable than others; the Edwardian actor-manager Sir Herbert Beerbohm Tree is said to have glowered at the camera and remarked, "I can't possibly act in front of that thing." The large screen required less sweeping gestures than the theatre and, with the advent of the CLOSE-UP, more subtle facial expressions. Similarly, with the coming of sound, stage actors had to reduce their theatrical voice projection. A number of silent stars failed to make the transition to sound owing to the poor quality of their speaking voices.

The technique known as METHOD acting, developed from the theories of Konstantin Stanislavsky (1863–1938) and taught by Lee Strasberg (1901–82) in his ACTORS' STUDIO in New York, was introduced to the screen by Marlon BRANDO in *A Streetcar Named Desire* (1951). More recent exponents include Al PACINO and Robert DE NIRO.

Keep it simple. Make a blank face and the music and the story will fill it in.
INGRID BERGMAN, advice to her daughter, Isabella Rossellini.

Don't sell it. Remember they're *peeking* at you.
CHARLIE CHAPLIN, advice to his actors.

Don't just do something, stand there.
CLINT EASTWOOD, quoting his drama coach.

The art of acting is not to act. Once you show them more, what you show them, in fact, is bad acting.
ANTHONY HOPKINS.

Don't act – think!
F. W. MURNAU.

You spend all your life trying to do something they put people in asylums for.
JANE FONDA.

Acting is a way of living out one's insanity.
ISABELLE HUPPERT.

I give myself to my parts as a lover. It's the only way.
VANESSA REDGRAVE.

Acting has been described as farting about in disguise.
PETER O'TOOLE.

Acting is like roller skating. Once you know how to do it, it is neither stimulating nor exciting.
GEORGE SANDERS.

Acting is the most minor of gifts. After all, Shirley Temple could do it when she was four.
KATHARINE HEPBURN.

It sounds pompous but it's the nearest thing I can do to being God.
ROD STEIGER.

First wipe your nose and check your flies.
SIR ALEC GUINNESS.

Acting is like sex. You should do it, not talk about it.
JOANNE WOODWARD.

actor A person who acts in a film, play, etc., especially one who does so professionally. The term used to be reserved for male actors but is now used increasingly of women also, in preference to **actress**.

In Europe, stage acting was long regarded as a raffish and disreputable profession; it did not achieve full social acceptance until the great Victorian actor Sir Henry Irving was knighted in 1895. This late-won respectability did not extend to the emergent profession of film acting, which continued to be regarded as a low and even scandalous activity. Numerous moralists of the 1920s and 1930s thundered at Hollywood as the modern Babylon, while even today film actors are readily suspected of loose morals, egomania, and lack of talent.

There's something wrong with actors, we've always been a suspect breed.
DIRK BOGARDE.

At one time I thought he wanted to be an actor. He had certain qualifications, including no money and a total lack of responsibility.
HEDDA HOPPER.

The only shot I had was either to become a crook, a dope dealer – or an actor.
JOE PANTOLIANO.

Actors are often thought of as talking props.
EMILIO ESTEVEZ.

Actors are cattle.
ALFRED HITCHCOCK, attrib.

A talented actor is as rare as an arsehole in the face.
THOMAS BERNHARD.

Actors are paid to be selfish and self-involved.
MICHAEL DOUGLAS.

Acting has never done anything for me except encourage my vanity and provoke my arrogance.
CANDICE BERGEN.

An actor's a guy who, if you ain't talking about him, ain't listening.
MARLON BRANDO.

An actor is like Jesus Christ; you have to suffer.
GÉRARD DEPARDIEU.

All actors are whores. We sell our bodies to the highest bidder.
WILLIAM HOLDEN.

Scratch an actor and you'll find an actress.
DOROTHY PARKER.

I'm an *actor*. An *actress* is someone who wears boa feathers.
SIGOURNEY WEAVER.

Actors' Studio The New York-based workshop for professional actors founded in 1947 by Elia KAZAN, Robert Lewis, and Cheryl Crawford. Under the artistic direction of Lee Strasberg (from 1948), the Studio became known as the US home of the METHOD school of acting and nurtured many leading stars of film and theatre, including Marlon BRANDO. The Studio is primarily a forum for exploration and experimentation, without the pressures of commercial production. The costs are met by voluntary subscription, and membership is by invitation following audition.

action Any activity that occurs as part of a filmed sequence. 'Action!' is the director's cue for actors to begin performing for the camera or for studio technicians to put props into motion.

actioner An informal term for a film with a fast-moving plot and plenty of physical action; such films are normally, though not necessarily, violent.

action still A single frame taken from a film sequence and reproduced as a still photograph, usually for publicity purposes. The term distinguishes such pictures from those specially posed for a still photographer (*see* PUBLICITY STILL).

ACTT Association of Cinematograph, Television, and Allied Technicians. The British film and television union that represents studio technicians. It was established in 1933 as the Association of Cine-Technicians (ACT), changing its name in 1956 to accommodate television and allied workers. ACTT negotiates on behalf of its members with such organizations as the Producers Association.

actual sound Film sound that relates to a person or object visible on the screen or to one whose presence is implied (e.g. another actor who is temporarily out of shot, a ringing telephone, etc.). The term is used to distinguish sound that has its source within the scene from COMMENTATIVE SOUND.

AD *See* ASSISTANT DIRECTOR.

Adjani, Isabelle (1955–) French actress, whose career has suffered through an injudicious choice of roles and the forceful assertion of her political views. Although many sources claim that Adjani was born in Paris to a German mother and a Turkish father, she stated in 1986 that her father was Algerian. This interview, given in response to the rise of the extreme Right in France, provoked outrage and Adjani was subjected to much racist abuse in the media, including the circulation of a rumour that she had AIDS. Although her work continues to enjoy critical and commercial success, her relationship with the French public remains, at best, ambivalent.

Having appeared in a number of amateur stage productions, she made her film debut in *Le Petit Bougnat* during the school holidays in 1970. Two years later she became the youngest-ever contracted player with the Comédie Française. Despite winning acclaim in productions of Molière, Lorca, and Giraudoux, she rejected a 20-year contract with the company for the lead in François TRUFFAUT's *The Story of Adèle H.* (1975). Her intense performance as Victor Hugo's daughter Adèle, whose passion for a British lieutenant led to madness, brought her a Best Actress Award from the New York Film Critics and an Oscar nomination. Truffaut praised her for acting "as though her life depended on it" and Adjani herself was convinced that things could never "happen so beautifully, so smoothly, and with such purity again."

Although her subsequent career has certainly been uneven, she has continued to collect awards on a regular basis. In 1981 she was named Best Actress at Cannes for her performances in Andrzej Zulawski's *Possession* (1980) and MERCHANT-IVORY's *Quartet* (1981). She has also scooped the Best Actress César on no less than four occasions, for *Possession*, Jean Becker's *One Deadly Summer* (1983), Bruno Nuytten's *Camille Claudel* (1988, also Oscar nominated), and Patrice Chéreau's historical epic *La Reine Margot* (1993). Her work in America, however, notably *The Driver* (1978) and *Ishtar* (1987), has been hugely disappointing.

Although Adjani has shown a more aggressive side to her screen personality in Claude Miller's *Mortelle randonée* (1983) and Luc Besson's *Subway* (1985), she is mainly associated with characters who suffer physically or emotionally, as in *The Story of Adèle H.*, Roman POLANSKI's *The Tenant* (1976), Werner HERZOG's *Nosferatu* (1979), *Camille Claudel*, and *La Reine Margot* (a film described by Adjani as "the first grunge costume drama"). This emphasis on solitude and suffering makes all the more revealing her remark that "one acts nothing but oneself, no matter how fiercely one denies it."

Adult Film Association of America An organization established in the late 1960s to promote the making of pornographic films (*see* PORNOGRAPHY) and to resist their censorship. Its members include producers, distributors, and exhibitors of sexually explicit movies.

advance On a film print with a soundtrack, the number of frames separating the image from the synchronous sound. This separation allows the soundtrack to pass through a scanning device at a continuous speed while the corresponding visuals are being advanced one frame at a time through the gate of the PROJECTOR. There is an advance of about 20 frames for 35mm film and one of about 26 frames for 16mm.

aerial cinematography The shooting of film sequences from cameras mounted on aeroplanes, helicopters, etc.; since the development of lightweight cameras, film-makers have also been able to use model aircraft. The first notable aerial film was the silent *Wings* (1927), about the Air Service during World War I. The director, William WELLMAN, who had flown in the war, mounted a camera in an aircraft to film simulated dogfights and bombings; the film won Oscars for Best Picture and Best Engineering Effects. The NATIONAL BOARD OF REVIEW reported that "so much in fact happens in the air that it is impossible to take it all in." During World War II aerial cinematography was used by both sides for reconnaisance and propaganda.

The first film to use a helicopter shot was *The Twisted Road* (1948), which featured two chase sequences filmed from the air. Other films to make striking use of aerial cinematography include Alfred HITCHCOCK's NORTH BY NORTHWEST (1959), in which Cary GRANT is pursued by a cropsprayer, John Guillermin's *The Blue Max* (1966), Francis Ford COPPOLA's Vietnam-War epic APOCALYPSE NOW (1979), and *Top Gun* (1986) starring Tom CRUISE as a naval fighter pilot.

AFI American Film Institute. An organization founded in 1967 to "preserve the heritage and advance the art of film in America." Based in Washington, DC, the AFI was created with funds supplied by the National Endowment for the Arts, the MOTION PICTURE ASSOCIATION OF AMERICA, and the Ford Foundation. Its film school offers a one-year Curriculum Program to film-makers or those in related fields (such as the theatre and music) and a Conservatory Program emphasizing individual creative work. The institute also maintains a library for researchers and publishes educational and reference material, including a catalogue giving details of all the US films ever made. It is probably best-known, however, for its annual presentations of a Life Achievement Award (the first recipient was John FORD, in 1973).

The AFI's first director was George Stevens Jnr (son of the director George STEVENS) and its first chairman Gregory PECK.

African Queen, The (1951) John HUSTON's film adaptation of the romantic adventure novel by C. S. Forester; the movie, a great box-office success, paired Humphrey BOGART with Katharine HEPBURN.

On the eve of World War I, Charlie Allnut (Bogart), the disreputable captain of the steamboat that gives the film its name, offers to take Rosie Sayer (Hepburn) down the Congo to safety after her missionary brother (Robert Morley) has been killed. After enduring numerous hardships on the way, these obdurate and ill-assorted characters learn to tolerate and finally love each other.

In adapting the novel, James AGEE produced a rather talky drama that was turned down by Charles LAUGHTON and Elsa LANCHESTER, David NIVEN and Bette DAVIS, and John MILLS and Deborah KERR before Bogart and Hepburn accepted the roles of the "wretched, sleazy, absurd, brave little man" and the "psalm-singing skinny old maid." Once the casting was settled, Huston quickly realized the potential for drama in the contrasting personalities of his stars (which he heightened by suggesting that Hepburn play Rosie in the manner of Eleanor Roosevelt). However, he remained unhappy with Forester's ending and Agee fell ill before he could supply one of his own. In the event, Huston and writer Peter Viertel produced four alternatives: Rosie proposing to Charlie; Charlie and Rosie being rescued by a British warship; Charlie recalling a long-forgotten wife; and, the one that was used, the couple being saved from hanging by the destruction of the German gunboat on which they are held prisoner.

According to Viertel's later novel *Roman à clef*, which is based on the making of the film, the director only undertook the project to pay off his debts and indulge his long-cherished ambition to go big-game hunting. (In 1990 Viertel's novel was itself filmed – as *White Hunter, Black Heart* – by Clint EASTWOOD.) Despite this, Huston travelled an exhausting 25,000 miles across Africa to find locations before settling on a 1000-mile stretch of the Congo near Ruiki. At various times the production was disrupted by wild boars, charging elephants, blood flukes, crocodiles, and soldier ants. When the film crew contracted malaria, Huston and Bogart escaped, largely, it is said, as a result of their preference for alcohol to the polluted bottled water. In fact, the only incident seriously to disturb Bogart was a scene in which he had to be covered in real leeches as he waded through the river pulling the steamer behind him; ironically, this was filmed in a vast water tank at Pinewood studios near London. His reward was his only Oscar for Best Actor; the film also proved the most commercially successful of Hepburn's long career.

In 1987 Hepburn published *The Making of* The African Queen, *or How I Went to Africa with Bogart, Bacall and Huston and Almost Lost My Mind*, which concluded:

Now, what do you suppose ever happened to Charlie and Rosie?...Did they stay in Africa? I always thought they must have. And had lots of little Charlies and Rosies. And lived happily ever after. Because that's what we wanted them to do. And every summer they take a trip in the old *Queen* – and laugh and laugh and laugh and laugh...

Age d'or, L' (1930) Luis BUÑUEL's outrageous essay in SURREALISM, an anarchic fantasia co-scripted by Salvador Dali. The slight plot concerns two lovers, Gaston Modot and Lya Lys; when the conventions of polite bourgeois society endanger their romance, they set out to undermine the religious, moral, social, and economic props that support it.

Buñuel described his earlier collaboration with Dali, *Un Chien andalou* (1929), as a work that "would plunge right into the heart of witty, elegant, and intellectualized Paris with all the weight of an Iberian dagger." Dali was equally delighted with the 17-minute film that "ruined in a single evening ten years of pseudo-intellectual postwar avant-guardism." *L'Age d'or*, planned with Dali but made without his active participation, is in some ways even more inflammatory. Indeed, such was the impact of the film's nihilism that its premiere resulted in the ransacking of the Studio 28 theatre in Paris; within days French fascists had succeeded in having it banned nationwide. Although the film lacked the sensational episodes that had earned *Un Chien andalou* its notoriety (most memorably, the slicing of a woman's eyeball), it still managed to offend, thanks to such incidents as the beating-up of a blind man, the slapping

of a dowager, the murder of a son by his father, and the erotic kissing of a statue's foot in parody of the veneration of St Peter's statue in Rome. The film even concluded with a salute to the Marquis de Sade.

Buñuel later described the way in which he and Dali had drawn on images from dreams and the subconscious:

When an image or idea appeared the collaborators discarded it immediately if it was derived from remembrance, or from their cultural pattern, or, if, simply, it had a conscious association with an earlier idea.

Remarkably, MGM was so impressed by the critical acclaim lavished on *L'Age d'or* that it offered Buñuel a contract, which he only rejected after an uncomfortable visit to the studio.

Agee, James (1910–55) US film critic, who helped to establish the Anglo-American tradition of cinema criticism. He also wrote five screenplays and three novels. Born in Knoxville, Tennessee, Agee was educated at Harvard, published some poetry, and wrote for *Fortune* magazine before beginning to review movies for *Time* and then *Nation* in the 1940s. He first went to Hollywood as a writer in 1948. His screenplays include THE AFRICAN QUEEN (1951), for which he was awarded an Oscar, and *The Night of the Hunter* (1955), Charles LAUGHTON's only film as a director. Agee's novel, *A Death in the Family*, won a posthumous Pulitzer Prize in 1958; five years later Philip Reisman adapted it as the film *All the Way Home*, starring Robert Preston and Jean SIMMONS.

Agee's reviews were often trenchant and memorable; of MGM's *Random Harvest* (1942) he wrote, "I would like to recommend this film to those...who could with pleasure eat a bowl of Yardley's shaving soap for breakfast", while of the musical *You Were Meant for Me* (1948) he commented simply, "That's what you think." Reviewing *The Miracle of Morgan's Creek* (1943), which satirized motherhood and other all-American values, he noted that the shock to the audience was "like taking a nun on a roller coaster." There was, however, far more to his criticism than smart one-liners; he wrote particularly sensitively of the silent comedian Harold LLOYD, aptly characterizing him as "funny from the inside." Agee sometimes got things badly wrong, as when he predicted that the wartime movie *The Clock* (1945), starring Robert Walker and Judy GARLAND would be remembered for 50 years.

agent   *See* FILM TALENT AGENT.

Aimée, Anouk   (Françoise Sorya Dreyfus; 1932–) Graceful French actress, who specialized in playing slightly mysterious women. She is best known for her starring role in Claude LELOUCH's *A Man and a Woman* (1966), France's greatest international film success of the 1960s and 1970s. Her fourth husband was Albert FINNEY.

Aimée was the daughter of theatrical parents who sent her to drama school in England. She made her screen debut at the age of 14 and two years later (billed only as 'Anouk') won acclaim in André CAYATTE's *The Lovers of Verona* (1948), playing a young actress who begins to live out her film role as Shakespeare's Juliet. In 1960 she played a call girl in FELLINI's LA DOLCE VITA and the title role in Jacques DEMY's *Lola* (another prostitute).

Aimée was nominated for an Oscar for her performance in *A Man and a Woman*, in which she played a widowed film script-girl who becomes involved with a racing driver (Jean-Louis Trintignant). This success led her to Hollywood in the late 1960s; in 1969 she starred in both George CUKOR's *Justine*, a misconceived adaptation of Lawrence Durrell's *The Alexandria Quartet*, and Sidney LUMET's *The Appointment*, in which she played a married woman suspected of prostitution by her husband, Omar SHARIF.

By the later 1970s Aimée had returned to France, where she made such films as *Si c'était à refaire* (1978), in which she attempts to seduce Catherine DENEUVE's adolescent son. Lelouch's *A Man and a Woman: Twenty Years Later* (1986), again with Trintignant, failed to match the great success of the original. In 1992 Aimée starred in *Docteur Norman Bethune.* ·

Ai No Corrida   (*Empire of the Senses*; 1976) Nagisa OSHIMA's complex and controversial film about sexual obsession. Based on a real-life love affair in 1930s Japan, the film was banned by the US customs on the eve of its screening at the New York Film Festival and refused certification in Britain until 1991 (although it had previously been shown at several private clubs).

Often described as the Japanese *Last Tango in Paris*, *Ai No Corrida* depicts an obsessive relationship between a maid, Sada (Eiko Matsudo), and her married employer, Kichi-zo (Fuji Tatsuya). The film graphically but sensitively shows how the couple create, and then retreat into, a private world of eroticism. The explicit sex scenes provoked considerable debate and outrage, including suggestions that some of the lovemaking had not been simulated. Perhaps the most controversial scene of all is the one in which Sada strangles Kichi-zo as he orgasms and, after his death, castrates him as a final act of devotion. The real-life maid was arrested for murder when she was found carrying her employer's severed penis.

Set during the most repressive period in recent Japanese history, *Ai No Corrida* gives a structured and intelligent view of the way in which social repression can lead to private obsession. In recent years the film has enjoyed something of a reappraisal; although still regarded as obscene by some, others have argued that it is one of the few erotic films not to be exploitative.

AIP   *See* AMERICAN INTERNATIONAL PICTURES.

Aldrich, Robert   (1918–83) US director, mainly of thrillers and action films, noted for his uneven work over three decades. An independent film-maker who disliked the Hollywood establishment, Aldrich was often accused of poor taste and excessive violence.

Born into a Rhode Island banking family, he studied economics at university before becoming a clerk at RKO; he later served as an assistant director to Jean RENOIR, Charles CHAPLIN, Lewis MILESTONE, and Joseph LOSEY, amongst others. After several years working for television, he made his debut feature, MGM's *The Big Leaguer*, in 1953; the film starred Edward G. ROBINSON as an ageing baseball player.

Aldrich made his name with *Vera Cruz* (1954), an action film starring Burt LANCASTER and Gary COOPER as adventurers in Mexico; the following year he directed Lancaster again in *Apache* (1954), notable for its sympathetic treatment of American Indians. In 1955 the thriller *Kiss Me Deadly* brought Aldrich his first accusations of sadistic violence. *The Big Knife* (1956), starring Jack PALANCE as a Hollywood star battling a brutal studio head, was the first film made for the director's own company, The Associates and Aldrich.

In 1962 Aldrich had a most embarrassing failure with the biblical epic *Sodom and*

Gomorrah. This was followed by the enjoyably over-the-top melodrama *Whatever Happened to Baby Jane?* (1962), about the poisonous relationship between two sisters (Bette DAVIS and Joan CRAWFORD). Davis played the title character, a grotesque ex-child star, and Crawford her victimized sister. The similarly gothic *Hush...Hush Sweet Charlotte* (1964) starred Davis as a demented Southern Belle and Olivia DE HAVILLAND as her prissy cousin.

Aldrich enjoyed his biggest box-office success with *The Dirty Dozen* (1967), about a group of convicts used in a commando raid behind Nazi lines. He used the profits to buy his own studio, but was soon obliged to sell it after making such flops as *The Killing of Sister George* (1968), about the decline of a lesbian actress (Beryl Reid).

In the 1970s Aldrich found renewed success with a series of films starring Burt REYNOLDS, who appeared as a prison football coach in *The Longest Yard* (British title *The Mean Machine*; 1974), as a corrupt cop in *Hustle* (1975), and as a deranged Vietnam War veteran in *Twilight's Last Gleaming* (1977). Subsequent films included *The Choirboys* (1978), about a particularly vicious gang of policemen, and *All the Marbles* (British title *The California Dolls*; 1981), with Peter Falk as the manager of a women's wrestling team.

Alexander Nevsky (1938) Sergei EISENSTEIN's celebrated film about the struggles of Prince Alexander Nevsky of Novgorod (Nikolai Cherkassov) to unify the Russian peoples in their struggle against an invading army of Teutonic knights.

When Eisenstein was offered the chance of directing this picture, he had not completed a film since *The Old and the New* in 1929. In the meantime he had endured an unhappy spell in Hollywood and been forced to abandon *Bezhin Meadow* (when it was 60% completed) at the insistence of Boris Shumyatsky, the head of the Soviet film industry. Shumyatsky had been entrusted with ensuring the triumph of Socialist Realism over formalism and his personal animosity towards Eisenstein was an open secret. However, following Shumyatsky's liquidation during the purges of 1936, Eisenstein was restored to favour and awarded this most prestigious project.

Although Eisenstein conceived his film as a "fugue on the theme of patriotism", *Alexander Nevsky*, with its score by Sergei Prokofiev, became more operatic than fugal. Freed from bureaucratic constraint, Eisenstein abandoned the heroic masses of his earlier films in favour of a powerful individual protagonist. He also forsook intellectual MONTAGE for a new style he termed "vertical montage", in which the visual image, dialogue, performance, score, and sound were all rigidly subjected to the director's artistic vision. *Alexander Nevsky* is a triumph of meticulously devised MISE-EN-SCÈNE and choreographed movement, with the celebrated 'Battle on the Ice' (actually shot in midsummer on artificial snow) as its centrepiece. Featuring thousands of extras, many of whom were drawn, at Stalin's insistence, from the Red Army, this complex sequence made pioneering use of hand-held cameras and SWISH PANs to place the viewer in the centre of the action.

Stalin was so delighted with the film that he awarded Eisenstein the Order of Lenin in 1939. However, with the signing of the Nazi-Soviet Pact later that year, the film became something of an embarrassment, as the Teutons were obviously supposed to represent the menace of Nazism (their uniforms evoke the Klansmen in THE BIRTH OF A NATION while their emblem clearly resembles the swastika). Following the German invasion of the Soviet Union in 1941, the film was reissued to renewed acclaim and Eisenstein received the Stalin Prize for his presentation of the indomitable spirit of the Motherland.

Alien (1979) Ridley SCOTT's hugely successful science-fiction horror thriller, which spawned two equally successful sequels. The original film starred Sigourney WEAVER as Lt Ripley, one of a spaceship crew pitted against a truly terrifying life-form that is intent upon their destruction. The film's mass appeal rested largely on Scott's brilliantly edited series of nasty surprises and some gory special effects – the most celebrated of these being the eruption of the embryonic alien from John Hurt's stomach, in which it has been incubating. Although critics pointed to dark metaphorical undertones, audiences were mainly content to enjoy the remorseless sequence of carefully managed shocks.

The alien itself was designed by the surrealist artist H. R. Giger and developed into a working model by Carlo Rambaldi, who three years later produced the lovable space creature ET. In its design and general appearance *Alien* had an enormous influence on film-making in the 1980s; the director Chris Jones has written:

> Every science-fiction film that has come after it seems to have that gritty, grimy, wet, steamy look, that kind of blue light and green darkness. It has totally changed the genre...

In 1986 James CAMERON's sequel *Aliens* pitted Weaver and a team of marines against a whole cohort of the nightmarish creatures. The Oscar-winning special effects were, if anything, even more impressive than those of the original film. Still more remarkable, perhaps, was the emergence of the supremely capable Ripley as a powerful feminist heroine for the late 1980s. A third film, *Alien 3*, was directed by the 28-year-old David Fincher in 1992; set in a grim penal colony in space, it repeats the formulae of the earlier films to diminishing effect.

> In space no-one can hear you scream.
> Slogan used in publicity for *Alien*.

all. *All About Eve* (1950) Twentieth Century-Fox's classic film about the jealousy between two actresses; the film was nominated for 14 Oscars (the most ever) and won six, leaving only minor awards for SUNSET BOULEVARD, the year's other great film about the acting profession. Joseph L. MANKIEWICZ directed and wrote the witty script, taking Oscars in both categories (as he had the previous year with *A Letter to Three Wives*). His screenplay was adapted from Mary Orr's short story, *The Wisdom of Eve*, based on true events involving the Austrian actress Elizabeth Bergner.

The film concerns the rivalry between fading film star Margo Channing and Eve Harrington, an ambitious young actress who plans her every move to capture the older woman's roles, love interest, and friends. Bette DAVIS excelled as the acidic Margo, determined to fight off the challenge from newcomer Anne BAXTER. During the party scene, Davis roars out her famous line "Fasten your seat belts, it's going to be a bumpy night!" Claudette COLBERT was scheduled to play the role but had to withdraw when she broke her back. Because she lowered her voice to play the part, some critics felt that Davis had based her performance on the husky Tallulah BANKHEAD; in reality, the change was owing to a broken blood vessel in her throat.

The Oscar for Best Supporting Actor went to George SANDERS for his performance as Addison de Witt, a malicious drama critic ("I am essential to the theatre – as ants to a picnic, as the boll weevil to a cotton field"). Nominations also went to Davis, Baxter, Celeste Holm, and Thelma Ritter. The as-yet-unknown Marilyn MONROE appeared in a bit part as the dumb blonde Miss Caswell, a graduate of the "Copacabana School of Dramatic Arts".

All Quiet on the Western Front (1930) Lewis MILESTONE's adaptation of Erich Maria Remarque's famous novel about World War I, as seen from the German trenches. Often described as the greatest anti-war film ever made, the picture attracted large audiences but was still a financial failure because of costs of nearly $2 million. *All Quiet* won the Oscar as Best Picture for Universal Studios, which then went 43 years before winning again with THE STING (1973).

Milestone, who took the Oscar as Best Director, also co-scripted. Two future directors were involved in the production: George CUKOR as dialogue director and Fred ZINNEMANN as an extra. Milestone used a giant crane to obtain his panoramic shots of the battlefield (actually a California mesa) and created battle smoke by burning old tyres. "Anytime we didn't like the background" he said, "we obscured it with smoke." His battle scenes were so realistic that footage was later used in war documentaries.

Lew AYRES, who starred as the soldier Paul Baumer, became a conscientious objector in World War II. The French soldier stabbed to death by Ayres was played by Raymond Griffith, a silent-film comedian whose career ended with the talkies because a vocal disease limited his voice to a whisper. For this, his final role, no words were required.

Universal also filmed Remarque's sequel, *The Road Back*, in 1937, with James WHALE directing. The company reissued *All Quiet on the Western Front* in 1939 and again in 1950 as the Korean War began.

The plot focuses on seven German schoolboys who enlist to fight for their Fatherland. Their dreams of glory are soon dispelled, however, as they face fear and death in the trenches. In the film's final moments, the soldier Baumer reaches for a butterfly and is shot dead by a sniper; as he dies, new recruits march forward. The hand seen clutching the butterfly actually belonged to Milestone rather than to Ayres.

all-star film A feature film that gathers together some of the best-known actors and actresses of the day. The all-star film was especially popular in the 1930s and 1940s, when the star power was often used to conceal a weaker-than-average plot.

The vogue for the all-star film was effectively launched by the success of MGM's *Grand Hotel* (1932), which brought together Greta GARBO, Joan CRAWFORD, and John and Lionel BARRYMORE. Although Paramount's *Alice in Wonderland* (1933) featured W. C. FIELDS as Humpty Dumpty, Cary GRANT as the Mock Turtle, and Gary COOPER as the White Knight, the film proved relatively unsuccessful, perhaps because most of the stars were unrecognizable under masks and make-up. World War II saw a rash of all-star morale-boosters such as *Hollywood Canteen* (1944), in which the stars played themselves entertaining soldiers. Many of the best-known all-star films have been war and action movies. *The Longest Day* (1962) about the D-Day invasion starred John WAYNE, Sean CONNERY, Richard BURTON, Robert MITCHUM, Henry FONDA, Kenneth MORE, Peter Lawford, Christopher LEE, and many others. Equally stellar was the cast of Richard ATTENBOROUGH's *A Bridge Too Far* (1977), which included Laurence OLIVIER, Dirk BOGARDE, Michael CAINE, Robert REDFORD, Anthony HOPKINS, and Gene HACKMAN.

A variation of the all-star movie is the film in which numerous well-known actors and actresses have CAMEO roles; perhaps the best known is UA's AROUND THE WORLD IN EIGHTY DAYS (1956). Occasionally, a movie becomes an all-star film in retrospect. Almost every member of the young cast of *The Big Chill* (1983) – which included Tom Berenger, Glenn CLOSE, William Hurt, and Kevin KLINE – subsequently became a star; even the corpse was played by a young and uncredited Kevin COSTNER.

Allefex machine A device formerly used in movie theatres to produce live sound effects to accompany silent films. The operator would pull the appropriate lever to produce such effects as 'smack', 'shot', 'thunder', 'telephone', etc.

Allen, Woody (Allen Stewart Konigsberg; 1935–) US director, writer, and actor, remarkable both for his output (approximately a film a year) and for the quality and diversity of his work.

Allen studied briefly at New York University and City College before becoming a gagwriter to such comedians as Sid Caesar and, later, a stand-up performer himself. The persona he developed – a neurotic, sexually insecure, Jewish atheist – and his gift for memorable phrases ("It's not that I'm afraid to die. I just don't want to be there when it happens") remain to this day.

Success in two Broadway plays, *Don't Drink the Water* and *Play it Again, Sam*, both of which he wrote, brought offers from Hollywood. His first film (as writer and actor) was the hectic farce *What's New Pussycat?* (1965); when this became a box-office hit, Allen was invited to participate in the spoof BOND FILM *Casino Royale* (1967). Neither of these films met with Allen's satisfaction, however, and he decided to work independently of the main studios, writing, directing, and starring in his own films.

Allen's first movies as a director, beginning with *Take the Money and Run* (1968), mixed slapstick with a style of verbal comedy sometimes reminiscent of the MARX BROTHERS. *Everything You Always Wanted to Know About Sex (but were Afraid to Ask)* (1972), and *Sleeper* (1973), a wicked science-fiction spoof, revealed a growing confidence. With *Love and Death* (1975) the jokes were still in evidence, but the parody (Tolstoy, BERGMAN) was becoming more highbrow.

Perhaps as a reaction to being seen purely as a funny man, Allen has produced a number of self-consciously 'difficult', almost Chekovian films, such as *Interiors* (1978) and *September* (1987). *Stardust Memories* (1980), in which Allen plays a lugubrious comedian turned film director, also suggested a limited patience with his public image.

Allen's most enduring films, however, are those in which his wry observations on love and angst fall from the lips of strong engaging characters, usually drawn from New York's chattering classes. ANNIE HALL (1977) still had the great one-liners ("Don't knock masturbation; it's sex with someone you love") but offered much more besides. It won Allen Oscars for Best Picture, Best Director, and Best Screenplay (with Marshall Brickman). MANHATTAN (1979) and *Hannah and Her Sisters* (1986), which again won Allen the Oscar for Best Screenplay, covered similar ground. *Broadway Danny*

Rose and *The Purple Rose of Cairo* (both 1984) saw Allen exploring the relationship between popular entertainment and reality, while ZELIG (1983), a tale of a human chameleon, was another hint that Allen wished to be seen as wide-ranging in his interests and styles. Subsequent films have included *Radio Days* (1987) and *Crimes and Misdemeanours* (1989).

Although Allen has always denied that his films are autobiographical, he frequently casts the women in his life (Diane KEATON, Mia FARROW) and his friends (Tony Roberts). Many likewise detected parallels between Allen's *Husbands and Wives* (1992) and his acrimonious divorce from Farrow. The serious allegations that emerged as the pair struggled for custody of their various (mainly adopted) children would have irreparably damaged the reputation and self-confidence of a lesser artist, but *Bullets over Broadway* (1994), nominated for no less than seven Oscars, seems to indicate that Allen's immense abilities remain unimpaired.

Allied Artists *See* MONOGRAM.

Allyson, June (Ella Geisman; 1917–)
Husky-voiced US actress, whose girl-next-door image brought her roles as cute teenagers in the 1940s and devoted wives in the 1950s.

Born in New York City, Allyson enjoyed a five-year career on Broadway before making her screen debut with the successful musical *Best Foot Forward* (1943). She subsequently became known as one of the 'MGM kids', a group of younger performers that also included Judy GARLAND and Mickey ROONEY. Her popular musicals included *Two Girls and a Sailor* (1944), with Gloria de Haven and Van JOHNSON, and *Good News* (1947), as the fellow college student of Peter Lawford. This was followed by straight acting roles in THE THREE MUSKETEERS (1948), with Gene KELLY, and *Little Women* (1949), in which she played Jo as a much softer character than Katharine HEPBURN had in the 1933 version.

In 1954 Allyson played the inspirational wife of the famous band-leader in *The Glenn Miller Story* (Miller being played by James STEWART). Allyson herself, who had married the actor Dick POWELL in 1945, claimed to be "anything but the perfect wife." The following year she gave one of her best dramatic performances as the nagging wife of Jose

Ferrer in *The Shrike*. She left MGM in 1956, later remarking:

> MGM was my mother and father, mentor and guide, my all-powerful and benevolent crutch. When I left them, it was like walking into space.

She subsequently worked mainly on television and the stage.

Almodóvar, Pedro (1949–) Spanish director, who emerged in the 1980s as one of the most colourful and controversial figures in European cinema.

Born in rural La Mancha, Almodóvar moved to Madrid when he was 17 and has made most of his films there. While working for the national telephone company, he became interested in the New Wave of Spanish cinema and began to write criticism. After teaching himself the rudiments of film-making, he made a series of outrageous underground films that earned comparisons with BUÑUEL and John WATERS amongst others. Such early films as *Pepi, Luci, Bom and Other Girls on the Heap* (1980) and *Dark Habits* (1983), a typically black farce about scandalous activities in a convent, were notable for their anarchic style and provocative concentration on female sexuality. A recurring theme is the clash between traditional Spanish attitudes and the demands of liberated young women. These films quickly established their director as a leading figure in *la movida*, the irreverent cultural movement that emerged in the wake of the death of General Franco (1975).

In the mid 1980s Almodóvar moved closer to the cinematic mainstream with such films as *What Have I Done to Deserve This?* (1984), a fast-moving comedy about a frustrated housewife, *Matador* (1985), *The Law of Desire* (1987), and *Women on the Verge of a Nervous Breakdown* (1988), all of which starred Carmen Maura. The last of these, a frenzied farce with an absurd plot involving Islamic terrorists and a pot of drug-laced gazpacho, won 50 awards and brought Almodóvar international fame. *Tie Me Up! Tie Me Down!* (1989), about a young actress (Victoria Abril) who falls in love with her kidnapper, caused a furore among feminists who mistakenly thought it condoned rape. Abril also starred in *High Heels* (1991). *Kika* (1993), a return to the kitschy melodramatic style of earlier work, received generally poor reviews and ran into censorship problems in America.

One of the few motion pictures in which you can see a woman in a leopardskin coat urinate on the head of a police sergeant's wife during a knitting class.

ROBERT CHALMERS, on *Pepi, Luci, Bom....*

alone. I want to be alone A catchphrase associated with the reclusive actress Greta GARBO, especially during her long retirement (1941–90). Garbo spoke the words in *Grand Hotel* (1932), in which she played an aloof and lonely ballerina.

I didn't say I wanted to be alone, I said I wanted to be *left* alone.

GRETA GARBO.

Altman, Robert (1922–) Maverick US director and screenwriter, best known for his landmark black comedy M*A*S*H (1970). He has maintained a prolific output of more than one film a year, mainly through his own production companies.

Born in Kansas City, Altman studied engineering at the University of Missouri and served as a bomber pilot during World War II. Having failed to become a Hollywood screenwriter, he spent six years producing industrial documentaries. He wrote, directed, and produced his first feature, *The Delinquents* in 1957, but it was a further ten years before he made his first major film, *Countdown* (1967) with James CAAN and Robert DUVALL as astronauts.

Altman's reputation was established three years later with the Oscar-nominated satire *M*A*S*H*, featuring Elliott Gould and Donald SUTHERLAND as doctors in a field hospital. His main technical achievement here was the use of improvisation and overlapping dialogue to achieve an effect of verisimilitude. These techniques were repeated in his masterpiece, *Nashville* (1975), which earned him another Oscar nomination for its satirical look at modern America through the country music business. The film cuts deftly between the stories of over 20 different characters and features brilliant ensemble scenes. The actors contributed to the script and in some cases wrote their own songs, with Keith CARRADINE winning an Oscar for his 'I'm Easy'.

Altman's other films of the 1970s were less well received. These included the atmospheric Western *McCabe and Mrs Miller* (1971), with Warren BEATTY and Julie Christie, and *Buffalo Bill and the Indians* (1976), an expensive flop with Paul NEWMAN as William Cody. In 1979 the critic Pauline KAEL

noted: "Altman has reached the point of wearing his failures like medals."

His more recent films have enjoyed greater success. *The Player* (1992) stars Tim ROBBINS as a Hollywood executive who is driven to murder by a series of threatening postcards from a writer whose calls he failed to return. The film is packed with Hollywood IN-JOKES and features CAMEOS by 65 stars, who agreed to take part for a nominal fee. Warren Beatty was allegedly excluded from this line-up because he failed to return Altman's calls. *Short Cuts* (1994), a film based on several stories by Raymond Carver, earned Altman another Oscar nomination and shared the Golden Lion at the Venice Film Festival (with Krzysztof KIEŚLOWSKI's *Blue*). By contrast *Prêt-à-porter* (1995), an all-star satire on the fashion world, was poorly received.

I don't think a really good film has been made yet.

ROBERT ALTMAN.

Amarcord (1973) Federico FELLINI's nostalgic film about his hometown of Rimini, which he re-created on the CINECITTÀ soundstage and lot. When the British director David LEAN dropped in on the production he was amazed to see Fellini film a gigantic ocean liner (constructed from papier-mâché) moving across the set in just two takes. *Amarcord* won the Oscar for Best Foreign Film and earned Fellini nominations for both his direction and his script.

The project began life as *Hammarcord – l'uomo invaso* (the profaned man) but was subsequently renamed *Amarcord*, a word of uncertain meaning. According to Fellini, its theme is the "isolation from reality" that Italians underwent during World War II. Although it features an outlandish dramatic personae including a midget nun, a perverted priest, and a royal prince, the film centres on the sexual awakening of the adolescent boy Titta (Bruno Zanin). Fellini tried by various means to persuade the retired actress Sandra Milo to play the voluptuous Gradisca, on one occasion sending her a hundred roses; when she refused, the part went to Magali Noël, the only established star in the cast.

Amarcord lacks a coherent plot, consisting rather of a series of kaleidoscopic vignettes, ranging from a snowball fight to a Fascist rally. In two famous scenes, the Fascists force Titta's father to swallow castor oil and Gradisca sexually amuses the prince in his room at Rimini's Grand Hotel.

Ameche, Don (Dominic Felix Amici; 1908–94) US light leading man, noted for his distinctive pencil moustache. Ameche, who had a background in radio and theatre, emerged as a star of comedies and musicals in the 1930s. Although much of his material was lightweight, his career outlasted that of most of his contemporaries; he won an Academy Award for his performance in *Cocoon* (1985).

Ameche made his screen debut in *Beauty at the World's Fair* (1933), a three-reel short. Supporting roles followed in several films, including *Dante's Inferno* (1935), Rita HAYWORTH's first movie. His first starring role was in *Ramona* (1936), a formulaic Western romance with Loretta YOUNG, whom he subsequently partnered in a number of romantic comedies. Later that year Ameche starred in *One in a Million*, the film that introduced Norwegian skating star Sonja Henje to the screen. This was followed by *In Old Chicago* (1938), a star-packed melodrama about the Chicago fire of 1871; with a budget of two million dollars, it was intended to top the earthquake movie *San Francisco*, a box-office hit of the previous year. It failed.

In 1939 Ameche played the lead role in the BIOPIC *The Story of Alexander Graham Bell*, a film that gave birth to a long-running joke that Ameche had invented the telephone; for some years afterwards the word 'Ameche' was used as a jocular name for this device. The 1940s and early 1950s brought numerous unremarkable comedies, romances, and musicals, a notable exception being Ernst LUBITSCH's *Heaven Can Wait* (1943), which provided Ameche with perhaps his finest role, that of a 19th-century Casanova seeking admission to Hell. His prolific output slowed in the 1950s and during the following decade he worked mainly in TV and on Broadway. His few films of the 1970s are best forgotten.

Ameche's career enjoyed a somewhat unexpected revival in the 1980s with a run of character roles in successful high-profile films, such as *Trading Places* (1983), *Cocoon* (1985), a comedy about alien-assisted rejuvenation, and *Bigfoot and the Hendersons* (1986). His last films included *Cocoon: The Return* (1988), and *Oscar* (1991), an indifferent comedy starring Sylvester STALLONE.

America.   American Film Institute *See* AFI.

American International Pictures (AIP) An independent US production company founded in 1955 by Samuel Z. Arkoff and James H. Nicolson to produce B-MOVIES for the new youth market. Its low-budget offerings, which were lambasted by critics but proved popular with their intended audience, included the tongue-in-cheek *I Was a Teenage Werewolf* (1957) and its sequel *I Was a Teenage Frankenstein* (1957). The former, with Michael Landon, was advertised as "The most amazing motion picture of our time!" Several California beach films followed, including *Bikini Beach* (1964) with Frankie Avalon and Annette Funicello.

At much the same time, AIP unleashed the cult horror director Roger CORMAN, maker of the Edgar Allen POE adaptations *The House of Usher* (British title *The Fall of the House of Usher*; 1960), *The Raven* (1963), and *Masque of the Red Death* (1964), all of which starred Vincent PRICE. Corman also produced the gangster movie *Boxcar Bertha* (1972), Martin SCORSESE's second film as director.

In the mid 1970s AIP made a half-hearted attempt to move upmarket with such films as *The Wild Party* (1975), starring James Coco and Raquel WELCH; however, when the film was released, director James Ivory (*see* MERCHANT-IVORY) claimed that the studio had reinserted his cuts in "a cheap attempt to over-exploit everything exploitable." In 1980 AIP was taken over by Filmways, which two years later became part of Orion.

American National Standards Institute (ANSI) A US non-profitmaking organization that sets technical standards for cinema and television work in such matters as film size, perforation, etc. ANSI, formerly the American Standards Association (*see* ASA), works with SMPTE to establish cinematographic standards that co-ordinate with those used in other parts of the world.

American Venus Nickname of the US actress Vera Ralston (Vera Hruba; 1919–), a former ice-skater from Czechoslovakia who starred in a series of low-budget films in the 1940s and 1950s. Ralston became the protégée of Herbert J. Yates, the head of REPUBLIC, who married her in 1952. The nickname was almost certainly the invention of the studio's publicity department.

America's Boy Friend Nickname of the US matinée idol Charles 'Buddy' Rogers (1904–). His films, which are now largely forgotten, include *Wings* (1927), the first winner of the Academy Award for Best Picture, *This Reckless Age* (1932), *This Way Please* (1937) with Betty GRABLE, and *Don't Trust Your Husband* (1948). Rogers, who was also known as the **love rouser**, became Mary PICKFORD's third husband in 1937.

America's Favourite Lovebirds Nickname bestowed on the US actors Janet GAYNOR and Charles Farrell (1901–90), who co-starred in a series of popular romances in the late 1920s and early 1930s. Both retired in early middle age; Farrell later became mayor of Palm Springs, Florida.

AMPTP Association of Motion Picture and Television Producers. An organization of major film and television production companies, founded in Hollywood as the Association of Motion Picture Producers (**AMPP**) in 1921. Its main purposes were to represent the producers in labour disputes and to settle any quarrels between its members – as when Samuel GOLDWYN hauled Jack WARNER before the association in 1938 for poaching his choreographer, Busby BERKELEY. It also tried to set moral standards; in the early 1930s, for example, it censured members for the violence of the early GANGSTERS films. It developed from and is affiliated to the Motion Picture Association of America (*see* MPAA).

anachronisms The appearance on film of an event, person, or object that is inappropriate to the period in which the action is set. There are three basic types. Firstly, there are those attributable to an incomplete knowledge of the period, such as the inclusion of a shot of the Pan Am building in New York (built in the 1960s) in Sidney LUMET's *The Group* (1966), which is set in the 1930s, a casual mention of the planet Pluto (discovered in 1930) in Sydney POLLACK's *The Scalphunters* (1968), which is set in the 1880s, or the inclusion of creatures that are not from the Jurassic period in Steven SPIELBERG's JURASSIC PARK (1993). Secondly, there are those caused by a failure to notice something until it is too late; this includes numerous appearances of such out-of-time phenomena as wristwatches on Vikings and Roman legionaires, television aerials in pre-television days, vapour trails left by aircraft (always most noticeable in Westerns), and sightings of newspapers and other publications from the wrong period. In *Camelot* (1967), Richard HARRIS, playing King Arthur, clearly has a sticking plaster on his neck in one shot. The third type of anachronism is the entirely deliberate one that is used to make a point. In Alex Cox's *Walker* (1987), based on the adventures of a US mercenary in Nicaragua in the 1850s, cars and helicopters are included to suggest the continuity of US foreign policy.

anaglyph The stereoscopic picture produced when two superimposed images of the same person or thing, shot from slightly different angles, are viewed through special glasses (known as **anaglyphoscopes**). The spectacles have lenses of two complementary colours, usually red and cyan (greenblue), which correspond to the colours of the two images on the screen, thereby producing a merging effect. The technique was much-used in the 3-D experiments of the 1950s.

anamorphic lens A type of lens used in such WIDESCREEN processes as CINEMASCOPE and PANAVISION. During shooting, an image of about twice the standard width is compressed onto 35mm film by the unequal magnification of an anamorphic lens in the camera. When the film is screened, this distortion is corrected by an anamorphic lens in the projector, thereby reproducing the original wide image on the wide screen. The anamorphic lens was first developed for use in tanks during World War I: it was subsequently used in aerial photography before being adopted by the cinema in 1928.

Anatomic Bomb The nickname given to the voluptuous Italian film actress Silvana Pampanini (1927–), who appeared in such light comedies as *Scandal in the Roman Bath* (1957).

Anderson, Lindsay (1923–94) British director and critic, who established his reputation as a prominent figure in the FREE CINEMA movement of the 1950s. He was associate artistic director with the Royal Court Theatre (1969–75) and governor of the British Film Institute (1969–70). As a critic, Anderson regularly attacked the British film industry for its complacency.

Anderson began his career as a filmmaker with a series of documentary shorts, including the Oscar-winning *Thursday's Children* (1954). His first feature, *This Sport-*

ing Life (1963), based on the novel by David Storey, gives a brutal picture of life in the industrial north of England. Starring Richard HARRIS as a professional rugby player who develops an unrequited love for his landlady (Rachel Roberts), the film made an enormous impact on British cinema and put Anderson at the forefront of the emerging social realist movement. After several years of theatre direction, he returned to the cinema with *The White Bus* (1967) and *If...* (1968), a poetic, violent, and often funny fantasy about a rebellion in an English public school, culminating in a machine-gun attack on the parents and staff on Speech Day. (Anderson gained permission to film on location at his old school, Cheltenham College, but has not subsequently featured among the famous Old Boys invited to distribute prizes on Speech Day.) The film won the Best Film Award at the Cannes Festival and became something of an instant classic.

Anderson maintained his criticism of the Establishment with *O Lucky Man!* (1973), in which the hero of *If...* (again played by Malcolm McDowell) makes a spiritual journey through contemporary British society. His bizarre adventures include a stay at a research centre where a human head has been attached to a pig's body and culminate in McDowell being offered the lead in the film we have just seen.

Anderson's subsequent offerings, including *Celebration* (1974), the bitter *Britannia Hospital* (1982), and *Glory! Glory!* (1989), failed to recapture the appeal of his early work; *The Whales of August* (1987), starring the veterans Bette DAVIS and Lillian GISH, also roused comparatively little interest. Davis summed up Anderson's problem: "I think he's a very talented man, but...a difficult man to work with. He really prefers theatre and not film." Anderson made a cameo appearance as an actor in CHARIOTS OF FIRE (1981).

> I suppose I'm the boy that stood on the burning deck whence all but he had fled. The trouble is I don't know whether the boy was a hero or a bloody idiot.
> LINDSAY ANDERSON.

Andrei Rublev (1966) Andrei TARKOVSKY's magnificent epic of medieval Russia, now recognized as one of the masterpieces of Soviet cinema. The screenplay (by Tarkovsky and Andrei KONCHALOVSKY) weaves a series of fictional episodes around the life of the 15th-century monk and icon-painter Andrei Rublev (a historical figure). Having observed the suffering of his native Russia at the hands of the Tatars, Rublev is so traumatized that he loses the power of speech. He later regains his voice and his ability to paint after seeing a young peasant boy supervising the casting of a giant church bell. In a stunning climax, the black-and-white film explodes into colour to show details from Rublev's icons.

The film was immediately recognized as an enigmatic parable about the role of the artist in society, especially during troubled times. Perhaps because of this, it was banned in the Soviet Union until 1971, when it was released with cuts. Shot in CINEMASCOPE, the film is remarkable for its detailed reconstruction of medieval life, its unusual episodic structure, and the stunning photography of Vadim Yusov.

Andrews. Julie Andrews (Julia Elizabeth Wells; 1935–) British actress and singer, who became stereotyped as the proper young Englishwoman of sterling principles and dauntless self-reliance following early success in such roles. Having made her debut in variety as a child, she won roles in the radio comedy series *Educating Archie* and in the stage musicals *The Boy Friend* (1954) and *My Fair Lady* (1956). To her chagrin, she was passed over in favour of Audrey HEPBURN (whose singing voice had to be dubbed) when the latter was filmed in 1964. She had her revenge on the casting directors when she won an Oscar for her starring role in Disney's MARY POPPINS (1964). Andrews went on to enjoy still greater success as Maria in THE SOUND OF MUSIC (1965), which broke box-office records and established its star's reputation for wholesomeness. Subsequent films included *Thoroughly Modern Millie* (1967), *Star!* (1968), in which she impersonated Gertrude Lawrence to somewhat mixed notices, and *Darling Lili* (1969).

After a US television series flopped in the early 1970s, Andrews developed a hit cabaret act that gave greater rein to her gifts as a comedienne. In the 1980s she sought to cast off her saccharine image in several films directed by her husband Blake EDWARDS (who complained that her fans assumed she had violets between her legs). Despite appearing topless in *S.O.B.* (1981), prompting journalistic quips about 'Mary Pop-out', and experimenting with cross-dressing in *Victor/Victoria* (1981), she continued to be identified with the stainless heroines of her earlier films. Other attempts to challenge her public image have included sporting a badge declaring "Mary Poppins is a junkie."

> She has that wonderful British strength that makes you wonder why they lost India.
>
> MOSS HART.

> Working with her is like being hit over the head with a Valentine's card.
>
> CHRISTOPHER PLUMMER.

Andrews Sisters, the US close-harmony trio, who starred in numerous Hollywood musicals of the 1940s and became the biggest-selling female vocal group of their time. Of Greco-Norwegian parentage, sisters Patty (1920–), Maxine (1918–), and Laverne (1915–67) Andrews appeared together in such films as *Give Out Sisters* (1942), *Hollywood Canteen* (1944), and the Bing CROSBY–Bob HOPE vehicle *Road to Rio* (1947). Their voices were also heard in the Disney cartoons *Make Mine Music* (1946) and *Melody Time* (1948). Among the many hits they sang on screen were the million-sellers 'Rhumboogie' and 'The Boogie Woogie Bugle Boy'. Their signature tune and biggest hit was '*Bei mir bist du schön*'.

One of the most popular of all acts with serving troops in World War II, the trio finally parted company in the 1950s but staged sporadic reunions for television and cabaret. After Laverne's death, Patty and Maxine appeared in the Broadway musical *Over Here* with a stand-in replacing their sister.

Angel Exterminador, El (*The Exterminating Angel*; 1962) A bitterly iconoclastic film by the Spanish director Luis BUÑUEL, attacking both bourgeois morality and organized religion. The key work of the director's middle period, it recalls the surrealist fantasia of his early film L'AGE D'OR (1930) while also looking forward to his more polished later productions.

Made in Mexico, the film stars Silvia Pinal, Enrique Rambal, Lucy Gallardo, Claudio Brook, Tito Junco, and Bertha Moss as a group of sophisticated dinner guests who find themselves mysteriously unable to leave at the end of the evening. As the hours stretch into days, the outwardly respectable guests descend into suicide, incest, drug-addiction, and witchcraft. When the char-

acters eventually escape, they go to a cathedral to give thanks – only to find themselves once more imprisoned. At times hilarious and yet also touching and disturbing, the film has been hailed as one of the few true masterpieces of the SURREALIST cinema. One key to its success is the simplicity of the central idea; as Buñuel himself commented:

> I simply see a group of people who couldn't do what they want to do.

angle on A script direction calling for a shot in which one constituent of the previous scene is filmed from a different camera position. This is generally used to emphasize a specific person or thing: if the previous shot showed a house with a visitor at the door, for example, the written direction might be 'angle on man knocking on door'. It is also used to eliminate 'dead' cinematic time while maintaining a sense of continuous action. For instance, a shot of a man entering a long room at one end may be followed by an 'angle on' the man farther down the room. *See also* CUTTING ON ACTION.

animals A perennially popular attraction at the box-office, animals have played starring roles both in fictional films and in such nature documentaries as Disney's THE LIVING DESERT (1953). In supporting roles they often upstage their human colleagues, confirming the show-business cliché: "Never work with animals or children." Animal characters are also the mainstay of cartoons and other animated films, from Disney's MICKEY MOUSE to the plasticine dog Grommit in Nick Park's *The Wrong Trousers*, which won the 1994 Oscar for Best Animated Short Film.

Dogs are undoubtedly the most popular screen animals. The early British film *Rescued by Rover* (1905) is regularly cited as the first movie to make use of the principles of continuity editing. Hollywood's first canine hero, the German shepherd RIN TIN TIN, was followed by the fox terrier ASTA and the screen's most popular animal of all time, the collie LASSIE, who starred in seven MGM films beginning with *Lassie Come Home* (1943). The mongrel in *Benji* (1974) and the St Bernard in *Beethoven* (1992) were also great box-office hits.

Horses have also proved popular protagonists. Roy ROGERS's Trigger and Gene AUTRY's Champion became almost as well known as their riders. In the much-loved *National Velvet* (1945) young Elizabeth TAY-

LOR trained a horse for the Grand National; the remake *International Velvet* (1978) starred Tatum O'NEAL. Anna Sewell's *Black Beauty* has been filmed several times, notably in 1946, 1971, and 1994, while the beautifully shot *The Black Stallion* (1980) proved equally popular with children and adults. Felines are less frequently given starring roles in live-action films, exceptions being the Siamese cat in Disney's *The Incredible Journey* (1963) and *That Darn Cat!* (1965), and the lions in *Born Free* (1965). Cats have sometimes featured as creatures of mystery or evil, as in the horror compendium *The Uncanny* (1977).

Budgies featured in *Bill and Coo* (1947), which won a special Oscar but was described by James AGEE as "the goddamnedest thing ever seen." A deer was the focus of *The Yearling* (1946), otters starred in *The Great Adventure* (1953) and *Ring of Bright Water* (1969), a dolphin in *Flipper* (1963), a fox in *The Belstone Fox* (1973), and an Orca whale in *Free Willy* (1993). The orang-utan Clyde held his own with Clint EASTWOOD in *Every Which Way But Loose* (1978) and its sequel, while a pig was the centre of attention in *A Private Function* (1985).

Animals as villains include the shark in JAWS (1975), a wild boar in *Razorback* (1984), piranhas in *Killer Fish* (1978), birds in Alfred HITCHCOCK's THE BIRDS (1963), ants in *Them!* (1954), and spiders in *Arachnophobia* (1990). *The Swarm* (1978) employed some 22 million bees, whose human co-stars were covered by a $70-million insurance policy against stings. Models were used for the giant gorilla in KING KONG (1933 and 1976) and for numerous dinosaur films, most notably in Steven SPIELBERG's JURASSIC PARK (1993). Humans have turned into animals (and vice versa) in such films as *You Never Can Tell* (1951), in which an Alsatian is reincarnated as private eye Dick POWELL, and *The Fly* (1958 and 1986). This kind of metamorphosis is also, of course, a staple of the numerous vampire and werewolf movies. *See also* MONSTERS.

animation The cinematic process by which an illusion of life and movement is imparted to drawings or inanimate objects. It involves photographing one or more frames and then making slight changes to the drawings or models before the next sequence of frames. The best-known method of animation involves photographing cartoon drawings; other techniques include drawing directly on film and the use of models or other concrete objects. Up to 14,400 individual drawings (or adjustments to models) may be required to produce ten minutes of animated film. In recent years, the advent of COMPUTER ANIMATION has removed much of the drudgery from the making of cartoon films.

Many pre-cinematic devices, such as the Zoetrope, exploited PERSISTENCE OF VISION to create 'moving' images from a series of drawings. The earliest known animated film, Albert E. Smith's *The Humpty Dumpy Circus* (?1898), used STOP-ACTION photography to give an appearance of motion to models from his daughter's toy circus. The first known cartoon film was J. Stuart Blackton's *Humorous Phases of Funny Faces* (1907) and the first cartoon character Winsor McKay's *Gertie the Dinosaur*, introduced in 1909. In France, a series of pioneering cartoons was produced by the artist Émile Cohl (1857–1938) from 1908 onwards. Animated films for cinema distribution soon began to appear in America, where popular newspaper COMIC STRIPS such as 'Mutt and Jeff' and 'The Katzenjammer Kids' were adapted for the new medium. The most successful cartoons of the silent black-and-white era were those featuring FELIX THE CAT, the creation of Australian cartoonist Pat Sullivan and animator Otto Mesmer. Meanwhile a separate tradition was developing in Eastern Europe, where the Russian Ladislav Starevich used stop-animation to film small puppets from 1911 onwards. The Eastern European tradition has remained very strong, its most remarkable contemporary exponent being the Czech Jan SVANKMAJER. The German Lotte Reiniger created the first full-length animated feature, *Adventures of Prince Achmed*, in 1926.

From the 1930s Walt DISNEY, the creator of MICKEY MOUSE and DONALD DUCK, dominated animation worldwide. Following the introduction of sound and colour the films became steadily more sophisticated; in 1937 Disney's first feature, SNOW WHITE AND THE SEVEN DWARFS, won an Oscar nomination for Best Film, while the musical FANTASIA (1940) was widely hailed as a landmark in the development of the art.

In the 1940s and 1950s such animators as Hanna and Barbera at MGM, and Tex Avery, Walter Lanz, and Chuck Jones at Warner Brothers developed a more anarchic and boisterous style of comedy in contrast to the increasingly bland Disney. The undoubted star of Warners' LOONEY TUNES series was Avery's BUGS BUNNY.

Animation has continued to develop both technically and artistically. The integration of animated characters and live action, pioneered by Aleksandr Ptushko in the 1930s, was taken to new heights of sophistication in Touchstone's WHO FRAMED ROGER RABBIT? (1988). Computer-aided techniques have been used to create the remarkable sense of depth and motion in recent Disney features, notably *Beauty and the Beast* (1991).

animation camera A camera used to take single-frame exposures of CARTOON drawings or other animated subjects. In the making of cartoons, the transparencies (CELLS) are placed one by one beneath the mounted camera and photographed at the rate of about eight feet of film an hour. It takes about two weeks to photograph the average cartoon short.

Année dernière à Marienbad, L' See LAST YEAR AT MARIENBAD.

Annie Hall (1977) Woody ALLEN's popular comedy of modern sexual manners. The film traces the relationship of TV gag-writer Alvy Singer (Allen) and aspiring vocalist Annie Hall (Diane KEATON) from its tentative beginnings to its acrimonious end, when she leaves him for pop star Tony Lacey (Paul Simon). Borrowing its flashback structure from Ingmar BERGMAN's WILD STRAWBERRIES, the film combines deft one-liners with such alienation devices as direct speech to the audience and the appearance of Marshall McLuhan during a dispute in a cinema queue. It also contains much autobiographical material drawn from the lives of both Allen and Keaton (the two were involved in an affair at the time).

Initially, Alvy and Annie's growing insecurities were to be only one part of the story; science fiction and thriller elements were among those cut at the suggestion of editor Ralph Rosenblum and co-writer Marshall Brickman. Although some 50 hours of film had been shot, additional scenes were then required to ensure narrative cohesion. Described by Allen himself as a "trivial middle-class comedy", *Annie Hall* grossed some $36 million worldwide and took the Academy Awards for Best Picture, Best Actress, Best Director, and Best Screenplay.

When United Artists objected to the film's original title *Anhedonia*, Marshall Brickman proposed a range of alternatives including *A Rollercoaster Named Desire*, *Me and My Goy*, and *It Had to be Jew*. The final title alludes to Keaton's real name, Diane Hall.

Ann-Margret (Ann-Margret Olsson; 1941–) Swedish-born actress, singer, and dancer who progressed from playing cute teenagers in 1960s musicals to mature sex roles in the 1970s.

A native of Stockholm, Ann-Margret made her screen debut with a small part in Frank CAPRA's *Pocketful of Miracles* (1961). The following year she appeared in the musical *State Fair* with clean-cut Pat Boone, who insisted that the script be rewritten so they would not have to kiss. Her first big hit was the youth musical *Bye Bye Birdie* (1963), about an Elvis Presley-type pop star (Bobby Rydell) who visits a small town.

By the early 1970s Ann-Margret's transformation into an adult sex symbol was complete. In 1971 she was nominated for an Oscar for her performance in Mike NICHOLS's *Carnal Knowledge*, in which she ages from college student to middle-aged wife. Her role in Ken RUSSELL's *Tommy* (1975), based on The Who's rock opera, involved bizarre close encounters with soap suds and a washing-machine full of baked beans.

Ann-Margret's more recent films have included the sex comedies *Middle Age Crazy* (1980), in which Bruce Dern suffers a mid-life crisis, and *A New Life* (1988), in which she is divorced by Alan Alda. She has also starred in her own cabaret act in Las Vegas and elsewhere.

answer or **approval print** The first complete colour-and-sound print of an edited film returned from the laboratory. The director and producer often call for changes in the colour, GRADING, or other technical adjustments.

anthology film A feature film that consists of EXCERPTS from earlier films. Successful examples include *The Golden Age of Comedy* (1957), composed of classic sequences from the silent films of LAUREL AND HARDY, Buster KEATON, and others, and *That's Entertainment!* (1974), a compilation of MGM musical sequences with performers ranging from Fred ASTAIRE to Frank SINATRA.

A number of feature-length documentaries have also been compiled from newsreel footage, notably Carol REED and Garson Kanin's *The True Glory* (1945), about the final year of World War II.

antihero or **antiheroine** A protagonist in a film, play, or novel who lacks the virtues of a traditional hero or heroine. In general, popular Hollywood genres such as the Western and the war movie continued to present attractive conventional heroes long after such figures had disappeared from most serious literature. Colourful or complex antiheroes have also enjoyed a long popularity, however, and are now perhaps the rule rather than the exception.

Screen antiheroes can be divided into two main categories – those who are powerful and attractive but corrupt, and those who are ordinary and ineffectual but likable. One of the first Hollywood films to present a rounded picture of a charismatic but morally ambiguous protagonist was Orson WELLES's CITIZEN KANE (1941). Glamorous antiheroes have long been the mainstay of the GANGSTER genre, from the early Warner Brothers classics starring James CAGNEY to BONNIE AND CLYDE in the 1960s and the GODFATHER FILMS of Francis Ford COPPOLA. The FILM NOIR style of the postwar years created another cinematic archetype – that of the cynical wise-cracking DETECTIVE. The antiheroes of the 1950s were more self-conscious in their rejection of conventional values; celebrated examples include Marlon BRANDO in *The Wild One* (1954) and James DEAN in REBEL WITHOUT A CAUSE (1956). During the anti-establishment 1960s and 1970s brutal, cynical, boorish, or passive heroes became widely accepted as did stars, such as Dustin HOFFMAN, who completely lacked conventional good looks. More disturbingly, several films have successfully encouraged the viewer to identify with a character whose morality must ultimately be rejected: examples include KUBRICK's *Lolita* (1962), starring James MASON as a child molester, and SCORSESE's TAXI DRIVER (1976), with Robert DE NIRO as the demented Travis Bickle.

Although the cinema has presented a long gallery of wayward women, from the VAMPs of the silent era to the promiscuous waifs of the 1960s and 1970s, strong and sympathetic antiheroines have been something of a rarity. Indeed, the term is seldom heard. Any definition of the cinematic antiheroine would have to embrace the larger-than-life bitches played by Bette DAVIS and Joan CRAWFORD in their heyday, the *femmes fatales* of such noir classics as DOUBLE INDEMNITY (1944), and the heroines of the feminist ROAD MOVIE *Thelma and Louise* (1991).

Antonioni, Michelangelo (1912–) Italian writer-director, whose intense slow-moving dramas brought him a large international audience in the 1960s. After studies at Bologna University, Antonioni found work as a film critic and wrote scripts for Roberto ROSSELLINI amongst others; he also acted as an assistant to Marcel CARNÉ on *Les Visiteurs du soir* (1942). A year later he made his own debut as a director with the documentary *The People of the Po Valley* (not completed until 1947). His first feature film, *Story of a Love Affair* (1950), is a brooding study of the guilt shared by two adulterous lovers when the cuckolded husband dies before the lovers have time to kill him.

Antonioni's reputation grew steadily with *Love in the City* (1953), *The Girl Friends* (1955), for which he won the Golden Lion at the Venice Film Festival, and *The Cry* (1957). L'AVVENTURA (1959) was the first part of a loosely linked trilogy completed by *La Notte* (1960) and *The Eclipse* (1962). This sequence of films – all languid studies of emotional sterility and isolation in which narrative plays only a minor role – established Antonioni as a leading commentator upon contemporary social mores and made a star of the actress Monica Vitti, who also appeared in several of his later films.

The Red Desert (1964) was the director's first English-language film and, many would argue, his last classic. Another haunting examination of guilt and futility, the film is remembered for its subtle and painterly use of colour. BLOW-UP (1966), starring David HEMMINGS, was both an enigmatic thriller and a meander through fashionable London during the 'Swinging Sixties'. Although it became one of the most successful art films ever made, the movie now appears horribly dated.

Antonioni's first US film, *Zabriskie Point* (1970), was an incoherent critique of modern materialism as seen through the eyes of a disaffected student. *The Passenger* (1975), a major return to form, explored issues of personal identity through the story of a journalist (Jack NICHOLSON) who assumes the persona of a deceased gun-runner. His more recent works include *The Oberwald Mystery* (1981), based on a story by Jean

COCTEAU, and *Identification of a Woman* (1982).

In 1985 Antonioni suffered a severe stroke that deprived him of the power of speech. Despite this handicap, he made a return to directing with *Lies* (1994) and *Beyond the Clouds* (1995; assisted by Wim WENDERS). In 1995 he was awarded a special Oscar for his lifetime achievement.

> Antonioni...tells the same story all the time in the same style. To me he is like a fly that tries to go out of a window and doesn't realize there is glass, and keeps banging against it, and never reaches the sky.
> FRANCO ZEFFIRELLI.

AOC Ass on Curb. In Hollywood, a jocular instruction given by an assistant director to members of the production crew; it is used to specify a time for transportation by the studio bus or other vehicle, as in: 'AOC by 7 a.m. at San Vicente Boulevard.'

aperture In a CAMERA, the opening that controls the amount of light admitted through the lens and hence the exposure of the film. The size of the aperture is generally adjusted by means of a diaphragm.

APO Action print only. A film print without a soundtrack.

Apocalypse Now (1979) Francis Ford COPPOLA's powerful fable about human corruption, set against the backdrop of the VIETNAM WAR. The film was nominated for eight Oscars and won two, for Sound and Cinematography; it also took the Grand Prix at Cannes and some $74 million worldwide. Originally to have been an impressionistic study of the Vietnam War directed by George LUCAS (who made STAR WARS instead), the film began to take firmer shape when Coppola took over and suggested that scriptwriter John Milius base his plot on Conrad's *Heart of Darkness*. In the screenplay Willard (Martin SHEEN), a ruthless army captain, is sent upriver into Cambodia to eliminate a maverick Green Beret, Kurtz (Marlon BRANDO), who is conducting his own campaign with the help of Montagnard warriors who believe him to be a god.

A $12 million budget was assigned to the picture, which was to be shot on location in the Philippines. When the US government refused to cooperate with the production, President Marcos loaned his entire fleet of 24 helicopter gunships. These, however, were regularly ordered away without notice to deal with insurgents in the hill country. The project was soon plagued by ill luck in more serious ways. During the filming of a raid involving over 450 actors, extras, and crew members, the action got out of hand and the unit prop store received a direct hit. Then, Hurricane Olga hit the islands, depositing 40 inches of rain in just six days and destroying most of the film sets. No sooner had shooting resumed, two months later, than Martin Sheen suffered a heart attack; for a time Coppola feared for the life of his star, let alone the future of his picture. Fortunately, Sheen made a remarkable recovery. By this time, costs had spiralled to over $30 million, some $18 million of which had been raised from Coppola's personal assets.

He still did not have an ending for his story, and ultimately issued two: in the 35mm version (which involved the biggest explosion ever staged for the screen), the credits roll over a napalm raid on what critics took to be Kurtz's village (although Coppola always denied this), while in the 70mm print, Willard leads his young accomplice Glean (Larry Fishburne) away from Kurtz's camp.

A full account of the drinking and drug-taking that fuelled the production, of Coppola's mounting megalomania, and of the impact on the cast and crew of the arrival of Dennis HOPPER (who played a sleazy journalist) is provided by Eleanor Coppola's documentary record of the shoot, *Hearts of Darkness: A Filmmaker's Apocalypse* (1991).

> It was crazy...we had access to too much money and too much equipment, and little by little we went insane.
> FRANCIS FORD COPPOLA.

Applause (1929) Paramount's melodramatic backstage musical, one of the most technically sophisticated of the early talkies. Garrett Fort's script, which was based on a novel by Beth Brown, concerns an ageing vaudeville star who sacrifices her daughter's love to keep her off the stage.

Applause was the film debut both for its star, Broadway singer Helen Morgan, and for director Rouben MAMOULIAN, who had made his name as a stage director. Although hired for his theatrical flair, he became intrigued by the versatility of the film medium and employed many of the techniques developed by the Russian and German cinema, including quick CLOSE-

UPS, extreme-angle and overhead shots, and EXPRESSIONIST designs. He also created a filming booth on wheels for cameraman George Folsey, who used it to achieve a flowing track-and-pan style. *Applause* is now acknowledged as the film that revived CAMERA MOVEMENT in the somewhat static and stage-bound era of the early talkies.

Although filmed mainly in Paramount's Long Island studios, the movie also used real New York City locations and street noises.

apple box A strong box used to raise the height of an actor or object during a shot. It was often used to make short actors appear taller, especially when playing romantic scenes with tall actresses. Some, however, found the apple box too demeaning: the diminutive Alan LADD, for instance, preferred to have his female co-stars stand in a trench. This brought protests from Shelley WINTERS during the shooting of *Saskatchewan* (1954) and from Sophia LOREN who appeared with Ladd in *Boy on a Dolphin* (1957). The **half-apple** is a smaller version used by not-so-short actors.

approach The director's instruction to move a camera towards the subject or action. The commands **dolly up**, **camera up**, and **come in** have the same meaning.

approval print *See* ANSWER PRINT.

Apted, Michael (1941–) British film and television director. Born in Aylesbury, Buckinghamshire, Apted studied law at Cambridge and entered television in 1963 as a researcher for Granada. His first film for the cinema was the curious *Triple Echo* (1972), starring Brian Deacon as a World-War-II deserter who poses as Glenda JACKSON's sister – only to become the object of lecherous advances from Oliver REED. The pop musical *Stardust* followed in 1974, with David Essex and Adam Faith as a singer and his manager. *Agatha* (1979), based on the real-life disappearance of mystery writer Agatha Christie in 1926, starred Vanessa REDGRAVE in the title role and Dustin HOFFMAN as a US reporter on her trail.

In 1980 Apted gained international recognition with the US-made *Coal Miner's Daughter*, a BIOPIC of country singer Loretta Lynn, in which he directed Sissy Spacek to an Oscar. His other Hollywood movies include the Moscow police story *Gorky Park* (1983), with Lee MARVIN and William Hurt, *Gorillas in the Mist* (1988), starring

Sigourney WEAVER as Dian Fossey, the anthropologist murdered while studying gorillas in Central Africa, *Class Action* (1990) about father-and-daughter attorneys (Gene HACKMAN and Mary Elizabeth Mastrantonio) who take opposite sides in a court case, and *Nell* (1995), with Jodie FOSTER.

Apu Trilogy, The Three films directed by Satyajit RAY – *Pather Panchali* (1955), *Aparajito* (1956), and *The World of Apu* (1959) – that have been ranked among the greatest achievements of world cinema. The trilogy traces the rites of passage of a Bengali village boy named Apu, played by Subir Bannerji, Pinaki Sen Gupta, Smaran Ghosal, and Soumitra Chatterjee at various stages of his life from childhood to parenthood. Ray had longed to film the story ever since being commissioned to illustrate a children's version of Bibbutibhusan Bannerji's novel in 1945.

Although a founder member of the Calcutta Film Society and a keen cineaste, Ray had no production experience and embarked on the shooting of *Pather Panchali* (*Little Song of the Road*) in 1950 with little more than a visit to Jean RENOIR, then working in India, to sustain him. Circumstances forced him to abandon the project until 1952, when he pawned his wife's and mother's jewellery to purchase stock and hire equipment. His 40-minute silent ROUGH CUT was seen by agents of the Museum of Modern Art in New York, who requested its inclusion in an exhibition, prompting the Prime Minister of West Bengal to divert funds from the road-improvement budget to permit the film's completion. Initial reaction was muted, but the feature recouped its costs after a 13-week run in Calcutta alone and was soon hailed throughout the subcontinent. One Bombay critic wrote:

> It is banal to compare it with any other Indian picture – for even the best of the pictures produced so far have been cluttered with clichés. *Pather Panchali* is pure cinema. There is no trace of the theatre in it. It does away with plot, with grease and paint, with the slinky charmer and sultry beauty, with the slapdash hero breaking into song on the slightest provocation or no provocation at all.

Making extensive use of long takes, REACTION SHOTS, multiple points of view, and enhanced lighting to convey the brilliance of Indian sunlight, Ray fashioned an unhurried style that was to inform the remainder of the trilogy. *Pather Panchali* astonished the film world by taking the Jury Prize at Cannes in 1956, while *Aparajito* (*The Unvanquished*) won the 1957 Golden Lion at Venice. *The World of Apu*, in which Apu's wife dies in childbirth, is considered by some critics to be the crowning glory of the trilogy. All three films boast striking monochrome photography by Subrata Mitra and a sitar score by Ravi Shankar.

Arbuckle, Fatty (Roscoe Arbuckle; 1887–1933) US actor and director, whose career as one of the great stars of the silent screen ended in sensational circumstances in 1921. His nickname refers, of course, to his considerable girth – Charlie CHAPLIN is said to have used a pair of Arbuckle's baggy trousers to create his original TRAMP costume.

According to Hollywood legend, Arbuckle, who began his working life as a plumber, was signed up by Mack SENNETT, America's 'king of comedy', after fixing his drains. A more prosaic version has it that he was discovered in the course of conventional auditions. After making his film debut with the KEYSTONE COMEDIES in 1913 he quickly rose to star status with his lovable fat-boy image.

Although such comedies as *Fatty and Mabel's Simple Life* (1915), one of several films in which he co-starred with Mabel Normand, *The Bell Boy* (1917), and *Gasoline Gus* (1921), proved big box-office hits, his career fell apart in the most spectacular way following the death of a starlet at a party in a San Francisco hotel in 1921. The dying girl's words, "He hurt me, Roscoe hurt me", led to lurid rumours of violent and unusual sexual practices and to Arbuckle's trial for rape and manslaughter. Although Arbuckle was eventually acquitted, his reputation was irredeemably damaged by details of his sexual philandering exposed during the trial. His acting career came to an immediate end, despite the defence of such loyal friends as Buster KEATON. The scandal led the studios to impose new restrictions on both the content of their films and the off-screen behaviour of the stars (*see* HAYS CODE).

One of the first notable casualties of the Hollywood star system, Arbuckle made a few half-hearted attempts at a comeback before his premature death. He remained in the film industry as a director, working

under the somewhat ironic pseudonym Will(iam) B. Good(rich).

arc. arc lamp or **arc light** A means of illumination formerly used for studio productions and in PROJECTORS. Its intense white light is produced by the electric current flowing between two carbon poles. Until the development of more sensitive film stocks in the early 1950s, the arc lamp was the only instrument powerful enough to illuminate indoor shots; the carbons in the lamp had to be replaced about every 40 minutes.

The most powerful arc lamp ever used on a Hollywood production was the 13,940 amp light used for *California* (1927); its beam could travel an estimated 90 miles.

arc out The director's instruction to move a filming camera away from a subject on a curved path.

archive *See* FILM ARCHIVE.

Arkin, Alan (1934–) US actor and director. Although best known for playing manic and vaguely surreal comic characters, Arkin is a versatile actor who has added lustre to a wide range of projects.

Born in Brooklyn, Arkin performed with a folk group before joining the Chicago Second City company. By the early 1960s he had appeared both on and off Broadway and in a couple of short films. His first sizable film role was in the Cold-War comedy *The Russians are Coming, The Russians are Coming* (1964), in which he played a Russian submarine commander. The film brought Arkin an Oscar nomination. The following year he played a psychopathic drug-smuggler who terrorizes a blind Audrey HEPBURN in the suspenser *Wait Until Dark*.

A second Oscar nomination came his way for a performance as a deaf-mute in *The Heart is a Lonely Hunter* (1968). Later that year he had the thankless task of playing a role already firmly associated with Peter SELLERS in *Inspector Clouseau*. Arkin's wife, the actress and screenwriter Barbara Dana (1937–) also had a minor role in the film.

In 1970 Arkin starred in Mike NICHOLS's screen adaptation of the antiwar satire *Catch-22*. Although the film was neither universally well received nor a great commercial success, Arkin's performance as the bewildered Captain Yossarian was recognized as a *tour de force*. He then made his debut as a director with the black comedy

Little Murders (1971), in which he also acted. Arkin's other films of the 1970s included *Last of the Red Hot Lovers* (1972), adapted by Neil Simon from his own play, *Freebie and the Bean* (1974), a comedy melodrama about two incompetent policemen, *The Seven Per Cent Solution* (1976), a very strange Sherlock HOLMES film in which Arkin played Sigmund Freud, and *Fire Sale* (1977), which he also directed.

In 1981 Arkin starred in *Chu Chu and the Philly Flash*, a comedy written by his wife and featuring his son, Adam (who co-wrote Arkin's next film, *Improper Channels*, 1981). *Big Trouble* (1986), in which Arkin co-starred with Peter Falk, was the last film to be directed by John CASSAVETES. In 1989 Arkin was cast to play a judge in *Bonfire of the Vanities* but was replaced at the last moment by the Black actor Morgan Freeman, in an attempt to counter the alleged racial bias in Tom Wolfe's novel. Arkin did appear that year in *Coup de ville*, an engaging and well-made ROAD MOVIE. His more recent films include *Havana* and *Edward Scissorhands* (both 1990). The all-star *Glengarry Glen Ross* (1992), based on David Mamet's play about the high-pressure existence of salesmen, saw Arkin give a deeply affecting performance.

Arkin is also the author of a number of children's books, a songwriter, and an exhibited photographer.

Arletty (Léonie Bathiat; 1898–1992) French actress, whose performance as the worldly-wise courtesan Garance in the classic LES ENFANTS DU PARADIS (1944) prompted comparisons with GARBO and DIETRICH. Her refusal to go to Hollywood, however, limited her international fame.

The daughter of a miner, whose death in an accident plunged the family into extreme poverty, she worked as a model for Matisse and other artists before establishing her reputation as a stage and film actress. Frequently cast as a prostitute or 'woman of the world', she made her name with her cool mocking performances in such films as *Le Petit Chose* (1938). Before making *Les Enfants du paradis*, she starred in three other films by its director, Marcel CARNÉ; these were the gloomy *Hôtel du nord* (1938) with Louis Jouvet, *Le Jour se lève* (1939) with Jean GABIN, and the allegorical *Les Visiteurs du soir* (1943). Like *Les Enfants*, the last was made under extremely difficult circumstances during the German Occupation.

At the end of World War II Arletty was condemned to death by a tribunal in Algiers because of her love affair with a German officer; she eventually served two months in prison as a collaborator. Her career never really recovered. In the 1960s she was reduced to supporting roles, having become virtually blind after an accident with her eye-drops. She was described by one journalist who met her at this time as "the loneliest woman I have ever met."

After seeing *Les Enfants du paradis* Marlon BRANDO fancied himself in love with Arletty, and on his first trip to Paris demanded to meet her. "Was that a mistake!" he later commented. "What a disillusionment! She was a tough article."

Arliss, George (George Augustus Andrews; 1868–1946) British actor, nicknamed the **First Gentleman of the Screen**, who established himself as a Hollywood star after many years as a stage performer on both sides of the Atlantic. Considered second only to Charlie CHAPLIN as a box-office draw in the mid 1920s, he commanded a huge salary and great critical respect, though his performances now seem mannered.

At his best playing royalty, statesmen, millionaires and other elevated roles, Arliss won high praise in such films as *The Green Goddess* (1923 and 1930), in which he played an Anglophobic rajah, and *Disraeli* (1921 and 1929), the later version of which brought him an Oscar and accolades as 'the Finest Actor of the Talking Screen'. In *The House of Rothschild* (1934) he gave one of his most memorable performances as the head of the banking dynasty.

Arliss's autocratic persona was an extension of his off-screen character: conditions laid down in his contract with any director brave enough to take him on included the stipulation that filming must end at 4.30 p.m. without fail, as he disliked working late.

In a court of law Arliss once described himself as the greatest living actor, justifying this immodest declaration with the excuse: "You see, I am on oath."

Armstrong, Gillian (1950–) Australian director who played a key role in the Australian New Wave of the 1970s and 1980s and has since alternated between home and Hollywood.

Although she had originally intended to become a film editor, Armstrong was encouraged to direct while studying at the Australian Film and Television School. One of her school films, *Gretel*, was the Australian entry at the Grenoble International Festival of Short Films in 1973. Among her earliest work was the documentary short *Smokes and Lollies* (1975), the first of a rites-of-passage trilogy that continued with *14's Good, 18's Better* (1980) and *Bingo, Bridesmaids and Braces* (1988).

With *My Brilliant Career* (1978) Armstrong became the first woman to direct an Australian feature since Paulette McDonagh in the early 1930s. Adapted from Miles Franklin's autobiographical novel, it starred Judy Davis as Sybella Melvyn, a headstrong 19th-century woman who is prepared to flaunt social convention to fulfil her literary ambitions. The picture won seven Australian Film Institute Awards, including Best Picture and Best Director. Armstrong also took the British Critics' Award for Best Newcomer.

Since making *Starstruck* (1982), a rock opera set in post-punk Sydney, Armstrong has switched from contemporary subjects to period drama with great facility. Turn-of-the-century Pittsburgh was the setting for *Mrs Soffel* (1984), her Hollywood debut; the film stars Diane KEATON as a prison warden's wife who abets Mel GIBSON and Matthew Modine in their escape. Back in Australia, Armstrong directed *High Tide* (1987), in which Judy Davis is reunited with the daughter she abandoned years before, and the powerful study of dysfunctional family life *The Last Days of Chez Nous* (1992). She disowned her drama about the Cuban 'raft people' *Fires Within* (1991) after it was recut by MGM to highlight the sex scenes between Jimmy Smits and Greta Scacchi. Nevertheless, she was lured back to America to direct a new version of Louisa M. Alcott's *Little Women* (1994), starring Susan SARANDON as Marmee and Winona RYDER as Jo. Although the film once more addresses women's issues, Armstrong resists the label 'feminist director':

> Of course I believe in women's rights, and of course I wouldn't do a film that was sexist, but that doesn't mean I want to make commercials for the women's movement. I've always thought that the best way to carry a message is with a bit of entertainment.

Arnold, Jack (1912–92) US director, one of the few to treat both FANTASY subjects and the 3-D process with respect. During World War II Arnold served in the signal corps and worked under the famous documentary maker Robert FLAHERTY. Following the end of hostilities he made the documentary *With These Hands*, which was nominated for an Academy Award and led to a contract with Universal. There he directed the studio's first 3-D science-fiction movie, *It Came from Outer Space* (1953), from a Ray Bradbury story. The film, which makes atmospheric use of desert locations, was a major influence on Steven SPIELBERG's *Close Encounters of the Third Kind* (1977). Its star Richard Carlson returned for Arnold's THE CREATURE FROM THE BLACK LAGOON (1954), while the amphibious 'gillman' from that film reappeared in *Revenge of the Creature* (1955).

Tarantula (1955) was followed by Arnold's masterpiece, *The Incredible Shrinking Man* (1957). This is the tale of a man, who, having been caught in radioactive fallout, shrinks over a period of weeks, encountering various perils suitable to his declining size before coming to a philosophical acceptance of his condition. It demonstrates Arnold's main strengths: an ability to combine outrageous fantasy with a sense of reality, and a talent for devising set pieces that illustrate the central concept of a movie – in this case an epic battle with a household spider.

Unfortunately, Arnold was soon diverted into such inferior projects as *The Space Children* and *Monster on the Campus* (both 1958). A year later he jumped at the chance to work with Peter SELLERS on *The Mouse that Roared* (1959), Arnold's first colour project and his favourite film. A satirical comedy in which Sellers plays three roles (including that of grand duchess Gloriana), the film was a massive international hit. Arnold subsequently moved into television, returning to the cinema for a handful of undistinguished films in the 1960s and 1970s.

Around the World in Eighty Days (1956) Michael Anderson's film adaptation of Jules Verne's novel; a big box-office success, it also picked up Oscars for Best Picture, Best Screenplay, Best Cinematography (colour), Best Score, and Best Film Editing.

The plot concerns the adventures of Phileas Fogg (David NIVEN), a Victorian gentleman who makes a wager with his fellow club members that he can circumnavigate the globe in a mere 80 days. He is accompanied on his travels by his valet Passpartout (played by the Mexican actor Cantinflas) and tracked by a detective (Robert NEWTON), who believes Fogg to be responsible for a robbery at the Bank of England.

In reality, this plot is little more than an excuse for an extravaganza. A consummate exercise in showmanship, the film made use of 150 sets, was shot in more than 100 locations in 13 countries, and featured 70,000 performers. Amongst the unusual or exotic modes of transport to be featured in the film are hot-air ballooning, elephant-riding in India, and even travelling by ostrich. The cinematography, with its luscious saturated colours, earned an Oscar for Lionel Lindon. The film also began a trend by having a series of major stars appear in CAMEO roles. Amongst the 45 'all-star-extras' appearing in the film were Marlene DIETRICH, John GIELGUD, Buster KEATON, John MILLS, Noël COWARD, George RAFT, and the US television broadcaster Ed Murrow.

arranger A person who adapts or orchestrates MUSIC for a film score. During Hollywood's Golden Era, music was usually arranged for a studio orchestra. One of the first important arrangers was MGM's Alfred Newman, who composed or arranged more than 250 scores, including the music for WUTHERING HEIGHTS (1939) with its haunting 'Cathy's Theme'.

Arriflex lens or **Arri** A light portable REFLEX CAMERA that can use either 16mm or 35mm film. Introduced in the late 1950s, it was named after its inventors, *Arn*old and *Ri*chter, and was widely imitated. It's introduction was essential to the HAND-HELD technique favoured by the directors of the French NEW WAVE and the makers of CINÉMA VÉRITÉ documentaries.

Arsenic and Old Lace (1944) Frank CAPRA's frenzied black comedy, an adaptation of Joseph Kesselrings popular Broadway play. The story revolves around the Brewster family: Mortimer (Cary GRANT), a confirmed bachelor who is about to marry; his spinster aunts Abby and Martha (Josephine Hull and Jean Adair), who murder elderly gentlemen with poisoned wine in order to end their supposed loneliness; their mad brother Teddy (John Alexander) who, thinking he is Teddy Roosevelt, hides the corpses in the cellar believing that he is burying yellow fever victims in the Panama Canal; and

Mortimer's psychotic brother Jonathan (Raymond MASSEY), a mass murderer who has returned home to hide from the police. Jonathan is accompanied by Dr Einstein (Peter LORRE), an alcoholic 'doctor' who has performed hideous plastic surgery on his charge. To say that mayhem ensues would be an understatement.

The film features a running joke in which people seeing police pictures of the remodelled Jonathan comment on his resemblance to Boris KARLOFF; each time this happens Jonathan goes into a psychotic fit. The joke refers to the fact that KARLOFF played the role of Jonathan in the Broadway production. One line from the play was removed by the film censors. When Mortimer discovers that he was adopted by the Brewsters and is not a blood relation, thereby allaying fears that he may also become insane, he shouts elatedly to his fiancée: "Elaine. Did you hear? Do you understand? I'm a bastard!"

Arsenic and Old Lace was a pet project for Capra, who, on seeing the Broadway play, allegedly ran backstage to buy the rights only to discover that they had already been purchased by Warner Brothers. Capra then went to Warners' and persuaded them to give him a $400,000 budget to make the film. Using minimal sets – most of the film takes place inside Abby and Martha's house or in the cemetery next door – Capra managed to create a world of deranged eccentricity that remains carefully insulated from reality.

art. **art department** The members of a production team who design, build, and paint the sets, scenery, and props used in a film. Their activities are supervised by the ART DIRECTOR.

art director or **production designer** The member of a production team who co-ordinates the work of the ART DEPARTMENT in creating the overall visual style of a film. He or she may take responsibility for costumes and for scouting out location sites as well as for decor and sets, etc. Oscar-winning art directors include Cedric Gibbons for THE WIZARD OF OZ (1939), Vincent Korda for THE THIEF OF BAGHDAD (1940), and John Stoll for LAWRENCE OF ARABIA (1962). Japan's Yoshiro Muraki and Shinobu Nuraki shared an Academy Award nomination for their work on RAN (1985).

art film An experimental, intellectual, or artistic film produced outside the Hollywood mainstream. Early examples of art cinema include the work of the German EXPRESSIONISTS after World War I, the films of the French AVANT-GARDE in the 1920s and 1930s, and those of EISENSTEIN and PUDOVKIN in the Soviet Union. The art film emerged as a distinct category in the 1950s, a decade that saw the emergence of such individualistic talents as Ingmar BERGMAN and Akira KUROSAWA, the establishment of international cinema festivals, and the spread of independent ART HOUSE theatres.

art house A cinema that presents ART FILMS and other non-commercial releases, such as foreign-language films and revivals of the classics. In 1950s America, such lightweight British comedies as *Doctor at Sea* (1955) and *Carry on Sergeant* (1958) were often relegated to art houses.

Arthur, Jean (Gladys Georgianna Greene; 1905–91) Vivacious US actress who made her name in Frank CAPRA's light comedies of the 1930s. Director George STEVENS called her "one of the greatest comediennes the screen has ever seen." Although Arthur broke down and cried at the sound of her first voice test, audiences loved the high-pitched tremulous quality of the voice that Derek Owen has described as "the sexiest...in the history of the talkies."

Born in New York city, the daughter of a photographer, Arthur left school at the age of 14 to become a model. Despite making her film debut as early as 1923, in John FORD's *Cameo Kirby* (1923), her genius for comedy did not emerge until she appeared in the same director's *The Whole Town's Talking* (1935) – some 12 years and 47 films later. Arthur then dazzled in three Capra comedies: MR DEEDS GOES TO TOWN (1936) with Gary COOPER, *You Can't Take It With You* (1938), in which she falls for wealthy James STEWART, and MR SMITH GOES TO WASHINGTON (1939), in which she played Stewart's secretary. At the time she was probably the biggest star amongst the numerous actresses tested for the role of Scarlett in GONE WITH THE WIND (1939); although she had an affair with the film's producer, David O. SELZNICK, Arthur did not get the part.

Her performance in *The More the Merrier* (1943), in which she shares a wartime flat with Joel MCCREA and Charles COBURN, earned her an Oscar nomination. However, this success was followed by a bitter dispute with Columbia Studios that led to her virtual retirement. Her final role was the homesteader wife of Van HEFLIN in the classic Western SHANE (1953). In later life she played a lawyer in the television series *The Jean Arthur Show* and taught drama at Vassar College.

> She'd stand in her dressing room and practically vomit every time she had to do a scene. And...out in the lights, turn the camera on and she'd blossom out into something wonderful. And when the scene was over, she'd go back into that dressing room and cry.
>
> FRANK CAPRA.

artificial light In a film production, light derived from any source other than natural daylight. Until the introduction of more sensitive film stocks in the 1950s, all indoor and many outdoor shots required extra illumination. Artificial light is also used to provide balance, to highlight details, and to create or remove shadows.

Arzner, Dorothy (1900–79) US director, the only female director of note to emerge during Hollywood's Golden Era. Listed as one of the top ten US directors of the 1930s, she helped to gain greater creative control for directors by taking a firm negotiating stance with producers and studios. Her independent heroines can also be seen as feminists before their time. In Arzner's *Christopher Strong* (1933), for example, Katharine HEPBURN plays an aviator who ends an affair with a married man in order to pursue her career; at one point Hepburn told the director "Isn't it wonderful you've had such a great career when you had no right to have a career at all?"

Before entering the cinema industry, Arzner was a waitress in her father's Hollywood restaurant, drove an ambulance in World War I, and worked for a newspaper. Initially employed as a typist in Paramount's story department, she soon moved into editing and won attention for her work on such films as the VALENTINO vehicle *Blood and Sand* (1922) and James Cruze's *The Covered Wagon* (1923).

When Arzner told Paramount she was leaving in order to direct, the studio appointed her writer-director of *Fashions for Women* (1927). Her subsequent films include *The Wild Party* (1929), starring 'It' girl Clara BOW, *Honor Among Lovers* (1931), with Claudette COLBERT as a secretary fighting off her boss Fredric MARCH, and *The Bride Wore Red* (1937), in which Joan CRAWFORD plays a cabaret singer posing as a society woman to win a rich husband.

Arzner's last film was *First Comes Courage* (1943), about a Norwegian woman who decides to join the Resistance against the Nazis rather than flee with her lover. Although she retired later that year she continued to make training films and television commercials; she also taught at UCLA in the 1960s. In 1975 Arzner received a special award from the Directors' Guild of America (*see* DGA).

ASA   American Standards Association. The former name of the AMERICAN NATIONAL STANDARDS INSTITUTE. ASA standards for the cinema industry were created in 1930. The best known of these is the **ASA rating** for film emulsion speed, an index of a film stock's sensitivity to light. Expressed numerically, this rating is also called the *ASA exposure index*, *ASA speed*, or simply *ASA*.

ASC   American Society of Cinematographers. An organization established in 1919 by Hollywood photographers "to advance the art of cinematography." It promotes the interests of the profession, distributes information, and allows members to put the initials ASC after their names on film credits. The organization admits associate members from allied crafts. *See also* BSC.

Ashby, Hal   (1936–88) US director, noted for his offbeat anti-establishment films of the 1970s. Born in Ogden, Utah, he entered the cinema as an editor and went on to win an Oscar for his work on Norman Jewison's racial drama IN THE HEAT OF THE NIGHT (1967). Ashby's first film as director was *The Landlord* (1970), which examines the developing relationship between a rich White man (Beau BRIDGES) and his Black Brooklyn tenants. He followed this with *Harold and Maude* (1971), a peculiar love story about a suicidal teenager given hope by an eccentric 80-year-old woman (Ruth GORDON), who eventually becomes his wife. The film became a cult on US campuses.

Ashby's first box-office hit was *The Last Detail* (1973), about two seamen escorting a naive teenage sailor to prison – with several stopovers for wine, women, and song. Jack NICHOLSON gained an Oscar nomination as the foul-mouthed petty officer 'Bad Ass' Buddusky. Still more successful was *Sham-poo* (1975), a satire on the Californian lifestyle that starred Warren BEATTY as a womanizing Beverly Hills hairdresser who combines business and pleasure with Julie Christie and Lee Grant.

A year later Ashby's *Bound for Glory*, the true story of legendary folk singer Woody Guthrie, earned six Oscar nominations including Best Picture. Ashby earned his only nomination as Best Director with *Coming Home* (1978), an emotional film about the problems faced by Vietnam veterans and their families. Jane FONDA gave an Oscar-winning performance as an army wife who falls for the paraplegic Jon Voight at a rehabilitation centre.

Ashby's last great success was *Being There* (1979), a satire on media power in which an illiterate gardener (Peter SELLERS in his final role) becomes a national figure by mouthing homilies learned from television.

Ashes and Diamonds   (*Popiol y Diament*; 1958) Andrzej WAJDA's film about the dilemmas of postwar Poland. On the day after World War II ends, Maciek Chelmicki (Zbigniew Cybulski) is ordered by his nationalist resistance commander to assassinate the new Communist Party district secretary. Vacillating between duty and conscience, Maciek carries out his orders only to be shot in reprisal and dies on top of a rubbish dump.

Adapted from Jerzy Andrzejewski's novel of the same name, *Ashes and Diamonds* completed Wajda's trilogy of films about the war, the earlier parts of the sequence being *A Generation* (1954) and *Kanal* (1956). The novel, a perceptive and perplexing insight into the difficulties facing the Polish people after World War II, had previously defeated the attempts of several film-makers to bring it to the screen. Wajda's approach was to condense the action into a single day and to use a series of complex symbols and metaphors to explore the plight of both Maciek and his nation. The theme is summed up in a few lines from the poet Cyprian Norwida:

Here nothing but ashes will remain,
The storm in an instant to oblivion will
 sweep them;
From the ashes perhaps a diamond will
 emerge,
Shining victoriously for centuries,
It will have blossomed for you.

Andrzejewski was delighted with Wajda's interpretation and Cybulski's performance:

The measure of my satisfaction is that during the writing of the book I pictured Maciek Chelmicki entirely differently. Now when I see the film, I see him only in this way, as Cybulski played him.

Cybulski, who played the part wearing anachronistic clothing (including pale green-tinted glasses) to provide an associative link with the youth of the late 1950s, became a major star as a result of his performance. Considered Poland's answer to James DEAN, he also died young, falling beneath a train as it pulled out of Wrocław station.

aspect ratio The width-to-height ratio of a film image when projected. This varies from the former standard of 1.33:1 (*see* ACADEMY FRAME) to 2.55:1 in some WIDESCREEN processes.

Asquith, Anthony (1902–68) British director of the 1930s and 1940s, noted for his elegant and restrained style. He was the son of the Liberal prime minister H. H. Asquith.

Asquith, who was usually known by his nickname 'Puffin', entered the film industry in 1925 and co-directed his first movie, the silent *Shooting Stars*, three years later. His first major success was the classic version of Shaw's PYGMALION (1937), starring Wendy Hiller and Leslie HOWARD (who also co-directed). This was followed by a series of well-crafted films, including the costume melodrama *Fanny by Gaslight* (1944), the war films *We Dive at Dawn* (1943) and *The Way to the Stars* (1945), the Rattigan adaptations *The Winslow Boy* (1948) and *The Browning Version* (1950), and *The Importance of Being Earnest* (1951). Asquith's films of this period now seem to encapsulate the understatement and stiff upper lip so long regarded as essentially British. His later all-star vehicles, among them *The VIPs* (1963) and *The Yellow Rolls Royce* (1964), were less successful than his earlier work.

assembly The first stage of EDITING, in which the various shots are spliced together in correct script sequence to create a ROUGH CUT.

assistant. **assistant cameraman** A member of the camera crew, who assists the CINEMATOGRAPHER or CAMERAMAN in such jobs as loading the film and checking equipment. He or she does not usually operate a camera.

assistant director (AD) or **production assistant** A person who carries out numerous duties assigned by the DIRECTOR, such as supervising rehearsals, drawing up shooting schedules, and organizing production crews. The position is an obvious training ground for future directors; former ADs include John FORD, Howard HAWKS, David LEAN, and Roman POLANSKI. The assistant director is not usually involved in the creative aspects of making a film.

associate. **Associated British (Picture Corporation)** (ABPC) A leading British production company in the years before and after World War II. John Maxwell, a Glasgow solicitor, founded British International Pictures (BIP) in 1926 and the Associated British Cinemas (ABC) chain two years later; the ABPC was created in 1932. Associated British films were distributed by PATHÉ and shown on the ABC circuit.

In the 1930s and 1940s, ABPC produced a steady stream of comedies, musicals, thrillers, and romantic costume films at its ELSTREE and Welwyn studios. It also supported Charles LAUGHTON and Erich Pommer's Mayflower Pictures, which produced Alfred HITCHCOCK's *Jamaica Inn* (1939). ABPC's own films included Herbert WILCOX's *Piccadilly Incident* (1946), Hitchcock's *Stage Fright* (1950), and Michael Anderson's *The Dam Busters* (1955).

Shortly after World War II WARNER BROTHERS bought 37½% of ABPC, giving the latter an outlet of some 800 cinemas in America; in 1956, the distribution arm became Warner-Pathé. That year Associated British-Pathé financed *The Door in the Wall*, the first DYNAMIC FRAME movie.

All ABPC feature production ended in the late 1950s. After a prolonged takeover bid Associated British was acquired in 1969 by EMI, who revived Elstree production and made Bryan FORBES managing director (1969–71). The company was bought by Cannon in the 1980s.

associate producer or **line producer** A person who supervises the day-to-day making of a film for the PRODUCER. At a large studio, the nominal producer may be involved with managing several projects at a time and have virtually no creative input. *Compare* EXECUTIVE PRODUCER.

Asta The feisty fox terrier that featured in MGM's comedy thriller THE THIN MAN (1934) and its five sequels. Played by several dogs,

Asta was the pet of the sleuthing couple Nick and Nora Charles (portrayed by William POWELL and Myrna LOY). His screen popularity led to a boom in ownership of Airedales and wire-haired fox terriers in America.

The original animal also appeared as George, the dog who buries Cary GRANT's priceless dinosaur bone, in *Bringing Up Baby* (1936).

Astaire, Fred (Frederick Austerlitz; 1899–1987) Legendary US dancer, singer, and actor. Although his screen career began inauspiciously with the celebrated audition verdict "Can't act. Can't sing. Slightly bald. Can dance a little", he went on to delight two generations of film-goers with his effortless elegance and inventive dance routines, which put him in a class of his own. No dancer of any kind has succeeded in emulating his gracefulness and sophistication. In 1969 he received a special Academy Award for his "unique artistry and contributions to the technique of musical pictures." More convincingly, both Balanchine and Nureyev described him as the world's greatest dancer, while other performers made no secret of their envy:

> I'd love to put on white tie and tails and look as thin as him and glide as smoothly. But I'm built like a blocking tackle.
> GENE KELLY.

> What do dancers think of Fred Astaire? It's no secret. We hate him. He gives us a complex because he's too perfect. His perfection is an absurdity.
> MIKHAIL BARYSHNIKOV.

Born in Omaha, Nebraska, Astaire took dancing lessons from the age of five and subsequently danced with his sister Adele in vaudeville and on Broadway. After Adele's marriage in 1932 he went to Hollywood, where he partnered Ginger ROGERS in a string of successful musical comedies including *Flying Down to Rio* (1933), TOP HAT (1935), *Swing Time* (1936), and *Carefree* (1938). In nearly all these films Astaire worked closely with the choreographer Hermes Pan (1905–90). His early retirement, announced in 1946, lasted just two years: he returned to the screen in *Easter Parade* (1948) with Judy GARLAND, following this with further musicals including *Funny Face* (1957), with Audrey HEPBURN, and *Silk Stockings* (1957), with Cyd CHARISSE. He made his straight drama debut as a nuclear

physicist in *On the Beach* (1959) and earned an Oscar nomination as Best Supporting Actor for his part in *The Towering Inferno* (1974). His last singing and dancing role – undertaken at the age of 69 – was in Francis Ford COPPOLA's disastrous *Finian's Rainbow* (1968); bizarrely, some of the dance routines are shot in such a fashion that Astaire's still lively feet are out of frame.

> In Astaire's loose legs, his shy grin, or perhaps the anxious diffidence of his manner, he has found the secret of persuading the world.
> C. A. LEJEUNE, film critic.

Astor, Mary (Lucille Vasconcellos Langhanke; 1906–87) Elegant US actress. Although equally at home playing good women and villainesses, her reputation rests almost entirely on the latter. In 1936 she became the centre of a Hollywood scandal when her personal diary, including details of her love affairs, was produced in court during a custody battle for her daughter. The four-times married star also battled against alcoholism and once attempted suicide; her stormy and self-destructive character is reflected in her famous line from *The Great Lie* (1941): "How I do love to do things I shouldn't."

Born in Quincy, Illinois, Astor entered a beauty contest at the age of 14 and made her film debut the following year (although her part was cut from the released film). Fourteen movies later, she found acclaim in *Beau Brummel* (1924) with John BARRYMORE, her off-screen lover. The best known of her early sound films was *Red Dust* (1932), in which she battled Jean HARLOW for the love of Clark GABLE.

Soon after making the excellent *Dodsworth* (1936), about a married couple's adulterous affairs, Astor became involved in the real-life custody case that involved producing her diary. Her lover, playwright George S. Kaufman, was arrested for forging a version of the diary in which he was not mentioned. Astor said she survived her court appearances by drawing on her dignified role as Walter HUSTON's wife in *Dodsworth*: "I sat a little straighter, I wore clean white gloves, and kept my hands quiet."

The bad publicity had little effect on her career. In 1941 she co-starred with Humphrey BOGART in THE MALTESE FALCON, playing the mysterious Brigid, a dame without a heart, and with Bette DAVIS in *The Great Lie*. Although her performance as a bitchy concert pianist in the latter won her the Oscar for Best Supporting Actress, she preferred the role of Brigid. In her acceptance speech she thanked Tchaikovsky for writing the music she played in the film.

In her middle age Astor played a number of warm-hearted matriarchal roles, notably in MEET ME IN ST LOUIS (1944), in which she was Judy GARLAND's mother, and in *Little Women* (1949). In *Act of Violence* (1948), however, she reverted to playing a "two-bit tart", Hollywood's first prostitute since the introduction of the HAYS CODE in 1934. After developing a heart problem in the 1950s she went into semi-retirement, returning to the screen as a fading Hollywood star in *Youngblood Hawke* (1964) and a lethal old lady in Robert ALDRICH's *Hush, Hush, Sweet Charlotte* (1964).

Attenborough, Richard, Baron (1923–) British director, producer, and actor, who became a star of the British cinema in the 1940s and subsequently emerged as a leading film-maker and spokesman for the industry.

Attenborough's film debut as a frightened sailor in Noël COWARD's war epic *In Which We Serve* (1942) established him as the British audience's favourite coward – a role that he was to recreate in several subsequent films. After playing the villainous Pinkie in *Brighton Rock* (1947), from the novel by Graham GREENE, he managed to diversify into a wider range of character parts. *Private's Progress* (1955), *The Angry Silence* (1959), *The Great Escape* (1963), *10 Rillington Place* (1971), *Loot* (1971), and *Conduct Unbecoming* (1975) were amongst his many subsequent films as an actor. In 1993 he played the mad Scottish owner of a dinosaur theme park in Steven SPIELBERG's JURASSIC PARK. At one point Attenborough asked Spielberg if he could have a "marvellous death scene". The director replied: "Do you want a marvellous death scene or a marvellous sequel?" The following year he starred as Kris Kringle, a benevolent department-store Santa, in John Hughes's remake of *Miracle on 34th Street*.

In the late 1950s Attenborough began to interest himself in film production and set up two companies with the writer and director Bryan FORBES. Early successes included *Whistle Down the Wind* (1961) and *The L-Shaped Room* (1962). In 1969 Attenborough won numerous awards for his first film as director, *Oh, What a Lovely War!*, an imaginative adaptation of the Theatre Workshop production by Joan Littlewood. *Young Winston* (1972) and *A Bridge Too Far* (1976) demonstrated his mastery of the epic adventure film and his ability to orchestrate huge numbers of extras, talents exercised to the full in the spectacular biopic GANDHI (1982), which was 20 years in the planning and won eight Oscars.

His other films as director include *Magic* (1978), starring Anthony HOPKINS as a murderous ventriloquist, the musical *A Chorus Line* (1985), and *Cry Freedom* (1987), based on the death in custody of the anti-apartheid campaigner Steve Biko. *Chaplin*, his long-awaited film biography of the silent clown, opened to somewhat mixed reviews in 1992. This was followed by *Shadowlands* (1993), a poignant drama based on the later life of the writer C. S. Lewis (played by Anthony HOPKINS).

Attenborough was knighted for his services to the national cinema in 1976 and raised to the peerage in 1993. He has chaired numerous cultural and charitable bodies, including the British Film Institute and Channel Four television (1987–92), and has held the post of goodwill ambassador for UNICEF since 1987. He has been married to the actress Sheila Sim since 1945.

> He has always been something of a Brutus of the British Establishment: loyal and loving, but not averse to sticking the knife in when it takes a step too far in the direction of authoritarianism.
> NEIL SINYARD.

audience Those who watch a particular film at the cinema, or those who regularly watch a particular type of film.

The largest cinema audience ever assembled was 110,000 at the Oval Amphitheater in Columbus, Ohio, for a showing of D. W. GRIFFITH's *Boots* on a giant screen.

audition The sample performance given by an actor before a talent scout, director, or studio executive to demonstrate his or her suitability for a particular role. Methods of auditioning vary widely. Ernest Borgnine recalled that when he auditioned for *Whistle at Eaton Falls* (1951), the director Robert SIODMAK's only instruction was "Walk across the room and say 'panhandle'." *See also* SCREEN TEST.

August, Joseph H. (1890–1947) US cinematographer, who was recognized as one of Hollywood's most distinguished photographers but never won an Oscar. His films of the silent era include his debut, *The Narrow Trail* (1917), the Western *Tumbleweeds* (1925), with William S. Hart, and *Dante's Inferno* (1924), which contained a remarkable 10-minute vision of Hell. During the Golden Age of Hollywood he photographed most of the cinema's greatest stars including Spencer TRACY in *Up the River* (1930), John BARRYMORE and Carole LOMBARD in *Twentieth Century* (1934), Katharine HEPBURN and Cary GRANT in *Sylvia Scarlett* (1935), Fred ASTAIRE in *A Damsel in Distress* (1937), and John WAYNE in *They Were Expendable* (1945). Films in which his atmospheric visuals made a particularly important contribution include John FORD's *The Informer* (1935), set in 1920s Dublin, and William DIETERLE's THE HUNCHBACK OF NOTRE DAME (1939).

August's last film was Dieterle's *Portrait of Jennie* (1948), an extraordinary ghost story produced by David O. SELZNICK. Selznick thought the long shots beautiful, but detested the close-ups of his actress wife Jennifer JONES, calling them "wretched beyond words". Unknown to the production crew, August was seriously ill and died a few months later while still working on the project. Ironically, he received his only Oscar nomination, a posthumous one, for this film.

Aurenche, Jean (1904–92) French screenwriter, whose best scripts were written in partnership with **Pierre Bost** (1901–75). "Screenwriters," he once remarked, "have made many a director believe he has talent."

After working as a director of commercials and documentaries, Aurenche began writing film scripts in the late 1930s, achieving his first great success with *Hôtel du nord* (1938) for Marcel CARNÉ. Although he collaborated with other writers, including Jean Anouilh and Marcel Achard, it is for his work with Bost, beginning in 1943, that he is mainly remembered. The pair wrote several memorable screenplays for the director Claude Autant-Lara (1901–), including *Le Diable au corps* (1947), about a married woman's affair with a teenage schoolboy, the macabre comedy *The Red Inn* (1951), which was banned in Britain, the Stendhal adaptation *Le Rouge et le noir* (1954), and the comedy *En Cas de malheur* (1958) with Jean GABIN and Brigitte BARDOT. Their work for other directors includes the screenplay for René CLÉMENT's JEUX INTERDITS (1951).

Aurenche and Bost's literate and well-crafted scripts belonged firmly to the so-called 'Tradition of Quality' that dominated French film-making in the early postwar period. In the mid 1950s, however, François TRUFFAUT denounced this tradition, and the work of Aurenche and Bost in particular, as old-fashioned and uncinematic – the "*cinéma du papa*". With the subsequent rise of the NEW WAVE they remained out of favour until the 1970s, when they returned with a series of scripts for Bertrand TAVERNIER, beginning with the Simenon adaptation *The Clockmaker* (1973). Aurenche and Tavernier also worked together on *Que la Fête commence* (1975), about decadence at the court of Louis XV, and *Coup de torchon* (*Clean Slate*; 1981), a black comedy about a murderous West African law officer. A year later, at the age of 78, Aurenche adapted another Simenon novel for the cinema as *L'Etoile du nord*.

auteur A director who exercises authority over all aspects of the film-making process in order to convey his own personal message or vision. The so-called **auteur policy** (*politique des auteurs*) was first expounded by François TRUFFAUT in the journal CAHIERS DU CINÉMA (January 1954). According to this view of film-making, a major film can be regarded as the work of a single individual in exactly the same sense as a novel or painting. The auteur policy, which differs radically from the collaborative and genre-based approach of Hollywood in its Golden Age, was adopted by many younger filmmakers of the 1960s and 1970s. *See also* CAMÉRA STYLO.

authenticator A member of the production team who checks the script, props, costumes, etc., for historical or factual accuracy. Nevertheless, errors and ANACHRONISMS frequently creep in. In the case of *Indiana Jones and the Last Crusade* (1989), Steven SPIELBERG's authenticator failed to notice that the hero crosses the Atlantic in 1938 – a year before such flights began.

Autry, Gene (Orvon Autry; 1907–) US singer and songwriter, the leading cowboy star of Western B-MOVIES in the late 1930s and early 1940s. With his tuneful Western ballads he changed the persona of the screen cowboy overnight; he is also credited with luring back rural audiences who had come to prefer the free entertainment provided by radio. He went on to become one of Hollywood's top businessmen, owning oil wells, ranches, and the California Angels baseball team.

Ironically, Autry, who was born on a ranch near Tioga, Texas, hated horse-riding; he nevertheless brought fame to his movie mount **Champion**, whose hoofprints can be seen in the pavement outside GRAUMAN'S CHINESE THEATER on Hollywood Boulevard. Discovered by cowboy entertainer Will ROGERS while employed as a railroad telegraph operator, Autry began singing on the radio in 1928 and two years later made his screen debut in the Western *In Old Santa Fe*. His first starring role was in *Tumblin' Tumbleweeds* (1935). With Smiley Burnette as his sidekick Frog, he went on to make dozens of films for Republic Pictures, including *Melody Ranch* (1940) and *Sunset in Wyoming* (1942).

During World War II Autry served with the Air Transport Command and travelled the country promoting War Bonds; in his absence, Republic replaced him with Roy ROGERS, who quickly overtook him in popularity. After the war Autry went to Columbia Pictures and eventually became a producer of films and television series.

avant-garde The schock-troops of ART CINEMA; those directors in the forefront of new stylistic and technical ideas. The term, from the French for a military vanguard, was first used in an artistic sense in the 1910s and soon became particularly associated with film-making.

The distinguishing feature of most avant-garde cinema is its rejection of the narrative structures developed by Hollywood during the 1910s and 1920s. The first country to develop a recognizable national style in opposition to the Hollywood mould was France, Germaine Dulac's Freudian *La Fête espagnole* (1919) being widely regarded as the first true avant-garde film. The outstanding technical innovator of the period was Abel GANCE, who developed SPLIT-SCREEN and 3-D processes for use in his epic NAPOLEON (1927). The radicalism of the *first avant-garde* – a loose association of French film-makers that included the impressionist Louis Delluc (1890–1924) as well as Gance

and Dulac – was soon overtaken by that of the so-called *second avant-garde*. This included the work of ABSTRACT FILM-makers such as Fernand Léger and that of the SURREALISTS, notably BUÑUEL, who drew much of their imagery from the subconscious.

Meanwhile Russia and Germany saw developments that were to have a more direct impact on international cinema style. German EXPRESSIONISM made use of skewed camera angles, harsh lighting, and idiosyncratic design to explore extreme subjective states. In Soviet Russia, the main development was the radical use of MONTAGE in the work of EISENSTEIN and others. Dziga Vertov's *The Man with the Movie Camera* (1929) introduced the idea of the camera as a protagonist in the film, a concern of much later avant-garde cinema.

In the post-World-War-II period the availability of cheap 16MM cameras, the growth of university film courses, and the rise of independent production companies have led to a boom in avant-garde film-making in America. Noted experimentalists include Kenneth Anger (1932–), director of *Scorpio Rising* (1964), and Maya Deren (1908–61), one of the first directors of UNDERGROUND FILMS. In Britain the avant-garde is represented by the work of art-school graduates Peter GREENAWAY and Derek JARMAN. The European avant-garde also flourished in the 1960s and 1970s, owing largely to the greater availability of funding and to a flourishing ART-HOUSE market; works by ANTONIONI, RESNAIS, FASSBINDER, and GODARD have all enjoyed a degree of commercial success, despite their uncompromising style. More recently the avant-garde has been exploring multi-media work and computer image-manipulation, as in Greenaway's *Prospero's Books* (1991).

Avventura, L' (1959) Michelangelo ANTONIONI's bleak parable about loneliness, disloyalty, and the fragility of human relationships. It has has been credited with changing the language of the cinema by emphasizing image and feeling over dialogue and plot. Antonioni both wrote and directed this semi-thriller, which he described as "a detective story back to front". The film was originally savaged by *The New Yorker* but has since been selected as one of the Ten Best Films ever made in *Sight and Sound*'s poll of world critics each decade since it appeared. It also won a Special Jury Prize at

Cannes in 1960, despite being greeted with boos and hisses when it was screened.

The plot concerns a group of rich and bored young people who set off on a yachting holiday to Sicily. When they go ashore on a volcanic island, Anna (Lea Massari) disappears following an argument. A search of the barren island (brilliantly photographed by Aldo Scavarda) proves fruitless and the group eventually leave, hoping that she has made her own way back. As the search continues in town, a love affair blossoms between Anna's lover, the architect Sandro (Gabriele Ferzetti), and her friend Claudia (Monica Vitti). Anna is never found.

awards Prizes given in recognition of achievement and excellence in the cinema, usually in the form of trophies or medallions. The earliest known awards were presented at a festival in Monte Carlo in 1898; the longest-running are those presented by America's NATIONAL BOARD OF REVIEW since 1917. The most famous and prestigious of all cinema awards are, of course, the Oscars or ACADEMY AWARDS.

Other US examples include the New York Film Critics' Awards, the Directors' Guild Awards, the Hollywood Foreign Press Association's Golden Globe Awards, and the PATSY AWARDS to animal performers. The most coveted awards in Britain are those presented by BAFTA, the BFI, and the London Film Critics' Circle, while the French film industry has its Césars.

Many international film festivals also select the best films, actors, directors, producers, and technicians. The most prestigious awards are considered to be the Palme d'or presented at the CANNES FILM FESTIVAL, the Golden Bear at BERLIN, and the Golden Lion at the VENICE FILM FESTIVAL. The newest annual ceremony is the EUROPEAN FILM AWARDS, established in 1989.

Aykroyd, Dan (Daniel Agraluscarsacra; 1950–) Canadian-born actor, writer, and director, who became a star during the 1980s. Despite his popularity, Aykroyd, who prefers working in collaboration with other performers, has not yet managed to carry a film by himself.

As a youth Aykroyd was expelled from several educational establishments, including a seminary. He later worked on the Canadian comedy circuit before moving to America in the mid 1970s. There he developed his writing and performing skills during a four-year stint with the TV series *Saturday Night Live*, which was also responsible for launching the careers of John BELUSHI, Chevy CHASE, Bill Murray, and Gilda Radner, performers with whom Aykroyd would subsequently co-star in several films.

Having made his film debut several years earlier in Canada, Aykroyd began his Hollywood career in 1979 with performances in *Mr Mike's Mondo Video* and *1941*, Steven SPIELBERG's notorious flop. His first success came with *The Blues Brothers* (1980), a high-speed romp featuring Belushi and Aykroyd as two deadpan blues performers the duo had created for *Saturday Night Live*. Aykroyd also co-wrote the script with director John LANDIS. Despite a critical mauling, the movie became one of the cult films of the 1980s. The two stars appeared together again in *Neighbours* (1981), a comedy that cast Belushi as a middle-aged suburbanite and Aykroyd as his 'wild-man' neighbour.

Following Belushi's death from a drug overdose in 1982 and the disastrous solo venture *Doctor Detroit* (1983), Aykroyd returned to prominence with the highly successful *Trading Places* (1983), in which he co-starred with Eddie MURPHY. In 1984 he appeared alongside Bill Murray and Harold Ramis in the comedy fantasy *Ghostbusters*, a huge box-office hit. The film, written by Aykroyd and Ramis, was originally conceived as a vehicle for Belushi and was heavily revised following his death.

The following year Aykroyd appeared in two John Landis films, *Into the Night* and *Spies Like Us*, a hit-and-miss comedy that he also co-wrote. Aykroyd was also responsible for co-writing *Dragnet* (1987), a spoof of the long-running US television series of the same name. The film made judicious use of Aykroyd's rather laconic personality in the role of police sergeant Joe Friday.

Several lacklustre comedies followed, including *Ghostbusters II* (1989), before Aykroyd appeared in a straight role in the charming *Driving Miss Daisy* (1989). Freed from the constraints of having to be funny, Aykroyd turned in a performance of warmth and maturity that brought him an Oscar nomination as Best Supporting Actor. In 1991 Aykroyd made his debut as a director with the comedy *Nothing But Trouble*, in which he starred with John Candy and Chevy Chase. The film was described by one critic as "one of the longest 94 minutes on record." Aykroyd has subsequently appeared in the enormously successful *My Girl* (1991) and (as Mack SENNETT) in Richard ATTENBOROUGH's *Chaplin* (1992).

Ayres, Lew (Lewis Ayer; 1908–) US actor, star of the classic war film ALL QUIET ON THE WESTERN FRONT (1930), numerous B-movies of the 1930s, and the popular Dr Kildare series. He was married to the actress Lola Lane from 1931 to 1933 and to Ginger ROGERS from 1934 to 1941.

Born in Minneapolis, Minnesota, Ayres studied medicine at the University of Arizona until 1928, when he was discovered playing with a band at a Hollywood night club. He co-starred with Greta GARBO in MGM's last silent film, *The Kiss* (1929), and a year later won fame as the disillusioned German soldier Paul Baumer in *All Quiet on the Western Front*. In 1938 he played Katharine HEPBURN's drunken brother in the comedy *Holiday*.

The first of many films to cast him as a medical man was *Young Dr Kildare* (1938), with Ayres as the title character and Lionel BARRYMORE as the crusty diagnostician Dr Gillespie. Ayres starred in eight sequels, ending with *Dr Kildare's Victory* (1942); after declaring himself a conscientious objector, he was removed from the series by MGM, who shifted the focus of attention to Barrymore's character. Other studios black-balled Ayres and cinemas refused his films. He restored his reputation by serving as a battlefield medic, however, and returned to Hollywood to make such films as *The Dark Mirror* (1946), with Olivia DE HAVILLAND, and *Johnny Belinda* (1948), in which he played a doctor to deaf-mute Jane WYMAN. His later films include *Battle for Planet of the Apes* (1973) and *Damien: Omen II* (1978). He has also appeared in numerous television films and series, including *Battlestar Galactica* and *Salem's Lot*.

B

B. B-hive From the mid 1930s to the mid 1950s, a production company that specialized in producing B-MOVIES for DOUBLE-FEATURES. The best known were probably REPUBLIC, which produced numerous cheap Westerns, and MONOGRAM, which specialized in crime films.

B-movie Formerly, a motion picture made to be shown as a companion to a main feature (*see* A-MOVIE) in a double-bill programme. B-movies were made on low budgets, usually with lesser-known stars, and often with formulaic plots. Although such films were frequently derided for their feeble special effects and wooden acting, a number of actors who featured in B-movies later became stars (including the future US president Ronald REAGAN). Some critics consider the US 'made-for-television' film to be the modern equivalent of the old B-movie. *See also* CO-FEATURE.

Babelsberg A film studio in Berlin, the oldest still in operation; its first production, *Der Toten Tanz*, was filmed there in 1912. Some 7700 features have been made on the site, including Fritz LANG's METROPOLIS (1926) and Josef VON STERNBERG's THE BLUE ANGEL (1930). After World War II it became the headquarters of DEFA, the organization that controlled all film production in communist East Germany. Although some $88 million is needed for modernization, the studios, which occupy nearly 500,000 square metres, have more production capacity than any other in the reunited Germany.

baby. baby or **the baby** An affectionate Hollywood nickname for the film camera.
Baby Doll (1956) Elia KAZAN's controversial black comedy set in the US South. Adapted from one of his own one-act plays by Tennessee Williams, the film revolves around three main characters: Archie (Karl MALDEN), a cotton-mill owner, his young wife Baby Doll (Carroll Baker, in her first major role), and Silva Vacarro (Eli WALLACH), a rival mill owner. Archie has been told not to consummate his marriage to Baby Doll until her 20th birthday, and when his advances are repelled on the eve of the big day he burns down Silva's mill in a fit of frustrated rage. Silva exacts his revenge through Baby Doll.

The film was shot on location in the town of Benoit, Mississippi, and featured a large number of local residents as extras; a large abandoned mansion was utilized as Archie's home.

Although the sex scenes are tame by modern standards, *Baby Doll* attracted considerable controversy at the time of its release, being described by one film magazine as "possibly the dirtiest American-made motion picture that has ever been legally exhibited" and condemned as "morally repellent" by the Catholic LEGION OF DECENCY. Kazan's response was that he "wasn't trying to be moral or immoral, only truthful." The controversy, unsurprisingly, did the film little damage at the box office, where takings were much higher than expected. For a time the film was even advertised with the publicity line "Condemned by Cardinal Spellman."

Baby Doll was nominated for four Oscars – Best Actress (Carroll Baker), Best Supporting Actress (Mildred Dunnock), Best Adapted Screenplay (Tennessee Williams), and Best Cinematography – but won none.

baby legs Nickname for a short-legged tripod used to support the camera for LOW-ANGLE SHOTS.

Baby LeRoy (LeRoy Winebrenner; 1932–) US CHILD STAR, who made his Hollywood debut at the age of one and retired at four after making nine films. His contract had to be signed by his grandfather, since both LeRoy and his teenage mother were under age. According to Hollywood legend, LeRoy had a running feud with W. C. FIELDS, whose child-hating screen image carried over to child-baiting on the set: a famous story had Fields spiking Baby LeRoy's orange juice with gin while filming *The Old-Fashioned Way* (1934) and then complaining "The kid's no trouper" when he fell asleep. In fact, Fields sustained baby LeRoy's brief career by writing him into scripts despite opposition from studio heads.

In 1933 LeRoy appeared in five films, including *A Bedtime Story*, with Maurice CHEVALIER and the ALL-STAR FILM *Alice in Wonderland*, his first movie with Fields. His final effort was *It's a Great Life* (1936).

baby spot A small SPOTLIGHT of 500, 750, or 1000 watts used especially for CLOSE-UPS and angle shots.

Bacall, Lauren (Betty Jean Perske; 1924–) Husky-voiced US actress, at her peak in the late 1940s and early 1950s. Her screen partnership with Humphrey BOGART began with her very first film, Howard HAWKS's *To Have and Have Not* (1944), and soon developed into an off-screen romance.

Bacall was not at first thrilled by the choice of co-star: "Howard Hawks said he would like to put me in a picture with Cary GRANT or Humphrey Bogart. I thought: Cary Grant – terrific. Humphrey Bogart – yuck." Despite this, a certain sexual chemistry is apparent throughout their scenes, especially in the delivery of Bacall's memorable lines: "You don't have to say anything...just whistle. You know how to whistle, don't you, Steve? You just put your lips together and blow." Bacall and Bogart were married the following year and remained together until his death in 1957. The publicity aroused by the couple's romance, together with the maturity and self-assurance of Bacall's performance in *To Have and Have Not*, ensured instant stardom for the newcomer. Her characteristic deep voice, however, caused problems when the script called for her to sing: the closest match for dubbing purposes was found to be that of the teenage Andy Williams.

Bacall's next film was an adaptation of Graham GREENE's *Confidential Agent* (1945), in which she co-starred with Charles BOYER. The following year she appeared opposite Bogart again in THE BIG SLEEP, a convoluted FILM NOIR based on Raymond CHANDLER's novel. Again the on-screen chemistry between Bogart and Bacall was exploited to the full, one reviewer noting that a "sullen atmosphere of sex saturates the film." The couple also co-starred in Bacall's next two films, *Dark Passage* (1947) and *Key Largo* (1948).

After appearing in a couple of less memorable movies, Bacall revealed a hitherto unsuspected talent for comedy playing a gold-digger in *How to Marry a Millionaire* (1953), in which she co-starred with Marilyn MONROE and Betty GRABLE. For the remainder of the 1950s her career was somewhat low-profile, with only Douglas SIRK's family melodrama *Written on the Wind* (1956) making much of an impact. After *Northwest Frontier* (1959) Bacall did not make another film until *Shock Treatment* (1964), a murder mystery set in a mental institution. Her subsequent screen appearances have been infrequent and largely disappointing, with the exception of *Harper* (1966), with Paul NEWMAN, *The Shootist* (1976), with John WAYNE, *Mr North* (1988), and *Misery* (1990), a thriller based on a Stephen King novel.

> She has a javelin-like vitality, a born dancer's eloquence in movement, a fierce female shrewdness and a special sweet sourness...plus a stone-crushing self-confidence and a trombone voice.
> JAMES AGEE.

back. **background** In a film shot, the area behind the main subject or action. The background may be a natural location, a studio set, or a BACK PROJECTION of the required setting. *See also* FOREGROUND.

background music *See* MUSIC.

background noises Secondary sounds dubbed onto a SOUNDTRACK to establish locale or atmosphere, etc. Continuous background sound can also play an important role in creating the sense that different shots belong to the same unfolding scene.

Recordings of background sound are obtained from the most varied and unlikely sources. For the amphitheatre scenes in *Spartacus* (1960), the sound of the crowd was actually recorded at a 1959 American football contest between the University of Notre Dame and Michigan State University. *See also* BUZZ TRACK; ROOM SOUND; WILD SOUND.

back lot or **lot** An outdoor area at a studio used for filming. With the addition of trompe l'oeil building and street frontages, vegetation, and other props, a variety of settings can be convincingly created.

When GONE WITH THE WIND (1939) began production, Selznick-International Studios had a 40-acre back lot covered with old sets from such films as KING KONG (1933) and *Little Lord Fauntleroy* (1936). To film the burning of Atlanta, David O. SELZNICK merely added some cheap false fronts and set fire to the lot at night.

back projection A technique for combining studio action with projected images. Usually, a film is projected onto a translucent screen from behind, while live action is shot in front of the screen, to create the illusion of a moving background. Typical back projections include passing scenery outside a train window or a receding street seen through a car's rear window. Still photographs may also be used to create a background. The technique has been superseded by FRONT PROJECTION.

backstage In film production, any area behind or around a set that is not shown on the screen. The term was adapted from its familiar theatrical meaning.

A **backstage musical** is one that deals with the lives, love affairs, rivalries, etc., of theatrical performers during a show. Typically, the actors find their real-life preoccupations mirrored in their stage roles. Examples of this subgenre, which became especially popular in the early talkie era, include 42ND STREET and *Footlight Parade* (both 1933). *See* MUSICAL.

Bacon, Lloyd (1890–1955) Prolific US director and actor, who turned out fast-paced hits for Warner Brothers in the 1930s and early 1940s. Born in San Jose, California, he acted on stage before moving into films in 1913; his early roles included heavies in a series of CHAPLIN two-reelers including *The Champion* (1915), *The Vagabond* (1916), and *The Fireman* (1916).

Bacon began directing comedy shorts in 1921 and made his first feature, *Private Izzy Murphy*, in 1926. Two years later, his reputation was established with the Warner Brothers musical *The Singing Fool*, starring Al JOLSON. The studio went on to use his talents on the Busby BERKELEY extravaganzas 42ND STREET (1933), *Footlight Parade* (1933), and *Gold Diggers of 1937* (1936). Bacon also worked with Warners' top stars on a series of crime films, including *Marked Woman* (1937), which paired Bette DAVIS and Humphrey BOGART. He brought a whimsical sense of humour to the gangster genre in such films as *A Slight Case of Murder* (1938), *Brother Orchid* (1940), and *Larceny Inc.* (1942), all of which starred Edward G. ROBINSON.

After making the war drama *Action in the North Atlantic* (1943), with Bogart and Raymond MASSEY, Bacon moved to 20th Century-Fox and directed *The Sullivans* (1944), based on the true story of a US family who lost five sons at sea during the war, and *Sunday Dinner for a Soldier* (1944), a sentimental flag-waver starring Anne BAXTER. His last offerings were RKO's *The French Line* (1954), a musical with Jane RUSSELL, and the comedy *She Couldn't Say No* (1934), starring Jean SIMMONS and Robert MITCHUM.

baffle On a SOUND STAGE, a movable wall or board used to control the reverberation of sound while recording.

BAFTA British Academy of Film and Television Arts. A British film and television organization, formed by the merger of the **British Film Academy** (founded 1946) with the Society of Film and Television Arts in 1959. The organization presents Britain's most prestigious film and television awards (sometimes called the **Stellas**). Winners of the Best Film category before 1969, when only British films were eligible, included Carol REED's *Odd Man Out* (1948) and THE THIRD MAN (1950), and David LEAN's *The Sound Barrier* (1953), THE BRIDGE ON THE RIVER KWAI (1958), and LAWRENCE OF ARABIA (1963). Prizewinners since 1969 have included John SCHLESINGER's MIDNIGHT COWBOY (1970) and *Sunday, Bloody Sunday* (1972), TRUFFAUT's *Day for Night* (1974), Miloš FORMAN's ONE FLEW OVER THE CUCKOO'S NEST (1977), Richard ATTENBOROUGH's GANDHI (1983), Claude BERRI's *Jean de Florette* (1988), BERTOLUCCI's *The Last Emperor* (1989), and the MERCHANT-IVORY film *Howards End* (1993).

> The American Oscar is the only award that carries any weight. Ours is just a load of shite.
> SARAH MILES.

Baker, Sir Stanley (1927–76) British actor. Baker made his screen debut in *Undercover* (1943), a propaganda piece about the Yugoslavian partisans. By the early 1950s he had moved up to supporting roles in such films as *The Cruel Sea* (1953), *The Red Beret* (1953), and *The Good Die Young* (1954); he also appeared as Henry Tudor in OLIVIER's RICHARD III (1955). After further strong supporting roles, Baker led the cast for the first time in *Hell Drivers* (1957), a funny and vicious film about road haulage that revealed his potential as a tough screen presence. That same year

Baker also appeared in *Campbell's Kingdom* with Dirk BOGARDE and the slum drama *Violent Playground*.

It was during the late 1950s and 1960s that Baker really came into his own, playing a number of hard-nosed roles that introduced a new realism to British crime films. These included Joseph LOSEY's thrillers *Blind Date* (1959) and *The Criminal* (1960), a dark and savage study of the British underworld. Subsequent films included the star-laden adventure movie *The Guns of Navarone*, the US-French production *In the French Style*, and Losey's disappointing *Eva* (all 1961). In 1963 Baker gave perhaps his finest performance as Lt John Chard in the historical war drama *Zulu*. The film, which Baker also co-produced, ran into considerable practical difficulties during the African shoot. These included getting the several thousand Zulu extras, none of whom had ever seen a film, to understand what was going on. Baker apparently solved the problem by showing them an old Gene AUTRY Western, after which they fully co-operated, lending a tremendous power to the battle scenes.

In 1967 Baker co-starred with Dirk Bogarde in another Losey film, *Accident*, before returning to crime drama in *Robbery*, a fictionalized account of the Great Train Robbery. Two years later he appeared in *Where's Jack*, a deliberately unromantic film about 18th-century highwaymen, and in *The Games*, Michael WINNER's film about the Olympic marathon. Baker's subsequent films were mostly unremarkable, perhaps the best of them being *Innocent Bystanders* (1972), in which he played an over-the-hill secret-service agent. He was knighted in 1976.

Balcon, Sir Michael (1896–1977) British producer, who was responsible for many of the classic British films of the 1940s and 1950s. Balcon entered the cinema in 1919, founding his own Gainsborough Pictures in 1928; he subsequently moved to Gaumont-British (1931) and MGM-British (1936) to make such films as HITCHCOCK's *The Man Who Knew Too Much* (1934) and THE THIRTY-NINE STEPS (1935).

In 1937 Balcon was appointed director and chief of productions at EALING STUDIOS, where he presided over the golden era that saw the creation of the 'Ealing Comedies', including KIND HEARTS AND CORONETS (1949), *Passport to Pimlico* (1949), and THE LAVENDER HILL MOB (1952). In recognition of his achievements at Ealing he received a knighthood in 1948. Later films, in which he continued to insist upon the highest production standards, included the war epics *The Cruel Sea* (1953) and *Dunkirk* (1958), as well as the Oscar-winning comedy TOM JONES (1963), starring Albert FINNEY and Susannah YORK. In 1964 he became chairman of BRITISH LION FILM CORPORATION. His autobiography, *A Lifetime of Films*, was published in 1969.

ballyhoo An older term for HYPE.

Bambi (1942) Classic DISNEY feature about the experiences of a young fawn. Based on a book by the German novelist and playwright Felix Salten, the film shows Bambi learning about life in a great forest, meeting its animal inhabitants, and braving the hazards of weather, fire, and man. It was much admired both for the quality of the animation and for the richly detailed backgrounds. Live deer were brought to the studios so that artists working on the project could learn to recreate their movements with the utmost realism; for similar reasons cameras were taken into the woods of Maine to capture the changing moods of the seasons. Such was the attention to detail, that Disney's previous average of ten feet of film a day was reduced to one of just six inches for *Bambi*; the whole feature took five years to complete.

Salten's original book was intended for adults and is much more harrowing than the Disney version, which omits scenes in which crows kill a baby hare, a ferret mauls a squirrel, and a fox dismembers a pheasant. The atmosphere of violence in the original novel was further defused by the introduction of such overtly sentimental characters as Thumper the rabbit and Flower the skunk. Somewhat oddly, both these characters were adopted as insignia by US military units serving in World War II; Thumper was depicted as a flying instructor and Flower equipped with a gas mask – while Friend Owl masqueraded as a machine-gunner.

Bancroft, Anne (Anna Maria Italiano; 1931–) US actress of Italian descent, who emerged as a major star in the early 1960s. Although she made her Hollywood debut as early as 1952, Bancroft found little success and returned to the theatre, explaining "I'm going back to New York, where an oversized bosom doesn't take priority over reading your lines." However, success on the stage persuaded the studios to give her a second chance and she went on to win acclaim for the integrity of her acting in such films as *The Miracle Worker* (1962), the moving story of Helen Keller (which brought Bancroft an Oscar for the role of Annie Sullivan, Keller's governess), the marital drama *The Pumpkin Eater* (1964), and *The Slender Thread* (1965). THE GRADUATE (1968) provided Bancroft with her best-known screen role, that of Dustin HOFFMAN's older lover, Mrs Robinson. The part only came to her after first-choice Jeanne MOREAU declined the role.

Subsequent films include *Young Winston* (1972), in which she played Churchill's mother, and the ballet movie *The Turning Point* (1977). In the spy comedy *To Be or Not To Be* (1983) she co-starred with her husband Mel BROOKS, who also produced. Although Brooks has extolled her as "a beautiful and talented woman who can lift your spirits just by looking at you", his Jewish mother was initially less impressed by the match: on learning that her son was to marry an Italian she allegedly said, "Bring her over. I'll be in the kitchen – with my head in the oven." Brooks was executive producer of one of Bancroft's more recent successes, *84 Charing Cross Road* (1987), in which she played a New York bibliophile corresponding with Anthony HOPKINS, a London bookseller.

The greatest actress of her generation.
RICHARD ATTENBOROUGH.

Bankhead, Tallulah (1902–68) Flamboyant US actress, whose screen performances never measured up to her brilliance on stage or her larger-than-life personality. Bankhead was witty and outrageous, called everyone 'dahling' in her deep husky voice, and was notorious for her exhibitionistic behaviour (such as playing the piano nude at parties). She had numerous lovers of both sexes and recklessly abused alcohol and drugs, claiming that cocaine was not habit-forming on the grounds that "I ought to know – I've been using it for years." The British actress Mrs Patrick Campbell once remarked, "Tallulah is always skating on thin ice. Everyone wants to be there when it breaks."

Largely because of this erratic reputation, film versions of her Broadway hits were usually handed over to others: Bette DAVIS, for example, took Bankhead's roles in both *Dark Victory* (1939) and *The Little Foxes* (1941). Having been forced to watch the stage version of the latter, Davis decided that Bankhead's "etched in acid" interpretation was the correct one and re-created it on screen, only to be criticized for plagiarism.

Bankhead was born in Huntsville, Alabama, the daughter of the speaker of the US House of Representatives. After winning a contest in a film magazine, she left for New York at the age of 15 and appeared in two silent films the following year. She made her London stage debut in 1923 and became an overnight sensation (police once had to disperse 2000 admirers from her stage door). She made two minor British films in the late 1920s, before returning to the New York stage and a Paramount contract in 1930. Her first major film was *Tarnished Lady* (1931), in which she played a socialite who marries for money. Posters proclaimed "This girl will shock you" – and cinemagoers who pulled the attached cord received a mild electric shock.

Bankhead gave such a poor performance in *The Cheat* (1931) that she forfeited her role in *Rain* (1932) to Joan CRAWFORD. She later failed to secure the role of Scarlett O'HARA in GONE WITH THE WIND (1939), having been voted third choice (behind Bette Davis and Katharine HEPBURN) by school groups. The highlight of her film career came with her critically acclaimed performance in Alfred HITCHCOCK's *Lifeboat* (1944), in which she played a selfish mink-wearing fashion journalist.

Bankhead's drinking cost her the role of Amanda Wingfield in *The Glass Menagerie* (1950), despite a brilliant screen test. In the words of director Irving Rapper: "It cost a fortune to do an Errol FLYNN picture because he was always drunk. And thanks to Errol Flynn, Tallulah lost the part." In her last film, Hammer's *Fanatic* (1965), she played a religious maniac who imprisons her dead son's fiancée (Stefanie Powers).

She was always a star, but only intermittently a good actress.
BRENDAN GILL; *The Times*, August 1973.

A day away from Tallulah is like a month in the country.
HOWARD DIETZ, film executive.

Banks, Leslie (1890–1952) British actor, who specialized in sophisticated or evil roles; he reversed the usual career pattern by making his name in Hollywood before moving to British films in the later 1930s.

Having studied at Oxford, Banks went on the stage in 1911 and served in World War I. The facial scars he received in the conflict actually enhanced his appeal in such roles as Zaroff, the mad baron who hunts human prey in *The Most Dangerous Game* (British title *The Hounds of Zaroff*; 1932).

Following his success in this role, Banks co-starred with Edna Best in Alfred HITCHCOCK's *The Man Who Knew Too Much* (1934), which also featured an early appearance by Peter LORRE as the villain. A year later he gave an acclaimed performance in the title role of *Sanders of the River*, a commissioner who keeps peace between two West African rulers, one played by Paul Robeson (who later regretted the stereotyped role) and the other by Jomo Kenyatta, later to become the real-life president of Kenya.

In 1937 Banks portrayed the Earl of Leicester in the Armada story *Fire Over England*, with Flora Robson as Elizabeth I; Vivien LEIGH and Laurence OLIVIER also featured as lovers in their first film together. During World War II he appeared as a treacherous squire in Ealing's invasion drama *Went the Day Well?* (1942), and as the Chorus in Olivier's *Henry V* (1944). He later starred in two stories about murder trials, *Madeleine* (1949), set in Victorian Glasgow, and *Your Witness* (1950), about a US lawyer who defends a suspect in an English court.

Bara, Theda (Theodosia Goodman; 1890–1955) US actress, Hollywood's first sex symbol and the first star to be artificially created by a studio. She made some 40 films in four years, turning out one a month at the peak of her career. Her wicked VAMP roles prompted a flurry of imitators and caused profound alarm in conservative America: Bara later recalled an occasion on which a passer-by "called the police because her child spoke to me."

Bara's publicity made much of her supposed Eastern origins, claiming that she was the daughter of a French artist and Arab princess (*see* HYPE). Her screen name was said to be an anagram of 'Arab Death'. She herself perpetuated this exotic image in her Californian mansion, where she lived among mummy cases, skulls, and tiger skins. Once she arrived at a Chicago hotel in a white limousine attended by 'Nubian' footmen and gave a press conference surrounded by incense and black velvet curtains. After fielding tough questions about her Egyptian past, Bara rushed to the window to rip down the curtains and gasp, "Give me air!"

She was, in fact, the demure daughter of a Jewish tailor in Cincinnati. After working on stage and as a film extra, she found overnight fame with her performance in Fox's *A Fool There Was* (1916), based on Kipling's poem 'The Vampire'; one of its captions, "Kiss me, my fool", became a catchphrase with a generation of filmgoers. Later roles included Carmen (1916), Cleopatra (1918), and the devil's daughter. Restricted by her contract from marrying (and, bizarrely, from going to a Turkish bath), she later rebelled against her image, leading Fox to drop her in 1918. After unsuccessful comebacks on stage and screen, including several films in which she burlesqued her vamp image, she retired from show business in the late 1920s.

> She is pretty bad, but not bad enough to be remembered always.
> ALEXANDER WOOLLCOTT, critic.

Bardem, Juan (1922–) Spanish director and screenwriter. Born to theatrical parents in Madrid, Bardem studied at the Spanish Institute of Cinema Research and Experimentation while writing film articles for magazines. In the late 1940s he worked with his former classmate Luis Berlanga (1921–) on several unproduced scripts and a short documentary, *Paseo Sobre una Guerra Antiqua* (1948). Three years later they had a major breakthrough with the co-written *Welcome, Mr Marshall* (directed by Berlanga). One of Spain's few international film successes during the Franco years, it told the story of a poor village's attempt to woo visiting administrators of the Marshall Plan. The film was denounced by US officials.

In 1953 Bardem founded the cinema magazine *Objectivo* and directed his first solo film, *Comedians*, which brought him international acclaim. He consolidated his reputation with two audacious political statements, *Death of a Cyclist* (1955), which won the Critics' Award at Cannes, and *Calle Mayor* (1956), a comedy about a cynical young man who pretends to be in love with a spinster. The Spanish authorities, disturbed by Bardem's sordid picture of life under Franco, arrested him; he was in jail when the Cannes award was announced.

The government also banned *Objectivo* and heavily censored Bardem's next film, *The Vengeance* (1958). Three years later his production company, Uninci, had its activity drastically curtailed after producing BUÑUEL's *Viridiana* (1961), an allegedly sacrilegious film about a young novice who is corrupted by her uncle. Bardem's later films, which he continued to script, include *The Uninhibited* (1965), *The Last Day of the War* (1969), *The Mysterious Island of Captain Nemo* (1973), *Seven Days in January* (1979), and *Lorca, Death of a Poet* (1987).

> Few film careers better suggest the trials, achievements and limitations of trying to make a political cinema under a dictatorship.
>
> JOHN HOPEWELL.

Bardot, Brigitte (Camille Javal; 1933–) Baby-faced French actress, who emerged as the sex symbol of an era in the mid 1950s. The daughter of an industrialist, she worked as a model before appearing in a series of French-made sex-comedies beginning with *Le Trou normand* (*Crazy for Love*; 1952). However, it was not until the release of *And God Created Woman* (1956) that she attracted international notice. Written and directed by her first husband, Roger VADIM, the film caused considerable moral outrage because it showed Bardot stripping on the beach at St Tropez. Amongst other denunciations, it was described by the Catholic LEGION OF DECENCY as "an open violation of conventional morality." Vadim himself commented:

> It was the first time on the screen that a woman was shown as really free on a sexual level with none of the guilt attached to nudity or carnal pleasure.

Her subsequent films, most of which capitalized on the 'Sex Kitten' image that Vadim had created, included *En Cas de malheur* (*Love is My Profession*, 1959) with Jean GABIN, *Henri Clouzot* (1960), *Love on a Pillow* (1962), and the all-star Western *Shalako* (1968). Although she made films for such distinguished directors as Jean-Luc GODARD (*Contempt*, 1963) and Louis MALLE (*Viva Maria*, 1965) she appeared unable to broaden her range and found few critical admirers.

Away from the cameras, Bardot seemed an increasingly unhappy woman in the later 1960s. Her unstable private life – a third marriage (to Gunther Sachs) collapsed in 1969 – was a continual target for scrutiny in the popular press and she is known to have made at least one suicide attempt. In 1973, shortly after her 40th birthday, Bardot announced her retirement from the cinema and withdrew abruptly from the public glare; she has since devoted her time to promoting animal rights. When asked about her old films in a 1990 interview she replied uncompromisingly:

> I don't give a damn about them. I care so little that you can't imagine. Everything I made can disappear for ever. I just don't care...Even when I was making the films, it didn't interest me.

barn doors An arrangement of hinged shutters around a studio lamp that can be adjusted to control the size and shape of the beam of light.

Barrault, Jean-Louis (1910–94) French actor. Although best known for his work in the theatre as actor, director, and manager, he also appeared in numerous films, most notably Marcel CARNÉ's epic of 19th-century theatrical life LES ENFANTS DU PARADIS (1944), in which he played the great mime artist Debureau.

Barrault made his first stage appearance in 1931 and his screen debut five years later, in the British war film *Mademoiselle docteur* (1936). That year he also appeared in Carné's black comedy *Drôle de drame* (US title *Bizarre, Bizarre*; 1936) as a murderous vegetarian. The great success of *Les Enfants du paradis*, was followed by starring roles in *La Symphonie fantastique* (1946), based on the early life of the composer Hector Berlioz, and *Le Puritan* (1947), a powerful moralistic drama that was banned on its original release. Subsequent film appearances included parts in Max OPHÜLS's *La Ronde* (1950) and the all-star war drama *The Longest Day* (1962), as well as an acclaimed performance (at the age of 72) in Ettore Scola's *La Nuit de Varennes* (1982), based on events of the French Revolution.

Barrymore family One of America's most celebrated acting families, consisting of Ethel Barrymore (1879–1959) and her brothers Lionel Barrymore (1878–1954) and John Barrymore (1882–1942). They were the children of the US actress Georgiana Drew (1856–93) and the British actor Maurice Barrymore (1847–1905).

Ethel Barrymore, one of the most distinguished performers of her generation, is chiefly remembered as a stage actress. She did, however, make a number of silent movies around the time of World War I and subsequently returned to Hollywood to play a series of difficult but warm-hearted matriarchs in the 1940s. Among her more notable screen appearances were *None but the Lonely Heart* (1944), for which she won an Oscar in the role of Cary GRANT's dying mother, *The Farmer's Daughter* (1947), and *Young at Heart* (1954).

Like other members of the Barrymore clan, Ethel was famous for her caustic wit. When a young actress attempted to apologize for not keeping an appointment with the words "I think I was invited to your house to dinner last Thursday night" the retort was immediate: "Oh, yes. Did you come?"

Lionel Barrymore, who called acting "the family curse", was one of the great Hollywood CHARACTER ACTORS. Although at his best playing crusty but endearing old gentlemen, he attempted a wide range of other roles and once suggested for his epitaph "I've played everything but the harp." He made his screen debut in 1909 and subsequently appeared in nearly 200 films, virtually abandoning the theatre after 1925. Amongst his most successful screen roles were those in *The Bells* (1926), *Sadie Thompson* (1928), *Madame X* (1929), which he also directed, *A Free Soul* (1931), for which he won an Oscar as Best Actor, *Grand Hotel* (1932), *Ah! Wilderness* (1935), and CAMILLE (1937). However, he is perhaps mainly remembered for playing the crusty Dr Gillespie in the Dr Kildare film series. Many of his later performances were conducted from a wheelchair, to which he was confined by arthritis and injuries resulting from a couple of falls.

Lionel also wrote a book about the history of the Barrymore family, *We Barrymores*, and composed a symphony, a section of which was used in the film *Dr Kildare's Wedding Day* (1941). His other claims to fame included securing Clark GABLE his first audition with MGM (although it did not immediately meet with success, Barrymore having persuaded him to dress up in Polynesian costume with a flower behind his ear).

John Barrymore had a more substantial film career than either his brother or his sister, despite being one of Hollywood's most notorious alcoholics. He made his first film in 1913 and for a time confined himself to light romantic parts on screen while continuing to play more serious roles in the theatre (he always regarded the cinema as the lesser art). After his success in *Dr Jekyll and Mr Hyde* (1920), however, he was cast in more debonair and self-confident roles, earning the nicknames the **Great Lover** and the **Great Profile** (a reference to the most striking aspect of a face that became familiar to cinemagoers worldwide).

His roles of the 1920s included the sleuth *Sherlock Holmes* (1922), the Regency dandy *Beau Brummell* (1924), and the notorious rake *Don Juan* (1926). The last film was advertised with the boast "The World's Greatest Actor as the Greatest Lover of all Ages" and required Barrymore to bestow a record 127 screen kisses on his female costars. After making the classic *Grand Hotel* (1932) with Greta GARBO (rumoured to have been one of his lovers), he teamed up with his brother and sister for *Rasputin and the Empress* (1932), the only film in which the three Barrymores appeared together. By this time, however, his drinking was becoming a serious problem. After completing work on *A Bill of Divorcement* (1932), Barrymore's co-star Katharine HEPBURN sighed: "Thank goodness I don't have to act with you any more", to which he cuttingly replied, "I didn't know you ever had, darling."

Although deepening alcoholism threatened Barrymore's career in the 1930s, he continued to please audiences in such films as *Dinner at Eight* (1933), *Counsellor at Law* (1933), *Bulldog Drummond Comes Back* (1937), and *Marie Antoinette* (1938). Attempts at teetotalism were doomed to failure and at one point he was reduced to drinking the perfume from his wife's dressing-table. Once, hopelessly drunk, he wandered by mistake into a ladies' lavatory and was greeted by the cry "This is for women!" Back came the undaunted reply, "And so, madam, is this!" Ultimately, Barrymore had to have CUE CARDS with his lines on hidden about the set. (He had, in fact, always been reluctant to learn his screen parts, explaining "My memory is full of beauty – Hamlet's soliloquies, the Queen Mab speech...most of the Sonnets – do you expect me to clutter up all that with this horse-shit?") In his last films, several of which featured him as a drink-sodden actor in decline, he appeared as little more than a caricature of his earlier self. He died penniless.

A bizarre tale told of Barrymore's death concerns his admirer and fellow-drinker Errol FLYNN: on hearing the news of the great actor's demise, Flynn went on a lengthy drinking spree and when he got home was stunned to find Barrymore sitting in a chair waiting for him, drink in hand. According to the story, friends had bribed the undertaker to let them have the body for a few hours as a joke.

The acting careers of John Barrymore's children, **Diana Barrymore** (1921–60) and **John Barrymore Jnr** (1932–), were also blighted by alcohol and drugs. Diana, whom her father once described as "a horse's arse, quite a pretty one, but still a horse's arse", made a handful of screen appearances in the 1940s and was the subject of the film *Too Much Too Soon* (1958), in which she was portrayed by Dorothy MALONE (with Errol Flynn as her father). John Jnr gave a number of unremarkable performances in films of the 1950s and 1960s. His daughter **Drew Barrymore** (1975–) also turned to drink and drugs after her early success in E.T.: THE EXTRA-TERRESTRIAL (1982), which was followed by juvenile roles in several forgettable films of the 1980s. By the tender age of 14 she had 'dried out'; the following year she published her autobiography, *Little Girl Lost*. She has recently made a comeback in the Western *Bad Girls* (1993).

Barthelmess, Richard (1985–1963) US actor of the silent screen, who starred in many of D. W. GRIFFITH's films. His co-star Lillian GISH described him as having "the most beautiful face of any man who ever went before the camera." The son of an actress, Barthelmess was discovered in a student production by the film star Alla Nazimova. After moving to Hollywood in 1916, he became Griffith's leading man in such melodramas as BROKEN BLOSSOMS (1919) and *Way Down East* (1920).

In 1921 he joined director Henry King to form a new production company, Inspiration Pictures; the two men made five films together, beginning with *Tol'able David* (1921), starring Barthelmess as a country boy who finally overcomes a bully in a showdown fight. The film, considered at the time to be Hollywood's best 'regional drama', includes a striking scene in which Barthelmess's mother hangs onto his legs to keep him from shooting a dog accused of killing sheep.

Barthelmess was nominated for an Oscar in 1929 (the first year of the Academy Awards) for his performances in *The Noose* and *The Patent Leather Kid*. His last major roles were in the talkies *The Dawn Patrol* (1930), directed by Howard HAWKS, and William DIETERLE's *The Last Flight* (1931), about US airmen in Paris. Thereafter he was cast mainly in supporting roles, as in *Only Angels Have Wings* (1939) with Cary GRANT and *The Spoilers* (1942) with John WAYNE; he retired from the cinema in 1942.

base side The side of a film that is not coated with emulsion; it is shiny in appearance, whereas the EMULSION SIDE is dull.

Basinger, Kim (1953–) Sensual US actress, who worked as a model and singer before emerging as a sex symbol in the mid 1980s. An appearance in the TV miniseries *From Here to Eternity* (1979) led to her film debut in *Hard Country* (1981), a contemporary Western. In 1985 Sam SHEPARD's *Fool for Love* provided her with one of her more demanding roles to date, while *No Mercy* cast her opposite Richard GERE. However, it was her third film of that year, the notorious *9½ Weeks* that shot her to stardom; the movie, which co-starred Mickey ROURKE, explored a sadomasochistic relationship and featured copious nudity. Subsequent roles included the disaster-prone blonde who creates mayhem for Bruce WILLIS in *Blind Date* (1987) and the love interest in BATMAN (1989). She later burlesqued her screen persona by supplying the voice of the blonde bombshell in the animated *Cool World* (1992).

Although she seldom pleased the critics, Basinger entered the 1990s as one of Hollywood's wealthiest female stars. Then disaster struck. In 1993 a court ordered Basinger to pay nearly $9 million in damages for breaking a verbal agreement to appear in *Boxing Helena*, the debut feature by Jennifer Lynch (daughter of David LYNCH). Basinger, who was forced to declare herself bankrupt, claimed in her defence that the film, about a woman who has all her limbs amputated and is kept in a box by an obsessed admirer, was deeply exploitative and that she had been misled as to its content. In 1994 she appeared in a remake of PECKINPAH's *The Getaway*, as half of a latter-day Bonnie and Clyde.

Bates, Alan (1934–) British actor, who came to prominence in the 'social realist' films of the early 1960s. Originally a stage actor, Bates made his screen debut in *The Entertainer* (1960), Tony RICHARDSON's screen adaptation of the John Osborne play. The following year he starred as the escaped convict in Bryan FORBES's *Whistle Down the Wind*, a poignant drama scripted by Keith Waterhouse and Willis Hall. Bates then starred in the remarkable *A Kind of Loving* (1962), adapted by Waterhouse and Hall from Stan Barstow's novel and directed by John SCHLESINGER. This landmark of the British cinema was followed by two rather disappointing films, Carol REED's *The Running Man* and a screen adaptation of Harold Pinter's *The Caretaker* (both 1963). Bates's other films of the 1960s included ZORBA THE GREEK (1964), in which he more than held his own against Anthony QUINN's expansive title character, GEORGY GIRL (1966), a now rather dated 'swinging sixties' film, Schlesinger's *Far From the Madding Crowd* (1967), John FRANKENHEIMER's *The Fixer* (1968), and Ken RUSSELL's *Women in Love* (1969). The last attracted much comment for the scene in which Bates and Oliver REED wrestled in the nude.

During the 1970s Bates's career seemed to lose momentum; certainly, such films as the crude 19th-century romp *Royal Flash* (1975) and *The Rose* (1979), in which he played the manager of rock star Bette MIDLER, added little to his reputation. There were, however, some notable exceptions, such as Joseph LOSEY's splendid *The Go-Between* (1971), the moving *A Day in the Death of Joe Egg* (1971), and Lindsay ANDERSON's *In Celebration* (1975). He also worked extensively in the theatre during this period.

Bates's more recent films, which have done little to revitalize his screen career, include Anderson's patchy *Britannia Hospital* (1982), *A Prayer for the Dying* (1987), the released version of which was disowned by its director Mike Hodges, and *Mister Frost* (1990), which was described by one reviewer as "staggeringly bad". However, both the understated *We Think the World of You* (1989) and Bates's performance as King Claudius in ZEFFIRELLI's *Hamlet* (1990) show that, given the right material, he is still capable of giving fine screen performances.

Batman   US COMIC-STRIP hero who has featured in a number of films, notably Tim BURTON's *Batman* (1989) and *Batman Returns* (1992). In the original comic strip, created in 1939 by Bob Kane for Detective Comics, Batman, the Caped Crusader of Gotham City, fought such criminal arch-

fiends as the Joker, the Penguin, and Catwoman. Unknown to anyone but his colleague Robin (the Boy Wonder) and his butler, the mysterious bat-masked vigilante was in reality the reclusive millionaire Bruce Wayne.

The subject was first filmed by Columbia Pictures as a 15-episode serial (1943) starring Lewis Wilson and Douglas Croft; this was followed five years later by the serial *Batman and Robin*, with Robert Lowery and John Duncan. The camp television series of the 1960s produced a spin-off movie, *Batman* (1966), starring Adam West and Burt Ward with Burgess Meredith and Cesar Romero as the villains.

Quite different was the $50-million version created for Warner Brothers by Tim Burton, a dark and EXPRESSIONISTIC movie in which Batman (Michael Keaton) appears as a sinister and driven figure. However, it is Jack NICHOLSON's outrageous portrayal of the Joker, with his grotesque fixed grin, that dominates the film. Nicholson made a record $50 million from the role, including a percentage of the $250-million gross and the merchandising of more than 160 products. The cast also included Kim BASINGER as Vicki and Michael Gough as Alfred the butler; Bob Kane, creator of the original character, made a cameo appearance. The film was America's top box-office hit of 1989 and won Academy Awards for art direction and score. Designer Anton Furst set out to make Gotham City, created on 18 sound stages at Pinewood Studios, look like "New York without planning permission for 300 years."

Burton's $80-million sequel, *Batman Returns*, set a record by opening simultaneously in 3700 cinemas in America and Canada. In the film, which was generally considered inferior to its predecessor, Keaton drives his Batmobile through Expressionist-style sets to battle the Penguin (Danny DEVITO) and the whip-wielding Catwoman (Michelle PFEIFFER).

Battleship Potemkin   (*Bronenosets Potemkin*; 1925) Sergei EISENSTEIN's silent masterpiece, a film commissioned by the Soviet authorities as one of a series of films to commemorate the 20th anniversary of the 1905 Revolution. One of the most influential works of international cinema, it has featured among the top ten films of all time in surveys conducted by *Sight and Sound* magazine from 1952 to 1992.

Eisenstein initially submitted a 100-page script chronicling the key events of 1905 and a proposal to shoot in 30 locations around the country. Filming began in Leningrad at the beginning of 1925, but bad weather soon forced Eisenstein to relocate to Odessa, where he intended to record a 42-shot sequence dealing with the mutiny on board the cruiser *Potemkin* and the massacre of civilians on the harbour steps that ensued. The director became so preoccupied with the cinematic possibilities offered by the steps that he abandoned the rest of his script to concentrate on the Odessa episode.

Although styled to resemble NEWSREELS, the film was structured in five acts like a traditional drama – Men and Maggots, Drama on the Quarterdeck, An Appeal from the Dead, The Odessa Steps, and Meeting the Squadron. Following a ten-week shoot, Eisenstein took just two weeks to edit the footage into an 86-minute film, comprising 1346 shots (compared to the average 600 that made up a contemporary Hollywood feature). The 'Odessa Steps' segment that had inspired the film, with its average shot length of two seconds, became the most influential sequence in cinema history and has been frequently imitated – a recent example being the shoot-out on the station steps at the climax of Brian DE PALMA's *The Untouchables* (1987).

Bava, Mario (1914–80) Italian director, writer, and cinematographer, who became a cult figure for his grisly horror tales. Born in San Remo, the son of a sculptor, Bava began to direct his own shorts while working as a cinematographer in the late 1930s. He moved into features in 1959 with *Black Sunday*, a sadistic story of witchcraft and vampirism that was heavily censored in Britain. *Hercules and the Haunted World* and *Erik the Conqueror* (both 1961) were muscleman adventures in the Italian style, the latter allegedly featuring a fleet of (model) viking ships made out of pasta. Bava then returned to horror with the outlandish *What!* (1963), also known as *The Whip and the Flesh*, a HAMMER-style film in which the usual undertones of sex and sadism are made alarmingly explicit. The film was mutilated by the studio and released with the director's credit given to one John M. Old. Hardly less shocking and bizarre were *Blood and Black Lace* (1964), *Planet of the Vampires* (1965), *Hatchet for a Honeymoon* (1969), and the truly deranged *Twitch of the Death Nerve* (1971). Bava's growing band of admirers detect a tongue-in-cheek approach to the mayhem, while also pointing to the superlative photography and lighting in all his films.

Baxter.   **Anne Baxter** (1923–85) US actress, often cast as innocent or seemingly innocent characters. She received an Oscar for her supporting role in *The Razor's Edge* (1946) but is best remembered as Eve, the two-faced young actress in ALL ABOUT EVE (1950).

Born in Michigan City, Indiana, she attended private schools in New York City and made her Broadway debut at the age of 13. Three years later she tested for the role of Scarlett O'HARA in GONE WITH THE WIND, giving a performance that George CUKOR considered the most touching of the auditions he saw. Her first film, the Western *Twenty Mule Team* (1940), was followed by parts in Jean RENOIR's *Swamp Water* (1941), Orson WELLES's THE MAGNIFICENT AMBERSONS (1942), and Billy WILDER's *Five Graves to Cairo* (1943), among others.

Baxter's Oscar-winning role in *The Razor's Edge*, based on a novel by Somerset Maugham, required her to change from an innocent young heiress into a drug-taking alcoholic. Four years later, in *All About Eve*, she was nominated for an Academy Award as the sugary schemer eager to supplant ageing Broadway star Bette DAVIS. Despite these two major successes, Alfred HITCHCOCK was reluctant to use Baxter in *I Confess* (1953); her other films of the 1950s included Fritz LANG's mystery drama *The Blue Gardenia* (1953) and the British suspense film *Chase a Crooked Shadow* (1957).

From the mid 1960s onwards Baxter's output was largely restricted to television movies. In 1971 she appeared on Broadway in *Applause*, a musical based on *All About Eve*, this time in the role of the older fading actress. Her later films for the cinema included *Fools Parade* (1971) with James STEWART and *Jane Austen in Manhattan* (1980) with Robert Powell.

Warner Baxter (1891–1951) Handsome US actor known for his serious (sometimes stodgy) roles in both silent films and talkies. Surprisingly, he was at one point considered for the part of Rhett Butler in GONE WITH THE WIND.

Baxter grew up in San Francisco, where he worked as an office boy and salesman before going on the stage. His film debut came with *Her Own Money* (1914). In 1929 he won an Oscar for portraying the Mexican bandit, the Cisco Kid, in his sound debut, *In Old Arizona*, ("The First Outdoor All-Talkie"). Baxter had only got the role after Raoul WALSH, the film's original director, lost an eye in a freak road accident involving a rabbit; he reprised the character in *The Cisco Kid* (1931) and *The Return of the Cisco Kid* (1939).

Baxter's other successes included the musical 42ND STREET (1933), in which he was particularly memorable as a tough Broadway producer who makes Ruby Keeler a star, Frank CAPRA's *Broadway Bill* (British title *Strictly Confidential*; 1934), in which he played a rich horse trainer (although he was actually afraid of horses), and *Robin Hood of Eldorado* (1935) as another Mexican outlaw.

In 1936 he starred as another Broadway producer in *The King of Burlesque* and as Dr Samuel Mudd, the man wrongly accused of complicity in Lincoln's assassination, in John FORD's *The Prisoner of Shark Island*. He later played the male lead in *Adam Had Four Sons* (1941), one of Ingrid BERGMAN's first US films. In the early 1940s Baxter suffered a serious nervous breakdown but continued to act in such B-movies as *Crime Doctor* (1943) and its seven sequels. He made his last film, *State Penitentiary*, in 1950, a year before his death following a lobotomy.

bay The area of the film studio in which set PROPS are stored.

bazooka A tubular support for an overhead studio light. The name comes from its resemblance to the wartime anti-tank weapon.

BCU Big close-up. *See* CLOSE-UP; EXTREME CLOSE-UP.

Beatles, The British rock group consisting of John Lennon (1940–80), Paul McCartney (1942–), George Harrison (1943–), and Ringo Starr (1940–). The group first appeared on film in Richard LESTER's *A Hard Day's Night* (1964), a black-and-white documentary-style film that gave a fictionalized account of 36 hours in their lives at the height of Beatlemania. There followed the more conventionally wacky *Help!* (1965), which, according to *Variety*, showed that the group had "a touch of the MARX BROTHERS." The group appeared in animated form in the surrealistic fantasy YELLOW SUBMARINE

(1968); the Liverpudlian voices were, however, supplied by actors. *Let It Be* (1970) was a documentary of the band's last days as a unit, with no attempt at scripted situations.

The members of the group have also appeared individually, beginning with Lennon, who featured as a misfit soldier in Lester's black comedy *How I Won the War* (1967). Of the four, Starr has enjoyed the most extensive acting career, appearing in *Candy* (1968) as a Mexican gardener, *The Magic Christian* (1969) with Peter SELLERS, *That'll be the Day* (1973) as David Essex's sidekick, *Lisztomania* (1975) as the pope, and (with his wife Barbara Bach) in *Caveman* (1981). McCartney wrote and starred in the disappointing thriller *Give My Regards to Broad Street* (1984), which also featured Starr and Bach as well as McCartney's wife Linda. It was supported by the delightful animated short *Rupert and the Frog Chorus* (1984), for which McCartney provided the music. Harrison's main contribution to the cinema has been as an executive of Hand Made Films, whose productions include *Monty Python's Life of Brian* (1979; *see* MONTY PYTHON) and *The Missionary* (1983), starring ex-Python Michael Palin.

The Beatles have themselves been the subject of several films, including *The Hours and the Times* (1992) and *Backbeat* (1994). *See also* POP STARS IN FILMS.

Beatty, Warren (Henry Warren Beaty; 1937–) US actor, producer, and director, who began his career hailed as the 'new BRANDO' but has since experienced mixed fortunes: in his own words, "My tides flow in and out." The younger brother of Shirley MACLAINE, Beatty supported himself in his early days with a variety of jobs, including rat-catcher, bricklayer, and pianist. Although he made an impact with sullen performances in such films as *Splendour in the Grass* (1961), *All Fall Down* (1962), and *Lilith* (1965), his big breakthrough came with the hugely successful BONNIE AND CLYDE (1967), with Faye DUNAWAY as his partner in crime. Curiously, US audiences gave *Bonnie and Clyde* a lukewarm reception at first; it was only when British critics greeted it as a classic that it became recognized as one of the films of the decade.

Beatty's subsequent films included *Shampoo* (1975), in which he appeared to spoof his own image as a womanizer, *Heaven Can Wait* (1978), and *Reds* (1981), which brought him an Oscar as Best Director. Like *Bonnie and Clyde*, all of these films were produced by Beatty himself. In *Reds* Beatty starred as the US journalist John Reed, with Diane KEATON as his free-thinking lover. During shooting he gave the extras a lecture on Reed's Marxist theories, including the capitalist exploitation of labour, and found himself with a strike on his hands: the extras demanded more pay – and got it.

In 1987 Beatty produced the disastrous comedy-thriller *Ishtar*, in which he co-starred with Dustin HOFFMAN; the film cost some $50 million and made virtually nothing at the box office. *Dick Tracy* (1990), which Beatty directed and co-starred in with Madonna, found a mixed reception from the critics but went on to win three Oscars. Films that Beatty has turned down include BUTCH CASSIDY AND THE SUNDANCE KID, THE GODFATHER, *The Great Gatsby*, *Last Tango in Paris*, and *The Way We Were*.

The press have always lavished great attention upon Beatty's love life, his name having been linked at various times with numerous screen stars, including Julie Christie, Diane KEATON, and Madonna. Singer Carly Simon, another former lover, is alleged to have written the song 'You're So Vain' with Beatty in mind. He finally silenced the gossipmongers – for a time, at least – when he married Annette Bening, his co-star in *Bugsy* (1992) and the mother of his children.

> Sex is the most important thing in his life. It's his hobby you could say.
> SHIRLEY MACLAINE.

> If I come back in another life, I want to be Warren Beatty's fingertips.
> WOODY ALLEN.

Becker, Jacques (1906–60) French director and screenwriter, known for his elegant comedies of the 1950s. An assistant of Jean RENOIR in the 1930s, Becker established himself as a director with *It Happened at the Inn* (*Goupi mains rouge*; 1942), a comedy melodrama set in a French village that provides an early example of his interest in characterization. Several of his later comedies dealt with Parisian society, among them *Antoine et Antoinette* (1949), which depicts the frustrations and despair of the young in postwar France, *Edouard et Caroline* (1951), about discord between two newly-weds, and *Casque d'or* (1952), starring Simone SIGNORET and Serge Reggiani as ill-fated lovers of the 1890s. Although now regarded as a classic of the French cinema, *Casque d'or*, was initially ill received, being pronounced "very feeble" when it opened in Brussels. *Honour Among Thieves* (*Touchez pas au Grisbi*; 1953), starring Jean GABIN and a young Jeanne MOREAU, was an unusual gangster film that greatly influenced the development of the genre in France. Its success was largely owing to the depth given to its central character: Gabin won the Best Actor Award at the 1954 Venice Film Festival for this role. Becker then directed a number of less significant films before embarking on his last project, *The Hole* (1959), which many consider his best work. Like his earlier films, it is simple in style yet acute in its observation of characters and relationships; the plot concerns an attempted escape by four convicts and their betrayal by another prisoner.

> He was – everyone said it – a most exceptional man, a man with constant ideas whose presence alone was enriching. Perhaps it's sufficient to say that I married him.
> FRANÇOISE FABIAN, Spanish actress.

Bellamy, Ralph (1904–91) Grave-looking soft-spoken US actor, who went from sophisticated film comedies to serious Broadway roles, later returning to Hollywood as an accomplished character actor. From 1952 to 1964 he served as president of US EQUITY.

Bellamy worked in the theatre as set designer, actor, and director (establishing his own Ralph Bellamy Players in 1927) before making his screen debut in the gangster film *The Secret Six* (1931). He was soon typecast as the 'other man', usually wealthy, who never gets the girl; his first such role was in *The Awful Truth* (1937), in which he lost Irene DUNNE to Cary GRANT (but won an Oscar nomination). In *Hands Across the Table* (1935) he lost Carole LOMBARD to Fred MACMURRAY, while in *Carefree* (1938) he lost his fiancée, played by Ginger ROGERS, to psychiatrist Fred ASTAIRE. Similarly, in HIS GIRL FRIDAY (1940) Rosalind RUSSELL abandons him to return to her charming but unscrupulous first husband, Cary Grant.

In 1940–41 Bellamy starred as the debonair sleuth Ellery QUEEN in four largely forgettable films made by Columbia Pictures. After World War II he left Hollywood for Broadway, returning some ten years later to appear in *The Court Martial of Billy Mitchell*

(1955). In 1960 he starred in *Sunrise at Campobello*, in which he re-created his award-winning Broadway role as President Franklin Roosevelt. He appeared as a sinister doctor in ROSEMARY'S BABY (1968), with George Burns in *Oh, God* (1977), and as a rich financier in *Trading Places* (1983). Bellamy also featured in numerous television movies and series.

Belle de jour (1967) Luis BUÑUEL's puzzling exploration of the fantasy life of a bored young woman. The screenplay (by Buñuel and Jean-Claude Carrière) is a loose adaptation of Joseph Kessel's 1928 novel about a sexually inhibited housewife, Séverine Sérizy (Catherine DENEUVE), who works part-time in a brothel to fulfil her masochistic fantasies, earning the nickname *belle de jour* (a pun on *belle du nuit*, a popular term for a prostitute). Buñuel, who rather disliked the book, set about replacing its linear narrative with a more ambiguous structure that includes several episodes that may or may not be erotic fantasies:

> As the film proceeds, I am going to increase the frequency of these interpolations, and at the end, in the final sequence, the audience will not be able to know if what is happening to her is actual or the heroine's subjective world – reality or nightmare.

Despite these drastic changes, Kessel was pleased with the result: "Buñuel's genius has exceeded by far all that I could hope for...We are in another dimension: that of the subconscious, of dreams and secret instincts suddenly laid bare. And what formal beauty in the images!"

The censors, however, were less enthusiastic, clipping footage from two of the brothel scenes and a sequence depicting a necrophiliac rite. Stunningly photographed by Sacha Vierny, the film has no music but makes inspired metaphorical use of natural sound. It contains two glimpses of the director – at the café where Séverine first meets the necrophiliac duke (Georges Marchal), and as a passer-by during the robbery on the Champs-Elysées. *Belle de jour* was awarded the Golden Lion at the Venice Film Festival in 1967.

Belmondo, Jean-Paul (1933–) French actor, whose handsome-ugly looks helped him to become a major star of the NEW WAVE of the late 1950s and 1960s. He successfully played a range of rebellious antiheroes in both crime and comedy films. Off-screen,

he served from 1963 to 1966 as president of the French Union of Actors.

The son of a sculptor, Belmondo was born in Neuilly-sur-Seine near Paris. He worked briefly as a boxer before studying drama at the Paris Conservatoire and going on the stage. Having made his film debut in *Dimanche...nous volerons* (1956), he went on to appear in a series of little-noticed roles before becoming an 'instant' hit in Jean-Luc GODARD's first feature, A BOUT DE SOUFFLE (1959); his performance as Michel Poiccard, a doomed murderer who idolizes Humphrey BOGART, effectively established his screen persona. Subsequent roles included a Hungarian murder suspect in Claude CHABROL's *Web of Passion* (1959) and the lover of his boss's wife (Jeanne MOREAU) in Peter Brook's *Moderato Cantabile* (1960). In *The Love Makers* (1961) he fell for a prostitute (Claudia CARDINALE), while in *L'Ainé des Ferchaux* (1963) he played the bodyguard of a French banker.

During the mid 1960s Belmondo's appearances in a series of sophisticated crime dramas made him France's favourite actor. He played a charismatic criminal in Godard's *Pierrot le Fou* (1965), while in Louis MALLE's *The Thief of Paris* (1967) he learned crime (from a priest) to bankroll an affair with Geneviève Bujold. After joining the all-star cast of the French-US production, *Is Paris Burning?* (1966), about the last days of the Nazi occupation, Belmondo played a man who suspects that his new wife (Catherine DENEUVE) is poisoning him in TRUFFAUT's *The Mississippi Mermaid* (1969), a man married to a disabled woman (Mia FARROW) in Chabrol's *Scoundrel in White* (*Docteur Popaul*; 1972), and a Jewish financier in Alain RESNAIS's *Stavisky* (1974).

His more recent films have included *Hold-up* (1985), *Itinéraire d'un enfant gate* (1988), for which he won a César as Best Actor, and *L'Inconnu dans la maison* (1992).

below the line *See* ABOVE THE LINE.

Belushi, John (1949–82) US actor and comedian, whose abrasive hard-hitting style helped to bring about a revolution in US humour in the late 1970s. Although he made only two successful films, his self-destructive lifestyle and early death have assured him of cult status.

The son of Albanian immigrants, Belushi began to appear in revues and clubs from the late 1960s onwards. He first found national fame on the innovative TV comedy series *Saturday Night Live* (1975–80), which also launched the careers of Chevy CHASE, Bill Murray, and his friend and frequent collaborator Dan AYKROYD.

Having made his screen debut in Jack NICHOLSON's Western *Goin' South* (1978), in which he played the tiny part of the sheriff's deputy, Belushi established himself as a box-office attraction with his performance as the slobbish Bluto in National Lampoon's college farce *Animal House* (1978). While this raucous comedy found a huge following amongst teenagers, Belushi's next two projects, *Old Boyfriends* (1979) and Steven SPIELBERG's *1941* (1979) were both dismal failures. In the meantime a popular series of sketches from *Saturday Night Live* provided the basis for another hit, *The Blues Brothers* (1980), in which Belushi and Aykroyd starred as deadpan rhythm-'n'-blues singers.

By this time, however, Belushi was leading a frenetic lifestyle and over-indulging in both alcohol and drugs. He made only two more films, in both of which he was bizarrely miscast; *Continental Divide* (1980) saw him playing the romantic lead, while *Neighbours* (1980) cast him as Aykroyd's staid suburban neighbour. Some 18 months later Belushi died of complications following a drug overdose; had he lived, he would have starred with Aykroyd in *Ghostbusters* (1984), one of the most successful comedies of the 1980s. The movie *Wired* (1989), starring Michael Chiklis, is based on Bob Woodward's book about Belushi's life and untimely death.

Ben-Hur (1959) William WYLER's sound version of the best-selling novel *Ben Hur – A Tale of the Christ* (1880) by Lew Wallace; MGM had already released a spectacular silent version in 1926. In the story Judah Ben-Hur, a 1st-century Roman Jew, is sent to the galleys for refusing to help the Roman Messala crush his people. On the way he meets CHRIST, who gives him water to drink. Having escaped during a sea battle, Ben-Hur later competes in a chariot race against Messala, who is killed. He meets Jesus again on the way to Calvary and returns his kindness.

The film won a record 11 Oscars, including Best Picture and Best Director. Filmed in TODD-AO PANAVISION with stereophonic sound, it cost $15 million to make and runs for three and a half hours. The most famous sequence in the film, the spectacular chariot race, was directed not by Wyler but by SECOND-UNIT DIRECTOR Andrew Marton. Charlton HESTON, who won the Oscar for Best Actor in the title role, was only taken on after the studio failed to secure either Marlon BRANDO or Rock HUDSON. The role was also coveted by Kirk DOUGLAS, who turned down the part of Messala, which Wyler offered him as an alternative. In the event Messala was played by Stephen Boyd, who acted the ruthless Roman so convincingly that children attacked him at a gala showing. Hugh Griffith won the Oscar for Best Supporting Actor in the role of an Arab sheikh. The face of Jesus is never seen.

MGM's earlier version of the story was the most expensive film of the silent era and arguably its greatest spectacle. Directed by Fred Niblo, it starred Ramon Novarro as Ben-Hur and Francis X. BUSHMAN as the evil Messala. Shooting began in Italy under the Goldwyn Company, but when this was subsumed into MGM in the early 1920s Louis B. MAYER moved the production home to the Culver City studios.

A still earlier version of *Ben-Hur*, a one-reeler produced by the Kalem Company in 1907, prompted a lawsuit by the publishers of Wallace's novel. Kalem argued that the film was good publicity for the book, but lost the case. *See* COPYRIGHT.

Bennett. Constance Bennett (1904–65) Glamorous US actress, whose success in romantic melodrama made her Hollywood's highest-paid performer in 1931. Having succeeded Gloria SWANSON as queen of the box office, she married Swanson's former husband, the Marquis de la Falaise; her five husbands also included the actor Gilbert Roland.

Bennett was born in New York, into an acting family that included father Richard Bennett, mother Adrienne Morrison, and sisters Barbara and Joan BENNETT. She made her screen debut at the age of 12 in her father's film, *The Valley of Decision*. In 1926 she abandoned acting to marry a wealthy man, but divorced him three years later to return as a major star of talkies in such films as *Three Faces East* (1930).

In her early career, Bennett often played a good girl wronged, being seduced in five films in less than a year in 1930–31. Her characters also tended to produce illegitimate babies, with Joel MCCREA being the most frequent culprit.

When Bennett's salary climbed to $30,000 a week (equalling that of John BARRYMORE), RKO informed her of the ruinous taxes to follow. "Oh, then you will have to pay the tax", she informed them, "for I must have $30,000 clear." In the later 1930s she made a successful transition to light comedy in TOPPER (1937), in which she played a frisky ghost, the sequel *Topper Takes a Trip* (1938), and *Merrily We Live* (1938).

Later films, such as *Two-Faced Woman* (1941), with Greta GARBO in her last screen role, proved less successful. In the early 1950s she left films for the stage and capitalized on her glamorous image by founding the Constance Bennett Cosmetics Company. She died shortly after making her first movie in 12 years, *Madame X* (1966), in which she wore the most expensive ($50,000) costume yet made for the screen.

Joan Bennett (1910–90) US actress, the sister of Constance BENNETT. Noted for her beauty and her soft voice, she played a wide range of roles from *femmes fatales* to doting mothers. She was one of the four actresses on the final shortlist for the part of Scarlett O'HARA in GONE WITH THE WIND but was rejected as too sentimental.

Her first film role, at the age of 13, was as a pageboy in GOLDWYN's *The Eternal City* (1923); her father, Richard Bennett, was also in the cast. Three years later she married her first husband (of four), the producer Walter Wanger, who did much to advance her career. Her first starring role came in *Bulldog Drummond* with Ronald COLMAN (1924). In 1932 she married another producer, Gene Markey, a jealous man who later caused a Hollywood scandal by shooting her agent (who survived the attack).

Although Bennett was a natural blonde, director Tay GARNETT dyed her hair for a vampish role in his *Trade Winds* (1939) and she appeared thereafter as a brunette. Later that year she played a gangster's moll in *The Housekeeper's Daughter* and officially protested (to no avail) at an advertisement that proclaimed, "She couldn't cook and she couldn't sew, but oh how she could so-and-so." Bennett gave perhaps her best performances in Fritz LANG's films of the 1940s, in which she was often cast as the victim. After Edward G. ROBINSON had murdered her with scissors in *The Woman in the Window* (1944) and with an ice pick in *Scarlet Street* (1945), he remarked: "I have nothing against Joan

Bennett, but if the script mentions that she must die, die she must."

Despite making a successful transition to comedy with *Father of the Bride* (1950), in which she and Spencer TRACY played the harassed parents of bride Elizabeth TAYLOR, Bennett's career faded in the 1950s. From 1966 to 1971 she starred in the hit television series *Dark Shadows*, about a vampire, making a film version in 1970. Her later made-for-TV movies included *Love* (1978) and *Divorce Wars* (1982).

Benny, Jack (Benjamin Kubelsky; 1894–1974) US comedian, who became a star of radio, television, and the movies (though he often boasted that he was a box-office flop). Benny, whose trademarks were his ever-present cigar and his violin, established himself as a top vaudeville entertainer in the 1920s. Unlike many of his contemporaries, he made a successful transition to the talkies in such productions as *Hollywood Revue of 1929* (1929). He went on to give memorable acting performances in *Charley's Aunt* (1941) and Ernst LUBITSCH's *To Be or Not To Be* (1942), in which he played an egotistical Polish actor involved in rescuing victims of the Nazis. In *The Horn Blows at Midnight* (1945), his last major screen appearance, he played a trumpeter who dreams that he is an angel sent to destroy the world.

Although in reality a generous man, Benny cultivated a popular image as a skinflint and many stories were told of his meanness. Among the most famous was one in which he was discovered attempting to crawl under a toilet cubicle door to avoid paying. (In fact, he had dropped his wallet inside the cubicle and had no coins with which to open the locked door.) On another occasion he refused all payment for a charity performance, then innocently inquired, "But just in case I *was* accepting money, how much was I refusing?" He was married to Mary Livingstone, his former radio co-star, and made provision in his will for her to receive a single red rose every day for the rest of her life.

> I don't deserve this, but I have arthritis, and I don't deserve that either.
> JACK BENNY, award acceptance speech.

> Jack was the sweetest sonofabitch in the world. He never said a mean word about anybody – but I suspect he did a lot of *thinking*.
> IRIS ADRIAN, actress.

Bergen, Candice (1946–) US actress, who achieved stardom with her first film but subsequently had difficulty finding suitable roles.

Bergen was born in Beverly Hills, the daughter of the ventriloquist Edgar Bergen (1903–78), a well-known radio entertainer who later made several films (he was awarded a special Oscar in 1937). A graduate of the University of Pennsylvania, Candice Bergen made a strong debut in Sidney LUMET's *The Group* (1966). The film, which launched a number of new talents, made a star of the 20-year-old actress in the role of the 'Sapphic' Lakey Eastlake. Later that year she appeared as Steve MCQUEEN's love interest in *The Sand Pebbles*, an epic film set during the Chinese Civil War of the 1920s. Her impact in the movie, in which she played a missionary, was, however, quite small.

Bergen then appeared in Michael CACOYANNIS's *The Day the Fish Came Out* (1967), an ill-conceived eco-satire, before starring as a fashion model to Yves MONTAND's reporter in the romantic drama *Live for Life* (1967). A string of ill-chosen projects followed, including an incoherent screen adaptation of John Fowles's novel *The Magus* (1968) and the pretentious *Soldier Blue* (1970). She did, however, appear to good effect as the 'love' interest of both Jack NICHOLSON and Art Garfunkel in Mike NICHOLS's *Carnal Knowledge* (1971). Other films of the 1970s included *The Hunting Party* (1971), a critically maligned melodrama with Gene HACKMAN and Oliver REED, the all-star comedy-caper *11 Harrowhouse* (1974), *Bite the Bullet* (1975), a well-photographed but muddled Western, and John Milius's *The Wind and the Lion* (1975), featuring Sean CONNERY as an Arab chief. This run of critical and commercial failures continued with *The End of the World (in our usual bed in a night full of rain)* (1977), a talkative drama that was less intriguing than its title, and *Oliver's Story* (1978), a lachrymose sequel to *Love Story*. However, *Starting Over* (1979), in which she played a singer who leaves husband Burt REYNOLDS to pursue her career, provided her with a role worthy of her talents and brought her an Oscar nomination.

Since her marriage to the director Louis MALLE in 1980 Bergen has not appeared in many films. Of her more recent outings perhaps the best-received was her performance as the photographer Margaret Bourke-White in ATTENBOROUGH's *GANDHI* (1982).

More recently, Bergen has enjoyed enormous success as the star of the Emmy award-winning TV series *Murphy Brown*.

Bergman, Ingmar Bergman (1918–) Swedish director and screenwriter. The son of a Lutheran clergyman, Bergman attended Stockholm University, where he began writing, directing, and acting in student theatre productions. He subsequently worked in the theatre until 1944, when Carl-Anders Dymling, the head of the Svensk Filmindustri, commissioned him to write a screenplay. The resulting film, Alf SJÖBERG's *Frenzy* (1944), was an international success that launched the career of Mai ZETTERLING. It also led to Bergman's debut as a director with *Crisis* (1945). Although he enjoyed some success with *Music is My Future* (1947), it was not until the melancholic *Summer Interlude* (1950) that Bergman began to attract any interest outside Sweden. His reputation continued to grow with *Summer with Monika* (1952) and the powerful *Sawdust and Tinsel* (1953), which utilized a shabby circus as the backdrop to a pessimistic examination of love and deceit.

Bergman's first real international success was the lyrical *Smiles of a Summer Night* (1955), an evocative comedy of manners set at the turn of the century. The film later inspired both Stephen Sondheim's *A Little Night Music* and Woody ALLEN's *A Midsummer Night's Sex Comedy*. The director's reputation as one of the high priests of ART CINEMA was then established with THE SEVENTH SEAL (1957), a sombre meditation on mortality and God set in the Middle Ages.

Following the success of WILD STRAWBERRIES (1957), a bitter-sweet film about ageing that interweaves memories, dreams, and reality, Bergman was idolized to a degree that few other directors have been before or since and many of his earlier films were reshown. In 1960 *The Virgin Spring*, a tale of rape and revenge based on a 14th-century ballad, won an Oscar for Best Foreign Film. Bergman's next three films, *Through a Glass Darkly* (1961), which also won the Oscar as Best Foreign Film, *Winter Darkness* (1962), and *The Silence* (1963), constitute a trilogy in which he explored religious belief and the fine line between sanity and madness. The three films are regarded by many as Bergman's finest achievement. At about this time he acquired a house on the Swedish island of Fårön, where he made several films including the complex *Persona* (1966), *Hour of the Wolf* (1967), and *The Shame* (1968), all of which are concerned with the relationship between art and reality.

With *The Touch* (1970) Bergman returned to the dissection of tortuous personal relationships that had characterized his earlier films. *Cries and Whispers* (1972), a harrowing tale of a woman dying of cancer, earned an Oscar for Bergman's longtime cinematographer Sven NYKVIST. In 1976 a dispute with the Swedish government over taxes forced Bergman into temporary exile in Germany, where he made *The Serpent's Egg* (1977) and *Autumn Sonata* (1978), both of which were considered disappointing. Bergman's last film as a director, the three-and-a-half-hour FANNY AND ALEXANDER (1982), marked a clear return to form, however. The film, about a Swedish family in the early years of the century, is a compendium of Bergmanesque themes and devices that stands as a suitable finale to one of the most original careers of the postwar cinema. It won a total of four Oscars, including Best Foreign Language Film. He has continued to write screenplays, including *The Best Intentions* (1992).

Taken as a whole, Bergman's work is remarkable for its overall cohesion in both themes and style – despite his many imitators, a Bergman film is recognizably a Bergman film and no-one else's. Although much of this is due to his repeated use of fine ensemble acting talent (notably Bibi Andersson, Liv ULLMANN, Max VON SYDOW, and Gunnar Björnstrand) and two highly talented cinematographers (Gunnar Fischer and Sven Nykvist), Bergman's own contribution as both writer and director cannot be overvalued.

Ingrid Bergman (1915–82) Swedish actress, who became an international star in the 1940s. Bergman was born in Stockholm and trained at the Royal Dramatic Theatre there. After making her screen debut in *Munkbrogreven* (1935) she appeared in several other Swedish films, including the original versions of both *Intermezzo* (1936) and *A Woman's Face* (1938; later remade with Joan CRAWFORD).

It was David O. SELZNICK who brought Bergman to Hollywood to appear alongside Leslie HOWARD in the 1939 remake of *Intermezzo* (British title *Escape to Happiness*). In 1941 Bergman appeared in three films, *Rage in Heaven, Adam Had Four Sons,* and the Spencer TRACY version of *Dr Jekyll and Mr Hyde,* none of which made a huge impact. A year later, however, Bergman gained screen immortality as Ilsa Lund Lazlo in Michael CURTIZ's CASABLANCA (1942), in which she played opposite Humphrey BOGART. Neither Bogart nor Bergman were first choices for the roles, which were originally to be played by Ronald REAGAN and Ann SHERIDAN. The film, which gave a boost to Bogart's career by showing that he could play characters with a romantic streak, prompted him to comment:

> I didn't do anything I've never done before, but when the camera moves in on the Bergman face, and she's saying she loves you, it would make anybody look romantic.

A string of box-office successes followed, including *For Whom the Bell Tolls* (1943) with Gary COOPER, George CUKOR's *Gaslight* (1944), for which she received her first Oscar, *The Bell's of St Mary's* (1945), in which Bergman played a nun to Bing CROSBY's priest, and Alfred HITCHCOCK's excellent suspenser *Notorious* (1946). However, *Arch of Triumph* (1948) proved something of a disaster, losing over $3 million at the box office, and *Joan of Arc* (1948) also enjoyed little commercial success (though producer Walter Wanger won a special Oscar for adding to the 'moral stature' of the film industry).

In 1950 Bergman, who was married to a Swedish doctor, bore a child to Roberto ROSSELLINI, the director of her film of that year, *Stromboli*. Although Bergman's husband divorced her and she married Rossellini, there was a huge scandal and the actress found herself not only ostracized in Hollywood but also morally condemned in the US Senate. Following this Bergman spent a period making films abroad, mostly in France and Italy, including Jean RENOIR's *Eléna et les hommes* (1956). The storm eventually died down sufficiently for Bergman to be awarded an Oscar for her comeback film *Anastasia* (1956). Two years later she appeared opposite Cary GRANT in Stanley DONEN's *Indiscreet* (1958) – a title that many found amusingly ironic. Bergman's subsequent films included *The Inn of the Sixth Happiness* (1958), *Cactus Flower* (1969), a romantic comedy with Walter MATTHAU and Goldie HAWN, and *Murder on the Orient Express* (1974), which brought her an Oscar as Best Supporting Actress (at the Awards ceremony Bergman announced that the statuette should really have gone to Valentina Cortese for *Day for Night*). From the 1960s onwards Bergman appeared with increasing regularity on both stage and television, winning particular acclaim for her portrayal of the Israeli prime minister Golda Meir in *A Woman Called Golda* (1982).

Berkeley, Busby (William Berkeley Enos; 1895–1976) US director and choreographer, whose name became a byword for lavishly choreographed MUSICALs featuring hundreds of DANCERs. Berkeley, who established his reputation on Broadway, subsequently stunned cinema audiences of the 1930s with the kaleidoscopic and often surreal mass dance sequences he produced for a series of Warner Brothers musicals. These were usually based on the 'putting on a show' formula, as in the groundbreaking 42ND STREET (1933), the *Gold Diggers* series (1933, 1935, and 1937), *Dames* (1934), and three films with the young Judy GARLAND and Mickey ROONEY – *Babes in Arms* (1939), *Strike Up the Band* (1940), and *Babes on Broadway* (1941). Whereas film musicals had previously been notoriously 'stagey', Berkeley revolutionized the genre by introducing camera movement, overhead shots, and a strong element of the bizarre. Idiosyncratic highlights of his routines included Ginger ROGERS performing 'We're in the Money' while dressed in dollar bills in *Gold Diggers of 1933* and Carmen Miranda singing 'The Lady in the Tutti Frutti Hat' in *The Gang's All Here* (1943); when Berkeley ruined the first take by dislodging her spectacular headpiece with his camera boom, she allegedly screamed at him "knock one banana off my head and I will make of you the flat pancake!"

Berkeley occasionally directed non-musical films, such as the drama *They Made Me a Criminal* (1939), about a boxer on the run, and the comedy *Cinderella Jones* (1946).

His vitality and ingenuity transcended the limitations of his sensibility, and he bequeathed to posterity an entertaining record of the audacity of an escapist era.
ANDREW SARRIS, film critic.

Berlin. Irving Berlin (Israel Baline; 1888–1989) Russian-born US songwriter, who provided the cinema with many enduring classics over the course of his long career. A prolific composer, he turned out nearly 1000 songs – despite the fact that he could

only play the piano in a single key (he eventually had a special instrument made that allowed him to play in different keys with the same fingering).

Berlin was born in the Siberian village of Temun, the son of a rabbi; at the age of four he saw his family home burned down during a pogrom. He arrived in America with his family in 1893 and worked as a street entertainer and singing waiter before making his mark as a songwriter with the huge hit 'Alexander's Ragtime Band' (1911). Having adopted the name Berlin after his real name was misprinted on a bill, he wrote extensively for the musical stage and for Hollywood. Successful films to feature his songs include TOP HAT (1935), *Follow the Fleet* (1936), *On the Avenue* (1937), *Holiday Inn* (1942), *Easter Parade* (1948), *Annie Get Your Gun* (1950), and *Call Me Madam* (1953). The Oscar-winning song 'White Christmas', which has sold over 30 million copies, was first heard in *Holiday Inn* and subsequently reappeared in other films, notably *White Christmas* (1954). Berlin's other hits included 'Cheek to Cheek', 'Let's Face the Music and Dance', 'Anything You Can Do', 'There's No Business Like Show Business', and 'Heat Wave'.

In 1943 Berlin himself was persuaded to appear in the film *This is the Army*, a morale-booster in which he sang his own 'Oh How I Hate to Get Up in the Morning'. When one of the crew heard Berlin's relatively weak voice he shook his head sadly and muttered, "If the guy who wrote this song could hear this guy singing it, he'd turn over in his grave."

Irving Berlin has no place in American music...he is American music.
JEROME KERN, songwriter.

Berlin Film Festival An international film festival founded in (West) Berlin in 1951. The most prestigious prize awarded is the Golden Bear for Best Film, inaugurated in 1956 (in earlier years the audience voted for the best movie). Winners have included LUMET'S TWELVE ANGRY MEN (1957), CHABROL'S *Les Cousins* (1959), SCHLESINGER'S *A Kind of Loving* (1962), POLANSKI'S *Cul de sac* (1966), DE SICA'S *The Garden of the Finzi-Continis* (1971), FASSBINDER'S *Veronika Voss* (1982), David Hare's *Wetherby* (1985), LEVINSON'S *Rain Man* (1989), and Lawrence Kasdan's *Grand Canyon* (1992). The 1976 award, for ALTMAN'S *Buffalo Bill and the Indians*, was declined by the director. For many years films from the Eastern bloc countries were excluded.

Berri, Claude (Claude Beri Langmann; 1934–) French director, screenwriter, and producer, who has also starred in several of his own films. The son of a Romanian Jewish mother and a Polish father, he acted in minor film roles for 12 years (1951–63) before turning his hand to direction with the highly praised short *Le Poulet* (1963). He subsequently consolidated his reputation with *The Two of Us* (*Le Vieil Homme et l'enfant*; 1966), which drew on his experiences as a Jew during the last months of World War II. *Marry Me! Marry Me!* (1968), a lively comedy in which Berri played a young Jewish bridegroom who falls for another woman shortly before his wedding, was also well received.

During the 1970s Berri's films were less successful: *The Sex Shop* (1972) brought accusations of voyeurism, while *A Summer Affair* (1977) was said by the critics to be too bland. In the 1980s, however, he found a new audience with two films adapted from books by Marcel PAGNOL: *Jean de Florette* (1986), a beautifully photographed story about a city-dweller's doomed attempt to make a new life in the French countryside, and *Manon des sources* (1986), in which the tragic story continues ten years later. The films, which starred Gérard DEPARDIEU and Yves MONTAND, were amongst the most expensive ever made in France and enjoyed enormous international success. Depardieu also starred in Berri's *Uranus* (1991), based on Marcel Ayme's novel about the ambiguities of wartime collaboration.

The Bear (1989), directed by Jean-Jacques Annaud and produced by Berri, had the highest ever budget – $25 million – for a French film. Such was Berri's faith in the project that he took the almost unprecedented step of financing it entirely from his own resources. A film with virtually no dialogue, about a bear chased by hunters, it was surprisingly successful at the box office, grossing $100 million worldwide. Berri has since produced the big-budget epics *Germinal* (1993) and *La Reine Margot* (1994).

Bertolucci, Bernardo (1940–) Italian director and screenwriter, who provoked international controversy with *Last Tango in Paris* (1972). Bertolucci was born in Parma, the son of a poet and film critic. It was as a result of attending screenings with

his father that he developed an early interest in the cinema, producing his first amateur films at the age of 15. In 1962 Bertolucci won a prestigious Italian literary award for his book *In cerca del mistero*.

After working as an assistant to Pier Paolo PASOLINI on the making of *Accatone* (1961), Bertolucci made his own debut as a director with *La commara seca* (1962). The film, about the murder of a prostitute, made little impact at the box office. For the rest of the 1960s, Bertolucci worked variously as a television film-maker, a writer (he co-wrote the story upon which Sergio LEONE's 1968 Western *Once Upon A Time in the West* was based), and a director. His best-known films of the decade are *Before the Revolution* (1964) and *The Spider's Stratagem* (1969), about a young man who discovers that his father, a supposed hero of the Resistance was actually a traitor; the film features stunning cinematography by Vittorio Storaro, with whom Bertolucci has often worked.

The Conformist (1970), a luscious adaptation of Alberto Moravia's novel, marked Bertolucci's cinematic coming of age and earned him an Oscar for Best Screenplay. Following his wife's inexplicable suicide in 1971, Bertolucci wrote and directed *Last Tango in Paris*, a sexually explicit film that features an extraordinary performance from Marlon BRANDO as a middle-aged widower who embarks on an anonymous affair with a young actress (Maria Schneider). A great admirer of the works of GODARD, Bertolucci gave the director a passing nod in the character of NEW WAVE film-maker Jean-Pierre Leaud.

Bertolucci then indulged his predeliction for epic in *1900* (1976), a survey of Italian history from the turn of the century to 1945 that featured an all-star cast including Burt LANCASTER, Robert DE NIRO, Gérard DEPARDIEU, and Donald SUTHERLAND. The film originally ran to nearly five and half hours but for international release was cut to nearly four. Reviews were mixed; although showing obvious signs of genius, the film was patchy, over-didactic, and often gave the impression of having sacrificed content to style. Similar criticisms were levelled at Bertolucci's next film *La luna* (1979), an Oedipal drama about an opera singer and her drug-addicted son. However, *Tragedy of a Ridiculous Man* (1982), an intelligent study of terrorism and moral responsibility, was better received.

Following a number of unrealized projects, Bertolucci enjoyed enormous success with *The Last Emperor* (1987), a visually arresting film about the life of Pu Yi, the last Chinese emperor. The film won a total of nine Oscars, including Best Director and Best Screenplay for Bertolucci and Best Cinematography for Vittorio Storaro. By comparison Bertolucci's 1990 adaptation of Paul Bowles's novel *The Sheltering Sky* was a disappointment. His most recent film is *Little Buddha* (1994), a lavish account of the life of Buddha starring Keanu REEVES.

best. **best boy** or **girl** A member of the film production crew, the chief assistant to the GAFFER.

The Best Years of Our Lives (1946) William WYLER's restrained and sensitive film about the problems faced by World-War-II heroes readjusting to civilian life. Produced by Samuel GOLDWYN, the film won eight Academy Awards, including Best Film, and set box-office records. The cast included Fredric MARCH, Myrna LOY, Dana Andrews, Teresa Wright, Viriginia Mayo, and Cathy O'Donnell. Robert Sherwood wrote the screenplay from MacKinlay Kantor's novel *Glory for Me.*

In contrast to Hollywood's wartime PROPAGANDA, *The Best Years of Our Lives* had a muted anti-war message, concentrating without sentimentality on the awkward reunions and painful readjustments of homecoming warriors and their families. The plot revolves around three servicemen: an army sergeant (March) has a loving reunion with his wife (Loy) but finds his bank job so confining that he turns to drink; an Air Force major (Andrews) is rejected by his unfaithful wife (Mayo) and finds comfort with the sergeant's daughter (Wright); a seaman (Harold Russell), who has lost both hands, worries about imposing his handicap on his girlfriend (O'Donnell).

Wyler, directing his first film since leaving the Air Force, won the Academy Award for Best Director and March was named as Best Actor. Harold Russell, a nonprofessional who had lost both hands during the war and had never previously acted, took the Oscar for Best Supporting Actor and received a special Academy Award "for bringing hope and courage to his fellow veterans." He went on to become a business executive and did not appear on screen again until 1980, when he featured in *Inside Moves*, Richard Donner's film about the

problems faced by the disabled. Oscars were also awarded for music and editing and for Sherwood's screenplay.

Betty Boop A cartoon character of the 1930s, a wide-eyed flapper with a childlike voice and her own catchphrase, 'Boop-boop-a-doop' (taken from Helen Kane's song 'I Wanna Be Loved By You', later made famous by Marilyn MONROE). Created for Max Fleischer's studio by 'Grim' Natwick (the man who later animated Snow White in Disney's SNOW WHITE AND THE SEVEN DWARFS, 1937), Betty first appeared in *Dizzy Dishes* (1930). She was initially drawn as a long-eared dog, only metamorphosing into a human being in 1932.

The Betty Boop series of cartoons ran until 1939, with Betty's voice being supplied by five different actresses, including Little Ann Little and Mae Questel. One of the secrets of Betty's sex appeal was that she was occasionally drawn naked (once in every ten frames in some cartoons), thereby creating a subliminal air of eroticism.

Along with many other cartoon characters, Betty made a brief comeback in 1988 in WHO FRAMED ROGER RABBIT?.

Beulah, peel me a grape A famous line from the Mae WEST comedy *I'm No Angel* (1933). Delivered by West to her Black maid with an air of insouciance after her lover has just walked out, the line was intended to indicate her emotional self-sufficiency.

Beverly Hills A town in SW California, close to Los Angeles. It has become the home town of many of America's leading film stars and other media celebrities. Tourists are taken on coach tours of the area to view (from a respectful distance) the often palatial houses belonging to their screen idols.

Until its annexation as a HOLLYWOOD suburb, Beverly Hills consisted largely of beanfields. Douglas FAIRBANKS was the first star to move there, renting a 36-room mansion in 1919. The following year he bought an adjacent house and had it rebuilt in palatial style as a wedding present for his new bride Mary PICKFORD. Between 1922 and 1930 the population of Beverly Hills rose by an estimated 2500%. *See also* SUNSET BOULEVARD.

BFFS British Federation of Film Societies. An organization that provides information on each British FILM SOCIETY and helps to arrange screenings. It also publishes the magazine *Film*. The BFFS, which is organized into Constituent Groups on a regional basis, is serviced by the Film Society Unit of the British Film Institute (*see* BFI).

BFI British Film Institute. A British organization founded in 1933 "to promote the 20th century's major new art form, the moving image." Today this includes the development, study, and appreciation of both film and television. Its headquarters are at 21 Stephen Street, London.

The BFI National Film Archive maintains a national repository of films and television programmes, while the BFI Library and Information Services has the world's largest collection of information on these subjects. BFI Distribution circulates copies of historic and new films, television programmes, and video items. The Institute also has a Communications Group engaged in research, an Education Unit working with schools, and Publishing Services that produce a range of books and periodicals including the *Monthly Film Bulletin* and the quarterly *Sight and Sound*. BFI Production acts as producer and co-investor for short films, features, and videos.

The BFI also runs the NATIONAL FILM THEATRE and the Museum of the Moving Image (MOMI), both on London's South Bank.

Bible films *See* CHRIST; EPIC.

Bicycle Thieves (*Ladri di biciclette*; 1948) A classic of Italian NEOREALISM, co-scripted by the movement's leading theorist, Cesare Zavattini, and directed by former matinée idol Vittorio DE SICA. Shot in the poorer areas of Rome in 1948, when unemployment had reached 22%, the film tells of a father (Lamberto Maggiorani) who pawns the family sheets to redeem his bicycle, so that he can take a job as a billsticker. While he is hanging a poster for a glamorous Rita HAYWORTH movie, his bicycle is stolen. He searches for it in the company of his hero-worshipping son (Enzo Staiola), but their relationship becomes increasingly strained as despair overtakes them.

Using a much-imitated 'flow of life' structure and unobtrusive camera and editing techniques, De Sica's multilayered film operates as a powerful realist drama, a parable of the dehumanizing effects of poverty, and a touching father-son story. Having spurned an offer from Hollywood of Cary GRANT for the leading role, De Sica cast Maggiorani, a metalworker, as the father. However, he rejected Maggiorani's son at audition and only spotted Staiola during the early days of shooting. The boy's screen mother was played by Lianella Carell, a journalist who wrote to the director asking for a part in one of his films.

Bicycle Thieves won a string of prizes including a Special Oscar as the Most Outstanding Foreign Film, the New York Critics' Award, the Grand Prix of the Belgium World Festival of Film and Arts, and the Social Prize at the Locarno Festival of Film. It was affectionately parodied by Maurizio Nichetti in *The Icicle Thief* (1989).

big. **big eye** Slang for a 10,000 watt light, as used to provide floodlighting during a shoot.

big head Slang for a head CLOSE-UP, i.e. one that shows the head or face of an actor.

The Big Sleep (1946) Howard HAWKS's celebrated film adaptation of Raymond CHANDLER's first novel. Filmed in stark black and white, *The Big Sleep* is one of the finest – and certainly one of the most convoluted – examples of the FILM NOIR genre.

The plot centres on Philip MARLOWE (Humphrey BOGART), a private detective who is hired by General Sternwood to track down a blackmailer who has obtained compromising photographs of his daughter Carmen (Martha Vickers). However, it transpires that the general's true intent is that Marlowe should locate his former confidante, Shawn Regan. From here the plot takes numerous intricate detours through an unsavoury world of extortion, pornography, and murder. During his adventures Marlowe falls in love with the general's eldest daughter, Vivian (Lauren BACALL).

It is not the plot, however, that makes *The Big Sleep* a great film – even Chandler himself, when asked by Hawks who the killer was, could only reply "How should I know? You figure it out." The film owes its classic status to a combination of elements – notably a strong sense of atmosphere, some sparkling and sexually charged dialogue between Bogart and Bacall (who got married during filming), striking photography (Sid Hickox), and some fine character acting, most notably from Elisha Cook as a small-time criminal. Above all, there is Hawks's deft and knowing direction, which puts the emphasis firmly upon the characters caught in this nightmarish little world.

MARLOWE: Speaking of horses...you've got a touch of class, but I don't know how far you can go.

VIVIAN: A lot depends on who's in the saddle. Go ahead Marlowe. I like the way you work.

Michael WINNER's 1977 remake, starring Robert MITCHUM, was described by one critic as the "big snooze".

bin A container, usually made of metal and lined with canvas, in which unwound film is kept during editing. A **trim bin** has a rack of hooks on which out-takes are hung, in case they are needed later.

Biograph Popular name for the American Mutoscope and Biograph Company. It was founded in 1895 by the British-born William Dickson (1860–1935), Herman Casler, Eugene Koopman, and Henry Marvin. In that year Dickson resigned as Thomas EDISON's assistant to join Casler in developing the MUTOSCOPE, a peepshow machine that became the main rival to Edison's KINETOSCOPE. They also manufactured a bulky camera and an equally large projector, both marketed under the Biograph name (see BIOSCOPE).

The New York company then began to produce popular films under its 'AB' symbol. In 1905 *The Lost Child* was photographed by G. W. 'Billy' Bitzer using a CLOSE-UP technique later claimed by D. W. GRIFFITH as his invention. Griffith joined Biograph in 1908 to make *The Adventures of Dollie*, about a girl kidnapped by gypsies. Later that year he was appointed head of production on $50 a week.

Griffith made about 460 shorts in his six years at Biograph, and they attracted record audiences. The *Musketeers of Pig Alley* (1912), in which the 15-year-old Lillian GISH played a married woman, is often described as the first GANGSTER film. Griffith's other teenage protégées included Mary PICKFORD, Mae Marsh, Mabel Normand, and Blanche Sweet. Mack SENNETT worked as an extra for $5 a day before leaving in 1912 to form the KEYSTONE Film Company.

Like other studios of the time, Biograph made only one- and two-reelers, thinking that anything longer would send audiences to sleep; in 1913 Griffith infuriated the executives by shooting an unauthorized four-reeler, *Judith of Bethulia*. Although the studio then began to produce five-reel versions of stage plays, Griffith was not allowed

to direct them. He responded by forming his own Mutual Film Corporation (1914), taking with him the Gish sisters, most of Biograph's other actors, and his cameraman, Billy Bitzer. Biograph's plays flopped and the company went into decline, sustained only by re-releasing the 'Griffith Biographs'.

Biograph Girl Nickname of the actress Florence Lawrence (1886–1938), who appeared in numerous films for the BIOGRAPH company in the 1900s. Lawrence, who like most film actors of the day appeared anonymously, became one of the first screen actors to win a following amongst the public. In 1910, when Biograph were paying her a mere $25 a week, Carl Laemmle lured her to his Independent Motion Picture Company (see IMP) for $1000 a week. She subsequently appeared under her own name until her retirement in the 1920s. Lawrence's much-publicized defection to IMP is widely credited with creating the Hollywood STAR system, under which famous performers could command vast salaries. She was replaced at Biograph by Gladys Smith, alias Mary PICKFORD, who also moved on to IMP.

biopic Biographical picture. A film based on the life of a real person. The heyday of the biopic was the 1930s and 1940s, when Hollywood turned out numerous films depicting the struggles and triumphs of painters, composers, scientists, and statesmen. These ranged in their approach from the triviality of *Love Time* (1934) and *A Song to Remember* (1944), based on the lives of Schubert and Chopin respectively, to the schoolroom seriousness of *The Story of Louis Pasteur* (1936) and *The Life of Emile Zola* (1937).

Thereafter the fashion for such films waned. Although biopics continued to be made, and some were successful, the studios learned to regard the genre with caution. Biopics were also unpopular with the critics, who mocked the sentimental distortions of the genre on the one hand, and its tendency to a dull worthiness on the other. It was largely owing to these prejudices that Richard ATTENBOROUGH's attempts to raise the money to make GANDHI met with such little enthusiasm for so long; when the film finally emerged in 1982 it did a great deal to rehabilitate the genre. In the 1980s and 1990s the biopic has seen a new lease of life with such films as Clint EASTWOOD's *Bird* (1988), about Charlie Parker, and

Spike LEE's *Malcolm X* (1992) amongst many others.

Over the decades, celebrities from all walks of life have received the biopic treatment; painters in *Rembrandt* (1936), with Charles LAUGHTON, *Lust for Life* (1956), starring Kirk DOUGLAS as Van Gogh, and *The Agony and the Ecstasy* (1965), with Charlton HESTON as Michelangelo; writers and poets in *The Bad Lord Byron* (1948), *Devotion* (1943), about the Brönte sisters, *The Trials of Oscar Wilde* (1960), and *Shadowlands* (1994) with Anthony HOPKINS as C. S. Lewis; scientists in *The Story of Alexander Bell* (1939), with Don AMECHE as the inventor of the telephone, and *Madame Curie* (1943), with Greer GARSON; sportsmen in *The Babe Ruth Story* (1948) and RAGING BULL (1980), about the boxer Jake LaMotta; soldiers in LAWRENCE OF ARABIA (1962) and *Patton: Lust for Glory* (1970), with George C. SCOTT; and politicians in *Young Mr Lincoln* (1939), starring Henry FONDA, and *Young Winston* (1972), with Simon Ward as Churchill. Ken RUSSELL made a series of controversial biopics about composers in the 1970s, notably *The Music Lovers* (1970) with Richard Chamberlain as Tchaikovsky, *Mahler* (1973), and *Lisztomania* (1975), in which Roger Daltrey played the composer as a Cockney rock star.

Not surprisingly, however, show business itself has provided the richest source of subjects for biopics. Although these have too often presented their subjects in a cliché-ridden fashion, the chance to portray a legend has attracted many of Hollywood's top stars; biopics of musicians have proved particularly popular – largely, no doubt, because a superior musical score comes ready supplied. Examples include *The Great Ziegfeld* (1936) with William POWELL, *The Jolson Story* (1946) with Larry PARKS, *The Glenn Miller Story* (1953) with James STEWART, *Funny Girl* (1968) with Barbra STREISAND as Fanny Brice, and *Lenny* (1974) with Dustin HOFFMAN as Lenny Bruce. Biopics of rock stars include Oliver STONE's *The Doors* (1991) and the 1994 release *Backbeat*, about the early days of the Beatles.

Biopics of the living, or those within living memory, often receive a cool response from those who knew the subject; of *The Eddie Cantor Story* (1953), CANTOR himself remarked: "If that was my life, I didn't live."

bioscope A name used by several pioneering camera/projection systems in the 1890s. The earliest of these was developed in 1891 by Georges Demeny (1850–1917) as a visual aid in training the deaf to speak; originally known as the Phonoscope, it was renamed in 1895. That same year the German Max Skladanowsky (1863–1939) patented the Bioskop, a system in which two loops of film were projected simultaneously. The need for a double-projector and the limitations of the loops ensured its commercial failure. The most influential bioscope was that developed in 1896 by the American Mutoscope and BIOGRAPH company. This had several advantages over EDISON's rival system, including a smoother frame-advance mechanism and a superior projector. Edison's victory in enforcing his patents in 1907 left the Biograph system as his only significant competitor. In 1909 the two companies pooled their technical resources by forming the MOTION PICTURE PATENTS CO.

bipack Any laboratory system in which two pieces of film are packed together in a camera, projector, or printer to produce a combined image. It is mainly used in the production of MATTE shots.

Birds, The (1963) Alfred HITCHCOCK's disturbing and much-discussed horror film, based on a short story by Daphne Du Maurier. Hoping to seduce lawyer Mitch Brenner (Rod Taylor), socialite Melanie Daniels (Tippi Hedren) brings a pair of lovebirds to Bodega Bay to present to his sister. In doing so she unleashes the jealousy of his mother (Jessica Tandy) and a devoted teacher (Susanne Pleshette), as well as the unexplained fury of the local bird population. After much trauma and destruction, this ends as suddenly and mysteriously as it began. Hitchcock makes his traditional CAMEO appearance in the opening scene at a San Francisco pet shop.

The film took three years to produce and contains over 370 trick shots. (One of these, in which a group of children are supposedly pursued by a flock of birds, may lose its impact for eagle-eyed viewers who notice that only the children have shadows.) The final sequence, in which the protagonists drive slowly away from the town through thousands of birds milling on the ground, was made up from 32 separate pieces of film. Hitchcock had intended the scene to fade to black as the car disappeared from view, but executives at Universal felt this was too ambiguous and insisted on the traditional 'The End' caption.

Bernard Herrmann (who had composed the scores for such Hitchcock classics as VERTIGO, NORTH BY NORTHWEST, and PSYCHO) was commissioned to produce an electronic soundtrack, consisting entirely of simulated bird cries and wing-flapping.

Initially, *The Birds* received very mixed reviews from the critics, many of whom found the film puzzling. The performances were also judged disappointing, particularly that of Hitchcock's new discovery, Tippi Hedren. *Variety* called *The Birds* "a Hitchcock-and-bull story that's essentially a fowl ball." Since then critics have never ceased to provide explanations of its meaning. The US film historian Charles Derry has summarized their diverse opinions:

> It has been discussed as a generic work of horror which inaugurated a whole series of apocalyptic films; as a film of special effects and state-of-the-art MATTE work representing the ingenuity of Hollywood; as the most sophisticated example of Hitchcock's ability to manipulate his audiences and to play upon the spectators' fears; as a profound and personal work concerning human frailty and the importance of commitment in human relationships; as a philosophical treatise – influenced by Kafka and Poe – on the existential human condition...and as the American film most influenced by and celebrative of the MONTAGE theories promulgated by the Russian cinema theorists.

Wherever the truth lies, it is clear that the message is deeper than that suggested by Arthur Knight in the *Saturday Review*: "Leave no tern unstoned."

Birth of a Nation, The (1915) D. W. GRIFFITH's controversial masterpiece, one of the most influential films in cinema history. In 1914 Frank E. Woods, one of Griffith's team of writers, suggested that Thomas E. Dixon's novel *The Clansman* might provide a worthy topic for the director's long-cherished ambition to produce 'the greatest picture ever made'. By filling out the plot with episodes from another Dixon story, *The Leopard's Spots*, Griffith and Woods came up with the basic screenplay for an epic work covering the Civil War and the troubled period of Reconstruction.

Although budgeted at $40,000, the film cost $110,000 – Griffith's entire personal fortune – to produce. It went on to become one of the top-grossing silent films. During a highly secret nine-week shoot, Griffith employed all the techniques that he had pioneered in his earlier films, spontaneously devising set-ups according to editorial strategies that he retained in his head. The film's female lead, Lillian GISH, later recalled that "all the 'writing' was done by Griffith as he moved groups of characters around...Very often we would play episodes without knowing the complete story...Only Griffith knew the continuity of *The Birth of a Nation* in its final form." Other leading roles were played by Henry B. Walthall, Mae Marsh, and Donald Crisp.

At a time when European features were composed of some 100 juxtaposed shots, Griffith took three months to construct a film of over 1500. With a score that combined US war songs with the music of Wagner, Tchaikovsky, Beethoven, and others, it was premiered as *The Clansman* in February 1915 and went on public release under its present title in March. President Wilson allegedly stated that the film was "like writing history with lightning", a statement that was rapidly withdrawn as a storm of protest gathered around the film's depiction of the liberated slaves (played by blackfaced Whites). The New York authorities and the National Association for the Advancement of Colored People insisted that racist footage – 169 shots – be excised, riots broke out at the premieres in Boston, Chicago, Atlanta, and elsewhere, and Wisconsin banned the picture altogether. The *Nation* labelled it "improper, immoral and injurious – a deliberate attempt to humiliate ten million American citizens and portray them as nothing but beasts", while Griffith sought to defend his film in a pamphlet entitled *The Rise and Fall of Free Speech in America*.

As technically sophisticated as it was politically crude, *The Birth of a Nation* had an incalculable influence on film-making worldwide. At the last count (in 1946) some 200 million people had seen it, but its stance has made it a dangerous film to admire.

> *The Birth of a Nation* was so clearly a work of genius, however flawed, that it conferred great prestige upon the new medium of the feature film when it most needed it. The first film ever to be widely acclaimed as a great work of art and simultaneously reviled as a pernicious distortion of the truth, *The Birth of a Nation* is the cinema's

seminal masterpiece, and its paradox is the parodox of cinematic narrative itself.

DAVID A. COOK, film historian.

Bisset, Jacqueline (1944–) British actress, who has appeared in numerous films on both sides of the Atlantic since making her screen debut in *The Knack* (1964). Usually cast for her stunning looks, she has complained "I'm either offered window-dressing parts in large movies – or little art films no one ever sees. People think the movies I end up in are my real choices. I do the best things I'm offered." Her more memorable appearances include those in the moralistic drama *The Grasshopper* (1970), TRUFFAUT's *Day For Night* (1974), the underwater spectacular *The Deep* (1977), and *Class* (1983), in which she played an older woman who has an affair with her son's room-mate. Of the publicity for this film, Bisset remarked: "The picture is called *Class* but the ad campaign is anything but. They've put my head onto another body and given me enormous bosoms. All the guys are going to be disappointed." In 1985 she played the title role in a TV version of *Anna Karenina*, with Christopher REEVE and Paul Scofield as the male leads. Shrewd investment in real estate has made her one of Hollywood's richest women.

> One of the greatest bodies I've ever worked with. But besides that she is...so damned intelligent. It's a strange combination, almost a double personality.
>
> EDITH HEAD, Hollywood dress designer.

> A movie star? I sure as hell don't feel like one.
>
> JACQUELINE BISSET.

bit player A film actor who plays minor roles. Stars to begin their careers as bit players include Marilyn MONROE, John WAYNE, Charles BRONSON, Meryl STREEP, and Clint EASTWOOD.

black. black-and-white (bw) Describing a film stock that renders all shades of COLOUR as tones of black, white, or grey, or a movie shot using such a stock. Although the first colour features were made as early as the mid 1910s, it was not until 1954 that Hollywood produced more colour films than black-and-white ones. To the horror of movie buffs, even classic monochrome films are now receiving computer-applied colour through the process of 'Colorization'.

Although few black-and-white features are now made, some directors continue to prefer the technical, dramatic, and atmospheric qualities of monochrome, at least for some purposes. Films of the last 25 years made wholly or partly in black-and-white include Peter BOGDANOVICH's *The Last Picture Show* (1971), Woody ALLEN's MANHATTAN (1979), Martin SCORSESE's RAGING BULL (1980), and Steven SPIELBERG's SCHINDLER'S LIST (1993). Other films have mixed monochrome and COLOUR SEQUENCES to emphasize differences in location or mood; in *Bonjour Tristesse* (1957), for example, Otto PREMINGER filmed the bustle of Paris in black-and-white and the opulence of the Riviera in colour.

The Blackboard Jungle (1955) A film set in a run-down New York high school, adapted from Evan Hunter's best-selling novel of the same name by Richard BROOKS, who also directed. A fierce indictment of certain aspects of the US state educational system, the film shocked cinemagoers of the 1950s with its graphic depiction of classroom strife (including vandalism and attempted rape). The term *blackboard jungle* was subsequently applied to schools in downtown New York (or elsewhere) in which delinquency was rife and discipline difficult to impose.

The film starred Glenn FORD as a well-meaning teacher struggling with pupils including Sidney POITIER (then aged 31) and Vic Morrow (in his screen debut). Poitier later starred as the harassed teacher in a British comedy with a similar theme, *To Sir With Love* (1967).

The Blackboard Jungle is also remembered as the first film to make use of rock-and-roll music, notably Bill Haley's 'Rock Around the Clock'.

blacklist *See* HOLLYWOOD BLACKLIST.

Black Maria The world's first purposely designed film studio, built for Thomas EDISON by his assistant William Dickson (1860–1935) at West Orange, New Jersey. It was opened in January 1893 to produce film loops for Edison's KINETOSCOPE machines. Edison's interest in electricity had induced him to develop an electrically powered camera, which, owing to its need for a large power source, was virtually immobile; hence the need for the studio. Basically a large shed covered in black tar-paper (from which it derived its nickname), it had a roof that opened up to let in the sunlight; the whole shed could also be rotated in order to make the best use of available light.

the Black Tower Hollywood nickname for the administration building at UNIVERSAL STUDIOS in Universal City, California.

blaxploitation film A type of film designed to exploit the new pride and spending power of the US Black community in the early 1970s. Although it had a number of predecessors, most notably *Cotton Comes to Harlem* (1970), the film that really launched this trend was *Shaft* (1971), a fast-moving action movie starring Richard Roundtree as a hip Black detective. The sexual prowess of the hero was proclaimed none too subtly in Isaac Hayes's hit theme song ("Who's the black private dick that's a sex machine to all the chicks? Shaft!"). *Shaft*'s success with both Black and White audiences prompted a series of low-budget urban dramas featuring violent, sexy, and amoral Black characters decked out in the most outlandish fashions of the era. The most memorable was probably *Superfly* (1972), starring Ron O'Neal as a swaggering flamboyant drug-pusher. Rather different was *Sweet Sweetback's Baadasssss Song* (1971), a militantly anti-White film directed by and starring Martin Van Peebles (who went on to become a Wall Street investment counsellor; his son Mario Van Peebles directed the Harlem gangster movie *New Jack City*, 1991).

When the formula began to wear thin, a number of similar films were made featuring voluptuous self-assured Black heroines – notably *Coffy* with Pam Grier and *Cleopatra Jones* with Tamara Dobson (both 1973). The blaxploitation craze also led to a reworking of familiar genres in such films as *The Godfather of Harlem* (1972), *Blacula* (1972), and *Black Frankenstein* (1973). Keenen Ivory Wayans's *I'm Gonna Git You Sucka* (1988) is a funny affectionate spoof of a genre that had begun to parody itself before the mid 1970s.

Blier, Bertrand (1939–) French director, noted for his stylish and sometimes surreal black comedies. The son of the film actor Bernard Blier, he worked as an assistant director and made several documentaries in the CINÉMA VÉRITÉ style (notably *Hitler? Connais pas!*, 1962) before graduating to feature films in the 1970s. His first major success was *Les Valseuses* (1974), a deliberately shocking story featuring the then

unknown Gérard DEPARDIEU and Patrick Dewaere as two petty criminals with a cavalier disregard for everything except their own sexual pleasure. (The title is French slang for testicles.) Depardieu and Dewaere reappeared in the Oscar-winning *Get Out Your Handkerchiefs* (1978), in which they played loutish young men totally unable to comprehend the emotions of the women in their lives. *Buffet froid* (1979), often considered Blier's best film, concerns the empathy between a confused psychotic (played by Depardieu), a mass murderer, and a callous police inspector (played by Blier's father). Blier continued to explore the weaknesses of the male psyche in such films as *Stepfather* (1981), starring Dewaere as a widower tempted by his 14-year-old stepdaughter, *My Best Friend's Girl* (1983), *Our Story* (1984), and *Evening Dress* (1986), a weird comedy featuring Depardieu as a burglar who forms a ménage-à-trois with a frustrated housewife and her meek husband.

Blier's recent films include *Trop belle pour toi* (1989), a black comedy about sexual obsession in which the influence of BUÑUEL is particularly apparent. Starring Depardieu as a rich businessman who spurns his beautiful wife for a dowdy secretary, the film won a Special Jury Prize at the Cannes Film Festival. Elements of SURREALISM were still more prominent in *Merci la vie* (1991), a dark comedy about the activities of two amoral girls in a seaside town. With its puzzling flashbacks to the Occupation era, the film appeared to be drawing an obscure parallel between wartime collaboration and contemporary reactions to the AIDS epidemic.

Bernard Blier (1916–89) appeared in numerous films from the 1930s onwards, including Marcel CARNÉ's *Hôtel du nord* (1938), *Quai des orfèvres* (1947), in which he played a killer facing the gallows, *Manèges* (1950) with Simone SIGNORET, and the British film *Catch Me a Spy* (1971).

blimp A soundproof casing for a camera that prevents the whirr of the motor from being picked up by the microphone BOOM. Most modern cameras are **self-blimped**, that is, designed to operate with virtually no noise.

blind bidding A system whereby Hollywood studios required cinema owners to bid for the right to show a particular film before they had seen it (sometimes, before it was even completed). Formerly much used by studios and distributors to get rid of indifferent or untested product, it is now generally outlawed.

block. block booking The practice whereby major Hollywood studios required exhibitors (often cinemas owned by the studios) to schedule secondary films in order to receive popular selections. Fox, Warner Brothers, and Paramount were amongst the studios that engaged in this practice, which was particularly rife in the 1920s and 1930s. In 1948 block booking was declared illegal in America because it restricted trade, a decision that contributed to the decline of the B-MOVIE.

blockbuster An expensively made film that is expected to be a great box-office hit and is usually HYPED as such in advance publicity. The first film to demonstrate that a huge financial outlay could bring even vaster returns was D. W. GRIFFITH's THE BIRTH OF A NATION (1915), which may have grossed as much as $100 million. As the producer William Wanger put it, "Nothing is as cheap as a hit, no matter how much it costs." With its unprecedented length, glossy TECHNICOLOR, and spectacular success at the box office GONE WITH THE WIND (1939) was the classic blockbuster of Hollywood's Golden Era.

It was in the mid 1970s, however, that a 'blockbuster mentality' began to exert its grip on industry thinking. Ever-rising production costs led the studios to make fewer but more expensive films, in the hope of securing a major international hit on the scale of COPPOLA's THE GODFATHER (1972) or SPIELBERG's JAWS (1975). In 1977 the success of 20th Century-Fox's STAR WARS showed that a single blockbuster could transform the financial position of a studio. It was, however, the unprecedented appeal of Spielberg's E.T.: THE EXTRA-TERRESTRIAL (1981) that established the trend for spectacular escapist entertainment, aimed mainly at the young, that would dominate commercial film-making in the 1980s. Other blockbusters of this kind include Spielberg's Indiana Jones films (1981, 1984, 1989) and JURASSIC PARK (1993), the comedy fantasies Ghostbusters (1984) and Back to the Future (1985), and Tim BURTON's BATMAN (1989). Occasionally the studios miscalculated badly; projected blockbusters that became multimillion-dollar FLOPS include the science-fiction epic Dune (1984) and George LUCAS's Howard the Duck (1986).

blocking the scene The process of deciding on the positions and movements of all those involved in a scene, including the actors, the camera operators, and other members of the production team. The positioning of large objects such as furniture, etc., is also decided. These movements are usually planned prior to shooting, using STAND-INS rather than actors.

Blonde Bombshell The nickname of Jean HARLOW, the US actress and sex symbol who starred in such films as Platinum Blonde (1931) and Bombshell (1933). The phrase has since been used of any attractive and vivacious blonde.

Blondell, Joan (1909–79) US comedy actress, who made her name playing lively roles in musicals and light comedies of the 1930s. The daughter of vaudeville performers, she toured widely on the stage before making her screen debut alongside James CAGNEY in Sinner's Holiday (1930). She appeared with Cagney again in the classic THE PUBLIC ENEMY (1931), in which she played a gangster's moll, the conman caper Blonde Crazy (1931), which provided her first starring role, and the Busby BERKELEY musical Footlight Parade (1933). Her other films of the 1930s include such frothy confections as The Greeks had a Word for Them (1932), Gold Diggers of 1933 (1933), Dames (1934), and Stage Struck (1936), in which she gave a memorable performance as a singularly dizzy actress. She married her co-star Dick POWELL just before the film was released, thereby greatly boosting the box-office receipts. Her other leading men included Douglas FAIRBANKS JNR, Errol FLYNN, and Leslie HOWARD.

In the 1940s Blondell grew tired of playing pert detectives and reporters and attempted to widen her range; thereafter she mixed light comedies such as Topper Returns (1941; see TOPPER), in which she played a sexually alluring ghost, with more serious dramas including the war film Cry Havoc (1943) and A Tree Grows in Brooklyn (1944). Despite stealing the limelight from Clark GABLE and Greer GARSON in Adventure (1946) she subsequently faded from view, later making a minor comeback with The Blue Veil (1951) and other films in the early 1950s. She continued to play supporting roles until the end of her life, highlights of her later career including The Opposite

Sex (1956), *Lizzie* (1957), and *The Cincinnati Kid* (1966).

For me the sexiest woman on the screen ever was Joan Blondell.
GEORGE C. SCOTT.

blood Artificial blood, that vital ingredient in horror, SLASHER and war movies, is usually made from a mixture of coffee, food colouring, and syrup.

Bloom, Claire (Claire Blume; 1931–) British actress, a classic beauty whose films range from Shakespeare and Ibsen to spy thrillers. She began her acting career with the Old Vic Company in the late 1940s. Having made her screen debut as a teenager in 1948, Bloom shot to stardom with her radiant performance in CHAPLIN's *Limelight* (1952), in which she played a young ballerina to the star's broken-down music-hall entertainer. Subsequent roles included Lady Anne in OLIVIER's RICHARD III (1955) and Helena in the Richard BURTON film of *Look Back in Anger* (1959). She later co-starred with Burton in the Le Carré adaptation *The Spy who Came in from the Cold* (1966). In the 1970s she largely deserted the cinema for television and the stage; her few films of the decade include an adaptation of Ibsen's *A Doll's House* (1973), in which she recreated her stage role of Nora. Her television work includes *Brideshead Revisted* (1979) and *Shadowlands* (1985). More recently she returned to the big screen for such films as *Separate Tables* (1983), Stephen FREARS's *Sammy and Rosie Get Laid* (1987), and Woody ALLEN's *Crimes and Misdemeanors* (1988).

She has been married three times, to the US actor Rod STEIGER, to the film producer Hillard Elkins, and to the US writer Philip Roth (since 1989).

bloop The noise that occurs when a SPLICE or break in a film SOUNDTRACK is read by the sound system during projection. The term is also given to the patch of tape or ink that is applied to the splice in order to eliminate the noise (a process known as *blooping* or *deblooping*).

blow. blow US slang for an actor's blunder while recording dialogue or during action shots.
blow-up (1) To make an enlarged copy of a film print for public exhibition; this usually involves blowing up an 8MM or 16MM print to 35MM. *See* GAUGE. (2) To enlarge part of a film frame, thereby eliminating other parts, during printing; this may be done either to emphasize a detail or to remove unwanted parts of the image.

Blow-Up (1966) Michaelangelo ANTONIONI's enigmatic film about the relationship between the photographic image and reality. Set in the 'swinging' London of the mid 1960s, the film was the first non-pornographic movie to feature full-frontal (female) nudity. Its *succès de scandale* marked Antonioni's move into international commercial cinema after a decade as an art-house favourite.

The slight plot revolves around Thomas (David HEMMINGS), a fashion photographer who, while wandering through a park, takes some photographs of a couple embracing. The woman (Vanessa REDGRAVE) chases after him and demands the return of the negative, but he refuses. Later, when he develops the film, Thomas thinks that he can make out a figure in the background of the photograph – a man pointing a gun at the back of the woman's partner. That evening Thomas goes back to the park and finds a man's corpse; however, when he returns the following morning, the body has gone. On re-examining the film, he can no longer make out the image of the gunman.

Although much of the film now appears as dated as the Herbie Hancock soundtrack, *Blow-Up* was, at the time, one of the most successful art films ever made (it still enjoys the status of a cult classic in some quarters). The film, which made a star of Hemmings, also marked the screen debut of Jane Birkin – as one of the two teenagers with whom Thomas romps in the nude.

Antonioni was nominated for Oscars as Best Director and for his screenplay (co-written with Tonino Guerra and the playwright Edward Bond).

blue. *The Blue Angel* (1930) Josef VON STERNBERG's classic melodrama, the film that made an international star of Marlene DIETRICH. Having been forced to resign from his post after being seen in the Blue Angel nightclub, Professor Immanuel Rath (Emil JANNINGS) marries Lola Frölich (Dietrich), the singer with whom he has become obsessed. When Mazeppa (Hans Albers) pays court to Lola, Rath tries unsuccessfully to kill him; he finally dies a broken man in his old classroom. As the sleazy but alluring Lola, Dietrich captivated audiences worldwide, though she herself disliked the role and feared the film would finish her career. Highlights of the movie include her much-imitated rendition of 'Falling in Love Again', a song that has remained associated with her name.

The film is based on Heinrich Mann's novel *Professor Unrat*. Although von Sternberg dispensed with two thirds of the text to concentrate on the professor's obsession with Lola, his script had Mann's unqualified approval: "These characters, bursting forth with life, have been transplanted just as they are. And even a few of my own lines have been salvaged." The film was shot simultaneously in German and English versions.

Despite their earlier collaboration on *The Last Command* (1928), von Sternberg found Jannings difficult to work with: "a thespian who was the equivalent of a dozen wild-cats." He found directing Dietrich a less onerous task, although 'Falling in Love Again' presented a particular problem as the line "Men cluster to me, like moths around a flame" kept coming out with 'moths' as 'moss'. Sternberg gave up after 253 takes; in the film the crucial word is masked by one of the customers in the bar loudly ordering a beer.

Lola had proved a difficult role to fill, with both Mann and UFA promoting their own favoured candidates. However, having seen Dietrich in Georg Kaiser's play *Zwei Krawatten*, von Sternberg was as bewitched as Rath and persuaded UFA to cast her, despite a mediocre screen test. Shooting was nearly completed when UFA passed into the control of Alfred Hugenberg, a right-winger who disapproved of Mann's politics and threatened to abandon the picture. However, when the director persuaded Mann to write a letter complaining about the misrepresentation of his novel, Hugenberg was appeased. Von Sternberg later recalled his sense of achievement as he returned to Hollywood with Dietrich (whom he was to direct in a further six features):

> By having made *The Blue Angel*, the most widely circulated German film, I had made a German woman the toast of many lands, and, if nothing else, had spread good will for the Germans at a time when they were not very popular.

A 1958 remake of the film, directed by Edward DMYTRYK with Curt Jurgens and May Britt, failed to impress the critics.

> I can only say that she makes reason totter on her throne.
>
> JAMES AGATE, of Dietrich in *The Blue Angel*.

blue movies Pornographic films not available for general public showing (*see* PORNOGRAPHY). Although the origin of the term has never been adequately explained, there is a longstanding and widespread connection between sexual activity and the colour blue. (The Chinese, for instance, have always painted their brothels blue.) Perhaps the most likely explanation, however, is an association with the censor's *blue pencil* (a term originating from the pencils wielded by military censors in the last century). In 1968 Andy WARHOL directed a film called *Blue Movie*, which featured a 35-minute sex scene, the longest on record.

blue pages Jargon for pages added to or substituted for part of the working script during filming. Revised scenes are sometimes printed on coloured paper to distinguish them from earlier versions.

blue-screen process A process used to combine separately filmed foreground and background action in a single composite print. First, the foreground action is photographed against a uniform blue background. Colour filters are then used to produce two **travelling mattes** from the negative (*see* MATTE): one with the foreground blank and the background dark; and one with the background blank and the foreground action rendered in silhouette. Using an OPTICAL PRINTER, the first matte is combined with the original film to block out the blue background, and the second matte with the separately filmed background scene. When the negatives so produced are combined in turn, there should be a perfect fit of foreground and background action. The system has several advantages over FRONT PROJECTION or BACK PROJECTION, in that it requires less preparation, allows greater camera movement, and permits the use of a greater range of special effects in printing.

A reverse blue-screen process has been developed for use with models. The paint used on the models contains phosphers, which emit a blue glow in ultra-violet light. The scene is filmed twice, with and without ultra-violet light, to produce the mattes. This process was developed for the film *Firefox* (1982).

board *See* CLAPPER BOARD; NUMBER BOARD.

body double *See* DOUBLES.

Bogarde, Sir Dirk (Derek van den Bogaerde; 1921–) British actor and author. Bogarde made his screen debut (as an extra) in the George FORMBY film *Come On George* (1940), but owing to war service was not seen on screen again until 1947. He first came to critical attention with his portrayal of a young spiv in Basil DEARDEN's police drama *The Blue Lamp* (1949).

Bogarde appeared in over 20 films during the 1950s, chiefly playing amiable characters in light comedies, such as *Doctor in the House* (1953) and its follow-ups; these films brought him wide popularity but did little to extend the range of his acting. His finest performances of this period were in villainous roles, notably in Charles Crichton's *Hunted* (1952) and Lewis GILBERT's *Cast a Dark Shadow* (1955).

In the 1960s Bogarde broadened his range, beginning with the courageous decision to play Melville Farr, the homosexual barrister in Dearden's *Victim* (1961). He also made a series of interesting films with the director Joseph LOSEY: THE SERVANT (1963), a searching examination of the British class system in which a working-class valet (Bogarde) subjugates his upper-class employer (James FOX), was followed by *King and Country* (1964), the high-camp *Modesty Blaise* (1966), and *Accident* (1967).

After moving to France in the late 1960s Bogarde appeared in a number of highly regarded European films including Luchino VISCONTI's *The Damned* (1969). Visconti's elegaic *Death in Venice* (1971) drew a particularly sensitive and powerful performance from Bogarde as an ageing German composer facing death, and is arguably his finest achievement. Subsequent films include *The Night Porter* (1973), a controversial story about the sadomasochistic relationship between a former SS concentration-camp commandant and one of his former prisoners, Alain RESNAIS's *Providence* (1977), and the all-star war movie *A Bridge Too Far* (1978).

In recent years Bogarde has appeared mainly on the small screen, having broken his earlier resolve never to work for television ("I don't want my audience going for a piss or making tea while I'm hard at work"). He has also written several novels and volumes of autobiography.

I owe the public nothing more than good entertainment. That's all they're paying me for.

DIRK BOGARDE, on his right to privacy in his off-screen life.

Bogarde doesn't care to hide his cruel streak. In part...it's a reaction born of the battles he's had to fight, for acceptance as an actor, for acceptance as a homosexual, for acceptance as a writer.

RICHARD RAYNER.

Bogart, Humphrey (1899–1957) US actor, best known for playing cynical wisecracking tough guys; one the of the most enduring of Hollywood cults. The diminutive (5′4″) star was noted for his crooked sardonic smile and slight lisp – both of which resulted from a bungled operation to remove a splinter from his lip as a child (although studio publicity attributed them to injuries sustained in World War I). Although he earned his only Oscar for his performance as Charlie Allnut in THE AFRICAN QUEEN (1951) he is best remembered for the wartime drama CASABLANCA (1942), in which he played Rick Blaine. His fourth wife was the actress Lauren BACALL.

Bogart was born in New York, the son of a surgeon. After serving in the Navy during World War I, he returned to New York to work as a broker's messenger, stage manager, and (from 1922) actor. Despite appearing in a series of routine comedy films from 1930 onwards, he made little immediate impression. In 1935, however, he won acclaim as the GANGSTER Duke Mantee in Robert Sherwood's play *The Petrified Forest*; although Warner Brothers wanted Edward G. ROBINSON to play the part in their 1936 film version, Leslie HOWARD, the film's star, insisted on appearing with Bogart. His performance in the film led to a series of gangster roles in such movies as *Dead End* (1937), *Angels with Dirty Faces* (1938), with James CAGNEY, and the gloomy *High Sierra* (1941), which gave him his first starring role.

The archetypal Bogart persona – that of a would-be cynic who cannot entirely suppress his more chivalrous instincts – emerged for the first time in John HUSTON's crime drama THE MALTESE FALCON (1941) and was further refined in Michael CURTIZ's ever-popular *Casablanca*. Bogart then co-starred with Bacall in two films by Howard HAWKS – *To Have and Have Not* and THE BIG SLEEP (1946), in which he played Philip Marlowe. His other films of the 1940s included THE

TREASURE OF THE SIERRA MADRE (1948), in which he played a gold prospector, and the thriller *Key Largo* (1948), both directed by John Huston.

To those who knew him, Bogart often seemed to be trying to live up to his hard-boiled hard-drinking image off-screen. He often commented, "I don't trust anyone who doesn't drink." In 1947, when Bacall threw a surprise party for his birthday, he arrived home drunk and hurled abuse at his waiting friends, yelling, "Who needs these bums! Get the bastards out of here!" "The trouble with Bogart", John Huston once said, "is that he thinks he's Bogart."

In 1951 Bogart teamed up with Huston once again to make *The African Queen*, in which he played a gritty boat owner lumbered with spinster Katharine HEPBURN. He was already ill with cancer when he made *The Caine Mutiny* (1954), a film that brought him an Oscar nomination for his performance as the psychotic Captain Queeg. When Bogart died, his wife placed his ashes in an urn with a gold whistle inscribed, "If you want anything, just whistle" – the famous line she had spoken to him in their first film together.

Bogdanovich, Peter (1939–) US director and screenwriter, who earned initial comparisons to Orson WELLES but was later jokingly nicknamed 'Peter Bogged-Down-A-Bit'. He received an Oscar nomination for directing *The Last Picture Show* (1971).

Bogdanovich was born in Kingston, New York, the son of a Yugoslavian immigrant painter. As a young man he played bit parts on stage, directed off-Broadway, and wrote film criticism, including monographs on his favourite directors, Welles, John FORD, Alfred HITCHCOCK, and Howard HAWKS.

In 1966 Roger CORMAN of American International Pictures gave Bogdanovich his first break in the cinema by using him as an uncredited SECOND-UNIT DIRECTOR on *The Wild Angels*. Corman then gave him two weeks to shoot the thriller *Targets* (1967), including only two days with the star, Boris KARLOFF. Bogdanovich's wife, Polly Platt, was production designer (and would later act as art director on all his films before their divorce in 1972).

His next three films were major critical successes. *The Last Picture Show*, which used a small Texas town in the 1950s as a microcosm of US life, featured newcomers Jeff BRIDGES and Cybill Shepherd (who became

the director's lover). Bogdanovich shot it in black-and-white because "Colour always has a tendency to prettify." *Newsweek* called the movie "the most important work by a young director since CITIZEN KANE." This was followed by *What's Up Doc?* (1972), a SCREWBALL COMEDY starring Barbra STREISAND and Ryan O'NEAL, and *Paper Moon* (1973), a black-and-white film about a travelling Bible salesman and his daughter (played by O'Neal and his real-life daughter Tatum). These early successes were followed by a string of failures. Shepherd starred in two, the Henry James adaptation *Daisy Miller* (1974) and the disastrous musical *At Long Last Love* (1975), with Burt REYNOLDS. When *Nickelodeon* (1976) – a nostalgic film about the early days of Hollywood starring Reynolds and the two O'Neals – also flopped, Bogdanovich did not make another film for three years. He returned with another box-office failure, the black comedy *Saint Jack* (1979).

With his career in deep disarray, Bogdanovich also suffered a grave personal trauma when his girlfriend, *Playboy* model Dorothy Stratten, was murdered by her jealous husband. He subsequently married Stratten's younger half-sister.

In 1985 Bogdanovich revived his reputation somewhat with *Mask* (1985), an emotional film starring CHER as the mother of a hideously deformed teenager. However, both *Texasville*, a downbeat sequel to *The Last Picture Show* that again starred Bridges and Shepherd, and *Noises Off* (1992), an adaptation of Michael Frayn's farce about a bumbling theatre company, proved flops.

Bolex Tradename of a lightweight Swiss camera. It is often used for news or DOCUMENTARY work.

Bollywood An informal term for the massive film industry based in Bombay, India, the centre of Hindi film production since the early 1930s. The term – a conflation of Bombay and Hollywood – is sometimes used more loosely of INDIAN CINEMA as a whole.

Bondarchuk, Sergei (1920–94) Russian director, screenwriter, and actor. A child actor, he studied at the Rostov Drama School and subsequenlty at Moscow's All-Union State Institute of Cinematography. After making his film debut in Sergei Gerasimov's *The Young Guard* (1948) he soon developed into a major star of the Soviet cinema. Amongst his leading roles were *Tara Shevchenko* (1951) and *Othello* (1956), in which he appeared opposite his future wife Irina Skobtseva.

In 1959 Bondarchuk made an impressive debut as a director with *Fate of a Man*, in which he also played the central character, a Russian soldier. An intimate and realistic look at the way in which individuals cope with war, the film is unusually free from propaganda for a Soviet film of this period. However, the crowning glory of Bondarchuk's career, and the most ambitious effort in Soviet cinema history, was his four-part screen version of Tolstoy's *War and Peace* (1966), which took five years to complete and cost up to $70 million. It was filmed in 168 different locations with a cast of 120,000, including Bondarchuk himself in the leading role. This was followed by another epic, the Soviet-Italian co-production *Waterloo* (1970), which culminated in a spectacular hour-long battle sequence featuring 20,000 extras from the Red Army. (For international release the film was cut from four hours to 132 minutes.) Bondarchuk then returned to Russian themes in the Chekhov adaptation *Uncle Vanya* (1974), *The Steppe*, which he also scripted, and *Ten Days That Shook the World* (1982), a remake of the EISENSTEIN epic about the Bolshevik Revolution. His last films included *Boris Godunov* (1987).

Bond films A series of spectacular action films featuring the British secret agent James Bond (codename 007). The suave, resourceful, and virile Bond was originally created by the novelist Ian Fleming (1908–64) – allegedly in an attempt to take his mind off his impending marriage. While Bond's name was taken by Fleming from that of an ornithologist neighbour, his adventures were loosely based on those of the British spy Sidney Reilly and the double-agent Dusko Popov, both notorious womanizers.

Bond first appeared on screen in 1954, when *Casino Royale* was adapted for US television with Barry Nelson in the lead. It was in 1961, however, that producers Albert R. ('Cubby') Broccoli and Harry Saltzman bought the rights to the Bond books and began work on a series of big-screen adventures that would continue to appear regularly for over 30 years. Despite a host of star contenders, the virtually unknown Sean CONNERY was cast in the role of Bond. Over the next five years Connery starred in *Dr No*

(1962) and *From Russia with Love* (1963; both directed by Terence YOUNG), *Goldfinger* (1964; directed by Guy Hamilton), *Thunderball* (1965; Young), and *You Only Live Twice* (1967; Lewis GILBERT), before abandoning the role for more challenging parts. That same year Charles K. Feldman produced the Bond spoof *Casino Royale*, directed by John HUSTON, Val GUEST and Joseph McGrath, amongst others. The film, starring David NIVEN as a stuttering sexless Bond, flopped badly, being neither an adequate parody nor a successful comedy in its own right.

In 1969 male model George Lazenby took the part in *On Her Majesty's Secret Service*, directed by former series editor Peter Hunt. Although one of the best Bond films, audiences missed Connery's charisma, and he was recalled for *Diamonds are Forever* (1971; Hamilton).

Roger MOORE's long stint as Bond began with *Live and Let Die* (1973; Hamilton). In some ways Moore was closer to Fleming's original idea of the character than Connery, but subsequent scripts came to rely too much on the star's charm and humour to mask their essential implausibility. Moore played Bond in *The Man with the Golden Gun* (1974; Hamilton); *The Spy Who Loved Me* (1977) and the STAR WARS-influenced *Moonraker* (1979; both Gilbert); and *For Your Eyes Only* (1981), *Octopussy* (1983), and *A View to a Kill* (1985; all directed by John Glen). Saltzman left the series after *The Man with the Golden Gun*, leaving Broccoli (who once said that "stumbling on Fleming and Bond was a piece of good luck – the rest was hard work") in sole charge of production. Despite the series' decline, the Roger Moore Bonds regularly appeared in the top-ten box-office hits of the 1980s. Even a further return to the role by Connery in *Never Say Never Again* (1983) failed to damage the earnings of the other Bond film released that year.

Indeed, the success of the Bond films should never be underrated. Until the late 1970s they were the top-grossing film series in the world; they created an international star in Connery and spawned such a host of copies that the SPY thriller became perhaps the dominant cinematic form in the COLD WAR 1960s.

In 1987 Shakespearean actor Timothy Dalton took on the role in *The Living Daylights*, with Glen once more directing. While returning to Fleming's books for inspiration on the one hand, Dalton brought Bond up to date on the other, playing him as a burnt-out assassin who (in Dalton's words) "lives on the edge". After Dalton's second and last Bond film, *Licence to Kill* (1989; Glen), legal complications brought the series to a stand-still, although these now appear to have been resolved. In the next Bond film, provisionally entitled *Goldeneye*, the role will be played by Pierce Brosnan. It remains to be seen if Bond can make an impression in the post-AIDS post-Cold War world of the 1990s.

> I don't think a single other role changes a man quite so much as Bond. It's a cross, a privilege, a joke, a challenge. And it's as bloody intrusive as a nightmare.
> SEAN CONNERY; *Sunday Mirror*, 1971.

Bonnie and Clyde (1967) Arthur Penn's landmark GANGSTER movie, based on the true story of Bonnie Parker (1911–34) and Clyde Barrow (1909–34), who went on a rampage of crime and violence across Texas, Oklahoma, New Mexico, and Missouri in the 1930s. Starring Faye DUNAWAY and Warren BEATTY in the title roles, it proved one of the most influential and popular films of the late 1960s. Its success did much to confirm Parker and Barrow (who were eventually gunned down in a police ambush after being betrayed by a confederate) as folk heroes.

Although in many ways reminiscent of the gangster movies of the pre-war era, the film broke new ground by mixing scenes of brutality and murder with comic and romantic episodes. Despite the graphic violence – Bonnie and Clyde are finally shot down in bloody slow motion – the story takes on the atmosphere of a fairytale. Much of the film's success was owing to the striking photography of Burnett Guffey, whose re-creation of the Depression era in dilapidated towns across southern America was recognized with an Academy Award. (Three of the banks featured in the film were those actually robbed by the real Bonnie and Clyde, meticulously restored to their original appearance.) The supporting cast included Gene HACKMAN, Estelle Parsons (who won an Oscar), and Michael J. Pollard; Beatty, Dunaway, Penn, and the film itself were among the unsuccessful Oscar nominees.

The film is associated in the minds of many with the hit single 'Ballad of Bonnie and Clyde', which was released by Georgie Fame in 1967: although the song was inspired by the film, it was not used on the soundtrack.

boom A lightweight telescopic arm used to suspend a microphone or camera over the action while remaining outside the frame. A hand-held boom is called a FISHPOLE. The most frequent of all technical mistakes is the dreaded appearance of the boom or its shadow on the final print.

Boorman, John (1933–) British film and television director, now resident in Ireland. Boorman began his career as a critic before making a number of documentaries for television in the early 1960s. His first feature, *Catch Us if You Can* (1965) a vehicle for the pop group the Dave Clark Five, was followed by *Point Blank* (1967), which showed an original creative approach to the traditional thriller. The theme of self-discovery, always important in Boorman's work, came to the fore in *Hell in the Pacific* (1969), a World-War-II drama in which a US and a Japanese soldier pursue their own private version of the larger conflict on a desert island, the curious fantasy *Leo the Last* (1970), and the Oscar-nominated *Deliverance* (1972). The last-named film, about four business executives who find their lives threatened by maniacal hillbillies while holidaying in a wilderness area of America, starred Burt REYNOLDS and Jon Voight as well as featuring an early appearance by Boorman's son Charley. This hugely popular movie is also remembered for its 'Duelling Banjos' theme music, which became a hit single.

In contrast such films as *Zardoz* (1974), a science-fiction epic, and *Exorcist II: The Heretic* (1977) failed to please either critics or audiences, while *Excalibur* (1981), a highly imaginative departure into Arthurian legend, had a mixed reception. More recent films include *The Emerald Forest* (1985), about a father's search for his son, who has been brought up by Indians in the Amazonian rainforest, and *Hope and Glory* (1987), a nostalgic re-creation of London during the Blitz. Charley Boorman appeared in both these films – as the missing son in *The Emerald Forest* and as a Luftwaffe pilot in *Hope and Glory*. In 1992 Boorman launched *Projections*, an annual magazine intended as a forum for film-makers.

> Movies are the repository of myth. Therein lies their power.
> JOHN BOORMAN.

booster light   A lamp used to augment day-light during outdoor location shooting. Its main purposes are to heighten details and block out shadows.

Bost, Pierre   *See* AURENCHE, JEAN.

Boulting brothers   The twin brothers John Boulting (1913–85) and Roy Boulting (1913–), British directors, producers, and screenwriters who are mainly remembered for their satirical comedies of the late 1950s and 1960s. The brothers set up their own independent film company in 1937 before serving in World War II. Subsequently, taking turns to fill the roles of producer and director, they made such films as *Fame is the Spur* (1946), *Brighton Rock* (1947), an adaptation of Graham GREENE's novel, and *The Guinea Pig* (1949).

Their next series of films satirized a number of British institutions – the army in *Private's Progress* (1955), with Ian Carmichael, the Bar in *Brothers in Law* (1956), and the diplomatic service in *Carlton-Browne of the FO*, with TERRY-THOMAS and Peter SELLERS. Perhaps their most successful film was *I'm All Right Jack* (1959), which made a star of Sellers while taking a swipe at the trade unions. Other films included *Lucky Jim* (1957), from the novel by Kingsley Amis, *The Family Way* (1966), starring Hayley MILLS (whom Roy later married), and *There's a Girl in My Soup* (1970), with Goldie HAWN. The brothers were directors of the BRITISH LION FILM CORPORATION from 1958 to 1972 and of Charter Film Productions from 1973.

Bow, Clara   (1905–65) US actress, the red-haired IT GIRL who was the premier film flapper of the Roaring Twenties and lived an even wilder life off screen. Also known as the **Brooklyn Bonfire**, she received over 30,000 fan letters in a single month at the height of her career.

Born in New York, the daughter of a waiter and a mentally unstable mother, Bow grew up in poverty. In 1920 victory in a beauty contest brought her a bit part in *Beyond the Rainbow*, her first film. The night she landed her first big role in *Down to the Sea in Ships* (1922), her mother woke her with a butcher's knife, saying "You'd be better off dead than in show business."

In 1925 producer B. P. Schulberg, who had signed Bow for $50 a week, took her with him to Paramount. Billing her as 'The Hottest Jazz Baby in Films', the studio capitalized on her bobbed hair, 'bee-stung' mouth, and zest for life in such movies as *Wings* (1927). Later that year she became a sensation in *It*, playing a pert shop girl who tells her boss, "I'll take the snap out of your garters!" The film was based on a notorious book by British novelist Elinor Glyn.

Bow made the transition to sound in *The Wild Party* (1927); unfortunately the stationary sound cameras put a halt to her frisky movements and revealed her nasal Brooklyn accent. She delivered her first line, "Hello everybody!" with such energy it burst a valve in the recording room.

Paramount offered Bow a $500,000 bonus if she avoided scandal, but she stood no chance of collecting. Her actor lovers included Fredric MARCH, Bela LUGOSI, and Gary COOPER, of whom she made the less-than-complimentary remark: "When he puts his arms around me I feel like a horse." She once played a nude football game with a squad from the University of Southern California (which included Marion Morrison, who later became John WAYNE).

In 1930 Bow sued her former secretary for embezzlement and the woman retaliated by giving details of the star's unbridled sex life. After a nervous collapse in 1931 Bow retired, marrying Western star Rex Bell to settle on his ranch and raise two sons. Fox paid her $125,000 for a two-film comeback in the early 1930s, but thereafter she retired for good. By 1939 her weight had risen to over 14 stone. Bow spent much of her later life in mental homes, dying in a Los Angeles sanatorium.

> She danced even when her feet were not moving.
> ADOLPH ZUKOR, film producer.

Bowery Boys, the   A gang of young street kids who featured in a series of comedies from the later 1940s onwards. Headed by their tough canny leader Leo Gorcey and the slow-witted Huntz Hall, they made 48 films in 13 years (1946–58), including five the first year. Other members of the gang were Bernard and David Gorcey, Bobby Jordan, Gabriel Dell, Billy Benedict, and Bernie Bartlett. By 1958 most of the 'kids' were in their forties.

The Bowery Boys grew out of the **Dead End Kids**, a team of young actors who appeared in a number of serious slum dramas beginning with Warners' *Dead End* (1937). The team then fragmented, with several members going to Universal to make *Little Tough Guy* and the *Little Tough Guys in Society* (both 1938) and others joining Monogram's copycat team the **East Side Kids**. In 1946 members of the three groups came together to form the Bowery Boys. The new team quickly became known for its rowdy comic antics in such films as *Spook Busters* (1946), *Hold that Baby* (1949), *Feudin' Fools* (1952), and *The Bowery Boys Meet the Monsters* (1954).

box office A small booth at a cinema from which tickets are purchased. In the 1960s Loew's 175th Street Theatre in New York made an unsuccessful attempt to replace the box office with an automatic ticket dispenser.

The term is also used of the revenue earned by a specific film, a shortening of the phrase *box-office receipts*. A star or film may be described as *good* or *bad box office*.

Boyer, Charles (1899–1978) French-born US actor. One of Hollywood's 'Great Lovers' of the 1930s and 1940s, he starred opposite such leading ladies as Jean HARLOW, Greta GARBO, Marlene DIETRICH, Ingrid BERGMAN, and Bette DAVIS. He received a special Oscar after World War II for founding the French Research Foundation in America.

Boyer studied philosophy at the Sorbonne and drama at the Paris Conservatoire before making his French stage and screen debut in 1920. He went to Hollywood in 1929 but achieved only moderate success in such roles as Jean HARLOW's chauffeur in *Red-Headed Woman* (1932). However, his 'romantic' accent, elegance, and charm won him a growing body of admirers from the mid 1930s onwards. His roles included a Trappist monk beloved by a devout socialite (Dietrich) in *The Garden of Allah* (1936), the tragic Archduke Rudolph of Austria in *Mayerling* (1937), the film that made his international reputation, Napoleon in *Conquest* (1937), with Garbo playing the Emperor's Polish mistress, a gangster in *Algiers* (1938), Ingrid BERGMAN's murderous husband in *Gaslight* (1944), and a German refugee surgeon in *Arch of Triumph* (1948). *Love Affair* (1939), in which Boyer was paired with Irene DUNNE, became the favourite film of both stars. Dunne later recalled, after Boyer's death: "The last time I saw *Love Affair*, I said to him, 'You know, Charles, you really were *good*.' 'Ah,' he said, 'so you finally looked at *me*.'"

In *Hold Back the Dawn* (1941), about a man who marries a schoolteacher to get a US visa, Boyer's character virtually disappears halfway through the film. When he refused to do a scene involving a cockroach, director Mitchell LEISEN was so infuriated that he had most of Boyer's later scenes written out.

Boyer joined Dick POWELL and David NIVEN to found Four Star Television in 1951 (they never found a fourth star) and appeared in their *Four Star Theatre* series through the 1950s. He continued to make films – including *The Happy Time* (1952), *A Very Special Favour* (1964), and *Barefoot in the Park* (1968) – until 1976, when he and director Vincente MINNELLI bowed out together with *A Matter of Time*, starring Liza MINNELLI and Ingrid Bergman.

Boyer was married to the British-born actress Patricia Paterson. Their only child, Michael, took his own life in 1965 and Boyer himself committed suicide in 1978, two days after his wife's death.

Branagh, Kenneth (1960–) British actor and director, born in Belfast, whose precocious talents first emerged in the mid 1980s. In 1984, at the age of 23, Branagh became the youngest actor to play the title role in *Henry V* with the Royal Shakespeare Company. Two years later he founded his own Shakespearean troupe, the Renaissance Theatre Company. He also starred in the television series *Fortunes of War* with Emma THOMPSON, whom he married in 1989. The 'Ken-and-Em' relationship, particularly Branagh's casting of Thompson in leading roles in most of his films, has been the subject of much media attention, not all of it generous. However, Thompson's recent successes outside her husband's films have largely silenced such criticism.

Branagh made his big-screen debut in *High Season* (1986), following this with a starring role in *A Month in the Country* (1987), about two World-War-I veterans. In 1989, with a seven-month shooting schedule and a budget of just $7.5 million, he directed his first feature, a naturalistic and surprisingly pacifist version of *Henry V*, in which he gave an Oscar-nominated performance in the title role. Comparisons with OLIVIER were inevitable and not always favourable: Richard Corliss in *Time* wrote that "Branagh seems as remote from Laurence Olivier as...Sandra Bernhard is from Sarah Bernhardt." However, the film is generally considered the cinematic equal of Olivier's version, and far more accessible to the modern audience (*see* SHAKESPEARE).

Branagh moved to Hollywood for his next directing project, the thriller *Dead Again* (1991), in which he and Thompson played two roles each and Robin WILLIAMS made an uncredited appearance. *Peter's Friends* (1992) was a wry comedy featuring Branagh's immediate circle of friends, including Stephen Fry as the aristocratic title character.

Branagh made an uncredited appearance as a Nazi villain in *Swing Kids* (1992) before directing and starring in another Shakespearean film, the comedy *Much Ado About Nothing* (1993), which saw his regular cast (Thompson, Richard Briers, and Branagh's mother-in-law Phyllida Law) appearing with Hollywood stars Denzel Washington and Keanu REEVES. *Mary Shelley's Frankenstein* (1994), his first movie without Thompson, was another transatlantic production, starring Robert DE NIRO as the monster, Branagh as his creator, and Briers as the blind hermit.

Brando, Marlon (1924–) US actor, who achieved international fame at the forefront of the METHOD movement in the 1950s; despite making only only a handful of screen appearances since the late 1960s, he has remained one of the most famous actors in the world.

The son of a salesman and an actress, Brando was sent to a military academy in Minnesota but was subsequently expelled. After a period of drifting he arrived in New York, where he studied with Stella Adler and with Elia KAZAN at the ACTORS' STUDIO. He was voted Broadway's Most Promising Actor for his role in *Truckline Café* (1946) and then confirmed his potential with an electrifying performance as Stanley in Tennessee Williams's *A Streetcar Named Desire* (1947).

To prepare for his first screen role as Ken, a paraplegic World-War-II veteran in *The Men* (1950), Brando spent weeks in a physical therapy ward observing the day-to-day difficulties of life in a wheelchair. The following year he repeated his Broadway triumph in the screen version of *A Streetcar Named Desire* (1951), earning his first Oscar nomination as Best Actor. Two further nominations followed: for *Viva Zapata!* (1952), in which Brando played the Mexican revolutionary leader, and for Joseph

MANKIEWICZ's *Julius Caesar* (1953), in which he played Mark Antony. Brando's next appearance was in Stanley KRAMER's *The Wild One* (1954), in which he starred as Johnny, the leader of a motorbike gang that terrorizes a small town. His brooding performance both added to his own off-screen reputation as a rebel and gave rise to a long line of moody teenage ANTIHEROES. The film's best-known lines of dialogue, between Brando and Mary Murphy as Kathie, have passed into screen legend:

KATHIE: What are you rebelling against?
JOHNNY: What've you got?

Brando's next film, ON THE WATERFRONT (1954), reunited him with Kazan to stunning effect. Brando played Terry Molloy, a one-time boxer now running errands for Johnny Friendly, a corrupt docker's union boss. An essay in gritty NEOREALISM, the film collected eight Oscars including one for Brando as Best Actor.

Subsequent roles included Sky Masterson in *Guys and Dolls* (1955) and the wily Sakini in *Teahouse of the August Moon* (1956), in which he demonstrated an ability to play comedy. In *Sayonara* (1957) Brando played a US Army major caught between regulations and matters of the heart; the part brought Brando another Oscar nomination. *The Young Lions* (1958), which also featured Montgomery CLIFT, saw Brando playing an idealistic German soldier.

By and large the 1960s were not good for Brando; his only film as director, the Western *One-Eyed Jacks* (1961), was not especially successful and his choice of roles seemed wayward. Although there was a so-so *Mutiny on the Bounty* (1962) and the well-observed *Reflections in a Golden Eye* (1967), there was also a string of box-office failures, including *The Chase* (1966) – described by one critic as "the worst thing that has happened to the movies since Lassie played a war veteran with amnesia" – and CHAPLIN's *A Countess from Hong Kong* (1967).

Although Brando made only six films during the 1970s, his reputation enjoyed a vast resurgence, largely owing to his extraordinary performance as the ageing Don Corleone in Francis Ford COPPOLA's THE GODFATHER and his no less compelling portrait of a man in crisis in BERTOLUCCI's *Last Tango in Paris* (both 1972). The former brought him his second Best Actor Oscar.

Brando subsequently co-starred with Jack NICHOLSON in *The Missouri Breaks* (1976), an eccentric Western, before appearing, in *Superman* (1978). His remuneration for the latter is thought to be the highest pro-rata salary ever paid to an actor (about $3 million for ten minutes screen time). Again, in Coppola's APOCALYPSE NOW (1979), he had a top-salaried top-billed role that amounted to less than 15 minutes of screen time.

Following a long break (nine years), a bulky Brando returned to the screen in Euzhan Palcy's anti-apartheid film *A Dry White Season* (1989). Palcy, the first Black woman to direct a feature for a major studio (MGM-UA), managed to secure Brando's talents for union rates. His performance as a liberal South African lawyer brought him an Oscar nomination for Best Supporting Actor. That same year Brando was unwillingly thrust into the headlines when his son, Christian, was arrested for the murder of his half-sister's boyfriend.

Brando's most recent films have been *The Freshman* (1990), in which he parodied his Don Corleone role, and *Christopher Columbus: The Discovery* (1992), in which he gave a subdued performance as Torquemada.

Brat Pack A group of young US film stars who emerged in the mid 1980s; they included Tom CRUISE, Matt DILLON, Emilio Estevez, his brother Charlie SHEEN, Kiefer SUTHERLAND, and Molly Ringwald. For a time, members of the group tended to be cast together in such teen dramas as *The Outsiders* (1983) and *Young Guns* (1988). The name *Brat Pack* was arrived at by analogy with the RAT PACK of the 1950s, a clique of Hollywood actors and singers led by Frank SINATRA. It is now commonly applied to any group of up-and-coming young people in a particular field.

Brazilian Bombshell The nickname of Carmen Miranda (1913–55), the extrovert Portuguese singer best known for wearing strange flower- and fruit-laden hats while performing South American songs in her many wartime films.

break. breakaway A PROP that is designed to break easily during action scenes without hurting the actors; typical examples include the bottles, chairs, and stair railings in Western saloon fights. Nevertheless, some performers have been injured by breakaways that proved too sturdy.

break figure A fixed amount of the box-office takings from a particular film, after which the exhibitor must pay the distributor a larger percentage of the receipts. Film rental contracts often involve a sliding scale in which the exhibitor pays between 25% and 50% of the gross ticket sales, depending on the film's success.

breath. breathing A blurring of the image on the screen, which appears to move in and out of focus. This is usually caused by a buckling of the film in the GATE of the projector.

Breathless *See* A BOUT DE SOUFFLE.

Brennan, Walter (1894–1974) Squawky-voiced US character actor, who appeared in more than 150 movies, including 14 in 1936 alone. He is usually remembered as a scruffy Western sidekick shuffling about in a near-scarecrow outfit. Contracted to Samuel GOLDWYN for most of his career, he won three Oscars as Best Supporting Actor in five years, including the first ever awarded (in 1936).

Born in Swampscott, Massachusetts, Brennan began his career in films as an extra and stuntman. His big break came in 1935, when Howard HAWKS tested him for the part of the grizzled Old Atrocity in *Barbary Coast* (1935). At the audition Brennan asked simply "With or without?"; when Hawks growled "With or without what?" Brennan replied "Teeth" and landed the role.

Brennan won his Oscars for *Come and Get It*, in which he played a lumberman, *Kentucky* (1938), in which he was a horse trainer, and *The Westerner* (1940), in which he supported Gary COOPER. Brennan, who could impersonate Goldwyn perfectly, once telephoned Cooper and raged convincingly, "You god-damned son-of-a-bitch, you're lousy and I want Brennan to have top billing!"

A year later Brennan was again Oscar-nominated for playing a hillbilly pastor in the war drama *Sergeant York* (1941). In the 1950s he made an easy transition to television comedy as a farmer in *The Real McCoys*. His later films include *Rio Bravo* (1959), as John WAYNE's crippled sidekick, and the comedy Western *Support Your Local Sheriff* (1969).

Bresson, Robert (1907–) French director and screenwriter, one of the most influential European film-makers to emerge since

World War II. Bresson had early aspirations to become a painter but entered the cinema as a writer of screenplays during the 1930s. After World War II (during which he spent a year as a prisoner-of-war) he made his debut as a director with *Angels of Sin* (1943), about a young nun's determination to save the soul of a murderess, even at the cost of her own life. The film set the tone for much of Bresson's later work, exploring the concept of salvation with characteristic austerity.

Les Dames du Bois du Boulogne (1945), a tragedy about a spurned lover's revenge, had a screenplay by Jean COCTEAU and a professional cast. In the films that followed, however, Bresson generally used non-professional actors and wrote the scripts himself. *Diary of a Country Priest* (1950), in which a priest comes to terms with his imminent death, *A Man Escaped* (1956), about a condemned man's escape from a Nazi prison, and *Pickpocket* (1959), concerning the redemption of a petty thief through love, are all closely observed studies of human suffering and resilience.

Among his films of the 1960s were *The Trial of Joan of Arc* (1962), *Au Hasard, Balthazar* (1966), a film about the sufferings of a donkey that has been interpreted as a Christian parable, *Mouchette* (1967), about the miseries of an unloved peasant girl, and *Une Femme douce* (1969), concerning a broken marriage that ends in suicide. An increasingly pessimistic tone pervaded his films of the 1970s, including *Four Nights of a Dreamer* (1971) and *The Devil Probably* (1977), both set in a bleak version of contemporary Paris, and *Lancelot du Lac* (1974), a violent excursion into Arthurian legend.

The most admired of Bresson's later films is *L'Argent* (1983), which traces the events linking a counterfeit 500-franc note with a motiveless axe murder; the film won the Grand Prix at the Cannes Film Festival. Bresson, whose many awards include the Légion d'honneur, has also published *Notes sur le cinématographe* (1975).

bridge. bridge music or **bridge** A short piece of background MUSIC used to connect one scene or shot to another. It is often only a few seconds long. In AROUND THE WORLD IN EIGHTY DAYS (1956), several transitions between images were accompanied by a mere eight notes of Victor Young's secondary theme music.

bridge plate *See* RISER.

bridging shot A shot used to indicate a change of time or place between one scene and the next. Traditional bridging shots for jumps in time include calendar pages flying away, the advancing hands of a clock, or images of seasonal change. A change of place may be indicated by a moving train or aeroplane or by an ESTABLISHING SHOT.

The Bridge on the River Kwai (1957) David LEAN's CINEMASCOPE war epic. Based on a novel by Pierre Boulle, the film won acclaim for its intimate profiles of a tough-minded British colonel (Alec GUINNESS) and his equally unbending Japanese captor (Sessue HAYAKAWA). Steven SPIELBERG has said, "I don't know of any director who doesn't go down on one knee whenever *The Bridge on the River Kwai* is discussed."

Set in a World-War-II Burmese prisoner-of-war camp (but shot in Ceylon), the film recounts the enforced building of the Siam Railway. Colonel Nicholson (Guinness) is ordered by the Japanese Colonel Saito (Hayakawa), to put his men to work on a strategic bridge. He heroically defends their rights under the Geneva Convention but, as construction progresses, Nicholson becomes proud of his creation and is horrified when his side blows up the bridge. Real-life British POWs condemned the film for failing to mention that some 116,000 prisoners died working on the project.

The film, produced by Sam Spiegel for Columbia, was the greatest box-office success of the decade; it won seven Oscars, including Best Picture, Best Director, and Best Actor (Guinness). Although an Oscar for Best Adaptation went to Pierre Boulle, the film was really scripted by two blacklisted Americans, Carl Foreman and Michael Wilson, who have since been credited for their contribution. Guinness was third choice for the role of Nicholson, after Humphrey BOGART and Laurence OLIVIER. Other major parts were played by William HOLDEN (replacing first choice Cary GRANT) and Jack HAWKINS. The wartime 'Colonel Bogey March' was used as a rousing background theme.

Bridges family The US actors Lloyd Bridges (1913–) and his sons Beau Bridges (Lloyd Vernet Bridges III; 1941–) and Jeff Bridges (1949–).

Lloyd Bridges was born in San Leandro, California, and made his Broadway debut in the late 1930s. He was signed by Columbia in 1941 and in four years made two dozen films, many of them Westerns. Subsequent films included *Home of the Brave* (1949), about racism in the army, and HIGH NOON (1952), in which he played Gary COOPER's eager deputy. During the investigations of the House Un-American Activities Committee in the early 1950s, Bridges confessed to past Communist Party membership. From the late 1950s he worked increasingly in television, starring in the hit underwater series *Sea Hunt* (1957–60) and making numerous TV movies, including the epic *Roots* (1977). He later moved into comedy, appearing in such films as the spoof disaster movie *Airplane* (1980) and *Hot Shots!* (1991), both of which had successful sequels. Bridges played supporting roles to his son Jeff in *Tucker: The Man and His Dream* (1988) and *Blown Away* (1994). He is married to the actress Dorothy Simpson.

Beau Bridges, born in Los Angeles, was a child actor in such films as *The Red Pony* (1949). During his schooldays, he was so embarrassed by his father's Cadillac that he insisted on being dropped off several blocks away from the school building. His adult acting career began on television in the early 1960s and continued on the big screen with *The Incident* (1967), in which he played a soldier terrorized by subway hoodlums. He was particularly acclaimed for his performance in Hal ASHBY's *The Landlord* (1970), in which he played a rich man who buys a ghetto apartment block and finds trouble. In 1989 he co-starred with younger brother Jeff as piano-playing brothers split apart by singer Michelle PFEIFFER in *The Fabulous Baker Boys*. At one point in the film Beau warmly refers to Jeff as "the unattractive one". He has also directed his parents in a television movie and appeared in many himself.

Jeff Bridges, also born in Los Angeles, made his screen debut at the age of eight months in *The Company She Keeps* (1950). In 1969 he composed music for the film *John and Mary* and was awarded his first major role as a White kid at an all-Black school, in *Halls of Anger*. Two years later he was nominated for an Oscar for his performance in Peter BOGDANOVICH's *The Last Picture Show*, in which he co-starred with Cybill Shepherd. The same performers returned as middle-aged lovers in the sequel *Texasville* (1990), their characters having aged 33 years in the interim (though only 19 years

of real time separate the two films). He also received Oscar nominations for both *Thunderbolt and Lightfoot* (1974), with Clint EASTWOOD, and *Starman* (1984), in which he played an alien who assumes the form of a young widow's dead husband. In 1989 he became the youngest actor ever honoured with a retrospective at Britain's National Film Theatre.

Bridges also starred in the courtroom drama *Jagged Edge* (1985) with Glenn CLOSE, *Tucker: The Man and His Dreams* (1988), about a revolutionary motor-car designer, Terry GILLIAM's *The Fisher King* (1991), and *The Vanishing* (1993), with Kiefer SUTHERLAND. In 1994 he made *Fearless*, in which he played a man who survives a plane crash, and *Blown Away*, his 34th film. This last title fittingly describes the real-life disasters that have recently afflicted Bridges: firestorms destroyed his Malibu retreat in 1993 and an earthquake demolished his Santa Monica home the following year.

Brief Encounter (1945) David LEAN's classic story of an illicit affair, adapted by Noël COWARD from his own one-act play *Still Life*. Coward had sold the rights to the play to MGM in the mid 1930s and had to buy them back (for £60,000 of the picture's £270,000 budget) in order to flesh out the plot for the screen. Described by one critic as "two characters in search of a bed", the film centres on the brief unconsummated affair between a doctor, Alec Harvey (Trevor HOWARD), and a middle-class housewife, Laura Jesson (Celia Johnson). On their first meeting, at a railway station, he removes a cinder from her eye, thereby initiating a friendship that leads to a series of clandestine meetings. Eventually, however, their sense of propriety demands that they end the relationship. The most lyrical passages of Rachmaninov's 2nd Piano Concerto heighten the emotional tension of this otherwise restrained drama.

Shot in Carnforth, Lancashire, in the depths of winter, the production was hampered by occasional air raids and by the local railway timetable, which meant that much of the filming had to be done at night. (Blackout restrictions in Kent, where the action of the film is set, necessitated the use of the Lancashire location.) Neither Johnson nor Howard (who were paid £1000 and £500 respectively for arguably the best performances of their careers) seems to have particularly enjoyed the experience.

The film was not an immediate success, being initially criticized for its excessive reserve. Following a preview in London's docklands, during which the audience dissolved into embarrassed laughter, Lean wanted to destroy the picture, distressed that his accumulation of everyday detail and authentic incident had been misconstrued as a stuffy portrait of suburban life and 'stiff upper lip'. Notwithstanding Oscar nominations for Best Director, Best Actress, and Best Screenplay, it was hailed as a masterpiece of intimate cinema only after its reissue in 1948. Regular television reruns have ensured its place among the most fondly remembered of British features, although its critical reputation continues to fluctuate.

British. British Academy of Film and Television Arts *See* BAFTA.

British Federation of Film Societies *See* BFFS.

British Film Institute *See* BFI.

British Lion Film Corporation A small production and distribution company founded in 1927 to film the crime stories of Edgar Wallace (1875–1932), its first chairman. The company's one stage (6235 square feet) was located at Beaconsfield, Buckinghamshire. Wallace directed the first film, *Red Aces* (1927), with the assistance of the young Carol REED, who had appeared in one of his plays. The first talkie was Wallace's *The Squeaker* (1929).

From the early 1930s British Lion concentrated mainly on importing and distributing US films. By this time the company was in debt, as was Wallace himself, who left for Hollywood in 1931 and died there shortly afterwards. In 1934 John HUSTON came over to Britain to make a joint Romulus–British Lion film, *Moulin Rouge* (1934), which proved a great success. During World War II George King made a series of melodramas for British Lion released with the production credit Pennant Pictures. The company also refinanced and distributed Noël COWARD's *In Which We Serve* (1942).

In 1946 Alexander KORDA bought out British Lion, which soon afterwards acquired SHEPPERTON STUDIOS. Despite making the hit comedy *The Belles of St Trinian's* with London Films in 1954, British Lion went bankrupt the same year. It was saved by the government's National Film Finance Corporation, which placed John and Roy BOULTING on the board. Richard ATTENBOROUGH and Bryan FORBES released their first film as producers, *The Angry Silence* (1960), through the new British Lion. The company was privatized in 1964, with Sir Michael BALCON as the new owner, and absorbed into EMI in 1976.

British Society of Cinematographers *See* BSC.

broad or **broadside**   A square 2000-watt FLOODLIGHT with a wide beam that is used to give general or diffuse illumination on a set. When shooting Scarlett O'Hara's famous corset-lacing scene in GONE WITH THE WIND, the cinematographer Lee Garmes alarmed Vivien LEIGH by yelling "Kill that broad" – meaning that he wanted the general lighting reduced so that a window frame would cast a shadow across the four-poster bed.

Broadway   A street in Manhattan that has become synonymous with New York's commercial theatre and that has exported many productions and performers to Hollywood. Some early film-makers saw the cinema as little more than a way of recording the best of the Broadway stage for posterity, but this approach proved commercially disastrous. In 1913 Adolph ZUKOR formed the company FAMOUS PLAYERS to make 'picturizations' of Broadway dramas, beginning with *The Count of Monte Cristo*. The trend was reversed later that year when the first popular feature film, Italy's QUO VADIS?, was shown in the Astor Theatre on Broadway to affluent audiences.

Film adaptations of Broadway productions have been impressive in both their number and their quality; the serious dramas of Eugene O'Neill and Tennessee Williams have transferred particularly well, as have the vast array of MUSICALs. Broadway's influence has been less solid in the field of casting, however, with studio executives mistrusting the box-office appeal of many stage stars. In 1964 Julie ANDREWS, the star of Broadway's long-running *My Fair Lady*, was passed over in favour of Audrey HEPBURN when the film version was cast; a year later, having established her screen credentials, Andrews took over Mary Martin's role in THE SOUND OF MUSIC. Other switches have been from Tallulah BANKHEAD to Bette DAVIS in *The Little Foxes* (1941), Jessica Tandy to Vivien LEIGH in *A Streetcar Named Desire* (1951), Carol Lawrence to Natalie WOOD in WEST SIDE STORY (1961), and Jill Haworth to

Liza MINNELLI in *Cabaret* (1972). Successful transfers of both play and leading players include *The Miracle Worker* (1962), in which Patty Duke and Anne BANCROFT won Oscars for re-creating their stage roles of Helen Keller and Annie Sullivan.

Broadway has also been the setting for numerous backstage films and musicals; examples include *Broadway Melody* (1929) and its sequels of 1936, 1938, and 1940.

Broken Blossoms (1919) D. W. GRIFFITH's silent melodrama about the doomed love between a Cockney girl and a young Chinese in London's Limehouse district. Her enraged stepfather, from whom she has run away, eventually kills her and is murdered in turn by the Chinese, who commits suicide. Griffith scripted the film from Thomas Burke's story 'The Chink and the Child' and cast Lillian GISH and Richard BARTHELMESS as the tragic lovers.

Griffith shot the film in 18 days without retakes and edited only 200 feet from the 5500 feet of total footage. Filmed entirely on set for just $88,000, it brought other directors rushing back from expensive locations. The beauty of Gish's face was enhanced by cinematographer Henrik Sartov, who filmed her through a series of gauzes. In one famous scene, having been ordered by her stepfather (Donald Crise) to smile through adversity, Gish slowly pushes her mouth up with her fingers. Although *Broken Blossoms* was made for Adolph ZUKOR's Famous Players, Zukor decided that the result was "too poetic" and sold it for $250,000 to the new United Artists Company, co-founded by Griffith with Mary PICKFORD, Douglas FAIRBANKS, and Charles CHAPLIN. The film went on to make a profit of $700,000.

In 1936 a talkie version of *Broken Blossoms* was made in Britain by J. H. Productions. Griffith, now aged 60 and an alcoholic, was brought over to direct but walked out after a squabble over casting. The German director Hans Brahm took over and cast his Austrian wife Dorothy Haas as the Cockney – opposite Welshman Emlyn WILLIAMS as the Chinese.

Bronenosets Potemkin *See* BATTLESHIP POTEMKIN.

Bronson, Charles (Charles Buchinski; 1922–) US actor noted for his scowling tough-guy roles in violent action films. He

has described his face as "a rock quarry that someone has dynamited."

Born in Pennsylvania, one of 15 children of a Lithuanian immigrant, he began work as a coal miner at the age of 16, earning $1 a ton. (By the mid 1970s he could command $2 million a film.) After World War II he studied art in Philadelphia, where he worked as a set designer and actor in a local company. He moved to Los Angeles in 1949 and made his screen debut in *You're in the Navy Now* (1951), later claiming "I got the job because I could belch on cue." During his early career, he adjusted his name from Buchinski to Buchinsky, finally changing it to Bronson in 1954.

In 1956 he played a bloodthirsty Indian in the Western *Run of the Arrow*, following this with the title role in *Machine Gun Kelly* (1957). He was one of the gunfighters led by Yul BRYNNER in *The Magnificent Seven* (1960), one of the POWs in *The Great Escape* (1963), and one of the 12 prisoners on a suicide mission in *The Dirty Dozen* (1967).

After leaving Hollywood to star in the French film *Guns for San Sebastian* (1968), Bronson worked mainly in France and Italy (where he became famous as 'Il Brutto'). In 1972 he returned to Hollywood, a star at last at the age of 50. Subsequent parts included the role for which he has become best known, that of the brutal urban vigilante in Michael WINNER's DEATH WISH (1974) and its numerous sequels, and a Secret Service man in *Assassination* (1986).

Bronson often co-starred with his second wife, the British actress Jill Ireland, who once said, "I think I'm in so many of his pictures because no other actress would work with him." In 1990 she died of cancer at the age of 54; they had six children. A 1991 television movie, *Reason for Living: The Jill Ireland Story*, was based on her book about their vain attempt to help their adopted son, Jason, conquer the drug habit that finally killed him. Jill Clayburgh portrayed Ireland and Lance Henriksen was Bronson.

> Some day I would like a part where I can lean my elbow against a mantelpiece and have a cocktail.
> CHARLES BRONSON.

Brooks. Louise Brooks (1906–85) US actress of the 1920s, remembered for her bobbed hairstyle and the air of vulnerability that she brought to her roles as a *femme fatale*.

Born in Cherryvale, Kansas, Brooks dropped out of high school to travel to New York with her dance teacher. After being sacked from a touring company for her disobedience, she danced on Broadway in the Ziegfeld Follies and in London at the Café de Paris.

Brooks's film debut in Paramount's *The Street of Forgotten Men* (1925) was quickly followed by a starring role as a beauty-contest winner in *The American Venus* (1926). Over the next two years Paramount cast her in a series of flapper comedies, including *It's the Old Army Game* (1926), with W. C. FIELDS; the director of this film, Edward Sutherland, briefly became her husband (1926–28).

In 1928 her performance in Howard HAWKS's *A Girl in Every Port* led the German director G. W. PABST to give her the lead in his classic *Pandora's Box*, after rejecting Marlene DIETRICH as too old. In the film, an adaptation of two plays by Wedekind, Brooks played the beautiful and promiscuous Lulu, a murderess who finally meets her nemesis at the hands of Jack the Ripper. Brooks also starred in Pabst's *Diary of a Lost Girl* (1928), as a seduced girl who ends up in a brothel.

After travelling to France to make Augusto Genina's *Miss Europe* (1930), Brooks returned to Hollywood to find only minor parts on offer. She then spent several years working as a nightclub dancer before making an attempted comeback in 1936. However, her refusal to become the mistress of Columbia boss Harry COHN led to her instant demotion to the chorus line in *When You're in Love* (1937). A year later Brooks made her final film, the John WAYNE Western *Overland Stage Raiders*.

After her retirement from the screen, Brooks taught dancing and appeared in radio soap operas as well as writing some excellent film reviews in the 1950s and 1960s. She also wrote and burned an explicit autobiography. Although her films were rediscovered in the mid 1950s, she chose to spend her later years living as a virtual recluse.

Mel Brooks (Melvin Kaminsky; 1926–) US writer, actor, director, and producer, noted for his raucous comedies. Brooks began his career in television in the 1950s, writing (with Neil Simon and Woody ALLEN amongst others) material for Sid Caesar in *Your Show of Shows*. He created the series *Get Smart* in 1965 and in 1967 won an Emmy for his writing. His first film as director was *The Producers* (1968), an outrageous black comedy starring Gene WILDER and Zero Mostel as theatrical con men who set out to produce a Broadway flop – only to achieve a surprise hit with the musical *Springtime For Hitler*.

Brooks followed this cult hit with *The Twelve Chairs* (1970), a farce adapted from a Russian novel, which he shot in Yugoslavia. He later remarked: "Never shoot a film in Belgrade...The whole town is illuminated by a 20-watt night light and there's nothing to do. You can't even go for a drive. Tito is always using the car." In 1973 came his most acclaimed film, the spoof Western *Blazing Saddles*, starring Cleavdon Little as a Black sheriff. With this film Brooks effectively invented the sketch movie, a format that has had a wide influence on subsequent Hollywood comedy. Next came *Young Frankenstein* (1974), a loving black-and-white parody of the Universal horror features of the 1930s. As FRANKENSTEIN (pronounced 'Franken*steeen*') Wilder reactivates his ancestor's monster using many of Universal's original props. Madeline Kahn, another of Brooks's regular players, provides the love interest, Marty Feldman plays Igor, and Gene HACKMAN makes a cameo appearance as a blind hermit. *Silent Movie* (1976) is a slapstick comedy in which the only line is spoken by mime artiste Marcel Marceau; the film includes a tango sequence featuring Brooks's wife Anne BANCROFT.

In 1977 Brooks directed and starred in the spoof thriller *High Anxiety*, which sends up all the best-known scenes from HITCHCOCK's movies. There followed what many have seen as an artistic decline, with such movies as *History of the World: Part One* (1981), Alan Johnson's *To Be Or Not To Be* (1983), a remake of the LUBITSCH classic produced by and starring Brooks, and *Spaceballs* (1987), a lame parody of the STAR WARS series, failing to match the inventiveness of earlier films. The downward trend continued with *Life Stinks* (1992), a misconceived comedy about homelessness, and was not really arrested by the 1993 hit *Robin Hood: Men in Tights*, starring Cary Elwes.

Vulgarity is in the hand of the beholder.
MEL BROOKS.

Richard Brooks (1912–92) US director and
screenwriter. Born in Philadelphia, Brooks
worked as a journalist and stage director
before being hired as a screenwriter by Universal. His early screenplays range from the
hokum of *Cobra Woman* (1944) to Jules
DASSIN's *Brute Force* (1947), a gripping
prison drama with Burt LANCASTER; he also
provided the script for John HUSTON's
acclaimed thriller *Key Largo* (1948), starring Humphrey BOGART and Lauren BACALL.

Meanwhile, Brooks's novel *The Brick
Foxhole* had been adapted by RKO as the
much-praised *Crossfire* (1947), with the
homosexual victim of the book changed
into a Jew. Following this success, he was
hired by MGM to write and direct *Crisis*
(1950), with Cary GRANT as a surgeon
forced to operate on a dictator. Brooks, who
remained at MGM for a decade, later said
that he learned his craft as a director
through the errors he made there, adding:
"The trouble today is that you don't make
mistakes any more, they're too expensive."

In 1955 THE BLACKBOARD JUNGLE, starring
Glenn FORD as a teacher facing violent students, earned Brooks his first Oscar nomination (as a writer). Three years later he
adapted Tennessee Williams's drama *Cat on
a Hot Tin Roof* (1958), receiving Oscar nominations for both writing and directing. His
only Oscar win came for the screenplay of
ELMER GANTRY (1960), which he also
directed; Brooks subsequently married one
of the film's stars, Jean SIMMONS. A year later
he directed Paul NEWMAN and Geraldine
PAGE in *Sweet Bird of Youth* (1961), another
Tennessee Williams adaptation.

His other films of the 1960s, including
the Conrad adaptation *Lord Jim* (1964), *In
Cold Blood* (1967), a true story about the
massacre of a Kansas farming family, and
The Happy Ending (1969), with Jean Simmons, were less successful. In 1968 the
critic Andrew Sarris summed up the prevailing view when he wrote of Brooks:
"Although most of his films display something of value on first viewing, none can
take the high ground in retrospect." Brooks
received greater credit for the disturbing
Looking for Mr Goodbar (1977), in which
Diane KEATON teaches deaf children by day
and picks up men in bars by night. His later
efforts included the gambling movie *Fever
Pitch* (1985), starring Ryan O'NEAL.

Brute Tradename for a high-intensity
10,000-watt SPOTLIGHT used to illuminate
dark locations or to light a large area. The
name is now used generically for this type of
lamp.

Brynner, Yul (Youl Bryner; 1915–85) US
actor, of obscure descent (though it is
thought he was born on the island of
Sakhalin off Siberia), who starred in a range
of musicals, Westerns, and thrillers.

Having worked in a circus and as a lifeguard, Brynner became an overnight star
after appearing in the Broadway version of
The King and I (1951). It was for this production that he shaved off what little hair he
had to create the distinctive bald pate of
virtually all his later appearances – a step he
was initially reluctant to take. The show
brought him numerous awards and was
filmed in 1956, bringing him an Oscar for
Best Actor.

His subsequent film roles included a
pharaoh in DE MILLE's THE TEN COMMANDMENTS
(1956), Dmitri in *The Brothers Karamazov*
(1958), and the gang leader in the classic
Western *The Magnificent Seven* (1960). In
Anastasia (1956) he played opposite Ingrid
BERGMAN, who later recalled:

> I realised at once that he was shorter...He
> turned round and said to me: "You think I
> want to play it standing on a box. I will
> show the world what a big horse you
> are."...I just laughed and laughed and I
> never had a complex about my height after
> that.

In Michael Crichton's *Westworld* (1973)
Brynner gave a terrifying performance as a
theme-park robot that goes out of control
and starts to kill the visitors. He died during
a triumphant revival of *The King and I* that
enjoyed long runs in both London and New
York.

Brynner turned his taste for dark clothes
into a trademark and wore nothing but
black for the last 45 years of his life. He once
defended this affectation by saying: "I don't
have any choices to make in the morning,
and shopping becomes so much easier."

BSC British Society of Cinematographers. A
body founded in the 1950s to recognize and
promote practitioners of cinema photography and to advance public knowledge of the
profession. It was closely modelled upon the
older ASC.

Buck Rogers US comic-strip hero, who has
appeared in various science-fiction films
and television series. First introduced in

Phil Nolan's novel *Armageddon 2419*, he appeared in a syndicated comic strip from 1929; the character is a US air-force officer who wakes up from a 500-year sleep in the 25th century to battle gangsters, mad scientists, and extra-terrestrials. In 1939 Universal made the serials *Planet Outlaws* and *Buck Rogers* to capitalize on the popularity of Buster Crabbe, who had become famous playing the futuristic hero FLASH GORDON. The low-budget serials were characterized by cheap sets and even cheaper props. Television series followed in 1950 and 1978 (starring Ken Dibbs and Gil Gerard respectively).

bug eye or **fish eye**   A camera lens that has an extremely WIDE ANGLE of view (almost 180°). The resulting distortion of the image is sometimes used for grotesque, eerie, or hallucinatory effects.

Bugs Bunny   A carrot-chewing rabbit with a Brooklyn accent, probably the most famous cartoon character not to emerge from Disney studios. Bugs first appeared, as a nameless hare, in the LOONEY TUNES short *Porky's Hare Hunt* (1938). Having metamorphosed into his current species, he was to have been called Happy Rabbit, but finally took the nickname of his creator Ben 'Bugs' Hardaway. Mel Blanc, who voiced Bugs for most of his career, improvised the rabbit's catchphrase: "Naaa, what's up doc?" from the scripted line "Hey, what's cooking?" Bugs's constant carrot crunchings were always recorded last and spliced in, as Blanc found that carrots made his throat tighten.

Bugs reached his greatest heights under animator Tex Avery (1907–80), whose anarchic style best suited the rabbit's personality. His most memorable adventures pitted him against farmer Elmer Fudd, whose characteristic speech impediment ("Kill the wabbit!") swiftly took over from Porky Pig's stammer. Bugs has so far appeared in 162 films, including a venture into 3-D – *Lumberjack Rabbit* (1953) – and the Oscar-winning *Knightly Knight Bugs* (1958).

Although Bugs went into semiretirement in the early 1960s, frequent showings of his films on television kept his memory alive and won him a new generation of fans. He made a big-screen comeback in 1988, when he appeared with many other cartoon stars in WHO FRAMED ROGER RABBIT? This led to his first new starring role for 28 years, in

Box Office Bunny (1990), as well as a cameo appearance in *Gremlins 2* (1990).

Bulldog Drummond   A former British army officer turned detective who featured in some 24 films between 1922 and 1970. The creation of Sapper (Hermann Cyril McNeile; 1888–1937), the character first appeared in his novel *Bulldog Drummond* (1920) – subtitled 'The Adventures of a Demobilized Officer who Found Peace Dull'. Many sequels followed; after McNeile's death the series was continued under the same pseudonym by G. T. Fairlie.

Having already proved successful in two silent British offerings, Drummond was revived for the Hollywood talkie *Bulldog Drummond* (1929). Ronald COLMAN's performance in the title role made him the first silent star to enhance his standing in sound films. "What Chaplin is to the silent film", Samuel GOLDWYN enthused at the premiere, "Colman will be to sound!"

Joan BENNETT also made her talkie debut in the film. When he first saw the finished print, Goldwyn objected to a scene in which a colonel complains of "the eternal din"; not knowing what 'din' meant, Goldwyn declared the word 'archaic', and ordered the large set rebuilt and actors hired to film the scene again.

Colman played the role for a second time in Fox's *Bulldog Drummond Strikes Back* (1934), in which Drummond's fiancée is kidnapped. (The series' running joke was the constant postponement of his forthcoming marriage.) Former silent star John BARRYMORE played Colonel Nielsen of Scotland Yard in both these films. Paramount continued the series in the late 1930s, with one film starring Ray MILLAND and seven with John Howard. Walter PIDGEON took the lead in *Calling Bulldog Drummond* (1951), while Richard Johnson was a Drummond in James BOND's image for Rank's *Deadlier than the Male* (1967) and its limp sequel *Some Girls Do* (1970).

bullet hit   A device used to simulate the impact of a bullet, especially in war films and Westerns. It is a low-level explosive device put behind or below an object (sometimes under the clothes of a person who is to be 'shot') and electrically discharged.

Buñuel, Luis   (Luis Buñuel Portoles; 1900–83) Spanish director, a pioneer of cinematic SURREALISM whose films fiercely attack organized religion and conventional morality. Buñuel was educated by the Jesuits in Zaragoza and subsequently at Madrid University, where he became friends with Salvador Dali and the writer García Lorca. He subsequently studied at the Acadèmie du Cinéma in Paris and collaborated with Dali on his first film the notorious *Un Chien Andalou* (1928), a series of nightmarish images described by Buñuel as "a despairing passionate call to murder." Another collaboration with Dali, L' AGE D'OR (1930), was widely banned because of its anticlericalism and alleged blasphemy.

After making *Las hurdes* (1932), a documentary about the poor in northern Spain, he was denied the opportunity to direct for 14 years, during which time he variously produced musical comedies and Republican newsreels in Civil War Spain, dubbed dialogue for Paramount and Warner Brothers, and re-edited documentary footage for Latin American consumption at the New York Museum of Modern Art. He was compelled to resign in 1942 on account of his left-wing sympathies (he always suspected that Dali had informed on him).

Having settled in Mexico in 1946, Buñuel reclaimed his position as a leading film-maker with *The Young and the Damned* (*Los olvidados*; 1950), which earned him the Grand Prix at Cannes. Other films of this period included *El* (1952), depicting the sexual jealousy and foot-fetishism of a devout church-goer, and *The Criminal Life of Archibaldo de la Cruz* (1955), a black comedy about a failed sex murderer.

Although *Viridiana* (1961) was filmed in Spain at the invitation of the Spanish government, a scene parodying the Last Supper led to the film being banned there. Subsequent films were no less subversive: in EL ANGEL EXTERMINADOR (1962) the conventional morality of a group of trapped dinner guests swiftly breaks down; in BELLE DE JOUR (1966) the demure Catherine DENEUVE plays a middle-class wife who takes up prostitution as an antidote to boredom; while in *Tristana* (1970) a young girl sets out to revenge herself on her seducer. The director's international reputation grew rapidly during the 1960s and 1970s. Both THE DISCREET CHARM OF THE BOURGEOISIE (1972) and *That Obscure Object of Desire* (1977), an exploration of frustrated lust, were awarded the Oscar for Best Foreign Film. Shortly before his death, Buñuel was awarded the Grand Cross of the Order of Isabella le

Catolica by the Spanish government as a gesture of reconciliation. He published an autobiography, *My Last Sigh*, in 1983.

> Religious education and surrealism have marked me for life.
> LUIS BUÑUEL.

Burton. Richard Burton (Richard Walter Jenkins; 1925–84) Welsh actor. The twelfth of 13 children of a miner, he took the stage name of Burton after an English teacher who helped to develop his love of language and to gain him an Oxford scholarship.

After making his stage debut in 1943, Burton spent three years with the RAF before returning to acting. His first film was *The Last Days of Dolwyn* (1948). Having made his reputation as a stage actor with Fry's *The Lady's not for Burning* (1949) and a highly successful 1951 season at Stratford, Burton made his Hollywood debut with *My Cousin Rachel* (1952), a routine melodrama that brought him an Oscar nomination for Best Supporting Actor. His films of the 1950s included the CINEMASCOPE epic, THE ROBE (1953), in which his performance as a Roman officer who turns to Christianity brought him a second Oscar nomination, *Alexander the Great* (1956), and the screen adaptation of John Osborne's *Look Back in Anger* (1959).

It was, however, the 1963 film *Cleopatra* that catapulted Burton to international fame. Although the film itself is no classic, public attention was caught by the adulterous affair of Burton and his co-star Elizabeth TAYLOR. After appearing together once more in the somewhat lacklustre *The VIPs*, Burton and Taylor married in 1964; their often stormy relationship – they divorced six years later and then briefly remarried (1975–76) – made them both international celebrities whose personal lives came to overshadow their professional fame. Of the films they made together Mike NICHOLS's *Who's Afraid of Virginia Woolf?* (1966) and *The Taming of the Shrew* (1967) are probably the best.

During the 1960s Burton gave some fine performances, notably in the Tennessee Williams adaptation *The Night of the Iguana* (1964), in which he played a defrocked priest, and *The Spy who Came in from the Cold* (1965), a low-tech spy thriller that brought him another Oscar nomination. In 1967 Burton co-directed a version of Marlowe's *Dr Faustus* featuring a splendidly miscast

Taylor as Helen of Troy; one critic cruelly noted that it turned out to be "the story of a man who sold his soul for Elizabeth Taylor."

Burton's subsequent career was one of rare highs and plentiful lows. Although films such as *Where Eagles Dare* (1969) and *The Wild Geese* (1978) enjoyed commercial success, they did little to stretch his abilities. Burton received a final Oscar nomination for playing the psychiatrist Dysart in *Equus* (1977). An alcoholic, he died in Switzerland from a cerebral haemorrhage.

Tim Burton (1959–   ) US producer-director, whose often macabre fantasy films have earned him the title **the Prince of Darkness**. He achieved great box-office success with Warner Brothers' atmospheric BATMAN (1989) and *Batman Returns* (1992).

Born in Burbank, California, the son of a city parks and recreation employee, Burton became an ardent fan of Vincent PRICE as a young boy. After studying animation at the California Institute of the Arts, he was hired by the DISNEY Studio and worked on *The Fox and the Hound* (1981) and *The Black Cauldron* (1985) amongst other films. However, Burton soon felt constricted by the studio, which he later accused of treating him like "a special retarded child."

Having left Disney, Burton made his debut as a director with *Pee-wee's Big Adventure* (1985), a comedy starring Paul Reubens as a child-like character in pursuit of his lost bicycle. He then made a larger impact with *Beetlejuice* (1988), a supernatural fantasy that featured some extraordinary special effects; Michael Keaton played the ghoulish title character.

The following year brought the $50-million *Batman*, starring Keaton in the title role, Jack NICHOLSON as The Joker, and Kim BASINGER as a female sidekick. *Variety* noted how Burton "effectively echoes the visual style of the original Bob Kane comics while conjuring up a nightmarish world of his own. It was a shrewd choice for Burton to emulate the jarring angles and creepy lighting of FILM NOIR."

Burton followed this success with the delightful fairy tale *Edward Scissorhands* (1990), about a boy (Johnny Depp) whose arms end in scissors. The director's childhood hero, Vincent Price, made his penultimate appearance before the cameras as the creator of this extraordinary lad. The $80-million *Batman Returns* saw Keaton facing Michelle PFEIFFER as Catwoman and

Danny DEVITO as the Penguin, with a role also going to Paul Reubens as the Penguin's father; *Variety* found the sequel "superior in several respects." Burton has subsequently produced the ghoulish Disney animation *The Nightmare Before Christmas* and *Ed Wood* (both 1994), a biopic of the man labelled "the world's worst director" (*see* WOOD JNR, ED).

Bushman, Francis X(avier) (1883–1966) US silent star, whose striking looks and powerful physique earned him the nickname **the Handsomest Man In The World**. Bushman and actress Beverly Bayne, who co-starred in such films as *Romeo and Juliet* (1916), were Hollywood's first romantic team; when their secret marriage was revealed in 1919, his career took a nose dive from which it never really recovered.

A former child actor, Bushman worked as a sculptor's model as a young man. After winning the *Ladies' World* Hero Contest in 1911, he signed a film contract with the Essanay company and made his debut later that year in *His Friend's Wife*. He went on to make 19 films in 1912 alone, including *The Fall of Montezuma*, in which he played Cortez.

Three years later, Louis B. MAYER launched Metro Pictures with a serial starring Bushman. The star, who posed for publicity photos in a leopard skin, drew a record number of female fans to this and subsequent films; he was soon earning an estimated $1 million a year. Following the subsequent decline in his career, he made a memorable comeback as the Roman Messala in MGM's silent BEN-HUR (1926), refusing a double for the famous chariot race with Ben-Hur (Ramon Novarro).

After losing his fortune in the 1929 stock market crash Bushman turned to radio soap operas as a source of income. His last major screen roles included King Saul in the lacklustre *David and Bathsheba* (1951) and Moses in the bizarre 1957 film *The Story of Mankind* (which also featured Harpo MARX as Isaac Newton and Hedy LAMARR as Joan of Arc). His career ended on a low note with a bit part in *The Ghost in the Invisible Bikini* (1966).

Bushman's son Ralph acted briefly under the name of Francis X. Bushman Jnr.

bust shot or chest shot   A MEDIUM CLOSE-UP shot of an actor from the waist upwards.

Butch Cassidy and the Sundance Kid
(1969) George Roy HILL's classic comedy
Western, the romanticized story of two
19th-century Wyoming outlaws. The title
characters were played by Paul NEWMAN and
Robert REDFORD respectively, with Katharine
Ross supplying the love interest. The film's
enormous success helped 20th Century-Fox
to survive losses of more than $100 million
in 1969–70. Surprisingly, the movie at first
received poor reviews but was rescued by
word-of-mouth. "The critics roasted the
film" said Hill, "If it had been a play, we'd
have closed in one night." Academy Awards
went to screenwriter William Goldman, cinematographer Conrad Hall, composer Burt
Bacharach, and the song 'Raindrops Keep
Falling on My Head', written by Bacharach
and Hal David.

Most of the events portrayed in the film
were based on fact. Butch Cassidy's real
name was Robert Le Roy Parker (1886–
1909) – he was called Butch for the good
reason that he was an ex-butcher. The Sundance Kid, real name Harry Longbaugh
(1860–1909), established his reputation
by robbing a bank in Sundance, Nevada. In
the film Butch, the leader of the Hole-in-
the-Wall Gang, teams up with Sundance to
rob the Union Pacific Express – twice. Afterwards they flee to Bolivia with schoolteacher Etta Place (Ross), where they 'go
straight' for a while; ironically, it is during
this period that Butch kills for the first time.
Having returned to robbing banks and a
fugitive life, they end up in a hut surrounded
by the militia. Butch and Sundance storm
out into a hail of bullets, but a FREEZE FRAME
spares audiences from seeing them die
(in contrast to the horrific closing moments
of BONNIE AND CLYDE).

Much of the film's appeal lay in the humour of the Oscar-winning screenplay and
the rapport between its ill-matched antiheroes, the impetuous Butch and the taciturn Sundance – a duo that director Hill
called "the LAUREL AND HARDY of Deadwood
Gulch." Earlier contenders for the title
roles had included Steve MCQUEEN, Marlon
BRANDO, and Warren BEATTY. The film made
the previously little-known Redford a superstar. (He later called his film base in Utah the
Sundance Institute.) In 1973 he rejoined
Newman for another popular buddy movie,
THE STING, also directed by Hill.

In 1979 Butch and Sundance returned
to the screen in Fox's PREQUEL *Butch and Sun-*
dance: The Early Years. With Tom Berenger
and William Katt in place of Newman and
Redford, and a weaker script, the film was
notably less successful than the original.

butterfly A SCRIM stretched over an oval
frame, used to reduce or diffuse the light
falling on a subject or an area of the set. It is
often used to decrease the intensity of sunlight in an outdoor scene.

butt splice *See* SPLICE.

buyer A member of the film crew who buys
(or rents) props and costumes for the production. When the Crown Film Unit made
Coastal Command in 1942, the buyer had to
ask the Ministry of Food for permission to
purchase seven pounds of lentils to be
painted and glued on a plane in place of
rivets, which could not be spared. (The Ministry was assured that any leftover lentils
would be used up in the canteen.) Buyers for
Laurence OLIVIER's *Henry V* (1944), another
wartime film, were spared the expense of
buying 1000 pairs of shoes when it was
discovered that 15th-century soldiers preferred to wrap their feet in cloth.

buzz track A soundtrack of general BACK-
GROUND NOISE or ROOM SOUND; recorded on the
set when actors are not present, it is later
mixed with the dialogue track to eliminate
the unnatural effect of total silence between
spoken lines.

bw The usual abbreviation for BLACK-AND-
WHITE.

Bwana Devil (1952) The first 3-D feature
film, a box-office hit that inspired a further
27 3-D movies the following year. The low-
budget movie was directed and produced by
Arch Oboler for his independent company
and released by United Artists; Oboler also
wrote the flimsy story about hunters tracking man-eating lions in Africa. Advertisements promised "a lion in your lap" while
audiences also had to dodge a few wild
spears hurled from the screen.

Robert STACK, Barbara Britton, and Nigel
BRUCE starred in this introduction to 'Natural Vision', an ANAGLYPH process that
required the audience to wear polarized
glasses to blend the superimposed images
from two projectors. Joseph Biroc directed
the camerawork and Gordon Jenkins wrote
the music.

C

Caan, James (1939–) US actor regularly cast in tough-guy roles. Born in the Bronx, Caan gained his earliest acting experience with the New York Neighborhood Playhouse and made a number of off-Broadway appearances in the early 1960s. His first major film role was as one of the bullying thugs who trap Olivia DE HAVILLAND in an elevator in the thriller *Lady in a Cage* (1964). A steady stream of work followed, including roles in the Westerns *The Glory Guys* (1965), directed by Sam PECKINPAH, *El Dorado* (1967), in which he starred with John WAYNE and Robert MITCHUM, and *Journey to Shiloh* (1968); other films of the period include Francis Ford COPPOLA's downbeat drama *The Rain People* (1969) and the Updike adaptation *Rabbit Run* (1970).

In 1972 he enjoyed a major success with Coppola's THE GODFATHER, in which he proved ideal as Marlon BRANDO's violent and self-destructive elder son. More violent roles followed in such film as *Rollerball* (1975), an Orwellian vision of a repressive future society in which Caan's sportsman character finds himself fighting his competitors to the death, and *The Killer Elite* (1975), in which he played a sadistic CIA man.

In the later 1970s Caan managed to escape this typecasting to play a wider range of characters in *The Gambler* (1975), the Barbra STREISAND vehicle *Funny Lady* (1975), and the modern Western *Comes a Horseman* (1978). He made his debut as a director with *Hide in Plain Sight* (1980), a thriller in which he also starred as a man searching for his missing children. In the 1980s, however, his career suffered a lull during which he made few films, and those not successful. A cameo role in Warren BEATTY's *Dick Tracy* (1990) was followed by a major comeback as the lead in Rob REINER's *Misery* (1990), in which he played an author held captive by a deranged admirer. *Honeymoon in Vegas* (1992) was a reasonably successful romantic comedy.

Cabaret (1972) Bob FOSSE's screen version of John Kander, Fred Ebb, and Joe Masteroff's successful 1966 Broadway musical about decadent 1930s Berlin. The film won eight Oscars, including awards for Fosse as Best Director, Liza MINNELLI as Best Actress (her first singing role on screen), and Joel Grey as Best Supporting Actor. Michael YORK played Minnelli's bisexual English admirer, Brian Roberts.

Critics praised *Cabaret* as the most original screen musical since WEST SIDE STORY (1961); it also proved the last Hollywood musical to enjoy an enormous success at the box-office. The film was co-produced by Allied Artists and ABC Television during the latter's brief flirtation with the big screen.

In some respects the script was closer to John Van Druten's play *I Am a Camera* (1951) and to Christopher Isherwood's original novel *Goodbye to Berlin* (1929) than to the stage musical. The plot centres on the sleazy Kit Kat Klub, with its leering white-faced MC (Grey) and its startling US chanteuse Sally Bowles (Minnelli; the character is an Englishwoman in the book). Despite the growing Nazi menace and the harrassment of her Jewish friends, Sally continues to escape to the make-believe world of the cabaret. When Brian decides to leave the city she declines to go with him.

The rousing Nazi song 'Tomorrow Belongs to Me' was cut from German prints to avoid inspiring neo-Nazi sentiments. Other songs include the title song, 'Willkommen', and 'The Money Song'.

Cabinet of Dr Caligari, The (1919) Robert Wiene's disturbing and innovative horror film, one of the key works in the development of German EXPRESSIONISM. The film introduced the classic horror formula of an insane doctor, his monster, and their innocent female victim. The narrator, Francis, describes how Dr Caligari, a fairground showman, uses the sleepwalker Cesare to carry out a series of murders. When instructed to kill the beautiful Jane, however, Cesare kidnaps her instead. The surprise ending reveals that this is the tale of a madman: Francis is a mental patient and Caligari his concerned doctor.

The film was written in six weeks by the Austrian Carl Mayer (who later wrote THE LAST LAUGH and *Sunrise* for F. W. MURNAU) and the Czech Hans Janowitz; the latter had seen a girl at a fairground who was later murdered by a sex maniac. The trick ending was not in the original screenplay, and was contrary to the writers' wishes. With striking sets designed by three German Expressionist painters, the film was shot in a deliberately non-naturalistic style to suggest a world of terror and madness (*see* CALIGARISME). The cast, which included Werner Krauss and Conrad VEIDT, were told to act with stiff mechanical movements. The resulting movie, which has often been described as the first ART FILM, was typically received either with enthusiastic admiration or utter hostility: it played continuously in the same Paris cinema from 1920 to 1927, although the audience at New York's Capitol Theater booed and demanded their money back.

The US remake (1962), starring Glynis Johns and Dan O'Herlity, bears little resemblance to the original and is considered inferior.

Cabin in the Sky (1943) MGM's all-Black musical, the first film to be directed by Vincente MINNELLI. Based on a hit Broadway play, it starred Ethel Waters from the stage version, Eddie Anderson (famous as Jack BENNY's servant Rochester), Lena Horne, and such renowned musicians as Louis Armstrong and the Duke Ellington Orchestra.

The story is based loosely on the Faust legend. Joe Jackson (Anderson) is a sucker for gambling, drinking, and women, especially the lovely Georgia Brown (Horne). He dreams that he has been killed in a bar-room brawl and given a six-month stay on earth because of the devotion of his wife (Waters). As the Devil battles with God for his soul, Joe awakes from his dream a reformed man. There is a spectacular stairway-to-heaven finale.

MGM commissioned three new songs for the screen version from Harold Arlen and E. Y. Harburg. One of these, 'Happiness is Just a Thing Called Joe', received an Oscar nomination but proved less popular with the public than 'Taking a Chance on Love',

one of the original stage numbers by Vernon Duke and John Latouche.

The scene in which a tornado destroys a nightclub was created by reusing footage from THE WIZARD OF OZ as a BACK PROJECTION.

Cabiria (1914) A 10-reel Italian 'super-spectacle', set in ancient Rome, directed by Giovanni Pastrone for Itala Film. Its length (originally about four hours) and budget ($210,000) were both records at the time; the film was also the first to make use of the camera DOLLY, a device invented by Pastrone's Spanish cameraman Segundo de Chomon.

Pastrone himself invented the TRACKING SHOT to show off the size and grandeur of Camillo Innocenti's sets, which included a vast Temple of Moloch. Ildebrando Pizetti composed his *Fire Symphony* to accompany the scene in which a sacrifice of maidens is made to the fire god. The scenario, co-written by the poet Gabrielle d'Annunzio, the first major literary figure to be involved in the cinema, centred on Rome's victorious Punic Wars against Carthage. (D. W. GRIFFITH allegedly copied the scene in which Carthage is stormed in his INTOLERANCE.) *Cabiria* was screened before President Woodrow Wilson and his Cabinet in the White House in June 1914.

In 1915 Pastrone made *Maciste*, a thin sequel, featuring the giant Black slave from *Cabiria*; the character later featured in numerous Italian muscle-man films. A shorter sound version was released in 1930 and a somewhat undistinguished remake in 1950. In 1957 Federico FELLINI made an unrelated film called *Cabiria* (originally *Le Notti di Cabiria*, or *Nights of Cabiria*) about an Italian prostitute.

cableman The crew member responsible for handling cables and their attachments during filming; the cables may belong either to sound equipment or to mobile cameras.

Cacoyannis, Michael (1922–) Greek director, actor, and screenwriter. Born in Cyprus, he took a law degree in Britain and practised as a barrister; he also produced Greek programmes for the BBC during World War II. After training as an actor and theatre director, he made his stage debut in 1946 at the Old Vic. He then travelled in America before returning to Greece to direct his first film, *Windfall in Athens*, in 1953. Two years later he won several international awards with *Stella*, starring Melina MERCOURI; he followed this with *A Girl in Black* (1956), about a writer's love for an unsophisticated island girl (Elle Lambetti) and its tragic aftermath. In 1957 he scripted and directed another melodrama, *A Matter of Dignity*, about a poor woman who marries a millionaire for her parents' sake. There followed *Our Last Spring* (1959), *Eroica* (1960), and the Italian film *The Wastrel* (1961). Cacoyannis became a star in his own right in his screen version of Sophocles's *Electra* (1961). He returned to the stage in 1963 with an off-Broadway production of *The Trojan Women*, which received excellent reviews.

Cacoyannis achieved his greatest commercial success with ZORBA THE GREEK (1964), from the novel by Nikos Kazantzakis. A celebration of the Greek spirit, it featured Alan BATES as a sensitive English writer in Crete who is befriended and overwhelmed by a local character (Anthony QUINN). Cacoyannis was nominated for Academy Awards for both his directing and his screenwriting. Since then, he has made the British film *The Day the Fish Came Out* (1967), about radioactive fallout contaminating a Mediterranean island, *The Trojan Women* (1971), the documentary *Attila 74* (1975), *Sweet Country* (1986), and the sex comedy *Up, Down, and Sideways* (1993).

Cagney, James (1899–1986) US actor, who became a top Hollywood star playing a succession of fast-talking pugnacious GANGSTERS; he later proved his versatility in a wide range of comic and musical roles.

Cagney, who started out in vaudeville, has been quoted as saying: "Once a song-and-dance man, always a song-and-dance man. Those few words tell as much about me professionally as there is to tell." In 1929 Cagney was discovered performing in *Penny Arcade*, a Broadway play that was adapted to become his first film, *Sinner's Holiday* (1930). He then established himself as the archetypal Hollywood mobster in THE PUBLIC ENEMY (1931), the film in which he rammed a grapefruit into the face of co-star Mae Clarke. (Clarke had been assured that the fruit would not touch her face, and her shocked expression was genuine.) Ironically, his potential as a screen baddie was only discovered by accident after Darryl F. ZANUCK, who had signed him up to play a different role, saw an out-take in which

Cagney snarled at the cameraman, "For God's sake, who wrote this crap?"

He went on to portray similar characters in *Blonde Crazy* (1931), *Taxi* (1931), and *Angels With Dirty Faces* (1938), which earned him an Oscar nomination. In later life, Cagney was to remark: "Where I come from, if there's a buck to be made, you don't ask questions, you go ahead and make it" and "With me, a career was the simple matter of putting groceries on the table." By 1941 he was the second-highest paid citizen of America (the first being Louis B. MAYER).

Cagney went on to demonstrate the breadth of his talent in such films as *A Midsummer Night's Dream* (1935), in which he played Bottom, *Yankee Doodle Dandy* (1942), in which he won an Oscar as Broadway impresario George M. Cohan, *Mister Roberts* (1955), as the captain of a wartime cargo ship, and the Billy WILDER comedy *One Two Three* (1961). He also tried his hand at directing with *A Short Cut to Hell* (1958). After *One Two Three* Cagney retired from films, but was tempted back 20 years later for his last cinema role, in Miloš FORMAN's *Ragtime* (1981).

Numerous fellow-actors have paid tribute to the honesty of Cagney's style: "There is no moment when he was not true" (Orson WELLES), "He was *real*, but not realistic" (Malcolm McDowell); "He was very theatrical, very intense, and yet always believable" (Gregory PECK). The tears he cried at his father's deathbed in *Yankee Doodle Dandy* were so convincing that director Michael CURTIZ could not help sobbing loudly as the cameras rolled.

> He can do nothing which is not worth watching.
> GRAHAM GREENE.

> He possessed...irresistible charm. It was a cocky, picaresque charm; the charm of pert urchins; the gaminerie of unlicked juvenile delinquents.
> KENNETH TYNAN.

Cahiers du cinéma French critical journal, founded in 1951 by André Bazin (1918–58), Lo Duca, and Jacques Dionol-Valcroze. The magazine combined an intellectual approach to the subject with an avowedly populist taste, thereby preparing the ground for the French NEW WAVE of the late 1950s. The impetus for this approach came from the vast influx of US movies in the post-war period, which revealed a far wider range of themes and treatments than the constricted cinema of the Occupation or the mannered and theatrical pre-war French cinema. Unkind comparisons with the Hollywood alternative led to a concerted attack on the bastions of French cinema and a rising demand for greater freedom for film-makers. The magazine's heyday was the mid 1950s, when such writers as TRUFFAUT, GODARD, CHABROL, ROHMER, and Rivette espoused the so-called AUTEUR theory of film-making by championing the work of (then) neglected directors, such as HITCHCOCK and FORD. All subsequently moved into directing themselves. After the death of Bazin the magazine lost its way, moving through structuralist, Marxist, and Maoist phases during the 1960s. It continues to appear, trading largely on its past reputation.

Caine, Michael (Maurice Joseph Micklewhite; 1933–) Versatile British actor, who found stardom after years of minor film and television roles. Caine is a former Smithfield meat porter who has never attempted to conceal his Cockney origins or accent – "I'll be a Cockney until I die," he told *Playboy* magazine in 1966 – but is equally at ease in the role of cultured elegant man-about-town. He took his name from his favourite film, *The Caine Mutiny* (1954).

Although Caine made his film debut as early as 1956, it was not until his appearance in the epic *Zulu* (1964) that he emerged as a star. He went on to play the leading role in the Harry Palmer trilogy – *The Ipcress File* (1965), *Funeral in Berlin* (1967), and *Billion Dollar Brain* (1967) – a series of downbeat SPY films created by James BOND producer Harry Saltzman as an antithesis to the dashing 007. Palmer wore glasses, often came off worse in a fight, and never seemed in control of events. Caine brought a wayward sexiness to the role that was also much in evidence in *Alfie* (1966), in which he excelled as the philandering Cockney. The film brought him an Oscar nomination and made him a household name.

Unlike his close friends Sean CONNERY and Roger MOORE, Caine took care never to be too closely identified with one role and always accepted a challenge. His roles have ranged from a vicious mobster in *Get Carter* (1971), to a Nazi paratrooper in *The Eagle Has Landed* (1976), a psychiatrist in *Dressed to Kill* (1980), a playwright with writer's

block in *Deathtrap* (1982), and a drunken academic in *Educating Rita* (1983). He has consistently honed his comic skills in such films as *California Suite* (1978) and *Dirty Rotten Scoundrels* (1988), and even managed to upstage the puppet stars of *The Muppet Christmas Carol* (1992).

A self-confessed workaholic, Caine makes on average two films a year. Inevitably, his willingness to tackle almost any role has led to appearances in some third-rate work, including *The Swarm* (1978), *The Hand* (1981), and *On Deadly Ground* (1993). However, among the routine films there are many gems, such as *The Italian Job* (1969), *Sleuth* (1972) with Laurence OLIVIER, *The Man Who Would Be King* (1976) with Sean Connery and Caine's wife Shakira, and *Without a Clue* (1988), in which he played a hapless Sherlock HOLMES. In 1986 he won an Oscar for Best Supporting Actor in Woody ALLEN's *Hannah and Her Sisters* (1986); ironically, his filming commitments for the forgettable *Jaws: The Revenge* (1987) prevented him from collecting the award in person.

A self-taught man with a passion for trivia, Caine has become associated with the catchphrase "Not many people know that" (or "Not a lot of people know that"). The phrase was first remarked upon by Peter SELLERS in the 1970s, long before Caine uttered it in *Educating Rita* (1983) and used it as the title of a charity book (1984).

> I'm a skilled, professional actor. Whether or not I've any talent is beside the point.
> MICHAEL CAINE.

> A brilliant actor.
> LAURENCE OLIVIER.

calibrations In the making of animated films (*see* ANIMATION), position points marked on art backgrounds to indicate the distance a figure should be moved between frames.

Caligarisme A term used by some French writers to describe the style and mood of Robert Wiene's EXPRESSIONIST masterpiece THE CABINET OF DR CALIGARI (1919). It is mainly used in reference to the film's visual style (flat painted sets, non-naturalistic lighting), its camera technique (distorted perspective, the use of shocking CAMERA ANGLES), and its concern with subjective reality (fantasy, dream imagery). The term is also sometimes used to refer to the state of confusion and despondency in post-war Germany from which Expressionism grew.

call or **shooting call** A timetable given to cast and crew, informing them of the times of shooting or rehearsal. The responsibility of the assistant director, it is either distributed as a **callsheet** or posted on the **callboard**. It will often give times at which the actors should be available for costume or make-up and spell out any technical requirements for the crew.

cameo A walk-on part played by a well-known actor or other celebrity. The word was first used in this sense by Mike Todd with reference to the 44 such appearances in his AROUND THE WORLD IN EIGHTY DAYS (1956). Apart from its main stars, the film contained cameo performances by Ronald COLMAN, Noël COWARD, Marlene DIETRICH, John GIELGUD, Trevor HOWARD, Buster KEATON, Peter LORRE, John MILLS, George RAFT, and Frank SINATRA. Other films that have used cameos, with varying degrees of success, include *The List of Adrian Messenger* (1963), *Won Ton Ton, the Dog who Saved Hollywood* (1976), *A Bridge Too Far* (1977) and *The Player* (1992).

Although cameos are generally used to boost a production's box-office appeal, they may be unannounced: Bob HOPE and Bing CROSBY sometimes made surprise appearances in each other's films. Director Alfred HITCHCOCK's cameo performances became so famous that he took care to "come on as early as possible – [I] don't want to hold them in suspense for the wrong reason!" For his cameo role as Superman's father in *Superman* (1978), Marlon BRANDO received $2,250,000 and 11% of the film's profits.

Non-actors to make brief appearances as themselves include Lord Baden-Powell in *The Woodpigeon Patrol* (1930), A. J. P. Taylor and Michael Foot in *Rockets Galore* (1958), Moshe Dayan and Yitzhak Rabin in *Operation Thunderbolt* (1958), Pelé in *Hotshot* (1987), and Mikhail Gorbachev in Wim WENDERS's *Faraway, So Close* (1994). *See also* DIRECTORS' CAMEOS.

cameo shot A shot in which a single subject (usually a performer) is filmed against a dark or neutral background with the minimum of surrounding props.

camera An optical apparatus used to capture images on light-sensitive film. Movie cameras differ from still cameras in containing a mechanism to advance the film automatically between photographs; when the film is printed and projected the images appear to move, owing to the phenomenon known as PERSISTENCE OF VISION.

The essential precondition for the development of the cine camera was the invention of the flexible film roll by George Eastman (1854–1932) in 1888. Over the next decade a number of pioneers – notably William Friese-Greene (1855–1921) in Britain and Thomas EDISON in America – began to develop methods of taking 'moving pictures'. Initially these involved combined camera-projector devices, such as the KINETOGRAPH or the LUMIÈRES' Cinèmatographe. Since the separation of these functions, developments have tended to focus on increased efficiency and portability, the only significant change occurring with the introduction of SOUND. The advent of the OPTICAL SOUNDTRACK meant that CAMERA SPEED needed to be increased and kept reliably constant; this necessitated the introduction of mechanical film-advance systems to replace hand-cranking while cameras also needed to be BLIMPED to counteract the noise.

The cine camera consists of five principal elements; a camera obscura, or light-proof box; a SHUTTER to control access of light; a lens to focus it; photosensitive film; and a mechanism to advance the film past the lens.

Although cameras differ in the detail of their design, the basic operation is always some variation on the following. Before shooting the camera is loaded with unexposed film, often in the form of a MAGAZINE. When the motor is started the teeth of a rotating SPROCKET engage with perforations in the sides of the film and pull it down towards the GATE. A loop of film is allowed to build up to provide some slack to compensate for changes in tension; a claw or other mechanism then pulls down a single frame, which is held taut behind the lens while the shutter is opened. Another frame follows. The exposed frames form another loop, again to prevent tearing, before being wound onto the take-up reel.

The frame-advance mechanism proved the greatest problem for early camera designers. While the film as a whole is in continual motion, each frame must be exposed individually (the principle of INTERMITTENT MOVEMENT). Early mechanisms could not easily prevent the film jerking or tearing when switching from continuous movement to single-frame advance.

Various broad categories of camera are now in use: studio cameras (large, 35mm, blimped); FIELD CAMERAS (non-blimped, portable, for location shooting); HAND-HELD CAMERAS (light, mainly for news/documentary work, often with built-in sound-recording system); and large format (65mm, originally for widescreen films, now mainly used for special effects). The major recent developments have been in CAMERA MOVEMENT, with remote control and video monitoring enabling cameras to film where this would once have been physically impossible and STEADICAM freeing cameras from tripods and DOLLIES. VIDEO cameras now offer a portable and inexpensive alternative to the traditional movie camera.

camera angle The angle from which a subject is filmed; the main variables are the elevation of the camera relative to the subject and the choice of an oblique or frontal view of it.

The camera is usually placed at eye-level to the subject, as this produces a relatively neutral image corresponding to the audience's normal view of the world. Placing the camera at other than eye-level will imbue the image with certain emotional qualities in the mind of the viewer. A LOW-ANGLE SHOT, in which the camera is placed below eye-level and tilted upwards, makes the subject appear larger, more imposing, and powerful – as if a child were staring up at its parent. The opposite of this is the HIGH-ANGLE SHOT; the camera is placed above eye-level and tilted downwards, making the subject appear more vulnerable or insignificant – literally beneath us. It can create a feeling of sympathy for an underdog, such as a child, or one of detached curiosity.

If the camera is angled at the subject from a position well to the left or right of it an **oblique-angle shot** is produced; when the camera is also tilted vertically the shot is known as a **dutch tilt**. Such shots tend to disorientate the viewer, creating an effect of tension or expectation; they are often the prelude to sudden movement or action. Dutch tilts and obliques can also be used to suggest extreme mental states, as in Robert DE NIRO's famous drunk scene in MEAN STREETS (1973). *See also* SUBJECTIVE CAMERA.

camera back *See* PULL BACK.

cameraman or **camera operator** A technician responsible for the operation of one or more cameras under the direction of the CINEMATOGRAPHER. He or she is responsible for the positioning of the camera, for ensuring that the image is correctly framed and in focus, and for any basic camera movements.

camera movement Moving the camera was one of the last basic principles of cinema to be exploited. Early US cinema had favoured static camera set-ups since the days of EDISON's studio-bound KINETOGRAPH; even such pioneers as D. W. GRIFFITH tended to move the action around the camera, rather than vice versa. It was in postwar Germany that camera movement really entered the film-maker's repertoire, with F. W. MURNAU's THE LAST LAUGH (1924) being the most important showpiece for such techniques. From the opening scene in which the camera rides down in a lift and glides through a hotel lobby, to the much-imitated sequence filmed from the point of view of a drunk, the camera used a freedom never before seen.

Although the technical limitations of early sound filming rendered the camera static once more in the late 1920s, the influence of the German EXPRESSIONISTS soon began to be felt, especially in horror and gangster movies. The vogue for camera movement reached its zenith, perhaps, in the improvised kitchen sequence of WELLES's THE MAGNIFICENT AMBERSONS (1942), in which the cast compose and recompose themselves in front of a fluid constantly moving camera. More recently, however, the cost and technical difficulties involved in rebalancing lighting, rehearsing cast and camera crews, and maintaining continuity, have again tended to favour the static camera.

When mounted on a rubber-tyred DOLLY, the camera can be moved towards, away from, or sideways to the subject; a crab dolly permits it to be moved in any direction. The camera can also be raised or lowered with the use of a CRANE. Any of these movements may be combined with movement on the part of the subject itself. The development of STEADICAM in the 1970s offered the cameraman a greater freedom of movement than ever before.

Camera movement can be used to shift audience attention from one subject or part of a subject to another; to follow the action of a scene that would otherwise pass out of the frame; or, more subtly, to withhold crucial information from the viewer until the moment it is required. Examples of all of these uses may be found in HITCHCOCK's extraordinary *tour de force* ROPE (1948), which is composed of eight extremely long takes shot using a fluid camera.

All these effects can be imitated to some extent by moving the head of a stationary camera (PANNING or TILTING) or using a ZOOM; the result is never precisely the same, however, owing to the laws of perspective. Some directors feel that camera movements give the audience a better sense of the physical environment in which a scene takes place. They can also add dynamism to a sequence that may otherwise be rather static, such as a dinner-table scene, etc.

camera rehearsal A RUN-THROUGH of a shot or scene, in which the cameras are moved and focused, etc., although no filming takes place. Its purpose is to practise the camera movements required and to discover any problems that may occur. STAND-INS may be used instead of actors.

camera right or **left** The right or left side of a frame as seen from the point of view of the cameraman (and hence that of the audience when the film is projected). The terms are also used as directions to the cameraman, indicating that he or she should move the camera to the right or the left.

camera speed The rate at which film is run through the camera, measured in frames per second (fps). The earliest movie cameras were hand-cranked with a variable speed; clockwork and electric motors later enabled camera speed to be standardized at 16 fps in silent cinema. In order to produce clarity on an OPTICAL SOUNDTRACK, however, the standard camera speed was increased to 24 fps after the arrival of talkies. Modern SUPER 8 film is run at a speed of 18 fps while video records at 25 fps. Some cameras allow the operator to vary the speed while filming, to create an effect of SLOW-MOTION or ACCELER- ATED MOTION when the film is projected.

> The cinema is truth, 24 times a second.
> JEAN-LUC GODARD.

caméra stylo or **camera pen** A term introduced by the film-maker and theoretician Alexander Astruc (1923–) in his essay 'Le Caméra Stylo' (1948). Astruc advocated a new style of film-making in which directors would be able to use their cameras in the same way that writers have traditionally used their pens – that is, to espouse a personal philosophy of life without regard for commercial criteria or studio pressures.

This idea, which is the direct ancestor of the so-called AUTEUR policy, found its greatest resonance amongst the CAHIERS DU CINÉMA group of writers and aspirant directors and greatly influenced the development of the French NEW WAVE.

camera trap A place of concealment in which a camera is placed during filming, usually to make it invisible to another camera shooting the scene simultaneously. It is often used to provide a CUTAWAY from a wider shot. GRIFFITH's THE BIRTH OF A NATION (1915), for example, features a scene in which a Confederate colonel charges the Union guns; the director cuts from a LONG-SHOT of the battlefield to a dramatic LOW-ANGLE SHOT of the officer thrusting his flag seemingly right into the camera – filmed from a camera concealed under the gun-barrel.

camera up *See* APPROACH.

Cameron, James (1954–) Canadian director and screenwriter, known for his high-tech action movies. Cameron began his career at New World Pictures, where he rose from miniature-set building to process production supervisor. After being appointed art director on *Battle Beyond the Stars* (1980), a tongue-in-cheek science-fiction epic, he made his debut as a director with the chaotic JAWS spoof *Piranha II* (1981), a hopeless failure at the box office. In 1984, however, Cameron directed and co-wrote THE TERMINATOR, a violent science-fiction thriller starring Arnold SCHWARZE-NEGGER as a cyborg sent back from the future with a mission to kill. Stylish, exciting, and completed on a remarkably low budget, the film became the surprise hit of 1984 and established both director and star as forces to be reckoned with in the cinema of the 1980s. After co-writing the much-reviled RAMBO: *First Blood Part II* (1985), which sent Sylvester STALLONE's demented veteran back to Vietnam, Cameron enjoyed another huge success with *Aliens* (1986), a sequel to Ridley SCOTT's ALIEN (1979). Part war movie and part science-fiction shocker, the film combined action, suspense, and terrifying special effects. In 1989 Cameron wrote and directed *The Abyss*, an ambitious underwater adventure made on a budget of $50 million; the remarkable visual effects were being imitated long before the film was released. *Terminator 2: Judgement Day* (1991) was even more expensive and spectacular, with a budget estimated at up to $100 million. Although the computer-generated visuals were more stunning than ever (*see* COMPUTER ANIMATION), many critics found the plot – with Schwarzenegger as a now-benign robot intent on saving the world from nuclear war – banal. Cameron followed this enormous success with *The Crowded Room* (1992) and *True Lies* (1994), an adventure-comedy that paired Schwarzenegger with Jamie-Lee CURTIS.

> Fear is a very strong reaction. It makes people realize that they're alive. Their hearts start to beat faster.
> JAMES CAMERON, 1988.

Camille (1936) George CUKOR's version of the classic TEARJERKER by Alexandre Dumas *fils*. Greta GARBO starred as Marguerite Gautier, a courtesan who is dying from tuberculosis but attains new self-knowledge through a last hopeless love affair. The film proved one of the highlights of Garbo's career, bringing her an Oscar nomination for Best Actress. Its success also owed much to fine performances from Robert TAYLOR as her lover and Lionel BARRYMORE as her father, as well as to William Daniels's moody camerawork. Garbo's rapt admirers little suspected that, beneath her lavish gowns, the actress generally sported a pair of well-worn bedroom slippers, finding them more comfortable than the elegant footwear originally intended for her. Producer Irving THALBERG died before the film was released, and in his honour Garbo consented to make one of her infrequent public appearances at the premiere.

The story, which originally appeared in novel form as *La Dame aux camélias* (1848), became a popular vehicle for tragic actresses in the late 19th century. Other film versions include those starring the 68-year-old Sarah Bernhardt (1912), Theda BARA (1917), Alla Nazimova (1920; with Rudolph VALENTINO), Norma TALMADGE (1927), and Isabelle HUPPERT (1981); *Camille 2000* (1969) was an attempted updating. The character of Marguerite was based on Dumas's own mistress, Marie Duplessis.

Campion, Jane (1954–) New Zealand writer-director; her features focus on strong women characters whose inarticulacy forces them to rely on their instincts.

Campion was born into a leading theatrical family (her mother Edith has a cameo reciting 'The Lady of Shalott' in *An Angel at My Table*). In spite of lodging with John O'Shea (the 'father of New Zealand cinema') while a student at the University of Wellington, she only became interested in film while studying art in London: "Somehow I wandered into the arthouse circuit and just fell in love with what film could do and mean and be", she later recalled.

Campion made her debut short, the award-winning *Peel* (1982), while attending the Australian School of Film, Television, and Radio. After making *A Girl's Story* and *Passionless Moments* (both 1984) and the TV-movie *Two Friends* (1985), she directed her debut feature, *Sweetie*, in 1989. Blending black comedy with bleak melodrama, it explored the suppressed paranoia of suburban family life in modern Australia with a raw intensity. Although it was booed at Cannes, *Sweetie* was critically acclaimed elsewhere. Campion then confirmed her reputation with another study of mental disorientation, *An Angel at My Table*. Based on Janet Frame's trilogy of autobiographical novels, this epic biopic was shown on New Zealand television as a three-part miniseries before its theatrical release in 1990.

With her next feature, *The Piano* (1993), Campion became the first woman to win the Palme d'Or at Cannes (shared with CHEN KAIGE's *Farewell, My Concubine*). The film, which traces the relationship between Ada (Holly Hunter), a 19th-century mute, and Baines (Harvey KEITEL), the estate manager of her husband (Sam Neill), brought Campion an Oscar nomination for Best Original Screenplay, as well as Academy Awards for Hunter and Ana Paquin (as Ada's nine-year-old daughter, Flora). Campion has compared the film's romanticism to that of Emily Brontë in *Wuthering Heights*: "It's very harsh and extreme, a gothic exploration of the romantic impulse. I wanted to respond to these ideas in my own century."

She is currently working on an adaptation of Henry James's *The Portrait of a Lady*, with Nicole Kidman in the role of Isabel Archer.

Cannes Film Festival An international film festival that takes place annually in May at Cannes in the South of France. Founded in 1946, the festival is regarded as the most important in Europe and attracts the jet set, the world's press, and other hangers-on as well as leading figures of the cinema industry. Winners of the prestigious Palme d'Or award for best film have included Carol REED's THE THIRD MAN (1949), FELLINI's LA DOLCE VITA (1960), BUÑUEL's *Viridiana* (1961), ANTONIONI's BLOW UP (1967), OLMI's *The Tree of Wooden Clogs* (1978), WAJDA's *Man of Iron* (1981), Steven Soderbergh's *sex, lies, and videotape* (1989), and Joel and Ethan COEN's *Barton Fink* (1991). The jury's choices have sometimes been unpopular; French director Maurice PIALAT was booed as he accepted the prize for *Under Satan's Sun* in 1987, as was Quentin TARANTINO whose *Pulp Fiction* won in 1994

The festival has been variously described as "Butlins on acid" by screenwriter Frank Clarke, "like a fight in a brothel during a fire" by director Eldar Riazanov, and "my idea of hell" by actor Dirk BOGARDE, who continued: "You see all the people you thought were dead and all the people who *deserve* to be dead. After a while, you start to think you might be dead, too."

Cantor, Eddie (Isidore Israel Itzkowitz; 1892–1964) US actor, comedian, and singer, who made a successful transition to the cinema in the late 1920s. His huge rolling eyes earned him the nickname 'Banjo Eyes'.

An orphan, Cantor sang on street corners and worked as a singing waiter before establishing himself in vaudeville, where he often appeared in blackface. Starring roles in Ziegfeld's *Follies* and other Broadway shows eventually brought him to the attention of the film studios; his early screen successes included versions of his stage hits *Kid Boots* (1926) and *Whoopee!* (1930). The latter includes a performance of his famous song 'Makin' Whoopee'. Among the films that followed were *The Kid from Spain* (1932), *Roman Scandals* (1933), *Kid Millions* (1934), *Strike Me Pink* (1936), *Thank Your Lucky Stars* (1942), and *If You Knew Susie* (1948).

The success of these movies allowed him to rebuild the fortune he had lost in the Wall Street Crash of 1929 (which was just as well, since the book he wrote on the subject – *Caught Short! A Story of Wailing Wall Street* – failed to make the money he had hoped for). In the late 1930s his career came under threat when he accused prominent public figures of being fascist sympathizers, but he was fully restored to favour when America subsequently entered World War II. In his later years he raised funds for the treatment of infant paralysis and won a special

Oscar (1956) for services to the film industry. *The Eddie Cantor Story* (1953) was a mostly inaccurate BIOPIC in which Keefe Brasselle played the title role.

The key to Cantor's success lay in his irrepressible energy, which often expressed itself in garrulity. When his wife Ida once told him to shut up, he observed coolly: "If I shut up, you and the kids would starve to death."

Capra, Frank (1897–1991) Sicilian-born US director, famous for his whimsical comedies of the Depression era. These typically involve a representative of the common man striving against corruption and vested interests with the assistance of an uncommon woman, who often proves stronger and smarter than the hero.

Capra began his career as a gagwriter for silent movies. Except for *The Platinum Blonde* (1931), which gave Jean HARLOW her nickname, and *The American Madness* (1932), a topical comedy about bank failure, his early films as a director are mainly unremarkable. The film that made his reputation was IT HAPPENED ONE NIGHT (1934), an inspired comedy starring Cary GRANT and Claudette COLBERT. A surprise hit, the film became the first to win all four major Oscars. MR DEEDS GOES TO TOWN (1936) and *You Can't Take It With You* (1938), both won Academy Awards for Best Director. In 1937 Capra made *Lost Horizon*, one of his most unusual and admired films. Scripted by Capra's close associate Robert Riskin from the novel by James Hilton, it took two years and cost $2 million to make. The final scenes, in which Ronald COLMAN struggles across icy wastes in search of the lost Shangri-La, are Capra's most moving. His final films of the period were MR SMITH GOES TO WASHINGTON (1939), with James STEWART as an idealistic senator, and *Meet John Doe* (1941).

Between 1942 and 1944 Capra directed the *Why We Fight* series of documentaries for the US government, including one about the contribution made by Black troops. His next feature, the Black comedy ARSENIC AND OLD LACE (1944), featured a performance from Cary Grant that was so over-the-top that he refused to watch the film in later years. Warner Brothers were initially reluctant to release this tale of serial killing, fearful that it would be shunned by war-weary audiences, but it proved to be a big hit.

By contrast IT'S A WONDERFUL LIFE (1946), with James Stewart as a small-town do-gooder contemplating suicide, was a commercial and critical failure when it was first released. The audiences who had made his films such a success in the Depression years had deserted Capra, and only in later years was *It's a Wonderful Life* regarded as a classic. Subsequent films were, however, so sentimental that critics took to deriding them as 'Capracorn'. The director's last film was *Pocketful of Miracles* (1961), a less successful remake of his 1933 hit *Lady for a Day*.

> I made mistakes in drama. I thought drama was when actors cried. But drama is when the audience cries.
> FRANK CAPRA.

caption or **label** A SUBTITLE used to supply information about a scene, usually the location or the passage of time (e.g. 'nine months later').

Cardinale, Claudia (1938–) Italian actress whose beauty, husky voice, and fiery personality captivated international audiences in the 1960s. Born in Tunis, she won a trip to the Venice Film Festival after coming first in a beauty contest at the age of 19. She studied briefly at Rome's Centro Sperimentale film school and made her Italian screen debut in 1958. After a minor role as an au pair girl in the British comedy *Upstairs and Downstairs* (1959), she came to the attention of wider audiences with *Rocco and his Brothers* (1960), Luchino VISCONTI's epic of Italian peasant life.

In the early 1960s the producer Franco CRISTALDI, her future husband, began to direct her career. Stardom arrived with two films released in 1963: Federico FELLINI's 8½ and Visconti's THE LEOPARD, in which she played a middle-class girl whose marriage to Alain Delon is opposed by his aristocratic father (Burt LANCASTER). In the mid 1960s she made a series of Hollywood movies beginning with THE PINK PANTHER (1964). This was followed by the spy spoof *Blindfold*, with Rock HUDSON, the war adventure *Lost Command*, and the Western *The Professionals* (all 1966). Cinematographer Conrad Hall, who worked with Cardinale on *The Professionals*, described her as "A cameraman's dream – a perfect piece of nature."

A starring part in Sergio LEONE's *Once Upon a Time in the West* (1969), in which Cardinale played a landowner terrorized by gunman Henry FONDA, was followed by a return to Italian films. Her subsequent output includes the British war film *Escape to Athena* (1979), Werner HERZOG's *Fitzcarraldo* (1982), *A Man in Love* (1987), about a group of Americans making a film in Italy, and *The French Revolution* (1989).

> I've never revealed my real self or even my body in my films. Mystery is very important.
> CLAUDIA CARDINALE.

Carné, Marcel (1906–) French director, best known for his historical fantasy LES ENFANTS DU PARADIS (1945). A leading exponent of French POETIC REALISM, he enjoyed long collaborations with screenwriter Jacques PRÉVERT, actor Jean GABIN, and art director Alexander Trauner.

The son of a Paris cabinetmaker, Carné served as his father's apprentice before studying film at night school. In 1928 he became an assistant cameraman to Jacques Feyder and a year later an assistant director to René CLAIR. He made his own debut as a director with *Jenny* (1936), about a nightclub owner with a prudish daughter.

In the late 1930s Carné established his reputation with a series of films scripted by Jacques Prévert, beginning with the black comedy *Drôle de drame* (*Bizarre Bizarre*; 1937). This was followed by the thrillers *Quai des brumes* (1938), featuring Gabin as an Army deserter, and *Le Jour se lève* (1939) with the same actor as a cornered murderer. The mood of romantic fatalism persisted in *Hotel du nord* (1938), a film scripted by Jean AURENCHE; the action is set in a rundown Paris hotel whose guests include a murderer (Louis Jouvet) and his mistress (ARLETTY).

During the Occupation Carné and Prévert turned to allegory in *Les Visiteurs du soir* (*The Devil's Envoys*; 1942), a medieval fantasy with an implicit anti-Nazi message, and the epic *Les Enfants du paradis*, a tribute to the 19th-century theatre that is also a tribute to the enduring spirit of France. After the war, Carné suffered a major disaster with *Les Portes de la nuit* (1946), a gloomy look at wartime collaboration that cost 80 million francs to make and flopped at the box office. He and Prévert ended their partnership halfway through filming the unfinished *La Fleur de l'age* in 1948. Thereafter Carné tended to script his own films, which included *La Marie du port* (1949), an unsuccessful film starring Gabin, and the well-received *Thérèse Raquin* (*The Adulteress*; 1953). Although he continued to make films during the 1960s and 1970s, his later work made little impression. In 1992 Carné, then in his mid eighties, returned to the cinema after a long absence to direct *Mouche*, from a story by Maupassant.

Caron, Leslie (1931–) French-American actress and dancer, remembered as the beguiling title character in the musical *Gigi* (1958) and for her Oscar-nominated performances in *Lili* (1953) and *The L-Shaped Room* (1962). She was married to the British theatre director Peter Hall from 1956 to 1966.

Leslie Caron was born in Boulogne-Billancourt, the daughter of a French chemist and a US dancer. Having seen her perform in Roland Petit's Ballets des Champs Elysées, which she had joined at the age of 16, Gene KELLY cast her as his love interest in the Gershwin musical *An American in Paris* (1951). The film ended with a lengthy ballet sequence that gave full rein to her dancing skills.

Caron's waiflike appearance enabled her to play a 16-year-old orphan in *Lili*, a carnival story featuring some innovative dream ballets. Against MGM's advice she wore drab costumes in the part, to excellent effect. She went on to dance opposite Fred ASTAIRE in *Daddy Long Legs* (1955), a musical about an orphan and her anonymous benefactor.

At the age of 27 Caron was cast as a teenager again in the Lerner and Loewe musical *Gigi*, having already played the role on stage in London. Her co-stars included Louis Jourdan, Maurice CHEVALIER, and Hermione Gingold. Bryan FORBES's *The L-Shaped Room* brought her a straight acting role as a pregnant French girl lodging in a run-down London house. In 1964 she played opposite Cary GRANT in the war comedy *Father Goose*, while in 1977 she co-starred with Rudolf Nureyev in Ken RUSSELL's *Valentino*.

More recently, Caron has appeared mainly in French and Italian films, including a Krzysztof ZANUSSI comedy, *The Contract* (1980), and *Dangerous Moves* (1983), which won an Oscar for Best Foreign Film.

> I'm not a ballerina. I'm a hoofer.
> LESLIE CARON.

Carpenter, John (1948–) US director of horror and suspense films. His enthusiasm for the pulp thrillers and space movies of the 1950s is reflected in many aspects of his work, not least his willingness to work with low budgets.

Carpenter studied film at the University of Southern California, where he wrote and directed several shorts including *The Resurrection of Bronco Billy* (1970), which won an Oscar for Best Short. In 1974 he made his feature debut with *Dark Star*, a low-budget space fantasy with a semi-professional cast, aspects of which were clearly intended to parody the lavish and intense 2001: A SPACE ODYSSEY; the film's quirky inventions included an alien that bears a striking resemblance to a beach ball and a bomb that enters into conversation with its victims.

Carpenter followed this cult success with *Assault on Precinct 13* (1976), a dark action film set in a besieged inner-city police station. In its situations and imagery the film draws equally on classic Westerns and George Romero's NIGHT OF THE LIVING DEAD (1968). Carpenter's breakthrough came with the horror movie *Halloween* (1978), about a small-town girl (Jamie Lee CURTIS) pursued by an escaped psychopath (Charles Cyphers). This independent low-budget feature took over $50 million at the box office and virtually created the 1980s subgenre of the SLASHER MOVIE. The mobile camera work and resourceful use of CINEMASCOPE testified to Carpenter's technical ability, while the Hitchcockian cutting style provoked inevitable comparison with PSYCHO (not least, one suspects, because the female lead is the daughter of the shower-scene victim, Janet Leigh). The sequels *Halloween II* and *III*, which were co-produced but not directed by Carpenter, are routine examples of the slasher genre.

The Fog (1979), in which the ghosts of wrecked sailors threaten a seaside town, was an unsuccessful attempt by Carpenter to bring an element of social comment into his work. Similarly, his remake of the 1950s monster classic *The Thing* (1982) failed to match Howard HAWKS's original, despite its extravagant special effects.

Carpenter continued to make violent thrillers throughout the 1980s. Although *Big Trouble in Little China* (1986), *Prince of Darkness* (1987), and the space movie *They Live* (1988) were all relative failures, *Starman* (1984), a gentler alien film with elements of romantic comedy, was better received. In 1992 *Memoirs of an Invisible Man*, starring Chevy CHASE, marked another venture into comedy. Apart from writing, directing, and producing Carpenter also composes the music for most of his films.

Carradine, John (Richmond Reed Carradine; 1906–88) Prolific US character actor closely associated with director John FORD. With his gaunt features and sonorous voice he graced more than 220 films, often in the role of the villain (he appeared three times as DRACULA). Carradine, a devoted Shakespearean, would loudly recite passages from the plays as he strolled the streets of Hollywood, earning himself the nickname the 'Bard of the Boulevard'. Three of his five sons – David, Keith, and Robert Carradine – became actors.

Born in New York City, John Carradine aspired to become a painter and sculptor before making his stage debut in 1925. Two years later, he hitchhiked to Hollywood and in 1930 appeared in his first film, *Tol'able David*. He acted under the name of John Peter Richmond until 1935. His roles for John Ford included Rizzio in *Mary of Scotland*(1936), an Indian brave in *Drums Along the Mohawk* (1939), a gentleman gambler in STAGECOACH (1939), and a preacher in THE GRAPES OF WRATH (1940). In 1938 Carradine showed his versatility in the contrasting roles of Abraham Lincoln in *Of Human Hearts* and Robert Ford in *Jesse James*. His rare starring roles included an artist who kills his models in *Bluebeard* (1944). Over the decades he appeared in numerous low-budget horror stories with such titles as *King of the Zombies* (1942), *Night of the Beast* (1967), and *Monster* (1978).

David Carradine (1936–) has been almost as prolific as his father, making some 95 films in the first 30 years of his screen career. These included *Boxcar Bertha* (1972), an early feature by Martin SCORSESE, the same director's MEAN STREETS (1973; with Robert Carradine), *Bound for Glory* (1976), in which he played folksinger Woody Guthrie, and *Bird on a Wire* (1990), with Mel GIBSON and Goldie HAWN. Nevertheless, he is probably best known for his role in the television series *Kung Fu* (1972–74). He has also directed several films including *You and Me* (1974) and *Americana* (1982).

Keith Carradine (1950–) made his screen debut in 1971 and enjoyed his first starring role in Robert ALTMAN's *Thieves Like Us* (1973). Subsequent films included *Pretty Baby* (1978), with Brooke Shields, Ridley SCOTT's *The Duellists* (1978), *Choose Me* (1984), and *The Ballad of the Sad Café* (1991), the directorial debut of Simon Callow.

David, Keith, and Robert Carradine, were among four sets of real-life siblings cast as on-screen brothers in the Western *The Long Riders* (1980), which also featured Stacy and James Keach as Frank and Jesse James.

> Never do anything you wouldn't want to be caught dead doing.
> JOHN CARRADINE's advice to his son DAVID CARRADINE.

Carry On films A long-running series of low-budget British farces, initiated in 1958 with *Carry On Sergeant*. Producer Peter Rogers, director Gerald Thomas, and writer Talbot Rothwell went on to make one or two films in the same bawdy vein every year until the mid 1970s. The films featured a regular team of comedians that included Sid James, Kenneth Williams, Charles Hawtrey, Kenneth Connor, Hattie Jacques, Barbara Windsor, Joan Sims, Bernard Bresslaw, and Liz Fraser. Never aspiring to be anything more than low farce, they eventually became a British institution with their appalling puns and vulgar innuendo.

After the death of such stalwarts as Sid James and Hattie Jacques in the mid 1970s, the quality of the series noticeably declined; the last film, *Carry On Emmanuelle* (1978), was but a pale shadow of such triumphs as *Carry On Cleo* (1965) and *Carry On up the Khyber* (1968).

In 1992 Gerald Thomas directed *Carry on Columbus*, an unsuccessful attempt to revive the Carry On format. This brought together a handful of survivors from the original series (Jim Dale in the title role, Bernard Cribbins, June Whitfield, Leslie Phillips, and Jack Douglas) with the 'alternative' comedians Alexei Sayle, Peter Richardson, Rik Mayall, and Julian Clary.

> Infamy! Infamy! They've all got it infamy!
> KENNETH WILLIAMS, as Julius Caesar in *Carry on Cleo*.

cartoon A film created by photographing a series of gradually changing drawings. *See* ANIMATION.

Casablanca (1942) Warner Brothers' classic wartime romance, one of the best-loved of all Hollywood films. Humphrey BOGART and Ingrid BERGMAN headed a strong cast and Michael CURTIZ directed. An immediate critical and commercial success, *Casablanca* won Academy Awards for Best Picture, Best Screenplay (by Julius J. Epstein, Philip

G. Epstein, and Howard Koch), and Best Director.

The film is set mainly in the nightclub owned by Rick Blaine (Bogart), a cynical American who has fled France for Nazi-occupied Casablanca. There he meets by chance his former lover Ilsa Lund (Bergman) – "Of all the gin joints in all the towns in all the world, she walks into mine" – who is now married to Resistance hero Victor Laszlo (Paul Henreid). Haunted by memories of their past love, Rick and Ilsa seem poised to rekindle the affair. Rick, however, realizes their union is doomed and begins to feel a commitment to the Allied cause. In the closing scene of the film the lovers part for ever on a misty airstrip.

The project began modestly enough when producer Hal B. WALLIS bought the play *Everybody Goes to Rick's* as a vehicle for Ronald REAGAN and Ann SHERIDAN. (The play, a somewhat creaky melodrama, was not staged until after the war; a 1991 revival in London proved a notable failure.) The mystery of *Casablanca* is how Bogart and Bergman, strongly supported by Claude RAINS (as Captain Louis Renault), Peter LORRE, Conrad VEIDT, and Sydney GREENSTREET, transformed a routine assignment into one of the great legends of the cinema. Other factors in the film's remarkable success must include the witty script, exotic setting, and timeless themes of romance, sacrifice, and moral responsibility. By a fortunate coincidence, the Allies had landed in North Africa and liberated Casablanca a week before the preview of the film, and it was on general release when Churchill and Roosevelt chose Casablanca for their next summit. Curiously, the bittersweet song 'As Time Goes By', which now seems inseparable from the film, was added as an afterthought. It was sung by Dooley Wilson (as Sam) but the piano was played on the soundtrack by studio musician Elliot Carpenter.

The ending, in which Bogart gives up Bergman and walks away with Rains – "Louis, I think this is the beginning of a beautiful friendship" – was not only kept a secret from the actors but remained undecided until a late stage of the shooting. This caused problems for Bergman: "I never knew how the picture was going to end, if I was really in love with my husband or Bogart. So I had no idea how I should play the character."

The enduring cult of *Casablanca* has proved a great surprise to many of those who were involved in making the film. Julius J. Epstein, one of the screenwriters, observed in 1984:

> Frankly, I can't understand its staying power. If it were made today, line for line, each performance as good, it'd be laughed off the screen. Its such a phoney picture. Not a word of truth in it. Its camp, kitsch. It's just...slick shit!

See also HERE'S LOOKING AT YOU, KID; PLAY IT AGAIN, SAM.

Cassavetes, John (1929–89) US actor and director of INDEPENDENT FILMS. A graduate of AADA, Cassavetes made his screen debut in *Taxi* (1953). (His performance in an earlier film, the documentary drama *Fourteen Hours*, 1951, ended up on the cutting-room floor.) In such early films as *The Night Holds Terror* (1955), *Crime in the Streets* (1956), and *Edge of the City* (1957), he was cast as a representative of the angry and alienated young.

In 1959 his success in the television series *Johnny Staccato* provided him with sufficient funds to make *Shadows*, his first film as a director. Considered by some to be "formless and dreary" and by others "powerful" and "startlingly immediate", the film broke new ground with its improvised script and CINÉMA VÉRITÉ technique. He subsequently made two films in Hollywood, *Too Late Blues* (1961) and *A Child is Waiting* (1962). The latter, starring Burt LANCASTER and Judy GARLAND, was disowned by Cassavetes after producer Stanley KRAMER recut it.

In the mid 1960s Cassavetes returned to acting for a while, appearing in Don SIEGEL's *The Killers* (1964), Robert ALDRICH's star-laden *The Dirty Dozen* (1967), for which he received an Oscar nomination, and Roman POLANSKI's occult thriller ROSEMARY'S BABY (1968). Having made enough money to finance another film, he directed *Faces* (1968), a drama of marital breakdown that featured the actress Gena Rowlands, Cassavetes's wife. The original version, some six hours long, was eventually cut down to just over two hours and earned three Oscar nominations including one for Cassavetes's screenplay.

In 1970 Cassavetes wrote, directed, and co-starred in the three-hander *Husbands* (1970), which also featured Peter Falk and Ben Gazzara. With its slight plot stretched over two and half hours, the film would almost certainly have benefited from trimming – as would many of Cassavetes's later works. Other films of the 1970s included *Minnie and Moskowitz* (1971), *A Woman under the Influence* (1974), which earned Oscar nominations for its star Gena Rowlands and director Cassavetes, and *The Killing of a Chinese Bookie* (1976). In the early 1980s he directed *Gloria*, which earned Rowlands another Oscar nomination, and *Love Streams* (1983), the story of the relationship between a brother and sister (Cassavetes and Rowlands). His last film as a director was *Big Trouble* (1985), an unsuccessful comedy version of the classic DOUBLE INDEMNITY. Cassavetes died, aged 59, from cirrhosis of the liver.

> As an artist I love him. As a husband I *hate* him.
> GENA ROWLANDS.

> As a director, too much of the time he is groping when he should be gripping.
> ANDREW SARRIS, film critic.

cast The actors appearing in a film. The term is also applied to the list of performers, usually with the names of the characters they portray, that forms part of the CREDITS. To cast a film is to hire performers for a production.

Films to feature a CAST OF THOUSANDS include Fritz LANG's METROPOLIS (1926), Cecil B. DE MILLE's THE TEN COMMANDMENTS (1956), Sergei BONDARCHUK's *War and Peace* (1967), and Richard ATTENBOROUGH's GANDHI (1982). At the other end of the scale, a number of films have been made with a cast of one, including *Give 'Em Hell, Harry* (1975) about Harry S. Truman, *Brontë* (1983), and the silent French film *The Last Battle* (1983), in which Pierre Jolivet plays the only survivor of the apocalypse. There have also been films with casts composed entirely of women, children, homosexuals, American Indians, animals, and even robots.

casting director The member of a production team responsible for the selection of actors or actresses to appear in a film (usually in other than the leading roles). His or her job may also include contractual negotiations.

a cast of thousands A phrase associated with the spectacular epics of Cecil B. DE MILLE and others, which regularly employed a whole army of EXTRAS. It is now used in a jocular manner of any enterprise involving many people. The phrase seems to have originated from the publicity for the first version of BEN-HUR (1927), which boasted "a cast of 125,000". One of many apocryphal stories about the producer Samuel GOLDWYN is that he once told a director shooting a scene of the Last Supper "only 12 disciples!...go out and get thousands!"

catchlight (1) The tiny highlight in the eye of a performer caused by the reflection of nearby light sources. (2) A light placed near an actor or actress to produce this effect in CLOSE-UPS.

cattle call A general audition for parts in a film or play. These are normally only held for minor roles, such as singers and dancers in the chorus. The agony of the cattle call has featured in a number of films, notably Richard ATTENBOROUGH's *A Chorus Line* (1985).

catwalk A narrow walk-way suspended above a set to allow electricians and other crew members access to the lighting, sound, or rigging equipment for maintenance or replacement.

Cavalcanti, Alberto (Alberto de Almeida-Cavalcanti; 1897–1983) Brazilian-born director and producer, whose work in Britain from 1933 to 1949 helped to develop both the art of DOCUMENTARY and the use of documentary realism in successful features.

Born in Rio de Janeiro, Cavalcanti studied law and architecture in Switzerland before travelling to Paris in the 1920s to design cinema sets. He made his own debut as a director in 1926. In 1933 his acclaimed documentary *Rien que les heures* earned him an invitation to become a producer-director for Britain's EMPIRE FILM BOARD, under whose auspices he made *The First Days*, about the rise of the Nazis, and *North Sea*, about the lives of trawlermen.

Cavalcanti joined Michael BALCON's EALING STUDIOS as a director-producer in 1940. For Ealing he produced *The Foreman Went to France* (1941), starring Tommy Trinder, and directed *Went the Day Well?* (1942), based on a Graham GREENE story about Nazi paratroopers occupying an English village. His other popular Ealing features included *Champagne Charlie* (1944), with Tommy Trinder and Stanley Holloway as Victorian music-hall rivals, and *Nicholas Nickleby* (1947) with Derek Bond, Cedric HARDWICKE, Stanley Holloway, and Sybil Thorndike.

In the late 1940s Cavalcanti returned to Brazil, only to move back to Europe in 1952 after being accused of communist activities. The Austrian film *Herr Puntila and his Servant Matti* (1955), based on a play by Bertolt Brecht, was directed and co-written by Cavalcanti with Brecht's active assistance. Cavalcanti later directed for British and French television and taught at UCLA in Los Angeles.

Cayatte, André (1909–89) French director and screenwriter, noted for a series of courtroom dramas that probe the relationship between law and morality. Cayatte practised as a lawyer before becoming a writer; after working as a journalist and novelist he turned to the cinema as a vehicle for his strong views on the injustices of French society. In 1942 he made his debut as a director with *La Fausse Maîtresse*, following this with *Les Amants de Vérone* (1949), a stylish reworking of the *Romeo and Juliet* story with Pierre Brasseur and Anouk AIMÉE.

Cayatte, who scripted or co-scripted all his own films, received growing international recognition in the 1950s. He took the Grand Prix at the Venice Film Festival with the courtroom drama *Justice est faite* (1950), showing how jurors are personally affected by a mercy-killing case, the Special Jury Prize at Cannes for *We Are All Murderers* (1952), and the International Critics' Prize at Cannes with *Avant le déluge* (1954). In the 1960s Cayatte directed *Anatomy of a Marriage* (1964), which looks at a strained marriage from the points of view of both partners, *The Crossing of the Rhine* (1960), a war film featuring Charles Aznavour, *Two are Guilty* (1963), and *A Trap for Cinderella* (1965). His later work included *Verdict* (1975), a melodrama starring Sophia LOREN as a gangster's widow who kidnaps a judge, and *Justice* (1978), in which he returned to the question of legal morality.

cell or **cel** One of the sheets of transparent material (generally cellulose ACETATE) on which the drawings that make up an ANIMATION are prepared. The technique of using separate transparent sheets for each part of an image was developed by J. R. Bray in 1914–15. The method has various advantages. Drawing the moving portions of the scene on separate cells means that the background need only be drawn once, thereby reducing costs and labour. It also produces an enhanced sense of depth in the filmed image.

celluloid A general term for cinema film. In fact, the use of celluloid (cellulose nitrate) in film stocks has long been superseded by that of flame-resistant cellulose ACETATE.

censorship The act of deciding which films, or parts of films, are unsuitable for showing to the public; also the system of regulation that enforces and informs this decision.

From the earliest days of the cinema, there has existed a fear of the power of motion pictures, prompted largely by the vividness and accessability of the medium. Demands for control were heard within months of its first public demonstration; the first recorded ban occurred in Russia in 1896, when newsreel footage showing Prince Napoleon dancing with a woman was seized by the police. That same year *Passion Dance* was banned in Atlantic City, thus becoming the first US film to be censored. The first call for statutory censorship in Britain came from the British cheese industry, in response to a CINEMICROGRAPHIC film of bacterial activity in Stilton. During the early 20th century most countries instituted some form of statutory censorship, with a system of pre-censorship by the industry becoming the norm elsewhere.

In Britain three acts cover censorship of films – the Cinematograph Acts of 1909 and 1952, and the 1994 Criminal Justice Act. Although the first of these was designed to ensure the safety of public cinemas, local authorities soon began to use it to withdraw the licences of theatres showing 'unacceptable' material. The need to find some kind of common standard led to the setting up of the British Board of Film Classification in 1912; it was agreed in principle that films passed by the board should prove acceptable to local councils. Loopholes in the system were exposed by the rise of private FILM SOCIETIES in the 1920s and the development of ACETATE (safety) film, which was not covered by the provisions of the 1909 Act. The 1952 Act was essentially a revision to cover these developments. By contrast, the 1994 Act is more far-reaching than either of its predecessors, setting out legislative guidelines for censorship and giving the state powers to compel the recall and reclassification of a film or video.

In America, the argument has centred on a film-maker's right to freedom of expression under the first and 14th amendments to the Constitution. Until this was established, films faced a variety of local and state regulations. In 1915 motion pictures were denied first-amendment protection in Mutual vs Ohio, when they were deemed items of commerce rather than works of art. In response to mounting public criticism, largely orchestrated by the Catholic Church, Hollywood opted for a stringent system of self-regulation with the setting-up of the HAYS office in the 1920s and the imposition of the Production Code. Demands for greater artistic freedom grew steadily after World War II, a major turning-point coming when (in Burstyn vs Wilson) the Supreme Court excluded blasphemy as grounds for suppression and effectively brought film under the first amendment. In the 1950s and 1960s the Production Code was gradually relaxed under the onslaught from directors (notably Otto PREMINGER), leading to its replacement by a RATINGS system in 1968. Legally, the issue of obscenity is still unresolved, with the 1973 ruling Miller vs California raising the thorny issue of "contemporary community standards".

The debate about the place of censorship in democratic countries shows no signs of abating, with home videos providing the latest focus for alarm. In America, sex is still the main worry, with such writers as Michael Medved accusing Hollywood of mounting a "war" on "American family values", while in Britain the debate centres on the level of violence – witness the outcry over *Childsplay 3* (1989) and *Natural Born Killers* (1994), both of which were condemned because of unsubstantiated links to real deaths.

Inevitably, the decisions of the censors have often looked arbitrary and ridiculous. In 1962, for instance, the Irish censor passed POLANSKI's *Knife in the Water* despite it's homosexual undertones – on the grounds that the Irish, knowing nothing of such matters, would fail to understand them. This attitude would not have recommended itself to the English censor, who refused a certificate to the surrealist film *The Seashell and the Clergyman* (1928) on the grounds that it was "so cryptic as to be almost meaningless. If there is a meaning it is no doubt objectionable." In 1979 New Zealand cut *The Muppet Movie* on grounds of gratuitous violence.

In non-democratic states, of course, film-makers have faced problems of infinitely greater severity, ranging from prolonged blacklisting to imprisonment or even death. Major Soviet directors whose careers suffered from state interference include EISENSTEIN, TARKOVSKY, and PARADJANOV.

Central Casting A casting agency maintained by the Alliance of Motion Picture and Television Producers (*see* AMPTP). Those accepted onto its books were classified according to 'type' (dumb blonde, elderly hick, etc.) and allocated bit parts accordingly. The phrase *right out of central casting* is now used of anyone or anything that seems absurdly stereotyped.

Chabrol, Claude (1930–) French director, a leading member of the NEW WAVE of the late 1950s. Chabrol trained as a pharmacist before working as a critic for the journal CAHIERS DU CINÉMA and writing (with Eric ROHMER) a book on Alfred HITCHCOCK. He made his debut as a director of feature films with *Le Beau Serge* (1958), a beautifully shot study of small-town France in which a young student attempts to redeem his childhood friend, now an alcoholic, at the cost of his own health. This film is generally regarded as the first expression of the New Wave in French cinema.

The success of *Le Beau Serge* enabled Chabrol to set up his own production company, a move that gave him greater scope to express his critical view of accepted bourgeois values. In *Les Cousins* (1959), about two cousins driven to violence by their desire for the same girl, *Les Bonnes Femmes* (1960), an exploration of the romantic daydreams of four Paris shop-girls, and *The Third Lover* (1962), in which a journalist destroys a happy marriage by informing the husband of the wife's adultery, Chabrol explored his favourite themes of guilt, jealousy, self-sacrifice, and redemption. Among the cast of *Les Bonnes Femmes* was Chabrol's future wife, Stéphane Audran (1939–), who starred in many of his subsequent films.

After a few years during which he produced only spy thrillers and other commercial projects, Chabrol returned to more serious film-making with *Les Biches* (1968), a study of the destructive effect of jealousy upon a lesbian love affair. Murder, and its effect on the relationships of those involved, was the central theme of *La Femme infidèle* (1968) and *Le Boucher* (1970), one of Chabrol's best-known and most admired films.

Chabrol's work of the mid 1970s was less remarkable and included several thrillers for television. Since then such films as *Violette Noizière* (1978), and the detective thrillers *Cop au vin* (*Poulet au vinaigre*; 1984) and *Inspecteur Lavardin* (1986) have enjoyed moderate box-office success while also pleasing the critics. Recent projects include a version of *Madame Bovary* (1991) starring Isabelle HUPPERT and *L'Enfer* (1994).

> Scriptwriting is like cooking. Shooting, the part I enjoy most, is like eating. Editing, therefore, is – well, the washing up.
> CLAUDE CHABROL.

Champions, the The US dancers Gower Champion (1919–81) and his wife Marge Champion (Marjorie Belcher; 1923–), who appeared together in numerous screen musicals of the 1950s. Films in which they featured include *Mr Music* (1950), a Bing CROSBY vehicle about a Hollywood songwriter, Jerome Kern's *Showboat* (1951), and *Give a Girl a Break* (1953), a backstage musical that provided them with starring roles. Gower went on to direct sentimental musicals and comedies such as *My Six Loves* (1963) and *Bank Shot* (1974), while Marge later appeared as a character actor in such films as *The Swimmer* (1967) and *The Party* (1968).

Chan, Charlie Fictional Chinese DETECTIVE created by the US writer Earl Derr Biggers, largely as a protest against the stereotyped depiction of the Chinese in America. The character was introduced in the novel *The House Without a Key* (1925) and featured in a Hollywood serial the following year (played by George Kawa).

Chan, who lived in Honolulu with Mrs Chan and his many children, was sometimes accompanied in his work by his 'number one' or 'number two' son. He was unfailingly dignified and polite, striving at all times to speak correct English. "You will do me the great honour to accompany me to the station, if you please" was his usual mode of arresting criminals.

The Swedish actor Warner Oland played the role of Chan in some 16 films between 1931 and 1938. Sidney Toler then took over for a further 22 films, moving from 20th Century-Fox to Monogram in 1944 with *Charlie Chan in the Secret Service*. Other actors to play the part include Roland Winters (1948–52) and Peter USTINOV, who revived the role in the slapstick spoof *Charlie Chan and the Curse of the Dragon Queen* (1980). The character has also appeared in TV movies and cartoons.

Chandler, Raymond (1888–1959) US novelist and screenwriter. One of the pioneers of the 'hard-boiled' school of DETECTIVE fiction, he is best known for creating the tough, cynical, but essentially decent private-eye Philip MARLOWE.

Born in Chicago of Quaker parents, Chandler was educated in England, France, and Germany. After returning to America in 1912 he tried a number of jobs, only turning to writing when he was sacked for drinking. The success of Chandler's novels and his ability to handle dialogue and characterization soon led to offers from Hollywood, though his experience there was not happy: he complained that writers were "treated like a cow, something to be milked and sent out to graze." His first screenplay was DOUBLE INDEMNITY (1942), an adaptation of a James M. Cain novel, which earned him an Oscar nomination. *And Now Tomorrow* (1944) was followed by *The Lady in the Lake* (1945), which Chandler described as "probably the worst picture ever made." Increasingly disenchanted, he claimed he only managed to write *The Unseen* (1946) by getting drunk. *The Blue Dahlia* (1946), which earned him another Oscar nomination, was Chandler's first original screenplay; his second, *Playback*, was abandoned and later resurfaced as his last novel. Chandler subsequently abandoned Hollywood, though he returned to work with HITCHCOCK, whom he admired, on *Strangers on a Train* (1951), his last and probably best film.

The first of Chandler's novels to be adapted for the screen was *Farewell My Lovely*, a version of which was released as *The Falcon Takes Over* in 1942. The novel was filmed under its original title in 1944 (with Dick POWELL) and 1975 (with Robert MITCHUM). Of all Chandler adaptations the finest is probably THE BIG SLEEP (1946), directed by Howard HAWKS, scripted by William Faulkner, and starring Humphrey BOGART as Marlowe. Other novels to be adapted include *The High Window*, filmed in 1947 as *The Brasher Doubloon*, and *The Little Sisters*, his Hollywood-inspired novel, filmed as *Marlowe* (1969).

> If my books had been any worse, I should not have been invited to Hollywood. If they had been any better, I should not have come.
> RAYMOND CHANDLER.

Chaney. Lon Chaney (1883–1930) US actor known as the **Man of a Thousand Faces** because of his remarkable use of make-up to create grotesque monsters and villains. (He wrote the entry on 'make-up' in contemporary editions of the *Encyclopaedia Britannica*.) Between 1913 and 1930 Chaney played more than 150 roles, many for the director Tod Browning; he was America's leading male box-office draw in 1928 and 1929.

Being the son of deaf-mute parents – his father a barber and his mother bedridden – the young Alonso Chaney soon learned to communicate through mime. After several years working as a stagehand at the local theatre and playing small roles, he co-wrote a play with his brother, John, and toured with it, still aged only 17.

In 1912 Chaney began a new career as a prop man in films when a musical he was touring with ran out of money near Los Angeles. Director Allan DWAN remembered, "He used to come around with funny teeth in his mouth and weird make-ups." After making his screen debut in the two-reeler *Poor Jake's Demise* (1913) Chaney appeared in a number of serials, usually as the villain. In 1915 he directed six films for Universal Pictures, scripting two of them.

When Paramount needed a contortionist to play the grotesque character of Frog, a bogus cripple, in *The Miracle Man* (1919), Chaney volunteered and became a star 'overnight'. His disguises and disfigurements often involved great hardships. To play the legless underworld boss in *The Penalty* (1920), he had his lower legs strapped behind him and walked on his knees. During his role as Quasimodo in THE HUNCHBACK OF NOTRE DAME (1923) he carried a 40-pound hump on his back and wore facial make-up that took nearly five hours to apply.

When Universal neglected to sign Chaney after this triumph, MGM stepped into the breach and nurtured him as their only 'ugly' star for the rest of his career. His subsequent roles included both a gangster and the Chinese who kills him in *Outside the Law* (1921), an insane waxworks attendant in *While Paris Sleeps* (1923), a scientist turned circus clown in *He Who Gets Slapped* (1924), and a criminal ventriloquist who dresses as an elderly woman in *The Unholy Three* (1925).

In 1925 Chaney found a new level of popular acclaim as the pathetic title character in Universal's $1-million *The Phantom of the Opera* (the studio paid MGM handsomely to borrow him for the role). His voice was added to a sound reissue five years later. Although initially suspicious of talkies, he agreed to remake a number of his films in sound, beginning with *The Unholy Three* (1930). Just after its successful release, he died of throat cancer at the age of 47. Doctors believed that Chaney's tortuous disguises may well have contributed to his early death.

Lon Chaney Jnr (Creighton Chaney; 1906–73) US actor, who trained as a plumber before following his father, Lon Chaney, into the movie business. He made his first films as Creighton Chaney, later adopting the name Lon Chaney Jnr to capitalize on his father's fame.

Although Chaney won critical acclaim for playing the simple Lennie in the Steinbeck adaptation *Of Mice and Men* (1939), he is mainly associated with horror roles. His most famous part was that of Lawrence Talbot, a sympathetic hero who turns into a werewolf in THE WOLF MAN (1941); the character was revived in three sequels: *Frankenstein Meets the Wolf Man* (1943), *House of Frankenstein* (1945), and *House of Dracula* (1945), as well as putting in an appearance in *Abbott and Costello Meet Frankenstein* (1948). Chaney also starred in Universal's 'Inner Sanctum' series, which gave him the opportunity to play a variety of horror roles; the six films began with *Calling Dr Death* (1943) and ended with *Pillow of Death* (1946). His other screen monsters include the Mummy in *The Mummy's Tomb* (1942) and its sequels, Frankenstein's monster in *Ghost of Frankenstein* (1942), and the son of Dracula in the 1943 film of that name.

A later highlight of Chaney's career was playing the old sheriff in HIGH NOON (1952). From then on, however, he languished in cheap horror movies and Westerns, perhaps the most memorable of these being Roger CORMAN's *The Haunted Palace* (1963), in which he appeared with Vincent PRICE. His final movies, *Dracula Versus Frankenstein* and the Western *The Female Bunch* (both 1971), were amongst the worst of his career.

changeover During the projection of a feature film, the transition from one reel to the next (loaded on a separate PROJECTOR) without any break in continuity.

changeover cue A dot or other mark in the top right-hand corner of the final frames of a film reel; a signal for the PROJECTIONIST to change projectors.

Chaplin, Charlie (Sir Charles Spencer Chaplin; 1889–1977) British comedian, actor, and director, one of the central figures in film history. As the little TRAMP with his moustache, bowler, and cane, he became the world's most popular comedian and one of the most enduring of 20th-century icons. His fame was so great that a right-wing group in the Japanese military, unaware that he was British, plotted his assassination when he visited Tokyo in 1931, believing that his death would bring certain war with America.

Born in London's East End, young Charlie was forced onto the stage to support his poverty-stricken family after the death of his father, a music-hall entertainer. His mother, also a music-hall singer, suffered from periodic insanity. While touring America with Fred Karno's theatrical troupe in 1913 he was spotted by Mack SENNETT of KEYSTONE Studios. *Making a Living* (1914) was the first of Chaplin's 35 Keystone films; others include *Kid Auto Races at Venice* (1914), which introduced the tramp character, and *Tillie's Punctured Romance* (1914), the first US feature film and the world's first feature-length comedy.

In 1915 Chaplin joined the Essanay company and began a 37-year collaboration with cameraman Roland Totheroh. After moving to Mutual in 1916 he made his most important two-reelers, notably *The Floorwalker* (1916), *The Immigrant* (1917), and *Easy Street* (1917). In 1918 First National gave him a million-dollar contract to make a series of films including *Shoulder Arms* (1918), about the ordinary man's reaction to war, and THE KID (1921), Chaplin's first feature. Soon afterwards he moved into independent production, releasing his films through UNITED ARTISTS, of which he was a co-founder.

The 1920s and 1930s saw the appearance of Chaplin's finest work, beginning with the sophisticated melodrama *A Woman of Paris* (1923), which he wrote and directed but did not star in, (confining himself to an uncredited cameo). This was followed by THE GOLD RUSH (1925), a hugely popular film in which Chaplin's blend of slapstick,

pathos, and balletic grace reached new levels of perfection. In *The Circus* (1928) and CITY LIGHTS (1931) he defied the coming of the talkies, preferring to refine his established visual style; Chaplin composed the score for *City Lights* and all his subsequent films. The element of social comment in his work became more explicit in MODERN TIMES (1936), the last tramp film and the first to feature his voice (in a nonsense song). In THE GREAT DICTATOR (1940) Chaplin played on his resemblance to Hitler and expressed his own romantic political credo in a long closing speech.

The black comedy *Monsieur Verdoux* (1947) marked a change in direction. For the first time Chaplin played a straight role, a bigamist who marries and murders rich widows to support his suburban family. The film was condemned by moralists and shunned by US audiences. In the elegaic *Limelight* (1952), a film that seems to reflect Chaplin's sense of belonging to an earlier era, he and Buster KEATON portrayed two declining vaudeville stars (with five of Chaplin's children in minor roles). This was to be Chaplin's last US film. A well-known supporter of left-wing causes, he fell foul of the virulent anti-communism of the period: his films were boycotted, and his right to residency revoked during a visit to Europe in 1952.

His case was not helped by a long-standing reputation for sexual scandal. Three failed marriages (including one to the actress Paulette GODDARD) and a string of affairs lay behind him when he married Eugene O'Neill's teenage daughter Oona in 1942 and finally settled into a marriage that endured until his death.

Chaplin retired to Vevey in Switzerland, making two further films in Britain: *A King in New York* (1957) – a satire on the US way of life – and *A Countess from Hong Kong* (1967). He returned to America in 1972 to collect an honorary Oscar, which he accepted with the words, "You're all sweet, wonderful people", later admitting "I hated all of them." Knighted in 1975, he died two years later in Switzerland. In 1992 Richard ATTENBOROUGH made the BIOPIC *Chaplin* with Robert Downey Jnr in the title role.

Great comedian, great actor, bad director.
WARREN BEATTY.

Chaplin means more to me than the idea of God.
FRANÇOIS TRUFFAUT.

character actor An actor with a well-known face and distinctive personality who usually plays a secondary or supporting role. Such actors often lack the good looks required of the romantic lead but are nonetheless much loved by film-goers; many enjoy longer careers than the stars because of their ability to play older or comic roles. Character actors of Hollywood's Golden Era include Walter BRENNAN, John CARRADINE, Margaret DUMONT, Charles Coburn, Hattie McDaniel, Franklin Pangborn, Buddy Ebsen, and Edward Everett Horton, all of whose faces are more familiar than their names.

Some character actors eventually become stars, an example being Britain's Margaret RUTHERFORD, who played Miss MARPLE in a number of Agatha Christie films after years in secondary roles. Conversely, some stars, such as John BARRYMORE, fade into character roles with age.

> I'm a character actor in a leading man's body.
>
> WILLIAM HURT

> I don't think of myself as a character actress – that's become a phrase which means you've had it.
>
> BETTE DAVIS

Chariots of Fire (1981) Oscar-winning British film produced by David PUTTNAM and directed by Hugh Hudson in his feature debut. The plot centres on the conflicts and pressures faced by two real-life British runners, the Scottish missionary Eric Liddell (Ian Charleson) and the Jewish undergraduate Harold Abrahams (Ben Cross), who were rivals in the 1924 Olympic Games. Charleson and Cross, both relative newcomers to the screen, were ably supported by Ian Holm, Nigel Havers, Cheryl Campbell, and Alice Krige, with John GIELGUD and Lindsay ANDERSON in CAMEO roles.

Despite mixed reviews – many critics found the film old-fashioned in both style and values – the film proved an unexpected success at the US box office, where it took some $62 million dollars (at that time a record for a non-US feature). The film also gave a welcome, if transient, boost to the British film industry by scooping the Oscar for Best Picture – the first UK product to be so honoured since *Oliver!*, 13 years earlier. Oscars were also awarded for Best Screenplay (Colin Welland), Best Score (Vangelis), and Best Costumes. On collecting his award, Welland delivered himself of the exultant and much-reported comment "You may have started something: the British are coming!" – a prophecy that has remained largely unfulfilled, despite the unprecedented success of GANDHI in 1982. The award for Best Costumes was particularly baffling to Puttnam, who later commented "What the heck were our costumes...? A few shorts and singlets."

Charisse, Cyd (Tula Finklea; 1921–) US actress and dancer, who starred in a series of MGM musicals in the 1950s. Having trained as a dancer from the age of eight, Charisse made her film debut in 1943 and went on to dance – and act a little – in such movies as *The Unfinished Dance* (1947), *East Side West Side* (1949), and *The Band Wagon* (1953), in which she partnered Fred ASTAIRE. Her films with Gene KELLY included Lerner and Loewe's *Brigadoon* (1954), *It's Always Fair Weather* (1955), and the ambitious ballet movie *Invitation to the Dance* (1957). Her cameo as a long-legged green-costumed vamp in the ballet sequence of Kelly's SINGIN' IN THE RAIN (1952) caused a sensation and remains her most famous role. She would have played the female lead in Kelly's *An American in Paris* had she not been pregnant at the time. Subsequent films ranged from *Silk Stockings* (1957), a musical reworking of the NINOTCHKA story, to the melodrama *Two Weeks in Another Town* (1962). In 1978 she made a guest appearance in the sci-fi adventure *Warlords of Atlantis* (1978).

> That Cyd! When you've danced with her you stay danced with.
>
> FRED ASTAIRE.

Charme discret de la bourgeoisie, Le See DISCREET CHARM OF THE BOURGEOISIE, THE.

Chase, Chevy (Cornelius Crane Chase; 1943–) US knockabout comedian, whose popular films have generally been slated by the critics. Born in New York City, he made his name as a regular on the television show *Saturday Night Live*, which brought him together with John BELUSHI and Dan AYKROYD. His usual comic persona is that of a banally ordinary US male. "I guess I look so straight and normal", he once said, "nobody expects me to pick my nose and fall."

Chase's first film was *Tunnelvision* (1976), a spoof about the television of the future. This was followed by the comedy-thriller *Foul Play* (1978), in which he and Goldie HAWN thwart a plot to assassinate the pope. In the 1980s Chase became a cult figure with teenage moviegoers in the role of Clark Griswold, the harrassed father who leads a tense family trip to 'Wally World' in *National Lampoon's Vacation* (1983). There followed the unsophisticated sequels *National Lampoon's European Vacation* (1985) and *National Lampoon's Christmas Vacation* (1989).

In 1985 Chase made *Spies Like Us*, in which he was reunited with Aykroyd, and *Fletch*, in which he played a wisecracking reporter who uses a series of disguises to trap a con man. A poor sequel, *Fletch Lives* (1989), had him embroiled in a Louisiana murder. Between these films Chase joined Steve MARTIN (another *Saturday Night Live* regular) and Martin Short for *Three Amigos!* (1986), a parody of *The Magnificent Seven*. In 1992 he starred in John CARPENTER'S *Memoirs of an Invisible Man* as a stock analyst who is accidentally made invisible.

Chase's attempt to host a late-night television chat show in 1993 proved an immediate disaster.

> I said that I didn't think Chevy Chase could ad-lib a fart after a baked-bean dinner. I think he took umbrage at that.
> JOHNNY CARSON, US chat-show host.

chase film or **chaser** A film in which the main plot or climax takes the form of a prolonged chase, as in numerous Westerns, comedies, police stories, and thrillers.

The chase has a long history in moving pictures, being one kind of action that cannot easily be represented in any other medium. One of the earliest chase films was Edwin S. PORTER'S *The Great Train Robbery* (1903), a film that helped to establish the convention of CROSS CUTTING between parallel action. Chase sequences soon became the mainstay of silent comedy, with classic examples including Buster KEATON's rail chase in THE GENERAL (1926) and the road chases of the KEYSTONE KOPS. The slapstick chase was memorably revived in Peter BOGDANOVICH's pastiche *What's Up, Doc?* (1972).

Numerous other comedies have been based on a prolonged pursuit in the form of a race; examples of this subgenre include GENEVIEVE (1953), *It's a Mad Mad Mad Mad World* (1963), *The Gumball Rally* (1976), and *The Cannonball Run* (1981). ROAD MOVIES, both comic and serious, also tend to involve an element of pursuit. Two wholly unserious examples are the trucker movies *Smokey and the Bandit* (1977), with Burt REYNOLDS, and *Convoy* (1978). In SPIELBERG's gripping *The Sugarland Express* (1974), based on a true story, Goldie HAWN and William Atherton are pursued across Texas in their quest to recover Hawn's baby from its foster parents.

Unforgettable car chases from serious thrillers include those in *Bullitt* (1968), with Steve MCQUEEN, *The French Connection* (1971), and Spielberg's classic short *Duel* (1971), in which Dennis Weaver is pursued by a menacing truck.

In the early days of the US cinema, a *chaser* was also the name given to an unappealing film used to clear the audience from a vaudeville house after live performances.

cheat. **cheater cut** In the CLIFFHANGER serials of the 1910s and 1920s, a type of footage frequently included at the beginning of an episode. This would show the hero or heroine escaping without too much difficulty from what had appeared, a week earlier, to be an impossible predicament. In fact, the 'cheat' footage often provided a means of escape that had not been present in the previous sequence.

cheat shot A shot that creates a simple illusion by leaving part of the action out of the frame. A common type of cheat shot is that in which a character apparently falls from a high building – only to land safely, off-camera, a few feet below. The roof that Oliver Hardy (*see* LAUREL AND HARDY) tumbled from in *Laughing Gravy* (1931) was in reality a few inches off the studio floor. The making of a Hollywood cheat shot, in which Meryl STREEP apparently hangs by her fingers from a high window ledge, is illustrated in the film *Postcards from the Edge* (1990).

Chen Kaige (1952–) Chinese director, the leading member of the so-called 'fifth generation' of directors who graduated from the reopened Beijing Film Academy in the early 1980s. Chen Kaige was born in Beijing, the son of the film-maker Chen Huai'ai. During the Cultural Revolution he was sent (1967–70) to work on the land in the poor province of Yünnan, an experience that did much to shape his view of the reality of life in communist China. After several years in the army he enrolled at the Beijing Film Academy, making his feature debut with the ambitious *Yellow Earth* (1984). Set in the years immediately preceding World War II, *Yellow Earth* examines the gulf between the idealistic communism of the industrial cities and the extreme conservatism of life in the Chinese countryside. The plot concerns a young communist scholar who visits a rural area to collect folk songs but finds communication with the local people almost impossible. This was followed by *The Big Parade* (1986), a film that explores the conflict between loyalty to the state and personal freedom through a story about young military cadets preparing for a parade, and *King of the Children* (1987), about the experiences of an enthusiastic young teacher at an impoverished rural school. *Life on a String* (1991) was a compassionate piece about the travels of a blind storyteller and his blind apprentice.

With his most recent work, the spectacular *Farewell, My Concubine* (1993), Chen found a degree of international recognition unequalled by any previous Chinese filmmaker. The film won both the Palme d'Or at the Cannes Festival (shared with Jane CAMPION's *The Piano*) and the prestigious International Critics' Award. Blending the epic with the intimate, *Farewell, My Concubine* follows the fortunes of two members of the Beijing Opera through the turbulent political events of half a century. Owing to both the awkward political questions it raises and to its frank treatment of homosexuality, the film was swiftly removed from circulation by the Chinese authorities. Although it was subsequently rereleased with cuts, the future of Chen's current project, a treatment of the Cultural Revolution, must remain in doubt.

Cher (Cherilyn Sarkasian, 1946–) US entertainer, who began her career as a pop singer but has more recently found success as a film actress. After working as a backing singer with the Crystals and the Ronettes, Cher became famous in the mid 1960s as the female half of the duo Sonny and Cher, the other half being her then husband, Sonny Bono. Although the couple made two unremarkable films – *Wild on the Beach* (1965) and *Good Times* (1967) – it was not until the 1980s that Cher's acting career was to begin in earnest. During the 1970s she worked as a cabaret singer, largely in Las Vegas.

Having persuaded Robert ALTMAN to give her a part in his 1982 off-Broadway production *Come Back to the Five and Dime, Jimmy Dean, Jimmy Dean*, Cher went on to play the same role in the film version a year later. Director Mike NICHOLS then offered her the role of Meryl STREEP's room-mate in *Silkwood* (1983), a performance that confirmed her abilities as a serious actress and brought her an Oscar nomination.

In Hollywood, however, Cher was still regarded as a lightweight – an image deriving mainly from her early career as a singer and her outrageous taste in clothes. Her impressive performance as a drug-addicted biker trying to help her handicapped son in *Mask* (1985) brought her the Best Actress award at Cannes (shared with Norma Aleandro), but, unaccountably, no Oscar nomination. In 1987 she did receive an Oscar, this time in the surprising role of a slightly dowdy young Italian widow in Norman Jewison's *Moonstruck*, a part that Jewison had himself persuaded her to take. Other successful films have included the black comedy *The Witches of Eastwick* (1987), with Susan SARANDON, Michelle PFEIFFER, and Jack NICHOLSON, and the charming *Mermaids* (1990), with Bob HOSKINS and Wynona RYDER.

> You don't have to be smart to act – look at the outgoing president of the United States.
> CHER, Dec. 1988.

chest shot   *See* BUST SHOT; MEDIUM CLOSE SHOT.

Chevalier, Maurice   (1888–1972) French singer and actor, whose sly charm carried him through 70 years as an entertainer. His trademarks were his lilting French accent, roguish rolling eyes, and famous straw boater. He achieved his biggest success in *Gigi* (1958), in which the 70-year-old Chevalier sang 'Thank Heaven For Little Girls' and (with Hermione Gingold) 'I Remember It Well'. That year, he received a special career Oscar and Jean COCTEAU's memorable compliment, "Paris has two monuments: the Eiffel tower and Maurice Chevalier."

Born in poverty, the youngest of nine children of a house painter and a lacemaker, he left school at 11 and by 13 was singing rude songs in Paris cafés and music halls. He appeared in his first film, *Trop crédule*, in 1908 and a year later joined the Folies-Bergère to appear with the famous Mistinguett, who became his lover. During World War I he spent more than two years in a German prisoner-of-war camp, where he learnt English from a British sergeant (he was subsequently awarded the Croix de Guerre). In 1919 he made his London stage debut, complete with straw hat, in *Hullo, America*.

Although Chevalier failed his MGM screen test, Paramount gave him a contract in 1928, stipulating that it would be cancelled if he lost his French accent. In *Innocents of Paris* (1929), his first Hollywood film, he sang 'Every Little Breeze Seems to Whisper Louise', a song that became one of his signature tunes. Over the next few years Ernst LUBITSCH directed Chevalier and Jeanette MACDONALD in several musicals, including *The Merry Widow* (1934); however, when Grace Moore was given top billing for his next movie Chevalier stormed back to Paris. His first dramatic role, as a murder suspect, was in the French film *Pièges* (1939).

During the Occupation, Chevalier entertained French prisoners, obtaining the release of ten of them in return for his services. However, he also performed on the German-controlled radio, leading to his denunciation as a collaborator (he was later exonerated). Besides *Gigi*, his later Hollywood films included *Love in the Afternoon* (1957) with Audrey HEPBURN, and *A New Kind of Love* (1963).

Al JOLSON called Chevalier "the greatest thing to come from France since Lafayette", but others were more equivocal in their praise. Director Rouben MAMOULIAN thought that "the whole of him was much bigger than the sum of his various talents", while Josephine Baker considered him "a great artiste, but a small human being". He unsuccessfully attempted suicide at the age of 82.

children.   *Children of Paradise See* ENFANTS DU PARADIS, LES.

child stars Youthful performers have been a feature of the cinema since the days of the GISH SISTERS and Mary PICKFORD, who became enormous stars while still in their teens. However, the heyday of the child star was undoubtedly the 1920s and 1930s, when Hollywood responded to the Depression with a steady stream of undemanding upbeat entertainment. During this period, the studios recruited a whole series of wide-eyed waifs to demonstrate to the adult world that honesty, innocence, and a sweet smile can overcome all obstacles.

The first true child star was Jackie Coogan (1914–84), who made a hugely suc-

cessful debut as a six-year-old in CHAPLIN's tearjerker THE KID (1921). A year later Hal ROACH initiated the OUR GANG comedy series, which ran for some 20 years. It was, however, in the 1930s that the biggest child stars appeared. Shirley TEMPLE became Fox's leading earner, Deanna DURBIN saved Universal from bankruptcy, while Mickey ROONEY and Judy GARLAND starred both separately and in tandem at MGM. Since the war relatively few child stars have appeared, Elizabeth TAYLOR and Jodie FOSTER being perhaps the most notable. More recently, the trend towards youth-orientated movies initiated by Steven SPIELBERG's E.T. (1982) has thrown up a number of high-earning juvenile performers – notably Macaulay CULKIN, the star of *Home Alone* (1990).

At their peak, child stars are as powerful as any other Hollywood player. Few, however, make the transition to teen or adult roles, a failure that must come hard after years of adulation. The later lives of former child stars tend to make sad reading; one thinks of Coogan suing his parents over his lost earnings, Freddie Bartholomew, star of MGM's *David Copperfield* (1934), watching as his million-dollar fortune was eaten away by adoption suits, and the well-documented drink and drug problems of Garland and Drew BARRYMORE. There appears to be much to be said for COWARD's advice: "Don't put your daughter on the (sound) stage Mrs Worthington." Perhaps Mrs Shirley Temple Black's successful diplomatic career is the exception that proves the rule.

Chinatown   (1974) Roman POLANSKI's evocative period detective drama. A brooding noir-style thriller, *Chinatown* earned a total of 11 Oscar nominations, though only Robert TOWNE, the scriptwriter, emerged victorious on the night.

Set in Los Angeles in 1937, the film concerns J. J. (Jake) Gittes (Jack NICHOLSON), a Chandleresque private detective specializing in divorce cases. Gittes accepts a job from the wife of a city water commissioner, only to discover that he has been duped when he meets the man's real wife, Evelyn Mulwray (Faye DUNAWAY) – who quickly becomes a widow. Gittes is then drawn into a dangerous and labyrinthine plot of murder, incest, and corruption spun by Dunaway's father Noah Cross (John HUSTON), who is involved in a scheme to divert the Los Angeles water supply for his personal gain.

The 1930s look is painstakingly recreated, the muted colour cinematography (John A. Alonso) is wonderfully evocative, and Towne's dialogue has just the right amount of acrimony. The role of Evelyn is said to have been turned down by Jane FONDA and forfeited by Ali McGraw, owing to her divorce from Robert Evans, the film's producer. Polanski appears in a cameo role as a knife-wielding thug who cuts Nicholson's nose – thus bringing the number of actor-directors in the film up to three (himself, Huston, and Nicholson). *The Two Jakes* (1990), a sequel to the film directed by Nicholson, was generally regarded as disappointing.

chinese dolly A shot in which the camera PULLS BACK and PANS at the same time; so-called by an analogy between the slanting movement and the supposed slanting eyes of the Chinese. *See* DOLLY.

chop socky *Variety's* humorous term for a MARTIAL-ARTS MOVIE; a blend of *chop suey*, karate *chop*, and *sock* (i.e. to strike).

choreographer The person who is responsible for devising and directing the DANCE in a film. Famous film choreographers include Busby BERKELEY and Bob FOSSE, both of whom began on Broadway. Action sequences of other kinds, such as fights or chases, may sometimes need to be 'choreographed' by a specialist. Indeed, some of the scenes of violence in Martin SCORSESE's *GoodFellas* (1990) were based on the choreography of the ballet movie THE RED SHOES (1948).

Christ. **Jesus Christ** Although the founder of Christianity has been the subject of numerous Bible EPICS and other films, actors and directors have faced many problems when portraying him on screen, not least the ease with which offence may be caused. The first film to provoke criticism on this score was D. W. GRIFFITH's INTOLERANCE (1916), which featured a rather rowdy wedding at Cana. Cecil B. DE MILLE was the first to film the entire life of Christ, in the captivating but often absurd *King of Kings* (1927), of which John Steinbeck remarked, "Saw the film – loved the book." Jesus spoke for the first time in the French film *Golgotha* (1935), although the British Board of Film Censors removed most of Robert Le Vigan's performance from the film. For many years afterwards the US film industry shied away from

making Jesus the the central character, preferring to use him as a peripheral presence in such widescreen epics as THE ROBE (1953) and BEN-HUR (1959).

The Gospel story became a popular subject for film-makers in the 1960s. In 1961 Nicholas RAY directed a new version of *King of Kings*, with Jeffrey Hunter as a very young and solemn Jesus. Four years later George STEVENS attempted the definitive account with *The Greatest Story Ever Told*, starring Max VON SYDOW as Christ, but the end result was overlong and marred by some woeful 'big name' casting (including John WAYNE as the Roman centurion at the crucifixion, who declares "Truly, this man was the Son of God"). By contrast, Pier Paolo PASOLINI's *The Gospel According to St Matthew* (1964), with its cast of unknowns, is generally regarded as the best film to be based on the Gospels. A gay Marxist, who was twice arrested for blasphemy, Pasolini produced a powerful film by taking his dialogue straight from the Bible and avoiding any false reverence.

A pair of hippy musicals, both based on stage shows, was released in 1973: *Jesus Christ Superstar* and *Godspell*. Most controversial of all was *Monty Python's Life of Brian* (1979), in which Graham Chapman played an ordinary man who is mistaken for the Messiah and, finally, crucified to the jaunty song 'Always Look on the Bright Side of Life' (*see* MONTY PYTHON). While not unexpected, the vitriolic protests that preceded the release of Martin SCORSESE's *The Last Temptation of Christ* (1988) were somewhat misplaced, as they mainly concerned the temptations faced (but rejected) by Willem DAFOE's very human Messiah. Denys Arcand's *Jesus of Montreal* (1989), about an actor whose role as Christ begins to take over his life, showed that it is sometimes easier to examine the subject through a modern parallel.

Christmas The festive season has frequently been used by film-makers as the setting either for a whole movie or for an important part of the action. It has variously been depicted as a time of romance (*I'll Be Seeing You*, 1944), supernatural intervention (*The Bishop's Wife*, 1947), and unfortunate family revelation (*The Holly and the Ivy*, 1952), but almost always Christmas means sentimentality. Festive scenes in such films as MEET ME IN ST LOUIS (1944), *Young at Heart* (1954), and IT'S A WONDERFUL LIFE (1946), perhaps the Christmas movie *par excellence*, inevitably tend towards dewy-eyed evocations of family, love, and the passing of time. By contrast, the disappointing *White Christmas* (1954), a remake of *Holiday Inn* (1942), is little more than an excuse for some pleasant songs. Sadder views of Christmas feature in *Meet John Doe* (1941) and *The Glenn Miller Story* (1953), while the timing of Dan AYKROYD's fall from grace in *Trading Places* (1983) is no coincidence. The comedy *National Lampoon's Christmas Vacation* (1989) presents the festive season as a potential disaster area, while in *Home Alone* (1990) Macaulay CULKIN's parents inadvertently leave him behind when they go away for Christmas.

Charles DICKENS's *A Christmas Carol* has inspired several films, though only the MGM version of 1938 (and a 1984 TV movie) kept the title intact. Three British films changed the title to *Scrooge*. Of these, the 1935 adaptation with Seymour Hicks is best passed over in favour of the classic 1951 version with Alastair SIM in the title role. The 1970 musical, featuring Albert FINNEY as Scrooge and Alec GUINNESS as one of the ghosts, was neither true to its own intentions nor faithful to the original, whereas Richard Donner's *Scrooged* (1988), starring Bill Murray, succeeded in transplanting the whole tale to contemporary America. (In true Dickensian spirit, Paramount refused to give the cast and crew a Christmas break from filming, but Donner got round this by firing them all on Christmas Eve and rehiring them at the end of the holiday period.) *The Muppet's Christmas Carol* (1992) has Michael CAINE as the miser and Kermit the frog as Bob Cratchit (with Miss Piggy as his wife).

Father Christmas has appeared in various films, notably *Miracle on 34th Street* (1947), in which a department store Santa Claus claims to be the real thing, *The Lemon Drop Kid* (1951), starring Bob HOPE, and the notorious *Santa Claus: The Movie* (1985), a box-office disaster featuring Dudley MOORE as one of Santa's little helpers. In late 1994 a furious row broke out between Disney and 20th Century-Fox, both of whom had produced new films about Father Christmas. When Disney held a preview in Los Angeles of its comedy *The Santa Clause*, Fox employees used subterfuge to gain access to the hotel bedrooms in which journalists were staying and left publicity material for their own film, a remake of *Miracle on 34th Street* starring Richard ATTENBOROUGH.

Christie, Agatha *See* MARPLE, JANE; POIROT, HERCULE.

Churchill, Sir Winston (1874–1965) British statesman and author, who led the free world in its opposition to Nazi Germany.

For most of his life, Churchill had other preoccupations than the cinema. However, while out of office during the 1930s, Churchill sought alternative outlets for his views, and alternative sources of income. Being an experienced writer with an enthusiasm for the cinema, this led him to embark on a brief career in films. In 1934 Alexander KORDA signed him as historical adviser for London Films and bought Churchill's script for *War and Peace: the Life of Marlborough*. Churchill subsequently worked on *Conquest of the Air* (1935), which advocated the use of strategic air power.

As war leader, Churchill showed a keen sense of the PROPAGANDA value of film, dispatching Korda to America with a secret brief to make pro-British movies. The best of these was *Lady Hamilton* (US title *That Hamilton Woman*; 1941), the theme of which was suggested by Churchill, who also wrote some of the dialogue. It has the distinction of being both Churchill's and Stalin's favourite film, and was the first British movie allowed on general release in the Soviet Union. In contrast, Churchill used all his powers to try to prevent the foreign release of POWELL and PRESSBURGER's THE LIFE AND DEATH OF COLONEL BLIMP (1943), which he considered detrimental to Britain's image. After the war Churchill's *History of the Second World War* became the basis for a number of documentaries, notably *Their Finest Hours* (1964). In the 1940s and 1950s his actress daughter Sarah featured in a number of films including *Royal Wedding* (1951).

Churchill himself has been portrayed on the big screen in over 20 films. Actors to play the great man include Patrick Wymark in *Operation Crossbow* (1965) and Simon Ward in *Young Winston* (1972). *The Eagle Has Landed* (1976), based on a novel by Jack Higgins, is an all-star film about a fictional attempt to kidnap Churchill in 1943. *See also* HITLER, ADOLF; WORLD WAR II.

Cimino, Michael (1943–) US director and screenwriter. A fine arts graduate from

Yale, Cimino studied acting and ballet and spent a time making industrial documentaries and TV commercials before moving to Hollywood in 1971. That same year he contributed to the script of *Silent Running*, the directorial debut of Donald Trumbull (who had provided the special effects for 2001: A SPACE ODYSSEY). Two years later he co-wrote the screenplay for the Clint EASTWOOD police thriller *Magnum Force* (1973). Eastwood was sufficiently impressed by Cimino's work to have him write and direct *Thunderbolt and Lightfoot* (1974), a brilliant multilayered HEIST MOVIE.

The success of *Thunderbolt and Lightfoot* led to Cimino being entrusted with a huge budget on his next film, *The Deer Hunter* (1978). The film, an examination of the effects of the VIETNAM WAR on the lives of three Pennsylvania steel workers, was brilliantly constructed and featured some stunning set pieces. It was released to both critical and commercial success and, for a time, it appeared that Cimino could do no wrong. However, this reputation was to collapse in the most dramatic way with his next film, the epic western HEAVEN'S GATE (1981), an account of the Johnson County Wars in Wyoming. The film opened to a critical mauling and – owing largely to drastic studio cuts that made it virtually incoherent – found little favour with the public. Having cost upwards of $35 million to make, *Heaven's Gate* is regarded as one of Hollywood's worst-ever disasters and is credited with effectively closing UNITED ARTISTS.

Cimino's subsequent films – *Year of the Dragon* (1985; scripted by Oliver STONE), *The Sicilian* (1987), and *Desperate Hours* (1991), a remake of William WYLER's 1955 film, have done little to retrieve his former reputation. Indeed, if anything they may have diminished it: *Heaven's Gate* may have been a failure, but it was a heroic failure, imbued with both a grand vision and with Cimino's ability to layer a film so as to create a multidimensional world. By comparison, his last three films are merely routine.

cinch marks The scratch marks that sometimes appear on films; they are usually caused either by dust particles or by layers of film rubbing against each other as a loose spool is tightened.

Cinderella film Another term for a SLEEPER.

cine. **cineaste** A serious and enthusiastic student of the cinema; a film buff. Of French origin, the term is also sometimes applied to those professionally involved in the making of films. The film journal *Cineaste*, published quarterly in America, deals chiefly with non-commercial and international films.

Cinecittà (Ital.: cinema city) The sprawling Italian studio complex whose 15 sound stages make it Europe's largest production centre. Built in 1936–37 on a site six miles from the centre of Rome, Cinecittà was originally designed as a monument to the glories of Fascism. It became known as **Hollywood on the Tiber** during the 1950s when US film-makers took advantage of Italy's low-cost facilities and cheap labour to produce such epics as QUO VADIS (1951) and BEN-HUR (1959). Federico FELLINI made virtually all his films at the studios. By the 1970s, however, the boom had ended and the empty Cinecittà stages had come to symbolize the crisis within the Italian film industry.

Although little filming has since taken place there, the complex has continued to offer full-service production facilities for features and television series. Recent productions have included three major films, Columbia's *The Adventures of Baron Munchhausen* (1989), Paramount's THE GODFATHER, PART III (1990), and Tri-Star's *Hudson Hawk* (1991). Following losses of $19 million in 1993, the government holding company, Ente Cinema, announced plans to privatize the complex.

cine-fi sound At some US DRIVE-IN theatres, the transmission on AM radio of the soundtrack of the film being shown. Cinemagoers can receive the soundtrack by tuning their car radio to the specified station; if the car radio does not operate with the ignition off, a transistor set can be used.

Cinema Exhibitors' Association (of Great Britain and Ireland) (CEA) The British union of cinema proprietors. Based in London, the CEA represents its members' interests within the industry and to parliament, the European Commission, and local governmental bodies.

The organization was founded in 1912 as the Cinematograph Exhibitor's Association, partly to oppose complaints by film producers that exhibitors were running individual films for too long, thereby reducing demand for new productions. Other early problems tackled by the Association included BLOCK BOOKING and the imposition of QUOTAS.

During World War II, members of the Association set aside ten minutes of each cinema programme for documentaries and other productions supplied by the Films Division of the Ministry of Information. By 1950 membership of the CEA had grown to some 4000; it now represents most British commercial cinemas, cinemas owned by local authorities, and Regional Film Theatres.

cinema nôvo (Port.: new cinema) A school of film-making that emerged in Brazil in the 1960s, noted especially for politically conscious fantasy and melodrama. Its exponents included the directors Glauber Rocha, Ruy Guerra, Nelson Pereira dos Santos, and Carlos Diégues. Although these directors generally used allegory and symbol to veil their political intent, the revolutionary nature of the movement led to its suppression by the government in the 1970s.

CinemaScope The first really successful WIDESCREEN process, introduced by 20th Century-Fox in THE ROBE (1953). The system employed an ANAMORPHIC LENS to compress a wide picture onto a standard 35-mm frame. When projected through a complementary lens, this produced an image with a width two and a half times its height. Although invented in the 1920s by Henri Chrétien, the process was not adopted by Hollywood until the 1950s, when it was seized upon in an attempt to counter the growing threat from television. Other studios introduced their own versions of the system, variously called Super-Scope, WarnerScope, etc. Initially, many directors disparaged the process, arguing that it narrowed the compositional possibilities available to the film maker. By the early 1960s it had been superseded by PANAVISION, a similar but more sophisticated process.

> There was a time when all I looked for was a good story, but nowadays everything has to look the size of Mount Rushmore, and the actors in close-up look as though they belong there.
> FRITZ LANG, director.

cinematheque In Britain, a small ART HOUSE or other cinema; US cinemas and film clubs sometimes use the word in their names to show that they are exhibitors of art films. In France a *cinémathèque* is a FILM ARCHIVE.

Cinémathèque Française A French film library founded in 1936 in Paris by Henri Langlois, whose private collection of films formed the core of the archive, with Georges FRANJU and Jean Metry. It played an important role in the concealment and protection of films from the Germans during the Occupation. Funded from 1945 to 1968 by the French government's Centre National du Cinéma, it has been privately supported since 1969, when the government established its own archive, the Service des Archives du Film. Langlois remained its director until his death in 1977.

Now the biggest such archive in the world, the Cinémathèque Française holds some 100,000 films, more than a million still photographs, and many thousands of books and documents. In 1972 it opened the Musée du Cinéma, a museum of movie artefacts that contains a number of reconstructed sets. The Cinématèque Française also runs two theatres, whose showings of Hollywood films influenced exponents of the AUTEUR theory and the NEW WAVE in the 1950s.

cinematic Relating to those aspects of film-making that do not involve the actual shooting of the film. The cinematic process includes financing, advertising, and distribution. *Compare* FILMIC.

Cinématographe *See* LUMIÈRE BROTHERS, THE.

cinematographer In a film production crew, the person responsible for the photography, lighting, and other technical elements involved in setting up shots, and for the processing of the exposed film. Also known as the **director of photography** or **lighting cameraman**, he or she is a major contributor to the overall visual effect of the film and works in close collaboration with the director. Among the outstanding cinematographers have been Billy Bitzer, chief cameraman to D. W. GRIFFITH, Gregg TOLAND, who filmed CITIZEN KANE (1941) and THE BEST YEARS OF OUR LIVES (1946), Joseph AUGUST, director of photography on numerous Hollywood films including *Portrait of Jenny* (1948), F. A. Young, who was responsible for filming the desert landscapes in LAWRENCE OF ARABIA (1962), Sven NYKVIST, best known for his long association with Ingmar BERGMAN, and Robert Krasker, responsible for the eerie night shots in THE THIRD MAN (1949).

cinéma vérité (Fr.: cinema truth) A style of DOCUMENTARY film-making that emerged in France in the 1960s. The aim was to convey a sense of real life, unrehearsed and unedited. Cameras were generally lightweight and hand-held, allowing cameramen to 'eavesdrop' on conversations; sound was recorded at the time of filming and subsequent editing kept to the minimum. Unlike the parallel US movement DIRECT CINEMA, however, there was no attempt to disguise the presence of the film crew or to pretend that it did not affect the behaviour of those filmed. Notable examples of the genre include *Chronicle of a Summer* (1961) by Jean Rouch, in which the camera records a series of interviews designed to reveal the preoccupations of Parisian society in the early 1960s. The term is now used more loosely to describe any realistic style of documentary.

cinemicrography or **microcinematography** Filming through a microscope to record subjects that are too small to be seen by the naked eye. Its main uses are in medicine and scientific research.

Cinemiracle A WIDESCREEN process that eliminated the wobbly joins between the images that were the chief defect of CINERAMA's three-projector system. 'Seamless Cinerama' was, however, soon superseded by CINEMASCOPE and other ANAMORPHIC LENS systems.

Cinemobile A vehicle resembling an enormous bus that is used both for transporting equipment and for various purposes on location. It can usually provide accommodation for a production crew of around 50, space for all the equipment required for filming, and several dressing-rooms and toilets. The Cinemobile was designed in America by Fouad Said in the 1960s; before its introduction (and the advent of lighter equipment) location shooting usually required a convoy of several trucks. If necessary, it can be transported by air.

Cinerama A WIDESCREEN process in which three synchronized projectors each project one third of a film image onto a large curved screen. The technique, which also required the use of three synchronized cameras, was invented by the New York photographer Fred Waller and given its first public showing in *This is Cinerama* (1952). The system's spectacular visual effects and stereo sound were restricted to travelogues until its first narrative use in *How the West was Won* (1962). Owing mainly to the expense of the cumbersome projection machinery, the system was superseded in the 1960s by such ANAMORPHIC systems as CINEMASCOPE and PANAVISION.

cinex strip A strip of developed film in which adjacent frames have been processed using a different printer light. This is returned with the dailies (*see* RUSHES) to show the cinematographer how a particular scene could look with a range of different printing effects.

Circarama A WIDESCREEN system involving the projection of a 360-degree image on a screen that completely surrounds the audience. Originally developed for Disneyland, the system was featured at the 1968 Hemisfair in San Antonio, Texas. It did not prove a very practical form of cinema.

circuit A chain of cinemas owned by the same organization. In America, the leading theatre circuits were all owned or controlled by the major studios until the late 1940s, when antitrust legislation was enforced. The main circuits in Britain were the ABC, ODEON, and GAUMONT chains; the first was controlled by ASSOCIATED BRITISH and the other two by the RANK ORGANIZATION. Today, the world's largest circuit is the United Artists Theater Circuit in America, which has some 2500 screens. Circuits are often able to negotiate special rates with distributors, putting independent exhibitors at a disadvantage.

Citizen Kane (1941) Orson WELLES's classic FILM À CLEF, based on the career of press baron William Randolph Hearst. In the plot a journalist (William Alland) interviews figures from the chequered past of Charles Foster Kane (Welles) in an attempt to discover the meaning of his dying word, ROSEBUD. As he talks to Kane's best friend (Joseph COTTEN) and second wife (Dorothy Commingore) the tycoon's rise and fall are depicted in a series of flashbacks. Rosebud is ultimately revealed to be the sledge Kane left in the snow the day he was parted from his mother to benefit from his inheritance.

Following a series of stage and radio triumphs, Welles came to Hollywood in 1939 on a six-film contract that guaranteed him total artistic freedom. He later remarked:

> That contract shattered all precedents and challenged for a brief moment the basic premise of the whole studio system. Quite simply, I was left alone.

In 1940 he and Herman J. MANKIEWICZ began work on a story entitled *American*, which ultimately became *Citizen Kane*; the extent of Welles's contribution to the Oscar-winning script has since been the subject of much debate. Although Welles claimed that his only preparation for directing was to watch John FORD's STAGECOACH 40 times, the film reveals many other influences, including Jean RENOIR's POETIC REALISM, MURNAU's SUBJECTIVE CAMERA technique, and the stylized sets associated with Josef VON STERNBERG. Welles was also indebted to cinematographer Gregg TOLAND, whose experiments with DEEP FOCUS photography, WIDE-ANGLE lenses, and high-intensity lighting contributed significantly to *Citizen Kane*'s fluidity and poetic texture. Toland pioneered the brighter sharper look that was to characterize the majority of Hollywood's black-and-white films in the 1940s and 1950s. Owing to a combination of Toland's expertise and budgetary constraint, almost 80% of the completed film involved process or trick photography.

Production took place behind closed doors, largely because Welles was afraid that Hearst would shut the film down if he discovered the subject matter. These fears proved justified, for while Hearst brushed aside the film's suggestions that he had sponsored the Spanish-American War to boost circulation, he was bitterly hurt by its thinly veiled assault on his mistress, the actress Marion DAVIES. Having failed in his attempt to buy the negative from RKO in order to destroy it, the 81-year-old tycoon ordered his papers not to carry advertisements for the picture; the influential gossip columnist Louella Parsons was also persuaded to denigrate the film and its precocious director at every opportunity.

Despite nine Oscar nominations, *Citizen Kane* enjoyed only limited release and was quickly withdrawn, losing $150,000. However, television airings restored the august reputation bestowed upon it by contemporary critics and it has topped every *Sight and Sound* 'Best Film of All Time' poll since 1962. *Citizen Kane* remained Welles's favourite film; reviewing his career in later life he said, "I started at the top and worked down."

City Lights (1931) Charlie CHAPLIN's sentimental comedy, a film that bucked the trend of the day by including music and sound effects but no dialogue. As well as starring, Chaplin scripted, directed, edited, produced, and wrote the music. Although he made the

$2-million film against the advice of his UNITED ARTISTS partners, it won rave reviews and earned $5 million worldwide. On its rerelease in 1950, *Time* magazine described it as the greatest film ever made.

The filming of *City Lights* took Chaplin an unprecedented 18 months. During editing he reduced 975,000 feet of film to 7784 feet, a SHOOTING RATIO of 125:1. One 70-second scene alone required five days of filming and a record 342 retakes. In it, a blind flower girl has to form the impression that the TRAMP character is rich, but Chaplin could not find a way of conveying this idea without dialogue. He solved the problem by having his character cross a busy street and slip through the open doors of a limousine parked at the kerb. When the girl hears the car door close, she assumes it is the wealthy occupant who has emerged.

During the premiere, which Chaplin attended with Albert Einstein, the film was halted at one point so that the management staff could show off its new theatre. Chaplin raced up the aisle fuming, "Where's that stupid son of a bitch of a manager? I'll kill him!" The screening soon recommenced. At the London premiere Chaplin sat with George Bernard Shaw.

After an opening scene in which the tramp is found asleep in the arms of a statue to Peace and Prosperity, two stories develop: in one Chaplin stops a drunken millionaire (Harry Myers) from committing suicide, while in the other he flirts with the blind girl (newcomer Virginia Cherrill), who believes him to be a glamorous figure. After her sight is restored (through an operation paid for by Chaplin) the two characters meet again by chance. In the film's last frames the girl realizes, through a stray touch, that her friend and benefactor was the grubby tramp in front of her. The critic James AGEE has described the long close-up of Chaplin that closes the movie as "The greatest piece of acting and the highest moment in movies"

Clair, René (René-Lucien Chomette; 1898–1981) French director, who established a reputation as one of cinema's most creative stylists with his whimsical comedy fantasies. Clair, who wrote short stories and three novels as well as co-scripting most of his films, was elected to the French Academy in the early 1960s.

Born in Paris, the son of a soap merchant, he served as an ambulance driver in World War I until a spinal injury forced his withdrawal. After living briefly in a monastery, he began to review films for newspapers and, in 1920, changed his name to René Clair to become a movie actor. Two years later he travelled to Brussels to work with his brother, Henri, an assistant director.

In 1923 he wrote (in one night) and directed the comedy short *Paris qui dort* (*A Crazy Ray*), about an invisible ray that brings life in Paris to a standstill. A year later he made *Entr'acte*, a nonsense piece featuring Man Ray, Marcel Duchamps, and various other luminaries of the SURREALIST movement. He then turned to pure comedy with *An Italian Straw Hat* (1927) and to the musical with *Sous les Toits de Paris* (1930) and *Le Million* (1931). In 1935 Clair moved to Britain to direct Alexander KORDA's fantasy-comedy *The Ghost Goes West* (1935), about an American (Robert DONAT) determined to ship a Scottish castle and its ghost back to the States. After directing a Jack Buchanan comedy, *Break the News* (1938), he returned to France to make a film about Paris children that was never completed owing to the Nazi occupation.

In the early 1940s Clair was allowed to go to Hollywood, where he directed Marlene DIETRICH in Universal's *The Flame of New Orleans* (1941). There followed the popular comedy *I Married a Witch* (1942), starring Veronica Lake and Fredric MARCH, and one episode of RKO's *Forever and a Day* (1943), a film comprising several separate stories set in one London house.

Clair regarded his next film, *It Happened Tomorrow* (1944), as the best of his US sojourn; Dick POWELL starred as a reporter who can see the next day's news in advance. His fourth and last Hollywood production, which he also produced, was an adaptation of an Agatha Christie thriller, *And Then There Were None* (British title *Ten Little Niggers*; 1945).

In 1946 Clair returned to France and directed *Le Silence est d'or*, a Maurice CHEVALIER comedy that proved a flop. *Le Beaute du diable* (1950), a retelling of the Faust story, brought accusations that his style had become old-fashioned. In the following decades Clair came under severe attack from the NEW WAVE critics, who criticized his rather literary style and preference for studio work rather than location shooting. His later films included the gangster movie *Port des lilas* (1957), which returned to the celebration of Paris that is such a feature of his 1930s work, and *Les Fêtes Galantes* (1965), the failure of which prompted his decision to retire.

clapper board or **clapboard** or **clapstick board** A NUMBER BOARD with a hinged wooden attachment known as a *clapstick* or *clapper*. This is clapped sharply against the board at the beginning of each shot as an audiovisual cue; the clap is recorded on the film and soundtrack simultaneously as an aid to synchronization. Although the device has been superseded by electronic synchronization systems, it is still sometimes used by nostalgic directors.

classification *See* RATINGS.

Clayton, Jack (1921–95) British director and producer, whose successful career was punctuated by long pauses. His relatively few films provided fine roles for such actresses as Simone SIGNORET, Maggie SMITH, and Deborah KERR. Born in Brighton, Clayton landed his first cinema job, with London Films at the age of 14 and slowly rose to assistant director and film editor. He directed documentaries for the RAF's Film Unit during World War II and subsequently worked as production manager to Alexander KORDA and associate producer to Anatole de Grunwald before joining Romulus as a producer.

Clayton made his debut as producer-director with a half-hour film, *The Bespoke Overcoat* (1955), in which a tailor steals a coat for a ghost. Starring Alfie Bass and David Kossoff, it won the Oscar for Best Short. His first full-length feature was ROOM AT THE TOP (1958), which took the BAFTA Award for Best Film, earned Clayton an Oscar nomination, and influenced a generation of British directors with its realistic approach to sex and social issues. Subsequent films included *The Innocents* (1961), a Gothic version of Henry James's *The Turn of the Screw* starring Deborah Kerr as the governess, *The Pumpkin Eater* (1964) with Maggie Smith and Peter FINCH, and *Our Mother's House* (1967), about a family of children who secretly bury their dead mother in the garden.

After several unproductive years, Clayton went to Hollywood in 1974 to direct a glossy adaptation of F. Scott Fitzgerald's *The Great Gatsby*; the film was scripted by Francis Ford COPPOLA and starred Robert REDFORD and Mia FARROW. A further gap was followed by the Disney fantasy *Something Wicked This Way Comes* (1983) and *The Lonely Passion of Judith Hearne* (1987), a British film in which Maggie Smith mistakes friendly overtures from Bob HOSKINS.

clean entrance During a shot, an actor's movement from out-of-camera range into the area being filmed. A **clean exit** is the reverse.

Cleese, John (1931–) Tall gangling British comedy actor and writer, best known as one of the MONTY PYTHON team and for his portrayal of the manic hotelier Basil Fawlty in the TV series *Fawlty Towers*.

A graduate of Cambridge University and its Footlights Revue, Cleese displayed his comic talents to a wider audience in his early television work, which included appearances in *The Frost Report* and *At Last the 1948 Show*. His first film, *Interlude* (1968), was followed later that year by a walk-on part in *The Best House in London*. He was also one of many familiar faces in the satirical comedy *The Magic Christian* (1969). Cleese's next film, *The Rise and Rise of Michael Rimmer* (1970), which he co-wrote with Peter Cook, Kevin Billington, and fellow-Python Graham Chapman, was an uneven satire about an efficiency expert who rises to become prime minister.

The success of *Monty Python's Flying Circus* on television was exploited in five films, most notably *Monty Python and the Holy Grail* (1974), *Monty Python's Life of Brian* (1979), and *Monty Python's Meaning of Life* (1983). Cleese's other film roles range from a foul-mouthed army officer in *Privates on Parade* (1982) to a sheriff in the revivalist Western *Silverado* (1985) and a scientist in *Mary Shelley's Frankenstein* (1994). In *Clockwise* (1985), a comedy written by Michael Frayn, Cleese starred as the headmaster of a large comprehensive school, whose calm and excessively ordered life is shattered by a train of accidents. According to Cleese, Frayn "was so flattered to have a film made of his own script that if we'd done it in Swahili he'd have been perfectly happy. The thrill of having us mangle his script was all he asked for."

During the 1980s and 1990s Cleese continued to appear in the films of his fellow Pythons, such as Terry GILLIAM's *Time Bandits* (1982), Graham Chapman's *Yellowbeard* (1983), Terry Jones's *Erik the Viking* (1989), and Eric Idle's *Splitting Hairs*

(1992). He finally established himself as an international film star with the outrageous comedy *A Fish Called Wanda* (1988), which also starred Jamie Lee CURTIS, Kevin KLINE, and Michael Palin. The script, which Cleese co-wrote with veteran EALING director Charles Crichton, earned an Oscar nomination.

Cleese has also produced a series of industrial training films for his company Video Arts Ltd, including the environmental comedy *Grimes Goes Green* (1990), which featured a guest appearance by Prince Charles.

Clément, René (1913–) French director, who established his reputation during the early 1950s. He first attracted attention with *La Bataille du rail* (1946), an experiment in NEOREALISM depicting the involvement of French railway workers in the Resistance during World War II, and went on to win four major awards at the Cannes Film Festival during the next decade. His films *Au-delà des Grilles* (*The Walls of Malapaga*; 1949) and LES JEUX INTERDITS (*Forbidden Games*; 1952), in which a group of children create macabre private rituals to mirror the horrors of World War II, also won Oscars for Best Foreign Film.

Knave of Hearts (*Monsieur Ripois*;1953) followed the romantic adventures of a Frenchman in London as he woos a succession of English ladies; the film's use of hidden cameras to capture the authentic life of the city caused a considerable stir when it was shown in Britain. *Gervaise* (1955), based on Emile Zola's novel *L'Assommoir*, took a third Oscar but proved to be the last of Clément's great successes. His subsequent films have been largely disappointing; they include *Quelle joie de vivre* (1962), *The Love Cage* (*Les Félins*; 1964), *Is Paris Burning?* (1966), an all-star epic of the Liberation with a script by Francis Ford COPPOLA and Gore Vidal, and *The Babysitter* (1975).

cliffhanger A suspense thriller that builds towards a life-or-death climax. Examples include Alfred HITCHCOCK'S NORTH BY NORTHWEST (1959), in the closing scenes of which Cary GRANT struggles with his pursuer on top of Mount Rushmore, and KING KONG (1933), in which the giant ape releases Fay WRAY just before being strafed off the Empire State Building.

The term originated from the silent SERIALS of the 1910s and 1920s, which invariably left one of the central characters in a life-threatening situation (sometimes, literally, hanging from a cliff) at the end of each episode. The character would then escape with suspicious ease at the beginning of the next instalment (*see* CHEATER CUT). Modern television soap operas use similar techniques to maintain viewing figures.

Clift, Montgomery (1920–66) US actor, who became famous for his sensitive handling of a wide range of roles. Following a period in summer stock as a teenager, Clift travelled to New York where he established a reputation as a fine stage actor over the next decade. His first film role was a supporting part in Howard HAWKS's *Red River* (1948), an epic Western starring John WAYNE. While Clift was making this film, he was approached to star in *The Search* (1948), about a US soldier caring for a war orphan. *The Search* (which was released before *Red River*), brought Clift the first of four Oscar nominations for Best Actor. The following year he appeared opposite Olivia DE HAVILLAND in *The Heiress* (1949), an adaptation of a Henry James novel. Clift earned his second Oscar nomination for his portrayal of the ambitious social climber George Eastman in *A Place in the Sun* (1951), in which he co-starred with Elizabeth TAYLOR and Shelley WINTERS. The following year Alfred HITCHCOCK's *I Confess* (1952) saw Clift playing a priest who is caught in a moral dillemma after hearing the confession of a murderer. He then received a third Oscar nomination for his role as the pacifist soldier Robert E. Lee Prewitt in FROM HERE TO ETERNITY (1953). During this period Clift turned down roles in SUNSET BOULEVARD (1950), ON THE WATERFRONT (1954), and EAST OF EDEN (1955) – films that certainly enhanced the reputations of the actors who eventually appeared in them (William HOLDEN, Marlon BRANDO, and James DEAN respectively).

It was during the filming of *Raintree County* (1957), a Civil War drama apparently conceived as a more downbeat GONE WITH THE WIND, that Clift was involved in a car accident that left him physically (and some say, emotionally) scarred. The film's director, Edward DMYTRYK noted:

We had a miserable time with him, particularly after the accident...He was the most sensitive man I've ever known. If somebody kicked a dog a mile away he'd feel it.

Despite appearing in a few outstanding films after this, such as *The Young Lions* (1958) with Marlon Brando, *The Misfits* (1961) with Clark GABLE and Marilyn MONROE, and *Judgment at Nuremburg* (1961), which brought him a final Oscar nomination, Clift's career never fulfilled the promise of his earlier performances.

Cline, Edward F. (1892–1961) US comedy director who made hundreds of silent shorts but is mainly remembered for his later work with W. C. FIELDS. Born in Kenosha, Wisconsin, Cline acted on stage before moving to Hollywood to join Mack SENNETT's KEYSTONE Comedy Company; in 1913 he became one of the KEYSTONE KOPS. He began his career as a director with a number of Sennett Bathing Beauties shorts.

Cline went on to work with Buster KEATON as co-director of *One Week* (1920) and the two-reelers *The Electric House* (1921) and *Baloonatic* (1923). In 1925 Sennett recalled him to make two-reelers with such stars as Carole LOMBARD and Ben Turpin. After the coming of sound, Cline directed the eccentric Fields for the first time in Paramount's comedy *Million Dollar Legs*. Fields, who liked the somewhat malleable Cline, later insisted that he replace the belligerent George MARSHALL on Universal's *You Can't Cheat an Honest Man* (1939). Although better able to deal with Fields's moods than most, Cline still suffered continuous humiliating insults from the great man throughout their subsequent association at Universal. Their partnership did, however, produce the classics *My Little Chickadee* (1939), with Mae WEST, *The Bank Dick* (1940), and *Never Give a Sucker an Even Break* (1941).

Cline had an easier, if less rewarding, time directing the madcap duo of (Ole) Olsen and (Chic) Johnson in *Crazy House* (1943), *Ghost Catchers* (1944), and other films; he ended his career turning out low-budget productions for MONOGRAM Pictures.

clip (1) A section of film removed in editing. (2) Another term for an EXTRACT.

Clockwork Orange, A (1971) Stanley KUBRICK's shocking depiction of violence and repression in a totalitarian society of the near future; the film was adapted from Anthony Burgess's parable about free will and social control. Following a feud within his gang of Droogs, Alex (Malcolm McDowell) is betrayed during a raid and left unconscious for the police. In prison he is subjected to a programme of aversion therapy that induces nausea whenever he sees violence, but also destroys his capacity for free choice and aesthetic enjoyment. Following his release, revenge is wreaked on him by his victims and his old comrades (now policemen). The viewer is left to wonder whether he will remain the 'model' citizen he has become or opt to resume his life of crime.

A Clockwork Orange earned Oscar nominations for Best Picture, Direction, and Screenplay, as well as taking the New York Critics' Prizes for Best Film and Direction. However, the critical acclaim was not unanimous, with many castigating the picture for its graphic depiction of physical and sexual violence. Particularly reviled were the brutal scenes in which Alex and the Droogs pulp a rival gang to the accompaniment of Rossini's 'The Thieving Magpie' and rape a woman to the strains of Gene KELLY's 'Singin' in the Rain'. With his use of SUBJECTIVE CAMERA, stylized MISE-EN-SCÈNE, and manipulative montage, Kubrick adroitly persuades the audience to align itself with Alex, in spite of his behaviour, and to accept the moral that it is better for one individual to act antisocially than for society to eliminate personal freedom.

An art-house success around the world in 1971, the film became a notorious cult hit in Britain when it reached London a year later. It was soon blamed for inspiring a spate of violent crimes, including the rape of a Dutch girl in Lancashire by assailants chanting 'Singin' in the Rain'. A teenager who had assaulted a younger boy while wearing the Droog uniform of white overalls and a bowler hat was told by the sentencing judge:

> We must stamp out this horrible trend which has been inspired by this wretched film. We appreciate that what you did was inspired by that wicked film, but that does not mean that you are not blameworthy.

Although Kubrick defended the artistry and intention of the film, saying "I think it is the most skilful movie I've ever made. I can see almost nothing wrong with it" he was totally unwilling to have his social satire held responsible for real-life acts of violence. In late 1973 he asked Warner Brothers to withdraw A Clockwork Orange from distribution in Britain, where it is now an offence to give a public exhibition of the film; in 1993 the Scala Cinema in London was prosecuted for screening it without the permission of the copyright holder. Despite periodic calls to reverse his decision, Kubrick remains adamant.

Close, Glenn (1947–) Strong-featured US actress who became one of the most successful stars of the 1980s; in 1987 she emerged as the top female box-office draw in the annual QUIGLEY POLL of exhibitors.

After studying drama and anthropology at William and Mary College, Virginia, Close toured in repertory theatre and appeared on Broadway. In 1981 her stage presence attracted the attention of George Roy HILL, who cast her as Garp's mother in The World According to Garp (1982), her first film. During the mid 1980s she went on to play a series of 'good' girls, including Sarah in The Big Chill (1983), and Robert REDFORD's childhood sweetheart in The Natural (1984). Of the latter role she remarked, "I'm probably quite proud that I'm the only woman on celluloid ever to have said 'no' to Robert Redford." Both parts brought her Oscar nominations. She also supplied the voice of Jane (played by Andie MacDowell) in Greystoke: the Legend of Tarzan, Lord of the Apes (1984).

Close then changed her image completely with the hugely successful Fatal Attraction (1987), in which she played the vengeful mistress of Michael DOUGLAS. After this tour de force, she went on to play a number of dangerous or ambiguous women, including the Marquise de Merteuil in Dangerous Liaisons (1988) and Gertrude in Franco ZEFFIRELLI's Hamlet (1990). Her other appearances have included a dual role in Maxie (1985), a lawyer defending Jeff BRIDGES in Jagged Edge (1985), a Swedish opera singer (dubbed by Kiri Te Kanawa) in Meeting Venus (1991), and a bearded pirate in Hook (1992).

close-up (CU) A shot taken at close range, in which part of an actor or other subject fills the frame. The most common subject for a close-up is the human face, usually in order to show a character's emotions, state of mind, or reaction to an event. The close-up is thus an important tool in creating audience identification with a character. Close-ups of actors can be subdivided into the **medium close-up**, which shows him or her from the waist upwards; the **close shot**

(CS), which shows head and shoulders; the **head close-up**; and the EXTREME CLOSE-UP, which shows only part of the face or head.

The close-up has a long history in the cinema. EDISON's *Fred Ott's Sneeze* (1891), reputedly the first film ever made, was shot entirely in close-up, while G. A. Smith and James Williamson's *Grandma's Reading Glass* (1900) featured a DETAIL SHOT of a single eye. It was, however, D. W. GRIFFITH and his cameraman Billy Bitzer who pioneered the use of close-ups to convey emotions and create empathy, in such films as *Friends* (1912) with Mary PICKFORD. At the time, Griffith's employers, the BIOGRAPH company resisted his use of the technique in the belief that audiences felt cheated if they did not see the entire actor, as on stage.

Clothes Horse, the A nickname for the actress Joan CRAWFORD, whose roles often required her to don glamorous creations by the designer Adrian. Her other nicknames included **Bow-Tie Mouth** (a reference to her full lips) and **the Empress of Emotion** (a name also bestowed on the Austrian-Italian actress Elissa Landi, 1904–48).

cloud wheel A device used to create a more realistic sky-effect when filming outdoor scenes on indoor sets. It consists of a slowly revolving disk through which light is projected on to a backdrop.

Clouzot, Henri-Georges (1907–77) French director and screenwriter, who established his reputation with a series of suspense thrillers in the 1940s. Clouzot began his career as a film critic and subsequently wrote several unremarkable screenplays. After making his debut as a director with the conventional thriller *L'Assassin habite au 21* (1942) he revealed himself as a major new talent with *Le Corbeau* (1943), in which a small French town is torn apart by a campaign of poison-pen letters. The film's bitter view of provincial French life led to false accusations that Clouzot was working on behalf of the occupying Germans; for some years thereafter he was given little work.

In 1947 he reaffirmed his power as a director with *Quai des orfèvres*, a somewhat traditional thriller distinguished by its atmospheric sets and pervasive air of tragedy, as well as by the performance of Louis Jouvet in the lead. Clouzot's best-known film remains, however, *The Wages of Fear* (1953), a tense story of greed and danger

set in a South American village. The film, which starred Yves MONTAND, has occasionally been described as the best suspense thriller ever made. Similarly gripping is *Les Diaboliques* (1955), about the murder of the sadistic headmaster of a down-at-heel boarding school. Other notable films include *The Picasso Mystery* (1956), *Les Espions* (1957), and *The Truth* (1960), a murder mystery starring Brigitte BARDOT, who later described it as the only valuable film of her career.

That red-fanged old marrow-freezer.
PAUL DEHN, film critic and screenwriter.

Coburn, James (1928–) US actor, known for his toothy smile and silver hair, who has specialized in playing tough-guy roles in Westerns and action films. Born in Laurel, Nebraska, Coburn trained as an actor in New York under Stella Adler. Before turning to films, he made his stage debut with Vincent PRICE in *Billy Budd* at the La Jolla Community Playhouse, California, and appeared in a number of television commercials.

His first film role was as a Western outlaw in *Ride Lonesome* (1959). A year later, he co-starred with Steve MCQUEEN, Charles BRONSON, and Yul BRYNNER in *The Magnificent Seven*, as a fighter who can throw a knife quicker than his gun-toting opponents can shoot. Coburn and McQueen went on to appear together in the war film *Hell is for Heroes* (1962), while Bronson joined them again for *The Great Escape* (1963). For the next few years Coburn continued to appear in supporting roles, including a heavy chasing Cary GRANT in *Charade* (1963) and Charlton HESTON's Indian scout in *Major Dundee* (1965).

He finally attained stardom in the spoof spy thrillers *Our Man Flint* (1965) and *In Like Flint* (1967), in which he played the engaging title character, a secret agent working for ZOWIE (Zonal Organization of World Intelligence Espionage). In the early 1970s he returned to the Western, costarring with Rod STEIGER in Sergio LEONE's *A Fistful of Dynamite* (1972) and with Kris Kristofferson in Sam PECKINPAH's *Pat Garrett and Billy the Kid* (1973). Coburn's more recent appearances have all been in minor films, including *The Baltimore Bullet* (1980), with Omar SHARIF, *Death of a Soldier* (1986), the true story of a GI who murdered three women, and the Bruce WILLIS flop *Hudson Hawk* (1991).

cobweb spinner A device used to produce artificial cobwebs for a set. It consists of an electric fan that blows filaments of rubber cement onto the ceiling, walls, furniture, etc.

Cocteau, Jean (1889–1963) French poet, novelist, and playwright, who made occasional startling ventures into the cinema. Although Cocteau, the son of two wealthy lawyers, was medically disqualified for military duty, he fought in World War I under an assumed name. In his early twenties he responded to a challenge from Diaghilev by collaborating on a work for the Ballet Russe in Paris, and helped to create *Parade*, which opened in 1917. He went on to make his name as a poet and writer in the 1920s.

Cocteau's first film, the SURREALIST fantasy *The Blood of a Poet* (1930), which he wrote and directed, was followed by a gap of ten years during which he concentrated on writing for the theatre. He returned to the cinema in the 1940s, scripting *La Comédie du bonheur* (1940) and *L'Eternel Retour* (1943), the first of many Cocteau films to star the actor Jean Marais, his long-term lover. Marais later commented "I was what he would like to have had for a son...At one point, he wanted to marry my mother so that I could become his son." This was followed by *La Belle et la bête* (1946), a version of the well-known fairy tale, with Josette Day as Beauty and Marais as the beast. C. A. Lejeune described the film, which was written and directed by Cocteau, as "absolute magic, diamond cold and lunar bright." Marais and Day reappeared in *Les Parents terribles* (1948), which Cocteau adapted from his own stage play. The film version of *Les Enfants terribles* (1950), based on Cocteau's novel of the same name with the author as narrator, was scripted and directed by Jean-Pierre MELVILLE.

Cocteau's last films as a director were ORPHÉE (1949), and *Le Testament d'Orphée* (1959), two extraordinary fantasies based on the myth of the poet Orpheus. He died of a heart attack after hearing that his friend Edith Piaf had died earlier that day.

> A film is a petrified fountain of thought.
> JEAN COCTEAU.

Coen Brothers The US film-making team Joel Coen (1954–) and Ethan Coen (1957–). Although Ethan produces and Joel directs, the distinction usually blurs in practice, especially as the brothers collaborate on their screenplays. The Coens are very much *auteurs*, overseeing every stage of production from scriptwriting and storyboarding to editing (sound as well as visuals). The actor Tim ROBBINS has commented on their "symbiotic" relationship: "They are completely on the same wavelength and will finish each other's sentences. I have never seen them argue."

Born in Minneapolis, the Coens made a few SUPER-8 films together before pursuing their studies – Joel taking film at New York University, Ethan philosophy at Yale. Joel then worked as an assistant editor on such horror pictures as Sam Raimi's *The Evil Dead* (1983) before the brothers began collaborating on screenplays. Raimi himself would film their *Crimewave* (1985); although the Coens later disowned the movie, this did not stop them hiring him as SECOND-UNIT DIRECTOR for *The Hudsucker Proxy* (which he had co-written).

The Coens' debut as a film-making team was *Blood Simple* (1984), a brooding FILM NOIR made on a shoestring budget of less than $1.5 million. Joel later married the film's star, Frances McDormand. With its clear debt to the crime novels of James M. Cain, the picture established the Coens' predilection for *hommage*: *Raising Arizona* (1987) managed to recall both the SCREWBALL COMEDIES of the 1930s and the LOONEY TUNES cartoons; *Miller's Crossing* (1990) was deeply indebted to Dashiell Hammett's *The Glass Key*; the Palme d'Or-winning *Barton Fink* (1991), a tale of the Hollywood STUDIO SYSTEM of the 1930s, owed much to the hallucinatory atmosphere of Roman POLANSKI's *The Tenant*; while *The Hudsucker Proxy* (1993) was an irresistible amalgam of the screwball styles of Frank CAPRA and Preston STURGES.

Raising Arizona, a frantic tale of baby-snatching starring Holly Hunter and Nicolas Cage, posed particular problems. As Joel recalls:

> We kept firing babies when they wouldn't behave. And they didn't even know they were being fired, that's what was so pathetic about it. Some of them took their first steps on the set. Ordinarily, you'd be pretty happy about something like that, but in this case it got them fired.

Although they are passionate about their work, the brothers often seem dismissive of it. When an earnest student writing a dissertation on *Miller's Crossing* sent the

Coens a questionnaire, Ethan was rather nonplussed:

> You make these stupid movies and then a year later you've got homework. It's really kind of alarming.

They are currently working on *Fargo*, another bungled kidnapping story, based on events that occurred in Minnesota in 1987. In spite of the box-office failure of *The Hudsucker Proxy*, they remain undaunted; as Barry Sonnenfeld, their cinematographer on *Blood Simple*, has put it:

> In the end, the only person Joel has to please is Ethan, and vice versa.

co-feature   A feature film shown as the second half of a DOUBLE BILL. Although this was usually a low-budget B-MOVIE specifically released for this purpose, standard features that flopped were also sometimes relegated to co-feature status.

Cohn, Harry   (1891–1958) US film executive, co-founder of COLUMBIA PICTURES and its head for 34 years. Proud of his reputation as Hollywood's most odious tycoon, he once boasted "I don't have ulcers, I give them." Gossip columnist Hedda HOPPER noted "You had to stand in line to hate him", while screenwriter Ben Hecht nicknamed him 'White Fang'. Cohn, a ruthless, grasping, and foul-tempered man, was also known for his vulgarity. He once told Columbia executives of his foolproof way of judging a film: "If my fanny squirms, it's bad. If my fanny doesn't squirm, it's good." Scriptwriter Herman J. MANKIEWICZ joked, "Imagine! The whole world wired to Harry Cohn's ass!" He was fired immediately.

Born in New York City, Cohn was the son of an immigrant German tailor and his Russian wife. He left school early to work as a shipping clerk, fur salesman, and vaudeville performer before his brother, Jack Cohn (1889–1956), got him a job in 1918 as secretary to their uncle Carl Laemmle, founder of Universal Pictures. Two years later the brothers founded CBC Sales Corporation (with Joe Brandt), changing its name to Columbia in 1924. Harry withstood his brother's attempt to oust him in 1932 and thereafter effectively ran the studio alone. His shrewd business sense led to two moves that ensured Columbia's success: hiring director Frank CAPRA in 1927 and promoting Rita HAYWORTH as a sex symbol in the 1940s.

Tales of Cohn's tyranny and paranoia abound. His staff endured a reign of terror that involved being snooped upon by informers and hidden microphones planted around the studio. He is said to have kept a large wall-chart behind his desk displaying the menstrual cycles of all Columbia's actresses, as he believed that women did not photograph well at certain times of the month. In 1930 Louise BROOKS unhesitatingly declined his promise to revive her career if she would become his mistress. On one occasion Cohn's yacht stalled at sea and Errol FLYNN towed it safely into harbour. As a joke, Flynn's passenger David NIVEN sent Cohn a letter claiming half the boat as salvage. He was promptly barred from ever working at Columbia.

Cohn eventually died of a heart attack, allegedly brought on by the shock of discovering that his protégée, Kim NOVAK was going out with a Black man, Sammy Davis Jnr. When Rabbi Magnin of the Wilshire Boulevard Temple was asked if he could say anything good about the deceased, he pondered for a minute and said, "He's dead."

cokuloris   A sheet of opaque material with various random holes cut in it; the device is placed between a light source and the set in order to reduce glare and to produce irregular shadows. It is known as a **cookie** or **cuke** for short.

Colbert, Claudette   (Claudette Lily Chauchoin; 1905–) French-born Hollywood actress, who specialized in pert sophisticated roles. She is best known for her performance in Frank CAPRA's comedy, IT HAPPENED ONE NIGHT (1934).

Born in Paris, she moved when six to New York, where she attended the Art Students' League, hoping to become a fashion designer. She was working as a typist when she met a Broadway dramatist and was given a bit part in *The Wild Westcotts* (1923). Her first film, Capra's *For the Love of Mike* (1927), led to a Paramount contract. Colbert began in serious roles, playing *femmes fatales* in Cecil B. DE MILLE's *The Sign of the Cross* (1932) and *Cleopatra* (1934). In *Imitation of Life* (1934), a film about racial attitudes, she played a woman who goes into business with her Black maid (Louise Beavers).

Capra only offered her the part of the eccentric heiress in *It Happened One Night* when he failed to land a big-name star. In

the event, both Colbert and her co-star Clark
GABLE won Academy Awards. She had so
little thought of winning, that she was
boarding a train for New York when Academy officials rushed up and sped her to the
ceremony to accept (still in her travelling
clothes).

Following this success, Colbert brought
her tongue-in-cheek style to such flighty
comedies as *She Married Her Boss* (1935)
with Melvyn DOUGLAS, *The Palm Beach Story*
(1942) opposite Joel MCCREA, and *The Egg
and I* (1947) with Fred MACMURRAY.

After retiring from the screen in 1961
she settled in Barbados, but was lured back
to New York for stage appearances with Rex
HARRISON in *The Kingfisher* (1978) and *Aren't
We All?* (1984). She also appeared in the
television mini-series *The Two Mrs Grenvilles*
(1987) at the age of 81.

Cold War The period of international tension between CHURCHILL's 'iron curtain'
speech in 1946 and the fall of the Berlin
Wall in 1989; the era was dominated by the
manoeuvring of the US and Soviet super-
powers and the threat of nuclear holocaust.
Directly or indirectly, the Cold War provided
the subject or setting for many films – most
notably a proliferation of SPY thrillers. The
tone of the films changed during the 1970s,
when Watergate and the Vietnam debacle
turned suspicion from the Kremlin to the
White House and Pentagon.

In the early 1950s anti-communist
hysteria gripped Hollywood as the House
Un-American Activities Committee began
its investigation into the film industry. The
witch-hunt that followed, and the climate
of suspicion it engendered, had a major
impact on the industry. Film-makers were
offered the choice of naming names or
never working again; in the case of the HOL-
LYWOOD TEN, the result was jail. With the
arrival of the blacklist many film-makers,
notably Charlie CHAPLIN, were forced into
exile, the alternative being to submit work
under pseudonyms or through friends – a
situation ridiculed by Woody ALLEN in *The
Front* (1976). A memorable injustice was
the award of the Oscar for scripting BRIDGE
ON THE RIVER KWAI to Pierre Boulle, author of
the original novel, rather than to the actual
screenwriters Carl Foreman and Michael
Wilson (one of the Hollywood Ten).

Hollywood showed its loyalty to Mc-
Carthyism by producing a number of films
with a 'reds under the bed' theme, such as

The Red Menace (1949), *I Married a Communist* (1950), and *Red Planet Mars* (1952).
The most ridiculous was probably Warners'
I was a Communist for the FBI (1951), which
received an Oscar nomination for Best *Documentary*. The critic James AGEE described
these films as "nominal nonfiction whose
responsibilities, whose power for good or
evil, enlightenment or deceit, are appalling."

In other genres the fear of enemy en-
croachment or takeover was dealt with alle-
gorically: Westerns underwent a revival
and SCIENCE FICTION entered a golden period.
Both *Invaders from Mars* (1953) and *Invasion of the Body Snatchers* (1957) raised the
spectre of brainwashing by alien powers
("You're next, you're next" was the warning). Similarly, *The Thing* (1951) cautioned
against trusting those who argue for learning from other cultures rather than eradi-
cating them. Few films tackled the threat of
nuclear war head-on; the best were DR
STRANGELOVE (1963), in which a mad USAF
colonel manages to launch a first strike,
Failsafe (1964), in which a similar situation
places President Henry FONDA in a dilemma,
and *On the Beach* (1959), which sets the
crew of a nuclear submarine wandering the
face of a post-holocaust planet. Fears of
nuclear catastrophe were also broached in
The Day the Earth Stood Still (1951) and *The
Incredible Shrinking Man* (1957).

With the arrival of détente in the 1970s
the fears reflected in these films gradually
subsided. Only the spy genre – which
became noticeably more downbeat and disenchanted – continued to reflect the tensions of the international situation. The
Reagan era saw a brief revival of the old-
style Cold War movie with such films as *Red
Dawn* (1984), in which teenagers rout a
Soviet invasion of Colorado.

Collins, Joan (1933–) British actress, a
second-rank starlet of the 1950s who successfully reinvented herself as a powerful
middle-aged sex symbol almost 30 years
later. The teenage Collins made her film
debut in Ealing's *I Believe in You* in 1952. By
trading on her sultry good looks, which won
comparisons with Elizabeth TAYLOR, she
went on to claim leading-lady status in such
lightweight British films as *Our Girl Friday*
(1953), *Land of the Pharaohs* (1955), and
Island in the Sun (1957).

Her career was in marked decline by the
late 1970s, when starring roles in the criti-

cally slated sex films *The Stud* (1978) and *The Bitch* (1979) – both written by her sister Jackie Collins – led to a sudden revival of public interest. Collins's new image as a powerful sharp-tongued glamour queen was then exploited to the full in her role as the villainess Alexis in the TV soap opera *Dynasty* (from 1981). "It's easy to play a bitch", Collins told *Playboy* magazine in 1984, while director Stephen FREARS observed: "Isn't that what Joan Collins's success is based on? People love bitches. The more dreadful they are, the more awful things they say, the more heavenly they are." Although she has made few subsequent films, constant press speculation about cosmetic surgery and the men in her life has kept her in the public eye; a frank autobiography, *Past Imperfect* (1978), and a number of sex n' shopping novels have also contributed to her continuing fame.

> She's common, she can't act – yet she's the hottest female property around these days. If that doesn't tell you something about the state of our industry today, what does?
> STEWART GRANGER, 1984.

Colman, Ronald (1891–1958) British actor, who established himself as Hollywood's archetypal English gentleman in a series of films made between the wars. Colman took to acting after being invalided out of the armed forces during World War I. He arrived in Hollywood in 1920 and soon proved a major box-office draw in such romantic melodramas as *The White Sister* (1923), opposite Lillian GISH, *The Dark Angel* (1925), and *Beau Geste* (1926). Thanks to his educated voice and impeccable manners, the advent of sound in the late 1920s proved no obstacle to Colman, who became one of the few stars of the era to enjoy equal success in both silent and talking films. His talking debut in BULLDOG DRUMMOND (1929) was followed by a long series of hits including *Raffles* (1930), *A Tale of Two Cities* (1935), as Sydney Carton, Frank CAPRA's *Lost Horizon* (1937), *The Prisoner of Zenda* (1937), *The Talk of the Town* (1942), with Cary GRANT and Jean ARTHUR, *Random Harvest* (1942), and *A Double Life* (1948), in which Colman won an Oscar for his performance as an actor obsessed with his role as Othello.

Among Colman's last roles was a guest cameo in AROUND THE WORLD IN EIGHTY DAYS (1956), for which he received payment in the form of a splendid Cadillac. When a journalist queried whether such a handsome reward was justified for just one day on the set, he retorted that the car came in exchange not for a day's work but for a lifetime's experience. His death from pneumonia was a consequence of the wounds he received in World War I.

> Beautiful of face and soul, sensitive to the fragile and gentle, responsive both to poetic visions and hard intellect...
> FRANK CAPRA.

> He has no personality of his own, only an appearance, and for that reason he is an almost perfect actor for the fictional screen.
> GRAHAM GREENE.

Colonel Blimp *See* LIFE AND DEATH OF COLONEL BLIMP, THE.

colour The use of colour has a much longer history in the cinema than is often supposed. The first colour film was probably EDISON's *Annabelle's Dance* (1896), which featured hand-painted scenes; by the time he made *A Trip to the Moon* (1902) the French pioneer George MÉLIÈS had developed a factory-line system for colouring using stencils. During the 1920s TINTING (dying a film's base) and toning (dying the silver particles in the emulsion, effectively the dark areas of the image) were often used to apply a single appropriate colour to a particular film or scene (e.g. red for a fire, straw for a sunny day, etc.).

None of these techniques proved satisfactory, however, owing to cost on the one hand and lack of range and flexibility on the other. More successful was the two-colour Kinemacolour process, developed in 1906 by Turner and Smith, which involved the use of a rotating red-blue filter when filming; owing to PERSISTENCE OF VISION the colours appeared to combine when the image was projected through a similar filter. Kinemacolour's biggest success was *The Durbar at Delhi* (1912), which showed the crowning of George V as King-Emperor of India. The main problem with the system was the difficulty of creating a sufficiently bright image when filming and projecting through filters.

During the 1920s processes using additive filters were gradually superseded by systems based on the principle of subtractive colour reproduction. The first important process of this kind was two-colour TECHNICOLOR, which used a beam-splitter camera to record two different negatives, which were then processed and attached back-to-back for projection; the high point of this system was the Douglas FAIRBANKS swashbuckler *The Black Pirate* (1926). Three-colour Technicolor was introduced in Disney's animation short *Flowers and Trees* (1932), made its feature debut with *Becky Sharp* (1935), and reached a high point of glossy sophistication with GONE WITH THE WIND (1939). In 1942 Technicolor introduced a system in which the three colour emulsions were combined on a single film base. 'Glorious Technicolor' remained the colour standard until the mid 1950s, when it was superseded by the Kodak company's EASTMAN COLOR (introduced in 1952). By the mid 1960s the majority of films were made in colour. *See also* BLACK-AND-WHITE.

colour sequence A scene from a film that has a colouring different to that of the film in general. In the early days of the cinema hand-painting, stencils, and rollers were sometimes used to produce colour sequences – a notable example being the eruption sequence of *The Last Days of Pompeii* (1913). After World War I the German EXPRESSIONISTS led the way in experimenting with TINTING and toning to impart a symbolic significance to certain sequences. With the arrival of reliable colour systems the range of expression available to filmmakers widened greatly. One common use of colour sequences has been to differentiate DREAMS, fantasies, or FLASHBACKS from the main body of the film. In the WIZARD OF OZ (1939), for example, colour is used to represent the fantasy land of Oz and BLACK-AND-WHITE the everyday world of Kansas; this is reversed in POWELL and PRESSBURGER'S A MATTER OF LIFE AND DEATH (1946), in which the earthbound scenes are in Technicolor and heaven in a rather chilly black-and-white.

Not all uses of colour sequences are this artistic. In the 1940s and 1950s film-makers would sometimes save money by reserving colour for spectacular sequences such as a fire or a lavish costume ball. It is also alleged that the puzzling alternation of black-and-white with colour in Lindsay ANDERSON'S *If* (1968) was the result of economic rather than artistic considerations.

Columbia Pictures US production and distribution company. In 1920 Harry COHN, his brother Jack, and Joe Brandt founded the CBC Sales Corporation, which became Columbia Pictures four years later. From 1932 until his death in 1958 Harry Cohn, the archetypal Hollywood tycoon, ran the company as his personal fiefdom.

For its first decade the tiny studio was a refuge for has-been stars such as John GILBERT, a victim of the talkies, who made his last film there. Its slogan, 'Gem of the Ocean' was soon corrupted by Hollywood wags to 'Germ of the Ocean'. Columbia finally lost its POVERTY ROW image in 1934, when Frank CAPRA, hired by Cohn in 1927, brought in a fistful of Oscars with IT HAPPENED ONE NIGHT, starring Clark GABLE and Claudette COLBERT. Capra went on to produce a string of hits for the studio in the 1930s, only walking out after Cohn put his name on another director's film in 1939.

Columbia created its first superstar when it changed Margarita Cansino's name to Rita HAYWORTH and launched her as a pin-up in such films as *Only Angels Have Wings* (1939). The studio's other hits of the 1940s included *The Jolson Story* (1946) and its sequel *Jolson Sings Again* (1949). Nevertheless the main emphasis remained on profitable B-movies until the late 1940s, when production executive Buddy Adler brought in such big successes as *All the King's Men* (1949), *Born Yesterday* (1950), and FROM HERE TO ETERNITY (1953).

In the early 1950s Columbia became the first major studio to create a television subsidiary, Screen Gems. It also became a leader in international CO-PRODUCTIONS. Producer Sam Spiegel joined forces with Columbia to make ON THE WATERFRONT (1954) as well as David LEAN'S THE BRIDGE ON THE RIVER KWAI (1957) and LAWRENCE OF ARABIA (1962). Other successes of the 1960s and 1970s included DR STRANGELOVE (1963), *A Man for All Seasons* (1966), *Oliver!* (1968), EASY RIDER (1969), *Close Encounters of the Third Kind* (1977), and *Kramer vs Kramer* (1979).

The company underwent major reorganization in 1968, when its name was changed to Columbia Pictures Industries. In the 1980s it was bought by Coca-Cola, then by Sony. Notoriously, the studio dropped E.T.: THE EXTRATERRESTRIAL (1982) after spending $1 million on it, letting Universal pick up the project and rake in the record receipts. In 1986 Britain's David PUTTNAM became chairman of Columbia only to be ousted after 13 unhappy months. The studio has enjoyed few recent successes.

combined print or **composite print** A film print on which the picture and the separately recorded SOUNDTRACK are combined in synchronization ('married').

come. comeback A performance in which an actor attempts to regain his or her star status after a decline in popularity or a long absence from the screen. One of the most celebrated of all Hollywood comebacks was that of Gloria SWANSON in SUNSET BOULEVARD (1950). Ironically, Swanson played a faded movie queen attempting a comeback, with the once-famous director Erich VON STROHEIM as her butler. In the film, Swanson is seen watching *Queen Kelly*, an unfinished movie she made with von Stroheim in 1928 that helped to wreck both their careers.

Bette DAVIS also played a faded star when she made her comeback in *Whatever Happened to Baby Jane?* (1962); after the film proved a success, she emphasized her employability by taking out a newspaper advertisement, "Experienced actress wants work", listing her name and telephone number. Joan CRAWFORD made a comeback in the same film. One of the most remarkable of all returns to the screen was that of the 86-year-old Mae WEST in *Sextette* (1978). Other notable comebacks include Henry FONDA in *Mister Roberts* (1955), Janet GAYNOR in *Bernardine* (1957), Joe E. Brown in SOME LIKE IT HOT (1959), and James CAGNEY in *Ragtime* (1981).

come in See APPROACH.

come up and see me some time A catchphrase associated with Mae WEST. The line, an obvious sexual innuendo, first appeared in her play *Diamond Lil* (1928) but gained wider currency from the film version *She Done Him Wrong* (1933); in this West says to the young Cary GRANT, "Why don't you come up some time and see me? I'm home every evening." It may be that the phrase was already used on the streets of New York before this, but if so it was certainly Mae West who immortalized it.

comedy. comedians In the early days of the cinema very few established comedians chose to make the transition from stage to screen, mainly because the new medium allowed no scope for verbal humour. Although there were exceptions to this rule (most notably Max Linder) film comedy in this period was largely self-inspired. However, with the introduction of sound, Hollywood was forced to turn back to the stage in search of new performers. For one thing, the technical limitations of sound filming at this time meant that many features of the established silent style had to be abandoned; for another, the demands of the audience were also changing – wisecracking humour was now expected, rather than mimed farce.

As Hollywood went to BROADWAY and started buying shows, some of cinema's greatest talents were discovered, including the MARX BROTHERS, W. C. FIELDS, and Mae WEST. Bob HOPE was one of the first comedians to make the move to pictures via radio. After the war, talent continued to be recruited from nightclubs, radio, and the new medium of television (although the greater security of TV lured many away from films in the 1950s and 1960s). Recent decades have seen a stream of performers, many of them with strong 'alternative' credentials, making the transition from stand-up to film stardom via national exposure on television. Appearances on the cult 1970s show *Saturday Night Live* led to film contracts for Dan AYKROYD, John BELUSHI, and Chevy CHASE, amongst several others. Such major stars of the 1980s as Robin WILLIAMS, Eddie MURPHY, Steve MARTIN, and Whoopi GOLDBERG are all ex-stand-up performers.

A similar pattern can be seen in the British cinema. Will HAY, Old Mother Riley, and the Crazy Gang all made the transition from the theatre to the cinema before the war, while in the postwar world many radio and TV comedians either entered the dwindling British film industry or tried their luck in Hollywood. On the whole, British comedians have been less successful than their US counterparts in finding suitable feature-length vehicles. Two British stars who made successful careers in Hollywood were Peter SELLERS and (briefly) Dudley MOORE.

comedy teams Two or more comedians acting in regular partnership as a means of increasing the range of comic situations. Often the comedy depends on the juxtaposition of widely differing physical or personality types, e.g. tall thin guy and his short fat friend, or the would-be sophisticate and his gauche hanger-on. The standard partnership of a mischievous clown and his STRAIGHT MAN or stooge can be traced back to the *Commedia dell'arte*, if not earlier.

The first successful comedy team in the cinema was Mack SENNETT'S KEYSTONE COPS, a bumbling squad of policemen who featured in numerous slapstick shorts from 1913. Their success was soon overshadowed by that of LAUREL AND HARDY, whose subtle comic interplay made them second only to CHAPLIN in popularity during the 1920s and 1930s. With the advent of sound a number of teams were brought in from vaudeville to provide quickfire verbal wit, chief among them being the MARX BROTHERS, probably the most anarchic team ever. Other double-acts to make the transition from the theatre included Olsen and Johnson and the regular partnership of George Burns and Gracie Allen. Two teams dominated the 1940s, Bob HOPE and Bing CROSBY in the popular series of 'Road' movies and Universal's ABBOTT AND COSTELLO. Since the heyday of the 1930s there have been fewer successful teams, Dean MARTIN and Jerry LEWIS being at best pale imitations of Abbott and Costello. More recently, there has been a return to farce with the work of the National Lampoon and *Saturday Night Live* teams in such films as *Animal House* (1978) and *The Blues Brothers* (1980).

comic strips A rich source of characters and stories for screen adaptation.

Many comic-strip characters have made the transition from newspaper to live-action film, with varying degrees of success. The first was Ginger Meggs, the artful dodger of an Australian comic strip, played in *Those Terrible Twins* (1925) by Ray Griffin. Meggs returned, played by Paul Daniel, in a film of 1982. In 1926 the first US comic-strip character made her live-action debut in *Ella Cinders*. Britain had to wait until 1949, when Christabel Leighton-Porter played the title role in *The Adventures of Jane*; the part was later revived by Kirsten Hughes in *Jane and the Lost City* (1987).

The most frequently portrayed comic-strip character is Blondie, who was played by Penny Singleton in 28 feature films (1938–50), with Arthur Lake as Dagwood. Other long runs include Joe Kirkwood as Joe Palooka in eight movies (1946–51), Johnny WEISSMULLER as JUNGLE JIM in eight movies (from 1948; a dieting clause was inserted in his contract after he had grown too fat to play TARZAN), and Johnny Sheffield as Bomba the Jungle Boy in 12 pictures (1949–55).

SUPERHEROES of comic-strip origin include BATMAN and SUPERMAN, while futuristic heroes include FLASH GORDON (played by ex-athlete Buster Crabbe in 1936–40 and by ex-footballer Sam J. Jones in 1980) and BUCK ROGERS (also played by Crabbe). The detective Dick Tracy was played by Ralph Byrd in three serials (1937–39) and two 1947 films, by Morgan Conway in two films of 1945 and 1946, and by Warren BEATTY in 1990. Robert Wagner played the title role in *Prince Valiant* (1954), and Monica Vitti the heroine of *Modesty Blaise*, a camp classic of 1966.

Other examples include *Little Orphan Annie* (1932) with Mitzi Green, *Li'l Abner* with Granville Owen (1940) and Peter Palmer (1957), the Jane FONDA vehicle *Barbarella* (1967), Barry Humphries's portrayal of his own creation in *The Adventures of Barry McKenzie* (1972; sequel1974), and *The Addams Family* (1991; sequel 1993). Big-budget flops of recent years include *Popeye* (1980), starring Robin WILLIAMS, and *Howard the Duck* (1986).

The numerous cartoon films to have been based on comic strips, include the *Gertie the Dinosaur* series (1919), the X-rated *Fritz the Cat* (1971), and the Peanuts films *A Boy Named Charlie Brown* (1969) and *Snoopy, Come Home!* (1972).

commentative sound Film sound that does not have its source, or implied source, in the scene it accompanies. The most familiar types are background MUSIC and NARRATION. *Compare* ACTUAL SOUND.

compilation film *See* ANTHOLOGY FILM.

composite. composite photography The SPECIAL EFFECTS technique of shooting two subjects separately and then combining their images so that they appear to be parts of the same scene. The most commonly used forms of composite photography are MATTE and BLUE-SCREEN shots, in which background and foreground are filmed separately and then merged. Similar forms of trickery have been used to create scenes in which the same actor plays more than one role, as in *The Parent Trap* (1961) with Hayley MILLS as identical twins. In Woody ALLEN's film *Zelig* (1983), Allen's character is superimposed on newsreel footage so that he appears with Hitler, Eugene O'Neill, and others; a similar technique was employed in *Forrest Gump* (1994). Other films, such as WHO FRAMED ROGER RABBIT? (1988), have combined cartoons and live action.

composite print *See* COMBINED PRINT.

computer animation Any method of ANI-MATION that involves the generation or manipulation of images by computer. A relatively new technique in the cinema, computer graphics were originally developed by commercial and educational institutions before being taken up by ABSTRACT FILM-makers, such as James Whitney and Stan Vanderbeek. It was some time before Hollywood began to take notice. The first feature film to make use of the new techniques was Disney's *Tron*, released on the strength of the video games boom in 1982; although the number of computer-generated sequences was actually quite small, its blend of live action and animation proved reasonably popular. Such films as *Ghostbusters* (1984) and WHO FRAMED ROGER RABBIT? (1988) have since used similar techniques with vastly greater sophistication. Since the mid 1980s the cinematic use of computer graphics has proceeded rapidly. Short animation pieces (many of them funded by the Canadian Film Board) are constantly redefining the limits of the medium, while makers of big-budget fantasy features are always on the look-out for the latest in spectacular SPECIAL EFFECTS. The development of the technique known as **morphing**, in which objects change form before the viewer's eyes, seems particularly worthy of mention; it was first exploited to the full in James CAMERON's *Terminator II* (1992; *see* TERMINATOR FILMS). As with previous technological developments, the question remains whether computer special effects will continue to be used mainly for their novelty value or genuinely to expand the artistic possibilities of the medium.

cone light A conical lamp, with a power of between 750 and 5000 watts, that gives off a wide beam, thereby creating a soft generally diffused light.

Connery, Sean (Thomas Connery; 1930–) British actor, best known as the first James BOND of the big screen. Now in his mid sixties, he regularly tops polls in women's magazines as the world's sexiest man.

Born in Edinburgh, Connery held a variety of odd jobs, including milkman, coffin-polisher, and male model, before making his stage debut in 1953. A Mr Universe competition in London then led to a small role in the first national tour of *South Pacific*. His early films, including *Lilacs in the Spring* (1954), *No Road Back* (1956), and *Tarzan's Greatest Adventure* (1959), are now largely forgotten with the exception of *Hell Drivers* (1957), starring Stanley BAKER.

Television provided him with his first big break in 1956, when the BBC offered him the lead role in *Requiem for a Heavyweight* after Jack PALANCE dropped out. Connery went on to star in two films of 1961, *Frightened City* and *On the Fiddle* (US title *Operation Snafu*). Strangely, it was his role as a dim-witted RAF recruit in the latter that encouraged Albert Broccoli and Harry Saltzman to cast him as 007 in the first of the Bond films, *Doctor No* (1962). His star status was consolidated by an appearance in the war film *The Longest Day* later that year.

Still widely regarded as *the* James Bond (he played the part five times between 1962 and 1967, and again in 1971 and 1983), Connery constantly struggled to free himself from the 007 image, even in the 1960s when Bond mania was at its height. His other films of this period included HITCHCOCK's *Marnie* (1964), *The Hill* (1965), and *Shalako* (1968), a rare example of a British Western. Despite his sterling performances in *The Molly Maguires* (1970) and John HUSTON's *The Man Who Would Be King* (1976), his popularity waned in the 1970s and early 1980s. He appeared in a number of science-fiction movies of varying quality, including *Zardoz* (1973), *Meteor* (1979), and *Time Bandits* (1981), and such films as *Robin and Marian* (1976) and *The First Great Train Robbery* (1978). In *The Wind and the Lion* (1975) John Milius cast him as an Arab chief: "His Arab speaks with a Scots accent, but we can assume he was taught English by a Scotsman."

Connery returned to form as the detective-monk in the 1986 adaptation of Umberto Eco's *The Name of the Rose*, which was a worldwide success. In 1988 he won the Oscar for Best Supporting Actor as an Irish cop in Brian DE PALMA's gangster thriller *The Untouchables*. Connery's rejuvenation continued apace with *Indiana Jones and the Last Crusade* (1989), in which he was cast as Harrison FORD's father, despite being just 12 years his senior. This was followed by *The Hunt for Red October* (1990), the last COLD WAR thriller to go into production before the fall of the Berlin Wall, and *The Russia House* (1990) with Michelle PFEIFFER. His fees for these two films – $10 million apiece – secured his position as Britain's highest-paid film actor.

There was nothing much in Fleming's Bond – English, public school, snobbish – that connected with him, but he took the character by the throat and shook some sense into it.

JOHN BOORMAN, director.

With the exception of Lassie, he's the only person I know who's never been spoiled by success.

TERENCE YOUNG, director.

continuity. **continuity girl** or **man** The person who ensures that every detail of costume, scenery, etc., is correctly repeated in successive shots of a film. As these shots may be filmed weeks or even months apart, and not necessarily in sequence, maintaining this continuity is not always a simple matter. The job was created by Sarah Y. Mason in 1917 and has been predominantly performed by women ever since.

Sometimes, inevitably, errors of continuity occur. In one of the best known films of its era, BRIEF ENCOUNTER (1945), Celia JOHNSON manages to remain completely dry after running through a downpour. In *The King and I* (1956) Yul BRYNNER's ear-ring comes and goes in successive shots and in *Jailhouse Rock* (1957) Elvis PRESLEY's prison number changes from 6239 to 6240. In *Anatomy of a Murder* (1959) Lee REMICK magically changes out of a dress into slacks as she leaves a café, while in *Sea of Love* (1989) Al PACINO puts on a second pair of underpants after making love to Ellen Barkin. One of the vehicles in the famous car chase in *Bullitt* (1968) loses a total of six hubcaps. In *Silkwood* (1983) CHER is driven away from Meryl STREEP's house but reappears there in the background. Inanimate objects mysteriously change positions – a bottle of beer in *Twins* (1988), the wheel of a boat in *Indiana Jones and the Last Crusade* (1989), a light switch in *Raising Cain* (1992) – while the level of liquid in actors' glasses frequently rises and falls without being replenished or consumed.

continuity sketches A series of quick sketches designed to illustrate a sequence from a script. These serve as a guide to the production designer in planning sets and to the director in composing shots. *Compare* STORYBOARD.

continuous action A scene that consists of a single long take (or that is edited to give this impression). The most famous example of uninterrupted action is Alfred HITCH-COCK's ROPE (1948), which consists of a series of ten-minute takes shot by a single camera in one room. In the long opening scene of Orson WELLES's TOUCH OF EVIL (1958), a single camera follows a car for several minutes through the streets of a Mexican town, while in the famous ending of Carol REED's THE THIRD MAN (1949) the camera waits for several minutes with Joseph COTTEN as Alida Valli slowly approaches and then walks past.

contract player An actor on a limited-term contract with a producer or studio, as opposed to one hired for a particular film. In the 1930s and 1940s the contract system gave the major Hollywood studios immense power over even their most famous stars.

Conway, Jack (1887–1952) Prolific US director, noted for his romantic comedies and action films of the 1930s and 1940s.

Born in Graceville, Minnesota, Conway left school early to work on the railway. In 1907 he joined a California stock company, and two years later made his screen debut in a Western for the Nestor Film Company, Hollywood's first studio. Having trained as a director under D. W. GRIFFITH, he directed his first film, *The Old Armchair*, in 1913.

Conway later joined MGM and made one of their first talkies, *The Unholy Three* (1930), a thriller with Lon CHANEY. Other hits included *Arsène Lupin* (1932) with John and Lionel BARRYMORE, *Red-Headed Woman* (1932) with Jean HARLOW, and *Viva Villa!* (1934) with Wallace Beery as the Mexican rebel. Howard HAWKS, who had intended to direct this last film himself, complained: "Conway's version had Wallace Beery playing Santa Claus." The DICKENS adaptation *A Tale of Two Cities* (1935) starred Ronald COLMAN, while *Saratoga* (1937) paired Clark GABLE and Jean Harlow for the last time; Harlow died towards the end of filming and had to be replaced by a double in some scenes. When Walter PIDGEON accidentally spilled cigarettes all over the floor in a scene from *Saratoga*, Conway, always reluctant to waste time on a retake, left it in. In 1937 he directed MGM's first film shot in Britain, *A Yank at Oxford*. It featured the little-known Vivien LEIGH, who created tension on set by rejecting Conway's direction in favour of suggestions from her lover, Laurence OLIVIER.

Conway's final films included *The Hucksters* (1947), with Gable and Deborah KERR, and *Julia Misbehaves* (1948), in which Walter Pidgeon and Greer GARSON patch up their marriage as their daughter (Elizabeth TAYLOR) prepares for her own wedding.

cookie *See* COKULORIS.

Gary Cooper (Frank James Cooper; 1901–61) US actor, mainly in WESTERNS, whose ability to suggest inward strength and resolution made him an all-American hero.

Cooper was born in Montana, the son of a judge. In the early 1920s he went to Hollywood and worked as an extra and stunt rider in silent Westerns, slowly making his way up to leading roles in smaller productions. He achieved fame with his performance as a terse cowboy in *The Virginian* (1929), one of the first talking Westerns. Over the next few years Cooper consolidated his stardom with roles in the Hemingway adaptation *A Farewell to Arms* (1932), *Design for Living* (1933), *The Lives of a Bengal Lancer* (1935), Frank CAPRA'S MR DEEDS GOES TO TOWN (1936), which earned him an Oscar nomination as Best Actor, *The Plainsman* (1937), *Beau Geste* (1939), and *The Westerner* (1940).

Cooper's characteristically noble performance as a Quaker war hero in *Sergeant York* (1941) brought him the Best Actor Oscar; the following year he was nominated once again for his portrayal of baseball star Lou Gehrig in *The Pride of the Yankees* (1942). A fourth nomination came his way for playing the taciturn hero in another Hemingway adaptation, *For Whom the Bell Tolls* (1943).

During the late 1940s Cooper's career went into something of a decline; however, his fortunes revived dramatically when he appeared in what is now regarded as his most memorable role, that of Sheriff Will Kane in HIGH NOON (1952). His performance as the reluctant hero Kane brought Cooper another Oscar and helped to make *High Noon* one of the handful of truly great Westerns. In subsequent films, notably *Vera Cruz* (1954), *Man of the West* (1958), and *The Hanging Tree* (1959) Cooper gave a tougher more determined edge to his characters. His last film was *The Naked Edge* (1961), a thriller.

In 1961 Cooper was presented with a special career Oscar; he died from cancer later that year.

> That guy just represents America to me. He's strong, he's able, he's kind, he wouldn't steal a penny from you, but if you cross his path – he'll kill you.
> FRANK CAPRA.

Coppola, Francis Ford (1939–) US director, writer, and producer who brought a spirit of independence and a renewed sense of ambition to mainstream Hollywood filmmaking in the 1970s.

Born to Italian parents in Detroit, Coppola made home movies as a child and studied film at UCLA. He has often been characterized as the first of a new generation of US directors with a background in film theory (*see* MOVIE BRATS). During the early 1960s he worked for Roger CORMAN as scriptwriter, dialogue director, and sound man on such low-budget productions as *Tower of London* (1962) and *The Young Racers* (1963). His first film as a director was Corman's *Dementia 13* (1963).

Over the next few years he worked mainly as a writer, churning out scripts and outlines for $300 a week. His ventures into direction ranged from the teen comedy *You're a Big Boy Now* (1967), to Fred ASTAIRE's last musical *Finian's Rainbow* (1968), and the more awkward and introspective *The Rain People* (1969). He won his first Oscar for the screenplay of *Patton* (1970).

Coppola finally advanced to the forefront of his generation of film-makers with his epic study of Mafia power and corruption, THE GODFATHER (1972), which won Oscars for Best Picture and Best Screenplay (with Mario Puzo). The saga of the Corleone clan continued with THE GODFATHER, PART II (1974), which won Academy Awards for Best Picture, Direction, and Screenplay, and the anticlimactic THE GODFATHER, PART III (1990). In 1974 Coppola made *The Conversation*, a smaller but no less incisive film about a bugging expert. His other major film of the 1970s was the stunning APOCALYPSE NOW (1979), a Vietnam-based exploration of the themes of Joseph Conrad's *Heart of Darkness*.

Coppola, who has always been particularly supportive of other directors, gave George LUCAS his first break in 1971 with *THX 1138*, a film co-produced by Coppola's American Zoetrope company. Two years later, in the first flush of fame from *The Godfather* he contributed to the huge success of Lucas's *American Graffiti* (1973) simply by adding his name as co-producer. However, Coppola's attempt to expand Zoetrope into a full-scale studio proved highly problematic. In the late 1970s he brought Wim WENDERS to Hollywood to make *Hammett*, but the film remained in pre-production for five years and then needed to be almost entirely reshot. Hugely expensive failures such as *One from the Heart* (1982) and *The Cotton Club* (1984) forced Coppola to become a jobbing director, working on such projects as *Peggy Sue Got Married* (1986). His contribution to *New York Stories* (1989) was coolly received, and few were surprised when *Bram Stoker's Dracula* (1992) had less to do with the original novel than any other version. When he followed this film by producing *Mary Shelley's Frankenstein* (1994; directed by Kenneth BRANAGH) some critics suggested that Coppola was gradually reverting to the style of his old mentor Corman. Nevertheless, his teen drama *Rumble Fish* (1983) and his biopic of maverick car designer Preston Tucker, *Tucker: The Man and His Dream* (1988), stand comparison with the best of Coppola's work.

> I probably have genius. But no talent.
>
> FRANCIS FORD COPPOLA: *Film Yearbook*, 1989.

co-production A film made through the collaboration of producers in two or more countries. It usually stars actors from different nations and is released in two or more languages. Successful examples include the SPAGHETTI WESTERN *A Fistful of Dollars* (1964) from Italy, Germany, and Spain, and BERTOLUCCI's *The Last Emperor* (1987) from Britain, Hong Kong, and Italy.

European co-productions became popular with US film-makers in the 1950s when financing was difficult and audiences in decline. Cheap labour and tax exemptions have also provided incentives for working in certain countries at certain times.

copter mount An attachment used to fix a camera to a helicopter for use in AERIAL CINEMATOGRAPHY. The mount will be designed for maximum freedom of movement with the minimum of vibration.

copyright The legal protection afforded to the owners of any intellectual property, provided that they have expressed it in an identifiable form. The first act to extend this protection explicitly to film was the 1912 Copyright Act in America. Worldwide copyright is now governed by the Universal Copyright Convention, drawn up by UNESCO in 1952, which harmonized the Berne Con-

vention with the Pan-American Union. Under this convention, copyright exists for 75 years in the case of a corporation or life plus 50 years in that of an individual. In countries with a nationalized film industry copyright resides with the state; the provisions of the UCC leave it unclear whether such copyright is subject to the usual time limits or granted in perpetuity.

In Britain three acts govern the use of film copyright; the 1911 act relating to works intended for performance, the 1956 act, which extended this explicitly to film and other modern media, and the Single Market Act of 1992. Under the 1956 act the screening of a film to a domestic, private, or school audience is exempt from copyright regulations.

The need for film-makers to obtain permission before adapting copyright material in other media was established by two landmark legal decisions. In 1907 the heirs of Lew Wallace successfully sued the makers of the silent BEN-HUR, while in 1922 Bram Stoker's widow forced the producers to withdraw copies of NOSFERATU.

Corman, Roger (1926–) US director whose infamous low-budget movies have obscured his status as a developer of talent and promoter of prestigious films. Corman resents the nickname **King of the B-Movies**, not least because the term is inaccurate: a Corman film, however small the budget, is always the main feature.

Corman's first job in the film industry was as a runner at 20th Century-Fox. Since the mid 1950s he has written, produced, directed, or distributed some 300 films through his own companies or others, most notably AMERICAN INTERNATIONAL PICTURES (AIP). His first film cost $12,000, took six days to make, and grossed $100,000. Much of Corman's earlier work was aimed at the teenage drive-in market and featured liberal doses of sex, violence, drugs, and alien menace. Typical titles include *Naked Paradise* (1956), *Attack of the Crab Monsters* (1956), *Not of this Earth* (1957), *Teenage Caveman* (1958), and *Bucket of Blood* (1959). It was only when he dabbled in politics with *The Intruder* (1961), in which a stranger stirs up racism in the Deep South, that Corman produced a flop.

His most popular films were the adaptations of Edgar Allen POE stories that he made for AIP in the 1960s, including *House of Usher* (1960), *The Pit and the Pendulum*

(1961), *The Raven* (1963), *The Masque of the Red Death* (1964), and *The Tomb of Ligeia* (1964). These films, most of which starred Vincent PRICE, were sumptuous examples of Corman's film-making abilities. His other well-known horror films of this period are *The Little Shop of Horrors* (1960), allegedly shot in two days, and *X – The Man with X-Ray Eyes* (1963), starring Ray MILLAND in the title role. *The Wild Angels* (1966) and *The Trip* (1967) were explorations of the biker and drug subcultures. The notoriety of such films has tended to eclipse his other work, including big-budget features such as *The St Valentine's Day Massacre* (1967) and the critically acclaimed *Bloody Mama* (1969).

In the 1970s Corman formed New World Films with the twin functions of producing features and releasing European art films in America. New World was behind such almost-forgotten films as *Piranha* (1978) and *Battle Beyond the Stars* (1980). In the 1990s he produced a few Poe remakes and returned to directing with *Frankenstein Unbound* (1990).

Corman's biggest contribution to mainstream cinema has been his willingness to provide a training ground for new talent, including Jack NICHOLSON, Martin SCORSESE, Francis Ford COPPOLA, Peter BOGDANOVICH, and Nicolas ROEG. In 1990 he published his autobiography *How I Made a Hundred Movies in Hollywood and Never Lost a Dime*.

Cornelius, Henry (1913–58) British director whose brief career produced two classic comedies, *Passport to Pimlico* (1949) and GENEVIEVE (1953). Born in South Africa, Cornelius trained under the theatre director Max Reinhardt in Berlin. With the rise of Nazism he left for Paris, where he studied at the Sorbonne while also working as an assistant editor on various French films. Having moved to Britain to assist René CLAIR in the editing of *The Ghost Goes West* (1935) for London Films, he remained to work on *Men are not Gods* (1936) and *The Drum* (1938).

During World War II, Cornelius went back to South Africa to write, direct, and produce documentaries. He then returned to Britain to work under Michael BALCON at EALING STUDIOS. Having co-scripted *It Always Rains on Sunday* (1947), the studios' first big hit, he made his directorial debut with *Passport to Pimlico*, a clever but gentle comedy that in many ways epitomizes the Ealing style. Two years later he directed and co-

scripted *The Galloping Major* (1951), a comedy about a neighbourhood syndicate that buys a racehorse, for British Lion. The ever-popular *Genevieve*, about the veteran car race from London to Brighton, was produced by Cornelius himself.

In 1955 Cornelius directed *I Am a Camera*, a rather disappointing adaptation of John Van Druten's play (based in turn on Christopher Isherwood's sketches of 1930s Berlin; *see* CABARET). The film prompted the famous three-word review "Me no Leica", attributed to C. A. Lejeune. He then wrote and directed the whimsical *Next to No Time* (1958), starring Kenneth MORE as an inventor who gains miraculous powers during an Atlantic crossing. Later that year, Cornelius died while filming the comedy *Law and Disorder* (1958), which was completed by Charles Crichton.

Costa-Gavras, Constantin (1933–) French director and screenwriter, born in Greece, who became well known for his political thrillers in the 1960s and 1970s. Of Russian descent, Costa-Gavras moved to Paris to study film and later worked as an assistant to such directors as René CLAIR and Jacques DEMY. He made his directorial debut in 1965 with *The Sleeping Car Murders*, an accomplished thriller; this was followed by a second suspense film, *Un Homme de trop* (1967).

In 1968 he established his international reputation with Z, a sharp political thriller that won the Oscar for Best Foreign Film. Although the film's setting was unspecified, parallels with the military coup in Greece were unmistakable. Costa-Gavras then continued to explore the official misuse of power in such films as *The Confession* (1970), about political trials in Stalinist Czechoslovakia, *State of Siege* (1972), about US involvement in atrocities in Uruguay, and *Special Section* (1975), which tackled wartime collaboration in Vichy France.

After directing *Clair de femme* (1979), Costa-Gavras went to Hollywood to make *Missing* (1982), which proved to be his most controversial work. Starring Jack LEMMON and Sissy Spacek, it explored America's role in the coup against Allende in Chile in 1973. Although its open criticism of US foreign policy aroused the wrath of the US government, Costa-Gavras was awarded an Oscar as co-author of the screenplay. The director continued to court controversy in his subsequent films, examining the Palestinian question in *Hannah K* (1983) and racism in the southern states of America in *Betrayed* (1988). *Music Box* (1991), a gripping thriller about the attempts of a US lawyer (Jessica Lange) to defend her Hungarian-born father on war-crimes charges, won the Golden Bear at the Berlin Film Festival. His most recent film is *Little Apocalypse* (1993).

Costello, Lou   *See* ABBOTT AND COSTELLO.

Costner, Kevin   (1955–   ) US actor, director, and screenwriter. On the flight home from his honeymoon, the young Costner spotted Richard BURTON on the aircraft and approached him for advice on getting into the movies. A month later he left his well-paid marketing job for a minor post in film-studio administration; his wife helped out financially by playing Snow White at Disneyland. By 1991, the year he headed the QUIGLEY POLL as America's top box-office draw, Costner was one of the highest paid actors in the film industry.

In his early career Costner was highly selective about the roles he accepted; in 1983, for instance, he gave up the lead in *War Games* to play a small part in *The Big Chill*, only to find his character virtually eliminated from the movie as released. A similar fate befell his character in *Frances* (1982). After minor roles in *Night Shift* (1982) and *Table for Five* (1983) Costner played his first real leads in *Fandango*, *American Flyers*, and *Silverado* (all 1985). The last of these, while not a hit at the time, teamed Costner with Kevin KLINE and John CLEESE and began the revitalization of the Western. Costner subsequently turned down leads in *Jagged Edge* (1985), *Platoon* (1986), and *Raising Arizona* (1987), all of which became big hits.

In the late 1980s a major role in Brian DE PALMA's gangster film *The Untouchables* (1987), was swiftly followed by starring parts in the thriller *No Way Out* (1987) and two baseball movies, *Bull Durham* (1988) and *Field of Dreams* (1989). *Bull Durham* contains a memorable speech in which Costner states: "I believe that Lee Harvey Oswald acted alone" – an assertion that his character in Oliver STONE's *JFK* (1991), lawyer Jim Garrison, dedicates his life to disproving. That year he also took the title role in *Robin Hood: Prince of Thieves*, only to be upstaged by Alan Rickman's Sheriff of Nottingham. Most of these films contributed to

Costner's rather serious clean-living image, a persona that some have found irritating. The concert documentary *In Bed with Madonna* (1991) features a scene with Costner in which the singer derides him as a bore: "Nobody says 'NEAT'!"

Costner made an impressive directorial debut with *Dances with Wolves* (1990), a three-hour epic in praise of Native American culture that won seven Oscars, including Best Picture and Best Director. The film was also a huge box-office success, although some critics disliked its highmindedness (Pauline KAEL called it "A New Age Social Studies lesson"). He released an even longer director's cut in 1992. More recently he has appeared in *The Bodyguard* (1992), the Western *Wyatt Earp* (1994), and *Waterworld* (1995), an extravagant marine fantasy.

costume. costume designer The person who designs the clothes worn by actors in a film. Hollywood's most famous costume designer was the legendary Edith Head (1907–81), who won a record eight Oscars, including one for Bette DAVIS's gowns in ALL ABOUT EVE (1950). Head also designed the most expensive costume ever made specially for a film, a $35,000 mink dancing dress for Ginger ROGERS in *Lady in the Dark* (1944). At the other end of the scale, Head initially chose an old shirt and a pair of men's trousers to dress Ingrid BERGMAN for her peasant role in *For Whom the Bell Tolls* (1943). On being ordered by the producer to design a new costume, she had the identical clothes made up in new fabric, which she then dyed and bleached to re-create the worn-out appearance of the originals.

Walter Plunkett, who designed costumes for *Little Women* (1933), *The Prisoner of Zenda* (1952), and many other films, was faced with a different problem on GONE WITH THE WIND (1939). The dress in which Vivien LEIGH flees the burning of Atlanta is her only article of clothing for a significant part of the film; 27 copies were made, which had to be progressively 'aged' with bleach and dye, and any accidental damage during the shooting of a scene had to be reproduced on all the remaining copies.

costume drama A film of a historical or literary subject, in which a period is re-created through the use of appropriate costumes. The term is often used in a slightly derogatory sense to suggest that a film is escapist fare that relies unduly on expensive tailoring and decor. Historical accuracy has not always been a major consideration; MGM's *Pride and Prejudice* (1940) was set some 50 years after the novel was written because the studio considered the costumes of the later era more attractive. The genre became particularly popular during the 1930s, when the Hollywood Production Code (*see* HAYS CODE) made the realistic depiction of contemporary subjects difficult. *See also* SWASHBUCKLERS.

Cotten, Joseph (1905–94) US actor, best known for his films with Orson WELLES in the 1940s. His later movies were mainly disappointing. Cotten, a handsome gentlemanly Southerner, admitted late in life "I was tall. I could talk. It was easy to do. I was in a lot of junk."

The son of a Virginia society family, Cotten worked variously as a paint salesman, football player, and drama critic in the 1930s. He first met Welles at a radio audition when they were both thrown out for laughing at an actor's mistake. Cotten joined Welles's Mercury Theater in 1937 and a year later took part in the notorious *War of the Worlds* broadcast that caused panic amongst listeners. "I'm afraid you'll never make it as an actor" Welles later told him, "but as a star, I think you well might hit the jackpot."

In 1941 the two men went to Hollywood to make CITIZEN KANE, in which Cotten played the important role of Jed Leland, Kane's best friend. "We made a classic without knowing it" he later wrote. The following year, Welles invited him to co-write and star in the thriller *Journey into Fear* and to play the inventor Eugene Morgan in THE MAGNIFICENT AMBERSONS. Cotten was then signed up by David O. SELZNICK, who almost immediately loaned him to HITCHCOCK for *Shadow of a Doubt* (1943), in which he played a serial killer. He later co-starred with Selznick's wife, Jennifer JONES, in the Western *Duel in the Sun* (1946) and *A Portrait of Jennie* (1948).

In 1949 he rejoined Welles for another classic, Carol REED's THE THIRD MAN, in which he played a writer hunting his black marketeer friend Harry LIME (Welles) through postwar Vienna. Selznick warned Reed beforehand that Cotten and Welles were frustrated writers and "experts at ridicule" who would compete in "tearing dialogue apart".

After his performance as Marilyn MONROE's murderous husband in *Niagara*

(1953), Cotten's career went into a long decline during which he made numerous Westerns in Hollywood and Italy. His later films also include *Hush...Hush, Sweet Charlotte* (1964) with Bette DAVIS and two monumental flops, *Tora! Tora! Tora!* (1970), about Pearl Harbor, and Michael CIMINO's HEAVEN'S GATE (1982).

cover shot Extra footage taken as an insurance policy in case part of a scene proves unusable for any reason.

Coward, Sir Noël (1899–1973) British stage actor, playwright, and songwriter who made his mark in cinema chiefly through adaptations of his witty plays; he also made occasional screen appearances.

Born in Teddington, the son of a travelling salesman, he made his stage debut at the age of ten and was writing plays by the time he was 20. In 1918 he made his screen debut as an extra in D. W. GRIFFITH's *Hearts of the World*. His first successful stage play was *The Vortex* (1924), a story of the decadent rich that was brought to the cinema by Michael BALCON in 1927. Although Coward thought the cinema "a soul-destroying industry", he later consented to further adaptations of his works, including Alfred HITCHCOCK's silent version of *Easy Virtue* (1927), Fox's *Cavalcade* (1933), filmed on stage by a Movietone News crew to preserve its vitality, and Ernst LUBITSCH's *Design for Living* (1933) with Gary COOPER, Fredric MARCH, and Miriam Hopkins.

During World War II, Coward worked in British intelligence in Paris until 1940. (A Gestapo list of those to be arrested at once following the Nazi invasion of Britain included his name.) In 1942 he co-produced, co-directed (with David LEAN), scored, scripted, and starred in the popular battleship drama *In Which We Serve*. For this multiple role Coward was awarded a special Oscar. His character in the film was based mainly on that of Louis Mountbatten, who commanded destroyers during the early part of the war. Because one scene showed a copy of the *Daily Express* proclaiming "No War This Year", the paper's owner, Lord Beaverbrook, used his position to disparage Coward for many years afterwards.

Over the next few years Coward and Lean collaborated on three more adaptations of his plays: *This Happy Breed* (1944), *Blithe Spirit* (1945) starring Rex HARRISON (who, after Coward's death, described him as "a lousy actor" who was "mannered and unmanly"), and BRIEF ENCOUNTER (1945), based on the play *Still Life*. In 1949 Coward was the first choice to play Harry Lime in THE THIRD MAN, but the part ultimately went to Orson WELLES. His later screen roles included a British official in *Our Man in Havana* (1959) and a criminal mastermind in *The Italian Job* (1969).

Coward was knighted for his services to the theatre in 1970.

Cowboy Philosopher, the A nickname for the actor, writer, and wit Will ROGERS.

Cox, Paul (Paulus Cox; 1940–) Australian director and screenwriter, born in the Netherlands. After studies at Melbourne University, Cox became a still photographer and held successful exhibitions in a number of countries. In 1965 he settled permanently in Australia and began to direct shorts; *The Journey* (1972) marked his debut as a feature director. He co-founded the production company Illumination Films (named after his film *Illuminations*, 1976) in the late 1970s.

Cox made his international reputation by directing and co-scripting *Lonely Hearts* (1981), which was named Best Film at the Australian Film Awards. This sensitive and witty comedy tells the story of a shy clerk (Wendy Hughes) and a piano tuner (Norman Kaye), two middle-aged people who meet through a marriage bureau. Cox then wrote, directed, and photographed *Man of Flowers* (1983), starring Kaye as a lonely painter whose love for a model (Alyson Best) leads to murder. The cast also included German director Werner HERZOG. Cox subsequently scripted and directed *My First Wife* (1984), about a composer who is deserted by his wife, and *Golden Braid* (1990), about a clock restorer who becomes obsessed with a braid of hair that he finds in a drawer. He has also directed a number of documentaries, including *The Secret Life of Trees* (1986) and *Exile* (1993).

crab dolly *See* DOLLY.

crane A mobile trolley on which a camera is mounted on a large BOOM in order to film from an elevated position. The camera platform also has seats for the camera operator and other members of the crew. As the boom can be raised, lowered, or turned while the trolley itself is in motion, the crane allows for a variety of complex cam-

era movements. A classic **crane shot** occurs in GONE WITH THE WIND (1939), during the scene in which Vivien LEIGH walks among the dead and wounded soldiers at the Atlanta railway depot.

Craven, Wes (Wesley Earl Craven; 1939–) US director who has so far worked exclusively in the horror genre. Craven grew up in a strictly religious household in which cinemagoing was forbidden: after studying education, psychology, and philosophy he began a career as an academic. It was only after making a film with a group of students, an experience he greatly enjoyed, that he decided to pursue a career in the cinema industry.

In 1970 he made a pornographic film, *Together*, with Sean Cunningham; its moderate success enabled Craven and Cunningham to find backers for their next enterprise, a reworking of Ingmar BERGMAN's 1959 classic *The Virgin Spring*. The result was a gory story of rape, murder, and butchery, which was released first as *Krog and Company* and subsequently as *Sex Crime of the Century*. Having failed totally under both these titles, it finally succeeded as *Last House on the Left* (1972), causing widespread outrage and making a fortune at the box office.

In 1977 Craven released his first really characteristic movie, *The Hills Have Eyes*, a disturbing film about a family of cannibals that attempted to subvert the stereotypes of North American middle-class life. It was followed in 1984 by an expensive but inferior sequel, *The Hills Have Eyes II*. *Deadly Blessing* (1981) was a less gory, more gothic, film, about the supernatural, whilst *Swamp Thing* (1981) was a camp 1950s-style monster movie.

Craven's fascination with dreams, which pervades all his work, culminated in *A Nightmare on Elm Street* (1984), the immensely popular 'teen terror' film that introduced Freddy Krueger (played by Robert Englund), the sinister slasher who became a cult villain of the 1980s. Craven was involved with only one of the four Elm Street sequels of the decade, *A Nightmare on Elm Street Part 3: Dream Warriors* (1987), which he co-wrote. His subsequent films have been less successful, despite bigger budgets: *Deadly Friend* (1987), *The Serpent and the Rainbow* (1988), and *The People Under the Stairs* (1991) made relatively little impression on the cinemagoing public. *Wes Craven's New Nightmare* (1994) was a sophisticated reworking of the Kreuger myth.

Crawford, Joan (Lucille Le Sueur, also known for a time as Billie Cassin; 1906–77) US actress who ranked amongst Hollywood's top female stars in the 1930s and 1940s. Having started out as a waitress (and according to some accounts, a prostitute), Crawford first attracted attention in flapper roles in such films as *Our Dancing Daughters* (1928). By dint of hard work and relentless self-improvement, she went on to establish herself as a major star and one of the few female leads to survive the advent of the talkies. She emerged as the top box-office draw in the QUIGLEY POLL of 1930. Her screen persona, that of the tough and ambitious career girl who makes it to the top, was in large part a reflection of her own character; visually, too, she made a profound impression with her large expressive eyes and the padded shoulders that were an essential part of the Crawford 'look'.

Crawford's most celebrated and successful films included *Grand Hotel* (1932), with Greta GARBO, *Dancing Lady* (1933), the all-female *The Women* (1939), *A Woman's Face* (1941), and Michael CURTIZ's *Mildred Pierce* (1945), which brought her an Oscar as Best Actress. After the lean years of the 1950s, *Whatever Happened to Baby Jane?* (1962) provided a memorable COMEBACK for both Crawford and her arch-rival Bette DAVIS. Shooting was punctuated by violent differences of opinion between the two stars; Davis later remarked, "The best time I ever had with Joan Crawford was when I pushed her down the stairs in *Whatever Happened to Baby Jane?*" When Davis and not Crawford was nominated for an Oscar, the latter threw all her energies into a successful campaign to secure the award for Anne BANCROFT.

Comparing Davis and Crawford, the German director Curtis Bernhardt commented "While Bette is an actress through and through, Joan is more a very talented motion-picture star." According to Rosalind RUSSELL, Crawford's co-star in *The Women*, "She lived the life of a star. When you walked into her house it looked as though a star lived there." That Crawford could be unforgiving and, on occasion, deliberately cruel was conceded by all who knew her; director Nicholas RAY spoke for many when he observed, "As a human being, Miss Crawford is a very great actress." Her private failings were cruelly exposed by her adopted daughter Christina in the biography *Mommie Dearest*, published in 1978. The book was filmed in 1981 with Faye DUNAWAY playing Crawford. Bette Davis remarked, "One area of life Joan should never have gotten into was children."

More endearingly, and contrary to her glamorous image, Crawford was well-known for her habit of knitting during breaks in filming and at every other opportunity. Oscar LEVANT once asked her, "Do you knit while you fuck?" She had four husbands, including Douglas FAIRBANKS JNR, and a lengthy on-off affair with Clark GABLE; in the end, however, she died alone – a recluse with a drink problem.

I was born in front of a camera and really don't know anything else.
JOAN CRAWFORD; *Variety*, April 1973.

A star is when someone says, "Let's leave the dishes in the sink and go see Joan Crawford."
CLARENCE BROWN, director.

crazy comedy *See* SCREWBALL COMEDY.

creature. creature-feature An informal term for a HORROR FILM, especially one involving MONSTERS.

Creature from the Black Lagoon, The (1954) Jack ARNOLD's 3-D horror movie, the tale of an expedition that sets out to capture a legendary underwater beast, the 'gill-man' (played on land by Ben Chapman and underwater by Ricou Browning). According to Arnold, the film plays deliberately on "the feeling when you are swimming and something touches your legs down below – it scares the hell out of you if you don't know what it is."

The film has been highly praised for its UNDERWATER CINEMATOGRAPHY, the scenes in which the gill-man swims under Julia Adams as she treads water being particularly effective. (Browning's costume did not permit the use of an aqualung, and he had to hold his breath for up to five minutes at a time.) Steven SPIELBERG is a confessed fan of the film, which clearly influenced his blockbuster JAWS (1975). Many would argue that Arnold's film is superior to Spielberg's, owing mainly to its atmosphere of mystery and to the sympathy the audience comes to feel for the tormented Creature.

A sequel, *Revenge of the Creature* (1955), has the gill-man captured and put on display in an oceanarium. Directed once more by Arnold, the film emphasized the

Creature's sexual curiosity and innocence, but lost much of its mystery in the process. It was shot in 3-D but released flat, the 3-D craze having passed. A further sequel, John Sherwood's *The Creature Walks Among Us* (1956), was decidedly inferior, largely because the new director treated the Creature as a standard monster (although the script revealed that it had human characteristics under the scales).

credits or **credit titles**   A full list of those involved in the making of a film, which usually appears on the screen at the beginning or end of the picture. It includes the names of actors, directors, producers, cinematographers, writers, designers, and all other artistic and technical personnel. The credits are occasionally spoken, as in THE MAGNIFICENT AMBERSONS (1942) and M*A*S*H (1970); those for PASOLINI's *Hawks and Sparrows* (1966) are sung.

In 1942 an attempt to do away with full credits proved, not surprisingly, unacceptable to the industry. Since then the length of credit sequences has tended to increase, especially on films with labour-intensive special effects: the 457 credits for *Superman* (1978) run for 12 minutes, nearly 10% of the film. The longest credits ever are those for Sergei LEONE's Western *Once Upon a Time in the West* (1969), which run to over 12 minutes.

The credits of spoof pictures, such as the *Airplane* series, are often worth reading for such joke items as "Worst Boy: Adolf Hitler". Other films with unusual credits include *Miranda* (1947), about a mermaid, which includes the title "Tail by Dunlop"; *Fatal Attraction* (1987), which credits James Dearden "For the screenplay based on his original screenplay"; and *Patti Rocks* (1989), which lists a "Spiritual Adviser" and a "Skunk Wrangler".

creeper title or **rolling title**   A title that moves up or across the screen at a slow reading pace. Its words are usually printed or painted on flexible material and rolled on a cylinder. A famous horizontal creeper-title was the MAIN TITLE for GONE WITH THE WIND (1939).

crew   Short for production crew, the people involved in the technical side of making a film, as opposed to the performers and creative personnel. The crew includes such specialists as the camera operators, GAFFER, BUYER, first PROP MAN, mike man, and technical advisor.

Cristaldi, Franco   (1924–92) Italian producer and executive, who was responsible for some of the most memorable films of the postwar Italian cinema. Cristaldi abandoned legal studies in Turin to set up his own production company, La Vides Cinematografica, at the age of 22. After several years making documentaries, he became Italy's youngest producer of features in 1953.

During his career he worked with such key figures of modern Italian cinema as VISCONTI (*White Nights*, 1957; *Of a Thousand Delights*, 1965), FELLINI (AMARCORD, 1974; *And the Ship Sailed on*, 1983), and Marco Bellocchio (*China is Near*, 1967; *In the Name of the Father*, 1971). He enjoyed a particularly successful partnership with Francesco ROSI, for whom he produced *Salvatore Giuliano* (1962), *Lucky Luciano* (1973), and the highly praised *Christ Stopped at Eboli* (1979), from the book by Carlo Levi. Other important productions include Pietro GERMI's stylish black comedy *Divorce Italian Style* (1961), Mario Monicelli's *Persons Unknown* (1958), and Gillo PONTECORVO's *Kapo* (1960).

In the 1970s Cristaldi worked on a number of international co-productions, including the British film *Lady Caroline Lamb* (1972), and became president of the International Federation of Film Producers Associations (IFFPA). Later successes included *The Name of the Rose* (1986), from the novel by Umberto Eco, and Giuseppe Tornatore's *Cinema Paradiso* (1988), which won an Oscar for Best Foreign Film. He was married to the actress Claudia CARDINALE.

Cronenberg, David   (1943–   ) Canadian director and occasional actor, known for his 'body horror' movies. According to Cronenberg, his films "have to do with physical existence and what happens when that breaks down in some radical way." His first feature was the disturbing *Stereo* (1969), in which a group of students submit to horrifying surgery to increase their telepathic abilities. The story was told in a clinical pseudo-documentary style quite unlike that of the traditional horror movie. *Crimes of the Future* (1970) introduced the director's obsession with the perils and pleasures of mutant biology, while *Shivers* (1974), his first attempt at a commercial movie, featured a surgically implanted (and mobile) parasite that is both an aphrodisiac and a cause of venereal disease. *The Brood* (1979) told the story of a woman (Samantha Eggar) who gives birth to "the children of her rage", mutant babies who act out her fantasies of revenge.

Cronenberg first came to public attention with *Scanners* (1980), a tense thriller in which rival telepaths use their powers to control other people's bodies. He followed this box-office success with his most personal movie, *Videodrome* (1982), featuring James Woods as a television addict who develops a new orifice in his stomach to receive living software. The following year, Cronenberg directed his first adaptation, a version of Stephen King's *The Dead Zone*. Perhaps aware that previous King films had erred on the side of spectacle, Cronenberg reined in his usual excesses and produced a near-bloodless thriller, the best of the King movies.

The Fly (1986), a remake of the 1958 horror classic, was a major breakthrough for Cronenberg. It is the beautiful and tragic tale of Jeff Goldblum, whose experiments in matter transportation lead to his genetic material becoming mixed up with that of a fly. As a result he slowly transforms into a hybrid of man and insect. The audience is shown both the humour of the scientist's predicament – he gets to walk on the ceiling – and the suffering it brings to him and his girlfriend (Geena Davis), who is finally forced to kill him. This love story, a big hit with audiences and critics alike, was followed by the complex *Dead Ringers* (1988), in which Jeremy IRONS plays twin gynaecologists who fall in love with the same woman (Genevieve Bujold). The success of these two films brought Cronenberg recognition as a mainstream director, though he has disputed this title: "A mainstream movie is one that isn't going to rattle too many cages. No horror film is truly mainstream."

Cronenberg made his acting debut in Clive Barker's *Nightbreed* (1990), in which he gave a restrained but chilling performance as a serial-killer psychiatrist. His two latest directorial projects have been a disappointing interpretation of William Burroughs's novel *The Naked Lunch* (1991) and an adaptation of the stage play *M. Butterfly* (1993).

> I don't have a moral plan. I'm a Canadian.
> DAVID CRONENBERG; *Film Yearbook*, 1985.

Crosby, Bing (Harry Lillis Crosby; 1904–77) US singer and actor, nicknamed the **Old Groaner**, who became one of the top box-office attractions of the 1930s and 1940s. He was called Bing after a cartoon character who, like him, had large ears. Having established his reputation as a singer with various big bands in the mid 1920s, he emerged as the foremost 'crooner' of his generation and one of the most successful recording artists of all time.

Crosby made his screen debut in *King of Jazz* (1930); his performance was cut from the original version of the film but restored after he had become a household name. He went on to star in such popular light musical comedies as *Mississippi* (1935), *Anything Goes* (1936), *Waikiki Wedding* (1937), *Sing You Sinners* (1938), and ROAD TO SINGAPORE (1940), the first of the seven 'Road' films in which he co-starred with Bob HOPE and Dorothy LAMOUR. Crosby sang the Irving BERLIN hit 'White Christmas' for the first time in *Holiday Inn* (1942), reprising it in *Blue Skies* (1946), *White Christmas* (1954), and on numerous Christmas television shows. *Going My Way* (1944), in which he won an Oscar in the unlikely role of a priest, was banned in a number of Catholic countries because of Crosby's unorthodox clerical attire of sweatshirt and baseball cap. Amongst his other films are *The Country Girl* (1954) and *High Society* (1956), a musical remake of THE PHILADELPHIA STORY that includes his memorable duet with Grace KELLY on 'True Love'. Crosby virtually retired from the cinema after *Road to Hong Kong* (1960); he died, as he might have chosen, on a Spanish golf course.

Although one of the best-loved stars of the day, Crosby was always modest about his abilities; he once confessed, "Honestly, I think I've stretched a talent which is so thin it's almost transparent over a quite unbelievable number of years." He was quite unruffled by Bob Hope's endless jibes: "There is nothing in the world I wouldn't do for Hope, and there is nothing he wouldn't do for me...we spend our lives doing nothing for each other." Crosby's easy-going nature did not extend to all areas of his life, however. Contrary to the popular image of the man, colleagues from his earlier days remembered his ruthless ambition and vanity: according to bandleader Phil Harris, "He was a tough guy. Make a wrong move and he'd never speak to you again."

He was an average guy who could carry a tune.

BING CROSBY, suggesting his own epitaph.

Bing Crosby sings like all people think they sing in the shower.

DINAH SHORE, singer and actress.

cross. cross-cutting The practice of cutting between two (or more) different scenes in separate locations, which are understood to be occurring simultaneously and to have a narrative relationship. This now familiar convention has no real precedents in literature or the theatre. The first film to make effective use of the technique is usually agreed to be Edwin S. PORTER's *The Great Train Robbery* (1904). Its main function has always been the creation of suspense, as in the numerous Western sequences in which shots of the wagon train being attacked by Indians are intercut with footage of the cavalry speeding to the rescue. The technique can also be used for irony, as in the closing moments of THE GODFATHER (1972), in which a baptism scene is intercut with a series of brutal killings; occasionally it is used to deliberately misdirect the audience, as in THE SILENCE OF THE LAMBS (1991), in which two unconnected scenes are cut together as an entrée to the main climax.

crossing the line Following one shot of a subject with another taken from the other side of an imaginary line connecting the principal elements in the scene. If the first shot featured a man talking to a woman on his left, their positions will appear reversed in the second shot. For the viewer, the effect is as if he or she had passed through the cinema screen to view the action from the other side. An example occurs during the ghost-town shoot-out in *The Good, the Bad and the Ugly* (1966), in which the cut is masked by a close-up of a wagon. Crossing the line is generally avoided as it risks confusing the audience; for example, if the cavalry exits frame left only to re-enter frame left, are they retreating?

Cruise, Tom (Thomas Cruise Mapother IV; 1962–) Boyish-looking US actor. He was the leading US box-office draw in 1986 and 1988 and ranked second to Clint EASTWOOD in 1993.

Born in New York State, Cruise made his screen debut in a bit part in *Endless Love* (1981), a teenage romance. His first leading role was as a high-school football star in *All the Right Moves* (1983); he also played a teenage gang member in Francis Ford COPPOLA's *The Outsiders* (1983). In his third film of the year, the comedy *Risky Business*, Cruise played a high-school youth who turns his parents' home into a bordello.

After several further films in which he played teenagers, including the fairytale *Legend* (1984), Cruise found international fame with his first adult role, that of a naval fighter pilot in the hugely successful *Top Gun* (1985). Cruise then teamed up with Paul NEWMAN in Martin SCORSESE's *The Colour of Money* (1986), a sequel to Newman's low-life movie *The Hustler* (1961). In *Rain Man* (1988) he played the sharp-dealing brother of Dustin HOFFMAN's autistic savant.

A year later Cruise won an Oscar nomination for his raw performance as a disabled Vietnam veteran in Oliver STONE's *Born on the Fourth of July*. Following this triumph he received $9 million plus a percentage for *Days of Thunder* (1990), about a stock-car racer, and $12 million for *Far and Away* (1992), in which he and his wife, Nicole Kidman, co-starred as Irish emigrants to America. His subsequent films have included *A Few Good Men* (1992), in which he played a naval lawyer defending marines on a murder charge, and another legal thriller, Sydney POLLACK's *The Firm* (1993). The latter earned $70 million at the box office in its first month. More recently, Cruise underwent a complete change of image (including dying his hair blonde) to play a bisexual vampire in *Interview with the Vampire* (1994), which was shot in Britain.

Crystal Award An annual award for women, presented by the organization Women in Films to those who have improved the image of women on the screen or have encouraged more women to enter the cinema profession.

CU *See* CLOSE-UP.

cue Any visual or sound signal used to prompt the beginning or end of action, such as the director's call of ACTION or CUT. The word also refers to words or lines whispered off-camera to prompt a performer, especially during rehearsals. In the silent era, the director could shout cues to performers in the midst of shooting.

cue card or **idiot card** A card displayed off-camera on which lines or words are written to prompt actors. Marilyn MONROE and

Marlon BRANDO are amongst the actors who are said to have needed cue cards.

cuke   *See* COKULORIS.

Cukor, George   (1899–1983) US director, best known for his comedies, literary adaptations, and 'women's pictures'. Cukor was nominated for five Oscars as Best Director but won only one, for *My Fair Lady* (1964). After more than half a century in the cinema industry, he made his last film at the age of 82.

Born in New York City of Jewish Hungarian parents, he made his stage debut as a teenager and became a Broadway director in his mid twenties. In 1929 he left the theatre to become a Hollywood dialogue director in the new era of sound. After co-directing several films for Paramount he made his debut as a solo director with *Tarnished Lady* (1931) starring Tallulah BANKHEAD. A year later Cukor moved to RKO with producer David O. SELZNICK and directed Katharine HEPBURN's debut performance in *A Bill of Divorcement* (1932). The three worked together again on RKO's great hit, *Little Women* (1933).

Later that year Cukor and Selznick moved on to MGM, where their first project was the Jean HARLOW film *Dinner at Eight*, which earned Cukor his first Oscar nomination. The Dickens adaptation *David Copperfield* followed in 1934; when Maureen O'SULLIVAN failed to produce real tears for the big deathbed scene, Cukor twisted her feet until she did so. In 1937 he directed Greta GARBO to one of her most acclaimed performances in CAMILLE, but their collaboration on the disastrous *Two-Faced Woman* four years later allegedly prompted Garbo's decision to retire.

A homosexual, Cukor was famous for his skill in handling actresses, especially those with a reputation for being 'difficult'. After Clark GABLE had Cukor removed from GONE WITH THE WIND (1939), Vivien LEIGH and Olivia DE HAVILLAND continued to visit him at home to discuss their scenes: "He was my last hope of ever enjoying the picture" Leigh noted. Later that year Cukor was chosen to direct the cast of 135 actresses – including the temperamental leading ladies Norma SHEARER, Joan CRAWFORD, and Rosalind RUSSELL – in MGM's all-female *The Women* (1939). Hollywood directors traditionally call the top star to the set first, but in this case Cukor had three stars of equal rank. He resolved the problem by announcing "Ready ladies!", at which all three would appear; when this system broke down he was obliged to send three underlings to knock simultaneously on three dressing-room doors.

The Women was followed by a string of classic comedies, including THE PHILADELPHIA STORY (1940) with Hepburn, Cary GRANT, and James STEWART, *Adam's Rib* (1949) with Hepburn and Spencer TRACY, *Born Yesterday* (1950) with Judy Holliday, and *Pat and Mike* (1952) with Hepburn and Tracy again. In 1954 Cukor directed Judy GARLAND in the powerful musical A STAR IS BORN; his other ventures into the genre include *Let's Make Love* (1960) with Marilyn MONROE and Yves MONTAND, and the lavish *My Fair Lady* with Audrey HEPBURN.

At the age of 77 Cukor directed the first US-Soviet co-production, a fantasy entitled *The Blue Bird*. Having told the head of the Leningrad studio how proud he was to be working where EISENSTEIN's BATTLESHIP POTEMKIN had been produced over 50 years earlier, Cukor was somewhat taken aback to learn that he would be using the same equipment. His last movie was *Rich and Famous* (1981), with Jacqueline BISSET and Candice BERGEN.

Culkin, Macaulay   (1980–) US actor, often described as the biggest CHILD STAR since Shirley TEMPLE. A string of successful films has established him as one of the most highly-paid stars in Hollywood, with a price tag of up to $8 million a movie.

After several stage appearances, the eight-year-old Culkin made his film debut in *Rocket Gibraltar* (1988), following this with John Hughes's *Uncle Buck* (1989) and the Adrian Lyne film *Jacob's Ladder* (1990). Hughes also wrote and produced the spectacularly successful *Home Alone* (1990), in which Culkin played Kevin McCallister, a pre-teen accidentally left behind to fend off burglars when his parents go on holiday. The combination of violent slapstick with Culkin's undeniable charm led to the film's becoming the surprise hit of 1990; it eventually grossed over $470 million.

The saccharine *My Girl* (1991), which treated audiences to the sight of Macaulay's first screen kiss, was followed by the inevitable *Home Alone II: Lost in New York*, which repeated most of the plot of the original film in a different location and at a higher price tag: Culkin now demanded $5 million and

5% of the gross. Only pedants drew attention to the contradiction in the title: the McCallister home is in Chicago. The youthful target audience was subjected to the most aggressive merchandising campaign since BATMAN (1989).

Of his subsequent projects the most interesting has been *The Good Son* (1993), a film scripted by Ian McEwan that saw Culkin playing an angel-faced but demonic child. In Britain, the film was temporarily denied a certificate in the moral panic following the murder of James Bulger. He has subsequently made *The Nutcracker* (1994), a version of the ballet, *Getting Even with Dad* (1995), and *Richie Rich* (1995).

A central role in all this has been played by Macaulay's father Kit Culkin, an ex-actor and dancer who serves as his son's manager. Hyperbolic stories of his ferocity in making and breaking deals are only matched by the fees he has secured for his young client. He is reported to have threatened to pull Macaulay from *Home Alone II* unless he was given the lead in *The Good Son*, which at the time was fully cast and only weeks away from principal photography. His displeasure at the addition of a narration to *The Nutcracker* led to his withdrawal of Macaulay from all promotional work for the movie.

Whether his father's uncompromising attitude will help Culkin junior to navigate the difficult transition between kiddie-sensation and fully fledged adult star remains to be seen.

cult film   A motion picture that draws a limited but devoted audience (often young). Cult movies will often continue to pack smaller theatres long after their original release. Examples include the horror classic THE NIGHT OF THE LIVING DEAD (1968), the counterculture monument EASY RIDER (1969), *The Rocky Horror Picture Show* (1975), and the critically lambasted comedy *The Blues Brothers* (1980). Outstandingly bad films, such as *The Attack of the 50-foot Woman* (1958) and the Japanese GODZILLA epics, can also achieve cult status.

Curly Top   A nickname of the US child star Shirley TEMPLE. *Curly Top* was also the title of a 1935 film that starred the six-year-old moppet and featured her famous rendering of the song 'Animal Crackers in My Soup'.

Curtis. Jamie Lee Curtis (1958–) US actress, who was initially typecast in shock horror films but revived her flagging career with two comedy successes, *Trading Places* (1983) and *A Fish Called Wanda* (1988).

The daughter of Hollywood stars Tony CURTIS and Janet Leigh, she was born in Los Angeles and educated at the University of the Pacific in Stockton, California. After appearing in the TV comedy series *Operation Petticoat* in 1978, she made her big-screen debut as the female lead in John CARPENTER's influential SLASHER movie *Halloween* (1979). More gore followed with *Prom Night*, about an axe murderer at large in a high school, *Terror Train*, and Carpenter's *The Fog* (all 1980), in which both Curtis and her mother played supporting roles. She continued to be stalked by bloodthirsty predators in *Halloween II* and *Road Games* (both 1981).

Her career then changed course with *Love Letters* (1983), an intimate low-key drama, and John LANDIS's *Trading Places*, in which she played the happy hooker loved by yuppie Dan AYKROYD. However, following the failure of *Perfect* (1985), a health-club drama with John TRAVOLTA, she remained in minor roles until 1988, when she starred as a seductive thief in *A Fish Called Wanda*. *Variety*, which had previously disparaged her work, noted how "Curtis steals the show with her keen sense of comic timing and sneaky little grins and asides."

Her more recent films have included *Blue Steel* (1990), in which she played a rookie cop, the comedy *My Girl* (1991), with Aykroyd again, *Mother's Boys* (1993), and *True Lies* (1994), with Arnold SCHWARZENEGGER.

Tony Curtis (Bernard Schwartz; 1925–) US actor with pretty-boy looks and visible nervous energy; he has played all his roles – which include a viking and an Arabian calif – with a straight Bronx accent.

Born in a poor section of New York, the son of an immigrant tailor, he joined a street gang at the age of 11. After serving in the navy during World War II, he studied at the City College of New York and took acting classes, leading to a number of off-Broadway appearances.

Curtis was signed by Universal in 1949, making his debut that year as a bit player in the Burt LANCASTER film *Criss Cross*. After playing the title roles in *Son of Ali Baba* (1952) and *Houdini* (1953) he gave perhaps the finest performance of his career as a sycophantic press agent grovelling to an important columnist (Lancaster again) in *Sweet Smell of Success* (1957). The next year he made *The Vikings*, a swashbuckler, with his then wife Janet Leigh.

In 1958 Curtis won an Oscar nomination for his performance as a bigoted White prisoner who escapes chained to a Black (Sidney POITIER) in *The Defiant Ones*. His greatest comedy success came a year later with SOME LIKE IT HOT (1959), in which Curtis and Jack LEMMON pose as women in order to escape the attentions of the mob. During the 1960s he co-starred with Natalie WOOD in two comedies, *Sex and the Single Girl* (1964) and *The Great Race* (1965), before appearing as a serial killer in *The Boston Strangler* (1968).

Curtis's career then declined sharply with appearances in such films as *The Bad News Bears Go to Japan* (1978) and a string of foreign productions. In 1977 he published a novel, *Kid Andrew Cody & Julie Sparow*; he is now a professional artist.

Curtiz, Michael (Mihaly Kertesz; 1888–1962) Hungarian-born Hollywood director, best known for his films with Errol FLYNN and for CASABLANCA. In his 25 years with Warner Brothers he made an average of four films a year.

Born in Budapest, Curtiz worked in the Hungarian film industry from 1912 onwards. In 1926 Jack Warner brought him to America, where he remained under contract to Warners until 1953. Curtiz quickly established a reputation as a tyrant on the set, wearing breeches and riding boots while flourishing a fly whisk; he once allegedly pinched a baby to make it cry for the camera. He was also a stickler for realism: when filming *Noah's Ark* (1929) he thought little of endangering the lives of extras during a flood scene. "Nothing delighted him more than real bloodshed" wrote Errol FLYNN, who once discovered that Curtiz had given the extras real spears to throw at him. Appalled, Flynn charged off the set in pursuit of the director, who yelled "Lunch!" and disappeared.

Curtiz's command of English remained fractured; his command "Bring on the empty horses!" while filming *The Charge of the Light Brigade* (1936) was used by David NIVEN (a supporting player in the film) as the title of one of his volumes of Hollywood reminiscences. When others laughed at this command, Curtiz raged: "You think I know

fuck nothing. Well, let me tell you, I know fuck all!" He was, however, an indisputably talented director, producing such thrillers as *Angels with Dirty Faces* (1938) with James CAGNEY and a series of 12 adventure films with Flynn, including *Captain Blood* (1935), the actor's first major film, *The Adventures of Robin Hood* (1938), and *Dodge City* (1939).

Curtiz's golden year was 1942, when he directed James Cagney to an Oscar in the musical *Yankee Doodle Dandy* and collected his own award for *Casablanca*, the romantic thriller with Humphrey BOGART and Ingrid BERGMAN. After finally leaving Warners, Curtiz directed the CINEMASCOPE spectacle *The Egyptian* (1954) with Edmund Purdom and Peter Ustinov for 20th Century-Fox. One particular shot required Ustinov to whisper secretly in Purdom's ear. According to Ustinov, Curtiz interrupted the scene yelling "No goot. Dis is Zinemascop, vide shkreen – ven you vispar muss be four feet apart." Curtiz's career subsequently declined with a series of Paramount musicals, the best known being *White Christmas* (1954) with Bing CROSBY and the Elvis PRESLEY vehicle *King Creole* (1958). His final film was the John WAYNE Western *The Comancheros* (1962).

Cushing, Peter (1913–94) British actor, known for his horror films, in which he was often teamed with his lifelong friend, Christopher LEE. Cushing went to Hollywood in 1939 and made his screen debut the same year in *The Man in the Iron Mask*. His first British role was that of the courtier Osric in OLIVIER's *Hamlet* (1948), which also featured an early screen appearance by Lee.

In 1957 Cushing entered the world of horror films in HAMMER's *The Curse of Frankenstein*, in which he played the Baron to Lee's monster. He played the same role in a further five films, including *The Revenge of Frankenstein* (1958) and *Frankenstein Must be Destroyed* (1969). One memorable scene in the latter has him flipping through the Bible as he waits to take the oath in a courtroom and frowning at the contents – a Cushing ad-lib. His other long-running role for Hammer was that of Dr Van Helsing to Lee's DRACULA, a part he played in four films, starting with *Dracula* (1957).

Cushing also gave memorable performances as Winston Smith in a TV version of *1984* (1954), as Sherlock HOLMES in Hammer's *The Hound of the Baskervilles* (1959), and as Doctor Who in *Dr Who and the Daleks* (1965) and its 1966 sequel. During the 1960s and 1970s he brought great professionalism and a surprising depth of characterization to a great many movies, becoming one of the 'big three' horror actors (together with Lee and Vincent PRICE). His talents were recognized by George LUCAS, who cast him as the villain in STAR WARS (1977).

In the 1980s Cushing's declining health – he was diagnosed as suffering from cancer in 1982 – forced him to curtail his film work. His death eventually came less than a year after that of Price. A revealing autobiography, in which he confessed his many behind-the-scenes affairs, also told of his enduring love for his dead wife Helen; he continued to sign letters to friends "with love from Peter and Helen" long after her death in 1971 and firmly believed that she was waiting for him.

He was indeed the gentle man of horror.
ROY SKEGGS, chairman of Hammer Films;
Daily Telegraph, 12 August 1994.

custard pie   A vital ingredient of SLAPSTICK comedy, relying on the fact that there are few funnier sights than the pompous and venerable being forced to lick the dignity from their faces. This familiar comic device was mainly developed by KEYSTONE; the cinema's first custard pie, thrown at Fatty ARBUCKLE in *A Noise from the Deep* (1913), was a blackcurrant and whipped cream tart ordered from the bakery opposite the studio. (Later pies were created specifically for filming, and usually consisted of shaving foam.) LAUREL AND HARDY's *The Battle of the Century* (1927) featured one of the biggest pie fights of all time, with some 24 protagonists and over 3000 pies. Other memorable fights include those in *The Great Race* (1965) and at the end of *Blazing Saddles* (1973).

cut   (1) The order given by the director to stop recording the scene. (2) A sudden transition from one shot to another, achieved by cutting and splicing the two pieces of film. (3) A portion of film removed from the print at the order of the studio or censor.

cutaway   A brief interpolated shot of something relevant, but not essential, to the main action of a scene. The device has several main uses: (1) to comment on the significance of what we have just seen; much the commonest form of cutaway is the REACTION SHOT, in which the editor cuts from the action to the horrified, amused, or quizzical expression of a bystander; (2) to generate suspense, e.g. by reminding us of another character who will shortly affect or be affected by the action; (3) to release tension by providing momentary relief from the main action; (4) to provide a transition between two shots when a straight cut from one to the other might be jarring.

cutting   Another name for EDITING.

cutting copy   *See* WORKPRINT.

cutting on action   In editing a film, managing the transition from one shot to the next so that the beginning of the second shot concludes a piece of action initiated at the end of the first shot. Cutting on action was a major tenet of the INVISIBLE EDITING style favoured by Hollywood from the 1920s onwards, which relied on the ability of movement to disguise small changes in camera angle or position. The extra footage required for cutting from one shot to another in this way can be obtained either by filming the whole scene with several cameras in different positions, or by shooting the scene more than once with a single camera.

cutting outline   The preliminary instructions given to the editors as to what footage is to be used and how it is to be assembled to produce the ROUGH CUT.

cutting room   The room in which the editor and his assistants cut and assemble film. A well-known fate of actors is to *end up on the cutting-room floor*, meaning that part or all of their performance has been deleted. After executives at 20th Century-Fox viewed Marilyn MONROE's debut in *Scudda-Hoo, Scudda-Hey* (1948) most of the footage (including her one line, "Hello") hit the cutting-room floor. Other stars who suffered the same ignominy in their early careers include Kevin COSTNER and Bing CROSBY.

cyclorama   A studio backdrop of a sky, distant landscape, etc., that is curved to give the illusion of depth.

D

Daffy Duck A Warner Brothers cartoon character, whose appearance is said to have been modelled on Harpo MARX. He was one of the stable of characters created for the LOONEY TUNES and Merrie Melodies cartoons by the Warners team of animators, which included Tex Avery, Chuck Jones, and Robert Clampett. The cantankerous Daffy's first real appearance came in *Porky's Duck Hunt* (1937); his spluttering speech was articulated by Mel Blanc, the voice behind nearly all the Looney Tunes characters.

Dafoe, Willem (1955–) US actor, often cast in malevolent or troubled roles. Having been expelled from college for making an allegedly pornographic video, Dafoe gained acting experience with Theatre X in Milwaukee and the avant-garde Wooster Group in New York. Although his screen debut was cut from the released version of CIMINO's HEAVEN'S GATE (1980), his next role as the Brandoesque leader of a vicious biker gang in *The Loveless* (1982) brought him considerable attention. Further roles in spectacularly nasty villains followed in *Streets of Fire* (1984) and William FRIEDKIN's *To Live And Die in L.A.* (1985). He then broke the pattern by playing the innocent foil to Tom Berenger's evil Sergeant Barnes in Oliver STONE's Vietnam drama, *Platoon* (1986). The film provided Dafoe with a particularly memorable death scene.

In 1988 Dafoe appeared in his most controversial role, that of CHRIST in Martin SCORSESE's much-reviled *The Last Temptation of Christ*. Dafoe imbued the role (originally intended for Robert DE NIRO) with a troubled humanity that makes the film one of the most moving screen versions of the New Testament story. His other films of 1988 were Alan PARKER's *Mississippi Burning*, in which he played an idealistic federal agent investigating the activities of the Ku Klux Klan, and *Off Limits*, a violent thriller in which he played a military policeman tracking down a serial killer in Vietnam. Although 1989 saw him playing another good guy, a resilient concentration-camp boxer in *Triumph of the Spirit*, he was better received as the psychotic villain Bobby Peru in David LYNCH's road movie *Wild at Heart* (1990). Subsequent films include the erotic thriller *Body of Evidence* (1993) and *Tom and Viv* (1994), in which he played the poet T. S. Eliot.

dailies *See* RUSHES.

damn. Frankly, my dear, I don't give a damn. The famous valediction of Rhett Butler (Clark GABLE) to Scarlett O'Hara (Vivien LEIGH) in GONE WITH THE WIND (1939). Although the HAYS Office insisted that the last word should be 'darn', David O. SELZNICK, the film's producer, refused and incurred a $4,000 fine for breaching the Production Code.

dance and dancers Although dance sequences are to be found in even the earliest silent movies, it was not until the mid 1930s that the world of dance and dancers became an important part of the Hollywood film-making tradition. The mass choreographed scenes introduced by Busby BERKELEY in such MUSICALS as 42ND STREET revolutionized screen dance, while the smoothly executed routines of Fred ASTAIRE and Ginger ROGERS became the highlights of every film in which they starred. By the late 1930s it was virtually obligatory for any big-scale Hollywood musical to incorporate a spectacular ballet sequence.

The immediate post-war years saw a shortlived vogue for films featuring classical ballet. The first and most popular of these was POWELL and PRESSBURGER's THE RED SHOES (1948), which combined a powerful backstage plot with stunning ballet sequences featuring Robert Helpmann, Leonide Massine, and Moira Shearer. Three years later the same directors made the still more elaborate *The Tales of Hoffman* (1951), with Shearer, Massine, and Frederick Ashton. Other films to draw inspiration from classical ballet released at this time included *Hans Christian Andersen* (1951), with choreography by Roland Petit, and Gene KELLY's lavish flop *Invitation to the Dance* (1952).

In the early 1950s the spirit of the pre-war song-and-dance spectaculars was successfully revived by Kelly in *An American in Paris* (1951), which culminated in a 17-minute ballet to Gershwin's music, and SINGIN' IN THE RAIN (1952), with its famous 'Broadway Ballet' sequence. Thereafter, however, the traditional Hollywood musical became much less popular with the studios, largely for reasons of cost.

Subsequent dance films have tended to fall into the categories of BIOPICs on the one hand and adaptations of classical ballets and stage musicals on the other. Margot Fonteyn and Rudolph Nureyev starred in several screen ballets in the 1960s and Nureyev subsequently appeared in the title role of *Nijinsky* (1980). *Isadora* (1968) presented Vanessa REDGRAVE as the great Isadora Duncan and included careful reconstructions of her technique (although one writer compared Redgrave's dancing to that of a "spastic carthorse"). In recent years, the only film with a ballet theme to achieve mainstream success has been *The Turning Point* (1987), a somewhat clichéd drama starring Anne BANCROFT, Shirley MACLAINE, and Mikhail Baryshnikov.

During the 1950s and 1960s the art of the film CHOREOGRAPHER was kept alive in a popular series of screen versions of stage musicals. At the same time it was being redefined by the commercial success of pop and rock music and the emergence of more energetic styles of modern dance, as showcased in WEST SIDE STORY (1961). Popular films of the 1970s and 1980s to be built around high-energy production numbers include *Saturday Night Fever* (1977), *Fame* (1980), *Flashdance* (1983), and *Dirty Dancing* (1987). Of recent US directors, the most preoccupied with the world of dance has been Bob FOSSE, himself a former dancer and Broadway choreographer. Another director who has continued to produce work of interest to the serious dance fan is the Spaniard Carlos SAURA, several of whose films celebrate the Spanish flamenco tradition, which he has done much to revive.

dancing divinity, the The nickname of Jessie MATTHEWS, the popular British singing and dancing star of the 1930s; it was presumably devised by her publicists.

Dassin, Jules (1911–) US director and actor, who established a cult reputation in the 1940s with such hard-hitting NEOREALIST thrillers as *Brute Force* (1947), *The Naked City* (1948), and *Thieves' Highway* (1949). Dassin, who insisted upon filming on location wherever possible and tackling such themes as fascism and corruption head on, suffered a setback to his career during the McCarthy era, when he was blacklisted and chose to move to Europe. Subsequently he reclaimed his audience with the tense heist movie RIFIFI (1954), one of several of his films in which he also appeared as an actor, and the popular comedy *Never on Sunday* (1960), featuring the Greek actress Melina MERCOURI, who became his wife. Dassin later alienated many critics by adopting a more self-conscious and undisciplined style for such films as *Topkapi* (1964; also with Mercouri), *10.30 P.M. Summer* (1966), *A Dream of Passion* (1978), and *Circle of Two* (1980). In the late 1960s Dassin and Mercouri were forced to leave Greece owing to their opposition to the military government.

> He has sacrificed a lot to his political beliefs...If he hasn't made many films recently, its because he devoted himself to the Greek cause and me.
> MELINA MERCOURI.

Davies, Marion (Marion Douras; 1897–1961) US actress, who owed her stardom largely to the patronage of newspaper tycoon William Randolph Hearst. Convinced that he could make his mistress a star, Hearst saw to it that she appeared in leading roles in numerous films between the wars. Most are now forgotten; among the few that won Davies a degree of praise from the critics were *Show People* (1928) and *Page Miss Glory* (1935). More typical was the review that ran "Miss Davies has two expressions – joy and indigestion." Her dressing-room was the most lavish ever constructed – a 14-room bungalow in the Spanish style that went with her whenever she changed studios. Despite a developing drink problem, her generosity and lack of illusions about her ability charmed many of those who worked with her. Having admitted that her career was based on "5% talent and 95% publicity", she retired from the screen after *Ever Since Eve* (1937). As Hearst's lover, Davies was the model for the hapless singer Susan Alexander in CITIZEN KANE (*see also* ROSEBUD).

Dorothy Parker and a friend once stayed at the Davies-Hearst household, only to find that guests were prohibited from sleeping together unless married (even though the hosts weren't). In pique, she wrote the following verse in the visitor's book as she left:

Upon my honour
I saw a madonna
Sitting alone in a niche
Above the door
Of the glamorous whore
Of a prominent son-of-a-bitch

Davis, Bette (Ruth Elizabeth Davis; 1908–89) US actress, whose powerful performances and notoriously acerbic temperament made her one of the great legends of Hollywood. Davis worked as an usherette in a Cape Cod summer theatre before embarking on an acting career. After making her film debut in *The Bad Sister* (1931) she established her reputation in such full-blooded melodramas as *Of Human Bondage* (1934) and *Front Page Woman* (1939). Although she played a wide range of roles, the public liked her best as a menacing, sometimes murderously intense, neurotic with a fearsome tongue. Her strong character compensated for her somewhat indifferent looks. David Zinman observed "All she had going for her was her talent", while Davis herself once commented:

I have eyes like a bullfrog, a neck like an ostrich, and limp hair. You have to be good to survive with that equipment.

According to one famous story, a studio man sent to meet Davis from her train failed to spot her, later explaining "No one faintly like an actress got off the train." Nevertheless, Oscars for *Dangerous* (1935) and *Jezebel* (1938) confirmed Davis's standing as one of the most sought-after stars of the silver screen. She remained in the top ranks of Hollywood's aristocracy for another decade or more, appearing in such memorable films as *Dark Victory* (1939), *The Private Lives of Elizabeth and Essex* (1939), *The Great Lie* (1941), *The Little Foxes* (1941), *The Man Who Came To Dinner* (1941), *Now Voyager* (1942), *The Corn is Green* (1945), and the classic ALL ABOUT EVE (1950).

Davis was well known for her vicious temper and for dominating both fellow-performers and directors. She was regarded by many as a gorgon and E. Arnot Robertson speculated that "she would probably have burned as a witch if she had lived two or three hundred years ago." Her wit was sharp, however; on being introduced to a young starlet with a scandalous reputation

she commented: "I see – she's the original good time that was had by all." Davis continued to appear in new movies into her late middle age, often playing embittered and eccentric elderly women, as in the cult classic *Whatever Happened to Baby Jane?* (1962), in which she terrorized fellow veteran Joan CRAWFORD. Davis retained her power to chill audiences to the end, notably as a suspected murderess in the thriller *The Nanny* (1965). In 1987 Davis was paired with another screen legend, Lillian GISH, in Lindsay ANDERSON's *The Whales of August*, which was to prove the swansong for two great stars. Her last years were darkened by a biography written by her beloved daughter, in which Davis was 'revealed' as a friendless evil-minded shrew, who was often the worse for drink.

Fasten your seat belts – it's going to be a bumpy night.
BETTE DAVIS, in *All About Eve*.

Dawn process *See* GLASS SHOT.

day. day-for-night Short for *day-for-night filming*, the practice of using special filters, exposures, and processing techniques to make a scene shot in daylight appear as though it is taking place at night. This is denoted in a film script by the instruction D/N.

Day For Night is also the usual English title of François TRUFFAUT's *La Nuit Américaine* (1973), one of the most revealing films ever made about film-making.

go ahead, make my day A catchphrase that derives from the Clint EASTWOOD film *Sudden Impact* (1983), in which the rogue cop 'Dirty' Harry Callahan (played by Eastwood) uses it twice; on both occasions while pointing a gun at an armed criminal. The implication is that Dirty Harry would like nothing better than an excuse for shooting the gunman. The line has now become a general catchphrase meaning 'go ahead if you dare'. It was popularized in this sense by President Ronald REAGAN, when speaking to a business conference about tax increases proposed by the US Senate (March 1985).

Day, Doris (Doris Von Kappelhoff; 1924–) US actress and singer, best known for her musicals and romantic comedies of the 1950s.

Day began her career as a singer with big bands, becoming a highly popular radio star in the 1940s. Her first screen appearance was in *Les Brown and His Orchestra* (1941), a three-reel short, while her first feature was *Romance on the High Seas* (1948), a lightweight musical set on a cruise ship. Although Day's early films, such as *Moonlight Bay* (1951) and *April in Paris* (1953), failed to provide her with outstanding roles, they successfully established her virginal girl-next-door image.

The musical *Calamity Jane* (1953), in which she co-starred with Howard Keel, provided Day with her first big success; one of the film's songs, 'Secret Love', earned an Oscar and gave her an international hit. The following year Day starred opposite Frank SINATRA in *Young at Heart*, a romantic musical drama based on *Four Daughters* (1938). Other musicals followed, including *Love Me or Leave Me* (1955) and the highly acclaimed *Pajama Game* (1957), with lively choreography by Bob FOSSE.

Day's career might easily have stalled at the end of the 1950s had it not been for the immense success of *Pillow Talk* (1959), which won an Oscar for Best Story and Screenplay. The film co-starred Rock HUDSON, who went on to appear opposite Day in a number of light romantic comedies, including the satirical *Lover Come Back* (1961).

Although Day's vocal talents and excellent comic timing made her a versatile star, her appeal as a straight actress was limited; this became clear from the critical and commercial failure of Alfred HITCHCOCK's 1956 remake of his own film *The Man Who Knew Too Much*, in which Day starred opposite James STEWART. She remained a top box-office star well into the 1960s, although later in the decade her choice of material, especially such films as *The Ballad of Josie* (1967) and *With Six You Get Egg Roll* (1968), left much to be desired. In 1967 she turned down the part of Mrs Robinson in THE GRADUATE. Her optimistic clean-living image (she is a devout Christian Scientist) also became increasingly out of key with the times. As one critic wrote in the mid 1960s:

> Her personality untouched by human emotions, her brow unclouded by human thought, her form unsmudged by the slightest evidence of femininity...until this spun-sugar zombie melts from our screens there is little chance of the American film's coming of age.
> JOHN SIMON.

In fact, her personal life has been far from serene. Her first husband, whom she divorced after two years, was a violent and disturbed man who later committed suicide, while her second marriage collapsed after eight months. On the death of her third husband, her agent Marty Melcher, she discovered that he had systematically defrauded her of millions of dollars. A fourth marriage failed in 1979.

Day retired from the cinema in 1968, although she has subsequently worked in television; "I never retired" she once told an interviewer "I just did something else." She is the founder of the Doris Day Animal League, an association for the protection of animal rights.

Day-Lewis, Daniel (1957–) British actor, the son of Poet Laureate Cecil Day-Lewis and the actress Jill Balcon (whose own father was the producer Sir Michael BALCON). His father's death in 1972 had a traumatic effect on the teenage Day-Lewis, who took an overdose of migraine pills ("I haven't had a migraine since") and was later institutionalized for heroin addiction. In 1989 he abandoned his stage role of Hamlet, disturbed by the similarities between his own situation and the father-son relationship in Shakespeare's play.

Following bit parts in *Sunday Bloody Sunday* (1971), GANDHI (1982), and *The Bounty* (1984), Day-Lewis established his reputation in two films of 1985 – MERCHANT-IVORY's costume drama A ROOM WITH A VIEW and Stephen FREARS's gritty *My Beautiful Laundrette*. These films in many ways epitomized the opposite poles of British filmmaking in the 1980s, and the characters played by Day-Lewis – the pompous Cecil Vyse and the gay punk Johnny – could not have been more different. He gave a further demonstration of his versatility as the sexually insatiable surgeon Tomas in Philip KAUFMAN's *The Unbearable Lightness of Being* (1988).

It was, however, Jim Sheridan's *My Left Foot* (1989) that proved to be the watershed of Day-Lewis's career. His performance as Christy Brown, the Irish author and artist born with cerebral palsy, not only brought him the Oscar for Best Actor, but also ten other awards – one Canadian, two Irish, three US, and four British. During shooting, Day-Lewis insisted on being wheeled or carried around the set at all times to keep himself in character. Similarly, to prepare for the part of Hawkeye in Michael Mann's *The Last of the Mohicans* (1992), his comeback picture after a three-year lay off, he spent a month at the Alabama Special Operations Center learning outdoor survival skills. Madeleine Stowe, who played Cora in the film, recalled:

> Daniel would carry his gun around *all the time*. When he went to lunch he'd have that gun with him, when he went to the bathroom he'd have that gun with him. He's sort of not-of-this-world, Daniel.

He next explored a very different aspect of US culture in SCORSESE's Edith Wharton adaptation *The Age of Innocence* (1993). Inevitably, however, it was his performance as Gerry Conlan, one of the Guildford Four, in Sheridan's *In the Name of the Father* that attracted the most media attention that year. Although Day-Lewis initially read the script out of mere curiosity

> The further I got into it the greater the sense of dread I had, because I could feel it had the kind of gravity I find hard to resist...which is pretty much what I thought when I first read *My Left Foot*. A tremendous enthusiasm mixed up with the sense that it was absolutely not the right thing for me to be doing.

Although his performance brought a second Oscar nomination, the film was bitterly attacked in the British press, with Day-Lewis (who has been an Irish citizen since 1987) being particularly vilified.

Dead End Kids, the   *See* BOWERY BOYS, THE.

Dean. Basil Dean (1888–1978) British film director and stage producer. He is mainly remembered as the founder of Associated Talking Pictures, the company that built EALING STUDIOS, and for discovering such stars as Gracie FIELDS and George FORMBY. He was later head of ENSA, the organization that co-ordinated entertainments for British troops during World War II. Films directed by Dean include the romantic drama *The Constant Nymph* (1933), which he also co-wrote, *Lorna Doone* (1935), from the classic romance by R. D. Blackmore, and *Twenty-One Days* (1937; not shown until 1940), a melodramatic vehicle for Laurence OLIVIER and Vivien LEIGH with a screenplay by Graham GREENE. He published an autobiography, *Mind's Eye*, in 1973.

James Dean (James Byron; 1931–55) US actor, who starred in only three films during a single year's work in Hollywood; his mete-

oric career was cut short by a fatal car crash that enshrined him as an icon of doomed and rebellious youth.

Born on an Indiana farm, Dean attended the University of California and (briefly) the ACTORS' STUDIO in New York. After playing small parts in such films as *Has Anybody Seen My Gal?* (1951) and *Fixed Bayonets* (1952) and appearing on Broadway, Dean secured a contract with Warner Brothers, who chose to present him as a more sensitive version of Marlon BRANDO.

His three famous roles were all as troubled loners. In the CinemaScope EAST OF EDEN (1955), directed by Elia KAZAN, Dean played a disturbed adolescent from a farming region of California who discovers that his mother is running a brothel. In Nicholas RAY's REBEL WITHOUT A CAUSE (1955), the film that did most to establish his image, he played a teenager from an affluent but loveless family who takes up with self-destructive delinquents. In *Giant* (1956), directed by George STEVENS and starring Rock HUDSON and Elizabeth TAYLOR, Dean played a reclusive ranch worker who strikes oil. He was killed a week after the completion of the film.

Nearly 40 years after his death, Dean's potency as a symbol of youthful rebellion remains curiously undiminished. Teenage fashions have come and gone but Dean's sullen features continue to glower from advertisements and the bedroom walls of his adolescent fans. His image was even used by the National Westminster Bank in an attempt to persuade teenagers that opening a bank account is a cool and rebellious thing to do. In the 1980s a James Dean Foundation was set up by the actor's relatives to control the use of his name and image – even the imitation by others of his characteristic poses.

> Maybe he's lucky he died when he did. His performance now is so stereotyped. All the bad imitations have destroyed James Dean. ANTHONY HOPKINS, 1980.

Dearden, Basil (1911–71) British director and producer, known for his stark World War II films, as well as for a string of successful thrillers and comedies. Born at Westcliff-on-Sea, Essex, Dearden worked for a while as an actor before becoming assistant to Basil DEAN at EALING STUDIOS in the 1930s. His early films included several Will HAY comedies, notably the anti-Nazi satire *The Goose Steps Out* (1942).

Dearden used a DOCUMENTARY style for *The Bells Go Down* (1943), about wartime fire brigades, and *The Captive Heart* (1946), a thriller starring Michael REDGRAVE as a prisoner of war in Germany. Three years later he directed the important British police film *The Blue Lamp*, in which Jack Warner's P.C. Dixon is killed in a shoot-out with criminals. (Warner's character was later revived for the long-running television series *Dixon of Dock Green*.) Continuing in this semidocumentary vein, Dearden made *I Believe in You* (1952), a drama about probation officers mainly notable for introducing the 18-year-old starlet Joan COLLINS as a youthful offender. *The League of Gentlemen* (1960) was a comedy thriller about a robbery carried out by eight ex-army officers. In 1964 he co-produced the thriller *Woman of Straw*, starring Sean CONNERY, Gina LOLLOBRIGIDA, and Ralph RICHARDSON.

Dearden's last film was *The Man Who Haunted Himself* (1970), a story about a man who recovers from a car crash to find that his role in life has been taken over by a doppelganger figure. A few months later Dearden himself was killed in a motorway accident.

Death Wish (1974) Michael WINNER's violent US thriller, starring Charles BRONSON as a ruthless vigilante. The plot revolves around the taciturn Paul Kersey (Bronson), who determines to revenge himself upon the gang of New York muggers who have killed his wife and reduced his daughter to an invalid state. Although liberal critics deplored the suggestion that taking the law into one's own hands was the solution for street crime, audiences cheered enthusiastically each time Bronson blew away another piece of New York low-life. The inevitable sequel, *Death Wish II* (1981), was even more brutal, beginning with the rape and murder of the still-traumatized daughter at the hands of thugs in Los Angeles. The welter of murder, explosions, and general mayhem continued with *Death Wish III* (1985) and *Death Wish IV: The Crackdown* (1987), neither of which wandered too far away from the initial premise – that the public would not hesitate to side with anyone who had it in for street criminals, as long as he pursued his revenge with sufficient mercilessness. At the age of 70, Bronson starred in *Death Wish V* (1994).

There's no moralistic side to *Death Wish*; it's a pleasant romp.
MICHAEL WINNER.

de Broca, Philippe (1933–) French director known for his brisk, witty, and stylish comedies, several of which starred Jean-Pierre Cassel and Jean-Paul BELMONDO. His tongue-in-cheek South American adventure *That Man from Rio* (1964), in which stolen Aztec statuettes are traced to a jungle temple, has been compared favourably to SPIELBERG's similar *Raiders of the Lost Ark* (1981).

Born in Paris, de Broca attended the Technical School of Photography and Cinematography in that city before starting work as a documentary cameraman. In the early 1950s he worked as an assistant to such directors as Claude CHABROL and François TRUFFAUT before making his first feature *Les Jeux de l'amour* (1959), a comedy about a man (Cassel) who is unwilling to give his mistress a baby. Belmondo starred in *Cartouche* (1962), about a French Robin Hood figure, and in *That Man from Rio*. De Broca tried unsuccessfully to repeat the formula of the latter film with *Up to his Ears* (1965) and *Le Magnifique* (1974).

The whimsical *King of Hearts* (1966), in which Alan BATES outwits both the German and British armies during World War I, became a cult film in America. *Louize* (1972) was a serious film about a divorcée (Jeanne MOREAU) who falls for an Italian half her age. De Broca enjoyed another US success with the comedy thriller *Dear Inspector* (*Tendre Poulet*; 1977), in which a woman detective and a professor join forces to pursue a murderer. Subsequent films have included *Psy* (1980), *Louisiana* (1984), and *The Gypsy* (1985).

debuts While a few Hollywood stars have enjoyed spectacular overnight success with their first screen roles, most have made their debuts in tiny, forgettable, or wildly uncharacteristic roles. Indeed, instant stardom is an even rarer phenomenon than it appears to be. Although many would cite Orson WELLES in CITIZEN KANE (1941) and Dustin HOFFMAN in THE GRADUATE (1967) as examples of triumphant movie debuts, both had in fact made unnoticed appearances beforehand. Similarly, many stars who do achieve success with their first films have already made their names on TV or the stage; examples include Grace KELLY and Barbra STREISAND. Examples of genuine overnight successes would have to include Lauren BACALL in *To Have and Have Not* (1944), Warren BEATTY in *Splendor in the*

Grass (1961), and Kathleen TURNER in *Body Heat* (1982). At the opposite extreme are the unheralded debuts of John WAYNE in the campus drama *Brown of Harvard* (1926), Meryl STREEP as Jane FONDA's friend in *Julia* (1976), Jack NICHOLSON as a hood in Roger CORMAN's *Cry Baby Killer* (1958), and Clint EASTWOOD as a lab assistant in *Revenge of the Creature* (1955).

Stars to make their debuts as children include Bruce LEE, aged six, in *The Birth of Mankind* (1946), Liza MINNELLI, aged three, in *In The Good Old Summertime* (1949), and Juliet MILLS, aged one, in *In Which We Serve* (1941). Debuts made at an advanced age include that of Sydney GREENSTREET, who was 61 when he appeared in THE MALTESE FALCON.

When Paul NEWMAN's first film, *The Silver Chalice* (1955), was shown on television years later, he was embarrassed enough to place a newspaper advertisement reading "Paul Newman apologizes every night this week."

De Carlo, Yvonne (Peggy Yvonne Middleton; 1922–) Canadian star of the 1940s and 1950s, who mainly appeared in Westerns. Born in Vancouver, she performed as a child dancer before making her feature film debut in *Harvard Here I Come!* (1942) Her first starring role was in the Western *Salome, Where She Danced* (1945); after appearing in *Criss-Cross* (1948), a tense FILM NOIR with Burt LANCASTER, she returned to the Western genre in *Calamity Jane and Sam Bass* (1949) with Howard Duff and *Tomahawk* (1951) with Van HEFLIN.

In the early 1950s De Carlo appeared in a series of British comedies, co-starring with Peter USTINOV in *Hotel Sahara* (1951), with Alec GUINNESS in *The Captain's Paradise* (1953), and with David NIVEN in *Happy Ever After* (1954). Subsequent films included the DE MILLE epic THE TEN COMMANDMENTS (1956) and the Western farce *McLintock* (1963) with John WAYNE. In the mid 1960s she appeared as the ghoulish Morticia in the television comedy series *The Munsters* and the film spin-off *Munster Go Home* (1966). Her later films have included *Satan's Cheerleaders* (1977), *The Man with Bogart's Face* (1980), and *Flesh and Bullets* (1985).

deck Hollywood jargon for the floor of a studio.

Dee, Sandra (Alexandra Zuck; 1942–) Petite US star of the 1950s and 1960s, who competed with Annette Funicello and Tuesday Weld for the new teenage audience. For most of the 1960s she was married to the singer Bobby Darin, with whom she co-starred in *That Funny Feeling* (1965).

Born in New Jersey, Dee modelled and acted on television as a child; at the age of 14 she made her film debut in *Until They Sail* (1957), in which she played the young sister of Jean SIMMONS, Joan FONTAINE, and Piper Laurie. Her films usually centred on puppy-love between clean-living youngsters. She played the daughter of Rex HARRISON and Kay Kendall in the British comedy *The Reluctant Debutante* (1958), of Lana TURNER in the melodrama *Imitation of Life* (1959), and of James STEWART in the comedy *Take Her, She's Mine* (1963). Dee initiated one teenage series with the beach movie GIDGET (1959) and took over Debbie REYNOLDS's role in another with the sugary *Tammy Tell Me True* (1961) and *Tammy and the Doctor* (1963).

By the late 1960s Dee's sweet and virginal screen persona had come to seem an anachronism and her box-office appeal declined sharply. Since making the rather wierd horror film *The Dunwich Horror* (1970) her screen appearances have been mainly restricted to foreign work and guest appearances in such television series as *Fantasy Island* (1977).

deep focus A shot in which objects close to the camera and others far away from it are held in sharp focus at the same time. Masters of deep-field cinematography include Gregg TOLAND, best known for his work on WELLES's CITIZEN KANE (1941).

DEFA Deutsche Film Aktien Gesellschaft. The former state-owned film organization of the German Democratic Republic (East Germany), which controlled all production from its base at the BABELSBERG Film Studio in East Berlin. Following World War II left-wing film-makers in East Germany set up **Filmaktiv**, an organization intended to renew the German cinema, under the auspices of the Soviet military administration. The first production, a newsreel, was followed by documentaries and, in 1946, Germany's first post-war feature, Wolfgang Staudte's anti-Nazi film *The Murderers Are Among Us*. That same year Filmaktiv became DEFA and began an ambitious period despite poor facilities and equipment. By the end of the 1940s, however, it had fallen under the control of the Soviet Union's ministry of film production, which insisted on fewer entertainment films and more political dogma and also imposed strict CENSORSHIP. This guaranteed limited distribution outside East Germany and drove the more creative film-makers to the West. The scant international approval that the East German cinema retained was mostly reserved for its many straight documentaries and animated productions.

Following German reunification and the restructuring of state-run industries, DEFA remains in limbo, with day-to-day decisions being made by a privatization agency, True-hand. DEFA is to receive government funding for certain essential renovations but is then expected to become a holding company. Although the organization's equipment is outdated and in disrepair, DEFA could be a force in the German cinema of the future if private investment is secured.

de Havilland, Olivia (1916–) US actress of British parentage, the older sister of Joan FONTAINE. Born in Tokyo, she came to America with her family while still a child. In the 1930s de Havilland became a star playing opposite Errol FLYNN in a series of Warner Brothers films directed by Michael CURTIZ, the first being *Captain Blood* (1935), made when she was 19. She adored Flynn and complained that during love scenes he gazed at her hairline rather than her face. Flynn later confessed that he had loved Olivia, but for once in his life had felt too shy to pursue a woman.

Her most famous role was as Melanie Hamilton in SELZNICK'S GONE WITH THE WIND (1939), a part she obtained through her sister's intervention. When de Havilland asked Jack WARNER to release her for the production, he laughed and said, "It's going to be the biggest bust in town." One of her lesser-known contributions to the film was providing the voice-over for Scarlett's retching scene, when Vivien LEIGH could not muster the unladylike sound.

In 1946 de Havilland won an Oscar for *To Each His Own*, in which a middle-aged woman meets her illegitimate son after many years of separation. In her acceptance speech she set a record by thanking 27 people. Two years later she was nominated for her performance as an asylum inmate in *The Snake Pit*, while in 1949 she

was again named Best Actress for *The Heiress*, a Henry James adaptation in which she appeared with Montgomery CLIFT and Ralph RICHARDSON.

Later films included *My Cousin Rachel* (1952) with Richard BURTON, the medical melodrama *Not as a Stranger* (1955) with Robert MITCHUM and Frank SINATRA, and *Hush, Hush, Sweet Charlotte* (1964), in which she played Bette DAVIS's evil cousin.

De Laurentiis, Dino (1919–) Italian producer, whose companies have enjoyed numerous international successes, although he himself exerts little creative influence on the films produced.

The son of a Naples pasta manufacturer, De Laurentiis studied at Rome's Centro Sperimentale di Cinematografia while working in any casual cinema job he could find: in a few years he graduated from extra to propman, unit manager, and assistant director. In 1941 he founded a production company, Real Cine, in Turin. After serving in World War II, he returned to producing and in 1949 won universal acclaim for the NEOREALIST *Bitter Rice*, about a thief's meeting with a girl in the rice fields of the Po Valley. This powerful film launched the career of the actress Silvana Mangano, who became De Laurentiis's wife a year later. In 1950 he and Carlo PONTI founded the Ponti-De Laurentiis production company, which during its seven-year existence was responsible for such box-office hits as FELLINI'S LA STRADA (1954) and *The Nights of Cabiria* (1956), both of which won the Oscar for Best Foreign Film. Other impressive films of the 1950s included the Kirk DOUGLAS epic *Ulysses* (1954) and *War and Peace* (1956), Paramount's first European co-production.

After this partnership dissolved, De Laurentiis built **Dinocittà**, a sprawling studio complex near Rome, which saw the making of several successful epics, including *Barabbas* (1961), John HUSTON's *The Bible* (1966), and *Waterloo* (1970). When the Italian film industry began to decline in the early 1970s he sold the studios to the government and moved to Beverly Hills, where his De Laurentiis Entertainment Group now has its headquarters. His US debut was *The Valachi Papers* (1972), a violent Mafia thriller starring Charles BRONSON. Subsequent Hollywood films have included *Serpico* (1973) with Al PACINO; a remake of KING KONG (1976); the *Serpent's Egg* (1977), one of Ingmar BERGMAN's few films in

English; Miloš FORMAN's *Ragtime* (1981), a $25-million flop about a Black pianist who becomes an urban terrorist; the comic-strip inspired *Conan the Barbarian* (1982) with Arnold SCHWARZENEGGER; David LYNCH's *Dune* (1985) and *Blue Velvet* (1986); and *Dracula's Widow* (1987).

Delfont, Bernard   *See* GRADE, LEW.

Del Ruth, Roy   (1895–1961) US director who began in silent comedies, moved into sound with a series of big-budget musicals, and ended his career directing B-MOVIES. Born in Philadelphia, Del Ruth worked as a journalist before writing scripts for Mack SENNETT and directing Ben Turpin and others in a series of slapstick shorts. In 1925 he moved to Warner Brothers, where he worked on the early Myrna LOY films and such comedies as *Ham and Eggs at the Front* (1927).

Del Ruth's career really took off when his friend Darryl F. ZANUCK became head of production at Warner Brothers and assigned him to musicals, including *The Desert Song* (1929), Hollywood's first sound operetta. He also helped to develop James CAGNEY's tough-guy image in such films as the hotel comedy *Blonde Crazy* (British title *Larceny Lane*; 1931). Between 1930 and 1933 he made 20 pictures.

In the later 1930s Del Ruth directed such spectacular MGM musicals as *Born to Dance* (1936), starring James STEWART (amazingly) as a singing and dancing sailor, and *Broadway Rhythm* (1944). He also directed William BENDIX as the baseball legend in *The Babe Ruth Story* (1948). However, after making several Doris DAY musicals in the 1950s he was only given such second features as *The Alligator People* (1959) and *Why Must I Die?* (1960).

De Mille, Cecil B.   (1881–1959) US director, who earned the title **the Greatest Showman on Earth**. The son of an Episcopalian minister, De Mille worked as a stage actor before deciding to travel West and make films with Jesse L. Lasky and Samuel Goldfish (later GOLDWYN). He intended to film his first feature in Flagstaff, Arizona, but disliked the weather and headed for the Los Angeles suburb of HOLLYWOOD, at that time filled with orange groves. De Mille's *The Squaw Man* (1913), about an English lord who marries a Red Indian, was Hollywood's first major film.

During the World War I period De Mille made over 20 films for FAMOUS PLAYERS-Lasky, the company that eventually became PARAMOUNT PICTURES. When Mary PICKFORD demanded a rise in 1919, De Mille persuaded the corporation to let her go, saying he would make films with unknowns. In the next four years his productions cost a total of $1,416,365 and grossed $9,719,666.

In the 1920s De Mille became known for his risqué sex comedies, which created the popular image of the 'Woman of the World'. He was the first to film scenes in bathrooms and bedrooms. His formulaic plots usually involved husbands or wives who strayed briefly before returning to the fold; the censors did not interfere because De Mille's lovers were always married men or women. The films were careful to maintain a moral façade, emphasized by such titles as *Don't Change Your Husband* (1919), *Why Change Your Wife?* (1920) and *Forbidden Fruit* (1921). Another De Mille ruse was to go back in history as a pretext for showing scenes of moral decadence; in *Male and Female* (1919), for instance, Gloria SWANSON, playing a woman in love with her butler, dreams that she is in ancient Babylon.

De Mille began to make the religious EPICS for which he is now best known in the 1920s but did not concentrate on the genre until later. As his brother William observed:

> Having attended to the underclothes, bathrooms, and matrimonial irregularities of his fellow citizens he now began to consider their salvation.

The original THE TEN COMMANDMENTS (1923) combined the biblical story with a contemporary tale of sin and redemption, while *King of Kings* (1927) was one of the first movies to portray CHRIST. *The Sign of the Cross* (1932), a tale of 1st-century Christianity, was enlivened by some spectacular orgy scenes. De Mille dominated the epic genre into the post-war era with such films as *Samson and Delilah* (1949), starring Victor MATURE and Hedy LAMARR. Perhaps his most famous epic was the sound remake of *The Ten Commandments* (1956), featuring an all-star cast headed by Charlton HESTON, Yul BRYNNER, and Edward G. ROBINSON. The film, which required some 12,000 extras and 15,000 animals, included such memorable special-effects sequences as the burning bush and the parting of the Red Sea.

> I have brought a certain sense of beauty and luxury into everyday existence; all

jokes about ornate bathrooms and de luxe boudoirs aside, I have done my bit toward lifting the level of daily life.

CECIL B. DE MILLE.

Demme, Jonathan (1944–) US director. Born in New York State, Demme abandoned a career as a vet to enter the film industry in the 1960s. After a period making promotional trailers, he sold a script, *The Hot Box*, to Roger CORMAN in 1972. The 'king of exploitation' also gave him the chance to direct; his debut feature, the women's prison drama *Caged Heat* (1974), was followed by *Crazy Mama* (1975), about a mother-daughter crime spree, and the revenge tale *Fighting Mad* (1976).

Demme's penchant for eccentric characters emerged more fully in *Citizens Band* (1977), a latter-day SCREWBALL COMEDY starring Paul Le Mat, and the delightful *Melvin and Howard* (1980), with the same actor as a nobody whose life is transformed by a chance encounter with Howard HUGHES (Jason Robards). Following the failure of the HITCHCOCK pastiche *Last Embrace* (1979) and the romance *Swing Shift* (1984), Demme directed a brace of concert films – *Stop Making Sense* (1984), featuring Talking Heads, and *Swimming to Cambodia* (1986), a record of Spalding Gray's one-man show.

Demme returned to the mainstream with *Something Wild* (1986), a fusion of screwball comedy and FILM NOIR that failed to hide the joins. *Married to the Mob* (1988), starring Michelle PFEIFFER as a Mafia widow who wants to flee the family, was a more successful blend of comedy and crime.

Demme's next film, THE SILENCE OF THE LAMBS (1991), was a major departure. Based on Thomas Harris's best-seller, the film followed FBI agent Clarice Starling (Jodie FOSTER) as she tracks down a mass murderer with the assistance of another killer, Hannibal Lecter (Anthony HOPKINS). The film became only the third in Oscar history (after IT HAPPENED ONE NIGHT and ONE FLEW OVER THE CUCKOO'S NEST) to scoop the 'big four' awards for Picture, Direction, Actor, and Actress. Despite its critical and commercial success, *The Silence of the Lambs* was attacked by some gay groups for its depiction of the murderous Jame Gumb. Demme's follow-up feature, *Philadelphia* (1993), was seen by many as an act of atonement. The first Hollywood blockbuster to tackle the subject of AIDS, it was nevertheless criticized for shying away from the gay relationship between

lawyer Tom HANKS and his lover Antonio Banderas. Demme countered by stressing the importance of bringing the picture's message to the widest possible audience:

> I feel that film directors are at least 1% anthropologists, and that they have a responsibility to reflect something about what the country is like. I'm *wallowing* in that with this film. It's rare that you get a chance to do a movie about something important.

Arguably, his sharpest portrait of contemporary America to date is *Cousin Bobby* (1982), a 16mm documentary about his long-lost cousin, an Episcopalian minister fighting poverty, prejudice, and drug-addiction in Harlem.

Demy, Jacques (1931–90) French director, best known for his surrealistic musical fantasies. As a teenager, Demy made simple animated films in the attic of his father's garage in Nantes. He subsequently studied art and film before making a number of shorts in the mid 1950s. Success came with his first full-length feature, *Lola* (1960), a love story about the reunion of an American and a French cabaret singer (Anouk AIMÉE). The film was admired for both its innovative camerawork and its emotional complexity. Like many of Demy's later works, it was shot in a lyrical style revealing the influence of BRESSON, COCTEAU, OPHÜLS, and VON STERNBERG.

Bay of Angels (1962), starring Jeanne MOREAU as a compulsive gambler, once again testified to Demy's inventiveness; the film uses the games of chance in the Nice casino as a metaphor for the element of luck in his characters' lives. Perhaps the best known of all his films is the charming fantasy *The Umbrellas of Cherbourg* (1964), in which Demy turned a drab French seaside town into a Hollywood-style setting for high romance (ultimately deflated). The bittersweet story concerns the young Genevieve (Catherine DENEUVE), an assistant in an umbrella shop, who on discovering that she is pregnant decides to marry a wealthy admirer rather than to await her lover's return from the army. All the dialogue is sung, to a score by Michel Legrand. The movie was named Best Film at Cannes and received six Oscar nominations, including Best Director. This success brought US backing for *The Young Girls of Rochefort* (1967), another Legrand musical, in which Gene

KELLY starred opposite Deneuve. The film was criticized for poor choreography.

Few of Demy's later films equalled the success of his 1960s work. In 1970 he went to America to make *Model Shop*, in which he revived the character of Lola, now a Los Angeles call girl. He then returned to Europe and made a series of unpretentious comedies and fairytale adaptations before turning to more serious themes with *A Room in the Town* (1982), a sombre musical set against the background of a dockers' strike. Another all-singing piece, it features a scene in which a character cuts his throat while singing. *Parking* (1985) was an unsuccessful rock opera based on the story of Orpheus and Eurydice.

In 1962 Demy married the film director **Agnès Varda** (1928–), whose work includes *Le Bonheur* (1965) and the highly praised *Vagabond* (*Sans toi ni loi*; 1985). In 1991 she released *Jacquot de Nantes*, a tender portrait of her husband's younger years, filmed mainly in the Nantes garage where he grew up and made his first shorts.

Deneuve, Catherine (Catherine Dorléac; 1943–) French actress, who came to international stardom in the late 1960s; a beautiful blonde, she was often cast in fragile or aloof roles. Deneuve had a child by Roger VADIM in 1963 and another by Marcello MASTROIANNI in 1972; in the later 1960s she was married to the British photographer David Bailey.

Born in Paris, the daughter of the actors Maurice Dorléac and Renée Deneuve, she made her screen debut at the age of 13 using her mother's maiden name. She first came to notice as the lead in Jacques DEMY's musical fantasy *The Umbrellas of Cherbourg* (1964). Four years later Deneuve and her real-life sister, Françoise Dorléac (1941– 67), played sisters in Demy's *The Young Girls of Rochefort* (1967); Dorléac was killed in a car accident later that year. Deneuve refused to appear in a third Demy musical, *A Room in the Town* (1982), when she learned that the director intended to dub her singing (*see* GHOSTING).

Deneuve came to worldwide attention in Roman POLANSKI's British film *Repulsion* (1965), in which she played a frigid psychopathic killer, and enhanced her somewhat enigmatic image in Luis BUÑUEL's BELLE DE JOUR (1967), in which she appeared as a middle-class housewife who plays at prostitution. The critic Dilys Powell commented on Deneuve's ability to look both "chilly and subterraneously debauched" at the same time. Her Hollywood films include Robert ALDRICH's *Hustle* (1975), in which she played a call girl who corrupts policeman Burt REYNOLDS. Of that part, she said; "I know girls like this. I understand them ...One is kept by a man and then discarded and then the process begins again. There's a market for that."

Later films have included TRUFFAUT's *The Last Metro* (1980), in which she shelters a Resistance fighter (Gérard DEPARDIEU), Tony Scott's *The Hunger* (1983), in which she played a bisexual vampire, *The White Queen* (1991), and *Indochine* (1992), which won the Oscar for Best Foreign Film.

In the late 1960s she replaced Brigitte BARDOT as the model for the head on France's coins.

Denham Studios A studio complex on the outskirts of north-west London that was a centre for film-making in Britain during the 1930s and 1940s. The studios were opened in 1936 and played a major part in the revitalization of the national film industry. This success was largely the result of the dynamism of Alexander KORDA, who filmed many of his lavish costume dramas at Denham, chiefly under the auspices of his own company, London Films. Other well-known movies made at these studios included the futuristic *Things to Come* (1936), the first film made there, *Gaslight* (1936), OLIVIER's *Henry V* (1944), and Carol REED's thriller *Odd Man Out* (1947). Among other landmarks, the studios made the first TECHNICOLOR film in the British cinema. After being taken over by the RANK ORGANIZATION, their use declined and they were finally closed in 1953, when activity was concentrated instead upon Pinewood Studios nearby.

De Niro, Robert (1943–) US actor, often regarded as the natural successor to Marlon BRANDO. A dedicated exponent of METHOD ACTING, he is famous for the startling way in which he changes his appearance from one film to the next. In 1981 his habit of disguise led to his arrest as a terrorist suspect in Rome. Although best known for playing gangsters and tough-guys he has also appeared in comedy and character roles. The director Bernardo BERTOLUCCI has described De Niro as "a very sensitive and probably neurotic person."

The son of two artists, he was born in New York's Greenwich Village and appeared in off-Broadway plays before making his film debut in Marcel CARNÉ's *Trois Chambres à Manhattan* (1966). His first sizable role came in Brian DE PALMA's *Greetings* (1968), about a young man's attempts to avoid the draft. However, De Niro owes his rather downbeat screen image mainly to his seven films for director Martin SCORSESE, the first being MEAN STREETS (1973), in which he portrayed a small-time hood. In TAXI DRIVER, his second film for Scorsese, De Niro gave a mesmerizing performance as Travis Bickle, a Vietnam veteran turned violent avenger. The film established the reputation of both actor and director.

His preparations for his film roles are legendary. Before playing the young Vito Corleone in THE GODFATHER, PART II (1974), he visited Sicily and had natives read his lines (almost all of which were in Italian dialect) into a tape recorder. The performance earned him the Oscar as Best Supporting Actor. For Scorsese's RAGING BULL (1980), based on the life of the boxer Jake LaMotta, he worked out in a gym to play the young fighter and then put on 60 pounds to age. This time his Oscar was for Best Actor. While making Scorsese's *The King of Comedy* (1982) De Niro refused to eat lunch with co-star Jerry LEWIS because their characters were at odds in the story.

De Niro's other films have included Michael CIMINO's Vietnam-War epic *The Deer Hunter* (1978), the sprawling crime saga *Once Upon a Time in America* (1984), Roland JOFFE's *The Mission* (1985), about Jesuit priests in South America, and De Palma's *The Untouchables* (1987), in which he played Al Capone. He has continued his collaboration with Scorsese in the gangster movie *GoodFellas* (1990) and a brutal remake of the thriller *Cape Fear* (1991). Other recent films include *Awakenings* (1990), *Guilty by Suspicion* (1991), and *Night and the City* (1992). He founded his own production company, TriBeca, in 1989 and directed his first film, *A Bronx Tale*, in 1993. A year later he appeared as the Creature in *Mary Shelley's Frankenstein*, directed by Kenneth BRANAGH.

[Being] a Hollywood star is death as far as acting is concerned. I don't want people to recognize me in the streets. I don't want to do what real stars have to do – repeat themselves in film after film, always being themselves.

ROBERT DE NIRO: *Screen International*, May 1976.

De Palma, Brian (1944–) Controversial US director, whose films have been widely criticized for graphic and gratuitous violence, particularly towards women. In his early career De Palma was usually associated with the so-called MOVIE BRATS, a group of young directors whose work shows them to have been steeped in Hollywood history (the others were Steven SPIELBERG, Martin SCORSESE, Francis Ford COPPOLA, and George LUCAS). Indeed, his rather derivative style has often been remarked upon; many of his films contain scenes and cinematography bearing a close similarity to work by HITCHCOCK in particular.

De Palma's first feature, *The Wedding Party* (1963), was made while he was still at college and financed by another student. No distributor was found for the film, which included an appearance by the then totally unknown Robert DE NIRO. After moving to New York, De Palma directed *Murder á la Mode* (1967), a Hitchcock pastiche that found a limited release. The satirical *Greetings* (1968) fared better, allowing De Palma to finance *Hi Mom!* (1969), a black comedy about voyeurism and pornography; both films starred De Niro.

When De Palma's first attempt at directing in Hollywood, the comedy *Get to Know Your Rabbit* (1970), attracted no attention from distributors, he returned to New York to make *Sisters* (1973), the first of a series of low-budget shockers. He continued in this vein with *Phantom of Paradise* (1974), a new version of the *Phantom of the Opera* story; *Obsession* (1976), a gruesome tale involving incest and necrophilia; *Carrie* (1976), a successful film based on the popular Stephen King horror novel; and *The Fury* (1978). Although *Dressed to Kill* (1980), a story of misogynistic violence that drew heavily on PSYCHO, appalled some critics, its technical brilliance could hardly be denied. This was equally true of *Blow Out* (1981), a fascinating reworking of ANTONIONI's BLOW-UP, and *Scarface* (1983), an ultra-violent GANGSTER movie starring Al PACINO. By contrast *Body Double* (1984), a particularly brutal piece in which a woman is attacked with an electric drill, found few defenders.

De Palma's work in the later 1980s and early 1990s has been more diverse. *Wise Guys* (1984) was a zany comedy starring Danny DEVITO, while *The Untouchables*

(1987) was a highly praised gangster film in which De Niro gave a bravura performance as Al Capone. While both this film and *Casualties of War* (1989), a Vietnam story starring Michael J. FOX, were undeniably bloody, their use of violence seemed both more sophisticated and more responsible than some of De Palma's earlier work. After the failure of *The Bonfire of the Vanities* (1990), a much-hyped but badly misjudged interpretation of the novel by Tom Wolfe, De Palma returned to thrillers with *Raising Cain* (1992) and *Carlito's Way* (1993).

Depardieu, Gérard (1948–) Burly French leading man, whose versatility in over 70 film roles has won him recognition as perhaps the finest film actor of recent decades. His appearance has been compared to a "handsome truck".

Depardieu had an unsettled youth that included a spell as a vagabond and petty thief. His own accounts of his background tend to be highly coloured; he has claimed that both his grandmothers were witches, his mother was a medium, and that he was raised by prostitutes. He also claims to have lost the power of speech for a long period during his teens, regaining it only by reading French Romantic poetry. He eventually went to gaol for stamping on a gendarme's hat and credits a prison psychiatrist with pointing him towards an acting career. Of these early experiences he has commented:

> Judges, juries, prison, and probation – they sharpen the imagination. You have to improvise at a moment's notice.

After studies at the Ecole d'Art Dramatique de Jean Laurent Cochet, Depardieu began to appear in minor film roles in the early 1970s. He first came to prominence starring as a loutish young criminal in Bertrand BLIER's *Les Valseuses* (1974). The two men have since worked together on *Get Out Your Handkerchiefs* (1978), in which Depardieu played a boorish husband who hires lovers for his wife, *Buffet froid* (1979), in which he played a psychotic, and the popular black comedies *Evening Dress* (1986), *Trop belle pour toi* (1988), and *Merci la vie* (1991). In the 1980s Depardieu was also closely associated with the films of Maurice PIALAT, appearing in the bleak love story *Loulou* (1980), *Police* (1985), and the acclaimed *Under Satan's Sun* (1987), in which he played a troubled priest.

Depardieu's other roles have included Robert DE NIRO's peasant friend in BERTOLUCCI's *1900* (1976), a mysterious stranger who may or may not be a returning prodigal in *The Return of Martin Guerre* (1982), a palaeontologist beloved by Sigourney WEAVER in *A Woman or Two* (1985), a hunchback in *Jean de Florette* (1986), the film that sealed his international fame, the sculptor Rodin in *Camille Claudel* (1989), a French immigrant in America in *Green Card* (1990), his first English-language film, the title role in *Cyrano de Bergerac* (1990), and Christopher Columbus in Ridley SCOTT's *The Conquest of Paradise* (1992). His most recent films include the US comedy *My Father, the Hero* (1993), an adaptation of Zola's *Germinal* (1993), and *Colonel Chabert* (1994).

Many Hollywood insiders believe that Depardieu would have won the Oscar for *Cyrano de Bergerac* had it not been for some foolish comments printed in *Time* magazine. In an interview dug up from years earlier he apparently claimed to have "assisted in several rapes" as a young man, including one when he was only nine. "The girls wanted to be raped", he said, "violence isn't committed by those who do the act but by the victims, the ones who permit it to happen." He subsequently disclaimed the remarks, saying he had been mistranslated. Despite the power of many of his French-language performances, his hesitant command of English has so far prevented his Hollywood career from taking off.

> To be an actor, it's not sufficient to make gestures, recite texts. It's also to provoke, to molest, to forget yourself, risk everything. One must see, listen, live – and go! And be good, bad, or bloody ridiculous.
> GÉRARD DEPARDIEU, 1972.

De Santis, Giuseppe (1917–) Italian director, screenwriter, and critic. De Santis studied literature and philosophy before enrolling at Rome's Centro Sperimentale de Cinematografia. He entered the film world as a critic for the magazine *Cinema*, where his calls for radical change in the style and content of Italian films anticipated many features of post-war NEOREALISM. He co-scripted *Obsessione* (1942), Luchino VISCONTI's first feature film, and worked as an assistant to several directors before making his own feature debut with *Tragic Hunt* (1947), which highlighted post-war Italy's desperate social conditions. He became famous with his second feature, the

NEOREALIST *Bitter Rice* (1949), starring Silvana Mangano as a girl who tries to steal from a thief (Vittorio Gassmann) as an antidote to the daily tedium of her life. A bleaker film was *Rome Eleven O'Clock* (1951), about the tragic collapse of a staircase under the weight of unemployed girls applying for a secretarial position. After the passing of the neorealist era, the director made a number of gentle films about personal relationships, notably *A Husband for Anna* (1953) and *Days of Love* (1954). Subsequent films, which have aroused comparatively little interest, include the Soviet-Italian co-production *Italiano brava gente* (1964) and *Un Apprezzato professionista di sicuro avvenire* (1972).

De Sica, Vittorio (1902–74) Italian director and actor, whose output ranged from stark NEOREALISM to slick commercial comedies. In the early 1960s he developed the career of Sophia LOREN, who once described the director as "my drama school." He himself appeared as an actor in about 150 films.

After a career as a matinée idol in the 1920s and 1930s, De Sica moved into directing with the comedies *Maddalena zero in condotta* (1941) and *Teresa Venerdì* (1941). These were followed by the neorealist *The Children are Watching Us* (1942), the first of several collaborations with the scriptwriter Cesare Zavattini (1902–89). The film introduced the style that characterized much of De Sica's subsequent work, being shot on location and employing nonprofessional actors to achieve a greater naturalistic impact.

Of his subsequent collaborations with Zavattini the most influential were *Shoeshine* (1946), about two teenage black marketeers who fall foul of the law in wartime Italy, and the classic BICYCLE THIEVES (1948), which won the Oscar for Best Foreign Film. The film provides a poignant examination of the injustices of Italian society, again seen through a child's eyes, as a young boy searches for the stolen bicycle that his father relies upon to do his job. Other films from this period included *Miracle in Milan* (1950), a fantasy in which the poor rise up against their oppressors, and *Umberto D* (1952), about a poverty-stricken pensioner who takes up begging.

During the 1950s and 1960s De Sica abandoned neorealism and concentrated upon more commercial films featuring professional performers. The first of these was *The Indiscretion of an American Wife* (1953), directed for David O. SELZNICK with Montgomery CLIFT and Jennifer JONES in the leads. De Sica also acted in comedies with Gina LOLLOBRIGIDA and Loren while turning out such hits as *Yesterday, Today and Tomorrow* (1963), a trilogy of stories starring Loren and Marcello MASTROIANNI that won the Oscar for Best Foreign Film.

More serious were *Two Women* (*La Ciociara*; 1960), about a mother (Loren) and daughter (Eleonara Brown) fleeing the war in northern Italy, and the Oscar-winning *The Garden of the Finzi-Continis* (1971), about the persecution of the Jews in Fascist Italy.

detail shot An EXTREME CLOSE-UP that reveals certain details of an object, such as a rope that is about to break, or something on an actor's body, such as a scar or tattoo.

detectives The private investigator has been a popular film protagonist since the earliest days of the cinema; the first to appear on screen was probably Nick Carter, who featured in a series of French shorts from 1910. The most celebrated of all detectives, Sherlock HOLMES, appeared in a number of silent shorts but only became a memorable screen presence when played by Arthur Wontner in the 1930s and Basil RATHBONE in the 1940s. The contemporary private eye was popularized by two series of the 1930s, the Charlie CHAN films, in which Warner Oland played the oriental detective, and the light-hearted THIN MAN series, featuring William POWELL and Myrna LOY as the married sleuths Nick and Nora Charles. In the 1940s George SANDERS sustained two series as the Saint and the FALCON.

Despite the popularity of these films, the enduring image of the hard-boiled laconic investigator was chiefly created by Humphrey BOGART's performances as Dashiell Hammett's Sam Spade in THE MALTESE FALCON (1941) and Raymond CHANDLER's Philip MARLOWE in THE BIG SLEEP (1946). The Chandler adaptation *Farewell My Lovely* (1944), in which Dick POWELL played Marlowe, set new standards of seediness and violence and helped to create the new genre of FILM NOIR.

The 1950s saw sleuths ranging from Mickey Spillane's hardened detective Mike Hammer, who appeared in such films as *My Gun is Quick* (1957), to G. K. Chesterton's benevolent priest *Father Brown* (US title *The Detective*; 1954), as played by Alec GUINNESS. Margaret RUTHERFORD carried Agatha Christie's nosy Miss MARPLE through a series of films in the 1960s, while Angela LANSBURY took on the role in *The Mirror Crack'd* (1980). The most highly acclaimed private-eye film of recent decades is probably POLANSKI's CHINATOWN (1974), in which Jack NICHOLSON starred as Los Angeles detective J. J. Gittes. More recently the entire genre was spoofed in Steve MARTIN's *Dead Men Don't Wear Plaid* (1982), which incorporates numerous EXCERPTS from classic crime films of the 1940s.

Police detectives have also proved popular, but more so on television than in the cinema. The big screen's most popular police investigator is Christie's Hercule POIROT, who has been played by such stars as Peter USTINOV in *Death on the Nile* (1978) and Albert FINNEY in *Murder on the Orient Express* (1974). The police genre has been sent up in the long-running PINK PANTHER series, starring Peter SELLERS as the monumentally incompetent Inspector Clouseau and in *The Naked Gun* (1988) and its sequels, starring Leslie NIELSEN as the maladroit Inspector Drebin.

deus ex machina (Lat. god out of a machine) In the plot of a film, play, or novel, a sudden and implausible turn of events that provides an easy solution to the protagonist's main problem. In TOM JONES (1963), for instance, the hero escapes the scaffold by a last-minute revelation of his noble birth. The *deus ex machina* was a popular convention of the silent serials, when someone left in a CLIFFHANGER situation one week would be saved with ridiculous ease at the start of the next episode (*see* CHEATER CUT). An extreme instance of the *deus ex machina* is the ending that shows a person awakening after having dreamed the entire plot, as in the Fritz LANG thriller *The Woman in the Window* (1944). The term derives from the ancient Greek theatre, in which the *deus ex machina* was traditionally a god who descended from Mount Olympus to right human wrongs.

devil, the The cinema has portrayed Satan in various guises, sometimes as a genuinely evil force but more often as a figure of harmless fantasy. Screen versions of the Faust story include the silent German film *Faust* (1926), with Emil JANNINGS as the evil one, and *Dr Faustus* (1967), with Andreas Teu-

ber as Mephistopholes and Richard BURTON in the title role. Of the many updated versions of the legend probably the most notable is *All That Money Can Buy* (1941), in which a hungry farmer succumbs to the temptings of 'Mr Scratch' (brilliantly played by Walter HUSTON). Other actors to appear as the fiend include Laird Cregar in the whimsical *Heaven Can Wait* (1943), Claude RAINS in *Angel on My Shoulder* (1946), in which Satan sends the spirit of a dead gangster back to earth to make mischief, Vincent PRICE in *The Story of Mankind* (1957), Donald PLEASENCE in the biblical epic *The Greatest Story Ever Told* (1965), Ralph RICHARDSON in *Tales From the Crypt* (1972), and Jack NICHOLSON as a lascivious devil in *The Witches of Eastwick* (1987). In *Oh God, You Devil* (1984) the veteran comic George Burns played both God and the devil, sometimes, through trick photography, in the same frame.

Although unseen, Satan is a potent presence in such occult shockers as ROSEMARY'S BABY (1968), THE EXORCIST (1973), and *The Omen* (1976).

DeVito, Danny (1944–) Short, plump, and balding US actor, who made his name playing irascible sharp-tongued characters. After an early career as a hairdresser, he studied at AADA in New York and began to work in the theatre. In 1971 he played a mental patient in the off-Broadway production of ONE FLEW OVER THE CUCKOO'S NEST, a role that led to his being cast in Miloš FORMAN's film version in 1975. Three years later Jack NICHOLSON, the star of *Cuckoo's Nest*, asked DeVito to appear with himself and John BELUSHI in the comedy Western *Goin' South* (1978).

In the late 1970s DeVito became well known to the public through his appearances in the television series *Taxi* (1978–83), in which he played the abrasive Louis. He then made a successful return to the cinema in *Terms of Endearment* (1983). The same year brought his first major film role, that of the snarling villain Ralph in the action comedy *Romancing the Stone*, with Michael DOUGLAS and Kathleen TURNER. He subsequently reprised the role in the sequel *The Jewel of the Nile* (1985). In 1986 he starred in *Ruthless People*, as the odious husband of loud-mouthed Bette MIDLER, who is overjoyed when she is kidnapped.

During the later 1980s DeVito enjoyed further box-office success with the comedies

Tin Men (1987) and *Twins* (1988), in which he plays the non-identical twin brother of Arnold SCHWARZENEGGER. He also made his debut as a director with *Throw Momma From the Train* (1987), a black farce in which he starred as a put-upon middle-aged bachelor who fantasizes about having his domineering mother assassinated by a stranger (Billy Crystal). Equally black was his next venture as a director, *The Wars of the Roses* (1989), a harsh comedy of marital breakdown starring Michael Douglas and Kathleen Turner. DeVito himself gave an uncharacteristically restrained performance as the narrator-lawyer.

DeVito's most recent films have included *Batman Returns* (1992), in which he played the Penguin, the biopic *Hoffa* (1992), which he also directed, and the army comedy *Renaissance Man* (1994).

DGA Directors Guild of America. An organization for professional film directors, founded in 1936; it now includes television directors amongst its members. The Guild provides directors with support in disputes with producers or stars; in extreme cases it can instruct members to boycott certain employers, as it did in 1958, when Samuel GOLDWYN was boycotted for firing Rouben MAMOULIAN from *Porgy and Bess*.

diagonal action Action that flows from one corner of the screen, through the central area, to the opposite corner. This type of movement is thought to enhance the impact of the action, since the subject moves both up or down the screen as well as across it. Examples include the helicopter shots of the fox-hunting chase in TOM JONES (1963).

dial (1) To adjust the sound level during filming. (2) To remove extraneous noise from the audio recording subsequently. A sound editor can *dial out* anything ranging from a cough to a jet flying overhead.

dialogue Any words spoken by characters in a film.

> For dialogue to be credible it must have enough faltering uncertainty – or foolish certainty – to be *lifelike*. This is why the *best written* dialogue will often *sound* like the *best improvised* dialogue – and may be mistaken for such by people who don't know about such things.
>
> TERRY SOUTHERN, screenwriter, 1972.

Perhaps the most famous line in movies is Clark GABLE's parting insult to Vivien LEIGH in GONE WITH THE WIND (1939); "Frankly, my dear, I don't give a damn" (*see under* DAMN). The most frequently used line in US films has been "Let's get outta here", found in 81% of 350 features dating from between 1938 and 1985. Audiences can have faulty memories concerning dialogue: Humphrey BOGART never said "Play it again, Sam" in CASABLANCA (1942) nor did Charles BOYER say "Come with me to the Casbah" in *Algiers* (1938).

dialogue coach A person hired to coach actors in the saying of their lines, paying particular attention to speech rhythms and any accents required. For GONE WITH THE WIND, the dialogue coach Susan Myrick made Clark GABLE repeat the phrase "Ah cain't affoahd a foah-doah Foahd" ("I can't afford a four-door Ford") to improve his Southern accent but never eliminated his Midwestern 'r'. Although frequently employed in the early sound era, full-time dialogue coaches are now a rarity.

Dickens, Charles (1812–70) British novelist, whose works have been a popular source for film adaptations since the early days of the cinema. Dickens's bustling theatrical plots and larger than-life characters have always appealed to filmgoers, who also seem to be endlessly fascinated by the shortcomings of the Victorian age.

Thomas Bentley's silent version of *Oliver Twist* (1912) was probably the cinema's first serious adaptation of a novel. Dickens adaptations boomed in America after 1934, when the Production Code (*see* HAYS CODE) made the realistic treatment of contemporary subjects more difficult. David O. SELZNICK was certainly influenced by the Code when he hired George CUKOR to direct *David Copperfield* (1934), the film that gave W. C. FIELDS his favourite role of Mr Micawber. Selznick followed this success with the classic *A Tale of Two Cities* a year later, while MGM produced the first of many versions of *A Christmas Carol* in 1938.

The most highly regarded of all Dickens adaptations is probably David LEAN's GREAT EXPECTATIONS (1946), which starred John MILLS and gave both Alec GUINNESS and Jean SIMMONS their first important film roles. Two years later, Lean adapted and directed *Oliver Twist* (1948) with Guinness as Fagin and Anthony Newley as the Artful Dodger. Despite the brilliance of both the acting and the direction, the film failed badly in America, where the depiction of Fagin was denounced as anti-Semitic.

Subsequent adaptations have included Rank's *A Tale of Two Cities* (1958) with Dirk BOGARDE, the Oscar-winning musical *Oliver!* (1968), directed by Carol REED with Ron Moody as Fagin, and Joseph Hardy's *Great Expectations* (1974), with an all-star cast headed by Sarah MILES, Michael YORK, and James MASON. Guinness reappeared in Ronald NEAME's *Scrooge* (1970), a musical starring Albert FINNEY, and in Christine Edzard's two-part *Little Dorrit* (1987), a lovingly detailed recreation of Dickens's London. Recent years have seen two further adaptations of the Scrooge story, *Scrooged* (1988), in which the action is updated to contemporary New York, and *The Muppets' Christmas Carol* (1992). *See also* CHRISTMAS.

Dieterle, William (Wilhelm Dieterle; 1893–1972) German director and actor, mainly remembered for his BIOPICs and for the classic RKO version of THE HUNCHBACK OF NOTRE DAME. Dieterle acted with Max Reinhardt's Berlin theatre company before beginning to direct silent films; these included the controversial *Sex in Chains* (1928), about homosexuals in prison, and his first biopic, *Ludwig II: King of Bavaria* (1929).

In 1930 Warner Brothers brought Dieterle to Hollywood to play Ahab in their German-language version of *Moby Dick*. During his early years in America he directed *The Last Flight* (1931), a dark comedy about US airmen who settle in Paris after World War I, and *Fog Over 'Frisco* (1934), a film famous for both its breakneck pace and for killing off its star, Bette DAVIS, after only 20 minutes. He also collaborated with Reinhardt on the latter's celebrated film version of *A Midsummer Night's Dream* (1935), which featured Mickey ROONEY and James CAGNEY.

In the later 1930s Dieterle directed Paul MUNI in two biopics, *The Story of Louis Pasteur* (1936), which won the star an Oscar, and *The Life of Emile Zola* (1937), which earned Warners its first Oscar for Best Film. After the success of *The Hunchback of Notre Dame* (1939), in which Charles LAUGHTON starred as Quasimodo, Dieterle made the daring *Dr Ehrlich's Magic Bullet* (1940), about the scientist who developed a cure for sexually transmitted disease, and *All That Money Can Buy* (1941), a brilliant variation

on the Faust theme. In 1948 he directed David O. SELZNICK's wife, Jennifer JONES, in the extraordinary ghost fantasy *Portrait of Jennie* (British title *Jennie*; 1948), about an artist who falls in love with a girl only to find that she is long dead.

Later US films included *Salome* (1953), with Rita HAYWORTH in the title role, and *Elephant Walk* (1953), starring Elizabeth TAYLOR. His Hollywood career was brought to a sudden end in the mid 1950s, when he was smeared by the House Un-American Activities Committee. Dieterle returned to Germany to make the Wagner biopic *Magic Fire* (1956) before retiring in 1960.

Dietrich, Marlene (Maria Magdalene von Losch; 1901–92) German-born US actress, famous for her long legs, icy beauty, and husky voice. Born in Berlin, she worked on stage in the early 1920s and appeared in German films from 1923 onwards. The following year she married a Czechoslovakian film-maker, whom she never divorced despite her numerous affairs. Although she was impressive as a royal mistress in Alexander KORDA's *A Modern Dubarry* (1927), G. W. PABST rejected her for the role of Lulu in *Pandora's Box* (1928) on the grounds that she was "too old and too obvious", giving the part to Louise BROOKS instead.

In 1930, however, Dietrich became an overnight sensation when Josef VON STERNBERG cast her as the cabaret singer Lola in THE BLUE ANGEL, the film in which she sings 'Falling in Love Again'. Lord Beaverbrook famously remarked that Dietrich in fishnet stockings in this film was a greater work of art than the Venus de Milo. Dietrich and von Sternberg, who became lovers, travelled to America soon after the film's release. Paramount signed her up at once when the producer Joe Pasternack predicted that "millions of guys would want to make love to her." However, for her first Hollywood film, von Sternberg's *Morocco* (1930), the studio made her shed 30 pounds. Director and star made another five films together, including *Shanghai Express* (1932), *The Scarlet Empress* (1934), about Catherine the Great, and *The Devil is a Woman* (1935).

Dietrich was often cast as a prostitute, as in *Dishonoured* (1931), *Destry Rides Again* (1939), in which she sang 'See What the Boys in the Back Room Will Have', and Orson WELLES's *A Touch of Evil* (1958). When she visited London's Soho district in 1939, she put on a veil and posed as a street-walker for 30 minutes without success, later commenting, "I'm a complete flop as a prostitute!" Off screen she is said to have maintained a bisexual lifestyle, with lovers ranging from Ernest Hemingway to the lesbian author Mercedes d'Acosta.

Despite her fame, Dietrich was never a great draw at the box office. From the mid 1950s onwards she made comparatively few films, but enhanced her legendary status with performances in cabaret and on record. Her later films included Billy WILDER's Christie adaptation *Witness for the Prosecution* (1957) and *Judgment at Nuremberg* (1961), about the 1948 war-crimes tribunals. During World War II Dietrich had entertained US troops and made pro-Allied broadcasts, something for which many Germans never forgave her. Soon after her death and burial in France, where she spent most of her later years, her gravestone was desecrated by Nazi sympathizers.

> Toulouse-Lautrec would have turned a couple of handsprings had he laid eyes on her.
> JOSEF VON STERNBERG.

> If she had nothing but her voice, she could break your heart with it. But she also has that beautiful body and the timeless loveliness of her face.
> ERNEST HEMINGWAY.

> I always thought that I was a very bad actress.
> MARLENE DIETRICH.

Dillon, Matt (1964–) US actor, who became a favourite with teenagers in the early 1980s. Born in New York State, Dillon made his first films, the comedy *Little Darlings* (1980), about teenage girls desperate to lose their virginity at summer camp, and *My Bodyguard* (1980), about troubled adolescents in Chicago, when he was only 16. In 1983 he leapt to stardom in two Francis Ford COPPOLA films based on novels by S. E. Hinton: *The Outsiders*, a sentimental melodrama about rival high-school gangs, and the black-and-white *Rumble Fish* (1983), about the rites of passage of a Tulsa teenager.

His subsequent films have included the beach-club comedy *The Flamingo Kid* (1984), *Target* (1985), a melodramatic spy story in which he co-starred with Gene HACKMAN, *Native Son* (1986), from the novel by Richard Wright, *Drugstore Cowboy* (1989), the thriller *A Kiss Before Dying*

(1991) with Max VON SYDOW, *Singles* (1992), and *Golden Gate* (1994).

Dinocittà *See* DE LAURENTIIS, DINO.

direct. **direct cinema** A style of US DOCUMENTARY cinema that emerged in the early 1960s. It was similar to CINÉMA VÉRITÉ in its use of light HAND-HELD CAMERAS and DIRECT SOUND recording but differed in its avoidance of narration or any involvement in the action by the film-maker. Examples include Albert and David Maysles's *Primary* (1960) and Donn PENNEBAKER's *Don't Look Now* (1966), which records a Bob Dylan tour.

direct cut A simple CUT from one shot to another, as opposed to some other more gradual transition, such as a DISSOLVE.

direct sound Film sound that is recorded as the action is shot, rather than dubbed on afterwards.

director The person who has overall responsibility for the creative and technical aspects of a film production. His or her major tasks include interpreting the SCREENPLAY in cinematic terms, coordinating the efforts of the actors, cameramen, technicians, and others during shooting, and supervising post-production EDITING and sound work. He or she is usually held responsible for the film's success of failure.

In the silent era, such directors as the Hollywood pioneers D. W. GRIFFITH and Allan DWAN took personal responsibility for editing, photography, sets, props, costumes, and many other tasks. Their assistants in these areas eventually became specialists, allowing the directors to concentrate on the actual filming if they wished. While many directors now give considerable creative freedom to writers, designers, CINEMATOGRAPHERs, and editors, others maintain a close personal involvement in some or all of these areas. Similarly, the extent to which a director will give precise instructions to the actors varies enormously.

Despite the autocratic tendencies of some directors, film-making during the classic Hollywood era of the 1930s and 1940s remained a largely collaborative venture. The director's own ideas usually had to be subordinated to the established style of the studio, the conventions of the genre, and the public image of his stars. The notion of the director as an artist with a distinct personal vision began to gain ground with the emergence of such individualistic talents as Orson WELLES in the 1940s and Ingmar BERGMAN in the 1950s. According to the AUTEUR theory of direction favoured by the exponents of the French NEW WAVE, the director creates a film in the same way and to the same extent that a writer creates a novel. Directors who have developed an unmistakable visual style of their own include Federico FELLINI and, more recently, Peter GREENAWAY. Despite their apparently god-like powers, directors do not usually have the right to decide the FINAL CUT; producers have often insisted on cuts, changes, or even a complete re-editing before the film is released (*see* DIRECTOR'S CUT).

We'd have better films if directors controlled them completely.
WOODY ALLEN, actor-director.

I direct as little as possible. I relieve myself of the ardours of direction, simply by casting it right.
JOHN HUSTON, director.

There are two kinds of directors – allies and judges.
JOHN HURT, actor.

It's the best job in the picture business because when you're a director, you're God. And you know, that's the best job in town.
BURT LANCASTER, actor-director.

I consider myself just another member of the crew, the highest-paid member of the crew.
WILLIAM FRIEDKIN, director.

Good directors don't direct actors.
GEORGE C. SCOTT, actor.

When you're working for a good director, you become...his concubine. All that you're seeking is his pleasure.
DONALD SUTHERLAND, actor.

In his present mode the director is wholly superfluous, an interfering parasite. His proper function – that is to say, a knowledge of lighting techniques and the use of lenses – has been taken over entirely by the director of photography.
TERRY SOUTHERN, screenwriter.

The best films are best because of nobody but the director.
ROMAN POLANSKI, director.

Film for me is a performing, communal art form, and not the work of a single individual. And I think this is still the case even if you've written it yourself, you're shooting it yourself, directing it yourself, and acting the leading part. It's in the nature of the medium.
SIDNEY LUMET, director.

If you can drive a car, you can direct a movie.
JOHN LANDIS, director.

director of photography *See* CINEMATOGRAPHER.

directors' cameos Directors have occasionally taken small roles in their own films or those of others. Alfred HITCHCOCK took walk-on parts in some 30 of his films, challenging audience members to spot his tubby figure strolling in a crowd or disappearing around a corner. Other directors to make uncredited appearances in their own work include Ingmar BERGMAN in *Waiting Women* (1952), Claude CHABROL in *Les Biches* (1968), and Tony RICHARDSON in *TOM JONES* (1963). John HUSTON played a tourist in THE TREASURE OF SIERRA MADRE (1948), which earned him an Oscar as Best Director. More unusual cameos include Jean COCTEAU's appearance as an old woman in ORPHÉE (1949) and Samuel FULLER's as a Japanese policeman in *House of Bamboo* (1955). The Jewish director Otto PREMINGER delighted in playing Nazis in such films as Billy WILDER's *Stalag 17* (1953). John LANDIS's road movie *Into the Night* (1985) featured a number of directors in small acting roles, notably Roger VADIM and Paul Mazursky; Landis himself appeared in *The Muppets Take Manhattan* (1984). Directors to appear as themselves include Cecil B. DE MILLE in SUNSET BOULEVARD (1950) and several other films.

More substantial acting roles have been taken by Jean RENOIR in LA RÈGLE DU JEU (1939), François TRUFFAUT in SPIELBERG's *Close Encounters of the Third Kind* (1977), and Roman POLANSKI in *Dance of the Vampires* (1967) and *The Tenant* (1976). *See also* CAMEOS.

director's cut A FINE CUT of a film made in accordance with the director's wishes, particularly when this differs significantly from the RELEASE PRINT authorized by the studio.

Unfortunately, pressure from the studio or distributor often means that a film is released in a form that travesties the intentions of the director. A film may simply be too long; VON STROHEIM's cut of GREED (1923) came in at a massive seven hours but MGM hacked it down to 140 minutes for release; the same director's *Foolish Wives* (1922) was cut from six to two hours. Von Stroheim was so bitter that he allegedly filmed expensive orgy scenes for *The Wedding March* (1928), knowing that the studio would have to ditch them to satisfy the HAYS Office. RKO slashed almost half of Orson WELLES's 148-minute-long THE MAGNIFICENT AMBERSONS (1942), while more recently Sergio LEONE's complex *Once Upon a Time in the West* (1968) was left almost incomprehensible after US cuts designed to permit an extra nightly showing.

PREVIEWS revealing unpopular narrative elements have also led to radical changes, as in *Fatal Attraction* (1987), the ending of which was reshot to satisfy the audience's vindictive feelings towards the Glen CLOSE character. Similarly, studios can demand cuts of scenes deemed too violent – as in most of PECKINPAH's films – or of overly sexual footage – Michael POWELL's *Peeping Tom* (1960) being one of many films thus ruined.

Recently, however, studio heads have realized that they can atone for past sins *and* make money by rereleasing films as 'director's cuts', a term now as much marketing- as production-speak. When Ridley SCOTT's *Blade Runner* (1982) was recut in 1992, the new editors restored missing footage, eliminated an insipid producer-imposed voice-over, and replaced an upbeat ending with Scott's original ambiguous finale. Similarly, LAWRENCE OF ARABIA (1962) was carefully recut by David LEAN and his original editor in 1989; some 35 minutes of footage was restored requiring Peter O'TOOLE to recreate his original vocal mannerisms in new dubbing sessions.

Thus a re-edit can placate a director, perhaps provide a richer filmic experience, and, crucially, offer new theatre or video earning capacity at a fraction of the cost of a new film or sequel. Other director's cuts include SPIELBERG's rather pointless 1980 revision of *Close Encounters of the Third Kind* (1977), the 1991 version of Jean-Jacques Beineix's *Betty Blue* (1986), which included an extra hour of footage, and a 1979 restoration of *Peeping Tom*.

Directors' Guild of America *See* DGA.

disaster film or **movie**   A type of suspense film that deals with the struggles of various characters to survive a natural or man-made disaster. The genre has been popular throughout Hollywood history, with such examples as *Tidal Wave* and *San Francisco* in the 1930s, *Titanic* in the 1950s, and *Krakatoa East of Java* in the 1960s. But the 1970s were the decade of the disaster movie, with such spectacular star-studded examples as *The Poseidon Adventure* (1972), set on board a capsized liner, *Airport '75* (1974), about a stricken aircraft, and *Towering Inferno* (1974), in which the world's tallest building catches fire; these and numerous others attracted huge audiences to the cinema. The two-dimensional characters, contrived situations, and platitudinous dialogue of many of these films were later spoofed in such parodies as *The Big Bus* (1976) and *Airplane* (1980) and its sequels.

discontinuity   *See* CONTINUITY.

discovery shot   A shot in which the camera tracks or pans to reveal something that was not in view when the shot began. If a ZOOM is used, the technique is called a **discovery zoom**. An example occurs in the ballroom scene in GONE WITH THE WIND, when the camera's gaze moves down Scarlett O'Hara in sombre mourning dress to show her feet moving gaily to the dance music.

Discreet Charm of the Bourgeoisie, The (*Le Charme discret de la bourgeoisie*; 1972) Writer and director Luis BUÑUEL's witty surrealistic attack on the upper classes, the clergy (always a favourite target), and politicians. The cast includes Fernando Rey, Delphine Seyrig, Stephane Audran, and Jean-Pierre Cassel.

The plot, such as it is, concerns a group of affluent friends who face continual frustration in their attempts to have a quiet dinner together. Either they meet on the wrong day, turn up at a restaurant only to discover the owner's corpse, or, more surreally, find themselves suddenly on stage in front of an angry audience. The failed dinner parties are intercut with other scenes that reveal more disturbing sides to their characters, such as involvement in drug-dealing or a predeliction for torture.

Owing largely to its surface sophistication, which belies the savagery of its assault on most accepted values, *The Discreet Charm of the Bourgeoisie* was nominated for an Oscar as Best Original Screenplay and took the award for Best Foreign Language Film.

disguise   Numerous comedies, thrillers, and adventure films have made use of disguise as a key element of the plot. In many other cases a star has been required to alter his or her appearance completely in order to play a particular role. The silent star Lon CHANEY was particularly famous for his disguises, becoming known as 'The Man of a Thousand Faces'; Chaney's son, Lon CHANEY JNR, likewise appeared heavily disguised in a number of monster and werewolf roles. Other actors famous for changing their appearance from one film to the next include Paul MUNI in the 1930s and Robert DE NIRO since the 1970s. Science fiction and horror movies have, of course, frequently required actors to transform their whole appearance through elaborate cosmetic effects (see MAKE-UP). Some low-budget films avoided expense and bother by adopting the plot device in which aliens or monsters cunningly disguise themselves as members of the human race.

Films in which a single actor has disguised his appearance to play MULTIPLE ROLES include Ealing's KIND HEARTS AND CORONETS, in which Alec GUINNESS played eight murder victims. The numerous comedies in which characters disguise themselves as members of the opposite sex include the classic SOME LIKE IT HOT (1959) and Mrs Doubtfire (1993), in which a separated husband impersonates a Scottish nanny in order to obtain access to his children. Less common are films in which actors have played characters of another race; two examples are The Watermelon Man (1970), in which a White bigot (Godfrey Cambridge) wakes up one morning to find that he has become Black, and Soul Man (1986), in which a White student (C. Thomas Howell) disguises himself in order to qualify for a Black scholarship at law school. Actors have often played roles considerably older than themselves; the 34-year-old Albert FINNEY, for instance, was unrecognizable as the decrepit miser Scrooge (1970).

Films in which disguise plays a minor or incidental role are, of course, far too numerous to mention. Those in which it is central to the plot include The Seven Faces of Dr Lao (1964), starring Tony Randall as a Chinese master of disguise, and The List of Adrian Messenger (1963), starring George C. SCOTT as a murderer with many faces. The latter also featured cameo performances from Robert MITCHUM, Frank SINATRA, Burt LANCASTER, and Tony CURTIS – all in impenetrable disguises. Popular film characters who make regular use of disguise include Sherlock HOLMES and the elusive Scarlet Pimpernel. Perhaps the most gruesome example of disguise in movie history occurs in the chiller THE SILENCE OF THE LAMBS (1989), in which a psychopath removes the face of one of his victims and uses it to cover his own features.

Disney, Walt (Walter Elias Disney; 1901–66) The world's most renowned ANIMATOR, whose films won 26 regular and six special Academy Awards. Although most Disney productions were not animated or directed by Disney himself, he provided overall vision and creative control until his death.

Disney himself cultivated a folksy avuncular image. When asked once how it felt to be a celebrity, he replied that it did not keep fleas off his dogs "and if being a celebrity won't give one an advantage over a couple of fleas, than I guess there can't be much in being a celebrity after all." A recent biography has hinted at a darker side to his character, accusing Uncle Walt of meanness, racism, and emotional cruelty.

Born in Chicago, Disney studied at the Kansas City Art Institute from the age of 14 and was a teenage ambulance driver in World War I. With Ub Iwerks, whom he met while working as a commercial artist in Kansas City, he moved to Hollywood to produce cartoons in 1923. Five years later they created MICKEY MOUSE, the most successful cartoon character of all time, with Iwerks providing the artwork and Disney supplying the squeaky voice. The Disney menagerie grew to include Minnie Mouse, DONALD DUCK, Goofy (originally named Dippy Dawg), and Pluto. Disney's cartoon shorts, which continued to be produced until 1965, are credited with killing off Hollywood's short live comedies.

In 1938 Disney released his first feature-length cartoon, SNOW WHITE AND THE SEVEN DWARFS. A great popular success, it demonstrated Disney's meticulous techniques (the rouge on Snow White's face was dabbed onto each separate frame). This was followed in 1940 by Pinocchio and FANTASIA, the latter matching animation to classical music; subsequent successes included DUMBO (1941), BAMBI (1942), Cinderella (1950), Peter Pan (1953), Lady and the Tramp (1955), 101 Dalmatians (1961), The Sword in the Stone (1963), and The Jungle Book (1967).

Disney's first non-cartoon film was Treasure Island (1950); this was followed by such live-action successes as The Shaggy Dog (1959) and MARY POPPINS (1964). The company's 'True-Life Adventures', a series of light-hearted natural-history documentaries for children, began in 1953 with THE LIVING DESERT. In 1954 Disney initiated a television series and a year later opened DISNEYLAND in Anaheim, California. After Disney's death in 1966, the film-making activities of the company were allowed to settle into a slow but inexorable decline from which they did not begin to recover until the mid 1980s. The renaissance began with the establishment of an adult production company, **Touchstone Films**, in 1984. Touchstone's first film, the mermaid comedy *Splash!* became the highest-grossing film in Disney's history and was followed by further hits including *Down and Out in Beverley Hills* (1985) and *Three Men and a Baby* (1987). Disney also led a revival of the animated feature with the highly acclaimed *The Black Cauldron* (1985) and *The Little Mermaid* (1989). Major hits of the 1990s have included *Beauty and the Beast* (1991), the first animation to receive an Oscar nomination as Best Film, *Aladdin* (1992), *The Lion King* (1994), and *The Santa Clause* (1995), the studio's most successful live-action feature.

Disneyland One of the world's most famous amusement parks, opened in Anaheim, California, in 1955. Disneyland incorporates all the fantasy elements of the cartoon world created by Walt Disney. Other Disney parks are Walt Disney World, Orlando, Florida (1971) and its companion the Experimental Prototype Community of Tomorrow (EPCOT) Center (1982), Lake Buenavista, Florida. Another Disneyland was opened in Tokyo in 1983; the most recent, EuroDisney, opened near Paris in 1992 and has proved less than successful.

dissolve or **lap dissolve** An effect used to link two scenes, in which the first appears to melt into the second. It is achieved by superimposing the two lengths of film. A dissolve is normally used to indicate either a change in place or a lapse of time; it may also be used to begin a FLASHBACK or DREAM sequence. By convention a **slow dissolve** indicates a greater interval of time or space than a **quick dissolve**.

distortion A misshapen film image, usually caused accidentally by a defective lens, unaligned optical system, or poor placement of the camera. Distortion is sometimes introduced deliberately in order to create a particular artistic effect, mainly by the use of optical attachments (**distortion optics**) on

a camera or printer. Sequences shot in this way include Fredric MARCH's transformation scenes in Paramount's *Doctor Jekyll and Mr Hyde* (1931). Strange camera angles were used by the German EXPRESSIONIST director F. W. MURNAU to create startling dramatic effects in THE LAST LAUGH (1924) and other films.

distributor A company that circulates films to EXHIBITORs through lease or rental agreements. In practice, this aspect of the film industry has always been tightly controlled by the major studios. The early days of Hollywood saw 10 production companies form the MOTION PICTURE PATENTS COMPANY (1909), a monopolistic consortium that charged theatres a $2 licence fee and then rented them films by the foot. The company was later ruled an illegal trust. In the 1930s such major producers as Paramount, Fox, and Warner Brothers insisted on BLOCK BOOKING of groups of films and BLIND BIDDING without prior screening, practices that were ruled illegal in 1950. Despite the advent of television in the 1950s and home video recorders in the 1980s, distribution is still effectively controlled by a small number of multinational entertainment conglomerates.

Dmytryk, Edward (1908–) Canadian director of low-budget FILM NOIR productions, who was blacklisted as a communist after World War II but returned to direct big-budget CINEMASCOPE films. Dmytryk began as a Hollywood messenger boy in the 1920s, later working his way up to become an editor and director at Paramount. He made his name with RKO's anti-Nazi film *Hitler's Children* (1943), which cost some $205,000 to make but earned over $1.5 million. *Farewell My Lovely* (1944), which cast the breezy singer Dick POWELL as Raymond CHANDLER's hard-boiled detective Philip MARLOWE, was Dmytryk's first film noir. Dmytryk received his only Oscar nomination as Best Director for *Crossfire* (1947), a film about an anti-Semitic murder that introduced the new stars Robert Young, Robert MITCHUM, and Robert RYAN.

A well-known left-winger, Dmytryk was investigated in 1947 by the House Un-American Activities Committee; his refusal to co-operate led to his becoming one of the HOLLYWOOD TEN. He subsequently fled the country, directing a British thriller *Obsession* (1948) before returning in 1950 to serve six months in prison for contempt. Later he named names and was able to resume his Hollywood career. In the 1950s and 1960s he directed four films for Stanley KRAMER, including *The Caine Mutiny* (1954), which starred Humphrey BOGART and was nominated for a Best Picture Oscar. This success brought him a number of big-budget projects, notably the Civil-War epic *Raintree County* (1956), a rather more downbeat GONE WITH THE WIND.

Dmytryk's later films included the British-produced Western *Shalako* (1968), starring Brigitte BARDOT and Sean CONNERY. In 1976 he retired from films to teach the subject; his autobiography, *It's a Hell of a Life but Not a Bad Living*, was published in 1978.

D/N *See* DAY-FOR-NIGHT.

Dr Strangelove (1963) A satirical black comedy directed by Stanley KUBRICK; it was one of the first movies to condemn the accelerating nuclear arms race. Entitled in full *Dr Strangelove: or, How I Learned to Stop Worrying and Love the Bomb* and based on a book by Peter George, the film starred Peter SELLERS in three roles: an RAF officer, US president Merkin Muffley, and the ex-Nazi scientist Dr Strangelove (*see* MULTIPLE ROLES). The movie also featured George C. SCOTT as a blustering US general and Sterling Hayden as Jack D. Ripper, the mad USAF commander who triggers the nuclear destruction of the world. At one point Scott's character remarks sagely:

> I don't say we wouldn't get our hair mussed, but I do say no more than ten to twenty million people killed.

The term *Strangelove* came to be applied to any fanatic or insane militarist who advocates large-scale pre-emptive nuclear strikes. Kubrick's original intention, fortunately abandoned, was to have the film climax in the sort of CUSTARD PIE throwing sequence beloved of silent movies. The film was nominated for four Oscars including Best Picture, Best Director, and Best Actor (Sellers).

documentary A film that depicts fact rather than fiction; the term was coined by John GRIERSON, a British pioneer of the genre, in 1929.

The use of film to record reality dates back to the earliest *actualité* shorts of the LUMIÈRE BROTHERS in the 1890s. An early US example recorded the 1898 Alaskan Gold Rush (at $40,000 this was then the costliest film yet made). Nevertheless, Robert FLAHERTY's *Nanook of the North* (1922) is usually seen as the first work to give the documentary real form. Having been sponsored by a US fur company, Flaherty lived and worked with the Canadian Eskimos before shooting over 20,000 metres of stock, which he later edited into a stark poetic film about the struggle for survival in the bleak north. He went on to make several other films about isolated communities, including *Man of Aran* (1934).

John Grierson began the strong British tradition with his founding of the EMPIRE FILM BOARD (which later became the GPO FILM UNIT) in 1929. His films include *Drifters* (1929), about North Sea herring fishermen, and *Night Mail* (1936), celebrated for its innovative night photography and W. H. Auden's soundtrack poem.

During the interwar period both the Soviet Union and Nazi Germany came to recognize the PROPAGANDA potential of documentaries. In Russia, an early period of creative experiment gave way to the crushing dogmas of Socialist Realism in the 1930s. Leni RIEFENSTAHL, the Führer's favourite film-maker, was allowed more freedom to demonstrate her virtuoso skills in *Triumph of the Will* (1935) and OLYMPIA (1938). The coming war saw the main protagonists produce hundreds of propaganda, information, and documentary films.

In the 1950s new HAND-HELD CAMERAS liberated film-makers from the tripod-bound heavyweights that had previously dominated quality photography, a development that made possible the fluid spontaneity of the DIRECT CINEMA style in America. Influenced more by NEWSREELS than by the studied, often staged, work of Flaherty or Grierson, its exponents aimed at all costs to avoid interfering with the action they were recording. The Maysles brothers' *Gimme Shelter* (1970), a film of the Rolling Stones in concert, heralded both 'non-fiction features' for cinema release, and created a new genre of 'rockumentary'. Later examples would include *Woodstock* (1970), SCORSESE's *The Last Waltz* (1978), and Jonathan DEMME's *Stop Making Sense* (1984). *This is Spinal Tap* (1984) spoofed the genre with such lethal accuracy that many assumed the featured heavy-metal band to be genuine.

In postwar Europe, Britain's FREE CINEMA movement, which nurtured the early careers of Linday ANDERSON and Karel REISZ, and the French CINÉMA VÉRITÉ style offer clear parallels to US Direct Cinema. A significant difference was the French directors' recognition that the camera's very presence affected what it documented. With its candid interviews and openly political intent, Marcel Ophüls's *The Sorrow and the Pity* (1969), a shocking document of France under the Occupation, exemplified the movement.

These styles of documentary had a profound effect on the cinema audience's notions of 'reality', making seamless Hollywood narrative look artificial by comparison. This led many film-makers to imitate documentary techniques in works of fiction; both COPPOLA's *The Conversation* (1974) and ALTMAN's *Nashville* (1975), for example, are suffused with a complex, often confusing, documentary immediacy. SPIELBERG'S SCHINDLER'S LIST (1994) owes much of its power to a black-and-white cinematography that skilfully evokes the harrowing newsreels of the concentration camps. *See also* FACTION; REALISM.

docudrama A film or television programme based on true events, presented in dramatized form. Such productions often make use of stylistic features associated with documentary film-making, leading to accusations that the format confuses fact and fiction to an intolerable degree. Works of FACTION are generally more blatant in their use of dramatic licence, while FILMS À CLEF alter names and other details while remaining close to fact.

dog Hollywood slang for a FLOP.

dogs *See* ANIMALS; ASTA; LASSIE; RIN TIN TIN.

Dolby system Tradename of a noise-reduction system used to reduce the hiss on SOUNDTRACK recordings, casette tapes, and video tapes. It operates by manipulating the high-frequency response during recording. Originally called the *S/N Stretcher*, it was invented in 1965 by the US-born scientist Ray Dolby at his London laboratory; it was initially used for disc recordings. The first film in Dolby sound was Stanley KUBRICK's A CLOCKWORK ORANGE (1971). Since 1977 all winners of the Academy Award for Best Achievement in Sound have used the system.

Dolce Vita, La (1959) Federico FELLINI's ambivalent exploration of 'the sweet life', as pursued by the idle rich in Roman high society at the dawn of the 'swinging sixties'. The film is essentially a series of tableaux, loosely connected by the presence of an unprincipled young reporter (Marcello MASTROIANNI) doing the rounds of parties and other social occasions. The cast also included Anouk AIMÉE as a bored young heiress and Anita EKBERG as a Hollywood starlet. Although the film was much admired for its striking visual motifs (ranging from lavish orgies to a famous shot of a statue of Christ being removed by helicopter) many found the work as a whole enigmatic. In particular, the director's avoidance of any direct moral comment on the empty hedonism of the main characters aroused criticism and perplexity. The film was a big hit in many countries, including America, and made Mastroianni a star. Its title introduced a new phrase to several languages, while the surname of the celebrity-chasing photographer *Paparazzo* also became a general term.

dolly A small mobile mount for a camera and its operator that is used for making TRACKING SHOTS (sometimes called *dolly shots*). A **crab dolly** is a dolly with an elaborate steering mechanism that enables it to be manoeuvred in all directions at once, while a **spider** or **spyder dolly** is one with projecting legs. A **velocilator** is a dolly mounted on a small CRANE. The term is also used as a verb, meaning to move the mount while filming.

dolly back *See* PULL BACK.

dolly up *See* APPROACH.

Donald Duck The popular DISNEY cartoon character, an irascible duck who was first seen in *The Wise Little Hen* (1934). The term is also British and Australian rhyming slang.

Donat, Robert (1905–58) British actor, who struggled with painful and debilitating asthma to continue his career, winning an Oscar for his portrayal of a shy schoolmaster in GOODBYE MR CHIPS (1939). Ironically, his asthma was largely responsible for his distinctive speaking voice, which contributed greatly to his appeal.

Donat also suffered from a stammer, which he corrected (along with his thick Lancashire accent) by elocution lessons. In the 1930s he found international stardom in such films as Alexander KORDA's THE PRI-

VATE LIFE OF HENRY VIII (1933) and Alfred HITCHCOCK'S THE THIRTY-NINE STEPS (1935). In the latter, one scene required him to be handcuffed to his co-star, Madeleine Carroll; Hitchcock, who was known for his unpleasant sense of humour, pretended to lose the key for the entire day (taking a particularly prurient interest in the couple's toilet arrangements).

Donat's versatility brought him parts ranging from a homesick Scottish ghost in *The Ghost Goes West* (1936) to the title character in the biopic *The Young Mr Pitt* (1942). Owing to his sober good looks he was often cast as professional men, including an idealistic doctor in King VIDOR's *The Citadel* (1938), a lawyer in *The Winslow Boy* (1948), and a vicar in *Lease of Life* (1951). Although never a star of the very first rank, Donat was greatly admired within the profession for his ability to absorb himself totally in a character. The actor Paul MUNI described Donat's appearance in *Goodbye Mr Chips* as:

> The most magnificent performance I've ever seen on any screen. Not a false motion – not a wasted gesture. He is the greatest actor we have today.

In 1949 Donat recovered his original Lancashire accent to play a soldier seeking a hometown bride in *The Cure For Love* (1949), a film he also wrote and directed. For the Festival of Britain in 1951, Donat overcame acute illness to star in *The Magic Box*, a film about the British cinema pioneer, William Friese-Greene. His last film was *The Inn of the Sixth Happiness* (1958), in which he appeared opposite Ingrid BERGMAN's English missionary.

> The gods gave him every grace and every gift but one, good health.
> CAMPBELL DIXON.

Donen, Stanley (1924–) US director best known for his musicals, which include the much-loved SINGIN' IN THE RAIN (1952). Donen worked closely with his co-director and star Gene KELLY, noting, "Anybody who says that every picture is not a collaboration is an idiot."

Born in Columbia, South Carolina, Donen appeared as a dancer in the Broadway chorus of *Pal Joey* (1940) at the age of 16; it was here that he met Kelly, the show's star. Their partnership at MGM began with *On the Town* (1949), an exuberant musical starring Kelly and Frank SINATRA as sailors

on leave in New York, and continued with the classic *Singin' in the Rain*, a satire on Hollywood's transition to sound. The film also featured Debbie REYNOLDS and Donald O'CONNOR. After making the popular *Seven Brides for Seven Brothers* (1954) with Howard Keel, Donen moved to Paramount to direct *Funny Face* (1956) with Fred ASTAIRE and Audrey HEPBURN. This was followed by two film versions of Broadway hits for Warner Brothers – *The Pyjama Game* (1957) with Doris DAY and *Damn Yankees* (co-directed with George Abbott; 1959), about an unsuccessful baseball team.

From the late 1950s Donen produced as well as directed, turning out such films as the comedy *Indiscreet* (1958), starring Ingrid BERGMAN and Cary GRANT, and the macabre *Charade* (1963), in which Grant plays a mysterious stranger protecting Audrey Hepburn from killers. Hepburn appeared again in the chic comedy *Two for the Road* (1967), in which she and Albert FINNEY played husband and wife. Donen's later comedies included the unsuccessful *Movie Movie* (1978) and *Blame It on Rio* (1984), which starred Michael CAINE.

dope sheet (1) A list, compiled by the cameraman or an assistant, of the shots taken on a particular reel of film. (2) A list of the contents of a reel kept in a film library.

Dors, Diana (Diana Fluck; 1931–84) British actress, a buxom blonde who was once considered Britain's answer to Marilyn MONROE. Dors, who was born in Swindon, began to appear in teenage roles from the mid 1940s onwards. Her image as a sex symbol was promoted by none-too-subtle publicity stunts, such as posing in a mink bikini at Cannes. She made several Hollywood films in the late 1950s.

Her true abilities as an actress first became apparent when, at 25, she starred in *Yield to the Night* (US title *Blonde Sinner*; 1956), a film in which a murderess recalls her story while awaiting execution. The drama, which took a firm stance against capital punishment, was clearly based on the case of Ruth Ellis, which had commanded widespread media interest at that time. Off screen, Dors was known for her humour and wit, qualities that were too rarely reflected in her performances. Her more successful comedies included Paramount's *On the Double* (1961) about a US soldier impersonating a British officer, which also starred Danny KAYE, Wilfrid Hyde White, and Margaret RUTHERFORD.

As Dors entered middle age and put on weight, she settled easily into character parts, including a cameo role in *Deep End* (1970) and the grotesque Mrs Wickens in *The Amazing Mr Blunden* (1972), a ghost story written and directed by Lionel Jeffries. Her last film was *Steaming* (1984), a study of the relationships between a group of women who meet in a London steam bath, in which she starred with Vanessa REDGRAVE and Sarah MILES.

double A person who looks like or has the same physical build as a leading actor and stands in for him or her in certain scenes. A STUNTMAN performs physical feats, especially those considered risky, a **photo double** appears in long shots or when only the performer's back is shown, while a **body double** is sometimes used in sex or nude scenes (either because the star is modest or because his or her nudity is considered unappealing). In GONE WITH THE WIND (1939), the famous carriage dash through Atlanta's burning streets used two doubles each for Clark GABLE and Vivien LEIGH. *See also* STAND IN.

double exposure *See* MULTIPLE EXPOSURE.

double feature Two feature-length films shown on the same programme for the price of one. In the 1930s Hollywood introduced the Saturday double-feature programme for young audiences. The double feature later became a staple of the DRIVE-IN, which expanded the concept to triple features and even all-night presentations of four or five films, often based on a common theme, such as horror. *See also* A-MOVIE; B-MOVIE; CO-FEATURE.

Double Indemnity (1944) Paramount's classic FILM NOIR, a chilling story of murder and betrayal directed by Billy WILDER with Fred MACMURRAY, Barbara STANWYCK, and Edward G. ROBINSON in the leads. This adaptation of James M. Cain's story *Three of a Kind* was one of the first films to feature an ANTIHERO as its central character; the tale is sarcastically narrated by MacMurray, who risked his all-American nice-guy image with this role. Although nominated for seven Oscars, including Best Film, Best Director, Best Actress, and Best Screenplay, it did not collect in any category. A lacklustre remake for television (1973) starred Richard Crenna, Samantha Eggar,

and Lee J. Cobb; Lawrence Kasdan's *Body Heat* (1981), a film clearly inspired by the 1944 classic, is a more worthy successor.

In the plot glamorous Mrs Dietrichson (Stanwyck) inspires insurance salesman Walter Neff (MacMurray) to murder her husband in an 'accident', so that they can collect the payout from his life-insurance policy, which has double indemnity (it pays double for accidental death). They are caught, however, by the insurance investigator (Robinson), who develops a liking for Neff. As the murderer lies dying, he tells his pursuer, "The guy you were looking for was too close, right across the desk from you." Replies the inspector, "Closer than that."

When Wilder's regular writing collaborator, Charles Brackett, turned down *Double Indemnity* because he thought the story immoral, the director brought in author Raymond CHANDLER (his first screenplay). According to Wilder their relationship was one of "hate at first sight". Chandler loathed the novel, which he labelled "the offal of literature", and Wilder literally threw his first draft back at him, suggesting he use it as a doorstop. Although Chandler, a heavy drinker, said that working with Wilder shortened his life, the experience seems to have been an inspiration for the director, whose next film, *The Lost Weekend* (1965), was about an alcoholic writer.

double take An actor's method of showing surprise or shock through a delayed reaction – usually a second startled look. This popular comic device was perfected by such film stars as James Finlayson (1877–1953), Bob HOPE, and Danny KAYE. Finlayson also developed the **double take and fade away**, in which the startled reaction is followed by a slow withdrawal of the head.

Douglas. Kirk Douglas (Issur Danielovitch, later Isidore Demsky; 1916–) US actor known for his tough-guy and heroic roles. His lengthy and successful career earned him the American Film Institute's Lifetime Achievement Award in 1991. More recently he has emerged as a writer, producing an acclaimed autobiography, *The Ragman's Son*, in 1988 and three novels since 1990. His son, Michael DOUGLAS, is an Oscar-winning actor.

Born in New York State, the son of Russian immigrants, Douglas financed his studies by working as a waiter, bellboy, usher, and professional wrestler. (He was later to remark: "My kids never had the advantage I had: I was born poor.") He made his film debut in the FILM NOIR *The Strange Love of Martha Ivers* (1946), and became a star three years later playing a cocky boxer in *Champion*, a performance that brought him an Oscar nomination. Major roles followed in such films as *Ace in the Hole* (1951), *Detective Story* (1951), and Disney's *Twenty Thousand Leagues Under the Sea* (1954).

In 1955, at the height of his career, Douglas formed his own production company, Bryna (his mother's first name). His famous roles of the mid 1950s include Vincent van Gogh in *Lust for Life* (1956), Doc Holliday in GUNFIGHT AT THE OK CORRAL (1957), and a World-War-I French officer defending the honour of his men in Stanley KUBRICK's controversial *Paths of Glory* (1957); the last named film only found financial backing because Douglas agreed to star in it.

Kubrick also directed the epic *Spartacus* (1960), in which Douglas played a Roman slave leading a hopeless revolt. In the 1970s Douglas began to direct some of his own films, such as *Scalawag* (1973), in which he played a one-legged pirate. Later films have included the space adventure *Saturn Three* (1979) and *Tough Guys* (1986), in which he and his great friend Burt LANCASTER co-star as over-the-hill train-robbers. This was the seventh time that Douglas had worked with Lancaster, who remarked somewhat later: "Kirk would be the first to tell you he's a difficult man. I would be the second."

Indeed, Douglas's arrogant and egotistical roles have often seemed a reflection of his own personality. "Kirk never makes much of an effort toward anyone else", Doris DAY once said, while Douglas himself has observed: "What is it to be a nice guy? To be nothing, that's what. A big fat zero with a smile for everybody."

Melvyn Douglas (Melvyn Edouard Hesselberg; 1901–81) Debonair US leading man in romantic comedies of the 1930s and 1940s. Douglas, who made his name on Broadway, often returned to live theatre work, complaining that his Hollywood roles were boring and stereotyped him as a "one-dimensional non-serious actor."

Born in Macon, Georgia, the son of a concert pianist, Douglas made his stage debut in 1919. He was already an established name by the time he went to Hollywood to reprise his Broadway role in the comedy *Tonight or Never* (1931), with Gloria

SWANSON. He subsequently starred with Greta GARBO in *As You Desire Me* (1932), Claudette COLBERT in *She Married Her Boss* (1935), Joan CRAWFORD in *The Gorgeous Hussy* (1936), and Marlene DIETRICH in *Angel* (1937). Douglas and Garbo teamed up again for NINOTCHKA (1939), in which he played the aristocratic playboy who finally thaws the icy commissar ("Garbo laughs!").

After a year during which he directed the Arts Council in Washington (1942–43), Douglas joined the army as a private, later rising to the rank of major. His post-war films included *Mr Blandings Builds His Dream House* (1948), in which Douglas gave a characteristically wry performance in support of Cary GRANT and Myrna LOY. Thereafter he worked largely on Broadway and television, although he sometimes took secondary roles in films such as *Hud* (1963) and *Being There* (1979), both of which earned him Academy Awards. In 1981, the year of his death, he starred with fellow veteran Fred ASTAIRE in *Ghost Story*; this was also Astaire's final role.

Michael K(irk) Douglas (1944–) US actor and film producer, the son of Kirk DOUGLAS. In 1987 he won the Academy Award for Best Actor playing the ruthless financial dealer Gordon Gekko in *Wall Street*. The QUIGLEY POLL of film exhibitors placed Douglas tenth among male box-office draws in the 1980s.

Born in New Jersey, Douglas appeared in several little-noticed films at the end of the 1960s before making his name in the TV police series *Streets of San Francisco*, some episodes of which he also directed. In 1975 he co-produced the screen version of ONE FLEW OVER THE CUCKOO'S NEST, a project that he took over from his father, who had failed to get it off the ground. The film took all four major Oscars. He also produced and acted in *The China Syndrome* (1979), a topical drama in which Douglas and Jane FONDA discover problems at a nuclear power plant run by Jack LEMMON.

Despite these successes, Douglas did not become a major star until his appearance in the comedy thriller *Romancing the Stone* (1984), which he also produced. The 40-year-old Douglas starred as an adventurer who rescues Kathleen TURNER in the jungles of South America. In 1987 he raised his profile still further with two enormously successful films, Oliver STONE's *Wall Street* and the controversial thriller *Fatal*

Attraction, in which he played a New York lawyer who is terrorized by his discarded mistress Glenn CLOSE.

His later films have included the black comedy *The War of the Roses* (1989) with Kathleen Turner, the sexually explicit *Basic Instinct* (1992) with Sharon STONE, for which Douglas received a multi-million-dollar fee, and *Disclosure* (1994) with Demi MOORE.

Douglas, who once remarked of his numerous on-screen love scenes: "Believe me, movie sex can be real tough", is reputed to have undergone treatment for 'sex addiction' in real life.

Dovzhenko, Alexander (1894–1956) Pioneering Soviet director, who combined commitment to the ideals of the Bolshevik Revolution with a lyrical and poetic style of film-making.

Born to an illiterate peasant family in the Ukraine, Dovzhenko worked as a teacher, a diplomatic clerk, and a book illustrator before turning to the cinema. Having directed several unremarkable comedies, he turned out a masterpiece with his fourth film, *Zvenigora* (1928). This epic of Ukrainian peasant life combines a semidocumentary style with elements of dream and symbolism (the chief symbol being that of a faraway treasure mountain). It starred Semyon Svashenko and Mikola Nademsky, both of whom Dovzhenko used in later films.

This triumph was followed by two further films about Ukrainian peasants: the romantic *Arsenal* (1929), which combines realism with poetry in its account of a Ukrainian workers' revolt, and *Earth* (1930), a hymn to life and nature that is usually considered Dovzhenko's masterpiece. Despite its beautiful photography, the film was attacked as 'counterrevolutionary' by Soviet officials. Dovzhenko later responded to Stalin's request for a more straightforward propaganda film by making *Shors* (1939), in which a Ukrainian intellectual liberates Kiev. As head of the Kiev studios he supervised the making of several documentaries and propaganda pieces during World War II. Following Stalin's death in 1953 he planned to return to his old themes but died too soon, leaving three projects to be completed by his widow, Yulia Solntseva.

down In a film script, an instruction to reduce the volume of sound, especially background music.

downstage The area of the set that is closest to the camera during a take; the foreground. *Compare* UPSTAGE.

dowser An automatic device that switches off a cinema projector's light during the CHANGEOVER between reels.

Dracula Bram Stoker's novel about the Transylvanian vampire, first published in 1897, has now inspired over 160 feature films. The best known is still Universal's 1931 *Dracula* starring Bela LUGOSI as an elegant hypnotic count. (Lon CHANEY was to have played the role but died before the film began production.) The plot, which owes more to the Broadway stage version than to Stoker's original novel, centres on the Englishman Renfield, who visits Count Dracula's Transylvanian castle, where he meets the count's three vampire sisters (who sleep in coffins in the dungeon). He becomes a victim himself and begins to eat insects. The story then moves to Whitby in Yorkshire, where Dracula has gone in search of fresh blood; he eventually meets his nemesis in the form of vampire-hunter Professor Van Helsing.

Critics agree that NOSFERATU, the first screen version of the Dracula story, filmed in 1921 in Germany, was more frightening than Universal's rather stagey film. Nevertheless *Dracula* marked a turning point in US horror films: its success directly inspired the making of Universal's FRANKENSTEIN later that year (the two films often appeared as a double bill).

Of the many later versions of the story, two of the best are HAMMER's 1958 *Dracula* (US title *Horror of Dracula*) with Christopher LEE and a more romantic Universal/Mirisch film (1979) starring Frank Langella and Laurence OLIVIER. The title of *Bram Stoker's Dracula* (1992), directed by Francis Ford COPPOLA with Gary Oldman as the count and Anthony HOPKINS as Van Helsing, suggested a more faithful interpretation of the original novel, but this is not borne out on the screen. Other versions of the legend, some of them none too serious, include *Dracula's Daughter* (1936), *Son of Dracula* (1943), *Billy the Kid Versus Dracula* (1965), *Dracula, Prince of Darkness* (1966), *Dracula Meets the Outer Space Chicks* (1968), *Countess Dracula* (1972), *Blacula* (1972), with a Black cast,

Dracula's Dog (1978), and *Love at First Bite* (1979).

dream. dream mode Action shots that reveal what a character is daydreaming or thinking about. These are often introduced by a wavy or blurred transition sequence. The device was used extensively in *The Seven Year Itch* (1955), in which married man Tom Ewell fantasizes about his beautiful neighbour Marilyn MONROE.

dreams Films have often used dream sequences to provide a change of pace, give psychological insight into a character, or simply to show off special effects. Hollywood musicals have also used dreams and fantasies as a means of introducing elaborate semi-surreal production numbers; the best-known example is perhaps the dream ballet in *Oklahoma!* (1955).

One of the first films to make dreams central to its plot was G. W. PABST'S EXPRESSIONIST drama *Secrets of the Soul* (1926), in which an academic goes to a psychiatrist because of recurrent nightmares about a knife. Lavish psychological dream sequences later featured in John HUSTON'S *Freud* (1963), starring Montgomery CLIFT.

A number of early films made use of the device by which the entire plot turns out to have been a dream; although this could provide the protagonist with a miraculous escape from danger, it usually left the audience (and critics) dissatisfied (*see* DEUS EX MACHINA). Will ROGERS escapes death in *A Connecticut Yankee* (1931) simply by waking up, and Fritz LANG'S *The Woman in the Window* (1944) is resolved in a similar fashion. Judy GARLAND'S whole adventure is apparently dreamed in THE WIZARD OF OZ (1939).

Other films in which dreams play an important part include Alfred HITCHCOCK'S SPELLBOUND (1945), set in a mental institution, and *The Secret Life of Walter Mitty* (1947), a comedy starring Danny KAYE as an incurable fantasist. In the 1940s and 1950s Ealing Studios produced several films based on dreams, including the aptly named *Dreaming* (1944), a comedy about a soldier who has been hit on the head, *The Dead of Night* (1945) in which a man is trapped in an endless series of murder dreams, and *The Night My Number Came Up* (1954), a suspense drama in which Michael REDGRAVE finds himself living out his own dream about a plane crash. The relationship between dreams and waking life was cleverly blurred in Wes CRAVEN's horror fantasy *A Nightmare on Elm Street* (1984), in which teenagers are murdered in their dreams only to die in reality.

dresser A person who assists the WARDROBE mistress or master. The term is also used of an actor's own personal wardrobe assistant; the relationship between actor and dresser is explored in the film *The Dresser* (1983), a screen adaptation of the play of the same name by Ronald Harwood.

Dreyer, Carl Theodor (1889–1968) Danish director and screenwriter, noted for his interest in the complexities of human psychology. Although he made few full-length films and enjoyed no commercial success, he gained a worldwide reputation as an innovator.

Born in Copenhagen, the illegitimate son of a farmer and his housekeeper, Dreyer worked as a pianist, sports journalist, and film critic before entering the Danish cinema industry as a scriptwriter. Having made his debut as a director in 1919, he aroused a measure of critical interest with his black comedy *The Parson's Widow* (1920) and other features before achieving international recognition with THE PASSION OF JOAN OF ARC (1927). This intense, fastidiously detailed, account of Joan's trial and martyrdom was widely hailed as a masterpiece but proved a disaster at the box office.

Dreyer's next film, the German-French *Vampyr* (1932), was also a commercial failure. A strange blend of fantasy and realism, the film contains unforgettable images, such as that of an evil doctor suffocating in flour. Although not appreciated by critics at the time, *Vampyr* is now regarded as a classic of the supernatural cinema. Dreyer lived for another 35 years but directed only four more features, three of which are considered masterpieces. The first of these, *Day of Wrath* (1943), is now his best-known film; the story of a woman's persecution as an alleged witch was clearly intended to parallel the Nazi occupation of Denmark. *Ordet* (1955) explored the world of a religious visionary, while *Gertrud* (1966) was a slow-moving drama about a married woman who abandons her husband for a young musician. The latter was particularly unpopular, its Parisian premiere being marred by shouts of disapproval.

Dreyfuss, Richard (1947–) US actor, who became especially popular in the 1970s. His short stature and antiheroic persona have led to frequent comparisons with Dustin HOFFMAN. One of Hollywood's most outspoken liberals, Dreyfuss refused military service during the Vietnam War, working instead as a hospital clerk. Of Hollywood itself, he has noted, "The motion picture business is run by corporate thieves."

Born in Brooklyn, New York, the son of an attorney, Dreyfuss appeared on Broadway before making his film debut with a small part in *Valley of the Dolls* (1967). He became a star playing a confused teenager in *American Graffiti* (1973) and went on to appear before vast international audiences in two of Steven SPIELBERG's early successes; JAWS (1975), in which he played the marine biologist Hooper, and *Close Encounters of the Third Kind* (1977), in which he is mysteriously drawn to the secret landing place of a UFO.

In 1977 Dreyfuss won the Oscar for Best Actor with his excellent performance in Neil Simon's comedy *The Goodbye Girl*; at 29 he was the youngest ever recipient of the award. Subsequent roles included a concert pianist in *The Competition* (1980) and a paralysed man in the moving *Whose Life is it Anyway?* (1981). In the early 1980s his career was interrupted by a period during which he struggled (successfully) with alcoholism and drug problems. His more recent films include the comedy *Down and Out in Beverly Hills* (1986), in which con man Nick Nolte moves in with Dreyfuss and Bette MIDLER, *Stakeout* (1987) with Emilio Estevez and Madeleine Stowe, the screen version of Stoppard's *Rosencrantz and Guildenstern are Dead* (1990), and *Lost in Yonkers* (1993).

drive-in An open-air cinema, chiefly in America, in which patrons remain in their cars, viewing the film through the windscreen. Each vehicle parks next to a loudspeaker that can be clipped onto the side window. Some drive-ins employ *carhops* who deliver refreshments, while many have playground equipment for children.

The US drive-in theatre originated in 1933 in Camden, New Jersey, and within 30 years about 4000 were in operation. By the 1950s most families had switched to television and dating couples took over the drive-ins, which became known as *passion pits*. Today, their numbers are counted in the hundreds.

drop A heavy canvas on which a background scene is painted. The earliest cinematic drops were crude paintings, such as the village scene in *The Gay Corinthian* (1924). By World War II the art of drop painting had become vastly more sophisticated, the sweeping background drops used by Michael POWELL in such films as *49th Parallel* (1941) being particularly worthy of mention.

Drummond, Bulldog *See* BULLDOG DRUMMOND.

dry run A rehearsal of actors or camera movements (often both together) before shooting begins.

dub To record dialogue to match the lip movements in a film that has already been shot. This is usually done to supply dialogue in a language other than the original for foreign release. In France, defenders of the French language have blamed the dubbing of US films for the introduction of anglicisms (which better match the movements of the actors' lips) into everyday language. The effect of poor dubbing can be intensely comic, as in English-language versions of the Japanese GODZILLA films. Woody ALLEN's spoof *What's Up, Tiger Lily?* (1966) dubs comic English dialogue onto a second-rate Japanese spy film.

Dubbing may also be used to rerecord words or lines that are unclear on the original track or to replace weak or inappropriate voices. In *Greystoke: The Legend of Tarzan, Lord of the Apes* (1984), for instance, the words of Andie MacDowell, who plays Jane, are spoken by Glenn CLOSE. The voice of Jack HAWKINS was dubbed in all his later films, his vocal cords having been removed in an operation for throat cancer in 1966. Songs are also dubbed for actors whose singing voices are not considered strong enough (*see* GHOSTING). The dialogue for many Italian films is dubbed at the post-production stage as a matter of routine. According to rumour, FELLINI would sometimes order his actors to recite numbers at random during shooting and write dialogue to match afterwards.

Duck Soup (1933) The anarchic MARX BROTHERS comedy, directed by Leo MCCAREY. When dowager Margaret DUMONT makes her donation of $20 million to the duchy of Freedonia dependent on its acceptance of Groucho as dictator, the result is comic mayhem. Although Mussolini was so offended by the film that he had it suppressed in Italy, the Brothers' biographer, Joe Adamson, doubts its anti-Fascist intent: "There are political satires and there are political satires. *Duck Soup* is neither." Groucho is said to have responded to objections from the inhabitants of Fredonia, New York, by instructing the Mayor to change the name of the town: "It is hurting our picture."

The title of the film was once explained by Groucho: "Take two turkeys, one goose, four cabbages but no duck and mix them together. After one taste you'll duck soup for the rest of your life." Widely considered the Brothers' fastest, funniest, and most irreverent film, *Duck Soup* was the product of adversity. Groucho had lost a fortune on the stock market, Zeppo had announced his plans to leave the act, and the Brothers lost their father, Frenchie, shortly before shooting began. Moreover, as each Marx Brothers picture since their debut in *The Cocoanuts* (1929) had suffered from diminishing returns, Paramount had intimated that *Duck Soup* would make or break the Brothers' contract. Thanks to their own inimitable clowning and the adroit comic skills of McCarey they produced what many critics hailed as their masterpiece; nevertheless, the film only grossed $1,500,000 and the Marx Brothers' contract was terminated.

In spite of its poor financial performance, *Duck Soup* contains a wealth of quips:

DUMONT: My husband is dead.
GROUCHO: I'll bet he's just using that as an excuse.
DUMONT: I was with him to the end.
GROUCHO: No wonder he passed away.
DUMONT: I held him in my arms and kissed him.
GROUCHO: So it was murder!

GROUCHO: I could dance with you till the cows come home. On second thoughts I'd rather dance with the cows till you come home.

GROUCHO: Go, and never darken my towels again!

GROUCHO: Remember, men, we're fighting for this woman's honour: which is probably more than she ever did.

Duke, the A nickname of the western star John WAYNE. Although it seems appropriate to Wayne's noble and authoritative screen persona, the name actually derived from that of a large dog he owned as a boy. The two were known as Big Duke and Little Duke – Wayne being the latter.

Dumbo (1941) Outstanding DISNEY animation, one of the most successful of the studio's early full-length releases. It is the story of a baby circus elephant who suffers the ridicule of performers and audiences alike because of his huge ears – but finally emerges as a star after learning to fly.

The film was admired not only for the high quality of the artwork, but also for the characterization and for the music, which won the Academy Award for Best Scoring of a Musical Picture; the songs include such classics as 'When I See an Elephant Fly'. Other highlights of the film include a sequence in which Dumbo – who never says a word – and his diminutive ally, a mouse called Timothy, get drunk on champagne and are terrorized by a herd of pink elephants in a surrealistic hallucination.

According to Hollywood legend, the faces of some of the clowns who threaten to strike for a rise after Dumbo's success were modelled on those of the organizers of a strike at the Disney studios. Plans to feature Dumbo on the front page of *Time* magazine were thwarted by the bombing of Pearl Harbor, which took place not long after the film's release.

Dumont, Margaret (Margaret Baker; 1889–1965) Stout and stately US character actress, best known as the butt of Groucho MARX in such comedy classics as *Animal Crackers* (1930), DUCK SOUP (1933), and *A Night at the Opera* (1935). The films required her to suffer a series of physical and verbal indignities, which left her confused but somehow undiminished; in *At the Circus* (1939) she was even fired from a cannon. Groucho, her chief tormentor, paid her the following tribute: "She was a wonderful woman. She was the same off the stage as she was on it – always the stuffy, dignified matron. And the funny thing about her was she never understood the jokes."

The critic Cecilia Ager once called for a statue, Congressional medal, or national holiday in honour of Dumont:

a lady who asks but little and gets it. Surrounded by brothers who are surely a little odd, she does not think so. To her, her world of Marx Brothers pictures is rational, comprehensible, secure. Calmly she surveys it, with infinite resource she fights to keep on her feet in it.

dump tank   A device used to simulate a flood or tidal wave on set. To create this illusion, several large tanks are elevated, connected to chutes, and filled with water. On cue, the water is released in a strong tumbling flow. The effect can be seen in such films as *When Worlds Collide* (1951), *The Dam Busters* (1954), *Earthquake* (1974), and *Indiana Jones and the Temple of Doom* (1984).

Dunaway, Faye   (1941–) US leading lady, who won the Oscar for Best Actress playing a ruthless television executive in the satire *Network* (1976). British photographer Terry O'Neill took pictures of Dunaway with her award, sparking a relationship that led to marriage in 1981 and the formation of their own film production company.

Born in Bascom, Florida, Dunaway financed her drama studies at the University of Florida by working as a waitress. She later refused a Fulbright Scholarship to London's RADA in order to act with the Lincoln Center Repertory Company in New York. Her screen debut in *The Happening* (1967) was followed by two more films in the same year: Otto PREMINGER's *Hurry Sundown* and the controversial BONNIE AND CLYDE. Her portrayal of the gun-toting cigar-chewing bank-robber Bonnie Parker in the latter brought her an Oscar nomination. A year later, she recorded the longest screen kiss ever (55 seconds) with Steve MCQUEEN in *The Thomas Crown Affair* (1968).

Dunaway received a second Oscar nomination for her performance as a woman having a daughter by her own father (John HUSTON) in Roman POLANSKI's CHINATOWN (1974). Of her portrayal of Joan CRAWFORD as a child-beater in *Mommie Dearest* (1981), Crawford's daughter Christina remarked: "Faye Dunaway says she is being haunted by mother's ghost. After her performance in *Mommie Dearest*, I can understand why." Later films have included Michael WINNER's remake of *The Wicked Lady* (1983), *The Handmaid's Tale* (1989), and *Faithful* (1991).

Opinions of Dunaway's talent and temperament vary considerably. Although Roman Polanski found her "a gigantic pain in the ass. She demonstrated certifiable proof of insanity", Frank Perry, director of *Mommie Dearest*, has commented "I adore Faye Dunaway. I love her and I feel she's one of the most underrated actresses." In 1994 she made the headlines when she sued the composer Andrew Lloyd-Webber after being sacked from the musical *Sunset Boulevard*.

Dunne, Irene   (1898–1990) Sophisticated US actress, who starred in numerous tearjerkers, comedies, and musicals of the 1930s and 1940s. By World War II, she was earning $100,000 a picture for such films as *The White Cliffs of Dover* (1944).

Born in Louisville, Kentucky, Dunne made her screen debut in *Leathernecking* (British title *Present Arms*; 1930), a comedy about a socialite's love for a marine. Her melodramatic roles of the 1930s included that of a pathetically self-effacing mistress in *Back Street* (1932) and a woman blinded and then cured by Robert TAYLOR in *Magnificent Obsession* (1935). Dunne also appeared opposite Cary GRANT in such comedies as *The Awful Truth* (1937), in which the two play a married couple who divorce and remarry each other, and *My Favourite Wife* (1940), in which she plays a shipwrecked explorer who returns home to find Grant remarried. Charles BOYER was her co-star in the romantic comedy *Love Affair* (1938). Her musicals included *Roberta* (1935), with rising stars Fred ASTAIRE and Ginger ROGERS, and the original film version of *Show Boat* (1936).

The 1940s saw Dunne slipping into more matronly roles: the governess to Rex HARRISON's children in *Anna and the King of Siam* (1946), the wife of William POWELL in *Life with Father* (1947), and the mother of a Norwegian immigrant family in *I Remember Mama* (1948), which earned her an Oscar nomination. Her last major role was that of Queen Victoria in *The Mudlark* (1950), with Alec GUINNESS as Disraeli.

> She's a first-class craftswoman...but instead of being dull and perfect, she's enchanting and perfect.
> DOUGLAS FAIRBANKS JR.

dupe   A duplicate negative made from a MASTER positive. This is then used to make RELEASE PRINTS for distribution. The purpose of *duping* is to protect the original negative from the effects of repeated reproduction.

Durante, Jimmy 'Schnozzle'   (James Francis Durante; 1893–1980) US comedian, known for his majestic nose and the explosive manner in which he delivered such catchphrases as "I'm mortified!", "Everybody wants to get into de act", and "Goodnight, Mrs Calabash, wherever you are". (Some believe that 'Mrs Calabash' was his late wife, but Durante would never confirm this.) A vaudeville star of the 1920s, Durante often simply performed his old routines on screen, pounding a piano and belting out such songs as 'Ink-a-Dink-a-Doo' and 'I'm the Guy that Found the Lost Chord'. He also became a popular radio and television star.

In 1932 Durante appeared with Buster KEATON in *Speak Easily*, having been groomed by MGM to replace the fading star; he subsequently became a regular face in MGM musical comedies. He was noted for saving films, including two productions with international stars: *The Phantom President* (1933) with George M. Cohan (advertised with the plea "Vote every schnozzle!") and *Land Without Music* (1936), Capitol Films' musical with Richard Tauber. When Durante was given the lead in *You're in the Army Now* (1940), however, the magic was missing. His later films included *The Man Who Came to Dinner* (1941), *The Milkman* (1950), and *Jumbo* (1962), which contains the classic exchange:

SHERIFF: Where are you going with that elephant?

DURANTE (innocently): What elephant?

Durbin, Deanna (Edna Mae Durbin; 1921–) Canadian singer, who enjoyed international stardom for a decade before overexposure and overweight brought her career to a premature end. In 1938 she received a special Oscar for "bringing to the screen the spirit and personification of youth." Twenty years later, she summed up her appeal to the cinemagoing public: "I represented the ideal daughter millions of fathers and mothers wished they had."

At the age of 15, Durbin made her debut in Henry Koster's musical *Three Smart Girls* (1936), about a trio of sisters who save their parents' marriage. Following this success, she starred in the same director's *One Hundred Men and a Girl* (1937), in which she marches an orchestra of unemployed musicians into the home of conductor Leopold Stokowski. Both films received Oscar nominations for Best Picture.

Durbin made three films in 1938, including *Mad About Music* and *That Certain Age*. Her popularity continued during the war years, with such hits as the Jerome Kern musical *Can't Help Singing* (1944), in which

she goes out West to join her soldier sweetheart. The same year saw Durbin miscast opposite Gene KELLY in a box-office failure, *Christmas Holiday*. Although she returned to form with *Because of Him* (1945), in which she played an aspiring singer helped by Charles LAUGHTON, her star began to wane in the latter half of the 1940s.

When she sings, there is no sense of the footlights about it. She sings for music, not for show.

C. A. LEJEUNE, film critic.

dutch tilt *See* CAMERA ANGLES *under* CAMERA.

Duvall, Robert (1931–) US character actor and occasional lead, mainly cast as gangsters, soldiers, and policemen; most of his roles are either corrupt or morally ambiguous. The son of a rear admiral, Duvall began his acting career with the New York Neighborhood Playhouse in the 1960s. After making his film debut as Boo in *To Kill a Mockingbird* (1963) he appeared in a series of supporting roles, including that of the priggish Major Burns in M*A*S*H (1969). A year later he landed his first leading role, in George LUCAS's *THX-1138* (1970) a futuristic action film. It was, however, his crucial performance as Tom Hagen, the family lawyer and adviser in COPPOLA's THE GODFATHER (1972) and THE GODFATHER, PART II (1974), that established his reputation as one of Hollywood's finest supporting players.

His other roles of the 1970s included an unheroic Jesse James in *The Great Northfield Minnesota Raid* (1971), a violent police detective in *Badge 373* (1973), a Nazi officer in *The Eagle Has Landed* (1976), and the demented Colonel Kilgore in Coppola's APOCALYPSE NOW (1979). In 1976 he broke briefly with stereotype to play Dr Watson in the Sherlock HOLMES spoof *The Seven Per Cent Solution*.

In 1983 Duvall fulfilled a longstanding ambition to play a more sympathetic character when he was cast as Mac Sledge, a country singer down on his luck, in Bruce Beresford's *Tender Mercies*. Duvall gave a warm and charming performance and was rewarded with an Oscar for Best Actor. His subsequent films have included Dennis HOPPER's *Colors* (1988), in which he played yet another streetwise cop, the motorracing story *Days of Thunder* (1990), with Tom CRUISE, and *Falling Down* (1993), as a policeman on the trail of Michael DOUGLAS.

His one film as a director, *Angelo, My Love* (1984), is a gentle story of gypsy life set in New York.

Dwan, Allan (Joseph Aloysius Dwan; 1885–1981) Pioneering Canadian director, producer, and screenwriter, who directed some 400 Hollywood films and claimed to have produced, scripted, or edited 1400 more. Most of these were one- or two-reel silent films made at the rate of two a week; few have survived.

Born in Toronto, Dwan entered the film industry in 1909 as a lighting engineer and soon began to write scripts. In 1911 he was handed his first assignment as a director when the maker of *Brandishing a Bad Man* disappeared on a drunken binge. Despite his inexperience, Dwan rapidly acquired a reputation for technical innovations; he devised the first TRACKING SHOT in 1915 and a year later created one of the first CRANE SHOTS, when he suggested that D. W. GRIFFITH use a 115-foot elevator to film the towering Babylonian set in INTOLERANCE.

In his early career Dwan worked for the American Film Co., a small company producing mainly one-reel Westerns. His crew frequently had to defend themselves from intimidation by the MOTION PICTURE PATENTS TRUST, who hired riflemen to shoot out his cameras; Dwan responded by giving his cowboys real weapons to ward off the snipers. These adventurous days helped to inspire Peter BOGDANOVICH's film *Nickelodeon* (1976).

From the mid 1910s Dwan was much in demand as a director and worked with many of the leading stars of the era, including Lon CHANEY, Mary PICKFORD, the GISH SISTERS, and Gloria SWANSON. When Swanson feuded with her rival Pola NEGRI, Dwan agreed to hire a 70-man brass band to drown out sounds from Negri's adjacent set. During this period he also directed Douglas FAIRBANKS in such rousing adventures as *Robin Hood* (1922). After the coming of sound he worked mainly for 20th Century-Fox, for whom he directed a string of B-pictures and several Shirley TEMPLE vehicles, including *Rebecca of Sunnybrook Farm* (1938). He left Fox to make the epic *Suez* (1938), starring Tyrone POWER, and such comedies as *Brewster's Millions* (1945).

Dwan's best-known post-war film is *Sands of Iwo Jima* (1949), a thundering war story starring John WAYNE and featuring convincing footage of military action. The film became Republic's top box-office hit of all time. In the 1950s he returned to Westerns with such films as *Cattle Queen of Montana* (1954) starring Barbara STANWYCK; his final offering was a science-fiction thriller, *The Most Dangerous Man Alive* (1961).

Dynalens Tradename for a camera mount that uses a water cushion to greatly reduce vibrations. It is chiefly used for shots taken from a van or other moving vehicle.

dynamic. **dynamic cutting** or **dynamic editing** A style of MONTAGE in which meaning is created by the selection and juxtaposition of images rather than through their individual content. It is a favourite technique of documentary and agit-prop film-makers, who often juxtapose contrasting images (e.g. of poverty and affluence) to make a polemical point.

dynamic frame An experimental technique of the late 1950s and early 1960s, in which a film was shot so that the size and shape of the frame varied from scene to scene. Individual shots were MASKED down to emphasize their particular visual qualities; a shot of a skyscraper, for example, would be tall and narrow and one of a funeral procession wide and low. The technique proved too distracting to audiences, however, and was soon abandoned.

E

Ealing Studios A small British studio complex in west London, where many successful British films of the 1940s and 1950s were made. Basil DEAN's Associated Talking Pictures built the studio – the first in Europe to be designed for sound – for a modest £140,000. Opening in 1931, it enjoyed an early success with *Looking on the Bright Side* (1932), in which Gracie FIELDS played a singing manicurist. Three George FORMBY vehicles were produced in 1937–38, while wartime propaganda films included *Went the Day Well?* (1942), in which Nazi paratroopers occupy an English village, and *Undercover* (1943), featuring Michael Wilding as a Yugoslav partisan.

The studios entered their golden era under the leadership of Michael BALCON, who became director and chief of productions in 1937. Lacking the financial resources available to the US film industry, Ealing concentrated on characterization, plotting, and scripts. Despite low budgets, production standards remained high. Ealing films often displayed a social conscience, too: in *The Proud Valley* (1939), a plea for the nationalization of the coal industry, Paul Robeson led Welsh miners in their struggle to reopen pits, while *Frieda* (1947) starred Mai ZETTERLING as a German war-bride who incurs hostility when she settles in England with her husband, a British prisoner of war (David Farrar).

The studios are now best known for the so-called **Ealing Comedies** – a series of whimsical comedies made in the late 1940s and early 1950s. These included Henry CORNELIUS's *Passport to Pimlico* (1948), Alexander MACKENDRICK's WHISKY GALORE! (US title *Tight Little Island*;1949), *The Man in the White Suit* (1951), and *The Ladykillers* (1955), Robert Hamer's KIND HEARTS AND CORONETS (1949), in which Alec GUINNESS played eight parts, and Charles Crichton's *The Titfield Thunderbolt* (1952). Typically, these films featured a cast of gentle eccentrics and golden-hearted rogues in mild revolt against authority. The appeal of this benevolent version of England and the English seems to have grown greater with the years.

Other notable films made at Ealing included the chiller *Dead of Night* (1945), consisting of five short stories of the supernatural, *Mandy* (1952), about a deaf-and-dumb girl (Mandy Miller) and her teacher (Jack Hawkins), and the epic *Scott of the Antarctic* (1948). The studios were closed in 1956 and sold to BBC television; the last film made there was *The Long Arm* (1956), featuring Jack HAWKINS as a Scotland Yard detective. Ealing films were made at the ELSTREE studios in Borehamwood for a further three years until the assets were sold to ASSOCIATED BRITISH.

> Here during a quarter of a century were made many films projecting Britain and the British character.
> Plaque put up at Ealing Studios in 1956.

east. *East of Eden* (1955) Elia KAZAN's powerful rural melodrama, mainly remembered as the film in which the 24-year-old James DEAN established his reputation as one of the cinema's legendary rebels. Based on the last third of a lengthy novel by John Steinbeck, *East of Eden* depicted the tensions between an unforgiving father (Raymond MASSEY) and his wayward son Cal (Dean), against the backdrop of California's Salinas Valley in the years before World War I. The film was an immediate success, winning an Oscar as Best Supporting Actress for Jo Van Fleet (as Kate) and nominations for Kazan, Dean, and screenwriter Paul Osborn. Kazan himself had no fondness for Dean as a person and once described him as "a pudding of hatred."

East Side Kids, the *See* BOWERY BOYS, THE.

Eastman Color Trade name for the three-colour process now used for nearly all films. TECHNICOLOR dominated the industry from 1932 until 1952, when Kodak introduced Eastman Color for the Canadian film *Royal Journey*. As it required less light for filming and was easier to process, Eastman Color soon became dominant; in 1955 it was used in 112 productions, 22 more than were made in Technicolor. Eastman Color stock is now used by other systems, such as Warnercolor and De Luxe; even the Technicolor laboratories process Eastman Color negative film. Early Technicolor films are now printed on Eastman Color stock. *See also* COLOUR.

Eastwood, Clint (1930–) US actor, director, and producer associated mainly with violent action movies. Eastwood, who has directed or starred in more than 50 films, is often called "the last of the great Western stars." In the 10 years 1975–85 his films earned a record $1,400 million and he is thought to be the richest actor in the world.

Eastwood worked as a firefighter, steel-furnace stoker, lumberjack, lifeguard, and US Army swimming instructor before making his acting debut (for $75 a week) in Universal's *Revenge of the Creature* (1955). His one line, "Oh there you are", caused a fist fight between the director, who wanted it cut, and the producer, who kept it in. The following year, the studio dropped Eastwood.

After a lengthy stint in the Western television series *Rawhide* (1958–65), Eastwood returned to the cinema in Sergio LEONE's *A Fistful of Dollars* (1964), the first of the SPAGHETTI WESTERNS. Eastwood starred as the violent and taciturn 'Man with No Name' a poncho-clad cheroot-chewing drifter who represented a new kind of Western hero. "I do everything that John WAYNE would never do" he once commented, "I play the hero, but I can shoot the guy in the back." The character returned for two equally brutal sequels before United Artists reclaimed Eastwood for Hollywood by offering him $40,000 and 25% of the box-office for *Hang 'Em High* (1967).

In 1969 he was cast in the World War II adventure *Where Eagles Dare* to add lustre to Richard BURTON's waning appeal. Burton praised the "dynamic lethargy" of Eastwood's style, commenting "He appears to do nothing and does everything." Eastwood made his debut as a director with *Play Misty for Me* (1971), about a DJ menaced by a female admirer. A year later he became even more firmly identified with brutal machismo by playing the title character in *Dirty Harry*, a rogue cop with the notorious catchphrase "Go ahead, make my day" (*see under* DAY). By now he was America's number-one box-office star. In 1978 he turned to comedy with *Every Which Way But Loose*, in which he co-starred with Clyde the orang-utan. His most successful film to date, it made $48 million at the box office. Eastwood's films of the 1980s include *Firefox* (1980), *Pale Rider* (1985), and *White Hunter Black Heart* (1990), all of which he also directed and produced. He served as mayor of the affluent town of Carmel, California, from 1985 to 1988.

A new level of critical respect came with *Unforgiven* (1993), a film about the return of a retired gunfighter that earned Oscars for Best Director, Best Picture, and Best Supporting Actor (Gene HACKMAN). Eastwood played another ageing action man in *In the Line of Fire* (1993), about a Secret Service agent who, having failed to prevent the Kennedy assassination, tries to recover his self-esteem by saving the current president from a copycat attempt. In 1994 Eastwood directed himself and Kevin COSTNER in *A Perfect World*. He was presented with the Irving G. Thalberg Award for producers at the 1995 Oscars ceremony.

Easy Rider (1969) An offbeat low-budget ROAD MOVIE that became a cult film by capturing the restless hedonism of the hippy era. The film's surprise success inspired a wave of youth-culture movies, few of which are now remembered. Its most lasting effect was to make a star of Jack NICHOLSON, who won an Oscar nomination for his portrayal of an aimless lawyer making his first experiments with drugs. The lead characters were played by Peter FONDA and Dennis HOPPER, who produced and directed respectively; both also collaborated on the script (with Terry Southern). The film, which cost only $375,000 to make, took some $50 million at the box office.

The episodic plot concerns two motorcyclists who take their profits from a drugs deal to head for the New Orleans Mardi Gras. In the course of their odyssey across America they meet frequent backwoods intolerance; eventually they are gunned down by Louisiana rednecks in a passing pickup truck. Athough the big studios attempted to imitate *Easy Rider*'s casual technique and rebellious attitudes, its impact was never equalled.

ECU   *See* EXTREME CLOSE-UP.

Eddie Awards   *See* ACE.

Eddy, Nelson (1901–67) US actor and singer, who succeeded Maurice CHEVALIER as Jeanette MACDONALD's partner in a series of film operettas. Having trained as an opera singer, Eddy made his film debut in *Broadway to Hollywood* (1931). He first co-starred with MacDonald in MGM's *Naughty Marietta* (1935), a musical about a French princess who falls in love with an American Indian scout. Although it now seems dated, the film was an attempt by producer Irving THALBERG and director W. S. Van Dyke to breathe new life into the implausible combination of plot and song that characterized film operettas.

Eddy and MacDonald continued their partnership in such films as *Rose Marie* (1936), in which Eddy played a Canadian Mountie, *Maytime* (1937), *Sweethearts* (1938), and *New Moon* (1940). In the late 1930s the two stars had an enormous following amongst that large constituency of filmgoers whose weekly visits to the cinema were made in search of an innocuous dose of escapism. Films made without MacDonald included *Phantom of the Opera* (1943) and Eddy's last operetta, *Northwest Outpost* (1947), in which he played a cavalryman. The couple later made guest appearances on television.

edge numbers Identification numbers printed at regular intervals in the margins of film stock and reproduced on the positive print during processing. They are especially useful in the process of creating a matching negative from the completed WORKPRINT.

Edinburgh International Film Festival A film festival held in Edinburgh for a fortnight each August and September. Founded in 1947 to focus on documentary films, it is now the world's longest-running film festival and presents new work in all genres from many countries. The programme also includes retrospective seasons, children's cinema, masterclasses with famous actors and directors, and the presentation of several awards, including the Michael Powell Prize for best British Feature Film, the Channel 4 Young Film-Maker of the Year Award, and the Charles Chaplin Young Film-Maker of the Year Competition. The festival's patron is the Scottish film actor Sean CONNERY.

Edison, Thomas A(lva) (1847–1931) US engineer, a prolific inventor who developed and exploited an early film-viewing apparatus and camera.

Edison thought sales of his phonograph would increase if it were complemented by a visual equivalent. As usual, he delegated development of the idea to one of his employees, and in 1889 W. K. L. Dickson (1860–1935), a Scot, began to experiment with moving pictures. After an initial period of failure, Dickson found success with a viewing device that used 15m celluloid film loops, which he demonstrated to Edison at the New Jersey laboratory in May 1891. In August Edison filed for patents on the KINETOGRAPH camera and KINETOSCOPE viewer and by 1892 he was ready to market both.

The electric camera used a 35mm celluloid film strip that was perforated to engage with sprockets (their first use), thereby ensuring accurate image register and effective INTERMITTENT MOVEMENT. The viewer was a box containing a continuously moving film loop that lasted about a minute. An intervening rotary shutter was used to break a beam of light directed through the film, producing a sequence of 'moving' pictures in a glass magnifier at the top of the box.

Although Edison tried to adapt this method so that the images could be projected onto a screen, the shutter obscured more light than it transmitted, resulting in dim blurry images at screen magnification. It never occurred to Edison to use his camera's intermittent movement in the projector, and he soon dropped the idea; his Kinetoscopes, sold for $200 each to arcade operators, who were also obliged to buy films produced by the Edison company, already provided a substantial income. By the time he saw the need for his own projector, his only option was to buy rights to Thomas Armat's device (in 1896).

Initially, Edison produced films only to entice exhibitors into buying his machines. To create a supply, Edison built the world's first film studio, a large hut covered in tarred paper known as the BLACK MARIA. Dancers, wrestlers, strongmen, and jugglers were filmed against a black wall at one end of the studio; the other end held a huge camera and dark room. A fight staged to end in a sixth-round knock-out took six hours to film, as each change of film took over half an hour: at one round per loop, however, viewers paid six times to see the whole match, so Edison's investment was soon repaid.

When rivals began using their own equipment to make or show films, Edison claimed patent infringement, forcing, in 1908, the major film producers to join him in a monopoly trust, the MOTION PICTURE PATENT COMPANY. With patents on raw film, projectors, and cameras, the trust levied $24,000-a-week royalties on users. Many producers avoided paying by filming in secrecy away from trust enforcement agents. One such site was open country near Mexico. Its name was HOLLYWOOD.

edit. editing The creative and technical process of assembling film footage in the most effective sequence.

The basic conventions of continuity editing were established, mainly by a process of trial and error, in the early years of the century; Edwin S. PORTER's *The Great Train Robbery* (1903) is often cited as the first landmark in the establishment of a new narrative language of film. This achievement was built upon by D. W. GRIFFITH, who introduced an unprecedented sophistication in the use of long, medium, and close shots to build up a scene, as well as pioneering the use of CROSS CUTTING between parallel actions (as in chase and rescue sequences). In the 1920s G. W. PABST established many of the conventions of so-called INVISIBLE CUTTING, such as CUTTING ON ACTION, which later became basic tenets of the classical Hollywood style. At much the same time a more self-conscious and experimental approach to editing was being developed by the Russian directors Sergei EISENSTEIN, Alexander DOVZHENKO, and Vsevelod PUDOVKIN. Eisenstein was chiefly responsible for developing the art of intellectual MONTAGE, in which shots are juxtaposed for symbolic rather than narrative reasons. The introduction of SOUND in the late 1920s posed severe practical problems for editors that were not fully resolved until the advent of multiple-channel mixing. In the 1950s many of the directors associated with the French NEW WAVE reacted against the seamless style of classic Hollywood editing by adopting abrupt or elliptical cutting techniques. In recent years the very painstaking and time-consuming process of editing has been greatly facilitated by the introduction of video editing systems.

The editing process begins with the viewing and cataloguing of RUSHES while the film is still being shot. These are sometimes edited in rough order during filming so that the director can see if changes are needed. The creative process of selecting, assembling, and trimming shots extends from the ROUGH CUT to the polished FINE CUT. At this stage the WORKPRINT is usually submitted to the director and producer for approval. Once this has been obtained, SOUND EDITING is completed and the original negative is cut to match the approved workprint. The ANSWER PRINT produced from this negative is again submitted for approval before the film is released.

Occasionally, a 'final' print is re-edited at a later date. When a PREVIEW audience watching SOME LIKE IT HOT (1959) laughed loudly at the sight of Jack LEMMON and Tony CURTIS struggling to walk in high heels, the director Billy WILDER extended the sequence by adding footage taken from other angles; the finished scene is made up of six views of the same walk past a railway carriage. Conversely, the preview audience's unfavourable reaction to the David NIVEN film *The Elusive Pimpernel* (1950), originally a musical, led to a decision to edit out all the songs. *See also* DIRECTOR'S CUT; FINAL CUT.

editing ratio *See* SHOOTING RATIO.

editor The person responsible for EDITING a film. He or she normally works under the control of the DIRECTOR, who has the final word if disputes arise.

> Shooting film is the director's way of talking to the editor – cutting film is the editor's way of answering.
> HARRY KERAMIDA, film editor.

> The notion that the director works continuously with the editor in cutting the film is a myth. It only happens that way when the director is also a cutter.
> ARAM AVAKIAN, film editor

Some directors, such as David LEAN, began as editors and continued to handle that aspect of their films.

educational films Films intended to inform and instruct. Some of the earliest known films come into this category: in the 1890s, for instance, a French scientist filmed bacteria through a microscope to demonstrate their behaviour patterns. In the 1930s Britain's EMPIRE FILM BOARD produced numerous DOCUMENTARIES with a strong educational content. Until the advent of VIDEO, training films for showing in schools, colleges, and workplaces were usually made in an 8MM or 16MM format. Some instructional films have reached a large audience via television, as through Britain's Open University series or America's National Educational Network (NET). In 1957 a complete high-school physics course was produced by Encyclopaedia Britannica Films.

Broadly defined, the category may be taken to include most forms of documentary film, ranging from commercial features like DISNEY's THE LIVING DESERT (1953) to historical footage such as that of the Wright brothers' flight (1908). Educational films may include a strong element of PROPAGANDA, especially when produced by totalitarian regimes or during wartime. Recently, many makers of sexually explicit videos for the British market have successfully evaded censorship by having their product classified as 'commercial education videos' (E classification).

Edwards, Blake (William Blake McEdwards; 1922–   ) US producer, director, and screenwriter of comedies. Edwards grew up in Hollywood, the son of a movie production manager. After acting briefly in the 1940s, he switched to screenwriting for the director Richard Quine. He made his own debut as a director in 1955, enjoying his first success with the naval comedy *Operation Petticoat* (1959), starring Cary GRANT and Tony CURTIS.

An even bigger success was *Breakfast at Tiffany's* (1961), a cleaned-up version of Truman Capote's novel featuring Audrey HEPBURN as an eccentric playgirl. The theme song, Henry MANCINI's 'Moon River' became an international hit. Mancini also scored *Days of Wine and Roses* (1962), starring Lee REMICK and Jack LEMMON as alcoholics, and provided the theme for THE PINK PANTHER (1963), the film that made Edwards's career. Peter SELLERS's bumbling Inspector Clouseau returned for a series of sequels, including *A Shot in the Dark* (1964) and *The Pink Panther Strikes Again* (1976). After Sellers's death, Edwards patched together old out-takes to create *The Trail of the Pink Panther* (1982), a flop that resulted in United Artists having to pay Sellers's widow $1,687,000 for infringement.

Edwards suffered a $22-million disaster with *Darling Lili* (1969) but married Julie ANDREWS, its star. Andrews subsequently played the longsuffering wife of Dudley MOORE in the popular sex comedy *'10'* (1979), showed her breasts in *S.O.B.*

(1981), a hit-and-miss satire on Hollywood greed, appeared as a cabaret artist who finds success by posing as a 'female impersonator' in the farce *Victor/Victoria* (1982), and played the ill wife of hypochondriac Jack Lemmon in *That's Life* (1986). Recent films, none of which has been very successful, include *Skin Deep* (1989) and *Son of the Pink Panther* (1993).

A man of many talents, all of them minor.
LESLIE HALLIWELL.

EFB   *See* EMPIRE FILM BOARD.

effects   (FX) A general term for all visual SPECIAL EFFECTS; sometimes also used of SOUND EFFECTS.

effect filter A FILTER placed over a camera lens to create a particular effect or atmosphere, such as a haziness to indicate a dream, etc.

effects track A separate SOUNDTRACK featuring SOUND EFFECTS, such as thunder or church bells; these are mixed with dialogue, music, etc. at a postproduction rerecording session.

eight.   *8½* (*Otto e mezzo*; 1963) Federico FELLINI's delightful semiautographical drama, often considered his finest and most influential work. Filmed in black-and-white, *8½* is a complex and intelligent account of a film director, Guido Anselmi (played by Marcello MASTROIANNI), who finds himself facing a creative crisis. Anselmi, who has just finished a highly successful film, is attempting to relax at a spa but finds himself constantly harried by his screenwriter and producer for details of his next project. He is also harassed by his wife (Anouk AIMÉE) and mistress (Sandra Milo). As the pressures on Anselmi mount – hundreds of people are depending on the success of his next film – he finds himself blocked and seeks to escape by retreating into fantastical dreams and memories.

The film featured a strong cast – with Aimee and Claudia CARDINALE giving particularly fine performances – and a memorable score from the Italian composer Nino Rota (who wrote the music for all of Fellini's early films and later provided the score for THE GODFATHER). Although not universally acclaimed upon release (one critic describing it as "not even like dogs dancing; it is not done well, nor does it surprise us that it is done at all") the film won Oscars for Best Costume Design and Best

Foreign-Language Film. It was also nominated for another three Oscars. The enigmatic title derives from Fellini's personal film-making history. Fellini had directed six films, co-directed another, and contributed to two anthology films; by his reckoning this added up to seven and a half films, making this one eight and a half.

8mm A narrow GAUGE of film used mainly by amateurs and others working outside the commercial mainstream. Sound was rarely used with 8mm film until the superior SUPER 8 gauge was developed in the 1970s. In the making of 'home movies' it has almost entirely been replaced by video. Being cheap, 8mm film has sometimes been used by makers of low-budget experimental films (notably Derek JARMAN). When projected onto the large screen, the 8mm image has a grainy quality that has sometimes been deliberately exploited by film-makers to create a sense of documentary REALISM.

Eisenstein, Sergei Mikhailovich (1898– 1948) Russian director, screenwriter, and theorist regarded as one of the great figures in cinema history. His most important technical innovation was his use of intellectual MONTAGE, the juxtaposition of images with no narrative connection to create a symbolic relationship. This device, which Eisenstein derived from Japanese ideograms and his own study of the psychology of perception, was later used by Alfred HITCHCOCK, Jean-Luc GODARD, and Alexander Kluge, amongst others.

Born in Latvia, the son of an architectural engineer, Eisenstein fought in the Red Army before becoming a stage designer; he made his first film, a five-minute short, in 1923. A year later he introduced his montage technique in the propaganda piece *Strike*, in which a scene of tsarist police massacring striking workers suddenly switches to a shot of a bull dying in an abattoir.

Eisenstein's most celebrated film is BATTLESHIP POTEMKIN (1925), about a naval mutiny during the revolution of 1905: it contains the famous sequence in which civilians are slaughtered on the Odessa Steps by tsarist troops. The film was shot in ten weeks using nonprofessional actors. It had a poor first run in America, but attracted growing audiences after Mary PICKFORD and Douglas FAIRBANKS described it as "the greatest film ever made." However, most European nations banned it as a work of communist propaganda.

Eisenstein followed this masterpiece with *October* (also called *Ten Days That Shook the World*; 1928), about the 1917 revolution. *The General Line* (also called *The Old and the New*; 1929), dealt with collective farming. Despite his reputation as a master, hard years were ahead for Eisenstein. In 1929 he visited Hollywood to film Thomas Dreiser's *An American Tragedy* for Paramount only to discover that Josef VON STERNBERG had been given the project. He returned home to find his work in disfavour owing to the new dogma of socialist realism in the arts. When his first sound project was squashed by the government, he made an abortive attempt to film in Mexico (1932–33).

Eisenstein returned to favour with his next production, ALEXANDER NEVSKY (1938), which was technically more conventional than his earlier work, if no less dazzling. Its story of a heroic 13th-century prince repelling German invaders was intentionally flattering to Stalin. Prokofiev composed scores for both this film and for Eisenstein's last project, the two-part IVAN THE TERRIBLE (1944 and 1946; a third part was destroyed). Although the first part, which implicitly compares Ivan's struggles with the Soviet dictator's fight against the Nazis, won the Stalin prize, officials banned the second part for depicting Ivan as "weak and indecisive, somewhat like Hamlet." A third episode, approved by Stalin, was abandoned by the director when his health began to fail. He spent the last year of his life lecturing and writing on the cinema. An Eisenstein Museum now exists in his widow's small flat in Moscow.

Ekberg, Anita (1931–) Statuesque Swedish actress, best remembered for kissing Marcello MASTROIANNI in a Roman fountain in FELLINI'S LA DOLCE VITA.

Ekberg, who represented Sweden in the 1951 Miss Universe competition, remained in America to model before making her film debut with a small role in *The Golden Blade* (1953), an Arabian Nights adventure. Her first major film appearance was in King VIDOR's *War and Peace* (1956). She also starred in such British offerings as the adventure film *Zarak* (1956) with Victor MATURE and the thriller *The Man Inside* (1958) with Nigel Patrick.

After burlesquing her own sexuality in Fellini's 'Temptation of Dr Antonio' episode in *Boccaccio '70* (1962), Ekberg continued to appear as a caricature blonde bombshell in such comedies as *Call Me Bwana* (1962) with Bob HOPE, *Four for Texas* (1963), with Frank SINATRA and Dean MARTIN, and *If It's Tuesday, This Must be Belgium* (1969). Her later films, such as the Italian cult shocker *Suor Omicidi* (*Killer Nun*; 1979), have been mainly European productions.

> I'm very much bigger than I was, so what? It's not really fatness, it's development.
>
> ANITA EKBERG: *Daily Mail*, 1972.

Ekland, Britt (Britt-Marie Eklund; 1942–) Swedish actress, who has made numerous international films, most of them in Britain. A beautiful blonde, she worked as a model before making her screen debut in 1962. Ekland was the second wife of the British actor Peter SELLERS, who called their marriage "just a mismatch."

Her films have included *After the Fox* (1966), in which she played Sellers's sister, and *The Bobo* (1967), in which she played the object of his desire. *The Night They Raided Minsky's* (1968) featured Ekland as an innocent Amish girl, who becomes a burlesque dancer. Other films have included the gangster movie *Get Carter* (1971), the cult chiller *The Wicker Man* (1973), the BOND extravaganza *The Man With the Golden Gun* (1974), the historical romp *Royal Flash* (1975), and Blake EDWARDS's sex comedy *Skin Deep* (1989).

> In order for there to be a Jane Fonda or a Vanessa Redgrave, there have to be people like me. That's the way it is.
>
> BRITT EKLAND, 1988.

electrician The member of a film crew who handles and maintains the lighting equipment on a set. He or she is usually supervised by the GAFFER or a lighting expert.

electronovision A process invented to convert videotapes into films for the big screen. It was deemed a technical failure after two television tapes were turned into feature films in 1965; a production of *Hamlet* with Richard BURTON in the lead and *Harlow*, a biopic of the actress Jean HARLOW, starring Carol Lynley and Ginger ROGERS (not to be confused with the 1965 cinema release of the same title featuring Carroll Baker).

elevation shot A shot in which the camera moves vertically but not horizontally. *See* CAMERA MOVEMENT.

Elliott, Denholm (1922–93) British actor, known originally for his supporting roles as a lovable, often drunk, bumbler, but later for more moving and sophisticated parts. Notorious for consistently stealing scenes from the stars, he provoked Gabriel Byrne to suggest that the old actors' adage be amended to "Never work with children, animals, or Denholm Elliott."

Born in London, Elliott spent three years as a prisoner of war in Germany during World War II. He made his stage debut in 1945 and four years later began his film career with a minor role in the comedy *Dear Mr Prohack*. By 1956 he was starring as a British colonial servant in *Pacific Destiny*. His screen character was established in two comedies directed by Clive Donner; in *Nothing But the Best* (1964) Elliott portrayed a debonair but seedy conman teaching Alan BATES the social tricks required to wed the boss's daughter, while in *Here We Go Round the Mulberry Bush* (1967) he played the inebriated father of a posh young lady wooed by a school-leaver.

In the 1970s and 1980s Elliott became a familiar international figure in such US films as the Nazi fantasy *The Boys from Brazil* (1978), in which he supported Gregory PECK and Laurence OLIVIER, the SPIELBERG adventure *Raiders of the Lost Ark* (1981), and the comedy *Trading Places*, starring Eddie MURPHY and Dan AYKROYD (1983). He also supplied the voice for the rabbit Cowslip in the cartoon feature *Watership Down* (1978).

In 1985 Elliott received an Oscar nomination for his role in MERCHANT-IVORY's E. M. Forster adaptation *A Room With a View* and won the BAFTA Award for Best Supporting Actor in the political melodrama *Defence of the Realm*. His last parts included roles in Merchant-Ivory's *Maurice* (1987), based on Forster's novel of homosexual love, and Woody ALLEN's *September* (1987). He died of AIDS.

Elmer Gantry (1960) Richard BROOKS's film version of the Sinclair Lewis novel about a Bible-bashing evangelist in 1920s America. Brooks received an Academy Award for his script, Burt LANCASTER won his only Oscar as the charismatic but hypocritical Gantry, and Shirley Jones was named Best Supporting Actress for playing the prostitute Lulu Baines. Jones recalled how this major departure from her usual sweet roles provoked angry letters from mothers: "You were my daughter's idol. How could you degrade yourself?" The strong cast also included Jean SIMMONS (who subsequently married

Brooks) as Sister Sharon Falconer, Arthur Kennedy, and Dean Jagger. Further Oscar nominations went to the film as Best Picture and to André Previn for his music.

The plot follows the rise and fall of Gantry, a Midwestern revivalist preacher with an appetite for liquor and women. One day he unexpectedly meets up again with Lulu, who had been an innocent preacher's daughter until he had seduced her years earlier. "He rammed the fear of God into me" Lulu recalls. Now a prostitute, Lulu seeks revenge by hiring a photographer to surprise Gantry during their intimate reunion and using the results to threaten him with exposure.

ELS *See* EXTREME LONG SHOT.

Elstree The site near Borehamwood, in outer London, of the famous British film studios. The complex was founded in the 1920s by British International Pictures, which after various mergers became ASSOCIATED BRITISH in 1933. The numerous films made at Elstree, sometimes called the 'British Hollywood,' include Alfred HITCHCOCK's *Blackmail* (1929), the first British all-talkie. At the height of its activity in the 1930s some 15 films a year were produced on the site. In 1969 the Borehamwood complex was acquired by Thorn-EMI, who sold out to Cannon in the 1980s. Although activity has been greatly reduced in recent decades, the facilities are still used from time to time by top producers.

Elvey, Maurice (William Seward Folkard; 1887–1967) Britain's most prolific director, who was responsible for more than 300 films, including 149 features, in a career spanning four decades. Amongst those who began their careers with Elvey were Carol REED, who assisted on *The Water Gypsies* (1932), and David LEAN, who worked as a clapper boy on *Quinneys* (1927). Elvey directed Gaumont's first talking feature, *High Treason* (1929), and the first British colour film, *Sons of the Sea* (1939).

Born in Darlington to poor parents, he had no formal education and was working from the age of nine. In his teens and early twenties he acted and directed for the stage, before making his first two films, *Maria Marten: A Murder in the Red Barn* and *The Great Gold Robbery*, for Motograph in 1913. Elvey's films of the 1920s included *Don Quixote* (1923), with George Robey as Sancho Panza, and the Gaumont comedy *You Know What Sailors Are* (1928). Gaumont's *High Treason*, which showed women of the future banding together to prevent war, was a remake of an earlier silent film by Elvey.

Elvey subsequently directed Gracie FIELDS in several films, including her first, *Sally in Our Alley* (1931). In 1932 he remade HITCHCOCK's silent film *The Lodger* (1926) as a talkie with the original star, Ivor NOVELLO. Three years later, he directed Leslie BANKS in *The Tunnel* (1935), about an attempt to build an undersea tunnel between Britain and America.

Elvey's wartime films included *Sons of the Sea*, in which Leslie BANKS attends the Royal Naval College, *For Freedom* (1940), about the sinking of the *Graf Spee*, and *The Lamp Still Burns* (1943), a tribute to the nursing services. After making *Second Fiddle* (1957) he retired, having lost the use of an eye.

empire. Empire Film Board (EFB) The familiar name for the British Empire Marketing Board Film Unit, a government body established in 1929 by John GRIERSON as part of the Empire Marketing Board. Under the direction of Sir Stephen Tallents the EFB produced nearly 100 films and made British DOCUMENTARIES world famous in the 1930s. The films sought both to educate and to advance the cause of democracy worldwide. Leading talents recruited by Grierson included the film-makers Alberto CAVALCANTI, Humphrey JENNINGS, Pat Jackson, Harry Watt, and Basil Wright, as well as the poet W. H. Auden, the composer Benjamin Britten, and the journalist Alistair Cooke.

When the Empire Marketing Board was dissolved in 1933, its Film Unit, still run by Grierson and Tallents, was put under the control of the General Post Office (*see* GPO FILM UNIT). Films from this period include the famous *Night Mail* (1936), a collaboration between Grierson, Wright, Britten, and Auden that gave a romantic account of the nightly journeys of the 'Postal Special' train between London and Edinburgh. In 1940 the unit was taken over by the Films Division of the Ministry of Information and renamed the **Crown Film Unit**. Under Jack Beddington it moved towards a blending of documentary and narrative form in such films as Pat Jackson's *Western Approaches* (1944), a story of torpedoed merchantmen adrift in the Atlantic.

Empire of the Senses *See* AI NO CORRIDA.

emulsion The suspension of photosensitive chemicals in gelatin that is used to coat one surface of cinematographic film (the **emulsion side**).

end title A TITLE that announces the conclusion of a film, usually 'The End' or 'Finis'.

Enfants du paradis, Les (*Children of Paradise*; 1945) Marcel CARNÉ's tribute to the theatre and the indomitable spirit of France. The film is set on the Boulevard du Temple, Paris, during the reigns of Charles X and Louis Philippe. A sprawling epic of 195 minutes, it tells of the impact on the lives of pantomimist Baptiste Debureau (Jean-Louis BARRAULT), Shakespearean actor Fréderick Lemaître (Pierre Brasseur), thief Pierre-François Lacenaire (Marcel Herrand), and Count Edouard de Montray (Louis Salou) of the adventuress Garance (ARLETTY).

Some 350 films were made in France during the Nazi Occupation, but this is by far the most ambitious and beloved. The idea for the picture, originally entitled *Les Funambules*, came from Barrault and was inspired by a sensational murder trial involving the historical Debureau. However, Carné and his regular collaborator, the poet Jacques PRÉVERT, saw in the exuberance of the milieu an opportunity for an allegorical celebration of the courage of the Free French. The 'children' of the title are those who sat in the cheapest seats of the theatre, known as 'Paradise', and by extension the French people as a whole.

Making the feature was something of an act of resistance in itself. The film's length was in flagrant contravention of Nazi curfew laws, which stipulated that no feature should run over 90 minutes. Composer Joseph Kosma and set designer Alexandre Trauner were employed despite the outlawing of Jews within the cinema, while several cast members were active in the Maquis and had to shoot their scenes secretly, causing much revision of the schedule. Carné was content to acquiesce in such delays as he hoped to premiere the film in a liberated Paris. Production began in Nice in August 1943, transferred to Joinville in September, and relocated to Nice in November. When one of the cast, Robert Le Vigan (who had made a number of broadcasts for the Germans), received death threats and refused to leave the capital, Carné was compelled to reshoot his scenes with Pierre Renoir. Electricity shortages contributed to further delays and the project was only completed in March 1944. Following D-Day, Carné deliberately slowed down the editing, hiding the negatives around Paris to prevent confiscation. *Les Enfants du paradis* finally opened on 9 March 1945, the first new film to appear after the Liberation. Critic Jacques Natanson wrote "Behold the monument of the French cinema" and *Les Enfants* remains one of its richest treasures.

English-language remakes The US film industry has often found it profitable to make English-language versions of successful foreign films. The first foreign feature to catch Hollywood's eye was the 12-reel Italian spectacle QUO VADIS? (1913; remade in 1925 and 1929), although it was not until 1951 that MGM made its own version. The process is usually much quicker. The French gangster movie *Pépé Le Moko* (1937) rapidly inspired two Hollywood remakes, *Algiers* (1938), with Charles BOYER and Hedy LAMARR, and the musical *Casbah* (1948), with Tony Martin and Yvonne DE CARLO. Similarly Marcel CARNÉ's *Le Jour se lève* (1939) was remade as the inferior *The Long Night* (1947), with Henry FONDA in Jean GABIN's original role of a cornered murderer. In 1960 Akira KUROSAWA's classic THE SEVEN SAMURAI (1954) was adapted as *The Magnificent Seven*, a Western starring Yul BRYNNER.

More recently Hollywood transformed Daniel Givne's 1982 film *Le Retour de Martin Guerre* into the successful *Sommersby* (1993), with Richard GERE replacing Gérard DEPARDIEU in the lead. That same year Luc Besson's stylish and violent thriller *Nikita* (1990) was remade as *Assassin* with Bridget FONDA in the lead. The process continued, fuelled mainly by the US public's notorious reluctance to watch foreign films.

epic A genre of film in which historical or legendary events provide a background for heroism and lavish spectacle. Epics are notorious for their extravagant sets, enormous casts (some 9000 extras being required for one scene alone in *Land of the Pharaohs* in 1955), and inflated budgets. As the humorist James Thurber remarked of DE MILLE's THE TEN COMMANDMENTS, "It makes you realize what God could have done if He'd had the money."

The lead in epics is generally a dashing hero, who displays a bronzed and muscular body clad in little more than a loincloth and sandals. Hollywood stars to find success in such roles have included Charlton HESTON (Moses), Victor MATURE (Samson), and Kirk DOUGLAS (Ulysses). Love interest has been supplied by such actresses as Hedy LAMARR (Delilah), Elizabeth TAYLOR (Cleopatra), and Susan Hayward (Bathsheba).

The epic arrived early in film history, the first major example being the Italian QUO VADIS? (1913), a 12-reel spectacular with a Christian theme that helped to convince Americans of the respectability of the new medium. D. W. GRIFFITH followed with the landmark productions BIRTH OF A NATION (1915), which cost over $100 million dollars, and INTOLERANCE (1916), with its mammoth Babylonian set. The most celebrated of all Hollywood epics are undoubtedly the biblical extravaganzas of Cecil B. De Mille, whose works include *King of Kings* (1927), *The Sign of the Cross* (1932), and *Samson and Delilah* (1949). All these films combine panoramic action, explicit brutality, and such stunning spectacles as the parting of the Red Sea in *The Ten Commandments* (1956); suggestive love scenes and a certain amount of religious moralizing complete the package. The genre found a new lease of life in the 1950s with the advent of the wide screen, which encouraged such productions as THE ROBE (1953), BEN-HUR (1959), *Spartacus* (1960), *El Cid* (1961), *Cleopatra* (1963), *Zulu* (1964), and *The Greatest Story Ever Told* (1964). More recently the term 'epic' has come to be applied to any lengthy and expensive film featuring a large cast and sweeping action.

> The easiest kind of picture to make badly.
> CHARLTON HESTON.

> Cecil B. De Mille
> Much against his will
> Was persuaded to keep Moses
> Out of the Wars of the Roses.
> ANON.

episodic film A film that contains several distinct stories. These are usually connected by a common theme, as in D. W. GRIFFITH'S INTOLERANCE (1915), or in some other way. Films presenting several stories by the same author include *Quartet* (1948), in which W. Somerset Maugham introduced four of his tales, and *O. Henry's Full House* (1952). PASOLINI's *The Canterbury Tales* (1971) anthologized the bawdier moments from Chaucer, while *Boccacio '70* (with episodes by FELLINI, VISCONTI, and DE SICA) consisted of stories that Boccacio *might* have told had he been alive in 1970. Film-makers have used

various devices to link episodes together: in the Ealing feature *Train of Events* (1949) the link was a train disaster in which all the characters are involved, while in *La Ronde* (1950; remade 1964) each story is linked to the next by a sexual encounter. The Neil Simon comedy *California Suite* (1978) and Jim Jarmusch's *Mystery Train* (1989) both deal with different groups of guests staying in the same hotel.

The term 'episodic' is also used of films in which the various incidents are only loosely related; examples include the cameo-filled AROUND THE WORLD IN EIGHTY DAYS and such ROAD MOVIES as EASY RIDER (1969) and David LYNCH's *Wild at Heart* (1990).

Equity. **(American) Actors' Equity Association** The US trade union for professional actors in the theatre, film, radio, and television founded in 1913. It was officially recognized in 1919 after calling a strike for better working conditions; in 1924 it became a closed shop. The union gained a minimum-wage scale for its members in 1933; a strike in 1960 resulted in further improvements in members' contracts, and the following year brought a commitment to racial equality in the theatre and cinema.

(British) Actors' Equity Association The trade union for Britain's professional actors. The strict rules surrounding membership have made the Equity card much sought-after (although it is not required to play speaking parts in the cinema). The union was formed in 1929 to deal with such concerns as pay and conditions of employment. It also subsidizes companies, protects its members from foreign actors seeking work in Britain, and conducts research: a 1992 survey found that actresses earn an average of 50% less than actors and even those actresses with top billing earn 30% less.

Eraserhead (1978) David LYNCH's extraordinary black-and-white debut feature. Beset by financial problems, Lynch produced, wrote, and edited the film himself as well as directing. Even so, lack of funds meant that *Eraserhead* was some five years in the making. In one sequence alone, a year-long gap ensued between a shot in which Jack Nance approaches a door and its successor, in which he emerges on the other side.

The film revolves around the character of Harry Spencer (Nance), a nondescript young man whose world is, from the very beginning of the film, more than a little frayed at the edges. Following a dinner with the family of his girlfriend, Mary X (Charlotte Stewart), the two set up home together and begin to raise their 'baby', a deformed screaming creature whose continual howling causes Mary to flee the apartment, leaving Henry to look after the child alone. As the film progresses, Henry's 'real' world disintegrates and the nightmarish creatures that exist at its peripheries, under the bed and behind the radiator, become more and more real.

The film's unique visual style is informed by Lynch's previous career as a painter and betrays many influences, including EXPRESSIONISM, SURREALISM, and the classic horror films. Lynch himself (once famously described by Mel BROOKS as "Jimmy STEWART from Mars") has emphasized the film's concern for "dark and troubling" things. Indeed, much of *Eraserhead* may be seen as a metaphor for a young man's fear of adulthood, parenthood, and responsibility. Although Lynch has since gone on to carve out a highly successful career in Hollywood, becoming something of the avant-gardist in residence, none of his subsequent films has managed to equal the fascinating repulsiveness of *Eraserhead*.

establishing shot A LONG SHOT used to establish the primary locale of a film or the setting of a particular scene. An establishing shot is often used at the very beginning of a movie; famous examples include the shot of the cotton fields at the start of GONE WITH THE WIND (1939). Some establishing shots have become so overworked as to become clichés – for instance the use of a PAN shot of a skyscraper to evoke New York or a view of Big Ben to denote London. By contrast a master of the device, such as Alfred HITCHCOCK, can use an establishing shot to convey in a moment information that would require paragraphs of prose. *See also* MASTER SHOT.

Estevez, Emilio *See* SHEEN FAMILY.

E.T.: the Extraterrestrial (1982) Steven SPIELBERG's science-fantasy tearjerker, which broke all previous records at the box-office during its first months on release. In the story, a spacecraft landing in California departs in such a hurry that one of its crew is left behind. Discovered, befriended, concealed, and loved by Elliott (Henry Thomas), a lonely young Californian boy, the extraterrestrial creature becomes involved in a series of escapades and comes close to death before being rescued by the returning spacecraft. The scene in which the creature nearly dies brought tears to the eyes of vast audiences throughout the world. One critic described *E.T.* as "the most moving science-fiction movie ever made"; another, with a sharper pen, declared that he refused to be moved by "a collection of Hoover parts."

In reality, the creature (designed by Carlo Rambaldi) consisted of an aluminium-and-steel frame covered in layers of polyurethane and rubber. Spielberg had quite specific ideas what his lovable alien should look like: the tail of DONALD DUCK, a long neck, and a face that resembled a newborn baby with the superimposed eyes and forehead of Albert Einstein. Three versions of this basic model were used in the film, two being controlled mechanically while the third (used for walking scenes) was operated by two midgets and a legless boy. The close-up head boasted 85 parts, which were made to move thanks to a diversity of electronic-, radio-, or hand-controlled cables. E.T.'s voice was provided by Pat Welsh and Debra Winger, although the howl that he emits when he first encounters Elliott was achieved by electronically manipulating the sound of an otter's cry. According to Spielberg, the technical problems involved in making the film were "torture. My pubic hairs turned grey."

Considering its apparently innocuous content, *E.T.* has been the subject of a surprisingly heated critical debate. While most saw the film as another enchanting and inexorable step in Spielberg's progress towards becoming the DISNEY of the 1980s, there were those who questioned its sexist and racist implications, its Reaganite politics, its attitude to parental control (which caused the film to be limited to children over the age of 11 in Sweden!), and even Spielberg's sincerity in alluding to the Christian doctrine of resurrection. However, even its most vehement detractors could not deny the film's cultural impact. As Robin Wood wrote:

> In itself, *E.T.* has no greater claim on the attention than countless other minor Hollywood movies. It does demand consideration as a cultural phenomenon: not merely the film itself and what it signifies, but the commercial hype, the American

critics' reviews, the public response, the T-shirts, the children's games, the candy advertisements. It represents a moment in American cultural history.

European Film Awards An international film ceremony at which awards are given in a number of categories to outstanding European films and film-makers. The Awards, established in 1989 by the European Film Academy in an attempt to raise the profile of European cinema, are closely modelled on the US OSCARS. Winners at the first European Film Awards ceremony included Theo Angelopoulos's *Landscape in a Mist*, which won the award for best film of the year, Géza Bereményi as best director for *The Midas Touch*, Ruth Sheen as best actress for *High Hopes*, and Philippe NOIRET as best actor for *Life and Nothing But* and *Cinema Paradiso*.

The concept of the Awards has provoked some scepticism both inside and outside the European film industry. In 1992 the president of the jury, Margaret Ménégoz, declared:

> I don't think European cinema exists...You will always have French films, German films, and Italian films, and so on.

The statuettes themselves are known as FELIXS.

excerpts Brief extracts from films. Perhaps the most common use of such clips is as publicity material for a new release, either to accompany interviews with the stars or in cinema and TV advertisements. Pieces of old footage have also been reused in new films for a variety of reasons. Sequels have frequently used clips from the original film as a convenient way of setting the scene, while footage of battle and crowd scenes has often been recycled for reasons of economy (action footage from KORDA's *The Four Feathers*, 1939, is known to have been used in at least five other films). Scenes from well-known films may also appear when characters visit the cinema or watch television; such extracts are often used to point up an ironic parallel with the action in the new film. Film-makers (and movie buffs) seem to delight in the kind of IN-JOKE that involves a star turning on the TV to be confronted by a scene from one of his or her earlier films. In some cases, the use of excerpts is part of the film's *raison d'être*; examples include Woody ALLEN's *Play It Again Sam* (1972), which incorporated clips from old Humphrey BOGART movies, and the same director's ZELIG (1983), which combined newsreel excerpts with new footage. For *Dead Men Don't Wear Plaid* (1982) the new scenes featuring Steve MARTIN's private detective were especially designed to dovetail with clips from 1940s crime movies featuring Bogart, BACALL, LAMOUR, and others. *See also* ANTHOLOGY FILM.

exchange A regional film distribution company in America. In the early days of the US cinema, exchange organizations were set up to act as middlemen between the theatres in their own area and the national production and distribution corporations.

executive producer A PRODUCER who concentrates on the business and financial sides of film-making, using an ASSOCIATE PRODUCER to co-ordinate the more general aspects of the production process. A successful executive producer, such as Dino DE LAURENTIIS, may supervise more than one production at the same time.

exhibitor A person or company who owns or operates a cinema.

existentialist films A 1940s Hollywood term for FILM NOIR, because the genre found a following among French existentialists in the post-war period. The followers of Sartre and Camus appear to have identified with the struggles of the individualistic and morally ambiguous heroes in such films and with the pervasive mood of menace and corruption.

Exorcist, The (1973) William FRIEDKIN's sensational story of demonic possession, with a script by William Peter Blatty from his own novel. The most successful horror movie of all time, it had grossed an estimated $89 million in North America by 1993.

In the story Regan (Linda Blair), the 13-year-old daughter of a movie star (Ellen Burstyn), develops grisly signs of demonic possession; these include levitating, barking obsceniies, spewing out jets of bilious ectoplasm, and, in the film's most notorious sequence, attacking her genitals with a crucifix. When the efforts of doctors and psychiatrists prove useless she is eventually cured by the offices of a saintly priest. Although Friedkin liked to claim that the film had a serious message about the conflict between good and evil, there is little doubt that audiences were mainly attracted by the stomach-churning special effects (Dick Smith), which were far in advance of anything previously seen in horror movies. Sequences such as that in which Regan's head swivels through 360 degrees had moviegoers fainting and rushing for the exits. Unlike earlier horror shockers, *The Exorcist* was big-budget, released by a mainstream studio, and achieved a degree of respectability through the award of one Oscar (for Blatty's screenplay) and nominations in five other categories. The film inspired two unsuccessful sequels, numerous imitations, and the parody *Repossessed* (1990), which also starred Linda Blair.

Owing to its notoriety, the film has never been issued on video in Britain (it was refused a certificate in the mid 1980s and has not been brought forward for release again). Such is the demand to see it, however, that London's MGM Trocadero hosts a special late-night screening of the film every Saturday.

expanded cinema A type of mixed media performance in which live actors and musicians interact with a film while it is being projected.

exploitation film A low-budget genre film of little or no artistic merit that is crudely targetted at a particular section of the moviegoing public. Examples include the rash of films aimed at the Black market in the early 1970s (*see* BLAXPLOITATION) and the numerous sex and horror movies aimed at teenagers in the 1980s. The term is sometimes used more generally of any film that depends on sensational sex or violence to draw an audience.

Although generally dismissed by critics, exploitation movies have recently been subjected to more serious examination by film students; it is argued that such films can reveal more about the attitudes and fears of the society that produces them than more self-conscious and artistic work.

expressionism An artistic style in which subjective ideas and emotions are allowed to distort the presentation of external reality. The cinema proved to be the ideal vehicle for the expressionist movement of the early 20th century, which first emerged in Germany in about 1910. Expressionism affected the design of sets, scenery, and costumes, and encouraged a new freedom and experimentation in the use of visual images.

Its hallmarks included the use of sinister shadowy sets, a preoccupation with abnormal psychological states, and a revelling in the grotesque and macabre.

The main exponents of cinematic expressionism were the Germans Fritz LANG, F. W. MURNAU, Paul Leni (1885–1929), and Robert Wiene (1881–1938), and the Austrian G. W. PABST. Masterpieces of the style include Wiene's THE CABINET OF DR CALIGARI (1919), which uses nightmarish imagery to convey a sense of psychological disturbance, Murnau's classic vampire film NOSFERATU (1922) and his Hollywood melodrama *Sunrise* (1927), which used a restlessly moving camera to tell the story of a husband bent on killing his wife, Leni's macabre *Waxworks* (1924), Pabst's *Secrets of a Soul* (1926), about a chemist with a phobia of knives, and Lang's METROPOLIS (1927), set in a robotic society of the future (with stunning sets indebted to Lang's training in art and architecture).

The influence of German expressionism can be traced in numerous horror and suspense films, notably the early works of Alfred HITCHCOCK and the FILMS NOIRS of the 1940s. More recent films to be influenced by the style include POLANSKI's *Repulsion* (1965) and David LYNCH's ERASERHEAD. Expressionist techniques are frequently used in DREAM sequences.

EXT The notation in a script that indicates **exterior action**, i.e., any scene that is supposed to take place out of doors. Such scenes may well be filmed on an indoor studio set.

Exterminating Angel, The *See* ANGEL EXTERMINADOR, EL.

extra A person who appears in a film in a very minor role, such as walking down a street, fighting in a battle, or participating in a crowd scene. Extras, who are rarely given lines to speak, may or may not be professional actors: when a production is shot on location, local people are often recruited for such parts. The as-yet-unknown Benito Mussolini can be glimpsed as an extra in *The Eternal City* (1914), as can Fidel Castro in *Holiday in Mexico* (1946).

Even when professional extras are given a few words, they sometimes blow them. During the filming of THE WIZARD OF OZ (1939) one of the Munchkins greeted Judy GARLAND with an enthusiastic "Hi, Judy!"

rather than by the name of her character. The gaffe was never cut from the film.

extreme. **extreme close-up** (ECU or XCU) or **big close-up** (BCU) A shot taken at very close range, especially one showing a detail of an actor's face or body. The extreme close-up was introduced by D. W. GRIFFITH, who pioneered the device with such shots as the clasped hands of Mae Marsh as she waits for the judge's pronouncement in INTOLERANCE (1916) and the terrified eyes of Lillian GISH in BROKEN BLOSSOMS (1919). At the time, the innovation was widely denounced as "barbaric." *See also* CLOSE-UP; DETAIL SHOT.

extreme high-angle shot A shot taken from a camera positioned high above the action and tilted down. Scenes shot in this way include Scarlett O'Hara's fall down the stairs in GONE WITH THE WIND (1939) and many battle scenes, including those in OLIVIER's *Henry V* (1945). *See also* CAMERA ANGLES; HIGH-ANGLE SHOT.

extreme long shot (ELS or XLS) A shot taken from a great distance away; famous examples include the sweeping vistas shot in Monument Valley for John FORD's STAGECOACH (1939). *See also* LONG SHOT.

extreme low-angle shot A shot taken from a camera positioned below the action and tilted upwards. Examples include the ground-level shots of the chariot race in BEN-HUR (1959) and those of the Manhattan air battles in *Superman 2* (1980). *See also* CAMERA ANGLES; LOW-ANGLE SHOT.

eye. **eye-level angle shot** A camera shot taken at the level of a character's eyes, in order to represent his or her POINT OF VIEW. It is one of the most frequently used devices in movie-making. *See also* CAMERA ANGLES.

eyes and ears of the world The motto of British Gaumont News; it became a common catchphrase after World War II. *See also* NEWSREELS.

F

facilities   *See* FAX.

faction   A film that blends fact and fiction; unlike a FILM À CLEF, a work of faction will use the names of real people and places. The genre has often been attacked, mainly on the grounds that the mixture of fact and dramatic licence allows film-makers to distort history to their own ends. Some recent works of faction to attract controversy include *In the Name of the Father* (1994), about the wrongful conviction of the Guildford Four, and Oliver STONE's *JFK* (1991), a highly speculative version of the Kennedy assassination that was labelled "Dallas in Wonderland" and "Dances with Facts" by its detractors.

fade.   fade-in (1) An effect in which an image slowly emerges on the darkened screen; it is traditionally used to open a film. The fade-in is also sometimes used to introduce a scene set apart, such as a daydream or FLASHBACK. (2) A gradual increase in the volume of a film's soundtrack, from inaudible to audible.
fade-out (1) An effect in which an image slowly disappears as the screen darkens to black; it is traditionally used to end a film. The fade-out was accidentally developed by D. W. GRIFFITH and G. W. 'Billy' Bitzer, the head cameraman at BIOGRAPH studios, when Bitzer mounted an IRIS diaphragm on his camera; during shooting, the weight of the camera's handle gradually closed the iris, creating a fade-out effect when the film was projected. According to Bitzer, this technique proved particularly useful because all of their films ended with a kiss. "We couldn't linger over the embrace, for then the yokels in the audience would make catcalls" he noted. "We couldn't cut abruptly – that would be crude. The fade-out gave a really dignified touch." (2) A gradual decrease in the volume of a film's soundtrack, from audible to inaudible.

Fairbanks.   Douglas Fairbanks (Douglas Elton Ulman; 1883–1939) Athletic US actor, famous for playing SWASHBUCKLING heroes and lovable rogues in a series of costume dramas.

Born in Denver, Colorado, Fairbanks made his stage debut while still a teenager; his first film appearance was in D. W. GRIFFITH's *The Lamb* (1915). His jokey acrobatics on the set greatly irritated Griffith, who suggested that he take up comedy. After forming his own production company, Fairbanks starred in such films as *He Comes Up Smiling* (1918) and *The Knickerbocker Buckaroo* (1919). His marriage to Anna Beth Sully, the mother of Douglas FAIRBANKS JNR, ended in 1918.

In 1919 Fairbanks, Mary PICKFORD, Charlie CHAPLIN, and D. W. Griffith founded the UNITED ARTISTS Film Corporation to produce and distribute their own pictures. In the same year Fairbanks led the exodus of stars from Hollywood to BEVERLY HILLS, when he bought a 36-room house in the area. Some months later he refurbished an adjoining hunting lodge as a wedding gift to Mary Pickford, whom he married in 1920. At **Pickfair**, as they named the house, the 'King and Queen of Hollywood' held court to Hollywood moguls and European nobility alike.

Once, when driving to Pickfair, Fairbanks saw an aristocratic-looking Englishman trudging along the road and invited him for a drink. When it became clear that the man knew most of his friends, Fairbanks whispered to his secretary, "I know he's Lord Somebody, but I just can't remember his name." The secretary smiled, "That's the English butler you fired last month for getting drunk."

Fairbanks, an intensely jealous man, was notorious for ordering his male guests from Pickfair on the slightest suspicion; it was, however, an affair of his own that destroyed the marriage in 1935. The two had only co-starred in one film, *The Taming of the Shrew* (1929).

Fairbanks played the first of his athletic swashbuckling roles in *The Mark of Zorro*

(1920), about a mysterious Mexican outlaw (*see* ZORRO). ROBIN HOOD (1922) featured more boisterous stunts and some extravagant sets, including a 450-foot banqueting hall, at that time the largest set ever created. THE THIEF OF BAGDAD (1924) contains the famous scene in which Fairbanks leapt in and out of a series of large jars, while in *Don Q, Son of Zorro* (1925), he lit a cigarette by cracking a bull-whip over an open fire. His later talkies, which include *The Private Life of Don Juan* (1934), made in England for Alexander KORDA, were mostly rather lacklustre. Fairbanks was awarded a posthumous Oscar for his lifetime's work in 1939.

> He was complete fantasy...unashamed and joyous. Balustrades were made to be vaulted, draperies to be a giant slide, chandeliers to swing from, citadels to be scaled.
> FRANK S. NUGENT.

Douglas Fairbanks Jnr (1909–) US actor, who became a popular matinée idol in the 1930s. The son of Douglas FAIRBANKS and his first wife, Fairbanks Jnr saw little of his father, who once admitted that his paternal feelings amounted to no more "than a tiger in the jungle for his cub." For his part, Fairbanks Jnr described his father as "a natural Peter Pan." The two became closer in later years.

Fairbanks was one of the few boys to attend the Hollywood School for Girls (where Jean HARLOW, amongst others, was educated). He made his screen debut at 13 in the title role of *Stephen Steps Out* (1922) and three years later played a wealthy husband in *Stella Dallas* (1925). For the latter role, the director Henry King had him grow a moustache. When Fairbanks's father, then 42, heard this, he rang King to protest: "Remember I'm still in pictures. Don't make Junior look too old."

Fairbanks Jnr's early attempts to cash in on the family name met with limited success; he once observed that trying to follow in his father's footsteps was difficult because they "were so light that they left no trace for anyone to follow." In 1929 his public profile was raised by his marriage to the up-and-coming Joan CRAWFORD. (That year studio publicity for *Our Modern Maidens* announced, "Reckless youth runs a race with death with Joan Crawford being chauffeured by Douglas Fairbanks Jnr, in her first starring picture.") The couple were divorced in 1933. Other names to be linked romantically with Fairbanks included the actress Gertrude Lawrence.

During the 1930s Fairbanks Jnr established himself as a star in his own right with roles that extended from the buccaneering parts associated with his father to more sophisticated roles in comedies of manners and thrillers. His most popular films included *The Dawn Patrol* (1930), *Catherine the Great* (1934), the classic *The Prisoner of Zenda* (1937), and *The Corsican Brothers* (1941), in which he played both brothers. In 1938 he was tested for Heathcliff in WUTHERING HEIGHTS but was considered too effete and the part went to Laurence OLIVIER. Instead, Fairbanks starred in *Gunga Din* (1939) with Cary GRANT.

Fairbanks served in the US Navy during World War II and emerged from the conflict one of the most decorated of the Hollywood stars to join the forces. He had previously (1940–41) undertaken a mission to Latin America as a special envoy of President Roosevelt. A keen Anglophile, who made a number of his films in Britain, he was awarded an honorary knighthood in 1949 for services to Anglo-US relations. In the early 1950s Fairbanks retired from the cinema and moved to London, where he presented and occasionally acted in the long-running television series *Douglas Fairbanks Presents* (1953–58).

He has subsequently appeared in television movies and in the film *Ghost Story* (1981), in which he swaps supernatural tales with fellow veterans Fred ASTAIRE, Melvyn DOUGLAS, and John Houseman.

Falcon, the A suave detective who appeared in some 16 second-feature films in the 1940s. The Falcon, who was invariably accompanied by his comic but muscular servant Goldie, was the creation of the novelist Michael Arlen (1895–1956). Originally played by George SANDERS, the detective was killed off in *The Falcon's Brother* (1942) to enable Sanders to retire. The Falcon's role was thereafter taken by the detective's brother, played by Sanders's real-life brother, Tom Conway. In nearly all the films Goldie was played by Edward Brophy.

Famous Players The US production company that developed into PARAMOUNT PICTURES. It was founded by Adolph ZUKOR in 1912. Using the slogan "Famous Players in Famous Plays", Zukor began to sign stage actors to appear in silent 'picturizations' of Broadway hits, his first big catch being James O'Neill, who took the lead in *The Count of Monte Cristo* (1913). His greatest find was Mary PICKFORD, who made 34 films between 1913 and 1919.

A merger with Jesse Lasky Feature Plays in 1916 created the Famous Players-Lasky Corporation, a powerful company that soon had Douglas FAIRBANKS, Mack SENNETT, William S. Hart, and Wallace Reid on its books. Those to direct films for the company included D. W. GRIFFITH, Cecil B. DE MILLE, and Allan DWAN.

Shortly after the merger the new corporation took over the distribution company Paramount; although *The Sheik* (1921) with Rudolph VALENTINO was still produced under the Famous Players-Lasky label the company was soon issuing films as Paramount Pictures. The Famous Players name disappeared entirely in the late 1920s.

In 1919 Famous Players-Lasky set up a studio in a former power station in Islington, London, in order to make a series of features with British themes. One of their first appointments was a 20-year-old designer of title cards named Alfred HITCHCOCK.

fan An enthusiastic admirer of an actor, film, or film genre. Letters written to the objects of such admiration are known as *fan mail*, while a *fan club* is an organization consisting of ardent devotees of a movie star or other famous person.

The term 'fan' is a shortening of 'fanatic' and there is no doubt that some obsessive fans pose a serious danger to themselves, their idols, and others. In 1981 John W. Hinckley Jnr wounded President Ronald REAGAN and three others in an assassination attempt designed to impress Jodie FOSTER. Another actress, Brooke Shields, lives under the close supervision of security guards owing to the number of deranged fans (apparently some 300) who have threatened her.

Fanny and Alexander (1982) Ingmar BERGMAN's last film for the cinema, a much-admired account of a Swedish childhood at the turn of the century. The film's magical opening scenes evoke the warmth and gaiety of Christmas with the Ekdahls, a large well-to-do Swedish family. However, when their father, an actor-manager, dies of a heart-attack, the children Fanny (Pernilla

Alwin) and Alexander (Bertil Guve) are removed from this happy environment and placed in the strictly regulated household of a Lutheran bishop (Jan Malmsjö). These scenes appear to draw heavily on the childhood of Bergman himself, whose own father was a Lutheran pastor who rose to the position of chaplain to the Swedish royal household. Although some scenes are harrowing, this exuberant three-hour movie is noticeably less austere and gloomy than most of the director's earlier work. One favourite Bergman theme to emerge clearly from the film is the deliberate artifice and deception employed by the artist at work. The fine cast includes Gunn Wållgren, Jarl Kulle, Erland Josephson, Harriet Andersson, Allan Edwall, Mats Bergman, and Gunnar Björnstrand.

Fantasia (1940) An animated feature by Walt DISNEY, in which various narrative and abstract techniques are used to interpret eight pieces of classical music. The film was orginally conceived as a two-reel version of Dukas's 'The Sorceror's Apprentice' starring Dopey, one of the Seven Dwarfs from SNOW WHITE. However, at an early stage of production, Disney decided to feature MICKEY MOUSE in the leading role; the studio has always denied that this was a conscious attempt to revive Mickey's flagging popularity in the face of competition from Goofy and DONALD DUCK. Disney himself was the live-action model for the Sorceror (who is called Yensid) and voiced Mickey for the last time in his career.

After consulting Leopold Stokowski, the conductor of the Philadelphia Symphony Orchestra, on the musical aspects of the project, Disney decided to expand the film into a 'Concert Feature' that ran for 126 minutes when complete (the British version lasted 105 minutes and the 1946 rerelease a mere 81 minutes). The German abstract film-maker Otto Fischinger was approached to make the 'Toccata and Fugue' segment, but walked out before filming began; nevertheless, the sequence bears his unmistakable influence. Members of the Ballet Russe posed as the models for the dancing hippopotami in the 'Dance of the Hours' section. The 'Night on a Bald Mountain' episode drew heavily on the opening movements of F. W. MURNAU's *Faust*, in which Emil JANNINGS's Mephistopholes menaces a small village. Although Bela LUGOSI was hired to pose for the artists working on this segment, animator Bill Tylta eventually based his images on the movements of a young Disney director, Wilfred Jackson.

Making extensive use of the multiplane camera (which enhanced the impression of depth of field) and stereophonic recording techniques, *Fantasia* cost $2,280,000 to complete. The expense of the specially designed Fantasound system and the film's mixed critical reception meant that it took some 15 years to break even. Amongst those to criticize the film was Stravinsky, who was scathing about the use of his *Rite of Spring*:

> I will say nothing about the visual complement as I do not wish to criticize an unresisting imbecility.

Fantasia proved more popular in the psychedelic phase of the 1960s and was reissued to considerable acclaim in 1982 with a new digital audio soundtrack conducted by Irwin Kostal. In the course of its recording it was discovered that the film had been two frames out of synch since its premiere.

fantasy   The creation of fantasy worlds and effects has been a major preoccupation of the cinema since the days of George MÉLIÈS, the ex-conjuror who used trick photography to astound audiences in the 1890s. In the late 20th century fantasy has lost none of its drawing power; a list of the most popular films of all time would include STAR WARS (1977), E.T.: THE EXTRATERRESTRIAL (1982), BATMAN (1989), *Ghost* (1990), and JURASSIC PARK (1993), none of which is a byword for cinematic REALISM.

Fantasy films fall into several main categories. The HORROR FILM explores the dark side of the human psyche, whether this is embodied in a human killer (e.g. PSYCHO, 1960) or a supernatural threat (e.g. DRACULA). SCIENCE FICTION films explore the use and abuse of technology, visions of the future, and the possibility of alien life-forms. Other categories include the MONSTER movie (e.g. KING KONG, 1933 and the GODZILLA series), the metaphysical fable (e.g. A MATTER OF LIFE AND DEATH, 1946), and the film derived from mythology (e.g. *Jason and the Argonauts*, 1963). Fairy tales have been presented more or less straight (*The Glass Slipper*, 1954), psychoanalysed (*The Company of Wolves*, 1984), or created from scratch (*Edward Scissorhands*, 1990). Jean COCTEAU's *La Belle et la Bête* (1946) successfully captured the haunting poetry of the original tale, while THE WIZARD OF OZ (1939) is a

deserved 20th-century classic that still has an ability to charm and beguile its audience.

Films of gods and heroes, such as *Sinbad and the Eye of the Tiger* (1977) and *Clash of the Titans* (1981), bring us closer to the modern literary genre known as fantasy, which was largely inspired by the success of J. R. R. Tolkein's *The Lord of the Rings* (made into an animated film in 1978). Other 'Sword and Sorcery' films include *Hawk the Slayer* (1980), *Conan the Barbarian* (1981) and its sequels, and *The Sword and the Sorcerer* and *The Beastmaster* (both 1982).

Of course, fantasy is by no means restricted to films dealing with the supernatural or the obviously impossible. Although outwardly realistic, *Rocky* (1976) is a rags-to-riches fable, *Trading Places* (1983) presents a fantasy of role-reversal between rich and poor, and *Die Hard* (1988) is a fantasy of impotence overcoming strength. Wish-fulfilment fantasies have been a mainstay of the cinema industry since the earliest days: James BOND is popular because deep down many men would like to be him; Michelle PFEIFFER is popular for similar reasons. Whatever its aspirations to realism, the film world is generally one of enhanced realities, populated by sexually attractive men and women, strikingly photographed, in evocative locations.

In the past the very act of going to a cinema, a building with colonnades, pillars, velvet drapes, and uniformed doormen, was itself like stepping into a different world. Now, with entertainment complexes and the advance of television and video technology in the home, going to see a film can be about as fantastical as stepping into the living room.

Farrow.   John Farrow (1904–63) Australian-born US director and screenwriter, whose strong Catholic beliefs influenced the mood of evil and corruption in his films. His harsh methods as a director prompted John Houseman to say that Farrow had "a reputation for sadism practised professionally and individually" on actors. He was married to the actress Maureen O'SULLIVAN, one of their seven children being Mia FARROW.

Born in Sydney, Farrow studied at Winchester College, England, and the Royal Naval Academy. After naval service, he travelled to Hollywood in the mid 1920s as a technical advisor for sea sequences. In 1927 he began scripting films himself, making his debut as a director ten years later with *Men in Exile* (1937). During World War II he directed *Wake Island* (1942), Hollywood's first film about US participation in the conflict, and *The Hitler Gang* (1944), about the Nazis' rise to power. After himself being wounded and discharged, Farrow directed Alan LADD in the naval drama *Two Years Before the Mast* (1946). In 1948 he made *Night Has a Thousand Eyes*, with Edward G. ROBINSON as a psychic, and the FILM NOIR *The Big Clock* with Ray MILLAND and Charles LAUGHTON. His best known film, *Alias Nick Beal* (British title *The Contract Man*; 1949) followed a year later; an updating of the Faust story, it starred Milland as a devilish stranger seeking to steal the soul of politician Thomas Mitchell.

In 1956 Farrow won an Oscar for co-scripting AROUND THE WORLD IN EIGHTY DAYS. He also wrote historical books about Thomas More and the Papacy and several novels.

Mia Farrow (1945–) Tiny lemon-haired US actress, whose long personal and professional association with Woody ALLEN ended acrimoniously in 1993. Before her involvement with Allen she had highly publicized marriages to Frank SINATRA (1966–68) and André Previn (1970–79). She is the daughter of John FARROW and Maureen O'SULLIVAN; her sister, Tisa Farrow, also acts.

Born in Los Angeles, Farrow contracted polio at the age of 9 and has remained physically fragile – a characteristic that has led to numerous roles as vulnerable women. She made her stage debut off-Broadway in 1963 and her first film appearance a year later. Having become known to a wider public through her role in the TV soap opera *Peyton Place*, she found stardom with her third film, POLANSKI's ROSEMARY'S BABY (1968), in which she played a young wife traumatized by the fear that she is giving birth to Satan's son.

Farrow's films of the 1970s included *The Great Gatsby* (1974), with Robert REDFORD, and the Christie mystery *Death on the Nile* (1978). She first joined Allen for *A Midsummer Night's Sex Comedy* (1982), following this with ZELIG (1983), in which she played the behavioural scientist who falls in love with the enigmatic title character. Her subsequent movies with Allen included *Broadway Danny Rose* (1984), *The Purple Rose of Cairo* (1985), *Hannah and Her Sisters* (1986), *September* (1988), *Shadows and Fog* (1992), and *Husbands and Wives* (1992), a

film that appeared to reflect the breakdown of their relationship.

In 1994 Farrow starred in the Irish comedy *Widow's Peak*, about a woman courted by a shy dentist. Ten years earlier Farrow's mother had appeared in the same part on stage, with Mia in a younger role (played by Natasha Richardson in the film). Farrow described the movie as therapy after the prolonged and very public court battle for custody of her and Allen's son, Satchel, which she eventually won; it was her first non-Woody film in ten years. She had brought the case after discovering that Allen was involved in an affair with her adopted teenaged daughter Soon Yi. She summed up: "I regret the day I met him, and I hope I never see him again."

far shot   *See* LONG SHOT.

Fassbinder, Rainer Werner (1946–82) German director, actor, and screenwriter, who established his reputation with a series of provocative melodramas during the 1970s. After working as a theatre director with fringe groups in Munich, Fassbinder made several shorts for the cinema, followed by his first feature, the gangster film *Love is Colder than Death* (1969). He first attracted attention with *Katzelmacher* (1969), a film based on his own stage play, in which he exposed racial prejudice in modern Germany as experienced by a Greek immigrant (played by Fassbinder himself). The film was notable both for its stylized dialogue and for its bleak view of modern society, traits which soon became hallmarks of his work.

Fassbinder's concern for the oppressed also inspired such films as *Why Does Herr R Run Amok?* (1969), in which a clerical worker is driven to mass murder, and *The Merchant of Four Seasons* (1971), which traces the decline of a fruit merchant into alcoholism and eventual death. Similar themes were explored in *The Bitter Tears of Petra von Kant* (1972), about the lesbian relationship of a fashion designer with one of her models, and *Fear Eats the Soul* (1973), about a doomed love affair between a Moroccan immigrant worker and an older woman.

Fassbinder's pessimism about human relationships is also apparent from such films as *Effi Briest* (1974), in which a young woman is trapped in a marriage to an old aristocrat, *Fox* (1975), in which Fassbinder (a homosexual himself) played a young man drawn into the exploitative world of a group of homosexuals, and the expressionistic *Satan's Brew* (1976).

For *Chinese Roulette* (1976), which explores the issue of the German people's collective guilt for the Nazi era, Fassbinder disbanded the team of actors he had previously used and experimented with innovative camera angles. The film was widely hailed as a *tour de force*. By contrast *Despair* (1978), a tale of obsession and schizophrenia starring Dirk BOGARDE, found only muted praise. His next film, *In a Year with 13 Moons* (1978), drew on the suicide of one of his homosexual lovers. *The Marriage of Maria Braun* (1978) and *Lola* (1981) were both fables about women who sacrifice their bodies to men in exchange for power, while in *Veronika Voss* (1982) Fassbinder delivered another attack on contemporary German society, this time through the story of the decline of a Third Reich movie star.

Fassbinder's last film was *Querelle* (1982), an adaptation of the novel by Jean Genet; he died of an overdose of drugs.

> Rainer's a little shit, but one can't help liking him. He...seems to feel this need to work in a permanent state of quarrel.
> PETER ZADEK, stage director.

fast motion *See* ACCELERATED MOTION.

favour In directing a scene, to give one actor prominence over the others by means of selective camera angles or better lighting.

fax Facilities. A general term for the technical equipment used in the production of a film, such as the cameras, lights, and sound system.

FBO Film Booking Office of America Inc. An early US production and distribution company that specialized in low-budget features. It was eventually absorbed into RKO.

The company began life in the first decade of the century as an East Coast releasing agency. It opened in Hollywood in 1920 as the Robertson-Cole studios and two years later changed its name to the Film Booking Office of America. In the 1920s it produced such features as *Kosher Kitty Kelly* (1926) and developed a former Presbyterian minister, Fred Thompson, into a Western hero.

In 1926 Joseph P. Kennedy, father of the future President John F. Kennedy, purchased FBO and placed it under the Radio Corporation of America (RCA), whose buyout of the Keith-Albee-Orpheum theatre chain created Radio-Keith-Orpheum (RKO).

feature. feature film A fictional film of some length designed for commercial release. Most feature films now run for 90 minutes or more, anything shorter than 34 minutes (3000 feet) being defined as a SHORT. Feature films usually have at least one well-known actor and provide the main item of a cinema programme. Formerly, it was usual for most suburban and provincial cinemas to show two feature-length films, the A-MOVIE or FIRST FEATURE and a low-budget production known as the B-MOVIE or SECOND FEATURE.

feature or **featured player** An actor who plays an important SUPPORTING role in a film, often as a sidekick to the hero. CHARACTER ACTORS can easily become typecast as feature players; examples include Peter LORRE and Stanley Holloway. Raymond Burr is an example of a feature player who later became a star on television.

feed. feed lines To CUE an actor with his or her lines; this is common during rehearsals and not unknown during filming.

feed reel A REEL from which film is fed into a camera or projector. *See also* TAKE-UP REEL.

Felix The name given to the statuettes presented at the EUROPEAN FILM AWARDS ceremony. They are so-named by analogy with the US OSCARS; Felix Ungar was *Oscar* Madison's incompatible flat-mate in the film *The Odd Couple* (1968).

Felix the Cat Hero of early animated films who first appeared in 1921 in a production by Pat Sullivan. Throughout his adventures the indestructible **Felix kept on walking**, thus originating a popular catchphrase. The character was revived for television in the 1950s and for *Felix the Cat: The Movie* in 1989.

Fellini, Federico (1920–93) Italian director and screenwriter, noted for his extravagant visual images.

Born in Rimini, he began his career as a cartoonist and theatre worker before entering films in 1940 as a gagwriter. His screenplays for ROSSELLINI'S ROME–OPEN CITY (1945) and other films were highly praised and in 1950 he made his debut as a director with *Variety Lights*, a satirical story about a humble touring theatre (on which he worked with Alberto Lattuada).

The White Sheik (1952) was a romantic comedy, while *I vitelloni* (*The Young and the Passionate*; 1953) reflected his love of the circus and his adolescent experiences of street life. This motif reappeared in LA STRADA (1955), a moving story about a young girl's travels with a circus, starring Fellini's wife, Giulietta Masina (1921–94); the film won the director an Oscar.

Fellini continued to explore themes of personal identity and the conflict between sexuality and innocence in such films as *The Nights of Cabiria* (1957), which again starred Masina, and LA DOLCE VITA (1960), starring Marcello MASTROIANNI. This story of moral disintegration in contemporary high society introduced Fellini's highly stylized cinematography to a wide international audience and confirmed his reputation.

Having contributed an episode to the film *Boccaccio '70* (1962), Fellini went on to make the film that many consider his masterpiece, 8½ (1963), in which Mastroianni again starred. The film had a strong autobiographical element and showed the director at his inventive best; it gathered several international awards, including the Oscar for Best Foreign Film. Thereafter Fellini indulged his growing predeliction for bizarre imagery and coarse humour in a series of less successful films that included *Juliet of the Spirits* (1965), *Fellini Satyricon* (1969), *The Clowns* (1970), and *Fellini Roma* (1972). The nostalgic AMARCORD (1974) and *Fellini's Casanova* (1976), a sombre portrait of the great lover in his declining years, attracted a renewed interest in his work.

Fellini's later films include *City of Women* (1980) and *Ginger and Fred* (1986), both of which starred Mastroianni, and the documentary-style *Intervista* (1987), in which Fellini developed themes suggested by his own career, even to the extent of incorporating scenes from *La Dolce Vita*. He was awarded a special Oscar for his lifetime achievement in 1993.

> His films are like the dreams of a country boy imagining what it's like to be in the big city. His greatest danger: to be a very great director with precious little to say.
> LUCHINO VISCONTI.

fg   *See* FOREGROUND.

field camera   A small portable CAMERA used for location filming.

Fields.   Dame Gracie Fields (Grace Stansfield; 1898–1979) British singer and comic actress of the 1930s and 1940s, known to her millions of fans as **Our Gracie** or the **Lassie from Lancashire**.

Born over a fish-and-chip shop in Rochdale, Lancashire, Fields began in music hall at the age of 12 and went on to enjoy huge success in the movies on the strength of her boisterous personality and powerful voice. Her films included the brightly optimistic musicals *Sally in Our Alley* (1931), her debut, *Sing As We Go* (1934), and *Shipyard Sally* (1939). She had equal success as a recording artist, her most popular hits including 'Sally', 'The Biggest Aspidistra in the World', and 'Wish Me Luck as You Wave Me Goodbye', which was taken up by British troops at the start of World War II.

By 1939 Fields was reputedly the highest-paid entertainer in the world; on one occasion parliament was adjourned so that members could listen to one of her rare radio broadcasts. The war years, however, witnessed an unexpected reversal in her fortunes as a result of her marriage to an Italian comedian and director, Monty Banks. To avoid his being interned after Italy entered the war, the couple moved to America – an act that was interpreted as a betrayal by many fans, who switched allegiance to Vera Lynn. In fact, Fields worked hard in America to raise funds for the war effort and returned to her homeland in 1941 – but the damage was done and she never reclaimed her old standing, a fact that caused her some bitterness.

After Banks died in 1950, Fields spent most of her time on Capri, making occasional visits to Britain to appear in a series of Royal Variety Command Performances. In the year before her death she was welcomed back to Rochdale, where a theatre was opened in her honour. She was made a DBE in 1979.

W. C. Fields (William Claude Dukenfield; 1879–1946) US comic genius, now better remembered for his eccentric behaviour and misanthropic one-liners than for his films. With his bulbous nose (a result of street fighting and drinking), nervous twitch, and nasal throwaway delivery, Fields specialized in playing disreputable and usually cantankerous characters with such names as Eustace McGargle, Larson E. Whipsnade, and Filthy McNasty. He also wrote scripts under such pseudonyms as Otis Criblecoblis and Mahatma Kane Jeeves (i.e. 'M' hat, m'cane, Jeeves').

Fields famously abhorred women, children, ballet dancers, and bankers, amongst many other categories of humanity. Asked once how he liked children, he replied "Parboiled". The well-known stories of his mistreatment of the child star BABY LE ROY seem, however, to be apocryphal.

Born in Philadelphia, Fields ran away from home at the age of 12 and became a novelty juggler in vaudeville, performing at Buckingham Palace in 1905. He reproduced many of his stage routines in his early silent films but did not attain stardom until the early 1930s, when he joined Mack SENNETT to appear in such shorts as *The Dentist* (1932) and *The Fatal Glass of Beer* (1933).

After a two-year retirement caused by excessive drinking, Fields joined Universal in 1938 for $125,000 a film plus $25,000 a script; scripts accepted allegedly included one plot written on the back of a postcard. His Universal roles included the eccentric Mr Micawber (his favourite part) in *David Copperfield* (1935), a circus owner in *You Can't Cheat An Honest Man* (1939), and a failed cardsharp in *My Little Chickadee* (1939), in which he co-starred with Mae WEST. The two stars were not friendly, and Fields ad-libbed shamelessly during the shoot in an attempt to steal the film.

When Fields's alcoholism became complicated by polyneuritis, his mistress, Carlotta Monti, sacrificed her career to care for him. He died on Christmas Day, which he had always professed to hate. A known agnostic, Fields was found thumbing through the Bible on his deathbed; "I'm looking for a loophole," he growled.

fill light or **fill-in light** or **filler**   A light used to supply overall illumination to a set to remove ('fill in') shadows created by the KEY LIGHTS. The term is also used for the illumination so provided.

film   (1) A strip of cellulose coated with light-sensitive emulsions, as used in still and cine photography. (2) The usual British name for a motion picture ('movie' being the more common expression in America).

film à clef (Fr. film with a key) A film based on fact but with names, locations, and other details changed. The most notorious *film à clef* was Orson WELLES'S CITIZEN KANE (1941), in which the character of Charles Foster Kane was based on the newspaper baron William Randolph Hearst (who attempted to prevent its release). There are numerous other examples. *Fame is the Spur* (1947) starred Michael REDGRAVE as a working-class politician not unlike the Labour Prime Minister Ramsey MacDonald, while *All the King's Men* (1949) featured Broderick Crawford in a role somewhat resembling the controversial Louisiana governor, Huey Long. *Compulsion* (1959) was based on the sensational Leopold and Loeb murder case, while *The Carpetbaggers* (1964) featured George Peppard as a Howard HUGHES-like film mogul.

The genre has since declined with the rise of FACTION, in which true stories are filmed using real names but great dramatic licence; examples include *In the Name of the Father* (1993), about the imprisonment of innocent people for the IRA Guildford pub bombings.

Filmaktiv *See* DEFA.

film archive A library in which films are stored and usually made available for academic research. Britain's National Film Archive was established in 1935 to "maintain a national repository of films of permanent value." Its collection contains more than 150,000 films as well as (since the 1950s) television productions. Safety film and videos are kept at the J. Paul Getty Jnr Conservation Centre at Berkhamsted, Hertfordshire, and some 140,000,000 feet of flammable nitrate film is stored in Warwickshire. The Imperial War Museum in London houses Britain's other major film archive.

Important European archives include the massive CINÉMATHÈQUE FRANÇAISE, and the Cineteca Italiana, established by the directors Alberto Lattuada and Luigi Comencini in 1940. America has numerous specialist collections; the Black Film Collection at Tyler, Texas, is devoted to films made by Blacks or featuring Black actors, while the National Center for Jewish Film at Brandeis University in Waltham, Massachusetts, has more than 2000 productions concerning Jewish subjects. The Library of Congress established a NATIONAL FILM REGISTRY in 1989. In 1982 an archive of 6506 productions was destroyed by fire at the Cineteca Nacional in Mexico City.

film base The thin flexible strip of cellulose onto which EMULSION is bonded to produce cinematographic film. It was introduced by Eastman-Kodak in 1889. Until 1950 the usual material for film bases was cellulose nitrate, a highly flammable substance; it was superseded by cellulose ACETATE.

Film Booking Office of America *See* FBO.

film club *See* FILM SOCIETY.

Film d'Art A French production company founded in 1908 to film important stage productions for a mass audience. Its popular successes included the 30-minute *Les Amours de la Reine Elizabeth*, shot in London with the legendary Sarah Bernhardt as Elizabeth I.

Although the Film d'Art productions were limited as cinema, being stiff and stage-bound, their international influence was profound. In Britain such famous actors as Herbert Beerbohm Tree and Johnston Forbes-Robertson were inspired to face the cameras. More importantly, the Film d'Arte Italiana company was established in 1909 to make serious costume spectacles; it was the US success of Enrico Guazzoni's QUO VADIS? (1912) that first convinced Hollywood that feature films could be commercially viable. A year later, inspired by the popularity of *Les Amours de la Reine Elizabeth*, which he distributed in America, Adolph ZUKOR formed Famous Players in Famous Plays (*see* FAMOUS PLAYERS), one of the first US companies to produce features.

The effect of the film d'art movement on the development of cinema was mixed. On the one hand, the slavish re-creation of stage plays on screen held back the development of the new medium for some years; on the other, it proved to audiences and actors alike that film could aspire to be something other than a vulgar sideshow.

Filmex The popular name for the Los Angeles International Film Exposition. The noncompetitive event is held annually for a fortnight in April at the Berwin Entertainment Complex on 6525 Sunset Boulevard in Hollywood. Domestic and foreign films are screened in the categories of features, first films, shorts, documentaries, animation films, and experimental films.

film festival An event held over a number of days in the same town, city, or region during which new films are premiered; awards are often presented to films in various categories, although noncompetitive festivals are also popular. Festivals provide an important opportunity for those who work in the different sides of the industry to meet and discuss new projects.

> Look at all the film buyers and sellers in Cannes and you're basically looking at a lot of shoe salesmen working out whether it should be sneakers or lace-ups next year.
> DAVID HEMMINGS, 1981.

The presence of leading stars usually attracts considerable media coverage. Major international film festivals are held at CANNES, BERLIN, EDINBURGH, LONDON, Florence, Moscow, Los Angeles, New York, Melbourne, Montreal, Toronto, Hong Kong, and Bombay.

The term is also sometimes used for a retrospective season during which films of a certain type or by a particular performer or director are shown.

filmic A word sometimes used to distinguish the technical and creative aspects of filmmaking from such related activities as the financing and distribution of films. A movie described as 'filmic' is one in which the techniques of editing, etc., that distinguish film from theatre or still photography are used in a particularly full or self-conscious way. *Compare* CINEMATIC.

filmic time and space The sense of time and space created by the editing of a film. This seldom has much relation to the 'real time' in which the movie was shot, or to the actual locations used. An audience may well see a character leaving one room and immediately entering another when the second shot was made months before the first and on the other side of the world.

film loader See LOADER BOY.

film-maker The DIRECTOR or PRODUCER of a film.

film noir (French; dark film) A style of film that enjoyed a considerable vogue on both sides of the Atlantic in the 1940s and 1950s. The term, reflecting both the dark nature of the subject matter and the sombre lighting effects employed, was first used by French critics to describe a new type of Hollywood GANGSTER thriller that had emerged during the war years. Film noir productions were characterized by their bleak view of society, with tangled plots focusing on murder, betrayal, corruption, and greed. Much of the action took place at night, contributing to the pervading atmosphere of menace and pessimism. In such matters as the predeliction for strong contrasts between light and dark in the framing of each scene the style is reminiscent of German EXPRESSIONISM, which is understandable, as many of the leading exponents of film noir, such as Billy WILDER, Fritz LANG, Otto PREMINGER, and Max OPHÜLS, were German émigres who began their careers in Europe during the 1930s. Perhaps the archetypal film noir is Wilder's DOUBLE INDEMNITY (1944). Key directors of the style in Europe included Jean-Pierre MELVILLE. *See also* EXISTENTIALIST FILMS.

filmography A list of the films made by a particular company, director, actor, cinematographer, etc. The cinematic equivalent of a bibliography.

filmology The study of films or film-making, especially when seen in their social, economic, and technological contexts rather than in purely aesthetic terms.

film society or **film club** A group of serious film lovers, who meet to view classic or favourite films as well as new productions not on general release. The meetings may include talks on the films seen or lectures about more general aspects of the cinema. Some of the most active film societies are based in colleges or other educational establishments.

In Britain, most film clubs belong to the British Federation of Film Societies (*see* BFFS). Local clubs with a national reputation include the Old Town Hall Film Society of Hemel Hempstead, the Avant-Garde Film Society of Ruislip, the Bank of Scotland Film Society, Eton College Film Society, and the Oscar Film Unit of Surrey University, Guildford.

film stock Unprocessed film, especially that which has been stored for future use. The term is also used to mean a specific type of stock, such as EASTMAN COLOR.

film strip A roll of film projected one frame at a time to produce still photographs or graphics. The role of film strips in audiovisual instruction, business meetings, and commercial presentations, has been largely taken over by VIDEO.

film talent agent A professional representative for actors and performers who negotiates deals with production companies, studios, and other employers. The agent receives a fee that is usually a percentage of his client's contracted payment or salary.

filter A transparent disc placed over a camera lens to absorb certain frequencies of light, thereby altering the colour balance. Filters can also be used to create such effects as FOG.

final cut The final right of decision about the form in which a movie is released to the public. This is usually reserved by the producers, who may order substantial re-editing against the wishes of the director. In recent years DIRECTOR'S CUTS of a number of well-known movies, often differing considerably from the versions originally released to theatres, have been made available.

Finch, Peter (William Mitchell; 1916–77) British actor, who emerged as a respected performer on both stage and screen in the 1950s but never achieved superstar status. Although born in London, Finch spent most of his early life in Australia, making his first stage appearances there in the mid 1930s. His earliest film roles were in such undistinguished Australian productions as *Dad and Dave came to Town* (1937). In 1948 Finch came to Britain as a protégé of Laurence OLIVIER, who was unaware that the up-and-coming actor had embarked on an affair with his wife, Vivien LEIGH; it lasted on and off for another ten years.

Finch's first notable screen role was as the Sheriff of Nottingham in *The Story of Robin Hood* (1951); major parts followed in the British war films *The Battle of the River Plate* and *A Town Like Alice* (both 1956). By the turn of the decade he had graduated to starring roles in *The Nun's Story* (1959), *The Trials of Oscar Wilde* (1960), and *No Love for Johnnie* (1961). He later gave memorable performances in John SCHLESINGER's Hardy adaptation *Far From the Madding Crowd* (1967) and the same director's *Sunday, Bloody Sunday* (1971), in which he played a homosexual doctor. Finch crowned his career with his portrayal of a troubled US news commentator in the satire *Network* (1976), a performance for which he received a posthumous Oscar.

fine. fine cut An advanced stage in the process of EDITING a film. The term may be applied to the last WORKPRINT before sound is mixed or to a composite print made by combining the action film and SOUNDTRACK. The fine cut, a version of the ROUGH CUT to which numerous adjustments and refinements have been made, usually corresponds approximately to the film as released.

fine-grain A term used to describe a film EMULSION in which the silver particles are smaller than normal. Such emulsions produce sharp images that can be enlarged with minimal loss of definition.

Finney, Albert (1936–) British film and stage actor, who has starred in both great hits and spectacular flops. Born in Lancashire, he studied at RADA and made his stage debut with the Birmingham Repertory Company in 1956. In the late 1950s and early 1960s he became particularly associated with the plays of the new wave of British dramatists, such as John Osborne and John Arden.

After making his screen debut in the film version of Osborne's *The Entertainer* (1959), Finney found success in *Saturday Night and Sunday Morning* (1960), in which he played a factory worker who has an affair with a married woman (Rachel Roberts). But it was his spirited performance in the title role of Tony RICHARDSON's TOM JONES (1963), that made him an international star and won him an Oscar nomination. A year later Finney starred in and co-produced a remake of the psychological thriller *Night Must Fall* (1964); he founded the production company Memorial Enterprises in 1965. After appearing opposite Audrey HEPBURN in the romantic comedy *Two for the Road* (1967), Finney made his debut as a director with the flop *Charlie Bubbles* (1968), in which he also starred. The film concerns a fashionable writer who unsuccessfully attempts to revisit his working-class roots.

Other parts have included the title role in the musical *Scrooge* (1970), Hercule POIROT in *Murder on the Orient Express* (1974), and 'Daddy' Warbucks in the disastrous screen version of the musical *Annie* (1982). His performances as an elderly actor-manager in *The Dresser* (1983) and as an alcoholic ex-British consul in John HUSTON's *Under the Volcano* (1984) brought him Oscar nominations. *Orphans* (1987), in which Finney played an outcast whose life is transformed by his meeting with a gangster, was one of Hollywood's worst ever flops, comparing budget to box-office. Later films have included *Miller's Crossing* (1989), *The Playboys* (1992), and *A Woman of No Importance* (1994).

first. first cameraman The principal camera operator on a production.

first feature The major film in a DOUBLE FEATURE programme; an A-MOVIE.

First Gentleman of the Screen Nickname of the British actor George ARLISS, whose aristocratic bearing brought him numerous parts as kings, rajahs, noblemen, and millionaires.

first grip The person in overall charge of the stagehands on a production. *See also* GRIP.

First Lady of the Screen Nickname of Norma SHEARER, the Canadian-born actress. She earned the nickname through being one of MGM's most coveted properties of the 1920s and 1930s, and particularly, perhaps, for her aristocratic performance in *Marie Antoinette* (1938). The title **First Lady of the Silent Screen** was sometimes given to Lillian GISH.

First National A Hollywood film company founded in 1917 as the First National Exhibitors' Circuit. It was set up by exhibitors angry at Adolph ZUKOR's imposition of BLOCK BOOKING; the name 'First National' was chosen because Zukor boasted of having established America's "first national theatre circuit." The new company soon moved into production, establishing First National Pictures to make films that would compete with Zukor's.

During its first year the company acquired both Mary PICKFORD, a former Zukor star, and Charlie CHAPLIN. Pickford's films for the company included her great success, *Daddy Long Legs* (1919), about an orphan and her unknown benefactor. In 1921 Chaplin fought with First National when they tried to reduce THE KID, his first feature, to another two-reel comedy. The studio's subsequent refusal to increase his budgets was a factor in Chaplin's decision to leave them in 1923. "They were inconsiderate, unsympathetic and short-sighted" he recalled, "and I wanted to be rid of them."

During the 1920s First National became one of the four most powerful Hollywood studios. It took over Associate Producers Inc. in 1922, bringing in Mack SENNETT, and a year later began to distribute Samuel GOLDWYN's films. Other famous names to work for First National included the director D. W. GRIFFITH, the future producer Alexander KORDA, the actresses Norma TALMADGE and Constance BENNETT, and Frank CAPRA, at the time an obscure screenwriter.

In 1929 the company was taken over by WARNER BROTHERS, which immediately moved into a new studio First National had built on Burbank farmland. Warners continued to produce First National films for another decade before retiring its flag logo. Ironically, First National had released Warner Brothers' first film, *My Four Years in Germany*, in 1918.

first prop man The person in overall charge of the prop crew on a production. *See also* PROP MAN.

first run The initial release of a film in selected cinemas before its general RELEASE. *The Super Fight* (1970), a film of an imaginary boxing match between Rocky Marciano and Muhammad Ali, was released worldwide for one showing before the US distributor burned all prints.

fish. **fish eye** *See* BUG EYE.

fishpole or **fishing rod** A long lightweight microphone BOOM manipulated by hand. It is used when the nature of the shooting space prevents the use of a regular boom.

Fitzgerald, Barry (William Joseph Shields; 1888–1961) Hollywood's favourite Irishman, whose accent became steadily more pronounced during his 30 years in supporting roles. His whimsical charm and scene-stealing abilities were seen at their best in his role of Father Fitzgibbon, a crusty old pastor who clashes with a younger priest (Bing CROSBY) in *Going My Way* (1940). Uniquely, the part brought him both an Oscar as Best Supporting Actor and a nomination for Best Actor.

Born in Dublin, Fitzgerald visited New York with the Abbey Theatre Players in the late 1920s. He made his film debut in HITCHCOCK's version of the Sean O'Casey classic *Juno and the Paycock* in 1930; six years later John FORD invited Fitzgerald and his brother, Arthur Shields, to Hollywood to reprise their stage roles in O'Casey's *The Plough and the Stars*.

Thereafter Fitzgerald appeared in numerous films of the late 1930s and 1940s, supporting Cary GRANT and Katherine HEPBURN in *Bringing Up Baby* (1938) and playing a New York policeman in *The Naked City* (1947). Following the success of *Going My Way*, he appeared again with Crosby in *Welcome Stranger* (1947), about two rival doctors, and *Top o' the Morning* (1949), about a theft of the Blarney Stone.

In 1952 he travelled to Ireland to appear in the John Ford classic *The Quiet Man* (1952), in which he played the village matchmaker who supervises the wooing of John WAYNE and Maureen O'HARA. Fitzgerald's brother played a priest. His last films included the British comedies *Happy Ever After* (1954), with David NIVEN and Yvonne DE CARLO, *Rooney* (1958), about an Irish dustman, and *Broth of a Boy* (1959), about a poacher's 110th birthday celebrations.

flag An opaque sheet used to block out undesired light from part of a set or from a camera lens. *See also* GOBO.

Flaherty, Robert J. (1884–1951) US explorer and film director, who has been called 'the father of the DOCUMENTARY', a title that always amused him. He photographed most of his films and was frequently assisted on location by his wife, Frances. Flaherty revolutionized travelogues by making them both more realistic and more personal; his usual method was to focus on the experience of an individual or family, whom he treated as characters in a story. The producer John Houseman once described his films as being "rooted in love".

The son of a gold prospector, Flaherty was raised in prospecting camps in Canada and attended Michigan College of Mines. His subsequent explorations took him to Hudson Bay, where the tall blond Flaherty lived among the Eskimos, wearing their clothes and observing their customs. He began to film them in 1913 but accidentally dropped a cigarette on his negatives and lost some 35,000 feet of film.

Undaunted, Flaherty tried again and in 1920 returned with the footage for *Nanook of the North*, a film documenting the harsh life of an Eskimo family. (Nanook starved to death soon after filming ended). Flaherty, a charismatic figure, persuaded the Roxy chain to book it into New York's Capitol Theater as the second half of a double bill. When Nanook received stunning reviews, PATHÉ distributed it worldwide to international acclaim.

In 1924 Jesse L. Lasky of Paramount gave Flaherty an unlimited budget to make a similar film about Samoa. On arriving in the islands for a 20-month stay, he told the Samoans: "Such pictures as this will create love and friendship among all the people of the world. Then misunderstanding and quarrels will end." The resulting film, *Moana* (1926), disappointed Paramount because Polynesian life seemed lacking in hardships. Largely because of poor marketing, the film failed at the box office. Several other projects proved abortive, partly owing to Flaherty's dislike of being tied to a script and partly to his tendency to squabble with collaborators. In 1928 he walked off projects with both MGM and 20th Century-Fox; a year later, while filming *Tabu* in the South Sea islands, he feuded with F. W. MURNAU, who bought him out.

In the 1930s John GRIERSON invited Flaherty to Britain, where he embarked on a three-year project, the influential *Man of Aran* (1934), about a fishing community on the remote Irish islands. He then travelled to India to co-direct the popular *Elephant Boy* (1937; with Zoltan Korda), featuring his young discovery SABU. In 1942 the US Department of Agriculture employed Flaherty to make *The Land*, a documentary about migrant farm workers; Standard Oil then funded *Louisiana Story* (1948), about an oil-drilling crew in the bayous. Flaherty died before starting work on two more State Department projects.

flare A bright patch on exposed film caused by extraneous light.

flash. flashback A shot or scene showing past events that is interpolated out of narrative sequence. This usually occurs when a character remembers an earlier incident or time; examples include the sequence in *Suddenly Last Summer* (1959) in which Elizabeth TAYLOR recalls a traumatic murder. Films in which the entire main story is told as a flashback include the noir classic DOUBLE INDEMNITY (1944) and Milŏs FORMAN's *Amadeus* (1983), in which the events leading to the death of Mozart are recalled by his former rival Salieri, who is now insane.

flash cutting Editing a sequence so that numerous brief shots follow each other in rapid succession. It is mainly used to create suspense. Flash cutting was used by Alfred HITCHCOCK for the famous shower scene in PSYCHO (1960) and for the scenes of birds attacking human beings in THE BIRDS (1963).

flash forward A shot or scene showing future events that is interpolated out of narrative sequence; the device is much less common than the FLASHBACK. The flash forward is mainly used to illustrate a character's hopes or fears for the future; in the comedy *Never Too Late* (1965), for example, a middle-aged man, told that his wife has become pregnant, envisions himself hobbling down the aisle at his daughter's future wedding. The device may also be used to create a sense of destiny or of the uncanny. In the thriller *The Eyes of Laura Mars* (1978), for example, a fashion photographer (Faye DUNAWAY) has premonitions of a series of murders.

flash frame A frame or short sequence of frames used to show an image for a split second only. The flash frame barely registers with an audience but helps to create an atmosphere of mystery or expectation. The technique was used memorably in the thriller *Don't Look Now* (1973), in which Donald SUTHERLAND repeatedly glimpses or imagines a small red-coated figure; at the end of the film he comes face to face with the figure, who stabs him to death.

The term is also used by film editors to mean a frame intentionally overexposed as a cue for editing.

Flash Gordon The hero of a series of science-fiction films of the late 1930s, introduced earlier that decade in a 13-part King Features newspaper COMIC STRIP. In *Flash Gordon* (1936), the first of the films, Flash (Larry 'Buster' Crabbe), his companion Dr Zarkov, and sweetheart Dale Arden blast off to rescue the Earth from collision with the Planet Mongo, ruled by the evil Ming the Merciless. The two sequels, *Flash Gordon's Trip to Mars* (1938) and *Flash Gordon Conquers the Universe* (1940), were in a similar vein. A faintly pornographic spoof version, *Flesh Gordon* ("Planet Porno bombards Earth with Sex Rays! Send for Flesh!"), appeared in 1974. In 1980 *Flash Gordon* itself was remade with Sam J. Jones and TOPOL in the cast; this was generally thought to lack the kitsch charm of the original.

flashing Exposing film briefly to light to increase the speed of its emulsion; this is often done if filming is to be carried out in dim light.

flash pan A rapid horizontal PAN shot that produces a slight blurring of the image. Also called a **swish pan** or a **zip pan**, the technique was formerly used to effect a transition between two scenes, especially when these were separated in space or time. The device was especially popular in the 1920s and 1930s.

flat A lightweight wooden or plywood frame supporting stretched canvas or other material, used as part of a studio set. Flats normally stand 18 feet high and up to eight feet wide, being supported by weights and braces. They have been used in the theatre since the 17th century.

flat lighting Lighting distributed evenly over a set; the opposite of high-contrast il-lumination.

flat print Traditional film PRINT as opposed to the 'squeezed print' used in such widescreen systems as CINEMASCOPE; the lat-ter has to be projected using an ANAMORPHIC lens.

Fleischer, Richard (1916–) Prolific US director, who has made some 40 features in as many years. His output includes several thrillers based on true crime stories.

Fleischer was born in Brooklyn, New York, the son of the animator Max Fleischer (of BETTY BOOP and POPEYE THE SAILOR fame). Having studied pre-med at Brown University and drama at Yale, he managed a stage company before joining RKO to direct news-reels and shorts in 1942. He was awarded his first feature, *Child of Divorce*, four years later.

Because he frequently refused the films that were assigned to him, Fleischer was often on suspension at RKO. Following his departure from the studio in 1952, he was picked up by Walt DISNEY for the big-budget CINEMASCOPE adventure, *20,000 Leagues Under the Sea* (1954). He then signed for several years with 20th Century-Fox.

Fleischer's true crime dramas included *The Girl on the Red Velvet Swing* (1955), based on a society murder, *Compulsion* (1959), about the notorious Leopold-Loeb murder case, *The Boston Strangler* (1968), starring Tony CURTIS, and the British film *10 Rillington Place* (1971), with Richard ATTENBOROUGH as the killer John Christie. His adventure films included *The Vikings* (1958), with Kirk DOUGLAS and Tony Curtis, and the all-star swashbuckler *The Prince and the Pauper* (1977). Unsurprisingly, his vast and varied output includes several disasters, notably the biblical story *Barabbas* (1961) with Anthony QUINN, the fantasy *Dr Dolittle* (1967) with Rex HARRISON, and the war epic *Tora! Tora! Tora!* (1970). Films like these led the critic Pauline KAEL to conclude that Fleischer had "no particular interests and no discernible style."

His more recent films have included *The New Centurions* (1972), with George C. SCOTT as an ageing cop, *Soylent Green*

(1973) with Charlton HESTON and Edward G. ROBINSON, the ghost story *Amityville 3-D* (1983), and two Arnold SCHWARZENEGGER offerings, *Conan The Destroyer* (1984) and *Red Sonja* (1985).

Fleming.   Rhonda Fleming (Marilyn Louis; 1923–) Glamorous US star of the 1940s and 1950s, who appeared in numerous Westerns, thrillers, and comedies. A red-head, she was often cast in temperamental roles. Towards the end of her career, she went through four husbands in five years (1966–71).

Born in Los Angeles, Fleming was signed up by David O. SELZNICK while still a senior at Beverly Hills High School. She failed to inform him that she was married with a baby, a fact Selznick only discovered when he called her at 1 a.m. and her husband answered. Selznick was so staggered that he never explained why he had called. After working for a while as an extra, Fleming graduated to second-female parts, such as a man-hating nymphomaniac in HITCHCOCK's SPELLBOUND (1945) and a friend to Dorothy McGuire in *The Spiral Staircase* (1946). In 1947 she was given a starring role opposite Bob HOPE, who chased her around an ocean liner in *The Great Lover*, while two years later she provided Bing CROSBY's love interest in *A Connecticut Yankee in King Arthur's Court*.

During the 1950s Fleming played op-posite Ronald REAGAN in the Western *Tennessee's Partner* (1955), with Joseph COTTEN in *The Killer is Loose* (1956), and with Burt LANCASTER and Kirk DOUGLAS in GUN-FIGHT AT THE OK CORRAL (1957). Her later films included the disaster movie *The Crowded Sky* (1960) and two Italian produc-tions.

Victor Fleming (1883–1949) US director best known for two films released in 1939: GONE WITH THE WIND and THE WIZARD OF OZ. His macho character is believed to have inspired Clark GABLE's screen image; the two men would go off together on wild motorcycle rides and brothel crawls. A keen big-game hunter, Fleming often threatened to leave the cinema and spend his time on perma-nent safari.

A former car mechanic, he was brought into the cinema by the director Allan DWAN, who took his car to Fleming for repair and noticed photographic equipment in his garage. Fleming worked on a couple of Douglas FAIRBANKS films in 1916–17 before serving in World War I as a pilot and cameraman. After the war, he joined Fairbanks's new United Artists company as a photographer and director. In 1922 he moved to Paramount to make *Mantrap* and began an affair with its star, Clara BOW.

Critical acclaim followed with *The Way Of All Flesh* (1926), which earned Emil JANNINGS the first-ever Academy Award for Best Actor. After making *The Virginian* (1929), his and Gary COOPER's first talkie, Fleming joined MGM to direct Jean HARLOW and Gable in *Red Dust* (1932). In 1936 he directed the first of five Spencer TRACY films, *Captains Courageous*, for which Tracy won his first Oscar.

In 1938 Fleming was called in to replace George CUKOR on *The Wizard of Oz*, only to be taken off the film when it was almost complete to replace Cukor once again on *Gone With The Wind*. Fleming greatly irritated the star, Vivien LEIGH, by calling her "Fiddle-dee-dee" and telling the costume designer in her presence: "For Christ's sake, let's get a good look at the girl's boobs!" She came to hate him and often went to Cukor's home to work on scenes privately. Fleming eventually became ill and was replaced by Sam WOOD. After the producer David O. SELZNICK bragged to the press about the way in which he 'supervised' his directors, Fleming boycotted the premiere and the Oscar ceremony, at which he won the award for Best Director.

In the 1940s he directed Tracy in *Dr Jekyll And Mr Hyde* (1941) and the Steinbeck adaptation *Tortilla Flat* (1942) before making *Adventure* (1945), Clark Gable's first movie after returning from the war. He ended his career with the unfortunate RKO epic *Joan Of Arc* (1949), which starred Ingrid BERGMAN, a former lover. Bergman blamed the flop for hastening Fleming's death, a few months after the film's release.

flick   Slang for a film. It derives from the flickering effect characteristic of early silent movies, a result of the relatively slow speed (16 fps) at which they were projected. The word was extremely widely used in the 1930s and 1940s, long after this defect was remedied, but is now rarely heard except in the phrase SKIN FLICK.

flies   The area above a film set where scenery or other equipment is kept, suspended by ropes or cables. To *fly* scenery is to lift or store it in this way. The term, which has a long history in the theatre, is probably nautical in origin.

flipover   A WIPE in which the image on screen appears to turn around from left to right or vice versa to show the next image on the 'reverse' side. It was a popular way of making a transition between two scenes in the 1930s. A **flopover** was a similar device in which the image appeared to turn over from top to bottom or vice versa.

floating release   A film distributed to all cinemas that wish to show it rather than being booked as a CIRCUIT release.

floodlight or flood   A high-powered lamp that gives diffuse lighting over a large area without casting shadows.

floor manager   The member of a production unit in charge of co-ordinating the various technical activities on a set. He or she supervises such crew members as stagehands, carpenters, painters, prop men, and technical advisers.

flop   A film that fails to recoup its costs at the box office. With the studios' growing concentration on big-budget BLOCKBUSTERS in the 1980s, the scope for huge financial losses became ever greater. Even when the figures are adjusted to account for inflation, it is a singular fact that the top ten money-losers in cinema history all belong to the last 15 years. They include HEAVEN'S GATE (1980; losses of $34.2M), COPPOLA's *The Cotton Club* (1985; 38.1M), *Ishtar* (1987; $47.3M), and Terry GILLIAM's *The Adventures of Baron Munchausen* (1988; $48.1M).

flopover   *See* FLIPOVER.

flop sweat   A Hollywood nickname for sweat on an actor's palms or brow caused by stage fright.

Florey, Robert   (1900–79) French director best known for his Hollywood horror films of the 1930s and 1940s, although he worked in many other genres. His most famous offerings were *Murders in the Rue Morgue* (1932) and *The Beast with Five Fingers* (1946), both of which show the influence of Weine's THE CABINET OF DR CALIGARI.

Born in Paris, Florey went to Hollywood in the late 1920s as a film critic but soon began scripting comedies and directing experimental shorts. He subsequently joined Paramount's studios in New York, where he worked with such stars as Edward

G. ROBINSON and Claudette COLBERT. In 1929 he directed the MARX BROTHERS' first film, *The Cocoanuts*, virtually a camera-in-the-theatre record of their popular Broadway musical. During this period he also began filming dance routines from a high angle, a technique later copied by Busby BERKELEY.

In the 1930s and 1940s Florey worked mainly at Warner Brothers and Paramount. Universal's *Murders in the Rue Morgue* starred Bela LUGOSI in a free adaptation of Edgar Allan Poe's story; an uncredited screenwriter on the production was the future director John HUSTON. During this period Florey also directed such stars as Errol FLYNN, Bette DAVIS, Peter LORRE, and Barbara STANWYCK. After making *The Beast With Five Fingers* with Lorre, Florey worked as an associate director on Charlie CHAPLIN's controversial black comedy *Monsieur Verdoux* (1947). In the early 1950s Florey was one of the first directors to move successfully into television.

Flynn, Errol (1909–59) US actor, born in Tasmania, whose swashbuckling roles and tempestuous private life made him one of Hollywood's greatest legends. Flynn's handsome looks and devil-may-care character equipped him for success in both spheres and ensured that his name was rarely out of the Hollywood gossip columns.

Born in Hobart, the son of a marine biologist and a mother descended from Fletcher Christian, Flynn was expelled from exclusive schools in Australia and England. He then worked variously as a shipping clerk, policeman, ship's cook, pearl diver, tobacco plantation manager, and (allegedly) diamond smuggler. His first film role, ironically, was as Fletcher Christian in the Australian production *In the Wake of the Bounty* (1931).

After a period performing in the Northampton Repertory Company he went to Hollywood, where he found instant success in Michael CURTIZ's *Captain Blood* (1935), the first of eight films in which he starred with Olivia DE HAVILLAND. A year later they appeared together in the same director's *The Charge of the Light Brigade*. Flynn was unpopular with the 600 extras, one of whom deliberately poked his horse, causing it to throw the actor to the ground. The subsequent fisticuffs ended with the burly bit player senseless on the floor.

Flynn's most famous roles were the title part in *The Adventures of Robin Hood* (1938),

with de Havilland as Maid Marian, and General Custer in *They Died with Their Boots On* (1941). Despite his screen heroics, he was classified 4F, unfit for service, during World War II because of a heart problem, malaria, and tuberculosis. He contributed to the war effort by making such propaganda films as *Edge of Darkness* (1943) and *Objective Burma* (1945), which caused a furore in Britain as it seemed to give the impression that Flynn had won the Burma campaign singlehanded.

Although he described himself as "a quiet reserved fellow", Flynn's off-screen life seems to have been a constant round of vodka, drugs, sex, and fighting. Despite the constant scandal, his happy-go-lucky demeanour largely protected him from his public's wrath. Amongst his other eccentricities, he was reputed to wear socks while making love and to put a pinch of cocaine on the end of his penis as an aphrodisiac. According to some reports he indulged in relations with both sexes, his male lovers including Tyrone POWER. Flynn found himself in serious trouble in 1942, when he was tried and acquitted of the statutory rape of two underage fans. Three years later he was hospitalized with broken ribs after a brawl with John HUSTON at a party.

After the war, he continued to throw himself with abandon into both his work and his leisure activities, though his appeal was evidently fading. With such exceptions as *That Forsyte Woman* (1949) and *Too Much Too Soon* (1958), most of his later films were unremarkable. He gave a sadly convincing performance as an alcoholic in *The Sun Also Rises* (1957). Two years later he travelled to Cuba to show his support for Fidel Castro's revolution, his final film, *Cuban Rebel Girls*, being a tribute to Castro. He died of a heart attack at the age of 50; an autobiography, *My Wicked, Wicked Ways* (1959), was published shortly after his death.

Despite Flynn's reputation as a hellraiser, David NIVEN and others close to the star have hinted at another side of his character, finding him emotionally insecure and confused. He often threw up behind the set because of stage-fright and always regretted that his passion for his co-star, Olivia de Havilland, had not been returned.

Nonetheless, it is the rabble-rousing Flynn who is cherished by Hollywood legend. Jack Warner spoke of Flynn as "all the heroes in one magnificent, sexy, animal package", a true star who "showered an audience with sparks when he laughed, when he fought, or when he loved." Flynn himself admitted he was a "Tasmanian Devil" and conceded "my difficulty is trying to reconcile my gross habits with my net income." His son Sean, a photographer, went missing, presumed killed, in the Vietnam War.

> The public has always expected me to be a playboy, and a decent chap never lets his public down.
>
> ERROL FLYNN.

in like Flynn A phrase meaning that the person so-described does not miss a chance to seduce a woman, or is quick to take advantage of anything else on offer. The phrase, which was particularly popular with the armed forces during World War II, derives from Errol Flynn's reputation as a Casanova. Flynn himself was not flattered by it.

Foch, Nina (Nina Consuelo Maud Fock; 1924–) Dutch-born US actress, who played a series of cool sophisticated blondes in the 1940s and 1950s. Born in Leyden, she was the daughter of a Dutch composer and the US actress Consuelo Flowerton. Foch, who moved to New York City with her family as a child, was briefly a concert pianist before making her stage debut at AADA. In 1943 Columbia Pictures signed her for horror films, casting her in *Cry of the Werewolf* and opposite Bela LUGOSI in *The Return of the Vampire*. Two years later Foch had her first real lead in *My Name is Julie Ross*, in which she played a kidnapped girl who is forced to impersonate an heiress. More psychological thrillers followed, notably *Escape in the Fog* (1945) and *The Dark Past* (1949), in which she appeared opposite William HOLDEN.

Foch's parts became more varied in the 1950s. In the musical *An American in Paris* (1951) she played a wealthy woman whose patronage is scorned by the poor artist Gene KELLY. After starring as Marie Antoinette in *Scaramouche* (1952), she again appeared with Holden in the boardroom drama *Executive Suite* (1954). Two biblical epics followed, THE TEN COMMANDMENTS (1956) and *Spartacus* (1960). Later films included the comedy, *Such Good Friends* (1971), in which she appeared as a friend of the mysteriously ill James Coco, and *Mahogany* (1975), a drama about modelling that starred Diana

Ross. Besides movies, she also acted on Broadway and on television.

focus puller The member of a camera crew responsible for refocusing the lens during a take. This adjustment may be required when the camera moves from one subject to another or to maintain a sharp focus during a FOLLOW SHOT.

fog (1) Unwanted density on a developed film; the most frequent causes are lens glare, extraneous light, poor storage, or incorrect processing. (2) An artificial fog created on a set by such means as a RUMBLE POT.

fog filter A diffusing FILTER placed over a camera lens to produce a softer image; it may be used for romantic effect, to hide the wrinkles on an ageing actor in a CLOSE-UP, or to create the illusion of fog.

Foley state A collection of devices used to create SOUND EFFECTS at a post-production dubbing session. These may consist of anything from paper to crumple to create a crackling fire sound to cement pavingstones for the sound of footsteps. The term derives from **Jack Foley**, the head of sound effects at Universal Studios in the 1930s, who once simulated the sound of Niagara Falls by directing a hose onto a tin advertising signboard. He became well known for removing the incidental sounds that occurred during shooting and redubbing them in perfect sync. In the US a sound-effects editor is known as a **Foley artist** or **Foley**; **Foley tracks** are the tapes on which Foley sounds are recorded.

follow. **follow focus** The readjustment of a lens during a FOLLOW SHOT to maintain a sharp focus. This task is the responsibility of the FOCUS PULLER, who will have made detailed calculations before the shot is taken.

follow shot A shot in which a camera moves to follow the subject or action. Famous examples include the title sequence of Orson WELLES'S TOUCH OF EVIL (1957), a one-camera unbroken follow shot through several blocks of a Mexican town.

Fonda. **Henry Fonda** (1905–82) US actor, who despite his naturally retiring character established himself as one of the most enduring stars of the cinema in a long series of demanding roles. Fonda's father initially opposed his son's ambition of becoming an actor but relented after attending his stage debut, calling him "perfect" and refusing to listen to even minor criticism. Fonda soon reached Broadway and in 1934 was recruited by Hollywood to make a film version of his stage success *The Farmer Takes a Wife*. Over the next few years he starred in such classic movies as *Young Mr Lincoln* (1939), the first of a series of collaborations with director John FORD, the same director's THE GRAPES OF WRATH (1940), and *The Lady Eve* (1941), which brought him together with Barbara STANWYCK, one of his favourite co-stars.

After distinguished service in the US Navy during World War II, Fonda continued his run of successes with Ford's *My Darling Clementine* (1946), *Mister Roberts* (1955), in which he had earlier triumphed on Broadway, *War and Peace* (1956), the courtroom drama TWELVE ANGRY MEN (1957), which he also co-produced, and *Fail Safe* (1964). Despite the consistently high quality of his performances over 40 years, Fonda did not win an Oscar until 1981, when the Academy chose to honour the dying actor for his performance opposite Katharine HEPBURN in *On Golden Pond*, a sentimental comedy in which his daughter Jane also played. (He had been given an honorary Academy Award the year before.)

A man of genuine integrity, if rather less lovable than his screen image might suggest, Fonda was always insistent on sticking closely to the scripts of the films on which he worked and clashed frequently with his directors. Nevertheless, he remained in demand to the end of his life. True to the undemonstrative vulnerable characters he often played, he was diffident about his art; when asked what he thought a young actor should try to find out, he replied simply "How to become an old actor."

Fonda married five times and his two children by his second wife (who killed herself on learning that he had fallen for another woman) were to establish their own reputations in the cinema.

Jane Fonda (1937–) US actress, the daughter of Henry FONDA, who inherited her father's fierce integrity as a performer. She made her film and Broadway debuts in 1960 after working for a time as a top model (even appearing on the cover of *Vogue*). Her films of the 1960s included *Cat Ballou* (1965), a spoof western, *Barefoot in the Park* (1967), a film version of Neil Simon's stage play that had her sparring with Robert

REDFORD, and the extraordinary science-fiction fantasy *Barbarella* (1968), which trod a thin line between fashion kitsch and soft pornography. Her deliberate rejection of sex-symbol roles in the late 1960s led to work on more challenging projects, notably the Depression-era tragedy *They Shoot Horses Don't They?* (1969), *Klute* (1971), in which she gave an Oscar-winning performance as a prostitute to Donald SUTHERLAND's stoic detective, *Julia* (1977), in which she took the role of playwright Lillian Hellman, *Coming Home* (1978), a depiction of the traumas suffered by Vietnam veterans that brought her the second Academy Award of her career, and the apocalyptic nuclear-disaster movie *The China Syndrome* (1980), for which she teamed up with Gene HACKMAN. Subsequent films have been less memorable; these include *On Golden Pond* (1981), which she deliberately selected as a vehicle for herself and her father, *Old Gringo* (1989), and *Stanley and Iris* (1991).

Away from the big screen, Fonda attracted controversy defending the rights of American Indians and as a figurehead of the anti-Vietnam War campaign of the late 1960s; more recently she has enjoyed highly lucrative success with fitness books and videos. She was married for some years to the French director Roger VADIM and subsequently to the US political activist Tom Hayden; in 1992 she announced her retirement from acting after marrying Ted Turner, the multi-millionaire president of CNN.

Peter Fonda (1939–) US actor, the son of Henry FONDA, remembered mainly for his role in the cult biker movie EASY RIDER (1969), which he starred in, co-wrote, and produced. Of his earlier films, only the bizarre motorcycle fantasy *Wild Angels* (1966) is memorable, while later work such as *Dirty Mary, Crazy Larry* (1974), another road movie, and the disappointing sci-fi epic *Futureworld* (1976), has been unfailingly mediocre. In the 1980s and 1990s Fonda's career became even more erratic, many of his roles being in low-budget co-productions made in Germany and Japan. His daughter **Bridget Fonda** (1964–) has recently emerged as a promising talent in such films as *Single White Female* (1992) and *Assassin* (1993).

Fontaine, Joan (Joan de Beauvoir de Havilland; 1917–) Elegant US actress of British parentage, the sister of Olivia DE

HAVILLAND, with whom she often feuded. Although Fontaine moved to America as a child, she tended to play demure, if sometimes scheming, English beauties on screen. Despite her decorous image, she was so difficult on set that some actors and directors refused to work on her films. Her autobiography was titled *No Bed of Roses*. Off screen, she was a licensed interior decorator and a keen pilot and balloonist.

Fontaine was married four times, her first husband being the actor Brian Aherne. One day she asked him, "How long have we been married?" When he replied that it must be nearly four years, Fontaine retorted, "My God! I never meant to stay married to you that long!" They divorced two years later.

Born in Tokyo, she began to act on the California stage under the names of Joan St John and Joan Burfield, using the latter for her 1935 film debut in *No More Ladies*. Two years later she played an English aristocrat opposite Fred ASTAIRE in *Damsel in Distress*. When Fontaine failed in her reading for the part of Scarlett in GONE WITH THE WIND (1939) she asked George CUKOR, "What about my sister?" to which the director responded, "Who's she?" As a result Olivia de Havilland was chosen for the part of Melanie.

Fontaine made her name in two Alfred HITCHCOCK movies. In the first of these, REBECCA (1940), her performance as the second Mrs de Winter brought her an Oscar nomination. Her erratic behaviour on set, however, meant that whole scenes had to be reshot and hundreds of her lines redubbed. A year later she won the Oscar for her performance in *Suspicion* (1941), in which she played a recently married woman who comes to suspect her husband (Cary GRANT) of murder.

Her other films included the costume dramas *Jane Eyre* (1943), in which she played the title character to Orson WELLES's Mr Rochester, *Frenchman's Creek* (1944), in which she played a married woman who becomes involved with a French pirate, and *Ivanhoe* (1952). Films of the 1960s included *Tender is the Night* (1961), Disney's *Voyage to the Bottom of the Sea* (1961), and the British movie *The Witches* (US title *The Devil's Own*; 1966), in which she played a schoolmistress who encounters black magic in an English village.

footage (1) The length of film shot or scheduled to be shot, measured in feet. The metrical equivalent is **métrage**. (2) More generally, any shot or sequence of shots from a film.

Forbes, Bryan (1926–) British director, screenwriter, producer, and actor. Born in London, Forbes attended RADA and began his acting career on the stage. After serving in Intelligence during World War II, he appeared in minor roles in a number of British films, including *An Inspector Calls* (1954) and *The Guns of Navarone* (1961). By the mid 1950s Forbes was scripting such war films as *Cockleshell Heroes* (1955) and *I Was Monty's Double* (1958). He also wrote the comedy thriller *The League of Gentlemen* (1959), the trade-union drama *The Angry Silence* (1960), which he co-produced with Richard ATTENBOROUGH, and the Peter SELLERS comedy *Only Two Can Play* (1962). He made his debut as a director with *Whistle Down the Wind* (1961), about three children who believe an escaped murderer to be Christ. A year later he found international acclaim with *The L-Shaped Room* (1962), a drama of London low-life. His other films, all of which he either scripted or co-scripted, include the melodrama *Seance on a Wet Afternoon* (1962), the US production *King Rat* (1965), *The Raging Moon* (1970), *The Stepford Wives* (1974), about a US suburb in which the men replace their wives with obedient androids, the comedy *Better Late Than Never* (1983), the mafia thriller *The Naked Face* (1985), and *The Endless Game* (1988) for television. He has also directed for the stage. Besides films, Forbes has written short stories, novels, and *Notes for a Life* (1976), an autobiography. He served from 1969 to 1971 as managing director and chief of production for ASSOCIATED BRITISH (EMI) and has been president of Britain's National Youth Theatre since 1984. His wife is the actress Nanette Newman.

> I may not have come up the hard way, but I have come up the whole way.
> BRYAN FORBES.

Forbidden Games See JEUX INTERDITS.

Ford. **Glenn Ford** (Gwyllyn Samuel Newton Ford; 1916–) Canadian-born US actor, whose kind face, relaxed style, and air of integrity brought him roles in dramas, Westerns, and comedies. He was married to the actress and dancer Eleanor Powell from 1943 to 1959.

Born in Quebec, the son of a railroad official, Ford moved to California with his family while still a child. He drove a bus before beginning to act professionally on stage. In 1939 he starred in his first film, *Heaven with a Barbed Wire Fence*, in which he played a New York clerk who settles in Arizona. His early movies ranged from the frivolity of *Blondie Plays Cupid* (1940) to the serious *So Ends Our Night* (1940), about refugees from the Nazis.

After wartime service in the US marines, Ford attained star status in two 1946 roles – Rita HAYWORTH's gambler lover in the FILM NOIR *Gilda* and the cuckolded husband of Bette DAVIS in *A Stolen Life*. In the 1950s he enjoyed a string of hits including the detective film *The Big Heat* (1953), THE BLACKBOARD JUNGLE (1955), in which he played a teacher struggling to control high school delinquents, *Teahouse of the August Moon* (1956), in which he played a GI in post-war Japan matching wits with a Japanese Marlon BRANDO, and *3:10 to Yuma* (1957), in which he played a prisoner being escorted to jail by sheriff Van HEFLIN.

In *Pocketful of Miracles* (1961) he again co-starred with Bette Davis. The shooting was disrupted by constant disputes between Ford and director Frank CAPRA, who later wrote that he lost his taste for movie-making "when Glenn Ford made me lick his boots." Later offerings included the French-Resistance drama *The Four Horsemen of the Apocalypse* (1962), the all-star *Is Paris Burning?* (1966), about the city's liberation in 1944, *Heaven with a Gun* (1969), in which he played a gun-fighter turned preacher, SUPERMAN (1978), *Happy Birthday to Me* (1981), and *Raw Nerve* (1991).

Harrison Ford (1942–) US actor, who made his name in a series of adventure fantasies in the late 1970s and early 1980s. In 1994 it was calculated that he had starred in six of the ten most successful films of all time.

After being expelled from his high school three days before graduation, Ford travelled to California, where a part in a stage play led to a seven-year contract with Columbia's new talent programme. His first movie role was as a bellboy, who delivers a message to James COBURN in *Dead Heat On A Merry-Go-Round* (1966). Minor parts in such movies as *Luv* (1967) and *Journey To Shiloh* (1968) followed, as well as television work in *Ironside* and *The Virginian*. The results were considered disappointing; one executive compared Ford unfavourably to the young Tony CURTIS, who had also started in small parts: "You knew that he was a star...you ain't got it, kid." On discovering that he had been cut from *Zabriskie Point* (1970), Ford decided to give up acting for carpentry, becoming well known for his work in the homes of Hollywood stars.

After several years away from the screen he auditioned successfully for George LUCAS's *American Graffiti* (1973) and then took the part of Robert DUVALL's gay henchman in Francis Ford COPPOLA's *The Conversation* (1974). While Ford was building a door to Coppola's office, Lucas walked in and asked the carpenter to audition for the role that became his breakthrough. Christopher Walken and Nick Nolte had both been considered for the role of Han Solo in the science-fiction spectacular STAR WARS (1977), but Ford was given the part, and a small percentage of the profits, which made him a multimillionaire; he reprised the role in *The Empire Strikes Back* (1980) and *Return of the Jedi* (1983). In the meantime, he was offered a number of other parts; he replaced Kris Kristofferson in *Hanover Street* (1979), appeared in the commando adventure *Force Ten From Navarone* (1978), and took a small role in Coppola's APOCALYPSE NOW (1979). When Tom Selleck proved unavailable, Lucas recommended Ford to Steven SPIELBERG for the part of Indiana Jones in RAIDERS OF THE LOST ARK (1981); Ford went on to consolidate his stardom in the sequels *Indiana Jones and the Temple of Doom* (1984) and *Indiana Jones and the Last Crusade* (1989).

After playing the lead in the futuristic *Blade Runner* (1982), Ford successfully broke out of fantasy roles by appearing in *Witness* (1985), a box-office success that also earned him an Oscar nomination. The following year he replaced Jack NICHOLSON in *The Mosquito Coast* (1986). *Working Girl* (1988) was a successful venture into comedy, while such hits as *Presumed Innocent* (1990) and *The Fugitive* (1993) have kept Ford's star status intact. Recently he has embarked on a new series of movies, playing CIA man Jack Ryan; *Patriot Games* (1992) was followed by the hugely successful *Clear and Present Danger* (1994).

John Ford (Sean Aloysius O'Fearna; 1895–1973) US director, who made more than 125 features over half a century and is always associated with his favourite actor,

John WAYNE. Ford, who greatly influenced the development of the WESTERN, has said of his contributions to the genre: "They weren't shoot-'em-ups, they were character stories." He won four Oscars for features and two more for wartime documentaries. Owing to eye problems, Ford usually wore sunglasses or an eye patch on location and never looked through a camera.

Born in Cape Elizabeth, Maine, Ford was the youngest of 13 children of Irish immigrants. At 19 he joined his brother, the actor-director Francis Ford, at Universal, where he worked as a propman, stuntman, and then as his brother's double and assistant director. One of his first screen roles was as a hooded Ku Klux Klan member in D. W. GRIFFITH'S THE BIRTH OF A NATION (1915).

Two years later Ford made his debut as a director with the Western *Straight Shooting* (1917). After making several more Westerns for Universal, he moved in 1920 to Fox, where he remained for the next 20 years. In 1935 he won his first Oscar as Best Director for *The Informer* (1935), about the betrayal of an IRA leader. By the late 1930s Ford's power and independence had become so strong that he could afford to eject Sam GOLDWYN from the sound stage for giving advice.

In 1939 Ford made a stunning return to the Western with STAGECOACH, a film that revolutionized the genre and made stars of both John Wayne and Monument Valley (ever since known as 'Ford Country' in Hollywood). He followed this masterpiece with two Oscar-winning triumphs, THE GRAPES OF WRATH (1940), an adaptation of the Steinbeck novel starring Henry FONDA, and *How Green Was My Valley* (1941), an intimate domestic drama set in a Welsh mining village (although most of the cast were Irish-American).

During World War II Ford made a series of propaganda documentaries for the Navy, eventually being awarded the rank of rear admiral. He returned to Hollywood to direct Wayne and Robert MITCHUM in the torpedo-boat saga *They Were Expendable* (1945) and Fonda as Wyatt Earp in *My Darling Clementine* (1946). Next followed a string of Wayne vs Indian Westerns: *Fort Apache* (1948), *She Wore a Yellow Ribbon* (1949), *Rio Grande* (1950), and the magnificent THE SEARCHERS (1956). As a change of pace, Ford directed Wayne and Maureen O'HARA in *The Quiet Man* (1952), a romantic comedy with an Irish setting that featured many of the

director's relatives in smaller parts; the film brought Ford his last Oscar. By 1962, Wayne was back as a gunman in *The Man Who Shot Liberty Valance* with James STEWART. Ford retired after making the flop *Seven Women* (1966), about a group of female missionaries held hostage in China.

foreground (fg) In a film shot, the part of the scene nearest to the camera. *Compare* BACKGROUND.

foreign. foreign release The international distribution of a film.

foreign version A film translated or edited for release in another country; in practice this usually means a Hollywood film dubbed or subtitled in another language. Changes may also be made to avoid giving offence or incurring a ban in countries where standards are different. The production of foreign versions boomed in the 1950s, when US films had to be edited for violence before they were shown in Europe and European productions had their sex scenes cut for US distribution. In 1945 two versions of the British film *The Wicked Lady* were shot because it was felt that US filmgoers might be offended by Margaret LOCKWOOD's décolletage. Similarly, Laurence OLIVIER had to dub *Henry V* (1944) for US audiences, changing the line "Norman bastards!" to "Norman dastards!" Bowdlerized versions of US films are still produced for distribution in some Third World countries, where stricter codes of CENSORSHIP apply.

Forman, Miloš (1932–) Czech director and screenwriter, who has worked in America since the late 1960s. Forman lost both parents in Nazi concentration camps. After training as a scriptwriter at the film college in Prague, he gained valuable experience with Josef Svoboda's Laterna Magika mixed-media group and worked on semi-documentary shorts. He made his debut as a director with *Audition* (1963) and *If There Was No Music* (1963), two medium-length films in a documentary style, which were released together as *Talent Competition*.

His first full-length feature was *Peter and Pavla* (1964), a wry depiction of the confusions faced by a trainee supermarket detective when he falls in love for the first time. Forman's use of nonprofessional actors and improvised dialogue brought him swift recognition as one of the leaders of the Czech New Wave; the film was awarded first prize at the Locarno Film Festival and the Czechoslovak Film Critics' Prize. *Loves of a Blonde* (1965), another mild comedy about the confusions wrought by a love affair, was equally successful.

In *The Fireman's Ball* (1967), however, Forman's satire took a more political turn, drawing parallels between the attempts of a small town's fire brigade to stage a beauty contest and the futile and corrupt management of the country by the Czech government. This audacious statement, a product of the shortlived 'liberal spring' in Czech politics, was banned when Soviet troops invaded the country in 1968. The director, who was in Paris at the time, thereafter took up permanent exile in the West.

Since settling in America in 1969, Forman has successfully found a mass audience for his work. His films of the 1970s included *Taking Off* (1971), a subversive comment on the gulf between the generations, ONE FLEW OVER THE CUCKOO'S NEST (1975), a multi-Oscar winning version of the novel by Ken Kesey, starring Jack NICHOLSON as a rebellious inmate of a mental institution, and *Hair* (1979), a screen version of the stage musical. Among more recent films have been *Ragtime* (1981), *Amadeus* (1983), a much acclaimed version of Peter Shaffer's play about the life and death of Mozart, which was awarded no less than eight Oscars, and *Valmont* (1989), based on Laclos's *Les Liaisons Dangereuses*. In 1994 he appeared as an actor in Barry LEVINSON's *Disclosure*, a film he was originally slated to direct.

format (1) The shape and size (ASPECT RATIO) of the frame when a film is projected; in the 1950s the standard ACADEMY FRAME was supplemented by various WIDESCREEN formats. (2) The physical arrangement of a scene to be photographed.

Formby, George (George Hoy Booth; 1904–61) British singer and comedian, born in Lancashire; the gormless ukelele-strumming hero of numerous comedies of the 1930s and early 1940s. Formby was the son of a celebrated stage comic – also billed as George Formby – but only began his performing career on his father's death, having worked previously as a jockey. He made his music-hall debut in 1921 (when he was 17) and his first film *Boots Boots!* in 1933. By the outbreak of World War II Formby had established himself as one of the most

popular British film performers of his era with such amiable low-budget comedies as *No Limit* (1935), *It's In The Air* (1938), and *Let George Do It* (1940); highlights included renditions of such saucy ditties as 'When I'm Cleaning Windows' (which was initially banned by the BBC), 'Leaning on a Lamp Post', and 'With My Little Stick of Blackpool Rock', all accompanied by his own ukelele playing. Among his most fervent admirers was George VI, who invited him to appear in the Royal Command Performance in 1937.

Although Formby was in constant demand entertaining the troops in World War II, his career went into something of a decline from the late 1940s. He has achieved cult status since his death, with a large fan club and numerous imitators devoted to keeping his old songs alive.

It seems that Formby, by nature shy and retiring, owed much of his success to his wife, the Accrington clog-dancer Beryl Ingham, who managed his career. Her drinking, bullying, and meanness allegedly made Formby's life a misery: at the peak of his career, when he was earning £30,000 per film, she allowed him just five shillings a day pocket money. He did not survive her long, dying just three months after her while making plans to marry again.

It's turned out nice again!
GEORGE FORMBY; one of his many catchphrases.

Forsyth, Bill (1947–) Scottish director and screenwriter, who established his reputation with several gentle perceptive comedies in the 1980s. Forsyth, who worked with the Glasgow Youth Theatre in the 1970s, began his film career with a series of industrial documentaries, making his first feature, *That Sinking Feeling*, in 1980. The delightful GREGORY'S GIRL (1980), about a teenage boy's infatuation with the girl who joins his school football team, brought his style of understated comedy to a wider audience, while *Local Hero* (1983), a whimsical piece about a small community's response to an oil company's plans for development, won glowing comparisons with the EALING comedies of the 1940s and 1950s. Forsyth's international standing was enhanced by the appearance of Burt LANCASTER in this film.

Subsequent films have included *Comfort and Joy* (1984), about a Glasgow DJ who finds himself embroiled in a clash between rival ice-cream companies, *Housekeeping*

(1987), Forsyth's first US film, about two sisters who have to come to terms with both the death of their mother and the eccentricities of the aunt who subsequently looks after them, *Breaking In* (1990), starring Burt REYNOLDS as an ageing safe-breaker, and *Rebecca's Daughters* (1992).

42nd Street (1933) One of Hollywood's classic backstage MUSICALS, directed by Lloyd BACON with dance routines by Busby BERKELEY. In the story, producer Julian Marsh (Warner BAXTER) is rehearsing a new show called *Pretty Lady*, which boasts Dorothy Brock (Bebe Daniels) as its star, Billy Lawler (Dick POWELL) as its lead juvenile, and Anytime Annie (Ginger ROGERS), Peggy Sawyer (Ruby Keeler), and Lorraine Fleming (Una Merkel) amongst its chorus. When Dorothy breaks an ankle on opening night, Peggy is sent on in her place after a stirring pep talk from Marsh: "Sawyer, you're going out a youngster but you've got to come back a star."

When Jack WARNER took an option on Bernard Ropes's novel (a downbeat work laced with alcoholism, homosexuality, and anti-Semitism), he expected it to provide a gritty backstage melodrama for director Mervyn LEROY (then dating Ginger Rogers, whom he recommended for the part of the sassy Anytime Annie). However, when LeRoy pulled out owing to exhaustion, the project was transformed into a fast-talking musical comedy interspersed with spectacular routines devised by Broadway choreographer Berkeley. After the initial excitement of the '100% all-talking, all-singing, all-dancing' productions of the early talkie era, musicals had come to be regarded as box-office poison. That Warners accepted the new line and then issued this hugely influential film was mainly a result of the faith in it expressed by Darryl F. ZANUCK, the producer, who allegedly ordered Berkeley to shoot his scenes only when Warner was off the lot. In these sequences Berkeley revolutionized screen dance by choreographing the camera as well as the chorines, laying suspension tracks to locate it at the centre of the action and mounting it on scaffolding high in the rafters (and even on the roof of the sound stage) to achieve his awesome kaleidoscopic overhead shots.

Released on the day of Franklin D. Roosevelt's inauguration, the film became Warner's biggest-grossing hit of the decade and prompted the rush-production of the imitative *Gold Diggers of 1933* and *Footlight Parade*. *42nd Street* enjoyed a new lease of life in 1980, when it opened on Broadway.

Fosse, Bob (1927–87) US choreographer, dancer, actor, and director. Born in Chicago, Fosse grew up in vaudeville, making his theatrical debut at the age of 13. After several years performing on stage with his first wife, Mary-Ann Niles, he went to Hollywood to assist with the choreography of MGM's *Kiss Me Kate* (1953), in which he also appeared. He subsequently divorced Niles to marry the dancer Joan McCracken; his third wife was the Broadway star Gwen Verdon. During the 1950s Fosse appeared as an actor or dancer in such films as *Give a Girl a Break* (1953), *My Sister Eileen* (1955), and *Damn Yankees* (1958), while also choreographing a number of highly successful Broadway shows, including *The Pajama Game* (1955).

In his forties and fifties Fosse went on to direct several impressive films, all concerned with the precarious world of dance and show business. The first of these was *Sweet Charity* (1969), a screen version of a musical that Fosse had already directed on Broadway; Shirley MACLAINE starred as the title character, a dance-hall hostess who proves repeatedly unlucky in love. Although Fosse's next film, the hugely successful CABARET (1972) was likewise adapted from a stage musical, the result was far more cinematic and benefited from the compelling central performance of Liza MINNELLI; the movie brought Fosse an Oscar as Best Director. *Lenny* (1974), a biopic of the doomed comedian Lenny Bruce, starred Dustin HOFFMAN in the title role and was shot in a striking quasi-documentary style.

In the mid 1970s Fosse suffered a near-fatal heart attack brought on by overwork and his abuse of alcohol and cocaine. He drew on this experience, and his troubled relationships with his wife, girlfriend, and daughter, in the extravagant FELLINI-influenced musical *All That Jazz* (1979), which he also co-wrote. This technically brilliant but deeply self-indulgent movie picked up Oscars for Editing, Score, Art Direction, and Costume Design as well as nominations in five other categories. Fosse's last film, *Playboy Star 80* (1983), was a poorly received piece about the tragic life of the murdered glamour model Dorothy Stratten.

Foster, Jodie (1962–) US actress and director, who began her film career at the age of ten. Born in Los Angeles, Foster appeared in several TV series, including *The Partridge Family*, before making her film debut in Disney's *Napoleon and Samantha* (1972), with Michael DOUGLAS. She remained with the studio for *One Little Indian* and *Tom Sawyer* (both 1973). As she entered her teens, however, Foster underwent a drastic change of image, playing a hard-drinking street kid in SCORSESE's *Alice Doesn't Live Here Anymore* (1975) and a drug-addicted child prostitute in the same director's TAXI DRIVER (1976). The latter role was to have dramatic repercussions when, five years later, an admirer tried to win her attention by making an assassination attempt on President Ronald REAGAN in imitation of an incident in the film.

In the later 1970s her roles ranged from the perky heroine of Disney's *Freaky Friday* (1977) to the seductive Tallulah of *Bugsy Malone* (1976) and the cool murderer Rynn in *The Little Girl Who Lives Down the Lane* (1977).

After several years during which she concentrated on her studies at Yale, Foster returned to Hollywood film-making in the mid 1980s. Her early adult roles included a series of traumatized victims in such films as *The Hotel New Hampshire* (1984), *Five Corners* (1988), and *Stealing Home* (1988). It was partly to break with this image that she chose to play a rape victim who fights back through the hostile judicial system in *The Accused* (1988), a performance that won critical acclaim and her first Best Actress Oscar. In 1991 she won a second Oscar for her part in Jonathan DEMME's thriller THE SILENCE OF THE LAMBS, having actively campaigned for the role of FBI trainee Clarice Starling (it was originally intended for Michelle PFEIFFER). Later that year she directed her first film, *Little Man Tate*, in which she also starred as the down-to-earth mother of a frustrated child prodigy. Subsequent films include *Sommersby* (1993), with Richard GERE, and the comedy-Western *Maverick* (1994); Michael APTED's *Nell* (1995), in which Foster plays a young woman who grows up without any contact with civilisation, brought her a further Oscar nomination.

four. **four-walling** An arrangement in which a DISTRIBUTOR pays an EXHIBITOR an agreed price to use his theatre. The distributor promotes and advertises the film or films, determines the ticket price, and receives any profits from the showings.

Four Weddings and a Funeral (1994) The most successful British film of all time, an unassuming romantic comedy that cost only $3.75 million to produce. It was jointly financed by Polygram Filmed Entertainment through its production company Working Title and by Channel 4 television. When *Four Weddings and a Funeral* proved a big success at Robert REDFORD's Sundance Film Festival, the opening date was advanced from April to March, a month in which US studios rarely release major movies. Following good reviews – *The New York Times* called the comedy "elegant, festive, and very, very funny" – the film went on to take $25 million in two months; it also picked up Oscar nominations for Best Picture and Best Screenplay.

Hugh Grant, the film's engaging lead, became an overnight sensation in America, with the *Washington Post* dubbing him "the new Cary GRANT." However, the actor confessed, "I was very unconfident doing the part." The cast also included Andie MacDowell, Kristin Scott-Thomas, Simon Callow, Charlotte Coleman, and Rowan Atkinson (scene-stealing as a bumbling vicar).

Mike Newell directed from a script by Richard Curtis, who had written for television's *Blackadder* and *Mr Bean* series. "We didn't think it would do any business in America at all" Curtis admitted. He had thought of the idea four years earlier, after attending 65 weddings in 11 years. The witty script takes in everything from a repeated use of the F-word in the film's opening minutes to a moving reading of W. H. Auden's *Funeral Blues* at the funeral of an Aids victim. (The film's success led to a popular revival of Auden's works.)

The story, shot in Surrey, follows a group of young people from one upper-class wedding to another. At the first of these, the bashful "serial monogamist" Charles (Grant) falls heavily for the American Carrie (MacDowell), who confesses to having slept with "less than Madonna, more than Princess Di." After several further meetings – one of them at Charles's own wedding – the two agree to live together without tying the knot.

400 Blows, The (*Les Quatre-cents coups*; 1959) François TRUFFAUT's semi-autobiographical first feature, one of the films that launched the French NEW WAVE at the end of the 1950s. Unhappy at school and unloved at home, 12 year-old Antoine Doinel (Jean-Pierre Léaud) runs away, only to be arrested for stealing a typewriter. He is then sent to the Observation Centre for Delinquent Minors, from which he escapes and heads for the Normandy coast.

"The adventures which Antoine Doinel experiences in *Les Quatre-cents coups* are mine" confessed Truffaut, who had been committed to a reformatory at the age of 16, only to be rescued by the film critic André Bazin (whom he had met during his attempt to run a Paris film club the previous year). Bazin later bailed Truffaut from a military prison where he was serving a sentence for desertion and gave him the opportunity to write for CAHIERS DU CINÉMA, the journal he had co-founded in 1951.

The 400 Blows was originally conceived as a 20-minute sketch designed to accompany four other episodes in a portmanteau study of childhood. However, Truffaut had developed the idea to feature-length by the time he began shooting in November 1958. Two days into the project, Bazin died and Truffaut dedicated the film to his memory. He later explained the title:

> Our main purpose was not to depict adolescence from the usual viewpoint of sentimental nostalgia but...to show it as the painful experience it is...During this stage, a simple disturbance, or upset, can spark off a revolt and this crisis is precisely described as adolescent rebellion...and one way to cope is to raise hell. In France this is known as *'faire les quatre-cents coups.'*

Truffaut had chosen Léaud for his physical resemblance to his teenage self; the boy's face, held in FREEZE FRAME as he approaches the sea at the end of the picture, became one of the most familiar images of the early New Wave.

Packed with references to Truffaut's favourite *auteurs* – RENOIR, HITCHCOCK, WELLES, and ROSSELLINI – *The 400 Blows* earned him the Best Director award at the Cannes Film Festival (which he had previously attacked for its commercialism). He went on to trace Antoine's rites of passage in four further films: *Love at Twenty* (1962); *Stolen Kisses* (1968); *Bed and Board* (1970) and *Love on the Run* (1979).

Fox. Fox Film Corporation *See* 20TH CENTURY-FOX.

Edward Fox (1937–) British actor of aristocratic appearance, often cast in cold or diffident roles. Born in London, he was the elder son of the theatrical agent Robin Fox and his wife Angela, a would-be actress best known for inspiring Nöel COWARD's song 'Don't Put Your Daughter on the Stage, Mrs Worthington'; their younger son is the actor James FOX. Edward's godfather was Rex HARRISON, who half a century later was disgusted to find himself supporting Fox's lead in the play *The Admirable Crichton* (1987).

Although he appeared regularly in films from 1962 onwards, Fox remained in the shadow of his younger brother for many years. After playing a pilot in the disastrous all-star vehicle, *The Battle of Britain* (1969), he came to international notice in Joseph LOSEY's *The Go-Between* (1970), in which he played an aristocrat whose fiancée (Julie Christie) has an affair with a young farmer (Alan BATES). The movie took the 1971 Grand Prix at the Cannes Film Festival. This was followed by another success, the thriller *The Day of the Jackal* (1973), in which Fox played a professional assassin hired to kill Charles De Gaulle.

Other roles have included a guest in *The Shooting Party* (1984), a military officer conducting the court-martial of Captain Bligh (Anthony HOPKINS) in *The Bounty* (1984), and a British officer in *Return from the River Kwai* (1989). His most recent films have included the cable production *Robin Hood* and *They Never Slept* (both 1991). Fox is probably still best known to British audiences for playing Edward VIII in the TV serial *Edward and Mrs Simpson* (1978).

James Fox (1939–) British actor, whose career was interrupted for a decade (1973–83) during which he concentrated on religious work. The younger brother of Edward FOX, he is often cast in sophisticated but weak or self-doubting parts. As a child actor, James used the name William Fox in such movies as Ealing's *The Magnet* (1950), a children's story.

After playing Tom Courtenay's public-school rival in *The Loneliness of the Long Distance Runner* (1962), Fox was given his first major part in Joseph LOSEY's THE SERVANT (1963), in which he played a weak master overwhelmed by his sinister man-servant (Dirk BOGARDE). His other films of the 1960s included the flapper musical *Thoroughly Modern Millie* (1967), in which he danced

'The Tapioca' with Julie ANDREWS, and *Isadora* (1968). In 1970 he starred in Nicholas ROEG's disturbing *Performance* as a gangster who falls in with ex-pop star Mick Jagger and assumes his drug-culture lifestyle.

After his ten-year retreat from the cinema, Fox was lured back to appear in David LEAN's last movie, *A Passage to India* (1984). His subsequent films have included three thrillers; *High Season* (1987), a spy caper filmed in Rhodes, John le Carré's *The Russia House* (1990), adapted by Tom Stoppard, and the IRA thriller *Patriot Games* (1991), in which he supported Harrison FORD. In 1993 he appeared in MERCHANT-IVORY's *The Remains of the Day*.

Michael J. Fox (1961–) Canadian-born US actor, whose boyish features and 5'4" height brought him a series of youth roles in the 1980s. At the end of that decade he was ranked seventh in world box-office appeal.

Fox began his screen career in such Canadian films as *Class of 84* (1983), about a school full of delinquents, before coming to US attention in the television sitcom *Family Ties*. In 1985 he leapt to international stardom in the hugely popular fantasy adventure *Back to the Future* (1985), in which a nutty scientist (Christopher Lloyd) helps the teenage hero (Fox) to return to the 1950s to arrange the marriage of his own parents. This was followed by starring roles in *Teen Wolf* (1985), about a high-school student whose discovery that he is a werewolf helps him to become a basketball star, *The Secret of My Success* (1987), a farce about a naive youth who moves to New York hoping to make his name, and the rock-and-roll musical *Light of Day* (1987). A year later Fox played his first adult character in *Bright Lights, Big City* (1988), about the dissolution of a New York magazine researcher who turns to cocaine. Neither critics nor audiences found it easy to accept the baby-faced Fox in the guise of a drugged debauchee. The star himself told the *Sunday Express*:

> The real trick was in snorting all those drugs and making it look convincing. Al PACINO told me to use powdered milk. What he didn't tell me was that the day after you've snorted a lot of this stuff, milk starts running down your nose...dripping all over the place.

At the end of the decade Fox rejoined Christopher Lloyd to make the sequels *Back to the Future II*, in which the duo visit the future but return to find the present in chaos, and *Back to the Future III* (1990), in which they travel back to the Wild West. Although these films retained much of the exuberant fun of the original, Fox, now close to 30, was becoming increasingly unconvincing in teenage roles. Faced with the problem of finding a more adult screen persona, Fox has since appeared in films ranging from Brian DE PALMA's *Casualties of War* (1989), in which he played a GI horrified at the rape of a Vietnamese girl by members of his own unit, to the mild comedies *The Hard Way* and *Doc Hollywood* (both 1991). More recent releases include *For Love or Money* (1993).

> I'm not a comedian. I'm just an actor who doesn't take myself too seriously.
> MICHAEL J. FOX.

frame (1) A single exposure on a cinema film. (2) The area that appears in a camera's viewfinder, and hence on the screen when the film is projected.

Franju, Georges (1912–87) French director and set designer, who made a series of idiosyncratic short documentaries before finding success as a maker of feature-length films. As a young critic Franju co-founded the CINÉMATHÈQUE FRANÇAISE, France's premier film archive, in 1936. He first attracted attention as a director with the documentary *Le Sang des bêtes* (1949), a harrowing investigation into the fate of animals in a Paris abattoir. Other powerful documentaries included *Hôtel des Invalides* (1951), in which Franju expressed his pacifist sympathies by juxtaposing shots of the Hôtel des Invalides in Paris with images of crippled soldiers. Amongst his other early films was *Le Grand Méliès* (1951), a tribute to the French cinema pioneer Georges MÉLIÈS.

Franju's first full-length feature, *The Keepers* (1958), dealt with the incarceration of a middle-class dropout in a mental asylum; the film marked its director out as a master of FILM NOIR with a poetic, if somewhat bizarre, insight into human oddity. Similarly *Eyes Without a Face* (1959), a horror story about a doctor who attempts to restore the beauty of his injured daughter by grafting onto her face the skin of other girls, whom he has murdered, was hailed for its challenging exploration of obsessive behaviour.

Subsequent films included the thriller *Spotlight on a Murderer* (1961), *Thérèse Desqueyroux* (1962), adapted from the novel by Mauriac, and *Judex* (1963), a highly surreal recreation of the adventure films of the silent era. Franju also adapted COCTEAU's *Thomas the Imposter* (1964), about life in the trenches during World War I, and Zola's anticlerical *The Demise of Father Mouret* (1970). His last major film for the cinema was *Shadowman* (*L'Homme sans visage*; 1973), in which he explored the world of the pulp thriller. In his later years he also made films for television.

Frankenheimer, John (1930–) US director, noted for his political thrillers. Following a spell in the US Air Force and several years working as a television director, Frankenheimer made his cinema debut for RKO with *The Young Stranger* (1957), an adaptation of a television play about a clueless young rebel. It was four years before Frankenheimer made his next cinema film, *The Young Savages* (1961), a melodrama about a district attorney based on the novel *A Matter of Conviction* by Evan Hunter (a pseudonym of Evan Lombino, who is better known as the crime writer Ed McBain). *The Young Savages* starred Burt LANCASTER, who went on to enjoy a long and rewarding film partnership with Frankenheimer; the two worked together on such films as *Birdman of Alcatraz* (1962), *Seven Days in May* (1964), an intelligent political thriller with a screenplay by Rod Serling of *Twilight Zone* fame, *The Train* (1964), and *The Gypsy Moths* (1969).

Frankenheimer's reputation as a filmmaker was firmly established by *The Manchurian Candidate* (1962), a thriller about a soldier who returns from imprisonment in Korea, where he has been brainwashed to assassinate a US presidential nominee. The film, which starred Frank SINATRA and Laurence Harvey, was a fast-moving blend of satire and suspense that came to seem all the more resonant in the conspiratorial atmosphere created by the assassination of John F. Kennedy the following year.

Seconds (1964), a mystery thriller about a secret society that offers middle-aged men a new life, was panned by some critics when first released but has since acquired minor cult status. *Grand Prix* (1967), about the tribulations of four racing drivers on and off the track, was technically inventive and featured some stunning camera work, although the story itself was not strong.

Considering the inventiveness of his earlier films, Frankenheimer's subsequent career has proved highly erratic and somehow disappointing. If *French Connection II* (1975) and *Black Sunday* (1976) showed that he could still make tight fast-paced thrillers, *The Horsemen* (1971), *99 and 44/100 Per Cent Dead* (1974), and *The Holcroft Covenant* (1985), a confusing political thriller that *Variety* described as "deficient in thrills or plausibility", have only detracted from his reputation. None of his more recent films, which include *Dead Bang* (1989), *The Fourth War* (1990) and *The Year of the Gun* (1991) rise above the routine.

Frankenstein The gothic horror story by Mary Shelley that has inspired countless films over the years, most notably the classic UNIVERSAL trilogy of the 1930s featuring Boris KARLOFF as the monster. Shelley, the wife of the poet Percy Bysshe Shelley, wrote her tale in 1816 while they were staying with Lord Byron in his rented villa on the shores of Lake Geneva. The three friends had agreed that each would write a ghost story. Mary's novel was suggested by a dream but also reflected contemporary evolutionary theory and public fascination with the properties of the recently discovered electricity. In the original story, which has been treated with scant respect by most directors, the idealistic scientist Frankenstein creates an immensely strong but unpredictable monster out of an assortment of body parts taken from fresh corpses and gives it life. A childlike being in a hostile world, Frankenstein's monster soon learns to respond to its persecutors with violence and finally has to be hunted down and destroyed.

Two silent versions of the story (1910 and 1920) were followed by James WHALE's classic *Frankenstein* (1931), one of the most influential horror films ever made. Karloff's performance as the lurching square-headed monster – a mixture of menace and pathos – established the popular image of the creature for all time; it also stole the movie so effectively that most people now believe that Frankenstein is the name of the monster, not its creator. The role was originally offered to Bela LUGOSI, who turned it down because he objected to the elaborate make-up and padded costume; it apparently took some four hours to dress Karloff for the part.

Karloff starred again in two memorable sequels, also directed by Whale, *The Bride of Frankenstein* (1935), in which Dr Frankenstein provides his creation with a mate (Elsa LANCHESTER, who also appeared as Mary Shelley in the film's prologue), and *Son of Frankenstein* (1939), featuring Basil RATHBONE as the late scientist's son and Lugosi as a grotesque Ygor.

Reworkings of the story – some very feeble and some definitely more straight-faced than others – have appeared at regular intervals ever since. These have included *Ghost of Frankenstein* (1941), *Frankenstein Meets the Wolf Man* (1943), *The House of Frankenstein* (1945), *Abbott and Costello Meet Frankenstein* (1948), *The Curse of Frankenstein* (1956), *I Was a Teenage Frankenstein* (1957), *Frankenstein 1970* (1958), *The Revenge of Frankenstein* (1958), *The Evil of Frankenstein* (1963), *Frankenstein Versus the Space Monsters* (1965), *Jesse James Meets Frankenstein's Daughter* (1966), *Frankenstein Created Woman* (1967), *Frankenstein Conquers the World* (1968), *Frankenstein Must Be Destroyed* (1969), *Lady Frankenstein* (1970), *Horror of Frankenstein* (1970), *Frankenstein and the Monster from Hell* (1973), *Frankenstein: The True Story* (1973), *Flesh for Frankenstein* (1973), *Re-Animator* (1985), *Re-Animator II* (1989), and *Roger Corman's Frankenstein Unbound* (1990). *Frankenhooker* (1990) is a bizarre reinterpretation of the myth in which a scientist reconstructs his dead fiancée using bits of murdered prostitutes (the result being described by one reviewer as "definitely less than the sum of its body parts"). The whole genre is sent up in Mel BROOKS's lovingly detailed spoof *Young Frankenstein* (1974), which even features the very laboratory equipment used in the 1931 original. The most recent version, Kenneth BRANAGH's *Mary Shelley's Frankenstein* (1993), stars Robert DE NIRO as the creature and claims (somewhat unjustifiably) to be a return to the original novel.

Franklin, Sidney (1893–1972) US director and producer at MGM during the 1930s and 1940s. Born in San Francisco, Franklin acted in small parts before becoming an assistant cameraman. With his brother, Chester, he began as an assistant to D. W. GRIFFITH in 1914, going solo in 1917. During the next few years he directed films starring Mary PICKFORD and Norma TALMADGE,

including the latter's box-office hit *Smilin' Through* (1921).

Franklin joined MGM in 1926, one of his first projects being a version of J. M. Barrie's costume drama *Quality Street* (1927), with Marion DAVIES and Conrad Nagel in the leads. He also worked as cameraman on the production, at one point donning roller skates to operate a hand-held camera while being pushed from behind by his assistant. During the 1930s he directed Norma SHEARER in several films, including *The Barretts of Wimpole Street* (1934), in which she played Elizabeth to Fredric MARCH's Browning. Franklin's only Oscar nomination came for *The Good Earth* (1937), about the turbulent life of a Chinese peasant couple (Paul MUNI and Louise Rainer); the film's most striking sequence featured a plague of locusts. He was given the film after the original director, George Hill, committed suicide while shooting footage in China and his replacement, Victor FLEMING, became ill.

In the later 1930s Franklin became increasingly involved in production. He enjoyed his most successful year in 1942, when he produced two hits starring Greer GARSON: MRS MINIVER, in which Garson and Walter PIDGEON survive World War II in the English countryside, won the Oscar as Best Film, while *Random Harvest* was nominated for Best Picture. That year Franklin was also awarded the Irving Thalberg Award for producers. He retired after directing a remake of *The Barretts of Wimpole Street* in CINEMASCOPE (1956).

Frears, Stephen (1941–) British director, noted for his fidelity to the script and his ability to coax exceptional performances from his casts.

Frears was born in Leicester and later directed *Prick Up Your Ears* (1987), adapted from the diaries of one of the city's other famous sons, Joe Orton. After law studies at Cambridge, he became an assistant director at the Royal Court Theatre, where he met such luminaries of the FREE CINEMA movement as Karel REISZ and Lindsay ANDERSON, whom he assisted on *Morgan: A Suitable Case for Treatment* (1966) and *If...* (1969) respectively. He spent much of the next 15 years working in television, learning from the period's top small-screen naturalists, among them Ken LOACH. His facility with character and setting were evident from his cinematic debut, *Gumshoe* (1971), an affectionate spoof of US detective films set in

Liverpool. *Bloody Kids* (1979) was originally made for television but received a belated theatrical release in 1983.

Frears began his cinematic career in earnest with *The Hit* (1984), which, together with *My Beautiful Laundrette* (1985) and *Sammy and Rosie Get Laid* (1987), can be regarded as a trilogy about the effects of Thatcherism on British society. He later compared John Hurt's role as a hitman in the first film to "some Thatcherite asset stripper, one of those blue-eyed incompetent killers. Cecil Parkinson could have played that part." *My Beautiful Laundrette* and *Sammy and Rosie*, which were both scripted by Hanif Kureishi and co-sponsored by Channel 4, dealt more explicitly with contemporary themes ranging from multiracialism to homosexuality and inner-city decay. The controversy provoked by these films would almost certainly have been surpassed had Frears carried out his threat to make a feature about the Royal Family:

> I was invited to a garden party at the Palace...people standing behind a rope to watch the Queen eat sandwiches. You realized this was a rich woman from the shires who all these people thought was descended from God.

Instead, he went to America to make *Dangerous Liaisons* (1988), scripted by Christopher Hampton from his stage adaptation of Laclos's novel about sexual intrigues amongst the 18th-century French aristocracy. This was followed by *The Grifters* (1990), a Martin SCORSESE production based on the racetrack thriller by Jim Thompson, which brought Frears an Oscar nomination for Best Director. By comparison *Hero* (British title *Accidental Hero*; 1992), a latter-day piece of 'CAPRA corn', was disappointing, in spite of the presence of Dustin HOFFMAN and Geena Davis. Frears then returned to contemporary realities with *The Snapper* (1993), adapted by Roddy Doyle from his own novel of Dublin life. Frears's latest, *Mary Reilly* (1995), retells the Jekyll and Hyde story from the viewpoint of the doctor's housekeeper; the project achieved a certain notoriety when the producers insisted that the ending be rewritten on 'feel good' lines more in keeping with the 1990s.

Free Cinema A British cinema movement of the 1950s, which emphasized the social relevance of film-making and attempted to deal with topical issues neglected by the commercial cinema. Although Free-Cinema films were essentially DOCUMENTARY, some contained fictionalized elements. Both Lindsay ANDERSON (*Every Day Except Christmas*; 1957) and Karel REISZ (*We Are the Lambeth Boys*; 1958) began their careers with the movement.

freeze frame An effect like a still photograph, achieved by printing a single frame of film many times in succession. It is normally used as a punctuation device; in Tony RICHARDSON's TOM JONES (1963), for instance, several of the scenes are concluded in this way. In the 1970s many police and comedy shows on US television ended with a freeze frame, a convention that rapidly became a cliché.

Fresnel or **Fresnel lens** A lightweight condenser lens whose surface consists of a number of smaller lenses, used to concentrate the beam from a spotlight. A spotlight having such a lens is called a **Fresnel spot**. The lens is named after the French physicist Augustin Jean Fresnel (1788–1827), who invented it.

Friedkin, William (1939–) US director, who achieved success with a number of technically brilliant but coldly exploitative films in the early 1970s. He was married to the actress Jean MOREAU (1977–80).

A precocious talent, Friedkin directed for television while still a teenager; he made his feature film debut in 1966 with the musical *Good Times*, starring pop duo Sony and CHER. After filming Pinter's *The Birthday Party* (1968) in Britain for Palomar, Friedkin was given *The Night They Raided Minsky's* (1968; British title *The Night They Invented Striptease*), a bustling period piece set in a 1920s burlesque theatre in New York. He consolidated his reputation as Hollywood's latest whizz-kid with *The Boys in the Band* (1970), a bitter comedy about an all-gay birthday party.

Friedkin's next film, *The French Connection* (1971), was a fast-paced police thriller based on a true case involving New York narcotics officers. It was named Best Picture at the Oscar awards, with additional honours going to Friedkin as Best Director and Gene HACKMAN for his performance as the eccentric cop Popeye Doyle. The film is remembered chiefly for its spectacular car CHASE sequence. Friedkin followed this success with the shocking special-effects spectacular THE EXORCIST (1973), which rapidly became the highest-grossing horror film of all time.

Friedkin's subsequent career has been something of an anticlimax. The $21-million flop *Sorcerer* (1977), a poor remake of *The Wages of Fear* (1953), was followed swiftly by *The Brinks Job* (1978), a moderately successful recreation of a 1950s Boston robbery. *Cruising* (1979), which starred Al PACINO as a ruthless cop hunting a psychopathic murderer in New York's homosexual bars, was widely condemned as exploitative. Friedkin's later films have included *Deal of the Century* (1983), about international arms dealing, and *To Live and Die in LA* (1985), about two cops chasing counterfeiters.

From Here to Eternity Fred ZINNEMANN's 1953 screen version of James Jones's sprawling bestseller. The film won a total of eight Academy Awards including Best Picture, Best Supporting Actor (Frank SINATRA), Best Supporting Actress (Donna Reed), Best Director, Best Screenplay, Best Editing, Best Cinematography, and Best Sound. It was also nominated for another four Awards.

The film opens with Robert E. Lee Prewitt (Montgomery CLIFT) being transferred to Schofield Barracks, Pearl Harbor, after having refused to continue as company boxer at his previous station. Prewitt's new commander, the misanthropic Capt. Holmes, wants Prewitt to box for the new company and attempts to bribe him with the offer of the post of bugler. When Prewitt refuses to comply, Holmes orders Sgt Warden (Burt LANCASTER) to ensure that he is detailed every dirty and demeaning task on the base. However, as Warden is having an affair with Holmes's wife (Deborah KERR) he has little inclination to cooperate. The victimized Prewitt is befriended by one other soldier, Angelo Maggio (Sinatra), a wisecracking loser who is continually hounded by the sadistic Sgt 'Fatso' Judson (Ernest Borgnine). While on a night's leave Prewitt meets and becomes entangled with Alma Lorene (Donna Reed), a hostess at a local club. He eventually goes AWOL and is fatally wounded while attempting to sneak back into the barracks.

From Here to Eternity is one of the most written-about of all Hollywood films and tales about its making abound. The novel had been considered unfilmable because of its violence and seedy realism. Many changes to the story were made at the behest of the army, who refused to allow Schofield Barracks to be used for filming if the original storyline was retained. Thus Holmes, who in the novel gets away with everything and is even promoted, is caught, punished, and discharged from the army in the film. In the same way the character of Alma Lorene was changed from a prostitute to a hostess.

Even the casting of the film was fraught with difficulties, director Zinnemann having to work hard to convince studio supremo Harry COHN that Clift was right for the role of Prewitt. Eli Wallach was the first choice for the role of Maggio and Sinatra virtually had to beg Cohn for the part, eventually agreeing to appear for next to nothing. The film lifted Sinatra, whose career was in slight decline, back into the ranks of major stardom. According to some industry rumours, the unforgettable 'horse's head' scene in THE GODFATHER (in which a filmmaker is intimidated into giving a part to a star with Mafia connections) offers a highly fictionalized account of the means by which Sinatra clinched the role.

front projection A technique for combining studio action with projected images that has largely superseded BACK PROJECTION. A half-silvered mirror set at a 45° angle is used to reflect a still or moving image from a projector onto a reflective screen behind the actors. As the mirror reflects the image precisely along the lens axis of the filming camera, the shadows cast by actors and props on the screen are invisible to the camera. Special lighting is used so that no sign of the projected image is visible on the actors. Front projection, which was first perfected for KUBRICK'S 2001: A SPACE ODYSSEY (1968), is mainly used for special effects.

frost On movie sets, a mixture used to simulate the effect of frost on windows, windscreens, and other surfaces. A popular choice of set designers is a concoction of left-over beer and epsom salts.

frying pan A round screen used to reduce or soften the light on a set.

Fuller, Samuel (1912–) Controversial US director, screenwriter, producer, and actor, whose films are noted for their brutal violence and amoral antiheroes. He has been praised for his direct visual style, unusual camera angles, harsh close-ups, and fast editing. A cult figure in France, he made an appearance in Jean-Luc GODARD's *Pierrot Le Fou* (1965), speaking a line that sums up his approach: "A film is like a battleground: love, hate, action, violence, death. In a word – emotion!"

Born in Worcester, Massachusetts, he began work as a newspaper copyboy at the age of 12, graduating to crime reporter by the time he was 17. He rode freight trains during the Depression and in 1935 published the first of several pulp novels, *Burn Baby Burn*. The following year he helped to write James Cruze's film, *Gangs of New York* (1938). After serving in the infantry during World War II, he returned to scriptwriting with Douglas SIRK's *Shockproof* (1948).

In 1949 he made his debut as a writer-director with the low-budget Western *I Shot Jesse James*; a string of black-and-white B-movies followed during the 1950s and 1960s. His first A-movie was Paramount's *Pick Up on South Street* (1953), starring Richard WIDMARK as a pickpocket who breaks a communist spy ring. Accustomed to working on the cheap, he shot the film in 20 days in a Los Angeles somehow disguised as New York. Another expensive project was *House of Bamboo* (1955), a CINEMASCOPE film starring Robert STACK as an undercover agent investigating Tokyo gangsters. A year later he made *China Gate*, the first US movie about France's Vietnam war. *Underworld USA* (1960) was a brutal movie about the FBI fighting a crime syndicate.

After a long interval during the 1970s, Fuller returned to feature-making with *The Big Red One* (1980), a film based on his own wartime experiences. Although widely hailed as his finest movie, *The Guardian* noted: "Like all Fuller movies, about an inch from cliché all the way." He followed this with *White Dog* (1981), a story in which an actress attempts to retrain a dog that has been taught to kill Blacks; the theme was considered so controversial that Paramount refused to give the film a proper release.

Fuller has also appeared as an actor in two films by the German director Wim WENDERS – as a movie director in *The American Friend* (1977) and as a cameraman in *The State of Things* (1982).

full shot or **full figure shot** A shot of an actor's body from the waist up. When introduced by D. W. GRIFFITH in the 1910s it disconcerted audiences used to films in which the entire body was kept in frame to reproduce the sense of watching a stage play.

The term full shot is also used of one taken up entirely by a single large subject, such as a crowd, an American Indian village, a hot-air balloon, etc.

fuzzy An out-of-focus image. These are sometimes created on purpose, usually to disguise the effects of ageing on an actor or actress.

G A US movie classification indicating that the film is considered suitable for a 'General Audience' (i.e. one of all ages) by the RATINGS Board of the Motion Picture Association of America (*see* MPAA). The ubiquity of violence, sex, swearing, and 'adult themes' in today's cinema means that G-rated films are now rare. Indeed, since the lucrative teenage audience is thought to shun G-rated films as a matter of principle, studios will often go out of their way to avoid such a rating, even for their most innocuous fare; a PG classification can usually be ensured by inserting one or two expletives.

Gabin, Jean (Jean-Alexis Moncorgé; 1904–76) French actor, whose burly physique and stoical features brought him numerous roles in crime films. He appeared in many of France's most distinguished productions in a career spanning four decades.

The son of a music-hall comedian, Gabin began his theatrical career as an extra at the Folies-Bergère. His early film roles included a thief in Jean RENOIR's Gorki adaptation *The Lower Depths* (1936) and a gangster in the melodrama *Pépé le Moko* (1936); he played an army deserter in Marcel CARNÉ's atmospheric *Quai des brumes* (1938) and a cornered killer in the same director's superb *Le Jour se léve* (*Daybreak*; 1939). Gabin made two other films for Renoir in the 1930s – *La Bête humaine* (1938), in which he starred as a train driver who plots with his lover (Simone Simon) to kill her husband, and the World-War-I classic LA GRANDE ILLUSION (1937), in which he played a French pilot held in captivity by German commandant Erich VON STROHEIM.

Gabin escaped to America during the Occupation and made his Hollywood debut playing a drunken seaman in *Moontide* (1942), an attempt at POETIC REALISM in the French style. A year later, RKO cancelled *The Temptress* when Gabin insisted that his co-star Louise Rainer be replaced by Marlene DIETRICH. After service with the Free French (1943–45) Gabin finally got to act with Dietrich in Carné's FILM NOIR *Les Portes de la nuit* (1947); however, she walked out because her role was too small and he was sacked for complaining about the script. They were replaced by Pierre Brasseur and Nathalie Nattier. The film, one of the most expensive ever made in France, was a commercial disaster.

Gabin continued to give strong performances throughout the 1950s. His portrayal of a bank robber in *Touchez pas au Grisbi* (*Honour Among Thieves*) earned him the Best Actor award at Venice in 1953, while five years later he took the Best Actor award at Berlin playing a hobo in *Archiméde le clochard* (*The Magnificent Tramp*; 1958). The following decade saw Gabin acting with many stars of the rising generation: Brigitte BARDOT was his love interest in *En cas de malheur* (*Love is My Profession*; 1958) and Alain Delon a fellow robber in *The Big Snatch* (*Any Number Can Win*; 1963). Later films included the two-hander *Le Chat* (1972), with Simone SIGNORET as his feuding wife, and *Verdict* (*Jury of One*; 1974) with Sophia LOREN. He also played Georges Simenon's Inspector Maigret in a series of films of the 1950s and 1960s.

At his best Gabin was the most magnetic actor the screen has ever known.
GEOFFREY MINISH.

Gable, Clark (William Clark Gable; 1901–60) US leading man of the 1930s and 1940s, known as **The King of Hollywood**. He usually played romantic rascals, his most famous role being the reckless Rhett Butler in GONE WITH THE WIND (1939). Offscreen, however, he was penny-pinching and shy with a reputation for dullness. His third wife, Carole LOMBARD, said of their life together: "Listen, he's no Clark Gable at home."

Born in Cadiz, Ohio, Gable left home at 14 to work as an oil-driller and lumberjack. He received his first acting tips from the actress Josephine Dillon, who became his wife in 1924. The couple moved to Hollywood but divorced in 1930. Gable failed screen tests at both Warner Brothers ("His ears are too big. He looks like an ape.") and MGM, who said he lacked machismo. The latter studio eventually signed him in 1931 and he was soon co-starring with Greta GARBO (*Susan Lenox*, 1931), Joan CRAWFORD (Possessed, 1931), and Jean HARLOW (Red Dust, 1932).

Gable got on poorly with Louis B. MAYER, who on one occasion 'punished' the actor by loaning him to Columbia for an unpromising comedy, Frank CAPRA's IT HAPPENED ONE NIGHT (1934). Although Gable and Claudette COLBERT began work on the film without much enthusiasm, they grew into their roles and became the first co-stars to win Oscars together. It is said that the scene in which Gable removed his shirt to reveal that he was not wearing a vest caused US sales of that item to plummet by 40%.

In 1935 he was nominated for a second Oscar for his performance as Fletcher Christian (to Charles LAUGHTON's Captain Bligh) in the classic *Mutiny on the Bounty*; the film confirmed Gable's status as Hollywood's top male star. Gable initially resisted the role of Rhett Butler in *Gone With the Wind* because of his disdain for the 'woman's director' George CUKOR. He eventually had Cukor removed from the film, supposedly because he felt the director was giving too much prominence to his co-star, Vivien LEIGH. Many years later, Cukor alleged that the real reason for Gable's animosity was that he knew about the star's scandalous past as a high-class rent-boy for Hollywood homosexuals. Although Gable got on better with Cukor's replacement, Victor FLEMING, relations remained poor with Vivien Leigh, who hated his bad breath (caused by his false teeth). The movie took most major Academy Awards and made him a superstar, but Gable himself received no Oscar.

He married Carole Lombard in 1939 but she was killed in a plane crash only three years later. After her death Gable enlisted in the air force, earning the Distinguished Flying Cross and Air Medal for bombing missions over Germany. His much-heralded return to the screen in *Adventure* (1945), in which he starred with Greer GARSON, proved a surprise flop. After making *Mogambo* (1953) with Ava GARDNER and *Betrayed* (1954) his contract was not renewed, and he became a heavy drinker. One fine role remained, as an ageing drifter in John HUSTON's *The Misfits* (1960); the film featured the last performances of both Gable

and Marilyn MONROE. Gable died of a heart attack shortly before the film was completed – some say as a direct result of the bare-back riding stunts he had insisted on performing himself.

> He was America's dream of itself, a symbol of courage, indomitable against the greatest of odds. But he was also a human being...a guy right out of the life all around the fans who worshipped him.
> BEN HECHT, screenwriter.

Gabor, Zsa Zsa (Sari Gabor; 1919–) Hungarian-born film actress of striking looks, whose fame rests as much upon her numerous marriages and her talent for appearing in gossip columns as her films. A former Miss Hungary, she appeared in various US, French, and British second features of the 1950s and 1960s. She played the part of Jane Avril in John HUSTON's Toulouse-Lautrec biopic *Moulin Rouge* (1953) and a small role in Orson WELLES's TOUCH OF EVIL (1958), but more typical were such B-movies as *Queen of Outer Space* (1959). In 1990 she was sentenced to perform 120 hours community service in a shelter for the homeless after slapping a policeman for being 'disrespectful'.

> I never hated a man enough to give him his diamonds back.
> ZSA ZSA GABOR.

> I'm a marvellous housekeeper – every time I leave a man I keep his house.
> ZSA ZSA GABOR.

gaffer The chief electrician in charge of lighting equipment on the set. His assistant is known as the **best boy** or **girl**.

gagman A person hired to write jokes for a comedy film or show. A number of screenwriters, actors, and directors began their careers in this way. The gag writers at Mack SENNETT's studio included the future directors Edward CLINE and Frank CAPRA. In the 1950s both Woody ALLEN and Mel BROOKS wrote gags for Sid Caesar's hit television programme *Your Show of Shows*.

Gance, Abel (1889–1981) Innovative French producer and director, who pioneered WIDESCREEN techniques in the 1920s. He was a disciple of the director Louis Delluc (1890–1924), who insisted that the French cinema must be distinctively French in style and content. Although Gance's career spanned 60 years none of his later work equalled the spectacular triumph of

NAPOLEON (1927), one of the greatest of silent epics. "A great film", he once said, "is a bridge of dreams thrown across from one epoch to another."

The son of a physician, Gance worked as a solicitor's clerk before making his first film, *Molière*, in 1909. Two years later he co-founded a production company for which he directed four short films. During World War I he enjoyed two successes with the FILM D'ART company, *Mater Dolorosa* (1917) and *Tenth Symphony* (1918).

Owing to ill health, Gance did not enter the war until its last stages and was soon invalided out. However, when Charles PATHÉ agreed to finance his film *J'Accuse* (1919), Gance returned to the front to shoot real battle footage. The film, an epic anti-war statement, employed SPLIT-SCREEN techniques and included a memorable scene in which the dead arise from the battlefields to accuse mankind. Gance said, "I was accusing the war, I was accusing men, I was accusing universal stupidity." The film's rapid cutting style influenced EISENSTEIN and other Soviet directors of the interwar years.

The eight-hour melodrama *La Roue* (1923) made innovative use of ACCELERATED MONTAGE and was the first film to end with a FREEZE FRAME. After completing this work Gance spent five months in America but disliked Hollywood and rejected a lucrative Metro contract. He returned to France to make *Napoleon*, a thrilling six-hour epic involving lavish historical reconstructions and thousands of extras. The film's concluding scenes were shot in 'Polyvision' and shown on triptych screens (30 years before CINERAMA).

Gance's first sound film, *The End of the World as Seen, Heard, and Rendered by Abel Gance* (1930), was a strange and somewhat megalomaniacal epic about the threatened destruction of the world by a comet. The director disowned the film after it was drastically cut by the producers. Gance's career never really recovered from this phenomenally expensive flop. In 1934 he cut *Napoleon*'s running time by two thirds and added stereophonic sound effects with his Pictographe system. By the 1950s he was using 'Magirama', a refinement of Polyvision, and working on more mainstream projects, such as the all-star battle movie *Austerlitz* (1959). His last film was *Bonaparte and the Revolution* (1971), although in 1978, at the age of 89, he was still planning new productions. The film historian Kevin

Brownlow reconstructed a five-hour version of *Napoleon* in 1981, the year Gance died.

Gandhi (1982) Richard ATTENBOROUGH's Oscar-sweeping epic of the life of Mohandas K. Gandhi (1869–1948), India's great nationalist leader and apostle of nonviolence. The $22-million BIOPIC is more than three hours long and has 430 speaking parts. Attenborough, who both produced and directed, nurtured his long-cherished project for 20 years and through 12 draft screenplays. He claims to have turned down about 40 acting parts during this time. *Gandhi* was finally shot on location in 26 weeks with the Indian government providing part of the finance.

A number of Hollywood studios shied away from the project (eventually released with the production credit Columbia/Goldcrest/Indo-British/National Film Development Corporation of India) when Attenborough refused to consider a major star for the lead. In the event the little-known Ben Kingsley won high praise as Gandhi; the cast also included Candice BERGEN, Edward FOX, and John GIELGUD. In addition, the film made use of more extras than any other in history – some 300,000 being employed for the scene of Gandhi's funeral.

The film's opening title announces its intention "to be faithful in spirit to the record and try to find one's way to the heart of the man." Gandhi's story is told from his early days in South Africa, where he led a campaign for Indian civil rights, through his rise to the leadership of the Indian National Congress, to his assassination. The film was criticized in some quarters for presenting an over-reverential view of its subject. However, confronted by Indian dignitaries who wanted Gandhi portrayed only as a moving light, Attenborough commented "I'm not making a film about bloody Tinkerbell!"

Gandhi won eight Oscars, the most ever received by a British film: Best Picture, Best Actor, Best Director, Best Original Screenplay, and technical awards for cinematography, film editing, art direction, and costume design.

gangsters Films about organized crime – an urgent contemporary problem in the era of Prohibition – first emerged as a distinct genre in the early 1930s. Although Warner

Brothers' LITTLE CAESAR (1931) was not the first crime talkie, it set the pattern for a series of violent urban thrillers that followed in its wake. Edward G. ROBINSON starred as Rico Bandello, a vicious mobster clearly based on Al Capone. The same year saw the release of THE PUBLIC ENEMY, a brutal film that made a star of James CAGNEY. Bleaker and more violent than either was Howard HAWKS's Scarface (1932), which features some 30 on-screen killings.

The early gangster films provoked much public unease, not only for their violence and apparent amorality, but also for their implied social criticism. The gangster was generally 'explained' in terms of his environment, and his rise through the criminal hierarchy presented as a twisted parody of the American Dream. By the mid 1930s the studios were under growing pressure to make sure that gangsters were not glamorized and that a clear anti-crime moral emerged from each screenplay.

One response was to shift the focus of interest from the gangsters to those charged with bringing them to book. Warners' G-Men (1935), for example, cast Cagney as an FBI man in pursuit of the hoods who killed his friend. The making of the film was closely monitored by J. Edgar Hoover. The rather similar Bullets or Ballots (1936), with Robinson and Humphrey BOGART, was released with the tag "Every real citizen should see it." Other film-makers softened the harsh realism of the first gangster classics by introducing elements of comedy, fantasy, and even romance. The last major gangster films of the decade were Angels with Dirty Faces (1938) and The Roaring Twenties (1939), both of which set up a contrast between Cagney as a hood with some altruistic tendencies and Bogart as a hood with none.

During World War II audiences preferred more escapist fare and the gangster movie languished until the rise of FILM NOIR in the late 1940s. Cagney himself made a memorable return to the genre in White Heat (1949), in which he played a psychotic killer with a mother fixation. A follow-up, Kiss Tomorrow Goodbye (1950), was equally brutal but less successful. Gangster movies of the 1950s included the noir-style Al Capone (1957), featuring a bravura performance from Rod STEIGER. In the early 1960s the popularity of television's The Untouchables, set in 1920s Chicago, prompted Warner Brothers to revisit the era in such

lacklustre offerings as King of the Roaring Twenties (1961).

A major landmark in the development of the genre was Warners' BONNIE AND CLYDE (1967), starring Warren BEATTY and Faye DUNAWAY as the leaders of the notorious Barrow gang. The film struck a chord with youthful audiences by depicting the title characters as glamorous nonconformists, who just happened to be mass murderers. It also set new standards for graphic on-screen violence. In the 1970s the gangster movie was effectively redefined by Francis Ford COPPOLA's THE GODFATHER and THE GODFATHER, PART II, which powerfully evoked a whole cultural milieu. Less subtle was Brian DE PALMA's shockingly violent updating of Scarface (1983), which starred Al PACINO (The Godfather's Michael Corleone). De Palma also directed Robert DE NIRO as Capone in The Untouchables (1987), a film based on the earlier television series. The same actor starred with Ray Liotta in Martin SCORSESE's GoodFellas (1990), perhaps the most highly praised gangster film of recent years.

The gangster movie has also flourished outside America. In particular, there has been a fascinating history of cross-fertilization between French and US examples of the genre; while the early Hollywood gangster films inspired such classics of POETIC REALISM as Pépé le Moko (1936), these in turn influenced the film noir style of the 1940s. Similarly, the distinctively French style of gangster film created by Jean-Pierre MELVILLE in the 1950s and 1960s has had an important impact on contemporary US directors. British gangster films include Get Carter (1971) with Michael CAINE, The Long Good Friday (1980) with Bob HOSKINS, and The Krays (1990).

Garbo, Greta (Greta Lorisa Gustafsson; 1905–90) Swedish film actress, famous for her melancholy beauty and avoidance of publicity. Born in Stockholm, Garbo studied acting at the Royal Dramatic Theatre there from the age of 17. She appeared as an extra and in tiny parts in a number of films before coming to the attention of the director Mauritz Stiller (1883–1928), who gave her the part of the Italian Countess in The Atonement of Gösta Berling (1924). When Stiller went to Hollywood in 1925, Garbo travelled with him. On first applying to MGM her agent was allegedly told by Louis B. MAYER "Tell her that in America men don't like fat women." Nevertheless, the studio signed Stiller and Garbo to make *The Temptress* (1927).

Garbo's off-screen shyness and her Swedish origins lent her an air of mystery that MGM turned to their advantage, promoting her as an aloof and enigmatic figure. From 1927 she was cast in a series of silent melodramas – including *Flesh and the Devil* (1927), *Love* (1927), and *A Woman of Affairs* (1928) – opposite the great screen lover John GILBERT. Such was her mystique that her first talking picture, *Anna Christie* (1930), was promoted with the simple slogan "Garbo talks!" and NINOTCHKA (1939) with "Garbo laughs!"

Her exotic image allowed her to be accepted in more emancipated and ambiguous roles than most of her US counterparts; there is even a hint of bisexuality in some of her performances. Her great successes of the 1930s included *Mata Hari* (1931), the all-star *Grand Hotel* (1932), and *Queen Christina* (1933), in which she gave a truly regal performance as the unconventional monarch. *Anna Karenina* (1935) and CAMILLE (1937), both of which won her Best Actress nominations from the New York film critics, show her gift for tragedy. One MGM executive commented:

> Garbo was the only one we could kill off. The Shearer and Crawford pictures had to end in a church, but the public seemed to enjoy watching Garbo die.

Despite these successes, she became increasingly reclusive and was absent from the screen for two years before making *Ninotchka*, a comedy, in 1939. This was followed by *Two-Faced Woman* (1941), another comedy, which received poor reviews and may have been the decisive factor in causing her to retire soon afterwards.

Garbo spent the remainder of her life refusing offers of new films and attempting to avoid publicity; her famous line from *Grand Hotel* "I want to be alone" came to epitomize the whole Garbo legend.

She received a special Academy Award in 1955 for her "unforgettable screen performances" but did not attend the awards ceremony.

> What, when drunk, one sees in other women, one sees in Garbo sober.
> KENNETH TYNAN, critic.

Gardner, Ava (1922–90) US actress, who filled the beauty-queen gap between Rita

HAYWORTH in the 1940s and Marilyn MONROE in the 1950s. Sloe-eyed, apple-cheeked, and dimple-chinned, Gardner was dubbed "a miniature Gloria SWANSON" early in her career and later proclaimed "the world's most beautiful woman." She had famous marriages to Mickey ROONEY (1942–43), band-leader Artie Shaw (1945–47), and Frank SINATRA (1951–57).

Gardner was born in Smithfield, North Carolina, one of six children of a poor tenant farmer. She was signed to an MGM contract at 18 after her brother-in-law sent her photo to the studio. Seeing her MGM test, Louis B. MAYER is reported to have said, "She can't talk. She can't act. She's terrific." Her debut was a bit part in the comedy *We Were Dancing* (1942). Four years later she played a major role in the Hemingway adaptation *The Killers*, as the woman who betrays Burt LANCASTER (in his first film).

She co-starred several times with Clark GABLE, although off-screen she found him a bore, confiding: "Clark is the sort of guy, if you say 'Hiya Clark, how are ya?' – he's stuck for an answer." She won an Oscar nomination for their safari film *Mogambo* (1953), directed by John FORD. After Gardner heard that her nude bathing scene had shocked the natives, she made a point of strolling around without clothes.

Gardner demonstrated a perhaps unexpected versatility when she portrayed the mixed-race Julie in the musical *Show Boat* (1951) and two years later Queen Guinevere in *Knights of the Round Table*, Britain's first CINEMASCOPE production. In the 1950s and 1960s she co-starred with Hollywood's best, including Humphrey BOGART in *The Barefoot Contessa* (1954), Errol FLYNN and Tyrone POWER in *The Sun Also Rises* (1957), Gregory PECK in *The Snows of Kilimanjaro* (1952), Charlton HESTON in *55 Days at Peking* (1962), and Richard BURTON in *Night of the Iguana* (1964).

Her later movies included the train disaster film *The Cassandra Crossing* (1976) with Burt Lancaster, the horror movie *The Sentinel* (1977), and the thriller *The Kidnapping of the President* (1980). After taking a small role in the D. H. Lawrence biopic *Priest of Love* (1981), Gardner moved to London where she lived quietly until her death.

Garland, Judy (Frances Ethel Gumm; 1922–69) US actress and singer. Born into a well-known vaudeville family, Garland had made her first stage appearance by the age of three. Four years later she and her elder sisters made their film debut as the Gumm Sisters, in the three-reel short *The Meglin Kiddie Revue* (1929). Several further shorts followed before Garland made her feature debut in *Pigskin Parade* (1936). Later that year she appeared in *Love Finds Andy Hardy* (1936), the first of many films with Mickey ROONEY. It was, however, the dazzling MGM musical THE WIZARD OF OZ (1939) that catapulted her to international stardom at the age of 17. Although Garland is forever associated with the film and its Oscar-winning song 'Over the Rainbow', she was not first choice for the role of Dorothy; had it not been for Jean HARLOW's death, which terminated an exchange deal between MGM and 20th Century-Fox, the role would have been played by Shirley TEMPLE. In the event, Garland was awarded a special Oscar for her enchantingly fresh performance.

Garland subsequently appeared in a string of juvenile musicals and films with Rooney, including *Babes in Arms* (1939), *Strike Up the Band* (1940), and *Babes on Broadway* (1941). In the mid 1940s she successfully made the transition to adult performer, starring in some of the finest MGM musicals of the period, notably MEET ME IN ST LOUIS (1944) and *Easter Parade* (1948). She also appeared in a non-musical role in *The Clock* (1945), a wartime romance directed by Vincente MINNELLI, whom she married that same year.

In the post-war years Garland was beset by a series of personal problems, including growing drug dependence, and, following her failure to fulfil her obligations on such films as *Annie Get Your Gun* (1950), MGM terminated her contract. One of the stars of the film, Howard Keel, later said: "It was the only tacky thing I knew MGM do...They should have closed it down till she was ready."

In the meantime Garland concentrated on live work, giving triumphant and emotionally charged concerts in London and New York. In 1954 she returned to the screen to star as Vikki Lester in George CUKOR's A STAR IS BORN, a musical remake of the 1937 film of the same name. The film, which featured superb central performances from Garland and James MASON, brought her an Oscar nomination for Best Actress. However, in a decision that many considered punishment for the earlier troubles she had caused, the award went to

Grace KELLY for her role in *The Country Girl*. This prompted Groucho MARX to send Garland a telegram denouncing the decision as "the biggest robbery since Brinks." Garland made no more films during the 1950s. The movies of her last years include the all-star *Judgment at Nuremberg* (1962), for which she received an Oscar nomination as Best Supporting Actress, John CASSAVETES's *A Child is Waiting* (1963), and *I Could Go on Singing* (1963).

Garland died in London in 1969 as a result of "an accidental overdose of sleeping pills." Her daughter by her second marriage (of five) is Liza MINNELLI.

> There wasn't a thing that gal couldn't do – except look after herself.
> BING CROSBY.

Garnett, Tay (1894–1977) US director, noted mainly for the classic FILM NOIR *The Postman Always Rings Twice* (1946) and for a series of shipboard movies. He was one of the few independent directors to thrive during Hollywood's Golden Era. After serving as a World War I flier, he entered movies in the early 1920s as a gagwriter for Mack SENNETT and subsequently wrote screenplays for Cecil B. DE MILLE amongst others. In 1931 he directed his first major production, *Bad Company*, an unusual GANGSTER film with a note of humour (the gang leader keeps a bust of himself and is paranoid about cats).

His shipboard films included *One Way Passage* (1932), about a doomed romance between murderer William POWELL and the terminally ill Kay Francis, *S.O.S. Iceberg* (1933), starring the German actress Leni RIEFENSTAHL (who later became Hitler's favourite film-maker), *China Seas* (1935), in which Clark GABLE rejects a society widow for the disreputable 'China Doll' Jean HARLOW, and *Seven Sinners* (1940), with Marlene DIETRICH as a South Seas cabaret singer vamping John WAYNE. In the latter Garnett parodied the style of Dietrich's former mentor, director Josef VON STERNBERG, by casting shadows over nearly every scene.

Garnett's other successes included the Hollywood satire *Stand In* (1937), with Leslie HOWARD as an accountant investigating an ailing studio and its alcoholic executive (Humphrey BOGART), the war films *Bataan* (1943) and *The Cross of Lorraine* (1944), and *The Valley of Decision* (1945), with Greer GARSON as a maid who weds her employer's son, Gregory PECK.

Garnett's most memorable film was *The Postman Always Rings Twice*, in which lovers John Garfield and Lana TURNER plot to murder her husband. Garnett prided himself on suggesting their torrid affair without obvious sex scenes; despite, or because of, this restraint the film is far more erotic than the 1980 remake. His later offerings, such as the Bing CROSBY vehicle *A Connecticut Yankee in King Arthur's Court* (1949), performed poorly at the box office. After making the CINERAMA film *Seven Wonders of the World* (1956), he turned to television work, directing for such series as *Wagon Train* and *Bonanza* in the 1960s.

Garson, Greer (1908–) Red-haired Anglo-Irish actress; her charm and wholesome beauty in a series of MGM features of the 1940s earned her the nickname **Metro's Glorified Mother**. These qualities were epitomized by her Oscar-winning performance in the wartime propaganda piece MRS MINIVER (1942). In 1945 she was the leading actress at the US box-office.

Born in County Down, Garson attended the University of London, meaning to become a teacher. Instead, she worked in advertising before making her stage debut with the Birmingham Repertory Company in 1932. After seeing her in the play *Golden Arrow* (1935) with Laurence OLIVIER, Louis B. MAYER cast her in GOODBYE, MR CHIPS (1939) as the young wife of the retiring schoolmaster Robert DONAT. When she received an Oscar nomination for her performance, Garson was rushed to Hollywood to make the classic *Pride and Prejudice* (1940), in which she played Elizabeth to Olivier's Darcy.

Garson was an obvious choice for the impeccably English heroine of *Mrs Miniver*, a role turned down by Norma SHEARER. An idealized picture of the British at war, the film was the first of eight in which she co-starred with Walter PIDGEON. Her acceptance speech at the Academy Awards dinner lasted 5½ minutes, the longest ever. In 1943 she married Richard Ney, the actor who played her son in the film; they divorced four years later.

Garson played the title role in *Madame Curie* (1943), a part originally intended for Greta GARBO, and the female lead in *Adventure* (1945), Clark GABLE's first film after military service (publicized with the line "Gable's back and Garson's got him!"). Her last great success was *Desire Me* (1947),

about a supposed widow whose husband returns after she remarries; her co-star, Robert MITCHUM, complained that in one scene she required 125 takes to say the word "No".

After appearing in such routine comedies as *Julia Misbehaves* (1948), which saw Walter Pidgeon as her husband once again, and *The Law and the Lady* (1951), in which she played a jewel thief, Garson retired in 1954. In 1960 she was lured back to play Eleanor Roosevelt to Ralph BELLAMY's FDR in *Sunrise at Campobello* (1960) but thereafter played only minor roles, in such offerings as *The Singing Nun* (1966) and *The Happiest Millionaire* (1967).

gate The component in a moving-picture CAMERA or PROJECTOR that holds each frame taut and stationary as it passes behind the lens. *See* INTERMITTENT MOVEMENT.

gattopardo, Il *See* LEOPARD, THE.

gauge The width of a FILM STOCK measured in millimetres. As a general rule, the wider the gauge the better a film stock is suited for projection onto the big screen; as less magnification is required, the loss of definition is also less. The standard gauge for commercial feature films is still 35MM, although developments in processing have led to a growing use of 16MM stock since the 1960s. Until the advent of video, amateur filmmakers generally used 8MM stock; being comparatively cheap, this has also been favoured by makers of low-budget avant-garde productions. Stocks with a gauge of 70mm or wider are sometimes used for expensive epic productions. *See also* 9.5MM; SUPER 8; SUPER 16.

Gaumont French cinema company that with PATHÉ dominated production and distribution in that country during the silent era. It was founded by the inventor Léon Gaumont (1863–1946), who developed (1901) an early method of synchronizing film and sound. Gaumont also established the film studios at Shepherd's Bush, London, and the **Gaumont circuit** of British cinemas, which owned some 300 theatres during its heyday. Gaumont-British remained independent for some years after the parent company's virtual absorption by MGM in the late 1920s; Michael BALCON was head of production between 1932 and 1936, while Alfred HITCHCOCK directed several features. The company was acquired by the RANK ORGANIZATION in 1942.

Gaynor, Janet (Laura Gainor; 1906–84) Tiny US star of the 1920s and 1930s, who won the first-ever Academy Award presented to an actress (1929). She was Hollywood's top box-office draw in 1931. Gaynor, only five-feet tall, was noted for her wholesome girl-next-door appeal and sentimental roles. She and Charles Farrell, "America's Favourite Lovebirds", co-starred in 12 Fox films.

Born in Philadelphia, Gaynor worked as a book-keeper and cinema usherette before becoming a Hollywood extra. After taking bit parts in Hal ROACH comedy shorts she starred as a doomed girl in *The Johnstown Flood* (1926). A year later, she appeared in F. W. MURNAU's expressionist masterpiece *Sunrise* (1927), with George O'Brien as the husband who plans to kill her but ends up loving her all the more. Her Oscar was awarded for cumulative performances in this and two films with Farrell: *Seventh Heaven* (1927), about a waif rescued from the Paris streets by a sewer sweeper, and the part-talkie *Street Angel* (1928), in which she played a prostitute who joins a circus. Both films were directed by Frank Borzage.

With the coming of sound many doubted Gaynor's ability to sustain her popularity. In the event, she enjoyed further successes with the maid-lodger romance *Merely Mary Ann* (1931), in which Farrell again co-starred, and *State Fair* (1933), in which Will ROGERS played her father. Her career was clearly winding down, however, by the time she won the Oscar nomination as the successful actress wife of fading actor Fredric MARCH in A STAR IS BORN (1937). Gaynor retired after making *Young in Heart* (1938), in which she and Douglas FAIRBANKS JNR played a couple trying to cheat an elderly lady.

gear head or **geared head** A camera head mounted on ballbearings so that it can be moved smoothly about its axis in PAN or TILT shots.

gel A sheet of coloured gelatin used as a camera FILTER.

Gemini A system in which a movie camera is linked to a small VIDEO camera so that both record the same image. This enables the image that appears in the cameraman's viewfinder to be simultaneously monitored by other members of the production crew, such as the director, editor, and continuity girl.

general. General Film Company *See* MOTION PICTURE PATENTS COMPANY.

general release or **showing** *See* RELEASE.

The General (1926) Buster KEATON's famous Civil War comedy; although some critics consider it the greatest of all silent comedies, it was a flop when first released. Keaton, who co-directed with Clyde Bruckman, acknowledged it as his own favourite amongst his films. The story was based on a true incident described in William Pittenger's *The Great Locomotive Chase* (the title of a 1956 Disney film on the same subject). Keaton altered the story so that the hero was a Southerner on the grounds that "you can always make villains out of the Northerners." His demand that the engines be fuelled with wood resulted in an Oregon forest fire, while a locomotive that crashed into a ravine during the filming supposedly remains there to this day.

In the plot, engineer Johnnie Gray (Keaton) sees his beloved engine, the General, hijacked by Union soldiers. As Johnnie's second love, Annabelle Lee (Marion Mack), is aboard he commandeers another engine to pursue the enemy. He rescues both the General and the girl, but finds the Yankees in hot pursuit in their own engine. As Annabelle sweeps and tidies up the cabin (and tosses away a valuable fuel log because it has a knot on it) Johnnie lures the pursuers over a burning bridge.

The film is considered a classic chiefly because of the skilful way in which the sight gags are integrated with the story. Keaton maintains his famous deadpan face throughout the hair-raising stunts; in one sequence he rode on the front of the locomotive, suspended over a wheel that could easily have killed him if too much steam had built up.

Genevieve (1953) Rank's vintage car caper; one of the best loved comedies of the period, the film holds the reissue record in Britain. Its success came as a surprise to the studio, who had released no advance publicity since the actors were hardly known. Henry CORNELIUS produced and directed, while the American William Rose won an Oscar nomination for his script.

During the course of the annual London-Brighton Vintage Car Rally, Alan McKim

(John Gregson) challenges his pal Ambrose (Kenneth MORE) to a race back to Westminster Bridge, with the car Genevieve as the prize. Despite the disgust of their respective partners, Wendy (Dinah Sheridan) and Rosalind (Kay Kendall), the race between Gregson's Genevieve, a 1904 Darracq, and More's 1904 Spyker goes ahead, with chaotic consequences.

Genevieve was filmed on 57 freezing days in the winter of 1952–53, with most of the road scenes being shot near Pinewood Studios in Buckinghamshire. When the time came to shoot the final scene on Westminster Bridge, Cornelius discovered that the tramlines essential to the drama had been removed and had to relocate to Lewisham. Such a casual approach was far from typical of the German-born Cornelius, who was a stickler for detail in other matters. Indeed, he insisted on devising family histories for each character – even though the fact that (for instance) Ambrose's father manufactured kidney pills never emerged during the film.

One curious aspect of the production was that John Gregson could not drive; he required a crash course (as it were) before principal photography. Kay Kendall also took music lessons to make her trumpet-playing sequence appear more convincing.

The appeal of the film was greatly enhanced by Larry Adler's catchy harmonica theme. In America the score and the Oscar nomination it received were credited to Muir Mathieson, because Adler was blacklisted during the McCarthy era.

Georgy Girl (1966) Bittersweet sex comedy starring Lynn REDGRAVE as the ugly-duckling flatmate of glamorous Charlotte Rampling. Georgy is a shy, ungainly, but charming girl, who suffers from the advances of her parents' employer (James MASON). More trouble comes from her oversexed selfish flatmate, whose affair with Alan BATES produces an unwanted baby that Georgy decides to look after as her own.

Scripted by Peter Nichols and Margaret Forster (from the latter's novel) and directed by Silvio Narrizano, *Georgy Girl* was one of the films that established the popular image of 'Swinging London' in the mid 1960s. The young stars, costumed by Mary Quant, cavort tirelessly about London, dancing in the rain and making mischief at parties. Owing largely to its risqué reputation, the film became a box-office hit in America,

while the catchy title song (performed by The Seekers) made the pop charts on both sides of the Atlantic. Following this success, the Canadian-born Narrizano was chosen to direct Paramount's heavily censored Western *Blue* (1968).

Gere, Richard (1949–) US actor, who emerged as a major sex symbol in the late 1970s. Following studies at the University of Massachusetts, Gere acted in repertory before appearing in the London version of *Grease* (1972). He remained in England to appear in a Young Vic production of *The Taming of the Shrew*. In 1974 he made his film debut with a bit part as a pimp in *Report to the Commissioner*. Theatre roles and some minor film parts followed but he attracted little attention until his edgy performance as a sadistic stud in the controversial *Looking for Mr Goodbar* (1977). Starring roles followed in *Bloodbrothers* (1978), Terence Malick's *Days of Heaven* (1978), and John SCHLESINGER's *Yanks* (1978). Gere's role as a male prostitute in *American Gigolo* (1979) was apparently turned down by both John TRAVOLTA and Christopher REEVE (who said of Gere: "Richard...has taken his shirt off in every movie he's made. He's falling out of his clothes").

His next film *An Officer and a Gentleman* (1981), in which he played a tough but vulnerable trainee navy pilot, proved an enormous success. He showed off his body once again in *Breathless* (1983), Jim McBride's inept remake of GODARD's classic A BOUT DE SOUFFLE, which seemed to miss the whole point of the original. That same year Gere also appeared with Michael CAINE and Bob HOSKINS in *The Honorary Consul*, a disappointing adaptation of the Graham GREENE novel. His next project was equally ill-fated; Francis Ford COPPOLA's *The Cotton Club* (1984), a story of gangsters and musicians in Harlem's legendary nightclub, was plagued by production troubles and achieved little commercial or critical success when finally released. Gere, a keen musician since childhood, played his own cornet solos in the film.

Gere's string of flops continued with Bruce Beresford's *King David* (1985), in preparation for which the star spent some weeks living with the Bedouin, Sidney LUMET's *Power* (1985), the routine police thriller *No Mercy* (1986), and *Miles from Home* (1988), an underrated rural drama. In 1990, however, Gere found astonishing box-office success in two contrasting films, the police drama *Internal Affairs*, in which he played a violent and corrupt policeman to chilling effect, and *Pretty Woman*, a Pygmalion-style romantic comedy in which he played a millionaire to Julia ROBERTS's prostitute. Following these two huge successes, Gere chose to appear in Akira KUROSAWA's personal examination of the after-effects of the bombing of Nagasaki, *Rhapsody in August* (1990). His subsequent films have included the Hitchcockian *Final Analysis* (1992); *Sommersby* (1993), an English-language version of *Le Retour de Martin Guerre* (1982), in which he starred opposite Jodie FOSTER; and *Intersection* (1994). His highly publicized marriage to the supermodel Cindy Crawford finally broke up in 1994.

German Expressionists *See* EXPRESSIONISM.

Germi, Pietro (1914–74) Italian director, screenwriter, and actor, whose career took him from post-war NEOREALISM to light comedy in the 1960s. Of Sicilian peasant origin, Germi worked as a messenger and took nautical studies before enrolling at Rome's Centro Sperimentale di Cinematografia. He worked as an extra, writer, and assistant director before making his debut as a director with *Il Testimone* (1945), like most of his early films a neorealist work with a strong social message. He maintained an ambivalent relationship with Sicily and its poor uneducated people, portraying them as tragic figures in his earlier social dramas and then more lightly in his satirical comedies. He returned repeatedly to the theme of crime in such films as *Mafia* and *In the Name of the Law* (both 1949).

Germi became internationally famous in 1961, when his *Divorce Italian Style*, a stylized comedy about a nobleman (Marcello MASTROIANNI) who arranges the murder of his wife (Daniella Rocca), won the Oscar for Best Script. Two more box-office successes followed: *Seduced and Abandoned* (1963) and *The Birds and the Bees and the Italians*, which won the 1966 Grand Prize at the Cannes Film Festival. Germi co-scripted all his films and acted in a number of them.

get in character The director's instruction to the actors to assume the characteristics of their roles in readiness for filming. Vivien LEIGH would often amaze her fellow actors by continuing to gossip on set after 'get in

character' was called, then instantly assuming her role when the cameras began. Since the advent of METHOD acting, such actors as Robert DE NIRO have often chosen to remain partly or wholly in character when off-camera.

ghosts Ghosts have been a popular subject since the earliest days of the cinema, largely, no doubt, because of the ease with which the medium can produce images of the supernatural. Techniques have ranged from the simple GHOST IMAGE to the elaborate state-of-the-art effects used in such films as *Ghostbusters* (1984). In terms of their content, films to feature ghosts have varied from lightweight thrillers and comedies on the one hand to HORROR FILMS and more serious treatments of the supernatural on the other. Such films are interesting not least for the range of popular attitudes to the afterlife that they reveal.

Many films have used ghosts to enforce a simple moral lesson. In the various adaptations of DICKENS's *A Christmas Carol* (*see* CHRISTMAS) ghosts provide humans with a reminder of their mortality and the need to spread goodwill on earth. Similarly, *The Scoundrel* (1935) starred Noël COWARD as a cynical publisher who, after his death in a plane crash, is forced to linger on earth until he finds someone who genuinely laments his passing. The most commercially successful ghost films of the 1930s and 1940s were TOPPER (1937) and its sequels, which turned on the clash of personalities between a strait-laced banker and some fun-loving spirits determined to show him the meaning of a good time.

One popular and undervalued subgenre is the 'old dark house' story, which mixes comedy, thriller, and horror. In *The Cat and the Canary* (1927; remade 1939 and 1979), *Seven Keys to Baldpate* (1935), *The Ghost Breakers* (1940), *The Ghost Train* (1931; remade 1941), *Ask a Policeman* (1938), *Band Waggon* (1939), and many others, criminals or spies pretend to be ghosts as a cover for their nefarious activities. Such films left metaphysics and theology to one side, spoofing the conventions of the gothic novel in a light-hearted manner later aped by the *Scooby Doo* cartoon series of the 1970s.

More serious explorations of the spirit world have often been treated with suspicion by the studios and the censors. While *The Uninvited* (1944) featured a genuinely frightening ghost that was cut by the British censor, Ealing's *Dead of Night* (1945) fared better and has a deserved reputation as one of cinema's classic nightmares. Two equally serious treatments of the supernatural are *The Haunting* (1963) and *The Legend of Hell House* (1973); in both films psychic investigators attempt to unravel the mystery of the haunted house, only to discover that the building itself has taken on the evil character of its former owners.

Other films have used ghosts simply as agents of terror and vengeance; in the peculiar *Ghost Story* (1981), for instance, a hideous spectre embodies the dark secret that haunts the lives of the principal characters. In *House* (1986) the threat is a RAMBO figure from beyond the grave, while in *Poltergeist* (1982) the problems are caused by the construction of a modern housing estate over an old graveyard. Tim BURTON's *Beetlejuice* (1988) has a pleasant New England couple, recently killed in a car crash, trying to scare off the ghastly yuppies who have come to buy and renovate their home. The film is unusual in that is suggests a terrifying afterlife, in which people squashed in road accidents remain in that state and where giant worms act as security guards.

For some reason the late 1980s and early 1990s saw a rash of films about life after death, much the most popular being *Ghost* (1990). Its plot – the ghost of a murdered man helps his former lover to deal with the murderer – was taken straight from the 1940 film *Earthbound*, but the film managed to be spooky and romantically satisfying at the same time. Unlike most ghost films, it presented a stark vision of the afterlife, in which the good go to heaven and the bad to hell. The theme of romantic love surviving even death was treated more maturely in Anthony Minghella's *Truly, Madly, Deeply* (1991).

ghost image A blurry semi-transparent image produced by double exposure or double printing, as used to create see-through ghost characters in films with a supernatural theme. The technique, which became popular in the 1930s, was used to turn Robert DONAT into a Scottish spook in *The Ghost Goes West* (1936) and Cary GRANT and Constance BENNETT into sprightly ghosts in *TOPPER* (1937).

ghosting Replacing the voice of one actor with that of another during post-production DUBBING sessions for any reason other than translation. The technique is mainly used in musical numbers: in *My Fair Lady* (1964), for example, Audrey HEPBURN's singing voice was ghosted (rather unconvincingly) by that of Marni Nixon. Other stars to be ghosted include Ava GARDNER in *Show Boat* (1951) and Christopher PLUMMER in THE SOUND OF MUSIC (1965). The plot of SINGIN' IN THE RAIN (1952) turns on the ghosting of Jean Hagen's shrill singing voice with that of Debbie REYNOLDS; ironically, in the real movie Reynolds's songs were dubbed by Betty Royce. After Jack HAWKINS had his voicebox removed in the mid 1960s his roles were always dubbed by another actor. For its initial US distribution the Australian film *Mad Max* (1979) was dubbed with American voices.

Gibson, Mel (1956–) Australian actor, noted for his handsome brooding looks. Although Gibson was born in New York his father emigrated to Australia in the 1960s to spare his sons the Vietnam draft. His first film role was an unpaid appearance in *Summer City* (1977), made while he was still at drama school. Having been badly beaten up one night, he went along to auditions held by the emerging Australian director George Miller, who decided that Gibson looked wrecked enough to play the hero of *Mad Max* (1979), his futuristic action movie. This fast-paced low-budget film enjoyed an extraordinary success in Australia. The following year Gibson's performance as *Tim* (1980), a mentally retarded boy, led to his being named Best Actor at the Australian Film Awards; he also made a cameo appearance in *The Chain Reaction* (1980), a comedy starring his ex-flatmate Steve Bisley. In 1981 he featured in both the commando adventure *Attack Force Z* and Peter WEIR's World War I epic *Gallipoli*, a film that set out self-consciously to demonstrate the health of Australian cinema. Gibson also appeared in a stage production of *Death of a Salesman* and took TV parts in such shows as *The Sullivans* before *Mad Max 2* (1981) brought him before international audiences again. Weir cast him for a second time in *The Year of Living Dangerously* (1982).

In 1983 Gibson went to Hollywood to film *The Bounty*, a picture that David LEAN had intended to make but abandoned to Roger Donaldson when the budget was slashed. Sting, Christopher REEVE, and David Essex had all been pencilled in for the role of Fletcher Christian (to Anthony HOPKINS's

Bligh) but it finally went to Gibson, who played the part with a perfect English accent. The following year he returned to Australia to make *Mad Max Beyond Thunderdome* (1985). Although Gibson's fame had been growing steadily, the breakthrough to real star status (and a $1-million fee) came with the stylish police thriller *Lethal Weapon* (1987). He reprised the role of jittery cop Riggs in two sequels (1989, 1992), only making the third movie on the condition that he was allowed to fulfil his dream of starring in a film version of *Hamlet*. Despite their initial scepticism, the critics were generally won over by his performance in ZEFFIRELLI's 1990 film of the Shakespeare classic. That same year Gibson was voted top movie star by *USA Today*. His subsequent films have included *Bird on a Wire* (1990), *Man Without a Face* (1992), which he also directed, and the comedy Western *Maverick* (1994).

Gidget The petite teenage heroine of a series of films made in the late 1950s and early 1960s; she is teasingly called Gidget by the boys because she is a 'girl midget'. In *Gidget* (1959), the first of the series, Sandra DEE's title character falls for a surfer (James Darren); this horrifies her parents until they discover that he is the son of their best friend. The character was subsequently played by Deborah Walley in *Gidget Goes Hawaiian* (1961) and by Cindy Carol in *Gidget Goes to Rome* (1962). Sally Field played the character in a television series of the later 1960s.

Gielgud, Sir John (1904–) British classical actor, who has appeared in numerous films and television movies. He is best known to general cinema audiences for his performance as Dudley MOORE's valet in *Arthur* (1981), which brought him an Oscar as Best Supporting Actor at the age of 77.

Born in London, Gielgud became recognized as one of the country's foremost Shakespearean actors in the 1920s and 1930s. His film debut came in the silent *Who is the Man?* (1924); he later had a bit part in Britain's first all-talking feature, *The Clue of the New Pin* (1929). Other early roles included the teacher in *The Good Companions* (1933), an unwilling spy in HITCHCOCK's *The Secret Agent* (1936), and Disraeli in *The Prime Minister* (1941).

During the 1950s Gielgud appeared in two memorable SHAKESPEARE films; Joseph MANKIEWICZ's *Julius Caesar* (1953), in which he effortlessly outshone Marlon BRANDO's mumbling Antony, and Laurence OLIVIER's RICHARD III, in which he played Clarence. He received an Oscar nomination for his performance as King Louis VII of France in *Becket* (1964) and was flawless as the moribund Henry IV in WELLES's *Chimes at Midnight* (1966). In 1977 he gave perhaps his best film performance as the dying novelist in Alain RESNAIS's *Providence*. For his last major film role the 87-year-old Gielgud appeared as Prospero in Peter GREENAWAY's extraordinary Shakespeare adaptation *Prospero's Books* (1992), a project the actor had himself suggested.

Interviewed shortly before his 90th birthday, Gielgud remarked:

> I never accept lengthy film roles nowadays, because I am always so afraid I will die in the middle of shooting and cause such awful problems.

Owing to the prestige of his name, Gielgud has been in constant demand as a supporting player; well-known films in which he has made brief appearances include the all-star *Murder on the Orient Express* (1974), the pornographic *Caligula* (1979), CHARIOTS OF FIRE (1981), and GANDHI (1982).

Gilbert. John Gilbert (John Pringle; 1895– 1936) US leading man who became the greatest lover of the silent screen following the death of Rudolph VALENTINO in 1926. A series of films with Greta GARBO established the couple as the sex symbols of their age (although one critic denounced their scenes as 'Gilbo-Garbage'). His career went into a tragic decline with the advent of sound.

The son of a stage comic, Gilbert sold rubber goods until 1916, when his father helped him to land a $15 a week bit-player's job with producer Thomas H. INCE. Five years later, he was earning $1,500 a week. He made his debut (as Jack Gilbert) in the crowd scenes of the Western *Hell's Hinges* (1916) and played his first leading role opposite Mary PICKFORD in First National's *Heart o' the Hills* (1919).

In 1920 his only solo attempt at direction resulted in a flop, *Love's Penalty*. When he joined 20th Century-Fox the following year, William FOX told him that his nose was too large, provoking Gilbert to grow his famous pencil moustache. After *Arabian Love* (1922), an attempt to emulate

Valentino's exotic image, Gilbert established his own style playing a riverboat gambler in John FORD's *Cameo Kirby* (1923). He signed with MGM in 1924 and soon afterwards established himself as a screen idol in King VIDOR's anti-war film *The Big Parade* (1925), the largest-grossing hit of the decade.

Gilbert reluctantly teamed up with Garbo in *Flesh and the Devil* (1927), thinking that she would dominate the picture; they subsequently co-starred in *Love* (1927) and *A Woman of Affairs* (1928). The two also enjoyed an off-screen affair. In 1929 Gilbert married the actress Ina Claire; asked what it was like being married to a celebrity, she retorted: "Why don't you ask my husband?" Gilbert married four times altogether and had various affairs, including one with the actress Clara BOW.

MGM renewed Gilbert's contract for $1 million in 1929, but three months later his first talkie, *His Glorious Night*, proved a disaster. The studio said that he suffered from 'white voice', a problem that could be cured, but Gilbert began to drink and went into a rapid decline. MGM tried to buy out his contract, but he resisted; in 1933 Garbo loyally demanded that he co-star with her in *Queen Christina*, having rejected Laurence OLIVIER. A year later Gilbert gave an acclaimed performance (ironically as an alcoholic) in the comedy *The Captain Hates the Sea* (1934) but died before he was able to rebuild his career.

Lewis Gilbert (1920–) British director, best known for his war and action movies, including several of the James BOND FILMS. He also made *Alfie* (1966), one of the archetypal 'Swinging London' films of the 1960s. Several of his best movies starred Kenneth MORE.

Born in London, Gilbert was introduced to film-making in the RAF Film Unit during World War II. After directing several short documentaries, he made his feature debut with *The Little Ballerina* (1947). Other early films include the GROUP 3 comedy *Time Gentlemen, Please!* (1952) and *Albert RN* (US title *Break to Freedom*; 1953), a POW comedy with Jack Warner.

Gilbert's first serious war film was the acclaimed *Reach for the Sky* (1956), with Kenneth More as legless fighter ace Douglas Bader; it took the BAFTA award as Best Film. Others included the biopic *Carve Her Name with Pride* (1958), starring Virginia McKenna as a war widow who decides to

spy against the Nazis, and the tense *Sink the Bismarck!* (1960), in which More plays a naval officer planning the destruction of the German battleship. More also starred in *The Admirable Crichton* (US title *Paradise Lagoon*; 1957) and *Greengage Summer* (US title *Loss of Innocence*; 1961).

Gilbert's *Alfie* (1966) made an overnight star of Michael CAINE in the role of the feckless womanizing title character. Three James Bond adventures followed: *You Only Live Twice* (1967) with Sean CONNERY as 007, and *The Spy Who Loved Me* (1977) and *Moonraker* (1979), with Roger MOORE.

In 1983 Gilbert earned another BAFTA award for *Educating Rita*, in which Julie Walters played the adult-education student of alcoholic tutor Michael Caine. He then returned to adventure with *Not Quite Jerusalem* (1985), about a terrorist attack on a kibbutz.

Gilliam, Terry (1940–) US director, writer, and animator. Gilliam was the only US member of the team that created MONTY PYTHON'S FLYING CIRCUS in the late 1960s; although he did not himself appear in the series, his surreal animated sequences made a huge contribution to its appeal. In 1975 he shared a director's credit with Terry Jones on the feature *Monty Python and the Holy Grail*; the Python connection continued when he cast Michael Palin as the hero of *Jabberwocky* (1977), a fantasy based on the Lewis Carroll poem. Palin also helped to script Gilliam's first major success *Time Bandits* (1981), a strange tale about a group of time-travelling dwarfs who drop in on Sean CONNERY's Agamemnon, Ian Holm's Napoleon, and John CLEESE's Robin Hood before meeting God in the business-suited form of Ralph RICHARDSON.

Gilliam's darkest work, and the highlight of his career so far, is undoubtedly the dystopian fantasy *Brazil* (1985), in which Jonathan Pryce stars as a romantic living in a hellish bureaucracy of the near future. Robert DE NIRO plays a heroic plumber and Palin a terrifyingly banal torturer. The stunning art direction and sets earned an Oscar nomination, as did the screenplay (by Gilliam, Tom Stoppard, and Charles McKeown). Before the film was released, however, Universal Pictures – who had last employed Gilliam as an advertising copywriter in 1967 – objected to its bleak ending and demanded severe edits. Gilliam resisted this pressure and eventually emerged as the victor in one of the longest-ever battles between a director and his producers.

The British-German co-production *The Adventures of Baron Munchausen* (1989) showed the negative side of Gilliam's independence; a wonderful but overblown epic, it became a byword for financial disaster in the industry. Now in desperate need of a Hollywood hit, Gilliam found one in *The Fisher King* (1992), a curious Arthurian fable that starred Robin WILLIAMS (who had also made an uncredited appearance in *Munchausen*). Although most critics felt that Gilliam's darker strengths had been diluted with too much whimsy, the film did earn Mercedes Ruehl an Oscar for Best Supporting Actress.

Gilliat, Sidney (1908–94) British screenwriter, director, and producer whose long collaboration with **Frank Launder** (1907–) produced some of the best comedies and suspense films of the 1930s and 1940s. The son of a newspaper editor, Gilliat entered films at 19 as an assistant to director Walter Mycroft. Five years later he produced his first successful screenplay, for Michael BALCON's thriller *Rome Express*.

In 1936 Gilliat teamed up with Launder, a former civil servant, to write the comedy-suspense film *Seven Sinners* and Michael POWELL's *Twelve Good Men*. They continued the collaboration with scripts for Balcon's *A Yank at Oxford* (1937), which made Vivien LEIGH a star, and Alfred HITCHCOCK'S THE LADY VANISHES (1938). For the next three years they worked with director Carol REED on a series of films that included *Night Train to Munich* (1940) and *The Young Mr Pitt* (1942); their attempt to show Pitt's flaws as well as his virtues displeased Reed and star Robert DONAT, who insisted on revisions.

Gilliat and Launder moved into direction in 1942 and three years later founded a production company, Individual Pictures; Gilliat's brother, the producer **Leslie Gilliat** (1917–), usually worked with them. However, the only film Gilliat and Launder directed together on the set was *Millions Like Us* (1943), a propaganda piece about a British family in wartime. Films directed by Gilliat alone included *The Rake's Progress* (US title *Notorious Gentlemen*; 1945) with Rex HARRISON as a 1930s playboy, *Green for Danger* (1946), a detective thriller starring Alastair SIM, and *London Belongs to Me* (1948), with Richard ATTENBOROUGH as a murderer. Launder's films included *The Blue Lagoon* (1949), Individual's most successful picture at the box office, and the school farce *The Happiest Days of Your Life* (1950). In 1954 Gilliat and Launder co-scripted *The Belles of St Trinian's*, based on Ronald Searle's cartoons of the appalling girls' school; the film starred Sim as both the headmistress and her bookmaker brother. Four sequels followed, all directed by Launder (*see* ST TRINIAN'S).

In 1958 Gilliat and Launder were named board members of the National Film Finance Corporation and three years later Gilliat became chairman of SHEPPERTON STUDIOS. Their last big hit was the excellent Peter SELLERS comedy *Only Two Can Play* (1962).

gimbal mount or **tripod** A camera mount fitted with two or three pivoted rings (*gimbals*) that enable the camera head to swing freely in all planes.

gimmicks Cinema history is strewn with shortlived gimmicks designed to attract interest and publicity. Although many now seem crude and naive, it is worth bearing in mind that moving pictures themselves were widely regarded as a nine-days' wonder when first presented at the turn of the century. Similarly, many within the industry dismissed both SOUND and COLOUR as transient gimmicks when they were first introduced.

The golden age of movie gimmicks was undoubtedly the 1950s, when film-makers sought desperately to provide cinema audiences with an experience not available from the new medium of television. The most productive area of experiment was the development of WIDESCREEN processes. CINERAMA, a system requiring a vast curved screen and three projectors, was swiftly superseded by more practical and cost-effective processes such as CINEMASCOPE and TODD-AO. In the meantime, however, a variety of other systems with such names as Naturama, Thrillerama, and Wonderama were tried out, often for one or two films only. Other attempts to add a new dimension to the cinema-going experience included 3-D and SMELL-O-VISION, in which various odours were released into the auditorium at appropriate moments. Some film-makers also experimented with the use of subliminal messages to increase fear or tension – a practice that is now illegal.

The same era saw a host of one-off gimmicks designed to attract audiences to particular films. The chief exponent of this kind of showmanship was the US director William Castle (1914–77), who devised a new publicity ploy for each of his movies. Castle's most notorious gimmicks included 'Emergo', in which a 12-foot plastic skeleton was hoisted over the audience's heads at a key moment in the film, and 'Percepto', in which selected moviegoers received tiny electric shocks from their seats in an attempt to set them screaming. For Castle's film 13 Ghosts (1960), made in 'Illusion-O', audiences were given coloured glasses that enabled them to see on-screen spectres invisible to the naked eye. Castle's introduction of a 'fright break' to allow nervous moviegoers to leave their seats before a supposedly terrifying scene was imitated by other film-makers, who incorporated such warning devices as the 'fear flasher' and a ringing bell to signal their most horrific sequences.

Gimmicks of a later era include the SPLIT-SCREEN technique Duo-Vision, introduced briefly in 1973, and SENSURROUND, the use of high decibel sound to create air vibrations within the theatre, a technique used in the disaster movie Earthquake (1974). See also HYPE.

Gish sisters. Dorothy Gish (Dorothy de Guiche; 1898–1968) US actress, the younger sister of the famous Lillian GISH. Dorothy's down-to-earth character was in marked contrast to Lillian's ethereal image. An accomplished light comedienne, she appeared in more films than her sister and became a star in her own right; at the height of her fame, her studio spent $10,000 a year posting photographs to her fans.

Born in Dayton, Ohio, she was appearing on stage as 'Baby Dorothy' (with 'Baby Lillian' and their mother) at the age of four. She was 14 when the sisters made their screen debut in D. W. GRIFFITH's An Uneasy Enemy (1912). He is said to have pinned red and blue ribbons on them to tell them apart.

After accompanying Griffith to Hollywood in 1913, they appeared together in THE BIRTH OF A NATION (1915), Hearts of the World (1918), for which Griffith had Dorothy watch and copy the walk of a prostitute, and BROKEN BLOSSOMS (1919). In 1920 Dorothy starred in Remodeling Her Husband, a film directed by her sister; later that year she married her screen spouse, James Rennie

(the couple subsequently divorced). In Orphans of the Storm (1922), her last film for Griffith, Dorothy played a blind girl with Lillian as her helping sister.

In the later 1920s Dorothy made five films in Britain for producer-director Herbert WILCOX; these included Madame Pompadour (1927), the first movie to be shot at Elstree Studios. Although she made a few minor talkies her career never recovered from the advent of sound.

Lillian Gish (Lillian de Guiche; 1896–1993) US actress, known as the **First Lady of the Silent Screen**, whose career spanned almost 90 years.

Gish began her stage career at the age of five, making her screen debut some ten years later in Biograph's An Unseen Enemy (1912). Mary PICKFORD had introduced the Gish sisters to the film's director, D. W. GRIFFITH, who supervised their careers for the remainder of the decade. Lillian played the principal female role of Elsie Stoneman in Griffith's epic THE BIRTH OF A NATION (1915) and the cradle-rocking 'Mother of the Ages' in INTOLERANCE (1916); she also starred as a series of waif-like heroines in such melodramas as BROKEN BLOSSOMS (1919) and Way Down East (1920).

After moving to MGM in the 1920s she was given slightly stronger roles in such productions as La Bohème (1926), The Scarlet Letter (1926), and the powerful melodrama The Wind (1928). Gish attempted to make the transition to sound with One Romantic Night (1930) and His Double Life (1933) but by now her acting style was perceived as dated by Hollywood directors. In the mid 1930s she returned to the stage, enjoying particular success as Ophelia to John GIELGUD's Hamlet in 1936.

For the remainder of her career Gish continued to work extensively for the live theatre, as well as making infrequent television appearances (notably in The Day Lincoln was Shot and Arsenic and Old Lace) and occasional films for the big screen. Her later movies included Charles LAUGHTON's fantasy-thriller Night of the Hunter (1955), Robert ALTMAN's A Wedding (1978), and her last film, Lindsay ANDERSON's The Whales of August (1987), in which the 92-year-old Gish co-starred with Bette DAVIS, a relative youngster at 79. She won an Oscar nomination for her part in the Western spectacular Duel in the Sun (1947), a Special Academy Award for her "superlative artistry" (1970), and, in 1984, the American Film Institute's Life Achievement Award.

> Her career is proof of the fact that the entire history of the feature film is contained within a lifetime.
>
> KEVIN BROWNLOW, film historian.

glass. glass filter A camera filter consisting of a coloured GEL between two sheets of glass.

glass shot A simple SPECIAL EFFECT in which a background, such as a town, forest, seascape, etc., is painted on a glass plate; this is then mounted in front of the camera so that it blends with the live action when the scene is shot. A glass shot can save enormous amounts of money that would otherwise be spent on sets or location filming. The technique is sometimes called the **Dawn process**, after the director and cameraman Norman Dawn, who invented it in about 1905.

gobo A masking device placed in front of a light to prevent it from illuminating particular areas of a set or subject. The term is also used in an audio sense to mean any device employed to absorb sound from a particular source.

Various unconvincing derivations have been offered for the term, including suggestions that it is an acronym of 'gel over blackout' or that it was devised by a lighting-man named Bo.

Godard, Jean-Luc (1930–) French director and screenwriter, who emerged at the forefront of the NEW WAVE of the early 1960s.

Godard spent much of his childhood in Switzerland, where his father ran a medical clinic. After studying ethnology at the University of Paris, he wrote for the influential film magazine CAHIERS DU CINÉMA, which also provided a vehicle for François TRUFFAUT, Claude CHABROL, and Eric ROHMER. In 1954 he directed his first short, *Operation Béton*, after which he worked in a variety of roles (editing, acting, publicizing, and producing) on the films of his *Cahiers* colleagues.

Godard directed his first feature, A BOUT DE SOUFFLE (*Breathless*), in 1959. The film, about a car thief and his US girlfriend, was made in a quasi-documentary style using HAND-HELD CAMERAS; it also introduced the JUMP CUTS, the monologues to camera, and the disconnected narrative style that were to become hallmarks of Godard's work.

He continued to develop his experimental techniques in such films as *Le Petit Soldat* (1960), which was banned in France, the light-hearted *Une Femme est une femme* (1961), *Vivre sa vie* (*It's My Life*; 1962), about a prostitute, and *Les Carabiniers* (*The Riflemen*; 1963), an anti-war film about two thuggish soldiers. Many of Godard's early films featured his then wife, the actress Anna Karina (1940–). The much-admired *Le Mépris* (*Contempt*; 1963) brought together two of Godard's central preoccupations: the relationship between film and life, and the difficulty of human communication. The story concerns an international film crew who can only speak to each other through interpreters; the veteran Fritz LANG plays the director while Godard appears as his assistant. Godard's films of the mid 1960s reveal a deepening pessimism, seen at its most extreme in the futuristic *Alphaville* (1965), a chilling blend of surrealism, FILM NOIR, and science fiction, and *Pierrot le Fou* (1966), a meditation on love, violence, futility, and suicide.

Following the break-up of his marriage to Karina, Godard's work became increasingly political; such films as *Masculin-Feminin* (1966), *Made in USA* (1966), and *Weekend* (1968) also took his exploration of the semantics of film to new extremes. This Marxist period culminated in the making of *Le Gai Savoir* (1968) and *Le Vent d'est* (1969). In 1971 Godard returned to more commercial film-making with *Tout va bien*, which starred Jane FONDA and Yves MONTAND. Following this, however, he spent several years in obscurity carrying out experimental work in television and video.

Godard made a vigorous return to the cinema with *Slow Motion* (*Suave qui peut*; 1980), which he described as "my second film...*Breathless* is the first film. This is the second first." Since then he has made *First Name: Carmen* (1983), a funny updating of the opera, *Hail Mary* (1984), a controversial retelling of the Nativity story in the setting of a petrol station, *Detective* (1985), a bizarre version of *King Lear* (1987) with a cast including Woody ALLEN and Norman Mailer, and *Nouvelle Vague* (1990).

Godard has enjoyed a prolific and controversial four decades in the cinema, during which he has never been less than unpredictable. Although his films have provoked a wide range of critical response, he has clearly had a profound effect on the nature of film-making; many of his techniques have now been incorporated – in less radical forms – into mainstream cinema. Godard has also displayed an undeniable love of the medium itself, apparent in the numerous cinematic allusions in his work.

Film is truth, 24 times a second.
JEAN-LUC GODARD.

Goddard, Paulette (Marion Levy; ?1911–1990) US actress, who became a top Paramount star playing vivacious, mischievous, and exotic roles, often in comedies. Her four husbands included Charlie CHAPLIN (1936–42) and the German novelist Erich Maria Remarque (1958–70).

Born on Long Island, New York State, Goddard began as a Ziegfeld Girl with the nickname 'Peaches'; in 1931 she drove to Hollywood to become a bit-part Goldwyn Girl with the nickname 'Sugar'. The following year Chaplin discovered her playing a minor role in the comedy *The Kid from Spain*. "Paulette struck me as being somewhat of a gamine" he later wrote, "This would be a wonderful quality for me to get on the screen." He cast her as the female lead in both MODERN TIMES (1936) and THE GREAT DICTATOR (1940).

In 1938 Goddard was a leading contender to play Scarlett O'HARA in GONE WITH THE WIND; indeed, the gossip columnist Louella Parsons began to refer to her as 'Scarlett O'Goddard'. When controversy arose over her relationship with Chaplin, she claimed that they had married in a shipboard ceremony off Singapore and that the yacht later came under guerrilla fire, leading to the loss of the marriage certificate. Although true, this story was widely ridiculed and probably lost her the part of Scarlett.

Subsequent films included the comedy-horror capers *The Cat and the Canary* (1939) and *The Ghost Breakers* (1940), George CUKOR's all-female *The Women* (1939), and Cecil B. DE MILLE's *Northwest Mounted Police* (1940), in which she co-starred with Gary COOPER. During World War II she entertained US troops in the China-Burma-India theatre. Although she excelled as a street urchin turned duchess in *Kitty* (1945) she was badly miscast in both Jean RENOIR's *Diary of a Chambermaid* (1946) and as Lucrezia Borgia in *Bride of Vengeance* (1948). By the 1950s her popularity was clearly waning and after *The Charge of the Lancers* (1954) she did not make another Hollywood film. In 1966 she attempted a comeback in an Italian production, *Time of Indifference*; she was also seen in a 1972 TV movie, *The Snoop Sisters*.

Godfather films, the *The Godfather* (1972) Francis Ford COPPOLA's epic saga about the New York Mafia (although that term is never used in the film); most critics would say that it has only one serious competitor for the title of the best GANGSTER film ever made – its sequel, THE GODFATHER, PART II. The plot centres on Vito Corleone (Marlon BRANDO), the ageing don who has ruled New York's mob for two generations. He mourns when one son, Sonny (James CAAN), is gunned down in an ambush and implores another, the sensitive Michael (Al PACINO), to take over when he dies of old age. Although he becomes head of the family with some misgivings, Michael quickly learns to become ruthless.

The film transformed the ailing career of director Coppola and provided a comeback for Marlon Brando, whose compelling performance earned him his second Oscar. He acted throughout with a gravelly voice and puffed cheeks, causing critic Rex Reed to complain, "Most of the time he sounds like he has a mouth full of wet toilet paper." Controversially, Brando stayed away from the Awards ceremony, sending an emissary to lecture the nation on the plight of the American Indians. The three-hour film also won the awards for Best Picture and Best Screenplay; Coppola was nominated for Best Director, while (remarkably) Pacino, Caan, and Robert DUVALL were all nominated as Best Supporting Actor. The nomination for Nino Rota's haunting score was withdrawn when the Academy learned that part of it had already been used in the Italian film *Fortunella* (1958).

In its time the most financially successful film ever made, *The Godfather* had earned more than $86 million by 1993. The movie was adapted from the best-seller by Mario Puzo, who had orginally conceived the story as a screenplay. Although most critics felt that Coppola's dark drama transcended the "trashy" novel, some remained troubled by its apparent glamorization of violence and its implied moral – that gangsters are businessmen much like any other.

The Godfather, Part II (1974) Francis Ford COPPOLA's sequel to THE GODFATHER, a film that surpasses the original in its epic scope, narrative power, and vivid sense of milieu; the performances are also quite outstanding. This is despite the absence of Marlon BRANDO, who was excluded from the project at an early stage, when he demanded an exorbitant fee.

The film interweaves two stories; that of the young immigrant Vito Corleone (Robert DE NIRO), making his way in Little Italy in the 1910s, and that of his son Michael (Al PACINO), consolidating his power as head of the New York Mafia 40 years later. Both stories show the corruption of idealism. The young Vito, rivetingly played by De Niro, changes gradually from a sympathetic underdog into the all-powerful don played by Brando in the earlier film. A generation later, Michael's aspiration to steer the Corleone clan into legitimate business is forgotten as the need to protect the family draws him deeper into bloodletting and betrayal.

Despite its complexity and length (well over three hours) the film was a resounding box-office success. It also swept the Oscars, winning awards for Best Picture, Best Director, Best Screenplay (Coppola and Mario Puzo), Best Supporting Actor (De Niro), Best Score (Nino Rota), and Best Art Direction. Pacino was nominated for Best Actor and three other performers – Talia Shire (the director's sister), Michael V. Gazzo, and Lee Strasberg – received nominations for Best Supporting Actress or Actor.

The Godfather, Part III The third and final instalment of COPPOLA's *Godfather* saga. Despite some powerful scenes (notably the violent climax in the La Scala opera house), the film fails to match the achievement of its predecessors. The somewhat unfocused plot deals with the doomed attempts of the ageing Michael Corleone (Al PACINO) to extricate himself and his family from their criminal past. In the event, he is drawn into a dangerous international conspiracy involving the Roman Catholic Church that leads to the destruction of all he holds dear.

The film was dogged by controversy and ill-fortune from the start. Although initially unwilling to add a third part to the saga, Coppola was finally unable to resist the huge fee offered by Paramount. He had previously remarked "I'm not really interested in gangsters any more." When Pacino and Robert DUVALL also demanded vast fees, Coppola threatened to write them out of the film. Pacino eventually lowered his price (to $5 million and a percentage) while Duvall was unceremoniously dropped.

Soon after filming began, Winona RYDER, cast in the important role of Michael's daughter Mary, left the set owing to exhaustion from overwork. Unwilling to accept further delays, Coppola replaced her with his daughter Sofia, an inexperienced actress whose performance was savaged by the critics.

Although nominated for seven Oscars, the film failed to win in any category.

Godzilla A 45m-high prehistoric monster, supposedly brought back to life by H-bomb tests, that has featured in a series of low-budget Japanese movies from the mid 1950s onwards. Despite being quite obviously a man in a rubber suit, Godzilla's popularity remains undiminished in Japan, where he was created as an Eastern answer to KING KONG (the monster's Japanese name *Gojira* is a compound of the words for gorilla and whale). With their primitive special effects, absurd stories, and comical dubbing, the films are regarded fondly by all afficionados of truly bad movies.

The Tokyo-based production company Toho began the cycle in 1954 – the same year that a Japanese fishing boat was affected by fallout from a bomb test on the Bikini atoll. In the original black-and-white *Godzilla* the creature rampages across Japan flattening cardboard cities, until finally laid to rest. Ever since, Godzilla has seemed to epitomize the vulnerable post-Hiroshima psyche of the Japanese. Despite his intended menace, Godzilla has often defended Japan against an alien (i.e. US) threat. Most explicitly, in *Godzilla vs King Gidorah* (1991) the monster routs a US attempt to force Japan to open its markets (while also jumping back through time to defeat some World-War-II Marines). The Godzilla cult also seems to represent an anarchic revolt against the materialism of contemporary Japanese life, with cities lobbying Toho for the privilege of being destroyed by the monster on screen. Following a campaign to bring Godzilla to the southern island of Kyushu for the first time, *Godzilla vs Space Godzilla* (1994) featured the destruction of Fukuoka.

Toho's usual formula is to pit Godzilla against some other creature; the conflict invariably ends in a prolonged sumo-wrestling bout. Although Godzilla's second film featured a battle with *Gigantis the Fire Monster* (1955), the real grudge match came with *King Kong vs Godzilla* (1962). Other masterpieces of the 1960s included

Ghidrah the Three-Headed Monster (1964), *Godzilla vs the Sea Monster* (1966), and *Destroy all Monsters* (1968), a co-production with AIP that gave the series an international flavour. Although these films were made in colour, the special effects remained as ordinary as before, with much clumsy use of BACK PROJECTION and stock footage.

Despite the simplicity of the plotting and the reliance on gimmicks (talking monsters in *Godzilla on Monster Island*, 1972, robot equivalents in *The Escape of Mechagodzilla*, 1975), some of the films tackle very pertinent issues. *Godzilla vs the Smog Monster* (1971) addressed the ecological damage caused by modern living (although the smog creature was just a man under a bit of old carpet), while *Return of Godzilla* (1984) saw the Japanese Prime Minister rejecting US and Soviet requests to use nuclear weapons against the monster.

Toho, now the largest film company in Japan, jealously guard their most famous creation (in 1982 they tried to sue US giant Sears and Roebuck over their 'Bagzilla' rubbish bags). However, no attempt has ever been made to update the 'special' effects; Godzilla is still an actor in a 90kg costume.

gofer or **gopher**   Originally US slang for the person on the set, sometimes a production assistant, who runs errands. The term, a pun on the name of the small burrowing rodent, comes from the idea that the person must 'go for' anything from scripts to coffee and doughnuts.

Goldberg,   Whoopi (Caryn Johnson; 1949–) Black US actress, who entered movies after making her name with a one-woman satirical act on stage and TV.

Goldberg found international fame with her role as the abused Southern Black woman in Steven SPIELBERG's *The Color Purple* (1985), a performance that earned her an Oscar nomination. Although some criticized the film for sentimentalizing the hardships endured by Black Americans in the late 19th century, Goldberg's performance brought out the pain and humiliation suffered by the heroine of Alice Walker's novel.

Since then, Goldberg has appeared in many films, most of them rather indifferent comedies. Although such offerings as *Fatal Beauty* and *Jumpin' Jack Flash* (both 1987) exploited her talent for quick-fire repartee, they failed to deliver in terms of plot or script, existing purely as star vehicles.

However, in films such as *Clara's Heart* (1987), which required much deeper characterization, Goldberg again demonstrated her talent for drama.

She revived her flagging career with *Ghost* (1990), in which she played a fake spiritualist who finds, to her horror, that she possesses genuine powers; the role brought her an Oscar as Best Supporting Actress. Success at the box office continued with *Sister Act* (1992), in which she played a nightclub singer who hides in a convent after witnessing a Mafia murder. Since then, her talents have again been squandered in so-so comedies, including *Sister Act 2* (1993), an unworthy sequel. Recent films include *Soapdish* (1991), Robert ALTMAN's Hollywood satire *The Player* (1992), and *Made in America* (1992). Between 1990 and 1994 Goldberg was a semi-regular in TV's *Star Trek: The Next Generation*.

Gold Rush, The   (1925) Charlie CHAPLIN's classic silent comedy about the Alaskan gold rush of 1898. A characteristic blend of slapstick and pathos, it starred Chaplin (who also wrote and directed) as the TRAMP, with Georgia Hale as his beloved and Mack Swain and Tom Murray as brutish prospectors. In 1942 Chaplin issued a slightly cut sound version, adding a spoken narrative and music.

Chaplin got the idea for the film at Pickfair, the home of Mary PICKFORD and Douglas FAIRBANKS, where he had been viewing stereoscopic slides of the Klondike. He began by shooting sight-gags such as the famous 'dance of the bread rolls', only supplying a script and storyline later. The scene in which the starving Chaplin eats his boot (actually made of licorice) was suggested by an account of how lost pioneers had once roasted and eaten their moccasins. Hundreds of hobos were hired to appear in the impressive opening shot of prospectors trekking across the snowy heights.

In the plot, Chaplin's lone prospector joins Big Jim McKay (Swain) and Black Larsen (Murray) to search for gold in the mountains. Food becomes so scarce that Thanksgiving dinner consists of a boot; Charlie's imagination turns the sole into meat, the laces into spaghetti, and the nails into succulent bones. The evil Larsen steals Big Jim's mining claim but dies in an avalanche; his companions strike gold soon afterwards. Back in town, Charlie falls for saloon girl Georgia Hale but Big Jim contracts amnesia and cannot remember the location of their gold strike. Eventually he recovers his memory and he and Charlie, now engaged to Georgia, become millionaires.

Goldwyn, Samuel (Schmuel Gelbfisz; ?1879–1974) Legendary Hollywood producer, who promoted the concept of 'family films' in the 1930s and 1940s. An intuitive salesman, he insisted that his movies should be acceptable to the whole family:

> Motion pictures should never embarrass a man when he brings his wife to the theatre.

> I seriously object to seeing on the screen what belongs in the bedroom.

These were less the utterances of a prude than of someone who understood how to fill cinemas. He was also genuinely dedicated to a notion of quality. On meeting George Bernard Shaw in 1921, Goldwyn tried to convince him of the high moral and artistic value of his films. Shaw finally interrupted: "It seems hardly necessary for us to continue, Mr Goldwyn. You see, you are interested in art, while I am interested only in money."

A Polish Jew, he was born in Warsaw at some time between 1879 and 1882. At the age of about 16 he travelled to England, where he slept in Hyde Park before relatives took him in. In 1898 he arrived penniless in New York (where immigration officials changed his name to Samuel Goldfish), found a job as a glove salesman, and enrolled in night school to learn English. His conversation remained riddled with solecisms for the rest of his life (*see* GOLDWYNISMS).

In 1913, inspired by a 'Bronco Billy' Western he had just seen, Goldfish talked his father-in-law Jesse L. Lasky into cofounding the Jesse L. Lasky Feature Play Company. The young Cecil B. DE MILLE became their principal director and Mary PICKFORD their leading lady. After their first film, *The Squaw Man* (1914), became a hit the company merged (1916) with Adolph ZUKOR's FAMOUS PLAYERS to become Famous Players-Lasky, which later evolved into PARAMOUNT PICTURES. However, later that year Goldfish left Lasky to start a new company with the brothers Archibald and Edgar Selwyn; the name Goldwyn Pictures was a blend of their names. He himself took the name Goldwyn two years later without consulting his partners.

When stockholders forced him out shortly before the company became part of Metro-Goldwyn-Mayer (*see* MGM) in 1923, Goldwyn formed his own Goldwyn Productions. His last silent productions included the original version of the epic BEN-HUR. With the advent of talkies, Goldwyn hired Florenz Ziegfeld to form the **Goldwyn Girls**, a troupe of singing and dancing beauties that included the 16-year-old Betty GRABLE. Other stars created by Goldwyn during the course of his career included Ronald COLMAN, Gary COOPER, David NIVEN, Susan Hayward, Merle OBERON, Danny KAYE, and Lucille Ball.

Goldwyn was well-known for his nononsense attitude to actors. One day in 1949, Niven sat in Goldwyn's office and turned down a film offer on the grounds that he had enough money in the bank. Goldwyn immediately flicked a switch on his desk and instructed someone: "Find out how much money Niven has in the bank." Within three minutes, he was informed that the account held $111. Niven starred in the film.

His most fruitful collaboration was with the director William WYLER, with whom he often argued. Their films together included WUTHERING HEIGHTS (1939), of which Goldwyn snapped, "I made *Wuthering Heights*, Wyler only directed it", and THE BEST YEARS OF OUR LIVES (1946), which won the Oscar as Best Picture.

Goldwyn's last films were all musical productions; *Hans Christian Andersen* (1952), starring Danny Kaye, *Guys and Dolls* (1955) with Frank SINATRA and Marlon BRANDO, and *Porgy and Bess* (1959) with a cast headed by Sidney POITIER.

Goldwynisms Verbal solecisms uttered by Samuel GOLDWYN, the US film producer. A non-native English speaker, he made eccentric use of his second language, perhaps not quite as naively as he pretended. "Gentlemen, kindly include me out", "Anyone who goes to a psychiatrist should have his head examined", "A verbal contract isn't worth the paper it's written on", "We have all passed a lot of water since then", "In two words IM-POSSIBLE", and "Directors are always biting the hand that lays the golden egg" are some of the fractured idioms attributed to him.

Goldwyn appears to have been a mixture of shrewdness and absurdity. For example, he had been told that Radclyffe Hall's

The Well of Loneliness was a controversial novel that would make a good film and gave instructions to buy the film rights. "But you can't make that into a film", said his rights man, "It's about lesbians." "That's not a problem", replied Goldwyn. "Where he's got lesbians we'll use Austrians." Goldwyn's showmanship was legendary:

> What we want is a story that starts with an earthquake and works its way up to a climax...

He told the assembled press at the release of THE BEST YEARS OF OUR LIVES (1946):

> I don't care if it doesn't make a nickel, I just want every man, woman, and child in America to see it.

The director Lindsay ANDERSON summed him up:

> Goldwyn is blessed with that divine confidence in the rightness (moral, aesthetic, commercial) of his own intuition – and that I suppose is the chief reason for his success.

Gone with the Wind (1939) Hollywood's epic romance of the American Civil War; its principal characters, the egotistic Scarlett O'HARA, the reckless Rhett Butler, and the steady Ashley Wilkes have entered 20th-century folklore.

No sooner had David O. SELZNICK acquired the rights to Margaret Mitchell's bestselling novel in 1936 than he began to receive thousands of letters begging him to secure Clark GABLE for the role of Butler. Selznick approached his father-in-law, Louis B. MAYER, the production chief at MGM, who approved the loan of Gable and a $1,125,000 investment in the picture – in return for distribution rights and half the profits. As soon as Selznick's distribution deal with United Artists lapsed he put his prize project into production with George CUKOR at the helm.

However, he still did not have a Scarlett O'Hara and began an exhaustive search during which he interviewed some 2000 hopefuls, tested 92 at a cost of $92,000 a time, and rejected actresses of the calibre of Jean ARTHUR, Tallulah BANKHEAD, Joan BENNETT, Claudette COLBERT, Joan CRAWFORD, Bette DAVIS, Irene DUNNE, Paulette GODDARD, Katharine HEPBURN, Carole LOMBARD, and Norma SHEARER before opting for a relatively unknown British actress, Vivien LEIGH.

The search for Scarlett was still in progress and writers still struggling with script revisions when Selznick ordered the shooting of the Atlanta fire sequence in December 1936. Using unwanted sets on the backlot at MGM, the sequence was directed by B. Reeves Eason, who had previously handled such spectacular action as the chariot race in the silent BEN-HUR (1925). When principal photography finally began in early 1939, Cukor was dismissed after only three weeks. Although the official story was that Gable had disapproved of his focusing too closely on Leigh and Olivia DE HAVILLAND (as Melanie), insiders confided that the star was unhappy at being directed by a homosexual – particularly one who might have known too much about his relationship with ex-star Billy Haines.

While Cukor continued to rehearse scenes in secret with Leigh and De Havilland, Victor FLEMING was hired to complete the picture (despite the fact that he was already working on THE WIZARD OF OZ). When a combination of tantrum and exhaustion caused Fleming to walk out on the production after two months, Selznick hired Sam WOOD (himself in the process of preparing GOODBYE, MR CHIPS) to keep the cameras rolling until Fleming returned. The picture was completed for $3.7 million after a seven-month shoot, with Wood occasionally working mornings and Fleming afternoons to meet deadlines.

Among the technical achievements of this three-hour-forty-minute feature (the longest yet produced by Hollywood and the first to require an intermission) were the extensive use of GLASS SHOTS and MATTES. The film also features a breathtaking CRANE shot, in which the camera pulls across the rail depot to reveal some 2000 extras and dummies posing as war wounded.

The film's record of ten Academy Awards was only overtaken by the remake of *Ben-Hur* in 1959, while its position atop the all-time box-office charts was secure until THE SOUND OF MUSIC in 1965.

Back in 1936, Louis B. Mayer had almost been persuaded to drop the project by his production chief Irving THALBERG, who told him:

> Forget it, Louis, no Civil War picture ever made a nickel.

Goodbye, Mr Chips (1939) MGM's poignant adaptation of James Hilton's story about the life of Charles Chipping, the shy classics master at an English public school. Robert DONAT won a well-deserved Oscar as Best

Actor (edging out Clark GABLE for GONE WITH THE WIND) in a role that required him to age over 60 years. The film made Greer GARSON into a star and featured John MILLS and Paul Henreid in supporting roles. Director Sam WOOD, who had previously made several MARX BROTHERS comedies, was nominated for an Oscar, as was the film itself.

Mr Chipping, the much loved headmaster of Brookwood school, is shown in flashback as a young teacher, unpopular with the boys because of his aloof manner. He marries a beautiful woman (Garson) who, before she dies in childbirth, gives him vision and social graces, encouraging him, for instance, to invite his pupils to tea. Once passed over as housemaster for lacking warmth, he now becomes an obvious choice for head. As he lies dying, the headmaster is told by a doctor that it is a great shame that he never had children. "Oh, but I did" he replies, "Thousands of them. And all boys..."

The original story had been written by Hilton in less than a week for publication in a magazine. He is said to have based the character of Mr Chips on his father, who was a headmaster, and on his old classics master, W. H. Balgarnie. Graham GREENE, himself the son of a headmaster, wrote of the film:

> The whole picture has an assurance, bears a glow of popularity like the face of a successful candidate on election day. And it is wrong to despise popularity in the cinema.

In 1969 MGM remade *Goodbye, Mr Chips* as a musical, with Peter O'TOOLE and Petula Clark in the leads. However, a new script by Terence Rattigan (author of a darker school drama, *The Browning Version*) turned Mr Chipping into a harsher figure and the film failed badly.

goose   Hollywood slang for a lorry used to transport cameras and other equipment to and from a location.

Gordon, Ruth   (Ruth Jones; 1896–1985) Vivacious pocket-sized US actress and screenwriter. She and her husband, Garson Kanin, wrote some of Hollywood's wittiest scripts of the 1940s and 1950s. As an actress, she is best known for her Oscar-winning role as Mia FARROW's sinister neighbour in ROSEMARY'S BABY (1968).

Born in Massachusetts, she went to New York to study acting as a teenager but was told she had no talent. Ignoring this advice, she took bit parts in a series of silent films shot in New Jersey, beginning with *Camille* (1915). Gordon used her early stage-struck life as the basis for a play, *Years Ago*, which she adapted for the screen as *The Actress* (1953); Jean SIMMONS played the young heroine and Spencer TRACY her father.

After appearing with Greta GARBO in *Two-Faced Woman* (1941), Gordon retired from the screen to concentrate on writing with Kanin. Between 1947 and 1953 they turned out a series of bright scripts for George CUKOR, winning Oscar nominations for *A Double Life* (1947), about a murderous actor, and *Adam's Rib* (1949), in which their friends Katharine HEPBURN and Spencer Tracy played husband-and-wife lawyers. They also scripted *Pat and Mike* (1952), in which Tracy played a sports promoter and Hepburn an athlete.

At the age of 69 Gordon returned to acting to play Natalie WOOD's mother in *Inside Daisy Clover* (1965), a part that won her an Oscar nomination. She followed POLANSKI's occult chiller *Rosemary's Baby* with two black comedies, *Where's Poppa?* (1970), in which she played George Segal's nutty mother, and *Harold and Maude* (1971), in which she appeared as an 80-year-old who marries a teenage boy. Gordon then joined Clint EASTWOOD and the orang-utan Clyde for *Every Which Way But Loose* (1978) and its sequel, *Any Which Way You Can* (1980). In the last year of her life, at the age of 89, she made a further four movies, her last role being another eccentric neighbour in *Maxie* (1985).

go to black   In a screenplay, a direction that a scene should FADE OUT until the screen is wholly dark.

GPO Film Unit   A British government-funded body that produced DOCUMENTARY films under the auspices of the General Post Office in the 1930s. It was created from John GRIERSON's EMPIRE FILM BOARD in 1933. Although its work was supervised by Sir Stephen Tallents, Grierson remained the driving force behind the Unit, which became the country's leading producer of documentaries and an important training ground for directors. Its acclaimed work included Basil Wright's *Night Mail* (1936), with a poetic text by W. H. Auden and music by Benjamin Britten.

In 1937 Grierson resigned to establish the advisory Film Centre. That year, the Unit created a new type of semidocumentary film with *The Saving of Bill Blewitt*, in which real Cornish fishermen acted out a scenario based on their daily lives. This was followed by the similar *North Sea* (1938), involving real trawlermen (who used the word 'bloody' without censorship). The GPO Film Unit's last production was Alberto CAV-ALCANTI's propaganda film *The First Days* (1940), about the Nazi threat; that year the Unit was placed under the control of the Ministry of Information's Film Division and retitled the Crown Film Unit.

Grable, Betty (Elizabeth Grable; 1916–73) US actress and dancer, famous for her 'peaches-and-cream' complexion and her 'million-dollar legs' (supposedly insured for that amount with a New York company). These attributes made her the favourite pin-up of US forces during World War II. She was apparently working as a chorus girl by the age of 12 and went on to star in light-hearted musicals and dramas throughout the 1930s and 1940s. Her debut in *Let's Go Places* (1930) was followed by small parts in *The Greeks Had a Word for Them* (1932), *Cavalcade* (1933), and the ASTAIRE-ROGERS musical *The Gay Divorcee* (1934). Starring roles then came her way in *Tin Pan Alley* (1940), in which she played a turn-of-the-century music-hall singer, *Coney Island* (1943), and *How to Marry a Millionaire* (1953), in which she appeared as one of a gold-digging trio of flatmates with Marilyn MONROE and Lauren BACALL.

> There are two reasons why I'm in show business, and I'm standing on both of them.
> BETTY GRABLE.

Grade, Lew (Louis Winogradsky; 1906–) Flamboyant British television executive, who turned to film-making with disastrous results. After his greatest flop, *Raise the Titanic!* (1980), which cost $40 million to make and earned only $7 million, Grade commented, "It would have been cheaper to have lowered the Atlantic!" His one hit was *On Golden Pond* (1981), with Katharine HEP-BURN and Henry FONDA. He was made a life peer (Baron Grade of Elstree) in 1976.

Born near Odessa, Russia, Grade came to Britain with his family in 1912. He and his younger brother, Boris (later Bernard Delf-ont), worked as dancers before setting up as theatrical agents and impresarios with their youngest brother, Leslie.

Grade became managing director of the ATV Network in 1962 and chairman in 1973. When his television-owned ITC company announced plans to make 20 films for the US market in 1975, Grade announced half tongue-in-cheek: "I intend to produce more feature films than any major studio in the world. I am only 68 and just beginning. By the time I am 70, British films will rule the world." In the event, Grade floundered badly with *The Boys from Brazil* (1978), in which Laurence OLIVIER confronts Nazi clones, *Raise the Titanic!*, which cost Grade his ITC post in 1981, and *The Legend of the Lone Ranger* (1981), described by *The Sunday Times* as "the kind of film that closes cinemas." Even the ever-popular Muppets drew modest crowds to *The Muppet Movie* (1979), in which the puppets travel to Hollywood to sign a film deal with a certain 'Lord Lew'. In 1995 Grade was reappointed as chairman of ITC following its acquisition by Poly-gram.

In the 1960s Grade's brother **Bernard Delfont** (1909–94) became chairman of EMI, which in 1969 bought ASSOCIATED BRIT-ISH to make international films. Such offerings as a remake of THE JAZZ SINGER (1980), pairing Laurence Olivier with pop singer Neil Diamond, and John SCHLESINGER's farce *Honky Tonk Freeway* (1981) proved no more successful than ITC's productions. Bernard was also made a life peer (Baron Delfont of Stepney) in 1976.

grader A lab technician who notes any undesired variations in density and colour on the negative so that they can be balanced during printing. A slight change in lighting conditions, as from morning to afternoon shooting, can cause big differences in brightness and tone between one shot and the next. Once the grader has noted these, the printer light can be adjusted wherever necessary to produce projection prints of more uniform density.

Graduate, The (1967) Mike NICHOLS's comedy of morals, sometimes described as the film that did for screen sex what BONNIE AND CLYDE did for violence. In the plot the diffident Benjamin Braddock (Dustin HOFFMAN) is seduced by old family friend Mrs Robinson (Anne BANCROFT) after his graduation party. Under pressure from his parents to forge a career, he lurches into simultaneous relationships with Mrs Robinson and her daughter Elaine (Katherine Ross). When he announces his engagement to Elaine, Mrs Robinson is determined to thwart the relationship. The film was based on Charles Webb's semiautobiographical novel.

Nichols, a highly successful stage director, had intended *The Graduate* to be his screen debut; in the event, however, circumstances dictated that he complete the TAYLOR-BURTON *Who's Afraid of Virginia Woolf?* instead. Several names had been associated with the roles of Benjamin and Mrs Robinson in preproduction, including Robert REDFORD, Patricia NEAL, and Doris DAY. The 30-year-old Dustin Hoffman was eventually given the role after he made a clumsy clutch at Katherine Ross's bottom during his screen test; Nichols instantly recognized the repressed aggression that was the key to Benjamin's personality. The part of Mr Robinson was initially secured by Hoffmann for his friend Gene HACKMAN – who was sacked during rehearsals for "not being capable of giving the director what he wanted." The part was played in the film by Murray Hamilton. Hoffmann received a mere $17,000 for his first major appearance and found the experience an unhappy one; he spent the succeeding months on both the dole and the psychiatrist's couch, vowing that he would never act in films again. Years later he would claim, "Looking back, I have no sense of achievement."

Although Nichols became the first director to command a $1-million fee for his services, the studio considered this money well spent as he guided the film, with its Simon and Garfunkel soundtrack, to seven Oscar nominations (for Best Picture, Direction, Script, Cinematography, and Hoffman, Bancroft, and Ross's performances) and, eventually, a worldwide box office of some $100 million. *The Graduate* is still a firm cult favourite for its depiction of juvenile alienation; its implied message – that the older generation is corrupt and hypocritical compared to the young – seems as popular now as in the late 1960s. Nichols, however, once commented, "I think Benjamin and Elaine will end up just like their parents; that's what I was trying to say in the last scene."

Grande Illusion, La (1937) Jean RENOIR's masterly exploration of war and the class system. During World War I, French pilots De Boildieu (Pierre Fresnay), Maréchal (Jean GABIN), and Rosenthal (Marcel Dalio) are brought to the POW camp for persistent escapees at Wintersborn. There De Boildieu forms a close friendship with camp commandant Von Rauffenstein (Erich VON STROHEIM), finding he has more in common with his fellow aristocrat than with his lower-class countrymen. However, when De Boildieu acts as a decoy to aid his compatriots' escape, the Prussian has no option but to shoot him. The symbols of the new France, the bourgeois Jew Rosenthal and the proletarian Maréchal, cross the Swiss border to safety.

Renoir's initial inspiration for the film was one General Pinsard, a World-War-I aviator who had managed to avoid capture on each of the seven occasions he had been downed in combat. With Charles Spaak, Renoir scripted a picture to be called *Les Evasions du Capitaine Maréchal* in 1934, although its scope soon broadened as Renoir sought to show that "the world is more divided by social conceptions than by the colour of flags" and to make a "statement of man's brotherhood beyond political borders." While he admitted that the title was open to various interpretations, Renoir said in an interview (1937) that the greatest illusion was "the war! With its hopes never realized, its promises never kept." Financial support was not forthcoming until Jean Gabin, an established star, expressed an interest in the project in 1936.

While remarkable as a pacifist statement, *La Grande Illusion* was also a landmark in film technique; Renoir's pioneering use of long takes, compositional depth, and DEEP FOCUS photography was a prime influence on André Bazin's concept of MISE-EN-SCÈNE. Branded "cinematographic enemy No. 1" by Goebbels, *La Grande Illusion* was also banned in Fascist Italy (despite winning a special prize at Venice) and ordered off Viennese screens following the Anschluss. Nevertheless, it won the New York Critics' Prize for Best Foreign Film and became the first French film to be nominated in the Best Picture category at the Academy Awards. During the war, the Nazis destroyed all the prints they could confiscate, while the negative was lost in an air raid. However, a surviving print was unearthed by the Americans in Munich and, after extensive restoration, the film was reissued in 1958.

Granger, Stewart (James Lablanche Stewart; 1913–1993) British-born leading man, whose tall powerful figure became familiar in costume films in the 1940s and 1950s; he conducted the longest swordfight ever filmed (about seven minutes) with Mel Ferrer in *Scaramouche* (1952). Granger, who changed his name to avoid confusion with James STEWART, consistently disparaged his roles, saying "I've never done a film I'm proud of." He was married (1950–60) to the actress Jean SIMMONS.

Born in London, he studied at the Webber-Douglas School of Dramatic Art, making his film debut as an extra in *A Southern Maid* (1933). During the 1940s he began to establish his screen image as a romantic hero in such British films as *The Man in Grey* (1943), *Love Story* (1944), *Caesar and Cleopatra* (1945) with Vivien LEIGH, and *Saraband for Dead Lovers* (1948).

After joining MGM in 1950, Granger made a series of adventure movies in which he was paired with many of the leading female stars of the era. He played opposite Deborah KERR in *King Solomon's Mines* (1950) and *The Prisoner of Zenda* (1952), Rita HAYWORTH in *Salome* (1953), Grace KELLY in *Green Fire*, Elizabeth TAYLOR in *Beau Brummell*, and Ava GARDNER in *Bhowani Junction* (1956) and the island comedy *The Little Hut* (1957).

Granger's later movies included the British film *Harry Black* (1958), the Italian-French co-production *Sodom and Gomorrah* (1962), a Biblical epic in which he played Lot, and Rank's *The Wild Geese* (1978). Among his television films were *The Hound of the Baskervilles* (1971), in which he played Holmes, and *The Royal Romance of Charles and Diana* (1982).

Grant, Cary (Archibald Alexander Leach; 1904–86) Urbane British-born US film star. Grant left school during his early teens to join an acrobatic troupe, with which he travelled to America in 1920. After appearing in stage musicals in both Britain and America he made his screen debut in the comedy *This is the Night* (1932). Grant played in several other films, including *Blonde Venus* with Marlene DIETRICH, before making his name in the Mae WEST vehicle *She Done Him Wrong* (1933). Although the film made Grant a star, many years later he commented: "I don't have a fond memory of Mae West. She did her own thing to the detriment of everyone around her."

Grant's other notable films of the 1930s included the fast-paced SCREWBALL COMEDIES *The Awful Truth* (1937), *Bringing Up Baby* (1938), with Katharine HEPBURN, and the classic HIS GIRL FRIDAY (1940), with Rosalind RUSSELL. *Only Angels Have Wings* (1939) and *Gunga Din* (1939) saw him in straight dramatic roles.

In 1940 Grant starred with Hepburn and James STEWART in George CUKOR's superlative comedy THE PHILADELPHIA STORY. Grant, who only appeared on the condition that he got top billing, donated his salary – reputedly $137,000 – to the British War Relief Fund. The following year he appeared (somewhat against type) as Joan FONTAINE's apparently villainous husband in HITCHCOCK's *Suspicion*. Grant starred in three further Hitchcock films, *Notorious* (1946), *To Catch a Thief* (1954), and the brilliant NORTH BY NORTHWEST (1959), each of which provided him with a strong role. While many actors have complained about working for Hitchcock, Grant spoke warmly of the director, saying he "couldn't have been a nicer fellow. I whistled coming to work on his films." Other major films of the 1940s included Frank CAPRA's black comedy ARSENIC AND OLD LACE (1944), the Cole PORTER biopic *Night and Day* (1946), *Mr Blandings Builds His Dream House* (1949), and *I Was a Male War Bride* (1949), a farce set in wartime Europe.

During the 1950s Grant made several strained and less-than-memorable films that relied a little too heavily upon his ability to carry a movie. Not even the added screen presence of Sophia LOREN and Frank SINATRA could bring much life to Stanley KRAMER's *The Pride and the Passion* (1957). Grant also formed his own production company, through which several of his later films were made. The name of the company changed slightly from production to production – being known as Grandon for Stanley DONEN's *Indiscreet* (1958), Granart for *Operation Petticoat* (1959), Granley for *That Touch of Mink* (1962), and Granox for *Father Goose* (1964). Grant's last film was *Walk, Don't Run* (1966), a flat comedy that most critics considered all too aptly named.

Following his retirement Grant became an executive for an internationally known cosmetics company. Although twice nominated for an Oscar – for *Penny Serenade* (1941) and *None But the Lonely Heart* (1944), neither of which were among his better films – Grant never won. In 1969 he received a Special Oscar for his contribution to motion pictures. Despite many offers of work he never returned to the screen.

One doesn't direct Cary Grant, one simply puts him in front of a camera.
ALFRED HITCHCOCK.

Grapes of Wrath, The (1940) John FORD's film adaptation of the epic Steinbeck novel about migrant farm workers during the Great Depression. The film, scripted by Nunnally JOHNSON, was widely hailed as a masterpiece of social realism. At a time when Congress was beginning to worry about communists in Hollywood, it bravely highlighted social injustices and capitalist exploitation – although an upbeat ending about family solidarity and the virtues of working people was tacked on.

Ford won an Oscar as Best Director, Henry FONDA received his first nomination for his performance as Tom Joad, and Jane Darwell, who played his mother, was named Best Actress. She spoke the film's optimistic last lines: "We're the people that live. Can't lick us. We'll go on forever, Pa, because we're the people."

The Joads, a family of sharecroppers, decide to leave their Oklahoma farm during the dustbowl days of the Depression. Led by Tom, they travel to the promised land of California only to find exploitation and more poverty. Finally they settle into a camp administered by the Department of Agriculture, but Tom poses the question, "Why aren't there more like it?"

Although *The Grapes of Wrath* was shown throughout the Soviet Union to highlight the miserable condition of US workers, this proved counterproductive; officials soon banned the film when they saw how impressed Russian audiences were at the fact that in America sharecroppers could own an automobile.

Grauman's Chinese Theater A famous Hollywood landmark (now renamed Mann's Chinese Theater) located at 6925 Hollywood Boulevard. The equally famous **Walk of Stars**, a pavement bearing the handprints and footprints of movie stars, runs in front of the cinema. It is also the departure point for tours to the stars' houses in BEVERLY HILLS and Bel Air.

Sid Grauman had built Hollywood's first exotic cinema, the Egyptian, on the other side of the boulevard in 1921. The pagoda-style Chinese Theater followed in 1927 and soon became known for its spectacular premieres. That same year, Grauman began the Hollywood tradition of getting the stars to leave their prints in wet cement when they attended the cinema (Norma SHEARER being the first).

grease. grease-glass technique A shot taken through a glass smeared with Vaseline or other petroleum-based product to create a blurred effect over all or part of a scene. In crowd shots it is sometimes used in order to blur out everyone except the person being concentrated upon; an example occurs in WEST SIDE STORY (1961), when Tony (Richard Beymer) spies Maria (Natalie WOOD) across a dance floor.

greasepaint Although MAKE-UP consisting of a mixture of grease and pigment had been used by actors for centuries, premixed greasepaint, in the form of numbered sticks, was only introduced in 1860. Until the widespread use of COLOUR in the late 1930s, the application of greasepaint (and other forms of make-up) was conditioned by the requirements of black-and-white photography. When Boris KARLOFF first played FRANKENSTEIN's Monster in 1931, he wore blue-green greasepaint that photographed a deathly grey. Max Factor introduced his Supreme Greasepaint for film use in 1914; The Max Factor Museum on Hollywood Boulevard displayed a collection of greasepaint until its closure in 1992.

great. Great Dictator, The (1940) Charlie CHAPLIN's satire on HITLER and Nazism. This was his last big hit with the public and the critics, winning him the New York Film Critics' Award for Best Actor and Oscar nominations for Best Actor, Best Screenplay, and Best Picture. Chaplin, well aware of the physical resemblance between his famous tramp and the German dictator, played both Adenoid Hynkel, a bullying tyrant based on Hitler, and a meek Jewish barber. When Hynkel has an accident, the barber is mistaken for him and obliged to address the crowd. He surprises them with a speech extolling progress, democracy, and common kindness, which is greeted with mass applause (created by Chaplin himself by shaking grapenuts on a tin tray). Although most critics found the six-minute speech naive and sentimental, the timeliness of the message could hardly be denied. By the time the film was released World War II had begun. Chaplin himself, who sometimes claimed to be part-Jewish, said later that he would never have made *The Great*

Dictator if he had known about Hitler's concentration camps.

The film contains some of Chaplin's most celebrated set pieces, notably the scenes in which Hynkel and Napaloni, dictator of Bacteria (Jack OAKIE), vie for prominence and the episode in which Hynkel dances a sublime dreamlike ballet with a globe of the world, which finally bursts in his arms. Although the film was inevitably banned in Germany, Hitler arranged for a private screening; he is said to have watched it twice through, absolutely alone.

Ironically, Chaplin the director could sometimes resemble the bullying Hynkel rather more than the meek barber he sentimentalized. Having cast his third wife, Paulette GODDARD, as a cleaner he instructed her to scrub the entire set as a rehearsal for the part. When she refused and walked off set, he sent the cast home until she complied.

Great Expectations (1946) David LEAN's much acclaimed adaptation of the classic DICKENS novel. A box-office hit in both Britain and America, it also gave Alec GUINNESS his first major screen role. Oscars went to art director John Bryan and cameraman Guy Green, while nominations were also received for Best Film, Best Director, and Best Screenplay.

As director and co-writer Lean received much praise for his intimate rendering of a long and complicated book. The plot concerns a poor youth, Pip, who falls in love with the beautiful but icy Estella and aspires to win her by becoming a gentleman. This seems within his grasp when he unexpectedly comes into money from an anonymous source. Pip moves to London and acquires sophisticated manners with the help of his friend Herbert Pocket (Guinness), only to find that his benefactor is an escaped convict he once aided as a boy. Much chastened, Pip eventually returns to Estella, who has herself suffered through marriage to an aristocratic boor.

The film remains essentially faithful to Dickens's novel, while interpreting it in genuinely cinematic terms. Especially memorable is the shock opening, in which the escaped convict Magwitch leaps out at the young Pip in a graveyard on the Kent Marshes. Bryan's atmospheric sets included the unforgettable cobwebbed dining room of the crazy recluse Miss Havisham. The cast includes John MILLS (as Pip), Valerie Hobson, Bernard Miles, the 17-year-old Jean SIMMONS (as Estella), Martita Hunt, and Francis L. Sullivan (who had also been in the 1934 Hollywood version).

Great Profile, the A nickname of the famously handsome actor John BARRYMORE.

Greed (1924) Erich VON STROHEIM's epic tale about the corrupting effects of avarice; in its uncut form it was the longest film ever made in Hollywood. The main plot concerns gold miner turned dentist McTeague (Gibson Gowland), who kills his wife Trina (Zasu Pitts) in order to secure what remains of a $5,000 lottery prize. After the murder he flees to California's Death Valley, with Trina's cousin Marcus (Jean Hersholt) in pursuit. McTeague kills Marcus, but dies handcuffed to his corpse in the parching sand.

Having explored the decadence of the upper classes in *Blind Husbands* (1918) and *English Wives* (1922), von Stroheim turned to his long-cherished ambition to produce a page-for-page adaptation of Frank Morris's novel, *McTeague* (1899). Shunning the studio realism of his earlier films for location shooting in Oakland, San Francisco Bay, and Death Valley, von Stroheim filled some 130 reels over nine months. For greater realism, one street scene, in which Zasu Pitts rushes out of a shop after finding a dead body, was filmed using a hidden camera. As Pitts grabbed passers-by and screamed hysterically about the murder, the camera caught the genuine look of horror on their faces. However, realism was compromised by the fact that some scenes had leading characters dressed for the 1890s and extras wearing 1923 fashions.

Von Stroheim finally presented producer Samuel GOLDWYN with a 42-reel nine-and-a-half-hour epic that had exceeded its budget three times over. Goldwyn requested that the film be edited down for release as a two-part feature, but von Stroheim was only able to cut 20 reels (four and a half hours), and was forced to seek the help of his director friend Rex INGRAM. After further cuts, both film-makers agreed that nothing more could be removed from the resulting four-hour epic without sacrificing meaning.

While this was going on, however, Goldwyn's company merged with Metro Pictures and Louis B. Mayer Productions to form MGM. The studio's new production chief was Irving THALBERG, who had formed a highly unfavourable opinion of von

Stroheim at Universal. He ordered a further revision of the film, telling screenwriter June Mathis and caption writer Joseph Farnham (who had read neither novel nor shooting script) to slash another eight reels and destroy the pared footage. Devoid of star names and filled with events and characters whose significance had been lost amidst the butchery, the film lost some $310,000 at the box office. The film's unforgettable scenes of gluttony and sexuality also raised hackles, provoking one critic to call it "the filthiest, vilest, most putrid picture in the history of the motion picture business." Many film-goers and critics seem to have been affronted by the un-American message that seeking money is immoral.

Von Stroheim, who had mortgaged his home in the course of production, refused to see the release print and ultimately disowned his most celebrated work. It testifies to his mastery of MISE-EN-SCÈNE and DEEP FOCUS photography that *Greed* remains one of the finest achievements of the silent screen, despite the loss of three quarters of its length. In 1971 Herman G. Weinberg attempted to convey the impression of the missing material with the aid of 348 photographs and 52 production stills.

Greenaway, Peter (1942–) British arthouse director, noted for his detached, sometimes macabre, examinations of sex, death, and flesh.

Greenaway trained as a painter, giving his first exhibition in 1964. Whilst working as a film editor at the Central Office of Information in the late 1960s he began to make his own shorts, including *Train* and *Tree* (both 1966) and *Windows* (1975). His perplexing originality was immediately apparent, and such films as *A Walk Through H* (1978) and *Act of God* (1981) were very successful at European film festivals.

Critical acclaim, and a surprising degree of popular interest, greeted *The Draughtsman's Contract* (1982), a film co-produced (like most of his subsequent work) for television's Film on Four. The piece is an elegant and puzzling game of allusions, in which the darker side of life in a Restoration household is gradually exposed by the artist commissioned to draw the estate. Critics praised both the brilliance of Greenaway's visual compositions and the striking minimalist music of Michael Nyman. Those who disliked the film pointed to its absence of emotional involvement, an aspect of film-

making that Greenaway has always treated with suspicion. This attitude has isolated Greenaway not only from British populist film-makers (Alan PARKER has been particularly vociferous in his criticisms) but also from such avant-garde directors as Derek JARMAN.

Greenaway's films have also been criticized for their reliance on Nyman's scores, which tend to alleviate the dryness of the visuals. A BBC arts programme once created its own 'Greenaway film' by combining footage from a nature documentary with a Nyman soundtrack. When Greenaway released *The Belly of an Architect* (1987) without a Nyman score, the absence was strongly felt. Despite this, the film is Greenaway's most accessible work, telling the story of the terminal decline of an architect against a lush Roman backdrop.

Between *The Draughtsman's Contract* and *The Belly of an Architect* came the bizarre *A Zed and Two Noughts* (1985). In the plot, twin brothers become involved with a beautiful amputee after losing their wives in a car crash caused by a low-flying swan. TIME-LAPSE photography of rotting animals and fruit is used to emphasize the theme of death and decay.

In *Drowning by Numbers* (1988), in which a coroner is baffled by three women all called Cissie Colpitts, each of whom has drowned her husband, Greenaway's game-playing again came to the fore; the numbers from one to 100 appear in various hidden forms throughout the course of the film. *The Cook, The Thief, His Wife and Her Lover* (1989) was a savage mock-Jacobean drama about a boorish gangster and his adulterous wife. Its lack of 'taste' (Ken RUSSELL walked out in disgust) was matched only by Greenaway's visual inventiveness.

The next year saw the screening of Greenaway's television film *A TV Dante*, which utilized the state-of-the-art computer-generated effects that have become a feature of his more recent work. The 1991 film meditation on *The Tempest*, *Prospero's Books*, was a special-effects film like no other. Liberated from the demands of realism, Greenaway seemed able to give his imagination free rein at last. *The Baby of Macon* (1993) was a grim and violent work with a Renaissance setting.

I'm not a film-maker. I'm a painter in cinema.

PETER GREENAWAY.

Greene, Graham (Henry Graham Greene; 1904–91) British novelist, screenwriter, and film critic. His most notable contribution to the cinema was the screenplay for Carol REED's THE THIRD MAN (1949). In 1973 he made a cameo appearance in François TRUFFAUT's *Day for Night* as 'Henry Graham', an insurance man who is seen viewing the rushes of an endangered movie.

Greene began his association with the cinema as film critic for *Night and Day* in the 1930s. Unfortunately, his outspokenness brought ruin on the publishers. After seeing Shirley TEMPLE in *Wee Willie Winkie* (1937), Greene suggested that her appeal was less innocent than it appeared, even accusing the studio of "procuring" the young star "for immoral purposes." The resulting libel suit closed the magazine.

Greene continued his career as a critic at *The Spectator*, where his trenchant reviews (collected in a 1972 volume, *Graham Greene on Film*) won a wide readership. He remained outspoken, claiming that THE THIRTY-NINE STEPS (1935) had been "inexcusably spoilt" by Alfred HITCHCOCK and calling the Crazy Gang "that rather repulsive troupe" in a review of *The Frozen Limits* (1939).

In 1948 Greene adapted his novella *The Basement Room* to create the screenplay for Carol Reed's film *The Fallen Idol* (US title *The Lost Illusion*; 1948). The two continued their collaboration with *The Third Man*, from a novella that Greene had written for screen adaptation. They co-wrote the script and fought off Orson WELLES's attempts to rewrite whole pages (although Welles managed to insert his famous 'cuckoo-clock' line). Greene and Reed later worked together on *Our Man in Havana* (1960), which starred Alec GUINNESS.

The novelist also adapted his own work for *This Gun for Hire* (1942), which starred Alan LADD, the BOULTING BROTHERS' *Brighton Rock* (US title *Young Scarface*; 1947), with Richard ATTENBOROUGH, and *The Comedians* (1967), with Guinness and Richard BURTON in Papa Doc's Haiti. His adaptations of works by others include a screenplay based on John Galsworthy's *The First and the Last*, filmed as *Twenty-One Days* (1937) by Alexander KORDA. Despite the presence of Laurence OLIVIER and Vivien LEIGH in starring roles, the film turned out badly; Greene himself reviewed it, saying the novel was unfilmable. In 1950 he volunteered to adapt *Brideshead Revisited* for his friend Evelyn Waugh, but funds could not be raised.

Films adapted from Greene novels by others include Fritz LANG's *The Ministry of Fear* (1944), *The Confidential Agent* (1945) with Charles BOYER and Lauren BACALL, *The Fugitive* (1947), adapted by John FORD from *The Power and the Glory*, *The End of the Affair* (1954) with Deborah KERR, George CUKOR's *Travels with My Aunt* (1972) with Maggie SMITH, *The Human Factor* (1979) with Richard Attenborough, and *The Honorary Consul* (US title *Beyond the Limit*; 1984) with Richard GERE and Michael CAINE.

One particularly flawed adaptation was Joseph MANKIEWICZ's version of *The Quiet American* (1957). Mankiewicz, who both directed and wrote the screenplay, transformed Greene's anti-American story into an anti-communist one. After the film flopped in America, Greene wrote an angry letter to *The Times* that ruined its chances in Britain.

greensmen Members of a production crew who maintain any real or artificial foliage – trees, bushes, or flowers – on a set or location.

Greenstreet, Sydney (1879–1954) Rotund British stage actor, who made his screen debut at the age of 61. Greenstreet, who specialized in playing mysterious master villains, went on to appear in a series of Warner Brothers melodramas in the 1940s, often with his friend Peter LORRE.

The son of a leather merchant, Greenstreet worked as a tea planter in Ceylon and the manager of a brewery before turning to the stage. After making his Broadway debut in 1904, he worked almost entirely in America. In his first film, the HUSTON classic THE MALTESE FALCON (1941), Greenstreet found immediate success as Kasper Guttman, the shady 'Fat Man' masterminding the search for the statuette. During filming Greenstreet struck up a close friendship with Peter Lorre, who played the part of his underling Joel Cairo (Lorre affectionately called him "the old man"). A year later the two appeared together again in CASABLANCA (1942), in which Greenstreet's character, Senor Ferrari, memorably remarks: "As the leader of all illegal activities in Casablanca, I am an influential and respected man." Their subsequent films included *Passage to Marseille* (1944), in which Greenstreet plays a Nazi sympathizer, *The Mask of Dimitrius* (1944), in which he completely outshines Lorre, and *Three Strangers* (1946).

Greenstreet also appeared in the comedies *Hollywood Canteen* (1944) and *Christmas in Connecticut* (1945), flawed films that nevertheless allowed a versatile talent to shine through. Other important appearances included those in *Across the Pacific* (1942), *Between Two Worlds* (1944), and *The Woman in White* (1948). His last film was *Malaya* (1950).

Gregory's Girl (1980) The internationally successful first feature by the Scottish director Bill FORSYTH. Produced on a tiny budget of £200,000 and shot in the new town of Cumbernauld, Scotland, the film starred John Gordon Sinclair as a gangling teenager in love and Dee Hepburn as the object of his desire.

In the slight story the shy and decent Gregory is displaced by a pretty girl as striker on his school soccer team. Instead of resenting this embarrassment, he decides that she is the girl of his dreams; dating her, however, proves a clumsy and confusing business. A gentle quirky comedy of irresistible charm, *Gregory's Girl* provided a refreshingly different view of adolescent mores to the crude teenage exploitation movies made on the other side of the Atlantic in the 1980s.

Grierson, John (1898–1972) British producer known as the 'father of the British DOCUMENTARY' for his work in that genre in the 1930s and 1940s. Credited with coining the very word 'documentary', he was a tireless advocate of the use of film as a medium of education and enlightenment.

Born in Kilmadock, Scotland, Grierson studied communications in America and embarked upon an academic career. In 1929 he established the Empire Marketing Board Film Unit (*see* EMPIRE FILM BOARD) and oversaw the making of the two-reel *Drifters*, about a North Sea herring catch. Other exceptional documentaries from this period included *Industrial Britain* (1931). In the early 1930s he also began a newspaper, *World Films News*, and made single-reel marionette movies for the new Associated Sound Film Industries.

When the Empire Film Unit became the GPO FILM UNIT in 1933, Grierson remained with it to produce such acclaimed documentaries as *Song of Ceylon* (1934) and *Night Mail* (1936). He resigned in 1937 to co-found the Film Centre, an advisory group on documentaries; the following year he was a leader of the successful campaign to establish an exhibition QUOTA for British films.

In 1939 Grierson moved to Canada to establish that country's National Film Board. He subsequently directed mass communications for UNESCO (1946–48) and was film controller for the Central Office of Information (1948–50). In the early 1950s he was executive producer of GROUP 3, a company that turned out quality second features. Grierson also appeared on Scottish TV as presenter of the series *This Wonderful World* (1957–65), a weekly anthology of clips from international documentaries.

Griffith, D(avid) W(ark) (1875–1948) US director of enormous influence during the early years of the film industry. He is credited with developing many of the basic techniques of film-making, including CLOSE-UPS, LONG SHOTS, FLASHBACKS, and CROSS-CUTTING. Although some of these techniques were already known, it was Griffith who discovered their particular emotional qualities and began to assemble them into a film language.

Griffith was born in Kentucky, the son of a former Confederate soldier. His formal education was cut short owing to the death of his father, after which he had to contribute to the family's finances. In the 1890s he began to act, later touring professionally with several stock companies.

In 1907 Griffith wrote some picture scenarios for the EDISON Film Company, also appearing as an actor in their film *Rescued from an Eagle's Nest*. The following year he was hired by the BIOGRAPH Company as a scriptwriter and director. Over the next five years Griffith made an estimated 400 to 500 one- or two-reel films for the company, including *The Adventures of Dolly* (1908), his first film as director, *The Violin Maker of Cremona* (1909), Mary PICKFORD's second film, and *The Unseen Enemy* (1912), the debut film of both Dorothy and Lillian GISH. After seeing the Italian feature QUO VADIS? (1912), Griffith began to experiment with longer films; his last film for Biograph, *Judith of Bethulia* (1913), ran to four reels. Biograph, however, thought the production too expensive and Griffith left to form his own company.

In 1915 Griffith's most successful and controversial film, THE BIRTH OF A NATION, was released. The Civil-War epic, which ran to over three hours, was made at a cost of over $100,000 – a then unprecedented sum. Despite grossing millions of dollars at the box-office, it was widely condemned for its heroic portrayal of the Ku Klux Klan and banned in some cities. The film's racism is, indeed, beyond apology. Nevertheless, with its narrative sweep and tumultuous cross-cut finale, *The Birth of a Nation* is undoubtedly the first master work of the fledgling US cinema industry.

Griffith's next major film was INTOLER-ANCE (1916), an ambitious work that interweaved four separate stories from different periods of history. The film enjoyed initial critical success, but was a commercial failure; audiences found it hard to understand and seem to have been put off by the moralizing tone. Technically, however, the film was a brilliant piece of work and its influence on later film-makers is hard to overestimate. Following *Intolerance* – on which Griffith had lost a great deal of his own money – he began to make films that were both simpler and less expensive, such as *Hearts of the World* (1918), a propaganda piece made at the request of the British government. The film, which incorporated newsreel footage, featured the Gish sisters, Erich VON STROHEIM, and Noël COWARD.

In 1919 Griffith formed UNITED ARTISTS with Charlie CHAPLIN, Douglas FAIRBANKS, and Mary Pickford, built his own studio, and released one of his most memorable films, the melodrama BROKEN BLOSSOMS. Thereafter, although his output continued to be as prolific as ever, both critical and commercial success by and large eluded him. *Way Down East* (1920), with Lillian Gish, proved to be a substantial hit at the box office but failed to restore his waning reputation; his Victorian style of moralizing had come to seem old-fashioned in the Jazz Age. Of Griffith's subsequent films perhaps the most noteworthy are *Orphans of the Storm* (1922), again with the Gish sisters, *The Sorrows of Satan* (1926), and *Abraham Lincoln* (1930), a biopic starring Walter HUSTON. His final film was *The Struggle* (1931), a tale of the horrors of alcoholism.

Despite receiving a special Oscar for his contribution to the film industry in 1936, Griffith could find neither financial backing nor employment (save a little work as a consultant director on Hal ROACH's *One*

Million BC) in the sound era. In more recent years, Griffith's work has undergone a major reappraisal and he is now seen as having been mistreated by the film industry. Perhaps owing to the generally higher level of film literacy today, audiences seem able to appreciate the technical mastery of his films even when their content is outdated or otherwise unacceptable.

grip A handyman on the set who performs such tasks as keeping the props in good condition, laying DOLLY tracks, and moving scenery.

Group 3 A British production company formed in 1951 to make SECOND-FEATURE films with budgets 25% below those of normal features; it aimed to use established stars while training young directors and technicians on the job. John GRIERSON, John Baxter, and Michael BALCON headed the company, which was established by the National Film Finance Corporation and funded by the British Film Production Fund.

Group 3 disbanded within two years, mainly because the movies, most of them sub-EALING comedies, were not great successes. The first film was Baxter's *Judgment Deferred* (1951), a story of drug smugglers captured by Dorset eccentrics that provided Joan COLLINS with her debut role; this was followed by John Eldridge's *Brandy for the Parson* (1951), in which Kenneth MORE fell in with smugglers.

The next year saw the release of Philip Leacock's *The Brave Don't Cry*, a documentary-style film about the Knockshinnock mining disaster, Terry Bishop's *You're Only Young Twice*, about an eccentric university head, C. M. Pennington-Richard's *The Oracle* (US title *The Horse's Mouth*) a whimsical tale about an oracle in an Irish well with Virginia McKenna, Eldridge's *Laxdale Hall* (US title *Scotch on the Rocks*), about a Scottish island that refuses to pay taxes, and Lewis GILBERT's *Time Gentlemen Please* (1952), in which a lazy tramp spoils the image of an otherwise well-kept village.

guerrilla film-making An informal term for the making of low-budget independent movies with a very light crew, often using HAND-HELD CAMERAS.

Guest, Val (1911–) British director and screenwriter with a wide range of film and TV credits, including two of HAMMER's *Quatermass* stories.

Guest worked as a newspaper reporter before writing a series of screen comedies for Arthur Askey (*Charley's Aunt*, 1940, and *Ghost Train*, 1941), the Crazy Gang (*Band Waggon*, 1939), and Will HAY (*Oh, Mr Porter*, 1938, and *Ask a Policeman*, 1940). He also wrote, directed, and produced *Miss London Ltd* (1943), featuring his wife, Yolande Donlan, and Frankie Howerd's first film, *The Runaway Bus* (1954).

In the later 1950s Guest showed his versatility by writing and directing some controversial hard-hitting films for Hammer. *Hell is a City* (1960) was a violent crime film with Stanley BAKER, while *The Camp on Blood Island* (1958) and *Yesterday's Enemy* (1959) subverted the popular image of the British soldier as a stiff upper-lip hero. Guest's greatest contributions to cinema, however, came within the SCIENCE-FICTION genre. He directed *The Quatermass Experiment* (1955) with such chilling bleakness that it can be regarded as the first Hammer horror film. His other films for Hammer included *Quatermass II* (1957) and *The Abominable Snowman* (1957), which likewise derived from a TV play by Nigel Kneale. His best film is probably British Lion's *The Day the Earth Caught Fire* (1962), which shows the end of the world through the eyes of *Daily Express* journalists. Guest made the most of his journalistic experience and even coaxed a performance from former Fleet Street editor Arthur Christiansen.

Guest's less successful efforts include the BOND spoof *Casino Royale* (1967), on which he collaborated with several other directors, *When Dinosaurs Ruled the Earth* (1968), and *The Boys in Blue* (1983), an attempt to remake *Ask a Policeman* with comedy duo Cannon and Ball. His TV credits include episodes of *The Persuaders* and *Space: 1999*.

guide track or **scratch track** A rough soundtrack recorded during filming despite background noise or other acoustic problems. It is used as a guide for editing and DUBBING.

Guinness, Sir Alec (1914–) British stage and screen actor, whose films have ranged from DICKENS and EALING comedies to STAR WARS; in 1957 he won the Academy Award for his portrayal of the austere Colonel Nicholson in THE BRIDGE ON THE RIVER KWAI. Peter USTINOV once called him "the outstanding poet of anonymity" for his ability to disappear into his characters. He was knighted in 1959.

Guinness began his working life as an advertising copywriter but found the work so boring that he telephoned John GIELGUD, then unknown to him, to ask his advice on becoming an actor. After taking voice lessons, Guinness won a scholarship to the Fay Compton Studio of Dramatic Art. Despite severe stage fright that afflicted him with crippling pain in his knees and back, Guinness began to make his name in Shakespearean roles in the later 1930s. He made his film debut as an extra in *Evensong* (1934).

After serving in the Royal Navy during World War II, he starred in two classic Dickens adaptations directed by David LEAN; in GREAT EXPECTATIONS (1946) he played Herbert Pocket, while his grotesque portrayal of Fagin in *Oliver Twist* (1948) led to accusations of anti-Semitism and a ban on the film in America. Guinness's films for Ealing included KIND HEARTS AND CORONETS (1949), in which he played eight members of the same family, and THE LAVENDER HILL MOB (1952), which earned him an Oscar nomination. Other roles of the 1950s included Disraeli in *The Mudlark* (1950), the title character in *Father Brown* (1954), and the bohemian artist Gilly Jimpson in *The Horse's Mouth* (1958), a film he also scripted. Guinness went to Hollywood in 1956 to make *The Swan*, a romantic comedy with Grace KELLY. Although he made his name in America with Lean's *The Bridge on the River Kwai* (1957), this was misspelled as 'Guiness' on the credits. During shooting he squabbled with the director, who refused to let him portray Colonel Nicholson with more humour.

In the 1960s Guinness took small roles in two more Lean films, LAWRENCE OF ARABIA (1962) and *Doctor Zhivago* (1965); he also appeared as Charles I in *Cromwell* (1970). When Guinness sought the title role in *Hitler – The Last Ten Days* (1973), he rented a Nazi uniform and strolled through London's streets to pose for a photographer. No one paid the slightest attention except a policeman, who warned him about his illegally parked car.

His role as the benign Obi-Wan Kenobi in *Star Wars* (1977) revitalized a somewhat flagging film career. In 1984 Lean cast him as an Indian mystic in *Passage to India*; the two feuded again, however, when the director cut his dancing scene. Guinness's recent work includes a return to Dickens in the excellent *Little Dorrit* (1987) and the film *Tales from Hollywood* (1991). His best-known television role was as the inscrutable spymaster George Smiley in *Tinker, Tailor, Soldier, Spy* (1979) and *Smiley's People* (1981–82).

> Olivier...ransacks the vaults of a part with a blowlamp, crowbar, and gunpowder; Guinness is the nocturnal burglar, the humble Houdini who knows the combination.
>
> KENNETH TYNAN, critic.

Gunfight at the OK Corral (1957) Paramount's ambitious widescreen Western, one of several films based on the historical shoot-out in Tombstone, Arizona, in 1881. John STURGES directed a strong cast headed by Burt LANCASTER as Sheriff Wyatt Earp, Kirk DOUGLAS, Rhonda FLEMING, and Jo Van Fleet. A minor role was played by future director Dennis HOPPER.

When one of the Earp brothers is killed in Tombstone, Marshal Virgil Earp and his brothers Wyatt and Morgan, along with 'Doc' Holliday, confront the two Clanton brothers and two McLowery brothers. In the ensuing gunfight Virgil and Morgan Earp are wounded; on the other side, only one member of the Clanton gang escapes with his life.

The film is more successful as drama than as history. Its departures from fact begin with the title; the real shoot-out took place in Fremont Street not at the OK Corral. The film also spreads the fight all over town to accommodate the sweep of VISTAVISION and makes it last five times as long as the real event to justify the long build-up. Lancaster plays Wyatt Earp as an upright figure who heroically faces down the Clanton gang for the public good; in fact, the grisly shooting spree was motivated mainly by vengeance and had no heroes. Kirk Douglas gave a more accurate impersonation of 'Doc' Holliday, the eccentric alcoholic dentist and gunfighter who changed to the side of the law when dying of TB.

Other films to treat the same events include Allan DWAN's *Frontier Marshal* (1939), the inferior *Tombstone* (1942), John FORD's *My Darling Clementine* (1946), *Tombstone* (1994) with Kurt Russell, and the Kevin COSTNER vehicle *Wyatt Earp* (1994). In 1967 Sturges directed *Hour of the Gun*, an antiheroic sequel to *Gunfight at the OK Corral*, in which James Garner played Earp as a cold-blooded vigilante.

H

Hackman, Gene (1930–) US actor. Considered by many the Spencer TRACY of his generation, Hackman was reputedly the busiest film star of the late 1980s. His strength as an actor lies in his ability to play, with complete conviction, average vulnerable flawed human beings.

Having lied about his age, Hackman enrolled in the US Marines at the age of 16; subsequent jobs included shoe salesman and truck driver. After working as a radio and television announcer, he enrolled in acting classes at the Pasadena Playhouse, where his classmates included Dustin HOFFMAN.

Despite regular appearances on Broadway and on television, Hackman did not make his big-screen debut until 1961. Three years later he took a small role in *Lillith* with Warren BEATTY, who was immediately impressed. Beatty later remarked "All I know is that it's impossible for me to be bad in a scene with Gene Hackman." Following a few more small roles, Hackman landed the part of Buck Barrow in the Beatty-produced BONNIE AND CLYDE (1967), which brought him an Oscar nomination for Best Supporting Actor. Roles followed in such high-profile films as *Downhill Racer* and *The Gypsy Moths* (both 1969). A year later Hackman was again nominated as Best Supporting Actor for his brilliant performance in *I Never Sang for My Father*. He finally broke through to the major league with his portrayal of Jimmy 'Popeye' Doyle in the police thriller *The French Connection* (1971), which brought him an Oscar as Best Actor. It is rumoured that Hackman, over 40 at the time, had been only sixth choice for the role.

Following this breakthrough, Hackman starred in *Scarecrow* (1973), with Al PACINO, and Francis Ford COPPOLA's celebrated *The Conversation* (1974), in which he played the surveillance expert Harry Caul ("the best bugger on the West Coast"). Despite critical praise, both these films proved commercially unsuccessful. Disillusioned, Hackman embarked on a policy of only appearing in films that seemed certain to make money. This resulted in a string of mostly bad films that conspicuously failed at the box office, including *Bite the Bullet* (1975) and *March or Die* (1977). Hackman managed to compound his losses during this period by turning down roles in ONE FLEW OVER THE CUCKOO'S NEST (1975), *Network* (1976), and *Close Encounters of the Third Kind* (1977). Following a lucrative appearance as Lex Luthor in SUPERMAN (1978), he went into semi-retirement for two years.

Having returned to the screen in the early 1980s, Hackman gave excellent performances in *Eureka* (1982), *Under Fire* (1983), *Hoosiers* (1986), and *No Way Out* (1987), amongst others. In Alan PARKER's *Mississippi Burning* (1988) he played an FBI agent investigating racial murders in the Deep South; the role brought him an Oscar nomination as Best Actor, some 18 years after his previous award. Subsequent films include *Another Woman* (1988), *Narrow Margin* (1990), and *Postcards from the Edge* (1990).

In 1990 Hackman suffered a near heart attack and underwent major surgery. He has since appeared in *Class Action* (1991), a courtroom drama, and as a brutal sheriff in Clint EASTWOOD's *Unforgiven* (1992).

hair stylist A person who devises and maintains the appropriate hair style for an actor performing a role. Elizabeth TAYLOR often insisted in her contract that her personal hair stylist from California be flown in during shooting.

halation A FOGged area on a film print, taking the form of a bright ring or halo around a light source. It is caused by excessive light reflecting from the FILM BASE.

half-apple *See* APPLE BOX.

Hammer Films British production company noted mainly for its low-budget HORROR FILMS.

Originally a subsidiary of Exclusive Films, Hammer was set up by Enrique Carreras and Will Hinds (who had acted under the pseudonym Will Hammer) in 1935. Although founded as a distribution company, Hammer made a number of films in the 1930s, the first being the comedy *The Public Life of Henry the Ninth* (1935).

From the late 1940s Hammer concentrated on making low-budget programme fillers for bigger distributors, who often provided part of the budget. The studio specialized in bringing BBC radio series to the big screen, including *Dick Barton, Special Agent* (1948) and *The Man in Black* (1950). With the advent of television in the 1950s, Hammer recognized another source of material. In 1955 the BBC sci-fi serial *The Quatermass Experiment* became Hammer's *The Quatermass Xperiment*, with both title and posters emphasizing its X certificate. When the film (directed by Val GUEST) proved a huge success, Hammer, never slow to exploit a trend, created another science-fiction-horror hybrid with *X – the Unknown* the following year.

Hammer then turned to the UNIVERSAL horror classics of the 1930s, seeking to recreate them in colour. With *The Curse of Frankenstein* (1957), *Dracula* (1958), and their numerous successors, Hammer created a lush gothic world full of mist-filled graveyards and Technicolor gore. Both the violence and the sexuality were more overt than in previous horror movies, and the public's interest proved in inverse proportion to the critics' scorn.

The films were made cheaply and quickly at the small studio at Down Place, Bray, near Windsor. The same personnel and locations were used again and again. Films such as *Plague of Zombies* and *The Reptile* (both 1966) were filmed back-to-back using the same sets and an almost identical crew. It is even said that Hammer sometimes came up with titles and posters before the script was written (*Zeppelin vs Pterodactyls* and *The Reluctant Virgin* being among the titles that never quite made it). Whatever the truth of this, much of Hammer's early output was equal to anything that Hollywood could produce. Directors of photography Jack Asher and Arthur Grant, editor James Needs, and directors Don Sharp, Terence Fisher, and John Gilling, all triumphed over limited budgets to produce technically remarkable films.

Over the next decade mummies, werewolves, *The Hound of the Baskervilles*, *The Phantom of the Opera*, *Dr Jekyll and Mr Hyde*, and the works of Dennis Wheatley all received the Hammer treatment. However, DRACULA and FRANKENSTEIN, starring Christopher LEE and Peter CUSHING respectively, proved to be Hammer's most enduring series. While Cushing continued to play both Baron Frankenstein and Dracula's nemesis, Van Helsing, Lee's irritation at the 'updating' of Bram Stoker's concept in *Dracula AD 1972* (1972) and *The Satanic Rites of Dracula* (1973) eventually led him to withdraw.

Even during its horror heyday, Hammer's output remained diverse, including war films, police thrillers, children's movies, and three ROBIN HOOD films. In 1966 the caveman film *One Million Years BC*, with Raquel WELCH, provided Hammer with another hit, which it exploited with a string of similar movies. The 1970s also saw a series of spin-offs from TV sit-coms, such as *On the Buses* (1971) and *Man about the House* (1974).

Such films were at best routine, and could not restore the fortunes of a company now in decline. Despite the Queen's Award for Export in 1968, Hammer found itself no less affected by the slump in the British film industry than any other company. In the 1970s it also had to accept that the horror genre had left it behind. Hammer's small budgets and its gothic rather than graphic approach meant that it could not compete with Hollywood films like THE EXORCIST (1973). The company's final horror outing was the Wheatley adaptation *To the Devil a Daughter* (1976). Following the remake of THE LADY VANISHES (1979), Hammer released no further features.

After years in the wilderness, Hammer has managed to secure financial backing from Hollywood director Richard Donner, which should lead to a remake of *The Quatermass Xperiment* and production of *Vlad the Impaler*, a film that has been in the pipeline since 1972.

hand. hand-held camera A film camera light enough to be operated by hand without the use of such mounts as a tripod or DOLLY. It allows for far greater flexibility and freedom of movement, as well as being relatively inexpensive to operate. The 35mm ARRIFLEX hand camera was introduced in the late 1950s and quickly became popular with the directors of the French NEW WAVE and makers of documentaries in the CINÉMA VÉRITÉ style. However, hand-held shots remained noticeably shaky until the introduction of the STEADICAM system of camera support in the 1970s. In 1977 it was estimated that more than 80% of Hollywood films made use of the light Panaflex camera.

hand props or **properties** Small objects handled or worn by actors in a film. They often play an important role in a film's plot or symbolism; examples include the lawman's badge Gary COOPER throws to the ground in HIGH NOON (1952). One hand prop, the Imperial Necklace from the jewellers Joseff of Hollywood, had been used in 125 films by 1950. *See* PROP.

handlebar mount A camera mount equipped with two handles like a bicycle, enabling the cameraman to change its direction with ease.

Handsomest Man in the World A promotional tag given to the US actor Francis X. BUSHMAN, the star of many silent films. His good looks and powerful physique brought him an enthusiastic female following.

Hanks, Tom (1956–) Baby-faced US actor, who progressed from unsophisticated comedy roles to take the 1994 Academy Award for his performance as an AIDS victim in *Philadelphia*. A year later he took a second Best Actor Award for *Forrest Gump* (1994), making him the only performer to equal Spencer TRACY's feat of winning Oscars in successive years.

Born in Oakland, California, Hanks began his screen career in teenage exploitation films, including the SLASHER MOVIE *He Knows You're Alone* (1980) and the raucous *Bachelor Party* (1983). Stardom came with Disney's *Splash* (1984), in which he played a vegetable wholesaler who falls for a mermaid (Darryl Hannah). Subsequent films included *Dragnet* (1987), a parody of the television police series, *Big* (1988), about a 13-year-old boy who is granted his wish to become a man, and *Turner & Hooch* (1989), about a policeman's relationship with the dog who is the only witness to a murder. A year later Hanks was rated the fourth most popular film personality in a poll devised by Marketing Evaluations of New York (which put him a place below BUGS BUNNY). Further successes followed with *A League of Their Own* (1992), a story

about a female baseball team, and the love story *Sleepless in Seattle* (1993), in which he appeared opposite Meg RYAN.

In *Philadelphia* (1993), directed by Jonathan DEMME, Hanks played Andrew Beckett, a homosexual lawyer who develops AIDS. After being sacked by his law firm, Beckett sues for unfair dismissal. In accepting his Oscar, Hanks made a much-publicized plea for tolerance for AIDS victims ("the streets of heaven are too crowded with angels"). He then enjoyed the greatest commercial success of his career playing the title character in *Forrest Gump*, a well-meaning simpleton who survives the 1960s, Vietnam, Watergate, and the troubled years thereafter through his very lack of intellectual sophistication. The film, which became one of the highest-grossing movies of all time in America, divided critics and commentators, who argued bitterly over its political implications.

hard-ticket attraction A film screening for which seats either can or must be reserved in advance. In the more formal days before World War II this was common for such blockbusters as GONE WITH THE WIND (1939). Today such arrangements occur mostly for premieres and special charity showings, although famous cinemas, such as New York's Radio City Music Hall, maintain the tradition.

Hardwicke, Sir Cedric (1893–1964) Distinguished British stage actor, who also played a wide range of historical and character roles in Hollywood films. Hardwicke, who was knighted in 1934, found acclaim as the evil Frollo in THE HUNCHBACK OF NOTRE DAME (1939) but was later attacked for lending his talents to such films as *The Ghost of Frankenstein* (1942). His autobiography was titled *A Victorian in Orbit* (1961).

Hardwicke's theatrical ambitions began in childhood, when he learnt pages of Shakespeare by heart. He subsequently attended RADA, making his stage debut in 1912. His sonorous voice enabled him to make an easy transition to British sound films in the 1930s, when he appeared in such roles as Charles II in *Nell Gwyn* (1934) and David Garrick in *Peg of Old Drury* (1935); he had previously appeared in the silent biopic *Nelson* (1926). After moving to Hollywood in the late 1930s his roles included Dr Livingstone to Spencer TRACY's Stanley in *Stanley and Livingstone* (1939), a

German commander in the Resistance story *The Moon is Down* (1943), the villainous Ralph in Ealing's *Nicholas Nickleby* (1947), the father of *The Winslow Boy* (1948), the ex-mayor of Stuttgart who warns Rommel (James MASON) of Hitler's paranoia in *The Desert Fox* (1951), Tiberius in *Salome* (1953), and King Priam in *Helen of Troy* (1955).

Hardwicke's theatrical successes included *Shadow and Substance* (1938), which he persuaded Charlie CHAPLIN to adapt for the cinema. Unfortunately, this was intended to be the first vehicle for Chaplin's discovery, Joan Barry, who soon afterwards took the clown to court, claiming that he had fathered her child; the film was never made.

George Bernard Shaw once called Hardwicke his fifth-favourite actor "after the MARX BROTHERS."

Hardy. Oliver Hardy *See* LAUREL AND HARDY.

Hardy family A fictional family that featured in some 15 Hollywood films between 1936 and 1946. Made by MGM on modest budgets, the films were financially extremely successful and won a special Academy Award (1942) for furthering the US way of life. The son Andy Hardy, played by the bouncy Mickey ROONEY, was every American's idea of the boy next door. His girlfriends, typifying the girl next door but one, included several starlets who later become stars in their own right – Judy GARLAND, Lana TURNER, Kathryn Grayson, and Esther WILLIAMS among them. The paterfamilias, a small-town judge with a fund of small-town wisdom, was played initially by Lionel BARRYMORE and subsequently by Lewis Stone. The mother was played endearingly, if a little too sweetly, by Fay Holden. A post-war revival of the family in *Andy Hardy Comes Home* (1958) suggested that their innocuous adventures belonged to another era.

Harlow, Jean (Harlean Carpenter; 1911–37) US actress, known as the **Blonde Bombshell**, who became the first sex symbol of the talkie era. Although she described herself as "the worst actress in Hollywood" she was a more than competent comedian, who brightened up a string of 1930s comedies with her brassy wisecracking style. Her promiscuous image was matched by her unstable private life, leading to the popular crack that her surname was spelt with a silent 't'.

Harlow was born to affluent parents, who divorced when she was still young. At the age of 16 she eloped with a millionaire's son who gave her a wedding present of $250,000, despite which the marriage soon failed. In the later 1920s she moved to Hollywood, where she worked as a bit player in various films, including CHAPLIN's CITY LIGHTS (1931).

One of Harlow's earliest appearances was in LAUREL AND HARDY's *Double Whoopee* (1929), in which Laurel accidentally rips off her skirt. When her grandfather phoned to say she had disgraced the family, Harlow told producer Hal ROACH that she was leaving the business. But not for long. Now using her screen name for the first time, Harlow quickly established her image in Howard HUGHES's World-War-I film *Hell's Angels* (1930), in which she lures Ben Lyon with the immortal line, "Excuse me while I slip into something more comfortable". Similarly, the early gangster movie PUBLIC ENEMY (1931) saw her trying to seduce James CAGNEY. Her first starring role came in Frank CAPRA's romantic comedy *Platinum Blonde* (1931).

In 1932 Harlow signed with MGM, who cast her in blonde temptress roles in such movies as *Red Dust* (1932) and *Dinner at Eight* (1933). Although *Bombshell* (1933) saw her playing a movie star who yearns to change her dumb-blonde persona, in reality MGM kept a tight control over her public image. The studio demanded, for instance, that she wear a girdle over her slim figure to keep her satin gowns from wrinkling. The peroxide-and-ammonia blonde look created for her eventually so injured her hair that she had to wear wigs.

Harlow married MGM producer Paul Bern in 1932 but embarked on an affair with Clark GABLE, her co-star in several comedies, almost immediately afterwards. Two months after the marriage Bern committed suicide by shooting himself, having first doused his naked body with perfume. The incident caused an immense scandal. Harlow later claimed that Bern was impotent and had beat her severely on their wedding night, causing chronic kidney damage. Three years later, she rather tactlessly made *Reckless* (1935), in which William POWELL helps Harlow's character to cope with her husband's suicide.

After a brief marriage to a cameraman, Harlow became engaged to Powell but the two were never to wed. Towards the end of shooting *Saratoga* (1937), a racing film in which she starred with Gable, Harlow collapsed with kidney failure; her mother, a Christian Scientist, prevented her from obtaining medical treatment and she died at the age of 26. In 1965 two films about her life were made, both entitled *Harlow* – a cinema release starring Carroll Baker and a made-for TV movie with Carol Lynley (later converted to film).

Harris, Richard (1932–) Robust Irish actor, known for his hell-raising persona both on and off the screen. Harris once spoke rapturously of "the clash of flesh, the entanglement of bodies, the wonderful sensation of a fist going into somebody's face." When he was given the role of Cain in John HUSTON's *The Bible* (1966) many saw this as typecasting.

Born in Limerick, Harris attended the London Academy of Music and Dramatic Art before making his stage debut in 1956. His first screen appearances came two years later, with a bit part in the British comedy *Alive and Kicking* (1958). He made his Hollywood debut playing the first mate of a salvage boat in *The Wreck of the Mary Deare* (1959).

In 1963 Harris became internationally known playing a rough-hewn rugby hero who woos a lonely widow (Rachel Roberts) in Lindsay ANDERSON's *This Sporting Life*; he was named Best Actor at the Cannes Festival and nominated for an Oscar. Other successes of the early 1960s included *Mutiny on the Bounty* (1962) with Marlon BRANDO, the war film *The Heroes of Telemark* (1965) with Kirk DOUGLAS, and *Hawaii* (1966) with Julie ANDREWS.

By this time Harris was becoming notorious for his furious temper and manic drinking bouts. His wife Elizabeth recalled that after a day's work on *Hawaii* he would sometimes run furiously into passing traffic and strike the cars with his fists until his knuckles bled.

In 1967 Harris landed the role of King Arthur in the film of Lerner and Loewe's *Camelot*, although critics noted that neither he nor his co-star Vanessa REDGRAVE could sing. Two years later he made his debut as a director with *Bloomfield*, the story of an Israeli boy and his football idol. In 1970 he took the title roles in both the epic *Cromwell* (1970) and the violent Western *A Man Called Horse*, in which he played an English lord captured by American Indians.

Harris gave up drinking in 1982 but is known to have occasional relapses. In 1990 he gave perhaps the finest performance of his career as the Lear-like patriarch of an Irish peasant family in *The Field*. His recent movies have included the IRA thriller *Patriot Games* (1992) with Harrison FORD, the Western *Unforgiven* (1992) with Clint EASTWOOD, and *Wrestling with Ernest Hemingway* (1994), in which he played a former Irish sea captain recalling his past conquests.

Harrison, Rex (Reginald Carey; 1908–90) Urbane British actor, best known for his Oscar-winning performance as the phonetician Henry Higgins in *My Fair Lady* (1964). In the 1930s he pursued a successful career on the London stage in such plays as Rattigan's *French Without Tears* and Eliot's *The Cocktail Party*. He also appeared in numerous prewar British films, of which only *Storm in a Teacup* (1937) with Vivien LEIGH and the medical drama *The Citadel* (1938) are very memorable. Before his wartime service with the RAF he also appeared in the excellent Shaw adaptation *Major Barbara* (1940) and Carol REED's comedy thriller *Night Train to Munich* (1940).

After the war Harrison went to Hollywood, where he starred in such films as *Anna and the King of Siam* (1946) and *King Richard and the Crusaders* (1954), in which he played Saladin. The highlight of his career was undoubtedly the Broadway production of Lerner and Loewe's *My Fair Lady* (1956) and its lavish film adaptation. His subsequent films included *The Agony and the Ecstasy* (1965), in which he played Pope Julius II to Charlton HESTON's Michelangelo (at one point confronting Heston with the line "Do you dare dicker with your pontiff?"), the flop musical *Doctor Dolittle* (1967), and the old-fashioned SWASHBUCKLER *Crossed Swords* (British title *The Prince and the Pauper*; 1977).

A debonair and charming man, Harrison was at his best in comedy; after seeing him in the film version of *Blithe Spirit* (1945), Noël COWARD is reported to have said to him:

After me, you're the best light comedian in the world.

According to some accounts he added:

If you weren't, all you'd be good for would be selling cars in Great Portland Street.

He married six times, his wives including the actresses Lili Palmer (1943–57), Kay Kendall (1957–59), and Rachel Roberts (1962–71).

Hathaway, Henry (1898–1985) US director, producer, and actor, who worked in Hollywood for 65 years. Noted for his Westerns, action films, and thrillers, Hathaway cultivated a macho image and was notorious for his rough handling of actors. "To be a good director you've got to be a bastard" he once said, "I'm a bastard and I know it."

Born in Sacramento, California, the son of a stage manager and an actress, he appeared in Westerns from the age of nine while also working as a prop boy at Universal. In 1923 he joined Paramount, where he worked as an art director to Josef VON STERNBERG and Victor FLEMING amongst others. He began his own career as a director with a series of B-Westerns starring Randolph Scott. His first major film was *Now and Forever* (1934), starring Gary COOPER as the con-man father of Shirley TEMPLE. Hathaway went on to direct Cooper in several films, including *Lives of a Bengal Lancer* (1935), which earned the director his only Oscar nomination.

In 1936 Hathaway made Paramount's first TECHNICOLOR movie, *The Trail of the Lonesome Pine*, with Henry FONDA. After a brief period at United Artists, he joined 20th Century-Fox in the late 1930s. One of his first films for Fox was *Brigham Young* (1940), a big-budget epic about the Mormon trek to Utah starring Tyrone POWER and Dean Jagger.

In the later 1940s Hathaway helped to develop the FILM NOIR style at Fox with such films as *The House on 92nd Street* (1945) and *Kiss of Death* (1947), with bad guys Richard WIDMARK and Victor MATURE. He then diversified somewhat with *The Desert Fox* (1951), in which James MASON starred as Rommel, and *Niagara* (1953), in which Marilyn MONROE plots to kill her husband Joseph COTTEN.

In 1962 Hathaway, John FORD, and George MARSHALL teamed up to direct *How the West was Won*, a CINEMASCOPE epic with an all-star cast. According to James STEWART the film was saved by Hathaway, who himself called Ford's work "shabby" and reshot Marshall's scenes, fuming about "that goddamn Cinerama".

Hathaway ended as he began, in Westerns; John WAYNE starred in both *The Sons of Katie Elder* (1965) and *True Grit* (1969), the director's last significant film. When his friend, the director George Seaton, became ill during the making of *Airport* (1970), Hathaway took over the film but refused billing and salary.

having had A phrase sometimes used in a Hollywood shooting CALL to warn actors and crew to eat lunch early because the normal break cannot be taken: 'Report at 11.45 having had'.

Hawkins, Jack (1910–73) British actor, best known for playing Scotland Yard detectives and authority figures in costume dramas. Following an operation for cancer of the larynx in 1966, he was unable to speak; although an electronic voice box was implanted, his later dialogue, mostly in small parts, was dubbed. His posthumously published autobiography was titled *Anything for a Quiet Life* (1975).

Hawkins made his stage debut at the age of 13 and his first film appearance in 1930. He played a Scotland Yard officer for the first time in *The Flying Squad* (1940). During World War II he appeared in *The Big Blockade* (1942) but was paid only his second lieutenant's wage of 11 shillings. When Hawkins discovered that the civilian actors were getting £15, he and David Hutcheson went to producer Michael BALCON asking for an increase. "My dear boys", Balcon explained, "I have given my word to the War Office that you will only get your basic pay."

Hawkin's post-war roles included a sensitive and moving performance as the teacher of a deaf child in the documentary-style *Mandy* (1952). He also appeared as the commander of HMS *Compass Rose* in *The Cruel Sea*, Britain's biggest box-office hit of 1953, and a totalitarian official who attempts to brainwash a Catholic cardinal (Alec GUINNESS) in *The Prisoner* (1955). He played a Scotland Yard superintendent again in *The Long Arm* (1956), the last film made at Ealing Studios, and in John FORD's *Gideon of Scotland Yard* (US title *Gideon's Day*; 1958).

Other notable roles included Pharaoh in Howard HAWKS's epic *Land of the Pharaohs* (1955), a Roman admiral in BEN-HUR (1959), a British officer in THE BRIDGE ON THE RIVER KWAI (1958), and General Allenby in LAWRENCE OF ARABIA (1962). His last film, released in the year of his death, was the macabre horror spoof *Theatre of Blood* (1973).

> Nobody else...can with such a three-dimensional effect draw for us the reliable chap, conscientious but no tortoise, harassed but wryly surmounting frustration.
> DILYS POWELL, film critic.

Hawks, Howard (1896–1977) US writer-director, who specialized in Westerns and comedies but worked in many genres during his 50-year career. His favourite stars were Cary GRANT, Gary COOPER, Humphrey BOGART, and John WAYNE. The women in his films were usually given strong independent roles; of the courtship ritual, Hawks noted, "I reverse it and let the girl do the chasing around."

Born in Goshen, Indiana, Hawks obtained an engineering degree at Cornell University before serving in the US Army Air Corps during World War I. He entered the cinema in 1918 as a prop boy for Famous Players-Lasky (later Paramount) and worked his way up to becoming a writer and editor. The film that made his name as a director was 20th Century-Fox's *The Road to Glory* (1936), about a French regiment during World War I.

Hawks introduced his characteristic style of fast overlapping dialogue in his first talkie, *The Dawn Patrol* (1930), about World-War-I fliers. In 1932 he directed Paul MUNI as the gangster Tony Camonte (Al Capone) in *Scarface*, an unsparing depiction of the US underworld often considered the masterpiece of the genre. *Ceiling Zero* (1935) was a pacey adventure movie starring James CAGNEY and Pat O'Brien as airline pilots, while the crazy comedies *Bringing Up Baby* (1938), in which Cary Grant fails to control wild socialite Katharine HEPBURN, and HIS GIRL FRIDAY (1940), again with Grant, were even more frantic. *Sergeant York* (1941) featured Cooper as a World-War-I pacifist turned hero; the role won him the Oscar as Best Actor, while Hawks was nominated as Best Director.

Hawks is once supposed to have bet Ernest Hemingway, "I can make a picture out of your worst story"; the result was *To Have and Have Not* (1945), for which Hemingway's novel was largely rewritten by William Faulkner. The film introduced its star, Humphrey BOGART, to his future wife Lauren BACALL, then 18, whom Hawks had seen on the cover of *Harper's Bazaar*. The following year, he again directed the pair in the classic CHANDLER adaptation THE BIG SLEEP (1946).

Hawks's first film with John Wayne was *Red River* (1948), a story about a cattle drive that also featured Montgomery CLIFT in his film debut. When director John FORD saw Wayne's performance, he fumed, "I never knew the sonofabitch could act!" Hawks then made the musical *Gentlemen Prefer Blondes* (1953), starring Marilyn MONROE and Jane RUSSELL as gold-diggers at large in Paris, before returning to the Western with two more Wayne pictures, *Rio Bravo* (1959) and *Rio Lobo* (1970). Hawks was awarded an honorary Oscar in 1974 for his lifetime's achievement.

Hawn, Goldie (1945–) US comedian, who combines an infectious giggle with warmth and beauty. Born in Washington, D.C., the daughter of a musician, Hawn played Juliet on stage at 16 but later dropped out of drama school to work as a go-go dancer.

In 1968 Hawn secured a small part in Disney's *The One and Only Genuine Original Family Band*. Later that year she came to national attention in the television comedy series *Laugh-in* (1968–73), in which she established her goofy image. Her first major role, as the mistress of nervous dentist Walter MATTHAU, in *Cactus Flower* (1969), brought her an Oscar as Best Supporting Actress.

Her films of the 1970s included *Butterflies are Free* (1972), in which she played an actress who falls in love with a blind man, *The Sugarland Express* (1974), as a woman encouraging her convict husband to escape, and *Foul Play* (1978), in which she helps Chevy CHASE to uncover a plot to assassinate the pope. With *Private Benjamin* (1980), a hugely popular comedy about a self-absorbed Jewish girl who joins the US Army, Hawn was suddenly elevated into the top rank of Hollywood stars. However, subsequent films, such as *Protocol* (1984) and *Overboard* (1987), suggested that she was unable to carry a movie by herself. Her recent work has included the comedy adventure *Bird on the Wire* (1990), with Mel GIBSON, the Steve MARTIN comedy *Housesitter* (1992), and the fantasy *Death Becomes Her* (1992), with Meryl STREEP.

> The brightest dumb blond since Queen Boadicea sliced Roman kneecaps.
> VICTOR DAVIS.

Hay, Will   (1888–1949) British music-hall comedian, who became a leading film star in the 1930s after some 20 years of success on stage. He specialized in playing incompetent, seedy, or crooked authority figures. "The character I play" he once said, "is really a very pathetic fellow." Off screen, Hay was a knowledgeable amateur astronomer.

Born in Stockton-on-Tees, he entered the halls in 1909 and quickly emerged as a master of comic timing; his first film, *Those Were the Days* (1934), was a nostalgic portrait of old-time music hall. Hay then established his screen image playing the disreputable Dr Twist of Narkover, a master at a school for the sons of criminals, in BIP's *Boys Will be Boys* (1935).

A year later Gainsborough's *Windbag the Sailor* teamed him with regulars Moore Marriott, playing the elderly Harbottle, and Graham Moffatt, as the fat boy Albert. *Good Morning, Boys* (1937) saw him playing a schoolmaster in charge of a chaotic trip to Paris, while *Oh, Mr Porter!* (1937), a minor masterpiece directed by the Frenchman Marcel Vernel, had stationmaster Hay harassing employees Marriott and Moffatt. Vernel then directed the trio in *Ask a Policeman* (1939) and *Where's That Fire?* (1940), in which they played inept firemen who foil an attempt to steal the crown jewels.

During World War II Hay co-directed two films with Basil DEARDEN: *The Goose Steps Out* (1942), in which he played a British spy disguised as a German schoolmaster (with Peter USTINOV as a pupil), and *My Learned Friend* (1944), a legal comedy. Later that year Hay retired owing to poor health.

Hayakawa, Sessue   (1889–1973) Hollywood's first Oriental star; his acting was once described as a combination of METHOD and Zen. Born in Chiba, Japan, Hayakawa joined his uncle's acting troupe before travelling to America in 1898 to study at the University of Chicago.

In 1913 he and his actress wife Tsuru Aoki returned to the States with the Japanese Imperial Company and visited Hollywood. The producer and director Thomas INCE constructed a Japanese village set in California's Santa Ynez Canyon and the company performed in *The Wrath of the Gods* and *The Typhoon* (both 1914); the latter gave Hayakawa a prominent role as a young doctor who strangles a showgirl. He first came to popular notice in Cecil B.

DE MILLE's *The Cheat* (1915), a sensational piece about a Burmese playboy who physically brands a society lady when she cannot pay back a loan. The film, a great popular success, became the first movie to be turned into a stage play.

Following his move to Europe in 1923 Hayakawa starred in such French films as *Yoshiwara* (1937), in which he played a coolie in love with a geisha. After World War II he played Japanese villains in numerous Hollywood war films. In 1957 his performance as an unbending Japanese POW camp commander in David LEAN's THE BRIDGE ON THE RIVER KWAI brought him an Oscar nomination.

Hays Code   The popular name for the **Production Code** administered by the Motion Picture Association of America (*see* MPAA) under the directorship of **Will H. Hays** (1879–1954). The MPAA was formed by the principal Hollywood studios in 1922 to impose self-censorship, a move prompted by growing public indignation at sexual boldness on the screen and the scandalous off-screen behaviour of some stars (notably Fatty ARBUCKLE). One of Hays's first moves was to insert morality clauses into players' contracts, enabling them to be dismissed for transgressions in their private lives. The **Hays Office**, as the MPAA was sometimes known, registered and collated complaints from the various local censorship boards and forwarded them to the studios. In 1930 a Production Code was issued detailing what could and could not be shown on the screen. For example:

> Excessive and lustful kissing, lustful embracing, suggestive postures and gestures, are not to be shown.
>
> Miscegenation (sex relationships between Black and White races) is forbidden.

The Code, formally implemented in 1934, became a constant source of friction between film producers and the Hays Office. Although it caused many tame and bowdlerized films to be produced, it had the effect of holding at bay calls for government censorship. One of the few flagrant breaches of the Code during Hollywood's Golden Era was the inclusion of the last word in Rhett Butler's line in GONE WITH THE WIND (1939): "Frankly, my dear, I don't give a damn." In time fewer and fewer people did give a damn; the Code was increasingly challenged by film-makers from the 1950s

onwards and eventually scrapped in 1968.
See also CENSORSHIP; RATINGS.

Hayworth, Rita (Margarita Carmen Cansino; 1918–87) Glamorous Hollywood
actress of the 1940s and 1950s, noted for
her long tawny hair and her vitality as a
dancer. Born in Brooklyn, Hayworth was
dancing in nightclubs by the age of 13 and
made her film debut three years later in
Dante's Inferno (1935). At 18 she married a
promoter, Edward Judson, who changed
her name, dyed her black hair auburn, and
made her take electrolysis treatments to
enhance her lovely forehead. When they
separated in 1941, he demanded and received $30,000 for his efforts.

Hayworth later said that the only two of
her films that she could watch without
laughing were *You'll Never Get Rich* (1941)
and *You Were Never Lovelier* (1942), in both
of which she appeared opposite Fred
ASTAIRE. When Astaire turned down a third
film, a version of the Gershwin hit *Cover Girl*
(1944), Gene KELLY joined Hayworth to
make Columbia's first Technicolor musical.

In 1943 Hayworth married Orson
WELLES, a match dubbed "Beauty and the
Brain" by the newspapers. When the couple
starred together in the thriller *The Lady from
Shanghai* (1948), Welles, who also directed,
cut her famous hair and dyed it blonde. This
so infuriated Harry COHN, the head of
Columbia, that he delayed the film's release
for two years. By then the stars were
divorced.

In the FILM NOIR *Gilda* (1946) Hayworth
played a married woman who resumes an
affair with old flame Glenn FORD; in the
film's most famous sequence she performed
a steamy mock striptease while singing
(dubbed) 'Put the Blame on Mame'. Later
she would say, "Every man I ever met fell in
love with Gilda and woke up with me." In
1949 she married the 'playboy prince'
Aly Kahn, a marriage condemned by the
Vatican. After they divorced, she made a
comeback in *Affair in Trinidad* (1952), again
with Ford. She was pregnant during filming
and had to hold her bag over her stomach
in many scenes.

By 1957 Hayworth, now 39, was playing the older woman in the Rodgers and
Hart musical *Pal Joey* (1957), which starred
Frank SINATRA. A year later she married her
fifth husband, the producer James Hill, who
cast her in the Rattigan adaptation *Separate
Tables* (1958). After this, however, major

roles dried up. By 1982 she was suffering
from Alzheimer's disease. "I haven't had
everything from life" she once said, "I've
had too much." Her life story was recreated
in a 1983 television film, *The Love Goddess*,
starring Lynda Carter.

haze A foggy effect on a LONG SHOT, caused by
dust or atmospheric conditions. The effect
can be partly eliminated by use of a **haze
filter** (or **haze-cutting filter**), which absorbs
ultraviolet light.

head. **head close-up** or **head shot** A shot in
which the frame contains only an actor's
head or face. *See* CLOSE-UP.

head gaffer The chief electrician on a film
production. *See* GAFFER.

head-on shot An action shot in which the
subject moves directly towards the camera. Well-known examples include the
approaching space station in 2001: A SPACE
ODYSSEY (1968), the racing chariots in BEN-
HUR (1959), and the long sequence in which
Omar SHARIF rides towards an oasis in LAW-
RENCE OF ARABIA (1962). Silent comedy films
often used the effect for near-misses in chase
scenes. The head-on shot was also a staple
of 3-D productions such as BWANA DEVIL
(1952), in which spears and lions seemed to
be coming straight at the audience.

head-up or **head-out** Term used to describe
a reel of film wound so that the start LEADER
is on the outside ready for projection. A reel
wound the opposite way is decribed as **tails-
up** or **tails-out**.

Heaven's Gate (1980) Michael CIMINO'S epic
Western, one of the most celebrated and
controversial failures in movie history. The
film starred Kris Kristofferson, Christopher
Walken, Isabelle HUPPERT, John Hurt, and
Jeff BRIDGES.

Based on the 1892 Johnson County
Wars, a land conflict between cattle ranch-
ers and settlers, *Heaven's Gate* was an epic
film in every sense; epic budget, epic vision,
and epic failure. Stories of Cimino's excesses
began to circulate long before the film was
released. Amongst other extravagances, the
arrogant young director of *The Deer Hunter*
(1978) was accused of rebuilding a period
train and moving it halfway across the continent and insisting on elaborately detailed
costumes for all the extras. Whatever the
truth of these tales, *Heaven's Gate* began
with a budget of $7.5 million and was com-
pleted at a final cost of over $35 million.

With its total failure at the box office and the ensuing collapse of UNITED ARTISTS, the film became not only cinema's most expensive flop to date but also a focus for earnest discussions about what had gone wrong with the industry as a whole.

One reason for the film's failure was almost certainly the cuts imposed by the studio, which rendered a complex story incoherent. Cimino's five-hour cut was reduced to about three-and-a-half hours for the movie's first showing in New York. Following vicious reviews, the film was withdrawn after only one day. A year later (1981) a mangled two-and-a-half-hour version was rereleased to total public indifference in America. In Europe, however, the film was more highly regarded and the DIRECTOR'S CUT (available on videocassette) has sometimes been hailed as a masterpiece.

As to what produced this division of opinion, the most plausible guess is the nature of the film itself. Westerns have generally provided a moral justification of the American Dream, showing how grit, determination, and a sense of justice have founded the land of the free. Cinimo's greatest sin, it seems, was to re-examine the foundations of the American Dream and represent it as a tangled web of moral compromise and vested interests from the start. A book, *Final Cut*, by Steven Bach, details the trials and tribulations of making the picture.

heavy   A villainous role in a film, or an actor who plays such a role. In the theatrical stock companies of the 19th century, the *heavy lead* was the actor who specialized in playing villains in melodrama. This tradition continued in the silent cinema, when such actors as the enormous bearded Scotsman Eric Campbell (1878–1912) were regularly cast as villains on the basis of their appearance. Famous heavies of the sound era have included James CAGNEY, Boris KARLOFF, Peter LORRE, Lee MARVIN, Oliver REED, and Jack NICHOLSON.

Heflin, Van   (Emmett Evan Heflin, Jnr; 1910–71) US supporting actor, noted for his burly glowering appearance. In 1941 Heflin won an Oscar playing Hollywood's first overtly homosexual character, the alcoholic friend of gangster Robert TAYLOR in *Johnny Eager*.

Born in Walters, Oklahoma, Heflin worked as a merchant seaman before attending the University of Oklahoma and Yale School of Drama. From 1928 he worked on Broadway where Katharine HEPBURN later discovered him, casting him as the father of her illegitimate child in *A Woman Rebels* (1936).

Subsequent roles included the husband of the ill-fated Emma (Jennifer JONES) in *Madame Bovary* (1940), the vice-president who succeeded Lincoln in *Tennessee Johnson* (1942), Athos in MGM's THE THREE MUSKETEERS (1948), a prison-camp informer pursued by Robert RYAN in *Act of Violence* (1948), a cop who helps a woman to murder her husband in Joseph LOSEY's *The Prowler* (1951), and a homesteader in SHANE (1953).

After appearing in several Italian films during the 1960s, Heflin returned to Hollywood in the box-office hit *Airport* (1970), in which he played a deranged bomber. He died the following year and, at his request, his ashes were scattered over an area of the Pacific Ocean where he had often sailed.

heist or **caper movie**   A film that depicts the planning, execution, and aftermath of a robbery from the viewpoint of its perpetrators.

John HUSTON effectively created the genre with the classic, possibly never bettered, *The Asphalt Jungle* (1950), in which a disparate rogues' gallery of characters assemble to steal a million-dollars' worth of jewellery. Later US examples include Stanley KUBRICK's *The Killing* (1956), *Odds Against Tomorrow* (1959), *The Anderson Tapes* (1971), *The Getaway* (1972), *The Taking of Pelham One, Two, Three* (1974), and Sidney LUMET's *Dog Day Afternoon* (1975).

In Europe, the key film was Jules DASSIN's tense RIFIFI (1955), about a massive jewellery heist. The movie spawned a long line of imitators in the later 1950s and 1960s. In general, European film-makers have brought a lighter touch to the subgenre, notably in such spoofs as the hilarious EALING comedies THE LAVENDER HILL MOB (1951) and *The Lady Killers* (1956) and Allied Film Makers' *The League of Gentlemen* (1961). In Italy, Mario Monicelli's *The Big Deal on Madonna Street (I soliti ignoti*; 1958) satirized the genre so effectively that it was remade twice. *Topkapi* (1964) was Dassin's own lighthearted return to his earlier theme.

Most heist movies have shown the plans of the thieves unravelling in the aftermath of their crime. Sometimes the cause is flawed planning; in *The Seven Thieves* (1960), for example, the criminals are obliged to return the unusably high-denomination notes to the casino they have robbed. More commonly, the isolated criminal microcosm disintegrates amidst greed, misunderstanding, and betrayal. This is seen most effectively in TARANTINO's claustrophobic *Reservoir Dogs* (1992), which skips both planning and execution; after the deed the protagonists, who are outlined in series of oblique flashbacks, converge on a warehouse, where their carefully laid plans collapse in bloody argument.

Hemmings, David (1941–) British actor, whose starring role in ANTONIONI'S BLOW-UP (1966) has made him a lasting symbol of London's 'swinging sixties'. When none of his subsequent movies made a comparable impact, Hemmings began to concentrate on writing and directing.

Born in Guildford, Hemmings began his career as a singer, performing with the English Opera Group at the age of nine and in nightclubs as a teenager. He made his movie debut as an extra in PREMINGER's *Saint Joan* (1957). His first substantial role was as a troublesome British youth in Clive Donner's *Some People* (1962), a film made to promote the Duke of Edinburgh's Award Scheme.

Four years later, Hemmings shot to international fame in *Blow-Up*, a film that seemed to epitomize the new freedoms of the era. Hemmings starred as a fashion photographer, who comes to believe that he has accidentally photographed a murder. Although his performance is characteristically bland, Antonioni skilfully emphasized his boyish good looks and enquiring eyes to create a memorable screen image. The scene that drew most comment, however, was the star's romp with two naked teenagers (Jane Birkin and Gillian Hills).

Hemmings subsequently played the evil Mordred in the musical *Camelot* (1967), a British officer in Tony RICHARDSON's *The Charge of the Light Brigade* (1968), and the title role in Donner's youth-oriented biopic *Alfred the Great* (1969). In the late 1970s he appeared in two Canadian films, *The Disappearance* (1977), a thriller that he also produced, and *Murder by Decree* (1979), in which Sherlock HOLMES investigates the Jack the Ripper murders. Hemmings's films as a director include *Running Scared* (1972), *Just a Gigolo* (1978), and *The Survivor* (1981).

Hepburn, Audrey Hepburn (Edda Hepburn van Heemstra Hepburn-Ruston; 1929–93) Belgian-born Hollywood star, with a sophisticated elfin quality that made her the screen's most elegant gamine. Her memorable roles include the call girl Holly Golightly in *Breakfast at Tiffany's* (1961) and the cockney Eliza Doolittle in *My Fair Lady* (1964).

Hepburn was born in Arnhem, the daughter of an Anglo-Irish banker and a Dutch baroness. After the Nazis invaded Belgium in 1940, she helped the Resistance by carrying messages in her shoes. Following the Liberation, she won a scholarship to the Ballet Rambert School in London and a minor part in a Dutch film. Her first English-speaking role was in the British *One Wild Oat* (1951). The following year, a chance meeting with the French novelist Colette brought her the title role in *Gigi*, a Broadway musical based on one of Colette's books. Rave reviews led to Hepburn making her Hollywood debut in *Roman Holiday* (1953), in which she played an overprotected princess who falls for newspaperman Gregory PECK. The role earned Hepburn her only Oscar.

In 1954 Hepburn married the actor Mel Ferrer, with whom she co-starred in King VIDOR's sprawling version of *War and Peace* (1956). The following year she sang and danced with Fred ASTAIRE in the enchanting *Funny Face* (1957) and appeared with Gary COOPER in Billy WILDER's comedy *Love in the Afternoon* (1957). She won Oscar nominations for both *The Nun's Story* (1959) and *Breakfast at Tiffany's*, and in 1963 joined the 60-year-old Cary GRANT in the Parisian thriller *Charade*.

In the same year Hepburn was chosen as the screen's Eliza Doolittle in preference to Julie ANDREWS, who had taken the part on Broadway; much to her chagrin, the producers decided that her singing would have to be dubbed. Although her fee was $1 million, five times that of her co-star Rex HARRISON, it was he who came away with the Oscar for Best Actor (presented by Hepburn). In 1966 the chic *Two for the Road* teamed her with Albert FINNEY as a couple recalling their early life together, while *Wait until Dark* (1967), about a terrorized blind woman, earned her another Oscar nomination.

After divorcing Ferrer in 1968 Hepburn married an Italian psychiatrist and retired for eight years. She returned to the screen in *Robin and Marian* (1976), playing a somewhat middle-aged Marian to Sean CONNERY's Robin Hood. Before appearing in the all-star thriller *Bloodline* (1979) she insisted on a $10,000 wardrobe designed by Givenchy, which would become her property after shooting. Her last major appearance was in the comic detective film *They All Laughed* (1982). She spent much of the last ten years of her life doing charitable work for UNESCO.

Katharine Hepburn (1907–) US actress, who has won a record four Oscars as Best Actress (the last at the age of 74) and 13 nominations. Born in Hartford, Connecticut, the daughter of a surgeon and a suffragette, she graduated from Bryn Mawr College before beginning a career on Broadway. This was not without its setbacks; Hepburn was sacked from her first starring role because the audience could not understand her unique delivery and dropped from *The Warrior's Husband* (1932) because of her rudeness. Luckily she was reinstated; it was this part that brought her a contract with RKO.

Hepburn made her film debut later that year in George CUKOR's *A Bill of Divorcement*. Producer David O. SELZNICK recalled his first reaction when she walked onto the set: "Ye gods, that horse face!" After completing the film she told her overbearing co-star, John BARRYMORE "Thank God I don't have to act with you anymore!" – to which he replied "I didn't know you ever had, darling." RKO came to know her as 'Katharine of Arrogance', while Lucille Ball noted "She ignored everyone equally."

A year later Hepburn won her first Oscar for *Morning Glory* (1933), in which she played a Broadway hopeful; it would be 34 years before her next Academy Award. After *Little Women* (1933) Hepburn was cast in a series of flops and became stigmatized as 'box-office poison'. Her career recovered when she formed a sparkling comedy partnership with Cary GRANT in *Bringing Up Baby* and *Holiday* (both 1938); Grant was also her co-star in Cukor's THE PHILADELPHIA STORY (1940), in which she played the headstrong heiress Tracy Lord.

In 1942 Hepburn sold the rights to *Woman of the Year* to MGM for $100,000 and demanded that Spencer TRACY appear as her co-star. To her blunt greeting, "I'm rather tall for you, Mr Tracy," he replied "Don't worry, I'll soon cut you down to size." This was her first of ten movies with Tracy, who became her friend and secret lover for 27 years. Their subsequent vehicles included such urbane comedies as *Adam's Rib* (1949) and *Pat and Mike* (1952). Tracy always received top billing; when urged that Hepburn, as a lady, might be allowed to come first, he replied "This is a movie, not a lifeboat."

During the 1950s Hepburn won Oscar nominations for THE AFRICAN QUEEN (1951) with Humphrey BOGART, *The Rainmaker* (1956) with Burt LANCASTER, and *Suddenly Last Summer* (1959). She then spent years helping to care for the seriously ill Tracy, even alternating with his wife as nurse. He died weeks after the completion of their last film together, *Guess Who's Coming to Dinner* (1967), which brought Hepburn her second Oscar. A year later she added a third for *The Lion in Winter*.

Hepburn's infrequent later films have included *Rooster Cogburn* (1975) with John WAYNE (who commented "She can't ride worth a damn") and the sentimental *On Golden Pond* (1981), which brought her a fourth Academy Award. The crumpled hat worn in the film by Henry FONDA had belonged to Tracy. In 1984 she played an old widow blackmailing a hit man (Nick Nolte) in *Grace Quigley*.

Hepworth, Cecil (1874–1953) British cinema pioneer. Apart from directing and producing hundreds of early shorts, Hepworth published the first film handbook, *The ABC of the Cinematograph* (1897), and began the British STAR system. He improved EDISON's projector by inventing a new arc lamp and in 1931 devised 'stretch printing', in which an effect of slow motion is achieved by printing some frames twice.

The son of a magic-lantern lecturer, Hepworth designed and sold photographic equipment before touring with his own film and magic-lantern show. In 1896 he opened a film laboratory at Walton-on-Thames and three years later produced his first film, *Express Trains in a Railway Cutting*. He filmed the 1898 Oxford and Cambridge boat race, the 1899 Derby (from the top of a horse-drawn bus), and the first British motorcar races.

Hepworth had made some 100 shorts by 1900 and double that number by 1906. Among the most popular was *Rescued by Rover* (1905), his first film to use professional actors; the hero, a collie dog, was billed as "Hepworth Picture Player Rover".

The film cost just over £7 to make, the actors being paid a half-guinea each.

Hepworth created the first English film star, Gladys Sylvani, and made Chrissie White and Alma Taylor into famous comediennes in his Tilly series. In 1920 two of his comedies found success in America: *The Amazing Quest of Mr Ernest Bliss* (1920) and *Alf's Button* (1920). As a result Hepworth sent his stars, Leslie Henson and Alma Taylor, on one of the first US promotional tours. Ronald COLMAN also appeared in several of Hepworth's films before going on to America and international fame.

Hepworth eventually bankrupted himself trying to generate electricity for his studios from diesel engines salvaged from a German U-boat. His last commercial film, the incomplete *Comin' Thro' the Rye*, was shown as part of British Film Week in 1924. The receivers took everything, wiping out 24 years of film-making by melting down master prints to recover chemicals. Hepworth spent the remainder of his career making trailers for the National Screen Service.

here's looking at you, kid   A line from CASABLANCA (1942), starring Ingrid BERGMAN and Humphrey BOGART, that became a popular catchphrase. It was based on a well-established US toast. Unlike the other catchphrase from the film, PLAY IT AGAIN, SAM, Bogart actually said it.

hero or **heroine**   The chief protagonist in a film, conventionally a plucky, attractive, and good-hearted character who triumphs over an evil opponent or an oppressive situation. Classic Hollywood good guys can conveniently be divided into three categories; action heroes (either strong and determined like John WAYNE or dashing like Errol FLYNN), romantic heroes (such as Tyrone POWER), and the earnest moral heroes (a type played to perfection by Henry FONDA). Clark GABLE may be said to combine the first and second categories and Gary COOPER the second and third. Strong heroines – as opposed to powerful bitches or appealing bad girls – were something of a rarity in pre-feminist Hollywood. Such actresses as Joan FONTAINE and Jane WYMAN specialized in playing sweet and vulnerable heroines, while Doris DAY later popularized the chirpy tomboy. Notions of screen heroism underwent a radical upheaval with the emergence of the ANTIHERO in the 1940s and 1950s.

Herzog, Werner (Werner Stipetic; 1942–)   German director, who emerged as one of the most original figures in European cinema in the 1970s. With its epic ambitions, intense lyricism, and general mood of despair, Herzog's work belongs firmly in the tradition of German Romanticism; indeed, the director has even compared himself to the 'mad' castle-building King Ludwig of Bavaria.

Herzog, who directed his first shorts while working as a welder in the mid 1960s, went on to make his feature debut with *Signs of Life* (1967), about the mental disintegration of a German soldier during World War II. In its exploration of man's relationship with the natural world and its sympathy with outcasts, the film anticipates Herzog's better-known works.

In *Even Dwarfs Started Small* (1970) and *Fata Morgana* (1971) Herzog further explored these themes; the first is set in a prison for dwarfs on a desolate island and the second on the edge of the Sahara desert, where a motley collection of eccentrics live amongst the debris of humanity. His next film, the documentary *Land of Silence and Darkness* (1972), was a sympathetic portrayal of a deaf and blind woman as she embarks on her first aeroplane trip.

Aguirre, Wrath of God (1973), starring Klaus KINSKI as a Spanish conquistador driven (like many of Herzog's central characters) to the edge of madness by his ambitions, brought the director international attention. In *The Enigma of Kaspar Hauser* (1974) the inhabitants of a 19th-century German town are presented with the mystery of a stranger with remarkable abilities, who can tell them nothing of his previous existence; *Heart of Glass* (1976) is an apocalyptic fable about the coming (and the implied doom) of modern industrial society, while in *Stroszek* (1977) three Germans decide to emigrate to America, where their ambitions of wealth are predictably disappointed.

Nosferatu the Vampyre (1979), a remake of the classic silent horror film, acquired cult status and brought Herzog a mass audience (*see* NOSFERATU). *Woyzeck* (1979) was a successful adaptation of the play by Büchner. *Fitzcarraldo* (1982), his most ambitious epic, concerns the efforts of a mad opera enthusiast (again played by Kinski) to bring opera to the natives of the Amazon basin. Both the bizarre plot and the sheer scale of the venture added to Herzog's already well-developed reputation for eccentricity. Subsequent films have been similarly unusual, including *Where the Green Ants Dream* (1984), about the conflict between the Aborigines and the Whites over land rights in Australia, *Cobra Verde* (1988), about an outcast slave trader in West Africa, and *Lessons of Darkness* (1992), a documentary-style film about Kuwait after the Gulf War.

Heston, Charlton (John Charlton Carter; 1923–) US actor, whose granite features and heroic physique made him the king of Hollywood's 'sword and sandal' EPICs of the 1950s and 1960s. Off-screen he served as president of the Screen Actors Guild (*see* SAG) and chairman of the American Film Institute (*see* AFI). At the 1977 Oscar ceremony, he was presented with the Jean Hersholt Humanitarian Award.

Born in Evanston, Illinois, Heston studied drama at Northwestern University, where he acted in two amateur films. After war service in the US Air Force, he made his Broadway debut in 1947; three years later he made his first professional film appearance in the thriller *Dark City* (1950). His first major role came in Cecil B. DE MILLE's circus drama *The Greatest Show on Earth* (1952), in which he played a circus owner, while the same director's THE TEN COMMANDMENTS (1956), in which he played Moses (and the voice of God), made him an international star.

US heroes played by Heston include Buffalo Bill in *Pony Express* (1953) and President Andrew Jackson in both *The President's Lady* (1953) and *The Buccaneer* (1958). In 1960 he won an Oscar for his performance in the title role of BEN-HUR. For his role as the Spanish hero *El Cid* (1961) he was required to age 20 years although his co-star Sophia LOREN refused to age a single day.

In *The Agony and the Ecstasy* (1965) Heston played an unlikely Michelangelo to Rex HARRISON's Pope Julius II. When Harrison put lifts in his shoes to match Heston's 6′3″ height, he found that his co-star had mysteriously grown taller again in the next scene. Historically minded critics pointed out that the real Michelangelo was virtually a dwarf. Harrison later complained that Heston "thinks the world is his supporting cast."

Later that year Heston undertook one of his least enjoyable assignments, playing an astronaut in the sci-fi film *The Planet of the Apes*; the star recorded that he had been "dragged, choked, netted, chased, doused, shipped, poked, shot, gagged, stoned, leaped on, and generally mistreated" during the shoot. His next role, General Charles Gordon in *Khartoum* (1966), was comparatively painless.

Less heroic parts followed: a middle-aged saddle tramp in *Will Penny* (1967) and a middle-aged football player in *Number One* (1969). In the 1970s he began a series of DISASTER FILMS with *Earthquake* (1974). *The Prince and the Pauper* (1977) teamed Heston, playing Henry VIII with his old antagonist, Rex Harrison, playing the Duke of Norfolk; Heston noted that "we didn't say much to each other except in front of the camera." His later films have included two Westerns, *The Mountain Men* (1980) and *Mother Lode* (1982), which he also directed.

high. high-angle shot A shot taken from a camera placed above the action. This can vary from a CLOSE-UP to an EXTREME HIGH-ANGLE SHOT, a LONG SHOT taken from hundreds of feet above. *See* CAMERA ANGLES.

high hat or **hi hat** Humorous nickname for a short tripod used to film LOW-ANGLE SHOTS. The high hat can also be used for filming action at or near ground-level and is therefore a staple of animal and nature documentaries.

high-key A term describing a lighting arrangement in which the KEY LIGHT is very intense. High-key illumination was popular for comedy and musical productions during Hollywood's Golden Era, when the bright effect was often enhanced by colourful costumes and sets.

highlighting The technique of using a thin beam of light to illuminate a small area of an actor's face, such as his eyes, for the camera. Highlighting is also used to emphasize details of props, such as the title of a book on a shelf, etc.

High Noon (1952) Classic Western directed by Fred ZINNEMANN from a script by Carl Foreman. With its focus on character and situation rather than action, *High Noon* is widely regarded as the first of the 'psychological' Westerns that appeared in the 1950s.

On the day he marries his Quaker fiancée Amy (Grace KELLY), Marshall Will Kane

(Gary COOPER) hears that desperado Frank Miller (Ian MacDonald) is returning to town with his gang to avenge his earlier arrest. Having failed to round up a posse from amongst the citizens of Hadleyville, Kane decides to slip away quietly, only to think better of it and return to face the music alone.

The role of Kane had been offered to Marlon BRANDO, Montgomery CLIFT, and Charlton HESTON before Cooper was approached at the insistence of the picture's major backer, a lettuce tycoon from Salinas, California. However, according to Zinnemann, "Cooper seemed absolutely right for the part. It seemed completely natural for him to be superimposed on Will Kane." Cooper was facing a number of problems of his own at the time of filming, including a crumbling marriage, a decline in box-office status, a bleeding duodenal ulcer, and a recurrent hip injury, all of which added to the realism of Kane's tortured expression and leaden gait as the burdens of treachery and isolation begin to weigh more heavily upon him. The performance earned Cooper his second Oscar as Best Actor.

Most critics applauded Zinnemann's taut control of the picture, which keeps close to the real time of the action between the 10.30 am wedding and the noonday shootout. However, rumours soon circulated that producer Stanley Kramer, unhappy with the preview, had ordered a recut that included many more close-ups of the suffering Cooper, numerous shots of clocks to heighten the suspense, and the inclusion of Dmitri Tiomkin and Ned Washington's 'Do Not Forsake Me' (which went on to win the Oscar for Best Song). Carl Foreman has always denied this, however. This was to be Foreman's last script before he was blacklisted during the McCarthyite witchhunt of the 1950s (see HOLLYWOOD BLACKLIST); at the time, the theme of a man adhering to principles when all around him take the easy option had powerful anti-McCarthy connotations. John WAYNE was reportedly so furious with the final scene, in which Kane throws his marshal's badge into the dust and rides away, that he made *Rio Bravo* (1958) in order to show a *real* lawman's devotion to duty.

high-speed camera A special camera used to achieve SLOW-MOTION effects. It films at a faster than normal speed so that the action appears to be slowed when the film is shown at standard speed. *Star Trek: The Wrath of Khan* (1982) featured an explosion scene filmed at 2500 frames per second (24 fps is standard for 35 mm), with the result that one second of shooting time was stretched out to one minute 44 seconds in the cinema.

Hill, George Roy (1922–) US director, who came to films relatively late in his career after working on Broadway and in television. He enjoyed several box-office hits with Paul NEWMAN and Robert REDFORD, including THE STING (1973), Universal's biggest ever money-maker.

Born in Minneapolis, Hill studied music at Yale and Trinity College, Dublin, where he acted with Cyril Cusack's repertory company. After serving as a Navy pilot in both World War II and the Korean conflict, he began to write for television in the mid 1950s, subsequently directing for both TV and the stage.

The 40-year-old Hill made his film debut with an adaptation of Tennessee Williams's *Period of Adjustment* (1962), a movie about a Korean War veteran that provided Jane FONDA with one of her first ingenue roles. When director Fred ZINNEMANN walked off *Hawaii* (1966), Hill stepped in to lead the cast, headed by Julie ANDREWS, to a box-office success. He and Andrews then enjoyed an even greater success with the lively flapper musical *Thoroughly Modern Millie* (1967). During shooting Hill barred temperamental producer Ross Hunter from the set, leading Hunter to fire him as soon as filming was over and to recut the film. "It was like putting a soufflé back into the oven for another hour" complained Hill.

In 1969 Hill directed the magical combination of Newman and Redford in BUTCH CASSIDY AND THE SUNDANCE KID (1969), a film that brought the director his first Oscar nomination. Four years later a second Hill-Newman-Redford romp, THE STING, took the Academy Award as Best Picture and earned Hill his only Oscar as Best Director. In 1972 he won the Special Jury Prize at Cannes for the anti-war fantasy *Slaughterhouse Five*.

Hill's films of the mid 1970s included *The Great Waldo Pepper* (1975), which starred Redford as a 1920s aerial daredevil and drew on Hill's flying experience, and the brutal *Slap Shot* (1977), with Newman as the player-coach of a professional ice-hockey team. At the end of the decade Hill went into semi-retirement to teach at Yale, but continued to make occasional films including *A Little Romance* (1979), *The World According to Garp* (1982) with Robin WILLIAMS, the Le Carré thriller *The Little Drummer Girl* (1984), and *Funny Farm* (1988), with Chevy CHASE as a would-be novelist.

Hiroshima, Mon Amour (1959) Alain RESNAIS's innovative first feature, an enigmatic love story with a screenplay by Marguerite Duras. A French actress, named only as She (Emmanuelle Riva), has a brief affair with a Japanese architect, known only as He (Eiji Okada), while shooting a peace film in Hiroshima. The couple discuss their experiences of the war, including her affair with a German soldier (Bernard Fresson), who was killed on the day of Liberation. He begs She to stay, but it is clear that she will return to her home in Nevers.

Impressed by Resnais's 1955 documentary *Night and Fog*, a Franco-Japanese consortium approached him to make a feature on a topic of his own choosing, providing that it touched on Hiroshima 12 years after the Bomb and featured performers and locations from both countries. Having failed to interest Françoise Sagan, Resnais persuaded Marguerite Duras to produce a spare script around which he could "compose a sort of poem in which the images would act as counterpoint to the text."

Resnais completed his picture after late summer shoots in Hiroshima and Tokyo and a pre-Christmas spell in Nevers, Paris, and Autun. His innovative use of FLASH CUTTING to suggest a transitory memory and his bold deployment of the SUBJECTIVE CAMERA to convey the woman's psychological state in some of the Nevers sequences established Resnais as the Proust of the screen. The opening sequence (over which a man's voice denies every statement made by a woman's) interweaves images of embracing bodies with shots of a museum, a hospital, and newsreel footage of the dropping of the Bomb (taken from Hideo Sekigawa's 1953 docudrama, *Hiroshima*). According to Resnais, this was designed as "a sort of dream, a voice coming from the unconscious, which is at one and the same time that of the authors and that of the spectators, which will only later become that of the principal characters."

Hiroshima, Mon Amour is primarily about memory and forgetfulness – and the way in which both enable people to deal with the pain of their past. However, Resnais was keen to emphasize that he was not equating the scale of the public and private tragedies:

> We contrast the immense, monstrous, incredible aspect of Hiroshima with the tiny little story of Nevers which to us is reflected through Hiroshima as the glimmer of a candle is magnified and reversed by a lens.

Shown out of competition at Cannes, the film was the undoubted hit of the festival, scooping the Film Writers' Award, the Prix Méliès (shared with Truffaut's THE 400 BLOWS), and the International Critics' Prize (shared with the Venezuelan feature *Araya*). It also earned Duras an Oscar nomination for Best Original Screenplay. Resnais would return to the theme of time's effect upon the memory in his second assault on the conventions of traditional screen narrative, LAST YEAR AT MARIENBAD (1961).

His Girl Friday (1940) Howard HAWKS's classic SCREWBALL COMEDY, famous for its breakneck pace and witty dialogue. Newspaper editor Walter Burns (Cary GRANT) is determined to prevent his ace reporter Hildy Johnson (Rosalind RUSSELL) from leaving his employ. As her ex-husband, he is equally intent on preventing her marriage to doltish millionaire Bruce Baldwin (Ralph BELLAMY). The escape of a framed 'killer' provides him with his opportunity.

Ben Hecht and Charles MacArthur's play had been filmed by Lewis MILESTONE under its original title, *The Front Page*, in 1931, with Adolphe Menjou as the scheming editor and Pat O'Brien as his crack newshound. The idea of changing the reporter's sex came to Hawks at a house party; the guests had decided to read through the play but a shortage of men left him no option but to give the role to a woman. He quickly contacted Hecht to propose the addition of a romantic twist to this already complex comedy. While agreeing to the amendment, Hecht pleaded prior commitments and suggested Hawks contact Charles Lederer, the author of the 1931 screenplay. In the end Hecht did contribute to the script but declined a credit.

Inspired by the change of emphasis, Lederer produced a screenplay crackling with one-liners. The film's celebrated IN-JOKES include Burns criticizing Baldwin because "he looks like that actor...Ralph Bellamy!" and Cary Grant's line, "The last man who said that to me was Archie Leach just a week before he cut his throat" – Archie Leach being Grant's original name. The rattling dialogue perhaps seemed funnier than it was owing to the rapid-fire delivery insisted on by Hawks: this has been timed at 240 words a minute, compared to the industry average of 100–140.

The first screwball comedy set in the world of work, the film provided a perfect vehicle for Cary Grant. Curiously, many of Grant's former co-stars, including Katharine HEPBURN, Jean ARTHUR, and Irene DUNNE, refused the part of Hildy, as did Claudette COLBERT and Carole LOMBARD. Convinced that Hawks was disappointed not to have landed a bigger name, Rosalind Russell is said to have told him: "You don't want me, do you? Well, you're stuck with me, so you might as well make the most of it." He did.

Billy WILDER and I. A. L. Diamond remade the 1931 original in 1974 with Walter MATTHAU and Jack LEMMON in the Burns and Johnson roles. While disappointing, this was considerably better than Ted Kotcheff's Switching Channels (1988), which restored the marital angle but transferred the action to a TV newsroom.

Hitchcock, Sir Alfred (1899–1980) British director and producer known as the **Master of Suspense** for his numerous expertly crafted thrillers. His portly figure and distinctive profile became familiar to a large public through his television series and CAMEOS in his own films. Notoriously, 'Hitch', who made 53 features in 53 years, never won an Oscar as Best Director despite receiving numerous other awards. His knighthood was bestowed only months before his death.

Born in London, the son of a poultry dealer, Hitchcock began his career in films designing titles for the London side of Hollywood's FAMOUS PLAYERS-Lasky company. When its studios were taken over by Gainsborough in the 1920s, Hitchcock remained, progressing from art director to assistant director and director. His first characteristic film was The Lodger (1926), a murder story in which he also appeared as an extra. His next success, and Britain's first feature talkie, was Blackmail (1929), a thriller starring Anny Ondra. She was the first of the icy blondes who would reoccur throughout his films, later examples being Grace KELLY, Janet LEIGH, Eva Marie Saint, Kim NOVAK, and Tippi Hedren.

Following the success of THE THIRTY-NINE STEPS (1935) and THE LADY VANISHES (1937), two of the cinema's greatest films of suspense, Hitchcock was invited to make his first US movie, REBECCA (1940). The film, which starred Laurence OLIVIER and Joan FONTAINE, was his only movie to win the Oscar for Best Picture. He apparently enhanced Fontaine's nervous performance by telling her, quite untruly, that she was hated by the rest of the cast. A year later he directed her to an Oscar in Suspicion (1941), having been obliged to change the ending when Cary GRANT's studio refused to let him play a murderer. The psychoanalytical SPELLBOUND (1945) starred Ingrid BERGMAN and Gregory PECK, while Notorious (1946) paired Bergman and Grant. His other triumphs of the immediate post-war years included the technical tour-de-force ROPE (1948) and the gripping Strangers on a Train (1951). The voyeuristic REAR WINDOW (1954) starred James STEWART and Grace Kelly, who reappeared in both Dial M for Murder (1954) and To Catch a Thief (1955). VERTIGO (1958), arguably the director's darkest and most self-revealing film, was followed by the comparatively amiable NORTH BY NORTHWEST (1959), a comedy-thriller with Cary Grant.

Hitchcock's films of the 1960s, which were seen at the time as something of a falling off, include three of his best-known and most-discussed works – PSYCHO (1960), THE BIRDS (1963), and Marnie (1964), which starred Tippi Hedren as a kleptomaniac. His final movie was Family Plot (1976). When he died, Hitchcock was the only director from the silent era still working.

Hitchcock was notorious for considering actors as mere chess pieces or, in his own alleged phrase, "cattle". However, Ingrid BERGMAN said that he gave her the best advice of her career when she complained of a difficult scene "I don't think I can do that naturally." After listening patiently to her long explanation, Hitchcock shrugged and said, "All right, if you can't do it naturally, fake it."

Hitler, Adolf (1889–1945) German dictator. First portrayed on sceeen in the satirical guise of Adenoid Hynkel in CHAPLIN's THE GREAT DICTATOR (1940), Hitler appeared as a character in several wartime propaganda films. The US actor Bobby Watson came to specialize in the role, playing Hitler seven times between 1942 and 1961, beginning with *The Devil with Hitler*. The plot of Ernst LUBITSCH's satire *To Be or Not to Be* (1942), involved a troupe of Polish actors impersonating Hitler and other leading Nazis; Mel BROOKS dressed up as the dictator in the inferior 1983 remake. Brooks's *The Producers* (1967) featured a hysterical scene in which massed hopefuls audition for the part of an all-singing all-dancing Hitler in a Broadway show. The first post-war Hitlers were the Soviet V. Savelyov in *The Fall of Berlin* (1950) and the American Luther Adler in *The Desert Fox* and *The Magic Face* (both 1951). Richard Basehart, better known as the star of TV's *Voyage to the Bottom of the Sea* (1964–68), took the role in the first full biopic *Hitler* (1962), a mainly sensational treatment. The historical, cultural, and moral significance of Nazism was explored at length in Hans-Jürgen SYBERBERG's *Hitler; a Film from Germany* (1977), a seven-hour art film in which the Führer is represented by photographs, dolls, and models rather than a live actor. A plot to clone hundreds of Hitlers was the subject of the far-fetched thriller *The Boys from Brazil* (1978). Perhaps the best serious portrayal was Alec GUINNESS's thoughtful depiction in *Hitler: the Last Ten Days* (1973), the oddest choice Peter SELLERS in *Soft Beds, Hard Battles* (1974), and the most unexpected success in the role that of sitcom veteran Colin Jeavons in *Hitler's SS: Portrait in Evil* (1985).

The real Hitler appears in Leni RIEFENSTAHL's documentary *Triumph of the Will* (1934), while newsreel footage of the man has been incorporated into numerous feature films. Often the real Hitler appears to be more of a demented caricature than the portrayals.

HMI lamp   A studio lamp used to produce the effect of bright sunlight.

Hoffman, Dustin   (1937–)   US film star, whose hesitant antiheroic image (he stands 5'6" tall) caught the mood of the late 1960s and early 1970s. Known for his remarkable versatility, Hoffman won Oscars as Best Actor for *Kramer vs Kramer* (1979) and *Rain Man* (1988). He has also taken occasional stage roles, including Shylock in the 1989 London production of *The Merchant of Venice*.

Born in Los Angeles, the son of a set-dresser at Columbia, Hoffman was named after the silent film star Dustin Farnum. He

originally wanted to be a jazz pianist but embarked on an acting career at the age of 19 "to meet pretty girls". He took classes at the Pasadena Playhouse, where he and Gene HACKMAN were voted "least likely to succeed". When his attempts to break into Broadway failed, Hoffman sold toys at Macy's and worked in a mental hospital before making his debut off-Broadway in 1965.

A year later, director Mike NICHOLS saw Hoffman in the British farce *Eh?* and cast the 30-year-old unknown in THE GRADUATE (1967), as an unsure 20-year-old who is seduced by one of his parents' friends (Anne BANCROFT). Hoffman was paid only $17,000 but the movie's huge critical and commercial success brought him overnight stardom and an Oscar nomination for Best Actor.

Two years later he earned a second Oscar nomination for his performance as the low-life Ratso in John SCHLESINGER's *Midnight Cowboy* (1969). Films of the 1970s included the American Indian story *Little Big Man* (1970), in which he ages to 121 (requiring five hours of make-up), *Lenny* (1974), a biopic of the doomed comedian Lenny Bruce that won the actor another Oscar nomination, *All the President's Men* (1976), in which he played the Watergate reporter Carl Bernstein, John Schlesinger's *Marathon Man* (1976), in which he was pursued by Nazi dentist Laurence OLIVIER, and Michael Apted's flop *Agatha* (1979), about the disappearance of the crime writer Agatha Christie (Vanessa REDGRAVE).

Hoffman finally clinched the Oscar with *Kramer vs. Kramer* (1979), in which he played a husband abandoned by his wife (Meryl STREEP), who then sues for custody of their child; the film was shot while Hoffman was himself going through a divorce. Subsequent roles have included an actor who pretends to be a woman in order to get work in *Tootsie* (1983), an autistic savant in *Rain Man* (1988), the title role in Steven SPIELBERG's $70-million Peter Pan story *Hook* (1991), and a petty crook who saves the victims of a plane crash in *Hero* (British title *Accidental Hero*; 1992).

Olivier, David PUTTNAM, and others have attested to the trials of working with Hoffman, a notorious perfectionist. When Sydney POLLACK earned an Oscar nomination for directing *Tootsie*, he is reported to have said, "I'd give it up, if I could have back the nine months of my life I spent with Dustin making it"; similarly Larry Gelbart, the film's writer, swore that he would "never work again for an Oscar-winner who was shorter than the statue."

Holden, William (William Franklin Beedle Jnr; 1918–81) US actor. Born into a wealthy family, who owned a chemical business, Holden was noticed by a talent spotter as a student and signed to a contract with Paramount. Following his appearance as an extra in *Prison Farm* (1938) and a single line in *Million Dollar Legs* (1939), he became a star playing the boxer-violinist hero of Clifford Odets's *Golden Boy* (1939). He subsequently played clean-cut roles in such films as Sam WOOD's *Our Town* (1940) and *The Remarkable Andrew* (1942).

Holden's screen image matured somewhat following his return from service in World War II. Having been cast against type as a vicious killer in *The Dark Past* (1948), he gave splendid performances as Judy Holliday's tutor in the George CUKOR comedy *Born Yesterday* (1950) and as Joe Gillis, the failed screenwriter turned kept man in SUNSET BOULEVARD (1950). Although the latter role brought him a Best Actor Oscar nomination, the real turning point of Holden's career came with his casting as the maverick hero Sefton in Wilder's *Stalag 17* (1953), a role that clinched him the Oscar. His other major films of the 1950s included Robert WISE's *Executive Suite* (1954) and the melodrama *Picnic* (1955); in the case of the latter he demanded an extra $8000 for his dancing scene with Kim NOVAK. He also starred as the escapee Shears in David LEAN's THE BRIDGE ON THE RIVER KWAI (1957). In 1956 Holden topped the QUIGLEY POLL as the top male US box-office draw.

Holden's work-rate slowed somewhat thereafter. During the 1960s and 1970s he travelled the world, amassing a large art collection and making some fairly terrible films in exotic locations. Notable among his later movies are Edward DMYTRYK's *Alvarez Kelly* (1966), Sam PEKINPAH's *The Wild Bunch* (1969), Clint EASTWOOD's *Breezy* (1973), and Sidney LUMET's *Network* (1976), for which Holden received his final Best Actor Oscar nomination. Although a resident of Geneva, Holden spent most of his later years in Africa, where he was the co-owner of a large safari club.

Holland, Agnieszka (1948–) Polish director, born in Warsaw. Her earlier films include *Provincial Actors* (1979), about the problems of achieving a successful career in a socialist state, and *Fever* (1980), about the rising tide of opposition towards tsarist Russia that preceded the 1906 Polish Revolution; the latter film was clearly meant to reflect the growing resistance to Soviet influence in Poland at the time it was made. Subsequent films have included *Woman on Her Own* (1981) and *Angry Harvest* (1985), a story loosely based on the events leading up to the murder of the dissident priest Father Jerzy Popieluszko. The ambitious *Europa, Europa* (1991), about a Jewish boy who spends the war years masquerading as a Hitler Youth, and *Olivier, Olivier* (1993), about the effect on a family of a son's return six years after his disappearance, were also based on true stories. *The Secret Garden* (1994), a sensitive version of the Edwardian children's classic, became a critical and commercial success in the West.

Hollywood A suburb of Los Angeles, California, famous as the centre of the US film-making industry. Founded in 1911, Hollywood had superseded New York as America's film-making capital by about 1914. Producers were attracted by cheap labour, constant sunlight, and the proximity of widely varied landscapes (including desert). Another undoubted attraction was the nearness of the Mexican border, which allowed independent film-makers to make a quick escape from the vigilantes employed by the MOTION PICTURE PATENTS COMPANY. By the 1920s Hollywood had become a magnet for European talent and a byword for glitz and glamour. Among the solid citizens of Middle America it had also earned a reputation for excess and immorality of all kinds – leading to the nickname **Sodom-by-the-Sea**. The **Golden Age of Hollywood** comprised the years of the STUDIO SYSTEM, roughly 1930 to 1949, when a handful of powerful producers dominated the US motion-picture output and the world mass-market entertainment business. By the mid 1950s a combination of factors, including the rise of television, McCarthyite blacklisting, the growing strength of European and world cinema, and the advent of the independent producer conspired to end the hegemony of the Hollywood 'dream factory'.

Many film professionals have commented bitterly on the greed, cynicism, and fickleness of Hollywood; the sheer unreality of **Tinseltown** has also been widely remarked upon:

> A town that has to be seen to be disbelieved.
> WALTER WINCHELL, journalist.

> The people are unreal. The flowers are unreal, they don't smell. The fruit is unreal, it doesn't taste of anything. The whole place is a glaring, gaudy, nightmarish set, built up in the desert.
> ETHEL BARRYMORE, actress.

> A place where they pay you $50,000 for a kiss and 50 cents for your soul.
> MARILYN MONROE, actress.

> A rotten, gold-plated sewer of a town. Guys who can't tie their own shoelaces are driving around Beverly Hills in $80,000 cars.
> JAMES WOODS, actor.

> To survive there, you need the ambition of a Latin-American revolutionary, the ego of a grand opera tenor, and the physical stamina of a cow pony.
> BILLIE BURKE, actress.

> It's only a village, you know. Village life around the pump.
> ANTHONY NEWLEY, actor.

See also BEVERLY HILLS; SUNSET BOULEVARD.

Hollywood blacklist A list of actors, directors, producers, and writers who were denied cinema work for years after the House Un-American Activities Committee accused them of being members or supporters of the Communist Party. *See also* COLD WAR; HOLLYWOOD TEN.

Hollywood High The Los Angeles high school located on SUNSET BOULEVARD less than 200 yards from the famous GRAUMAN'S CHINESE THEATER. It provided the prototype for high schools seen in such films as REBEL WITHOUT A CAUSE (1955), *Grease* (1978), and *Back to the Future* (1985). Former students include Lana TURNER, James Garner, Sue Lyons, Linda Evans, Carol Burnett, and Ricky Nelson (whose name is carved into his old desk). Hollywood High's sports teams are nicknamed 'The Sheiks', after the VALENTINO movie.

Today, the school is graffiti-covered and its neighbourhood taken over by drunks, prostitutes, and drug-pushers. Students have occasionally been caught trading guns and drugs by the school's ten-man security force.

Hollywood on the Tiber A nickname for the CINECITTÀ studio complex near Rome. *See under* CINE.

Hollywood Ten The group of ten US screenwriters, producers, and directors who refused to either confirm or deny their affiliation to the Communist Party during the investigations of the House Un-American Activities Committee in 1947. The ten were Alvah Bessie, Herbert Biberman, Lester Cole, Edward DMYTRYK, Ring Lardner Jnr, John Howard Lawson, Albert Maltz, Sam Ornitz, Adrian Scott, and Dalton Trumbo. All were subsequently imprisoned for a short time for contempt of court and on their release were blacklisted and unable to work in Hollywood for several years. Many did not return to the film industry.

Holmes, Sherlock Sir Arthur Conan Doyle's DETECTIVE has appeared on screen more often than any other fictional character; to date, he has been played by 75 actors, in 211 films (including TV movies), from 14 countries. The first screen version was *Sherlock Holmes Baffled*, a US silent short of 1900 (actor unknown), and the first British version *The Speckled Band* (starring George Treville) in 1912. The first, and as yet only, Black Holmes was Sam Robinson, who played the role in *Black Sherlock Holmes* (1918).

Long-running Sherlocks include the Dane Viggo Larsen, who starred in 13 (mainly German) Holmes movies, starting with *Sherlock Holmes i livsfare* (1908); Ellie Norwood, who appeared in 47 British shorts in the early 1920s, starting with *The Dying Detective*; and Basil RATHBONE, the star of 14 US movies made between 1939 and 1945, starting with *The Hound of the Baskervilles*. Rathbone's later movies brought Holmes into the modern era. Rathbone also sent up his role in *Crazy House* (1943) and did a Holmesian voice-over for Disney's *The Great Mouse Detective* (1986).

Other actors to play the sleuth include: John BARRYMORE (*Sherlock Holmes*, 1922); Peter CUSHING (*The Hound of the Baskervilles*, 1959, the first colour Holmes movie); Christopher LEE (three times, beginning with *Sherlock Holmes und das Halsband des Todes*, 1962); Harry Reems (in the pornographic *Sherlock Holmes*, 1975); Peter Cook (*The Hound of the Baskervilles*, 1978); and Charlton HESTON (*The Crucifer of Blood*, 1991).

Only two actors have appeared as both Holmes and Dr Watson: Reginald Owen, who played the former in *A Study in Scarlet* (1933) and the latter in *Sherlock Holmes*

(1932), and television's long-running Sherlock, Jeremy Brett, who played Watson in *The Crucifer of Blood*.

The only two films found in Hitler's bunker after his death were *Der Hund von Baskerville* and *Der Mann, der Sherlock Holmes* (both 1937).

homosexuality Despite a significant, if largely covert, homosexual population, Hollywood has generally approached this subject with caution, largely through a fear of alienating mainstream audiences.

Two of the earliest treatments of the theme originated in Weimar Germany: *Anders als die Andern* (1919) presented love amongst gay men as "Neither a vice nor a crime, nor even a sickness, but a variation", while the tender *Mädchen in Uniform* (1931), set in a girls' boarding school, has a teacher defending her love for a pupil with the words "what you call sins, Principal, I call the great spirit of love which has a thousand forms." Less overtly, the US film *Wild Party* (1929) – directed by Dorothy ARZNER, herself a lesbian – presented an idyllic view of the close relationships in a women's college.

However, owing to the strict enforcement of the HAYS CODE from the 1930s onwards, homosexuality could only be presented in a highly oblique or coded fashion in the movies of Hollywood's Golden Era. Characteristic was Paramount's promotion of DIETRICH as "the woman all women want to see" in *Morocco* (1930), in which the bisexual star, cross-dressed in top hat and tails, kisses another woman on the lips. Similarly, GARBO, another bisexual, hinted at the lesbianism of the 'pure' Swedish queen in *Queen Christina* (1933). Male homosexuality was suggested through overt effeminacy, as with Peter LORRE's character in THE MALTESE FALCON (1941), whose 'sin' is signposted by his perfumed visiting card.

After the war, homosexuality began to be treated explicitly in such UNDERGROUND FILMS as Kenneth Anger's *Fireworks* (1947) and Jean Genet's lyrical *Un Chant d'amour* (1950). With their passionate gay aesthetic, these films anticipate later European art movies such as FASSBINDER's emotional *Querelle* (1982) and Derek JARMAN's *Sebastiane* (1976) and *Caravaggio* (1986).

Mainstream cinema lagged far behind, however. In Britain A TASTE OF HONEY (1961) showed a sympathetic young gay befriending a lonely pregnant girl, while the black-mail story *Victim* (1961) presented a case for legalizing homosexuality. In America, versions of the classic stage plays *Cat on a Hot Tin Roof* (1958) and *The Children's Hour* (1961), which allude to male homosexuality and lesbianism respectively, forced a slight relaxing of the Code. By the 1960s directors could present Peter O'TOOLE's homosexual rape in LAWRENCE OF ARABIA (1962), BRANDO as a repressed gay in *Reflections in a Golden Eye* (1967), and Mick Jagger as a bisexual in *Performance* (1970). Nevertheless, despite a growing confidence in the depiction of homosexuality, the tone of most films remained negative. Lesbians continued to be stereotyped as predatory dykes in such films as *From Russia With Love* (1963) and *The Killing of Sister George* (1968), or presented for male titillation in e.g. Hammer's *Vampire Lovers* (1970). Depictions of male homosexuals have ranged from the shrieking queens of *La Cage aux folles* (1978) or *Privates on Parade* (1982) to the seediness of *Cruising* (1980), which showed an unsavoury gay milieu terrorized by a serial killer. When successive Hollywood blockbusters presented a psychotic killer transvestite (THE SILENCE OF THE LAMBS, 1991) and a crazed killer-dyke (*Basic Instinct*, 1992) militant gay groups organized boycotts and demonstrations.

The 1980s and 1990s have seen a number of exceptions to this stereotyped treatment, notably *Making Love* (1982), which shows a married man coming to terms with his gayness, Donna Deitch's honest lesbian love story *Desert Hearts* (1985), MERCHANT-IVORY's *Maurice* (1987), and Gus Van Sant's gay road movie *My Own Private Idaho* (1991). *Go Fish* (1994) was a romantic comedy in which the protagonists just happened to be lesbians. Despite reasonable distribution, such films have not been able to attract a mass heterosexual audience. One film that did achieve mainstream success was *Philadelphia* (1994), Hollywood's first serious attempt to deal with the AIDS epidemic.

Take out the homosexuals and there's no Hollywood!
ELIZABETH TAYLOR.

Hope, Bob (Leslie Townes Hope; 1903–) Wisecracking US comedian, whose show-business career has lasted nearly 70 years. Hope was Hollywood's top male box-office draw in 1943 and 1949. Although his star declined in the 1960s, he remains a US institution. He acted as MC for the ACADEMY AWARDS ceremonies for four decades and himself received five special Oscars for his charity work and for entertaining US troops abroad. In 1994 the 91-year-old Hope performed for the veterans visiting D-Day commemorations. One of the world's richest entertainers, Hope is known for his friendships with US presidents.

Born in the London suburb of Eltham, he moved to Cleveland, Ohio, with his family at the age of four. He later worked as a newsboy, soda jerk, and boxer (under the name of Packy East). In 1927 Hope travelled to New York but could only find work dancing with a pair of Siamese twins. By 1933 he was appearing in the Broadway musical *Roberta*, where he met his wife the singer Dolores Read; the couple are still married. Although Hope's earliest comedy shorts, made in New York, were unsuccessful he soon became a hit on radio, leading to an appearance in *The Big Broadcast of 1938*, an all-star revue in which he first sang his signature tune, 'Thanks for the Memory'.

His first starring role came in the comedy thriller *The Cat and the Canary* (1939), in which he attempted to safeguard Paulette GODDARD's sanity in the archetypal spooky old house. Such lines as "I'm not really frightened, I'm just naturally nervous" and "Even my goosepimples have goosepimples" helped to establish Hope's screen image as an amiable coward, which he continued to play upon into the 1960s.

Having become accustomed to hurling friendly insults at each other during golf matches, Hope and Bing CROSBY decided to pair up in a film. Their opportunity came with THE ROAD TO SINGAPORE (1940), the first of seven song and comedy 'Road films' that also featured Dorothy LAMOUR (the film had originally been intended for George Burns and Gracie Allen). The series became known for its IN-JOKES, running gags, and asides to the audience. In *The Road to Utopia* (1946) Hope finally wins Lamour but their son, when we see him, looks curiously like Crosby.

Excluding the 'Road' series, Hope's most successful film was *The Paleface* (1948), in which Jane RUSSELL plays Calamity Jane to his cowardly dentist. As Russell is finally dragged off by a galloping horse Hope turns to ask the audience: "Well, what did you expect? A happy ending?" In 1950 he became the first major Hollywood star to sign a long-term television contract, with CBS.

His later movies included *Fancy Pants* (1950) with Lucille Ball, *Call Me Bwana* (1963) with Anita EKBERG, *Cancel My Reservation* (1972), and, at the age of 87, *Don't Shoot, It's Only Me* (1990).

> If I wanted to have a weekend of pure pleasure, it would be to have a half-dozen Bob Hope films and watch them...He is a great, great talent.
> WOODY ALLEN.

Hopkins, Sir Anthony (1937–) Intense British film and stage actor, who has progressed from character roles to international stardom. He was knighted in 1992, a year after winning the Oscar for his performance as a serial killer in THE SILENCE OF THE LAMBS. In 1994 the cinema magazine *Premiere* called him "quite simply the finest screen actor in the world today."

Born in South Wales, Hopkins trained at the Cardiff College of Drama and at RADA. After making his stage debut in 1960 he spent seven years with the National Theatre Company at the Old Vic. His first film role was that of Richard I in *The Lion in Winter* (1968), a historical drama in which he supported Katharine HEPBURN and Peter O'TOOLE.

After playing Lloyd George in Richard ATTENBOROUGH's *Young Winston* (1972), Hopkins began to work mainly in US television. His feature films of the later 1970s included the all-star war drama *A Bridge Too Far* (1977) and Attenborough's horror story *Magic* (1978), in which he played a ventriloquist taken over by his dummy. Hopkins then received excellent notices as Captain Bligh (to Mel GIBSON's Christian) in Dino DE LAURENTIIS's $20-million *The Bounty* (1984). In *84 Charing Cross Road* (1987) he played a reserved English bookseller swapping almost-love letters with US bibliophile Anne BANCROFT.

Hopkins found a new level of international fame with his performance as the terrifying cannabalistic Dr Hannibal Lecter in *The Silence of the Lambs* (1991). His tense head-to-head meetings with FBI recruit Jody FOSTER provide the most gripping moments of the film. Hopkins went on to play the bullying husband of Vanessa REDGRAVE in MERCHANT-IVORY's *Howards End* (1992) and the repressed butler Stevens in the same team's *The Remains of the Day* (1993). Subsequent roles include C. S. Lewis in Attenborough's moving *Shadowlands* (1994), based on the writer's brief marriage to a dying American (Debra Winger), and the health crank Dr John Kellogg in Alan PARKER's *The Road to Wellville* (1994). In 1995 he made his directorial debut with *August*, an adaptation of Chekhov's *Uncle Vanya*.

Hopper. Dennis Hopper (1936–   ) US actor and director, best known for playing menacing or demented characters. An actor since his teenage years, Hopper made his film debut in Nicholas RAY's *Johnny Guitar* (1954) and went on to play small parts in the James DEAN vehicles REBEL WITHOUT A CAUSE (1955) and *Giant* (1956). However, a reputation for being difficult severely limited his early screen career – from 1958 to 1963 he made only four films. During the mid-to-late 1960s Hopper played small roles in big films, such as *The Sons of Katie Elder* (1965), *Cool Hand Luke* (1967), and *True Grit* (1969), while also appearing in 'counterculture' movies, such as Roger CORMAN's *The Trip* (1967) and *Head* (1968).

Hopper's great breakthrough came in 1969, when he teamed up with Peter FONDA, his co-star from *The Trip*, to write, finance, and star in the biker movie EASY RIDER, which Hopper also directed. The huge success of this low-budget film – it took some $16 million at the box office – caused a major rethink in Hollywood, where Hopper had previously been ignored. In 1970 Hopper, armed with $1 million from Columbia, headed for the jungles of Peru to make *The Last Movie* (1971), a film that he also wrote and starred in. He returned with over 40 hours of footage, which he then spent a year editing. Although the resulting film was widely condemned as pretentious and incomprehensible (the credits appear 30 minutes into the film), Hopper has resolutely defended it. *The Last Movie* set the seal on his reputation as the 'madman of the movies' and led to a period outside the Hollywood mainstream.

Hopper, however, continued to work steadily, appearing in such films as *Kid Blue* (1973) and *Tracks* (1976); in 1977 he starred as the psychotic Ripley in Wim WENDER's *The American Friend*, an adaptation of a novel by Patricia Highsmith. His appearance as a photojournalist in COPPOLA's APOCALYPSE NOW (1979) then led to something of a resurgence in his career. The next year he returned to direction with *Out of the Blue*, an examination of dysfunctional family relationships.

During the 1980s Hopper made a spectacular return to the Hollywood mainstream with a series of striking roles in commercially successful films (he made six movies in 1986 alone). Particularly notable were his performances in *Rumble Fish* (1983), *Hoosiers* (1986), which brought him an Oscar nomination for his portrayal of an alcoholic, and David LYNCH's *Blue Velvet* (1986), in which he played the foulmouthed psychopath Frank Booth. In 1988 Hopper directed the hit movie *Colors*, a film about Los Angeles street gangs that co-starred Sean Penn and Robert DUVALL. However, his next film as a director, *Catchfire* (1990), was released in a version of which Hopper did not approve; consequently he insisted on his name being removed from the credits (the film's direction being credited to 'Alan Smithee').

Hopper's more recent films as an actor have included *Paris Trout* (1991), *True Romance* (1993), and *Speed* (1994), in which he plays an embittered ex-policeman with a penchant for unusual bombs. He has also directed *Flashback*, in which he appeared with Kiefer SUTHERLAND, and *The Hot Spot* (both 1990).

Hedda Hopper (Elda Furry; 1890–1966) Hollywood gossip columnist, noted for her acid wit and flamboyant hats. She is credited with helping to create and destroy numerous stars during her 28-year career.

Born in Hollidaysburg, Pennsylvania, Hopper was working as a Broadway chorus girl when she married the actor DeWolf Hopper (1868–1935) in 1913. While he became a popular matinée idol, she moved on from VAMP roles to playing society women in such films as *Wings* (1927), *The Last of Mrs Cheyney* (1929), and *Speak Easily* (1932), with Buster KEATON and Jimmy DURANTE.

Hopper began to host a chatty radio show in 1936 and two years later was a syndicated columnist challenging the reign of the veteran Hollywood gossip Louella Parsons. S. J. Perelman once described their rivalry as "sugar and strychnine". Hopper was the first to identify the title character in CITIZEN KANE (1941) with newspaper tycoon William Randolph Hearst, who happened to be Parsons's employer.

When David O. SELZNICK chose the British actress Vivien LEIGH to play Scarlett in GONE WITH THE WIND (1939), Hopper wrote furiously that "out of millions of American women, David couldn't find *one* to suit him." She also persecuted such stars as Constance BENNETT and Rex HARRISON, whose career she continually described as finished. In 1949 she reluctantly had to present him with the Tony Award for his performance in *Anne of the Thousand Days*; Harrison later commented "It was better than a beheading."

Her son, William Hopper Jnr, (1915–1970) appeared in such movies as THE MALTESE FALCON (1941), REBEL WITHOUT A CAUSE (1955), and *Myra Breckinridge* (1970).

horror films   Like the thriller, the horror film is defined in terms of its intended emotional impact. While its outward form may range from SCIENCE FICTION to gothic FANTASY or psychological crime drama, the horror film will always strive to generate fear or revulsion. Its major themes are death, sex, and religion (preferably all three at once).

Horror has been an important genre throughout cinema history, with many early silent films testifying to the new medium's power to disturb. The first important examples hailed from Germany; these included Robert Weine's EXPRESSIONIST fable THE CABINET OF DR CALIGARI (1919), and F. W. MURNAU's NOSFERATU (1922), an unauthorized reworking of Bram Stoker's DRACULA. Like most vampire films, *Nosferatu* projects the fears of a society onto the outcast MONSTER. Later Dracula films – particularly those made by HAMMER – show the vampire penetrating the bastions of society (church and family) to offer a grotesque form of immortality.

In the 1930s UNIVERSAL brought such themes to American audiences with seminal versions of *Dracula* and FRANKENSTEIN (both 1931), starring Bela LUGOSI and Boris KARLOFF respectively. Although the EDISON Company had produced a version of Mary Shelley's story in 1910, *Frankenstein*'s true forebear was another German film, Paul Wegener's *The Golem* (1920), in which an artificial human being is created and goes on the rampage. The message of such created-monster films is clear: there are areas in which humans are not meant to dabble.

Unlike most of the Universal classics, which externalize the monster, such films as *Dr Jekyll and Mr Hyde* (1932) and THE WOLF MAN (1941) show the beast erupting from within. Feminist or post-Freudian readings of such films – that lycanthropy offers men the chance to act out their deepest and most repressed desires – seem quite appropriate. Subsequent werewolf films, such as Hammer's *The Curse of the Werewolf* (1960), explicitly linked lycanthropy with deviant sexuality. In 1957 American International released *I Was a Teenage Frankenstein* ("Body of a boy...Mind of a monster...Soul of an unearthly thing!") and *I Was a Teenage Werewolf*. These films recognized that, for young people, horror films often provided both an escape from reality and an adroit comment on their own perceived problems. The teenage monster in the first film is ugly (read: acne) while that in the second suffers perplexing biological changes (read: puberty).

By the 1960s Roger CORMAN's POE adaptations and Hammer's gothic classics were vieing for popular attention with more 'realistic' examinations of the monster within. Michael POWELL's *Peeping Tom* (1959) and HITCHCOCK's PSYCHO (1960) explored the deadly desires of apparently nice young men in a manner far removed from Hammer's fantasy world.

Over the next few years the boundaries of 'taste' were pushed back by such low-budget independent productions as *Blood Feast* (1963), in which a young woman's leg is sawn off in the bath, and George Romero's zombie classic NIGHT OF THE LIVING DEAD (1968). In 1972 THE EXORCIST used a vast special-effects budget to create scenes of horror unprecedented in the mainstream cinema. Meanwhile the explicit gore of such non-horror films as PECKINPAH's *Straw Dogs* (1971) and WINNER's DEATH WISH series directly influenced vengeance dramas such as *Last House on the Left* (1972), directed by Wes CRAVEN, and the notorious *I Spit on Your Grave* (1979). Tobe Hooper's *The Texas Chainsaw Massacre* (1974) was one of the first SLASHER MOVIES, a blood-soaked genre that came to dominate horror production in the 1980s. Films of this type, featuring scenes of graphic mayhem in which teenagers met a variety of hideous deaths, included John CARPENTER's *Halloween* (1978), *Friday the 13th* (1980), and Craven's *A Nightmare on Elm Street* (1984).

Somewhat surprisingly, the 1990s saw a return to the gothic roots of the genre with *Bram Stoker's Dracula* (1993) and *Mary Shelley's Frankenstein* (1994). However, as THE SILENCE OF THE LAMBS (1990) had clearly demonstrated, the ultimate horror was not a man in a cape or a creature with bolts through his neck but the depravity of the human mind.

horses. *See* ANIMALS.

horse opera A humorous nickname for a WESTERN film.

Hoskins, Bob (1942–) Stocky British leading man, best known in tough-guy roles. A Londoner of working-class origin, he began his acting career in fringe theatre; his later work for the stage includes appearances with the RSC and in musicals, notably an acclaimed production of *Guys and Dolls* at the National Theatre. He made his film debut in *The National Health* (1973) but first became known to a wider public in the Dennis Potter television series *Pennies from Heaven* (1978), in which he played a travelling sheet-music salesman. His starring role in the London gangland drama *The Long Good Friday* (1980) led to his US debut in *The Honorary Consul* (1983), a disappointing Graham GREENE adaptation. Films of the mid 1980s included COPPOLA's *The Cotton Club* (1984), in which he played a tough nightclub owner, and Neil JORDAN's *Mona Lisa* (1986), as a petty criminal who becomes infatuated with a beautiful prostitute (Cathy Tyson); the part brought him an Oscar nomination for Best Actor.

Hoskins went on to enjoy his greatest commercial success to date as the parody gumshoe stooge to the animated hero of WHO FRAMED ROGER RABBIT? (1988). He himself commented on the blending of live-action and animated footage in this hugely successful film:

> It's verging on insanity. I spend all my time talking to characters who are not there, fighting weasels, and being thrown out of clubs by gorillas.

Subsequent roles have included CHER's handyman admirer in *Mermaids* (1990), and Mario the Brooklyn plumber, a computer-game superhero, in *Super Mario Brothers* (1992).

Howard. Leslie Howard (Leslie Stainer; 1893–1943) British actor best known for his gentle brooding roles, especially that of Ashley Wilkes in GONE WITH THE WIND (1939). He also directed and produced a number of features. Born in London, the son of Hungarian immigrants, Howard worked as a bank clerk before going on the stage in 1918. In the early 1920s he was a founder of Minerva Films, a small unsuccessful production company. He made his Hollywood debut in the curious life-after-death fable *Outward Bound* (1930); a some-

what similar film, *Berkeley Square* (1933), earned him an Oscar nomination for Best Actor. By the later 1930s Howard's low-key romantic style had established him as Hollywood's idea of the perfect Englishman (despite being a Hungarian Jew). He starred as the English hero of the French Revolution in Baroness Orczy's *The Scarlet Pimpernel* (1935) and subsequently appeared with Norma SHEARER in *Romeo and Juliet* (1936), with Bette DAVIS and Humphrey BOGART in *The Petrified Forest* (1936), and with Ingrid BERGMAN in *Intermezzo* (British title *Escape to Happiness*; 1939).

Howard was given the job of associate producer of the latter as an inducement to appear in *Gone with the Wind*. At 45 the actor felt he was too old for the part of Ashley (22 years younger in the book). He wrote, "I hate the damn part" and called the film "a terrible lot of nonsense."

Howard also played the role of Henry Higgins in the original version of Shaw's PYGMALION (1938), a film that he co-directed with Anthony ASQUITH. During the war he starred in such films as *The First of the Few* (US title *Spitfire*; 1942), a biography of R. J. Mitchell, the Spitfire designer. A year later he was killed in an air crash off Portugal. Rumours spread that he had been on a special mission for the British government or, alternatively, that his plane was downed by the Germans because they believed that Churchill was on board.

Trevor Howard (1916–88) British actor, who belied his gruff appearance by playing sensitive restrained characters. He began as a romantic lead and ended as a respected character actor, often playing the shabby Englishman abroad. A cricket fanatic, Howard insisted that his contracts contain a clause excusing him from filming during Test Matches.

Born in Kent, he made his debut on the London stage while a student at RADA. He served in the Royal Artillery during World War II but was invalided out. A year after making his first film, the war drama *The Way Ahead* (US title *Immortal Battalion*; 1944), Howard became an international star in David LEAN's classic BRIEF ENCOUNTER. The film starred Howard as the married doctor involved in a chaste affair with housewife Celia Johnson, whose shoulder he gamely squeezes when they finally part.

In 1947 Howard took the lead in Britain's first gangster film, *They Made Me A*

Fugitive (US title *I Became a Criminal*). He played the terse British major in Carol REED's THE THIRD MAN and later starred in the same director's Conrad adaptation *An Outcast of the Islands* (1951) – a movie *The Observer* called "the most powerful film ever made in this country". Further acclaim followed for *The Heart of the Matter* (1953), a Graham GREENE adaptation that starred Howard as the tormented deputy police commissioner in an African township. Another film with an African setting was John HUSTON's *The Roots of Heaven* (1958), in which Howard played a White Man trying to protect elephants.

Howard's roles of the 1960s and 1970s included the miner father in *Sons and Lovers* (1960), a performance that earned him an Oscar nomination, Captain Bligh in *Mutiny on the Bounty* (1962), the worldly wise priest in David Lean's *Ryan's Daughter* (1970), and Richard Wagner in VISCONTI's *Ludwig* (1973). Later films included SUPER-MAN (1978), GANDHI (1982), the comedies *The Missionary* (1982) and *Foreign Body* (1985), and *White Mischief* (1988), another film with a colonial setting.

The greatest screen actor Britain has ever produced.
BRIAN BAXTER.

Howe, James Wong (Wong Tung Jim; 1899–1976) Chinese-born cinematographer, whose LOW-KEY photography helped to set Warner Brothers' style in the 1940s. He was a pioneer of both the HAND-HELD CAMERA and the use of DEEP FOCUS. Howe won Academy Awards late in his career for *The Rose Tattoo* (1955) and *Hud* (1963).

Born in Kwantung, Canton, he moved to America with his family at the age of five. After a brief career as a teenage boxer, he settled in Los Angeles and worked as a delivery boy for a photographer. In 1917 he joined Cecil B. DE MILLE as a cutting-room helper and was quickly promoted to slate boy and then assistant cameraman.

Having photographed his first film, *Drums of Fate*, in 1923 he went on to make his name (then simply James Howe) with Paramount's *The Trail of the Lonesome Pine* that same year. For Victor FLEMING's *Mantrap* (1926) he carried out extensive location shooting in the wilds of Canada, while the Western *Viva Villa!* (1934) owed much of its impact to Howe's dark landscapes with brilliant clouds. Howe's other films of the 1930s included THE THIN MAN (1934), *The*

Prisoner of Zenda (1937), and the gangster drama *Algiers* (1938), which brought him an Oscar nomination.

During his association with Warners, which lasted from 1938 until 1947, Howe photographed a long series of melodramas and biopics. His moody photography for *King's Row* brought another Oscar nomination in 1942. When the director Robert ROSSEN wondered how to film the climactic prizefight in *Body and Soul* (1947), Howe struck on the idea of moving around the ring on roller skates with a hand-held camera. Similarly, he took some shots in *He Ran All the Way* (1951) while being pushed in a wheelchair.

After his Oscar for *The Rose Tattoo* (1955), Howe won a nomination for *The Old Man and the Sea* (1958), a second Oscar for the black-and-white *Hud*, and nominations for John FRANKENHEIMER's *Seconds* (1966) and his last film, *Funny Lady* (1975).

How many pages? A phrase used by a member of a film production team to enquire how much of the script will be shot that day.

Hudson, Rock (Roy Scherer Jnr; 1925–85) US actor. A major star of the late 1950s and early 1960s, he is best remembered for his bedroom comedies with Doris DAY. Although married for three years to his secretary Phyllis Gates, Hudson was homosexual; he later became the first Hollywood star to announce he was dying of AIDS.

Born in Winnetka, Illinois, Hudson served as a naval aircraft mechanic during World War II and returned to civilian life as a truck driver. After changing his name to Rock Hudson, he moved into films on the strength of his rugged good looks alone, having no acting experience. During the shooting of his first picture, Warner Brothers' *Fighter Squadron* (1948), he required 38 takes for his one line.

Hudson subsequently joined Universal, whose publicity department labelled him the 'Baron of Beefcake'. In the mid 1950s he became a star in three tearjerkers directed by Douglas SIRK: *Magnificent Obsession* (1954) and *All that Heaven Allows* (1955), both with Jane WYMAN, and *Written on the Wind* (1956), with Lauren BACALL. He was then loaned to Warners for *Giant* (1956), in which he played a rich Texas rancher opposed by his former employee (James DEAN). The part brought him his only Oscar nomination.

Hudson co-starred with Jennifer JONES in *A Farewell to Arms* (1957), a box-office failure, before joining Day in three successes, *Pillow Talk* (1959), *Lover Come Back* (1961), and *Send Me No Flowers* (1964). When these mild sex comedies began to look tame in the swinging 1960s, he made a radical departure from his usual screen image in John FRANKENHEIMER's terrifying science-fiction film *Seconds* (1966); although both Hudson and the critics considered this his best performance, the film flopped. Later movies included the adventure film *Ice Station Zebra* (1968), the sci-fi *Embryo* (1976), the disaster film *Avalanche* (1978), and a political thriller, *The Ambassador* (1984). Hudson also starred in the television series *McMillan and Wife* (1971–75) and appeared in the soap opera *Dynasty* (1985).

Hughes, Howard (1905–76) Eccentric US producer, director, aviator, and businessman, who helped to turn both Jean HARLOW and Jane RUSSELL into sex symbols. Although he enjoyed early success with *Hell's Angels* (1930) and *Scarface* (1932), Hughes's tendency to interfere with productions made him unpopular with directors. He was married to the actress Jean PETERS from 1957 to 1971.

Born in Houston, Texas, Hughes acquired the basis of his fortune when he inherited his father's oil-drilling tool company at the age of 18. Three years later he began to produce films with *Everybody's Acting* (1926) and the comedy *Two Arabian Knights* (1927), which brought Lewis MILESTONE an Oscar for Best Director.

The World-War-I fighter-pilot drama *Hell's Angels* is remembered for its flying sequences and for giving Jean Harlow her first starring role. When the director, Marshall Neiland, walked out after continual interference from Hughes, the latter took over in his place. Further success followed with *The Front Page* (1931), a brilliant comedy that won Oscar nominations as Best Picture and for director Milestone, and Howard HAWKS's *Scarface*, one of the first gangster classics.

Having become a major force in Hollywood, Hughes abandoned his film career to train under an assumed name as a co-pilot with American Airways. In the mid 1930s he broke several air-speed records, leading to the award of a Congressional Medal. After ten years away from the cinema, he

returned to launch Jane Russell and her cleavage in THE OUTLAW (1943); once again he fired the director (Hawks) and assumed that role himself. The release was delayed for years by censorship battles. In 1944 Hughes established the shortlived California Pictures with Preston STURGES and produced the melodrama *Vendetta*, a vehicle for his new protégée, Faith Domergue.

During the 1930s and 1940s Hughes was well known for dating such stars as Ginger ROGERS, Ava GARDNER, Lana TURNER, and Olivia DE HAVILLAND. When the last-named was erroneously linked to him by gossip columnist Louella Parsons, Hughes phoned de Havilland to say, "Now that we're engaged, don't you think we ought to meet?"

Following an air crash in 1946, Hughes became steadily more reclusive, disappearing completely from public view in the late 1940s. When he bought RKO for $9 million in 1948 many of its top staff deserted, a factor that contributed to the studio's $40-million losses over the next six years. In 1954 Hughes bought the outstanding stock and sold the studio to General Teleradio at a $10-million profit; by 1958 his film days had ended.

When Jean Peters divorced Hughes in 1971 she had not seen him for over ten years. Stories abounded about his living in a single Kleenex-lined room, his terror of flies and disease, and the length of his fingernails and hair. When he died 30 different wills were produced, leading to prolonged legal battles and the freezing of his fortune.

Huillet, Daniele *See* STRAUB, JEAN-MARIE.

Hulot, Monsieur The eccentric accident-prone character made famous by the French actor-director Jacques TATI. Hulot is a gangling pipe-smoking bachelor with a remarkable tennis style; his tangles with the modern machine age provide a number of very funny film sequences. In MONSIEUR HULOT'S HOLIDAY (1953) he causes havoc in a quiet seaside resort. The subsequent films – *Mon Oncle* (1958), *Playtime* (1968), and *Traffic* (1971) – have an element of social satire, with Hulot often playing a peripheral role.

Hunchback of Notre Dame, The *Notre Dame de Paris* (1831), Victor Hugo's tale of medieval Paris, has inspired at least six screen versions. The plot concerns Quasimodo, the deformed bellringer of Notre

Dame cathedral, and his love for the beautiful gypsy Esmeralda; when she is falsely accused of murdering her lover, Quasimodo rescues her and hides her within the cathedral, before losing his own life to the vengeful mob.

Three early versions of the story filmed under various titles were followed by Universal's silent *The Hunchback of Notre Dame* (1923), which starred Lon CHANEY as the grotesque bellringer and Patsy Ruth Miller as the gypsy girl. The movie made Chaney an international star but Universal somehow forgot to sign him and he moved on to MGM. The young William WYLER worked as an assistant director on the film, his only task being to yell a cue to hundreds of extras: "Pull up your tights and light your torches."

In 1939 RKO remade the film as a lavish sound spectacle with Charles LAUGHTON in the lead. The movie featured huge crowds of extras and elaborate medieval sets (compared to Universal's unconvincing backlot cathedral). Laughton, whose make-up put one eye two inches above the other, co-starred with Maureen O'HARA; able support was provided by Cedric HARDWICKE as the King's High Justice and Thomas Mitchell as the King of Beggars. William DIETERLE directed with aplomb while future director Robert WISE was co-editor.

Inferior in every respect was the French-Italian co-production *Notre Dame de Paris* (1956), starring Anthony QUINN and Gina LOLLOBRIGIDA.

Huppert, Isabelle (1955–) Freckle-faced French actress, who is equally comfortable playing exploited innocents, worldly women, and pitiless *femmes fatales*.

Born in Paris, Huppert trained at the Conservatoire National d'Art Dramatique. Although she made her screen debut at 16 in *Faustine et le bel été* (1971), she first drew critical attention as the teenager who gleefully loses her virginity in Bertrand BLIER's *Les Valseuses* (1974). She became an international star three years later in Claude Goretta's *The Lacemaker*, in which she played Pomme, a gentle girl whose sense of cultural and sexual inadequacy results in her mental breakdown. Goretta said of this character:

> She finds a sort of refuge in madness, in silence, because society isn't the way she hoped it would be. Still, when she looks into the camera...there is something peaceful and strong inside her, with a sort of defiance.

This quiet defiance can also be seen in many other Huppert characterizations: as Anne Brontë in André Téchiné's *Les Soeurs Brontë* (1978); as the victim of the class war in Maurice PIALAT's *Loulou* (1980); as Marguerite Gauthier in Mauro Bolognini's *The True Story of the Lady of the Camelias* (1981); as the blinded wife in Paul COX's *Cactus* (1986); as Emma in Claude CHABROL's *Madame Bovary* (1991); and as the nun turned pornographer in Hal Hartley's *Amateur* (1994). A touch of steel was added to her persona in Michael CIMINO's HEAVEN'S GATE (1980), Jean-Luc GODARD's *Slow Motion* (*Sauve qui peut*; 1980), and Chabrol's *Une Affaire des femmes* (1989), in which she played a madame, a prostitute, and a surrogate mother respectively.

She also took delight in tormenting the mistress of her lately dead husband in Jacques Doillon's *La Vengeance d'une femme* (1990). This cruel streak had been evident since her chilling performance as a teenage murderess in Chabrol's *Violette Nozière* (1977), which won her the Best Actress prize at Cannes. It was to recur in Bertrand TAVERNIER's *Clean Slate* (*Coup de torchon*; 1981), Joseph LOSEY's *The Trout* (1982), Blier's *My Best Friend's Girl* (1982), and Curtis Hanson's *The Bedroom Window* (1987). This collection of killers, *femmes fatales*, and good-time girls was a far cry indeed from the shy and sheepish Pomme.

Huston family The Canadian-born character actor Walter Huston (Walter Houghston; 1884–1950), his son the writer-director John Huston (1906–87), and John's daughter the actress Anjelica Huston (1952–). In 1947 THE TREASURE OF THE SIERRA MADRE produced Oscars for both father (Supporting Actor) and son (Director), while nearly 40 years later Anjelica Huston was named Best Supporting Actress for *Prizzi's Honour* (1985), which her father directed.

Walter Huston was born in Toronto and studied engineering before appearing in vaudeville. He made his Broadway debut in 1924 and five years later moved to Hollywood, where he won acclaim in the title role of D. W. GRIFFITH's *Abraham Lincoln* (1930). In 1936 he revived one of his most famous Broadway roles for the screen in *Dodsworth*, which his son John co-scripted.

Huston often played eccentric characters and rogues, including Mr Scratch (the devil) in *All That Money Can Buy* (1941) and the grumpy gold-seeker in *The Treasure of the Sierra Madre*. During World War II he made cameo appearances in two of his son's films, THE MALTESE FALCON (1941) and *In This Our Life* (1942); he also played opposite Katharine HEPBURN in *Dragon Seed* (1944), a propaganda piece about Chinese peasants fighting the Japanese. Despite his son's expertise as a screenwriter, Huston once proudly declared: "Hell, I ain't paid to make good lines sound good. I'm paid to make bad lines sound good."

John Huston was born in Nevada, Missouri, and appeared on stage at the age of three. He left school at 14 in order to box (in 1945 he put Errol FLYNN in hospital after a famous off-screen fistfight) and later served as a Mexican cavalry officer. In 1930 he followed his father to Hollywood, where he worked as a scriptwriter; two years later he travelled to Britain to write for Gaumont but was reduced to performing on the streets when the job fell through. After joining Warner Brothers in 1937, Huston won Oscar nominations for co-scripting *Dr Ehrlich's Magic Bullet* (1940) and *Sergeant York* (1941). That same year, he made his debut as a director with the brilliant Hammett adaptation THE MALTESE FALCON, which starred Humphrey BOGART as the private eye Sam Spade; the movie is often considered the first FILM NOIR.

When Huston received his military call-up by telephone in 1942, he was directing a scene from *All Around the Pacific*, in which Bogart is trapped in a building besieged by Japanese soldiers. Before departing, Huston ordered that the number of Japanese extras should be trebled, and all exits from the building boarded up; his note for his replacement (Vincent Sherman) read simply: "I'm in the army – Bogie will know how to get out."

For the next three years Huston served in the Signal Corps and made official war documentaries. After returning to Warner Brothers, he wrote and directed THE TREASURE OF THE SIERRA MADRE (1947), a fable about the destructive power of greed in which Bogart portrayed a drifter. When Huston promised the Mexican extras more money for falling off their horses, their representative made an offer: "For 50 pesos, señor, you can shoot them in the arms and legs. But, mind you, no killing." The director made two further movies with Bogart, the gangster melodrama *Key Largo* (1948) and the riverboat adventure THE AFRICAN QUEEN (1951), in which he co-starred with Katharine HEPBURN.

In the early 1950s Huston led the Committee for the First Amendment, a group that outspokenly attacked the House Un-American Activities Committee hearings as "morally wrong". After two decades spent mainly in Ireland, where he painted and bred horses in his spare time, he moved on to Mexico in the mid 1970s.

Huston's later movies are peculiarly varied in genre and style; he himself commented once, "I fail to see any continuity in my work from picture to picture." They include *Moby Dick* (1956) with Gregory PECK as Ahab, *The Misfits* (1961) with Clark GABLE and Marilyn MONROE, the biopic *Freud* (1962), the Old Testament epic *The Bible* (1966), the Western *Judge Roy Bean* (1972), the $35-million disaster *Annie* (1982), and the acclaimed Mafia comedy *Prizzi's Honour* (1985), starring Jack NICHOLSON and Kathleen TURNER. He died shortly after completing his last film, a sombre version of James Joyce's story *The Dead* (1988).

Huston also enjoyed an occasional career as an actor, graduating from bit parts in his own films to more substantial roles in *The Cardinal* (1963), CHINATOWN (1974), and a number of TV movies.

At the age of 16 **Anjelica Huston** appeared as a medieval nobleman's daughter in her father's flop, *A Walk with Love and Death* (1969); she later featured in both *Prizzi's Honour* (1985) and *The Dead* (1987). Her other films have included *The Last Tycoon* (1976), *Frances* (1982), about the tragic film actress Frances Farmer, *A Handful of Dust* (1988), and *The Addams Family* (1991). She was nominated for the Best Actress Oscar for both *Enemies, a Love Story* (1989) and Stephen FREARS's low-life drama *The Grifters* (1990). Her long and stormy love affair with the actor Jack NICHOLSON aroused considerable publicity in the 1980s.

hype The intense promotion, usually by a studio press office, of a film or star. Hype is always exaggerated and sometimes completely untrue. In the 1920s the aristocratic Delores del Rio was said to be "the richest girl in Mexico" while the silent star Theda BARA, actually a native of Ohio, was publicized as an exotic Egyptian who was born beneath the Sphinx. Nicknames were a popular form of hype: Clark GABLE was billed as "the King", Rita HAYWORTH as "the Love Goddess", Corinne Griffiths as "the Orchid Lady of the Screen", and Lon CHANEY as "the Man of a Thousand Faces". By the 1920s, Hollywood was hyping itself as "the Magic Empire of the 20th Century" and "the Mecca of the World."

Hollywood publicists have never been shy of making inflated claims, no matter how absurd; Cecil B. DE MILLE'S THE TEN COMMANDMENTS (1923) was advertised as "The mightiest dramatic spectacle of all the ages!" while the bland fantasy *Gabriel over the White House* (1933) carried the tag-line "It comes like a marching army to thrill the nation!...The picture that will make 1933 famous!" The Hal ROACH studio touted *One Million BC* (1940) as "The most exciting adventure in a million years!" while Universal International's publicity for THE CREATURE FROM THE BLACK LAGOON (1954) stated: "Not since the beginning of time has the world beheld terror like this!" For the masters of hype, bigger is always better: BEN-HUR (1959) boasted "a cast of 125,000!" while for *The Egyptian* (1954), 20th Century-Fox promised "10,965 pyramids, 5,337 dancing girls, one million swaying bulrushes, 802 sacred bulls." Busby BERKELEY claimed that his chorus girls sported "miles of silk, tons of feathers, and gallons of glitter."

In the pre-permissive era publicists delighted in raising salacious expectations that were invariably disappointed by the film itself. In 1943 *Devotion*, an innocuous biopic about the Brontë household, laboured under such publicity lines as "It tells ALL about those Brontë sisters!...the sweetness of love and the meaning of torment – she [Charlotte] learned them both together!" Similarly, the publicity for Universal's original DRACULA (1931)

screamed: "So evil, so fantastic, so degrading...Innocent girls lured to a fate truly worse than death!"

Bogus 'warnings' for the nervous or sensitive have been a favourite device for those publicizing horror films. During screening of the 1959 B-movie *Terror is a Man* a bell would be rung before the most 'terrifying' scenes, so that the squeamish could close their eyes. Similarly William Castle, the director of *Macabre* (1958), took out a policy insuring members of the audience for $1000 against death by fright. (This echoes the earlier publicity gimmick of ABBOTT AND COSTELLO, who insured themselves against claims from the families of anyone who died from laughing at their films.)

In the 1950s film-makers responded to the threat of television with a number of much-hyped GIMMICKS intended to enhance the cinematic experience; these included CINERAMA and other widescreen processes, 3-D, and SMELL-O-VISION.

Although such techniques appear primitive and laughable in today's sophisticated public-relations world, hype is plainly far from dead. Indeed, makers of BLOCKBUSTER movies in the 1980s and 1990s have been able to achieve feats of saturation coverage across the media that would have amazed earlier publicists. With its relentless advance publicity and numerous merchandizing spin-offs, Tim BURTON'S BATMAN (1989) has often been described as the most-hyped movie of all time, although JURASSIC PARK (1993) and *The Flintstones* (1994) must run it fairly close.

hyphen or **hyphenate** Hollywood nickname for someone who has two or more functions on a film production team, such as a writer-director or actor-director-producer.

I

IAIP *See* INTERNATIONAL ASSOCIATION OF INDEPENDENT PRODUCERS.

IATSE International Alliance of Theatrical and Stage Employees. A US and Canadian craft union for behind-the-scenes staff in the cinema; its members include camera and editing personnel, set-designers, make-up and costume artists, electricians, lab technicians, etc.

Iceberg Nickname of the US actress Grace KELLY, presumably a reflection of her cool beauty and aloof persona.

> A Dresden doll with a kind of platinum beneath the delicate porcelain, a beautiful girl who I felt was always in control of her world.
> MAURICE CHEVALIER.

idiot card *See* CUE CARD.

Ikiru (British title *Living*, US title *To Live*; 1952) Akira KUROSAWA's subtle exploration of the sterility of postwar Japanese life. In the plot a widowed civil servant, Watanabe (Takashi Shimura), discovers that he is suffering from terminal cancer with only a short time to live. This sudden realization forces him to re-examine his shallow over-structured life. The film follows him as he makes a series of uncomprehending anticlimactic attempts to live a life of pure hedonism. Meanwhile, flashbacks show the course of his earlier career and his growing alienation from his family.

Through Watanabe's predicament, Kurosawa asks questions about the purpose of living in a world apparently without meaning. For the postwar Japanese this is a world in the shadow of the mushroom cloud, in which the emperor has surrendered his divinity, and the pursuit of pleasure and success has largely replaced religion. Like the European existentialists, however, Kurosawa, finds a value in the struggle to be good despite, or perhaps because of, its absurdity. Eventually Watanabe forces through the building of a children's playground in the slums and dies content.

A rare example of a Kurosawa film in a modern setting, *Ikiru* is remarkable for its low-key photography (Asaichi Nakai), touching acting, and masterly depiction of bureaucracy.

Imax A WIDESCREEN system boasting the largest frame size in cinema history (71.09mm by 52.63mm, ten times the size of a standard 35mm frame). The film also incorporates six sound tracks. First exhibited at Expo 70 in Osaka, Japan, in 1970, Imax is now used mainly at theme parks and similar sites, where it is projected onto a dome or curved screen to provide a giant 'surround' picture.

IMP Independent Motion Picture Company. The US production company that was the main ancestor of UNIVERSAL studios. It was founded in 1909 by Carl Laemmle (1867–1939) in response to the attempts of the MOTION PICTURE PATENTS COMPANY to impose a monopoly on production and distribution. As Laemmle and other independent exhibitors held around half the market and were loath to pay for the Patent Company's licences, the obvious solution was to move into production and distribution. After creating IMP, Laemmle went on to organize a number of independents into the Motion Picture Distributing and Sales Company, which aggressively marketed their products to cinemas.

In his career with IMP Laemmle effectively invented two things that have become synonymous with US cinema – HOLLYWOOD and the STAR system. The creation of Hollywood was largely a result of the independents' attempts to find locations outside the reach of the East-Coast based Patents Company. Declaring that "Local color is the order of the day in motion picture making", IMP filmed in Cuba and Mexico before settling in Hollywood, then a small suburb of Los Angeles, in 1912. Los Angeles was chosen in preference to San

Francisco as it allowed a quick escape to Mexico if the Patent Company's agents came snooping. It was, however, the invention of stars that ensured the success of the company. While most producers kept their actors' profiles as low as possible in order to keep salaries down, Laemmle (as an exhibitor) recognized the value of a familiar face in drawing the public back to the cinema. In 1910 he poached Florence Lawrence, the popular but still anonymous BIOGRAPH GIRL, from the Biograph company by offering her a 40-fold pay rise. To maximize publicity, he planted a false story that the Biograph girl had died tragically, only to 'expose' this lie as an invention of Biograph, jealous of IMP's coup. In 1910 she became the first actor to receive a screen credit, in other words the first star. Later that year he achieved an even greater coup by poaching Mary PICKFORD, "The girl with the curls" from Biograph.

As the war with the Patents Company heated up in 1912, the battle lines were redrawn. That year Majestic left Laemmle's Sales Company and, with others, formed Mutual, a vertically integrated conglomerate. In response, Laemmle united IMP with Pat Powers Picture Plays, Bison, The New York Motion Picture Co., and others to create his own conglomerate – Hollywood's first major studio, Universal.

in. in-betweener In the making of ANIMATED films, a junior artist who provides *in-betweens*, i.e. the drawings that fill out the gaps between the pictures showing key actions or events. The latter are the work of the principal artist.

in camera or **in frame** or **in shot** Used of any person or thing that appears within the camera's field of view, and hence on the exposed film if the camera is taking.

in-camera effects SPECIAL EFFECTS that are created by the manipulation of the camera during filming rather than in post-production. These include changing film feed or speed to produce REVERSE, ACCELERATED, or SLOW motion and the use of FILTERS or special lenses to distort the images. Before the development of the OPTICAL PRINTER, DISSOLVES, MATTE shots, and other forms of MULTIPLE EXPOSURE were created by running the same piece of film through the camera more than once.

in-joke A joke included in a film for the benefit of a small group of people with special knowledge – normally either those involved in the production or obsessive movie buffs who can spot obscure cinematic allusions.

In-jokes are often included to honour behind-the-scenes staff who would not otherwise receive much prominence. For example, the villain of *Bill And Ted's Bogus Journey* (1992) was named De Nomolos after writer Ed Solomon. CAMEOS and uncredited appearances are a fertile source of in-jokes; in KING KONG (1933) the flight commander and chief observer of the aircraft that attack the giant ape are Ernest Schoedsack and Merian Cooper, the director and producer of the film.

Such jokes may also be included to increase the film's appeal to a particular, often genre, audience, who feel flattered by getting the point. For example, the opening sequence of the Stephen King movie *Cat's Eye* includes miniature homages to several earlier King films. The MOVIE BRAT generation of directors – SPIELBERG, COPPOLA, and their contemporaries – often refer to their own, each others', and older films in this manner. Close observers will notice that part of the undercarriage of the giant spacecraft at the end of Spielberg's *Close Encounters of the Third Kind* (1977) is made up of R2D2, the robot from STAR WARS (1977).

In recent years, whole films have evolved out of a culture of in-jokes; the *Wayne's World* (1992, 1993) and *Gremlins* (1984, 1990) movies, for example, feature extended pastiche sequences. The first of the *Gremlins* films – directed by Joe Dante, an inveterate in-joker – features one of the best. At an inventors' convention, a man is seen speaking on the telephone in the background, while a replica of the time-travel device from *The Time Machine* (1960) is starting up behind him. When, a few minutes later, we cut back to him, the machine has vanished, leaving gawping spectators.

In recent years, no film has included more Hollywood in-jokes than Robert ALTMAN's satire on the movie business *The Player* (1991). When Whoopi GOLDBERG, playing a police inspector, visits a studio on business she picks up an Oscar statuette and makes a brief mock speech; Goldberg had in fact made a similar speech when accepting the Oscar for *Ghost* the previous year. More obscurely, the film begins with an eight-minute TRACKING SHOT through the studio's offices, during which a character is overheard to complain that film directors never use long takes nowadays.

in the can A phrase used to indicate that the shooting of a scene has been satisfactorily completed and that the film is ready to be developed. It is also used to mean that *all* shooting on a production is finished and that the film is ready for post-production. The phrase alludes to the cans in which exposed film is taken from the set or location to the lab.

In the Heat of the Night (1967) Norman Jewison's dramatic thriller about the relationship between a bigoted Southern sheriff and a Northern Black detective working together on a murder case. It won the Academy Award as Best Picture, with Oscars also going to Rod STEIGER as the sheriff, screenwriter Sterling Silliphant (who adapted John Ball's novel *Heat*), and editor Hal ASHBY.

The police chief of Sparta, Mississippi, desperate to solve the murder of a prominent industrialist, is shocked to find that the Black suspect he has arrested is Virgil Tibbs (Sidney POITIER), a homicide lieutenant from Philadelphia. Tibbs is assigned to the case over the head of the chief, whose initial prejudice is eventually replaced by respect for his cool companion.

While full of praise for the idea of a thriller in which the crime is solved by racial collaboration, Steiger added realistically, "It's not going to stop the riots in Chicago." Poitier carried his detective character through two sequels, *They Call Me Mister Tibbs!* (1970) and *The Organization* (1971), both set in San Francisco.

Four years earlier, MGM made *In the Cool of the Day*, an unrelated film set in Greece.

Ince, Thomas H(arper) (1882–1924) Early US producer and director generally credited with formalizing the STUDIO SYSTEM.

Having begun as a child actor, Ince followed a vaudeville and theatre career that led to some film roles for IMP in 1910; he also directed for the company before moving on to New York Motion Pictures a year later. Having established his **Inceville** studio outside Los Angeles, he specialized in making Westerns and epics, working with a Wild West show of "350 people, including riders, actors, cowboys, and girls, Indians, horses, steers, mules, equipment and paraphernalia." *Custer's Last Raid* (1912) restaged the Battle of Little Big Horn with Sioux extras, while *The Battle of Gettysburg* (1914) required 800 extras to recreate the battle

scenes, which were shot from different angles by eight cameras.

Such complex undertakings taught Ince the necessity of production schedules and detailed SHOOTING SCRIPTS; from 1912 onwards he increasingly turned his organizational and entrepreneurial skills to rationalizing an industry hitherto characterized by spontaneity and a degree of chaos. Although he has been called "a routine director and a mediocre editor" his all-round knowledge of the industry equipped him to become, in effect, the first modern PRODUCER.

By 1915 he had ceased directing. Working with a team of eight directors, he produced a steady stream of films, gradually formalizing a system in which producers scheduled and budgeted a range of simultaneous productions, marshalling creative teams to each film. He nevertheless remained intimately involved with all his productions, determining camera positions, writing dialogue, and editing the footage. His showman's eye for talent soon spotted William S. Hart (1870–1946), solemn-faced star of many silent Westerns, and leading man Charles Ray (1891–1943), both of whom became popular stars; he also recognized in Frank Borzage (1893–1962) a talent for directing sentimental romantic dramas.

Ince's last major production was *Civilisation* (1916), a pacifist epic of war and peace. Thereafter he produced mainly pot-boilers before dying in suspicious circumstances while on board the yacht of William Randolph Hearst.

incidental music *See* MUSIC.

incident light The light that falls on a subject, as opposed to that reflected from it. Although amateur film-making requires only the use of reflected-light metres (usually incorporated within the camera), professional cinematography demands the use of metres to read incident light as well.

independent. independent film-making The production of films without the financial backing of a major Hollywood studio. Although obtaining finance from banks, government agencies, friends or relatives, etc. can be extremely problematic, such an arrangement often allows the film-maker a greater choice of subject and treatment than is usually provided by the Hollywood system.

In practice, independent film-making falls into two main categories. Firstly, there is the production of AVANT-GARDE or minority-interest films by a director who himself takes responsibility for raising finance. Since movies that employ radically new techniques or that deal with marginalized communities are unlikely to get mainstream funding, going independent is often the only option available. Some independent films have achieved considerable success through addressing markets that Hollywood has traditionally neglected, e.g. ethnic minorities, (Spike LEE's *She's Gotta Have It*, 1986), the HOMOSEXUAL community (*Go Fish*, 1994), or disaffected youth (EASY RIDER, 1969). The second type of independent film-making is the production of broadly commercial films by smaller companies. Since the decline of the major studios in the 1950s, this has become an increasingly important part of the industry. Independent films of this type range from the high-budget spectaculars of James CAMERON (e.g. the TERMINATOR movies) to the low-budget shockers of Roger CORMAN or Russ Meyer (1922–); the more high-brow works of John Sayles (1950–) or David Mamet (1947–) also come into this category. Works produced in this sector are often harder-hitting than the product of the major studios, as there is less fear of offending corporate sponsors or middle America.

The earlier 1980s saw a boom in independent film-making, with the role of the big studios dwindling increasingly to the provision of development finance, the rental of facilities, and, most importantly, the marketing and distribution of movies. Many independent companies did not, however, survive the recession of the later 1980s.

Independent Motion Picture Company. *See* IMP.

Indian cinema The history of the Indian cinema – now the largest in the world – begins with a show by representatives of the LUMIÈRE BROTHERS in Bombay on 7 July 1896. Although *actualité* shorts were being produced within a year, it was not until 1912 that *Pundalik*, India's first fiction short, was released (the film was made using imported equipment with a British director and crew). Indian cinema proper can be said to begin with *Raja Harischandra* (1913), the subcontinent's first feature; the director, Dabasheb Phalke (1870–1944), went on to make over 100 films in which he established many of the conventions followed by later movie-makers, notably in the fields of subject matter (mythical), length (epic), and style (gaudy).

While World War I brought about a temporary boom, the opening of the market in peacetime effectively wrecked the fledgling industry. In 1927–28 the Indian Cinematograph Committee reported that while distribution and exhibition were well advanced, Indian films held only 15% of the market. Although India already produced more films than Britain, these were judged "generally crude" and "defective in composition, acting, and every respect." Most Indian silent films were destroyed for recycling in World War II.

Sound came late to Indian cinema with *Alma Ara* (1931), directed by Ardeshir M. Ivani (who also made India's first colour film in 1937). This had the effect of fragmenting the vast Indian market into a number of smaller markets based on language, while at the same time squeezing out Western competition. As in the West, the result was the consolidation of the dominant-language cinema (Hindi) and the rise of a number of smaller regional cinemas (Bengali, Tamil, etc.). Sound also encouraged exhibitors to go into production, resulting in the formation of three large studios – Prabhat, New Theatres Ltd, and Bombay Talkies. In this highly creative period, film acted as a unifying force in an amazingly diverse society, providing almost the only form of widespread popular entertainment. Bombay soon became the centre of the Hindi industry, with hundreds of mythological and social dramas being produced every year by the mid 1940s. Among the many notable directors to begin their careers in the 1930s and 1940s were Bimal Roy (1909–66), K. A. Abbas (1914–87), Raj Kapoor (1924–88), and Prince P. C. Barua (1903–51).

A serious blow to artistic standards came in the aftermath of World War II, when an influx of black-market cash lured stars away from the studios into independent productions. The result has been described as "A star system without studio control, formula film-making without Hollywood's variety of formulas." In order to appeal to as wide an audience as possible, Hindi films aimed at the lowest common denominator, eschewing social drama for soap-operas set amongst India's Westernized middle classes. The moral of these stories is invariably conservative, with the hero rejecting new-fangled city ways and returning to the bosom of his family. The other standard genre was the mythological melodrama, the ingredients of which have been itemized as:

Songs (six or seven) in voices we know and trust; dance, solo or ensemble – the more frenzied the better; bad girl, good girl, bad guy, good guy, romance but no kisses; tears, guffaws, fights, chases, melodrama.

The unifying role of Indian cinema declined rapidly in the post-independence period, as anti-British sentiment was replaced by regional feeling. The regional cinemas also received a major boost from government funding policy in the 1950s, which aimed to stimulate production outside Bombay. By the mid 1980s three other languages had outstripped Hindi in terms of the numbers of films produced, with Madras becoming the new capital of the industry.

Although the number of films continued to increase during the post-war era, the general quality was little improved. The most notable exception was provided by the work of Satjavit RAY, the most acclaimed director yet to emerge in the Indian (Bengali) cinema. The international success of Ray's *Pather Panchali* (1955) showed that it was possible for a non-Hindi film to recoup its costs from the Western film-festival circuit. This proved a vital factor for many smaller language cinemas, especially Bengali, which lost half its market through partition. Other notable directors of the 'Indian New Wave' include Guru Dutt (1925–64), Ritwik Ghatak (1925–76), and Mrinal Sen (1923–   ).

More recently, increased competition from TV and satellite seems to be shaking Indian cinema from its complacency. The plots have become more violent, the heroes more antiheroic, and the heroines more sexual. Although this trend can be traced back to *Deewar* (1976), it has intensified in the 1990s with the Westernizing influence of TV. In 1994 the film *Bandit Queen* became a *cause célèbre* with its realistic exploration of the caste system.

ingénue A young and ingenuous female character in a film or play; also an actress who specializes in such roles. Notable screen ingénues include Leslie CARON in the

title role of *Gigi* (1958), Audrey HEPBURN in *Roman Holiday* (1953) and *Funny Face* (1957), Jane FONDA in such early films as *Cat Ballou* (1965) and *Barbarella* (1968), and Goldie HAWN in her earlier films.

Ingram. Rex Ingram (1895–1969) US Black actor, best known for playing De Lawd (i.e. God) in *The Green Pastures* (1936). Born aboard the riverboat *Robert E. Lee*, on which his father was a stoker, Ingram was educated at a military school in Chicago and later obtained a medical degree from Northwestern University.

At the age of 19 he suddenly decided to enter films, moving to Hollywood to make his debut in the silent short *Snatched from a Burning Death* (1915). Three years later he played an African native in *Tarzan of the Apes* (1918), the first of the TARZAN films. Equally small roles came his way in THE TEN COMMANDMENTS (1923), *The Thief of Bagdad* (1924), and KING KONG (1933). In the early 1930s he began appearing on Broadway.

Ingram became famous in the all-Black *The Green Pastures*, a charming retelling of Old Testament stories in a rural Louisiana setting. In addition to De Lawd – played as a cigar-smoking Black gentleman who encourages his people to live it up – Ingram also took the parts of Adam and Hezdrel. Ingram later played Lucifer in the all-Black CABIN IN THE SKY (1943), based on the 1940 Broadway musical. Other notable roles included Jim in *The Adventures of Huckleberry Finn* (1939) and the menacing but jovial Genie in the classic 1940 version of THE THIEF OF BAGHDAD.

Sadly, however, Black roles were few in the Hollywood of the 1940s and 1950s, and Ingram's promising career dissolved into a series of stereotyped parts in such films as *King Solomon's Mines* (1950), *Watusi* (1959), and ELMER GANTRY (1960). His last films included Otto PREMINGER's racial melodrama *Hurry Sundown* (1967) and the Western *Journey to Shiloh* (1968).

Rex Ingram (Reginald Ingram Montgomery Hitchcock; 1892–1950) Irish director of silent Hollywood spectaculars, who launched the 'Latin lovers' Rudolph VALENTINO and Ramon Novarro in the 1920s. Erich VON STROHEIM called him "the world's greatest director", while James Joyce mentioned "Rex Ingram, pageant-master" in *Finnegans Wake*. Both David LEAN and Michael POWELL have acknowledged his influence.

A clergyman's son, Ingram studied law in Dublin before emigrating to America at the age of 18. After several years during which he worked as a clerk in railway stockyards and took a sculpture class at Yale, he joined the Edison Company in New York as an actor, scriptwriter, and set designer. He then moved on to Vitagraph and to Fox, where he wrote scripts for Theda BARA. In 1916 he joined Universal to direct *The Great Problem* but was fired a year later after disagreements.

During World War I Ingram enlisted in Canada's Royal Flying Corps but the conflict ended before he saw action. In 1920 he joined Metro and decided to take a chance on the little-known Valentino in the lead role of *The Four Horsemen of the Apocalypse*; the film (which Ingram directed wearing a top hat) made the names of both director and star. It also starred Alice Terry, whom Ingram married in 1922; the three teamed up again to make *The Conquering Power* (1921). Ingram's other great discovery of the early 1920s, Ramon Novarro, starred in *The Prisoner of Zenda* (1922), *Scaramouche* (1923), and *The Arab* (1924), the latter shot in North Africa.

When Metro became part of MGM, Louis B. MAYER reneged on his promise that Ingram could direct BEN-HUR (1925). In disgust, Ingram established his own Victorine Studios in Nice; although his later films were released through MGM, the director always referred to the company as 'Metro-Goldwyn', pointedly omitting Mayer. These late works included Ingram's personal favourite *Mare Nostrum* (1926) and an adaptation of Somerset Maugham's *The Magician* (1926), a key film in the development of the horror genre.

Following the arrival of sound, Ingram made one talkie in Morocco, *Baroud* (1932), in which he himself played the lead, before retiring from films. He lived for a while in Cairo, then returned to America to write, sketch, and sculpt.

ink. inker In the making of ANIMATED films, the artist who uses acetate ink to trace onto the CELLS the drawings supplied by the animator.

inky-dinky A small (hence *dinky*) lighting device that supplies incandescent (hence *inky*) light for studio work. Their power usually ranges from 100 to 250w.

insert A brief self-contained shot that is INTERCUT with other material at the editing stage, usually as a means of conveying some relevant information; one of the commonest forms of insert is the sudden CLOSE-UP on a newspaper headline.

insert stage A small studio for the filming of INSERTS; these are usually DETAIL SHOTS of inanimate objects, e.g. a close-up of the protagonist's wristwatch (although the wrist we see is unlikely to belong to the star).

INT Interior. The notation in a script that indicates an indoor shot. The term *interior action* refers to anything filmed indoors, whether in a studio or on location.

intercutting Cutting back and forward between two or more different pieces of action to build up a single film scene. Simple examples include the use of REACTION SHOTS or other CUTAWAYS. When the editor cuts between PARALLEL ACTION in different locations (e.g. a racing train and a speeding car heading for the same level crossing), the term CROSS-CUTTING is generally used in preference.

intermittent movement The stop-go action of film as it is fed through a CAMERA or PROJECTOR; while the film as a whole needs to pass the aperture at a regular speed, there must be a brief pause as each frame is exposed or projected individually. The development of a mechanism that could produce this stop-go effect without jerking or tearing the film proved a stumbling block in the early days of cinema. Two innovations were particularly important, the **Maltese cross** and the **Latham loop**; the former is a type of gear (originally used in Swiss watch-making) that converts the regular motion of a constantly revolving drive shaft into single-frame advance as the film passes the GATE, while the latter is simply a loop of film that is allowed to build up on either side of the gate, thus providing enough slack to prevent damage to the film.

International Association of Independent Producers (IAIP) A Hollywood-based organization of INDEPENDENT FILM producers and production companies. Its members collaborate on projects, exchange ideas and information and share equipment; the Association also conducts workshops and seminars in America, Europe, and other parts of the world.

intertitle A TITLE card introduced during a film sequence to provide information in written form. In silent films intertitles were widely used to summarize dialogue or plot developments that could not readily be inferred from the action. Early sound films sometimes used them to indicate time or place or set the mood of a story; they are now rarely employed except for comic effect (as in Kaurismäki's eccentric *Leningrad Cowboys Go America*, 1989). *See also* CAPTION; SUBTITLE.

Intolerance (1916) D. W. GRIFFITH's epic treatment of intolerance through the ages. In *The Rise and Fall of Free Speech in America*, the pamphlet Griffith issued in defence of THE BIRTH OF A NATION in 1915, he wrote:

> The integrity of free speech and publication was not attacked seriously in this country until the arrival of the *motion picture*, when this new art was seized by the powers of intolerance as an excuse for an assault on our liberties...Intolerance is the root of all censorship. Intolerance martyred Joan of Arc. Intolerance smashed the first printing press. Intolerance invented Salem witchcraft.

Ultimately he chose four other examples to illustrate his theme in the film: the conquest of Babylon by Cyrus the Persian, the St Bartholomew's Day Massacre, the Crucifixion of Christ, and a modern tale of New York tenement life called 'The Mother and the Law', which Griffith had already been working on when the idea for his grander design occurred to him.

Intolerance was far and away the most ambitious project ever attempted in Hollywood. In addition to 60 named characters and thousands of extras, the film boasted eight assistant directors, four of whom would become well known in their own right during the 1920s: Allan DWAN, Tod Browning, Erich VON STROHEIM, and Christy Cabanne. Fourteen months in preparation, the film allegedly cost some $2 million, with the Belshazzar's feast sequence alone costing more than twice the entire budget of *The Birth of a Nation*. The set for this episode was inspired by the Tower of Jewels exhibit that Griffith and his cameraman Billy Bitzer had seen at the San Francisco Exposition in 1915. The TAVIANI BROTHERS' 1987 film *Good Morning, Babylon* was a fantasy on the part played in the construction of these sets by Italian immigrant workers.

Griffith originally planned to release an eight-hour version of the film in two parts, but eventually cut it down to a single three-and-a-half hour print; in its final form the film featured a number of sequences TINTED according to their atmosphere or content. Although *Intolerance* was later to inspire film-makers as diverse as EISENSTEIN, PUDOVKIN, Fritz LANG, Abel GANCE, and Cecil B. DE MILLE, it was a critical and commercial failure on its initial release. Critics pointed out that its complex narrative structure led to confusion within the individual tales, while the Huguenot story was accorded too little screen time. The film also flopped at the US box office, being withdrawn after just 22 weeks. Griffith spent the rest of his life paying off the colossal debt that the picture had incurred.

invisible. invisible cutting The 'seamless' style of EDITING that has dominated mainstream cinema since its adoption by Hollywood in the 1920s. Its invention is usually credited to the German director G. W. PABST. While the MONTAGE technique of Pabst's contemporary EISENSTEIN aimed to stimulate an intellectual response by the juxtaposition of obviously discrete images, Pabst's invisible cutting aimed to be as unobtrusive as possible, so that nothing should distract the audience from character and narrative. The general rule is to cut on action (*see* CUTTING ON ACTION), as the audience tends to be sufficiently intent upon the action not to notice the change from one camera angle or position to another. Such cuts are often used to compress inert cinematic time, as when a character has to walk down a long street or room, without the audience noticing. Hollywood later developed a whole series of rules of thumb, such as the convention of beginning a scene with an ESTABLISHING SHOT, then moving in to a MEDIUM SHOT of the principals, then using REACTION SHOTS to illustrate their dialogue, etc., from these basic principles.

The Invisible Man The protagonist of H. G. Wells's novel of 1897, an inventor who discovers a means of becoming invisible only to develop criminal inclinations. The character, whose name is Griffin, was first brought to the screen in James WHALE's *The Invisible Man* (1933). Claude RAINS, who played the part, became an overnight star despite being unseen for virtually the whole of the film; Boris KARLOFF had earlier turned the role down for this reason. The story gave scope for some of the most imaginative special effects yet seen. The sequence in which the scientist removes his bandages and appears to be invisible beneath them was created by filming the scene against a black velvet background, underneath the bandages being a stuntman covered in black velvet. The 1940 'sequel' *The Invisible Man Returns* featured Vincent PRICE in his first starring role; this time around the protagonist was an honest invisible man, trying to clear his name. The same year saw the release of a poor SCREWBALL COMEDY *The Invisible Woman*, with John BARRYMORE as a scientist who makes Virginia Bruce disappear. In the wartime *The Invisible Agent* (1942), Griffin's son (Jon Hall), having inherited his father's secret, uses it to thwart Peter LORRE's Japanese villain. Hall returned in 1944 for *The Invisible Man's Revenge*.

Invisibility played only a minor part in the plot of *The Invisible Boy* (1957), which was really a starring vehicle for Robby the Robot of *Forbidden Planet* (1956) fame. In 1958 a freely adapted Mexican version of the original story starred Arturo de Cordova; a similarly loose West German version starring Ivan Desny appeared in 1963. The 1933 German movie *An Invisible Man Goes through the City* was a comedy with no connection at all to the other films.

Memoirs of an Invisible Man (1992) was a flop Chevy CHASE comedy that attempted to show the lighter side of the invisible predicament.

iris (1) An adjustable mask-like device placed over the lens of a camera and used to control the size of the aperture; so-called because its action resembles that of the iris in the human eye. (2) A type of FADE, mainly used to open or close a scene in silent films, that was created by adjusting an iris. In the **iris-in**, a small circle of light appears in the centre of a dark screen and expands to reveal the scene; the process is reversed in the **iris-out**. An iris-out could also be used to concentrate the audience's attention on a particular character, while the iris-in could provide ironic or dramatic effects, as the image expanded to reveal something unexpected.

Iron Butterfly The Hollywood nickname for Jeanette MACDONALD, a US star of the 1930s best known for the series of screen operettas in which she appeared with Nelson EDDY. The pair were sometimes known as the **Singing Capon** and the Iron Butterfly, especially by those who found their popularity inexplicable. The nickname Iron Butterfly has also been used occasionally of Julie ANDREWS.

Irons, Jeremy (1948–) British actor with a theatrical background; while greatly admired in America, he has still to secure the status of a major screen star in his homeland. Born on the Isle of Wight, Irons trained at the Old Vic School in Bristol and achieved his first break playing John the Baptist to David Essex's Christ in *Godspell*. Having made his film debut as the choreographer Fokine in Ken RUSSELL's *Nijinsky* (1980), he became internationally known as Charles Ryder in the TV adaptation of *Brideshead Revisited*.

Over the next few years Irons brought suitable gravitas to Karel REISZ's *The French Lieutenant's Woman* (1981), in which he played opposite Meryl STREEP, Harold Pinter's screen adaptation of his stage hit *Betrayal* (1983) and *Swann in Love* (1984), Volker SCHLÖNDORFF's skilful Proust adaptation. His most impressive early roles were the foreman of a Polish building gang in Jerzy SKOLIMOWSKI's *Moonlighting* (1982) and the Jesuit Gabriel in Roland JOFFE's *The Mission* (1986).

Just as his film career was taking off, Irons took a sabbatical from the screen to join the Royal Shakespeare Company (alongside his wife Sinead Cusack) in 1987. His only film in this period was *Danny, Champion of the World* (1987) – another family affair featuring his son Sam and father-in-law Cyril Cusack. Still unwilling to take the Hollywood plunge, Irons next went to Canada to play the twin gynaecologists Beverly and Elliot Mantle in David CRONENBERG's *Dead Ringers* (1988). Five years later he rejoined the director to play a diplomat who falls for a Chinese transvestite in the resistible *M. Butterfly* (1993).

Following a disappointing outing in Michael WINNER's Ayckbourn adaptation *A Chorus of Disapproval* (1988), Irons was finally lured to Hollywood by Barbet Schroeder for *Reversal of Fortune* (1990). His performance as Claus von Bülow, the aristocratic émigré accused of the attempted murder of his wife (Glenn CLOSE), brought him an Oscar as Best Actor. Since then he has been tempted back into the Hollywood mainstream only once, when he rejoined Close and Streep for Bille August's *House of the Spirits* (1993). As he himself has commented:

> I find working for money and nothing else just *totally* soul destroying. I've *always* wanted to work with the best directors and on material that interests *me*.

In 1992 alone he played the title role in Steven Soderbergh's *Kafka*, the fenland schoolteacher reliving his past in *Waterland*, and the Tory MP who seduces his son's fiancée in Louis MALLE's *Damage*. More recently he voiced the would-be usurper Mufasa in Disney's *The Lion King* (1994).

it. **It Girl** One of the best-known Hollywood nicknames; it was given to Clara BOW, a leading actress of the silent era, who was widely considered the sexiest woman in films. *It* was a humorous synonym for sex appeal popularized by the writer Elinor Glyn in her novel of that name. Bow acquired the name after appearing in *It* (1927), the film version of Glyn's story, in which she portrayed a vivacious pouting flapper. Redhaired and exuberant, Bow epitomized the spirit of the Jazz Age, hence another of her nicknames, the **Jazz Baby**.

It Happened One Night (1934) The SCREWBALL COMEDY that established the reputation of its director, Frank CAPRA. In the plot, runaway heiress Claudette COLBERT sets off across America to marry an indolent playboy, only to find romance with abrasive reporter Clark GABLE – whose interest in her is initially sparked by the $10,000 reward offered for her return. Adapted by Robert Riskin from Samuel Hopkins Adams's story 'Night Bus', *It Happened One Night* was the SLEEPER of 1934 and became the first movie to sweep the Big Five Oscars – Best Picture, Director, Actor, Actress and Screenplay (an achievement only matched since by ONE FLEW OVER THE CUCKOO'S NEST, 1974, and THE SILENCE OF THE LAMBS, 1992).

Yet this was the film that no-one really wanted to make. Overcoming a conviction that bus movies were box-office poison, Harry COHN, the detested boss of Columbia, set about acquiring loaned stars in the studio's customary manner. Having been turned down by Robert Montgomery, Myrna LOY, Constance BENNETT, Miriam Hopkins and Margaret Sullavan, he finally landed Gable and Colbert, both of whom were in disfavour with their own studios. Gable was assigned to the project by MGM as part of his punishment for refusing to attend

reshoots for *Dancing Lady*, while Paramount was keen to see some return on Colbert's contract after a run of disappointments. Understandably, neither star was particularly enthusiastic about the project. Demanding double her usual fee, Colbert reported for work shortly after Thanksgiving insisting that she should be released by Christmas. For his part, Gable (who had recently undergone surgery to remove his appendix and tonsils) arrived on the back of a heavy drinking spree brought on by persistent toothache and the collapse of his second marriage. However, their eventual enjoyment is clear from such classic scenes as the lessons in hitchhiking, dunking doughnuts, and how men undress – not to mention the 'wall of Jericho' episode, in which Gable uses a blanket to divide their motel room to observe the proprieties.

Nevertheless, Colbert still told friends that she had "just finished the worst picture in the world" and her judgment seemed sound when the film closed after just a week in New York. Appropriately, however, it proved to be a blockbuster on the road, reviving Colbert's flagging career and setting Gable on his way to becoming 'King of Hollywood'.

Perhaps the most surprising consequence of *It Happened One Night* was the creation of BUGS BUNNY, who, animator Bob Clampett claimed, had been inspired by the sight of Gable eating a carrot in the film.

It's a Wonderful Life (1946) Frank CAPRA's sentimental story about a suicidal bankmanager who comes to realize the true value of his life to those around him; for many, it is the archetypal piece of 'Capra corn'. Capra later recalled his reaction on first seeing the story:

> It was the story I had been looking for all my life! Small town. A man. A good man, ambitious. But so busy helping others, life seems to pass him by. Despondent. He wishes he'd never been born. He gets his wish. Through the eyes of a guardian angel he sees the world as it would have been had he not been born. Wow! What an idea.

The 'idea' belonged to Philip Van Doren Stern, who had circulated a privately printed edition of the story as a Christmas greeting in 1939. RKO had failed three times to develop the tale into a filmable script for Cary GRANT and Jean ARTHUR before Capra took an option to make it for his own Liberty Films.

Capra had not completed a feature since 1942, although he had supervised the production of the seven films in the acclaimed *Why We Fight* series. He was keen to use James STEWART, his leading man in MR SMITH GOES TO WASHINGTON (1939), but the actor (who had served in the USAF during the war and had not made a feature since 1941) was undergoing a crisis of confidence. Even though he accepted the role of George Bailey, it was not until Lionel BARRYMORE (who played his chief adversary, Mr Potter) assured him that his talent had not deserted him that Stewart began to enjoy the experience: "After a week or so of working I just knew I was going to be all right." In fact, Stewart emerged as a much-improved actor. While *It's a Wonderful Life* gave him the chance to demonstrate the decency that had characterized his prewar roles, it was also the first film to reveal a darker side. This would later be exploited in the thrillers of Alfred HITCHCOCK and the psychological Westerns of Anthony MANN.

While for Stewart the picture was the start of a new phase, for Capra it signalled the beginning of the end, as his brand of sentimental Americana went out of fashion in a new age of cynicism. As Stewart recalled decades later: "I don't think it was the type of story people wanted just after the war...Our movie just got lost." Yet the film did have its adherents, including Humphrey BOGART, who apparently screened his personal copy for family and friends every Christmas Day. The film's Yuletide setting and 'auld lang syne' sentiments soon made it an essential part of television schedules over the festive season, with George's impassioned plea to the angel Clarence (Henry Travers) bringing lumps to the throat of viewers worldwide:

> Get me back. Get me back. I don't care what happens to me. Get me back to my wife and kids. Help me, Clarence. Please! Please! I wanna live again. I wanna live again! I wanna live again! Please, God, let me live again!

See also CHRISTMAS.

Ivan the Terrible (Part One, 1944; Part Two, *The Boyars' Plot*, 1945; Part Three, *Ivan's Struggles*, 1945 – destroyed) Sergei EISENSTEIN's uncompleted trilogy about the reign of Tsar Ivan IV, who did much to forge the Russian empire in the 16th century. In 1928 Eisenstein wrote that if he ever made a film about the despotic Ivan he would

depict him as a "merchant-tsar" and not as "a personality in the manner of Edgar Allen Poe" as this "would hardly interest the young Soviet worker." His eventual portrait counterpoised the traditional view of "a Mephistophelian figure, a Tsar who was a wild beast", with a more analytical view of the relationship between Ivan the ruler and Ivan the man.

Considering that "the grandeur of our theme necessitated a grandiose design", Eisenstein abandoned the MONTAGE aesthetic that had informed his earlier films. Instead, he drew on the art of El Greco and the stylized expression of Wagnerian opera, Marinskian ballet, and Japanese Kabuki theatre to achieve a total fusion of sound and image, lighting and colour. Even the cast, led by Nikolai Cherkasov, was asked to adapt the angular postures proposed by Vsevolod Meyerhold in his biomechanical theory of acting in order to complement the MISE-EN-SCÈNE. Production began on all three films simultaneously at the Alma-Ata studios in central Asia in 1943. Rather than a SHOOTING SCRIPT, Eisenstein used a series of STORYBOARD sketches. It was from these alone that Sergei Prokofiev scored the films, the director insisting that his music should be "an active participant in the drama...filling it with a parallel developing action of emotional sound."

Part One was released in late 1944 and was awarded the Stalin Prize for its artistic achievement. Eisenstein suffered a heart attack at the party thrown to celebrate and friends kept from him the news that Part Two had incurred Stalin's wrath for its ambivalent attitude towards Ivan's secret police, the *oprichniki*. In August 1946 it was banned by the Party Central Committee for "ignorance in the presentation of historical fact." Six months later Eisenstein, still only partially recovered, appealed personally to Stalin for an opportunity to emend the offending scenes. Although this was granted, all he completed before his death was the reshooting of the concluding sequence on Agfacolor stock, which had been confiscated from the retreating Nazi forces. The film was withheld until 1958 and the completed reels of Part Three were destroyed. In the circumstances, it seems little short of miraculous that *The Boyars' Plot* survives in the form in which Eisenstein intended it to be shown.

Ivory, James   *See* MERCHANT-IVORY.

J

Jackson, Glenda (1936–) British actress, who abandoned her dramatic career on being elected a Labour MP in 1992. Of working-class origins, Jackson worked as an assistant on the cosmetics counter at Boots before enrolling at RADA. She first came to public attention in 1961, when she inherited Diana Rigg's place in the Royal Shakespeare Company after the latter left to star in television's *The Avengers*. Her film debut followed in 1967, when she appeared in the screen version of the RSC's *Marat/Sade*. She went on to combine theatre work with regular roles on both television and in the cinema; despite her somewhat unglamorous looks she tended initially to be cast in 'sexy' roles (even being described at one point as "Britain's First Lady of the Flesh").

Although *Women in Love* (1969), Ken RUSSELL's film of the D. H. Lawrence classic, brought Jackson an Academy Award, her next film, Russell's *The Music Lovers* (1971), was slated. Both contained controversial nude scenes. Controversy also attended John SCHLESINGER's *Sunday Bloody Sunday* (1971), in which she and Peter FINCH compete for the affections of a bisexual designer (Murray Head). That same year Jackson played the role most closely associated with her name – that of Elizabeth I – in the television series *Elizabeth R*. In the quest for authenticity, she was filmed entering the Tower of London through the real Traitor's Gate, the first time the gate had been opened for some 100 years. Though some thought her miscast as the Virgin Queen, Jackson was invited to recreate the role for the big screen in *Mary Queen of Scots* (1971), with Vanessa REDGRAVE as Mary.

Having won an Emmy Award for *Elizabeth R*, Jackson collected a second Oscar the following year for the romantic comedy *A Touch of Class* (1972). Subsequent films included *A Bequest to the Nation* (1973), about the relationship of Nelson and Lady Hamilton, Joseph LOSEY's *The Romantic Englishwoman* (1974), and *Hedda* (1976), a screen version of her stage performance as Ibsen's tragic heroine. *The Incredible Sarah* (1976) saw her playing the legendary Sarah Bernhardt, while in *Stevie* (1978) she portrayed the eccentric poet Stevie Smith. Her films of the 1980s included *Hopscotch* (1980), *Turtle Diary* (1985), and *Business as Usual* (1987). In Ken Russell's adaptation of Lawrence's *The Rainbow* (1989) Jackson played the mother of the character she had played 18 years earlier in *Women in Love*.

According to Jackson herself, however, the high point of her acting career was an appearance with the television double-act Morecambe and Wise, in which she memorably lampooned her stage success as Shakespeare's Cleopatra.

Jancsó, Miklós (1921–) Hungarian director, who emerged as one of Hungary's leading film-makers in the 1960s. Having begun as a director of documentary shorts, Jancsó directed his first full-length feature film, *The Bells Have Gone to Rome*, in 1958. This was followed by *Cantata* (1963) and *My Way Home* (1964), works that combine revolutionary fervour with great technical skill. International recognition came with *The Round-Up* (1965), a detailed account of atrocities perpetrated against the peasant population during the days of the Austro-Hungarian Empire. The film was particularly admired for Jancsó's handling of huge set-pieces. In *The Red and the White* (1967), an epic recreation of the Russian Civil War, the two opposing armies are seen locked in a futile struggle to dominate a vast empty landscape.

Jancsó drew on memories of his own youth in *The Confrontation* (1968), while in *Agnus Dei* (1971) he portrayed the conflict between religion and revolution. *Red Psalm* (1971) was praised for its sympathetic analysis of the plight of the Hungarian peasantry at the turn of the century and won Jancsó the Best Director award at the Cannes Film Festival. In the 1970s Jancsó also worked outside Hungary, making *The Pacifist* (1971) and several other films for

Italian television. In *Elektreia* (1975) he adapted Greek myth to explore the concept of revolution, while in *Private Vices and Public Virtues* (1976) he interpreted the Mayerling scandal as a case of youthful rebellion against patriarchal tyranny.

Jancsó's more recent works have been somewhat coolly received, partly owing to changes in the political climate; they include *Hungarian Rhapsody* (1979), *The Tyrant's Heart* (1981), and *Season of Monsters* (1987).

Jannings, Emil (Theodor Emil Janenz; 1884–1950) German actor, born in Switzerland, who in the late 1920s was perhaps the most admired of all screen performers. Jannings, who made his theatrical debut when just 10 years old, worked as a touring actor before joining Max Reinhardt's company in Berlin. In 1913 he switched to films in search of a higher salary, making his first appearance on the big screen a year later. His breakthrough came when he teamed up with his old friend Ernst LUBITSCH in 1917; after appearances in *Wenn Vier Dasselbe Machen* and *Ein Fideles Gefängnis* (both 1917), he quickly graduated to leading roles. Though originally cast in a different part, Jannings persuaded Lubitsch to let him play Louis XV in *Madame Dubarry* (1919), the film that established the international reputations of both men. Jannings thereafter forsook the theatre permanently in favour of the cinema.

Formidable both in frame and in terms of his screen presence, Jannings was usually cast in tragic domineering roles, such as Henry VIII in *Anne Boleyn* (1920), and the title characters in *Danton* (1921), and *Othello* (1923). In fact, his film technique was restricted and to modern eyes his performances seem 'hammy' in the extreme. His other German films included *Peter the Great* (1923), *Waxworks* (1924), QUO VADIS? (1924), in which Jannings played a Nero "repulsive in his utter bestiality", *Tartuffe* (1925), and *Faust* (1926), as Mephisto. Perhaps his finest performance from this era was his *tour de force* as a pompous hotel doorman in MURNAU'S THE LAST LAUGH. After being lured to Hollywood in 1926 Janning's continued in much the same vein, winning the first ever Oscar for Best Actor with his performances in *The Way of All Flesh* (1927) and Josef VON STERNBERG's *The Last Command* (1928). However, *The Betrayal* (1929), in which he was cast alongside Gary COOPER,

was not a success and with the coming of sound Jannings decided to return to Germany, his English not being particularly good.

Jannings gave perhaps the most memorable performance of his career in von Sternberg's THE BLUE ANGEL (1930), in which he played a professor whose downfall is triggered by his passion for Marlene DIETRICH. In the mid 1930s the Nazis appointed him to a senior post in German cinema, leading to his appearance in such vehicles as *The Old and the Young King* (1935), *The Broken Jug* (1937), and *Die Entlassing* (1942), in which he portrayed Bismarck. Janning's connections with the Nazi regime meant that he was prohibited from making further films after World War II and he retired to Austria, where he died in disgrace.

> One of the world's great actors...is there any film actor living today who is possessed of the sheer power of Jannings?
> JAMES AGATE, critic.

Jarman, Derek (1942–94) British director, artist, and writer. A product of the Slade School of Art during its 1960s heyday, Jarman began his career in films after a chance meeting with a friend of Ken RUSSELL's on a train journey. Two days later Russell asked him to work as a designer on *The Devils* (1971), a role he took again on *Savage Messiah* (1972). Excited by the possibilities of film, Jarman began directing SUPER 8 home movies, including *In the Shadow of the Sun* (1973, not shown until 1980). Jarman's first feature, *Sebastiane* (1975), is typical of all his work in its stylistic triumph over a tiny budget (one reason for the copious nudity in the film was the lack of costumes), and its concern with themes of history, power, and sexual identity. In *Jubilee* (1977) similar themes are aired as Elizabeth I tours a futuristic and decaying Britain populated by such punk luminaries as Toyah and Adam Ant. Toyah reappeared in *The Tempest* (1979), an eccentric version of Shakespeare's play set in a crumbling mansion. Having failed to persuade TERRY-THOMAS to play Prospero, Jarman cast the poet Heathcote Williams; the film also featured the androgynous Tilda Swinton (soon to become a Jarman regular), Daniel DAY-LEWIS, and the blues singer Elizabeth Welch.

At about this time, Jarman began work on his most ambitious project, *Caravaggio* (1986), a fantasy about the turbulent life of the Renaissance artist. The fight to fund this work, as well as the struggle to get his earlier films a screening on Channel 4, led to Jarman's emergence as a public figure in the 1980s; he would become one of the decade's most outspoken champions of gay rights. While struggling with *Caravaggio*, Jarman also returned to Super 8; some of his films of this time were later blown up to 35mm and collected as *The Angelic Conversation* and *Imagining October* (both 1985). Eventually, shooting for *Caravaggio* was completed with an East End warehouse doubling for Renaissance Rome. Much of the film is shot in a chiaroscuro style imitating that of the painting's themselves. Before the premiere in Berlin in 1986, Jarman took the HIV test. It was, as he expected, positive.

Jarman responded by putting his career into overdrive. There followed in quick succession the bitter *The Last of England* (1987), a segment of the multi-director opera movie *Aria* (1987), and a powerful visualization of Benjamin Britten's *War Requiem* (1988), with Wilfred Owen's poems spoken by Lord OLIVIER. Faced once again with a cash crisis, Jarman reduced his own fee for this film to £1. *The Garden* (1990) was a series of tableaux set in the extraordinary garden Jarman had constructed around his house in the shadow of Dungeness power station. *Edward II* (1991), an arthouse hit, was a (nearly) faithful adaptation of Marlowe's play, while *Wittgenstein* (1993) was a bold attempt to illuminate the ideas of the philosopher.

Jarman's final film, *Blue* (1993) is in many ways his most extreme; the audience is given an unvarying blue screen to contemplate while listening to a soundtrack dealing with themes of illness and mortality. Radio audiences were sent a blue postcard to stare at while they listened.

Having asked to be taken off his medication, Jarman died in hospital surrounded by followers and those inspired by his work.

Jaws (1975) Steven SPIELBERG's hugely successful shocker about a great white shark that terrorizes a small seaside resort on Cape Cod. Based on the bestseller by Peter Benchley, the film was the first to demonstrate Spielberg's ability to play on the nerves and emotions of vast audiences. While the sequences in which swimmers are menaced and mauled by the shark exploit primordial anxieties, their impact is greatly heightened by brilliant editing (Verna Fields) and the unnerving music of John Williams. The plot, as several critics pointed out, is essentially an updating of Ibsen's *An Enemy of the People*; when the chief-of-police (Roy Scheider) raises the alarm about the presence of a deadly shark he is opposed by the town's mayor (Murray Hamilton), who fears for the tourist trade. The movie culminates in a battle to the death between the monster and veteran shark hunter Quint (Robert Shaw). Richard DREYFUSS played the part of marine biologist Matt Hooper.

Jaws did little for the reputation of the shark, leading conservation groups to point out that shark attacks are much rarer than the film suggests and that certain species are dwindling alarmingly as a result of persecution by hunters. The sharks seen in the film were in fact mechanical replicas, built at a cost of thousands of dollars each. *Jaws 2*, the first of three inferior sequels, was released with the famous slogan "Just when you thought it was safe to go back in the water."

Jazz Singer, The (1927) WARNER BROTHERS' pioneering talkie feature, the film that sparked the SOUND revolution of the late 1920s. The movie, which made use of the VITAPHONE sound-on-disc system, consisted mainly of songs from its star, Al JOLSON, but also contained a few lines of dialogue. Following a sensational premiere on 6 October 1927 at Warners' Theater in New York, the film went on to take in more than $3.5 million. The Academy gave a special award to Warners for making "the pioneer outstanding talking picture."

The vaudeville performer George Jessel had originally turned down the lead when Warners refused his demand for an extra $10,000 for the use of his voice. Eddie CANTOR also rejected it, not wanting to pick up Jessel's discarded roles. Third-choice Jolson signed for $75,000 and some Warners' stock.

Once cast, *The Jazz Singer* was filmed on Warners' Stage Three, the industry's first purpose-built sound stage, with Alan Crosland directing. Al Cohn scripted from the play by Samson Raphaelson, a non-musical work adapted from his own short story, *The Day of Atonement*. The plot is a sentimental Jewish melodrama about Jakie Rabinowitz, a cantor's son (Jolson was the son of a rabbi) who breaks with family tradition to become a show-business star.

The cast also featured May McAvoy, Warner Oland (who would later portray

Charlie CHAN), and Eugenia Besserer. Mc-Avoy sneaked into cinemas on several occasions and was amazed at the audiences' reaction to Jolson. "A miracle occurred" she said, "You'd have thought they were listening to the voice of God."

The six songs included 'Mammy', 'Toot-toot-tootsie', and 'Mother I Still Have You', the first song composed specifically for a movie. The story was mostly told in titles, with the two talking sequences containing a total of 354 words. The dialogue was improvised. The first voice heard was that of Bobbie Gordon, who played the Jolson character as a child.

The Jazz singer has been remade twice; in 1953 Michael CURTIZ directed Danny Thomas and Peggy Lee (in her first feature lead), while in 1980 Neil Diamond, Laurence OLIVIER, and Lucie Arnaz took the leads with Richard FLEISCHER at the helm.

jelly Short for gelatin: *see* GEL.

Jennings, Humphrey (1907–50) British film-maker, best known for his documentary work during World War II. Born in Suffolk, Jennings studied literature at Cambridge before beginning a career in the theatre as a set designer. During the 1930s he developed an interest in both the Mass Observation and the Surrealist movements, influences that were later reflected in his work. In 1934 he joined the GPO FILM UNIT, where he assisted Alberto CAVALCANTI before directing *Locomotives* (1934) and *Post Haste* (1934), possibly the first non-animated film composed entirely of prints and drawings. In 1936 he left the Unit to make the avant-garde *Birth of a Robot* (1936), a puppet film that he co-directed with Len Lye. After returning to the GPO in 1938, he ran into controversy with *Spare Time* (1939), an unsentimental portrayal of working-class life with a commentary by Laurie Lee. The film was criticized by fellow members of the documentary movement for its satirical tone and lack of educational value.

Professionally, World War II proved lucky for Jennings, supplying him with both copious government funding and a focus for his disparate talents. The result was his finest work, probably the best record of the war made by any film-maker in any country. Early work such as *The First Days* (1939) and *London Can Take It* (1940) – both co-directed by Harry Watt (1906–87) – were blatantly propagandist, the latter being aimed specifically at US opinion. His best work was more impressionistic, combining sound and images with a minimum of commentary; in *Words for Battle* (1942), for example, images showing the stoic courage of the home front unfold to the voice of OLIVIER reading a selection of poetry and prose. His earlier interest in Mass Observation emerges in *Listen to Britain* (1942), in which workers and servicemen go about their daily business to a soundtrack of natural and found sound, including popular songs of the day. *Fires were Started* (1943), Jennings's only feature-length film, shows his ability to handle dramatic narrative; following a night in the life of a typical fire crew, it used real firemen to re-enact actual fires. At the end, after seeing a fireman die we cut to his wife listening to a news broadcast about the bombing: "Fires were started, casualties light." *Diary for Timothy* (1945), a record of Britain in the period after D-Day, reflected the hopes for a better society prevalent at the time. The film's main weakness was the over-written commentary, provided by E. M. Forster.

With the end of the war, Jennings's almost mystical belief in the unity of the British people came to seem old-fashioned and such films as *The Cumberland Story* (1947) and *Dim Little Island* (1949) aroused little public interest. His last film, *Family Portrait* (1950), was made for the Festival of Britain. Having been commissioned to make a film for 'The Changing Face of Europe' series, he died after falling off a cliff while researching locations in Greece.

Jeux interdits (*Forbidden Games*; 1952) René CLÉMENT's disturbing film about the impact of World War II on young minds. When five year-old Paulette (Brigitte Fossey) loses her parents in a Luftwaffe attack on a refugee column, she is befriended by an eleven year-old farm boy, Michel (Georges Poujouly), whose parents shelter her. The experience of burying her pet dog and witnessing the funeral of his older brother prompts them to create a secret cemetery of their own in the barn; eventually they begin to kill small creatures and steal crucifixes for their innocent ceremonies or 'forbidden games'.

Although Clément had intended his third feature film to be a portmanteau of three stories about children, he soon chose to focus solely on the first segment, adapted from François Boyer's novel *Les Jeux inconnus.* Rejecting the book's melodramatic ending, in which Michel is crushed by the weight of a stone cross stolen from the church belfry, Clément opted for a more authentic denouement; in the film, Paulette is sent to an orphanage despite the promises of Michel's father that she would not be punished for her part in their 'games'.

Clément co-scripted the film with Jean AURENCHE and Pierre Bost, both prominent figures in the rather literary film style known as the 'Tradition of Quality'; indeed, *Jeux interdits* emphasizes its literary origins by setting out its credits on the pages of a book. Yet the film also had roots in NEOREALISM. Although he styled his lighting on the paintings of the Dutch artists Jan Vermeer and Pieter de Hooch, Clément insisted on shooting the exteriors on location and exclusively cast nonprofessionals. Having found Poujouly in a holiday camp for underprivileged Parisians and Fossey vacationing in Cannes with her aunt, he proceeded to cast her mother and father as her screen parents. The film also anticipated the NEW WAVE with its use of long takes and lingering close-ups.

Jeux interdits took major prizes at Cannes and Venice as well as the Oscar for Best Foreign Language Film. Although it is also a powerful satire on rural life and religion, the film remains primarily a pacifist statement. As Clément remarked: "For me, foremost of the forbidden games is war."

Joffe, Roland (1945–) British film director, also noted for his work in television. Joffe made his cinema debut with THE KILLING FIELDS (1984), a harrowing depiction of the horrors of Pol Pot's Kampuchea, as experienced by a US journalist (Sam Waterston). The film won Oscars for editing, photography, and Best Supporting Actor (the nonprofessional Haing S. Ngor) and received further nominations for Best Director, Best Film and Best Actor (Waterston). Joffe also received an Oscar nomination for the $22-million epic *The Mission* (1985), a beautifully photographed story about the attempts of Jesuit priests to resist the colonial exploitation of the natives in 18th-century South America. The distinguished cast was headed by Robert DE NIRO and Jeremy IRONS, while Ennio Morricone supplied the memorable music. *Fat Man and Little Boy* (1989) was a controversial film about the development of the atomic bomb during World War II, a theme Joffe returned to in the television

film *Shadow Makers* (1990). His most recent feature film was *City of Joy* (1992). Other work for television has included *Spongers* (1978), an indignant account of poverty in modern Britain that won the Prix Italia, *United Kingdom* (1981), and a version of the Jacobean revenge tragedy *'Tis Pity She's a Whore* (1982).

Johnson. **Nunnally Johnson** (1897–1977) Prolific US screenwriter, who also produced and directed. Many of his later films were comedies, including the first CINEMASCOPE comedy, *How to Marry a Millionaire* (1956). When asked how he would write for the wide screen, Johnson said, "Very simple. I'll just put the paper in sideways."

Johnson began as a journalist, working his way up from Georgia dailies to the *New York Herald Tribune.* His introduction to films came in 1927, when one of his short stories was adapted as the Clara BOW vehicle *Rough House Rosie.* Five years later he travelled to Hollywood to become a scriptwriter. After joining Darryl F. ZANUCK's 20th Century-Fox in 1934 he combined writing with producing. His scripts of this period include those for three John FORD films, *The Prisoner of Shark Island* (1936), THE GRAPES OF WRATH (1940), which brought Johnson an Oscar nomination, and *Tobacco Road* (1941). In 1943 he co-founded International Pictures, the company's first offering being his own comedy *Casanova Brown* (1944), with Gary COOPER. Johnson moved into directing in the mid 1950s but thereafter concentrated on screenwriting once more.

Other films written by Johnson in the 1940s and 1950s include Fritz LANG's *The Woman in the Window* (1944), *The Dark Mirror* (1946), in which Olivia DE HAVILLAND played identical twins, *The Desert Fox* (1951), starring James MASON as Rommel, and *My Cousin Rachel* (1952), with Richard BURTON and de Havilland. In 1957 Johnson directed Joanne WOODWARD to an Oscar in the psychological study *The Three Faces of Eve* (1957), which he also wrote. His last scripts included two James STEWART comedies, *Mr Hobbs Takes a Vacation* (1962) and *Take Her, She's Mine* (1963), the Peter SELLERS vehicle *The World of Henry Orient* (1964), and the war film *The Dirty Dozen* (1967).

Van Johnson (Charles Van Johnson; 1916–) US actor, whose cheerful boy-next-door appeal brought him matinee-idol status in the 1940s. When Hollywood's top male stars left to fight in World War II, Johnson filled the gap, charming his way through musicals and war films, often in the company of June ALLYSON. Although he aspired to become a serious actor, he was dogged by his freckled boyish image.

Born in Newport, Rhode Island, Johnson worked as a chorus boy on Broadway before earning a bit part in RKO's *Too Many Girls* (1942). After signing with MGM he found immediate success as *Dr Gillespie's New Assistant* (1942); his character had been created to replace the popular Dr Kildare when the studio dropped Lew AYRES for being a conscientious objector.

Johnson went on to star in *A Guy Named Joe* (1943), in which he wins Irene DUNNE with the help of a ghost (Spencer TRACY). His films with Allyson included *Two Girls and a Sailor* (1944) and *Till Clouds Roll By* (1946), which also featured Judy GARLAND and Frank SINATRA; for *In the Good Old Summertime* (1949) Garland replaced Allyson, who had become pregnant.

Although he took the lead in the successful *Battleground* (1949), Johnson tended to find himself back in supporting roles once MGM's top stars had returned from the war. He supported Clark GABLE in *Command Decision* (1948) and Tracy in *Plymouth Adventure* (1952), for example. He did star in three 1954 roles, as a soldier's ghost visiting Jane WYMAN in *Miracle in the Rain*, a writer in love with Deborah KERR in *The End of the Affair*, and as Gene KELLY's wisecracking friend in the musical *Brigadoon*. In the mid 1950s Johnson left MGM to work independently, sometimes in Italy. His later movies included *Divorce American Style* (1967) and *Yours Mine and Ours* (1968); he returned to the stage in the 1970s, and appeared in the 1984 television series *Glitter*.

Jolson, Al (Asa Yoelson; 1886–1950) US star of blackface revue, who earned undying fame as the first man to speak audibly in a feature film. Jolson combined magnetic stage presence with overpowering enthusiasm and an unquenchable thirst for public acclaim; by the late 1920s he was able to use the self-bestowed title **The World's Greatest Entertainer** without ridicule. This was all in the face of debilitating stage fright and without benefit of musical training (he only had six singing lessons in his life, undertaken at the age of 35 and quickly abandoned when he suspected them of harming his voice).

Born in Russia, the son of a rabbi, Jolson settled in America with his parents in 1894. After running away from home, he worked initially in the circus and then in vaudeville. In 1911 he made his Broadway debut and his first recording – a process complicated by the fact that he found it virtually impossible to keep still while singing. Such songs as 'Mammy' – which he delivered on one knee, imploring his audience's sympathy with outstretched hands – 'Swanee', and 'California Here I Come' were among the biggest hits of the interwar period. However, Jolson doubted his chances of success on the silent screen and turned down offers of film roles (his refusal to finish D. W. GRIFFITH's *Mammy's Boy* in 1923 led to a protracted legal dispute).

In 1926, after appearing in the sound short *April Showers*, Jolson agreed to take part in a full-length talking feature for Warner Brothers. His first words in THE JAZZ SINGER (1927) – "Wait a minute! Wait a minute! You ain't heard nothin' yet" – rank among the most famous utterances of the century. Tradition has it that the line was an unscripted aside addressed by Jolson to a stage technician. He had in fact used the line as a catchphrase for many years – notably at a concert in 1918, when he took the stage after Caruso. Amongst his subsequent films were *The Singing Fool* (1928), which made more money than any other movie before GONE WITH THE WIND (1939), *Hallelujah, I'm a Bum* (1933), *Rose of Washington Square* (1939), and *Swanee River* (1940). In 1946 Jolson's somewhat fading career was revived, when his singing voice was used in Columbia's biopic *The Jolson Story* (the role was acted by Larry PARKS). A sequel, *Jolson Sings Again* (1949), was also extremely popular with the public.

This must have been greatly to Jolson's satisfaction, his craving for public adulation being intense. On one occasion, during the first night of the Broadway revue *Show Girl* in 1929, he chafed so much at being a mere member of the audience that he stood up and joined in from the auditorium, to thunderous applause. On another occasion, when appearing in the stage show *Bombo* (1921), he tired of his role and stepped to the front of the stage to enquire if the audience wouldn't prefer to hear him sing a few songs; they concurred, the rest of the cast was dismissed, and Jolson performed until the early hours, when the audience were finally persuaded to go home.

You've never heard of me, but you will.
AL JOLSON; advertisement placed in *Variety*
c. 1910.

Jones, Jennifer (Phyllis Isley; 1919–) US
star of the 1940s and 1950s, who won an
Oscar in her first major film, *The Song of
Bernadette* (1943). She was the wife of producer David O. SELZNICK.

Born in Tulsa, Oklahoma, she appeared
on stage as a child with her parents' stock
company. After studies at AADA she married
another student, Robert Walker, in 1939.
Later that year the couple travelled to
Hollywood, where Jones appeared in the B-
Western *New Frontier* and a serial, *Dick
Tracy's G-Men*.

In 1940 Selznick signed her to a long-
term contract with MGM. When he tried to
change her name she at first resisted, but
finally wired: "JENNIFER JONES IS OKAY. LOVE.
JENNIFER JONES." After three years during
which Selznick groomed her for stardom
(and became her lover), she made her MGM
debut in *The Song of Bernadette*, playing the
peasant girl whose vision of the Virgin
Mary (an uncredited appearance by Linda
Darnell) established Lourdes as a pilgrim-
age site.

The day after receiving her Oscar, Jones
began divorce proceedings against Walker.
In 1945 she took an overdose in an attempt
to get Selznick to marry her, which he eventually did four years later. Her former husband, now an acclaimed actor, suffered a
series of nervous breakdowns and died
in 1951. Their son, Robert Walker Jnr
(1941–), is also an actor.

Jones's other roles included the love
interest of brothers Gregory PECK and Joseph
COTTEN in the steamy *Duel in the Sun* (1946),
the ghost love of Cotten in *Portrait of Jennie*
(British title *Jennie*; 1948), and the tragic
heroine of *Madame Bovary* (1949). She won
the last-named part after the censors suggested that this tale of adultery was more
likely to gain their approval with Jones in
the role instead of the sexy Lana TURNER.

In the 1950s she appeared as a wild
Shropshire girl in POWELL and PRESSBURGER'S
Gone to Earth (US title *The Wild Heart*; 1950),
with Laurence OLIVIER in William WYLER'S
Carrie (1952), and as a World-War-I nurse
in the 1957 remake of *A Farewell to Arms*.
This last proved the most ill-fated project
of her career. Not only did the original
director, John HUSTON, abandon the film
when Selznick insisted on using it to

spotlight his wife, but its total failure at the
box-office persuaded the producer to make
no more films. Jones's later appearances
were few and far between; she played a
divorced woman falling for her son's friend
in the British sex comedy *The Idol* (1966)
and had a small part in the all-star disaster
film *The Towering Inferno* (1974).

Jordan, Neil (1950–) Irish director and
writer. Modern Ireland provided the setting
for Jordan's first film, *Angel* (1982), in
which a saxophone player sets out to
avenge a terrorist murder that he has witnessed; like his subsequent films this
thriller, influenced by both BUÑUEL and
SCORSESE, has a surreal and apocalyptic
edge. He then established his name in the
cinema with *The Company of Wolves* (1984),
an adaptation of Angela Carter's reworking
of the Little Red Riding Hood story. The film,
which blends elements of fairytale with horror and sexual fantasy, was much praised
for the quality of its photography and its
special effects.

Jordan enjoyed even greater commercial
success with his third film, *Mona Lisa*
(1986), which follows the developing relationship between a small-time villain (Bob
HOSKINS) and a prostitute (Cathy Tyson)
in London's underworld. Less successful
was the supernatural comedy *High Spirits*
(1988), starring Peter O'TOOLE, although the
special effects were once again remarkable.
The Crying Game (1992) was a powerful
story of love and murder set in Northern
Ireland and London. The plot contains one
of the least anticipated twists in movie history; audiences were incredulous when,
towards the end of the film, the beautiful
female lead stripped naked revealing herself
to be, quite unmistakably, a man (Jaye Davi-
son).

In 1994 Jordan enjoyed the biggest box-
office success of his career with *Interview
with the Vampire*, an adaptation of Anne
Rice's neo-gothic novels starring Tom
CRUISE.

juicer Slang for an electrician on a film set.

Jules et Jim (1961) François TRUFFAUT'S
masterly depiction of a doomed *ménage à
trois*. The film, scripted by Truffaut and Jean
Gruault from a novel by Henri-Pierre Roche,
starred Jeanne MOREAU, Oskar Werner, and
Henri Serre as the three friends who attempt
to live lives unshackled by convention.

Miraculously, the film manages to convey all the joy of friendship and young love while also recognizing the self-deception of the protagonists. Although *Jules et Jim* is a showcase for many of the techniques associated with the burgeoning NEW WAVE – mobile camerawork and quick cutting, overlapping scenes, slow motion, and freeze-frames – this virtuosity never distracts from the story and the characters.

The Bohemians Jules (Werner), an Austrian, and Jim (Serre), a Frenchman, are inseparable companions. When both fall for the vivacious but enigmatic Catherine (Moreau), this seems to deepen, rather than disrupt, their friendship. A period of idyllic togetherness for all three comes to an end when Catherine agrees to marry Jules on the eve of World War I. After the war, during which the two men are obliged to fight on opposing sides, Jim joins Jules and Catherine in Austria to renew their triangular relationship. Despite moments of the old happiness, the three find themselves caught in a downward spiral of jealousy and despair, culminating in the deaths of Catherine and Jim. In 1980 US director Paul Mazursky unsuccessfully attempted to remake the story in a contemporary US setting as *Willie and Phil*.

jump cut An effect in which a moving subject appears to 'jump' abruptly from one position to another on the screen. When this is intended rather than accidental, it is achieved by removing unwanted middle portions of a continuous shot during editing. Although traditional INVISIBLE EDITING always masked jump cuts by changing the camera angle or interpolating a CUTAWAY, some modern directors have used them to disorientate and disturb the viewer or to heighten the drama. The revolutionary jump cuts in GODARD's A BOUT DE SOUFFLE (1959) were used both to quicken the pace and to cut costs.

Junge, Alfred (1886–1964) German art director who settled in Britain. Junge designed sets for the Berlin State Opera and State Theatre before becoming (1920) art director for UFA, the government-supported film production conglomerate. At UFA he worked on such silent classics as Paul Leni's *Backstairs* (1921) and *Waxworks* (1924), an EXPRESSIONIST shocker set in a fairground waxworks museum. In the late 1920s he came to Britain to assist the director E. A.

Dupont with the silent melodrama *Piccadilly* (1928); he subsequently remained in this country, adding imaginative decor to numerous films for Gaumont and other companies. His pictures of the 1930s included the screen version of Priestley's *The Good Companions* (1933), the early HITCHCOCK film *The Man Who Knew Too Much* (1934), and the poignant GOODBYE, MR CHIPS (1939).

Junge's most notable work, however, came in the 1940s when he created sets for several productions by Michael POWELL and Emeric PRESSBURGER, including THE LIFE AND DEATH OF COLONEL BLIMP (1943), and *A Canterbury Tale* (1944). His work on the visually sumptuous *Black Narcissus* (1947) earned him an Oscar, while his sets for the heavenly sequences in A MATTER OF LIFE AND DEATH (1946) are perhaps the most stunning he produced. In the late 1940s Junge moved to MGM's British studios, where he served for a decade as head of the art department. During this era he created settings as varied as medieval England for *Ivanhoe* (1952), Kenya for *Mogambo* (1953), Regency Bath for *Beau Brummel* (1954), and Victorian London for *The Barretts of Wimpole Street* (1957). He also devised the settings for Gene KELLY's lavish ballet film *Invitation to the Dance* (1956).

Jungle Jim US COMIC STRIP hero created by Alex Raymond in the 1930s. The character appeared in a film serial, *Jungle Jim* (1937), and was later played by Johnny WEISSMULLER in a series of low-budget films (1948–55). He was accurately described as "Tarzan with clothes".

junior or **junior spot** A 1000 or 2000w SPOTLIGHT. *Compare* SENIOR.

Jurassic Park (1993) Steven SPIELBERG's spectacular dinosaur film; the most commercially successful movie of all time, it cost about $58.7 million to make and took nearly $1 billion at the box office. During its first year on release in America, it grossed more than twice its nearest rival, *The Fugitive*. Spielberg tempted Richard ATTENBOROUGH out of retirement as an actor to play the role of the wealthy entrepreneur John Hammond, who has cloned live dinosaurs from fossilized DNA.

The story was co-scripted by Michael Crichton from his best-selling novel (1991) about a dinosaur theme park created by genetic engineers on a remote jungle island. A combination of ingenious models and COMPUTER ANIMATION was used to create the screen's most realistic prehistoric animals. Vivid scenes of dinosaurs eating human beings provoked debate as to whether the film was too frightening to be seen by the children who formed its natural constituency.

The plot shows Hammond welcoming a group of experts to see and approve his new dinosaur safari park. Amongst the visitors are palaeontologists Dr Alan Grant (Sam Neill) and Elli Sattler (Laura Dern), as well as the wisecracking mathematician Ian Malcolm (Jeff Goldblum), who believes in an unpredictable universe ruled by chaos. His theory seems to be proved correct when a storm maroons two carloads of guests in the park at night and a tyrannosaurus rex goes on the rampage...

A sequel has been planned for 1997.

K

Kadár, Ján (1918–79) Czechoslovakian director and screenwriter. Born in Budapest, he abandoned his legal training to study at the Bratislava Film School; during World War II he was forced into a Nazi labour camp. After the war, he returned to Bratislava to direct his first film, *Life is Rising from the Ruins* (1945), a documentary short; he subsequently joined the Barrandov Studios in Prague as a writer and assistant director. In 1950 he directed his first feature, *Katya*, a comedy that displeased the state authorities. Two years later he began a rewarding 17-year collaboration with **Elmar Klos** (1910–93), with whom he co-directed and co-scripted a string of documentary and feature films that have been much praised for their craftsmanship. Several won international prizes, notably *The Shop on Main Street* (1965), a tragicomic tale about a carpenter's disastrous attempt to protect a Jewish woman during the German occupation, which won the Oscar for Best Foreign Film in 1965. Other films of the 1950s and 1960s included *Kidnap* (1952), *The House at the Terminus* (1957), *Three Wishes* (1958), the documentary *Youth* (1960), *Death is Called Engelchen* (1963), and *The Accused* (1964).

Kadár and Klos were often called in by the communist authorities to answer questions about the submerged political content of their films. This resulted in one suspension of two years, while the Soviet invasion of Czechoslovakia in 1968 delayed the release of their Czech-US co-production *Adrift* for three years. Kadár emigrated to America in 1969 and a year later made his first US film, *The Angel Levine*, a parable about an elderly Jewish tailor's visitation by a black angel. In 1975 he made *Lies My Father Told Me*, a sentimental Canadian film about a poor Jewish boy and his grandfather in 1920s Montreal. In his last years Kadár worked mainly for television, making such documentaries as *The Other Side of Hell* (1977) and *Freedom Road* (1978).

Kael, Pauline (1919–) Acerbic US film critic, whose provocative reviews appeared in *The New Yorker* magazine for 23 years. Her writings have been collected in such volumes as *I Lost it at the Movies* (1965), *Kiss Kiss Bang Bang* (1968), *Reeling* (1976), *5001 Nights at the Movies* (1982), and *Movie Love* (1991).

Born in Petaluma, California, she majored in philosophy at Berkeley before beginning her career in the cinema as the manager of a movie theatre. Although her first reviews appeared in the mid 1940s, Kael made her name some 15 years later with a series of stinging attacks on pretentious avant-garde critics and the excesses of the fashionable AUTEUR theory. After becoming *The New Yorker*'s film critic in 1968 she continued her campaign against auteurism, notably with her claim that scriptwriter Herman MANKIEWICZ contributed as much to the success of CITIZEN KANE as did Orson WELLES.

By the mid 1970s her trenchant judgements, expressed in a conversational, even slangy, style had made her the most influential film critic of her generation. Never awed by the presence of distinguished talent, she labelled *Eleven Harrowhouse* (1974), starring James MASON and John GIELGUD, "a bumbling and stupid romp." She also called David LEAN's *Ryan's Daughter* (1970) "gush made respectable by millions of dollars tastefully wasted", *Airport 1975* (1974) "processed schlock", *Return of the Jedi* (1983) a "junky piece of moviemaking", and *Greystoke: The Legend of Tarzan, Lord of the Apes* (1984), "a unique mixture of pomposity and ineptitude." Neither did she worry about being out of step with popular sentiment. Of Kevin COSTNER's *Dances with Wolves* (1990), which won seven Oscars including Best Picture and Best Director, Kael remarked, "Costner has feathers in his hair and feathers in his head." In 1991 she retired from regular journalism at the age of 72.

Karloff, Boris (William Henry Pratt; 1887–1969) British actor, best known for his HORROR roles. The son of a civil servant, Karloff was originally destined for a diplomatic career. However, in 1909 he emigrated to Canada, where he later began to work with touring theatre groups. His screen debut came with *The Dumb Girl of Partici* (1916).

Over the next decade and a half Karloff appeared in small parts in dozens of undistinguished silent films and serials. In 1930, however, he gave a memorable performance as a convict turned killer in *The Criminal Code*; this led to a number of character roles including the part that made his name, that of the monster in James WHALE's FRANKENSTEIN (1931) – one of 16 films in which Karloff appeared that year.

Although he did not speak in the part, Karloff's classic portrayal of the monster, who is made to seem at once terrifying and pathetic, brought him overnight stardom. Whatever else happened in his career, this was the role for which the public and casting directors remembered him and, as a result, he remained typecast in the horror genre for the rest of his days. Karloff repeated the role of the monster twice, in Whale's masterful *Bride of Frankenstein* (1935) and in the weaker *Son of Frankenstein* (1939).

His other major horror films included Whale's *The Old Dark House* (1932), which provided Karloff with his first real starring role (although, again, he did not speak), *The Mummy* (1932), *The Raven* (1935), *The Body Snatcher* (1945), and *Bedlam* (1946). Outside the horror genre, Karloff appeared in the Mr Wong series of detective films and as the criminally minded psychiatrist Dr Hollingshead in *The Secret Life of Walter Mitty* (1947). During the 1940s he also worked on stage, including the Broadway run of ARSENIC AND OLD LACE, in which he played the murderous Jonathan.

In his later career Karloff played in a large number of routine films and spoofed his sinister persona in a couple of ABBOTT AND COSTELLO vehicles (but not *Abbott and Costello Meet Frankenstein*). Roger CORMAN's *The Raven* (1963) teamed him up with fellow heavies Vincent PRICE, Peter LORRE, and Jack NICHOLSON, while *Targets* (1967), directed by Peter BOGDANOVICH, brought his career full circle by casting him as an ageing former star of horror films. During his last years arthritis confined Karloff to a wheelchair; he died from a respiratory ailment.

Kaufman, Philip (1936–) US director, screenwriter, and producer, whose relatively small output has established him as one of Hollywood's true mavericks. Born in Chicago, he attended Harvard Law School and taught in Italy before beginning to make low-budget independent films. At the age of 26 he co-produced, co-directed, and co-wrote *Goldstein* (1963), an eccentric satire that won the Prix de la Nouvelle Critique at Cannes in 1964. The following year, he directed, produced, and scripted *Fearless Frank* (1965; not shown until 1967) an even stranger film starring the then unknown Jon Voight.

Kaufman made his mark in Hollywood in 1971, when he wrote and directed Universal's *The Great Northfield Minnesota Raid*, an unromantic Western starring Robert DUVALL as Jesse James and Cliff Robertson as Cole Younger. After directing *White Dawn* (1974), a harsh film about the conflict between whalers and eskimos at the turn of the century, he returned to the Western with *The Outlaw Josey Wales*, an extravagantly violent film starring Clint EASTWOOD. Kaufman was to have directed as well as supplying the screenplay, but was fired after a dispute with Eastwood, who took over the direction. His films of the late 1970s include an acclaimed remake of the 1956 horror classic *Invasion of the Body Snatchers* (1977) and *The Wanderers* (1979), a violent film about teenage gangs that became a cult favourite. The latter is one of several films that he has co-written with his wife, Rose Kaufman.

Kaufman suffered another setback in 1980, when he saw Steven SPIELBERG take over *Raiders of the Lost Ark* (1981), a project he had been developing for some time with George LUCAS. In 1983, however, he achieved the biggest commercial and critical success of his career with *The Right Stuff*, an epic film about the Mercury astronauts that won four Oscars.

Always a slow worker, Kaufman took three years to complete *The Unbearable Lightness of Being* (1987), a sly sex comedy starring Daniel DAY-LEWIS as a womanizing Czech physician caught up in the Prague Spring of 1968. Kaufman's adaptation of Milan Kundera's complex novel brought him an Oscar nomination for Best Screenplay. He then produced, directed, and co-wrote *Henry & June* (1990), about the triangular relationship between the writers Anaïs Nin and Henry Miller and Miller's wife June. *Rising Sun* (1993) was a thriller set amongst the Japanese business community in Los Angeles.

Kaye, Danny (Daniel David Kaminsky; 1913–87) US actor, singer, and dancer, of Russian descent, who became a Hollywood star in the 1940s and 1950s. Kaye made his film debut in the 1930s but only achieved screen fame after being taken up by Sam GOLDWYN, who recognized his potential as a singing-and-dancing light comedian. Other studio executives felt that Kaye was too Jewish in appearance and insisted that he dye his hair red-blonde.

A qualified airline pilot, Kaye began his show-business career in vaudeville, where he specialized in fast tongue-twisting novelty songs and slapstick dance routines. He was given full rein in such stage shows as *Lady in the Dark* (1941), featuring the extraordinary song 'Tchaikovsky', which lists the names of 54 Russian composers in 34 seconds, and Cole Porter's *Let's Face It* (1941). His first film for Goldwyn was the army comedy *Up in Arms* (1944); among the movies that followed were *Wonder Man* (1945), *The Secret Life of Walter Mitty* (1947), in which he played Thurber's daydreaming simpleton, and *A Song is Born* (1948). In *Hans Christian Andersen* (1952) he sang such favourites as 'The Ugly Duckling' and 'Thumbelina' in the guise of the celebrated children's writer, while *The Court Jester* (1956), provided another excellent vehicle for his talents. His later films, which were mainly disappointing, included *On the Double* (1961) and *Peter Pan* (1976), in which he played both Mr Darling and Captain Hook. Several of his songs were the work of his wife, Sylvia Fine.

Kay's contribution to Hollywood was acknowledged in 1954, when he was awarded a special Oscar. He made fewer films in the late 1950s and 1960s, devoting much of his time to humanitarian work for UNICEF. Somewhat contrary to his image as a warm and caring personality, however, Kaye was disliked by many colleagues, who found him difficult to get on with; there were even reports of the star slapping children who pressed him for his autograph.

Kaye is not naturally funny but more of a stuntman of humour, who relies on glib footwork, a glibber tongue, and a foxy aptitude for facial contortions.
Time review, 1970.

Kazan, Elia (Elia Kazanjoglou; 1909–) Turkish-born US director. Kazan's family moved from Constantinople to New York when he was four. After studies at Yale Drama School, he worked in the theatre as a property manager and later as an actor. He made his film-acting debut with *Pie in the Sky* (1934) and his directorial debut with *The People of the Cumberlands* (1937), a short. During the 1930s Kazan was briefly a member of the Communist Party and worked mainly with left-wing theatre groups. He later became well known for his Broadway productions of plays by Tennessee Williams, Arthur Miller, and Thornton Wilder. In 1947 he co-founded the ACTORS' STUDIO in New York, a workshop that became known as the principal home of the METHOD.

Kazan's early feature films included *A Tree Grows in Brooklyn* (1945) and *Gentleman's Agreement* (1947), an attack on anti-Semitism that earned him an Oscar as Best Director. Ironically, the film was produced by Darryl F. ZANUCK, one of the few non-Jewish film moguls. Zanuck also produced *Pinky* (1949), which tackled the problem of racism against Black Americans. When the original director, John FORD, asked to be replaced after only two week's shooting, Kazan stepped in, scrapped Ford's footage, and finished the film in eight weeks. *Panic in the Streets* (1950), starring Richard WIDMARK and Jack PALANCE was a thriller with a public-health theme.

In the early 1950s Kazan began a run of triumphs with the Tennessee Williams adaptation *A Streetcar Named Desire* (1951), the film that popularized the Method style of acting, earned Kazan a Best Director Oscar, and made a star of Marlon BRANDO. The film won a total of four Oscars, out of 12 nominations. Following *Viva Zapata!* (1952), which starred Brando as the doomed Mexican revolutionary, Kazan appeared before the House Un-American Activities Committee, where he confessed to earlier Communist Party membership and, ignominiously, supplied the names of other members. Interestingly, his next film, ON THE WATERFRONT (1954), dealt with the issue of betrayal; Terry Malloy (Brando) is persuaded by a priest (Karl MALDEN, another Kazan regular) to inform on a corrupt union boss and his henchmen. Whatever its politics, *On the Waterfront* featured excellent performances, stunning cinematography, and strong direction: the film earned a total of eight Oscars, including Best Film and Best Director. The following year Kazan directed James DEAN in EAST OF EDEN (1955), a Cain and Abel story that earned him a Best Director nomination.

BABY DOLL (1956), another adaptation of a Tennessee Williams play, was a black sex comedy that attracted much controversy after being condemned by the Catholic LEGION OF DECENCY. Kazan then rounded off the decade with A Face in the Crowd (1957), an early satire on the power of television that launched the film careers of Andy Griffith and Lee REMICK, and the excellent Wild River (1960), with Remick, Jo Van Fleet, and Montgomery CLIFT. Fleet played an 80-year-old widow being forced off her land by the Tennessee Valley Authority, who want to flood the valley.

During the 1960s Kazan gradually withdrew from the cinema. Both America, America (1963), about a young Turk's dream of emigration, and The Arrangement (1969), about a businessman's attempted suicide, were also scripted by Kazan (in the latter case, from one of his own novels). His last film was The Last Tycoon (1976), an all-star movie about Hollywood during the 1930s; despite featuring a script by Harold Pinter and the combined talents of Robert DE NIRO, Robert MITCHUM, Tony CURTIS, Jeanne MOREAU, and Jack NICHOLSON, the film proved a crashing failure. It was described by one critic as: "So enervated it's like a vampire movie after the vampires have left." Kazan published an autobiorgaphy, My Life, in 1982.

Keaton. Buster Keaton (Joseph Francis Keaton; 1895–1966) US comedian and director, one of the great stars of the silent era. Indomitable, unspeaking, and sublimely straightfaced, Keaton was the master of the slapstick stunt, always performing his own tricks himself. Appropriately enough, he was nicknamed 'Buster' – by the legendary escapologist Houdini – after surviving a fall downstairs as a baby.

Keaton began to appear on stage as part of his parents' comedy act at the age of three. Although he soon established himself as the undisputed star of the troupe, the family act fell apart after Buster's father started to drink heavily, thereby endangering his partners in their acrobatic stunts. The young Keaton turned to films in 1917 after a chance invitation to watch the filming of a Fatty ARBUCKLE comedy. Keaton was captivated by the medium of film and, rejecting lucrative offers from Broadway, quickly formed a partnership with Arbuckle.

After 14 shorts with Arbuckle, solo stardom came his way with The Saphead (1920); this was followed by such classics as The Playhouse (1921), The Boat (1922), The Paleface (1922), Cops (1922), Our Hospitality (1923), The Navigator (1924), Sherlock Junior (1924), Seven Chances (1925), THE GENERAL (1927), and The Cameraman (1928). Typically crowned by a natty straw hat and always the victim of accident and misunderstanding, Keaton was rapidly hailed as the only serious rival to Charlie CHAPLIN. In retrospect, many have judged his brand of stoical clowning superior to Chaplin's, which is often too sentimental for modern tastes.

Keaton's career tailed off somewhat with the advent of the talkies and the ill-advised decision to leave his own film company for MGM, who never understood the nature of his genius. The studio even considered trying him in straight dramatic roles (specifically in the part played by Lionel BARRYMORE in Grand Hotel). Having overcome the alcoholism that plagued him in the 1930s, he continued to make occasional appearances until his death, the most notable of these being his vaudeville double-act with Chaplin in the latter's Limelight (1953). According to rumour, his part in the film was drastically cut when he threatened to outclass Chaplin himself. Cameos followed in AROUND THE WORLD IN EIGHTY DAYS (1956), It's a Mad Mad Mad Mad World (1963), and A Funny Thing Happened on the Way to the Forum (1966). He was awarded a special Oscar for his lifetime achievement in 1959.

Keaton's unchanging expression in the face of the most bizarre perils earned him the nickname **Old Stoneface**; his contract with MGM allegedly stipulated that he must never smile on camera, in order to preserve his unique persona. In fact, he laughed just once in all his films – in the Arbuckle short Fatty at Coney Island. A shot of Keaton smiling at the close of Steamboat Bill Jr (1927) was cut after audiences objected.

> With the humour, the craftsmanship and the action there was often, besides, a fine, still and dreamlike beauty.
> JAMES AGEE, of Keaton.

Diane Keaton (Diane Hall; 1946–) US actress particularly associated with the films of Woody ALLEN. "She increased my affection, feelings and understanding for women and made me see how appealing the female sex is" Allen once said. Despite a variety of other roles, Keaton has found it difficult to shake off her image as Allen's eccentric but charming leading lady. She has recently turned to directing.

The daughter of a civil engineer, she left college to study acting at the Neighborhood Playhouse in New York. In 1968 she made her Broadway debut in the musical *Hair*, attracting a certain amount of attention as the only member of the cast not to remove her clothes. A year later, she played opposite Allen for the first time in his Broadway production of *Play It Again, Sam*; Keaton also appeared in the film version (1972). Her first movie role was in the sex farce *Lovers and Other Strangers* (1970).

Having become Allen's live-in lover in the early 1970s, Keaton took the female lead in his films *Sleeper* (1973) and *Love and Death* (1975). However, the role that brought her fame (and an Oscar for Best Actress) was the title character in Allen's much-loved ANNIE HALL (1977). The film was clearly based on Keaton's own personality and lifestyle (her original name being Hall) and her unstable relationship with Allen. Annie's baggy masculine clothes – again reflecting Keaton's preferred off-screen dress – set a new fashion trend in the late 1970s. Despite having separated, Keaton and Allen worked together on *Interiors* (1978) and MANHATTAN (1979); she also starred in his *Manhattan Murder Mystery* (1993) after the departure of Mia FARROW.

Her other films include THE GODFATHER (1972) and its two sequels (1974 and 1990), in which she played Al PACINO's WASP wife, the thriller *Looking for Mr Goodbar* (1977), and Warren BEATTY's *Reds* (1981). In 1986 she made her debut as a director with *Heaven*, in which members of the public are interviewed about their ideas of the next world. She played a devoted yuppie mother in *Baby Boom* (1987) and a neglectful parent in *The Good Mother* (1988), a story of sexual abuse.

Keitel, Harvey (1947–) US actor. Having left the US Marines to study at the ACTORS' STUDIO under Stella Adler and Lee Strasberg, Keitel made his film debut in Martin SCORSESE's first feature, *Who's That Knocking*

on My Door (1968). He has since appeared in the debuts of a whole string of promising film-makers, including Ridley SCOTT (*The Duellists*, 1977), Paul SCHRADER (*Blue Collar*, 1978), Quentin TARANTINO (*Reservoir Dogs*, 1991) and Danny Cannon (*The Young Americans*, 1993).

Keitel also collaborated with Scorsese on MEAN STREETS (1973), in which he played the idealistic Charlie, *Alice Doesn't Live Here Anymore* (1975), and TAXI DRIVER (1976). Despite consistently strong performances, his career dipped in the wake of a series of highly public rows. Francis Ford COPPOLA turfed him off the set of APOCALYPSE NOW, Stanley DONEN had his voice dubbed when he refused to accept changes to the script of *Saturn 3*, and Keitel himself acrimoniously quit Scorsese's *The King of Comedy*. Although a series of mundane, mainly European, assignments followed in the 1980s, there were still some sterling supporting performances, notably in Nicolas ROEG's *Bad Timing* (1980) and Tony RICHARDSON's *The Border* (1982).

Ironically, it was Scorsese who offered Keitel a lifeline with the role of Judas in *The Last Temptation of Christ* (1988). Subsequently, he has become almost ubiquitous, featuring in an astonishing 20 movies in the first four years of the 1990s. The majority of these films have seen him playing abrasive streetwise characters operating on one or other side of the law: the long list includes *The Two Jakes* (1990), *Bugsy* (1991), which brought him an Oscar nomination as gangster Warren BEATTY's abusive West Coast contact, *Reservoir Dogs*, Abel Ferrara's lurid *Bad Lieutenant* (1992), *Rising Sun* (1993), and Tarantino's *Pulp Fiction* (1994). Despite this roll call, Keitel insists that:

> I've *never* played a violent character. I've played people who are in conflict and had a need sometimes to commit violence as a result...I don't look upon it as playing Mr Nice Guy or playing Mr Bad Guy, an actor...has to investigate all aspects of himself.

He went some way to prove his point as the understanding cop in Ridley SCOTT's *Thelma and Louise* (1991) and as Baines, the gone-native estate manager who gives Holly Hunter the chance to redeem her beloved piano in return for sexual favours, in Jane CAMPION's *The Piano* (1993).

Kelly. Gene Kelly (Eugene Curran Kelly; 1912–) US actor, dancer, singer, choreographer, and director, who revitalized the Hollywood MUSICAL after World War II. Having worked as a bricklayer and soda-fountain attendant, Kelly began his Broadway career as a member of the chorus line in *Leave It to Me* (1938). Within two years he was being cast in starring roles, his first being in the stage musical *Pal Joey*. This success led to his first film appearance, in *For Me and My Gal* (1942), with Judy GARLAND; he made his debut as a choreographer with *Cover Girl* (1944), in which he danced and acted opposite Rita HAYWORTH. As a choreographer he acquired a reputation for innovatory dance sequences, which were at once both strongly balletic and seemingly spontaneous (despite Kelly's own notorious perfectionism).

Anchors Away (1945) saw him teamed with Frank SINATRA and the cartoon character Jerry the Mouse, while highlights of *The Pirate* (1948) included Kelly's rendition of Cole Porter's 'Be a Clown'. He appeared with Sinatra again in the innovative location musical *On the Town* (1949), a film co-directed by Kelly and his friend Stanley DONEN. The same partnership was responsible for the enduring favourite SINGIN' IN THE RAIN (1952), which provided an unsurpassable showcase for Kelly's talents as dancer and choreographer. The film provided Hollywood with one of its most cherished images, that of Kelly dancing and singing his way through the rain-soaked streets (and looking marvellously cheerful despite the fact that he was suffering a heavy cold). Kelly gave another virtuoso performance in Vincente MINELLI's *An American in Paris* (1951), which culminated in a sensational 20-minute ballet to the music of Gershwin. Minelli also directed Kelly in the somewhat disappointing screen version of Lerner and Loewe's *Brigadoon* (1954).

In 1956 Kelly suffered a severe setback with the failure of his ambitious wordless musical *Invitation to the Dance*, a film that he wrote, directed, and choreographed. By this time the era of the great Hollywood musicals was drawing to a close and Kelly's career never really recovered. He continued to busy himself as a director, with credits including *Gigot* (1962) and *Hello Dolly* (1969), while straight acting roles included a supporting part in *Inherit the Wind* (1960); he also narrated the MGM compilation *That's Entertainment* (1974). At the age of 68 he sang and danced in *Xanadu* (1980), a feeble disco musical. He was awarded a special Oscar for his contribution to the Hollywood musical in 1951.

> I can think of no one in Hollywood, just now, who is more satisfying or more hopeful to watch for singing, dancing or straight acting.
> JAMES AGEE, critic, 1944.

Grace Kelly (1928–82) US actress, noted for her cool regal beauty; her career came to a perfect climax when her 'fairytale romance' with Prince Rainier III (1923–) of Monaco led to a royal wedding in 1956.

The product of a wealthy and well-connected family, Kelly trained at AADA and worked as a model and on TV before making her Broadway debut in 1949. An acclaimed screen debut, in the documentary drama *Fourteen Hours*, followed in 1951; a year later she consolidated her stardom playing opposite Gary COOPER in the Western HIGH NOON (1952). In 1953 her performance in *Mogambo* earned her an Oscar nomination, while the Best Actress Award became hers a year later for *The Country Girl* (1954), in which she played the long-suffering wife of alcoholic Bing CROSBY.

Having reached the heights of Hollywood's aristocracy, she mixed with the top stars of her day and for millions came to epitomize the glamour of the movies. Her somewhat glacial good looks appealed greatly to Alfred HITCHCOCK, who cast her in his classic thrillers *Dial M for Murder* (1954), REAR WINDOW (1954), and *To Catch a Thief* (1955); the last was filmed in Monaco and brought her into contact with her future husband. The musical *High Society* (1956) saw her in the company of Bing Crosby, Frank SINATRA, and Louis Armstrong.

Kelly's marriage to Prince Rainier spelt the end of her film career at a point when she was the second-biggest box-office draw in Hollywood. Although she never returned to film-making, she was tempted by the title role in Hitchcock's *Marnie* (1962) and was considered for *The Turning Point* a few years later. She continued to attract the attentions of the world's press as the dignified and supremely elegant real-life princess until her death in a car accident on the Corniche above Monte Carlo.

> Writing about her is like trying to wrap up 115 pounds of smoke.
> PETE MARTIN.

Kerr, Deborah (Deborah Kerr-Trimmer; 1921–) British actress, born in Scotland, who made her reputation playing a series of reserved heroines from English upper middle-class backgrounds. Having trained for the stage under her aunt, who ran a theatre school, Kerr started out as a ballet dancer but quickly forsook dance for acting, making her film debut in 1940. Good notices for her performance in *Major Barbara* (1941) brought Kerr her first leading roles; she finally made her big breakthrough playing three parts in POWELL and PRESSBURGER'S THE LIFE AND DEATH OF COLONEL BLIMP (1943). Having played opposite Robert DONAT in the comedy *Perfect Strangers* (1945) she went on to please the critics with understated performances in *I See a Dark Stranger* (1946), a thriller in which she starred with Trevor HOWARD, and Powell and Pressburger's *Black Narcissus* (1947), in which she played the head of a convent in the Himalayas. After being lured to Hollywood in the late 1940s she made *Edward My Son* (1949), which added Spencer TRACY to her list of leading men, *King Solomon's Mines* (1950), *The Prisoner of Zenda* (1952), and *Dream Wife* (1953), in which she partnered Cary GRANT.

Her career, by this time somewhat in decline, revived with a vengeance when she gave a passionate performance in Fred ZINNEMANN'S FROM HERE TO ETERNITY (1953). She was rewarded with further strong roles in the Graham GREENE adaptation *The End of the Affair* (1955), and Rodgers and Hammerstein's *The King and I* (1956), in which she played a resilient English governess faced with the chauvinism of Yul BRYNNER'S King. Subsequent films include *Tea and Sympathy* (1956), *An Affair to Remember* (1957), *Separate Tables* (1958), *The Sundowners* (1960), *The Innocents* (1961), *The Night of the Iguana* (1964), and *Prudence and the Pill* (1968). She went into semi-retirement in Switzerland in the 1960s but has continued to make occasional film and theatre appearances, as well as featuring in the television mini-series *A Woman of Substance* (1984) and *Hold the Dream* (1986).

Kerr has received no less than six Oscar nominations as Best Actress – a record for any female performer who has not gone on to win an Award.

Kettle, Ma and Pa A hillbilly couple, played by Marjorie Main (1890–1975) and Percy Kilbride (1888–1964), who first appeared on the screen in *The Egg and I* (1947), based on the novel of the same name by Betty Macdonald. The Kettles and their numerous offspring went on to feature in a further nine cheap but popular film comedies, which continued until the late 1950s. The legacy of hayseed humour embodied by the Kettles was later revived in the popular US television series *The Beverley Hillbillies* (1962–71).

key. **key grip** The person in charge of the stagehands (GRIPS), who are responsible for setting up and moving the camera tracks, props, scenery, etc., on a film shoot.

key light The dominant source of illumination on a film set. The level of the key lighting plays a vital role in establishing the mood and atmosphere of a scene. HIGH-KEY lighting creates a generally bright effect with few areas of contrast, whereas LOW-KEY illumination produces deep dramatic shadows (as in FILM NOIR). Once the main lighting has been determined by the cinematographer, supplementary lights, such as FILLERS or back lighting, are used to complete the illumination without changing the prevailing mood.

Keystone Comedies The silent film comedies made by Mack SENNETT's Keystone Comedy Company in Hollywood. The first of these slapstick burlesques appeared in 1913. Charlie CHAPLIN worked with the company between 1913 and 1915, donning his famous TRAMP outfit for the first time in *Kid Auto Races* at Venice (1914). The company's leading lady was Mabel Normand (1894–1930). One of the most popular features of the Keystone Comedies was the hectic CHASE sequences involving the **Keystone Kops**, a chaotic team of comedians (led by Ford Sterling) who executed daring comic stunts dressed in oversized police uniforms.

kid. *The Kid* (1921) Charlie CHAPLIN's first feature-length film, often considered his most perfect blend of slapstick and pathos. The opening title announced: "A picture with a smile – perhaps a tear." Chaplin, who also scripted and directed the film, starred with the six-year-old Jackie Coogan, who played a lovable waif. Under Chaplin's direction, Coogan gave one of the most remarkable screen performances ever given by a child (*see* CHILD STARS). "He could apply emotion to the action" said Chaplin, "and action to the emotion." When Chaplin could not get Jackie to cry for a scene, his father, the actor Jack Coogan, threatened to pull him off the film and put him in a workhouse. When young Coogan began bawling, his father told Chaplin, "He's all ready." To his dismay, Coogan was popularly dubbed 'the kid' for the rest of his fading career.

Chaplin, whose previous works had all been one- or two-reelers, spent an unprecedented amount of time and care on the film. It took him two weeks to perfect a single one-minute scene of a pancake breakfast. In the end, he spent nearly $500,000 shooting over 400,000 feet of film, later edited down to 6000 feet. The producers, FIRST NATIONAL, wanted the six reels released as three two-reel comedies. Chaplin refused and, when they sought court action, smuggled the film to Salt Lake City to cut and preview it. Nearly 50 years later, one of Chaplin's last creative acts was to reissue it with new music he had composed.

When an unmarried mother abandons her child, Chaplin's Tramp reluctantly takes him in. The two soon strike up a business arrangement; the kid roams the streets breaking windows and Chaplin, the glazier, follows offering repairs. (The state of Illinois cut this scene, fearing that it might encourage delinquency.) Eventually, the authorities arrive to take the boy away to an institution. In the film's most memorable sequence, Chaplin races across the rooftops, rescues the child, and chases off his abductors. The scene almost certainly draws its emotional power from Chaplin's own traumatic childhood, during which he was forcibly separated from his mother and taken to a workhouse. Years later, the mother now rich, recovers her child; unexpectedly, she sends for the Tramp to join them.

the Kid A nickname of the US actor and director Warren BEATTY (1937–), who is the 'kid' brother of the actress Shirley MACLAINE (1934–).

Kieślowski, Krzysztof (1941–) Polish director, who made several of his later films in France. Kieślowski was born in Warsaw and attended the School of Cinema and Theatre in Łódź. In the late 1960s he began to direct for Polish television, winning the Golden Dragon at the International Festival of Short Films in Cracow with his *First Love* (1974). He followed his first film for the

cinema, *The Scar* (1976), with the satirical *Camera Buff* (1979), which won the Moscow film Festival Grand Prix despite its implicit anti-authoritarian message. In 1988–89 Kieślowski came to international attention with *Decalogue*, a powerful series of television films, each of which is based on one of the Ten Commandments. Two of these were also released to cinemas. *A Short Film about Killing* (1988), a grim piece about a man who commits a motiveless murder and is then – equally pointlessly – executed won the Oscar for Best Foreign Film and a Special Jury Prize at Cannes. Its companion piece, *A Short Film about Love* (1988), is a bleak film about a teenage voyeur. Other films of the 1980s and early 1990s include *Blind Chance* (1982), *No End* (1984), and *City Life* (1990).

The Double Life of Véronique (1992) consolidated Kieślowski's reputation as perhaps the most imaginative and accomplished director in Europe. It tells a story of two parallel lives: Veronika, a beautiful singer, sees her double among a busload of French tourists in a Cracow square; she dies early in the film from a mysterious illness, while her French double, Véronique, lives on. Both parts are played by Irene Jacob. The film received rapturous, if rather baffled, reviews and took the International Critics' Jury Award at Cannes. In 1993 Kieślowski released *Blue*, the first part of a trilogy based on the French tricolour and the associated values of Liberty, Equality, and Fraternity. This was followed by *White* (1993) and *Red* (1994); the latter earned three Oscar nominations including Best Director. Having completed this highly praised sequence, Kieślowski dismayed his admirers by announcing his intention to make no more films. His intention, he said, was to sit at home and smoke cigarettes.

Killing Fields, The (1984) Roland JOFFE's film about a cross-cultural friendship in war-torn Cambodia. Based on a true story, the film was produced by David PUTTNAM for Enigma/Goldcrest and shot in Thailand. *The Killing Fields* won the BFA's Best Film Award and received an Oscar nomination as Best Picture. Joffe, who had previously worked in theatre and television, also earned an Oscar nomination as Best Director. The stunning cinematography of Chris Menges was recognized by an Academy Award, as was the editing of Jim Clark.

The screenplay was based on 'The Death and Life of Dith Pran' (1980), an article in which Sydney H. Schanberg, a correspondent for the *New York Times*, described the ordeal of Dith, his former guide, under the Khmer Rouge. In the film Schanberg was played by Sam Waterston, who won an Oscar nomination. Dith was played by a Cambodian refugee doctor, Haing S. Ngor, who received the Oscar as Best Supporting Actor, becoming only the second non-professional to win an Award (the other was Harold Russell in THE BEST YEARS OF OUR LIVES, 1946). Dr Haing had been in the middle of an operation when Khmer Rouge guerrillas took over his hospital; he escaped to Thailand and worked as a doctor in refugee camps before leaving for America.

In the story Schanberg arrives in Cambodia in 1973 and is assisted by Dith, a local photographer who acts as his guide and translator. When Schanberg is captured by the Khmer Rouge, Dith intercedes to save his life. After the American is evacuated from Pnom Penh, Dith is interned in a brutal 're-education' camp, from which he later escapes. His subsequent flight through a silent landscape of death and horror provides the film with its most powerful sequences. Although Schanberg believes his friend to be dead, he returns to Cambodia after the Vietnamese invasion in an attempt to find him. The two men are eventually reunited.

Kind Hearts and Coronets (1949) Robert Hamer's elegant comedy of murder, a film usually considered the finest of the EALING comedies. The witty literate screenplay was adapted from Roy Horniman's novel *Noblesse Oblige* by Hamer and John Dighton. The film's title derives from Tennyson's couplet "Kind hearts are more than coronets, And simple faith than Norman blood." According to his own account, Hamer deliberately set out to make a film that disregarded normal moral conventions; while the British ending leaves the viewer in some doubt as to whether the villain will be caught, the US version adds a scene in which his fate is made explicit.

The strong cast included Alec GUINNESS, Dennis Price, Valerie Hobson, and Joan Greenwood. Guinness emerged as a major star from this, his third film. He was asked to play three of the eight murder victims but decided to portray all eight.

The story is set in the Edwardian era. Louis Mazzini (Price), a haberdasher with aristocratic connections, decides to claim his 'rightful' inheritance by killing the eight D'Ascoyne relatives who stand in his way. His victims include Lady Agatha (Guinness), who dies when an arrow punctures her hot-air balloon. "I shot an arrow in the air", recites Louis, "She fell to earth in Berkeley Square." Although he is finally arrested and led to prison, two of his sweethearts (Greenwood and Hobson) secure his release. Louis, however, leaves an incriminating diary in his cell (in the US version this is clearly shown in the authorities' hands).

kineto-. **Kinetograph** One of the first camera-projector systems devised to show moving photographs to a theatre audience. It was invented in 1891 by W. K. L. Dickson (an Englishman) for his employer, Thomas A. EDISON. The Edison company gave its first screening of moving pictures for a public audience at Koster and Bial's Music Hall on Broadway in 1896. *Compare* KINETOSCOPE.

Kinetoscope A peep-show machine in which moving drawings or photographs could be viewed by one person at a time. Developed in 1891 by Thomas A. EDISON's assistant, W. K. L. Dickson, it consisted of a small pine cabinet with a viewing hole at the top; the images, on a 50-foot loop of celluloid film, moved as the viewer turned a handle. Edison patented the device in his own name and, after Dickson left following an argument, claimed he had invented it himself.

In 1893 Edison built a workshop, called the BLACK MARIA, to produce pictures for the Kinetoscope. His first film, copyrighted the following year, was *Fred Ott's Sneeze* (Ott being his assistant).

By 1895 the machine had a rival, Dickson's own MUTOSCOPE. In Britain, Birt Acres and Robert William Paul pirated the Kinetoscope and patented their own moving-picture camera in 1895. They presented *The Oxford and Cambridge University Boat Race* in a Kinetoscope machine at the 1896 India Exhibition at Earls Court.

The first Kinetoscope Parlor had opened in 1894 in New York. By 1899 San Francisco had a Kinetoscope Arcade with **Kinetophones**, headphones that supplied music and sound effects to the viewer. However, it was soon apparent that the future of moving pictures lay with communal rather than private viewing; the success of the

LUMIÈRE BROTHERS's Cinématographe and Edison's own KINETOGRAPH quickly rendered the Kinetoscope obsolete.

king. King and Queen of Hollywood A title bestowed on the US actor Douglas FAIRBANKS and his wife Mary PICKFORD, both of whom enjoyed huge popularity in the 1920s. Their Beverly Hills mansion Pickfair was the venue for numerous glittering parties attended by the Hollywood aristocracy.

King Kong (1933) RKO's classic giant-ape tale, a film that displayed the very latest in Hollywood SPECIAL EFFECTS. The process work stretched production out to 55 weeks and pushed the budget up to a then massive $670,000. Despite the Depression and some lukewarm notices (James AGEE called the movie "just amusing nonsense"), *King Kong* established a world record in its first four days, taking nearly $90,000. Strangely, it received no Oscar nominations.

The cast included Fay WRAY, Robert Armstrong, and Bruce Cabot. *Variety* called Wray's part "a film-long screaming session...too much for any actress and any audience." When extras playing African natives devised their own nonsense language, the suspicious HAYS office demanded an English translation before approving the film.

The idea for the film (and the name of the ape) originated with Merian C. Cooper, a remarkable adventurer and explorer who had already collaborated on two documentaries about African wildlife. However, the project failed to take off until Cooper interested David O. SELZNICK in 1931. The original idea of putting an actor in a gorilla suit was abandoned when special-effects man Willis O'Brien successfully created an 18-inch Kong of wire, rubber, and rabbit fur (in some scenes he carries an animated doll representing Wray).

In the story a film crew begins work on the remote Skull Island only to have their actress (Wray) abducted by a gigantic ape. Although Kong is captured and taken to New York as an exhibit, he escapes with Wray in his grasp and climbs the Empire State Building; he is eventually shot down by biplanes. "It wasn't the airplanes", marvels Wray's friend Carl (Armstrong), "It was beauty killed the beast."

Although the sequel *Son of Kong* (1933) featured O'Brien's special effects once again, poor production work and a feeble script meant that it was received as a comedy by cinema audiences. In 1976 Dino DE LAURENTIIS spent over $22 million remaking *King Kong* in colour, with Jeff BRIDGES, Charles Grodin, and Jessica Lange; it received an honorary Oscar for visual effects. A weak sequel, *King Kong Lives*, followed in 1986.

King of Hollywood The title conferred on the US actor Clark GABLE in the 1930s. A ruggedly handsome man with an air of self-assurance, he specialized in portraying macho heroes with charm.

King of the Cowboys A title bestowed on two US stars of cowboy films, Tom Mix and Roy ROGERS (the so-called 'Singing Cowboy').

Tom Mix (1880–1940) was, by his own (disputed) account, a US marshal and war hero before turning to acting in 1909. His films, over 400 B-feature Westerns, idealized the American West. In his private life he maintained the role of cowboy hero, invariably dressing in boots and a white suit; his car was a huge vehicle embellished with a saddle and steer horns.

Kinski. Klaus Kinski (Claus Gunther Nakszynski; 1926–91) German actor, who emerged as a leading star of his country's revitalized film industry in the 1970s. Indeed for many, Kinski, who specialized in playing tortured souls driven to the verge of madness, came to personify the seriousness and intensity of modern German cinema. He also became notorious as one of the most difficult actors of his generation, storming out of press conferences in a blind rage almost as a matter of habit.

Kinski made his film debut in *Ludwig II* (1954) but attracted little attention until the mid 1960s, when his roles included a pathological hunchbacked killer in the cult SPAGHETTI WESTERN *For a Few Dollars More* (1965). After appearances in *Dr Zhivago* (1965) and *Circus of Fear* (1967), he starred in the powerful *Aguirre, Wrath of God* (1972), the first of a series of much admired films for the German director Werner HERZOG. Here Kinski gave a compelling performance as the leader of a doomed band of conquistadors in the jungles of South America. Herzog also cast Kinski to great effect as a menacing but also strangely sympathetic Dracula figure in his NOSFERATU (1978), and as the deranged protagonist of *Woyzeck* (1979). In Herzog's extraordinary *Fitzcarraldo* (1982) the actor gave a towering performance as a crazed opera-lover obsessed with the idea of bringing the music of Caruso to the Indians of the remote Amazon basin. The role was given to Kinski after it had been refused by Mick Jagger.

Having resisted the lure of Hollywood for some 20 years, Kinski finally succumbed in 1982, when he appeared in the cult science-fiction film *Android*. He subsequently squandered his talents in such mediocre English-language films as *Codename Wildgeese* (1984), commenting that he now chose movies "with the shortest schedule and the most money."

Nastassia Kinski (1959–   ) German-born actress, the daughter of Klaus KINSKI. A striking ethereal beauty, she became a star on both sides of the Atlantic in the 1980s. Having made her debut as a juggler in Wim WENDERS's *Wrong Movement* (1975), she went on to appear in HAMMER's *To the Devil a Daughter* (1976), in which she is threatened by the forces of evil in the person of Christopher LEE. She first emerged as a star playing the doomed heroine of Roman POLANSKI's *TESS* (1980), from the novel by Thomas Hardy. Subsequent films included the erotic thriller *Cat People* (1982), Francis Ford COPPOLA's *One From the Heart* (1982), *Exposed* (1983), in which she appeared with Rudolf Nureyev, and Jean-Jacques Beneix's *The Moon in the Gutter* (1983) with Gérard DEPARDIEU. In 1984 she gave one of her best performances in Wenders's epic road movie *Paris, Texas*. A year later, however, her career suffered a setback when she starred with Al PACINO in the American War of Independence epic *Revolution*, which was slated by the critics and proved a disaster at the box office. The mid 1980s saw her beset with mounting personal problems, including the much-publicized breakdown of her marriage. Her more recent films, made for the most part in France and Italy, have achieved little commercial success.

Klimov, Elem (1933–   ) Russian director, who emerged as a leading spokesman for the Soviet film industry in the 1980s; he is now regarded as one of his country's most prominent film-makers. After training as an aviation engineer and studies at the State Cinematography Institute, Klimov directed a series of short allegorical films satirizing the Soviet system; unsurprisingly, they were banned. With Alexei Petrenko he made *Agony* (1975), a fantastic portrayal of the relationship between Rasputin and the Romanov family, which likewise remained

unshown for several years. This was the first Soviet film to depict the mad monk. Klimov did not make another film until *Larisa* (1980), a tribute to his wife **Larisa Shepitko** (1939–   ), also a noted director, who had been killed in a car accident in 1979. Klimov then completed his wife's *Farewell* (1981), a haunting account of the destruction of a Siberian village to make way for a new dam. The film was acclaimed as a masterpiece by many Western critics.

Further praise came his way for *Come and See* (1985), in which Klimov dwelt upon the atrocities committed during the Nazi invasion of Byelorussia in World War II. The film, which won the Grand Prix at the Moscow Film Festival, is one of the most overwhelming depictions of war ever produced. During the Gorbachov era the director was appointed first secretary of the Film-Makers' Union while his work found a steadily growing audience in the West.

Kline, Kevin (1947–   ) US leading man and character actor. Kline began his career as an understudy with the New York Shakespeare Festival Company. In 1979 he won a Tony Award after replacing Raul Julia as the Pirate King in Joseph Papp's updated *The Pirates of Penzance* (1979). Although he lost the lead in Lawrence Kasdan's *Body Heat* (1981) to William Hurt, he made his film debut a year later in *Sophie's Choice* (1982), with Meryl STREEP. His first starring part came in a film adaptation of Papp's *The Pirates of Penzance* (1983); the film was as big a flop as the stage show had been a success.

That year Kasdan gave Kline another chance in *The Big Chill* (1983) and was sufficiently impressed to cast him in the lead of the Western *Silverado* (1985). Although a failure at the time, the film has been hugely influential in both its style and the stars it helped to create (Kevin COSTNER and Danny Glover amongst them). In characteristic style, Kline followed this major film with *Violets are Blue* (1986), a forgettable romance with Sissy Spacek. He also took on a role that Harrison FORD had turned down, that of the journalist Donald Woods in ATTENBOROUGH's *Cry Freedom!* (1987); unhappy with the angle of the script, he commendably underplayed his scenes with Denzil Washington's Steve Biko to give the latter more prominence.

John CLEESE, who had worked with Kline on *Silverado*, then asked him to play the role of Otto in *A Fish Called Wanda* (1988), a part that brought him an Oscar for Best Supporting Actor. Kline, never the careerist, followed this hit with *The January Man* (1989), a film that he summed up as: "A murder mystery-comedy-thriller-film noir-absurdist-theatrical-naturalistic mess." Kasdan's sweet comedy *I Love You To Death* (1990) and the ambitious *Soapdish* (1991) were also notable flops. Although Attenborough rescued him for the swashbuckling role of Douglas FAIRBANKS in *Chaplin* (1992), he followed this with the poorly judged *Consenting Adults* (1993).

Kline's continuing attempt to balance being a Hollywood star with being a serious actor bore better fruit with *Dave* (1993), in which he played both a corrupt US president and the naive lookalike who is asked to stand in for him. The film's success suggested that at long last Kline may have consolidated his relations with the cinemagoing public.

Klos, Elmar   *See* KADÁR, JÁN.

Konchalovsky, Andrei   (Andrei Mikhalkov-Konchalovsky; 1937–   ) Russian director, living in America, who emerged as a leading film-maker in the 1960s. The son of a poet, Konchalovsky began his career in the cinema writing screenplays for TARKOVSKY; he subsequently made his debut as a director of full-length features with *The First Teacher* (1965). This story of a young soldier's attempts to educate a rural community in revolutionary theory marked Konchalovsky out as one of the most promising new talents in Soviet cinema. However, his second feature, *Asya's Happiness* (1967), about life on a collective farm, fell foul of the Soviet censors and was banned for 20 years; thereafter he was obliged to tackle less challenging subjects.

After making a number of uncontroversial adaptations of works by such writers as Chekhov and Turgenev, Konchalovsky emigrated to America. Here, he revived his reputation with *Maria's Lovers* (1984), a moving depiction of the emotional difficulties faced by veterans of World War II on their return home. Also well received was *Runaway Train* (1985), a gripping thriller starring Jon Voight as an escaped convict who becomes involved in an attempt to prevent a rail disaster; eventually he sacrifices himself to dissuade another young man from turning to crime. Subsequently

Konchalovsky's reputation has declined somewhat owing to a series of misjudged ventures intended to attract a mass commercial audience. These included *Duet for One* (1986), starring Julie ANDREWS as a concert violinist who develops multiple sclerosis. *The Inner Circle* (1992), a film about Stalin and his coterie as seen through the eyes of his personal projectionist, was the first US movie to be shot inside the Kremlin and the former KGB headquarters. Konchalovsky's brother, Nikita Mikhalkov (1945–   ), is also a film director.

> Hollywood is a corporate mentality – like Socialist mentality. All the people are paid to say no.
> ANDREI KONCHALOVSKY.

Korda, Sir Alexander   (Sándor Kellner; 1893–1956) Flamboyant Hungarian-born director and producer, who became a leading figure in British cinema in the 1930s and 1940s. Korda, who started out as a journalist, began his career in cinema as a writer of intertitles for imported US films; he first tried his hand at directing in 1916. Having fled Hungary in the wake of the White Terror that followed World War I, he made several films in Germany before travelling on to America. However, he failed to make much impact in Hollywood and moved to Britain in 1930, establishing his own London Films at DENHAM STUDIOS. Korda then quickly attracted attention with a series of lavish productions starring some of the biggest names in British cinema. Films directed by Korda himself include the comedy *Service for Ladies* (1932), his first real success, and THE PRIVATE LIFE OF HENRY VIII (1932), which featured Merle OBERON– the second of his three wives – as Anne Boleyn to Charles LAUGHTON's Henry. Other memorable films produced by London in the 1930s and 1940s include *The Scarlet Pimpernel* (1934), the H. G. Wells adaptation *Things to Come* (1936), *The Four Feathers* (1939), and *Anna Karenina* (1948). Amongst the studio's later successes were THE THIRD MAN (1949), David LEAN's *Hobson's Choice* (1954), and Laurence OLIVIER's *Richard III* (1954).

A popular socialite who enjoyed an extravagant lifestyle, Korda managed to steer his company through choppy financial waters with aplomb. Despite his reputation, many of his films lost money for his backers, largely because he attempted to rival the excesses of the Hollywood that had

rejected him as a young man. His fascination with English history often exceeded his
judgement in choosing good box-office
material, leading to such disasters as *Bonnie
Prince Charlie* (1948), starring David NIVEN.
At the same time the ambitious scale of his
movies and the high production standards
achieved did a great deal to raise the international profile of British cinema. Whatever the crisis, Korda managed to rise above
it and to continue enjoying himself. He was
particularly proud of his successes with the
opposite sex, boasting that he had seduced
many beautiful women by pretending to be
impotent and thus goading them into making amorous advances.

In his later years Korda was much
honoured, being knighted in 1942 and
appointed to the Légion d'honneur in 1950.
On one occasion, after a poker game, Samuel GOLDWYN wrote Korda a cheque in red
ink for $10,000 with the acerbic note
"Signed with my blood"; he subsequently
received from Korda a cheque in blue ink
covering losses in another game, to which
was added the legend "This is signed in my
blood, too". Korda's brothers **Vincent Korda**
(1896–1979) and **Zoltan Korda** (1895–
1961) also worked as directors, often in collaboration with their more famous sibling.

> It's not enough to be Hungarian, you must
> have talent too.
> ALEXANDER KORDA.

Korngold, Erich Wolfgang (1897–1957)
Czech-born musical prodigy who became
Hollywood's highest-paid film composer in
the 1930s and 1940s. During his 12 years
in Hollywood, he turned out 18 scores,
ranging from the rousing music for *Anthony
Adverse* (1936) and *The Adventures of Robin
Hood* (1938), both of which brought him
Oscars, to the haunting theme for *King's
Row* (1942). He also wrote operas and sym-
phonies.

Born in Brno, Czechoslovakia, he had
operas and ballets performed in Vienna and
Berlin while he was still a teenager. Richard
Strauss labelled him "a second Mozart." In
the early 1930s he collaborated with the
theatre director Max Reinhardt, who helped
to get him a place with Warner Brothers in
1935. His first Hollywood score was for
Michael CURTIZ's *Captain Blood*.

Korngold went on to score Reinhardt's
A Midsummer Night's Dream (1936), William DIETERLE's *The Story of Louis Pasteur*
(1936) and *Another Dawn* (1937), and

Curtiz's *The Private Lives of Elizabeth and
Essex* (1939), *The Sea Hawk* (1940), and
The Sea Wolf (1941). His other films
included *The Constant Nymph* (1943),
Between Two Worlds (1944), *Deception*
(1946), *Of Human Bondage* (1946), and
Escape Me Never (1947).

After World War II, Korngold went back
to Vienna to concentrate on his career as a
serious composer. However, after the failure
of two operas, he returned to Hollywood
and scored such movies as Dieterle's *Magic
Fire* (1956), a biopic of Richard Wagner.
When a producer suggested that his earlier
music had been more effective, Korngold
explained, "When I first came here, I
couldn't understand the dialogue." After his
death, a black flag was flown over the
Vienna Opera House.

Kramer, Stanley (1913–) US director
and producer, noted especially for his 'social
issue' movies of the 1950s and 1960s. One
New York Times reviewer complained: "All
those big ideas – race hatred, nuclear war,
evolution, genocide – running around in
that tiny mind gives me cramps." One of
Hollywood's first independent producers, he
was awarded the Irving Thalberg Award for
his "consistently high quality in film-
making" in 1961.

Born in New York City, Kramer joined
MGM as a researcher in the mid 1930s, and
worked his way up to associate producer
before World War II. After serving in the
Army Signal Corps, he established his independent Screen Plays Inc. in 1948. His early
films, released through United Artists,
included *Champion* (1949), an exposé of the
boxing world starring Kirk DOUGLAS, and
Home of the Brave (1949), an attack on
racial discrimination that became a hit
without provoking the predicted riots. *The
Men* (1950) featured Marlon BRANDO in his
screen debut as a paraplegic World-War-II
veteran, while the Western HIGH NOON
(1952), which focused on community apa-
thy towards a man in danger (Gary COOPER),
was widely understood as a comment on
McCarthyism.

In the early 1950s money problems
forced Kramer to renounce his independence and become an associate producer at
Columbia. His films for the company
included the first biker movie, *The Wild One*
(1954), starring Brando as a moody gang-
leader. After a string of failures, he left Columbia in 1954, just as *The Caine Mutiny*, a

shipboard drama with Humphrey BOGART, became a box-office hit.

Kramer subsequently became an independent producer-director who released his films through United Artists. In 1958 his racial drama *The Defiant Ones*, starring Tony CURTIS and Sidney POITIER as escaped convicts, earned six Oscar nominations. *On the Beach* (1959) dealt with the aftermath of a nuclear attack, *Inherit the Wind* (1960) was a courtroom drama based on Tennessee's famous Darwinian 'monkey trial', and *Judgment at Nuremberg* (1961) a powerful all-star film about the Nazi war-crime tribunals. For Columbia, he made *Guess Who's Coming to Dinner* (1967), a picture about a mixed-race marriage in which Spencer TRACY and Katharine HEPBURN appeared together for the last time.

The 1960s also saw Kramer move into comedy with the all-star romp *It's a Mad Mad Mad Mad World* (1963) and *The Secret of Santa Vittoria* (1969). Later films, such as *Bless the Beasts and the Children* (1971) and *The Runner Stumbles* (1979), found little success at the box office.

Kubrick, Stanley (1928–) British director, writer, and producer. Formerly a magazine photographer, Kubrick made an ambitious debut with *Fear and Desire* (1953), a story about GIs stranded behind enemy lines that he produced, directed, photographed, and edited himself. Although made for a mere $100,000, it was, as *Variety* noted, "definitely out of the potboiler class one would expect from a shoestring budget." Kubrick then added screenwriter to his credits for *Killer's Kiss* (1955), another low-budget thriller, and *The Killing* (1956), a HEIST MOVIE made in a semidocumentary style that proved hugely influential. It was Kirk DOUGLAS who persuaded United Artists to back Kubrick's next picture, the epic World-War-I drama *Paths of Glory* (1957). The film's depiction of the blinkered inhumanity of the French generals and the subsequent suffering of their men led to its being banned in France until 1970. *Spartacus* (1960), starring Douglas and Laurence OLIVIER, was Kubrick's first colour picture, a historical EPIC about a slave revolt in 1st-century Rome; the strong cast also included Peter USTINOV, who won an Oscar as Best Supporting Actor. A scene that suggested a homosexual relationship between Olivier and Tony CURTIS was dropped from the released film but restored

in the 1992 DIRECTOR'S CUT (with Olivier's lost voice track dubbed by Anthony HOPKINS).

If *Spartacus* gave the impression that Kubrick was moving into the mainstream, LOLITA (1962) changed all that. Even if the impact of Nabokov's novel was tremendously toned down, the taboo subject matter and the hip 1960s style were a million miles from Hollywood epic. DR STRANGELOVE: *or How I Learned to Stop Worrying and Love the Bomb* (1964) confirmed that Kubrick's career had indeed taken an unconventional turn. This savage anti-war comedy, a delirious travesty of the serious source novel *Two Hours to Doom*, earned Kubrick his first Best Picture nomination at the Oscars. 2001: A SPACE ODYSSEY (1968) was Kubrick's coldest and most beautiful movie. Written by Kubrick and Arthur C. Clarke, the picture is both an attempt to instil a sense of wonder at human development (from apes to embryonic starchildren) and a concerted experiment in CINERAMA and SPECIAL-EFFECTS technology. "The ultimate trip" proclaimed the posters, much to Clarke's chagrin.

In 1971 Kubrick released A CLOCKWORK ORANGE, a frightening depiction of a futuristic society that focuses upon Alex (Malcolm McDowell), a teenage psychopath who leads his uniformed Droogs on a crusade of violence. Although the film contains less on-screen violence than its reputation would suggest, the atmosphere is continuously menacing. Following reports of acts of copycat violence, Kubrick withdrew his permission to show the film in Britain and it remains banned there to this day. Despite the nature of the material, the film was nominated for Best Picture at the Oscars, as was the staid period piece *Barry Lyndon* (1975).

Kubrick's *The Shining* (1980) angered Stephen King enthusiasts with its departures from the original novel, but is still a uniquely disturbing movie. The first mainstream feature to use STEADICAM, *The Shining* takes viewers on a nerve-wracking tour of the isolated hotel in which Jack NICHOLSON struggles to complete a novel while becoming possessed by malign forces from the past. In *Full Metal Jacket* (1987) Kubrick returned to his obsession with war; the Vietnamese setting was replicated mainly on London's Isle of Dogs.

Kubrick has since largely retired from direction but plans to make another science-fiction movie, called *A.I.*, when the effects technology is adequate.

Kurosawa, Akira (1910–) Japanese director and screenwriter. Kurosawa studied Western painting and worked as an illustrator before becoming (via a newspaper advert) an assistant director with the Toho company. He was already a skilled editor and screenwriter when he made his directorial debut with *Judo Saga* (1943), a martial-arts story that focused on a master-pupil relationship (a recurrent theme in his work). His subsequent films of the 1940s – these include *The Most Beautiful* (1943), *They who Step on the Tiger's Tail* (1945, released 1952), and *Drunken Angel* (1948), a gangster melodrama that began a long collaboration with the actor Toshiro Mifune – reveal wide thematic interests and an eclectic visual style.

It was, however, RASHOMON (1950), again featuring Mifune, that brought Kurosawa to an international audience. The film, which explored a story of rape and murder from several different viewpoints, won the Best Film prize at the Venice Film Festival. In doing so it became the first Japanese film to gain Western interest.

Kurosawa's successes of the 1950s were exceptionally varied; they range from adaptations of Western literature, such as *Hakuchi* (1950), based on Dostoevski's *The Idiot*, and *Donzoko* (1957), based on Gorki's *The Lower Depths*, to IKIRU (1952), a poignant examination of Japan's postwar malaise. THE SEVEN SAMURAI (1954) was a visually innovative reworking of the classic Hollywood Western, while *Throne of Blood* (1957) was a head-on fusion of Noh theatre and Shakespeare's *Macbeth*. As if to underline his versatility, *The Bad Sleep Well* (1960), about business corruption, was based on an Ed McBain thriller.

Yojimbo (1961), one of Clint EASTWOOD's favourite films, and *Sanjuro* (1962), in which Mifune played a lazy mercenary, introduced an element of parody and dark humour to the samurai genre and were highly influential to the development of the SPAGHETTI WESTERN in the later 1960s. *Red Beard* (1965), which again focused on a master-pupil relationship, was Kurosawa's last film with Mifune.

Following several abortive projects in America, Kurosawa returned to Japan to make *Dodes Ka-Den* (1970), about the lives and dreams of the inhabitants of a shanty town. The film enjoyed little success and the following year Kurosawa made a failed attempt at suicide. The mid 1970s saw a return to form with *Derzu Uzala* (1975), an epic adventure about a trapper, much of which was filmed in Siberia; the film won an Oscar as Best Foreign Language film and a Gold Medal at the Moscow Film Festival.

Kagemusha (1980), a powerful return to the samurai genre, shared the Palme d' Or at the Cannes Festival and enjoyed considerable box-office success. Following this triumph, he was at last able to raise finance for RAN (1985), an adaptation of *King Lear* set in 16th-century Japan that he had wanted to make for at least a decade. With a budget of $11 million (small by present-day Hollywood standards), *Ran* was the most expensive Japanese film ever made. The film, which was nominated for four Oscars, including one for Kurosawa as Best Director, is often regarded as his masterpiece. His most recent films have been *Dreams* (1990), *Rhapsody in August* (1991), with Richard GERE, and *Not Yet* (1993), which he directed at the age of 82.

Kurosawa's place in the history of cinema is unique; in fusing two distinct traditions he influenced not only subsequent generations of Japanese directors, but also numerous US film-makers, especially in the field of the modern Western.

L

label *See* CAPTION; SUBTITLE.

Ladd, Alan (1913–64) US actor, who specialized in tough-guy roles despite his short (5′5″) stature. Raymond CHANDLER once called him "a small boy's idea of a tough guy", while Ladd, whose leading ladies often had to stand in a trench on the set, described himself as "the most insecure guy in Hollywood." He was the father of Alan Ladd Jnr, president of 20th Century-Fox from 1977 to 1979, and of the child stars David and Alana Ladd.

Born in Hot Springs, Arkansas, Ladd spent much of his childhood living in a mobile home with his alcoholic mother. He began to act at high school, where his nickname was 'Tiny', before working as a lifeguard, service-station attendant, and hotdog vendor.

In 1932 Universal placed Ladd in their school for young actors but dropped him after his bit part in *Once in a Lifetime*. He then worked for two years as a GRIP at Warner Brothers and took a succession of small roles, including a reporter in CITIZEN KANE (1941) who speaks the single line "Or Rosebud". His big break came when he met agent Sue Carol. "He looked like a young Greek god" recalled Carol, who became his second wife in 1942.

It was Carol who landed his first major role, as an airman in RKO's *Joan of Paris* (1942). Later that year he attained stardom playing a killer in the Graham GREENE adaptation *This Gun for Hire*; his co-star was Veronica Lake, one of the few actresses who was shorter than him. Although their relations were frosty on set, they teamed up again in *The Glass Key* (1942) and the film noir *The Blue Dahlia* (1946). The partnership of the stone-faced melancholy Ladd and the slinky Lake in many ways foreshadowed that of Humphrey BOGART and Lauren BACALL a few years later.

Ladd served in the Army Air Force during World War II but was invalided out and returned to the screen in such films as *And Now Tomorrow* (1944) and *Two Years Before the Mast* (1946). Although he tried to change his image with his performance as a rich playboy in *The Great Gatsby* (1949), the film flopped. His outstanding role came in George STEVENS's SHANE (1953), in which he played the mysterious gunfighter who protects a frontier family. However, the film's six Oscar nominations did not include one for Ladd.

Ladd's later movies included the British-made *The Black Knight* (1954) and Fox's *Boy on a Dolphin* (1957) with Sophia LOREN (who found standing in the Ladd trench particularly objectionable). He gave one of his best performances as the ageing cowboy star in *The Carpetbaggers* (1964) but died of an overdose of sedatives and alcohol shortly before its release.

Ladri di biciclette *See* BICYCLE THIEVES.

Lady Vanishes, The (1938) Alfred HITCHCOCK's popular comedy thriller. Adapted from Ethel Lina White's novel *The Wheel Spins* by Frank Launder and Sidney GILLIAT, *The Lady Vanishes* is one of Hitchcock's least plausible but most entertaining films. Returning by train from a holiday in the Balkans, Iris Henderson (Margaret LOCKWOOD) enlists the help of music scholar Gilbert Redman (Michael REDGRAVE) to rescue fellow passenger Miss Froy (May Witty), who has mysteriously disappeared, from an international spy ring.

Shot on a minuscule budget and on a principal set measuring just 90 feet, the film made much use of BACK PROJECTION, painted transparencies, and models. Its success owed much to both Hitchcock's assured touch and the superb ensemble playing, with Paul LUKAS excelling as lead villain Dr Hartz, Catherine Lacey making a supremely sinister nun, and Basil Radford and Naunton Wayne entering British film folklore as Charters and Caldicott – the archetypally English pair whose participation in the escapade is prompted less by patriotism than their desire not to miss a cricket match.

The feature won Hitchcock not only the New York Critics' Award for Best Direction, but also a lucrative invitation to Hollywood to direct a version of Daphne Du Maurier's REBECCA. The critics were almost unanimous in their praise: *The New York Herald Tribune* considered the film "a product of individual imagination and artistry quite as much as a Cézanne canvas or a Stravinsky score", while *Newsweek* noted "Hitchcock lets his audience in on his secret early and piles one thrilling sequence on another as his characters grope slowly and dangerously toward the truth." Orson WELLES claimed to have seen *The Lady Vanishes* at least 11 times.

In 1979 *The Lady Vanishes* was remade as a screwball thriller by Anthony Page; Cybill Shepherd was cast as an eccentric heiress, Elliott Gould as a *Life* photojournalist, and Angela LANSBURY as Miss Froy – this time travelling on a train passing through prewar Nazi Germany. Overwritten and overplayed, the film was a far cry from the original.

Lamarr, Hedy (Hedwig Kiesler; 1914–) US actress, born in Austria, who became one of the most glamorous Hollywood stars of the 1940s. She began her career (as Hedy Kiesler) in Vienna around 1930 and became famous, or rather notorious, after appearing completely naked in the Czech film *Ecstasy* (1933). Such was the furore raised by the film that the man who became her husband shortly afterwards spent a fortune trying to buy up every copy (he failed, as did the marriage).

Having been recruited by Hollywood and renamed by MGM, Lamarr found glamorous roles in such films as *Algiers* (1938), *Boom Town* (1940) and *Comrade X* (1940), both with Clark GABLE, *White Cargo* (1942), and the DE MILLE epic *Samson and Delilah* (1949), in which she appeared opposite Victor MATURE. Films she turned down included CASABLANCA (1942) and George CUKOR's *Gaslight* (1944); both roles went to Ingrid BERGMAN. She never made any pretence of being a great actress (though MGM touted her initially as the new GARBO); King VIDOR noted that "Acting probably didn't come naturally to her" while John Cromwell remarked, "She...didn't have an ego problem. The problem was that she couldn't act."

The decline in her film career from the early 1950s onwards was accompanied by further misfortunes, including repeated marital problems (she was married six times), the loss of virtually all her money, and a well-publicized trial in 1965 for shoplifting (she was acquitted). Publication of a risqué autobiography, *Ecstasy and Me*, in 1966 resulted in Hollywood turning its back on her; in an attempt to limit the damage Lamarr tried to sue her ghostwriters for getting the story wrong.

You too will be "Hedy" with delight and your verdict will be "Lamarrvellous".
Advertising slogan for *Lady of the Tropics* (1939).

Lamour, Dorothy (Mary Leta Dorothy Kaumeyer; 1914–) US actress, whose early Paramount films stereotyped her as a native girl wearing a sarong. She later spoofed this image in the 'Road' comedies of Bob HOPE and Bing CROSBY.

A striking beauty, Lamour was named Miss New Orleans when 17; she subsequently worked as a band singer and made a number of radio appearances that brought her a Paramount contract in 1936. Later that year she made her screen debut as a female TARZAN in *The Jungle Princess*; her sarong started a US fashion trend that lasted for a decade.

When the pre-production crew of her next film, *The Hurricane* (1937), watched *Jungle Princess*, they all agreed that Lamour looked like a 'tart', except director John FORD, who mused, "I can do something for her." After this second role as a scantily clad native girl, Paramount put her in 'sarongers' at every opportunity, even one entitled *Typhoon* (1940).

ROAD TO SINGAPORE (1940) was originally planned as a Lamour vehicle with Fred MACMURRAY and George Burns as comic relief. However, with Hope and Crosby as the male leads, it became the first of an increasingly madcap series that continued with *Road to Zanzibar* (1941), *Road to Morocco* (1942), *Road to Utopia* (1945), *Road to Rio* (1947), *Road to Bali* (1952), and *Road to Hong Kong* (1962). In the last of these, which was filmed in Britain, Lamour made only a guest appearance, having yielded her role as the boys' main love interest to Joan COLLINS.

Lamour made a number of other comedies with Hope, including *Caught in the Draft* (1941), an army farce ("What a bundle", Hope exclaims on seeing the Colonel's daughter, "She looks like Dorothy Lamour with clothes on"). She later played supporting roles in *Donovan's Reef* (1963),

The Phynx (1970), *Won Ton Ton* (1975), and *Creepshow 2* (1987).

Lancaster, Burt (Stephen Burton Lancaster; 1913–94) US actor and occasional director, known for his athletic physique. After leaving New York University, Lancaster spent several years working as an acrobat in circus and vaudeville before an injury forced him to quit. He then worked in a variety of jobs (including singing waiter and lingerie salesman), before joining the army in 1942. It was during his war service that he developed an interest in acting. Following his Broadway debut in 1945, Lancaster received a number of offers from Hollywood, leading to his first screen role in *The Killers* (1946), Robert SIODMAK's seminal FILM NOIR.

Starring roles followed in a number of action films, such as the savage prison drama *Brute Force* (1947) and *I Walk Alone* (1948), of which the critic James AGEE wrote: "The picture deserves, like four out of five other movies, to walk alone, tinkle a little bell, and cry 'Unclean, unclean!'" The same year, however, Lancaster cast aside his tough-guy image to play Chris in *All My Sons* (1948), a screen adaptation of Arthur Miller's play, and took more control of his career by forming his own production company, Hecht-Hill-Lancaster. Lancaster was one of the first actors to make this move, contributing in the process to the downfall of the old STUDIO SYSTEM. His company was later responsible for the innovative and trendsetting *Marty* (1955), which won four Oscars.

In the early 1950s Lancaster made two hugely successful and highly acrobatic SWASHBUCKLERS with his old circus partner Nick Cravat, *The Flame and the Arrow* (1950) and *The Crimson Pirate* (1952). FROM HERE TO ETERNITY (1953) brought Lancaster his first Oscar nomination, in the role of Sergeant Milton Warden. In *The Sweet Smell of Success* (1957) director Alexander MACKENDRICK drew a wonderfully chilling performance from Lancaster as the megalomaniacal gossip columnist J. J. Hunsecker, with Tony CURTIS as his servile agent.

In 1960 Lancaster won the Oscar as Best Actor for his portrayal of an evangelical preacher in the acclaimed ELMER GANTRY. He received a further nomination for his portrayal of Robert Stroud, a convicted murderer who becomes an ornithological expert, in *The Birdman of Alcatraz* (1962).

The following year he starred in VISCONTI's THE LEOPARD, a stunning adaptation of Lampedusa's novel about the decline of the Italian aristocracy. Other notable films of the 1960s included John FRANKENHEIMER's political thriller *Seven Days in May* (1964), the commercially successful *The Professionals* (1966), the enigmatic and definitely uncommercial *The Swimmer* (1967), and Sydney POLLACK's strange war film *Castle Keep* (1969).

During the 1970s Lancaster's production company closed and his career appeared to be coming to an end. However, the 1980s brought him a fresh lease of life: his Oscar-nominated performance as an ageing small-time crook in Louis MALLE's *Atlantic City* (1981) was followed by appearances in *Local Hero* (1983), *Tough Guys* (1986), which paired Lancaster with Kirk DOUGLAS for the eighth time, and *Field of Dreams* (1989). Lancaster was also lined up to play opposite Jane FONDA in *Old Gringo* (1989), a role that eventually went to Gregory PECK.

> The living proof that you can be a sensitive actor and macho at the same time.
> KIRK DOUGLAS.

Lanchester, Elsa (Elizabeth Sullivan; 1902–86) Red-haired British character actress, who specialized in eccentric roles. She earned Oscar nominations as Best Supporting Actress for *Come to the Stable* (1949), in which she played a religious painter, and *Witness for the Prosecution* (1957), one of several films in which she co-starred with her husband Charles LAUGHTON. Lanchester and Laughton became US citizens in 1950.

Born in Lewisham, Lanchester danced with Isadora Duncan's company as a child. She met Laughton on the London stage in 1926; they were living together when she made her film debut in *One of the Best* (1927) and married two years later. Although Laughton later confessed his homosexuality, and both had extramarital affairs, their marriage lasted until his death in 1962.

In 1933 Lanchester's comic portrayal of Anne of Cleves in KORDA'S THE PRIVATE LIFE OF HENRY VIII, gave a major boost to her career; the film starred Laughton in the title role. The couple went to Hollywood the following year. Lanchester's best-known US film was Universal's classic *The Bride of Frankenstein* (1935), in which she played both author Mary Shelley and the eccentrically coiffured

female created for the monster (*see* FRANK-
ENSTEIN). After appearing as Clickett in
George CUKOR's *David Copperfield* (1935) she
joined her husband again for Korda's *Rembrandt* (1936) and the comedy *Vessel of
Wrath* (US title *The Beachcomber*; 1937),
about a prudish woman missionary who
falls for an alcoholic. In the 1940s and
1950s she continued to display her versatility with the thriller *The Spiral Staircase* (1945), the heartwarming *Come to the
Stable* (1949), and *Witness for the Prosecution*, in which she played Laughton's
over-protective nurse.

Apart from MARY POPPINS (1964), in
which she played a small role, Lanchester's
later films were mostly horror movies and
comedy thrillers; they included *Willard*
(1971), *Terror in the Wax Museum* (1973),
Murder by Death (1976), and *Die Laughing*
(1980).

Landis, John (1950–) US director and
screenwriter noted for his quirky comedies,
often with juvenile appeal. Many of his films
have featured comedians from the long-
running US television series *Saturday
Night Live*, (among them John BELUSHI, Dan
AYKROYD, and Chevy CHASE). One of Landis's
directorial whims was the inclusion of the
words "See you next Wednesday" in all his
films up to the mid 1980s (when the audience began to notice). Another is his passion for CAMEOS: no less than nine fellow
directors make fleeting appearances in *Spies
Like Us* (1985).

After his 1976 debut with the little-
known comedy *Schlock*, Landis came to public attention with *Kentucky Fried Movie*
(1977), a series of sketches satirizing TV
commercials, pornographic movies, and
MARTIAL ARTS MOVIES amongst much else. His
big break followed in 1978 with *National
Lampoon's Animal House*, a raucous parody
of college life starring John Belushi. The
romp featured a food fight that was later
imitated on many real campuses. *The Blues
Brothers* (1980) was an expensive $33-
million flop that went on to become a cult
film, with Belushi and Aykroyd reprising
their Blues Brothers act from *Saturday Night
Live*. The script was by Landis and Aykroyd.
Landis also scripted his successful horror
spoof *An American Werewolf in London*
(1981), a film featuring Oscar-winning special effects by Rick Baker. The critic Roger
Ebert noted that Landis clearly "didn't want

to bother with things like transitions, character development, or an ending."

In 1983 Landis directed one of the four
segments of *Twilight Zone: The Movie*. During filming, the actor Vic Morrow and two
children were killed in a helicopter crash;
Landis was subsequently acquitted of manslaughter charges. Later that year, he made
the box-office hit *Trading Places* in which
tramp Eddie MURPHY swaps lives with yuppie Aykroyd. This was followed by *Spies Like
Us*, a homage to the 'Road' films of Bing
CROSBY and Bob HOPE, with Aykroyd and
Chase as bumbling intelligence men and a
cameo appearance by Hope himself. *Three
Amigos!* (1986), a spoof of THE MAGNIFICENT
SEVEN featuring Chase, Steve MARTIN, and
Martin Short, was rather coolly received.
Landis enjoyed greater success with the
comedy *Coming to America* (1988), in which
Murphy played an African prince who ends
up cleaning floors in New York. His latest
film is *Innocent Blood* (1992).

> If you can drive a car, you can direct a
> movie.
> JOHN LANDIS; *Film Yearbook*, 1990.

Lang, Fritz (1890–1976) Austrian-born
director and screenwriter who was prominent in the German EXPRESSIONIST movement before embarking on a successful
20-year Hollywood career. His thrillers,
melodramas, and SCIENCE-FICTION films explored the psychology of violence and the
destructive power of love. "The fight of the
individual against destiny", he once said,
"is probably the basis of all my films."

Born in Vienna, Lang studied architecture and art before travelling to the Far East
as an itinerant painter. In 1919 he wrote
and directed his first film, *The Half-Breed*, in
Berlin. The following year he began to collaborate on scripts with Thea von Harbou,
whom he subsequently married. Their successes included *Destiny* (1921), an expressionist allegory about death, *Dr Mabuse the
Gambler* (1922), which introduced Lang's
famous master criminal, and the two-part
epic *The Nibelungen* (1924). On a visit to
New York Lang conceived METROPOLIS
(1927), a film about a futuristic society controlled by robots. Scripted by von Harbou, it
was the most expensive film that had ever
been produced in Germany.

Lang followed this with *The Girl in the
Moon* (1928), a somewhat muddled science-fiction movie; curiously the film provided the origin of the rocket countdown

later used for real-life launches. His first sound film, and his own favourite, was the expressionistic M (1931) starring Peter LORRE as a child murderer. Because *The Testament of Dr Mabuse* (1932) put Nazi slogans into the mouths of heavies it was banned when Hitler came to power. Bizarrely, Joseph Goebbels then asked Lang, a Jew, to head Germany's film industry. Lang immediately fled to France and then America; his wife, who remained in Germany, later divorced him and directed Nazi films.

In 1936 Lang made his Hollywood debut with *Fury*, a film about mob violence. After America's entry into the war he collaborated with Bertolt Brecht on the anti-Nazi film *Hangmen Also Die* (1943), although Brecht considered the end result to be so far from his original idea that he insisted the credits indicate that his script was not used. Lang later made *Scarlet Street* (1945), Hollywood's first movie to leave a crime unpunished, *Rancho Notorious* (1952), starring Marlene DIETRICH, and *The Big Heat* (1953), a successful thriller. He left Hollywood in 1957 and returned to Germany, saying, "I think I'll step out of this rat race." In 1960 he directed his last film, *The 1000 Eyes of Dr Mabuse*. After appearing as himself in Jean-Luc GODARD's *Le Mépris* (1963), he retired to Beverly Hills.

Lansbury, Angela (1925–) British-born US actress and singer, who has frequently appeared in unsympathetic or villainous parts; more recently, this image has been tempered by her television role as a kindly sleuth in the series *Murder She Wrote*. Lansbury has also appeared on Broadway in such musicals as *Gypsy* (1974) and *Sweeney Todd* (1979).

The daughter of an actress (and the granddaughter of Labour Party leader George Lansbury), she went on the stage as a child and studied drama in London and New York. In 1943 she moved to Hollywood to sign an MGM contract; a year later, at the age of 18, she won an Oscar nomination for Best Supporting Actress in her first screen role, as a lovestruck servant in the thriller *Gaslight*. Lansbury also played Elizabeth TAYLOR's friend in *National Velvet* (1944). She made several musicals in her early career, playing a music-hall singer in *The Picture of Dorian Gray* (1945) and a saloon hussy in *The Harvey Girls* (1946). More varied parts followed, such as Queen Anne in

THE THREE MUSKETEERS (1948) and Samson's wife in *Samson and Delilah* (1949). Her comedies included *The Court Jester* (1955) with Danny KAYE.

In the early 1960s, Lansbury began to be cast as the dominating mother: in 1962 she bullied her sons Warren BEATTY and Brandon de Wilde in *All Fall Down* and appeared as the monstrous mother of Laurence Harvey (just three years her junior) in the political thriller *The Manchurian Candidate*. The latter role brought her an Oscar nomination. Her later parts have included a bumbling witch in DISNEY's *Bedknobs and Broomsticks* (1971), Agatha Christie's Miss MARPLE in *The Mirror Crack'd* (1981), the pirates' nursemaid in *The Pirates of Penzance* (1983), and Granny in Neil JORDAN's *The Company of Wolves* (1984). She also supplied one of the voices in Disney's *Beauty and the Beast* (1991).

lap. **lap dissolve** *See* DISSOLVE.

lap splice *See* SPLICE.

Lassie The doughty collie-dog heroine of Eric Knight's *Lassie Come Home* (1940), a novel for children, who went on to feature in a series of MGM films of the 1940s. *Lassie Come Home* (1943) was followed by *The Courage of Lassie* (1946), *Son of Lassie* (1945), and *The Sun Comes Up* (1949). Later adaptations have included *Lassie*, a popular and long-running US television series, *Lassie's Rescue Rangers* (1973–75), an animated series, and the TV movie *Lassie: The New Beginning* (1978). Lassie returned to the big screen in the musical *The Magic of Lassie* (1978), a reworking of the story of *Lassie Come Home*.

The part of Lassie in the early films was actually played by a male dog called Pal; among his co-stars were Roddy McDowell, Elizabeth TAYLOR, and Jeanette MACDONALD, who made her last screen appearance in *The Sun Comes Up*. Like all animal stars, Pal often required edible incentives to perform, such as a dog biscuit on the far side of a door that he was to scratch at, and ice cream smeared on a cheek that he was to lick. On one occasion, he limped so convincingly (thanks to a piece of chewing gum under his paw) that cinema-goers complained in their thousands about cruelty to animals.

last. *The Last Laugh* (*Der leztze Mann*; 1924) F. W. MURNAU's silent classic, a landmark in the development of CAMERA MOVEMENT. Considered too old to cope with the demands of his job, the pompous uniformed doorman of the Hotel Atlantis (Emil JANNINGS) is demoted to the post of lavatory attendant; his humiliation is soon alleviated by the sizeable bequest left to him by a US millionaire for being the last man to serve him. This most visual of silents (it has just one explanatory caption) became one of the key films of the age owing to its innovative camerawork. Screenwriter Carl Mayer devised with Murnau the idea of the 'unchained camera', which allowed events to be depicted from the point of view of the protagonist (*see* SUBJECTIVE CAMERA). The most celebrated example was the opening TRAVELLING SHOT, in which the camera was attached to a bicycle and made to descend to the hotel vestibule, cross the hall, and then (with a cut between shots) continue into the street.

Later, in order to depict Jannings's drunken delirium, the camera was strapped to the chest of cinematographer Karl Freund, who proceeded to stagger about the room; on other occasions it was mounted on the ladder of a fire engine, suspended from overhead cables, and swung through the air attached to a piece of scaffolding. The famous dream sequence was shot using distorting mirrors, while the episode in which the doorman juggles the heavy cases was achieved by means of a series of pulleys and invisible wires. Jannings had considerable difficulty acquiring the deft touch required to complete this illusion, but Murnau kept him at it until he got his shot at around two a.m. Murnau's biographer, Lotte Eisner, declares that "it was the almost universal decision of Hollywood that this was the greatest picture ever made."

Last Year in Marienbad (*L'Anée dernière à Marienbad*; 1961) Alain RESNAIS's enigmatic art-house drama, a film scripted by the experimental novelist Alain Robbe-Grillet. Never in the history of cinema has the action of a film been open to so many widely differing interpretations: "We never really know if the scenes are occurring in the man's mind or the woman's", said Resnais. Did X (Giorgio Albertazzi) really meet A (Delphine Seyrig) in the Frederiksbad gardens the previous year and did she really promise to elope with him? Is the film really taking place in the mind of A, as she wonders whether to leave M (Sacha Pitoëff), the

man who may be her husband, or to heed her recurrent premonitions of disaster? Or, if the assault we see M perpetrate on A really did result in her death, is the entire picture merely X's painful memory? Does the film's circular structure mean that it actually starts at the point where it appears to end?

According to Resnais, "*Marienbad* is an 'open' film which proposes to everyone an involvement, or a choice." Shot in Paris and on location in the Schleissheim, Nymphenburg, and Amalienburg castles near Munich, it questions both the reliability of memory and the nature of reality. The film relies on stylized TRACKING SHOTS and meticulously composed MISE-EN-SCÈNE to recreate the complex chain of images past, present, and future that pass through the minds of the characters – a sort of cinematic stream of consciousness. Indeed, the critic Dwight McDonald considers it to be "the *Finnegans Wake* of the movies". Resnais wrote:

> We hope that the lyrical dream world that is to be found in this picture will appeal to the collective unconscious of people in all countries.

The film won the Golden Lion at the Venice Film Festival and an Oscar nomination for Best Original Screenplay. Yet not everyone has concurred with these accolades: Harry and Michael Medved, instigators of the Golden Turkey awards, deemed it one of the 50 worst movies of all time.

Latham loop *See* CAMERA; INTERMITTENT MOVEMENT.

Laughton, Charles (1899–1962) British-born US actor, who established his reputation with a series of character roles on the London stage. He made his first film appearances in the British shorts *Bluebottles* (1928) and *Daydreams* (1928), both of which also featured his future wife Elsa LANCHESTER.

Following success on Broadway in the early 1930s, Laughton went to Hollywood, where he quickly impressed in such films as James WHALE's *The Old Dark House* (1932), with Boris KARLOFF, and Cecil B. DE MILLE's *The Sign of the Cross* (1932), in which he played the emperor Nero. It was however, his outstanding portrayal of the title figure in Alexander KORDA's THE PRIVATE LIFE OF HENRY VIII (1933) that made his name in the cinema (Lanchester played Anne of Cleves). The film brought him a Best Actor Oscar, the first ever Academy Award for a British movie.

Laughton followed this triumph with a run of brilliant performances, mainly in vicious or bullying roles; these included Dr Moreau in the classic chiller *Island of Lost Souls* (1933), the tyrannical father in *The Barretts of Wimpole Street* (1934), a marvellously self-righteous Captain Bligh in *Mutiny on the Bounty* (1935), for which he was Oscar nominated, and the merciless Javert in *Les Misérables* (1935). More sympathetic parts included the painter in *Rembrandt* (1936) and Quasimodo in THE HUNCHBACK OF NOTRE DAME (1939).

Judged against the brilliance of these films, Laughton's movies of the 1940s and early 1950s were a disappointment. He himself was having grave personal problems at the time, feeling insecure about both his physical appearance and his homosexuality. Even during this troubled period he turned in the occasional strong performance, however, notably as Georges Simenon's Inspector Maigret in *The Man on the Eiffel Tower* (1949). From the mid 1950s Laughton once again shone in such roles as the belligerent title character in David LEAN's *Hobson's Choice* (1957), the barrister Sir Wilfred Roberts in Billy WILDER's *Witness for the Prosecution* (1957), which brought him another Best Actor nomination, and the senator Gracchus in KUBRICK's *Spartacus* (1960). His last role was that of a sneaky Southern senator in Otto PREMINGER's *Advise and Consent* (1962).

Laughton made only one film as a director, the haunting, beautiful, and downright chilling *The Night of the Hunter* (1955), a tale of murder and religious mania set in the US South during the Great Depression. The film, which was scripted by James AGEE, features a wonderful performance from Robert MITCHUM as Preacher Harry Powell, a psycho with 'love' tattooed on one hand and 'hate' on the other. The relative failure of this minor masterpiece discouraged Laughton from further directorial projects, which apparently included a planned adaptation of Mailer's *The Naked and the Dead*.

Launder, Frank See GILLIAT, SIDNEY.

Laura (1944) Otto PREMINGER's atmospheric thriller, described by Pauline KAEL as "everybody's favourite chic murder mystery." The spare script was based on a novel by Vera Caspary and greatly enhanced by David Raskin's haunting theme music. With its obsessive characters, devious plot, and moody ambience, *Laura* was an important forerunner of the FILM NOIR genre of the later 1940s.

Preminger, the film's producer, took over as director when Rouben MAMOULIAN was sacked after a few days of shooting. The film made Preminger's reputation: his long takes, flashbacks, and light drifting pace created a strange tension, earning him his first Academy Award nomination. The film's only Oscar went to Joseph LaShelle for Best Black-and-White Cinematography. Gene TIERNEY starred in the title role (refused by Jennifer JONES, whom 20th Century-Fox unsuccessfully sued for $613,000). Clifton Webb received an Oscar nomination for Best Supporting Actor in his first sound film and first screen appearance for 20 years. (He opens the film with a soliloquy.) The small cast also included Dana Andrews in his first major role, Judith Anderson, and Vincent PRICE.

A body found in a New York apartment is identified as that of Laura, a beautiful art executive. The investigating police lieutenant (Andrews) becomes increasingly obsessed with the case as he falls in love with her mysterious portrait and begins to interview those close to her, including her aunt (Anderson), a debonair acerbic critic (Webb), and her weak fiancé (Price). Midway through the film, however, the real Laura suddenly appears.

Laurel and Hardy Hollywood's most successful COMEDY TEAM, the thin British-born Stan Laurel (Arthur Stanley Jefferson; 1890–1965) and the tubby Oliver Hardy (1892–1957). Despite making over 100 films together, including 27 features, the duo did not socialize off set. Their fans ranged from Winston CHURCHILL to Joseph Stalin. The driving force of the team was Laurel, who often scripted and helped to direct. In 1960 he received a special Academy Award for his "creative pioneering in the field of cinema comedy."

Their comedy, which translated easily from silent to sound movies, depended on the universal appeal of their characters (known in Germany as 'Dick und Doof' – fat and dumb). When trouble arrived, the simple-minded Laurel would give a blank look, blink his eyes, scratch the top of his head, and weep like a baby; the sharper Ollie would twiddle his tie, gaze helplessly at the camera, and complain to his partner, "Here's another nice mess you've gotten me into."

The son of actors, Laurel was born in Ulverston, Lancashire, and made his stage debut at the age of 16. Having become Charlie CHAPLIN's understudy in Fred Karno's vaudeville troupe, he remained in America after their 1912 tour. Five years later he made his screen debut in *Nuts in May* and appeared in *Lucky Dog*, a film that also featured Hardy. However, the two did not team up until 1926, the year Laurel signed with Hal ROACH.

Hardy was a lawyer's son from Harlem, Georgia (where a Laurel and Hardy Museum now exists) and began his performing career with a minstrel show at the age of eight. In 1910 he abandoned his law studies to open a cinema, making his film debut in *Outwitting Dad* four years later. He went on to play villains and character parts in such comedies as Buster KEATON's *The Three Ages* (1923) before becoming a fellow Hal Roach All Star with Laurel.

Their best known shorts, most of which were directed by James Parrott, included *The Battle of the Century* (1927), in which a record 3,000 pies are thrown, *Unaccustomed as We Are* (1929), their first talkie, the Oscar-winning *The Music Box* (1932), in which the duo suffer multiple disasters carrying a piano up a long flight of stairs, and *Their First Mistake* (1932), in which Stan tells Olly, "You know, I'm not so dumb as you look."

Among their features were *Fra Diavolo* (1933), in which they get giggling drunk in a wine cellar, the excellent *Sons of the Desert* (1933), *Blockheads* (1938), *A Chump at Oxford* (1940), and *Great Guns* (1941), remembered for the sight gag in which Stan crosses the screen carrying the front end of a long plank and then reappears carrying the rear end.

Laurel and Hardy left Roach in 1940; most of their later, inferior, films were made for 20th Century-Fox or MGM. After abandoning the screen in 1945 to tour Britain in music hall, they made only one more film, the disastrous French-Italian *Atoll K* (US title *Robinson Crusoeland*; 1950); they made another British tour in 1954. Although a comeback was planned, Hardy died following a stroke and Laurel never performed again.

Lavender Hill Mob, The (1951) Charles Crichton's tongue-in-cheek HEIST MOVIE, one of the best-loved of the EALING comedies. It tells of a bullion raid masterminded by a mild-mannered bank clerk (Alec GUINNESS); following the robbery, Guinness and his gang (comprising Stanley Holloway, Sid James, and Alfie Bass) attempt, unsuccessfully, to smuggle the gold to the Continent in the form of souvenir Eiffel Towers.

Michael BALCON had originally detailed scriptwriter T. E. B. Clarke to research a serious thriller to be called *Pool of London*. However, following visits to a small docklands foundry and the Bank of England (during which a number of senior officials had provided him with several ingenious robbery stratagems), Clarke became convinced that he had the material for a comedy. Liberally spoofing his own script for Basil DEARDEN's 1949 classic *The Blue Lamp* (which made a star of Dirk BOGARDE and gave the world Dixon of Dock Green), Clarke produced a 112-minute screenplay, which the precise Crichton honed to just 78 minutes. Balcon was reportedly furious that Clarke had disregarded his orders, but scheduled the shooting of *The Lavender Hill Mob* on the same locations as *Pool of London* (which had gone ahead anyway); during one chase sequence, Guinness stumbled onto the *Pool of London* set and ruined a take.

Guinness received an Oscar nomination for his performance as Dutch Holland, while Clarke took the Academy Award for Best Original Screenplay. The film also contains early screen appearances by James FOX (then 12 years old, and billed as William Fox) and Audrey HEPBURN (as Guinness's escort, Chiquita, in the opening bar sequence).

Lawrence of Arabia (1962) David LEAN's sweeping BIOPIC of the desert adventurer T. E. Lawrence, a film that cost $15 million and took three years to make. It won seven Academy Awards, including Best Picture and Best Director. Maurice Jarre took an Oscar for his stirring music, and screenwriter Robert Bolt was nominated for his script, a loose adaptation of Lawrence's *The Seven Pillars of Wisdom*. The *New York Times* critic, however, called it "just a huge thundering camel opera."

The film starred two unknowns, Peter O'TOOLE (as Lawrence) and Omar SHARIF, both of whom were nominated for Academy Awards. Albert FINNEY refused the title role, and Sharif replaced first-choice Alain

Delon. Cary GRANT was to have played General Allenby, a role that ultimately went to Jack HAWKINS. The cast also included Alec GUINNESS, Anthony QUAYLE, Anthony QUINN, and Jose Ferrer. The locations, including Saudia Arabia, Jordan, Morocco, and Spain, were filmed strikingly in Super-PANAVISION by Freddie Young, who won an Oscar. A re-edited and fully restored version of the film was released in 1989, with much missing footage reinstated (including cuts made in Sharif's famous long entrance by camel). Some of the dialogue had to be re-recorded as a result of damage to the master negative.

Over three and a half hours long in the 1989 version, the film opens with Lawrence's death in a motorcycle accident then flashes back to 1916, when we see him as an obscure intelligence officer in Cairo. Having been assigned to observe the Arab revolt against the Turks, Germany's ally in World War I, Lawrence persuades Prince Feisal (Guinness) to let him lead a raid on the strategic port of Aqaba. Although Lawrence's Arabs eventually sweep into Damascus, he is disillusioned by the Allies' failure to honour promises to give the Arabs independence and returns home a broken and bewildered man.

While Lean admired Lawrence greatly, Bolt, a pacifist, was determined to present him as a more ambiguous figure, corrupted by power and bloodshed. Arguably, the resulting portrait is less complex than incoherent. Following the film's release, relatives of Lawrence, Allenby, and some of the Arab characters protested bitterly at its historical misrepresentations. The film is banned in most Arab countries and has never been shown in Turkey.

lead The principal role in a film. The term is also applied to the actor or actress who plays this part, also known as the **leading man** or **leading lady** (especially when a film has two leads, male and female).

leader The blank length of film at the head or tail of a reel; its function is to protect the film proper from wear or damage in threading. An Academy leader, i.e. one that conforms to standards set by the ACADEMY OF MOTION PICTURE ARTS AND SCIENCES, provides a projectionist with the film title, the reel number, and a numbered countdown to the start of the action.

Lean, Sir David (1908–91) British director and screenwriter, noted for his expensive epic productions. Lean began his career as a studio teaboy, gradually working his way up to become an editor for such directors as Paul Czinner, Anthony ASQUITH, and Michael POWELL. In 1942 he co-directed Noël COWARD's wartime adventure *In Which We Serve*, beginning a collaboration that continued with *This Happy Breed* (1944), *Blithe Spirit* (1945), and the much-loved BRIEF ENCOUNTER (1945), one of the classic romances of the British cinema.

In 1946 Lean established his international reputation with GREAT EXPECTATIONS, a masterly adaptation of the novel by Charles DICKENS. A further Dickens adaptation, *Oliver Twist*, followed in 1948. During the 1950s he made a number of relatively small-budget films, such as *The Sound Barrier* (1952), which co-starred Ralph RICHARDSON and Lean's wife Ann Todd, and *Hobson's Choice* (1953), with Charles LAUGHTON and John MILLS. The lavish romance *Summer Madness*, with Katharine HEPBURN, followed in 1955. This led to the first of his big-budget epics, THE BRIDGE ON THE RIVER KWAI (1957), a World-War-II drama starring Alec GUINNESS as an obsessive British officer in a Japanese prisoner-of-war camp. This moving, intelligent, and beautifully photographed film earned Lean an Oscar as Best Director.

During the 1960s Lean continued to make spectacular larger-than-life movies including LAWRENCE OF ARABIA (1962), with Peter O'TOOLE as T. E. Lawrence, and *Doctor Zhivago* (1965), starring Omar SHARIF and Julie Christie in a love story set in post-revolutionary Russia. *Ryan's Daughter* (1970), an intimate story of adultery in an Irish village in 1916, was somewhat swamped by Lean's epic treatment and was coolly received; Lean later remarked, "No one caught on that *Ryan's Daughter* was actually an adaptation of *Madame Bovary*."

After a break of 14 years, Lean, now 76, returned to the cinema with *A Passage to India* (1984), a sensitive interpretation of the novel by E. M. Forster. With this, his last film, Lean largely re-established his earlier reputation.

Lee. **Bruce Lee** (Lee Yuan Kam; 1940–73) US film star, who demonstrated his mastery of the MARTIAL ARTS in a series of action-packed low-budget movies. His films enjoyed an enormous box-office success and inspired the kung-fu cult of the 1970s.

Born in San Francisco, the son of a Chinese opera star, he was brought up in Hong Kong, where he received his first instruction in the martial arts. Although he later returned to America as a student and worked briefly as a television actor there, the films that brought him fame were all made in Hong Kong; these include *Fist of Fury* (1972), *Enter the Dragon* (1973), and *The Way of the Dragon* (1973). After his sudden death in mysterious circumstances at the age of 33, he became something of a cult figure. The US BIOPIC *A Dragon Story* (British title *The Bruce Lee Story*; 1974) was followed by a number of Hong Kong films supposedly based on his life, including *Bruce Lee – True Story* (1976) and *Bruce Lee: the Man, the Myth* (1978). Another US biopic, *Dragon: The Bruce Lee Story*, was released in 1993.

His son **Brandon Lee** (1966–94), who appeared in *Kung Fu: The Movie* (1986) and went on to star in *Rapid Fire* (1992), died at the age of 28 while filming *The Crow* (1994).

> His fans say things like: "Hey, I loved your dad. C'mon, tell the truth – he's still alive, isn't he?"
> BRANDON LEE.

Christopher Lee (1922–) British actor best known for his horror roles, especially that of DRACULA. Born in London, Lee made his screen debut in *Corridor of Mirrors* (1948), following this with a small part in Laurence OLIVIER's *Hamlet*; coincidentally, the film also featured his frequent screen partner Peter CUSHING. His first horror role was that of the monster in HAMMER's *The Curse of Frankenstein* (1957), for which one critic suggested a new certificate: SO, for sadists only. It was also in 1957 that he first donned the cape to play the title role in *Dracula*. Initially he was given very few lines, perhaps because his voice – a suburban English drone – did not match his gaunt aristocratic presence. He went on to play the part 11 times, mostly for Hammer, who also cast him in the title roles of *The Mummy* (1959), *Rasputin, The Mad Monk* (1965), and a series of six films starting with *The Face of Fu Manchu* (1965).

During the past 45 years Lee has appeared in over 200 movies from 12 different countries (he is an accomplished linguist). In the 1970s alone, his films ranged from the grim *Starship Invasions* (1977) to the glorious *Julius Caesar* (1970), from the BOND film *The Man with the Golden Gun* (1974) to self-parody in SPIELBERG's *1941* (1979), and from Robin Hardy's sinister *The Wicker Man* (1973) to Richard LESTER's spoof version of THE THREE MUSKETEERS (1973). His more recent films include *Gremlins 2* (1990) and *Death Train* (1992).

Lee is also a writer, and has had many of his plays broadcast on British radio.

> There are many vampires in the world today – you only have to think of the film business.
> CHRISTOPHER LEE; *Films Illustrated*, 1971.

Spike Lee (Shelton Jackson Lee; 1957–) US producer, director, actor, and screenwriter, whose polemical films about Black life in contemporary America have aroused both admiration and anger. Lee, who works from his own 40 Acres and a Mule Filmworks in Brooklyn, has also directed music videos and commercials, as well as writing several books about his films.

Born in Atlanta, Georgia, he was educated at New York University and the Institute of Film and Television. In the early 1980s he wrote scripts for several New York films before directing the short *Joe's Bed-Study Barbershop: We Cut Heads* (1983). Two years later, he directed, produced, wrote, edited, and acted in his award-winning *She's Gotta Have It*, shot in Super 16MM in 15 days. The story concerns an independent young Black woman (Tracy Camilla Johns), who is unable to decide between three very different men.

The success of this film led Columbia to back Lee's next project, *School Daze* (1988), a musical set in a Black university; the director himself plays Half-Pint, a diminutive freshman. *Do the Right Thing* (1989), a provocative look at relations between Blacks and Italian-Americans in a Brooklyn neighbourhood, won Oscar nominations for Lee's screenplay and for Danny Aiello as Best Supporting Actor. *Mo' Better Blues* (1990) starred Denzel Washington as a New York jazz musician and Lee as his manager, while *Jungle Fever* (1991) explored an interracial romance between Black yuppie Wesley Snipes and working-class Italian Annabella Sciorra.

In 1992 Lee made *Malcolm X*, a three-and-a-half hour biopic of the controversial Black leader, for Warner Brothers; Denzel Washington received an Oscar nomination for his performance in the title role. Lee's most recent film is *Crooklyn* (1994), starring

Alfre Woodard, Delroy Lindon, and Zelda Harris.

Legion of Decency Familiar title of the **National Legion of Decency**, a Catholic body founded by a group of US bishops in 1933 to campaign against immorality in US films. Supported by many Protestant and Jewish groups, it exerted enormous pressure on the industry until the 1960s. A year after the Legion was founded, Hollywood arranged for a Catholic priest and a layman to rewrite its self-regulatory Production Code (*see* HAYS CODE).

The Legion's board reviewed films before their release and classified them as 'Passed', 'Objectionable in Part', or 'Condemned'. Findings were then announced from pulpits. Catholics were advised to stay away from partly objectionable films and told it was a venial sin to view a condemned movie. Studios regularly submitted films and even scripts for the Legion's approval, although Darryl F. ZANUCK ignored its advice not to produce *Forever Amber* in 1947, as did Otto PREMINGER with *The Moon is Blue* in 1953. Amongst the films condemned by the Legion were Ingmar BERGMAN's *The Silence* (1963), which it described as "dangerously close to pornography", and Sidney LUMET's *The Pawnbroker* (1965), which contained female nudity. In the latter half of the 1960s the Legion lost influence and became more lenient, changing its name in 1966 to the National Catholic Office for Motion Pictures.

Leigh. **Mike Leigh** (1943–) British director, one of the sharpest and most sardonic observers of the contemporary British scene.

Having dropped out of RADA and a series of art colleges, Leigh, a native of Salford, enrolled at the London Film School and began to direct for the stage. In 1971 he adapted his own play *Bleak Moments* for the cinema (with financial backing from Albert FINNEY). Although the picture, about the futile attempts of a London typist to escape from the drudgery of caring for her disturbed sister, was critically acclaimed, Leigh would not work in film again for another 17 years. During this period he directed some of the most memorable plays ever whown on British television, including *Nuts in May* (1976), the cult comedy *Abigail's Party* (1977), and *Meantime* (1983). He also perfected his celebrated method of working, in

which he devises a situation, selects his cast, and then spends weeks in improvisational rehearsal before shooting.

In 1988 Leigh returned to the cinema with *High Hopes*, a poignant depiction of changing social attitudes in Thatcherite Britain. Presenting Englishness as a sort of incurable ailment, the film made the everyday lives of ordinary people seem utterly compelling. *Life is Sweet* (1990), a cosier comedy, focused on the cruelties and embarrassments of family life and the failure of most attempts at meaningful communication. The picture, which starred Leigh's wife and regular collaborator Alison Steadman, drew the usual accusations that he was patronizing his working-class characters. He responded:

> My job is to put characters on the screen the way people are...Of course there are characters who are depicted unsympathetically, but that's because there are people in society who are deeply dangerous and disgusting. But this thing about being patronizing to the working class, I have never heard that from someone with a working-class background, ever.

In 1993 Leigh won the Directors' Prize at Cannes with *Naked*, a film that marked a clear departure from the measured satire of his earlier work. This relentless (and, according to many critics, misogynistic) film presents Leigh's bleakest vision of Britain, with David Thewlis quite magnificent as a foul-mouthed Mancunian loose on the streets of London.

Vivien Leigh (Vivian Mary Hartley; 1913–67) Beautiful British actress, best known as Scarlett O'HARA in GONE WITH THE WIND (1939). The second wife of Laurence OLIVIER, she suffered from tuberculosis throughout her career and later developed a manic-depressive condition.

Born in Darjeeling, India, the daughter of a British exchange broker, Leigh was educated at convents in Britain and Europe before enrolling at RADA. She made her film debut in *Things Are Looking Up* (1934); although her agent suggested she took the name of 'April Morn', she decided to adopt the middle name of her first husband, barrister Herbert Leigh Holman. In 1937 she starred with Olivier on stage and in Alexander KORDA's *Fire Over England* and they began an affair. Both were married at the time.

After co-starring with Robert TAYLOR in *A Yank at Oxford* (1938), Leigh followed Olivier to Hollywood, where he made WUTHERING HEIGHTS (1939). When she lost the part of Cathy to Merle OBERON, Leigh turned down a secondary role in the film, despite being warned by director William WYLER that as a virtual unknown in America she would be offered nothing better. Shortly afterwards David O. SELZNICK chose her over some 1400 candidates (including such stars as Bette DAVIS, Norma SHEARER, Katharine HEPBURN, and Paulette GODDARD) for the role of Scarlett. Although she received only $15,000, was billed fourth, and suffered various indignities from director Victor FLEMING (including having to stuff cotton wool into her dress to enhance her bosom), the role brought her an Academy Award and overnight stardom.

In 1941 Leigh and Olivier, who had married the previous year, co-starred in *Lady Hamilton* (British title *That Hamilton Woman*). Leigh went on to play Cleopatra in *Caesar and Cleopatra* (1945) and the title role of *Anna Karenina* (1948). In 1951 she recovered from a severe attack of tuberculosis to earn a second Oscar playing the fragile Southerner Blanche Dubois in *A Streetcar Named Desire*. She had previously played the part in a 1949 stage production directed by Olivier.

While shooting *Elephant Walk* (1953), Leigh suffered a breakdown and was replaced by Elizabeth TAYLOR (the original star is clearly visible in some of the film's long shots). Her increasingly unbalanced (and openly promiscuous) behaviour led to the end of her marriage to Olivier in 1961. Leigh made her last screen appearance in *Ship of Fools* (1965). On her death from tuberculosis the exterior lights of West End theatres were dimmed for an hour as a mark of respect.

Leisen, Mitchell (1898–1972) US director, who moved from romantic comedies to costume dramas during his 20 years at Paramount. In the 1940s he drew on his background in costume and set design to create such glamorous productions as *Lady in the Dark* (1945) with Ginger ROGERS.

Born in Menominee, Michigan, Leisen studied architecture and worked for a Chicago practice until 1919, when he left for Hollywood. He designed costumes for Cecil B. DE MILLE and won an Oscar nomination as set designer for *Dynamite* (1929) before making his debut as a solo director with *Cradle Song* in 1933. This was followed by such witty SCREWBALL COMEDIES as *Easy Living* (1937) with Jean ARTHUR, and the excellent *Midnight* (1939) with Claudette COLBERT. The former was written by Preston STURGES and the latter co-scripted by Billy WILDER and Charles Brackett; according to Hollywood rumour, Leisen's flippant handling of their scripts provoked both Sturges and Wilder to become directors themselves.

Wilder also supplied the script for Leisen's *Hold Back the Dawn* (1941), a touching romance starring Charles BOYER and Paulette GODDARD. The film begins with a scene in which Boyer's character sells his story to Leisen, who is seen directing actors on set. *Frenchman's Creek* (1944) with Joan FONTAINE cost $4 million, making it the most expensive production of its time; Leisen later described it as "lousy". *Kitty* (1945), was a *Pygmalion*-style story starring Paulette Goddard as a cockney girl who is transformed into a lady by Ray MILLAND. In the late 1940s and 1950s Leisen's career declined; he directed some television episodes, before retiring from films to become an interior decorator.

> He found himself in the unenviable position of a diamond cutter working with lumpy coal.
> ANDREW SARRIS, film critic.

Lelouch, Claude (1937–) French director. Although Lelouch made his debut as a director in 1960 and continues to work today, audiences still know him almost entirely for the hugely successful *A Man and a Woman* (1966). The film, which won both the Palme d'Or at the Cannes Film Festival and the Oscar as Best Foreign Film, attracted wide international audiences by applying the stylistic innovations of the French NEW WAVE to a rather conventional love story. Anouk AIMÉE plays a widowed film script girl and Jean-Louis Trintignant the racing driver with whom she begins a romance.

Critics have generally found Lelouch's subsequent films – beginning with *Life for Life* (1967), a melodramatic treatment of similar themes set in New York and Vietnam – disappointing. Lelouch was one of the directors who collaborated on *Far from Vietnam* (1969), a protest against the Vietnam War. In 1973 he wrote, produced, and directed *Happy New Year*, another variant on the theme of *A Man and a Woman*, this time about the relationship between a jewellery thief and an antiques dealer. This was followed by *And Now My Love* (1975) and the Western *Another Man, Another Chance* (1977).

Bolero (1981), starring James CAAN in the dual role of a 1930s bandleader and his gay son, was a hit in France but flopped in America (to the dismay of Caan, who was to have received the film's US earnings as his fee). *Edith and Marcel* (1983), a BIOPIC sentimentalizing the affair between Edith Piaf and the boxer Marcel Cerdan, also had a cool reception. In *A Man and a Woman: 20 Years Later* (1986) the stars of the original film play the same characters two decades on; Lelouch has threatened to produce a further sequel in 2006. *Attention Bandits!* (1987) starred Marie-Sophie Pochat, who became Lelouch's wife at the end of shooting (she is credited in the titles as Marie-Sophie L.).

> Film-making is like spermatozoa. Only one in a million makes it.
> CLAUDE LELOUCH; *Film Yearbook*, 1985.

Lemmon, Jack (1925–) US actor, who is known mainly for such comedies as SOME LIKE IT HOT (1959) and *The Odd Couple* (1967), although he has also appeared in serious roles. The son of a doughnut salesman, Lemmon was born in a stuck hospital lift in Boston. After graduating from Harvard in 1947, he moved to New York City, where he took a variety of jobs (including piano player and singing waiter) while also appearing in some 400 bit parts on television. His first film role was a small part in *It Should Happen to You* (1954); the following year he won the Oscar for Best Supporting Actor as Ensign Frank Thurlowe Pulver in *Mister Roberts*.

In 1959 Lemmon co-starred with Tony CURTIS and Marilyn MONROE in the masterly *Some Like It Hot*, which brought Lemmon an Oscar nomination for Best Actor. Thus began a seven-film collaboration with director Billy WILDER that would furnish him with some of his finest screen roles. The following year he earned another Oscar nomination as a put-upon office worker, C. C. Baxter, in Wilder's *The Apartment*.

Having established himself as one of the cinema's more individual comedy talents, Lemmon sought recognition as a serious actor by playing an alcoholic in Blake EDWARDS's *The Days of Wine and Roses* (1962); this powerful performance brought

him a third Oscar nomination. A number of routine comedies followed, such as *How to Murder Your Wife* (1964) and *The Great Race* (1965). In *The Fortune Cookie* (British title *Meet Whiplash Willie*; 1966), Lemmon was paired with Walter MATTHAU for the first time in a sparklingly cynical Wilder comedy. Lemmon and Matthau created their most famous screen partnership the following year in *The Odd Couple*, an adaptation of a Neil Simon play.

Lemmon returned to straight drama in *Save the Tiger* (1973), winning the Oscar as Best Actor for his portrayal of Harry Stoner, a businessman with nowhere left to go but down. The following year he co-starred with Matthau once again in *The Front Page*, a remake of the 1931 comedy of the same name. Lemmon received yet another Oscar nomination for his role in *The China Syndrome* (1979), a tale of negligence and cover-up at a nuclear power plant. The film, which also featured Jane FONDA and Michael DOUGLAS, was released just weeks before the accident at Three Mile Island. *Tribute* (1980), a father-and-son comedy about an ailing press agent, was followed by Constantin COSTA-GAVRAS's politically charged drama *Missing* (1982). Lemmon played a conservative American in search of his son, who has gone missing after a coup in an unnamed South American country.

Lemmon's more recent films include *That's Life* (1986), which also featured his son Chris Lemmon, *Dad* (1989), Oliver STONE's *JFK* (1991), and *Glengarry Glen Ross* (1992) about the dog-eat-dog world of real-estate sales. In 1994 he teamed up with Walter Mathau yet again in *Grumpy Old Men*. Lemmon has made one film as director, the comedy *Kotch* (1971), which starred Matthau as an eccentric grandfather.

> Just by looking at him people can tell what goes on in his heart.
> BILLY WILDER.

Leone, Sergio (1921–89) Italian director, who established his reputation with his popular SPAGHETTI WESTERNS in the 1970s. Leone began his career in the cinema as an assistant director and screenwriter; he made his own debut as a director in the late 1950s. His first major success came with *A Fistful of Dollars* (1964), a reworking of KUROSAWA's *Yojimbo* in which the action was relocated to the Wild West. Unlike many earlier Westerns, the film avoided sentimentality by combining brutality with black humour; it was also notable for its striking musical score by Ennio Morricone.

Leone repeated this success with two further instalments in what became known as the 'Man with no Name' trilogy, all featuring the US actor Clint EASTWOOD in the role of the tight-lipped fast-shooting ANTIHERO. Both *For a Few Dollars More* (1965) and *The Good, the Bad and the Ugly* (1967) became cult films. Critical recognition then arrived with *Once Upon a Time in the West* (1969), a sweeping panoramic film hailed by many as the best Western ever made; the strong cast included Henry FONDA (cast against type as a ruthless killer), Claudia CARDINALE, and Charles BRONSON. *A Fistful of Dynamite* (1972), a variant on the Spaghetti Western theme, traced the involvement of an exiled IRA terrorist with a bandit at the time of the Mexican Revolution.

After almost 12 years absence from the cinema Leone returned to direct his final film, the highly praised *Once Upon a Time in America* (1983), a gangster epic exploring themes of betrayal, guilt, and self-discovery. The original version of the film runs for nearly four hours; it was cut by some 90 minutes for US release and consequently seemed incoherent to critics and audiences.

> They call me the father of the Spaghetti Western. If so, how many sons of bitches have I spawned?
> SERGIO LEONE; *Film Yearbook*, 1990.

Leopard, The (*Il Gattopardo*; 1963) Luchino VISCONTI's luscious adaptation of Prince Giuseppe Tomasi di Lampedusa's elegiac novel about the decline of the Italian aristocracy. Set against the turbulent background of the Risorgimento, the plot revolves around Prince Don Fabrizio Salina (Burt LANCASTER), an elderly Sicilian nobleman struggling to come to terms with a society racked by changes that question the very validity of his existence. Eventually Lancaster accommodates himself to the new order by arranging for his impecunious nephew Tancredi (Alain Delon) to wed Angelica (Claudia CARDINALE), the daughter of a prosperous merchant. The final third of the film is given over to the wedding ball, a scene that took over five weeks to shoot and is widely considered to be one of the finest set pieces ever filmed.

The film's major strength is the way it evokes a sense of yearning for the era that is drawing to a close, while making clear the inevitability of social change. In this it reflects a dilemma faced by the director, an avowed communist sympathizer who was born into the Milanese aristocracy. (Lancaster claimed to have based his characterization on Visconti.) The film also provides an insight into one of the basic dynamics of the human condition: intellectually change is recognized as irresistible, but emotionally there is always a desire to retain what is known.

The Leopard was released in Europe to great critical acclaim, winning the Palme d'Or at the Cannes Film Festival. However, it was drastically cut (from nearly three and a half hours to just over two and a half) for the US audience. 20th Century-Fox, who had financed the film only because it starred Lancaster, were baffled by it and released it in an inferior form (badly dubbed and in poor colour) that made little impact. In 1983 a partly restored version was released in America and enjoyed considerable success.

LeRoy, Mervyn (1900–87) US director and producer, whose films ranged from powerful social dramas to romances and costume spectacles. He received two special Academy Awards, one in 1945 for *The House I Live In*, a documentary short about prejudice, and the 1975 Irving Thalberg Memorial Award for his lifetime achievement.

Born in San Francisco, LeRoy began his working life delivering newspapers at the age of 10 and went on stage two years later as 'The Singing Newsboy'. In 1919 he arrived in Hollywood to work in the wardrobe department of his cousin Jesse F. Lasky's company, FAMOUS PLAYERS-Lasky. After working as an assistant cameraman and writing scripts and gags for FIRST NATIONAL, he began to direct his own films in 1927.

LeRoy's early successes included Samuel GOLDWYN's *Tonight or Never* – Gloria SWANSON's last major film for 20 years and Melvyn DOUGLAS's screen debut. That same year, he made his name with LITTLE CAESAR, the film that initiated WARNER BROTHERS' gangster cycle and made a star of Edward G. ROBINSON (who called LeRoy "that cheery, bubbling, joking director"). He enjoyed another triumph with the social drama *I am a Fugitive from a Chain Gang* (1932), which starred Paul MUNI and was nominated for Best Picture at the Academy Awards.

In 1938 LeRoy joined MGM and produced a number of films, including THE WIZARD OF OZ (1939), before returning to directing with *Waterloo Bridge* (1940), a wartime romance starring Vivien LEIGH and Robert TAYLOR. He then directed Greer GARSON in three consecutive films nominated for Best Picture Oscars: *Blossoms in the Dust* (1941), *Random Harvest* (1942), and the biopic *Madame Curie* (1943). LeRoy's major war drama, *30 Seconds Over Tokyo* (1944), starred Spencer TRACY.

After making the $10 million costume epic QUO VADIS? (1951), with Robert Taylor and Deborah KERR, LeRoy set up as an independent producer-director; his subsequent successes included the navy comedy *Mister Roberts* (1955; completed for John FORD), the musical *Gypsy* (1962), and the melodrama *Moment to Moment* (1965) with Jean Seberg.

Lester, Richard (1932–) British-based US director, who made fashionable 'Swinging London' films in the 1960s and action movies in the 1970s. His frenzied quick-cutting comic style helped to disguise the BEATLES' lack of acting ability in two films.

Born in Philadelphia, Lester studied clinical psychology at the University of Pennsylvania while also writing music and singing on television. After leaving his job as a CBS television director to travel round Europe, he settled in England to direct comedy and commercials for the new ITV network in 1956. Peter SELLERS and Spike Milligan starred in Lester's first short film, *The Running, Jumping and Standing Still Film* (1959), which was shot in one day. His first feature, *It's Trad, Dad* (1962), was followed by the comedy *The Mouse on the Moon* (1963), also with Sellers.

Lester's third feature was the Beatles' first, the semidocumentary *A Hard Day's Night* (1964), this was followed a year later by the zany *Help!*. Lester then directed Rita Tushingham in *The Knack* (1965), a sexual romp with strong visual jokes that won the Palme d'Or for Best Film at Cannes. Although his next three films – the musical *A Funny Thing Happened on the Way to the Forum* (1966) and the comedies *How I Won the War* (1967) and *The Bed Sitting Room* (1969) – were less successful, he returned to form with the all-star version of THE THREE MUSKETEERS (1973) that spawned two sequels (1974 and 1989).

Columbia's *Robin and Marian* (1976), with Sean CONNERY as a middle-aged Robin and Audrey HEPBURN as Maid Marian, marked a change of pace for Lester; according to Connery "*Robin and Marian* was supposed to be called *The Death of Robin Hood* but Americans don't like heroes who die." *Butch and Sundance: The Early Days* (1979), a PREQUEL to BUTCH CASSIDY AND THE SUNDANCE KID, was followed by two SUPERMAN sequels, *Superman II* (1980) and *Superman III* (1983). In 1990, Lester made *Get Back*, documenting a world tour by Paul McCartney's band.

Levant, Oscar (1906–72) US pianist, humorist, and actor who appeared in character parts in over a dozen films. He was invariably cast in cynical, sarcastic, and bad-tempered roles, which mainly entailed being himself. Reviewing his film career, he noted "In some situations I was difficult, in odd moments impossible, on rare occasions loathsome, but at my best unapproachably great." His books included the autobiographies *The Memoirs of an Amnesiac* (1965) and *The Unimportance of Being Oscar* (1968).

The son of a Pittsburgh watch repairman, Levant studied to become a concert pianist but thereafter played mainly with dance bands and in Broadway shows. After making his film debut in *The Dance of Life* (1929) he stayed in Hollywood to score films. He also appeared in the Ginger ROGERS vehicle *In Person* (1935), and alongside Bing CROSBY in *Rhythm on the River* (1940).

During the 1930s he became the close friend of composer George Gershwin and a leading interpreter of his music. After Gershwin's death, Levant played himself in a tribute, *Rhapsody in Blue* (1945), contributing several piano solos and most of the best lines. The following year he appeared in *Humoresque*, a story about an ambitious violinist (John Garfield); and his patroness (Joan CRAWFORD); of his role in the film, Levant commented "I played an unsympathetic part – myself." The same could be said of Levant's appearance as Gene KELLY's sarcastic piano-playing friend in *An American in Paris* (1951). The film features a memorable nightmare sequence in which every member of an orchestra is revealed in turn as the gloomy-looking Levant. His last films were the Fred ASTAIRE musical *The Band Wagon* (1953), in which he played the grumpy half of a songwriting team, *The I Don't Care Girl* (1953), and *The Cobweb*

(1955), in which he played a psychiatric patient.

The possessor of a lethal wit, Levant once described himself as a "verbal vampire". When the playwright Moss Hart, a committed bachelor, arrived at a party escorting the actress Edith Atwater, Levant cracked, "Ah, here comes Moss Hart and the future Miss Atwater."

> A tortured man who sprayed his loathing on anyone within range.
> SHELLEY WINTERS.

Levinson, Barry (1942–) US writer-director, who began his career scripting TV comedy shows in the early 1970s. After considerable success with *The Carol Burnett Show*, he moved into cinema with the thriller *The Internecine Project* (1974, co-written by Jonathan Lynn). The later 1970s saw him collaborating on the scripts of *Silent Movie* (1976) and *High Anxiety* (1977) with director Mel BROOKS (the deranged bellboy who attacks Brooks with a rolled-up newspaper in the latter is played by Levinson).

He next co-wrote a trio of scripts with his wife Valerie Curtin. In spite of an Oscar nomination for *And Justice for All* (1979), neither this film nor *Inside Moves* (1980) or *Best Friends* (1982) enjoyed much critical or commercial success. With the encouragement of Brooks, Levinson finally made his debut as a director with *Diner* in 1982. Based on incidents from his own adolescence in the 1950s, the picture helped to establish the reputations of such newcomers as Micky ROURKE, Ellen Barkin, Steve Guttenberg, and Kevin Bacon. Levinson completed his 'Baltimore trilogy' (which he also scripted) with *Tin Men* (1987), about the rivalry between two aluminium salesmen (Richard DREYFUSS and Danny DEVITO) and *Avalon* (1990), based on the history of his own immigrant family (with the character of Michael representing the director himself).

Apart from *Jimmy Hollywood* (1994), Levinson's other outings as director have employed scripts written by others. Despite this, they all have at their core a male character whose individuality sets him apart from his immediate community. In *The Natural* (1984), for instance, Robert REDFORD plays a gifted baseball player with a troubled personal life, while in *Young Sherlock Holmes* (1985) Nicholas Rowe displays the nascent genius of the future sleuth.

Equally nonconformist are Robin WILLIAMS as the radio DJ whose broadcasts anger the military authorities in *Good Morning, Vietnam* (1987) and Dustin HOFFMAN as the 'idiot savant' exploited and then protected by his wheeler-dealing brother (Tom CRUISE) in *Rain Man* (1988).

Levinson followed his Best Director Oscar for *Rain Man* with a second nomination for *Bugsy* (1991), a stylish biopic of Benjamin Siegel, the gangster who brought gambling to Las Vegas. Although his form has dipped since with *Toys* (1992), a multi-million-dollar flop, and *Jimmy Hollywood*, an unsuccessful satire, Levinson's stock remains high. He was personally chosen by scriptwriter Michael Crichton to direct *Disclosure* (1994), a drama of sexual harassment in the workplace starring Michael DOUGLAS and Demi MOORE.

Lewis, Jerry (Joseph Levitch; 1926–) US comedian, director, screenwriter, and producer. Although their work was frequently dismissed by critics as infantile nonsense, Lewis and his partner Dean MARTIN were the top box-office comedy team of the 1950s. They split up after making 18 films. Lewis went on to enjoy solo success in the 1960s, especially in France ('Le Roi du Crazy') and Germany, where he is regarded as a comic genius.

Born in Newark, New Jersey, Lewis performed with his show-business parents from the age of five. After leaving school he worked as a soda jerk, bellboy (gaining experience he later put to good use in his 1960 film, *The Bellboy*), and cinema usher, before becoming a stand-up comic. In 1946 he teamed up with nightclub crooner Dean Martin to make a triumphant debut at the 500 Club in Atlantic City. Three years later producer Hal WALLIS signed them for Paramount, and gave the duo supporting roles in the comedy *My Friend Irma*. *At War with the Army* (1951), their first starring feature, was followed by a string of successful farces, such as *The Caddy* (1953), *Artists and Models* (1955), and *Hollywood or Bust* (1956). The two were never close friends. Martin noted, "At some point Jerry Lewis said to himself, 'I'm extraordinary, like CHAPLIN.' From then on, nobody could tell him anything." Martin also spoke of "Two of the greatest turning points in my career: first, meeting Jerry Lewis; second, leaving Jerry Lewis."

Lewis's first solo comedy, *The Delicate Delinquent* (1956), was well received and he went on to write, direct, and star in such successes as *The Bellboy* and *The Nutty Professor* (1963), his best film. Frank Tashlin wrote and directed several other hits, including *Cinderfella* (1960) and *The Disorderly Orderly* (1964). Lewis's career faltered in the late 1960s. After ten years in retirement he attempted a comeback with the ironically entitled *Hardly Working* (1980) and a straight role in Martin SCORSESE's flop *The King of Comedy* (1982). Lewis is also well known for heading the annual muscular dystrophy telethon for 'Jerry's Kids'.

> I like me, I like what I've become. I'm proud of what I've achieved, and I don't really believe I've scratched the surface yet.
> JERRY LEWIS.

leztze Mann, Der *See* LAST LAUGH, THE.

library shot *See* STOCK SHOT.

life. *Life and Death of Colonel Blimp, The* (US title *Colonel Blimp*; 1943) POWELL and PRESSBURGER's romantic and witty film about the life and loves of a career officer in the British army. Its gentle satire of the British military mentality was bound to arouse controversy during wartime, as was its inclusion of a good German (albeit one who calls Nazism "the most devilish invention of the human brain"). CHURCHILL wanted to ban the export of the film as "detrimental to the morale of the army" but relented when Minister of Information Brendan Bracken said it was too boring to cause any harm.

Almost three hours long, the film was the first offering of Powell and Pressburger's new company, The Archers, and the second of seven British wartime films made in TECHNICOLOR. The title alludes to the famous cartoon character created by Low in the *Evening Standard* – a pompous simpleminded reactionary opposed to all forms of change. However, the film's central character is neither called Blimp nor much like him, being fundamentally well-meaning, if rather obtuse.

In the story Colonel Clive Wynne-Candy, VC (Roger Livesey) survives three wars and three women (all played by Deborah KERR, who was having an affair with Powell at the time). After serving as a young subaltern in the Boer War, he travels unofficially to Berlin to fight anti-British propaganda; he sees action once more at Flanders and, as an old man, experiences total warfare in the

Blitz. He ends up as an anachronistic but by no means despicable figure, refusing to end his long friendship with his former German duelling opponent (Anton Walbrook) and continuing to believe that the Germans are decent chaps badly misled by Hitler.

Life of O-Haru (Japanese title *Sikaku Ichidai Onna*; 1952) The first of Kenji Mizoguchi's four masterpieces of the 1950s. The screenplay was adapted from the novel by Saikaku Ihara by Mizoguchi, Yoshikata Yoda, and Kaneto Shindo (who later said he put everything he had into this script and would never be able to equal it). The tragic story raises questions about the role of women in society and the value of human existence itself.

Released a year after RASHOMON (1951), *Life of O-Haru* was only the second post-war Japanese film to be seen in the West; it was awarded the Silver Lion at the 1952 Venice Festival. The striking black-and-white cinematography was by Yoshima Kono and Yoshimi Hirano.

Set in the 17th century, the story concerns a samurai's daughter (Kinuyo Tanaka), who has an affair with a servant (Toshiro Mifune); when this is discovered, her lover is executed and she and her family banished. Thereafter her life is one of poverty and prostitution, with only occasional interludes of happiness.

The Shochiku film company turned down the story and the rival Shintoho studios only backed it after Mizoguchi first agreed to direct their *Portrait of Madame Yuki* (1950).

light. **light 'em out** The usual command from a director or GAFFER asking electricians to position lights to eliminate microphone shadows on the set.

lighting cameraman *See* CINEMATOGRAPHER *under* CINE.

lighting plot A diagram that indicates the location of any lighting needed for a take. The plot marks different light types and may also include the output level of each unit.

Lime, Harry The unscrupulous character played by Orson WELLES in THE THIRD MAN (1949), Carol REED's thriller. Lime, a shady figure who appears only briefly in the doorways, fairgrounds, and sewers of post-war Vienna, has a hospital contact who supplies him with penicillin, which he then sells on the black market. As a result, the diluted penicillin left in the hospital fails to cure the sick children to whom it is administered. Welles's appearances in the film are accompanied by the 'Harry Lime theme', an insidious zither tune played and composed by Anton Karas.

Despite claiming to "hate Harry Lime: he has no passion; he is cold; he is Lucifer, the fallen angel", Welles agreed to resurrect him for a radio series, which ran for 52 episodes, each of which began with the lines:

> That was the shot that killed Harry Lime. He died in the sewers beneath Vienna, but before he died he lived many lives. How do I know? I know because my name is Harry Lime.

Welles later merged two instalments into a novel, *Mr Arkadin*, which he adapted for the screen in 1955 as *Confidential Report*.

line producer   *See* ASSOCIATE PRODUCER *under* ASSOCIATE.

Little Caesar   (1930) The classic GANGSTER film that made the names of both its star Edward G. ROBINSON and its director Mervyn LEROY. Described by *Variety* simply as "a swell picture", the film became one of Warner Brothers' first talkie successes. Oscar nominations went to writers Francis Faragoh and Robert E. Lee for their work in adapting the novel by W. R. Burnett (who two years later co-scripted Howard HAWKS's *Scarface*).

Little Caesar established a new trend in raw topical crime films "torn from today's headlines", as Warners put it. *The New York Herald Tribune* praised the film for its emphasis on character, for ignoring the usual romantic conventions, and for Robinson's "genuinely brilliant performance".

The film shows how Rico, a young tough, rises through the gangster ranks to become a mob leader in the era of Prohibition. He survives the brutal gang warfare but is finally shot down in the street by police. "Mother of God", cries the boss, "is this the end of little Rico?" The central character was based on Al Capone, whose homosexuality is hinted at in Rico's loyalty to his friend (Douglas FAIRBANKS JNR). Robinson was forever afterwards identified with the role and went on to play a succession of sneering gangsters.

Litvak, Anatole   (Michael Anatol Litwak; 1902–74) Russian-born US director and producer, noted for his suspense films and romantic dramas. Born in Kiev, he worked as a stagehand from the age of 14 before studying philosophy and drama. He joined the Nordkino Studios in 1923 and a year later directed his first film, *Tatiana*.

From the late 1920s he worked mainly in Germany, but left when the Nazis came to power to make the comedy *Sleeping Car* (1933) in Britain. He subsequently joined Pathé in Paris to make a series of films including the romantic melodrama *Mayerling* (1936), with Charles BOYER. Its success took him to Hollywood, where his early films included the topical *Confessions of a Nazi Spy* (1939) and the box-office hit *All This and Heaven Too* (1940), with Boyer and Bette DAVIS.

During World War II Litvak helped to direct photography of the D-Day landings, an enterprise that earned him several military decorations. In 1948 he directed and co-produced the thriller *Sorry Wrong Number*, with Barbara STANWYCK, and earned his only Oscar nomination as Best Director with *The Snake Pit*, an exposé of conditions in US mental institutions starring Olivia DE HAVILLAND. For *Anastasia* (1956), Litvak brought Ingrid BERGMAN out of semi-retirement to win an Oscar; she also starred in his Parisian drama *Goodbye Again* (1961). In the 1960s Litvak settled in Paris and directed a number of US-European co-productions including his last film, the thriller *The Lady in the Car with Glasses and a Gun* (1970).

live.   live action A film sequence featuring people, animals, or real locations, as opposed to animation or titles. The term is mainly used when much of a movie is *not* live action, as in Walt DISNEY's *Song of the South* (1946), which comprises about one third animation and two thirds live action.

livestock man The member of a production crew who looks after the animals appearing in a film. A gang of livestock men were hired for AROUND THE WORLD IN EIGHTY DAYS (1956), which used 8552 animals, including 512 monkeys and six skunks.

Living See IKIRU.

Living Desert, The (1953) Walt DISNEY's 'True Life Adventure' depicting the daily lives of animals and insects in the deserts of the US West. The film won an Oscar as Best Documentary. A facetious commentary lightened the mood, while many of the more entertaining sequences (such as the famous 'square dance' of the scorpions) were orchestrated rather than spontaneous. James Algar co-wrote and directed, with photography by N. Paul Kenworthy Jnr and Robert H. Grandall. The cartoon-style music was supplied by Paul Smith.

The Living Desert was the first feature-length film in the Disney live animal series, which had begun in 1948. Later True Life offerings included *The Vanishing Prairie* (1954), *White Wilderness* (1958), and *Jungle Cat* (1960).

Lloyd, Harold (1893–1971) US comedian, one of the great stars of the silent screen. Born in Nebraska, Lloyd made his stage debut as a child, playing Fleance in *Macbeth*. He broke into the movies in 1912 and quickly made his mark as a slapstick comedian in a series of films for Hal ROACH and Mack SENNETT. In a number of his early films he appeared in the character of Lonesome Luke, a figure of CHAPLINesque pathos that Lloyd himself hated. It was, however, in the far more congenial role of the 'Glasses Man', a shy, bespectacled, and straw-hatted innocent who gets into all manner of life-endangering scrapes, that he became a major star. Such films as *Grandma's Boy* (1922), *Safety Last* (1923), *The Freshman* (1925), and *The Kid Brother* (1927) established Lloyd as a serious rival to both Chaplin and KEATON and remain classics of the era. Amongst those to appreciate the subtlety beneath the slapstick was James AGEE, who observed that "out of his thesaurus of smiles he could at a moment's notice bland prissiness, breeziness, and asininity, and still remain tremendously likeable."

Nevertheless, the highlights of every Lloyd comedy were invariably the spectacular and death-defying stunts. He always performed these himself, maintaining his hapless screen persona with complete assurance as he dodged animals, policemen, trolley-cars, and trains or, most famously of all, dangled in mid-air from the hands of a sagging clockface halfway up a skyscraper (in *Safety Last*). Ironically, his only serious injury occurred in 1920, while he was posing for a publicity shot with what he thought was a dummy stunt bomb; he lost his right thumb and forefinger when the device exploded.

After a string of box-office hits, Lloyd's name began to fade with the coming of sound in the late 1920s. In 1948 the failure of *Mad Wednesday*, produced by Howard HUGHES, led him to sue (successfully) for $30,000 as compensation for the damage to his reputation. Years later the compilations *Harold Lloyd's World of Comedy* (1962) and *The Funny Side of Life* (1963), which Lloyd put together himself, did much to revive interest in his work. He was awarded a special Oscar in 1952.

Among Lloyd's many fans was the last emperor of China, P'u Yi, who to honour his screen idol wore a pair of round horn-rimmed spectacles in the style made famous by the star.

Loach, Ken (1936–) British director and screenwriter, who made his reputation in television during the 1960s; he subsequently became known for his harshly realistic films about social problems in Britain. Loach's work belongs to the FREE CINEMA tradition of British film-making, combining a powerful semidocumentary style with radical political comment. His early work for television included *Up the Junction* (1965) and *Cathy Come Home* (1966), a play about homelessness in British cities that caused a considerable stir. He made his first feature film, the poignant *Poor Cow*, in 1967. High praise followed for *Kes* (1970), a sympathetic account of a young boy's attempts to train a kestrel, which becomes a symbol of his desire to escape from the brutality and hopelessness of life in the industrial north of England.

More controversial was *Family Life* (1972), a harrowing depiction of the mental breakdown of a young woman: the screenplay (by David Mercer) followed the then-fashionable theories of R. D. Laing in presenting her schizophrenia as a response to her stifling environment. Loach continued to express his radical views in the television films *The Price of Coal* (1977), about the mining industry, and *The Gamekeeper* (1979), which explored class divisions in modern British society; the feature film *Looks and Smiles* (1981) dealt with a doomed teenage romance in Thatcherite Britain.

Other films of the 1980s included *Fatherland* (1987), which compares capitalist West Germany and communist East Germany, finding faults with both, and *Hidden Agenda* (1990), a highly controversial drama about the British presence in Northern Ireland. *Riff-Raff* (1991), a bleak comedy about workers on a building site, initially failed to find a distributor in Britain; it was subsequently given a limited release after winning the International Critics' Award at the Cannes Film Festival. *Ladybird, Ladybird* (1994) was a painful film about the struggles of a single mother (Crissie Rock).

loader boy or **girl** The member of a production crew responsible for loading the cameras.

location Any shooting site outside the confines of studio buildings or BACK LOT.

The earliest films had to be shot in sunlight. However, as film stock and lighting improved, film-makers increasingly shot outdoor scenes indoors, where they had more control and bad weather would not interrupt. Where scale precluded indoor work, sets were erected on vast studio backlots. As far as Hollywood was concerned, *anything* could be conjured on the lot and there was little need to stray outside to make a film. Heavy cumbersome equipment did little to encourage location work, which was only used *in extremis*, as in Westerns; even here studio artifice often marred films like *The Plainsman* (1936), in which actors in close-up fire at blatantly back-projected Indians.

Even when outdoor filming was essential, producers were loathe to travel abroad in search of authentic locations. The moors in WUTHERING HEIGHTS (1939) were faked in 540 acres of hills near Hollywood: at a cost of $100,000, inappropriate vegetation was removed and thousands of tumbleweeds, sprinkled with purple sawdust, stood in for heather in the long shots (1000 real plants were used in close-up work).

After the war, Hollywood could no longer afford its extravagant studio-based production style. As it happened, the need for economy coincided with a trend towards documentary REALISM, heralded by such influential Italian films as ROME – OPEN CITY (1945). *Naked City* (1948), filmed entirely on over a hundred New York locations (often from behind one-way mirrors in a van to avoid curious stares), painted a grim unglamourized picture of the city and inhabitants. Its success, and the arrival of improved lightweight cameras, better film stock, and more flexible sound recording methods, prompted a gradual move away from the studio.

In Britain, interiors for A TASTE OF HONEY (1961) were shot in a real flat, rented for the period of filming. During one scene Tony RICHARDSON directed Rita Tushingham and Dora Bryan from the end of the bed while a cameraman was squeezed between the bed and the wall. In this way the film-makers avoided the common situation in which a purportedly humble dwelling's studio interiors look bigger than its exterior – as well as saving over £1700 a week in studio rentals.

Despite the inevitable logistic problems of providing lighting, generators, shelter, and food for actors and crew, location shooting is a vital aspect of modern film production.

Lockwood, Margaret (Margaret Day; ?1911–) British actress, who is now mainly remembered for her starring role as a female highwayman in *The Wicked Lady* (1945). In contrast to this glamorous but deadly role were the parts she played in the 1930s, when she was generally cast as an ingenue.

Born in Karachi, Lockwood trained for the stage before making her film debut with a supporting part in *Lorna Doone* (1934). She went on to play opposite Douglas FAIRBANKS JNR, Maurice CHEVALIER, and others in a series of forgettable British films of the mid 1930s. However, good notices for her performance in Carol REED's *Bank Holiday* (1938) confirmed her as the leading British starlet of the time and brought her the leading role in HITCHCOCK's THE LADY VANISHES (1938). Her arrival in Hollywood in 1939 was followed by appearances with Randolph SCOTT, Shirley TEMPLE, and Fairbanks. She resumed her British career shortly afterwards with the highly successful *Night Train to Munich* (1940). Having played her first baddie in *The Stars Look Down* (1939), Lockwood continued the trend in the Regency romance *The Man in Grey* (1943), in which she steals her best friend's husband and then kills her into the bargain. The great success of *The Wicked Lady* led to several rather derivative films of the same type.

As the Wicked Lady Lockwood caused quite a stir in conservative America. In particular, some of the plunging dresses that she wore in the film were deemed too risqué for US audiences, causing several scenes to be reshot with Lockwood in more modest attire. Inevitably, this furore did much to promote the film on both sides of the Atlantic. In Britain, Lockwood replaced Greer GARSON as the top film actress of the mid 1940s and seemed assured of a lasting reign. In the event, quarrels with the Rank Organization, together with poor choice of roles, led to a decline in her popularity. Apart from a strong performance in the Dirk BOGARDE film *Cast a Dark Shadow* (1955), all her subsequent appearances proved disappointing. Undeterred, she returned to the live theatre and also had some success in character roles on television. Echoes of her former role as a star villainess were sounded in 1976, when she played the Wicked Stepmother in the film musical *The Slipper and the Rose*.

Logan, Josh(ua) (1908–88) US director and screenwriter, who was also a leading figure on Broadway in the 1940s and 1950s. Logan made his first foray into the movies as director of *I Met My Love Again* (1938), a sentimental romance starring Henry FONDA. He was not involved in the cinema again until 1955, when he helped to adapt his World War II drama *Mister Roberts* for the screen (the film again starred Fonda). He followed this success with the melodramatic *Picnic* (1956), adapted from a play he had directed and co-produced on the stage three years earlier, the sex comedy *Bus Stop* (1956), which starred Marilyn MONROE, and *Sayonara* (1957), a powerful if rather stagey tale of racial prejudice that earned ten Oscar nominations (including Best Picture and Best Director). In 1958 Logan directed the film version of Rodgers and Hammerstein's *South Pacific*; he himself had contributed to the libretto of the stage show, which was first presented in 1949. The following decade saw him bring two Lerner and Loewe musicals to the screen – *Camelot* (1967), which according to one reviewer "drowns the Arthurian legend in a sea of pink blancmange and leaves one desperately scanning the horizon for flotsam", and *Paint Your Wagon* (1969).

Among Logan's more curious efforts was the play *The Wisteria Tree* (1950), which transplanted Chekhov's *The Cherry Orchard* to the US South. Wags labelled it "Southern fried Chekhov".

Lolita (1962) Stanley KUBRICK's film version of the controversial novel about paedophilia by Vladimir Nabokov, who earned an Oscar nomination for the screenplay. The movie introduced the word 'nymphet' to the English language, although it is only used once.

MGM's publicity posed the question, "How did they ever make a film of *Lolita?*" In order to avoid protests and censorship, Nabokov raised the age of the girl from 12 to

14 and made the lustfulness of her suitor less explicit. For his part, Kubrick chose to shoot the film in more liberal Britain, even though this meant that most of the book's satire of middle America was lost.

Although Hayley MILLS was considered for the title role, it eventually went to 15-year-old newcomer Sue Lyon; a number of critics felt that she was too sexually mature for the part. Shelley WINTERS, who played the confused mother, said of the pretty and sophisticated Lyon: "Damn it, she makes me look like Marjorie Main" (the veteran actress best known for playing hillbilly matriarch Ma KETTLE). Lolita's middle-aged lover was played by James MASON, after both Noël COWARD and Laurence OLIVIER turned the part down. The performance revived Mason's languishing career. The film also introduced Peter SELLERS to US audiences as Clare Quilty, an eccentric playwright who disguises himself as an Austrian psychiatrist and other amusing characters. Impressed by this performance, Kubrick gave Sellers a multiple role in his next film, the satirical DR STRANGELOVE (1963).

In the plot Humbert Humbert, a middle-aged university lecturer, moves into a rooming house and falls for Lolita, the budding daughter of widowed Charlotte Haze. He marries the mother to be near Lolita and, to Humbert's delight, Mrs Haze soon dies. Although he takes Lolita with him on his journeys, the writer Clare Quilty soon becomes a serious rival for the girl.

Lollobrigida, Gina (1928–) Italian actress, who became an international sex symbol in the 1950s and 1960s. Born near Rome, the daughter of a carpenter, she made her film debut in 1946 after being spotted in the street by director Mario Costa. She subsequently became well known in Italy (where she was nicknamed **La Lollo**) with performances in such films as *The Bride Couldn't Wait* (1949) and *Achtung! Banditi!* (1951). Thereafter the generous size of Lollobrigida's bust probably did as much as any acting talent to further her career; after relatively unremarked appearances with Errol FLYNN and Humphrey BOGART amongst others, she at last became an international name starring opposite Vittorio DE SICA in the Italian-made *Bread, Love, and Dreams* (1953). She went on to partner De Sica in a sequel (1955), Vittorio Gassmann in *The Most Beautiful Girl in the World* (1955), Tony CURTIS and Burt LANCASTER in Carol

REED's *Trapeze* (1956), Anthony QUINN in the remake of THE HUNCHBACK OF NOTRE DAME (1956), Yul BRYNNER in *Solomon and Sheba* (1959), Frank SINATRA in *Never So Few* (1960), Rock HUDSON in *Come September* (1961), and Sean CONNERY in *Woman of Straw* (1964). Her range remained limited however, and her career tailed off with appearances in minor SPAGHETTI WESTERNS and comedies. In the early 1970s she forsook the big screen altogether to pursue her interest in photography. A 1977 comeback proved abortive owing to quarrels over her contract; indeed, the irascible Lollobrigida clashed with several of her co-stars over the years and particularly resented the success of her rival Sophia LOREN. In more recent years she has appeared in the television mini-series *Deceptions* (1985) and a remake of the film *La Romana* (1988).

Lom, Herbert (Herbert Charles Angelo Kuchacevich ze Schluderpacheru; 1917–) Czech actor, who has enjoyed a long career as one of the most reliable and versatile of supporting players; he was often cast in suave or sinister roles. Having made his debut in Czech films in 1937, Lom fled to Britain on the Nazi takeover of his country. During the 1940s and 1950s he gradually emerged as one of the stalwarts of the British cinema, his parts ranging from Napoleon, whom he impersonated in both *The Young Mr Pitt* (1941) and *War and Peace* (1956), to a psychiatrist in *The Seventh Veil* (1945) and a psychotic gangster in *The Ladykillers* (1955). He is now mainly known, however, as the luckless police chief in the PINK PANTHER SERIES, driven literally insane by the bumbling antics of his subordinate, Inspector Clouseau. His other credits include *Dual Alibi* (1947), *State Secret* (1950), Hammer's *Phantom of the Opera* (1962), in which he was the Phantom, *Murders in the Rue Morgue* (1971), *The Dead Zone* (1983), and *The Pope Must Die* (1990).

Lombard, Carole (Jane Alice Peters; 1908– 42) US actress, a blue-eyed blonde whose performances combined sex appeal with a fine comic intelligence. Her long affair with the married Clark GABLE led eventually to their wedding in 1938, making them Hollywood's most glamorous couple.

Lombard was born in Fort Wayne, Indiana, but brought up in Los Angeles. At the age of 12 she was spotted playing neighbourhood baseball by director Allan DWAN, who cast her in *A Perfect Crime* (1921). After a spell as a Mack SENNETT bathing beauty in 1926 she signed with Paramount in 1930. Some months later she married the actor William POWELL, who was 17 years her senior; they divorced after only two years but remained friends.

During the next ten years Lombard excelled in a series of sophisticated SCREWBALL COMEDIES that included Howard HAWKS's *Twentieth Century* (1934) with John BARRYMORE, *My Man Godfrey* (1936) with William Powell, and Alfred HITCHCOCK's *Mr and Mrs Smith* (1941) with Robert Montgomery. She also starred in the brilliant black satire *Nothing Sacred* (1937) and in Ernst LUBITSCH's anti-Nazi comedy *To Be or Not to Be* (1942), with Jack BENNY.

Lombard clearly relished the Hollywood lifestyle, taking numerous lovers, throwing expensive parties, and engaging in elaborate practical jokes. At the same time her high spirits, kindliness, and professionalism made her genuinely loved within the industry. When Culver City, California, named her honorary mayor, she gave Hollywood bosses a headache by declaring a one-day holiday for all studio employees.

She first met Gable when they appeared together in *No Man of Her Own* (1932) but their affair did not get under way until later. When he was filming GONE WITH THE WIND, she left a wrapped gift on his dressing-room table with the note: "Don't let it get cold. Bring it home hot for me." The gift was a knitted codpiece.

At the age of only 34, Lombard was killed (with her mother) when her plane crashed into Table Rock Mountain near Las Vegas during a tour to promote war bonds. *To Be or Not to Be*, usually considered her best work, was released a few weeks later.

London Film Festival One of Europe's leading festivals of cinema; it has taken place annually since 1958, when it was founded by the critics Derek Prouse and Dilys Powell. Among the 15 films screened during the first festival were premieres of KUROSAWA's *Throne of Blood* and BERGMAN's THE SEVENTH SEAL. By the 30th anniversary of the festival in 1988 the programme had grown to include 150 films; by 1992 this figure had increased to over 200 films from 40 countries. In recent years the festival has attempted to shed its somewhat elitist image by presenting films in leading commercial cinemas in London, as well as in its home base at the NATIONAL FILM THEATRE.

long shot (LS) A shot giving a general view of a whole subject or scene. Along with the MEDIUM SHOT and the CLOSE-UP, the long shot is one of the standard tools of cinematography. Such terms do not neccessarily refer to the distance between camera and subject (which is rendered fairly meaningless by lenses of different focal lengths) but to what is seen in the camera viewfinder. No theoretician has attempted to define the precise dividing line between 'medium' and 'long', but it is usually accepted that a long shot incudes at least the full figures of subjects, occupying perhaps one-third of the frame depth. Long shots and EXTREME LONG SHOTS, are often used as ESTABLISHING SHOTS, conveying essential content to locate the sequence for a viewer.

A classic example occurs at the end of *Oh! What a Lovely War* (1969): the start of the shot shows a few figures by a war grave. The helicopter-mounted camera slowly rises to reveal more graves. As the camera retreats further, more and more graves appear, until finally, in extreme long shot, the screen is crammed with numberless graves.

Looney Tunes and **Merrie Melodies** Two long-running series of cartoon shorts produced by Warner Brothers from the mid 1930s until the 1960s. The best-known characters are Porky Pig, created by Bob Clampett for *I Haven't Got a Hat* (1935); BUGS BUNNY, who made his debut in *Porky's Hare Hunt* (1938) and was later perfected by Tex Avery; DAFFY DUCK, first drawn by Avery for *Porky's Duck Hunt* (1937); Tweetie Pie, who was introduced in *Birdie and the Beast* (1944); his feline pursuer SYLVESTER, first seen a year later in *Kitty Kornered*; and Speedy Gonzales, "the fastest mouse in all Mexico", who debuted in the Oscar-winning *Speedy Gonzales* (1955). Academy Awards also went to *Tweetie Pie* (1947), *For Sentimental Reasons* (1949), *Birds Anonymous* (1957), and *Knightly Knight Bugs* (1958).

The voices were all supplied by Mel Blanc, who invented Bugs's famous and seldom answered question, "What's up Doc?" He gave lisps to Bugs's enemy Elmer Fudd ("That wascally wabbit!") and to Sylvester ("Sufferin' succotash!"), a stutter to Porky ("Tha-tha-tha-that's all folks!"), a speech impediment to Tweetie ("I taught I taw a putty tat!"), a French accent to the skunk Pepe le Pew, and a Mexican accent to Speedy.

loop (1) Short for **Latham loop**. *See* CAMERA; INTERMITTENT MOVEMENT. (2) A loop of film or tape used to provide endless repetition of a soundtrack element during mixing or DUBBING.

looping The DUBBING technique in which an actor attempts to record dialogue to match the action on a repeating film loop.

Loren, Sophia (Sophia Scicolone; 1934–) Italian-born actress, who emerged as an international sex symbol on the strength of her generous figure and Mediterranean looks. Loren herself once remarked "Everything you see, I owe to spaghetti." In the 1960s and 1970s, however, her abilities as an actress won increasing recognition.

Raised in the slums of Naples, Loren was pushed into a film career by her mother after winning a beauty contest at the age of 15. Over the next few years she appeared in a series of films produced by Carlo PONTI, who became her mentor and subsequently her husband. She quickly attracted attention for her beauty, which she inherited from her mother (who had once won a Greta GARBO look-alike competition). Opinion as to her potential was mixed, however, and the conclusion of one cameraman damning:

> She is quite impossible to photograph, too tall, too big-boned, too heavy all round. The face is too short, the mouth is too wide, the nose is too long.

Nevertheless, Loren went on to star in such Italian films as *Aida* (1953) and *Woman of the River* (1955), a film expressly designed to show off her voluptuous beauty. This won her an invitation to Hollywood, where she showed her developing talents as an actress in such films as *Boy on a Dolphin* (1957), *The Black Orchid* (1959), which brought her a Venice Festival Award and *The Millionnairess* (1960), in which she partnered Peter SELLERS. Her powerful performance in Vittorio DE SICA's *Two Women* (*La Ciociara*; 1961) brought her an Oscar, the first ever awarded to a performer in a foreign-language film. She also appeared in the same director's *Marriage Italian Style* (1964). Other movies have included *It Started in Naples* (1960), in which she starred opposite Clark GABLE, the epic *El Cid* (1961), *Man of La Mancha* (1972),

The Cassandra Crossing (1977), and *Firepower* (1979). After a long absence during the 1980s, she resumed her cinematic career in Lina WERTMULLER's *Saturday, Sunday, and Monday* (1990) and Robert ALTMAN's *Prêt à porter* (1994).

Her career has not been without its mishaps, however; among the oddest of these was the bizarre miscasting that placed her opposite Richard BURTON in a remake of BRIEF ENCOUNTER for US television in 1974 (a production that was quickly withdrawn after initial reactions). In 1982 Loren was nearly persuaded to embark on a new career as a television baddie, when she was approached by the makers of the soap opera *Dynasty*; she proved too expensive even for US television, however, and Joan COLLINS got the part. That same year a low point in Loren's fortunes was sounded when she served a brief term in an Italian gaol for tax offences (she was treated with such deference by her captors, however, that many considered the sentence no punishment at all). A naturalized French citizen, she was admitted to the Légion d'Honneur in 1991, a year that also saw the award of a special Oscar for her lifetime achievement.

Lorre, Peter (Lazlo Lowenstein; 1904–64) Hungarian-born actor, who made films in Germany, Britain, and Hollywood. His bulging eyes and menacing voice brought him numerous roles as villains in melodrama.

After several years playing bit parts in a German theatrical troupe, Lorre made his screen debut in *Bomben auf Monte Carlo* (1931). He found international fame with only his second film, Fritz LANG's provocative M (1931), in which he played a child murderer hunted through Berlin by both the police and the criminal underworld. Owing to his effectively chilling performance in this film, Lorre continued to be cast in sinister roles for the rest of his 30-year career. Following a few more films in Germany, Lorre appeared in Alfred HITCHCOCK's early British suspenser *The Man Who Knew Too Much* (1934), about the kidnapping of a small child.

Lorre's first Hollywood film was the bizarre *Mad Love* (British title *The Hands of Orlac*; 1935), in which a pianist's hands are amputated and replaced by those of a murderer by an insane surgeon. Other notable films of the 1930s include the Dostoevski adaptation *Crime and Punishment* (1935) and Hitchcock's *The Secret Agent* (1936).

Between 1937 and 1939 Lorre also appeared as the Japanese sleuth in no less than eight MR MOTO films.

During the early 1940s Lorre appeared in three of the roles for which he is now best remembered: the slightly effeminate Joel Cairo in John HUSTON's THE MALTESE FALCON (1941), the slimy Ugarte in CASABLANCA (1942), and the drunken Dr Einstein in Frank CAPRA's black comedy ARSENIC AND OLD LACE (1944). Both *The Maltese Falcon* and *Casablanca* saw Lorre appearing with the British stage actor Sidney GREENSTREET; the two subsequently played together in the melodramas *Background to Danger* (1943), *Passage to Marseilles* (1943), *The Mask of Dimitrios* (1944), *The Conspirators* (1944), *Three Strangers* (1946), and *The Verdict* (1946). Owing to their contrasting physical types the pair have been described, most appropriately, as a kind of unholy LAUREL AND HARDY.

In 1950 Lorre returned to Germany to script and direct *Der Verlorene* (US title *The Lost One*), an expressionist-style drama in which he also starred. His subsequent Hollywood career was anticlimatic, being limited to character and supporting roles in such films as *The Story of Mankind* (1957), in which he played Nero, and *Voyage to the Bottom of the Sea* (1961). In his last years he appeared in several independent horror productions, including Roger CORMAN's *Tales of Terror* (1962) and *The Raven* (1963).

Losey, Joseph (1909–84) US director, working in Europe and Britain from the early 1950s.

A Harvard graduate, Losey worked in the theatre and radio before studying film with EISENSTEIN in Moscow. After directing several educational shorts, Losey made his feature debut with *The Boy with Green Hair* (1948), an antiwar fantasy. Other early films include *The Lawless* (1949), which dealt with racism, and a remake of Fritz LANG's classic M (1951). After making *The Prowler* (1951) Losey fell victim to the McCarthy witch-hunts and found himself blacklisted.

Losey subsequently moved to Europe, where he directed a number of films under the pseudonyms of Victor Hanbury and Joseph Walton. His early British work, which was mainly unremarkable, included *The Sleeping Tiger* (1954), a melodrama that began his long association with the actor Dirk BOGARDE. *Blind Date* (1959) and *The*

Criminal (1960) were gritty crime films starring Stanley BAKER – another Losey regular – who also appeared in *Eva* (1962) as a writer ensnared by a *femme fatale* (Jeanne MOREAU). *The Damned* (1961) was one of Losey's most grandiose and peculiar films; set in Weymouth, it featured a plot about a scientist who keeps radioactive children in a cave and a subplot about teddy boys.

By contrast THE SERVANT (1963), which reunited Losey with Bogarde, was an absorbing story about a master-servant relationship with a script by Harold Pinter. Losey's other films with Bogarde included *King and Country* (1964), an antiwar courtroom drama, *Modesty Blaise* (1966), a camp spy spoof, and *Accident* (1967), an examination of class and adultery.

In the late 1960s Losey's critical reputation went into a serious decline, with *Boom!* (1968), a Tennessee Williams adaptation featuring Richard BURTON and Elizabeth TAYLOR, *Secret Ceremony* (1969), and *Figures in a Landscape* (1970) all being widely condemned as pretentious nonsense. Although *The Go-Between* (1971), a Pinter adaptation of L. P. Hartley's novel, was much better received (and took the Best Film award at Cannes), such films as *The Assassination of Trotsky* (1972) and *The Romantic Englishwoman* (1975) did little to revive his former reputation. Following a move to France, Losey retrieved his standing a little with *Mr Klein* (1976) and a powerful version of Mozart's *Don Giovanni* (1979). However, *The Trout* (1982) and *Steaming* (1984, released posthumously) went largely unnoticed.

lot   *See* BACK LOT.

low.   low-angle shot A shot taken from below EYE LEVEL with the camera pointing upwards. Its effect is to distort normal perspective, so that elements closer to the lens appear enlarged and those further away seem reduced; distortion increases as the camera angle tilts closer to the vertical. The psychological repercussions of this can be important; figures filmed from a low angle appear bigger, and in movement seem to accelerate faster, giving them a heroic or menacing quality. A low-angle shot may also be used to eliminate extraneous detail, especially outdoors, when the camera can concentrate on an actor shot against an appropriately moody sky.

Orson WELLES'S CITIZEN KANE (1941) made effective use of low camera angles to dramatize its larger-than-life protagonist, while few can forget Norman Bates's home in PSYCHO (1960), first revealed in all its gothic menace in a much-imitated low-angle shot.

low-budget production A relatively inexpensive film, such as a B MOVIE or SECOND FEATURE. Many INDEPENDENT and AVANT-GARDE films are necessarily made on a very low budget. The US actor-director John CASSAVETES has produced several low-budget films, such as *The Killing of a Chinese Bookie* (1976), for which his actors accepted deferred payments. Another director to show persistence and imagination in the face of crippling financial constraints was Britain's Derek JARMAN. Low-budget productions to achieve box-office success have included the early space-monster movie *The Thing* (1951), Hitchcock's PSYCHO (1960), and Steven Soderbergh's *sex, lies and videotape* (1989).

low key A term describing a lighting arrangement in which the KEY LIGHT is kept very low. The effect is to produce deep mysterious shadows, as in the FILMS NOIRS of the 1940s.

Loy, Myrna (Myrna Williams; 1905–93) US actress, who became known as the **Queen of Hollywood** during the 1930s. Loy began her career as a stage dancer; amongst those to spot her potential at this time was VALENTINO, who screentested her as early as 1925. After making her film debut in 1926, she went on to appear in some 60 silent movies, mainly in VAMP roles.

With the coming of sound, however, she redefined her screen persona in a series of light comedies and dramas, in which she played the perfect wife to such stars as Clark GABLE and William POWELL. The films that lifted her to stardom in the early 1930s included *The Mask of Fu Manchu* (1932), *When Ladies Meet* (1933), and *Night Flight* (1933), her first film with Gable. Her new success was consolidated by her partnership with Powell in the comedy-thriller THE THIN MAN (1934) and its sequels; the pair soon became one of the chief attractions in the MGM stable. Other notable films included CAPRA's *Broadway Bill* (1934), *Wings in the Dark* (1935), in which she played opposite Cary GRANT, *Whipsaw* (1935), which paired her with Spencer TRACY, *Love Crazy* (1941), and THE BEST YEARS OF OUR LIVES (1946). Two of her best post-war films, *The Bachelor and the Bobby Soxer* (1947) and *Mr Blandings Builds His Dream House* (1948) paired her once again with Cary Grant. Loy continued to appear in a wide range of roles throughout the 1950s. After several years in which she concentrated upon her stage career, she returned to the big screen to join Jack LEMMON and Charles BOYER in *April Fools* (1969); thereafter she appeared mainly on television. Her last films included *Airport 1975* (1974) and *Just Tell Me What You Want* (1980).

Unlike many of the more extrovert female stars of the day, Loy was shy in public and normally lived quietly with her mother when not on the set (her four marriages all failed). During World War II she worked full-time for the Red Cross and when peace came acted as an observer for America at the United Nations.

It was while watching *Manhattan Melodrama* (1934), starring Loy, Gable, and Powell, that the gangster John Dillinger was cornered and shot dead by police.

Lubitsch, Ernst (1892–1947) US director, born in Germany, who became one of the most revered Hollywood film-makers of the 1930s and 1940s. Born in Berlin, Lubitsch appeared as a comic actor with Max Reinhardt's company before moving into films. Although his role as Meyer, a comical Jewish businessman in a series of German-made shorts, brought him a degree of fame, it soon became apparent that his real talent lay in direction. Having made such German films as *Carmen* (1918) and *Madame Dubarry* (1919), he moved to Hollywood in 1922. Despite an initial flop with *Rosita* (1923), starring Mary PICKFORD, he soon consolidated his reputation with such silent classics as *The Marriage Circle* (1924) and *Lady Windermere's Fan* (1925).

Lubitsch made his sound debut with *The Love Parade* (1930), a musical; *One Hour With You*, the first of several operettas starring Maurice CHEVALIER and Jeanette MACDONALD followed two years later. His reputation for ultra-sophisticated light comedy with a strong sexual undercurrent was first established with *Trouble in Paradise* (1932), starring Herbert Marshall and Miriam Hopkins. *Angel* teamed Marshall with Marlene DIETRICH and Melvyn DOUGLAS, while NINOTCHKA (1939) prospered on the promise of a laughing Greta GARBO. Subsequent

films included *The Shop Around the Corner* (1940), *To Be or Not to Be* (1942), with Jack BENNY and Carole LOMBARD, and the whimsical *Heaven Can Wait* (1943).

Apart from directing, Lubitsch was also influential as head of production at Paramount during the 1930s. His glossy films, with their arch cynical lovers and witty dialogue, have retained the status of classics; critics still talk of the **Lubitsch touch**, in which elegance and innuendo are seamlessly blended (although some of his later films were flawed by a Lubisch touch that had become more like a hammer blow). He was awarded a special Oscar in 1937 and was appointed to the Légion d'honneur in 1938.

Like some other celebrated Hollywood figures, Lubitsch was notorious for his shaky grasp of the English language. Once, when trying to crush a playwright with whom he was having a difference of opinion, he rounded on him fiercely with the retort "How do you do!"

Lucas, George (1944–) US director, producer, and writer. Although Lucas has only directed three movies, the proceeds from the third enabled him to become a major independent film executive. His first film, *THX1138* (1971), an extended version of his student film project, presented a dystopian picture of the future. His second, the nostalgic *American Graffiti* (1973), was the first picture to have a greatest-hits soundtrack, gave Harrison FORD his first break, made stars of Richard DREYFUSS and Ron Howard (who went on to exploit his 1950s image in TV's *Happy Days*), and was nominated for Best Picture at the Oscars. His third was STAR WARS (1977).

A homage to the FLASH GORDON serials that Lucas adored (the movie declares itself in its opening credits to be "Part Four, A New Hope"), *Star Wars* must have seemed an unlikely candidate for success in the cynical 1970s; indeed 20th Century-Fox had so little faith in the project that they willingly gave Lucas 40% of net profits in lieu of a higher salary, as well as all merchandising rights. The movie sparked off a recession-era FANTASY boom that has not yet abated, and remained all-time box-office champion until the advent of SPIELBERG'S E.T.: THE EXTRA-TERRESTRIAL (1981). It also received an Oscar nomination for Best Picture. Lucas invested his $50 million personal profit in Lucasfilm, his production company, and in establishing the SPECIAL-EFFECTS outfit Industrial Light And Magic. He never directed again, limiting himself to writing and producing the two sequels in 1980 and 1983. The original film contains a tiny homage to Lucas's origins: one of the stormtroopers uses the radio callsign THX1138.

His new power enabled Lucas to produce a number of films of his own choosing, ranging from *More American Graffiti* (1979) to such diverse projects as the Japanese-language biopic *Mishima* (1985), Michael Jackson's *Captain Eo* (1986), the Philip Glass video montage *Powaqqatsi* (1988), and the disastrous *Howard the Duck* (1986). He also provided Spielberg with the storylines and characters for the Indiana Jones movies, starting with RAIDERS OF THE LOST ARK (1981). In the mid 1980s he acknowledged one of his major influences by producing a series of TV interviews with the mythologist Joseph Campbell, whose books on folklore had helped to suggest the universal storylines that had made Lucas so successful. He also assisted with Spielberg's *first* dinosaur movie, the animated *The Land Before Time* (1988).

There are rumours that Lucas is considering expanding his *Star Wars* trilogy to the nine episodes he had originally intended.

Lugosi, Bela (Bela Ferenc Dezso Blasko; 1882–1956) Hungarian-born US actor, best known for his sinister roles. Born in Lugos, Transylvania, Lugosi began his stage career as a matinée idol; he first appeared in Hungarian pictures (under the name Arisztid Olt) in 1917. His first film as Bela Lugosi was *Az Ezredes* (1917), and his first horror film *Az Elet Kiralya* (1918), a version of *The Portrait of Dorian Gray*. Following the arrival of communism in 1919, Lugosi fled to Germany, where his film work included an appearance as the American Indian Chingachgook in *Lederstrumpf* (1920).

In 1922 he emigrated to America, making his first US movie, *The Silent Command*, a year later. Lugosi first played DRACULA on Broadway in 1927; Universal's film version, the movie that made him a household name, followed in 1931. He quickly became a horror icon, receiving more fan mail than Clark GABLE in the mid 1930s. In 1934 he appeared with Boris KARLOFF (a man he disliked, but would work with five more times) in *The Black Cat*, and played the hero in the serial *The Return of Chandu*, having been the villain in the original feature. By the late

1930s his star was fading rather and he went to Britain to make the early Hammer picture, *The Mystery of the Marie Celeste* (1936). But things were soon looking up again. A re-release of FRANKENSTEIN (1931) and *Dracula* on the same bill rekindled interest in horror, leading Universal to employ him as Ygor, the hunchback servant, in the *Son of Frankenstein* (1938) and *Ghost of Frankenstein* (1942). He also appeared in a straight acting role in the GARBO vehicle NINOTCHKA (1939). Further horror roles included the original lycanthropic peasant who bites Lon CHANEY JNR in *The Wolfman* (1941) and the part he had always previously turned down, that of Frankenstein's monster, in *Frankenstein Meets the Wolfman*. In the released film Lugosi's dialogue was erased, although you can see the creature's lips moving.

In the mid 1940s Lugosi starred in the radio series *Mystery House* and numerous inferior horror movies for low-budget producer Sam Katzman. From this time on his career went into an irreversible decline. He was soon reduced to burlesquing his screen persona in such films as *Abbott and Costello Meet Frankenstein* (1948), the British *Old Mother Riley Meets the Vampire* (1952), and *Bela Lugosi Meets a Brooklyn Gorilla* (1952). During the 1950s Lugosi descended into alcoholism and drug addiction and began an association with legendary 'bad movie' director Ed WOOD, beginning with the beserk transvestite drama *Glen or Glenda* (1953). The *Bela Lugosi Revue* proved a huge hit in Los Angeles, but ill health soon forced the actor to abandon it. In 1956 he committed himself to hospital and emerged cured of his addition. His last complete movie was *The Black Sheep* (1956), with Lon Chaney Jnr and Basil RATHBONE; he also achieved some dignity by introducing *Lock Up Your Daughters* (1956), a compilation of his movies, and appearing in the anti-drug play *The Devil's Paradise*. Only tiny segments of his performance were used in Ed Wood's wonderfully terrible *Plan 9 from Outer Space* (1959).

Lukas, Paul (Pal Lukacs; 1885–1971) Hungarian-born actor, who played a long series of debonair villains (and some heroes) from the 1930s onwards. Born on a train near Budapest, Lukas worked in the Hungarian theatre and cinema before joining the Berlin-based company of Max Reinhardt. He was subsequently taken up by director Alexander KORDA, then working in Germany, who featured him in such movies as *Samson und Delila* (1922). In the late 1920s fellow-Hungarian Adolph ZUKOR brought Lukas to Hollywood, where he made his US debut in the silent *Three Sinners* (1928), with Pola NEGRI. He quickly established himself as a useful supporting actor, generally in the role of a suave middle-European seducer or other rogue. In the mid 1930s he extended his range in such films as *Little Women* (1934), in which he played a shy professor and THE THREE MUSKETEERS (1935), in which he was Athos; *Dodsworth* (1936) saw him playing yet another charming European adventurer.

Although Lukas subsequently moved to Britain in search of bigger roles, he was obliged to revert to type as the sinister Dr Nartz in HITCHCOCK's THE LADY VANISHES (1938). Similar roles came his way in Warner Brothers' *Confessions of a Nazi Spy* (1939) and the British-made *The Chinese Bungalow* (1940). Having enjoyed success on the stage in Lillian Hellman's *Watch on the Rhine*, he was cast in the same role when the play was filmed in 1943; his performance as a committed opponent of the Nazis brought him his only Oscar. This triumph led to several parts of a similar nature, including that of a German Jew in *Address Unknown* (1944). Henceforth, however, he was mainly confined to villains and supporting parts once more. His postwar films included *Experiment Perilous* (1945), *Kim* (1950), in which he played a lama, Disney's *20,000 Leagues Under the Sea* (1954), *The Four Horsemen of the Apocalypse* (1961), and *Lord Jim* (1965). He made a concession to the passing years in *Tender is the Night* (1961), when he appeared for the first time without his customary hairpiece.

Lumet, Sidney (1924–) US director, producer, and actor, whose numerous films range from straightforward thrillers to psychological dramas. Lumet began his career in the movies as a child actor but subsequently branched out as a director, beginning with a number of plays for television. In 1957 he won instant recognition with his first feature, TWELVE ANGRY MEN (1957), a courtroom drama starring Henry FONDA as the principled jury member who finds himself in a minority of one. Fonda featured again in *Stage Struck* (1958), which starred Susan Strasberg as an aspiring actress. During the 1960s Lumet consolidated his repu-

tation with a series of thrillers that dealt powerfully (if not always very coherently) with urgent contemporary issues. These included *Fail Safe* (1964), a nuclear-war thriller with Fonda once again, *The Pawnbroker* (1965), with Rod STEIGER as a Jewish pawnbroker haunted by his war memories, and *The Hill* (1965), with Sean CONNERY as a rebellious British soldier in North Africa. *The Group* (1966) was an adaptation of Mary MacCarthy's novel about the subsequent lives of eight women who graduated in the 1930s.

Thereafter Lumet was able to draw on the best of Hollywood talent. James MASON starred in *The Deadly Affair* (1966), *The Seagull* (1968), and *Child's Play* (1972), Al PACINO took the lead in *Serpico* (1974) and *Dog Day Afternoon* (1975), while an all-star cast was gathered for Agatha Christie's *Murder on the Orient Express* (1974). Peter FINCH won a posthumous Oscar for his performance in the satire *Network* (1976) and Richard BURTON starred in *Equus* (1977); *The Wiz* (1978) was an all-Black version of THE WIZARD OF OZ, with a cast led by Diana Ross and Michael Jackson. Lumet's films of the 1980s included *Deathtrap* (1982), starring Christopher REEVE and Michael CAINE, the legal thriller *The Verdict* (1982), with Paul NEWMAN, and *Running on Empty* (1988), the film that made a star of the teenage River PHOENIX. In *Family Business* (1989), Sean Connery starred as Dustin HOFFMAN's father, despite being only seven years older in reality. Particularly admired have been Lumet's exposés of corruption in the New York police system, *Prince of the City* (1981) and *Q&A* (1990).

Lumière brothers The French cinema pioneers Auguste Lumière (1864–1954) and Louis Lumière (1864–1948), who were the first to project technically successful films to a paying public. Their father, Antoine, manufactured photographic paper and roll film. In 1894 Louis saw Edison's KINETOSCOPE in Paris and immediately hit on a way of improving this peepshow device.

Unaware that his idea was not new, Louis wondered if by projecting film and momentarily stopping each frame to register it distinctly on the screen he could create a convincing illusion of movement. Excitedly, he explained the idea to Auguste; on 13 February 1895 they patented their Cinématographe, a hand-cranked camera-cum-projector that used a claw mechanism to achieve INTERMITTENT MOVEMENT. On 22 March they gave a private screening of *Workers Leaving the Lumière Factory* and on 28 December showed 12 short films in the basement of the Grand Café, Paris, in what is regarded as the first technically mature screening for a paying audience. The half-hour show included the forerunner of all slapstick cinema, *Watering the Gardener* (in which a boy steps on a hose, the gardener inspects the nozzle, and is promptly drenched when the boy removes his foot), and *Arrival of a Train at Ciotat Station*, which sent frightened viewers fleeing to the exit!

At one franc a head, the first night's takings barely covered the room's rent. However, within weeks daily takings rose to 2500 francs and by the end of 1896 Lumière films had been shown all over the world.

The Lumières' achievement was fundamental. If Edison's Kinetescope had become the norm, cinema would have been a private experience, more akin to TV, and the nature of cinema production and distribution would have been very different. But the Lumières' foresight did not match their inventiveness; owing to their photographic background, they saw the Cinématographe as an improved means of recording reality and nothing more. Both brothers subsequently abandoned film-making: Louis went on to improve film stock and develop colour photography, while Auguste became a research biologist.

> This invention is not for sale, but if it were it would ruin you. It can be exploited for a while as a scientific curiosity; beyond that it has no commercial future.
> ANTOINE LUMIÈRE, rejecting George MÉLIÈS's desperate attempt to buy a Cinématographe.

Lupin, Arsène Fictional criminal turned DETECTIVE, who appeared in a series of novels and stories by the French author Maurice Leblanc, beginning with *The Seven of Hearts* (1907). The character has been compared to both Sherlock HOLMES and the upper-crust criminal Raffles. Films about the *cambrioleur* include a German-made series of shorts starring Paul Otto (1910–11), a US silent movie with Earle Williams in the lead (1917), and various talkies made in the 1930s and 1940s. Actors to play the role have included John BARRYMORE (1932), Melvyn DOUGLAS (1938), and Jean-Claude Brialy in a 1962 French film. The character

also featured in a French television series of the 1970s.

Lupino, Ida (1918–) British-born actress, who was groomed by Warner Brothers as a rival to Bette DAVIS; she later moved into writing and direction. The daughter of the comedian Stanley Lupino (1894–1942), Ida was the last of a theatrical dynasty that can be traced back to the 17th century. Her first film role came her way when a producer rejected her mother, the actress Connie Emerald, as too old for a part but decided to try the 15-year-old Ida. She was soon signed by Paramount, who considered her for the lead in *Alice in Wonderland* (1933) before concluding that she was too sexually attractive. Various supporting roles followed, before she found stardom as the Machievellian murderess in *They Drive by Night* (1940), a melodrama that also featured George RAFT and Humphrey BOGART. A year later she appeared as a moll to Bogart's gangster in *High Sierra* (1941).

Other roles of the early 1940s included a former gaolbird in *The Sea Wolf* (1941), a housekeeper who murders her callous employer in *Ladies in Retirement* (1942), and an unscrupulous schemer determined to get to the top in *The Hard Way* (1943). Now established as a top Hollywood attraction, she appeared in the glossy all-star vehicles *Forever and a Day* and *Thank Your Lucky Stars* (both 1943) before extending her range in such films as *Devotion* (1946), in which she played Emily Brontë, *Deep Valley* (1947), in which she played a woman with a speech defect, and *Road House* (1948), in which she appeared as a torch singer.

Lupino made her debut as a director with *Not Wanted* (1949), a drama about an unwanted pregnancy that she also wrote and produced. She went on to write and direct a number of unusual melodramas in the early 1950s, although these were never very successful, before switching to television for a time. Her later appearances included roles in the horror films *The Devil's Rain* (1975) and *The Food of the Gods* (1976).

Lupino was not always the easiest star to handle, as Warners discovered soon after they signed her in 1940; the making of *They Drive By Night* was much disrupted when she refused to turn up on the advice of her astrologer, who warned her that the film would bring bad luck.

Lynch, David (1946–) US director, writer, producer, and occasional actor. Lynch's bizarre vision was first displayed at feature length in ERASERHEAD (1978), a film that the director had worked on for five years, aided by a grant from the AFI. Although *Variety* described it as a "sickening bad taste exercise", this nightmarish story of a man doing his best to take care of a horrible, but somehow engaging, mutant baby soon became a cult. The title refers to the character's eccentric hairstyle. *The Elephant Man* (1980), also made in black-and-white, dealt with a similar theme – the life of the historical circus freak John Merrick, played by John Hurt under heavy make-up; however, Lynch's direction was mainstream enough to earn three Oscar nominations (including Best Picture). Following this success, he was chosen to direct the oft-proposed screen version of Frank Herbert's science-fiction epic *Dune* (1985), and proved exactly the wrong choice. After shooting a reported eight-hour version of the book, he was obliged to cut the footage to two hours; the final movie managed to be both banal and over-complicated, if visually stunning. On the positive side, it introduced Lynch's favourite leading man, Kyle MacLachlan.

The deeply disturbing *Blue Velvet* (1986) was Lynch's first outing into the Middle American wierdness that he has since made his own. In the plot, MacLachlan's innocent hero gradually uncovers the oddness underneath the everyday exterior of his town, eventually coming face to face with the terrifying evil represented by Dennis HOPPER. Although some critics found the film sick and degrading, it won Lynch an Oscar nomination for Best Director. The late 1980s saw Lynch make an acting appearance in *Zelly and Me* (1988) and begin work on his successful television 'soap opera' *Twin Peaks*. Lynch's obsession with the dark side of American culture also informed his violent and passionate road movie *Wild at Heart* (1990). *Twin Peaks: Fire Walk with Me* (1992) is both the final solution to the mystery of the TV series, and an astonishing and frightening exploration of its leading character, Sheryl Lee's Laura Palmer.

Lynch's daughter, Jennifer, who had written the Laura Palmer diaries upon which this movie was based, made one of the most reviled directorial debuts of all time with *Boxing Helena* (1993).

M

M. *M* (1931) Fritz LANG's first sound film, a powerful drama about the crimes of a child murderer, Franz Becker (Peter LORRE), and his capture and 'trial' by a kangaroo court comprising members of the Berlin underworld. One of the last classics of German EXPRESSIONIST cinema, the film features claustrophobic sets and murky lighting that recall the 'studio realism' of G. W. PABST's 'street films' of the 1920s. Although critics have traditionally associated the story with that of the Düsseldorf murderer Peter Kürten, a serial killer of the late 1920s, Lang always insisted that he hit on the idea while studying suspects at the Berlin Alexanderplatz police station.

Peter Lorre gives a compelling performance throughout, whether stalking his victims (while whistling a tune from Grieg's *Peer Gynt*) or pleading for his life before the court of criminals: "I can't help myself! I haven't any control over this evil that's inside me." Many of the 'jurors' trying Becker were real-life hoodlums; on one occasion Lang was forced to post lookouts to warn of an impending police raid on the set.

The version of the film most widely available today has the screen fade to black after Becker is saved from lynching by policeman Otto Wernicke; on the soundtrack, one of the neighbourhood mothers urges greater vigilance over their children as the Grieg theme strikes up. In another version the court is dispersed with an off-screen voice pronouncing the words "In the name of the law..." Neither version corresponds with Lang's original intention, which was to dissolve from the warehouse to a legitimate courtroom where one of the mourning mothers laments, "We should learn to look after our children more."

In 1951 *M* was remade by director Joseph LOSEY, with David Wayne in the lead. Losey transferred the action to Los Angeles and made the murderer a far more sympathetic character: "I consciously repeated only one shot...essentially Lang's villain was my hero."

M and E Music and (sound) effects. A soundtrack including music, sound effects, and background noise but no dialogue. It is produced to accompany foreign releases, in order that native-language dialogue may be added to form a final mix.

McCarey, Leo (1898–1969) US director, producer, and screenwriter. A former boxer, mine manager, and lawyer, McCarey entered the film industry in 1918. Five years later he joined Hal ROACH to write and direct comedy shorts, including several starring LAUREL AND HARDY. After making his feature debut with *The Sophomore* in 1929, he went on to work with Eddie CANTOR in *The Kid from Spain* (1932), the MARX BROTHERS in DUCK SOUP (1933), Charles LAUGHTON in *Ruggles of Red Gap* (1935), and Cary GRANT and Irene DUNNE in *The Awful Truth* (1937), a fast-paced romantic comedy that brought him an Oscar as Best Director.

Further acclaim followed with the romance *Love Affair* (1939), which teamed Dunne with Charles BOYER and brought McCarey an Oscar for the screenplay; five years later the sentimental *Going My Way* (1944), starring Bing CROSBY as the irredeemably good-hearted Father O'Malley, earned McCarey Oscars as both writer and director. Subsequent films included another Father O'Malley film, *The Bells of St Mary's* (1945), which paired Crosby with Ingrid BERGMAN, and *An Affair to Remember* (1957), a remake of *Love Affair* with Cary Grant and Deborah KERR. His last film was another story about priests, the curious anti-communist tale *Satan Never Sleeps* (British title *The Devil Never Sleeps*; 1962).

McCrea, Joel (1905–90) Tall handsome US actor, one of Hollywood's most popular leading men in the 1930s and 1940s. McCrea moved into the cinema from the theatre, making his screen debut in *The Jazz Age* (1929). His first major role, in Cecil B. DE MILLE's *Dynamite* (1929), led to a series of films with Constance BENNETT for RKO, including *Born to Love* (1931), *Rockabye*

(1932), and *Bed of Roses* (1933). Other partners from his early career included Dolores del Rio in *Bird of Paradise* (1932), Fay WRAY in *The Most Dangerous Game* (1932), and Ginger ROGERS in *Chance in Heaven* (1933).

He went on to work with such famous names as Shirley TEMPLE, Merle OBERON, and Humphrey BOGART, who played a murderous gangster to McCrea's honest architect in *Dead End* (1937). Although McCrea was sometimes cast in roles that had been turned down by Cary GRANT or Gary COOPER (such as the lead in HITCHCOCK's *Foreign Correspondent*, 1940), he was often first choice, being a particular favourite of Preston STURGES, who used him in such comedies as *Sullivan's Travels* (1941) and *The Palm Beach Story* (1942). De Mille cast him opposite Barbara STANWYCK in the Western *Union Pacific* (1939), while George STEVENS paired him with Jean ARTHUR in *The More the Merrier* (1943).

From the mid 1940s McCrea confined himself largely to Westerns, including *The Virginian* (1946), *Stars in My Crown* (1950), and Sam PECKINPAH's *Ride the High Country* (1962), his last film before retirement. He returned to the cinema for final appearances in *Cry Blood Apache* (1971) and *Mustang Country* (1976).

McCrea was one of the many stars whose names were habitually mangled by Sam GOLDWYN, who always called him Joe McRail. When McCrea attempted to correct him, the producer complained, "Look! He's telling me how to pronounce his name, and I've got him under contract!" McCrea himself never acted the part of a Hollywood star and remained modest about his talents, once remarking: "Acting? I never attempt it. A placid sort of fellow, that's me."

MacDonald, Jeanette (c. 1901–65) US actress and singer, who starred with Nelson EDDY in a series of popular film operettas of the 1930s. After extensive experience on stage, MacDonald made her screen debut as the Queen of Sylvania in LUBITSCH's *The Love Parade* (1929). Several unremarkable films followed before Lubitsch persuaded Paramount to match MacDonald with Maurice CHEVALIER in the musical *One Hour With You* (1932), which proved her first big hit. They were paired again for MAMOULIAN's *Love Me Tonight* (1932), with songs by Rodgers and Hart, and *The Merry Widow* (1934) which, according to Clive Hirschhorn, "marked the

end of what many consider the most interesting part of Jeanette MacDonald's career, when she was the only singer in pictures who could sing with her tongue in the cheek."

In 1935 she appeared with Eddy for the first time in *Naughty Marietta*, which cast MacDonald as a princess and Eddy as a backwoods scout. A year later they made their most successful film together, the lush musical *Rose Marie* (1936), which entered cinema legend with its 'Indian Love Call' sequence. MacDonald then co-starred with Clark GABLE in *San Francisco* (1936), a film memorable chiefly for the spectacular earthquake with which it concludes, before returning to Eddy for *Maytime* (1937). Now established as a regular partnership, MacDonald and Eddy co-starred in *The Girl of the Golden West* (1938), *Sweethearts* (1939), *New Moon* (1940), *Bitter Sweet* (1940) – a version loathed by author Noël COWARD – and *I Married an Angel* (1942).

MacDonald's film career tailed off in the 1940s, partly as a result of a clash with Louis B. MAYER over the dubbing of her voice for foreign-language versions of her films. Thereafter she opted to develop her talents as a singer of grand opera – with mixed results. Her last screen appearance was in the LASSIE film *The Sun Comes Up* (1949).

macguffin or **McGuffin**   A word used by the director Alfred HITCHCOCK to describe something that sparks off the action of a film plot but subsequently turns out to be irrelevant; an example is the case of mistaken identity in his NORTH BY NORTHWEST (1959). Hitchcock claimed to have taken both the name and the idea from a Scottish shaggy-dog story in which a train passenger carrying a large odd-looking parcel is asked what it contains. He replies that it is a macguffin and goes on to explain that a macguffin is a lion in the Highlands. When it is pointed out to him that there are no lions in the Highlands, he replies that there are no macguffins either.

Mackendrick, Alexander   (1912–93) US director and screenwriter, who created some of the best-loved EALING comedies. Mackendrick, who entered the British film industry in 1937, worked mainly in documentaries until after World War II. Having co-scripted Ealing's *Saraband for Dead Lovers* (1948), he enjoyed great success as director of the classic farce WHISKY GALORE! (1949), which depicted the subterfuges of a small Scottish community when a shipwreck brings a cargo of whisky to their shores. Mackendrick subsequently presided over another Ealing classic, *The Man in the White Suit* (1951), a darkly comic tale starring Alec GUINNESS as the inventor of an indestructible fibre that threatens the commercial livelihood of northern England.

Mandy (1952), also made at Ealing, was not a comedy but the moving story of a young deaf-and-dumb girl (played by Mandy Miller), while *The Maggie* (US title *High and Dry*; 1954) was an amusing exploration of the clash of old and new cultures revolving around an ancient Scottish cargo boat. Mackendrick completed his quintet of Ealing films with another classic comedy, *The Ladykillers* (1955). The film starred Alec GUINNESS as the leader of a gang of robbers whose crime is discovered by a little old lady (Katie Johnson), whom they cannot bring themselves to kill.

Mackendrick then went to Hollywood to make *Sweet Smell of Success* (1957), a savage study of the cynical ways of the newspaper world starring Burt LANCASTER and Tony CURTIS. This was followed by *Sammy Going South* (1963), about the wanderings of a young orphan in Africa, and the pirate adventure *A High Wind in Jamaica* (1965).

MacLaine, Shirley (Shirley Maclean Beaty; 1934–) US actress, who emerged as a popular leading lady in the 1950s and has since played a variety of roles in musicals, straight dramas, and comedies. The sister of actor Warren BEATTY, MacLaine began her career as a Broadway dancer. Her breakthrough into the movies is the stuff of cinema legend. While appearing in the chorus of *The Pajama Game*, MacLaine was chosen as a last-minute replacement for the female lead, who had hurt her leg. As luck would have it, the audience that night included the film producer Hal WALLIS.

MacLaine made her film debut in HITCHCOCK's *The Trouble with Harry* (1955) and instantly established herself as a fresh new talent. After appearances in AROUND THE WORLD IN EIGHTY DAYS (1956) and several other movies, she earned her first Oscar nomination for *Some Came Running* (1958), in which she co-starred with Frank SINATRA and Dean MARTIN. *Ask Any Girl* (1959) brought her a British Film Academy award, as did Billy WILDER's *The Apartment* (1959), in which she was teamed with Jack LEMMON.

In 1963 she played a Paris street-walker to Lemmon's naive *flic* in the Wilder musical *Irma la douce*, a role that brought her another Oscar nomination. This was the first of several occasions on which she played the stereotype 'tart with a heart'; Maclaine later remarked, "I'm certain I was a prostitute in some other life. I just have empathy for them."

Her films of the mid 1960s, such as *Gambit* (1966) and *Woman Times Seven* (1967), were generally less successful and met with mixed reviews. In 1968, however, Maclaine surprised the critics with her best performance yet, as a dance-hall hostess in the lavish musical *Sweet Charity*.

After *Desperate Characters* (1971), in which she gave a strong performance as an 'ordinary' housewife, Maclaine took a break from the cinema to concentrate on her club act. In the late 1970s she returned to the big screen in the ballet movie *The Turning Point* (1977) with Anne BANCROFT and *Being There* (1979), a black comedy with Peter SELLERS. The successful comedy-tearjerker *Terms of Endearment* (1983), brought Maclaine an Oscar for her performance as the domineering mother of Debra Winger.

Her more recent films include John SCHLESINGER's *Madame Sousatzka* (1988), in which she played a somewhat overbearing piano-teacher, *Steel Magnolias* (1989), as one of the friends who share each other's woes in a Southern beauty salon, and *Postcards from the Edge* (1991), in which she played Meryl STREEP's alcoholic mother.

In the 1980s MacLaine became known for her belief in reincarnation and other New Age nostrums, claiming that "You do not die, you just change form. You are divine, as is everything."

> Shirley – I love her, but her oars aren't touching the water these days.
> DEAN MARTIN.

MacMurray, Fred (1908–91) US actor, the amiable leading man of numerous Hollywood comedies and thrillers of the 1930s and 1940s, who went on to become a DISNEY star in the 1960s. The son of a concert violinist, he toyed with a career as a saxophonist before entering films in the late 1920s and continued to work as an instrumentalist and singer for some years. After being signed by Paramount in the mid 1930s he co-starred with Claudette COLBERT in a series of popular comedies beginning with *The Gilded Lady* (1935) and *The Bride Comes*

Home (1935). That year he also partnered Katharine HEPBURN in *Alice Adams* and Carole LOMBARD in *Hands Across the Table*. After extending his range in the drama *The Trail of the Lonesome Pine* (1936), with Henry FONDA, and the Western *The Texas Rangers* (1936), he went on to co-star with Ray MILLAND in *Men with Wings* (1938), Bing CROSBY in *Sing You Sinners* (1938), and Madeleine Carroll in *Café Society* (1939) and several other movies.

MacMurray's venture into more serious drama included *Remember the Night* (1940) and the Billy WILDER classic DOUBLE INDEMNITY (1944), in both of which he appeared with Barbara STANWYCK. For the latter, he shed his nice-guy image to play an insurance agent turned murderer – a role that had been turned down by no less than 11 other performers. He tried his hand at production with *Pardon My Past* (1946), in which he also starred, but from then on confined himself to acting.

In the 1950s MacMurray's flagging career received something of a boost with good notices for *The Caine Mutiny* (1954), while towards the end of the decade Disney Studios identified him as ideal material for their live-action pictures. He went on to find new stardom in such films as *The Shaggy Dog* (1959), *The Absent-Minded Professor* (1961), *The Happiest Millionaire* (1967), and *Charley and the Angel* (1973). MacMurray closed his career with appearances in television movies and in the disaster thriller *The Swarm* (1978).

McQueen, Steve (Terence Steven McQueen; 1930–80) US actor.

During his youth McQueen spent time in a reform school and served for a period in the US Marines. Later, he took acting classes at the New York Neighborhood Playhouse, while working variously as a bartender and docker. He made his Broadway debut in *The Gap* (1954) and his first film appearance (as an extra) in *Somebody Up There Likes Me* (1956). By his fourth film, the B-movie *The Blob* (1958), he had graduated to starring roles.

A popular television series *Wanted – Dead or Alive* (1958) then led to a high-profile role in John STURGES's *The Magnificent Seven* (1960). Three years later McQueen gave a truly great performance as 'Cooler King' Kilts in Sturges's *The Great Escape*, the film that made him a major star. He went on to consolidate his image as a quiet loner with an inimitable coolness in such films as *Love With the Proper Stranger* (1963), in which he played a jazz musician, *The Cincinnati Kid* (1965), and *The Sand Pebbles* (1966), for which he received his only Oscar nomination.

His films of the late 1960s included *The Thomas Crown Affair* (1968), a gimmick-laden heist movie, and *Bullitt* (1968), an enormously popular police drama that featured one of the cinema's most celebrated car CHASES. *Le Mans* (1971) was a virtually plotless film about a driver in the 24-hour race; although not a great commercial success, the film delighted McQueen, a keen motor-racing fan. Sam PECKINPAH's *The Getaway* (1972), a violent crime drama, saw McQueen co-starring with Ali MacGraw, whom he married a year later.

During the period of his marriage to MacGraw, McQueen made only a few films, notably *Papillon* (1973), a prison drama with Dustin HOFFMAN, and *Towering Inferno* (1974), a disaster movie that saw McQueen billed above Paul NEWMAN – an ambition of his since *Somebody Up There Likes Me* nearly 20 years earlier. *An Enemy of the People* (1977) was a screen adaptation of the Ibsen play that McQueen made through First Artists, a production company he had founded with Newman, Sidney POITIER, and Barbra STREISAND. Following his separation from MacGraw in 1978, McQueen lost much of the weight he had put on and made another two films – *Tom Horn* (1980), an elegiac Western, and *The Hunter* (1980), a thriller about a modern-day bounty hunter. He died of a heart attack following surgery for cancer.

macrocinematography The filming of objects that are too small for conventional cinematography but not small enough to require the use of a microscope. A camera used for macrocinematography is fitted with a special lens, sometimes combined with extension devices. A **macro lens** can focus clearly on objects as close as 1mm, while a **macrozoom lens** can focus at any distance from 1mm to infinity. *See also* CINEMATOGRAPHY.

magazine A lightproof container for film that is mounted on the camera during shooting. The unexposed film is initially fed manually from the magazine into the camera, usually in a double-layered black bag designed specifically for this purpose; the exposed film passes back into the magazine onto a second reel situated directly behind the first. The FEED and TAKE-UP reels usually form twin humps on the top of the camera.

magnetic. **magnetic film** or **mag film** Perforated film coated with a ferromagnetic substance, used to record sound in SYNCHRONIZATION with the images recorded simultaneously on photographic film. Since the 1950s the use of magnetic film has largely superseded the practice of OPTICAL SOUND recording.

magnetic master or **master soundtrack** The finished mix of the SOUNDTRACK, combining dialogue, sound effects, background noise, and music. This is created and held on magnetic tape before being optically transferred to the release print.

magnetic stripe or **mag stripe** A band of iron oxide on the outer edge of a photographic film, used for recording sound simultaneously with the pictures. Such film is often used in 16MM documentary work.

magnetic tape or **mag tape** Tape coated with a ferromagnetic substance used to record sound (audio tape) or sound and pictures (videotape). *Compare* MAGNETIC FILM.

magoptical release print A RELEASE PRINT of a film that has both MAGNETIC and OPTICAL soundtracks. While MULTIPLEXES and other modern cinemas are equipped for magnetic stereo sound, others are not; a magoptical release print can therefore be shown at a larger number of cinemas. In the case of foreign-language films, a magoptical release print offers the choice of either the optical-sound original or a magnetic dubbed version.

magnificent. *The Magnificent Ambersons* (1942) Orson WELLES's dramatic portrait of US society at the end of the 19th century. Inventor Eugene Morgan (Joseph COTTEN) returns to the town where he lost his beloved Isabel Amberson (Dolores Costello) to a wealthy rival. Although Isabel's pompous son, George Minafer (Tim Holt), courts Morgan's daughter (Anne BAXTER), he is determined that his mother shall never marry Morgan, whom he considers beneath her dignity.

Following the commercial failure of CITIZEN KANE, RKO insisted that Welles select a more popular subject for his next picture. When plans to film *The Pickwick Papers* fell through, Welles opted for an adaptation of Booth Tarkington's 1919 novel about the downfall of a landed family at the onset of the industrial revolution of the 1890s. A silent version of the story, *Pampered Youth*, had been released in 1924 and Welles himself had produced an adaptation for radio in 1939. Removing much of the original's melodramatic excess, Welles completed his script during a nine-day retreat on King VIDOR's yacht. Having briefly considered casting himself as Morgan, he decided to concentrate on direction (although he did provide the voice-over).

Production began after six weeks of rehearsal. Refining the techniques he had pioneered in *Kane*, Welles made extensive use of DEEP-FOCUS cinematography and atmospheric lighting (modelled on that commonly used in turn-of-the-century photography). He also devised a number of innovative sound strategies, including overlapping dialogue, natural sound, and the use of neighbours as a Greek chorus, commenting on the principal characters and their actions.

Welles was already on location in Brazil shooting *It's All True* when the time came for editing. Having viewed the RUSHES, he would write long notes to editor Robert WISE detailing the order of shots, ideas for improving scenes (often requiring reshooting), and changes to the dialogue and soundtrack. Jack Moss, Freddie Fleck, and Vernon Walker all directed new footage, attempting both to incorporate Welles's ideas and to emulate his style. However, after two disastrous preview showings RKO boss George Schaefer demanded that the 130-minute film be cut by a third. In a series of lengthy telephone calls from Brazil, Welles tried in vain to preserve the integrity of his picture; with entire scenes excised and a melodramatic new ending tacked on, *The Magnificent Ambersons* was released as the second half of a double bill looking "as though somebody had run a lawnmower through the celluloid", according to Welles. Despite positive reviews from critics such as James AGATE, who called Welles a "cinemaestro", and four Oscar nominations including Best Picture and Best Supporting Actress (Agnes Moorehead, as George's aunt), the film was a box-office disaster.

the Magnificent Wildcat Nickname of the Polish-born US silent film actress Pola NEGRI, who cultivated an exotic passionate image.

main. **main feature** *See* A-MOVIE; FEATURE FILM.

main title The TITLE that announces the name of a film. Although this usually appears at the very beginning of a movie, there is sometimes a PRE-CREDITS SEQUENCE. In the opening sequence of GONE WITH THE WIND (1939) each word of the title moves slowly across the screen (in fact, the camera had moved past the letters in a DOLLY shot). In the main title of *Crime Without Passion* (1934) the words are gradually spelt out in shattered glass from the windows of a skyscraper.

Makavejev, Dušan (1932–) Yugoslav (Serbian) writer-director, who attracted much attention in the 1960s with his challenging films on political and sexual themes.

Born in Belgrade, Makavejev made various shorts and documentaries before releasing his first feature, *Man is Not a Bird*, in 1965. The film, a provocative picture of the doomed love between a girl and a factory worker, incorporates flash forwards, documentary footage, and other devices of the Western avant-garde. Still more daring was *Love Affair; or the Case of the Missing Switchboard Operator* (1966), an exposé of contemporary sexual mores that also raised questions about personal freedom under communism. Both films were admired for their robust wit and unconventional editing.

Innocence Unprotected (1968) was a curious reworking of Dragolijub Aleksic's film of the same name, the first Serbian talkie. Makavejev combined footage from the original film, which had been shot during the German occupation, with extracts from contemporary newsreels to create an ironic collage. The radical political and sexual theories of Wilhelm Reich were the subject of the equally free-form *WR: Mysteries of the Organism* (1971), a film that was banned in Yugoslavia. After going into voluntary exile in the 1970s, Makavejev made the Canadian-French-German *Sweet Movie* (1974), a film that was banned not only in his homeland but also in many Western countries. His next film, the Swedish-British *Montenegro*, a witty depiction of the sexual liberation of a frustrated housewife, did not appear until 1981. Subsequent films have been somewhat poorly received, with the political and sexual themes of *The Coca-Cola Kid* (1985) and *Manifesto* (1988) failing to arouse the interest that they did in the 1960s.

make-up The use of cosmetics, false hair, or more recently prosthetics to alter or enhance a performer's appearance on screen. Make-up was almost ignored in the cinema until close-up work revealed primitive film stock's inability to depict realistic flesh tones. Because early orthochromatic film was insensitive to reds, rendering rosy cheeks grey and freckles black, performers masked any such facial colouring with yellowish make-up, which produced acceptable black-and-white tones. Max Factor formulated the first make-up designed specifically for film work in 1914, and by 1920 most studios had special departments to ensure that performers looked natural under the powerful arc lights, which otherwise rendered their complexions a ghastly white relieved with ashen greys.

In the 1920s the introduction of superpanchromatic film, a highly sensitive stock that accurately resolved all of the spectrum into an evenly graduated black-and-white scale, made life easier for the make-up departments, though the advent of COLOUR photography brought its own problems.

Make-up artists have also created many fantastic monster or freak effects for the screen. For THE HUNCHBACK OF NOTRE DAME (1923) Lon CHANEY needed four and a half hours in make-up before he was ready for the cameras, while Charles LAUGHTON required an hour longer in the 1939 remake; these were rapid make-overs compared to the ten hours it took eight artists to 'tattoo' all of Rod STEIGER's upper body for *The Illustrated Man* (1968).

Elaborate make-up is both expensive – over $1,000,000 was spent creating apes capable of facial expressions for *Planet of the Apes* (1968) – and inconvenient. Long hours in the make-up studio restrict the time available for acting, while temporarily crippling disguises or swelteringly hot layers of latex inevitably impair endurance and ability. Elsa LANCHESTER's make-up in *The Bride of Frankenstein* (1935) restricted her to eating through a tube, while John Hurt's horrific appearance in *The Elephant Man* (1980) prevented him from eating at all. An Oscar for make-up was introduced in 1981, the first winner being *An American Werewolf in London*.

Malden, Karl (Mladen Sekulovich; 1913–) US character actor, who established his reputation in the theatre but also appeared in a wide range of drama and adventure films. The son of Yugoslav immigrants, he made his screen debut in *They Knew What They Wanted* (1940) and went on to appear in such powerful tales as *Kiss of Death* (1947), with Richard WID-MARK, and *The Gunfighter* (1950), in which Gregory PECK played a doomed outlaw in the Wild West.

In 1952 Elia KAZAN's celebrated screen adaptation of the Tennessee Williams play *A Streetcar Named Desire* brought Malden an Oscar as Best Supporting Actor for his performance as Marlon BRANDO's bachelor friend Mitch. His subsequent films included two more Kazan classics, ON THE WATERFRONT (1954), again with Brando, and the controversial BABY DOLL (1956), in which he played the boorish husband of a young sexually alluring Carroll Baker. In 1953 he starred as the police officer dealing with a tight-lipped Catholic priest (Montgomery CLIFT) in HITCHCOCK's *I Confess*. *Time Limit* (1957), a tense courtroom drama starring Richard Widmark and Richard Basehart, was Malden's first and only film as director. His later credits include *The Adventures of Bull-whip Griffin* (1967), *Hotel* (1967), *Beyond the Poseidon Adventure* (1979), *The Sting II* (1982), and *Nuts* (1987). He also joined the ranks of the television detectives in the series *The Streets of San Francisco* (1972–76).

Malkovich, John (1953–) US actor who turned to film in the mid 1980s, having already earned a reputation as one of the finest stage performers of his generation. In 1975 he co-founded the Steppenwolf Theater Company in Chicago, which became renowned for its provocative productions. As well as directing many stage shows, Malkovich has also contributed costume and set designs.

Following his film debut as a war photographer in THE KILLING FIELDS (1984), Malkovich won an Oscar nomination for his performance as Sally Field's blind tenant in *Places in the Heart* (1985). However, he then stumbled into a succession of poor pictures, including *Eleni* (1985) and *Making Mr Right* (1987), before his star rose once more with strong performances in SPIELBERG's *Empire of the Sun* (1987) and Stephen FREARS's *Dangerous Liaisons* (1988), in which he played the scheming Vicomte de Valmont. Subsequent films have been highly uneven. While *Object of Beauty* and *Queens Logic* (both 1991) were relatively small projects,

BERTOLUCCI's *The Sheltering Sky* (1990) and Woody ALLEN's *Shadows and Fog* (1991) were far more prestigious, thus making his mixed reviews all the more disappointing. He himself is philosophical about his position within the US cinema, commenting: "I think I am probably seen as someone who can play a leading role if they can't get Kevin COSTNER or Mel GIBSON or maybe Bill Hurt."

In 1994 Malkovich was nominated for a Best Supporting Actor Oscar for his performance as an assassin in the Clint EASTWOOD actioner *In the Line of Fire* (1993). Many of his recent roles have been in adaptations of literary classics: he played Lennie in *Of Mice and Men* (1992), Kurtz to Tim Roth's Marlow in *Heart of Darkness* (1994), and Dr Jekyll in Frears's *Mary Reilly* (1995). He has also been much in demand in Europe, working with Manuel de Oliveira on *Pierre de Touche* (1994) and Michelangelo ANTONIONI on *Lies* (1994).

Malle, Louis (1932–) French director of the NEW WAVE. After studying at the Sorbonne and the Institute of Advanced Cinematographic Studies, Malle worked as an assistant to the director Robert BRESSON. The documentary *World of Silence* (1956), co-directed with the oceanographer Jacques Cousteau, was followed by Malle's first feature, the moody thriller *Ascenseur pour l'echafaud* (*Frantic*; 1957) with Jeanne MOREAU. A year later *The Lovers* (1958), an exploration of bourgeois sexuality, achieved international notoriety and made a star of Moreau. Other early films by Malle include *Zazie dans le métro* (1961), adapted from the novel by Raymond Queneau, and the highly acclaimed *Le Feu follet* (*The Fire Within*; 1963), a sombre depiction of the last hours in the life of a suicidal playboy.

In 1967 Malle visited India, where he directed the documentaries *Calcutta* (1968) and *Phantom India* (1971). On his return to France he made the controversial *Le Souffle au coeur* (1971), containing scenes of incest between a son and his mother, and the masterly *Lacombe, Lucien* (1974), which probed the equally taboo subject of collaboration during the German occupation. The reaction to this film was so hostile that Malle decided to continue his film-making career in America. His first US-made film, *Pretty Baby* (1978), the story of a 12-year-old girl (Brooke Shields) growing up in a New Orleans brothel, was followed by *Atlantic*

City (1980), starring Burt LANCASTER as an ageing petty criminal. *My Dinner with André* (1981) consisted almost entirely of a cerebral dinner-party conversation between two characters.

Malle's films of the later 1980s included *And the Pursuit of Happiness* (1986) and the semiautobiographical *Au revoir les enfants* (1987), about the friendship between a young French boy and a Jewish boy during the Nazi occupation. While the latter proved a great critical and popular success, *Damage* (1992), an erotic drama starring Jeremy IRONS as a Conservative minister who has an affair with his son's girlfriend (Juliette Binoche) was poorly received. *Vanya on 42nd Street* (1994) recorded the Broadway production of David Mamet's version of Chekhov's *Uncle Vanya*. In 1980 Malle married the actress Candice BERGEN, who has appeared in a number of his films.

> It takes a long time to learn simplicity.
> LOUIS MALLE.

Malone, Dorothy (Dorothy Maloney; 1925–) US actress, who played *femme fatale* roles in numerous Hollywood films of the 1950s. Having made her screen debut in 1943, she first attracted attention with a small role in the Howard HAWKS classic THE BIG SLEEP (1946). Over the next few years she played supporting roles in a wide range of adventure films and Westerns, including *Colorado Territory* (1949) with Joel MCCREA.

In 1956 Malone won the Oscar for Best Supporting Actress playing Robert STACK's nymphomaniac sister, in the Texas oil drama *Written on the Wind* (1956); Rock HUDSON played her lover and Douglas SIRK directed. She went on to give acclaimed performances in *Man of a Thousand Faces* (1957), a biopic of Lon CHANEY Snr, *The Tarnished Angels* (1957), which reunited her with Sirk, Hudson, and Stack, and *Too Much Too Soon* (1958), in which she played the tragic actress Diana BARRYMORE. Her subsequent credits have included various films for television and the thriller *Winter Kills* (1979), a black comedy with an all-star cast led by Jeff BRIDGES and John HUSTON. In 1992 she had a small role as a murderess in the erotic thriller *Basic Instinct*.

However, Malone's most famous role was probably that of Constance Mackenzie in the television soap opera *Peyton Place*, which became a firm favourite on both sides of the Atlantic in the 1960s. She responded defensively to criticism of the series: "People

say the series was overdone, but after all that has happened to me in my life it reflected a great deal of reality." In 1985 Malone joined fellow veterans of the series in the television movie *Peyton Place: The Next Generation*.

Maltese. Maltese cross. *See* INTERMITTENT MOVEMENT.

The Maltese Falcon (1941) John HUSTON's first film as a director, a crime mystery based on the novel by Dashiell Hammett. In pursuit of the man who murdered his partner, private eye Sam Spade (Humphrey BOGART) encounters Mary ASTOR, Sydney GREENSTREET, Peter LORRE and Elisha Cook Jnr, who are all on the trail of the Maltese Falcon, a jewel-encrusted statue.

This was the third screen adaptation of Hammett's 1929 novel: *The Maltese Falcon* (1931) was directed by Roy DEL RUTH and *Satan Met a Lady* (1936) by William DIETERLE. (A weak parody, *The Black Bird*, appeared in 1975.) Huston's claustrophobic version was remarkably faithful to its source, although the HAYS office insisted that the more overt references to homosexuality and to Spade's relationship with his partner's widow be removed. Studio boss Jack WARNER also suggested that Huston abandon the book's ending for one in which Spade watches the murderer disappear behind the barred door of an elevator. Warner later had the opening sequences reshot after the preview audience complained that the action was too confusing.

Huston had previously worked with Bogart as a scriptwriter, and this was to be the first of seven collaborations in their new roles of director and star. Bogart was only offered the part of the cynical private eye when George RAFT, the studio's first choice, refused to have anything to do with a B-MOVIE remake in the hands of a novice. Huston was not the film's only debutant: Broadway veteran Sydney GREENSTREET made his first screen appearance at the age of 61. Walter HUSTON, John's father, had an unbilled CAMEO role as Captain Jacobi, the dying ship's officer who hands the falcon to Spade; he was made to repeat the scene several times before his son was satisfied.

Huston's film, which was completed two days ahead of its month-long schedule, was nominated for three Academy Awards, including Best Picture. *The Maltese Falcon* was the first of the MGM/UA film library to be colorized by Turner Broadcasting in

1986. Huston was disgusted with the result, which he said looked like a roast that had been basted with "teaspoon after teaspoon of syrup."

> The actors were all in their places – looking at me expectantly. I'd no idea what was required. Finally, my assistant...whispered: "Say action!" I did so and *The Maltese Falcon* was underway.
> JOHN HUSTON, 1983.

Mamoulian, Rouben (1897–1987) US director, born in Russia of Armenian descent. After training as an actor at the Moscow Art Theatre, Mamoulian directed plays in London and elsewhere before travelling to America in 1923. A series of Broadway triumphs then led to an invitation to direct the musical APPLAUSE (1929), a film that revolutionized the making of talkies with its innovative camera work. This was followed by *City Streets* (1931), a tale of gangsters and bootlegging that was rumoured to be a particular favourite of Al Capone, *Dr Jekyll and Mr Hyde* (1932), with Fredric MARCH in the title role, and the Rodgers and Hart musical *Love Me Tonight* (1932), which paired Maurice CHEVALIER and Jeanette MACDONALD. These early films won Mamoulian immediate recognition as a director with a wonderfully fluent style and an inventive attitude to film-making: the transformation of March from Jekyll to Hyde, for instance, was achieved by making different parts of the actor's make-up sensitive to a succession of light filters.

In 1933 Mamoulian presided over two films, the historical romance *Queen Christina*, which proved one of the highlights of Greta GARBO's career, and *Song of Songs* with Marlene DIETRICH. His other films of the 1930s included *Becky Sharp* (1935), the first feature-length film to employ three-strip TECHNICOLOR, *The Gay Desperado* (1936), the boxing drama *Golden Boy* (1939), and *The Mark of Zorro* (1940), with Tyrone POWER as the masked swashbuckler and Basil RATHBONE as his adversary (*see* ZORRO). Mamoulian's career continued with less remarkable results through the 1940s and 1950s; in 1962 he was invited to direct the ill-fated epic *Cleopatra*, but was soon dismissed and replaced by Joseph L. MANKIEWICZ.

> His tragedy is that of the innovator who runs out of innovations.
> ANDREW SARRIS, film critic.

man. Man of a Thousand Faces Nickname of the actor Lon CHANEY Snr, who was known for appearing in heavy DISGUISE in macabre roles. *Man of a Thousand Faces* was also the title of a biographical film about him made in 1957 and starring James CAGNEY.

a man's gotta do what a man's gotta do A catchphrase that is widely thought to have originated from a John WAYNE Western, although nobody seems sure which. The line *is* spoken verbatim by Alan LADD in SHANE (1953). Later that year Wayne spoke the words "A man oughta do what he thinks is right" in the rather similar *Hondo*.

The Man You Love to Hate A nickname associated originally with the actor Erich VON STROHEIM, but subsequently with many other screen heavies. It was first used in publicity for the 1918 propaganda film *The Heart of Humanity*, in which von Stroheim played a particularly unpleasant German officer. In 1979 it became the title of a film commemorating the life and work of von Stroheim, who had gone on to become an admired Hollywood director.

Mancini, Henry (1924–94) US film composer, songwriter, and arranger, whose music has won four Oscars and 20 Grammy Awards. His Academy Award-winning compositions include 'Moon River' from *Breakfast at Tiffany's* (1961) and the title song from *Days of Wine and Roses* (1962), both of which were directed by Blake EDWARDS. His theme for Edwards's THE PINK PANTHER (1963) also earned an Oscar nomination.

Mancini was an intensely private man who prided himself on not having an identifiable style; he once commented, "If anyone could recognize that it was my writing, I shouldn't have been doing the job." He was also a workaholic who dashed off his compositions at top speed. After seeing a photograph of the waif-like Audrey HEPBURN in *Breakfast at Tiffany's*, he wrote 'Moon River' in 30 minutes on a rented piano in his garage. The mischievous Pink Panther theme was created just as quickly.

Mancini's father, an Italian immigrant, taught him to play the flute as a child. He later studied at the prestigious Julliard School of Music in New York and after World War II was hired as a pianist and arranger for the Glenn Miller orchestra. Subsequently Mancini followed his wife, the singer Ginny O'Connor, to Hollywood, where he arranged library music for Universal Studios. He was known as 'Big Hank' because of his gangster-like image: tall, bald, and burly. His work with Miller's band made him the ideal arranger for *The Glenn Miller Story* (1953), which brought his first Oscar nomination. He also arranged *The Benny Goodman Story* (1956).

In 1958 Mancini provided a nervous jazz score for Orson WELLES'S TOUCH OF EVIL (1958) and a throbbing theme for the television series *Peter Gunn*. It was the latter that began his long association with Blake Edwards. Other Edwards films to feature music by Mancini include *High Time* (1960), *Darling Lili* (1970), and *Victor Victoria* (1982), the score for which brought the composer another Oscar.

Manhattan (1979) A bittersweet comedy directed by Woody ALLEN, who also co-wrote the Oscar-nominated screenplay and appeared in the lead role. The plot concerns Isaac Davies (Allen), a TV comedy writer anxious to prove that he can produce a serious novel. However, he is unable to concentrate on his work because of his tangled relationships with three women: ex-wife Jill (Meryl STREEP), who is writing a book revealing why she left him for a lesbian; teenage drama student Tracy (Mariel Hemingway), whose devotion to him is a source of much guilt; and Mary (Diane KEATON), the former mistress of a friend, whom Isaac hopes to liberate from her pseudo-intellectual pretensions.

A tribute to Allen's home city, *Manhattan* begins with a series of views of its most celebrated landmarks accompanied by the strains of Gershwin's 'Rhapsody in Blue'. Isaac is then heard speaking into a tape recorder:

> "Chapter One. He adored New York. He idolized it all out of proportion." Uh, no, make that: "He–he...romanticized it all out of proportion. Now...to him...no matter what the season was, this was still a town that existed in black and white and pulsated to the great tunes of George Gershwin."

The most sentimental of Allen's films, *Manhattan* contains some of the tenderest lines he ever wrote, as when Isaac tells Tracy: "You're God's answer to Job. He would've pointed to you, and said 'I do a lot of terrible things, but I can also make one of these.'" It also allows the audience to get closer than

ever before to the film-maker; when Isaac delivers the following speech to his tape recorder, we know we are gaining an insight into Allen himself:

> Well, all right, why is life worth living? That's a very good question. Um. Well, there are certain things I – I guess that make it worthwhile. Uh, like what? Okay, um, for me...oh, I would say...what, Groucho Marx to name one thing...uh, ummmm, and Willie Mays, and um, uh, the second movement of the Jupiter Symphony, and ummmm...Louis Armstrong's recording of 'Potatohead Blues'...umm, Swedish movies, naturally...*Sentimental Education* by Flaubert...uh, Marlon Brando, Frank Sinatra...ummmm, those incredible apples and pears by Cézanne...uh, the crabs at Sam Wo's...tsch, uh...Tracy's face.

Originally shot in PANAVISION on Technicolor stock, the film was transferred to monochrome for its release print.

Mankiewicz, Herman J. Mankiewicz (1897–1953) US screenwriter and journalist, brother of Joseph L. MANKIEWICZ. Celebrated as one of the great wits of Hollywood, he scripted a host of successful movies in the 1930s and 1940s, his first screenplay being the silent *Road to Mandalay* (1926). He is known to have made uncredited contributions to both DUCK SOUP (1936) and THE WIZARD OF OZ (1939), amongst many others. It was, however, his work on Orson WELLES'S CITIZEN KANE (1941) that was to earn him a permanent place in Hollywood history. Although Welles claimed a credit (and accepted an Oscar) as co-writer, Pauline KAEL and others have argued that the witty poignant screenplay was essentially Mankiewicz's work. Having collaborated with Welles at the hour of his greatest glory, Mankiewicz is alleged to have remarked once as the actor-director went by: "There, but for the grace of God, goes God." (This line has also been attributed to Winston Churchill, of Stafford Cripps.)

Mankiewicz's other screenplays included *Christmas Holiday* (1944), adapted from the novel by Somerset Maugham, *Spanish Main* (1945), and *Pride of St Louis* (1952). Despite his track record, he was forever being sacked for his irreverent attitude to studio bosses, while his career was further disrupted by a weakness for alcohol. Between screenplays, he wrote drama criticism for *The New York Times* and also ventured into theatre production. When a stage production of *Love 'Em and Leave 'Em* by John Weaver got into financial trouble and Mankiewicz found himself unable to meet the author's fee, his solution to the problem was audacious: he borrowed the money from Weaver's wife, who happened to be a friend of his. Mankiewicz's own wife Sara bore the brunt of her husband's misdemeanours – when a friend inquired after her health, asking "How's Sara?", Mankiewicz couldn't place the name until the friend prompted him "Sara – your wife." Back came the reply "Ah, you mean Poor Sara."

Joseph L. Mankiewicz (1909–93) US screenwriter, producer, and director, brother of Herman J. MANKIEWICZ. A former journalist, Joseph Mankiewicz began writing screenplays in 1929 with Paramount's *The Mysterious Dr Fu Manchu*. He later branched out into production with *Fury* (1936), directed by Fritz LANG and made his debut as a writer-director with *Dragonwyck* (1946). His most successful films included the acerbic *A Letter for Three Wives* (1949) and the classic ALL ABOUT EVE (1950), both of which brought him Academy Award doubles as Best Screenplay and Best Director. *The Barefoot Contessa* (1954) was allegedly closely modelled on the romance between Rita HAYWORTH and Prince Aly Khan. In 1963 he replaced Rouben MAMOULIAN as director of the ill-fated epic *Cleopatra*, starring Elizabeth TAYLOR and Richard BURTON; the movie, which proved the most expensive film of its time, prompted Mankiewicz himself to admit that it was "shot in a state of emergency...and wound up in blind panic."

Among his later credits were *There was a Crooked Man* (1970) and the thriller *Sleuth* (1972), which paired Laurence OLIVIER and Michael CAINE. Of all his films, the one that gave him the most pleasure was the SHAKE-SPEARE adaptation *Julius Caesar* (1953), starring John GIELGUD, Marlon BRANDO, and James MASON, which Mankiewicz expected to be a huge flop. So certain was he that it would fail, that he fled Britain when the notices were due; much to his surprise, they were all enthusiastic.

> His wit scratches more than it bites.
> ANDREW SARRIS, film critic.

> For Joe Mankiewicz –
> Always at my back I hear,
> Winged release dates hurrying near.
> I'm glad my producer's literate,

> Gentle, kindly and considerate.
> OGDEN NASH, poet.

Mann, Anthony (Emil Bundesmann; 1906–67) US director of numerous WESTERNS, war adventures, and thrillers in the FILM NOIR tradition. Mann made his debut in 1942 with *Dr Broadway* and subsequently established his reputation with such highly stylized crime thrillers as *Desperate* (1947) and *T-Men* (1947). *Reign of Terror* (British title *The Black Book*; 1949), was the first of several historical ventures, while *Devil's Doorway* (1950) was Mann's first Western. The latter film broke new ground by having an American Indian character (Robert TAYLOR) as its hero. Later that year James STEWART's performance in Mann's psychological Western *Winchester '73* (1950) initiated a partnership that continued with *Bend of the River* (1952), in which Stewart guides a wagon train of settlers to Oregon, and *The Naked Spur* (1953), with Stewart as a bounty hunter. After the popular biopic *The Glenn Miller Story* (1953), in which Stewart played the title role, the duo returned to a Wild West setting for *The Far Country* (1954) and *The Man from Laramie* (1955).

Among Mann's later credits were *Men in War* (1957), about a lost patrol in the Korean War; the Western *The Tin Star* (1957), starring Henry FONDA; the family drama *God's Little Acre* (1958); *Man of the West* (1958), a Western with Gary COOPER; and the spectacular epics *El Cid* (1961) and *The Fall of the Roman Empire* (1964). *The Heroes of Telemark* (1965), like many of Mann's previous works, set the deeds of the central characters against the backdrop of breathtaking landscapes. Mann's last film, *A Dandy in Aspic* (1968), was completed after his death by its star, Laurence Harvey.

Mansfield, Jayne (Vera Jane Palmer; 1933–67) US actress, one of the most the most celebrated Hollywood sex symbols of her generation. Owing largely to her remarkable physique, Mansfield achieved greater fame than was merited by her performances in some 20 rather mediocre films. Her generously sized breasts inspired many Hollywood jokes: Alan King once observed "She'll never drown", while Kenneth MORE, her co-star in *The Sheriff of Fractured Jaw* (1959), gave her the nickname "Miss United Dairies".

Having launched her screen career in *The Female Jungle* (1955), Mansfield went on to appear in such movies as *The Girl Can't Help It* (1957), remembered chiefly for the performances of various rock 'n' roll greats, *Will Success Spoil Rock Hunter?* (1957), *Too Hot to Handle* (1960), and *A Guide for the Married Man* (1967). She revelled in her star status and became one of the legends of Hollywood, with a palatial home and a well-publicized fetish for pink: her house, her car, and even her poodle were pink and she was once photographed bathing in pink champagne. For a British television interview in 1957 she wore a stunning leopard-skin dress that left very little room for movement – when offered a chair to sit down, she said she would remain standing, explaining, "This dress ain't for sittin', this dress ain't for walkin', all this dress is for is leanin'."

Mansfield's private life was darker than many were aware: she married at 16, had a baby a year later, suffered three failed marriages, and was devastated when her career went into decline in the 1960s. In 1967 she and her new fiancé were decapitated when their sports car collided with a lorry near New Orleans. It was rumoured at the time that their deaths were owing to their involvement with satanism, in which Mansfield had dabbled since 1965. Her occultist, Anton La Vey, had allegedly placed a ritual curse on her lover a month before the accident. (La Vey himself went on to play the Devil in ROSEMARY'S BABY and enjoyed success on the cabaret circuit with his act 'Anton La Vey and his Topless Witches'.)

March. Fredric March (Frederick McIntyre Bickel; 1897–1975) Stylish US actor, one of Hollywood's most respected leading men of the 1930s and 1940s. Having rejected a career in banking, March developed a reputation as a stage actor before making his film debut in one of the very first talkies, *The Dummy* (1929). That same year, he played a supporting role in the Clara BOW picture *The Wild Party* (1929) and appeared in five other films. After reprising his stage impersonation of John BARRYMORE in *The Royal Family of Broadway* (1930), he went on to achieve stardom with his performance in Rouben MAMOULIAN's classic horror film *Dr Jekyll and Mr Hyde* (1932), which brought him an Oscar for Best Actor.

Subsequent starring roles included Death in *Death Takes a Holiday* (1934) and Valjean in *Les Misérables* (1935). In the original A STAR IS BORN (1937) he portrayed a movie star well past his best, while in *Nothing Sacred* (1937), he played a sleazy journalist attempting to exploit a supposedly dying girl (Carole LOMBARD). Other films of the period include several collaborations with his wife, the actress Florence Eldridge. In 1940 he played Joan CRAWFORD's long-suffering husband in *Susan and God*, following this with such wartime movies as *One Foot in Heaven* (1941), *I Married a Witch* (1942), and *The Adventures of Mark Twain* (1944).

In 1946 William WYLER's THE BEST YEARS OF OUR LIVES brought March a second Academy Award for his performance as a war veteran returning to civilian life. During his later career he gave outstanding performances as Willy Loman in *Death of a Salesman* (1952), as Spencer TRACY's Bible-bashing courtroom opponent in *Inherit the Wind* (1960), and as a conspired-against US president in *Seven Days in May* (1964). He bowed out in style in his last film, *The Iceman Cometh* (1973), an acclaimed adaptation of the play by Eugene O'Neill.

> Fredric March's laborious stylishness...always made up in persistence what it lacked in persuasiveness.
> ANDREW SARRIS, film critic.

The March of Time A series of semidocumentary shorts created and sponsored by *Time* magazine with film-maker Louis de Rochemont at the helm. Introduced in 1935, the series was developed from an existing *March of Time* radio programme. The films, which were narrated by Westbrook van Voorhis, combined newsreel footage with interviews and dramatized reconstructions of current events. Over the next decade the *March of Time* two-reelers became an authoritative voice of US opinion throughout the world, especially during World War II. Their popularity declined in the early 1950s with the advent of daily television news and TV documentary programmes.

In the early 1960s a 13-part series of excerpts was put together for television, but no buyers were found. In 1965 *Time* magazine attempted to revive *The March of Time* as a weekly television show on current topics, but a *New York Times* headline announced "Time Marches On, Awkwardly" and the series was cancelled after eight weeks.

mark (1) A chalk mark or piece of tape placed on the floor where a performer is to stand during a take. Before shooting begins these marks are used to focus the cameras for the scene (a procedure that usually involves STAND-INS rather than the stars themselves). Scenes involving complex character and/or camera movements may require an elaborate system of marks so that all principals remain in focus. When an actor fails to move to the prearranged position at the correct time, he or she is said to *miss the mark*, a phrase that has entered the language. (2) The order given to the CLAPPER BOARD operator to bang the clapsticks together, thereby enabling the later SYN-CHRONIZATION of sound and picture.

Marlowe, Philip A Los Angeles private DETECTIVE created by the US writer Raymond CHANDLER, who introduced the character in his 1939 novel THE BIG SLEEP. The book was adapted for the cinema in 1946, with Humphrey BOGART as the private eye. Some months earlier Dick POWELL had taken the role in *Farewell, My Lovely* (1945); both films were later remade (in 1978 and 1975 respectively) with Robert MITCHUM as Marlowe. A number of Chandler's other Marlowe stories have been filmed, including *The Long Goodbye* (1973) with Elliot Gould. *Marlowe* (1969), starring James Garner in the title role, was based on Chandler's *The Little Sister*.

Marlowe is a cool tough guy, attractive to women, and never short of a cynical wisecrack; at the same time he is often revealed as a solitary and unexpectedly moral character. Typical of Marlowe are the following lines from the Bogart version of *The Big Sleep*:

I don't mind if you don't like my manners. I don't like 'em myself. They're pretty bad. I grieve over 'em on long winter evenings.

Marple, Jane An amateur DETECTIVE created by the British crime writer Agatha Christie (1891–1976). Miss Marple, whose gentle manner disguises a capacity for powerful deductive reasoning, has been played on the big screen by Margaret RUTHERFORD in *Murder She Said* (1961), *Murder at the Gallop* (1963), *Murder Most Foul* (1964), and *Murder Ahoy* (1964); Angela LANSBURY in *The Mirror Crack'd* (1980); and Helen Hayes in *Murder is Easy* (1982) and *Murder with Mirrors* (1985). Hayes went on to play Miss Marple on US television, while the veteran actress Joan Hickson endeared

herself to thousands of viewers in the title role of a British television series.

marquee A canvas projection over the entrance of the cinema giving the title, stars, etc. of the film being shown. A star whose name is likely to attract the public to a movie is sometimes said to have *marquee appeal*.

married A British term describing a COMBINED PRINT carrying both picture and synchronized sound.

Marshall. George Marshall (1891–1975) US director, whose numerous credits over an immensely long career included Westerns, comedies, and thrillers. Born in Chicago, Marshall worked as a labourer, baseball player, and portrait painter before entering the cinema as an extra in 1912. He was soon playing larger roles in a host of silent comedies and adventure serials. He began directing in 1917, when he made the first of a string of popular Westerns starring Harry Carey. In 1932 he directed one of the first LAUREL AND HARDY features, *Pack Up Your Troubles*, in which he also appeared in the role of an irascible army cook; he continued his association with leading comedians of the day with the W. C. FIELDS movie *You Can't Cheat an Honest Man* (1939).

That same year Marshall drew on his previous experience in both genres to create the classic comedy Western *Destry Rides Again*, which starred James STEWART as a pacifist marshal and featured Marlene DIETRICH singing 'See What the Boys in the Back Room Will Have'. In 1940 he directed one of the funniest Bob HOPE movies, *The Ghost Breakers*; also well received was *Murder, He Says* (1944), starring Fred MACMURRAY as a hapless public-opinion pollster terrorized by an eccentric hillbilly family. After demonstrating his versatility with the taut thriller *The Blue Dahlia* (1943), starring Alan LADD and Veronica Lake, he went on to direct a mixed bag of thrillers and comedies, including the spoof Western musical *Red Garters* (1954). Among the more notable achievements of his later career was his contribution to the epic *How the West was Won* (1962).

Herbert Marshall (1890–1966) British actor, who played cultured English gentlemen in Hollywood movies of the 1930s and 1940s. The sets of his films were always specially designed to conceal the limp that was a permanent legacy of his wartime injuries (he lost a leg while serving with the merchant marine during World War I).

Marshall made his stage debut in 1911 and his first film *Mumsie*, in 1927. Other early films included *The Letter* (1929), from a story by Somerset Maugham, HITCHCOCK's *Murder* (1930), and *Blonde Venus* (1932), in which he played Marlene DIETRICH's husband. That same year his sparkling performance in the LUBITSCH comedy *Trouble in Paradise* (1932), confirmed him as one of the most reliable leading men in the Paramount stable. The studio had originally intended to market him as a Great Lover, but he preferred to play more demure roles, supporting rather than overshadowing the talents of his co-stars. He went on to appear in such films as *The Painted Veil* (1934) with Greta GARBO, *The Dark Angel* (1935) with Merle OBERON, and *Breakfast for Two* (1937) with Barbara STANWYCK. In 1940 he enjoyed one of his biggest triumphs in a remake of *The Letter*, this time as the husband rather than the lover, the role he played in the 1929 version. After being cast against type as a villainous Nazi sympathizer in Hitchcock's *Foreign Correspondent* (1940), he returned to form as Bette DAVIS's long-suffering husband in *The Little Foxes* (1941).

Marshall's last major role was that of Somerset Maugham in *The Moon and Sixpence* (1942). Thereafter his career went into a slow decline, despite comebacks in such movies as *The Enchanted Cottage* (1944), in which he was seen with limp and stick for the first time. Highlights of his later career included *Stage Struck* (1957), with Henry FONDA.

martial-arts movies Films of minimal plot and maximum violence featuring various Far Eastern combat sports and self-defence styles. More popularly known as kung-fu (or, in *Variety*'s phraseology, 'chop-socky') movies, the genre emerged from an older tradition of Cantonese melodrama that inspired such early films as *The Burning of the Red Lotus Monastery* series (1928–31).

Having been largely forgotten, the genre was revived during the Hong Kong cinema boom of the 1960s by the Golden Harvest and Shaw Brothers studios. Leading exponents of the style included the directors Chang Cheh and King Hu, whose *Come Drink with Me* (1966) was an early success.

Such films as *A Touch of Zen* (1969), *The Fate of Lee Khan* (1973), and *The Valiant Ones* (1974) provided Shaws' with a steady income in the 1970s. However, it was the diminutive Sino-American BRUCE LEE who really put the genre on the map, by evolving his own distinctive *jeet kune do* form of balletic but bone-crunching violence. His physical skills were truly extraordinary; it is said that some of Lee's high-speed flying kicks had to be shot in slow motion to avoid the appearance of blurred fakery that 24 fps would have given them. *The Big Boss* (1971), *Fist of Fury* (1972), *The Way of the Dragon* (1973) and *Enter the Dragon* (1973), the latter US-produced, brought Lee international fame and led to David CARRADINE's popular TV series *Kung Fu* (1972–74).

Lee's untimely death made him a cult figure and spawned a plethora of dubious tributes. These, incidently, provided brief careers for sound-alikes Bruce Li, Bruce Lei, Bruce Le, Tiger Lee, Dragon Lee, and Bronson Lee. Despite Hong Kong's many other stars – Sonny Chiba, Jimmy Wang Yu, and Alexander Fu Sheng to name only a few – no performer has approached Lee's success. The only star to come close is Jackie Chan in the 1990s. The American Chuck Norris, a former world middleweight karate champion, found success with a number of violent martial-arts movies in the 1980s.

Martin. **Dean Martin** (Dino Paul Crocetti; 1917–   ) US actor and singer, who made his name as straight man to Jerry LEWIS in the 1950s; he subsequently emerged as a solo star, making a virtue of his easygoing charm and self-deprecating humour. Having worked as a coal-miner, a boxer, a gambling-house croupier, and a garage forecourt attendant, Martin first attracted attention as a nightclub singer in the late 1930s, modelling his relaxed style on that of Bing CROSBY. He met Lewis in 1946 and their comedy singing act quickly caught on. They made their film debut in *My Friend Irma* (1949) and went on to collaborate on a series of 16 zany comedies ending with *Hollywood or Bust* (1956); the partnership allegedly broke up when Lewis took exception to Martin's casual attitude.

In the late 1950s and 1960s he extended his range with serious roles in such films as *The Young Lions* (1958), *Rio Bravo* (1959), *Toys in the Attic* (1963), and *Sons of Katie Elder* (1965). He also hosted a very popular television series. Other credits included a series of films – starting with *The Silencers* (1966) – in which he played private detective Matt Helm, the disaster movie *Airport* (1970), which brought him some seven million dollars as his share of the gross receipts (believed to be a record at the time for earnings from a single movie), and CAMEO parts in *The Cannonball Run* (1981) and its sequel (1983).

Off screen, Martin attracted notoriety as one of the RAT PACK of high-living stars who associated with Frank SINATRA in the 1950s. He also became well known for his excessive indulgence in alcohol, a failing that provided him with much comic material. He once memorably denounced teetotalism with the adage "Imagine getting up in the morning and knowing that's as good as you're going to feel all day."

Steve Martin (1945–) US actor, comedian, writer, and producer. Martin began his career in entertainment at Disneyland, where he learnt magic, juggling, and banjo playing, while also studying symbolic logic at Long Beach State University. In the late 1960s he started to write material for such television shows as *The Smothers Brothers Comedy Hour*, on which he later became a regular, and to develop his own stand-up act.

Martin's brand of manic humour brought him growing fame in the mid 1970s, leading to his first venture into film in the Oscar-nominated short *The Absent-Minded Waiter* (1977); he later played the same character in *The Muppet Movie* (1979). Although CAMEOS followed in the flop *Sergeant Pepper's Lonely Hearts Club Band* and the Who documentary *The Kids are Alright* (both 1978) his screen career was slow in taking off. In 1979, however, Universal agreed to take his feature screenplay *The Jerk* (1979); the film, which was directed by Carl Reiner, also gave Martin his first starring role. Martin also starred in the unsuccessful film adaptation of Dennis Potter's *Pennies From Heaven* (1981). He then continued the partnership with Reiner in *Dead Men Don't Wear Plaid* (1982), a FILM NOIR spoof in which Martin appeared to be acting alongside various 1940s stars, and *The Man with Two Brains* (1983), in which he played the mad scientist Dr Hfuhruhurr. Neither film was a great box-office success, and *The Lonely Guy* (1984) sank without trace.

Martin and Reiner's first great success came with *All of Me* (1985), in which he played a man forced to share his body with the spirit of the deceased Lily Tomlin. Martin's bravura physical performance gained him the New York Critics' Award as the year's best actor. A year later he married his co-star Victoria Tennant and appeared as one of the *Three Amigos!* (1986) in John LANDIS's patchy cowboy spoof.

A wonderful cameo as the sadistic dentist in *Little Shop of Horrors* (1986) preceded Martin's biggest role to date, that of the nasally challenged fireman hero of *Roxanne* (1987), an updating of the Cyrano de Bergerac story that he also wrote and co-produced. In subsequent films Martin deliberately stretched his range, appearing as a virtual straight man to John Candy in *Planes, Trains and Automobiles* (1987), and taking on with Michael CAINE in *Dirty Rotten Scoundrels* (1988). After taking another virtually straight role in *Parenthood* (1989), Martin appeared with Robin WILLIAMS in a stage production of *Waiting For Godot*. Recent films, such as *My Blue Heaven* (1990), the remake of *Father of the Bride* (1991), and his own *LA Story* (1991) have been only moderately successful. His search for rewarding parts has continued in *Grand Canyon* (1992) and the flop *Leap of Faith* (1993) but appears to have affected his ability to draw big audiences.

Marvin, Lee (1924–87) US actor. The son of an advertising executive, Marvin began his acting career almost by accident. Having been invalided out of the US Marines, he worked as a plumber's asisstant before being asked to replace an ill bit-part player in summer stock. In 1951 he appeared in a Broadway production of Billy Budd and made his screen debut with a small role in *You're in the Navy Now*, a Gary COOPER film. Abetted by his tall, ugly, and menacing presence, Marvin went on to establish himself as a heavy in Westerns and crime thrillers. His more notable films of the 1950s include Elia KAZAN's *The Wild One* (1953), Fritz LANG's *The Big Heat* (1953), in which he played a sadistic killer, *Bad Days at Black Rock* (1955), and *Attack!* (1956).

Following appearances in a couple of John WAYNE films, *The Comancheros* (1962) and *Donovan's Reef* (1963), Marvin gave a strong performance as a hitman in Don SIEGEL's remake of *The Killers* (1964). It was, however, the spoof Western *Cat Ballou* (1965), in which he appeared opposite Jane FONDA, that really lifted him to stardom. The film brought him a Best Actor Oscar and launched him on a new career as a versatile leading man capable of both menace and comedy. That same year he appeared as a drunken ex-baseball player in Stanley KRAMER's *Ship of Fools*, while *The Professionals* (1966), John BOORMAN's *Point Blank* (1967), and *The Dirty Dozen* (1967) all saw him returning to hard-man roles. In 1968 he appeared with Clint EASTWOOD in the popular comedy-Western musical *Paint Your Wagon*, a highlight of which was Marvin's *basso profundo* rendition of 'I was Born under a Wandering Star.'

During the early 1970s Marvin continued this varied output at a slightly more leisurely pace. Notable films of the period include John FRANKENHEIMER's Eugene O'Neill adaptation *The Iceman Cometh* and Robert ALDRICH's *Emperor of the North* (both 1973). From the mid 1970s onward he found few good roles, playing in such standard fare as *Shout at the Devil* (1976), *The Big Red One* (1980), and even *The Dirty Dozen: The Next Mission* (1976) for television. A noted exception was *Gorky Park* (1983).

In 1979 Marvin appeared in the headlines when a landmark legal case was brought against him for 'palimony' by a woman he had lived with, but never married. The claim was eventually rejected.

Marx Brothers The famous comedy team consisting of the brothers Chico (Leonard Marx; 1886–1961), Harpo (Adolph Marx; 1888–1964), and Groucho (Julius Marx; 1890–1977). Two other brothers were Gummo (Milton Marx; 1893–1977), who appeared with the team in their early stage years, and Zeppo (Herbert Marx; 1901–79), who joined them in their first four films.

Each of the three main brothers had a clearly defined persona. Groucho sported a black moustache (greasepaint until 1948), leered through heavy glasses, fingered a cigar, had a stooped walk, and specialized in innuendo, insults, and bad puns ("You go Uruguay and I'll go mine"). Harpo never spoke on film (although he was not, as their publicity material suggested, dumb), played the harp beautifully, whistled messages, honked a horn, wore a red wig, and chased blondes. Chico spoke with an Italian accent, played butter-fingered piano, and wore a Tyrolean outfit with a pointed hat.

The brothers were born in New York City, sons of a poor Jewish tailor (such a bad one, Groucho said, that "he preferred not to measure his customers") and a madcap mother who launched them into vaudeville. After beginning as a musical act, they switched to comedy and in 1924 hit Broadway in their smash revue *I'll Say She Is*. A year later *The Cocoanuts* introduced the matronly Margaret DUMONT, who would become their constant foil. Screen versions of this revue and its follow-up, *Animal Crackers*, were made in 1929 and 1930.

The first Marx Brothers film to feature a specially written screenplay was *Monkey Business* (1931), in which they play stowaways. However, S. J. Perelman's script was frequently ignored by Groucho and Chico, who adlibbed with abandon (when Chico says "I come up to see the Captain's bridge"; Groucho replies, "I'm sorry, but he keeps it in a glass of water while he's eating.") *Horse Feathers* (1932) was followed by the great DUCK SOUP (1933), a film banned in Italy because Groucho's depiction of the dictator Rufus T. Firefly annoyed Mussolini.

Zeppo left the team before *A Night at the Opera* (1935), their first MGM film. Its follow-up, *A Day at the Races* (1937) was banned in Latvia as 'worthless' (to the brothers' joy). Later films included *At the Circus* (1939), *A Night in Casablanca* (1946), and *Love Happy* (1950), their last as a team.

Most of the brothers' sharpest quips were spoken by Groucho:

> One morning I shot an elephant in my pajamas. How he got into my pajamas I'll never know.
> *Animal Crackers*, 1930.

> GROUCHO I want to register a complaint. Do you know who sneaked into my room at three o'clock this morning?
> RECEPTIONIST Who?
> GROUCHO Nobody, and that's my complaint.
> *Monkey Business*, 1931.

Groucho was also celebrated for his off-screen remarks. When a woman contestant on his television quiz show, *You Bet Your Life*, revealed that she had 22 children and cooed "I love my husband", Groucho immediately responded "I like my cigar, too, but I take it out once in a while." Chico also produced some off-screen gems. It is said that when his wife caught him kissing a chorus girl, he protested that he wasn't doing any such thing – "I was whispering in her mouth" he said.

After the act broke up, Chico retired, Harpo wrote his autobiography, *Harpo*

Speaks! (1961), and Groucho worked on television and published various books. At the age of 82, he performed a one-man show at Carnegie Hall. His son, Arthur Marx, later alleged that Groucho's companion, Erin Fleming, drugged and bullied him during his last increasingly senile years.

Mary Poppins (1964) DISNEY's popular family musical about an ideal children's nanny with magical powers (Julie ANDREWS). Based on the stories by the British author P. L. Travers, Robert STEVENSON's film proved a huge success for Disney and an enduring children's classic. The film is memorable both for the clever songs, which include 'Supercalifragilisticexpialidocious' and 'Chim-chim-cheree', and for the special effects, which include Andrews sailing through the London skies underneath a black umbrella, tidying rooms at the flick of her fingers, exploring the cartoon world behind a series of chalked pavement pictures, and sliding up banisters. The film was nominated for 13 Oscars and won five, including Original Score, Special Effects, and Best Actress (Andrews). The cast had no weak links, Andrews being ably supported by Dick VAN DYKE as the chimney sweep Bert and David Tomlinson as the children's father (though critics had their reservations about Van Dyke's cockney accent).

Walt Disney had first come across the Mary Poppins books when his young daughters read them. He subsequently pursued the author for over ten years before she agreed to give him the film rights (she had mixed feelings about the end result, which lacked the subtlety of her original books). Other actresses considered for the leading role included Mary Martin and, somewhat curiously, Bette DAVIS. Andrews allegedly clinched the part when Disney decided that she had the best whistle. Filming the story was not without its mishaps: during one flying sequence Andrews was dumped unceremoniously on the floor and to the ensuing inquiry from a technician "Is Miss Andrews down yet?" came the distinctly un-Poppins-like response "Down? I'm bloody nearly through the floor!"

M*A*S*H (1970) Robert ALTMAN's black comedy about military surgeons in the Korean War zone; the initials stand for 'Mobile Army Surgical Hospital'. This savage, brilliant, and often tasteless antiwar satire was aimed squarely at young audiences of the Vietnam era (one critic described it as "Sergeant Bilko in Vietnam"). Amongst its other distinctions, *M*A*S*H* was the first mainstream film to include the word 'fuck' in its script. The film spawned the record-breaking CBS television series that ran from 1974 until 1983 with Alan Alda in the lead. Altman himself hated the series, which became increasingly soft-centred as it went on.

Stylistically, the film's greatest triumph is the effect of spontaneity achieved through overlapping dialogue, fast editing, and brilliant ensemble work. The film, which had been turned down by 12 other directors, made the name of Altman (whose 14-year-old son wrote the lyrics for the movie's theme tune 'Suicide is Painless'). It also made stars of the virtually unknown Elliott Gould, Donald SUTHERLAND, and Sally Kellerman, and helped to establish the careers of Robert DUVALL and Tom Skerritt. Altman and Kellerman received Oscar nominations, as did the film itself, which also took the Best Film Award at Cannes. Ring Lardner Jnr, formerly best known as one of the HOLLYWOOD TEN, won an Oscar for his adaption of Richard Hooker's novel.

The episodic story concerns a group of army medics who remain sane amidst the carnage by swapping one-liners while operating, dodging military discipline, and spending their free time chasing women.

mask (1) A device placed over the camera lens in order to change the shape or size of the picture. The use of masks was popular during the silent era, when an IRIS shot might be used to open or close a scene or a keyhole-shaped picture to suggest voyeurism. Masks can also be used to change the ASPECT RATIO. (2) Another name for a MATTE.

Mason, James (1909–84) Distinguished British actor, who appeared in over 100 films of widely varying quality. After taking a degree in architecture from Cambridge, Mason began acting on the stage from 1931; he subsequently appeared at the Old Vic and the Gate Theatre in Dublin. Having made his film debut in *Late Extra* (1935), he starred in numerous British QUOTA QUICKIES, making a further 12 films before the end of the decade. He then achieved prominence playing saturnine villains in a series of wartime costume dramas, notably *The Man in Grey* (1943), *Fanny by Gaslight* (1944),

The Seventh Veil (1945), memorably described by Pauline KAEL as a "sadomasochistic sundae", and the Regency shocker *The Wicked Lady* (1945). Following his success in Carol REED's *Odd Man Out* (1947), which presented him with perhaps his finest role, that of a hunted IRA man, Mason moved to Hollywood, where his distinctive voice and manner brought him a series of plum parts. His roles of the 1950s included Rommel in both *The Desert Fox* (1952) and *The Desert Rats* (1953), Judy GARLAND's alcoholic husband in A STAR IS BORN (1954), a part that brought him his only Oscar nomination as Best Actor, Captain Nemo in Disney's *20,000 Leagues Under the Sea* (1955), and a drug-addicted schoolteacher in Nicholas RAY's *Bigger Than Life* (1956). The end of the decade saw Mason in fine form as the suave villain in Alfred HITCHCOCK's NORTH BY NORTHWEST (1959).

Among Mason's more notable films of the 1960s were Stanley KUBRICK's LOLITA (1962), in which he played the lecherous Humbert Humbert, Richard BROOKS's *Lord Jim* (1965), and the British-made GEORGY GIRL (1966), for which he received a nomination as Best Supporting Actor. During the following decade Mason kept up a prolific work rate, appearing almost indiscriminately in British, US, and European films that ranged from good to awful. Some of the better films of this period include John HUSTON's *The Mackintosh Man* (1973), *Heaven Can Wait* (1978), and *The Boys from Brazil* (1978). Notable among his last films were Sidney LUMET's *The Verdict* (1982), for which Mason received his second Best Supporting Actor Oscar nomination, and *The Shooting Party* (1984).

Massey, Raymond (1896–1983) US actor and producer, born in Canada, who made his reputation in a series of British and US films of the 1930s. After active service in France with the Canadian army, Massey travelled to London, where he launched his acting career. He made his screen debut playing Sherlock HOLMES in *The Speckled Band* (1931). In the 1930s and 1940s Massey became a memorable screen presence with his large build and expressive voice. Amongst his early successes were the comedy-horror film *The Old Dark House* (1932), Alexander KORDA's *The Scarlet Pimpernel* (1934) and *Things to Come* (1936), and *The Prisoner of Zenda* (1937), in which he played the usurper Black Michael. Later hits included the film version of his stage success *Abe Lincoln in Illinois* (1940), POWELL and PRESSBURGER's *The 49th Parallel* (1941), ARSENIC AND OLD LACE (1944), in which he played the psychotic Jonathan, *Mourning Becomes Electra* (1947), and EAST OF EDEN (1955), in which he played James DEAN's puritanical father. Many knew him best, however, as Dr Gillespie in the US television series *Dr Kildare* (1961–65).

Massey particularly enjoyed impersonating Lincoln, to the point that the celebrated wit George S. Kaufman once remarked that "Massey won't be satisfied until he's assassinated."

His son **Daniel Massey** (1933–) became a respected stage and television actor, as well as appearing in a handful of films – notably *Star!* (1968), in which he portrayed Noël COWARD. His more recent television credits include the central role in *Intimate Contact* (1987), a much-discussed drama about a businessman who contracts AIDS after a fling in New York. Raymond Massey's daughter **Anna Massey** (1937–) has also enjoyed a lengthy career on both stage and screen. Her work for the cinema includes *Frenzy* (1972) and *A Doll's House* (1973), while her television credits have included *Rebecca* (1979), in which she played Mrs Danvers, and *Hotel du Lac* (1986).

master. **master positive** A fine-grain positive print of the original negative. It is created for the purpose of producing duplicate negatives (DUPES).

master shot A LONG SHOT used to establish our overall sense of a scene. Other specified shots, such as CLOSE-UPS and MEDIUM SHOTS, are inserted during editing. The term **master scene** is sometimes used for a moving long shot of a scene in which much action occurs over a wide area. Examples include the epic battle scenes in Sergei BONDARCHUK's *Waterloo* (1970), filmed over a two-mile front using 20,000 extras from the Red Army.

Mastroianni, Marcello (1923–) Italian actor, who became one of Europe's best known leading men in the 1960s. Mastroianni, who escaped from a German prison camp during the war, gave up his employment as a draughtsman to make his movie debut in *I Miserabili* (1947), an adaptation of Hugo's *Les Misérables*. He went on to distinguish himself as a stage actor and to star in such movies as VISCONTI's *Le Notti* *bianche* (1957) and FELLINI's LA DOLCE VITA (1960), the film that established him as an international sex symbol. He also played the leading role – a surrogate for the director himself – in Fellini's 8½ (1963).

During the early 1960s Mastroianni was much in demand as a leading man, playing opposite Claudia CARDINALE in *Il Bell' Antonio* (1960), Jeanne MOREAU in ANTONIONI's *La Notte* (1961), Brigitte BARDOT in *Private View* (1962), and Sophia LOREN in *Yesterday, Today and Tomorrow* (1963) and *Marriage Italian Style* (1964). International audiences also flocked to see him as a murderous husband in Pietro GERMI's *Divorce Italian Style* (1961), which earned him an Oscar nomination as Best Actor.

When later films were less well received, Mastroianni reluctantly set about learning English in an attempt to win US parts; however, initial releases in which he spoke English lines that he had learnt phonetically did not go down well and the great majority of his films continued to be in Italian. In 1970 he picked up the Best Actor Award at Cannes for his role in *Drama of Jealousy*. His credits since then have included *The Priest's Wife* (1971), Fellini's *La Cittá delle donne* (1981) and *Intervista* (1987), the English-language *Macaroni* (1985), *Dark Eyes* (1987), which brought him another Oscar nomination, and *The Broken Flight of the Swan* (1991).

One well-known story illustrates Mastroianni's natural charm: having been presented with a gold watch by the producer Joseph Levine, who did not know that Mastroianni was already wearing one, the actor nonchalantly removed the watch he had on and dropped it in a convenient waste-bin.

match. match cut A CUT in which the two shots are linked by some form of visual (occasionally aural) resemblance. Essentially a type of visual pun, the match cut can be used either light-heartedly or to make a complex symbolic point. An example of the latter is the famous moment in 2001: A SPACE ODYSSEY (1969) in which KUBRICK cuts from a whirling bone thrown into the air by a prehistoric man to a space station rotating gracefully in space. In the early scenes of LAWRENCE OF ARABIA (1962) David LEAN added a verbal pun to the visual parallel by cutting from a flaring *match* in the hand of Lawrence to a spectacular desert sunrise. "In one cut" commented Steven SPIELBERG,

"he creates the entire scope of the Arabian Desert."

match dissolve A DISSOLVE in which the two shots are linked by some form of resemblance in either subject or action. The effect is often used to evoke the passage of time, as when a shot of a young character dissolves to one of the same actor in different make-up to suggest ageing. It is also used for the transformation scenes in werewolf films or the various versions of *Dr Jekyll and Mr Hyde*.

matte A device placed over the lens of a camera or the aperture in an OPTICAL PRINTER to prevent the access of light to a part of the film image, thereby leaving it unexposed. A composite picture can then be created by filming or printing another image onto the previously unexposed area, while using a second matte to protect the already exposed film. The technique was developed in the silent era to allow such SPECIAL EFFECTS as the combining of separately shot backgrounds and foregrounds or the enhancement of a set by drawn material. Originally, a MASK was placed in front of the camera lens and the same film run through the camera twice. This procedure was later superseded by a BIPACK method in which the original shot is taken in the normal fashion and then used to produce a second negative with the required area masked out; an optical printer is then used to combine this image with a similar negative containing the additional material. However, these techniques are only possible with stationary subjects. More sophisticated procedures are required to produce a **travelling matte**, in which the matted area of the film changes from frame to frame, the most common of these being the BLUE-SCREEN PROCESS.

matte artist An artist who specializes in the painting of MATTES for the creation of composite pictures.

matte box A box-like attachment placed in front of a camera lens into which are slotted MATTES, MASKS, FILTERS, or similar devices used to create simple special effects.

Matter of Life and Death, A (US title *Stairway to Heaven*; 1946) Michael POWELL and Emeric PRESSBURGER's classic fantasy, a film made to promote goodwill between Britain and America in the immediate aftermath of World War II. The plot concerns a wartime British pilot (David NIVEN), who is forced to jump from his burning plane without a parachute. Before he jumps, Niven has a last conversation with a US radio operator, (Kim Hunter) and falls in love with her voice. Having miraculously survived the fall, Niven meets Hunter and the two embark on a romance. Niven, however, is suffering from brain damage for which he must undergo an operation.

Meanwhile, in heaven, Conductor 71 (Marius Goring) realizes that Niven was, in fact, scheduled to die. When summoned, Niven argues that as a mistake has been made that permitted him to fall in love, he should be allowed to live. A heavenly court is convened to decide his fate, Niven's case being argued by his recently deceased doctor (Roger Livesy), and opposed by Abraham Farley, an 18th-century American patriot (Raymond MASSEY).

The heavenly scenes – which can be rationalized as a product of Niven's brain damage and a metaphor for his fight for survival – feature a stunning set designed by Powell and Pressburger's regular art director, Hein Heckroth (1897–1970). These sequences are shot in a chilly black-and-white, while the earthly scenes are filmed in vivid Technicolor (see COLOUR SEQUENCES. The film, which was chosen for the first Royal Command Film Performance, aroused a certain amount of controversy amongst those who considered it anti-British. Despite or because of this, the film did well in America.

Matthau, Walter (Walter Matas-schanskayasky, 1920–) US actor, best known for playing grouches with a heart of gold. Having worked as a filing clerk, boxing instructor, and basketball coach, Matthau trained for the stage under Erwin Piscator and began a career on Broadway. After making his film debut in 1955 he went on to play a series of baddies, drunks, and other supporting roles in such movies as *Charade* (1963), *Goodbye Charlie* (1964), and *Mirage* (1965). In 1965 his award-winning performance in Neil Simon's stage play *The Odd Couple* led Billy WILDER to cast him as the conman Whiplash Willie in *The Fortune Cookie* (1966); the film earned Matthau an Oscar for Best Supporting Actor and initiated his screen partnership with Jack LEMMON, who was to appear with him in some of the most effective comedies of the following decades.

Matthau's lugubrious features and irascible persona served him well in both *A Guide for the Married Man* (1967) and the film adaptation of *The Odd Couple* (1968), in which he played the slob Oscar, whose life is turned upside down by the fastidious Felix (Lemmon). Further plaudits came with the musical *Hello Dolly!* (1969), the irreverent *A New Leaf* (1970), in which he starred as a playboy trying to dispose of the wife he has acquired for the sake of her wealth, and Neil Simon's *Plaza Suite* (1971), in which he played three separate roles. After taking a relatively straight role in the thriller *The Taking of Pelham One Two Three* (1974), Matthau was reunited with Lemmon for Wilder's remake of the classic newspaper comedy *The Front Page* (1975) and appeared with George Burns in *The Sunshine Boys* (1975), about two ageing vaudeville artists. He subsequently appeared in Simon's *California Suite* (1978), teamed up with Lemmon again in *Buddy Buddy* (1981), and starred in Roman POLANSKI's ill-fated *Pirates* (1986). In 1994 he resumed business with Lemmon after a break of some 14 years in *Grumpy Old Men* and appeared as Albert Einstein in the comedy *IQ*.

The grown-ups' Yogi Bear.
JOHN COLEMAN: *New Statesman*, 1968.

Matthews, Jessie (1907–81) British actress, singer, and dancer, who starred in a series of popular romantic musicals in the 1930s. The daughter of an impoverished street trader, Matthews is said to have danced in the street as a young girl to earn coppers from passers-by. She made her stage debut at the age of 12 and first ventured into films in 1923. In classic showbusiness style, she became a star after going on for the sick Gertrude Lawrence in *Charlot's Revue* in New York (1924). Much loved for her high spirits, delicate dancing, and fragile voice, she went on to star in further stage musicals and revues on both sides of the Atlantic. She also emerged as one of Britain's first talkie stars in such movies as *Out of the Blue* (1931), *The Good Companions* (1932), in which she co-starred with John GIELGUD, and *Evergreen* (1934), highlights of which included the song 'Over My Shoulder' and a famous dance on the ceiling. In *It's Love Again* (1936) she appeared with Sonnie Hale who later became her husband and directed her in *Head Over Heels* (1937) and *Sailing Along* (1938). She made 17 films in all, ten of them musicals.

After World War II she spent some time in Australia before returning to Britain to star as Mrs Dale in the long-running radio series *Mrs Dale's Diary*; she continued to make occasional appearances in film and on television until her death. Her personal life remained very much the stuff of soap operas, her poverty-stricken childhood being followed by three failed marriages, clashes with the film companies who employed her, nervous breakdowns (she came out in nervous rashes during the making of her most celebrated film, *Evergreen*), and bitterness at the way the public lost interest in her frivolous style during and after World War II.

Mature, Victor (1916–) US actor, who became a Hollywood sex symbol in the 1940s and 1950s, generally playing muscle-bound heroes in romances and EPICS. After a few years in the theatre, Mature broke into the movies in 1939, having been spotted by producer Hal ROACH. Billed initially as **The Hunk**, Mature made an effective hero in the prehistoric drama *One Million BC* (1940) and went on to co-star with Betty GRABLE, Rita HAYWORTH, and Lucille Ball during the war years. He was Doc Holliday in the FORD Western *My Darling Clementine* (1946), a policeman in the thriller *Cry of the City* (1948), a theatre director in *Red Hot and Blue* (1949), and the biblical hero in Cecil B. DE MILLE's *Samson and Delilah* (1949). It was of the last-named epic that Groucho MARX made the observation: "I have one major criticism – you can't expect the public to get excited about a film where the leading man's bust is bigger than the leading lady's."

Subsequent roles included a Roman centurion in *Androcles and the Lion* (1952), an army officer in the Korean War drama *The Glory Brigade* (1953), the Christian convert Demetrius in THE ROBE (1953) and its sequel *Demetrius and the Gladiators* (1954), and the title part in *Chief Crazy Horse* (1955). Mature's career then went into something of a decline with a series of adventure films set against a variety of backgrounds. In 1966, however, he disarmed many of his critics by sending himself up mercilessly as a preening film star in the Italian comedy *After the Fox*. On another occasion he admitted "I'm no actor and I've 64 pictures to prove it." Occasional returns to the cinema since then have included the Monkees film *Head* (1968), Michael WINNER's *Won Ton Ton, the Dog who Saved Hollywood* (1976), and a television remake of *Samson and*

Delilah (1984), in which he played Samson's father.

> Actually, I am a golfer. That is my real occupation. I never was an actor, ask anybody, particularly my critics.
> VICTOR MATURE, 1968.

Mayer, Louis B. (Eliezer Lazar Mayer; 1885–1957) Russian-born film executive, who as head of MGM became Hollywood's most powerful boss in the 1930s and 1940s. With an annual salary of $1.25 million, he was reputedly America's highest-paid executive. The prime mover in the founding of the ACADEMY OF MOTION PICTURE ARTS AND SCIENCES in 1927, Mayer himself received a special Oscar in 1950 for "distinguished service to the motion picture industry." However, *Variety* wrote: "One does not remember his achievements so much as his monumental pettiness, his savage retaliation, the humiliations he heaped on old associates."

Born in Minsk, he was still a child when his parents emigrated to Canada, where his father sold scrap metal. By 1904 he had his own junk business in Boston. Having bought his first cinema in Haverhill, Massachusetts, in 1907, he soon owned the largest chain in New England and began distributing. In 1917 he went into production in Los Angeles with Louis B. Mayer Pictures; at that time the company's one star was Anita Stewart, whom Mayer had lured from VITAGRAPH.

In 1924 Mayer became vice president and general manager of the new combine Metro-Goldwyn-Mayer. GOLDWYN, pushed out that year, came to hate Mayer so much that for the rest of his life he referred to MGM as the 'Metro-Goldwyn Company' (as did director Rex INGRAM).

With his production chief Irving THALBERG, Mayer was responsible for making the letters MGM synonymous with Hollywood's most glossy and polished product. The company, which boasted "more stars than there are in the heavens", could draw on the talents of Greta GARBO, Clark GABLE, Judy GARLAND, Mickey ROONEY, and Greer GARSON amongst many others. Though frequently ruthless, Mayer liked to think of employees as family members. When Robert TAYLOR was seen emerging from Mayer's office one day a friend asked him if he had got the rise he was no doubt seeking. "No", Taylor replied "but I gained a father."

Mistakes were sometimes made. In 1928 Mayer refused to hire Walt DISNEY because he thought MICKEY MOUSE would frighten pregnant women in the audience.

In 1951 Mayer was ousted from MGM by his former aide, Dore Schary. Although he found a new role as advisor to the CINERAMA Corporation he continued to encourage stockholders to overthrow MGM's management. Hollywood insiders joked "The old grey Mayer, he ain't what he used to be." He died of leukaemia six years after losing his job.

mcu   *See* MEDIUM CLOSE-UP.

Mean Streets   (1973) Martin SCORSESE's powerful film about the lives of four young Italian-Americans in the streets, bars, and pool halls of New York's Little Italy. The film, a low-budget affair shot mainly on New York locations, signalled Scorsese's arrival as a major new director.

The plot centres on four protagonists, Tony (David Proval), who runs the local bar, Mike (Richard Romanus), a small-time con artist, the reckless Johnny Boy (Robert DE NIRO), who has fallen into the clutches of loan sharks, and Charlie (Harvey KEITEL), the nephew of a Mafia boss who finds himself torn between the life his uncle can offer him and his desire to run a restaurant. Charlie, who is also deeply religious, becomes obsessed with the idea that he has a duty to 'save' his mad friend Johnny Boy and to take care of Johnny's epileptic sister Teresa (Amy Robinson), to whom he finds himself attracted.

The film, which features startling jittery camera work and brilliant performances all round, marked the beginning of the long partnership between Scorsese and De Niro. Rather than focusing on the slight narrative, it concentrates heavily on characterization and inter-character relationships, a hallmark of much of Scorsese's subsequent work. *Mean Streets* is also typical of its director in its use of filmic references; in one scene the four protagonists sit in a cinema watching John FORD's THE SEARCHERS, while at other points posters for John BOORMAN's *Point Blank* and John CASSAVETES's *Husbands* are clearly seen. Scorsese himself appears in a small role as an assassin, while the elderly lady who looks after Teresa while Charlie chases after Johnny Boy is played by the director's mother.

meat axe   A long pole with a piece of blacked wood or cardboard attached to one end, used to block out light or cast shade when required. So called because of its shape.

medium.   **medium close-up** (mcu) A shot somewhere between a CLOSE-UP and a MEDIUM SHOT. When the subject is a person, it may be considered to include the area from the waist to the top of the head.

medium long shot (mls) A shot somewhere between a LONG SHOT and a MEDIUM SHOT. While not giving the expansive vistas of the long shot, it will include the relevant terrain in its entirety.

medium shot or **mid shot** (ms) A shot somewhere between a LONG SHOT and a CLOSE-UP, generally used to focus on one or more characters to the exclusion of their environment. The shot will usually show a standing subject from the knees upwards or a seated character in his or her entirety. A medium shot is often used as a bridge between a long shot and a close-up; e.g., a character walks into a bank (ls), we see his hand reach into his pocket (ms), a gun is withdrawn (cu).

Meet Me in St Louis   (1944) MGM's wartime musical about a devoted Southern family. In the plot Alonzo Smith (Leon Ames) is delighted with his promotion, but his wife (Mary ASTOR), children (Judy GARLAND, Margaret O'BRIEN, Lucille Bremer, Joan Carroll, and Henry H. Daniels) and cook (Marjorie Main) have no intention of leaving St Louis for New York. The film was directed by Vincente MINNELLI and gave Garland her first adult role.

Set in a 1903 that recalls the paintings of Thomas Eakins, the film was conceived by MGM as a nostalgic flagwaver on the virtues of family life. In Minnelli's hands, however, it became a perceptive analysis of the social changes that the war had wrought on US life. Based on a series of *New Yorker* pieces by Sally Benson, the first draft of the script cast Esther Smith (Garland) as the victim of blackmail. In ordering a rewrite Minnelli nearly lost his star, who, at 21, was keen to move away from teenage roles.

Minnelli's handling of his young cast was occasionally unconventional. In order to arouse a convincingly tearful rage in Margaret O'Brien for the scene in which she demolishes a snowman, he described in graphic detail how someone was going to kill her pet dog. The seven-year-old completed the scene in a single take. Judy

Garland, however, proved more of a problem. In the throes of her divorce from David Rose, she was already addicted to the drugs the studio had been feeding her since childhood to help her cope with her rigorous schedule. In spite of this, she had never looked more radiant on the screen, largely thanks to make-up artist Dotty Ponedal, who dispensed with the rubber discs and caps that had altered the shape of Judy's nose and teeth since her first films. Early in the shoot, she became convinced that she could no longer act, and it was partly in an attempt to restore her confidence that Minnelli began to see her socially. By the time editing began, they were lovers.

When the final print was judged too long, it was suggested that the famous Hallowe'en scene that had first attracted Minnelli to Benson's stories should be cut. Ultimately, a scene set during the construction of the 1904 World's Fair (including a Rodgers and Hammerstein song, 'Boys and Girls Like You and Me') was excised instead. Of the other songs, the title number, 'The Boy Next Door', 'Have Yourself a Merry Little Christmas' and 'The Trolley Song' remain among the most popular in the Garland repertoire. *Meet Me in St Louis* became, for a while, the second most successful picture in MGM history (after GONE WITH THE WIND).

Méliès, Georges (1861–1938) Pioneering French film-maker, who virtually invented the SCIENCE FICTION and FANTASY genres. Unlike the LUMIÈRE BROTHERS, who used their cinématographe purely for the passive documentation of reality, Méliès saw how film could be manipulated creatively to provide a new form of narrative entertainment. This arguably earns him a place as the cinema's first true 'director'.

Méliès worked variously as a painter, carpenter, cartoonist, and mechanic before buying (1888) a Paris magic theatre, in which he staged elaborate bills of conjuring, puppets, *tableaux vivants*, and electrical trickery. After seeing the Lumières' Paris shows of the mid 1890s, he bought a projector from Robert Paul (1869–1943) and devised his own camera. Méliès claimed to have discovered trick photography when his camera jammed during the filming of a street scene; when he projected the film, a bus magically mutated into a hearse. Inadvertently, he had stumbled on the STOP-ACTION technique. In 1896 he used double exposure to change a woman into a skeleton in *The Vanishing Lady*.

Having built his own specially designed studio in 1897, Méliès went on to develop a whole series of tricks that would become commonplace, including DISSOLVES, MULTIPLE EXPOSURES, and SPLIT SCREEN images. Some of his effects are still not understood today. The fantasy elements in *The Four Troublesome Heads* (1898) (self-propelled dismembered body parts), *The Astronomer's Dream* (1898) (old astronomer visited by comic moon that becomes buxom maiden), and other films culminated in the masterpiece *A Trip to the Moon* (1902); as usual, Méliès directed, wrote the script, built and painted the props, and played the lead.

At a time when few films ran over a minute or two, *A Trip to the Moon* was a 21-minute epic. Mixing live action with model work, the film opens with the casting of a huge cannon to fire a shell carrying astronauts to the moon. To the accompaniment of fanfares and dancing girls, the gun is fired and the explorers reach their target. On taking shelter from a snowstorm in a crater, the astronauts are captured by moon-men; nevertheless, all ends well with a sea splashdown on earth. There, awaiting rescue and a heroes' welcome in Paris, the intrepid voyagers marvel at the wonders of ocean life. The film's narrative complexity and inventiveness delighted audiences, who had seen nothing to compare with it.

Méliès's output was vast (precisely how large is unknown; hundreds of negatives were melted down in the 1920s), and includes early 'blue' films, adverts, a fake NEWSREEL of Edward VII's coronation, and such fantasies as *An Impossible Voyage* (1904), *200,000 Leagues Under the Sea* (1907), and *Tunnelling the English Channel* (1907). However, he was a poor businessman and lost money from pirating and plagiarism; by the 1910s his work looked dated beside new US films and he retired into obscurity.

A veritable alchemist of light.
CHARLIE CHAPLIN.

Melville, Jean-Pierre (Jean-Pierre Grumbach; 1917–73) French writer-director, noted for his original GANGSTER films, which often transcend their US models in both style and content. Having fought with the Free French during World War II, Melville made shorts with his own production company before embarking upon a career as a director of feature films. He assumed the name Melville in homage to his favourite author. His first full-length film was *Le Silence de la mer* (1947), about the love-hate relationship between a German officer and the two French people with whom he is billeted. This was followed by a powerful adaptation of Jean COCTEAU's *Les Enfants terribles* (1948), in which he explored for the first time the themes of loyalty and betrayal that dominate his later films.

His first gangster thriller was *Bob the Gambler* (1955), in which the conventions of US gangster films of the 1930s and 1940s were translated to Paris with enormous success; the effectiveness of his Parisian night scenes influenced several directors of the NEW WAVE. For the rest of the decade Melville continued to explore a range of subjects. In *Leon Morin, Priest* (1961) he examines the moral issues arising when a priest attempts to convert a young girl who is in love with him. In this film he developed the austere stylized manner that was to charactertize all his subsequent work.

Second Breath (1966), a striking and poetic FILM NOIR in which Melville once more probed the complex loyalties of the gangster world, consolidated the director's reputation and remains one of his most admired works. Similar themes of honour amongst thieves and outlaws resurfaced in *The Samurai* (1967), a moody thriller starring Alain Delon as a contract killer, and *Army in the Shadow* (1969), about the French Resistance.

Melville's last films, *The Red Circle* (1970) and *Dirty Money* (1972), are amongst the best examples of the distinctive French gangster genre he had created. They were noticeably darker than his earlier work, being somewhat bleak in both style and philosophy. Since his death, Melville's reinterpretation of the Hollywood gangster tradition has had a pronounced effect upon such US film-makers as Martin SCORSESE.

Menzel, Jiří (1938–) Czech director and occasional actor, who was a leading figure in the brief 'liberal spring' of the Czech cinema in the late 1960s. A graduate of FAMU, the Prague film school, he made a striking feature debut with *Closely Observed Trains* (1966), a sometimes black comedy about World-War-II saboteurs, which went on to win the 1968 Oscar for Best Foreign Film. Menzel also co-scripted and acted in the film, which is notable for its somewhat static

and theatrical camera style. His eye for the ridiculous in socialist society hindered his career after the 1968 Soviet invasion: his *Larks on a String* (1969) was banned and he retreated for a while to the stage. Later films were less controversial; in 1979, for example, he wrote, directed and acted in *Those Wonderful Film Cranks*, a nostalgic comedy about the early days of film-making in Prague. *My Sweet Little Village* (1985) was nominated for the Oscar for Best Foreign Film.

Since the fall of communism in Czechoslovakia, Menzel's career has enjoyed a renaissance. In 1990 his *End of the Old Times* took the Grand Prize of the International Film Producers' Meeting in Cannes and he himself received the Akira Kurosawa Prize for Lifelong Merit in Cinematography. *Larks on a String* was finally released in 1991 to commercial and critical success, winning the Czech Film Critics' Prize and a Berlin Festival award. He was head of the department of film directing at FAMU from 1990 until 1992.

In 1993 he took a starring role in the French film *La Petite Apocalypse*.

Merchant-Ivory The independent production company established in 1961 by the US director James Ivory (1930–) and the Indian-born producer Ismail Merchant (1936–). The two men have become internationally known for their prestigious literary adaptations, their first great success being with E. M. Forster's A ROOM WITH A VIEW (1985). Their work has drawn on the cultures of India, Britain, and America; "We have the luck of all three countries" noted Merchant.

Ivory, who was born in Berkeley, California, studied fine arts at the University of Oregon and was awarded a master's degree in cinema by the University of Southern California. In 1960 he was commissioned by the Asia Society of New York to make a documentary about India. There he met Merchant, who was born in Bombay and graduated from New York University with a master's in business administration.

In the early 1960s the two men began to make films about the changing face of Indian culture, with Merchant handling the financial side and Ivory directing and co-writing with Ruth Prawer Jhabvala, a German-born Indian by marriage. The early fruits of this collaboration include *The Householder* (1963), about the first year of a marriage, and the acclaimed *Shakespeare Wallah* (1965), about a troupe of English actors in post-colonial India.

In the 1970s they moved away from Indian subjects with *Savages* (1972) and *The Wild Party* (1974), a film loosely based on the Fatty ARBUCKLE case. Merchant-Ivory then enjoyed its biggest success so far with Jhabvala's Henry James adaptation *The Europeans* (1979), which starred Lee REMICK. She went onto adapt Jean Rhys's *Quartet* (1981), a tale of Anglo-Americans in Paris starring Alan BATES and Maggie SMITH, and James's *The Bostonians* (1984), which starred Christopher REEVE and Vanessa REDGRAVE.

In 1985 A ROOM WITH A VIEW, from E. M. Forster's story of an English girl (Helena Bonham Carter) finding romance in Italy, earned three Oscars, including one for Ivory as Best Director. Another elegant Forster adaptation, *Howards End* (1992), proved equally successful at the box-office, although some critics began to murmur that the formula was wearing thin. The film, which starred Vanessa Redgrave, Emma THOMPSON, and Anthony HOPKINS, earned Oscar nominations for Best Picture and Best Director. Hopkins and Thompson also gave fine performances in *The Remains of the Day* (1993), Jhabvala's adaptation of the novel by Kazuo Ishiguro; the film received four Oscar nominations.

In 1994 Merchant made his debut as a feature director with Jhabvala's adaptation of Anita Desai's *In Custody*, about the relationship between an Urdu poet and a journalist. That same year Merchant-Ivory completed a deal to make movies for Disney, beginning with *Jefferson In Paris* with Nick Nolte.

Mercouri, Melina (1923–94) Greek actress and politician, who emerged as a top European star in the 1950s and went on to ruffle feathers in several quarters with her political activities. The daughter of a prominent Greek politician, she trained for the stage and landed big parts in both Athens and in Paris before making her film debut in *Stella* (1955). Two years later she appeared in the successful *He Who Must Die* (1957), a parable about a village putting on a Passion play; the film was directed by Jules DASSIN, who became her husband and mentor. Mercouri enjoyed her biggest success to date in Dassin's *Never on Sunday* (1960), in which she played a carefree prostitute who

wins the love of a visiting American (played by Dassin). The role brought her a Best Actress Award at Cannes and an Oscar nomination. Now established as an international star, Mercouri gave another flamboyant performance in Dassin's lively HEIST MOVIE *Topkapi* (1964). Subsequent films made far less impact. Moreover, her co-stars, who included George Peppard, James MASON, and James Garner, amongst others often seemed visibly uneasy in the face of her florid acting style.

Mercouri's political interests dominated her career from the late 1960s onwards. A leading opponent of the ruling military junta in Greece, she went into exile at the end of the decade but returned when civilian rule was restored in 1974. In the 1980s she served several terms as the country's minister of culture, becoming particularly notorious in Britain on account of her repeated calls for the return of the Elgin Marbles.

The Attic Danny La Rue.

PENELOPE GILLIATT.

Merrie Melodies   *See* LOONEY TUNES.

Method, the   An acting technique developed from the theories of the Russian theatre director Konstantin Stanislavsky (1863–1938) and taught from 1950 onwards at the ACTORS' STUDIO, New York, under the directorship of Lee Strasberg. Strasberg was a former pupil of Richard Boleslavsky, who had brought Stanislavsky's ideas to America in the 1920s. The most important principle of the Method is the actor's total understanding of and identification with his character's motivation; to grasp this, he or she is encouraged to draw on comparable experiences in his or her own life, including painful ones that have been buried in the subconscious. This is intended to produce a greater realism in the actor's subsequent portrayal of the character. The technique has been widely criticized on both psychological and artistic grounds, but remains an important influence on stage and screen acting. Notable exponents of the Method in the cinema have included Marlon BRANDO, Dustin HOFFMAN, and Robert DE NIRO.

Keen method actors have often gone to bizarre lengths to 'find' their characters. Brando spent several weeks in bed to weaken his legs before playing a crippled war veteran in *The Men* (1950), while Sean Penn stubbed a cigarette out on his hand to get into the character of a teenage drop-out in *Fast Times at Ridgemont High* (1982).

métrage See FOOTAGE.

Metro The short name for Metro Pictures Corporation, a New York-based production company founded in 1915 by Richard Rowland, a Pittsburgh distributor. Having initially rented Hollywood facilities, the company took over the Mutual 'Lone Star' studio (where a number of Charlie CHAPLIN's two-reel comedies had been made) in 1917. Many of Metro's early films were low-budget 'programme fillers' shown between main features.

In 1918 the company closed its New York office and moved into impressive green-shuttered buildings in Hollywood. A year later Rowland suggested to Adolph ZUKOR that Metro become part of his growing empire. "The only reason I'd have to take you in", Zukor said, "would be to put you out of business." Instead, Metro was bought for $3 million by Lowe's Incorporated, which owned a string of cinemas.

In the early 1920s Metro became a major studio by releasing several Buster KEATON comedies and Rex INGRAM's *The Four Horsemen of the Apocalypse* (1921), the film that introduced Rudolph VALENTINO. Valentino also starred in Metro's *The Conquering Power* and *Camille* before moving to Famous Players-Lasky to make *The Sheik* (1921). Over the next few years Metro's star list grew to include Alla Nazimova, Mae Murray, Harold Lockwood, Renee Adoree, Ramon Novarro, and the child actor Jackie Coogan. Directors included Ingram, who specialized in such costume dramas as *The Prisoner of Zenda* (1922) and *Scaramouche* (1923), and Fred Niblo. The producer-director Thomas INCE also began releasing his films through Metro in 1919.

In 1924 Metro merged with the GOLDWYN Company and Louis B. MAYER Pictures to form Metro-Goldwyn-Mayer (MGM), which is still sometimes called Metro for short. One of its first triumphs was Niblo's BEN-HUR (1926).

Metropolis (1927) Fritz LANG's silent classic about a futuristic underground city. This chilling vision of the year 2000 was inspired by Lang's first visit to New York in 1924. One of the screen's first SCIENCE FICTION stories, it was denounced by H. G. Wells as "quite the silliest film"; Lang later agreed that the theme of love conquering all was "a fairy tale".

Lang wrote the film with his wife, Thea von Harbou, basing the script on her novel of the same name. With its spectacular EXPRESSIONIST sets and huge cast (some 1100 bald extras were used in the 'Tower of Babel' sequence alone), *Metropolis* was the most expensive film made by the German UFA studios. The SHOOTING RATIO of 149:1 – some 1,960,000 feet of film were cut to 13,165 feet – was also highly extravagant. Despite this cutting, the finished film ran for over three hours (a shorter version was shown in America and Britain). In 1984 an 83-minute version with tinted sequences and a soundtrack by Girogio Moroder was released to critical howls.

The somewhat weak cast was led by Alfred Abel, Gustav Fröhlich, Brigitte Helm, and Rudolf Klein-Rogge. Karl Freund and Günther Rittau were the cinematographers, while the massive sets were created by art directors Otto Hunte, Erich Kettelhut, and Karl Vollbrecht.

The film depicts a futuristic society in which slave workers toil underground while their rulers, led by John Fredersen (Abel), dwell above in "eternal gardens". However, Fredersen's young son, Freder (Fröhlich), falls for Maria (Helm), a beautiful and infuential worker. Fearing for the status quo, Fredersen has the evil scientist-cum-magician Rotwang (Klein-Rogge) make a robot of Maria to rouse the workers to a self-destructive revolt. When Freder and the real Maria act to rescue the children, Fredersen repents, seeing their love unite capital and labour.

metteur-en-scène A director, especially one who is not considered an AUTEUR. The term, which means literally 'he who puts (a production) on stage', originated in French theatrical criticism. In film writing, it often has a slightly pejorative air, implying that a director has failed to impose an individual style or signature on his or her work.

MGM Metro-Goldwyn-Mayer. The famous Hollywood studio that dominated the industry through its golden era of the 1930s and 1940s. Leo the Lion, its roaring mascot, was recognized worldwide as a sign of glamorous entertainment of superior technical quality.

In its heyday the studio could draw on an incomparable range of talent. Over the years its stars included Lillian GISH, Lon CHANEY, Gloria SWANSON, Jean HARLOW, Greta GARBO, John GILBERT, Norma SHEARER, Clark GABLE, Joan CRAWFORD, William POWELL, Myrna LOY, Fred ASTAIRE, LAUREL AND HARDY, the MARX BROTHERS, Greer GARSON, Spencer TRACY, Gene KELLY, Frank SINATRA, Judy GARLAND, Mickey ROONEY, and Elizabeth TAYLOR. Directors included Erich VON STROHEIM, King VIDOR, Fritz LANG, Cecil B. DE MILLE, George CUKOR, Victor FLEMING, and Vincente MINNELLI.

MGM was formed in 1924 by the merger of the METRO Picture Corporation, Louis B. MAYER Pictures, and the GOLDWYN Picture Corporation. Mayer was made studio head, and the young 'genius' Irving THALBERG became his production chief. In 1926 Thalberg turned out both BEN-HUR, which lost $700,000, and The Big Parade, which made nearly $3.5 million. During the early talkie era MGM emerged as the largest and most consistently successful of the Hollywood studios, partly owing to its links with the extensive Lowe cinema chain. Triumphs of this period included David Copperfield (1934), Mutiny on the Bounty (1935), and The Good Earth (1937).

With its motto of Ars Gratia Artis ('Art for Art's Sake'), MGM was making 40 to 50 films a year by the mid 1930s. After Thalberg's early death, success continued with such classics as THE WIZARD OF OZ (1939), GOODBYE, MR CHIPS (1939), and MRS MINIVER (1942), as well as with the popular series featuring the HARDY FAMILY and Dr Kildare. The company also distributed David O. SELZNICK'S GONE WITH THE WIND (1939). In 1948 Dore Schary assumed Thalberg's old job and four years later ousted Mayer in a boardroom coup. Although Schary himself preferred literate films like Julius Caesar (1953), he also made such comedies as Father of the Bride (1950) and the spectacular QUO VADIS? (1951).

The growth of television in the early 1950s seriously damaged MGM's pre-eminence, as did the antitrust action (1952) that forced Lowe to break its links with the studio. MGM survived largely on the strength of the incomparable musicals produced by Arthur Freed; directed by Minnelli, Charles Walters, and Stanley DONEN amongst others, these featured such talents as Astaire, Kelly, and Garland. The long list included MEET ME IN ST LOUIS (1944), Easter Parade (1948), Show Boat (1951), An American in Paris (1951), SINGIN' IN THE RAIN

(1952), Seven Brides for Seven Brothers (1954), High Society (1956), and Gigi (1958).

In 1969 the studio was bought up by businessman Kirk Kerkorian, who sold its props and costumes to an auctioneer for $1.5 million; the items, which included Garland's ruby slippers from The Wizard of Oz, were then auctioned separately for a total of $12 million. Despite such successes as Doctor Zhivago (1965) and Network (1976), MGM stopped making movies in the 1970s to concentrate on its Las Vegas casino-hotel. In 1986 its film library was bought by United Artists and the Turner Broadcasting System, who computer-coloured the black-and-white classics for television. MGM has since established a growing cinema chain.

Mickey Mouse The happy-go-lucky cartoon character created by Walt DISNEY in the late 1920s. Originally named Mortimer, the mischievous but good-natured mouse made his debut in a 1928 short. The character's high-pitched voice was supplied by Disney himself. Mickey subsequently appeared in numerous shorts, often with his girlfriend Minnie Mouse and his friends Goofy and Pluto. He was redesigned somewhat in the early 1930s, since when he has remained the most universally recognized cartoon figure in the world. The character's finest hour was undoubtedly the 'Sorcerer's Apprentice' sequence in FANTASIA (1940). Disney, who once declared "I love Mickey Mouse more than any woman I've ever known", was awarded a special Oscar for creating him in 1932.

The term 'Mickey Mouse' is now often used to describe something small, inferior, and trivial. This usage derives from the Mickey Mouse wristwatches introduced in America in the 1940s, which had a picture of Mickey on the dial with his outspread arms functioning as the watch-hands.

microcinematography See CINEMICROGRAPHY.

microphone or **mic** or **mike** An electroacoustical device that converts sound waves into electrical impulses so that they can be recorded magnetically. In filmmaking, the type of microphone used depends on the requirements of the shot. Omnidirectional and cardiod mikes are used to pick up general BACKGROUND NOISE, while the highly directional shotgun mike is used to record sound from a specific source, such as dialogue.

microphone boom *See* BOOM.

mic or **mike man** The technician responsible for the correct positioning of the microphones and for ensuring that they are functioning properly.

midget A small (50–200w) SPOTLIGHT with a 4 inch FRESNEL lens.

Midler, Bette (1945–) Ebullient US actress, who came to the movies as an established recording and cabaret artist. A native of Honolulu, Midler travelled to the mainland with the crew after playing a bit part in *Hawaii* (1966). She studied at the Berghof Studio and starred in a number of Broadway and fringe productions before signing a recording contract in 1971. The brash, frequently coarse, style that she had developed on the cabaret stage was then brought to the screen in Midler's full-feature debut, *The Rose* (1979), a film about a self-destructive rock star that earned her an Oscar nomination. Unfortunately, the temperamental personality revealed in both that film and the concert movie *Divine Madness* (1980) came to the fore off-screen during the production of *Jinxed!* (1982). Midler's feuds with veteran director Don SIEGEL and co-star Ken Wahl made headlines and helped to sink the picture. Wahl apparently spoke for many when he said:

> In one scene I have to hit her in the face, and I thought we could save some money on sound effects here.

Midler's movie career was rescued by the DISNEY subsidiary Touchstone Pictures, who offered her a big-money contract following the success of *Down and Out in Beverly Hills* (1986), a reworking of RENOIR's classic *Boudu Saved from Drowning* (1932). The actress presented the same irascible if finally engaging persona in *Ruthless People* (1986), *Outrageous Fortune* (1987), *Big Business* (1988), and *Scenes from a Mall* (1991). By the 1990s, however, Midler had undergone an image transformation; in *Beaches* (1989), *Stella* (1990), and *For the Boys* (1991), which brought her a second Oscar nomination, she was cast in the mould of one of the suffering stars of the 1940s 'woman's picture'. Her performance in the children's comedy *Hocus Pocus* (1993) and her playing of Mother Earth

in a television programme to celebrate Earth Day in 1990 would suggest that the reinvention of Bette Midler is an ongoing process.

Midnight Cowboy (1969) John SCHLESINGER's tragicomedy about two homeless drifters trying to survive in New York. The film was the first X-rated movie to win a Best Picture Oscar (a rating later changed to an R in America). Oscars also went to Schlesinger as Best Director and Waldo Salt (whose daughter appears in the film) for Best Adapted Screenplay.

The film's protagonists are Joe Buck (Jon Voight), a well-built dishwasher from Texas who is convinced that he can make money as a stud to rich women, and Enrico 'Ratso' Rizzo (Dustin HOFFMAN), a tubercular pimp who convinces Buck that he needs a manager. The film chronicles the pair's adventures in the grubby New York night world. Eventually the two men form a close and highly dependent relationship that only ends with Rizzo's death on a coach as they near Florida.

Voight, who had appeared in only a couple of unremarkable films before this, made his name for his portrayal of Buck. Acting honours, however, must go to Hoffman, who, after the success of THE GRADUATE and the failure of *Madigan's Millions*, was being very selective about his choice of roles. Hoffman said that the part was not character acting but "...just an autobiography of subjective feelings about oneself." Also notable was the film's soundtrack, which featured a melancholy harmonica track by jazz player Jean 'Toots' Thielsman and the song 'Everybody's Talking', sung by Harry Nielson, which became a hit.

Miles, Sarah (1941–) British actress, who played neurotic young seductresses in the 1960s before graduating to more varied roles. She received an Oscar nomination as the cheating wife of schoolmaster Robert MITCHUM in David LEAN's *Ryan's Daughter* (1970). In 1967 Miles married the dramatist and screenwriter Robert Bolt (1924–95); they divorced in 1976 but later remarried. She is the sister of the director Christopher Miles (1939–), who appeared with her in his short *The Six-Sided Triangle* (1963).

Born in Ingatestone, Essex, Miles attended RADA from the age of 15. Six years later she made her screen debut in *Term of*

Trial (1962), playing a 15-year-old student who accuses her teacher (Laurence OLIVIER) of indecent assault. Her success in this role brought her the part of the seductive maid Vera in Joseph LOSEY's THE SERVANT (1963). In the mid 1960s Miles turned to comedy with *Those Magnificent Men in Their Flying Machines* (1964), appeared on stage with the National Theatre Company, and took a supporting role in ANTONIONI's BLOW-UP (1966). After *Ryan's Daughter*, a lush Irish epic scripted by Bolt, she played the histrionic title character in *Lady Caroline Lamb* (1972), a somewhat unhistorical biopic written and directed by her husband.

In 1973 Miles went to Hollywood to make the Western *The Man Who Loved Cat Dancing* with Burt REYNOLDS. Her other films of the 1970s include *The Hireling* (1973) and the bizarre Mishima adaptation *The Sailor Who Fell from Grace with the Sea* (1976). There followed five lost years during which Miles, who had become notorious for her unstable behaviour, made only one film, a remake of THE BIG SLEEP (1978). The later 1980s saw a revival in her career with prominent roles in John BOORMAN's *Hope and Glory*, Losey's *Steaming*, and *White Mischief* (all 1987). In 1992 Miles penned her first play, *Charlemagne*.

Milestone, Lewis (Levis Milstein; 1895–1980) US director, who is mainly remembered for the handful of Hollywood classics he made in the 1930s. Having begun his career as a film editor, Milestone made his debut as a director with *Seven Sinners* in 1925. He confirmed his talents in that capacity with *Two Arabian Knights* (1927), which earned him an Oscar as Best Director. His most enduring achievement, however, was the masterly ALL QUIET ON THE WESTERN FRONT (1930), a technically brilliant and deeply compassionate work that remains the most evocative of all films depicting the horrors of World War I. The film earned Oscars as Best Picture and for Milestone as Best Director. Also nominated as Best Picture was the fast-paced comedy *The Front Page* (1931), starring Adolphe Menjou as a scheming newspaper editor; the film was later remade as the even faster HIS GIRL FRIDAY. The whimsical Al JOLSON vehicle *Hallelujah, I'm a Bum* (1933), with songs by Rodgers and Hart, also did good business with Depression-era audiences.

The best of Milestone's subsequent movies were probably the thriller *The General Died at Dawn* (1936), the hugely admired *Of Mice and Men* (1939), based on the novel by John Steinbeck, and *A Walk in the Sun* (1946), a highly effective war parable following the fate of a US army patrol in Italy in World War II. Films from the later stages of his career included the Korean War drama *Pork Chop Hill* (1959), with Gregory PECK, and *Mutiny on the Bounty* (1962), an uneven remake of the 1935 MGM classic with Marlon BRANDO as Fletcher Christian and Trevor HOWARD as Bligh.

Milland, Ray (Reginald Truscott-Jones; 1905–86) Welsh actor and director, who starred in a host of light comedies and thrillers in the 1930s and 1940s. Having served as a Royal Guardsman, he began his stage career touring in a dance act with the then-unknown Anna NEAGLE. Milland made his film debut in 1929 and quickly attracted the attention of MGM, who signed him up the following year. In 1934 he was selected at the last minute to play Carole LOMBARD's fiancé in *Bolero*, after the original choice was stabbed by his male lover. Subsequent films saw him sparring with Bing CROSBY in *We're Not Dressing* (1934), playing rival to Fred MACMURRAY in *The Gilded Lily* (1935), and rescuing Dorothy LAMOUR in *The Jungle Princess* (1936).

After securing his first leading role in the comedy *Easy Living* (1937), Milland went on to play big parts in *Beau Geste* (1939), *French Without Tears* (1940), *Arise My Love* (1941), the ghost story *The Uninvited* (1944), and Fritz LANG's *The Ministry of Fear* (1944). In 1945 his career reached a high point when he gave perhaps his strongest performance as the alcoholic writer in Billy WILDER's *The Lost Weekend* (1945) – a role that brought him an Oscar for Best Actor. Although many of his subsequent films were unremarkable, he made effective appearances in *Alias Nick Beale* (1949), a crime story with a supernatural element, the Western *Bugles in the Afternoon* (1952), the almost wordless *The Thief* (1952), Alfred HITCHCOCK's *Dial M for Murder* (1954), in which he plotted the death of his wife, Grace KELLY, and *The Girl in the Red Velvet Swing* (1955).

As big parts became rarer, Milland took to directing himself in a series of vehicles, which ranged from Westerns and crime thrillers to the nuclear-war drama *Panic in Year Zero* (1962). Amongst his later credits were Roger CORMAN's *Premature Burial*

(1962), *The Man with X-Ray Eyes* (1963), *Love Story* (1970), in which he appeared as Ryan O'NEAL's father (and acted without his toupee for the first time), and Disney's *Escape to Witch Mountain* (1976). He also appeared in numerous TV movies of the 1970s and 1980s.

Miller, Arthur (1894–1971) US cinematographer, who won three Oscars in the 1940s. A master of black-and-white composition, he always preferred monochrome to colour, explaining later "I liked crisp, sharp, solid images."

Born on Long Island, Miller worked as an assistant cameraman from the age of 13 and also played a number of bit parts. He worked for pioneer director Edwin S. PORTER before World War I and helped to photograph PATHÉ's famous serial THE PERILS OF PAULINE (1914). The following year saw the making of *At Bay*, his first film as director of photography.

In the 1920s Miller worked for several years with the Irish director George Fitzmaurice. When Samuel GOLDWYN sent Fitzmaurice to Rome to film *The Eternal City* in 1923, Miller filmed a crowd scene that also included shots of Mussolini on a balcony with King Victor Emmanuel. After the Fascists tried to confiscate the film, Fitzmaurice and his cast fled the country, leaving Miller to smuggle the negative out. (Goldwyn never filmed abroad again.)

Miller achieved his greatest commercial success with the seven Shirley TEMPLE films he made for 20th Century-Fox in the 1930s; these included the expensive *Wee Willie Winkie* (1937) and (as co-photographer) *The Little Princess* (1939), an early TECHNICOLOR movie. His finest work, however, came in the next decade, when his credits included the stark *How Green was My Valley* (1941), the sensitively lighted *The Song of Bernadette* (1943), and the lavish but black-and-white *Anna and the King of Siam* (1946), all three of which won Oscars for their cinematography.

Miller's distinguished work in the Western genre included *The Ox-Bow Incident* (1943) and *The Gunfighter* (1950), a film shot in sepia greys to suggest the effect of old photographs. His last movie was the FILM NOIR *The Prowler* (1951). After his early retirement (owing to tuberculosis) Miller became president of the American Society of Cinematographers (ASC).

Mills, Sir John (Lewis Ernest Watts; 1908–) British actor, a popular leading man of the 1940s and 1950s.

Mills was inspired to go on the stage by his older sister Annette, who had revived the Charleston in New York (and later partnered Muffin the Mule on British television). He made his debut in 1929 and two years later starred in the first production of Noël COWARD's *Cavalcade* (becoming the first actor to sing 'Mad Dogs and Englishmen'). After making his film debut in *The Midshipmaid* (1932), he played supporting parts in numerous comedies and dramas, including *Those were the Days* (1934), in which he played Will HAY's schoolboy son, the Hornblower adventure *Forever England* (1935), and GOODBYE, MR CHIPS (1939).

Mills really came into his own during World War II, when he was cast as a series of unassuming gentlemen heroes. He played a sailor in Coward's *In Which We Serve* (1942), a submarine commander in *We Dive at Dawn* (1943), the central role in Coward's *This Happy Breed* (1944), a soldier in *Waterloo Road* (1944), and an RAF pilot in *The Way to the Stars* (1945). He stepped out of uniform for David LEAN's GREAT EXPECTATIONS (1946), in which he played the leading role of Pip. Two years later he starred in Ealing's *Scott of the Antarctic* (1948).

Mills began a second career as a producer with *The History of Mr Polly* (1949), in which he also starred, but concentrated on acting again after the failure of *The Rocking Horse Winner* (1950). His next big success came as the timid Willie Mossop in Lean's *Hobson's Choice* (1954), after which he appeared in further war stories, among them *Dunkirk* (1958) and *Tunes of Glory* (1960). Other roles included character parts ranging from a cab-driver in AROUND THE WORLD IN EIGHTY DAYS to a Russian peasant in *War and Peace* (both 1956). Notable films of the 1960s included Disney's *The Swiss Family Robinson* (1961), *The Wrong Box* (1966), and *Oh, What a Lovely War!* (1969), in which he portrayed Field-Marshal Haig. In 1970 Lean chose Mills to play the deaf-mute idiot in his Irish drama *Ryan's Daughter*; the role brought him a wholly unexpected Oscar for Best Supporting Actor. Since then he has confined himself largely to supporting parts, notably in the historical epics *Young Winston* (1972), *Lady Caroline Lamb* (1972), *Zulu Dawn* (1979), and GANDHI (1982); he also provided one of the voices for the animation *When the Wind Blows* (1987). He was knighted in 1976.

His daughter, **Hayley Mills** (1946–), profited by her father's fame to become a leading child star of the early 1960s. She was 14 when she made her film debut in *Tiger Bay*, a melodramatic piece in which her father also starred. Her warm but serious demeanour then won her starring roles in *Pollyanna* (1960), for which she earned an Oscar as Best Child Actress, *The Parent Trap* (1961), *Whistle Down the Wind* (1961), and *Sky West and Crooked* (US title *Gypsy Girl*; 1966), directed by her father. Although she has continued to appear in films and on television, she remains best known for her childhood roles. More recent credits have included television's *The Flame Trees of Thika* (1981).

Sir John's elder daughter **Juliet Mills** (1941–) also developed a career in the cinema, although she never became as popular as Hayley. She made her debut in the comedy *No, My Darling Daughter* (1961) and went on to appear in *Carry On Jack* (1964), *Oh, What a Lovely War!* (1969), and other films.

miniature A small-scale replica of a location or object that is used in preference to a life-sized version, usually for reasons of economy. Miniatures are often used in scenes of spectacular destruction, such as earthquakes, conflagations, etc. Footage involving models is frequently combined with live action, as in KING KONG (1930) and numerous other monster movies. In photographing moving miniatures it is usually necessary to adjust the camera speed, so that their motion is correct relative to any other action.

minimal cinema (1) A form of extreme REALISM in which cinematic conventions and techniques are kept to an absolute minimum. Ideally, the audience will forget that they are watching a movie. Examples of this kind of minimal cinema include Robert BRESSON's *Diary of a Country Priest* (1951). (2) A type of ABSTRACT or absolute film that stresses the material aspects of the cinematic process rather than subject matter or technique. Examples include *Film in which there Appear Sprocket Holes, Edge Lettering, Dirt Particles, etc.* (1966) by George Landow.

Minnelli. Liza Minnelli (1946–) Vivacious US singer and actress, the daughter of Judy GARLAND and her third husband Vincente MINNELLI. Her gamine features, spontaneity, and air of vulnerability helped her to an Oscar-winning triumph in CABARET (1972). Like her mother, she proved equally at home with electrifying showstoppers and plaintive ballads, prompting the French to label her 'La petite Piaf americaine'.

Liza first appeared on screen at the age of two and a half, when she joined her mother for *In the Good Old Summertime* (1949). Five years later she danced on the New York stage as her mother sang. Minnelli made her acting debut off-Broadway in 1963 and two years later, when 29, became the youngest-ever Tony Award winner with her performance in *Flora, the Red Menace*.

Her screen acting debut came with *Charlie Bubbles* (1968), in which she played Albert FINNEY's secretary; not all the critics were convinced, with one calling her presence "supreme deadweight". The following year, Minnelli's performance as a neurotic college girl in Alan PAKULA's *The Sterile Cuckoo* (British title *Pookie*) brought her an Oscar nomination. In 1970 she played a disfigured girl in the tragicomedy *Tell Me That You Love Me, Junie Moon*.

Minnelli revealed the full range of her talents for the first time in Bob FOSSE's *Cabaret*, in which she sang and danced with aplomb as well as giving a sensitive performance as Sally Bowles, a US nightclub singer in 1930s Berlin. However, with the decline of the screen musical as a genre, her career had no obvious place to go. Both *A Matter of Time* (1976), a melodrama directed by her father, and Martin SCORSESE's expensive *New York, New York* (1977), in which she played a singer to Robert DE NIRO's jazz musician, failed at the box office. She later found success as Dudley MOORE's girlfriend in *Arthur* (1981), taking a larger role as his wife in the sequel *Arthur II: On the Rocks* (1988). *Stepping Out* (1991) was a 'feel-good' movie about a class of amateur tap-dancers.

Minnelli has continued to record and perform concerts. She returned to Broadway in 1978 to win another Tony in *The Act* and made a 1985 television film, *A Time to Live*.

Vincente Minnelli (1910–86) US director, best known for his classic MGM musicals, although he also made melodramas and comedies. He wrought a quiet revolution in the musical genre by weaving songs into situations from daily life, rather than using the traditional show-business based plots. In 1958 he won an Oscar as Best Director for *Gigi*. He was married from 1945–51 to Judy GARLAND, their daughter being Liza MINNELLI.

Born in Chicago, he began to perform with his family's Minnelli Brothers Dramatic Tent Show at the age of three. He left school at 16 to become a photographer's apprentice, then worked for a cinema chain as an assistant stage manager and costume designer for live programmes. After several years as set and costume designer to New York's Paramount Theatre, he was named art director of Radio City Music Hall in 1933.

Minnelli was signed up by MGM producer Arthur Freed in 1940 and made his first feature as a solo director, the all-Black musical CABIN IN THE SKY, in 1943. He followed this with the marvellous MEET ME IN ST LOUIS (1944), set during the 1904 World's Fair. The film starred Garland, whom he married the following year.

Minnelli's other musicals included the Oscar-winning *An American in Paris* (1951), with music by George Gershwin and choreography by Gene KELLY, who also starred, Lerner and Loewe's *Brigadoon* (1954), with Kelly and Van JOHNSON in a ghostly Scottish village, and the same writers' *Gigi*, a Parisian romp starring Louis Jourdan and Leslie CARON (Gene Kelly's love interest in *An American in Paris*).

His non-musical films included the comedy *Father of the Bride* (1950), starring Spencer TRACY and Joan BENNETT, the biopic *Lust for Life* (1956), with Kirk DOUGLAS as Vincent Van Gogh, and the World-War-II melodrama *The Four Horsemen of the Apocalypse* (1961), with Charles BOYER. Being used to the Californian climate, Minnelli was shocked to see leaves falling from the trees when he shot sections of the last-named film in Paris in November. He immediately ordered his stagehands to nail the leaves back onto the boughs, only desisting when city officials protested.

Minnelli disliked both CINEMASCOPE and adaptations of Broadway musicals; *Kismet* (1955) was both, and he accepted the film only after MGM promised to back his pet project, *Lust for Life*. *Kismet* flopped as did another Broadway adaptation, *Bells are Ringing* (1960). His last musical was a version of Alan Jay Lerner's Broadway hit *On a Clear Day You Can See Forever* (1970), with Barbra STREISAND in the lead. Minnelli retired after making the disastrous *A Matter of Time* (1976), co-starring Ingrid BERGMAN and his daughter Liza.

Mirisch Brothers The US producers Harold Mirisch (1907–68), Marvin Mirisch (1918–), and Walter Mirisch (1921–), who co-founded the Mirisch Company in 1957. With its popular quality films, this became the most successful independent production company of the 1960s and 1970s. Harold and Walter were brothers and Marvin their half-brother.

Walter Mirisch had previously been a producer of low-budget films for MONOGRAM and Allied Artists, while Harold and Marvin were former exhibitors. On founding the new company, Walter became vice president in charge of production with Harold as president and Marvin vice president and director.

Their success was built on financing the films of major directors and producers while giving them creative freedom. Mirisch films were distributed by Allied Artists until it folded in 1957 and thereafter by United Artists. The company's best-known films were all early productions, such as Billy WILDER'S SOME LIKE IT HOT (1959), John STURGES's Western *The Magnificent Seven* (1960), and two winners of the Oscar for Best Picture, Wilder's *The Apartment* (1960) and the musical WEST SIDE STORY (1961). Later Mirisch films included Sturges's *The Great Escape* (1963), George Roy HILL's *Hawaii* (1966), Norman Jewison's IN THE HEAT OF THE NIGHT (1968), and *Dracula* (1979).

When Harold died in 1968, Samuel GOLDWYN, who often worked with the company, was appalled by the motley crowd who turned out for his funeral. When Zsa Zsa GABOR flounced by, Goldwyn fumed, "Whores, lawyers, and agents! That's all that showed up for this wonderful man."

Walter became president of the Academy of Motion Picture Arts and Sciences in 1973; the Academy presented him with its Irving Thalberg Memorial Award in 1978 and its Jean Hersholt Humanitarian Award five years later.

miscasting Casting an actor in a role to which he or she is not suited. There is often a thin line between 'casting against type', which can yield interesting results, and sheer incongruity. Some of the most glaring instances of miscasting have occurred in historical films; examples include Paulette GODDARD as Lucrezia Borgia in *Bride of Vengeance* (1948), Cary GRANT and Frank SINATRA as Peninsular War soldiers in *The Pride and the Passion* (1957), Tony CURTIS as a viking in *The Vikings* (1958), Raquel WELCH as a cavewoman in *One Million Years BC* (1966), and Al PACINO as a fur trapper caught up in the US War of Independence in *Revolution* (1985).

mise-en-scène The visual characteristics of a film that are created by the director's activity on set, as opposed to those created subsequently by MONTAGE. The French term translates literally as 'putting into the scene'. In cinematic usage, it covers not only the physical arrangement of the scene (deployment of actors, objects, and decor, choice of colour, interplay of light and shade, etc.) but also the way in which it is filmed (camera angles and movement, choice of lens, composition of the frame, etc.). Although critics have traditionally associated *mise en scène* with REALISM and montage with EXPRESSIONISM, others have pointed out that there is no necessary connection.

Mr and Mrs. *Mr Deeds Goes to Town* (1936) Frank CAPRA's classic comedy about a humble man's attempts to give away his fortune in Depression-wracked New York. An enormous popular success, it brought Capra an Oscar as Best Director and nominations for Gary COOPER in the title role and screenwriter Robert Riskin. The film itself was nominated for an Oscar as Best Picture. Graham GREENE felt that *Mr Deeds* was Capra's best film and "a comedy quite unmatched on screen", but Alistair Cooke criticized the director for "starting to make pictures about themes instead of people."

The plot centres on Longfellow Deeds (Cooper), who arrives in New York to collect his unexpected $20-million inheritance. Deeds, a simple small-town man with simple pleasures (sliding down banisters, following fire engines, playing his tuba in bed), finds New York wholly uncongenial until he meets the pretty Babe Bennett (Jean ARTHUR), who plays on his compassion by claiming to be unemployed. In reality, however, she is a hard-nosed newspaper reporter with instructions to expose the 'Cinderella Man' as a phoney. When he discovers her duplicity, he begins to distribute his fortune to the have-nots; by this stage Babe has genuinely fallen for him. Hauled before a lunacy commission, Deeds is ruled sane on the dubious testimony of hometown witnesses.

The movie established Cooper's image as an incorruptible 'man of the people' and gave Jean Arthur her first major role. The ludicrous court-room finale provided brief but memorable roles for the character actresses Margaret Seddon and Margaret McWade; their description of the eccentric Cooper as 'pixilated' added a new word to the English language.

Mr Magoo The short-sighted bumbling hero of numerous animated shorts produced by UPA from the early 1950s onwards. He was created by the animator Stephen Bosustow. The humour revolved largely around Magoo's failure to recognize everyday objects and situations; he talks to hatstands and mistakes the face in a portrait for his own reflection in a mirror, etc. His distinctive voice was provided by Jim Backus (1913–89), the US character actor, otherwise best known for playing James DEAN's father in REBEL WITHOUT A CAUSE.

Mr Moto The Japanese DETECTIVE hero of a popular Hollywood film series of the late 1930s. The character was created by John P. Marquand and played by Peter LORRE – usually a classic villain. The first film in the series was *Think Fast Mr Moto* (1937); the title of the last, *Mr Moto Takes a Vacation* (1939), proved prophetic since with Pearl Harbor, America's interest in Japanese heroes disappeared overnight. (This development seems to have prolonged the career of Hollywood's Chinese detective, Charlie CHAN, who appeared in some 20 films during the 1940s.) A nostalgic revival, *The Return of Mr Moto*, was released in 1965 with Henry Silva in the title role.

Mr Smith Goes to Washington (1939) Frank CAPRA's inspiring story about the trials and eventual triumph of an average honest man (James STEWART) in his struggle against government corruption. Capra, who produced and directed for Columbia, described the film as his best work because "Stewart *is* Mr Smith." Others in the strong cast included Jean ARTHUR, Claude RAINS, Thomas Mitchell, and Harry Carey.

The screenplay won Oscars for both writer Sidney Buchman and Lewis R. Foster, the author of the original story. The film received 11 other nominations, including Best Picture, Best Director, and Best Actor. When Stewart won the Oscar a year later for THE PHILADELPHIA STORY, many felt that this was intended to compensate for his failure to win for *Mr Smith Goes to Washington*.

The movie, which alleged that "you have to check your ideals outside the door" of the US Senate, was popular everywhere except in government. Although *The New York Times* called it an "inspiring testament to liberty and freedom", Joseph Kennedy, the US ambassador to London, predicted that it would do "inestimable harm to American prestige all over the world."

The plot concerns the naive but idealistic Jefferson Smith (Stewart), who is induced to step into the shoes of a recently deceased senator. Little does Smith realize that he has been chosen solely because the state's respected, though crooked, senior senator Joseph Paine (Rains) believes him gullible enough to rubber-stamp the construction of a dam – the profits from which will line the pockets of Paine and his corrupt associates. Smith, however, proves more than a match for Washington and, with the aid of his secretary, Saunders (Jean Arthur in splendidly cynical form), devises tactics that force Paine to confess all before the entire Senate.

Mrs Miniver (1942) MGM's celebrated morale-booster about life in a rosily evoked wartime Britain. Directed by William WYLER, the film starred Greer GARSON as the impeccably English Kaye Miniver, with Walter PIDGEON, Richard Ney, Christopher Severn, and Clare Sanders as the other members of her exemplary family. The screenplay was adapted from Jan Struther's book *Mrs Miniver*, which collected the previously serialized 'diaries' of the title character.

In her journals Mrs Miniver, an upper-middle-class housewife, records her reactions to international events, both before and during the war, and the details of daily life in the English village of Belham. Despite its patent sentimentality and its absurdly inaccurate picture of rural England, the film made a powerful and lasting contribution to the mythology of wartime Britain. On seeing the film Winston CHURCHILL declared that its effect on US opinion would be worth six divisions in the field. Although it now seems an unremarkable piece of work, *Mrs Miniver* picked up Oscars for Best

Picture, Best Script, Best Director, Best Actress (Garson), and Best Supporting Actress (Teresa Wright, as the daughter of the lady of the manor) as well as nominations in four other categories. The message of the piece is summarized in the sermon preached by the Vicar (Henry Wilcoxon) in the bombed church as the film draws to a close:

> This is not only a war of soldiers in uniforms. It is a war of the people – of all the people – and it must be fought not only on the battlefield but in the cities and in the villages, in the factories and on the farms, in the home and in the heart of freedom...This is the people's war. It is our war. We are the fighters. Fight it, then. Fight it with all that is in us. And may God defend the right.

Mitchum, Robert (1917–) US actor, who has proved an enduringly popular leading man despite frequent criticisms of his 'wooden' acting. In reality, Mitchum has been highly professional in his approach to his roles, taking great pride in giving a perfect performance on the first take. Directors have noted his ability to make the most of even the plainest parts and learned to discount protestations that he was only interested in acting on the grounds that "it sure beats working".

After an unsettled youth, during which he was in frequent trouble with the law, Mitchum worked at various times as a ditch-digger, coalminer, and professional boxer. His film career began humbly enough, with a series of bit parts in Westerns and war adventures from 1943 onwards. In 1945 he was a surprise nomination for a Best Supporting Actor Oscar for his performance in *The Story of GI Joe*. Now recognized as a rising star, Mitchum found himself perfectly suited to playing doomed FILM NOIR protagonists in such movies as *The Locket* (1946), *Crossfire* (1947), *Out of the Past* (British title *Build My Gallows High*; 1947) and *Where Danger Lives* (1950). In 1948 his future was temporarily clouded when he was arrested and gaoled for smoking marijuana, but the charges were later dropped.

In the 1950s Howard HUGHES cast Mitchum opposite Jane RUSSELL in *His Kind of Woman* (1951) and *Macao* (1952), hoping that the couple would become an established team. When the chemistry failed to work, Russell was replaced by Susan

Hayward in *The Lusty Men* (1952), Jean SIM-MONS in *Angel Face* (1953), and Marilyn MONROE in *River of No Return* (1954). Mitchum's best notices to date came with his performance as a murderous preacher in *The Night of the Hunter* (1955), which led the film's director Charles LAUGHTON to describe him as "one of the best actors in the world." However, Mitchum's subsequent films, a host of second-rate Westerns and thrillers, did little to enhance his reputation. Somewhat better than the rest were John HUSTON's *Heaven Knows Mr Allison* (1957) and Fred ZINNEMANN's *The Sundowners* (1960), in both of which he co-starred with Deborah KERR. In 1962 he played the terrifying psychopath Max Cady in the original *Cape Fear*.

The 1970s brought some good roles, notably the country schoolteacher in David LEAN's *Ryan's Daughter* (1970), a veteran criminal in *The Friends of Eddie Coyle* (1973), and the private detective repaying a debt of honour in *The Yakuza* (1975). In the remake of *Farewell My Lovely* (1975) Mitchum brought both a world-weary integrity and the full weight of his own past as a film noir icon to the part of MARLOWE.

More recently he has worked mainly on television. In 1983 he starred in he starred in the long-running World-War-II series *The Winds of War*, explaining that he was attracted by the prospect of a year's free lunches; however, the sequel, *War and Remembrance* (1989) proved such a flop that US advertisers demanded their money back. His later film roles have included a joyously mad television executive in *Scrooged* (1988) and a benevolent millionaire in *Mr North* (1988); the latter part was originally intended for John Huston, who bequeathed it to Mitchum when he became terminally ill. He also took a small role in Martin SCORSESE's remake of *Cape Fear* (1991), which saw Robert DE NIRO in Mitchum's original part.

> Movies bore me, especially my own.
> ROBERT MITCHUM.

Mix, Tom *See* KING OF THE COWBOYS *under* KING.

mixer (1) A technician in the sound department who is responsible for blending the various separate SOUND TRACKS (e.g., dialogue, music, effects) into a single MAGNETIC MASTER. (2) One of the various consoles used to create the final mix.

mob scene Slang for a scene involving a large number of EXTRAS, especially one involving a good deal of action and noise.

Modern Times (1936) Charles CHAPLIN's comedy about the dehumanizing effect of the machine age. Many have pointed to the irony of the film's title; although released at the height of the talkie boom, *Modern Times* was virtually silent. When movie-goers finally got to hear Chaplin's voice, it was in a song composed entirely of nonsense syllables. As usual, the star also directed, produced, and wrote both the script and the music. The film, his first since CITY LIGHTS five years before, was the last appearance for the TRAMP. Chaplin's wife, Paulette GODDARD, played a charming waif.

The film begins with a sequence juxtaposing a crowd of workers entering a factory with a herd of sheep. One (Chaplin) eventually becomes deranged by the maddening tempo of his machinery and flees into the street. He makes hopeless attempts to become a shipbuilder, nightwatchman, and singing waiter before settling onto the dole. Soon he meets a gamine (Goddard), who has been arrested for stealing bread, and their love survives strikes, riots, and other problems of 'modern times'.

A number of the movie's situations are similar to those in René CLAIR's *A Nous la liberté* (US title *Freedom for Us*; 1931) and Chaplin only escaped a plagiarism suit because Clair generously insisted on his wider debt to the master. For his part, Chaplin claimed to have got the basic idea for the film from "a bright young reporter" who told him of farm workers lured to Detroit's factory-belts and turned into nervous wrecks.

Though hardly profound in its sociological analysis, the film remains a classic for its brilliantly executed sight gags. It was banned as 'communist' propaganda by the fascist authorites in both Italy and Germany. Chaplin's own comment on the mounting political accusations against him emerges in the film; in one scene his character plays idly with a red flag he has found in the street, only to be swept up in a riot and arrested as an agitator.

moguls The all-powerful and often autocratic men who controlled Hollywood before World War II. The term derives from the Moguls, Muslim conquerors of India in the 16th century.

Under the STUDIO SYSTEM, virtually all actors, directors, writers, composers, and technicians were contracted to one of the studios, which, in the case of the majors, also owned theatre chains to distribute their films. At the pinnacle of these huge empires, which in some cases were producing a film a week, were men like Darryl F. ZANUCK at 20th Century-Fox, Louis B. MAYER at MGM, and the detested Harry COHN at Columbia. Often flamboyant and brash, they were also shrewd showmen: one commentator described them as "monsters and pirates and bastards right down to the bottom of their feet but they loved movies."

The breed gradually became extinct after World War II when, under onslaughts from all directions, the studio system gradually collapsed.

There was only one boss I believed in, and that was me.
DARRYL F. ZANUCK.

A producer shouldn't get ulcers: he should give them.

I am willing to admit that I may not always be right, but I am never wrong.
SAMUEL GOLDWYN.

Monogram   Monogram Pictures Corporation. A Hollywood studio established in 1930 from Rayart Productions, a company founded six years earlier by W. Ray Johnston. In the 1930s Monogram became known as a B-MOVIE factory specializing in serials, WESTERNS, and other action films, many of them shot on its extensive ranch location. Jean-Luc GODARD was a devoted fan of the studio's output and dedicated his first feature, A BOUT DE SOUFFLE, to Monogram.

During its first decade, Monogram turned out films featuring such cowboy heroes as John WAYNE, who made a dozen movies for the studio, Colonel Tim McCoy, Tex Ritter, Bill Cody, and Bob Steele. It also distributed foreign productions, such as the British musical *Break the News* (1938), with Jack Buchanan and Maurice CHEVALIER.

Better films were made in the 1940s, including the gangster story *Dillinger* (1945), which won an Oscar nomination for its script (by Philip Yordan). In 1946 the studio created a subsidiary, **Allied Artists Productions**, for its more expensive ventures but continued to crank out low-budget Monogram products, including the popular series featuring the EAST END KIDS

and six Charlie CHAN films starring Roland Winters.

Fearing that television would mean the doom of the cheap B-movie, Monogram changed its name to the **Allied Artists Pictures Corporation** in 1952 and began to improve production standards. Two successes of the mid 1950s were Walter Wanger and Don SIEGEL's *Riot in Cell Block II* (1954), based on Wanger's own prison experience, and the classic horror movie *Invasion of the Body Snatchers* (1956). The distinguished director William WYLER made his first independent production, *Friendly Persuasion*, for Allied Artists in 1956.

monopole   A single overhead light suspended from a grid that enables it to be moved both laterally and vertically.

Monroe, Marilyn   (Norma Jean Mortenson; 1926–62) US actress, whose short unhappy life began in an orphanage, included rape as a child and marriage at 14, and ended with an overdose of sleeping pills at the age of 36. During the last decade of her life she starred in half a dozen films that established her as both the greatest sex symbol of the era and a comedienne of genuine, if limited, abilities.

Born Norma Jean Mortenson, she later changed her surname to Baker. Amongst those who knew her in the early days was Robert MITCHUM:

When Pearl Harbor was attacked, I was working at the Lockheed airplane factory in the sheet-metal department. My partner was a guy named Jim Dougherty, married to a girl named Norma Jean Baker...She was not a very sexy girl. She had no sex appeal whatsoever. She had a lot of serious physical problems. Yes, really. And very shy.

When the marriage broke up five years later she was still only 20; by this time, however, she had changed from the gawky adolescent Mitchum remembers into someone who had at least the confidence to attempt modelling. It was in this period that she posed nude for the now famous calendar. Asked later by a journalist whether she had anything on at the time, she replied famously: "Oh yes, I had the radio on."

At the end of the 1940s Monroe entered the film industry as a bit player, first attracting attention with two films of 1950, *The Asphalt Jungle* and ALL ABOUT EVE. Her first starring role came in the thriller *Don't*

Bother to Knock in 1952. It was at this point in her career that the Hollywood press discovered her nude calendar. Regardless of her claim that she had only posed for it because she was hungry, the publicity transformed the emerging starlet into a major sex symbol. It was in this role that she starred in her best-known films – Howard HAWKS's *Gentlemen Prefer Blondes* (1953), *The Seven Year Itch* (1954), *Bus Stop* (1956), *The Prince and the Showgirl* (1957), in which she held her own opposite Laurence OLIVIER, and the marvellous SOME LIKE IT HOT (1959). The director of three of these films, Billy WILDER, was less than charitable about the mythical creature he had helped to create:

> She had breasts like granite and a brain like Swiss cheese, full of holes. Extracting a performance from her is like pulling teeth.

Otto PREMINGER was equally caustic:

> Directing her was like directing Lassie. You needed 14 takes to get each one right.

The public, however, remained devotedly on her side, as did most of the critics, who were enchanted by her freshness, spontaneity, and instinctive comic talent.

Monroe's second marriage, to baseball star Joe DiMaggio in 1954, lasted only nine months, although they remained friends for the rest of her life. A year later she surprised the world by marrying the playwright Arthur Miller, who later wrote the screenplay of HUSTON's *The Misfits* (1961) as a vehicle for her. By the time the film was released, the couple had divorced, leading to a further deterioration in her fragile mental condition. The movie proved to be her last (coincidentally; it was also the last to feature her co-star Clark GABLE). When she died, Miller did not attend the funeral. Asked why, he said:

> Why should I, *she* won't be there!

Whether or not she intended to take her own life has never been established. In recent years, various conspiracy theorists have attempted to draw links between her death and her alleged affairs with both President John F. Kennedy and his brother Robert.

Since her death, Monroe's myth has far outstripped that of any other Hollywood sex goddess, including even the enigmatic GARBO. Clearly, her extraordinary appeal can be partly but not wholly explained by the combination of rare beauty, blatant sexuality, and an almost childlike innocence.

Although most of her problems had little to do with her choice of career, the popular imagination has also cast her as the archetypal Hollywood victim. The industry can perhaps be blamed for creating the myth of the sex symbol, exploiting it, and then failing to support the vulnerable woman around whom it was constructed. Her life and death have been the subject, of numerous books, films, plays, and songs.

Monsieur Hulot's Holiday (*Les Vacances de Monsieur Hulot*; 1953) The film in which Jacques TATI introduced the immortal bungler M. HULOT. With his bounding gait, angular gestures, ankle-length trousers, and inept charm, Hulot was an amalgam of two men (an architect and a soldier) whom Tati recalled meeting. He intended the character to be "simple and honest and also a little bit out of control...He is different. When people say 'Go right,' he nods nicely and goes left, because it happens his mind is on the moon at the time." While holidaying in St Marc-sur-Mer in Brittany, Hulot causes untold chaos in his guest house, on the beach, and around the town, while remaining blissfully ignorant of it all.

Although the piece may seem an unassuming comedy, a number of critics have made high claims for its place in cinema history. According to Dave Kehr, *Monsieur Hulot's Holiday* is "the *Sacre du printemps* of the movies...without [it] there would be no Jean-Luc GODARD, no Jean-Marie STRAUB, no Marguerite Duras – no modern cinema." In order to overthrow the tyranny of conventional narrative, Tati returned to the style and structure of early films by the LUMIÈRE BROTHERS and Georges MÉLIÈS. He also drew inspiration from Max Linder, Charlie CHAPLIN, Buster KEATON, and Harold LLOYD, while aiming to devise a wholly new brand of screen SLAPSTICK. Rejecting the close-up ("I have no right to bang anyone's nose against the screen") and the usual alternation of different camera distances, he opted instead for repeated WIDE-ANGLE SHOTS ("because they allow the audience to participate and choose what to look at"). A leisurely pace also enabled his meticulously planned gags to develop in their own time.

Significantly, the English version of the film opened with the caption: "Don't look for a plot, for a holiday is meant purely for fun." Tati later commented "People's seriousness when they are having fun is funny. Why do they approach holidays so seriously?" Yet his intention was to persuade the viewer to have fun with the episodic nature of his film and take a holiday from the traditional narrative form as it had existed since D. W. GRIFFITH.

Tati began shooting in July 1951 but did not complete the picture until October 1952. Although he wanted to make the picture in colour, this was precluded by financial problems. On its release, the film became an immediate hit with the public and critics alike, largely owing to the character of Hulot himself. Indeed, such was his popularity that Tati reprised the role in *Mon Oncle* (1958), *Playtime* (1967), and *Traffic* (1971).

monsters Cinema's fascination with grotesque FANTASY and visual trickery can be traced back to the early experiments of George MÉLIÈS in the 1890s. In particular, the medium has revelled in its ability to produce nightmarish and semi-human creatures; the roll-call extends from the FRANKENSTEIN monster and KING KONG in the 1930s to such gruesome creations as Freddy Kreuger in *A Nightmare on Elm Street* (1984), Pinhead in *Hellraiser* (1987), and the giant bugs in David CRONENBERG's *The Naked Lunch* (1991).

Alert to charges of mere sensationalism, makers of early monster movies usually took care to establish a moral dimension to their tales. Classic HORROR FILMS, such as those in Universal's DRACULA and WOLF MAN series, have often made a powerful point about the 'monster within' by showing human beings transformed into sinister beasts. Likewise, many films in the SCIENCE FICTION genre have used the creation of a monster or monsters by humans to point a moral about the arrogance of science. Examples include *Frankenstein* (1931) and its sequels as well as Earle C. Kenton's *Island of Lost Souls* (1933), a grim adaptation of H. G. Wells's *The Island of Dr Moreau*. Similarly, the creation of a destructive robot to mislead the workers in Fritz LANG's METROPOLIS (1926) shows both a crude mistrust of science and a rather ambivalent political attitude.

The other principal type of science-fiction monster is the alien who comes to earth, often to invade or destroy it. Such films have also provided a focus for contemporary anxieties – it seems no coincidence that *The Thing* (1951), *The War of the Worlds* (1953), *It Came from Outer Space* (1953), and *Invasion of the Body Snatchers* (1956) should all have been produced at the height of the COLD WAR era. Very occasionally the aliens show a benign nature that puts our own to shame (*The Day the Earth Stood Still*, 1951). In another large class of films, the monster emerges not from space but from an obscure or exotic part of the earth: thus *King Kong* (1933), *The Beast from Twenty Thousand Fathoms* (1953), and THE CREATURE FROM THE BLACK LAGOON (1954). In GODZILLA (1954) and JURASSIC PARK (1993) the monsters, though 'natural', are brought back to life by science, thus linking both strands.

The cyclops and gorgons of older legend have also inspired a number of film-makers, most notably Ray Harryhausen's work, whose works include *Jason and the Argonauts* (1963), *Sinbad and the Eye of the Tiger* (1977), and *Clash of the Titans* (1981).

Sympathetic or likable 'monsters' include the cute robots of *Forbidden Planet* (1956), *Silent Running* (1971), STAR WARS (1977) and *The Black Hole* (1979). The grotesque circus performers in Tod Browning's notorious *Freaks* (1932) are also presented sympathetically, the villains of the piece being the beautiful ('normal') high-wire artist and strongman. As in Jean COCTEAU's *La Belle et la Bête* (1946), perhaps the ultimate 'monster' film, appearances can be deceptive. When Beauty believes Beast to be dying, she exclaims "My Beast! I'm the monster, Beast. You shall live!"

montage (Fr: assembling) Originally a general term for EDITING, now used more specifically to mean those forms of cutting that deliberately draw attention to the juxtapositions of image they create. In this sense, montage is the antithesis of the INVISIBLE CUTTING traditionally favoured by Hollywood.

The term is particularly associated with the theories of editing that emerged from Lev Kuleshov's Moscow Film School in the 1920s. Owing to the shortage of film in the post-revolutionary period, students were obliged to work largely with found film, thus forcing them to concentrate on the principles of editing. Kuleshov's two star pupils, Vsevold (PUDOVKIN and Sergei EISENSTEIN, developed his notion of **associational montage** in different directions. While the former developed a style in which the viewer's thoughts and feelings are led seemingly inevitably from one shot to the next, Eisenstein relied on the dramatic juxtaposition of disparate images to create a certain rhetorical effect. To explain his idea of **intellectual montage** Eisenstein often used the analogy of Chinese calligraphy, in which the characters 'dog' and 'mouth', for example, are juxtaposed to express the concept 'bark'.

During the 1920s and 1930s Hollywood developed its own less radical conventions of montage. The most common of these was the use of a rapid succession of cuts, fades, superimpositions, etc., as a form of narrative shorthand. For example, the progress of a campaigning politician might be indicated by a montage consisting of brief shots of a steaming train, a map on which a line is moving, and a series of superimposed newspaper headlines. Hollywood has also used various forms of impressionistic montage to create hallucinatory or dreamlike effects, or to reflect the extreme emotional state of a character. An example is the famous shower scene in PSYCHO (1960), which uses about 60 increasingly short cuts to convey the frenzy and violence of the attack.

Montand, Yves (Yvo Livi; 1921–93) Italian-born French actor and singer, a stalwart of the French cinema industry for 45 years. He was married to the actress Simone SIGNORET from 1951 until her death in 1985.

Born in Tuscany, Montand fled with his Jewish family to Marseille after the Fascists came to power. As a young man he knew poverty, leaving school at 11 to work as a barman and labourer before becoming a singer in his late teens. Having met Edith Piaf at the Moulin Rouge, he became her protégé in the 1940s, making his film debut with her in *Star Without Light* (1946). A year later, he starred as the lover of a married woman in Marcel CARNÉ's gloomy *Les Portes de la nuit*.

In 1953 Montand became internationally known with his performance in Henri-Georges CLOUZOT's suspense thriller *The Wages of Fear*. He and Signoret co-starred for the first time in *The Witches of Salem* (1957), a version of Arthur Miller's *The Crucible*. After taking his one-man show to Broadway in 1959, Montand went to Hollywood to make George CUKOR's *Let's Make Love*, in which he played a millionaire falling for singer Marilyn MONROE (the two stars also enjoyed an off-screen affair).

Montand's films of the early 1960s included Tony RICHARDSON's disastrous *Sanctuary* (1961) and Anatole LITVAK's

Goodbye Again (1962), with Ingrid BERGMAN. At the end of the decade he expressed his left-wing sympathies by joining the Greek director Constantin COSTA-GAVRAS for a series of political thrillers beginning with z (1968), which won the Oscar as Best Foreign Film, and continuing with the *The Confession* (1970), about the show trial of an Eastern European politician, and *State of Siege* (1973), in which Montand played a CIA agent held hostage. He also appeared with Jane FONDA in Jean-Luc GODARD's highly political *Tout va bien* (1972), about striking workers in a sausage factory.

After a lengthy period during which he made few film appearances, Montand returned to the limelight with his starring role in Claude BERRI's popular PAGNOL adaptations *Jean de Florette* (1986) and its sequel *Manon des Sources* (1986). In the two-part story Montand plays a grasping peasant battling for water rights with incomer Gérard DEPARDIEU, whose daughter finally avenges his death. Montand's last film was Jean-Jacques Beneix's *IP5* (1992).

Monty Python A team of writers and performers who created the groundbreaking BBC television comedy series *Monty Python's Flying Circus* (1969–74) and went on to appear together in a number of films. The original team comprised the British comedians Graham Chapman, John CLEESE, Eric Idle, Terry Jones, and Michael Palin, and the US animator Terry GILLIAM. With its idiosyncratic blend of satire, absurdism, and elements of the English nonsense tradition, the show became an unexpected cult success, especially among students and the young. It later scored a still more unlikely success in America. Favourite targets for its satire included bureaucracy, English reserve and deference, and the conventions of television itself.

The first Python film, *And Now For Something Completely Different* (1971), was simply an anthology of sketches from the first series. In 1975, however, Gilliam and Jones directed the team in *Monty Python and the Holy Grail*, a feature-length narrative in which the clichés of medieval romance and Hollywood COSTUME DRAMAS are gleefully debunked. The film featured such unforgettable characters as Tim the Wizard, Roger the Shrubber, a Village Ne'er-do-well Very Keen on Burning Witches, and Page Crushed by a Rabbit. In general, the humour is darker and less whimsical than that in the TV series. Equally funny, if less focused, was *Monty Python's Life of Brian* (1979), a spoof of biblical EPICs that enraged some Christian spokesmen. *Monty Python's the Meaning of Life* (1983) was a series of sketches.

Since the early 1980s the members of the Python team have all pursued solo careers in the cinema with varying degrees of success. Most notably, Cleese has starred in the comedies *Clockwise* (1985) and the hugely popular *A Fish Called Wanda* (1988), while Gilliam has emerged as a marvellously imaginative writer-director of fantasy adventures. Palin took major roles in both Gilliam's *Brazil* (1985) and *A Fish Called Wanda* as well as his own *American Friends* (1991). This was one of several films backed by Prominent Features, a production company founded by the ex-Pythons.

Moore. **Colleen Moore** (Kathleen Morrison; 1900–88) US star of silent films, who popularized the bobbed hair-style for women when she appeared as the perfect Jazz-Age flapper in *Flaming Youth* (1923). The top box-office draw of 1926, she received some 15,000 fan letters a month for the next year. She also became one of Hollywood's richest performers, earning $12,500 a week in 1929. The film A STAR IS BORN (1937; remade 1954) was partly based on her life.

The daughter of an irrigation engineer, she attended convent school and studied piano at the Detroit Conservatory. In 1916 D. W. GRIFFITH offered her an opening in movies to repay her uncle, a Chicago editor, for his help in persuading the censors to approve his films. Her early films, which were chiefly undistinguished Westerns, saw her wearing long curly hair like Mary PICK-FORD.

Stardom only came when she moved to FIRST NATIONAL and developed a new image as an emancipated young woman. The studio's production head, John McCormick, became her husband. After the success of *Flaming Youth*, she built on her risqué reputation with such titles as *Flirting with Love* (1924), *Naughty but Nice* (1927), and *Why Be Good?* (1929). For *Naughty but Nice*, Moore persuaded the 14-year-old Gretchen YOUNG to change her name to Loretta – the name of Moore's most beautiful doll.

Despite the success of these films, First National let her contract expire when the flapper vogue had run its course. Moore spent some time on Broadway before returning to the cinema for a fraction of her former salary. Although she got to play opposite Spencer TRACY in *The Power and the Glory* (1933), her comeback stalled as she refused parts. She was too rich to care. At the height of her success she had invested wisely in the markets, and later wrote a book on financial dealings.

Demi Moore (Demi Guynes; 1962–) Beautiful husky-voiced US actress, who became a sex symbol in the 1990s. In 1991 she obtained enormous publicity by appearing nude on the cover of *Vanity Fair* magazine when heavily pregnant. She is married to the actor Bruce WILLIS.

Born in New Mexico, Moore acquired an agent at the age of 15 and began a modelling career in Los Angeles. A few appearances on television in the late 1970s then led to a regular role in the soap opera *General Hospital*. Soon after making her film debut in *Blame it on Rio* (1984), she won her first starring role as a beauty with a 16-year-old admirer in *No Small Affair* (1984). Other early films included the college-graduate drama *St Elmo's Fire* (1985) and *About Last Night...* (1986), in both of which she co-starred with Rob Lowe.

Moore achieved her first great success with the romantic fantasy *Ghost* (1990), in which Patrick SWAYZE played the ghost of her murdered lover. The following year she co-produced the thriller *Mortal Thoughts* (1991), in which she played one of two women implicated in the murder of Bruce Willis, and appeared as a clairvoyant in the comedy *The Butcher's Wife* (1991).

Although Moore lost the lead in *Basic Instinct* (1992) to Sharon STONE, her performance in the legal drama *A Few Good Men* won her some of the best notices of her career. *Indecent Proposal* (1993), in which she played a married woman offered $1 million for sex by Robert REDFORD, was another big box-office hit. In 1995 she co-starred with Michael DOUGLAS in *Disclosure*, a torrid story of boardroom politics and sexual harassment.

Dudley Moore (1935–) Diminutive (5'2½") British comedian, actor, and cabaret pianist, whose cuddly image made him a top Hollywood star in the late 1970s and early 1980s. He is mainly remembered as the bumbling suitor of Bo Derek in '*10*' (1979) and the drunk playboy in *Arthur* (1981).

Born in the London suburb of Dagenham, he studied the piano and won an organ scholarship to Oxford University. Moore first came to notice in 1959, when he co-starred with Peter Cook, Jonathan Miller, and Alan Bennett in the satirical revue *Beyond the Fringe*. In one memorable skit, Moore (who has a club foot) played a one-legged actor seeking the role of Tarzan.

Moore went on to star with Cook in the popular television series *Not only...but also* (1965–66). After making their screen debut in the British farce *The Wrong Box* (1966), the pair appeared together in *Those Daring Young Men in Their Jaunty Jalopies* (British title *Monte Carlo or Bust*) and in Richard LESTER's *The Bed Sitting Room* (both 1969). Moore moved to Hollywood in 1973 but returned to Britain to play Watson to Cook's Sherlock Holmes in the spoof *The Hound of the Baskervilles* (1977).

Moore's Hollywood break finally came with the comedy mystery *Foul Play* (1978), in which he supported Chevy CHASE and Goldie HAWN; he found stardom the following year in Blake EDWARDS's sex comedy *'10'*. Edwards cast Moore in the part (which George Segal had already turned down) after they met in group therapy; "he irked me week after week" the director confessed, "because of his obvious appeal to the females in the group."

Moore's last major success was in *Arthur* (1981), a film turned down by Richard DREYFUSS. The comedy won a Golden Globe Award, as did Edwards's farce *Micki and Maude* (1984), in which Moore impregnates both wife and mistress. His later movies include the sequel *Arthur II: On the Rocks* (1988), *Crazy People* (1990) with Daryl Hannah, and *Blame It on the Bellboy* (1992).

In 1994 Moore was arrested following a fracas with his girlfriend, Nicole Rothschild, as they watched the Oscar ceremony on television. Their reconciliation was followed by an immediate wedding. His previous marriages were to actresses Suzy Kendall (1968) and Tuesday Weld (1975) and to model Brogan Lane (1988).

Roger Moore (1927–   ) British actor, best known for his portrayals of Simon Templar in television's *The Saint* and of James BOND in films between 1973 and 1985.

Moore, who was spotted as star material while working as a film extra, went on to train at RADA. After National Service, he went to Hollywood and appeared in a series of minor roles before making his name in the TV Western *Maverick*, in which he co-starred with James Garner. With his good looks, suave voice, and boyish sense of humour, he was a natural leading man in lightweight adventure roles. On British TV he took the lead in *Ivanhoe*, *The Saint*, and *The Persuaders* (with Tony CURTIS).

Although Moore starred in *Crossplot* (1969) and *The Man Who Haunted Himself* (1970), it was not until he was cast as 007 that he became a major film star. Of his seven films as Bond the most memorable are probably *Live and Let Die* (1973), *The Man with the Golden Gun* (1974), and *For Your Eyes Only* (1981). Despite the box-office success of these films, the critics were generally unkind, comparing Moore unfavourably with Sean CONNERY. The Bond years were Moore's busiest; during this period he also starred in *Gold* (1974), *That Lucky Touch* (1975), *Shout at the Devil* (1976), *Escape to Athena* (1979), and *The Naked Face* (1980).

Although Moore never tried to extend his limited range as an actor, films like *The Cannonball Run* (1980) showed that he was quite willing to send himself up. Somewhat inactive in recent years, Moore is planning a big-screen comeback as Simon Templar in *The Saint's Son*.

More, Kenneth (1914–82) British actor, who enjoyed wide popularity in the 1950s; his bluff easy-going manner proved adaptable to both comic and adventure roles.

More worked as an engineer's apprentice and a fur trapper in Canada before taking a bit part in the Gracie FIELDS vehicle *Look Up and Laugh* (1935). A series of small roles in films and plays followed. After war service in the Royal Navy, he demonstrated his versatility in such films as the submarine drama *Morning Departure* (1950), the comedy *Brandy for the Parson* (1951), and the thriller *The Yellow Balloon* (1952).

In the mid 1950s More made his name as a comic actor in the hugely popular GENEVIEVE (1953) and *Doctor in the House* (1954). In the first he played a braggart racing a 1904 Spyker back from the Brighton veteran car run and in the second a somewhat confused medical student (a role that won him a British Film Academy Award as Best Actor). A year later he was named Best Actor at Venice for his performance in the Rattigan adaptation *The Deep Blue Sea*, in which he co-starred with Vivien LEIGH.

More's run of successful roles continued with the legless fighter ace Douglas Bader in *Reach for the Sky* (1956), the title character in *The Admirable Crichton* (US title *Paradise Lagoon*; 1957), the first mate on the *Titanic* in *A Night to Remember* (1958), and an English officer in *Northwest Frontier* (US title *Flame over India*; 1959). As the fashion for breezy stiff-upper-lip heroes declined in the 1960s, More found himself with fewer film offers. His later roles included the Director of Naval Operations in *Sink the Bismarck!* (1960), Kaiser Wilhelm II in the satirical *Oh, What a Lovely War!* (1969), and the Ghost of Christmas Present in *Scrooge* (1970). He also appeared before an audience of millions in television's *The Forsyte Saga* (1968).

Moreau, Jeanne (1928–) French actress, often seen in *femme fatale* roles; she is chiefly remembered as the free-spirited Catherine in TRUFFAUT'S JULES ET JIM (1961). Her sophisticated sensual image has been mirrored by her off-screen life (she has described herself as "a passionate woman who falls in love very easily"). In her 40-year career Moreau has performed for some of the world's great directors, including Louis MALLE, Michelangelo ANTONIONI, Jacques DEMY, Joseph LOSEY, Luis BUÑUEL, Orson WELLES, Elia KAZAN, and Rainer Werner FASSBINDER.

Born in Paris, she studied at the Conservatoire and appeared with the Comédie Française before making her screen debut in *Dernier Amour* (1948). She then made some 20 films before winning her first major role in Malle's thriller *Lift to the Scaffold* (US title *Frantic*; 1957). A year later the same director's controversial *The Lovers* (1958) made her a star. The film, in which Moreau played a bored housewife who deserts her husband for a younger man, was banned in some US cities. Her next film, Roger VADIM's updated version of *Les Liaisons dangereuses* (1959), was briefly banned from export for its unflattering picture of French diplomats.

In 1960 Moreau won the Best Actress award at Cannes for her starring role in Peter Brook's art movie *Moderato Cantabile* (1960). The following year she gave the greatest performance of her career as the amoral woman loved by two men in *Jules et Jim*. Other roles of the 1960s included a compulsive gambler in Demy's *Bay of Angels* (1962), a gold-digger in Losey's *Eva* (1962), an amoral serving-girl in Buñuel's *Diary of a Chambermaid* (1964), the whore Doll

Tearsheet in Welles's *Chimes at Midnight* (1966), and a vengeful widow in Truffaut's *The Bride Wore Black* (1967).

In the later 1970s Moreau tried her hand at writing and directing with *La Lumière* (1976), a film in which she also acted, and *The Adolescent* (1979). In 1977 she married the US director William FRIEDKIN. Her later films have included the thriller *Nikita* (1990), *The Old Woman Who Walked in the Sea* (1991), and the Canadian *Map of the Human Heart* (1992).

morphing See COMPUTER ANIMATION; TERMINATOR FILMS.

MOS Hollywood jargon indicating that a particular shot is silent. It is thought to derive from the guttural cry of the many German-born directors who worked in Hollywood in the 1930s, calling for a scene 'mit out sound'.

motion picture. Motion Picture Patents Company A monopoly trust established in 1908 in New York by eight US and two French film companies; its effect was to restrict film production, distribution, and exhibition for nearly a decade.

When Thomas EDISON's attempts to sue his competitors failed because they also had patents, he invited them to join him in the Motion Picture Patents Company, known informally as the Edison Trust. Apart from Edison's, the US companies involved were VITAGRAPH, BIOGRAPH, Kalem, Lubin, Selig, Essanay, and Klein; France's PATHÉ and MÉLIÈS also joined. The Trust members announced that only they could make motion pictures and that no one could distribute or exhibit films without obtaining a licence and paying a fee. The charge for films, good or bad, was set at ten cents a foot. In 1910 the Trust tightened its stranglehold by forming the **General Film Company** to distribute films to licensed exhibitors, who had to pay $2 a week every week of the year to use the MPPC's patented projectors.

The Trust's main opponents were William Fox and Carl Laemmle, two independent exhibitors who owned exchanges that bought and rented films to NICKELODEONS. When General Film took over the leading exchanges and warned others to close, Fox ignored them and Laemmle showed his defiance by creating the bullying cartoon character 'General Filmco'. Both formed their own production companies to make films in the early 1910s.

Fox eventually filed a suit against the General Film Company that led to its abolition in 1915 and the dissolution of the Motion Picture Patents Company two years later. By then, the rise of independent filmmaking on the West Coast had already rendered both organizations powerless.

Motion Picture Association of America *See* MPAA.

motor cue   *See* CHANGEOVER CUE.

movie   The usual US term for a moving picture (the normal British term being FILM).

movie brats   A group of US directors, principally George LUCAS, Francis Ford COPPOLA, Martin SCORSESE, John CARPENTER, and Steven SPIELBERG, who emerged in the early 1970s. The nickname reflects their profound love and knowledge of film and their then youthful precocity.

By the 1960s Hollywood was in crisis: TV was baying at the door, veteran directors such as FORD and HAWKS were retiring, and a burgeoning youth culture was rejecting the 'mom and pop' values of mainstream cinema. Hollywood's imprudent response was bigger, glossier, and more expensive spectaculars; with a few exceptions, these were dismal failures. But EASY RIDER (1969) gave unexpected hope, showing that original but low-budget films, made outside the stifling STUDIO SYSTEM, could attract the all-important youth audience.

Significantly, the movie brats did not pursue the usual career path through the big studios; instead, Coppola, Lucas, Spielberg, De Palma, Scorsese, and Carpenter learned their craft and theory at university or film school. Several, notably Scorsese and Coppola, further honed their skills making cheap youth-orientated quickies under Roger CORMAN at American International Pictures. This background revealed itself in several ways, most notably an ability to rethink old themes in a new manner for modern audiences. Although many of the directors later commanded huge budgets, all initially showed an ability to make exciting films at low cost – Coppola's *You're a Big Boy Now* (1966), scripted and directed for his UCLA graduate thesis, Spielberg's *Duel* (1971), and Scorsese's MEAN STREETS (1973) being classic examples.

The new directors' love of film tradition often revealed itself in references, parodies, IN-JOKES, and affectionate tributes: De Palma showed his indebtedness to HITCHCOCK in such horror thrillers as *Dressed to Kill* (1980), Scorsese evoked Frank CAPRA's sentimental comedies, in *Alice Doesn't Live here Anymore* (1974), while Spielberg strove to reawaken the wonder of earlier cinema audiences with *Close Encounters of the Third Kind* (1977), E.T.: THE EXTRATERRESTRIAL (1982), and RAIDERS OF THE LOST ARK (1981), a spectacular reworking of prewar adventure serials. Peter BOGDANOVICH – "I have more affection, more affinity for the past" – looked back more than any. *The Last Picture Show* (1971) paid black-and-white homage to HAWKS and FORD; *What's Up Doc?* (1972) revived the SCREWBALL COMEDIES of the 1930s, while *Nickelodeon* (1976) harked back to the silent era.

Movietone   An early form of sound-on-film recording, developed by T. W. Case and E. I. Sponable for Western Electric in the late 1920s. The system, which was used in a series of Fox shorts from 1927, provided a far more reliable synchronization of sound and picture than the VITAPHONE sound-on-disc system being developed at Warner Brothers. In 1927 Movietone News, the first sound NEWSREEL, gripped the public imagination with footage of Lindbergh's trans-Atlantic flight. By 1930 Movietone had been successfully used in several features, leading to the immediate obsolescence of sound-on-disc systems.

Moviola   The tradename of a portable EDITING device, often used generically for all such equipment. It is basically a simplified projector equipped with a foot pedal that enables the operator to stop or start the film at will, as well as to control its speed. Picture and sound can be run separately or in synchronization. Owing to its poor reproduction, the Moviola is not now used in professional editing, although it is still sometimes used for viewing RUSHES on location. It is also a basic piece of equipment in film schools.

moving shot   *See* CAMERA MOVEMENT; DOLLY; TRACKING SHOT.

MPAA   Motion Picture Association of America. A trade association of major Hollywood producers and distributors that oversees the industry's artistic and moral standards. It is affiliated with the Association of Motion Picture and Television Producers (AMPTP).

The organization was founded in 1922 as the Motion Picture Producers and Distributors of America (MPPDA). Among the 14 founding fathers were Samuel GOLDWYN, William Fox, Carl Laemmle, Lewis and Myron Selznick, and Adolph ZUKOR. The first president was Will H. Hays, a former US Postmaster General.

The MPPDA immediately formed a public-relations committee to counteract the effect of scandals among film stars and the growing calls for government censorship. The Association's attempts to impose a "dictatorship of virtue" on the screen were eventually formalized in the self-regulatory Motion Picture Production Code, or HAYS CODE. It also set standards in other areas, such as ensuring fair contracts between distributors and exhibitors.

The organization changed its name to the present one when Eric Johnston replaced Hays in 1945. In 1968 MPPA president Jack Valenti oversaw the replacement of the production code by the present RATINGS system.

multi-. multiplex A cinema with several screening rooms, enabling it to show more than one film at the same time. Multiplex cinemas began to be introduced in America in the 1970s and have since become the norm throughout the Western world; many older movie theatres were converted during this period, often to the dismay of those who appreciated their aesthetic qualities. The arrangement has obvious economic advantages for the cinema owner, most notably in mitigating the effect of a flop on any one screen. The multiplex system can be seen as a sign of the fragmentation of the cinema audience since the 1950s.

multiscreen A projection system requiring the use of two or more projectors and several screens; this may be used to present a MULTIPLE-IMAGE or to create a WIDESCREEN effect. The first such system was the 11-screen Cineorama, developed by Raoul Grimoin-Sanson (1860–1941) in 1897. In the 1920s the British Widescope system used two 35mm films threaded together in the same projector, while Abel GANCE's 'Polyvision' version of NAPOLEON (1927) used three screens to create spectacular multiple-image effects. In general, however, multiscreen has remained a novelty attraction restricted to the various World Fairs and similar events.

multiple. multiple exposure An effect in which two or more images appear superimposed, achieved by exposing the same piece of film more than once. This is mainly done to create such effects as a GHOST, a DREAM sequence, or a DISSOLVE from one scene to another. *See* SPECIAL EFFECTS.

multiple-image shot A SPLIT SCREEN effect, more particularly one consisting of several images of the same subject. These may either be identical, or shot from different angles, etc.

multiple roles The nature of film makes it relatively easy for the same actor or actress to play more than one part in a movie. The most extreme case of multiple roles was that of Rolf Leslie, who played 27 parts in an early biopic of Queen Victoria in *Sixty Years a Queen* (1913). Artistically, Ealing Studio's black comedy KIND HEARTS AND CORONETS (1949) is probably the finest essay in multiple-role playing; the film stars Alec GUINNESS as eight superbly characterized members of the same aristocratic family.

One actor who specialized in multiple roles was Peter SELLERS, whose sublime minicry enabled him to play six parts in *Soft Beds and Hard Battles* (1973) and three each in *The Mouse that Roared* (1959) and DR STRANGELOVE (1964) – the former triple role including one in drag. More recently, *Coming to America* (1988) included four roles each for Eddie MURPHY and Arsenio Hall. Other examples include Tony Randall's and Jerry LEWIS's seven roles in, respectively, *Seven Faces of Dr Lao* (1964) and *Family Jewels* (1965), Alan Young's four in *Gentlemen Marry Brunettes* (1955), and Deborah KERR's three in THE LIFE AND DEATH OF COLONEL BLIMP (1943). Although multiple roles usually occur in comedy or fantasy, some darker films have used the device; doubles or split personalities were played by Louis Hayward in *The Man in the Iron Mask* (1939), Fredric MARCH in *Dr Jekyll and Mr Hyde* (1932), and Jeremy IRONS in *Dead Ringers* (1988). *See also* DISGUISE.

multiple-story film *See* EPISODIC FILM.

Muni, Paul (Muni Weisenfreund; 1895–1967) Austrian-born US actor, noted especially for playing historical characters in Warner Brothers' BIOPICS of the 1930s. He won an Oscar for his performance in the title role of *The Story of Louis Pasteur* (1936). Although his style now seems old-fashioned, he was widely considered the finest actor in Hollywood at the time; uniquely, the studio always called him 'Mr Paul Muni' in their publicity and advertisements.

Muni's parents were strolling actors who emigrated to New York when he was seven. His first appearances were all on the Yiddish-speaking stage. He did not act in English until 1926, when he made his Broadway debut in *We Americans*; he was signed by Fox three years later.

Remarkably, Muni was nominated for a Best Actor Oscar for his first film, *The Valiant* (1929). In his next, *Seven Faces* (1929), he demonstrated his versatility by playing seven roles, including Napoleon and Don Juan. In 1932 he earned another Oscar nomination for his performance in Warners' social-issue movie *I am a Fugitive from a Chain Gang* and starred as a Capone-like figure in *Scarface*, one of the early gangster classics.

When he signed with Warners, Muni was given a contract allowing him to choose a film of his own if the studio failed to come up with congenial projects. This led to the making of the Pasteur story, which Warners' regarded with despair until it became a surprise hit and Muni won the Oscar. Subsequent parts included a Chinese peasant in *The Good Earth* (1937) and the title roles in *The Life of Emile Zola* (1937) and *Juarez* (1939), about the liberator of Mexico. Bette DAVIS, who played the Empress Carlota in *Juarez*, noted Muni's love of physical DISGUISE, commenting "He seemed intent on submerging himself so completely that he disappeared." The House Committee on Un-American Activities would later cite his preference for playing non-US heroes as evidence of his anti-American views. When Warners rejected Muni's idea of a Beethoven biopic, he countered by refusing the gangster movie *High Sierra* (1941); the part went to Humphrey BOGART, making him a major star. After parting company with Warners in 1940, Muni appeared in *Hudson's Bay* (1940), as the French explorer Pierre Radisson, and *A Song to Remember* (1944), as Chopin's music teacher. He received a last Oscar nomination for his final role as an elderly doctor in *The Last Angry Man* (1959).

Murnau, F(reidrich) W(ilhelm) (Friedrich Wilhelm Plumpe; 1888–1931) German director, who pioneered the EXPRESSIONIST style after World War I. Murnau's use of oblique-angle shots and an ever-moving camera influenced Alfred HITCHCOCK and Orson WELLES amongst others.

After studying in Berlin and Heidelberg, Murnau won a scholarship place with Max Reinhardt's famous Berlin theatre company. During World War I he served as a fighter pilot and was interned after making a forced landing in Switzerland. On his return to Germany in 1919, he made his debut as a film director with *The Boy in Blue*.

In 1922 Murnau came to international notice with the vampire film NOSFERATU, A SYMPHONY OF HORROR, in which Max Schreck's terrifying Dracula visits Bremen. It is the only one of Murnau's first 12 films to survive. His reputation was confirmed by THE LAST LAUGH (1924), a comedy starring Emil JANNINGS as a pompous doorman who is suddenly demoted to lavatory attendant. The film is remarkable for its daring use of the SUBJECTIVE CAMERA technique; for one scene, Murnau put cameraman Karl Freund on roller skates to give the central character's drunken impression of a wedding party.

On the strength of these films, Murnau was signed by Fox in 1927. His first US film was the lyrical masterpiece *Sunrise* (1927); the movie's use of a moving camera and dream-like contrasts of light and shade made it unlike anything previously produced in Hollywood. The story involves a man (George O'Brien) who plans to kill his wife (Janet GAYNOR) but then realizes that she is his true love. Although *Sunrise* flopped at the box office, the film won Oscars for Best Actress (Gaynor), photography, and "unique artistic achievement" at the first-ever Academy Awards. CAHIERS DU CINÉMA later rated *Sunrise* the best movie ever made.

Murnau followed this triumph with the less remarkable *The Four Devils* (1928) and *Our Daily Bread* (1929). He then joined the celebrated documentary director Robert FLAHERTY to make *Tabu* (1931), a story about a pearl diver filmed in the South Seas. When the two directors argued, Murnau bought out Flaherty. A week before its premiere, Murnau died in an automobile crash at the age of 42.

Murphy. Audie Murphy (1924–71) Boyish US star of low-budget Westerns, who occasionally handled more serious roles. He is mainly remembered for his off-screen life, which was more dramatic and remarkable than most of his films.

Born in Texas, the son of poor sharecroppers, Murphy found national fame as America's most decorated soldier in World War II. His 28 awards included the Congressional Medal of Honor. Although lauded as a "one-man army", the diminutive and battle-traumatized Murphy later had difficulty in living up to his public image.

It was Murphy's military renown, rather than any obvious acting ability, that led to his film debut in *Beyond Glory* (1948). In 1950 he played both Billy the Kid in *The Kid from Texas* and Jesse James in *Kansas Raiders*. A year later he won unexpected critical acclaim for his sensitive portrayal of an American Civil War private in John HUSTON's *The Red Badge of Courage*. Subsequent films included George MARSHALL's comedy-Western *Destry* (1954) and *To Hell and Back* (1955), a movie based on Murphy's own war exploits. His non-Western roles also included the naive title character in *The Quiet American* (1958), from Graham GREENE's novel.

During the 1960s, however, Murphy became trapped in a series of barely distinguishable Western roles; he himself commented that only the horses seemed to change from one film to the next. By 1968 he was bankrupt. In 1970 his fortunes declined even further, when he was charged with killing a man in a bar fight. Only months after his acquittal, he died when his private plane crashed during a business trip. His last film, in which he again played Jesse James, was named *A Time for Dying*.

Eddie Murphy (Edward Regan Murphy; 1961–) Black US comic actor, who began as a stand-up comedian on television and in night-clubs. In America he was the biggest box-office draw of the 1980s after Clint EASTWOOD. Murphy has acknowledged Richard Pryor, the Black comedian and actor, as his inspiration.

Born in Brooklyn, New York, he first came to national attention on the anarchic TV show *Saturday Night Live* (1980–84). He then made a memorable film debut as the wisecracking foul-mouthed criminal who helps cop Nick Nolte in *48 Hours* (1982). In John LANDIS's comedy *Trading Places* (1983) Murphy plays a streetwise conman who swaps lives with yuppie Dan AYKROYD (also from *Saturday Night Live*) for the sake of a bet.

A year later Murphy enjoyed an immense success with the raucous comedy-action film *Beverly Hills Cop* (1984), in which he plays a Detroit police detective manhunting in Los Angeles. The role had originally been intended for Sylvester STALLONE. In 1987 he made *Beverly Hills Cop II*, a somewhat formulaic sequel, and released an uncensored film of his night-club act, *Eddie Murphy Raw*. For his next film, Landis's *Coming to America* (1988), Murphy abandoned his usual streetwise persona to play a naive African prince who comes to New York in search of a bride. Murphy also supplied the original story and appeared in several cameo roles.

In 1989 he made his debut as screenwriter and director with the disappointing *Harlem Nights*, in which he appeared with Richard Pryor as a pair of Harlem nightclub owners. His more recent films include *Boomerang* (1992), in which he plays a cosmetics executive who is irresistible to women, *The Distinguished Gentleman* (1992), a political satire about a con man posing as a congressman, and *Beverly Hills Cop III* (1994).

music   Music has been an important part of the experience of film-going since the earliest days of the cinema. During the silent era, live music (usually provided by a single pianist, a small orchestra, or the WURLITZER ORGAN), was used both to underscore the action and to mask the sound of the projector. The arrival of synchronized SOUND in the late 1920s presented a host of new challenges, many of which are still being wrestled with today.

Clearly, the composer of film music has to work within a number of constraints that other composers do not. Most obviously, there are the disciplines of timing and synchronization. The music must fit the image – but not too literally or heavyhandedly. During the 1930s there was a tendency for Hollywood composers to underline the slightest nuance of dialogue or emotion in a manner that now seems excessive. Film music must also strike a fine balance between being memorable and being functional. Much film music is designed to enhance the mood of a particular scene – romantic, ominous, or comic – without itself being obtrusive. In horror and suspense films, the skilful use of music can impart a sense of menace or expectation to otherwise innocuous images. Classic examples of the use of music to heighten tension include the shrieking strings of Bernard Herrmann's score for PSYCHO (1960) and the throbbing ostinati of John Williams's music for JAWS (1975).

Perhaps the most successful movie scores of all are those that seem completely integrated with the film while also being striking in their own right. The zither music of Anton Karas in Carol REED'S THE THIRD MAN (1949), for example, became almost as well known as the film itself, as did Vangelis's highly appropriate music to CHARIOTS OF FIRE (1981). Other examples of movie tunes that went on to become popular hits include Maurice Jarre's balalaika theme from *Doctor Zhivago* and Mikis Theodorakis's bazouki music from ZORBA THE GREEK (both 1965). In some cases the music may prove more enduring than the film. The wartime *Dangerous Moonlight* (1941), is now largely forgotten, but Addinsell's *Warsaw Concerto* is still familiar. More recently Jean-Jacques Beneix's *Diva* (1981) and KIEŚLOWSKI'S *The Double Life of Veronique* (1991) – both of which are about singers – have set new standards for the subtle integration of music and image.

Given its specialized demands, it is not surprising that most film music has been written by composers who have devoted themselves to the genre almost exclusively. Amongst the best known and most prolific of the composers to work in Hollywood during its Golden Era were Erich KORNGOLD (*The Adventures of Robin Hood*, 1938; *King's Row*, 1941) and Max STEINER (GONE WITH THE WIND, 1939). More recent practitioners include Elmer Bernstein (*The Magnificent Seven*, 1960), Nino Rota (LA STRADA, 1954; THE GODFATHER, 1972), and Ennio Morricone (*Once Upon a Time in the West*, 1969). A number of distinguished classical composers have also supplied music for the cinema, notably Sergei Prokofiev (ALEXANDER NEVSKY, 1938; IVAN THE TERRIBLE, 1944, 1946), Aaron Copland (*Of Mice and Men*, 1939), and Malcolm Arnold (THE BRIDGE ON THE RIVER KWAI, 1957).

Rather than employ a composer to provide new music, many film-makers have used established classics. Examples include the use of Rachmaninov's 2nd Piano Concerto in BRIEF ENCOUNTER (1945) and that of Beethoven's Violin Concerto in SELZNICK'S *Intermezzo* (British title *Escape to Happiness*; 1939); in both cases the music provided a muted background for most of the film, with the strongly lyrical passages being used to heighten the most emotional moments. A piece of music can become so closely associated with its use in a particular film that it subsequently becomes difficult to think of one without the other. Examples include the use of Richard Strauss's *Also sprach Zarathustra* in 2001: A SPACE ODYSSEY (1968), of Mahler's 5th Symphony in *Death in Venice* (1971), and of Mozart's Piano Concerto No. 21 in *Elvira Madigan* (1967). Concert programmes and record sleeves now often refer to the Mozart piece by the name of the film. In the mid 1970s the piano rags of Scott Joplin, especially 'The Entertainer', experienced an enormous leap in popularity, purely as a result of their revival in the film THE STING (1975).

One clear trend of the last few decades has been the use of familiar pop songs to evoke a whole era (the 1950s in *American Graffiti*, the 1960s in *The Big Chill*) and with it the shared experiences of a generation. Another trend has been the commissioning of pop stars to supply a hit song, even when this has little obvious connection with the film; in this way, every time the song (or better still, the video) is played it provides free publicity for the film, which in turn boosts record sales.

The convention of background music has been sent up in a number of films, usually by the sudden appearance of the source of the music in an incongruous location, as in Mel BROOKS's spoof Western *Blazing Saddles* (1974).

musical A film that tells a story using a mixture of dialogue, songs, and dance routines. By coincidence, the movies discovered sound just as the Broadway musical entered its golden age in the late 1920s; in the subsequent decade, the musical established itself as one of the most popular of all Hollywood genres, a position it would retain for over 30 years.

The success of THE JAZZ SINGER (1927) encouraged the studios to produce a flood of musicals in the early years of sound. Initially, these were mainly screen adaptations of established stage shows, often with the same casts; primitive film versions of both *The Desert Song* and *Show Boat* were released in 1929. That year also saw the advent of the first original screen musical, MGM's *Broadway Melody*. Like most of its immediate successors, this was essentially a revue-style show based around a thin plot about BACKSTAGE goings-on. Once the novelty of sound had worn off audiences began to desert such formulaic material and it seemed as if the musical vogue had run its course. It had also become apparent that the integration of song with dialogue and action on screen raised a number of artistic problems that had not yet been solved.

The artist who did most to restore the fortunes of the genre in the 1930s was the Broadway choreographer Busby BERKELEY. His startling production numbers in 42ND STREET and *Gold Diggers of 1933* (both 1933) made the musical a truly cinematic form for the first time. The immense success of these films led to a boom in the musical spectacular in the mid 1930s. Fred ASTAIRE and Ginger ROGERS brought high style to the dance vehicles created for them, while MGM's Jeannette MACDONALD and Nelson EDDY starred in a series of rather conventional operettas. Other stars to have emerged by the end of the decade included Bing CROSBY and the juvenile Shirley TEMPLE. Judy GARLAND followed her triumph in THE WIZARD OF OZ (1939) with a series of backstage musicals in which she co-starred with the teenage Mickey ROONEY. The MARX BROTHERS, meanwhile, perfected their own style of anarchic musical entertainment, turning the accepted conventions of the genre on their head.

The popularity of the musical remained undiminished during the war years, which saw the emergence of such glamorous stars as Betty GRABLE and Carmen Miranda. It was during this period that MGM emerged as the undisputed leader in the field. Vincente MINNELLI, a former art director, combined style and colour with a new emphasis on realism in such films as MEET ME IN ST LOUIS (1944). Gene KELLY then raised standards of choreography to new heights in the MGM classics *On the Town* (1949), *An American in Paris*. (1951), and SINGIN' IN THE RAIN (1951). The other major musical star of the era, Frank SINATRA, was also an MGM player during this period.

Despite the emergence of a new generation of stars, including Doris DAY, Howard Keel, and Mario Lanza, the musical had already passed its heyday by the mid 1950s. In particular, escalating costs, and a number of expensive flops, discouraged the studios from taking a chance with original material. Virtually all the well-known film musicals of the 1950s and 1960s were based on stage shows that had already

proved successful. Examples include Cole Porter's *Kiss Me Kate* (1953), Irving BERLIN's *Call Me Madam* (1953), *Guys and Dolls* (1955), Lerner and Loewe's *Gigi* (1958) and *My Fair Lady* (1964), Lionel Bart's *Oliver!* (1968), and *Fiddler on the Roof* (1970). The musicals of Rodgers and Hammerstein proved particularly successful in the cinema; the screen version of *Oklahoma!* (1955), described by Ernst LUBITSCH as "the first musical I ever saw...where the people were not complete idiots", was followed by films of *The King and I* (1956), *Carousel* (1956), *South Pacific* (1958), and the enormously popular THE SOUND OF MUSIC (1964).

The story of the film musical in the last three decades has been one of more or less continuous decline. The fashion for 'rock opera' in the early 1970s, as represented by *Jesus Christ Superstar* (filmed 1973) and *Tommy* (filmed 1975) failed to start a significant trend. Meanwhile the older Broadway tradition was continued by Bob FOSSE's *Sweet Charity* (1969) and CABARET (1972) and the rather old-fashioned *A Chorus Line* (1984). Various films of recent decades have featured energetic production numbers without being in the strict sense musicals; these would include the disco-dance movie *Saturday Night Fever* (1977) and Alan PARKER's *Fame* (1980) and *The Commitments* (1991).

Mutoscope The peep-show viewing machine that emerged as the first serious rival to EDISON's KINETOSCOPE. It was developed by the British-born W.K.L. Dickson, a former Edison assistant, with the help of Herman Casler; the two joined others to form the American Mutoscope and BIOGRAPH Company in 1895. A year later, the machine was demonstrated in Pittsburgh and at Koster and Bial's Music Hall in New York. By the late 1890s Mutoscope Parlors were a common sight in US towns; some machines remained in use until after World War II.

The Mutoscope contained photographs of continuous action mounted on cards. When the viewer inserted a coin and operated a hand crank the pictures were rapidly flipped over to create the illusion of (jerky) movement.

Muybridge, Eadweard *See* ZOOPRAXISCOPE.

N

Napoleon (1927) Abel GANCE's epic account of the youth and early career of Bonaparte; it was originally intended to be the first of a six-part biography – *Napoléon vu par Abel Gance* – that would continue the story to Waterloo and St Helena.

The result of over one year's research, *Napoleon* cost over 17 million francs and took more than two years to shoot and edit. Production was fraught with difficulties: credit was withdrawn after only a quarter of the picture had been completed; the star, Albert Dieudonné, nearly drowned on location in Corsica; Gance and his crew were badly burned in an explosion during the filming of the Siege of Toulon; and the director himself suffered a detached retina during editing.

The film is famous for its technical innovations. In particular, Gance and his team of a dozen cinematographers and assistant directors pioneered a wealth of SUBJECTIVE CAMERA techniques; at various times the camera was attached to a guillotine blade, a galloping horse, a swinging pendulum, and a football (to simulate the flight of a snowball and later a cannonball). The sequence depicting Napoleon's triumphal entry into Italy was simultaneously filmed in colour, 3-D, and 'Polyvision', although, ultimately, only the latter process was used to project the action in triptych. Gance explained: "The story one is telling is on the central screen. The story is prose, and the wings, the side screens, are poetry." He also made innovative use of superimposition and SPLIT SCREEN techniques so that the action "burst the restrictive limits of that mean little rectangle which is the ordinary cinema screen."

A 220-minute version of *Napoleon* was premiered at the Paris Opéra in April 1927, while the full seven-hour cut was shown episodically on successive nights. Gance re-edited the film as the much shorter *Napoleon Bonaparte* in 1935 but it was coolly received. In 1969, as part of the Emperor's bicentenary celebrations, he was awarded a grant to produce a new version of his masterpiece; while *Bonaparte et la Révolution* (1971) contained new scenes and a number of recut sequences, it lacked the triptychs, largely because much of the footage had been burned by the director during a fit of depression. The film historian Kevin Brownlow issued a restored print in 1979 with a score by Carl Davis, which lasted five hours. Two years later, Francis Ford COPPOLA also released an edited version. While neither film exactly reproduces Gance's vision, they give modern audiences an insight into the picture Charles Champlin considered "the film against which all others have to be measured, now and forever."

narration or **voice-over** The use of an off-screen voice to describe or analyse the action of a film. Most non-fiction films use a commentary of this kind to supply information necessary for the interpretation of the images. The tone and content of the narration, and the manner in which it is delivered, can be crucial factors in persuading us to accept the veracity of the film-makers' viewpoint. The US DIRECT CINEMA movement of the 1960s developed largely as a reaction against the manipulative use of voice-overs in many documentaries. Exponents of the movement abandoned narration and other overt directorial devices in favour of a fly-on-the-wall approach that allowed the images to 'speak for themselves.'

Fiction films have used narration in a number of ways. Much the most familiar is the voice-over in which a character reminisces, sums up, or thinks aloud. Such soliloquies can enhance an audience's identification with the character, as well as providing information that it might be difficult to convey through images or dialogue. On the other hand, they can slow the action and risk confusing the audience with over-laboured explanations. Narration by an off-screen voice that does not belong to any of the characters is rare; the device is occasionally used to give a flavour of the author's style in literary adaptations (the best known example is probably TOM JONES, 1963). Voice-over has sometimes been added to a film at a late stage to explain matters that do not emerge clearly enough from the action – a surprisingly common fault in crime dramas. Notoriously, it has also been used to 're-write' the film at the demand of the studio, as seen in the different versions of *Blade Runner* (1982 and 1992).

narrow-gauge film Any film stock with a GAUGE of less than 35MM. Such stocks are mainly used for amateur, experimental, and independent productions. *See* 8MM; 9.5MM; 16MM; SUPER 8MM; SUPER 16MM.

national. National Board of Review America's first body for the CENSORSHIP of films. The panel, founded in 1909 in New York as the National Board of Censorship of Motion Pictures, was set up by the People's Institute of New York under the aegis of the MOTION PICTURE PATENTS COMPANY. The Board had few powers, its main function being to issue a semi-official report on each movie prior to its release. Its true purpose was to head off government censorship of films.

The Board assumed its current name in 1921. Its judgments were invariably liberal; in 1930, for instance, it praised Josef VON STERNBERG's violent *Underworld* (1927), describing the director as a creative experimentalist. That year, it also began its practice of selecting the year's 'Ten Best Films'. The Board still publishes *Films in Review* and presents annual awards, including citations for five foreign films.

National Film Registry The US national FILM ARCHIVES, established in 1989 by the Library of Congress and maintained by that body. More than 125 "culturally, historically, or aesthetically significant" films have been placed on the Registry. At present, the 1940s lead with 27 titles, followed by the 1930s with 25, and the 1950s with 23. The oldest film in the collection is Edwin S. PORTER's *The Great Train Robbery* (1903) and the most recent *Blade Runner* (1982).

Among the 26 titles added in 1993 were *The Black Pirate* (1926), IT HAPPENED ONE NIGHT (1934), the MARCH OF TIME documentary *Inside Nazi Germany – 1938*, *Cat People* (1942), *Lassie Come Home* (1943), and SHANE (1953).

National Film Theatre A cinema complex on the South Bank in London, one of the most important venues for new films in Britain. Originally known as the Telekinema, it was founded in 1951 by the British Film Institute (BFI) as part of the Festival of Britain. In 1958 the present cinema was built nearby, a second screen being added in 1970. The annual LONDON FILM FESTIVAL is based here.

National Legion of Decency *See* LEGION OF DECENCY.

NC-17 *See* RATINGS.

Neagle, Dame Anna (Marjorie Robertson; 1904–86) British leading lady, who starred in numerous films made by her husband, the producer-director Herbert WILCOX. Although best known for portraying historical figures, she also starred in MUSICALS and comedies. She was created a DBE in 1969.

Born in London, she danced on stage from the age of 14 and went on to appear in revues and a number of undistinguished films. Having been discovered by Wilcox in the early 1930s, she starred in his *Nell Gwyn* (1934), which was banned in America until cuts were made. A few years later she came to international notice as Queen Victoria in Wilcox's *Victoria the Great* (1937) and its TECHNICOLOR sequel, *Sixty Glorious Years* (US title *Queen of Destiny*; 1938). The couple travelled to Hollywood in 1939 but suffered a series of flops with the RKO musicals *Irene* (1940), *No, No, Nanette* (1940), and *Sunny* (1941). *The New York Times* even suggested that Neagle was destroying the US musical.

After their return to London, Neagle launched a comeback with the romantic comedy, *I Live in Grosvenor Square* (US title *A Yank in London*; 1945), in which she played a duke's daughter courted by RAF officer Rex HARRISON and GI Dean Jagger. She then co-starred with Michael Wilding in several similar films with titles drawn from London street names. Their successful partnership began when Harrison proved too busy to make *Piccadilly Incident* (1946) and continued with *Spring in Park Lane* (1948) and the Technicolor *Maytime in Mayfair* amongst others.

Neagle later played a Resistance heroine in *Odette* (1950) and Florence Nightingale in *The Lady with the Lamp* (1951). *Lilacs in the Spring* (US title *Let's Make Up*; 1954), in which she co-starred with Errol FLYNN, was the first of several disasters that eventually bankrupted Wilcox. After making her last movie, the musical *The Lady is a Square* (1958), she returned to the stage. In 1965 she opened in the musical *Charlie Girl*, which ran for five years.

Neal, Patricia (1926–) US actress who suffered a series of crippling strokes in 1965 but fought back to win a 1968 Oscar nomination. In the 1981 television BIOPIC *The Patricia Neal Story* Glenda JACKSON played Neal and Dirk BOGARDE her British husband, the writer Roald Dahl.

After studying drama at Northwestern University, Neal worked as a model and appeared in shows. Her performance in *Another Part of the Forest* (1946) led to dinner with producer David O. SELZNICK, who, as Neal later reported, "got very drunk, told me how much he loved Jennifer JONES, and then tried to get me into bed."

In 1949 she signed with Warner Brothers to make the comedy *John Loves Mary*, in which she co-starred with Ronald REAGAN, *The Fountainhead*, in which she played a journalist who smears architect Gary COOPER, and *The Day the Earth Stood Still*, about an alien landing. Off-screen, she had a stormy affair with Cooper that led to her nervous breakdown. After marrying Dahl in 1953 she virtually retired; her comeback film was *A Face in the Crowd* (1957), Elia KAZAN's satire on the power of television. The early 1960s brought Neal two of her most memorable roles – the rich sponsor of writer George Peppard in *Breakfast at Tiffany's* (1961) and the housekeeper assaulted by Paul NEWMAN in *Hud*. The latter earned her an Oscar as Best Supporting Actor.

After making the naval film *In Harm's Way* (1965) with John WAYNE, Neal suffered the near-fatal strokes that left her semi-paralysed and barely able to speak. With her husband's help, she made an amazing recovery to return to the screen three years later in *The Subject was Roses*; her performance as the anguished mother of an unhappy family brought her an Oscar nomination. Neal and Dahl divorced in 1983.

Her later films included *The Night Digger* (1971), an unsuccessful thriller scripted by Dahl, *Ghost Story* (1981), and *An Unremarkable Life* (1989).

Neame, Ronald (1911–) British director, cinematographer, producer, and screenwriter, who has latterly worked mainly in America.

The son of film director Elwin Neame and actress Ivy Close, Neame began as a

14-year-old messenger and tea boy at the British International Film Studios. After working as an assistant cameraman on Alfred HITCHCOCK's *Blackmail*, he graduated to director of photography in the 1930s, when he filmed several George FORMBY comedies. While photographing *Major Barbara* (1941), he was constantly badgered by Rex HARRISON, who insisted that he film his hairpiece from its best side.

Neame's big break came as part of the team put together by Noël COWARD to film *In Which We Serve* (1942). Having formed the production company Cineguild, the same team made several further films, including *This Happy Breed* (1944), which Neame photographed and co-scripted with David LEAN; unusually in that era of over-brilliant colour, the film is made in a realistic muted TECHNICOLOR.

Neame's debut as a director came with the successful thriller, *Take My Life* (1947). The following year, he produced David LEAN's *Oliver Twist* and the flop *The Passionate Friends* (US title: *One Woman's Story*) for Cineguild, which disbanded soon afterwards. His association with Alec GUINNESS, who had played Fagin in *Oliver Twist*, continued with *The Card* (US title *The Promoter*; 1952), *The Horse's Mouth* (1959), and *Tunes of Glory* (1960).

From 1957 Neame worked mainly in Hollywood, where his films included Judy GARLAND's last movie, *I Could Go on Singing* (1963), *The Prime of Miss Jean Brodie* (1969), featuring an Oscar-winning performance from Maggie SMITH, and the musical *Scrooge* (1970), with Albert FINNEY. His greatest box-office success, however, was the trend-setting DISASTER FILM, *The Poseidon Adventure* (1972), about passengers trapped in a capsized liner; another commercial triumph was the thriller, *The Odessa File* (1975). Later films include the comedies *First Monday in October* (1981), with Jill Clayburgh as a Supreme Court judge, and *Foreign Body* (1986), with Victor Banerjee as a fake London doctor. In 1992 the 81-year-old Neame took up a teaching post at the University of California in Los Angeles (UCLA).

Neeson, Liam (1956–) Northern Irish actor. Neeson's earliest experience of acting was in a school play written in Gaelic, a language he did not understand. He subsequently abandoned a promising boxing career (although he later played a bare-knuckle bruiser in *The Big Man*, 1990) to join first the Lyric Players of Belfast and then the Abbey Theatre in Dublin.

It was here that he was spotted by John BOORMAN, who gave him the part of Sir Gawain in *Excalibur* (1981); this was followed by a series of supporting roles in such features as *Krull* (1983) and *The Bounty* (1984). Neeson then took the lead in *Lamb* (1986), playing a kindly Christian Brother who absconds to London with an epileptic scallywag in an attempt to relieve the misery of the boy's existence. Although he played another priest, one of Jeremy IRONS's Jesuits, in *The Mission* (1986), film-makers thereafter showed more interest in his physicality than his spirituality. From the late 1980s he played a series of villainous types, including a mute on trial for murder in *Suspect* (1987), a sensationalist film-maker in the 'Dirty Harry' movie *The Dead Pool* (1988), a murderous ghost in *High Spirits* (1988), and a detective with an ulterior motive in *Under Suspicion* (1991).

Despite good notices, stardom remained elusive. In 1989 he lost the chance to play the lead in *Dead Poets Society* when Jeff Kanew was replaced as director by Peter WEIR, who wanted Robin WILLIAMS for the part. Although Neeson impressed as the comic-book avenger in Sam Raimi's *Darkman* (1990) and in Woody ALLEN's *Husbands and Wives* (1992), all that ensued were such humdrum assignments as *Shining Through* and *Ruby Cairo* (both 1992). As a result, Neeson made for Broadway. His big break followed when Steven SPIELBERG noticed him in an O'Neil play and cast him as the profiteer-cum-philanthropist Oskar Schindler in SCHINDLER'S LIST (1993). Despite capturing the character's moral ambiguity to a nicety, Neeson was denied a merited Oscar nomination. He prepared for the role in a curious manner:

> When I got the part, I started watching a lot of George SANDERS films, because it's a period film and there's a way to wear suits that we, as a jeans and t-shirt culture, have lost. To watch Sanders in a tuxedo is like a lesson in how to move.

Neeson took another philanthropic role in *Nell* (1994), playing the doctor who introduces backwoodswoman Jodie FOSTER to the dubious benefits of civilisation. He has since returned to the action genre as the 17th-century Scottish clan leader *Rob Roy* (1995).

negative A piece of exposed and developed film in which the colour tones are the reverse of those in the original subject (and in the subsequent positive print). In black-and-white photography the areas of light and shade are reversed, while in colour photography the colours are complementary to those of the original scene. The system of recording a negative from which subsequent positives are printed has the advantage of allowing unlimited replication of the original image.

negative cost The total money spent on the production of a movie, excluding the costs of extra prints, publicity, distribution, and exhibition.

Negri, Pola (Appolonia Chalupiec; 1897–1987) Fiery Polish-born Hollywood star, known as **the Magnificent Wildcat**, who had a long-running feud with her Paramount rival Gloria SWANSON. Off-screen, she had affairs with Charlie CHAPLIN and Rudolph VALENTINO. In 1926 she sent 4000 roses to Valentino's funeral and fainted at his bier, but soon recovered to wed a Russian prince.

The daughter of a gypsy violinist, she was raised mainly in Russia. After making her stage debut in 1913, she appeared in her first film, the Polish *Love and Passion*, a year later. Max Reinhardt then invited her to Berlin, where she performed on stage and in Ernst LUBITSCH's *Madame Dubarry* (US title *Passion*; 1919). When Paramount took Negri to Hollywood in 1923, she immediately challenged Swanson's supremacy. Their feud became so intense that Adolph ZUKOR moved all Swanson's productions to New York.

Negri's US successes included *Bella Donna* (1923), the Lubitsch satire *Forbidden Paradise* (British title *Czarina*; 1924), about Catherine the Great, and the romantic thriller *Hotel Imperial* (1927), in which she played a hotel maid. However, her stylized acting and thick Polish accent meant that her US career did not survive the coming of the talkies. Off-screen, she lost fans by expounding on the superiority of German culture. By 1928, when she made *Three Sinners*, exhibitors were refusing to feature her name in advertisements.

Thereafter she returned to European film-making. One great fan was Adolf Hitler, who reportedly watched her film *Mazurka* (1935) several times a week. Asked in a 1936 interview if she had

Hitler's support, she replied: "Why not; after all there have been many important men in my life." She later successfully sued a French magazine for claiming that she was Hitler's mistress.

On the fall of France in 1940, Negri returned penniless to Hollywood, where she made the comedy *Hi Diddle Diddle* (1943). She then disappeared from the screen for over 20 years before returning in a character role in Disney's *The Moon-Spinners* (1964).

Negulesco, Jean (1900–84) Romanian-born US director, who pioneered the FILM NOIR style in the 1940s. After World War II his output changed from tough thrillers and melodramas to so-called 'Women's pictures'. Cameramen often had difficulty following his directions because, as Negulseco acknowledged: "my accent is so thick that when I get excited or nervous, nobody can understand me."

Born in Craiova, he spent some years painting in Paris before moving to New York in 1927. After entering films as an artistic adviser on Paramount's *The Story of Temple Drake* (1933), he quickly advanced to associate director. In 1941 he was assigned to direct Warner Brothers' THE MALTESE FALCON, but the project was taken from him by another novice, John HUSTON; he made his directorial debut later that year with *Singapore Woman*.

Negulesco's first real success was *The Mask of Dimitrios* (1944), a spy-thriller starring Peter LORRE and Sydney GREENSTREET that is sometimes considered the first film noir. The three worked together again on *The Conspirators* (1944) and *Three Strangers* (1946). *Humoresque* (1946) was a melodrama about an ambitious violinist (John Garfield).

Negulesco's greatest critical success came with *Johnny Belinda* (1948), a powerful film starring Jane WYMAN as a deaf mute who is raped. Although Jack WARNER disliked the movie so much that he delayed the release date and fired Negulesco, it went on to receive 12 Oscar nominations, including one for Best Director (Wyman was the single winner).

Negulesco's reputation for location work brought him his next job, Fox's film noir *Road House* (1948); he subsequently remained with the studio to direct such popular movies as *The Mudlark* (1950), with Irene DUNNE as Queen Victoria and Alec

GUINNESS as Disraeli. His greatest box-office triumph, however, was the CINEMASCOPE comedy *How to Marry a Millionaire* (1953), which teamed Marilyn MONROE with Laren BACALL and Betty GRABLE.

Other successes included the romantic THREE COINS IN THE FOUNTAIN (1954), the comedy *Woman's World* (1954), the musical *Daddy Long Legs* with Fred ASTAIRE and Leslie CARON (1955), and *Boy on a Dolphin* (1957) with Sophia LOREN. His later films were generally less memorable; they included *Jessica* (1962), about a sex strike by Sicilian women, and *The Heroes* (1979).

neorealism A movement in the Italian cinema of the 1940s and 1950s, characterized by an emphasis on REALISM and a concern for the social condition of the poor. Neorealism began to emerge as a distinct style during the mid 1940s, when the harsh reality of the war and its aftermath seemed to demand that the cinema should reflect the suffering of the people. Accordingly, such directors as Vittorio DE SICA and Roberto ROSSELLINI employed nonprofessional casts and undertook much filming on location in order to make their work as real and immediate as possible. In general, directors tried not to draw attention to the presence of the camera or to the editing process. Classics of the neorealist style include Luchino VISCONTI's *Ossesione* (1942), Rossellini's ROME OPEN CITY (1945), De Sica's BICYCLE THIEVES (1948), and Giuseppe DE SANTIS's *Bitter Rice* (1949). Other major figures in the movement were the directors Renato Castellani (1913–81), Alberto Lattuada (1914–), and Luigi Zampa (1905–91) and the screenwriters Suso Cecchi D'Amico (1914–) and Cesare Zavattini (1902–89). Although the ideals of neorealism faded somewhat during the 1950s, when Italian film-makers turned increasingly to comedy and glamour, a whole generation of directors had by this time been influenced by its techniques, among them PASOLINI and FELLINI as well as many Hollywood figures.

new. New American Cinema *See* UNDERGROUND FILMS.

New Cinema or *Neue Kino* A movement that revitalized German cinema in the 1960s and 1970s, influencing international film-makers through its intellectual rigour and political commitment. It was launched in 1962 with the signing of the **Oberhausen manifesto** by a group of young directors who determined to break away from West Germany's moribund commercial cinema. With financial help from the Kuratorium Junger Deutscher Film organization, founded in 1964 to help young film-makers, such directors as Alexander Kluge (1932–), Volker SCHLÖNDORFF, Jean-Marie STRAUB, and Werner HERZOG began to forge a new cinema of intellectual seriousness and high artistic standards. With the critical success of such films as Kluge's *Yesterday Girl* (1966), Schlöndorff's *Young Törless* (1966), and Straub's *The Chronicle of Anna Magdalena Bach* (1967), the New Cinema came to be recognized as an important new departure for European film. In the 1970s and 1980s budgets were increased and directors like Rainer Werner FASSBINDER and Wim WENDERS were able to tackle more ambitious subjects while remaining faithful to the ideals of the 1962 manifesto. Several of the later films to come out of the movement have enjoyed international success, among them Herzog's *Nosferatu the Vampyre* (1979) and *Fitzcarraldo* (1982) and Schlöndorff's *The Tin Drum* (1979), which became the first postwar German film to win an Oscar (as Best Foreign Film). In his speech Schlöndorff accepted the award not only for himself but for a whole generation of German film-makers.

New Wave or *Nouvelle Vague* An influential movement in French film-making that began in the late 1950s. Several of the directors associated with the movement developed their ideas about film while working as critics for the journal CAHIERS DU CINÉMA, the most prominent among them being Jean-Luc GODARD and François TRUFFAUT. The group rejected many established Hollywood conventions in order to develop the more challenging narrative and editing techniques pioneered a generation earlier by such figures as HITCHCOCK, Jean RENOIR, and Jean VIGO.

The first masterpiece of the movement was Godard's debut feature À BOUT DE SOUFFLE (1959), a fast-moving, unpredictable, technically adventurous, and self-consciously filmic piece of work that seemed to announce a radically new approach to film-making. The sense of a coherent movement was created by the release of Truffaut's THE 400 BLOWS and Alain RESNAIS's HIROSHIMA MON AMOUR that same year. Other directors associated with the New Wave include Claude CHABROL, Eric ROHMER, Jacques DEMY, and Louis MALLE. These film-makers soon developed their own highly distinctive styles and it is arguable whether the New Wave ever really existed as a defined movement. Nevertheless, it exerted a permanent and liberating influence upon European cinema – not least by proving that it was possible to produce innovative and stimulating films on the smallest of budgets. Chabrol himself once observed:

There is no new wave, only the sea.

Newman, Paul (1925–) US actor and director. Following service in World War II, Newman enrolled in college on a sports scholarship; however, owing to a knee injury he soon switched to a drama programme.

After considerable stage and television work, Newman was signed by Warner Brothers and tried out for the James DEAN role in EAST OF EDEN. Instead, he was launched in *The Silver Chalice* (1955), which Newman himself has described as "the worst motion picture filmed during the 1950s." Following this debacle, which almost ended his career, Newman bounced back in *The Rack* (1956) and Robert WISE's *Somebody Up There Likes Me* (1956), a popular biopic of boxer Rocky Graziano; the role would have been played by Dean, had he still been alive. He went on to star in *Cat on a Hot Tin Roof* (1958), which brought him an Oscar nomination as Best Actor, and *The Left-Handed Gun* (1958), in which he played Billy the Kid.

Although *From the Terrace* and *Exodus* (both 1960) were popular successes, it was Robert ROSSEN's *The Hustler* (1962) that provided Newman with his finest early role, as pool shark 'Fast' Eddie Felson. The film brought him a second Oscar nomination. Over the next few years Newman gave some truly exceptional performances, notably as the amoral title character in *Hud* (1963), which brought him a third nomination, as a Chandleresque private eye in *Harper* (1966), and as the eponymous antihero of *Cool Hand Luke* (1967). Newman's biggest success of the decade, however, was as Butch to Robert REDFORD's Sundance in the hugely popular BUTCH CASSIDY AND THE SUNDANCE KID (1969).

In 1968 Newman made his directorial debut with *Rachel, Rachel*, which featured Joanne WOODWARD, his second wife. Newman has subsequently directed her in several other films, including *The Effect of Gamma Rays on Man-in-the-Moon Marigolds* (1972) and *The Glass Menagerie* (1987).

During the 1970s Newman gave notable performances as a disillusioned disc-jockey in *WUSA* (1970), the 'hanging judge' in John HUSTON's *The Life and Times of Judge Roy Bean* (1972), and a con-man in the enormously popular THE STING (1973), which again teamed him with Redford. Following a rather quiet period at the end of the decade, Newman returned as a commanding and slightly underplayed presence in such films as *Fort Apache, The Bronx* (1980), *Absence of Malice* (1980), and *The Verdict* (1982). The last two films brought his tally of Oscar nominations to six; he received an honorary Oscar in 1985 and then, at last, the real thing for his appearance in Martin SCORSESE's sequel to *The Hustler*, *The Color of Money* (1986). Newman's more recent films have included *Fat Man and Little Boy* (1989), *Mr and Mrs Bridge* (1990), which co-starred Joanne Woodward, and the COEN BROTHERS' *The Hudsucker Proxy* (1994). His performance as an old codger in *Nobody's Fool* (1994) brought a seventh Oscar nomination.

Apart from his film career, Newman supports various foundations with the profits – in 1994 over 6 million dollars – of 'Newman's Own', a range of food products.

newsreels Short films documenting current affairs. These have a long history: Kaiser Wilhelm II was filmed opening the Kiel Canal as early as June 1895, while a year later Queen Victoria noted: "we were all photographed by Downey by the new cinematograph process." By 1906 a daily newsreel, *Day by Day*, was showing in London, while the French *Pathé-Faits Divers* (soon renamed *Pathé-Journal*) initiated newsreel for general release. Although most early newsreels were genuine, others, such as battle reports, were faked or restaged after the event; in 1901 Georges MÉLIÈS used a double in his purported documentation of King Edward VII's coronation.

By the 1920s, however, cameramen were scouring the world, often at great personal risk, for material to fill *Movietone News*, *Pathé News* or *Universal Newsreel*. Cinema programmes contained regular short slots for round-ups of national and international events, sports reports, celebrity gossip, and anything else deemed newsworthy or entertaining. The MARCH OF TIME two-reelers became particularly important during World War II.

By the mid 1950s television and cheap mass transport had rendered newsreel largely obsolete; the final deathblow was the advent of international satellite transmission. By 1979 the last newsreels had vanished from US and British screens. However, much priceless archive material survives, and continues to resurface in a variety of contexts. The Australian tribute to the newsreel business, *Newsfront* (1979), contains an excellent blend of fiction and archive footage. *See* MOVIETONE; PATHÉ.

Newton, Robert (1905–56) British character actor, noted for his imposing and often scene-stealing performances. After making his debut in *Reunion* (1932), it was four years before Newton next appeared, in *Fire Over England* (1936), a swashbuckler with Laurence OLIVIER. By his fourth film, *Farewell Again* (1937), Newton had moved up to billed roles. Particularly notable among his films of this period are *Vessel of Wrath* (1938), with Charles LAUGHTON, *Jamaica Inn* (1939), again with Laughton, *Gaslight* (1939), and *Busman's Holiday* (1940).

Newton's popularity continued to grow throughout the 1940s, owing to strong roles in such films as Vincent Korda's *Major Barbara* (1941), *Hatter's Castle* (1941), in which he gave a barnstorming performance as a Scottish hat-maker, David LEAN's *This Happy Breed* (1944), Olivier's *Henry V* (1944), in which he played the bombastic Pistol, and *Odd Man Out* (1947), in which he played a mad painter determined to catch the look of death in the eyes of hunted IRA man James MASON. At the end of the decade he starred as Bill Sikes in Lean's *Oliver Twist* (1948) and as an eye-rolling Long John Silver in *Treasure Island* (1950), Disney's first totally live-action film. The role was to prove lucrative for Newton, who reprised it for a short-lived television series and another film, *Long John Silver* (1955).

Among his later films are *Tom Brown's Schooldays* (1951), an unremarkable remake only distinguished by Newton's performance as an understanding teacher, *Blackbeard the Pirate* (1952), for which he wheeled out his eye-rolling Long John Silver act once again, *Androcles and the Lion* (1952), and *The Desert Rats* (1953). His last role was as Inspector Fix, the pursuer of Phileas Fogg, in the star-laden AROUND THE WORLD IN EIGHTY DAYS (1956).

NG No good. An abbreviation used to indicate that for whatever reason (poor acting, bad lighting, a technical or continuity error, directorial caprice, etc.) a shot must not be used.

Nichols, Mike (Michael Igor Peschkowsky; 1931–) US director, who won an Oscar for his second film, THE GRADUATE (1967). He is known for his remarkable empathy with actors.

Nichols, who was born in Berlin to Jewish parents, fled to New York with his family in 1938. After working as a janitor, post office clerk, and truck driver, he attended the University of Chicago and trained at Lee Strasberg's ACTORS' STUDIO in New York.

Back in Chicago, he helped to form an improvisational group, the Compass Players, which included Elaine May and Alan ARKIN. In 1960 Nichols and May won acclaim on Broadway with their satirical revue *An Evening with Mike Nichols and Elaine May*. Three years later, he made his debut as a Broadway director with Neil Simon's *Barefoot in the Park*.

Nichols's move into films came when Richard BURTON and Elizabeth TAYLOR asked him to direct them as the warring couple in *Who's Afraid of Virginia Woolf?* (1966); Nichols noted, "the poor Burtons had to spit at each other and hit each other for days." A year later he became the first director to earn $1 million from a single movie with *The Graduate* (1967), in which he introduced his New York stage discovery, Dustin HOFFMAN.

Nichols then continued in the same offbeat vein with the anti-war satire *Catch-22* (1970), which flopped badly, and *Carnal Knowledge* (1971), a painful sex comedy starring Jack NICHOLSON. His other films of the 1970s were *The Day of the Dolphin* (1973), an unsuccessful thriller starring George C. SCOTT, and *The Fortune* (1975), a black comedy in which Nicholson and Warren BEATTY plot to murder the latter's fiancée. When another film was abandoned in mid-production, Nichols went back to Broadway.

In the mid 1980s he made a successful return to the screen with *Silkwood* (1983), a film based on the mysterious death of the plutonium-plant employee Karen Silkwood (Meryl STREEP). Subsequent films included *Heartburn* (1986), again with Nicholson and Streep, and Neil Simon's *Biloxi Blues* (1988). *Working Girl* (1988), a Cinderella story for the 1980s, starred Melanie Griffith

as a secretary who rises to the top of the executive ladder. The modern corporate world was also the setting for *Wolf* (1994), which stars Nicholson as a mild-mannered book editor who revitalizes his career when he turns into a werewolf.

Nicholson, Jack (1937–) US actor and occasional director. Although he did not realize it until many years later, Nicholson's childhood was remarkably strange. The son of a young unmarried woman, he was brought up to believe his grandmother to be his mother and his mother and aunt to be his sisters. His 'father' (actually his grandfather) was an alcoholic sign painter, who abandoned the family when Nicholson was an infant.

While visiting one of his 'sisters' in California, Nicholson landed a job in the cartoon department at MGM. He then acted in television soaps before making his film debut as a delinquent in Roger CORMAN's *Cry Baby Killer* (1958). Nicholson's association with Corman continued for a decade, bringing him both work as a screenwriter (notably with *The Trip*, 1967) and numerous roles in teenage exploitation and horror films.

Stardom came belatedly to Nicholson with the role of George Hanson, the alcohol-soaked Southern lawyer in EASY RIDER. In his hands the small role stole the film, bringing him an Oscar nomination as Best Supporting Actor. Nicholson then consolidated his stardom with an edgy depiction of a middle-class dropout in Bob RAFELSON's *Five Easy Pieces* (1970); this time the role brought him a Best Actor nomination. Following an excellent performance in Mike NICHOLS's *Carnal Knowledge* (1971), Nicholson worked with Rafelson again on *The King of Marvin Gardens* (1972), in which he played a weary disc jockey. Starring roles in Hal ASHBY's *The Last Detail* (1973) and (as private detective J. J. Gittes) in Roman POLANSKI's CHINATOWN (1974) also brought Oscar nominations.

After taking the lead in ANTONIONI's enigmatic *The Passenger* (1975), Nicholson finally won the Oscar for his towering performance as the quintessential free spirit, Randle Patrick McMurphy, in Miloš FORMAN's ONE FLEW OVER THE CUCKOO'S NEST (1975). The later 1970s brought major roles in Elia KAZAN's *The Last Tycoon* (1976), Arthur Penn's weird Western *The Missouri Breaks* (1976), and the self-directed comedy Western *Goin' South* (1978). Nicholson then burst into the 1980s with a thrillingly over-the-top performance in Stanley KUBRICK's *The Shining* (1980) and an acclaimed depiction of Eugene O'Neill in Warren BEATTY's *Reds* (1981). His portrayal of an ex-astronaut in *Terms of Endearment* (1983) brought him a second Oscar.

Nicholson's other roles of the 1980s included a dim-witted hitman in John HUSTON's *Prizzi's Honor* (1985), the "horny little devil" in *The Witches of Eastwick* (1987), and an alcoholic tormented by his past in *Ironweed* (1987). More recently he has been seen as The Joker in Tim BURTON's BATMAN (1989), as J. J. Gittes in his self-directed sequel to *Chinatown*, *The Two Jakes* (1990), and as the title character in the biopic *Hoffa* (1991). His performance as the terrifying Col. Nathan R. Jessep in *A Few Good Men* (1992) brought him another Best Supporting Actor nomination. In 1994 he starred as a gentleman-publisher turned lycanthrope in *Wolf*.

Presently Nicholson is in an almost unique position, still having the drawing power of a major star but often preferring to work at a supporting level – mainly, he claims, because he becomes bored easily. Nicholson's long relationship (1973–90) with the actress Angelica HUSTON ended when he had a child by a young waitress.

nickelodeon A former name for a cheap movie theatre; it derived from the usual price of admission (five cents) plus *odeon*, a name for a small hall for music, etc. The original Nickelodeon was the cinema opened by John P. Harris and Harry Davis at McKeesport, near Pittsburgh, Pennsylvania, in 1905. The first picture shown was Edwin S. PORTER's *The Great Train Robbery*. Following the success of this venture, thousands of nickelodeons sprang up throughout America; in 1908 it was estimated that some 80 million tickets were being sold every week. The name was later used of other forms of cheap mechanized entertainment, such as a pianola or jukebox.

Nielsen, Leslie (1926–) Canadian-born Hollywood actor, whose unusual career has taken him from wooden roles in B-films to even more wooden roles in a series of hugely successful comedy spoofs. He is best known as the bungling police detective Frank Drebin in the *Naked Gun* series.

The son of a mountie, Nielsen served in the Canadian airforce and worked as a disc jockey before going on the stage. His film debut came in *Ransom* (1955), starring Glenn FORD. Subsequent roles included the space-cruiser commander in *Forbidden Planet* (1956), the older love interest of Debbie REYNOLDS in *Tammy and the Bachelor* (1957), and General Custer in *The Plainsman* (1966). As his career slowed down in the 1970s, Nielsen took small parts in the DISASTER FILMS *The Poseidon Adventure* (1972) and *City on Fire* (1979).

The extraordinary revival in Nielsen's fortunes began when he appeared in *Airplane!* (1979), a frenetic spoof of the disaster genre from the writing and directing team of Jim Abrahams, David Zucker, and Jerry Zucker. Nielsen then starred as Drebin in the same team's *Police Squad* (1982), a short-lived television cop spoof that subsequently spawned the international hit *The Naked Gun: From the Files of Police Squad!* (1988). The plot, which is the merest excuse for a barrage of gags and pratfalls, has Nielsen saving Queen Elizabeth II from an assassination attempt; Priscilla Presley played his love interest, George Kennedy his associate, and O. J. Simpson his accident-prone assistant. The cast remained together for *Naked Gun 2½: The Smell of Fear* (1991) and *Naked Gun 33⅓: The Final Insult* (1993).

night. **night filter** A camera FILTER used to give the appearance of night-time to scenes filmed in the daytime (*see* DAY-FOR-NIGHT). In black-and-white photography this is usually a red filter; in colour photography, a graduated neutral density filter may be used.

night-for-night Filming a location scene that requires a night-time setting at night, rather than using a DAY-FOR-NIGHT simulation; the practice requires a fast film stock and sufficient lighting.

Night of the Living Dead (1968) Cult HORROR movie, made by industrial film-maker George Romero (1939–) on a shoestring budget of $150,000. Although it featured a largely non-professional cast and was shot at weekends using grainy black-and-white film and homemade special effects, *Night of the Living Dead* revolutionized the horror genre; not merely with its explicit gore (which now seems tame), but also for its revelation that the good do not always triumph and, indeed, often meet unpleasant ends.

The plot revolves around flesh-eating zombies brought back to life by radiation from a space rocket to terrorize the living. Described as "the best film ever made in Pittsburgh", *Night of the Living Dead* is one of the most successful INDEPENDENT FILMS ever made. Romero went on to make *Dawn of the Dead* (1979) and the inferior *Day of the Dead* (1985). An expensive colour remake of *Night of the Living Dead* (1990) failed to equal the nightmarish power of the original.

9.5 mm A narrow-gauge film stock introduced by the PATHÉ company in 1922 for amateur use. It had 40 frames per foot with one perforation between each frame. Once highly popular with amateur European film-makers, it was subsequently replaced by 8MM film. Other now-obsolete GAUGES produced by Pathé were 17.5mm and 28mm.

Ninotchka (1939) Ernst LUBITSCH's romantic satire on the communist-capitalist divide, best remembered for the famous publicity line "Garbo laughs!" Although she had laughed on screen a number of times before, this was her first light comedy role after a series of tragedies and other intense pieces; the change of image was prompted by the dwindling of her US audiences in the late 1930s. *Ninotchka* briefly turned the tide, with Garbo winning an Oscar nomination for her performance as a stern Soviet emissary; after the failure of another comedy, however, she forsook the cinema never to return.

The film co-starred Melvyn DOUGLAS as a suave French count who becomes infatuated with Garbo, a part for which William POWELL and Robert Montgomery were both considered; Bela LUGOSI also has a supporting role. Lubitsch produced as well as directed, while Billy WILDER, Charles Brackett, and Walter Reisch, collaborated on the witty Oscar-nominated screenplay. *Ninotchka* also won nominations for Best Picture and Best Original Story (by Melchior Lengyel). In 1957 the story was remade as the musical *Silk Stockings*, starring Fred ASTAIRE and Cyd CHARISSE.

Nina Yakushova, known as Ninotchka, is the severe and efficient commissar sent to Paris to bring home three comrades who have been seduced by the Western lifestyle. However, an aristocratic playboy (Douglas) gradually converts her both to materialism and to romantic love ("Never did I dream I could feel like this toward a sergeant" he confesses at one point). Ironically, Ninotchka's rival for the count's love was played by Ina Claire – the wife of Garbo's lover and long-time screen partner John GILBERT.

nipple count Industry jargon for the number of exposed female breasts appearing in a film, considered as a selling-point.

Niven, David (James David Nevins 1909– 83) Urbane British actor, who remained popular with film-goers for over 40 years. Niven himself was somewhat puzzled by his appeal, describing his features as "a cross between two pounds of halibut and an explosion in an old clothes closet." He wrote two best-selling memoirs, *The Moon's a Balloon* (1972) and *Bring on the Empty Horses* (1975).

The son of a Scottish army officer, who was killed in World War I, Niven attended the Royal Military College at Sandhurst and served with the Highland Light Infantry. After travelling to America in the 1930s he had various jobs, including technical adviser to a group of Cuban insurgents and deliveryman (in a Rolls Royce) for a Chinese laundry.

In 1935 Niven made his Hollywood debut as an extra thrown from a saloon in GOLDWYN's *Barbary Coast*. Over the next few years he graduated to supporting roles and joined the roistering social set of Errol FLYNN, Douglas FAIRBANKS JNR, and Clark GABLE. In 1936 he appeared with Flynn in Warners' *The Charge of the Light Brigade*; during one battle sequence the Hungarian-born director Michael CURTIZ gave the inept order "bring on the empty [i.e. riderless] horses" – a phrase that gave Niven a title for his book. Three years later Goldwyn cast him as Linton to Laurence OLIVIER's Heathcliff in WUTHERING HEIGHTS. After he became a star, Niven insisted that every film in which he appeared contain a reference to a character named Trubshawe, a former military friend.

Niven was one of the first stars to volunteer for World War II, during which he served in the British army and made propaganda films. He also starred in POWELL and PRESSBURGER's fantasy A MATTER OF LIFE AND DEATH (1946), playing a brain-damaged RAF pilot who is given another chance at life by the heavenly powers. For his war efforts, he received the American Legion of Merit.

After his return to Hollywood, Niven signed up again with Goldwyn, who forced him to star in the great British disaster *Bonnie Prince Charlie* (1947). His career declined somewhat thereafter, but recovered with AROUND THE WORLD IN EIGHTY DAYS (1956), in which he played the debonair Phineas Fogg. In 1958 his performance as a bogus army major in *Separate Tables* brought him his only Oscar. Later roles included an explosives expert in *The Guns of Navarone* (1961), an aristocratic jewel thief in THE PINK PANTHER (1964), and James Bond in the spoof BOND FILM *Casino Royale* (1967).

Throughout it all, Niven never lost his dry wit. When the 1974 Academy Awards ceremony was disrupted by a male streaker, Niven, then on the platform, quipped instantly "Just think, probably the only laugh that man will ever get is for stripping and showing his shortcomings." He died in Switzerland after a long battle with the wasting disease amytrophic lateral sclerosis. Shortly before his death, he filmed scenes for *The Curse of the Pink Panther* (1983).

Noiret, Philippe (1930–) Prolific French actor, who has starred in both French and international productions; he is noted for his versatility and for the many fine character roles of his later years.

Born in Lille, Noiret trained under Roger Blin, the avant-garde theatre director. After working as a nightclub entertainer, he moved into theatre and film, making his screen debut with a bit part in *Gigi* (1948). During the 1950s he joined the Théâtre National Populaire and worked in cabaret, his only film of the decade being Agnes Varda's *La Pointe Court*. He then began to achieve prominence in such films as Louis MALLE's *Zazie dans le Métro* (1961), in which he played a transvestite, Georges FRANJU's *Thérèse Desqueroux* (1963), for which he won a Best Actor prize at the Venice Film Festival, and Yves ROBERT's *Alexandre le bienheureux* (1968). In 1965 Noiret made his English-language debut in Peter Ustinov's *Lady L* (1965), following this with roles in the British production *Night of the Generals* (1967) and Alfred HITCHCOCK's *Topaz* (1969).

During the 1970s his popularity as a versatile and distinguished actor continued to grow, as did his prodigious workrate.

Notable films of the period include *La Grande Bouffe* (1973), *The Clockmaker* (*L'Horloger de St Paul*; 1973), his first film with the director Bertrand TAVERNIER, and Robert Enrico's *Le Vieux Fusil* (1975), for which he won a César. Noiret's other films for Tavernier, with whom he has enjoyed a long and fruitful relationship, include *Let Joy Reign Supreme* (*Que la Fête commence*; 1975), *The Judge and the Assassin* (1976), the Oscar-nominated *Coup de torchon* (*Clean Slate*; 1981), about a colonial police officer, and *Life and Nothing But* (1989), in which he gave a towering performance as an army officer trying to make sense of the fatalities of World War I.

During the 1980s he appeared in a number of highly successful films including *Le Cop* (1984) and Giuseppe Tornatore's *Cinema Paradiso* (1988), in which he played an ageing projectionist. His most recent movies include *Les Ripoux Contre les ripoux* (1990), a sequel to *Le Cop*, *Especially on Sunday* (1991), and the Dumas adaptation *La Fille d'Artagnan* (1994).

North by Northwest (1959) Alfred HITCHCOCK's comedy spy thriller. The film is effectively a cross country CHASE; following a case of mistaken identity, Roger Thornhill (Cary GRANT) is pursued both by spies (James MASON and Martin Landau), who are intent on killing him, and by FBI agents, who want to arrest him. He is accompanied by the mysterious Eve Kendall (Eve Marie Saint).

The film features several set pieces that have entered screen legend, notably the crop-dusting sequence, in which Grant (on foot) is chased by a plane, and his desperate escape across the giant faces of Mount Rushmore at the film's climax. Hitchcock's request to film these scenes on location at the Mount Rushmore National Memorial was turned down by the US Department of the Interior, so life-size replicas were used instead.

MGM had originally wanted their contract star Cyd CHARISSE to play the part of Eve Kendall, but Hitchcock (who preferred blonde leading ladies) insisted on Saint. The director appears in his customary CAMEO as a man rushing to catch a bus, only to have the doors shut in his face.

The film's title derives from an enigmatic aside in *Hamlet*:

I am but mad north-northwest; when the wind is southerly I know a hawk from a handsaw.

Nosferatu, a Symphony of Horror (1922). F. W. MURNAU's classic vampire film, the first to feature Bram Stoker's bloodsucking Count DRACULA. It was scripted by Henrik Galeen, whose 1914 film *The Golem* (co-directed by Paul Wegener) was one of the first works in the German tradition of fantasy horror that also included such classics as Weine's THE CABINET OF DR CALIGARI (1919), LANG's *Destiny* (1922), and Wegener and Galeen's *The Student of Prague* (1926). Shot on location in Bremen to make the vampire's activities appear more realistic, the film also made effective use of such trickery as negative footage (to convey the sinister nature of the forest around the count's castle) and convulsive STOP-ACTION photography (to suggest his strength). While *Nosferatu* established many of the conventions of the Dracula movie, Max Schreck's hideously ugly count, with his pointed features and bird-like claws, was far removed from the suave sensual vampires of Bela LUGOSI or Christopher LEE, and others. Unlike most of its successors, the film remains genuinely frightening today; the Hungarian critic Béla Bélázs has written that "a chilly draught from doomsday" whistles through every scene.

"*Nosferatu* is the most visionary of all German films" wrote Werner HERZOG, who in 1979 remade the picture as *Nosferatu the Vampyre* with Klaus KINSKI in the lead. "In Murnau's film the vampire is without a soul, he is like an insect, a crab. My vampire...is so suffering, so human, so sad, so desperately longing for love that you don't see the claws and fangs any more." Herzog had hoped to follow Murnau by shooting in Bremen, but was obliged to settle for Delft in Holland. However, the *burgomeister* refused to allow the release of 11,000 rats into the streets for the scene in which Nosferatu's ship docks because the town had only just completed its own vermin-control programme. The animals were white rats from a laboratory in Hungary, laboriously painted grey for the sequence. Eventually, the city of Schiedam agreed to host the production.

notch Any cut or mark made on the edge of a film as a cue. The main types are: (1) The CHANGEOVER CUE for projectionists. (2) A mark used to identify a particular sequence of frames during editing. (3) A cut or mark introduced during the process of grading. This triggers a mechanism in the printer that alters the amount of light supplied and thus the density of the printed picture.

Nouvelle Vague *See* NEW WAVE.

Novak, Kim (Marilyn Pauline Novak; 1933–) Blonde US actress. Although she was uncomfortable before the camera and critics deplored her acting, Novak's cool sensuality helped her to become a major star in the 1950s. In 1957 she was America's top female box-office draw, replacing the previous year's winner, Marilyn MONROE. At various times she was romantically linked with Cary GRANT and Frank SINATRA.

The daughter of Czech immigrants, Novak began to model at the age of 11 and later demonstrated refrigerators as 'Miss Deepfreeze'. She was discovered by Columbia's casting director Max Arnow after studio boss Harry COHN ordered "Get me another blonde!" His star Rita HAYWORTH had defected to another studio and 20th Century-Fox had just made a sex symbol out of Monroe. Novak changed her name to Kim thinking that Hollywood only had room for one Marilyn.

After making her Columbia debut wth a bit part in *The French Line* (1954), Novak co-starred with Fred MACMURRAY in *Pushover*; director Richard Quine characterized her appeal as "the proverbial lady in the parlour and the whore in the bedroom." She became a major star with Joshua LOGAN's *Picnic* (1955), in which she played William HOLDEN's fiancée. The scene in which the couple dance slowly and sensually to the music of 'Moonglow' became one of the most famous of the decade. Despite her new fame, she was paid only her normal salary of $100 a week when she made *The Man with the Golden Gun* (1956) with Frank Sinatra.

After receiving the best reviews of her career for the biopic *Jeanne Eagels* (1957), Novak made the musical *Pal Joey* (1957) with Sinatra and Hayworth. The following year she confused James STEWART in both HITCHCOCK's VERTIGO and the comedy *Bell, Book and Candle*, in which she played a modern-day witch. That year, Cohn had a heart attack and died after reading press reports about her close involvement with Sammy Davis Jnr (shocking at the time because Davis was Black).

Novak's popularity began to fade in the mid 1960s, when her roles included the prostitute Polly the Pistol in Billy WILDER's *Kiss Me Stupid* (1964) and the title character in *The Amorous Adventures of Moll Flanders* (1965); her British co-star in the latter, Richard Johnson, briefly became her husband (1965–66). When the melodrama *The Legend of Lylah Clare* (1968) flopped dismally, its director Robert ALDRICH, asked pointedly "Is Kim Novak a joke in her own time?" By the mid 1970s she was appearing in undistinguished TV movies and such films as *Massacre at Blood Bath Drive-In*. Despite a strong comeback in *Just a Gigolo* (1979) few roles came her way in the 1980s and 1990s.

Novello, Ivor (Ivor Novello Davies; 1893–1951) British actor, composer, and writer, whose successes on the West End stage launched him into British and Hollywood films. As a silent star, the handsome dark-haired Novello was often compared to the 'Latin lover' Ramon Novarro. He also wrote 'Keep the Home Fires Burning', the most popular song of World War I.

Novello was born in Cardiff, the son of the singer and teacher Dame Clara Novello Davies; after training as a chorister, he wrote his first play in 1916 and made his stage debut in 1921. A year later he travelled to Hollywood to appear in *Carnival* and *The Bohemian Girl*, in which he co-starred with Gladys COOPER. He was an established matinée idol by the time he came to play a Parisian thief in *The Rat* (1925), adapted from his own successful play.

In 1926 Novello played a man wrongly suspected of being Jack the Ripper in *The Lodger* (US title *The Case of Jonathan Drew*; 1926), a film that made the name of its young director Alfred HITCHCOCK. Six years later Novello wrote and starred in a sound remake of the story with Maurice ELVEY directing. He stayed with Hitchcock to make *Downhill* (US title *When Boys Leave Home*; 1927), in which he played an expelled schoolboy (at the age of 34).

By 1929 Novello was Britain's top movie star. In the early 1930s, he demonstrated his versatility by composing music for Hitchcock's *Elstree Calling* (1930), co-scripting *Tarzan, the Ape Man* (1932) for MGM, and co-starring with Madeleine Carroll in Anatole LITVAK's *Sleeping Car*. Films adapted from Novello's plays and musicals include *Glamorous Night* (1937), *The Dancing Years* (1949), and a CINEMASCOPE version of *King's Rhapsody* (1955) starring Errol

FLYNN and Anna NEAGLE. Novello was close to Viven LEIGH, who co-starred with him in the London play *The Happy Hypocrite* (1936). Shortly after Laurence OLIVIER had been knighted, Novello visited the couple and irritated Leigh by continually called her 'Lady Olivier'. Finally she snapped "Oh, you bloody fool, will you have some fucking tea?"

Novello died while appearing in a stage revival of his *King's Rhapsody*.

nudity *See* SEX.

number.   number board The slate or board held in front of a filming camera immediately before the commencement of a shot; it contains such necessary information as the film title, the number of the shot and take, the names of the director, cinematographer, etc., whether the scene is interior or exterior, and the date. *See also* CLAPPER BOARD.

numbered sequels Although the first numbered SEQUEL, Hammer's *Quatermass II*, appeared as early as 1957, this way of selling a film by emphasizing its similarity to an earlier success only really took off during the 1980s. *Rocky 2* (1979) began the trend and *Superman 2* (1980) followed. Numbered sequels have a generally poor reputation with cinephiles, largely because they are so often the product of mere commercial calculation without fresh creative input. The longest series of sequels in the mainstream cinema is the *Star Trek* saga (1979–94); when the sixth and supposedly final part was released in 1991 most critics commented on the visible ageing of the cast. (*Star Trek; Generations*, with new actors, appeared in 1995.) In the field of schlock-horror, the prize must go to *Friday The Thirteenth Part VIII: Jason Takes Manhattan* (1989) – despite the fact that we were promised *Friday The Thirteenth: The Final Chapter* back in 1984. Numbered sequels particularly abound in straight-to-video releases.

Nykvist, Sven (1922–   ) Swedish cinematographer and occasional director, who won two Oscars for his work with Ingmar BERGMAN. Having begun his career as a 19-year-old assistant cameraman, he graduated to director of photography for *13 Chairs* (1945). *Under the Southern Cross* (1952), a documentary about Albert Schweitzer, was also co-directed and co-scripted by Nykvist.

It was, however, through his long association with Bergman that Nykvist made his name. This began with *The Virgin Spring* (1960), a medieval tale filmed in stark black-and-white. His distinctive photography, with its strong contrasts of light and dark, helped to establish the sombre mood of such films as *Through a Glass Darkly* (1961), *Winter Light* (1963), and *The Silence* (1963). In 1972 Nykvist won the Oscar for Best Cinematography with his bleak but beautiful work on Bergman's *Cries and Whispers*. His last Bergman films were *Autumn Sonata* (1978) and FANNY AND ALEXANDER (1982), which brought Nykvist his second Academy Award.

As his reputation grew, Nykvist was brought to Hollywood to make a series of films, beginning with Richard FLEISCHER's gangster story *The Last Run* (1971). This was followed by *The Dove* (1974), a beautifully filmed sea adventure, Louis MALLE's *Pretty Baby* (1978), and the Dino DE LAURENTIIS films *King of the Gypsies* (1978) and *Hurricane* (1979). His subsequent US work has included Alan J. PAKULA's *Starting Over* (1979), Paul Mazursky's *Willie and Phil* (1980), the remake of *The Postman Always Rings Twice* (1981), Philip KAUFMAN's *The Unbearable Lightness of Being* (1988), Woody ALLEN's *Crimes and Misdemeanours* (1989), Richard ATTENBOROUGH's *Chaplin* (1992), and *Sleepless in Seattle* (1993). In 1991 he directed the Swedish film *The Ox*, starring Bergman's old company players Liv ULLMANN and Max VON SYDOW.

O

Oakie, Jack (Lewis Delaney Offield; 1903–78) Plump US comic actor, who usually played happy dim-witted characters. Amongst his other achievements, he is credited with expanding the traditional DOUBLE TAKE into a triple take. He won an Oscar nomination as Best Supporting Actor for his performance as Napaloni, dictator of Bacteria, a caricature of Mussolini, in CHAPLIN'S THE GREAT DICTATOR (1940).

Born in Sedalia, Missouri, he grew up in Oklahoma (his screen name, Oakie, being the nickname for an Oklahoman). After working as a clerk in a New York brokerage firm, he made his stage debut in George M. Cohan's musical *Little Nellie Kelly* (1922). His first film role was a bit part in *Finders Keepers* (1928). Thereafter he rose quickly to stardom. Several of his films were scripted by Joseph MANKIEWICZ, the future writer-director, notably *Million Dollar Legs* (1932), a lively spoof of the 1932 Olympics that also starred W. C. FIELDS.

Oakie's best-known roles included an idiotic vaudevillian in *Once in a Lifetime* (1932) and Tweedledum in the all-star *Alice in Wonderland* (1933). He often played a college student, as in *College Humour* (1933), *College Rhythm* (1934), and *Collegiate* (1936). By the 1940s he was back in secondary roles and made only a handful of movies thereafter; in his last film, *Love Come Back* (1962), he supported Doris DAY and Rock HUDSON.

Oberhausen Manifesto *See* NEW CINEMA *under* NEW.

Oberon, Merle (Estelle Merle O'Brien Thompson 1911–79) British actress, who became one of the most glamorous Hollywood stars of the late 1930s and 1940s. Oberon owed her break in the movies to Alexander KORDA, who discovered her working as a dance hostess at the Café de Paris in London. From 1932 onwards he groomed her for stardom, largely on the strength of her lustrous beauty (the couple married in 1939 and divorced five years later). Her first major role, as Anne Boleyn in THE PRIVATE LIFE OF HENRY VIII, brought her to the attention of Sam GOLDWYN, who enticed her to Hollywood a few years later. Not all her subsequent roles were judiciously chosen, however; she was uneasy in the role of Cathy in WUTHERING HEIGHTS (1939) and even more so as Georges Sand in *A Song to Remember* (1944), an unconvincing BIOPIC about the private life of Chopin. Among her other credits were *The Scarlet Pimpernel* (1934), in which she played opposite Leslie HOWARD, her real-life lover at the time, *Beloved Enemy* (1936), *The Divorce of Lady X* (1938), and *Raffles* (1939), in which she starred opposite the "gentleman cracksman" David NIVEN. Filming of *I Claudius* (1936), arguably one of the most intriguing Hollywood projects never completed, was abandoned after Oberon was involved in a car accident (though the true reason for the film being stopped had more to do with the difficult behaviour of her co-star, Charles LAUGHTON).

In the 1940s Warner Brothers tried to groom Oberon as successor to Bette DAVIS but she failed to make much impression in a series of thrillers and tearjerkers. Thereafter her appearances became more occasional; her later films included *Desirée* (1954), in which she played Josephine to the Napoleon of Marlon BRANDO, *The Oscar* (1965), in which she played an over-the-hill film star, and *Hotel* (1966).

The details of Oberon's birth were kept deliberately obscure by her studios, the official version being that she was born in Tasmania. In fact, she was born in Bombay to a Singhalese mother (whom she later passed off as her maid) and spent her childhood in India, a background that might have threatened her career if it had become known. The truth was not revealed until some years after the star's death.

oblique-angle shot *See* CAMERA ANGLES *under* CAMERA.

O'Brien, Margaret (Angela Maxine O'Brien; 1937–) US actress, who created a sensation as a CHILD STAR in the 1940s. Making her film debut at the age of just four, O'Brien startled many observers with the professionalism that was to become a hallmark of her shortlived career. When a part required her to shed tears, the six-year-old O'Brien allegedly asked the director "When I cry, do you want the tears to run all the way or shall I stop halfway down?" Second only to Shirley TEMPLE as the most adored screen youngster of her generation, O'Brien proved a huge money-maker for MGM, who showcased her in such films as *Journey for Margaret* (1942), *Lost Angel* (1943), in which she played a child genius, and MEET ME IN ST LOUIS, in which she played Judy GARLAND's younger sister. Her popularity was officially acknowledged by the award of a Special Oscar in 1944. Despite further success with *Our Vines Have Tender Grapes* (1945), in which she starred with Edward G. ROBINSON, *Little Women* (1949), and *The Secret Garden* (1949), her refusal to be loaned to Disney for *Alice in Wonderland* led to her suspension by MGM. O'Brien switched to Columbia and, looking noticeably older, was kissed for the first time on screen in *Her First Romance* (1951). Thereafter her star waned fast and her few adult roles were all supporting parts. She finally received the earnings she had made as a child following a court case in 1977.

O'Connor, Donald (1925–) US actor, dancer, and singer, one of the top stars of the Hollywood MUSICAL during its golden age. Having made his film debut in *Sing You Sinners* (1938), O'Connor became well known to the public while still a teenager. Perky, energetic, and immensely inventive as a dancer and comedian, he played a range of supporting roles in the late 1930s and early 1940s, often with his own song-and-dance spot. His early credits include *Tom Sawyer Detective* (1938), *Chip off the Old Block* (1944), and *Patrick the Great* (1945). In 1949 he began one of Hollywood's most unlikely partnerships when he co-starred with Francis the Talking Mule in *Francis*, the first of six Universal comedies featuring the duo (O'Connor was replaced by Mickey ROONEY in 1955).

It was however, O'Connor's sparkling performance in SINGIN' IN THE RAIN (1952) that best demonstrated his precocity as a comedian, singer, and eccentric dancer. His acrobatic rendition of 'Make 'Em Laugh' is for many the highlight of the film. Large parts followed in *Call Me Madam* (1953) and *I Love Melvin* (1953), which included an inventive football ballet with Debbie REYNOLDS as the ball, *There's No Business Like Show Business* (1954), in which he shared top billing with Ethel Merman, Dan Dailey, and Marilyn MONROE, and *Anything Goes* (1956). In 1957 he took the title role in *The Buster Keaton Story*. Thereafter, the decline of the Hollywood musical left him with fewer opportunities; with Gene KELLY, he narrated the history of the genre in the popular compilation *That's Entertainment* (1974). Other more recent appearances have included those in Miloš FORMAN's *Ragtime* (1981) and *Pandemonium* (1982).

Odeon Tradename of a British cinema chain founded in 1933. The name derived from the Greek *odeion*, meaning a hall for music; in Britain, it had become almost synonymous with movie theatre itself by the time the controlling company was taken over by the RANK ORGANIZATION in 1941. The flagship of the chain was the Odeon in London's Leicester Square.

O'Hara, Maureen O'Hara (Maureen Fitzsimmons; 1920–) Irish actress, a popular leading lady of the 1940s and 1950s. A red-haired Dublin beauty, O'Hara distinguished herself at the Abbey Theatre School and made her screen debut in the British comedy *Kicking the Moon Around* (1938). A year later Alfred HITCHCOCK cast her as the heroine in his *Jamaica Inn* (1938), the first of many historical adventures.

Having been signed by RKO, she made a striking Hollywood debut as Esmeralda in the classic Charles LAUGHTON version of THE HUNCHBACK OF NOTRE DAME (1939). Although the limits of her range were cruelly revealed when she attempted more ambitious things in *A Bill of Divorcement* (1940), a major role in John FORD's *How Green was My Valley* (1941) restored her to favour. Subsequent films included the SWASHBUCKLER *The Black Swan* (1942), with Tyrone POWER, the wartime thriller *This Land is Mine* (1943), in which she appeared once more with Laughton, *Miracle on 34th Street* (1947), and the romantic yarn *At Sword's Point* (1952). In the 1950s Ford cast her opposite John WAYNE in three films – the Western *Rio Grande* (1950), *The Quiet Man* (1952), a much-loved romantic comedy set against the backdrop of rural Ireland, and the war story *The Wings of Eagles* (1957).

Dubbed the **Queen of Technicolor** largely because of the cinematic impact of her red hair, O'Hara remained popular throughout the 1950s, although the critics were rarely impressed. Later films included Carol REED's *Our Man in Havana* (1959), Disney's *The Parent Trap* (1961), in which she played Hayley MILLS's mother, and Sam PECKINPAH's *The Deadly Companions* (1962). She went on to partner James STEWART in *Mr Hobbs Takes a Vacation* (1962) and *The Rare Breed* (1966), Henry FONDA in *Spencer's Mountain* (1963), and Wayne again in *McLintock!* (1963) and *Big Jake* (1971).

Although considered a reliable choice by the studios, O'Hara's demure performances led some critics to accuse her of lacking a certain something when it came to more passionate scenes. Elsa LANCHESTER summed it up with the oft-repeated observation: "She looks as though butter wouldn't melt in her mouth – or anywhere else."

Scarlett O'Hara The headstrong heroine of David O. SELZNICK's Civil War epic GONE WITH THE WIND (1939). First introduced in Margaret Mitchell's best-selling novel of the same name (1936), Scarlett was based on the author's maternal grandmother, Annie Fitzgerald Stephens (1844–1934). Annie, the daughter of a Southern plantation owner, witnessed the burning of Atlanta in 1864 before returning to the neglected family farm. Selznick's long search for the perfect screen Scarlett quickly became part of Hollywood legend: after some 90 screen tests, much fevered speculation, and some heated wrangling, the part went to the little-known Vivien LEIGH.

Olivier, Laurence, Baron (1907–89) British actor and director, generally considered the leading classical actor of his generation. He was awarded a special Oscar for his lifetime achievement in 1979.

The son of an Anglican clergyman, Olivier won special praise from the actress Ellen Terry when he appeared in a school play at the age of ten. He went on to establish his reputation as a stage actor playing Shakespearean and other roles in the 1930s. His long screen career began humbly enough with a part in the German-made short *Hocus Pocus* (1930). In his early film roles he deliberately modelled himself on such matinée idols as John BARRYMORE and Ronald COLMAN; the films, most of which were made in

Britain, flopped badly and have rarely been revived.

Olivier's first Hollywood success came with GOLDWYN's classic WUTHERING HEIGHTS (1939), in which he played Heathcliff to Maureen O'HARA's Cathy; this was followed quickly by Alfred HITCHCOCK's REBECCA (1939), in which he co-starred with Joan FONTAINE, and MGM's *Pride and Prejudice* (1940) in which he was Darcy to Greer GARSON's Elizabeth. In *That Hamilton Woman* (British title *Lady Hamilton*; 1941), a film about Nelson and his mistress, he co-starred with Vivien LEIGH, whom he had recently married.

Olivier's finest achievements in the cinema were his remarkable versions of Shakespeare's *Henry V* (1944), *Hamlet* (1948), and RICHARD III (1956), all of which he both starred in and directed. Both his stirring wartime *Henry V* and his downbeat black-and-white *Hamlet* were duly honoured with Oscars.

His films of the 1950s included the moving *Carrie* (1952), about a man destroyed by love, and *The Prince and the Showgirl* (1958), in which the 'dream' combination of Olivier and Marilyn MONROE proved somewhat uneasy. The outstanding successes of his later career were *The Entertainer* (1960), in which he revived his triumphant stage performance as John Osborne's Archie Rice, and the convoluted thriller *Sleuth* (1972), in which he co-starred with Michael CAINE. The latter earned him his highest-ever fee, $200,000. Olivier cheerfully admitted that many of the roles he accepted in his later years – notably that of Zeus in the fantasy movie *Clash of the Titans* (1981) – were potboilers for his old age. His last appearance was in Derek JARMAN's *War Requiem* (1989).

Almost universally acknowledged as "the greatest of them all" (as Spencer TRACY put it), Olivier was knighted in 1947 and became the first actor to be created a life peer in 1970; one of the stages at the Royal National Theatre, of which he was a co-founder, is named in his honour.

In many ways a throwback to the great tradition of the English actor-managers, Olivier had little time for those younger performers who espoused the METHOD acting of Stanislavsky and Strasberg. When Dustin HOFFMAN, his co-star in *Marathon Man* (1976), insisted on staying awake for days on end because his character had to, Olivier merely suggested "Why don't you try acting, dear boy – it's so much easier."

Olmi, Ermanno (1931–) Italian director and screenwriter. Olmi was born into a peasant family and began work as a clerk in the Edison-Volta electric plant, where he took part in stage and film projects sponsored by the company. Between 1952 and 1959 he made some 40 short documentaries about the electricity industry. His first commercial release, the semidocumentary *Time Stood Still* (1959), was followed by a series of features notable for the realism and dignity with which they depict the lives of working-class characters.

Olmi's almost NEOREALISTIC style is characterized by straightforward camerawork and the use of nonprofessional actors. By the late 1960s he was working mainly in Italian television, although such films as *The Scavengers* (1969), *During the Summer* (1971), and *The Circumstance* (1974) were subsequently released to cinemas. In 1978 he was awarded the Palm d'or at the Cannes Film Festival for *The Tree of Wooden Clogs*, a three-hour epic about a peasant family in 19th-century Lombardy that has come to be regarded as a classic of modern Italian cinema. Since founding the innovative film school, Ipotesi Cinema, in 1980 Olmi has supervised the making of many shorts by young film-makers. In 1987 he directed *Long Live the Lady*, an allegory about capitalism and freedom. A year later, Olmi was awarded the Golden Lion at the Venice Festival for *The Legend of the Holy Drinker*, adapted from Joseph Roth's novel. His latest films are *Down the River* (1991), a documentary about the pollution of the river Po, and the biblical film *Genesis: the Creation and the Flood* (1995).

Olympia (*Olympische Spiele*; 1938) The official film of the XI Olympiad, held in HITLER's Berlin in 1936. Although initially reluctant, director Leni RIEFENSTAHL was persuaded to undertake the project by the secretary general of the German Olympic Committee and Hitler himself. Both had admired the mass choreography of *Triumph of the Will* (1935), her film of the Nuremberg rallies.

Having been assured that she could spend 18 months on postproduction work, Riefenstahl began to train her crew in the filming of sporting activity and to assess the various technical problems involved. During the 16 days of competition, Riefenstahl and her crews worked tirelessly, making innovative use of slow-motion photography and telephoto lenses to shoot 1.3 million feet of film. While Willy Zielke directed the Prologue in Olympia, Greece, Riefenstahl began to edit the footage singlehanded. The undoubted star of the main *Festival of the People* section was the Black US athlete Jesse Owens, who won gold in four events. Riefenstahl's favourite sequence was the marathon, which she cut to suggest the growing exhaustion of the runners. Highlights of the more lyrical *Festival of Beauty* section include the opening sequence in the Olympic Village and the yachting, gymnastics, and springboard diving competitions.

Although Hitler himself was delighted with the film, it immediately caused controversy elsewhere. At the 1938 Venice Festival British and US jurors tried to have it disqualified from the Best Feature Award on the grounds that it was a documentary. Despite accusations that she had produced a work of Nazi propaganda, the director was invited to subsequent Olympiads in gratitude for her often exhilirating achievement. As the critic Frederick W. Ott wrote:

> *Olympia* is nothing less than an education in the art of the motion picture.

one. *One Flew Over the Cuckoo's Nest* (1975) Miloš FORMAN's satirical fantasy about rebellion and repression in a mental asylum. Hoping to escape work on a prison farm, Randle McMurphy (Jack NICHOLSON) has himself committed to the local asylum, where he finds himself subjected to the even more rigorous regime of Nurse Mildred Ratched (Louise Fletcher). His attempts to subvert the system end in tragedy.

Kirk DOUGLAS had bought the rights to a stage adaptation of Ken Kesey's novel in the mid 1960s and had enjoyed considerable Broadway success as McMurphy. However, his schedule had prevented him from bringing the role to the screen and in 1975 he presented the property to his son Michael DOUGLAS, then better known as a producer than as a movie star. To direct the film, Douglas hired the Czech Miloš Forman, whose anti-authoritarian satires had attracted Western attention in the 1960s. The cast was led by Jack Nicholson, who had already demonstrated a facility for playing manic antiheroes in such pictures as *Five Easy Pieces* (1970), and Louise Fletcher, a relative newcomer. Other parts were played by then largely unknown actors, such as Brad Dourif, Christopher Lloyd,

Danny DE VITO, and the Cree Indian artist and ex-rodeo rider Will Sampson. Two non-professionals also appeared – Dean R. Brooks, superintendent of the hospital in which the film was shot, and former state governor Tim McCall, who played a TV newsreader.

Having checked into the hospital while he completed the shooting script, Forman encouraged the supporting cast to sit in on group therapy sessions. During the filming itself, one of the patients took advantage of the removal of protective window bars to throw himself from a third-storey window. The local paper's report was headlined "One Flew Out of the Cuckoo's Nest."

An enormous critical and commercial success ($120 million receipts worldwide), the film swept the Oscars, being the first picture since IT HAPPENED ONE NIGHT to take the four topline Awards.

While *Cuckoo's Nest* confirmed the growing reputations of Nicholson and Forman, it proved something of a millstone for Fletcher, who has yet to emerge from Nurse Ratched's shadow.

one-reeler A short movie that could be shot on a single REEL of film. One-reelers, which generally ran for 10–12 minutes, were standard in the early years of the movie industry. D. W. GRIFFITH directed more than 100 such films in 1909, his first year with BIOGRAPH Studios. The one-reeler was also the standard vehicle for the early Mack SENNETT comedies starring Charlie CHAPLIN, Buster KEATON, and the KEYSTONE Kops. *See also* SHORT SUBJECT; TWO-REELER.

O'Neal. Ryan O'Neal (1941–) Square-jawed US actor, a popular leading man in the early 1970s whose career subsequently stalled. A former lifeguard, he entered television as a stuntman, later becoming well known in the TV soap opera *Peyton Place* (1964–68), in which he played the handsome Rodney Harrington (his love interest, Allison, was played by another unknown, Mia FARROW). It was as the male lead in the lachrymose *Love Story* (1970), however, that he became a star; the part also brought him an Oscar nomination. Luck was definitely on O'Neal's side when he landed the role: it had already been turned down by Beau BRIDGES, Jon Voight, Michael YORK, and Michael DOUGLAS, amongst others. He went on to star in such movies as *What's Up Doc?* (1972), a madcap comedy created as a vehicle for him and Barbra STREISAND, and the

touching *Paper Moon* (1973), which also launched the film career of his daughter Tatum.

Thereafter his popularity declined sharply, though he acquitted himself well enough in KUBRICK's *Barry Lyndon* (1975), the all-star *A Bridge Too Far* (1977), and the crime melodrama *Driver* (1978). *Oliver's Story* (1979), a sequel to the film in which he made his name, seemed like a desperate move to revive a flagging career. More recent releases have included two notable disasters, *Fever Pitch* (1985) and Norman Mailer's *Tough Guys Don't Dance* (1987). Although his stormy relationships with Farrah Fawcett and his own children have kept him in the gossip columns, O'Neal has found very little work in recent years.

Tatum O'Neal (1962–) US actress, the daughter of Ryan O'Neal and Joanna Moore. At the age of 11 Tatum O'Neal found sudden fame in Peter BOGDANOVICH's *Paper Moon* (1973), a Depression-era comedy in which she appears with her father. Her performance as a streetwise orphan brought her an Oscar for Best Supporting Actress, making her the youngest-ever Award winner. Despite protestations that she did not like acting, she adjusted easily enough to her new-found status as a movie star. Asked by a school inspector whether she was afraid that her maths might suffer owing to the demands of stardom, she replied: "No, I'll have an accountant." Her subsequent credits have included Bogdanovich's *Nickelodeon* (1976), the misconceived remake *International Velvet* (1978), and the teen comedy *Little Darlings* (1980). Since the 1980s public attention has focused less on her film work than on her relationship and eventual marriage to maverick tennis star John McEnroe (a match about which father Ryan expressed some reservations). She played a small role in *Little Noises* (1991).

On the Waterfront (1954) Elia KAZAN's intense drama about corruption on the New York waterfront. In the plot, failed boxer Terry Malloy (Marlon BRANDO) works for Johnny Friendly (Lee J. Cobb), a union boss whose strongarm tactics result in the death of a troublesome longshoreman. Terry is persuaded by the murdered man's sister (Eva Marie Saint) and her priest (Karl MALDEN) to inform, even though it will implicate his own brother, Charley (Rod STEIGER), who is Friendly's lawyer.

Following the murder of a dockland hiring boss in 1948, *New York Sun* journalist Malcolm Johnson began a Pulitzer Prize-winning series of articles exposing corruption in the shipping industry. Budd Schulberg, who had produced a hard-hitting exposé of boxing in *The Harder They Fall*, was already working on a script based on Johnson's journalism when Kazan contacted him about making a film set in New York. Columbia boss Harry COHN was initially reluctant to back a picture on such a topic, particularly one that intended to deal with it in such a realistic way; in the event, he passed the project over to independent producer Sam Spiegel but retained distribution rights.

Having become something of a location specialist, Kazan opted to shoot on the Hoboken waterfront and the bleakness of this setting added considerably to the film's power. He offered the lead to Marlon Brando, who had been nominated for an Oscar on both the previous occasions they had worked together (*A Streetcar Named Desire*, 1951; *Viva Zapata*, 1952). This time he would go one better and take the Best Actor Award – although his hesitation over accepting the role nearly led to Kazan casting Frank SINATRA. Brando was allegedly unhappy with the film's most famous scene (completed after many retakes in a small downtown studio), in which he confronts his brother about his detrimental impact on his life:

I coulda been a contender. I coulda had class and been somebody. Real class. Instead of a bum, let's face it, which is what I am. It was you, Charley.

Apart from Brando's Oscar, the film picked up another seven Academy Awards, including those for Best Picture, Best Director, and Best Screenplay.

While the critics applauded the performances, the documentary realism of Boris Kaufman's photography, and Leonard Bernstein's score, they were divided on the film's message. Both Kazan and Schulberg had testified before the House UnAmerican Activities Commission and many saw the film, with its suggestion that informing was a democratic duty, as a thinly veiled justification of their actions. In the novelization of his script, Schulberg altered the ending; Terry is butchered with an ice-pick, packed into a barrel of quicklime, and deposited in a swamp.

Oomph Girl   The nickname of the US actress Ann SHERIDAN, reflecting the tough but optimistic roles she often played, especially during World War II. She herself disliked the name, saying that Oomph was "the sound a fat man makes when he bends over to tie his laces in a phone booth."

Open City   *See* ROMA, CITTA APERTA.

Ophüls, Max   (1902–57) German-born director, who won wide praise for his sophisticated and visually gorgeous romances in the 1940s and 1950s. Ophüls, who began his career in the German theatre, made his feature debut in 1930 with *Rather Cod Liver Oil*. The most significant of his German films was *Liebelei* (1932), about the doomed love of a young girl and a soldier; the contrast between the visual extravagance of the film and the harsh reality of the story is typical of his work.

After Hitler's rise to power, Ophüls left Germany and worked in France, the Netherlands, and Italy on such films as *La Signora di tutti* (1934), in which he demonstrated both his mastery of the moving camera and his fascination with female sexuality. With the German invasion of France in 1940 Ophüls departed to America, but failed to find employment there until 1947, when Douglas FAIRBANKS JNR invited him to direct *The Exile*, a swashbuckling adventure about the young Charles II. His most notable US film, however, was *Letter from an Unknown Woman* (1948), starring Joan FONTAINE and Louis Jourdan in a love affair that gradually turns sour; like a number of Ophüls's films, it is set in 19th-century Vienna, allowing the director free rein to indulge his taste for lavish settings and decor.

After further US success with *Caught* (1949) and *The Reckless Moment* (1949), Ophüls returned to France to direct *La Ronde* (1950), a highly stylized examination of the many faces of love, and *Le Plaisir* (1951), a collection of three stories by Maupassant. Paris was also the setting for *The Earrings of Madame de...* (1953), an ornate drama about the tangled affairs of a fashionable lady (Danielle Darrieux) and her husband (Charles BOYER). The central character's earrings become a symbol of the materialism and hollow values of the world she inhabits.

Ophüls's last film, *Lola Montès* (1955), rivals *The Earrings of Madame de...* as his most accomplished work. The film contrasts the romantic memories of the 19th-century adventuress Lola Montès with the degrading reality of her life as a circus attraction.

optical. optical printer A projector-camera combination used to copy and manipulate pre-shot images. First introduced in the 1920s, the device consists basically of a projector, loaded with exposed and processed film, pointed at a camera, loaded with unexposed film; when the two machines are synchronized, projected frames are photographed through the camera lens and duplicated on raw stock.

In practice, there are many variables that can be used to alter or combine images, making the optical printer an extraordinarily flexible tool for the film-maker. Most use two or more projectors, the images from which are directed onto the camera lens by mirrors or prisms. This permits the creation of a whole range of SPECIAL EFFECTS in which images from two or more sources are combined. Such effects as DISSOLVES, MULTIPLE EXPOSURES, stationary and travelling MATTES, and the combination of live-action with miniatures or animation can all be produced in this way.

Special lenses can be used to distort proportions or alter perspectives in the printer, while filters can correct colour or contrast values in processed footage. By reducing the distance between camera and projector, a film-maker can zoom in on the main subject, effectively changing e.g. a medium shot into a close-up. Increasing the distance between camera and projector has the opposite effect. Similarly, reducing or increasing the speed of the projector relative to that of the camera can be used to create such effects as FREEZE FRAMES or PIXILLATION. By opening or closing the camera shutter, images can be faded in or out.

With so many complex variables to manipulate, professional optical printers are usually computer-controlled.

optical sound A method of recording SOUND on photographic film. Although Eugene Lauste had devised the essentials of recording sound on film as early as 1910, his process could not be used owing to a lack of effective amplification. In the event, early sound systems all depended on cumbersome gramophone-projector combinations that were difficult to synchronize in cinemas. Having been introduced in the feature *The Air Circus* (1928), optically recorded sound soon made all such sound-on-disc systems obsolete.

During filming microphones convert sound into electrical impulses of varying strength; these power a lamp that converts them into equivalently varying light beams. The sound has now been translated into a form recordable on a photo-sensitive track adjacent to the film frames (the two main types being the VARIABLE-DENSITY TRACK and the VARIABLE-AREA TRACK).

To reproduce the sound during screening, the system is put into reverse; the beam from a constant-intensity 'exciter lamp' is focused onto the soundtrack and emerges on the other side as a beam of varying intensity. This modulated beam excites a photo-electric cell to emit electric impulses, which are converted into sound by a loudspeaker.

Owing to its technical superiority and its flexibility in mixing and editing, MAGNETIC sound has been favoured for most recording since the 1950s. The magnetic master is usually converted into optical form for release to cinemas.

option An exclusive right, lasting a set period, to develop a 'property' (a novel, play, OUTLINE or any other copyright material) for possible filming. An option, which can usually be bought for 5–10% of the outright cost of a property, gives its purchaser time to prepare a TREATMENT and raise funding, while preventing anyone else from using it during the period of the agreement.

Lapsed options can be sold to any other interested party or renewed for a further payment; if a production results, full rights are usually payable on the first day of PRINCIPAL PHOTOGRAPHY.

original screenplay A SCREENPLAY that owes nothing to an original novel, play, TV production, or other source. The annual ACADEMY AWARDS ceremony distinguishes between Oscars for screenplays "written directly for the screen" and those "based on material from another medium."

Many regard a film made from an original screenplay as the purest form of cinema, since it is conceived from the start in filmic 'language', suffering none of the compromises inherent in literary or theatrical adaptations. During Hollywood's Golden Era, contracted teams of studio writers ensured a steady stream of original screenplays; today they are speculatively written or specially commissioned from an OUTLINE.

Orphée (1949) Jean COCTEAU's extraordinary poetic fantasy, a personal allegory about love, death, and the creative process. Adapted from Cocteau's prewar stage play (1924), the film is a loose reworking of the myth of the poet Orpheus and his journey into hell to retrieve his dead wife, Eurydice. Cocteau uses startling contemporary imagery (Death's followers are leather-clad bikers) and special effects, including an entry through a mirror into a modern Hades reminiscent of Nazi-occupied Paris. Although much of its symbolism is impenetrable, the film remains a fascinating adventure in cinematic devices. "It is a drama of the visible and the invisible," said Cocteau, "I interwove many myths." Jean Marais (Cocteau's long-time companion) starred as Orpheus and Maria Casares as the Princess of Death. The superb photography and art design were by Nicholas Hayer and Jean d'Eaubonne respectively. The film, which took first prize at the Venice Festival, was dedicated to Christian Berard (1902–49), its designer.

In 1959 Cocteau rounded off his cinematic career with *Le Testament d'Orphée*, a still more bizarre piece about the death and resurrection of a poet. The amazing cast included not only Marais and Casares but also Pablo Picasso, Brigitte BARDOT, Yul BRYNNER, Françoise Sagan, Charles Aznavour, and Cocteau himself.

Oscar A gold-plated figurine, properly known as the ACADEMY AWARD statuette, awarded annually by the ACADEMY OF MOTION PICTURE ARTS AND SCIENCES for the best film work in various categories. According to one account, Bette DAVIS named the figure after her husband, Harman O(scar) Nelson, because she thought its buttocks resembled his. According to another, it owes its nickname to a long-forgotten secretary who, on seeing the newly cast figure in 1929, remarked that it reminded her of her uncle Oscar.

> The statuette is a perfect symbol of the movie business – a powerful athletic body clutching a gleaming sword, with half of his head, the part that holds his brains, completely sliced off.
> FRANCES MARION, 1928.

Oshima, Nagisa (1932–) Japanese director and screen-writer. The son of a government official, Oshima studied law and political science at the University of Kyoto.

In the 1950s he entered the film industry as an assistant director at Shochiku's Ofuna studios and founded the magazine *Eiga Hihyo*, which was noted for its highly critical attitude to most Japanese filmmaking of the time.

Oshima made his debut as a director with *A Town of Love and Hope* (1959), a film remarkable for its open hostility towards traditional Japanese values. A year later he earned praise from the critics for *Night and Fog in Japan* (1960). However, following the commercial failure of *The Christian Rebel* (1962), Oshima left the Shochiku studios and worked freelance for a time, also undertaking some television and documentary work. In 1965 he formed an independent production company with his wife Akiko Koyama, who was to become a regular performer in his films.

In the later 1960s Oshima gradually began to attract international attention, especially with *Death by Hanging* (1968), a film about the execution of a Korean for the rape and murder of two Japanese girls. The film was both an attack on capital punishment and an indictment of Japanese attitudes towards ethnic minorities. Oshima, who co-scripted the film, was also the narrator. *Diary of a Shinjuku Thief* (1968), which he again co-scripted, linked a couple's personal quest for sexual freedom to a wider desire for social freedom, while *Boy* (1969) was a black comedy about a child whose parents force him to feign injury from car accidents so that they can blackmail the drivers. *The Ceremony* (1971), in which a traditional wedding must proceed despite the absence of the bride, and *Dear Summer Sisters* (1973) were further attacks on Japanese ways; the latter begins as a film about a holiday romance and then moves to an examination of the atrocities committed by the Japanese during World War II.

In 1975 Oshima founded Oshima Productions and began to move into bigger-budget international film-making. The following year saw the release of his controversial Japanese-French co-production AI NO CORRIDA (*Empire of the Senses*). The film, a masterly examination of sexual obsession and violence, was initially banned by US customs and led to Oshima being prosecuted for obscenity in Japan (the charges were later dropped). *Empire of Passion* (1978), a tale of an adulterous couple haunted by the ghost of the woman's husband, lacked the depth of its predecessor and was much more open to charges of exploitative eroticism.

Oshima's subsequent films include *Merry Christmas, Mr Lawrence* (1983), an English-language film about a World-War-II Japanese prisoner-of-war camp, and *Max Mon Amour* (1986), an odd tale of a British diplomat's wife in Paris who falls in love with a chimpanzee. He has also published several books of film criticism and analysis.

O'Sullivan, Maureen (1911–) Irish actress, who specialized in reserved and gentle roles (often as the heroine's friend or sister). Having made her screen debut in 1930, O'Sullivan became famous playing Jane to Johnny WEISSMULLER'S TARZAN in a series of jungle movies that began with *Tarzan the Ape Man* (1932) and continued with the likes of *Tarzan and His Mate* (1934), *Tarzan Finds a Son* (1939), etc. Although she appeared in over 60 features, mainly in supporting roles, few of these are now remembered. Exceptions include *The Barretts of Wimpole Street* (1934), the GARBO version of *Anna Karenina* (1935), the MARX BROTHERS' *A Day at the Races* (1937), *Pride and Prejudice* (1940), and the comedy *Never Too Late* (1965). After a long hiatus she returned to the big screen in her mid seventies, with parts in Francis Ford COPPOLA'S *Peggy Sue Got Married* and Woody ALLEN'S *Hannah and her Sisters* (both 1986). In the latter she played the mother of her real-life daughter, Mia FARROW.

O'Toole, Peter (1932–) Lanky Irish-born British actor, who usually plays eccentric or dissipated characters. He was an overnight success in his first major part, the title role of LAWRENCE OF ARABIA (1962), and a leading box-office draw in the late 1960s and early 1970s.

The son of a bookie, O'Toole was born in Connemara and raised in Leeds. Having left school at 14 to join the Yorkshire *Evening Post* as an office boy, he subsequently worked as a reporter before winning a scholarship to RADA.

O'Toole made his first professional stage appearance in 1955 and his screen debut with a minor role in Walt DISNEY'S *Kidnapped* (1959). Three years later, David LEAN took a chance on the unknown actor after Albert FINNEY declined the role of T. E. Lawrence in the $25-million epic. The part brought him an Oscar nomination as Best Actor. Further

acclaim followed for his role as Henry II in *Becket*, with Richard BURTON as the martyred bishop. To play the scene in which the drunken Henry asks "Will no one rid me of this meddlesome priest?", O'Toole, a notoriously hard drinker, became genuinely inebriated.

His other roles of the 1960s included the title character in *Lord Jim* (1965), a private detective in William WYLER'S *How to Steal a Million* (1966), Henry II once again in *The Lion in Winter* (1968), with Katharine HEPBURN, and the title role in the musical remake of GOODBYE, MR CHIPS (1969).

Owing largely to problems caused by his drinking, O'Toole's career became far more erratic during the 1970s. In 1972 he won another Oscar nomination as a dotty earl in *The Ruling Class* but also suffered a flop with *Man of La Mancha*, with Sophia LOREN. After several rather barren years he made a comeback with Oscar-nominated performances in two films about Hollywood, *The Stuntman* (1980) and *My Favourite Year* (1982); the latter saw him playing a drunken hellraising actor based mainly on Errol FLYNN. Thereafter he moved into secondary parts in such films as *Supergirl* (1984), *The Last Emperor* (1986), and *King Ralph* (1990), in each of which he played the mentor to the main character. Both *High Spirits* (1988) and *Rebecca's Daughters* (1992) saw him starring in his familiar role as a dissipated aristocrat.

otto e mezzo   *See 8½ under* EIGHT.

Our Gang A group of child actors who appeared in a number of slapstick shorts produced by Hal ROACH in the 1920s. Its best known members were the fat Spanky McFarland (1928–93) and the dog Pete. None of the Gang went on to find success in adult roles. With frequent changes of personnel, the team survived until the mid 1940s.

out. out-take Any footage that is not included in the final version of a movie, usually because it contains technical or performing errors or because it is considered less effective than an alternative TAKE of the same shot. The ratio of footage shot to that used (SHOOTING RATIO) will depend very much on the nature of the movie and the perfectionism of the director. Because of their unpredictable nature, high-speed action scenes usually produce numerous out-takes: the famous chariot-race sequence in BEN-HUR (1925) was edited down from over 200,000 ft of footage to just 750 ft in the final film.

Some film-makers, including the so-called 'one-shot' directors GRIFFITH, PABST, and DE MILLE, seem to envisage the final film better than others, in effect editing in the camera rather than in the cutting room. At the other extreme, Michael CIMINO's two-and-a-half-hour HEAVEN'S GATE (1981) was the result of 220 hours of filmed material.

Out-takes may also result from a studio or distributor forcing a director to remove scenes deemed too violent or sexually explicit.

out of sync Out of SYNCHRONIZATION; the situation in which a film's sound and picture do not match. This is especially noticeable when lip movements do not coincide with what is said. The phenomenon is to some extent unavoidable when DUBBING from one language to another; otherwise, it is caused by poor printing.

Outlaw, The (1943) Howard HUGHES's once-controversial Western, now mainly remembered for the outrage provoked by Jane RUSSELL's cleavage. Having completed the film in 1941, Hughes fought the Production Code Administration for a seal of approval for six years (*see* HAYS CODE). In 1943 the film was given a brief showing in San Francisco but hostile public reaction seemed to rule out a general release. Hughes finally distributed the film nationwide without the seal in 1947.

Having produced the story as a debut showpiece for Russell, his new discovery, Hughes insisted on taking over from the original director, Howard HAWKS. During principal photography he shot some 470,000 feet of film, which he was then obliged to reduced by a ratio of 45:1.

Although the story centres upon Billy the Kid (Jack Beutel), Hughes had little doubt about the real sources of its appeal and personally built a specially engineered brassiere to enhance Russell's charms (in the event she did not wear it). Russell also posed straddling a haystack with a gun in each hand for a poster with the slogan 'Mean, Moody, and Magnificent'. Another provocative publicity shot showed her on a bale sucking a piece of straw.

The film also starred Walter HUSTON as Doc Holliday and Thomas Mitchell as Sheriff Pat Garrett. Russell played Rio, Billy's half-breed love, who causes dissension among the male characters. The plot, which is mostly a prolonged chase, is based on the premise that Billy the Kid was not killed as supposed but lived to fight again.

outline A brief plot synopsis, including the main characters, that may form the basis of a film. If accepted or OPTIONED for development, an outline will be turned into a TREATMENT.

over-the-shoulder shot (OSS) A shot taken from behind a performer's shoulder to show what his or her character sees. By including part of the shoulder in frame, the shot indicates clearly that it is supposed to represent that character's POINT OF VIEW. Its most common application is to show facial reactions to dialogue. Most conversation scenes are built up by CROSS-CUTTING back and forth from listener to speaker as the discussion develops.

P

Pabst, G(eorg) W(ilhelm) (1885–1967)
Austrian director and producer, who led the
German cinema's move towards pessimistic
realism in the 1920s. Born in Bohemia,
Pabst studied engineering before enrolling
at Vienna's Academy of Decorative Arts.
After graduating he worked as an actor
(from 1906) and stage director (from
1918). In 1921 he moved to Berlin to assist
Carl Froelich with the direction of two films,
later making his own directorial debut with
The Treasure (1923). *Joyless Street* (1925), a
story of poverty in postwar Vienna, introduced the stark realism and leftist social
commitment that would mark Pabst's later
works; it also gave Greta GARBO one of her
first major roles. A more subjective and
EXPRESSIONIST style characterized *Secrets of a
Soul* (1926), a study of phobia and obsession. One of the first films to show the influence of Freudian ideas, it also included
an innovative multiple-exposure DREAM
sequence.

The Love of Jeanne Ney (1927), set against
the backdrop of contemporary Paris, proved
a rehearsal for Pabst's masterpiece,
Pandora's Box (1928), a brilliant screen
adaptation of the Lulu plays of Wedekind.
Louise BROOKS starred as the promiscuous
femme fatale Lulu, who finally meets her
nemesis at the hands of Jack the Ripper. The
classic *Diary of a Lost Girl* (1929) used the
career of another provocative innocent
(again played by Brooks) to cast a highly
critical eye upon contemporary German
society. Pabst then ventured into sound
with *Comrades of 1918* (1930), a chilling
antiwar film that brought protests from the
National Socialist Party.

When the Nazis came to power Pabst
worked in France for a while before moving
on to Hollywood, where he directed
Warners' *A Modern Hero* (1934), a moral
tale about a greedy tycoon, but received no
further offers. On the outbreak of World
War II he declared his wish to become a US
citizen but soon afterwards returned to Germany to make films for the Nazis. After the

war, however, he made *The Trial* (1948)
an Austrian film that denounced anti-
Semitism and won the Best Direction prize
at the Venice Film Festival. Nazism was also
attacked in *The Last Ten Days* (1955), about
the final days of Hitler's life, and *The Jackboot
Mutiny* (1955). Pabst retired a year later
after suffering a stroke.

Pacino, Al (1940–) US actor of Sicilian
descent, best known for playing GANGSTERS
and low-life characters. After an extremely
sheltered childhood, during which he was
allowed out of the house only to go to school
and to the cinema, Pacino quickly developed a taste for performing in public and
worked as a dancer, stage actor, and stand-
up comedian. Appearances as a gigolo in
Me, Natalie (1969) and a drug pusher in *The
Panic in Needle Park* (1971) led to his breakthrough role as Marlon BRANDO's sensitive
son Michael in THE GODFATHER (1972). The
metamorphosis of Pacino's character from
a likeable youth into a frightening cold-
blooded manipulator provides the central
thread of the film and its sequel, THE GODFA-
THER, PART II (1974).

An exponent of METHOD acting, Pacino
established a reputation for the lengths he
would go to identify with his characters
in such movies as Sidney LUMET's *Serpico*
(1973), in which he played a seedy detective, and the same director's *Dog Day
Afternoon* (1975), in which he played a
homosexual driven to rob a bank.

After another gangster part in the brutal
Scarface (1983), Pacino's career took a serious nosedive with the disastrous epic *Revolution* (1985), which saw him badly miscast
in a historical role. Pacino subsequently
avoided the cinema for several years before
bouncing back with admired peformances
in the thriller *Sea of Love* (1989) and the
comic-book adventure *Dick Tracy* (1990),
for which he donned grotesque make-up to
play the villain Big Boy. He also reclaimed
his status as a major box-office draw with
THE GODFATHER, PART III (1990) – in preparation for which he had his teeth filed down to

make him look older (they were capped after the film was made). Subsequent films include *Glengarry Glen Ross* (1992), in which he played a ruthless real-estate salesman, and *Scent of a Woman* (1992), which earned him an Oscar for his performance as a blind army veteran on a spree in New York. He prepared himself for this role by wearing a black hood over his head for hours on end; he later told his co-star Chris O'Donnell "I didn't see it, but I hear you gave a great performance." His most recent film is *Carlito's Way* (1993).

Page, Geraldine (1924–87) US actress, who made her name on Broadway and subsequently divided her time between the live stage, the cinema, and television. Page, who made her film debut in 1947, became particularly associated with the plays of Tennessee Williams in the 1950s. In 1954 she was cast opposite John WAYNE in the Western *Hondo* after the role was refused by Katharine HEPBURN; although Warner Brothers were so unhappy with her performance in one scene that they demanded a re-shoot, she was rewarded with an Oscar nomination. After further Broadway success, she starred in screen versions of Williams's *Summer and Smoke* (1961) and *Sweet Bird of Youth* (1962). Although the first was judged disappointing, her performance opposite Paul NEWMAN in the latter drew comparisons with Bette DAVIS. Despite her prestige as an actress, subsequent films received mixed notices and Page never quite realized her promise on the screen.

Her movies of the 1960s and 1970s included *Dear Heart* (1965), Francis Ford COPPOLA's *You're a Big Boy Now* (1967), Disney's *The Happiest Millionaire* (1968), the Muriel Spark adaptation *Nasty Habits* (1976), in which she starred with Glenda JACKSON, and Woody ALLEN's *Interiors* (1978). Her starring role in *The Trip to Bountiful* (1985) finally won her an Oscar on her eighth nomination. Page, who was married to the actor Rip Torn, died of a heart attack while appearing in *Blithe Spirit* on Broadway.

Pagnol, Marcel (1895–1974) French director, producer, and writer. The son of a schoolmaster, Pagnol grew up in Marseilles and rural Provence. After serving in World War I he too worked as a schoolteacher, writing novels and plays in his spare time. His breakthrough as a dramatist came with the comedy *Topaze* (1928), after which he enjoyed further success with the trilogy of plays *Marius* (1929), *Fanny* (1931), and *César* (1936), about waterfront life in Marseilles.

Pagnol began his involvement in the film business in the 1930s, starting the journal *Cahiers du film* in 1931 and opening his own studios near Marseilles in 1934. After adapting the first two parts of his Marseilles trilogy into screenplays for Alexander KORDA and Marc Allégret respectively, he filmed the third part himself. In collaboration with the Provençal novelist Jean Giono, Pagnol went on to create a series of classic films set in the South of France: *Harvest* (*Regain*; 1937), *The Baker's Wife* (1938), and *The Well-Digger's Daughter* (1940). His most successful postwar film was his adaptation of Daudet's *Lettres de mon moulin* (1954).

In 1946 Pagnol became the first filmmaker to be elected to the Académie Française. He published a memoir evoking his idyllic childhood in Provence, *La Gloire de mon père*, in 1957, following this with a similar volume, *Le Château de ma mère*, a year later.

Recent years have seen a remarkable upsurge of interest in Pagnol's work. In the late 1980s Claude BERRI's two-part film *Jean de Florette* (1986) and *Manon des Sources* (1987), adapted from two novels that Pagnol had based on his own earlier film *Manon des Sources* (1953), played to packed houses in France and abroad. This was followed by the Yves ROBERT films *La Gloire de mon père* and *Le Château de ma mère* (both 1991), which dramatized incidents from Pagnol's memoirs.

Paisá (1946) Roberto ROSSELLINI's pioneering NEOREALIST film about the defeat of Italy in World War II. It consists of six unrelated vignettes tracing the Allied advance, from the invasion of Sicily in 1943 to the battle for the Po delta in 1945. The title is a colloquial form of the Italian for 'peasant'; during the war, this had come to serve as a patriotic greeting, meaning 'countryman'.

Using the same neorealist techniques Rossellini had employed on ROME, OPEN CITY the previous year, the film creates a sense of immediacy described by the US critic James AGEE as "the illusion of the present tense." Although loosely scripted by Rossellini, FELLINI, and others, much of the action was improvised. The film, shot on locations throughout Italy, employed only nonprofessionals and adhered closely to newsreel methods.

Among the cast was a Black GI, Dots M. Johnson, whose character was used to equate the injustices suffered by Black Americans with those inflicted on ordinary Italians by the war. Similar characters (invariably played by John Kitzmiller) featured in several other neorealist pictures, including Luigi Zampa's *Vivere in pace* (1947) and Alberto Lattuada's *Without Pity* (1948).

At the time, the film was less warmly received than its predecessor; Rossellini concluded his wartime trilogy a year later with *Germany, Year Zero*. Despite its lack of commercial success, *Paisá* has been cited as a key influence by such directors as Gillo PONTECORVO, Ermanno OLMI, and the TAVIANI BROTHERS. It also inspired Ingrid BERGMAN to abandon her Hollywood career to make a film with Rossellini. Their personal and professional liaison, which began during the filming of *Stromboli* (1949), scandalized Hollywood, which blacklisted the actress until the mid 1950s.

Pakula, Alan J. (1928–) US director and screenwriter, who has also produced most of his films. Pakula studied drama at Yale before becoming an assistant in the cartoon department at Warner Brothers. In 1950 he joined MGM as an apprentice, being promoted to production assistant the following year. Later, while working as an associate producer at Paramount, he began a long association with the director Richard Mulligan, producing *Fear Strikes Out* (1957), *To Kill a Mockingbird* (1962), and *Up the Down Staircase* (1967) amongst others.

Pakula came late to directing, having passed the age of 40 when he made his debut with *The Sterile Cuckoo* (British title *Pookie*; 1969), a sex comedy starring Liza MINNELLI; the film was not rapturously received. His second film, *Klute* (1971), an adult thriller starring Jane FONDA (in an Oscar-winning performance as a prostitute) and Donald SUTHERLAND fared much better. However, *Love and Pain and the Whole Damn Thing* (1972), which conspicuously failed to live up to the interest of its title, proved another also-ran.

Pakula then directed two of the finest political thrillers of the 1970s. *The Parallax View* (1974), starring Warren BEATTY, was a stylish conspiracy thriller that reflected, in a highly oblique manner, on the Kennedy assassination. A startling array of extreme camera angles and other alienation devices are used to create a disorientating effect. *All the President's Men* (1976), an account of the press investigation that broke the Watergate scandal, featured Dustin HOFFMAN and Robert REDFORD as *Washington Post* journalists Bernstein and Woodward; the film successfully fused elements from such diverse genres as the political thriller, the detective story, the reporter film, and the 'buddy-buddy' movie. Frank Wills, the security guard who discovered the Watergate break-in, appears in the film as himself.

Pakula's other films of the 1970s were *Comes a Horseman*, an offbeat modern Western starring James CAAN and Jane Fonda, and *Starting Over* (1979), a romantic comedy in which Burt REYNOLDS was cast interestingly against type. Neither was a huge success at the box office. After making *Rollover* (1981), Pakula enjoyed another hit when he directed Meryl STREEP to an Oscar in *Sophie's Choice* (1982), a film about the dreadful secret of a Polish refugee in America; Pakula also co-wrote the Oscar-nominated screenplay. Although his next few films, *Dream Lover* (1986), *Orphans* (1987), and *See You in the Morning* (1989), found little critical or commercial success, he returned to form with *Presumed Innocent* (1990), a claustrophobic murder-mystery featuring Harrison FORD and Brian Dennehy. He has since directed and produced *Consenting Adults* (1992) and *The Pelican Brief* (1993).

Palance, Jack (Vladimir, later Walter, Palahnuik; 1919–) US actor. The son of a coal miner, Palance himself worked briefly in the mines before concentrating on athletics and boxing. He then served as a bomber pilot during World War II; it was plastic surgery for burns following a crash that gave him the taut-skinned face so familiar to filmgoers.

Following stage work, Palance made his screen debut in Elia KAZAN's *Panic in the Street* (1950), in which he played a gangster carrying bubonic plague. He received Oscar nominations for playing villains in both *Sudden Fear* (1952) and SHANE (1953). For the remainder of the decade he continued to play mainly sinister characters in both films and on television. Other movies of the 1950s include *The Silver Chalice* (1954), Paul NEWMAN's debut flop, Robert ALDRICH's

The Big Knife (1955), and the same director's *Attack!* (1956), a brutal war film. Palance also won an Emmy for *Requiem for a Heavyweight* (1956).

Having worked increasingly in television during the late 1950s, Palance turned to European – mainly Italian – productions during the following decade. His films of the 1960s include the Italian-US production *Barabbas* (1962), the only film ever to feature a real eclipse of the sun, *The Professionals* (1966), *Torture Garden* (1967), and *They Came to Rob Las Vegas* (1969), a Spanish-German-Italian-French HEIST MOVIE. The 1970s continued in much the same vein, with Palance appearing in US and foreign films ranging from *Oklahoma Crude* (1974) to *Godzilla vs the Cosmic Monster* (1976).

Although Palance began the 1980s with *Hawk the Slayer* (1980), a lacklustre sword-and-sorcery film, his splendid performance as a dotty painter in *Bagdad Cafe* (1987) led to some very high-profile US work at the end of the decade. Recent films include *Young Guns* (1988), BATMAN (1989), *Tango and Cash* (1989), and *City Slickers* (1991), for which he earned a Best Supporting Actor Oscar. At the Awards ceremony Palance, now in his seventies, demonstrated his vigour by performing a number of one-arm push-ups. Although his character died in *City Slickers*, Palance was asked to appear in *City Slickers II* (1994) – playing that character's brother.

> He's brilliant – but nuts...He's Mr Method, and its like he's got Tourette's disease. You'd say "Would you mind just taking your hat off?" and he'd say "What the fuck d'you want me to do that for?"
>
> PAUL WEILAND, director of *City Slickers II*.

Palmer, Lillie (Lilli Peiser; 1914–86) German leading lady, who starred in numerous US, British, and European films over a half a century. She began in the live theatre, making her stage debut as a child in Germany. Her first film appearance, in the British *Crime Unlimited* (1935), led to supporting roles in HITCHCOCK's *Secret Agent* (1936), and Will HAY's *Good Morning Boys* (1937). Success in the live theatre was then rewarded with more substantial parts in such films as *Thunder Rock* (1942), and *The Rake's Progress* (US title *Notorious Gentlemen*; 1945), in which she co-starred with her husband, Rex HARRISON. While filming the latter she had furious rows with the director Sidney

GILLIAT, who commented "Give her an inch and she'd take a furlong."

After the war, Palmer accompanied Harrison to America, where she appeared in such films as the period comedy-drama *My Girl Tisa* (1947) and on Broadway. When her stormy marriage to Harrison finally collapsed she moved restlessly from country to country, making films in Britain, Germany, and France. Hollywood recalled her for *But Not for Me* (1959), in which she played opposite Clark GABLE, and *The Pleasure of His Company* (1961), in which she appeared with Fred ASTAIRE.

Her films of the 1960s and 1970s rarely gave her a chance to display her undoubted gifts as an actress. Later screen credits included Disney's *Miracle of the White Stallions* (1963), *Operation Crossbow* (1965), in which she teamed up with Sophia LOREN, *Le Voyage du père* (1966), in which she co-starred with Fernandel, *Lotte in Weimar* (1975), from the novel by Thomas Mann, *The Boys from Brazil* (1978), and her last film, *The Holcroft Covenant* (1985).

pan or **pan shot**   A shot in which the camera sweeps in a horizontal arc across a scene, pivoting around its vertical axis. It enables the camera to take in the full breadth of a scene while also registering details that would be lost in a LONG SHOT. The device also enables a director to focus our attention on some aspect of a scene without disrupting our sense of that scene as a whole. It is frequently used to track a moving object across a landscape or to represent the changing POINT OF VIEW of a character as his or her head turns.

Panavision   A WIDESCREEN process developed by MGM in the 1950s. Owing to its improved ANAMORPHIC LENS, it superseded CINEMASCOPE as the most generally used widescreen system. Panavision films were initially shot on 65mm stock; when theatre owners balked at buying new projectors, however, they were reduced to 35mm for general release. Some films are still given special pre-release showings in **Super-Panavision** or **Ultra-Panavision**, which use 65mm or 70mm stock.

paparazzo   A freelance photographer who aggressively and intrusively pursues famous people in order to photograph them. The word derives from the surname of such a photographer in FELLINI's LA DOLCE VITA

(1959). In Italy, street photographers were commonly seen in pursuit of film celebrities before the practice caught on elsewhere. The word is usually used in the plural, as *paparazzi* tend to hunt in packs.

paper prints An early way of registering the copyright of a film under US law, which did not cover the concept of moving pictures on celluloid until 1912. To establish copyright the film-maker had to supply paper prints of each frame, which were held at the Library of Congress. Owing to this legal anomaly over 3500 films that might otherwise have been destroyed or lost forever were preserved for reshooting in 16mm for the Motion Picture Academy archives.

Paradjanov, Sergei (1924–90) Russian film director. Born in Georgia of Armenian parents, Paradjanov studied both music and cinema before joining the Dovzhenko Studios in Kiev as an assistant director. After making several shorts and features in the 1950s he attracted greater attention with the poetic *Shadows of Our Forgotten Ancestors* (1964), in which young love overcomes a quarrel between families. Paradjanov's rejection of Socialist Realism resulted in the Soviet authorities turning down ten of his suggested scripts in five years. Although he finally received permission to make *The Colour of Pomegranates* (1969), the first of a trilogy of 'tableaux films', this surrealistic treatment of the life of the 18th-century poet Sayat Nova was subsequently banned.

In 1973 Paradjanov was sentenced to six years hard labour for allegedly speculating in art and being a homosexual, amongst other offences. He served five years before worldwide protests secured his release. In 1984 he returned to the cinema with *The Legend of the Suram Fortress*, the second part of his trilogy. The story of a young man who is buried alive when the walls of a crumbling fortress collapse on him, the film carried an obvious political symbolism. Nevertheless, the gathering cultural thaw in the Soviet Union permitted its release in the West. In 1986 Paradjanov completed his trilogy with *Ashik Kerib* and made the short *Arabesques on the Pirosmanashvili Theme*, a warm tribute to the Georgian folk painter Niko Pirosmanashvili (1863–1918).

parallel action A sequence that cuts back and forth between two or more separate actions to indicate that they are taking place at the same time. The technique is particularly common in CHASE sequences. *See also* CROSS-CUTTING.

Paramount Pictures Major Hollywood studio, known for its comedies, musicals, and melodramas. Its slogan in the 1930s was "If it's a Paramount picture, it's the best show in town." The company's box-office triumphs have stretched from *The Sheik* (1921), starring Rudolph VALENTINO, to *Forrest Gump* (1994), with Tom HANKS.

The driving force behind the creation of Paramount was Adolph ZUKOR, who founded the FAMOUS PLAYERS Film Company in 1912. About that time, W. W. Hodkinson began a distributing company, Paramount Corporation, which in 1914 began representing Famous Players and the Jesse L. Lasky Feature Play Company. In 1916 Zukor and Lasky merged to form the Famous Players-Lasky Corporation with Zukor as president. The next year, Hodkinson was forced out and Paramount was absorbed along with 12 small production companies.

From 1923 the corporation began to release films (including Cecil B. DE MILLE's epic THE TEN COMMANDMENTS) with the production credit Paramount/Famous Players-Lasky. The studio was renamed Paramount Publix Corporation in 1926. During the 1920s, it developed a chain of hundreds of cinemas throughout America.

Paramount's silent stars included Mary PICKFORD, Douglas FAIRBANKS, John BARRYMORE, Clara BOW, and Gloria SWANSON. B. P. Schulberg, who became production head in 1925 then discovered Gary COOPER, Claudette COLBERT, Fredric MARCH, and George RAFT, amongst others. He also recruited Marlene DIETRICH and Emil JANNINGS from Germany, and the noted European directors Josef VON STERNBERG, Ernst LUBITSCH, and Rouben MAMOULIAN. As a result, Paramount's films of the 1930s and 1940s were often recognizably European in style, while remaining American in theme.

Despite its successes, which included a series of MARX BROTHERS comedies, the company was financially troubled. In the early 1930s Lasky and Schulberg were ousted and Paramount Publix went bankrupt before reorganizing as Paramount Pictures, Inc. The studio recovered by producing popular light movies starring W. C. FIELDS, Mae WEST, Fred MACMURRAY, and Jean

ARTHUR, and the 'Road' films of Bing CROSBY and Bob HOPE.

Zukor, meanwhile, was gaining a reputation as a tightfisted mogul. When he offered playwright George S. Kaufman only $30,000 for one of his works, Kaufman responded by offering $40,000 for Paramount.

New Paramount stars of the 1940s included Alan LADD, Veronica Lake, Paulette GODDARD, Burt LANCASTER, and Kirk DOUGLAS. The studios greatest success of the decade was the multi-Oscar winning *Going My Way* (1944), which starred Bing Crosby. Paramount also nurtured Billy WILDER's creative output, Preston STURGES's sophisticated comedies, and Hal WALLIS's melodramas during this period.

Like other studios, Paramount suffered from the advent of television in the 1950s and from being forced to relinquish its cinema chain under anti-trust legislation. The studio introduced its WIDESCREEN VISTA-VISION process in 1954. The successful comedy team of Dean MARTIN and Jerry LEWIS kept the studio going during the 1950s; other notable films of the period include George STEVENS's SHANE (1953), and Alfred HITCHCOCK's REAR WINDOW (1954), VERTIGO (1958), and PSYCHO (1960).

In 1966 Paramount became a subsidiary of Gulf & Western Industries. Its run of successes continued throughout the 1970s with *Love Story* (1970), THE GODFATHER (1972), *Saturday Night Fever* (1977), and *Grease* (1978). Later blockbusters have included *Star Trek* (1979) and its seven sequels, Steven SPIELBERG's RAIDERS OF THE LOST ARK (1981) and its two sequels, the supernatural thriller *Ghost* (1990), *Indecent Proposal* (1992), with Robert REDFORD and Demi MOORE, and the controversial *Forrest Gump*, which became Paramount's biggest-ever box-office success in 1994. That same year the studio was taken over by Viacom, the world's second-largest media conglomerate, in a $10.5 billion deal.

Parker. Alan Parker (1944–) British director and screenwriter. Parker worked in television advertising and wrote several screenplays before beginning to direct. His first successful feature was the popular gangster-film parody *Bugsy Malone* (1975), made with a cast of children. He enjoyed further commercial success with *Midnight Express* (1978), a harrowing movie about the experience of a drug smuggler in a

Turkish prison; the film featured an Oscar-winning screenplay by Oliver STONE and fine performances from Brad Davis, Randy Quaid, and John Hurt. It also aroused fierce criticism for its alleged racism. Since then Parker, a severe critic of the British film scene, has worked mainly in America. *Fame* (1979), set in New York's High School for the Performing Arts, was notable mainly for its exuberant production numbers, while *The Wall* (1982) was based on the album by Pink Floyd. *Birdy* (1987) was a sensitive depiction of postwar trauma and *Mississippi Burning* (1988) a controversial thriller about an investigation into the murder of three civil rights workers in Mississippi in 1964. Although Parker's films are admired for their style and technical virtuosity, they have sometimes been criticized for sensationalism and lack of intellectual content. One movie to receive uniformly good reviews was *The Commitments* (1991), an exhilarating depiction of an aspiring soul combo in working-class Dublin based on the novel by Roddy Doyle. *The Road to Wellville* (1994) is an outrageous scatological comedy set at a health-spa.

Eleanor Parker (1922–) Red-haired US actress, who was among the most popular leading ladies of the late 1940s and early 1950s. Having started out as a stage actress, Parker made her film debut as an extra in 1941. During the war she established herself as a useful supporting player in such films as *Mission to Moscow* (1943) before graduating to leading roles. She was cast opposite John Garfield in *Pride of the Marines* (1945), took the role previously played by Bette DAVIS in the remade *Of Human Bondage* (1946), earned an Oscar nomination for her role in William WYLER's *Detective Story* (1951), and was Charlton HESTON's wife in *The Naked Jungle* (1954). Miscasting as Frank SINATRA's wheelchair-bound wife in *The Man With the Golden Arm* (1955) did little for her subsequent career, though she was reunited with Sinatra in CAPRA's *A Hole in the Head* (1959). Few of her later films excited much interest, though she made the most of her brief role as Christopher PLUMMER's rejected fiancée in THE SOUND OF MUSIC (1965); other parts included Stuart Whitman's alcoholic ex-wife in *An American Dream* (1966) and a wealthy invalid in the horror film *Eye of the Cat* (1969). She appeared in various television movies during the 1970s.

Parks, Larry (Sam Kleusman Lawrence Parks; 1914–75) US actor, who is mainly remembered for his impersonation of Al JOLSON in two celebrated BIOPICS. Parks established himself as a B-MOVIE stalwart in the early 1940s, when he appeared in some 35 films in five years. Stardom finally arrived when he was cast as the lead in *The Jolson Story* (1946) and its successor in *Jolson Sings Again* (1949). The success of the two pictures did much to revive interest in Jolson, whose own films had become a fading memory. Parks was justly acclaimed for his energetic on-stage performances, though Jolson himself sang the songs on the soundtrack. Fame proved fleeting, however, and Parks failed to find further suitable roles. His career was effectively destroyed by his decision to name names to the notorious House Un-American Activities Committee, after which few actors would work with him (at the time one Hollywood newspaper carried the derisive headline "Jolson Sings Again"). His last appearance was in the British biopic *Freud* (1962).

Pasolini, Pier Paolo (1922–75) Italian director, writer, and artist, whose films dealt provocatively with social, religious, and sexual themes. A native of Bologna, he established his reputation with a series of poems and novels about life in the slums of Rome, where he lived during the 1940s. His sympathy for the poor and his Marxist leanings were also apparent from his first screenplays, which included those for FELLINI's *Nights of Cabiria* (1957) and BERTOLUCCI's *The Grim Reaper* (1962). Pasolini made his debut as a director with *Accattone* (1961), a NEOREALIST exploration of the Roman underworld, which made effective use of nonprofessional actors. The film, which was widely praised, provided the director with an opportunity to expose the conflicts in a society that embraces both Catholicism and Marxism.

His second film, *Mamma Roma* (1962), dealt with similar themes but failed to match the confident style of its predecessor, despite a powerful performance by Anna Magnani. Far more successful was his third film, *The Gospel According to St Matthew* (1964), in which Pasolini again examined the relationship between Christian and Marxist values, this time by filming the story of CHRIST with a peasant cast in poverty-stricken southern Italy.

Subsequent films were more diverse and eclectic. After *Hawks and Sparrows* (1966), a strange fantasy in which a talking crow discusses Marxist theory with two peasants, Pasolini made *Oedipus Rex* (1967), a virtually silent film in which the Freudian aspects of the tragedy are brought to the fore. *Theorem* (1968) was a provocative attack on the shallowness of bourgeois values, while *Pigsty* (1969) ran together the stories of a medieval cannibal and a decadent rebel in contemporary Italy, apparently to demonstrate that modern morality is even less appealing than that of previous ages. His main work of the 1970s was a trilogy of films adapted from the tales of sexual intrigue in *The Decameron* (1970), *The Canterbury Tales* (1971), and *The Arabian Nights* (1974). Pasolini's last film was *Salò, or the 120 Days of Sodom* (1975), an odyssey into the extreme limits of sexual perversion, in which a notorious work by the Marquis de Sade is updated to Mussolini's Salò Republic. Pasolini's murder – he was found brutally beaten to death in the slums of Rome – was probably an outcome of his homosexual private life (although others have suggested that his allegations of corruption in the Italian Establishment may have had some bearing on the matter).

Passion of Joan of Arc, The (*La Passion de Jeanne d'arc*; 1928) Carl Theodor DREYER's remarkable silent film about the trial and death of Joan of Arc, based on the actual records of the proceedings. Shot in exact sequence against simple white backgrounds, the film consists mainly of a series of extreme CLOSE-UPS of the performers' unmade-up faces. Dreyer later justified this unprecedented technique by arguing that the true nature of the trial could be conveyed

> ...only through huge close-ups that exposed, with merciless realism, the callous cynicism of the judges behind hypocritical compassion...on the other hand there had to be equally huge close-ups of Joan, whose pure features would reveal that she alone found strength in her faith in God.

Much of the $350,000 budget went on a vast cement castle, erected in the Paris suburbs. Although little of it was actually seen in the picture, Dreyer considered it money well spent as it helped the cast to summon up a sense of period and place. By contrast, the interiors were filmed in a disused car assembly plant at Billancourt. Trenches were dug beneath the sets to enable Dreyer to achieve his remarkable camera angles.

Lillian GISH was orginally approached to play Joan, but Dreyer insisted on an inexperienced vaudeville performer named Renée Falconetti. Rigorously rehearsed by Dreyer throughout the production, she had to endure such humiliations as the shaving of her head to ensure an authentic emotional response. He later had nothing but praise for this remarkable actress in her only film role: "She *lived* the part. There was something indefinable about her – something that was not of this earth."

Premiered in Copenhagen, the film was withheld in France until the numerous cuts recommended by the Archbishop of Paris had been carried out. Owing to the film's depiction of the English soldiery, the British censors banned it altogether until 1930. Although many critics attacked its over-reliance on captions (Dreyer had hoped to make a sound film but was thwarted by a lack of recording equipment), Jean COCTEAU was among those who recognized it as an important work of art. Doomed to commercial failure in the face of competition from the talkies, the film was shown in various bowdlerized forms until a new print (which Dreyer disowned) was issued in 1951 with a soundtrack including music by Vivaldi, Bach, and others. Although the original negative was destroyed in a fire, work is currently in progress to piece together the film as Dreyer intended it to be seen.

Pathé, Charles (1863–1957) French producer and businessman, who applied mass-production to film-making. Today he is best remembered for the Pathé NEWSREELS that continued into the 1950s, although these were a relatively minor adjunct to the huge enterprise that he had developed before World War I.

Pathé began by hawking EDISON phonographs and cylinders at Paris fairs. Although he sold a few KINETOSCOPES in 1895, he soon realized that the LUMIÈRE system was the future of film and employed Henri Joly to design a camera-projector. This was marketed by Pathé Frères, the company he set up with his brothers, in 1896.

Three years later Ferdinand Zecca (1864–1947) was put in charge of Pathé film production. By declining to get involved at every production stage, as most

earlier film-makers had done, Zecca managed to turn films round in a matter of days, and to minimize costs. As a result, most films broke even after only 15 prints had been sold; with average sales of about 350 prints per film, Pathé's profits were correspondingly enormous. Though quality inevitably suffered, it mattered little to the unsophisticated audiences who eagerly handed over their centimes to the travelling showmen who usually screened films in France. In 1902, having acquired the Lumière patents, Pathé began manufacturing a new camera which soon became an industry standard; in the same year he built his first studio in Vincennes.

Pathé's output embraced all genres. From the mid 1900s he made a series of popular comedies with such established stars as the clown André Deed and Max Linder (1883–1925), whose debonair character influenced CHAPLIN. Linder became the first international film star, earning over a million francs in 1912. Pathé also formed the Société Cinématographique des Auteurs et Gens de Lettres (SCAGL) to bring classics to the screen, notably a two-part adaptation of *Les Misérables* (1912) that ran an astonishing three and a half hours. Despite the scale of such films, Pathé's output remained essentially backward-looking in technique.

At its 1908 peak, Pathé Frères produced more than the whole US industry, taking a third of global cinema business. Pathé's empire included cinemas, studios, factories manufacturing cinematic equipment and film stock, and agencies in Britain, Spain, Russia, Italy, and America. These agencies not only distributed French Pathé films, but also made their own; US productions included the phenomenally popular serial THE PERILS OF PAULINE.

However, the success of US subsidiary productions obscured the fact that Pathé's French films were losing their appeal in America. As costs rose, it became clear that Pathé had failed to develop enough cinemas in France to support the production of what were essentially *French* films (a problem French and other European film industries would recognise today).

The end came in 1914, when key personnel and materials were diverted to the French war effort. By the time commercial film-making began again in 1915, French audiences had developed a taste for Chaplin and the early works of DE MILLE and GRIFFITH. Pathé never regained its pre-eminence:

although the company continued to finance, distribute, and exhibit films, production had virtually ceased by the 1930s.

Patsy Awards The animal 'Oscars', awards presented annually since 1951 to Hollywood's best performing ANIMALS (including, since 1958, those on television). The American Humane Association created the Patsy, which takes its name from the initials of the full title 'Picture Animal Top Star of the Year'. The first winner was the 'talking' mule who played the title role of *Francis* (1950), with Donald O'CONNOR as his co-star. Other Patsy winners have ranged from the dolphin star of *Flipper* (1963) to the mongrel hero of *Benji* (1974).

Peck, Gregory (1916–) US actor, who became one of Hollywood's most popular romantic heroes in the years after World War II. Having started out as a stage actor, Peck made his film debut in 1943 in *Days of Glory*. His first starring role, as an ageing priest in *The Keys of the Kingdom* (1944), earned him an Oscar nomination, and he went on to co-star with Greer GARSON in *The Valley of Decision* (1945), Ingrid BERGMAN in HITCHCOCK's SPELLBOUND (1945), and Jane WYMAN in *The Yearling* (1946). Among the most successful of his early films were *Duel in the Sun* (1946), *The Macomber Affair* (1947), the war drama *Twelve O'Clock High* (1949), and the Western *The Gunfighter* (1950).

In 1951 Peck crossed the Atlantic to make *Captain Horatio Hornblower*, based on C. S. Forester's seafaring novels. Having turned down HIGH NOON, he won further acclaim in *The Snows of Kilimanjaro* (1952), *Roman Holiday* (1953) with Audrey HEPBURN, and *The Man in the Gray Flannel Suit* (1956). That year he also starred as the demented Captain Ahab in John HUSTON's valiant attempt to bring *Moby Dick* to the screen. Co-writer Ray Bradbury had really wanted Laurence OLIVIER to fill the role: "It [the film] misses because Peck couldn't bring madness to it. A dear sweet gentleman, but he's not mad. Olivier is a madman to begin with." *Moby Dick* was very nearly Peck's last film: shooting of the epic sequence in which he clambers onto the 80-foot 'whale' was disrupted by a sudden squall, the tow rope parted in the rough sea, and the whale – complete with star – disappeared into a bank of fog. Fortunately the crew managed to find the missing leviathan

after a brief search and Peck was spared Captain Ahab's watery fate.

Peck enjoyed greater success in William WYLER's Western *The Big Country* (1958), the World-War-II thriller *The Guns of Navarone* (1961), and *To Kill a Mocking Bird* (1963), for which he won an Oscar. Among his subsequent credits are the comedy *Arabesque* (1966), the Western *Shootout* (1971), the cult horror classic *The Omen* (1976), and *The Boys from Brazil* (1978), in which he appeared as a villain for the first time. More recent films have included *The Sea Wolves* (1980), with fellow veterans David NIVEN and Trevor HOWARD, and *Old Gringo* (1989).

> Solid, kindly, dignified, likable, and somewhat self-effacing, he is at his best in roles that match these qualities. When miscast, he has gone down with a dull thud.
> CASEY ROBINSON, screenwriter.

Peckinpah, Sam (1925–84) US director and screenwriter, noted for his handling of explicit violence.

Peckinpah was born and raised on a ranch in California. After service in the US Marines, he worked as a theatre director, a prop manager for a television station, and an assistant editor at CBS, before becoming an assistant to director Don SIEGEL on *Riot in Cell Block 11* (1954). He then worked with Siegel on a number of features, including *Invasion of the Body Snatchers* (1956), which he co-wrote and played a small role in. During the late 1950s he returned to television, writing and directing for such classic Western series as *The Westerner* and *The Rifleman*.

Peckinpah made his feature film debut with *The Deadly Companions* (1961), an unremarkable though thoroughly competent Western. That same year he also directed *Ride the High Country* (British title *Guns in the Afternoon*), a thoughtful film that examined one of his favourite themes, the predicament of men who have outlasted their time. Fittingly enough, the leads were taken by the veteran Western stars Randolph Scott and Joel MCCREA, both of whom retired after making the film.

A recurring feature of Peckinpah's career has been his conflicts with the studios who employed him. In 1964 he was removed as director from *The Cincinnatti Kid*. Later that year he disowned *Major Dundee* (1964), a film he had co-written and directed, following conflict with Paramount about the form in which it was released.

Peckinpah's next film as director was *The Wild Bunch* (1969), which he again co-wrote. The movie, arguably one of his finest, once more concerned men who had out-lived their own age and could not adapt to the strictures of the new one. The bloody slow-motion climax set new levels in the graphic depiction of violence. Following the elegiac comedy Western *The Ballad of Cable Hogue* (1970), Peckinpah directed Dustin HOFFMAN in the highly controversial and often unpleasant *Straw Dogs* (1971), which attempted to show how primitive violent instincts always triumph over civility and rationality. If *Junior Bonner* (1972), which featured Steve MCQUEEN as a rodeo rider, was somewhat gentler, violence returned to the forefront in *Pat Garrett and Billy the Kid* (1973), Peckinpah's last Western. MGM cut, re-edited, and restructured the film to such an extent that the director attempted to have his name removed from the credits.

According to Peckinpah, *Bring Me The Head of Alfredo Garcia* (1974) was the only one of his films over which he had complete artistic control. The movie, which again features Peckinpah's trademark slow-motion violence, is regarded by some as a cult clas-sic and by others as a gruesome curiosity (one critic remarked: "The only kind of analysis it really invites is psychoanalysis"). Peckinpah's last films, *The Killer Elite* (1975), *Cross of Iron* (1977), *Convoy* (1978), and *The Osterman Weekend* (1983), were generally considered disappointing. Despite the unevenness of his work, Peckinpah's uncompromising style has had a profound influence on later directors, notably Walter Hill and, more recently, Quentin TARANTINO.

Peekaboo Girl, the A nickname for the US actress Veronica Lake (1919–73), who wore her blonde hair in a style that covered one eye. An actress of limited ability, she is best remembered for the films she made with Alan LADD in the 1940s.

Pennebaker, D(on) A(lan) (1930–) US DOCUMENTARY film-maker, a leading expo-nent of the DIRECT CINEMA movement. Pen-nebaker trained as an engineer, served in the US Navy, and worked as an advertising copywriter before making his film debut with *Daybreak Express* (1953), a collage of New York images set to a Duke Ellington soundtrack. In 1959 he joined Filmakers, a co-operative venture that also included the

documentarists Richard Leacock and Albert Maysles. Employing new technology, such as lightweight cameras and improved sound-recording equipment, the group began to move away from the structured style of traditional documentary towards the fly-on-the-wall technique that remains popular today.

While *Primary* (1959) followed the elec-tion campaigns of John F. Kennedy and Hubert Humphrey, *Jane* (1961), which showed Jane FONDA in rehearsal for a new play, and *Lambert and Co* (1963) were both performance orientated, exploring the rela-tionship between the artists' on-stage and off-stage activities. This was further explored in *Don't Look Back* (1966), an account of Bob Dylan's 1965 British tour that focused on the media circus and Dylan's off-stage interaction with both the public and other celebrities. *Monterrey Pop* (1968) contained some fine performance footage while also managing to capture the atmosphere at one of the first major rock festivals of the hippy era. Both *Keep on Rockin'* (1971), featuring Chuck Berry and Little Richard among others, and *Ziggy Star-dust and the Spiders From Mars* (1973), with David Bowie, concentrated more on the per-formance itself.

Among Pennebaker's more eccentric projects are *One P.M.* (1971), which inter-cuts film of Jean-Luc GODARD at work with rejected footage from a Godard project called *One A.M.*, and *Town Bloody Hall* (1972, released 1979), a record of a debate on feminism involving Germaine Greer and – seconds out – Norman Mailer. His more recent works include *DeLorean* (1981), *Dance Black America* (1985) and a slew of music-led films including *Depeche Mode 101* (1989), *Jerry Lee Lewis: The Story of Rock 'n' Roll* (1990), and *Wynford Marsalis* (1992).

Perils of Pauline, The (1914) The hugely popular film SERIAL starring Pearl WHITE and directed by Donald Mackenzie. The melo-dramatic plot revolved around a series of CLIFFHANGING attempts on the heroine's life by her evil guardian. There have been two further films of the same title: the 1947 ver-sion was a biopic of Pearl White, starring Betty Hutton, while the 1967 version was based on the original serial, with Pamela Austin taking the role of Pauline.

Perkins, Anthony (1932–92) US actor, who was unable to escape from the shadow of his most memorable role, that of Norman Bates, the psychopathic motel owner in HITCHCOCK's PSYCHO (1960).

The son of an actor, Perkins began working in summer stock at the age of 15 and made his film debut six years later in *The Actress* (1953). He then spent a period working on Broadway and in television before making his next film *Friendly Persuasion* (1956), for which he received a Best Supporting Actor nomination at the Oscars. The next year he gave a notable performance in the baseball film *Fear Strikes Out* (1957).

After a couple of years in which he was cast mainly in adolescent roles, Perkins made his name with an unforgettable performance as Bates in the horror-thriller *Psycho*. Although the film's success catapulted him to international fame, he spent the rest of the decade appearing in a series of European co-productions, few of which were at all beneficial to his career. During the 1970s he did rather better, appearing in such notable films as *WUSA* (1970), Mike NICHOLS's *Catch 22* (1970), in which he played Chaplain Tappman, John HUSTON's *The Life and Times of Judge Roy Bean* (1972), the star-laden *Murder on the Orient Express* (1974), and *Winter Kills* (1977, released 1979).

However, his inability to reproduce the success of his role as Bates led Perkins to appear in two inferior sequels, *Psycho II* (1983) and *Psycho III* (1986), with which he made his debut as a director. A television movie, *Psycho IV*, followed in 1990. He made one other film as director, *Lucky Stiff* (1988). In 1984 Perkins was offered the role of a psychopathic clergyman in Ken RUSSELL's *Crimes of Passion*, with Kathleen TURNER. Intent on actually being the part, Perkins had himself ordained as a minister of the Universal Life Church of America – in which capacity he later officiated at Russell's wedding. Perkins died of an AIDS-related illness.

persistence of vision "A clever trick by the optic nerve in collusion with the brain", whereby an image is retained for a fraction of a second after the object viewed is removed or changed. The phenomenon, which is still not completely understood, is essential to the illusion of movement in film; during projection each individual frame is held just long enough in the brain to blend imperceptibly with the next, thus creating the sensation of smooth continuous motion.

Peters, Jean (Elizabeth Jean Peters; 1926–) Dark-haired US star of the late 1940s and early 1950s. In 1957 she secretly married the millionaire producer Howard HUGHES, though they lived apart for most of their 14-year marriage, which ended in divorce.

Born in Canton, Ohio, Peters studied at Ohio State University. In 1946, having been voted the most popular student on campus, she won a trip to Hollywood, where her looks persuaded 20TH CENTURY-FOX to give her a contract. She made her screen debut a year later in the $4.5-million COSTUME DRAMA *Captain from Castile*, with Tyrone POWER. Her subsequent co-stars included Marlon BRANDO in *Viva Zapata!* (1952), Darryl F. ZANUCK's story of the Mexican revolutionary. In *Pickup on South Street* (1953) she was given a role intended for Marilyn MONROE, that of a prostitute who joins Richard WIDMARK to expose a communist spy ring. That same year, however, Peters was outshone by Monroe in the offbeat thriller *Niagara*.

In 1954 Peters starred in the popular romance THREE COINS IN THE FOUNTAIN, perhaps her best remembered film, and the Western *Apache*, in which she and Burt LANCASTER played Indian lovers. She retired after co-starring with Richard Todd in *A Man Called Peter* (1955), but returned in the mid 1970s with the television movie *The Moneychangers* (1974) and Universal's *The Great Waldo Pepper* (1975), starring Robert REDFORD.

Pfeiffer, Michelle (1957–) US actress, a striking beauty who became a major star in the late 1980s. Pfeiffer's first full-time job was as a checkout girl in a supermarket; however, victory in a California beauty contest led to work in TV commercials and an acting debut in the television series *Fantasy Island*. She made her big-screen debut with a small part in *Falling in Love Again* (1980).

After appearances in such unremarkable films as *Charlie Chan and the Curse of the Dragon Queen* (1981), Pfeiffer attracted a little attention with her role in *Grease 2* (1982), an unsuccessful sequel. She followed this with the major role of Elvira, the cocaine-addicted wife of a drugs baron, in Brian DE PALMA's brutal *Scarface* (1983). Although she went on to play the female lead in films ranging from John LANDIS's *Into the Night* (1985) to the fantasy *Ladyhawke* (1985), it was her performance as the sex-starved Sukie Ridgemont in *The Witches of Eastwick* (1987) that launched her to real stardom. She has subsequently given notable performances in Jonathan DEMME's *Married to the Mob* (1988), *Tequila Sunrise* (1988), with Mel GIBSON, and Stephen FREARS's *Dangerous Liaisons* (1988), in which she played the innocent Madame de Tourvel, a part that brought her an Oscar nomination as Best Supporting Actress. *The Fabulous Baker Boys* (1989), in which she played nightclub singer Susie Diamond opposite Jeff and Beau BRIDGES, saw her nominated for a Best Actress Oscar. Her more recent films include *The Russia House* (1990), a spy thriller in which she co-starred with Sean CONNERY, *Frankie and Johnny* (1991), a romantic drama that reunited her with *Scarface* star Al PACINO, *Batman Returns* (1992), in which she played a leather-clad Catwoman, and *The Age of Innocence* (1993), Martin SCORSESE's adaptation of the Edith Wharton novel.

PG Parental Guidance. In Britain and America, a cinema certification used to indicate that a film contains scenes that some parents may consider unsuitable for younger children. America also has a **PG-13** RATING, which strongly cautions parents about allowing children under that age to attend. This was introduced in 1984 as a response to parental concern about the frightening scenes in several of the Steven SPIELBERG movies of that era.

Philadelphia Story, The (1940) George CUKOR's classic comedy about life amongst the rich of Philadelphia. The film stars Katharine HEPBURN as the rich and head-strong Tracy Lord, Cary GRANT as her ex-husband C. K. Dexter Haven, and James STEWART as Mike Connor, the gossip journalist who ultimately succumbs to her charms. (Hepburn had hoped to have Spencer TRACY as her co-star, but happily accepted Cukor's choice of Grant.) The strong supporting cast included Ruth Hussey, Roland YOUNG, and John Howard.

The film brought to the screen the witty stage play by Philip Barry, in which Hepburn had already enjoyed acclaim on Broadway; the cinema version proved one of the highlights of her screen career, as well as providing Cukor with perhaps his

finest hour. Stewart earned an Oscar as Best Actor and the film received four other nominations – for Best Picture, Best Actress, Best Director, and Best Screenplay. Grant donated his salary – an impressive $137,000 – to British war relief.

High Society (1956), a musical remake in which the sparkling dialogue was cut to make room for some Cole Porter numbers, only served to emphasize how good the original film had been (despite competent performances from Grace KELLY, Bing CROSBY, and Frank SINATRA in the leading roles).

Philipe, Gérard (1922–59) Dashing French actor, whose spectacular career was cut short by his tragically premature death. Philipe, who specialized in playing romantic leads, made his first appearances on both stage and screen in 1943. His first notable success in the cinema came with a version of Dostoevsky's *The Idiot* in 1946. International recognition followed for his role in Claude Autant-Lara's love story *Le Diable au corps* (1947) with Micheline Presle, though he subsequently turned down invitations from Hollywood. He consolidated his following with strong performances in such films as *Une si jolie petite plage* (1949), in which he played a murderer, *La Beauté du diable* (1950), as the devil, the swashbuckler *Fanfan la tulipe* (1951), and the fantasy *Les Belles de nuit* (1952).

After making the British film *Knave of Hearts* (*Monsieur Ripois et son nemesis*; 1954), in which he played a French philanderer in London, Philipe went on to star in further French-made films including *Le Rouge et le noir* (1954) and *Les Grandes Manoeuvres* (1955). His debut as a director with *Les Aventures de Till l'Espiègle* (1957) failed to impress the critics, however, and he had mixed reviews for both *Montparnasse 19* (1957), in which he played the painter Modigliani, and *Les Liaisons dangereuses* (1959). His sudden death from a heart attack at the age of 37 caused both shock and grief; he was buried in the costume he had worn in Corneille's play *Le Cid*. In 1961 he became one of the very few film stars to be depicted on a French postage stamp.

> He was an angel searching avidly, wildly, to become a man.
>
> MARIA CASARES, film actress.

Phoenix, River (1971–93) US actor, whose premature death from a drug overdose established him as a cult figure with teenagers. His winsome good looks, air of vulnerability, and early demise have invited comparisons with James DEAN.

Phoenix was born in a log cabin in Oregon to highly unorthodox parents. As the growing family (there would eventually be four siblings with equally exotic names: Rain, Leaf, Liberty, and Summer) became missionaries for The Children of God, a controversial sect, River spent much of his early life on the road and received no formal education.

After leaving the sect and moving to California, the family began to rely for its income on River's appearances in TV commercials (he refused to continue these at the age of ten as they were "numbing me to my as yet undeveloped craft"). His big-screen debut followed in *Explorers* (1985), a children's sci-fi fantasy. After attracting the attention of the critics in *Stand By Me* (1986), a nostalgic account of four boys' friendship in the 1950s, Phoenix starred with Harrison FORD in *The Mosquito Coast* (1986), a difficult film that saw him giving an impressively sustained performance.

Major stardom came to Phoenix with *Running on Empty* (1988), a story about a family of ex-Vietnam protesters on the run from the FBI that bore similarities to his own early life (though Phoenix denied any connection). The film earned him an Oscar for Best Supporting Actor. A cameo as the young Indy in *Indiana Jones and the Last Crusade* (1989) was followed by *I Love You to Death* (1990) and *Dog Fight* (1991). Phoenix then gave his most impressive performance, as a narcoleptic gay prostitute, in *My Own Private Idaho*, a film that co-starred Keanu REEVES. *Sneakers* (1992) was a return to teen territory.

A vegan and a committed environmentalist, Phoenix became known for issuing sincere but often incoherent lectures on a range of spiritual and ecological subjects (a habit that gave rise to the common magazine headline 'River's Deep'). His public advocacy of healthy lifestyles made his drug-induced collapse at the Viper Rooms, a now infamous Hollywood nightclub, and subsequent death, an even greater shock to fans. However, his capacity for youthful humbug is illustrated by Peter WEIR's memory of his eating Mars Bars and quaffing Coke on the set of *The Mosquito Coast* when he thought no-one was looking.

His last completed film, *The Thing Called Love* (1993), was given only a limited release in America. *The Sunday Times* commented "Phoenix looks drunk or tranquillized most of the time, and shows none of the gifts he once had to burn." Another posthumous release, Sam SHEPARD's *Silent Tongue*, appeared in 1994.

photo double   *See* DOUBLE.

Pialat, Maurice   (1925–   ) French director and occasional actor. A painter by training, Pialat entered the cinema in the late 1950s with a series of shorts. After several years working in French television, he embarked on his first full-length feature, *L'Enfance nue* (1968), a semiautobiographical piece about a young delinquent. In this and subsequent films he depicted everyday emotional traumas in a supremely naturalistic style, often employing nonprofessional actors. *We Won't Grow Old Together* (1972) traced the break-up of two lovers, while *The Mouth Agape* (1973) was a sensitive portrayal of a woman's slow death from cancer. The uncharacteristically cheerful *Passe ton bac d'abord* (1976) studied the preoccupations of a group of teenagers.

Pialat first came to international attention with *Loulou* (1980), starring Gérard DEPARDIEU and Isabelle HUPPERT as lovers in the run-down suburbs of Paris. A similarly bleak view of the world characterizes *A nos amours* (1984), in which a promiscuous 15-year-old falls out with her family; Pialat played her sympathetic father. *Police* (1985), another drama of emotional conflict, starred Depardieu once again, as did the acclaimed *Under Satan's Sun* (1987). Based on the novel by Bernanos, the latter film is an intense analysis of the nature of evil and religious faith, with Depardieu as a self-doubting priest and Pialat as his superior. In 1992 Pialat released *Van Gogh*, a highly praised biopic of the artist.

Pickford, Mary   (Gladys Mary Smith; 1893–1979) Canadian-born US actress, who became known as the **World's Sweetheart** in the 1910s. Having begun to act as a child, Pickford made her film debut at the age of 16, under the direction of D. W. GRIFFITH (who warned that she was "too little and too fat" to be a star). Griffith initially paid her the princely sum of five dollars a day. After some 24 movies she began to be cast in the 'little girl' roles that made her the top box-office attraction of her era: adorned with long golden ringlets, she captivated audiences around the globe with her innocence and youthful charm. Highlights of her early career included *The Little Teacher* (1910), *Cinderella* (1914), *The Little American* (1917), *Rebecca of Sunnybrook Farm* (1917), and *Daddy Long Legs* (1919).

By this time Pickford was the indisputable queen of Hollywood, commanding immense fees and receiving some 18,000 fan letters a month. Despite her wide-eyed image she became known as a shrewd businesswoman; victims of her financial acumen took to calling her 'Attila of Sunnybrook Farm' while Samuel GOLDWYN once remarked: "It took longer to make one of Mary's contracts than it did to make one of Mary's pictures." She consolidated her status by marrying fellow screen idol Douglas FAIRBANKS and forming a business partnership with him, Griffith, and Charlie CHAPLIN that led to the birth of UNITED ARTISTS. Among her films for the company were the hugely popular *Pollyanna* (1920), which she hated, *Little Lord Fauntleroy* (1921), and *Little Annie Rooney* (1925). In *Little Lord Fauntleroy* she played both the title character and his mother; the scenes in which they appear together (including one in which the 'boy' jumps into her arms) are remarkable examples of the early use of MULTIPLE EXPOSURE. As the mother, Pickford had to stand nine inches taller than her son and frequently fell off the ramp constructed for this purpose.

Although increasingly bored with her image, Pickford continued to don ringlets and girlish frocks to welcome important guests at United Artists and at Pickfair, the palatial home where she and Fairbanks lived. During the 1920s she made several attempts to break out of the 'Little Mary' stereotype, playing adults in *Rosita* (1923) and *Dorothy Vernon of Haddon Hall* (1924). Her career finally faltered with the coming of sound at the end of the decade – despite initial success with the talkie *Coquette* (1929), for which she won an Oscar. After co-starring with Leslie HOWARD in *Secrets* (1933) she retired from the screen to write various books, including an autobiography. She was awarded a special Oscar for her achievements in 1976.

Although Pickford remained one of the richest women in America, her last years were a far cry from the great days of the 1920s: she became a bedridden recluse at Pickfair, seeking solace in whisky and demanding that any pessimistic news be cut out of her daily paper before it was handed to her.

Pidgeon, Walter (1897–1984) Handsome Canadian leading man of the 1930s and 1940s, mainly remembered for his screen partnership with Greer GARSON. Pidgeon's screen career was launched after Fred ASTAIRE heard him singing at a party and encouraged him to try for the movies. He made his film debut in 1926 and soon established his place among the romantic leading men of the day with such films as *Turn Back the Hours* (1928) with Myrna LOY.

With his rich baritone voice, Pidgeon found himself much in demand for operettas and musical melodramas in the early talkie era. The latter part of the decade saw him in a variety of supporting and lead roles in such films as *The Girl of the Golden West* (1938), *Too Hot to Handle* (1938), and *Society Lawyer* (1939). He subsequently concentrated on playing more mature leading men, finally securing star status during the 1940s. In 1941 he co-starred with Greer Garson for the first time in *Blossoms in the Dust*. His acclaimed performance as a Welsh preacher in John FORD's *How Green was My Valley* (1942) was followed by another film with Garson, the hugely popular MRS MINIVER (1942). The Garson-Pidgeon team was re-formed for *Madame Curie* (1943) and *Mrs Parkington* (1944), while other projects paired him with Ginger ROGERS, Claudette COLBERT, and Deborah KERR. After co-starring with Clark GABLE in *Command Decision* (1948), he was teamed with Garson again for *That Forsyte Woman* (1950) and the sequel *The Miniver Story* (1950).

Although Pidgeon disappeared from the front rank of Hollywood stars in the 1950s, he continued to take leading roles in such films as *Forbidden Planet* (1956), as a mad scientist, and *Voyage to the Bottom of the Sea* (1961). His last major film was the political melodrama *Advise and Consent* (1962), though he continued to work in the cinema and television until the late 1970s.

> That handsome piece of screen furniture.
> JAMES AGATE, film critic.

***Pink Panther* Series**   Blake EDWARDS's long-running series of films about the bumbling French sleuth Inspector Clouseau. Peter SELLERS played the detective with an exaggerated French accent that became one of the films' best-loved trademarks. Other running gags had the accident-prone Clouseau leaving a trail of physical mayhem every-time he stirred, ineptly romancing gorgeous suspects, and warding off surprise attacks by Cato, his oriental valet. Edwards co-scripted and directed seven of the eight United Artists films and produced all but two; the role of Clouseau, turned down by Peter USTINOV, made Sellers a millionaire.

The original Pink Panther was a price-less diamond stolen by David NIVEN in the first film of the series, *The Pink Panther* (1963). (The opening credits featured an animated pink panther who went on to become a cartoon character in his own right.) Henri MANCINI won an Oscar nomi-nation for the insidious theme music, which remains closely identified with both the live-action and the cartoon series. The first sequel, *A Shot in the Dark* (1964), intro-duced Clouseau's arch-antagonist Chief Inspector Dreyfus, played by Herbert LOM: "Give me 10 men like Clouseau, and I could destroy the world!"

In 1964 Sellers had a heart attack and vowed never to play Clouseau again. Con-sequently the inferior *Inspector Clouseau* (1968), directed by Bud Yorkin, had Alan ARKIN in the title role, this time investigat-ing the Great Train Robbery. Sellers then bounced back for three more Panthers: *The Return of the Pink Panther* (1974), in which the original jewel is stolen from a museum; *The Pink Panther Strikes Again* (1976), with Clouseau tracking Dreyfus who has escaped from a mental home; and *The Revenge of the Pink Panther* (1978), in which Clouseau attempts to foil an international drug ring.

After Sellers's death in 1980, Edwards attempted to prolong the series with *Trail of the Pink Panther* (1982), using old clips, OUT-TAKES, and a double who is seen only at a distance or in heavy disguise. The film flopped and UA had to pay Sellers's widow Lynne Frederick $1,687,000 and costs of $214,000 for infringement of his rights. In *Curse of the Pink Panther* (1983) Clouseau is replaced by an equally incompetent detec-tive played by Ted Wass: *Sight and Sound* called it "film-making as grave-robbing". Edwards has plans for future films using a new Clouseau.

pixillation A technique in which real objects or people are shot frame by frame (STOP-ACTION) to produce an effect of broken motion. The technique was used in various trick films of the silent era. The Canadian animator Norman McLaren (1914–87)

employed pixillation to great effect in *Neigh-bours* (1952), in which he and a collabora-tor were shot in a series of poses that changed slightly from frame to frame, thereby producing a strange automated effect. A similar result can be obtained by removing frames from a normally filmed sequence during editing; this produces a comic jerky effect, as in the KEYSTONE KOPS-style sequences in TOM JONES (1963).

play it again, Sam A well-known misquota-tion from CASABLANCA (1942), starring Humphrey BOGART and Ingrid BERGMAN. The film also features Dooley Wilson as the pia-nist Sam, who plays and sings 'As Time Goes By' so evocatively that it reminds Bogart and Bergman of their prewar liaison in Paris. The closest the screenplay comes to the phrase is Bergman's line "Play it Sam, play 'As Time Goes By'".

By 1969 the misquotation was well enough established for Woody ALLEN to use it as the title of his play about a critic who is helped by the 'ghost' of Humphrey Bogart. The play was filmed in 1972 with lookalike Jerry Lacy as Bogart.

Pleasence, Donald (1919–95) British actor, whose quiet voice and unblinking gaze brought menace to such sinister roles as that of Dr Crippen, in the 1962 film about the Edwardian killer. Pleasence was also an experienced stage actor and made numer-ous television appearances in Britain and America.

Born in Worksop, Pleasence made his stage debut in 1939 before serving with the RAF during World War II. He began his film career with a bit part in *The Beachcomber* (1954) and remained in supporting roles for the next eight years. For his role in *The Great Escape* (1963) he drew effectively on his experience as a prisoner of war from 1944 to 1946.

By this time the title role in *Dr Crippen* had stereotyped him as a villain: he went on to play the devious tramp Davies in the screen version of Pinter's *The Caretaker* (1964), the DEVIL to Max VON SYDOW's CHRIST in *The Greatest Story Ever Told* (1965), a menacing stranger in Roman POLANSKI's black comedy *Cul-de-Sac* (1966), a German heavy in the BOND FILM *You Only Live Twice* (1967), the Nazi Heinrich Himmler in *The Eagle Has Landed* (1976), and Pontius Pilate in *The Passover Plot* (1976). However, in the best-known of his later films, John

CARPENTER's horror thriller *Halloween* (1979), Pleasence played a hero, the psychiatrist Dr Loomis. He reprised the role in the sequels of 1981 and 1988. His last roles included a CAMEO appearance in Woody ALLEN's *Shadows and Fog* (1992).

Plummer, Christopher (Arthur Christopher Orme Plummer, 1927–) Canadian actor, often cast in distinguished but chilly roles; he is best remembered as Captain Von Trapp in the record-breaking Rodgers and Hammerstein musical THE SOUND OF MUSIC (1965).

Born in Toronto, Plummer made his stage debut in Ottawa in 1950; his first film role was as a playwright in Sidney LUMET's *Stage Struck* (1957). Despite acclaim as the cruel emperor Commodus in *The Fall of the Roman Empire* (1964), he remained best known as a Shakespearean actor until his appearance as Von Trapp (with his singing dubbed) in *The Sound of Music*. In *Inside Daisy Clover* (1965) Plummer played a sadistic studio head creating a star out of Natalie WOOD, while *The Night of the Generals* (1967) saw him in the role of Field Marshal Rommel. That same year, he was replaced by Rex HARRISON as the title character in *Dr Dolittle*: the film flopped disastrously and almost ruined 20th Century-Fox, but Plummer kept his fee.

Plummer's varied roles of the 1970s include the Duke of Wellington in Sergei BONDARCHUK's epic *Waterloo* (1970), a retired jewel thief in *The Return of the Pink Panther* (1974), Rudyard Kipling in *The Man Who Would Be King* (1975), and Sherlock HOLMES to James MASON's Dr Watson in *Murder by Decree* (1978). Among his later movies are the thriller *Eyewitness* (British title *The Janitor*; 1981), the comedy *Lily in Love* (1985), with Maggie SMITH, the police spoof *Dragnet* (1987), in which he plays a televangelist, and *Star Trek VI: The Undiscovered Country* (1991).

Poe, Edgar Allan (1809–49) US writer, whose macabre stories have inspired no less than 111 films, though many of these, such as *The Black Cat* (1934), owe nothing more to Poe than the title and a sinister atmosphere. Among the best-known Poe adaptations are a series of films of the 1960s directed by Roger CORMAN and starring Vincent PRICE: *The Fall of the House of Usher* (1960), *The Pit and the Pendulum* (1961), and *The Raven* (1963) were all scripted by

Richard Matheson, while *The Masque of the Red Death* (1964) was stylishly photographed by Nicholas ROEG. So great was the subsequent demand for Poe that the film *Witchfinder General* (1968), with Price in the title role, was retitled *The Conquerer Worm* in America, although it had nothing to do with the tale of that name.

Other popular Poe stories include *The Tell-Tale Heart*, with five screen adaptations (including a cartoon version), and *The Murders in the Rue Morgue*, filmed four times (including the 1954 3-D version *Phantom of the Rue Morgue*). The life of Poe, a manic-depressive alcoholic, has also been the subject of a number of movies, including *The Loves of Edgar Allan Poe* (1942).

poetic realism A style that emerged in the work of several French directors of the 1930s. Although their films focused on the commonplace realities of everyday life, these were suffused with a marked lyricism, mainly through the use of softly gradated black-and-white cinematography. Jean RENOIR spoke of: "a certain style. It was called French realism. It was, however, really a matter of showing – through this realism – a kind of poetry."

Although René CLAIR's *Sous les Toits de Paris* (1930) can be seen as a precursor of the style, its most important exponent was undoubtedly Renoir, the son of the impressionist painter. His nine films from *Toni* (1935) through to the masterpieces LA GRANDE ILLUSION (1937) and LA RÈGLE DU JEU (1939) show the style at its very best, combining a moving and sensitive humanity on the one hand with a mastery of DEEP FOCUS, long takes, and strong frame composition on the other.

Other directors associated with the style include Jacques Feyder (1888–1948), best known for *Le Grand Jeu* (1934) and *Carnival in Flanders* (*La Kermesse héroique*; 1935), and Julien Duvivier (1896–1967), maker of the gangster film *Pépé le Moko* (1937). Another master was Marcel CARNÉ, whose fatalistic *Quai des brumes* (1938) foreshadowed FILM NOIR; his incomparable LES ENFANTS DU PARADIS (1945) concluded the movement in classic style.

point-of-view shot (POV) A camera shot that presents a scene through the eyes of a particular character, thereby encouraging us to identify with him or her. An EYE-LEVEL ANGLE SHOT or OVER-THE-SHOULDER SHOT is often deployed to create this effect. Point-of-view shots are usually combined seamlessly with standard shots of the character in the context of the scene. When the effect is kept up over an extended period, the term SUBJECTIVE CAMERA sequence or technique tends to be used instead.

Poirot, Hercule The dapper Belgian DETECTIVE created by Agatha Christie in her first crime novel, *The Mysterious Affair at Styles* (1920); he went on to appear in some 33 books, 56 stories, and various film adaptations. The slightly plump ex-policeman is famous for the fastidious grooming of his waxed moustache and his insistence that crimes are best solved by the use of one's "little grey cells". In recent decades he has been played on screen by Albert FINNEY in *Murder on the Orient Express* (1974) and by Peter USTINOV in *Death on the Nile* (1978), *Evil Under the Sun* (1982), and *Appointment with Death* (1988). Ustinov has also taken the role in three US television movies, including *Murder in Three Acts* (1986), while for many British viewers David Suchet's impersonation of Poirot in a TV series of the early 1990s is the definitive portrayal. Christie, who was generally allergic to screen versions of her stories, took a particular dislike to Finney's characterization, finding his moustache seriously below standard.

Poitier, Sidney (1924–) US actor and director, the first Black to win an Oscar in a leading role.

The son of impoverished tomato growers, Poitier dropped out of school at the age of 13 and worked in a variety of menial jobs. After war service in the army, he joined the American Negro Theater and made his Broadway debut in 1946. Having already appeared in a US Army documentary, he made his feature-film debut in *No Way Out* (1950), in which he played a doctor treating a racist patient. His more notable films of the 1950s include THE BLACKBOARD JUNGLE (1955), *Edge of the City* (1957), which dealt with racial tensions in the brutal world of New York's waterfront, and *The Defiant Ones* (1958), which brought him an Oscar nomination as Best Actor for his role as a convict on the run chained to racist fellow con Tony CURTIS. He also appeared (with his singing voice dubbed) in GOLDWYN's *Porgy and Bess* (1959).

By the 1960s Poitier was firmly established as Hollywood's premier Black actor. *Lillies of the Field* (1963) brought him the Best Actor Oscar, making him only the second Black performer to win an Academy Award (the first was Hattie McDaniel, who played Mammy in GONE WITH THE WIND). His popularity reached a peak in the late 1960s with roles in Norman Jewison's IN THE HEAT OF THE NIGHT (1967), in which he gave a superb performance as Virgil Tibbs, a Philadelphia police detective, the British film *To Sir, with Love* (1967), and *Guess Who's Coming to Dinner* (1967), a miscegenation drama that also starred Spencer TRACY and Katharine HEPBURN. In 1968 he became the first Black actor to top the QUIGLEY POLL as the top US box-office draw.

In the 1970s, with his popularity now somewhat in decline, Poitier directed himself in a number of vehicles, including *Let's Do It Again* (1975) and *A Piece of the Action* (1977). By the early 1980s he was directing films for other actors, notably *Stir Crazy* (1980) and *Hanky Panky* (1982), both of which starred Gene WILDER. He returned to acting later in the decade and has recently appeared in *Sneakers* (1992), with Robert REDFORD and River PHOENIX. His latest film as director is *Ghost Dad* (1990).

Polanski, Roman (1933–) French director, screenwriter, and actor of Polish-Jewish descent, noted for the macabre and obsessive qualities of his work. Born in Paris, Polanski accompanied his family to Poland before World War II; his parents were subsequently imprisoned in Nazi concentration camps and his mother died in Auschwitz. After the war, he directed a number of imaginative shorts while studying at the Polish Film School in Łodz and working as an actor. His first feature, the thriller *Knife in the Water* (1962), in which a couple play out a series of dangerous emotional games with a complete stranger, won a prize at the Venice Film Festival. He then made two films in Britain that won major prizes at the Berlin Film Festival: *Repulsion* (1965), with Catherine DENEUVE, which was acclaimed as a horror film of rare intelligence, and *Cul-de-Sac* (1966), portraying the destruction of the ordered life of a couple on a remote island.

Polanski then moved to America to make ROSEMARY'S BABY (1968), a supernatural chiller starring Mia FARROW. A year later his private life was shattered when his pregnant wife, the US actress Sharon Tate, was murdered by members of the notorious Manson gang. Some critics interpreted the violence of Polanski's next film, *Macbeth* (1971), as a reflection of this tragedy. The acclaimed thriller CHINATOWN (1974), with Jack NICHOLSON in the lead, brought Polanski an Oscar nomination as Best Director. After making *The Tenant* (1976), a macabre fantasy in which he himself took the lead, Polanski became headline news once more when he was convicted of raping a 13-year-old girl; he fled to France for his next major project, TESS (1979), an accomplished adaptation of Thomas Hardy's *Tess of the D'Urbervilles* that brought him another Oscar nomination. He remains a fugitive from US justice. His more recent films include *Pirates* (1986), a parody of the SWASHBUCKLER genre, the Hitchcockian *Frantic* (1988), *Bitter Moon* (1992), and *Death and the Maiden* (1994), from the play by Ariel Dorfman. Polanski's autobiography, *Roman*, was published in 1984.

His talent is as undeniable as his intentions are dubious.

ANDREW SARRIS, film critic.

Pollack, Sidney (1934–) US director, producer, and actor, who has long been associated with Robert REDFORD, directing seven of his films. One of these, *Out of Africa* (1985), earned Pollack an Oscar for Best Director.

Born in South Bend, Indiana, Pollack trained at New York's Neighborhood Playhouse Theater School before making his Broadway debut in 1954. He then spent several years serving in the army and working in television. Both Pollack and Redford made their film debuts in *War Hunt* (1961); his first movie as a director was *The Slender Thread* (1964), in which Sidney POITIER tries to save potential suicide Anne BANCROFT. He then filmed Tennessee Williams's *This Property is Condemned* (1966), with Redford and Natalie WOOD. *They Shoot Horses, Don't They?* (1969), a film about the marathon dances of the Depression era starring Jane FONDA, earned Pollack an Oscar nomination as Best Director. His films of the 1970s included four with Redford – *Jeremiah Johnson* (1972), about a trapper, *The Way We Were* (1973), co-starring Barbra STREISAND as a political activist, the thriller *Three Days of the Condor* (1975), and *The Electric Horseman* (1978), a comedy Western.

In 1982 Pollack enjoyed a major box-office triumph with *Tootsie*, starring Dustin HOFFMAN as an unemployed actor forced into drag. Pollack directed and produced the film and also acted in it, as Hoffman's agent. He later told John BOORMAN that "if he could get back the 18 months of his life which were total misery making it, he would gladly give back the money [his $14-million share of the profits]. He said it was the worst experience of his life." His second triumph of the decade was the Oscar-winning *Out of Africa*, also named Best Picture, a biopic of writer Isak Dinesen with Redford and Meryl STREEP.

His more recent films include the hit comedy *The Fabulous Baker Boys* (1989), starring Jeff and Beau BRIDGES and Michelle PFEIFFER, *Presumed Innocent* (1990), with Harrison FORD, *Havana* (1990), in which Redford becomes involved in the Cuban revolution, and *The Firm* (1993), with Tom CRUISE as a lawyer who suspects his firm of corruption and murder.

Pontecorvo, Gillo (Gilberto Pontecorvo; 1919–) Italian director, born in Pisa. The younger brother of the physicist Bruno Pontecorvo (later notorious for betraying nuclear secrets to the Soviets), he took a degree in chemistry but subsequently worked in journalism. His career in the cinema began after World War II, when he worked as an assistant to such directors as Yves Allégret and Mario Monicelli; in 1953 he directed the first of several documentary shorts. Four years later he made his first feature, *La Grande Strada Azzurra*, following this with *Kapo* (1960), about the experiences of a young girl in a Nazi concentration camp.

Pontecorvo's reputation depends almost entirely on the historical epic *The Battle of Algiers* (1966). Subsidized by the Algerian government, it told the story of that country's rebellion against the French. Critics applauded the use of grainy images and nonprofessional actors to achieve the realistic look of newsreel footage and the film won the Golden Lion at the VENICE FILM FESTIVAL. His next film, the Italian-French *Burn!* (1969), starred Marlon BRANDO as a diplomat who becomes involved with revolutionaries on a Caribbean island; after the failure of this film Pontecorvo was little heard of until the late 1980s, when there was a revival of interest in his work. His other credits include *Operation Ogro* (1979), about the struggle of Basque terrorists against the Franco regime, and *The Devil's Bishop* (1988). Despite his meagre output, he is now regarded as one of the masters of post-war European film-making.

Ponti, Carlo (1910–) Italian-born French producer, husband of the actress Sophia LOREN. Ponti practised law before moving into film production in the 1940s, when he worked with such NEOREALIST directors as Luigi Zampa, Luigi Comencini, and Alberto Lattuada. ROSSELLINI'S ROME, OPEN CITY (1945), one of his early productions, won the New York Critics' Prize in 1947. In 1950 he established with Dino DE LAURENTIIS the Ponti-De Laurentiis production company, which was responsible for such films as FELLINI'S LA STRADA (1954) and *The Nights of Cabiria* (1956), *Ulysses* (1954), and the US-Italian co-production *War and Peace* (1956). After the partnership dissolved in 1957 Ponti produced films in Britain, France, and Hollywood.

His personal life has often loomed larger than his films. In 1957 he married Sophia Loren in Mexico; the union was not recognized in his native country and in 1964 Ponti became a French citizen. In 1979 an Italian court convicted him in absentia of smuggling art and curency abroad and, although he could not be extradited from France, sentenced him to four years' imprisonment and a fine of $25 million. Loren has appeared in many of Ponti's films including the romantic melodrama *The Black Orchid* (1958), the Western spoof *Heller in Pink Tights* (1960), Vittorio DE SICA'S *Two Women* (*La Ciociara*; 1960), a World-War-II tale that won her an Oscar for Best Actress, *Yesterday, Today, Tomorrow* (1963), named Best Foreign Film at the Academy Awards, and the rail-disaster film *The Cassandra Crossing* (1977). Ponti's other productions include LEAN'S *Doctor Zhivago* (1965), the ANTONIONI films BLOW-UP (1966), *Zabriskie Point* (1970), and *The Passenger* (1975), and *Andy Warhol's Frankenstein* (1975).

Popeye the Sailor An irascible tattooed cartoon character who enjoyed great popularity in the 1930s and 1940s. He was created by Max Fleischer (1889–1972) in about 1933. When Popeye the tough sailorman needed to defend his girlfriend Olive Oyl against the villainous Bluto, he fortified himself with a tin of spinach – a ploy said to have been inspired by the marketing department of a tinned-spinach manufacturer.

In 1980 the character was revived for the unsuccessful live-action feature *Popeye*, starring Robin WILLIAMS and directed by Robert ALTMAN.

Popiol y Diament See ASHES AND DIAMONDS.

pop stars in films Film-makers have long recognized the publicity potential of casting pop or rock stars in screen roles, even though the resulting performances are often unremarkable. The first popular recording artists to make films were Al JOLSON, star of the first talkie, THE JAZZ SINGER (1927), and Bing CROSBY, who began his film career in a series of comedy musicals. Frank SINATRA first appeared on screen in 1941, his most popular films being those made with Gene KELLY, beginning with *Anchors Aweigh* (1945). Sinatra proved a strong enough actor to resurrect his career through the cinema, winning an Oscar for FROM HERE TO ETERNITY (1953).

The first star of the rock-and-roll era to make the move from music to films was Elvis PRESLEY. Over 30 vehicles were created for him, starting with the Western *Love Me Tender* (1956). His subsequent films, which included *Jailhouse Rock* (1957) and *Frankie and Johnny* (1966), tended to concentrate on the songs and Presley's charisma at the expense of plot or character. The British pop singer Tommy Steele (Tommy Hicks; 1936–) appeared in a number of films, such as *The Tommy Steele Story* (1957), *The Happiest Millionaire* (1967), *Half a Sixpence* (1967), and *Finian's Rainbow* (1968). The films of Cliff Richard (Harold Webb; 1940–), including *The Young Ones* (1961) and *Summer Holiday* (1962), were light song-based features in the tradition of the earlier Presley movies.

The two major BEATLES films, Dick LESTER's *A Hard Day's Night* (1964) and *Help!* (1965), were a strong influence on the London-based spy and comedy films of the later 1960s. Individual members of the group have appeared in such films as *How I Won the War* (1967; John Lennon) and *That'll Be the Day* (1973; Ringo Starr); Paul McCartney wrote and starred in *Give My Regards to Broad Street* (1984).

Roger Daltrey (1944–) of The Who starred in *Tommy* (1974), Ken RUSSELL's version of Pete Townsend's musical fantasy, and played Liszt in the same director's

Lisztomania (1975). Daltrey's subsequent films include *McVicar* (1980) and *Buddy's Song* (1990), in which he played an ageing rocker. The films of Bob Dylan (Robert Zimmerman; 1941–) include D. A. PENNEBAKER's groundbreaking rock documentary *Don't Look Back* (1966), Sam PECKINPAH's *Pat Garrett and Billy the Kid* (1973), and the self-directed *Renaldo and Clara* (1978). Mick Jagger (1943–) of the Rolling Stones has appeared in *Ned Kelly* (1969) and Nicholas ROEG's *Performance* (1970).

As Jagger showed in *Performance*, rock stars tend to perform best on screen when their role is close to their perceived public image. David Bowie (David Jones; 1947–) is still best remembered as the alien in *The Man Who Fell to Earth* (1976), despite subsequent appearances in *Merry Christmas, Mr Lawrence* (1982) and *The Last Temptation of Christ* (1988). Phil Collins (1951–), who appeared in a number of films as a child actor, was well cast in the title role of *Buster* (1988), which portrayed the Great Train Robber as a lovable Cockney lad. The films made by Prince (Prince Rogers Nelson; 1958–) – *Purple Rain* (1984), *Under the Cherry Moon* (1986), and *Graffiti Bridge* (1990) – also trade on the public's perception of the star. Sting (Gordon Summers; 1951–) has appeared in over ten films, including *Quadrophenia* (1978), *Brimstone and Treacle* (1982), and *Dune* (1984).

Pop stars' performances occasionally confound expectations: the glamorous Spandau Ballet hardly seemed an appropriate choice for *The Krays* (1990), but the brothers Gary (1960–) and Martin Kemp (1961–) impressed critics with their chilling brutality. CHER, of the 1960s singing duo Sonny and Cher, carved out a new career as a successful actress in such films as *Silkwood* (1983), *Mask* (1985), and *Moonstruck* (1987), for which she won an Oscar. Madonna (Madonna Louise Veronica Ciccone, 1961–) has found the transition more difficult; of her performance in *Desperately Seeking Susan* (1985) co-star Rosanna Arquette remarked, "She's jumped right into the movie game...but I think people should learn to act first, you know what I mean?" Her more recent films include *Dick Tracy* (1990), *A League of Their Own* (1992), and *Body of Evidence* (1993).

pornography Films made solely to arouse sexual excitement in the (usually male) viewer. Such movies differ from mainstream films with an explicitly sexual content mainly by showing, or purporting to show, unsimulated sex acts.

The erotic potential of moving pictures was recognized from the earliest days. In the 1890s such pioneers as MÉLIÈS and Eugène Pirou introduced screen nudity into films intended for all-male 'smoking concerts' or stag parties. By 1910 short porn movies were showing in brothels and men-only gatherings in Argentina, America, and France.

Indeed, technical advances aside, there is very little to differentiate the smut of the 1950s from that of the 1900s. Although pornographers readily embraced any technical advances their budgets allowed (the close-up being a particularly important development), plots, dialogue, and acting skills remained primitive. With anything beyond the most discreet titillation proscribed in the mainstream cinema, pornographers chose to concentrate on the unique selling point of their product. As late as 1973, a porn director listed just five basic plots – woman and visiting salesman/plumber; woman (aroused by animals copulating) and farm worker; doctor/dentist and patient; burglar and woman; Peeping Tom and bather: with few exceptions, 'scripts' got to the nitty-gritty as soon as possible.

After World War II, the availability of cheap reliable equipment and film stock meant that colour and sound became more common. By the late 1960s, relaxations in CENSORSHIP and changing public attitudes led to an increased blurring of the line between porn and mainstream entertainment. Purportedly 'documentary' films – *Sexual Freedom in Denmark: a New Approach* (1969), *A History of the Blue Movie* (1971) – opportunistically illustrated their theses with hard-core clips. Russ "I always had a tremendous interest in big tits" Meyer's soft-porn fantasies *Mondo Topless* (1966) and *Beyond the Valley of the Dolls* (1970), were hitherto unimaginable outside a peep-show ghetto. Finally *Deep Throat* (1972), featuring Linda Lovelace's attempts to stimulate a clitoris located where anatomy usually dictates a set of tonsils, brought hard-core to mainstream New York cinemas. Superior production values and the publicity of a failed prosecution helped *Deep Throat* to gross over $1,000,000 and led to a rash of similar films, such as *The Devil in Miss Jones* (1973).

Briefly, pornography was chic, a counter-culture rallying cry. However, once the public could see nudity and love-making in well-made Hollywood films with proper stories, the attractions of the old-style BLUE MOVIE dwindled dramatically. Pornographers responded by catering for ever more specialized tastes, such as sado-masochism and bestiality, that remained taboo in the mainstream cinema.

The final death blow to pornography in the cinema came with the advent of the home VIDEO. Today, uncensored videos to satisfy any front-room predilection are legal in most of the West (Britain notably excepted). *See also* SEX.

Porter, Edwin S(tratton) (1869–1941) Pioneering US director, one of the first to use 'modern' techniques of film-making and editing. Present at the very birth of the film industry, he organized a New York screening in 1896, devised various projectors, and made such early NEWSREELS as *The America's Cup* (1899). In 1900 he began working for EDISON as a camera designer but soon moved over into direction, producing most of the Edison Company's films. In *The Life of an American Fireman* (1902) Porter combined existing *actualité* footage of firemen at work with specially staged scenes to produce an integrated narrative about a child rescued from a fire. This and other Edison shorts boasted the then novel use of CLOSE-UPS, DISSOLVES, and PAN shots.

His *The Great Train Robbery* (1903), at 12-minutes an epic of its time, brought together effects developed in earlier films to create a narrative that was at once exciting, coherent, and wholly cinematic. One of its more revolutionary sequences CROSS-CUT back and forth between the rescue of a telegraph operator, the assembly of a posse, and the train-robbers' escape with the money, prompting an excited response in the audience. The film ends in a close-up of the bandit leader firing a gun at the camera. Primitive though it seems today, *The Great Train Robbery* was one of the first pictures to break away from the prevailing style of film-making, in which each scene consisted of a single (usually long) shot, with the action unfolding laboriously in front of a static camera. Other film-makers immediately began to use its techniques in their own work.

Porter continued to direct prolifically until 1916, after which he concentrated on manufacturing his Simplex projector.

positive *See* PRINT.

post-. **post-production** Any work done on a film after shooting has been completed. This includes EDITING, the creation of SPECIAL EFFECTS using an OPTICAL PRINTER, DUBBING and mixing soundtracks, musical scoring, and the addition of credits.

post-synchronization *See* DUB.

Poverty Row A collective term for the smaller Hollywood studios, such as REPUBLIC and MONOGRAM, which specialized in the production of B MOVIES in the 1930s and 1940s.

Powell. **Dick Powell** (1904–63) US actor, singer, director, and producer, who made a surprise transition from sweet-voiced crooner to tough private-eye in the mid 1940s. He was played by his son, the actor Dick Powell Jnr, in John SCHLESINGER's Hollywood story *The Day of the Locust* (1975).

Born in Arkansas, Powell worked for a telephone company and as a band vocalist before making his film debut in Warners' comedy *Blessed Event* (1932). A year later he appeared in the first of several Busby BERKELEY musicals, the famous 42ND STREET (1933), with Ruby Keeler and Ginger ROGERS. The three teamed up again for Berkeley's *Gold Diggers of 1933*, while *Gold Diggers of 1937* saw Powell co-starring with his wife Joan BLONDELL. After their divorce in 1945 he married the actress June ALLYSON.

In 1944 Powell hit the screen as the hard-boiled detective Philip MARLOWE in Edward DMYTRYK's trend-setting FILM NOIR *Murder My Sweet* (1944); the title of Raymond CHANDLER's novel *Farewell My Lovely* was altered because it was thought to suggest another musical. Chandler himself preferred Powell's Marlowe to that of Humphrey BOGART. More tough-guy roles followed in the slick Columbia thrillers *Johnny O'Clock* (1946) and *To the Ends of the Earth* (1948).

In 1952 Powell began a second career as a director with the suspense film *Split Second*; four years later he produced and directed *The Conqueror*, a misconceived epic starring John WAYNE as Genghis Khan. With David NIVEN and Charles BOYER he founded Four Star Television, Inc. in 1952 (a fourth star was never found); Powell himself became president and appeared regularly in the *Four Star Playhouse* series and *The Dick Powell Theatre* (1959–61). Live drama before millions of viewers presented a nightmare for an actor used to short takes, but Powell became adept at survival. When he forgot his lines, he continued to mouth silent words so that viewers would believe there was a technical problem with the sound.

Michael Powell (1905–90) British director, producer, and screenwriter, who in collaboration with Emeric PRESSBURGER created some of the most inventive films to issue from the British cinema in the 1940s and 1950s.

Powell worked as an actor and assistant director from the mid 1920s; he began to contribute screenplays from 1930 and directed his first film, *Two Crowded Hours*, a year later. After a number of unambitious comedy-thrillers, his mature directorial style emerged with *The Edge of the World* (1937), which led to work with Alexander KORDA and his meeting with Pressburger.

In his first film with a Pressburger screenplay, the thriller *The Spy in Black* (1938), Powell experimented with the mystical, fantastical, and witty style that became a hallmark of his later films. The war years saw the making of several of the pair's most memorable works (usually under the auspices of **The Archers**, the company they founded in 1942). These included *49th Parallel* (1941), a skilful propaganda piece calling for US intervention in the war, *One of Our Aircraft is Missing* (1942), THE LIFE AND DEATH OF COLONEL BLIMP (1943), which traced the changing nature of warfare in the 20th century, and the curious *A Canterbury Tale* (1944). *I Know Where I'm Going* (1945) and A MATTER OF LIFE AND DEATH (1946) were both highly unusual dramas making clever use of the supernatural.

Outstanding among the films that followed were *Black Narcissus* (1946), a torrid tale set in the Himalayas, THE RED SHOES (1948), a tragedy set in the world of ballet that featured many leading dance figures, and *The Small Back Room* (1948). Later films, among them *The Tales of Hoffman* (1951) and *The Battle of the River Plate* (US title *Pursuit of the Graf Spee*; 1956), lacked the brilliance of their earlier work.

Of the films made by Powell after the break-up of the partnership in 1956, the most interesting was *Peeping Tom* (1960), a movie about a sadistic murderer that raised disturbing questions about the voyeuristic nature of cinema; the director himself played the killer's father. The film's hostile reception in the British press effectively ended Powell's career as a director of major features. Martin SCORSESE later described *Peeping Tom* as the "greatest intellectual influence" on his own work. In the 1960s Powell travelled to Australia and made such films as *They're a Weird Mob* (1966) and *Age of Consent* (1969) before returning to Britain for one last collaboration with Pressburger, the children's fantasy *The Boy Who Turned Yellow* (1972). Shortly before his 80th birthday Powell married Martin Scorsese's editor Thelma Schoonmaker, a woman 40 years his junior. He published two outstanding volumes of autobiography, *A Life in Movies* (1986) and *A Million Dollar Movie* (1992).

William Powell (1892–1984) Suave US actor best remembered as Nick Charles in the THIN MAN detective series of the 1930s and 1940s. Powell began by playing heavies in silent films, but with the coming of sound his cultured voice made him more suited to debonair roles. When he first heard his voice on a soundtrack he ran from the room shouting that he was going into hiding.

A student of AADA, Powell appeared on Broadway from 1912 onwards and made his screen debut ten years later as Moriarty in *Sherlock Holmes*. Other villainous roles included the sadistic film director in Josef VON STERNBERG's *The Last Command* (1928); Powell found von Sternberg so difficult that he later demanded contracts specifying that he would never have to work with him again. He played his first detective, Philo Vance, in *The Canary Murder Case* (1929) and went on to make three sequels.

Powell was married to Carole LOMBARD from 1931 to 1933; when she walked off the set of *The Greeks Had a Word for Them* (1932), rumour said that she had aborted their child.

In 1934 Powell began his long-running screen partnership with Myrna LOY in *Manhattan Melodrama*. Later that year they co-starred as wise-cracking husband-and-wife detectives in *The Thin Man* (1934), a low-budget adaptation of Dashiell Hammett's mystery novel. The film became a great box-office success, made the principals major stars, and gained Powell an Oscar nomination. They went on to co-star in five sequels and six other movies, including *Libeled Lady* (1936), a comedy that also featured Spencer TRACY and Jean HARLOW (Powell's fiancée when she died in 1937). That same year Powell starred in the musical biopic *The Great Ziegfeld*, with Loy as his wife, and the comedy *My Man Godfrey* (1936), as Carole Lombard's butler. In 1940 Powell was just edged out by Laurence OLIVIER for the lead in HITCHCOCK's REBECCA.

Later roles included the eccentric husband of Irene DUNNE in *Life with Father* (1947), a rich Texan in *How to Marry a Millionaire* (1953), and the ship's doctor in *Mister Roberts* (1955).

Power, Tyrone   (1913–58) Handsome US actor who was 20th Century-Fox's top romantic lead before World War II. He generally played sincere gentle characters but was also known for his SWASHBUCKLING roles. Power was married three times; his daughter, Romina Power, also became an actress.

Born in Cincinnati, he was the third actor in his family to be named Tyrone Power, the others being his Irish great-grandfather and his father, a British matinée idol who emigrated to America. Tyrone Power Jnr, as he was initially billed, made his stage debut as a page in *Hamlet* (1931) and his screen debut a year later in Universal's *Tom Brown of Culver*. In the later 1930s he emerged as a star in four diverse films directed by Henry KING: *Lloyds of London* (1936), *In Old Chicago* (1937) about the famous fire, the Irving BERLIN musical *Alexander's Ragtime Band* (1938), and *Jesse James* (1938), in which he co-starred with Henry FONDA.

Subsequent films included Rouben MAMOULIAN's remake of *The Mark of Zorro* (1940), in which he played the masked title character, and another swashbuckler, King's pirate drama *The Black Swan* (1942). Power, who starred in *A Yank in the RAF* (1941), fought in the US Marines during World War II. After demobilization, he favoured more serious roles, such as the tragic carnival barker in *Nightmare Alley* (1947), but continued to appear in such expensive costume dramas as King's *Captain from Castile*.

As Power's popularity waned in the 1950s, he returned to the stage. His last completed films were King's Hemingway adaptation *The Sun Also Rises* (1957) and

Billy WILDER's *Witness for the Prosecution* (1958). He died of a heart attack while filming *Solomon and Sheba* in Madrid.

Power was also known for his practical jokes. One day in 1947 an attractive young lady invited Rex HARRISON home for 'tea'. With Harrison in a state of undress, her mother suddenly appeared in a rage. Panicking, he pulled on his trousers, only to see Power, David NIVEN, and other male friends peering through the window convulsed with laughter. Power had hired both women from CENTRAL CASTING.

pre-.   pre-credits sequence Any action that appears before the MAIN TITLE and opening CREDITS of a film. Such sequences are generally used as a prologue, either setting the scene or whetting the appetite for what follows. An early example is *Crime Without Passion* (1934), which opens with close-ups of a gun firing and a pool of blood forming on the floor.

The device became fashionable to the point of cliché in the 1970s: *The Last Movie* (1971) and *The Return of a Man Called Horse* (1976) have, respectively, 30- and 17-minute pre-credits sequences. *Papillon* (1973) and *Cruising* (1980) dispense with opening credits altogether, reserving all credits for the end.

pre-production Any work carried out on a film before shooting commences. Pre-production includes script preparation; casting; contracting production personnel, actors, and actresses; budgeting and scheduling the film; designing and building sets; costume design and purchase or tailoring; finding and selecting locations; prop manufacture or purchase; preparation of lighting plots, and so on. Given that Elizabeth TAYLOR's costumes for *Cleopatra* (1963) cost a record $194,800, that the galleon used on *Pirates* (1986) cost £7,000,000, and that $3,000,000 were spent acquiring film rights to make *Basic Instinct* (1992), pre-production can be extremely expensive.

premiere The first public showing of a film, usually in a single theatre. The glitzy event is attended by the star performers, director, producer, and others involved with the production. Important premieres also attract scores of journalists and photographers and crowds of sightseers. The premiere of GONE WITH THE WIND (1939) at the Grand Theatre in Atlanta drew five Southern governors, temporarily increased the city's population from some 300,000 to one million, and led the governor of Georgia to declare a state-wide holiday.

Preminger, Otto (1906–86) Austrian-born director and producer, who made a successful career out of breaking Hollywood taboos.

The son of Austria's attorney general, he studied acting with Max Reinhardt while earning a law degree in Vienna; he directed his first film, *Die Grosse Liege*, in 1931. After directing on Broadway he travelled to Hollywood to make *Under Your Spell* (1936) for 20th Century-Fox but was sacked soon afterwards for arguing with Darryl F. ZANUCK. He returned to stage direction with *Margin for Error* (1938), in which the Jewish Preminger played a Nazi villain. When Fox asked him to repeat the role for their 1943 screen version, he agreed on condition that they also allowed him to direct.

After appearing as another Nazi heavy in *They Got Me Covered* (1943), Preminger produced and directed LAURA (1944), the most acclaimed film of his career; his adult handling of a classic murder story laid the groundwork for the FILM NOIR genre and brought him an Oscar nomination as Best Director.

In 1953 Preminger formed his own company, Carlyle Productions. His films of the 1950s wre pioneering and controversial efforts. *The Moon is Blue* (1953) caused a sensation by using the taboo words 'virgin' and 'pregnant' and became the first commercial feature to be released without a seal of approval from the MPAA. More controversy accompanied *The Man with the Golden Arm* (1956), which was Hollywood's first close look at drug addiction. Preminger enjoyed further success with the all-Black musical *Carmen Jones* (1954) but was less lucky with *Saint Joan* (1957), starring Jean Seberg, and with Samuel GOLDWYN's *Porgy and Bess* (1959). During the production Goldwyn and Preminger, who was notorious for his on-set sarcasm and shouting, argued about every detail. At one point Preminger gestured at an expensive costume and yelled at Goldwyn, "Look, you've got a two-dollar whore in a $2,000 dress!"

That same year, Preminger produced and directed the box-office success *Anatomy of a Murder* (1959), with the unusual casting of James STEWART as a lawyer in a murder case. It was again controversial for its realistic description of a rape, in which 'panties', 'contraception', and 'spermatogenesis' were mentioned on screen. His later films, which were increasingly melodramatic in style and content, included *Exodus* (1960), about the founding of modern Israel, the political thriller *Advise and Consent* (1962), *The Cardinal* (1963), and *Hurry Sundown* (1966), an overwrought drama about racism. His last film was Graham GREENE's spy story *The Human Factor* (1979).

When the stripper Gypsy Rose Lee died in 1971, Preminger revealed that he had been the father of her son, the 26-year-old Erik Kirkland, whom he then adopted. Kirkland changed his name to Preminger and became his father's associate producer and screenwriter.

prequel The reverse of a SEQUEL; a film dealing with the earlier lives of characters who have already appeared in a successful movie. The prequel is a way of extending the potential of a saga-like story, especially when a sequel is not possible because a major character dies in the original film. For example, 20th Century-Fox capitalized on the phenomenal success of BUTCH CASSIDY AND THE SUNDANCE KID (1969), in which the title characters are both killed, by making *Butch and Sundance: the Early Days* (1979) ten years later. Francis Ford COPPOLA's THE GODFATHER, PART II (1974) is both a prequel and a sequel to the original film.

Presley, Elvis (1935–77) US rock-and-roll idol, who starred in over 30 formulaic films in the 1950s and 1960s. Although they grossed more than $150 million and made Presley the tenth ranking box-office draw of the 1960s, the critics remained unimpressed.

Presley worked as a cinema usher and truck driver before making his first recordings for Sun Records in 1954. By 1956 his fusion of country music with rhythm and blues and his exciting performance style had made him America's top-selling singer, a position he retained until his death.

That year Paramount's Hal B. WALLIS signed Presley to a seven-year contract only to loan him to 20th Century-Fox for his first film, the Western *Love Me Tender* (originally titled *The Reno Brothers* but renamed after one of the songs). Actresses on the set smiled when the shy newcomer addressed them as 'Ma'am'. Next came the semi-autobiographical story *Loving You* (1957), which followed Elvis on tour, *Jailhouse Rock* (1957), in which his tight trousers began a teenage trend, and the superior *King Creole* (1958).

His return from two years' overseas service in the US Army was marked by *G. I. Blues* (1960), about a soldier stationed in West Germany. He followed this with Don SIEGEL's *Flaming Star* (1960), in which he gave his best film performance as an American Indian. Later films included such routine vehicles, as *Girls! Girls! Girls!* (1962), *Viva Las Vegas* (1964), and *Change of Habit* (1969).

In 1969 Presley abandoned his film career and returned to the stage. Despite continuing success as a recording artist, his later years were marked by weight problems, drug addiction, and reclusiveness. He died of a heart attack at the age of 42.

Pressburger, Emeric (1902–88) Hungarian-born British screenwriter, director, and producer best known for his collaborations with Michael POWELL. Pressburger attended the universities of Prague and Stuttgart and worked as a journalist before beginning to write scripts for Austrian and German films. Following Hitler's rise to power, he worked in France before moving to Britain in 1935. He met Powell in 1937 and the two collaborated for the first time on Alexander KORDA's *The Spy in Black* (1938).

Having formed a production partnership in 1942 as **The Archers**. Powell and Pressburger worked together on the writing and direction of their films until 1956. Although none of their films was a great commercial success all were marked by high artistic and technical qualities. The first of their movies on which Pressburger shared the credit for direction was *One of Our Aircraft is Missing* (1942). Other remarkable features included THE LIFE AND DEATH OF COLONEL BLIMP (1943), A MATTER OF LIFE AND DEATH (1946), an ambitious film about the trial of a British airman in heaven, *Black Narcissus* (1947), set in an Anglo-Catholic convent in the Himalayas, the ballet story THE RED SHOES (1948), which received an Oscar nomination for best film, and *The Battle of the River Plate* (US title *Pursuit of the Graf Spree*; 1956).

After the break-up of the partnership, Pressburger wrote, produced, and directed *Miracle in Soho* (1957), about the romance between a roadworker and a barmaid, and scripted and produced the US film *Behold a Pale Horse* (1964), an adaptation of his own novel *Killing a Mouse on Sunday*. He also wrote the Carlo PONTI release *Operation Crossbow* (1965), about a World War II mission to destroy a Nazi rocket plant. In 1983 the British Film Institute awarded BFI Fellowships to Pressburger and Powell.

Prévert, Jacques (1900–77) French poet and screenwriter, best known for his popular ballads and for scripting Marcel CARNÉ's LES ENFANTS DU PARADIS. He was France's leading screenwriter from the mid 1930s to the mid 1940s.

Born in Neuilly-sur-Seine, Prévert became associated with the surrealist movement in the late 1920s and began to publish poetry. In 1932 he co-scripted the comedy *L'Affaire est dans le sac* (1932) with his brother Pierre, who directed. Prévert went on to write the comedy drama *The Crime of Monsieur Lange* (1935) for Jean RENOIR and Carné's *comédie noire*, *Bizarre bizarre* (1937).

The writing-directing team of Prévert and Carné first came to international attention with *Quai des brumes* (1938), a fatalistic drama about an army deserter (Jean GABIN) and his lover. Their collaboration continued with *Le Jour se lève* (1939), a story of jealousy and murder that also starred Gabin. The film's pessimism led to a government ban on its export.

During the Occupation, Prévert and Pierre Laroche co-scripted Carné's *Les Visiteurs du soir* (US title *The Devil's Envoys*; 1942), a supernatural fable in which the Devil clearly represented Hitler. Next came the masterpiece *Les Enfants du paradis* (1945) a romantic epic about the Parisian theatre of the 1820s that can also be seen as an allegory of the Occupation. Their collaboration ended with an expensive flop, *Gates of the Night* (1946), based on a ballet co-written by Prévert, who also contributed lyrics to its popular song, 'Autumn Leaves'.

Prévert subsequently wrote little for the cinema; his later screenplays include *The Lovers of Verona* (1948) for André CAYATTE, *The Hunchback of Notre Dame* (1956), and *Les Amours célèbres* (1961).

preview A showing of a film before its official PREMIERE. These are often arranged to allow critics to publish their reviews before the film's release. Audiences may also include members of special-interest groups or 'opinion-makers', whose word-of-mouth endorsement of a film can encourage a positive attitude before release.

Previews are increasingly used at a still earlier stage to test audience reaction to big-budget films. This may result in last-minute editing revisions or, more rarely, in major plot changes that require the shooting of new material. The original ending of *Fatal Attraction* (1987) had Alex (Glenn CLOSE) commit suicide, implicating Dan (Michael DOUGLAS) as her killer; however, outraged preview audiences screaming "Kill the bitch!" persuaded the producers to shoot a new ending, in which Alex is killed by Dan's righteous wife, Beth.

Price, Vincent (1911–93) US actor, who became typecast in HORROR FILMS during the 1950s. Price was heir to a fortune, his grandfather being head of the Price Baking Powder Co. and his father a jelly-bean magnate. In 1935 he gained an MA Arts from the University of London but, finding that he was a mediocre painter, gave it up and began to act on the British stage. His breakthrough came when he was cast (because he could speak German) as Prince Albert in *Victoria Regina* (1935). The play later ran for 517 weeks on Broadway and led to Price's first film role, in the screwball comedy *Service de Luxe* (1938).

The nightmarish *Tower of London* (1939) was Price's first venture into horror; he subsequently appeared in *The Invisible Man Returns* (1940) and became well known as radio's The Saint in the 1940s. After a long interval, Price returned to horror with the big-budget 3-D feature *House of Wax* (1953). As the Devil in *The Story of Mankind* (1957), he argued powerfully for humanity's inherent evil, making a "much better case" than Ronald COLMAN for the defence, according to *Variety*. In the 1950s his career ranged from the heights of *The Fly* (1958) to the depths of the GIMMICK movie *The Tingler* (1959). His non-horror roles included a memorable performance as an Egyptian architect in DE MILLE'S THE TEN COMMANDMENTS (1956).

House of Usher (1960) began Price's long association with Roger CORMAN and the tales of Edgar Allen POE, which continued for another six movies; the high point of the series was his performance as a decadent nobleman in *The Masque of the Red Death* (1964). Few of Price's films were of this calibre, however. During the making of *Witchfinder General* (1968), the actor fell out

with director Michael Reeves, and, listing his numerous credits, demanded to know how many pictures Reeves had made. "Two good ones" he replied.

From then on, Price concentrated on the camper end of the horror market, appearing with Peter CUSHING and Christopher LEE in *Scream and Scream Again* (1970) and as the villain in *The Abominable Doctor Phibes* (1971). In *Theatre of Blood* (1973) he played a Shakespearean actor who takes revenge on his critics by murdering them in ways suggested by Shakespeare plays. His last horror movie was *The Monster Club* (1980). In his old age Price married actress Coral Browne, wrote two cookbooks, became a noted art critic, and won a Grammy award for his spoken-word album *Tales of Witches, Ghosts and Goblins*. He also appeared with Bette DAVIS and Lillian GISH in the gentle *The Whales of August* (1987). In his final film Price played the creator of *Edward Scissorhands* (1990).

principal photography The most important photography on a SHOOTING SCRIPT, generally that involving work with the main performers. The SECOND UNIT is relegated to shooting less-demanding background footage. Other secondary units may have responsibility for special effects or for action scenes.

print Positive film printed from an original or duplicate negative (DUPE). The main types are the WORKPRINT used in editing, the MASTER PRINT struck from the original negative once this has been cut to match the approved final version of the film, and the RELEASE PRINTS struck from dupes and circulated to cinemas.

print it! A director's call indicating his or her satisfaction with a TAKE; this version of the shot can now be processed. The decision is usually noted in the production log.

Private Life of Henry VIII, The (1933) Alexander KORDA's lighthearted BIOPIC of the infamous monarch. The movie launched the British film industry into the world market and established producer-director Korda as its premier figure. It also made Charles LAUGHTON an international star and boosted the careers of Robert DONAT, Merle OBERON (who became Korda's wife), and Elsa LANCHESTER (Laughton's wife).

Korda reportedly conceived the film after hearing a taxi-driver singing the music-hall number 'I'm 'Enery the Eighth, I am'. It was made quickly for about £60,000. When Paramount, who had Laughton under contract, refused to advance funds so that filming could be completed United Artists helped out. The film premiered to record-breaking crowds at New York's Radio City Music Hall, two weeks before opening at London's Leicester Square Theatre. After it earned £500,000 on its first release, UA signed up Korda for a further 16 films. Laughton's roistering depiction of Henry earned him the Oscar as Best Actor, while the film itself was Britain's first to be nominated as Best Picture.

The plot reviews the king's extensive marital life, summarized in Henry's classic line "The things I do for England!" Of his six wives, five are featured: Catherine of Aragon is ignored because, as the film announces, she was "a respectable woman and therefore not very interesting." The film opens with intercuts of Jane Seymour (Wendy Barrie) preparing for her wedding and Anne Boleyn (Oberon) preparing for the executioner. Highlights include the banquet scene, in which Henry belches and throws chicken bones over his shoulder, his card game with the giddy Anne of Cleves (Lanchester), and his grief at the supposed affair between Catherine Howard (Binnie Barnes) and Culpepper (Donat).

producer The person responsible for a film budget and in overall charge of all creative and production personnel. A producer will follow a film through every stage of its development, from the initial idea, through scripting and shooting, to the marketing and distribution of the completed picture.

In the 1910s many exhibitors and distributors began to produce movies in order to keep hungry audiences filling their theatres. Knowing little about the artistic and technical sides of film-making, they generally assumed the role of 'moneymen', making alliances with directors and performers as required. In this way the business and creative aspects of film-making became separated.

It was Thomas INCE who formalized the system in which studio-contracted producers, reporting to production heads or EXECUTIVE PRODUCERS, became responsible for costing and scheduling a number of productions and assembling the teams to make them. This STUDIO SYSTEM of production prevailed throughout Hollywood's Golden Era. A handful of independent producers,

such as David O. SELZNICK or Sam GOLDWYN, also ran studios whose output was distributed by the majors. Nowadays most producers work independently, financing and distributing films on a one-off basis with different companies.

Although the idea for a film may not originate with its producer, the decision to take it into production depends ultimately on his or her hunch. This will be based on an evaluation of current public taste, the track record of any similar films, and the creative team that he or she can assemble. If a 'hot' director or performer can be associated with a production, this will help to attract finance to the 'package' the producer has to offer.

The producer's true function is to create an environment in which film-making is possible. Once a film goes into production, some delegate all creative decisions, giving an ASSOCIATE PRODUCER day-to-day responsibility; others are notorious for their constant interference.

> The producer must be a prophet and a general, a diplomat and a peacemaker, a miser and a spendthrift. He must have vision tempered by hindsight, daring governed by caution, the patience of a saint and the iron of a Cromwell.
> JESSE L. LASKY, producer.

> Producers are assholes...They know all the tricks of the trade but they don't know the trade itself.
> JAMES WOODS, actor.

production. production assistant *See* ASSISTANT DIRECTOR.

Production Code *See* HAYS CODE.

production credits *See* CREDITS.

production designer *See* ART DIRECTOR.

production manager *See* UNIT MANAGER.

project. projectionist A person who operates a film PROJECTOR. Working from a projection booth, the projectionist must operate the two quite different audio and visual mechanisms, keeping the picture in focus, the image steady, the frame edges out of sight, and the soundtrack audible and clear. In an era of less reliable equipment, projectionists needed strong nerves to be able to restart a film in the face of an irate audience's boos and hisses when things went wrong!

Though complete movies can now be wound on huge reels holding up to four and a half hours of film, traditionally a projectionist had to ensure a smooth CHANGEOVER from the end of a reel on one projector to the start of the next reel on a second projector. More fundamentally, the projectionist had to ensure that the correct reels were shown in the correct order.

The advent of computerized systems has greatly simplified the projectionist's task. Interval lighting, background music, and adverts or TRAILERS are all now automatically triggered. Had MULTIPLEX cinemas existed 50 years ago, they would have required a small army of projectionists to run them; nowadays the whole complex can be run by one man or woman.

projector The machine used to project enlarged images from a moving film strip onto a screen; owing to PERSISTENCE OF VISION, the rapid succession of still frames is perceived as a moving sequence.

A projector is essentially a camera in reverse; instead of receiving images, focused by a lens, onto camera film, a projector uses a powerful light source to cast images from positive film, focused by a lens, onto a screen. As with the cine camera, the heart of the cine projector is the film transport mechanism; this intermittently moves film into the picture gate, holds a single frame there for a fraction of a second for projection, and then advances the next frame. As light shone through film in transport would project a blur, a synchronized rotary shutter is used to cut off the beam until the frame is ready for projection. To prevent a flickering effect, the shutter has two blades that break the light source 48 times a second (i.e. twice for each frame with films shown at the standard sound speed of 24 fps).

In large theatres, a picture on the screen can be 500,000 times bigger than the frame in the projector. With magnification on this scale, an extremely strong light source is needed if the picture is to be adequately bright; originally high-temperature carbon ARC LAMPS needing constant attention were used, but cooler longer-lasting xenon lamps are now the norm.

Although projection is intermittent, OPTICAL SOUND must be read continuously, like the tape in a tape recorder. To surmount this problem, the soundtrack is displaced 20 frames in ADVANCE of its visual equivalent; this enables it to be read in a separate mechanism some inches beyond the picture gate,

where the film flows continuously past an exciter lamp beam.

Over the years, various special systems have been devised to project WIDESCREEN images. The main types have been multiprojector systems, such as CINERAMA, ANAMORPHIC processes, such as CINEMASCOPE, which squeeze a wider-than-normal image into a standard frame, and the use of wide-gauge film, as in TODD-AO.

prop Any movable object used in a film scene, excluding costumes, furniture, or sections of the set. Props can range from simple HAND PROPS, such as glasses and cigarettes, to the £7,000,000 galleon constructed for *Pirates* (1986) or the artworks worth $10,000,000 hired for *Legal Eagles* (1986). Some 11,250,000 different items were required for *Gone With the Wind* (1939).

prop man or **woman** A person who purchases, hires, or arranges the manufacture of any props needed for a production. He or she generally runs a **property department**, which must ensure that every prop, from vintage cars to bunches of red roses or specific dishes of food, is in the right place at the right time.

propaganda Films, usually government instigated, intended to manipulate mass opinion for political ends. The power of cinema as a tool of propaganda first became apparent during WORLD WAR I, when most of the belligerents made recruiting vehicles (*England Expects*, 1914, *The Fatherland Calls*, 1914) or films vilifying the enemy (*The Kaiser, the Beast of Berlin*, 1918). It was left to the totalitarian regimes of the interwar era to systematize the use of film to spread and enforce ideology.

During the Russian Civil War, Lenin's 'agit trains' took revolutionary film to illiterate peasants. Although early Bolshevik propaganda, such as the DOCUMENTARIES of Dziga Vertov (1896–1934), was often technically inventive, creative freedom was severely limited from the late 1920s onwards. Thereafter, Soviet production was mainly restricted to uplifting works of Socialist Realism or such essays in beatification as *Lenin in 1918* (1939).

In Fascist Italy, the regime encouraged the making of films of a "patriotic nature...to correct public taste...corrupted by films whose moral and aesthetic qualities...left much to be desired." These included *Path of the Heroes* (1936), glorying Italy's Abyssinian invasion, and Silvio Gallone's *Scipio Africanus* (1937), an epic equating heroic Roman imperialism with that of Il Duce. The screenplay of the latter film is rumoured to have been written by Mussolini himself.

If Italian or Soviet propaganda was often comically blatant, Goebbels (who argued that propaganda must "invisibly...penetrate the whole of life without the public having any knowledge at all of the ...initiative") favoured a more insidious approach. Drumbeating gospels of Aryanism, anti-Semitism, and a heroic *Volk* loyal to Fatherland and Führer, were generally limited to newsreels or documentaries, thereby avoiding the alienating effect of propaganda posing as entertainment. Leni RIEFENSTAHL's powerful *Triumph of the Will* (1934) imbued a Nuremburg Rally with almost medieval mysticism, while the same director's OLYMPIA (1938) used the Berlin Olympics to glorify Aryan athleticism. A few feature films were more overt, notably the rabidly anti-Semitic *Jud Süss* and *The Eternal Jew* (both 1940): *Titanic* (1943) blamed the ship's sinking on a reckless Anglo-Jewish bid for a transatlantic record, while *Ohm Krüger* (1941) showed valiant Boers struggling against the British oppressors and their brutal concentration camps.

Although initially unprepared for war, Britain was soon producing such uplifting documentaries as Humphrey JENNINGS's *London Can Take It* (1940) and *Fires Were Started* (1943). Such features as *In Which We Serve* (1941) extolled British heroism and decency, while OLIVIER's stirring *Henry V* (1944) prepared the public for D-Day. In America, such films as *Lady Hamilton* (1941) – England resists Napoleonic invasion – and *Sergeant York* (1941) – Quaker becomes war hero – helped to sway public opinion against isolationism. Once America had entered the war, Hollywood played a major role in the war effort: *Hitler's Children* (1942) showed Nazi tyranny; CASABLANCA (1942) emphasized the need for personal sacrifice; and MRS MINIVER (1942) painted a heroic picture of the British home front. Similar films helped in the war against Japan (*See* WORLD WAR II).

After the war, such pro-Soviet films as *Mission to Moscow* (1943) proved highly embarrassing to Hollywood in the era of the communist witch-hunts. The COLD WAR years elicited a rich harvest of propaganda from US film-makers; approaches ranged from the direct (*I Was a Communist for the FBI*, 1952) to the allegorical (*Red Planet Mars*, 1952). Soviet anti-Americana included *The Russian Question* (1948) and *Conspiracy of the Damned* (1950), about a Vatican-CIA plot to destabilise Eastern Europe.

> The cinema is the greatest means of mass propaganda.
> JOSEPH STALIN.

Psycho (1960) Alfred HITCHCOCK's shocking suspense thriller. The 45-second scene in which Janet LEIGH is murdered in the shower is still considered one of the most frightening ever filmed. The impact of the scene owes less to any graphic violence – the knife plunging through the shower curtain never connects – than to the ultra-rapid cutting style and Bernard Herrmann's screechy music. The blood seen flowing down the drain was actually chocolate sauce (the film was made in black-and-white).

Adapted from Robert Bloch's horror novel, *Psycho* was originally intended for the director's weekly television show *Alfred Hitchcock Presents*. He apparently considered it a half-humorous spoof of the horror genre. However, the shift from his established style of psychological suspense to a more direct treatment of violence and perversity led to miserable reviews from the British press, with the *Daily Mail* calling it the director's worst film ever.

In the plot Marion Crane (Leigh) steals $40,000 from her employer and spends the night at a rundown motel. The shy manager Norman Bates (Anthony PERKINS) calms her nerves by chatting amiably about his invalid mother and his hobby of taxidermy. Minutes later, Marion is murdered in the shower. When Detective Milton Arbogast (Martin Balsam) noses about, he is also killed. It is left to Marion's sister, Lila (Vera Miles), to discover Norman dressed in his mother's clothes and the old woman herself sitting embalmed in the cellar.

Perkins reprised the role of the mother-fixated psychopath in two inferior sequels, *Psycho 2* (1983) and *Psycho 3* (1986). The film must also be considered the ancestor of all the sadistic SLASHER MOVIES of the 1980s.

Psycho's famous hilltop gothic house, two-thirds lifesize, is now a star attraction of the Universal Studios tour.

Public Enemy, The (1931) Warner Brothers' trend-setting GANGSTER movie, featuring James CAGNEY as a vicious but charismatic hoodlum. Cagney was originally cast in the main supporting role, but three days into shooting director William WELLMAN gave him the lead in place of Edward Woods. The other principals were Joan BLONDELL, Mae Clarke, and Jean HARLOW, whose performance was so weak that many of her lines were cut.

Wellman himself admitted "The thing that made it a success was one word: Cagney." The actor's rivetingly brutal performance made him a star overnight. Even his rough handling of women won devoted female fans; the scene in which he shoved a grapefruit into Clarke's face over the breakfast table soon became the film's most celebrated moment. To deflect criticism, Warners' added both a foreword and a postscript making it clear that it did not intend to "glorify the hoodlum or the criminal."

Harvey Thew's script was based on a hard-hitting story by Kubec Glasmon and John Bright, two former Chicago reporters who won Oscar nominations for Best Original Screenplay. Wellman's direction was determinedly realistic: for one scene, an expert marksman on a raised platform fired a submachinegun towards Cagney so that the camera could film the slugs striking the building inches from his head.

The story begins with two rowdy slum boys, Tom Powers and Matt Doyle, growing up in 1909 Chicago. By 1920 they have graduated from petty theft to armed robbery and bootlegging. Powers, played as an adult by Cagney, becomes ever more ruthless and arrogant as he rises in the criminal world. After killing Doyle, a rival mob eventually kidnaps and executes Powers, dumping his body on his mother's doorstep.

publicity. **publicist** The person responsible for disseminating publicity about a movie. The publicist plays a vital role in the marketing of a film, a process that starts long before posters appear and that can cost more than the film itself (publicity for JURASSIC PARK, 1993, was budgeted at $8,000,000 more than its $60,000,000 production cost).

A publicist usually controls a publicity department or works with a public relations firm, whose staff will prepare press releases, encourage media interest in the creative or technical aspects of a film, take journalists to exotic locations, arrange interviews or photo-opportunities, and even seed rumour to arouse curiosity. The price of a property is an early opportunity for a press release, as is the signing of major stars or a director; stories about the complexity and expense of the special effects, or gossip about the stars' antics on and off camera can also be guaranteed to arouse interest. Scope for publicity grows as a film nears release and is shown to PREVIEW audiences – lurid tales of audiences fainting, vomiting, or even having heart attacks have long been used to HYPE horror films, for instance.

Publicity stunts are as old as the industry and have sometimes included the use of rent-a-mob picketers 'protesting' at a controversial screening. Nothing, however, beats the interest aroused by a ban: Oliver STONE's *Natural Born Killers* (1994) was refused classification for some months by the British Board of Film Classification while claims of several copy-cat killings were investigated. By the time it was passed in 1995, hype had effectively blurred with independent comment to create a publicity gale that no budget could buy.

publicity still A photograph used for publicity or advertising purposes, usually just before a movie is released. This may be either an ACTION STILL, a posed shot of the stars, or a candid shot of on-set work.

Pudovkin, Vsevolod (1893–1953) Soviet director, theorist, and actor who ranks with EISENSTEIN and DOVZHENKO as one of the three great Russian film-makers of the silent era. A disciple of D. W. GRIFFITH, Pudovkin developed a form of MONTAGE that was less aggressive though no less technically accomplished than Eisenstein's celebrated technique. His theoretical writings also advocate AUTEUR-style directors and restraint in acting. Although Pudovkin's films are full of propaganda for the Soviet regime this is generally presented through individual characterization rather than an emphasis on the masses. He was awarded the Stalin Prize for *Suvorov* (1941) and *Admiral Nakhimov* (1946).

The son of a travelling salesman, Pudovkin was raised in Moscow and studied physics and chemistry at the university there. During World War I he was wounded and imprisoned by the Germans but escaped. Having become intrigued by Griffith's INTOLERANCE (1916) he enrolled at Moscow's State Institute of Cinematography in 1920 and joined Lev Kuleshov's 'experimental laboratory' two years later.

For Kuleshov's first experimental film, *The Extraordinary Adventures of Mr West in the Land of the Bolsheviks* (1924), Pudovkin acted as co-writer, assistant director, and art director as well as playing the part of a Russian conman who fleeces a US tourist. A year later, he directed his first film, the documentary *Mechanics of the Brain* (released in 1926, after his two-reel slapstick comedy *Chess Fever*, 1925).

Pudovkin's masterpiece *Mother* (1926) was adapted from Maxim Gorki's story about a mother (Vera Baranovskaya) who becomes a communist after betraying her strike-breaking son. The film is seen as a *tour-de-force* of editing technique. His subsequent silent films included *The End of St Petersburg* (1927), which features spectacular scenes in which the mob attack the Winter Palace, *Storm Over Asia* (1928), about the Red Army's battle with a small British force in Mongolia, and the moralistic *A Simple Case* (1932), which condemns adultery.

Pudovkin made 13 talkies, mostly collaborations, beginning with *The Deserter* (1933) about a fleeing Red Army soldier. In 1935 he was badly injured in a car accident that killed his screenwriter, Nathan Zarkhi. After three years' recuperation, Pudovkin co-directed *Victory* (1938); he later returned to acting in Eisenstein's IVAN THE TERRIBLE (*Part One*; 1944) in which he played the fanatic Nikolai. He completed *Vasili's Return* (1953) shortly before his death.

pull. pull back The director's instruction to move a filming camera away from the subject or action. The direction **dolly back** or **camera back** may also be used.

pull-down mechanism *See* CAMERA; INTERMITTENT MOVEMENT.

push-off or **push-over wipe** *See* WIPE.

Puttnam, David (1941–) British producer, whose film CHARIOTS OF FIRE (1981) became the most successful British movie to date at the US box-office. At the 1982 BAFTA Awards ceremony he was presented with the Michael Balcon Award for his outstanding contribution to the British Film Industry.

Puttnam worked in advertising and photojournalism before entering the film industry in 1968. His first film as a producer was the teenage comedy-drama *Melody* (also released as *S.W.A.L.K.*; 1971). In the later 1970s Puttnam attracted attention with such major features as Alan PARKER's *Bugsy Malone* (1976) and *Midnight Express* (1978), which won two Oscars, and Ridley SCOTT's *The Duellists* (1977). After becoming chairman of Enigma productions in 1978 Puttnam enjoyed a run of successes that established him as Britain's leading producer. Hugh Hudson's *Chariots of Fire*, a story about the rivalry of two British runners, won four Oscars, while Roland JOFFE's *The Killing Fields* (1985), winner of three Oscars, and *The Mission* (1986), one Oscar, were both awarded major European prizes, as was Bill FORSYTH's *Local Hero* (1982).

In 1986 Puttnam became the first Briton to head a major US studio when he was given control of COLUMBIA PICTURES. His attempts to raise artistic standards while also slashing budgets were not always well received, however, and he quickly ran into opposition. In particular, he made enemies of Dustin HOFFMAN and Warren BEATTY by cutting the publicity budget for their expensive flop *Ishtar* (1987). Within a year he had brought the average cost of a Columbia picture down to $14.5 million, the lowest in Hollywood. His Columbia films included John BOORMAN's nostalgic wartime story *Hope and Glory* (1987) and Bernardo BERTOLUCCI's *The Last Emperor* (1987), which won nine Oscars including Best Picture. Despite these successes his position became untenable and he resigned after only 13 months.

In 1988 Puttnam returned to Britain and relaunched Enigma. Among his subsequent productions have been *Memphis Belle* (1990), about a US bomber crew stationed in Britain during World War II, Istvan SZABÓ's *Meeting Venus* (1991), and *Being Human* (1993).

Pygmalion (1938) The first film adaptation of George Bernard Shaw's comedy of linguistic manners. One of the most successful British films of its time, *Pygmalion* became the year's top moneymaker in Britain and a box-office hit in America, where it was distributed by MGM.

In 1936 Samuel GOLDWYN had tried unsuccessfully to buy the rights from Shaw, who replied that Hollywood had no more notion of telling a story than "a blind puppy has of composing a symphony." A year later, however, he allowed the British producer Gabriel Pascal to talk him into adapting the play for the screen. His main condition was that:

Not the least regard will be paid to American ideas, except to avoid them as much as possible.

In the event Shaw, Ian Dalrymple, Cecil Lewis, and W. P. Lipscomb, won an Oscar for the script, which was the first to get the word 'bloody' into a film. Shaw himself was unimpressed by the award, commenting "It's an insult for them to offer me any honour, as if they have never heard of me before."

In the plot, Henry Higgins, a professor of phonetics, undertakes to transform a cockney flower girl, Eliza Doolittle, into a 'duchess' in order to demonstrate his point about the role of accent in the English class system. Although he succeeds, Eliza is soon at odds with the overbearing Higgins, who persists in treating her as an experimental subject rather than as a human being. Unlike the original play, the film ends with a romantic reconciliation between Eliza and Higgins (a change that Shaw approved).

The film starred Leslie HOWARD as Higgins and Wendy Hiller, in her first leading role, as Eliza. Both received Oscar nominations, as did the picture itself. Howard co-directed with Anthony ASQUITH, who established his international reputation with the film. The brilliant pacing of the comedy is thought to owe much to the work of a young editor, David LEAN. When the musical version of the story, *My Fair Lady*, was released in 1964, *Pygmalion* was withdrawn from circulation.

Q

Q-score A rating sometimes used in America to indicate the popular appeal of a film star or other celebrity. Arrived at by marketing research, it is of keen interest to film producers, advertisers, etc. Fictional characters have been assessed in the same way: in 1990 advertising researchers correctly predicted only modest success for Warren BEATTY's *Dick Tracy*, on the grounds that the hero had a Q-score of only 19 – some way below Wonder Woman and a children's puppet called Howdy Dowdy.

Quatre-cents coups, Les See 400 BLOWS, THE.

Quayle, Sir Anthony (1913–89) British Shakespearean actor, who often played forceful characters in costume dramas or war films. He was nominated for an Oscar as Best Supporting Actor for his performance as Cardinal Wolsey in *Anne of the Thousand Days* (1969).

Quayle studied at RADA and made his first stage appearance in 1931; a year later he joined the Old Vic Company. After wartime service with the Royal Artillery he returned to the theatre as director of the Shakespeare Memorial Theatre Company in Stratford-upon-Avon (1948–56).

Quayle, who made his screen debut as the officer Marcellus in Laurence OLIVIER's *Hamlet* (1948), has often been cast in military roles. He was a Russian general in POWELL and PRESSBURGER's *Oh Rosalinda!* (1955), a naval commander in their *The Battle of the River Plate* (US title *Pursuit of the Graf Spree*; 1956), a British major in the successful Anglo-US production *The Guns of Navarone* (1961), and a staff officer in LAWRENCE OF ARABIA (1962). His other films include Alfred HITCHCOCK's *The Wrong Man* (1956), the Western *Mackenna's Gold* (1969), and Woody ALLEN's comedy *Everything You Always Wanted to Know About Sex but were Afraid to Ask* (1972). He also appeared in numerous television movies in the 1970s and 1980s.

queen. **Ellery Queen** The DETECTIVE hero of numerous films and stories of the 1930s and 1940s. The name was also used as a pseudonym by the authors of the stories in which he appeared, actually written by the cousins Frederic Dannay (1905–71) and Manfred Lee (1905–   ). First introduced in the novel *The Roman Hat Mystery* (1929), the sleuth made his screen debut in *The Spanish Cape Mystery* (1935), in which he was played by Donald Cook. In the 1940s Ralph BELLAMY and William Gargan both made frequent appearances in the role. The character was later revived for several television series.

Queen of Hollywood A title bestowed on Mary PICKFORD, in the 1920s and Myrna LOY in the 1930s.

quickie A cheaply produced film designed to catch the less discriminating and make a quick return on the money invested. Hundreds of quickies were turned out by such B-HIVES as Monogram and Republic in the 1940s and 1950s. *See also* QUOTA QUICKIE.

Quigley Poll A US poll of exhibitors that determines the top box-office stars of each year; the most frequent name in the top ten has been that of John WAYNE who appeared 25 times between 1949 and 1974. Since 1967, when Julie ANDREWS was named top box-office draw for the second year running, the list has been consistently headed by male stars, including Clint EASTWOOD (1972–73; 1983–84), Robert REDFORD (1974–76), Burt REYNOLDS (1978–82), and Tom CRUISE (1986; 1988; 1992).

Quinn, Anthony (1915–   ) US actor of Mexican-Irish parentage, who has appeared in over 100 films, often as larger-than-life rascals. After a brief period on the stage, Quinn began working in films in 1936, making his debut in *The Milky Way*. Despite marrying Cecil B. DE MILLE's adopted daughter the following year, he continued in small roles throughout the 1930s and 1940s, often as a foreign heavy.

453

QUO VADIS

Following a period on Broadway after World War II, his film career began to gather pace. Quinn won two Oscars during the 1950s, one for Best Supporting Actor in Elia KAZAN's *Viva Zapata!* (1952) and the second for his brief appearance as the artist Gaugin in *Lust for Life* (1956). He also appeared in such noted films as FELLINI's LA STRADA (1954), in which he played Zampano the strongman, George CUKOR's *Wild is the Wind* (1957), and John STURGES's *Last Train from Gun Hill* (1959). Following a failed attempt to move into directing with *The Buccaneer* (1958) he returned to acting.

During the early 1960s Quinn became a household name with striking performances as a Greek patriot in *The Guns of Navarone* (1961), a wild tribal leader in LAWRENCE OF ARABIA (1962), and the lusty title character in ZORBA THE GREEK (1964). The role of Zorba, a life-loving Greek peasant, brought Quinn an Oscar nomination as Best Actor; it has sometimes been suggested that he has played the same character, with variations, ever since. Other films from the 1960s include *A High Wind in Jamaica* (1965) and *The Magus* (1968), in which he played another larger-than-life Greek; Quinn, who had to shave his head for the role, insured himself against the risk of his hair not growing back.

After a less active period during the 1970s and early 1980s, Quinn reappeared in character roles in such films as the Kevin COSTNER flop *Revenge* (1989), Spike LEE's *Jungle Fever* (1991), and the Arnold SCHWARZENEGGER vehicle *Last Action Hero* (1993).

quonking Extraneous sounds, such as passing cars or jet planes, that are picked up by on-set microphones. They are usually removed in post-production sound work. Quonking was a serious problem in the early days of sound, when the noise of the cameras themselves had to be masked (*see* BLIMP).

quota quickie In the 1920s and 1930s, a type of inferior B-MOVIE churned out by British studios in order to take advantage of the **quota system**. This was a well-intentioned measure requiring British cinemas to show a certain percentage of home-produced films. In practice, however, the dearth of good British material meant that cinemas could only make up the quota by accepting substandard products. As a result, poor-quality low-budget films acquired a distribution they would never have gained on their own merits; this made them commercially attractive to produce.

Quo Vadis (1951) MGM's three-hour EPIC of 1st-century Rome, one of the studio's biggest ever hits. Directed by Mervyn LEROY, it was advertised with the memorable line: "Ancient Rome is going to the dogs, Robert TAYLOR is going to the lions, and Peter USTINOV is going crazy!" John HUSTON was orginally scheduled to direct but walked out after failing to get approval for a more serious treatment. The eventual $10-million spectacular received eight Oscar nominations, including Best Picture, but failed to win in any category; both Ustinov and Leo Genn were nominated for Best Supporting Actor.

Taylor starred as Roman commander Marcus Vinicius, a role originally intended for Gregory PECK and then for Stewart GRANGER; to help Taylor prepare, producer Sam Zimbalist showed him Granger's screen test. His love interest, the Christian Lygia, was played by Deborah KERR (LeRoy wanted Audrey HEPBURN but was overruled). It is, however, Ustinov, as a wonderfully loony Nero, who steals the film; Genn plays his adviser, Petronius Arbiter, and Finley Currie is St Peter. The young Elizabeth TAYLOR has a tiny role as a Christian martyr.

Quo Vadis owed much of its appeal to the spectacular scenes of the burning of Rome and of Christians being eaten by lions (which resulted in an A rating in Britain). It was the fourth screen adaptation of the 1895 novel by Polish writer Henryk Sienkiewicz. The others were silent: a French film of 1901, Enrico Guazzoni's Italian 12-reeler (1912), one of the first feature-length movies, and a 1924 Italian remake with Emil JANNINGS as Nero.

The familiar-sounding plot concerns an arrogant Roman commander who falls in love with a Christian girl; he remains contemptuous of her religion until the jealous empress Poppea orders them both thrown to the lions. There is a happy Hollywood ending.

R

R Restricted. A US film classification introduced in 1968, meaning that in the opinion of the MPAA the film is unsuitable for anyone under 17, unless accompanied by a parent or guardian. *See* RATINGS.

rack (1) An arrangement of rollers and sprockets used to advance the film in a processing machine. (2) To thread the film into any viewing, editing, or projecting machine so that the frame is properly aligned with the picture gate. (3) Another name for a trim bin (*see* BIN).

RADA The Royal Academy of Dramatic Art. The best-known British drama school, founded in 1904 by Herbert Beerbohm Tree, manager of His Majesty's Theatre. Later that year he handed the Academy over to an independent governing body and it moved to the present Gower Street site. RADA has trained such luminaries of the British cinema as Margaret LOCKWOOD, Richard ATTENBOROUGH, Alan BATES, Glenda JACKSON, and Kenneth BRANAGH.

Rafelson, Bob (1934–) US producer, director, and screenwriter, best known for creating the Monkees pop group and for advancing the career of Jack NICHOLSON. He has made relatively few films, largely because he considers the work so stressful.

Rafelson worked as a rodeo hand, a crew member on an ocean-liner, and a jazz drummer while still a teenager. He later studied philosophy before dropping out to write for television. With Bert Schneider he originated and co-produced *The Monkees* TV series in the 1960s, also writing and directing the individual episodes. This led to Rafelson directing the group in his first movie, *Head* (1968), a psychedelic farrago that he produced and scripted with Nicholson (who has a cameo). Later that year, he co-founded the short-lived BBS Productions, which produced EASY RIDER in 1969; it was on Rafelson's recommendation that Nicholson joined the cast.

In 1970 Rafelson made his name with *Five Easy Pieces*, which won him the New York Film Critics' Award as Best Director. The film, starring Nicholson as a former classical pianist who becomes a drifter, epitomizes the anti-establishment mood of the late 1960s. Star and director then teamed up again for *The King of Marvin Gardens* (1972), a critical and commercial flop.

In *Stay Hungry* (1976) Jeff BRIDGES played a rich Southerner who uses his money in unconventional ways. Rafelson, who always shoots in proper sequence, chose the happy ending on the final day of filming. The director then remade the classic FILM NOIR *The Postman Always Rings Twice* (1981), adding explicit sex scenes between Nicholson and Jessica Lange.

Rafelson's more recent movies have included *Black Widow* (1987), starring Theresa Russell as a woman who kills her husbands, *Mountains of the Moon* (1989), about the explorers Richard Burton and John Hanning, and the comedy-thriller *Man Trouble* (1992), with Nicholson as a guard-dog trainer helping a harassed Ellen Barkin.

Raft, George (George Ranft; 1895–1980) Poker-faced US actor who played gangsters for Paramount in the 1930s and 1940s. He is chiefly remembered as the coin-flipping mobster Guido Rinaldo in Howard HAWKS's *Scarface* (1932). His career suffered from terrible judgment: Raft turned down the leads in THE MALTESE FALCON (1941) and CASABLANCA (1942), both of which went to Humphrey BOGART. Billy WILDER later joked that he knew he had a good film when Raft refused his DOUBLE INDEMNITY (1944). A notoriously extravagant man, Raft squandered some $10 million at the height of his career, explaining "Part of the loot went for gambling, part for horses, and part for women. The rest I spent foolishly."

Born and raised in New York's infamous Hell's Kitchen, Raft worked as a boxer and racketeer before becoming a Broadway dancer. He made his screen debut in *Queen of the Nightclubs* (1929), having (allegedly) secured the role as a pay-off when under-world connections sent him to threaten the producers. With his slick black hair and exciting dancing ("the world's fastest Charleston dancer") he was quickly dubbed the 'New VALENTINO'. After finding stardom in *Scarface*, he encouraged the studio to sign up his old Broadway friend Mae WEST, who made her movie debut alongside Raft in *Night after Night* (1932).

In 1933 Paramount loaned Raft for 20th Century-Fox's first production, *The Bowery*. Four years later he turned down the lead in *Dead End* (1937) because the story showed the killer being idolized by teenagers (the famous DEAD END KIDS). He then co-starred with James CAGNEY in the prison drama *Each Dawn I Die* and with William HOLDEN in the crime story *Invisible Stripes* (both 1939). *Broadway* (1942), about a hoofer who becomes a movie star, was virtually a Raft biopic.

After World War II Raft's Hollywood career declined and attempts to move into European films proved unsuccessful. His casino investments were also in crisis: Fidel Castro closed his Havana club in 1959 and Britain, where he managed a plush London casino, banned him in the mid 1960s because of supposed criminal connections. Raft was subsequently confined to cameos in which he spoofed his gangster image (most notably in SOME LIKE IT HOT, 1959). In 1961 Ray Danton portrayed him in the biopic *The George Raft Story*. Fittingly, his last cameo was alongside the 86-year-old Mae West in *Sextette* (1978).

Raging Bull (1980) Martin SCORSESE's tough-minded BIOPIC of the boxer Jake LaMotta, middleweight champion of the world from 1949 to 1951. Robert DE NIRO's unflattering portrait of the brutal LaMotta brought him the Oscar for Best Actor, with nominations also going to the film itself, to Scorsese as director, and to supporting players Cathy Moriarty and Joe Pesci. Ten years after its release *Raging Bull* was voted the best movie of the 1980s by US film critics.

De Niro's absorption in the role was extraordinary, even by his standards. In order to put on brawn he spent his days working on a road gang and his nights training in a gymnasium. His greatest challenge, however, was adding 60 pounds to his 160-pound weight for the later scenes depicting the bloated ex-boxer; shooting of the film was halted for four months while De

Niro went on a pasta binge in Italy, rising early each morning in order to eat three large meals.

Raging Bull was De Niro's fourth film with Scorsese. Highlights of the movie include the impressive boxing sequences, hailed by *Variety* as "possibly the best ever filmed." The sound effect of punches being landed was created from rifle shots and the sound of melons being smashed open. Except for several home-movie sequences depicting the boxer's domestic life, Scorsese filmed in black-and-white.

The story follows LaMotta from Bronx slum kid to title contender and champion. Employing realistically ugly language throughout, it is unsparing in its depiction of the boxer's obsessive jealousy for his teen-age wife (Moriarty) and his decline into a fat has-been who is reduced to working as a stand-up comedian in cheap nightclubs. Part of his act includes reciting Marlon BRANDO's famous lines about his boxing career from ON THE WATERFRONT (1954): "I coulda been a contender."

Raiders of the Lost Ark (1981) Steven SPIELBERG's homage to the action adventure serials that had thrilled him as a boy. In the fantastic plot archaeologist Indiana Jones (Harrison FORD) and his old flame Marion Ravenwood (Karen Allen) outwit scheming Nazi agents in their search for the Ark of the Covenant.

Conceived by George LUCAS during a five-hour script conference, *Raiders* was originally to be directed by Philip KAUFMAN, who suggested that the Ark should be the subject of Indie's search. When Kaufman dropped out, Lucas turned to his old friend Spielberg, who was still smarting from the failure of his war comedy *1941*.

The film's story, supplied by Lawrence Kasdan, bore more than a passing resemblance to Leslie HOWARD's *Pimpernel Smith* (1941), in which a professor abandons academia to confound the Nazis in true swashbuckling style. Howard had played his own leading man, but 'Lucasberger' had more trouble casting their hero, with Tom Selleck committed to TV work and Harrison Ford reluctant to play another Han Solo-esque role. He finally signed up when assured that he could alter his lines whenever he saw fit; in the event, his best-remembered amendment, in which he phlegmatically shoots an Arab swordsman rather than become involved in an extended fight scene, was prompted by a sudden attack of dysentery.

Shot in France, Hawaii, Tunisia, and Elstree Studios, the film was assigned an 87-day schedule, with stiff fines threatened by Paramount if it overran. The team allegedly cut some corners by including preshot footage, including excerpts from *Lost Horizon* (1972) and *The Hindenberg* (1975). More seriously, the speed imposed on the production nearly resulted in several accidents; Ford, who performed many of his own stunts, almost had his legs crushed by the wheels of an aircraft during one sequence. Because Karen Allen was reluctant to stand in a pit of snakes some shots contain not her ankles but those of the snakes' male trainer. Six thousand grass snakes were imported from Holland for the scene, although a third of them vanished from Elstree and were never recovered.

The winner of Academy Awards for Art Direction, Sound, Editing, and Visual Effects (as well as nominations for Best Picture, Direction, Score, and Cinematography), the film scooped more than $200 million on its release and spawned two sequels, *Indiana Jones and the Temple of Doom* (1984) and *Indiana Jones and the Last Crusade* (1989).

rails Slang term for an overhead grid from which lighting equipment may be hung, either on set or in storage.

rain cluster A group of sprinklers suspended above the set, used to give the impression of heavy rainfall during filming.

Rains, Claude (1889–1967) British-born Hollywood actor, who often played sophisticated charming villains. A compact plain-looking man with a rich voice and restrained manner, Rains is best remembered as the corrupt police chief in CASABLANCA (1942).

Born in London, he was working on the British stage at the age of 11. Having performed on Broadway for several years, he made his screen debut (at the age of 44) in the title role of THE INVISIBLE MAN (1933). Although his face was never seen in the film, Rains spoke the part so memorably that he became a big star.

Rains went on to play a series of devious characters including a murderous lawyer in *Crime Without Passion* (1935) and the evil Prince John in *The Adventures of Robin Hood* (1938). Oscar nominations came his way

for portraying a corrupt senator in MR SMITH GOES TO WASHINGTON (1939) and the conniving Louis Renault in *Casablanca*. He earned a third nomination (opposite Bette DAVIS) in the title role of *Mr Skeffington* (1944) and a fourth as a Nazi spy in HITCHCOCK's *Notorious* (1946).

After George Bernard Shaw visited Denham Studios in 1944 to watch Rains and Vivien LEIGH make *Caesar and Cleopatra*, he wrote to the actress saying that he had better change the line in which she calls Caesar "thin and stringy". Although Leigh protested that she could make the line believable, Shaw insisted on the change.

Rains co-starred with Davis again in the melodrama *Deception* (1946). His last major role was as the cuckolded husband of Ann Todd in David LEAN's *The Passionate Friends* (1949). He later made minor appearances in LAWRENCE OF ARABIA (1962) and as the dying Herod in *The Greatest Story Ever Told* (1965).

Rambo The brutal muscle-bound hero played by Sylvester STALLONE in a series of violently jingoistic films of the 1980s. Stallone was offered the part after it had been turned down by Paul NEWMAN and others. The original Rambo film was *First Blood* (1982), an adaptation of David Morrell's novel about a Vietnam veteran's battle with a petty small-town sheriff. Although Morrell killed off his hero, Stallone returned to the part in the ultra-violent *Rambo: First Blood Part II* (1985), in which the machine-gun toting hero rescues US prisoners-of-war in Vietnam. The film caught the nationalistic mood of mid-1980s America, earned the approval of President REAGAN, and made the central character into a folk hero. A third instalment, the $85-million *Rambo III*, saw Rambo fighting the Soviets in Afghanistan. The films have added two new words to the language: *Ramboesque* and *Ramboism*.

Ran (1985) Akira KUROSAWA's stunning adaptation of Shakespeare's *King Lear*; the story is transposed to feudal Japan, with Lear's unfilial daughters being replaced by sons. The title is a transliteration of the Japanese character for 'chaos' or 'madness'; Kurosawa himself glossed its meaning as "human deeds as viewed from heaven." Almost 30 years after his triumphant adaptation of *Macbeth* as *Throne of Blood* (1958), Kurosawa returned to Shakespeare at the age of 75. It had taken him nearly a decade to raise the finances for the project from Japanese and French investors (with Francis Ford COPPOLA also providing funds).

The visually sumptuous film won an Oscar for Best Costume Design for Emi Wada, who used traditional Samurai costumes and make-up from Noh drama. Nominations were also received for Best Director, Best Art Direction (Yoshiro Muraki and Shinobu Nuraki), and Best Cinematography (Takao Saito).

The tragic plot centres on the ageing warlord Hidetora (Tatsuya Nakadai), who divides his lands among his three sons and demands an oath of loyalty. The youngest (Daisuke Ryu), who loves his father most, is the only one to refuse. The elder brothers eventually destroy each other in the stupendous battle scene, while the warlord is driven to madness.

Rank Organization A commercial enterprise that dominated the British film industry in the 1940s and 1950s, founded and headed by **J. Arthur Rank** (1888–1972). The product of a wealthy flour-milling family with strong Methodist convictions, Rank entered the film business largely because he saw it as the most effective way of spreading his Christian beliefs. His earliest films were instructional aids for Sunday schools and he later used his influence to promote material of a religious or edifying character, often to the dismay of his accountants. During the 1930s and 1940s he extended his activities from film production into distribution and exhibition; by the time he founded the Rank Organization in 1946, he controlled not only Pinewood and DENHAM STUDIOS but also the ODEON and GAUMONT cinema chains. The Organization later diversified into such areas as hotels, Xerox copying, etc. Rank himself never lost his early sense of mission, claiming that if he gave a full account of his experiences in the film world "it would be as plain to you as it is to me that I was being led by God."

The Organization's trademark, a huge metal gong struck by a bare-torsoed muscleman at the start of each film, was in reality made of cardboard.

Rashomon (1950) Akira KUROSAWA's exploration of the complex nature of truth. The first modern Japanese film to make an impact on Western audiences, it made the reputations of both Kurosawa, who directed and scripted, and his leading actor,

Toshiro Mifune, who played the bandit Tajomaru. In rehearsals, Kurosawa showed Mifune a film of a jungle lion and told him to act in a similar fashion. Hollywood remade the film as a Western, *The Outrage*, in 1964.

Kurosawa spent two years trying to find a studio that would produce the film, a complex adaptation of two stories by Ryunosuke Akutagawa. Although Daiei eventually agreed, the result was not much to their liking; its head walked out of the first screening and the studio subsequently hired a commentator to explain the film to cinema audiences. Daiei also opposed the film's entry in the 1951 Venice Film Festival, and was shocked when it came away with the Grand Prix. Kurosawa was not even informed that his film had been entered. *Rashomon* went on to win a special Oscar as the best foreign-language film (a category not officially created until 1956).

The story, set in medieval Japan, concerns a mysterious incident in a forest, during which a woman (Machiko Kyo) is raped and her husband murdered. At the subsequent trial, the incident is retold by the woman, the dead husband's ghost, a bandit, and a woodcutter. All the versions are different, calling the nature of truth itself into question. The four versions of the murder story are framed by scenes in which the trial is discussed years later by the woodcutter, a priest, and a peasant, who have taken shelter under the ruined Rashomon gate.

rat.   the Rat Pack The clique of film actors and entertainers who surrounded Frank SINATRA in the 1950s; other members of the group, who became notorious for their wild social life, included Dean MARTIN and Sammy Davis Jnr. *See also* BRAT PACK.

you dirty rat A phrase always associated with the tough-guy roles of James CAGNEY, and used frequently by impersonators. In fact, he never said it. The closest he came to saying something like it was: "a dirty double-crossing rat" in *Blonde Crazy*, and "You dirty yellow-bellied rat" in *Taxi* (both 1931).

Rathbone, Basil (Philip St John Basil Rathbone; 1892–1967) Hollywood actor of British parentage, who played sneering villains in the 1930s and a wry aloof Sherlock HOLMES in the 1940s. His gaunt figure and impressive profile appeared in numerous costume films, with Rathbone usually being dispatched in swordplay by Errol FLYNN or Tyrone POWER. Margaret Mitchell, author of GONE WITH THE WIND, said privately that she would have chosen Rathbone instead of Clark GABLE to play Rhett Butler in the 1939 film.

Born in Johannesburg, he attended school in England and made his stage debut in 1911; he first appeared on screen in the British film *Innocent* (1921) and moved to Hollywood three years later. When talkies arrived, his rich voice brought him such roles as the evil Mr Murdstone in *David Copperfield* (1934) and villains in the swashbucklers *Captain Blood* (1935) and *The Adventures of Robin Hood* (1938).

In 1939 20th Century-Fox paired Rathbone with Nigel Bruce (as Watson) in the Sherlock Holmes story *The Hound of the Baskervilles*. Although critic Graham GREENE complained that the famous detective now had a sense of humour, the public loved it, turning out again for Fox's sequel *The Adventures of Sherlock Holmes* (1939) and a further 12 films from Universal.

Rathbone took up the sword once more in *The Mark of Zorro* (1940), while the costume drama *Frenchman's Creek* (1944) saw him playing the caddish husband of Joan FONTAINE. After his last Holmes outing, *Dressed to Kill* (1946), Rathbone suffered a period of inactivity but stormed back duelling (at the age of 63) in *The Court Jester* (1955). In the 1960s he played camp horror in such movies as *Tales of Terror* (1962) and *The Comedy of Terrors* (1963), both with Vincent PRICE, and (the final indignity) *Hillbillies in a Haunted House* (1967).

ratings Official film classifications, based mainly on the incidence of sex, violence, and bad language in a movie. The current British ratings, determined by the British Board of Film Censors, are U (Universal), PG (Parental Guidance), 12, 15, and 18 (ages for admission), and 18R (for specially licensed cinemas). In America, classifications are issued by the Code and Rating Administration of the Motion Picture Association of America (MPAA); the current system involves six ratings – G (General), PG (Parental Guidance), PG-13 requiring "special guidance" from parents of children under 13, R (Restricted) requiring children under 17 to be accompanied by an adult, and two ratings, NC-17 and X, that bar anyone under 17.

Britain introduced ratings in 1913, the original advisory categories being U and A (Adult). An H rating for 'horrific' films was introduced in 1933 and replaced by the X certificate in 1951; a new AA rating barring those under 14 was added in 1970. The current rating system was introduced in 1982 and extended to videos three years later (except for the 12 rating, which was added in 1989).

In America classifications were not introduced until 1968, when they superseded the notorious Production Code (*see* HAYS CODE). The original M (Mature Audiences) rating was briefly replaced by GP in the early 1970s and then by PG. PG-13 was added in 1984 and NC-17 in 1990 (because the X classification made no allowance for more artistic films). *See also* CENSORSHIP.

> Oh, I get it. PG means the hero gets the girl, 15 means that the villain gets the girl – and 18 means that everybody gets the girl.
> MICHAEL DOUGLAS, on British film ratings.

Ray. Nicholas Ray (Raymond Nicholas Kienzie; 1911–79) US director. The son of a builder, Ray studied architecture under Frank Lloyd Wright before developing an interest in the theatre. After moving to New York in 1932, he worked with left-wing theatre groups and appeared in several early productions by Elia KAZAN. He subsequently joined John Houseman's Phoenix Theater Company and wrote and directed radio propaganda broadcasts during World War II.

After assisting on several films, including Kazan's *A Tree Grows in Brooklyn* (1945), Ray made his debut as a director with *The Twisted Road* (1948), a FILM NOIR about two young lovers on the run from the law. This was withdrawn after a short release, but reissued a year later under the title *They Live by Night*. The film, which attracted little attention at the time but was later much acclaimed, was the first to feature aerial shots from a helicopter. Ray's films of the early 1950s ranged from *In a Lonely Place* (1950), a melodrama with Humphrey BOGART, to the flamboyant *Johnny Guitar* (1954), a truly peculiar Western starring Joan CRAWFORD at her most camp. He then created the ultimate teenage angst movie in REBEL WITHOUT A CAUSE (1955), a vehicle for James DEAN; the film brought its director his only Oscar nomination, for supplying the original story. His other films of the decade included *Hot Blood* (1956), *The True Story of Jesse James* (1957), and *Wind Across the Everglades* (1958).

Ray made only three films during the 1960s: *The Savage Innocents* (1960), *King of Kings* (1961), and *55 Days in Peking* (1963), in which he also acted. After this he was assigned no more Hollywood features, although his cult standing as a director continued to grow.

In 1971 Ray became professor of cinema studies at the New York State University, where he completed the film *You Can Never Go Home Again* (1973) with his students. His only other directing work of the 1970s was a contribution, as one of 11 directors, to a Dutch soft porn film, *Dreams of 13* (1974). *I'm a Stranger Here Myself* (1974), a documentary about Ray, derived its name from a line delivered by Sterling Hayden in *Johnny Guitar*. In 1977 he appeared as an actor in Wim WENDER's *The American Friend*, a film that featured several other directors in acting roles. This led to a collaboration with Wenders on *Lightning Over Water/Nick's Film* (released 1980), a bizarre film that documented the last days of Ray's life as he died of cancer.

Ray was married four times, his second wife being the actress Gloria GRAHAME. In 1961 Grahame married Ray's son from another marriage, Anthony Ray, an actor turned producer who worked on several of Paul Mazursky's films of the 1970s.

Satjavit Ray (1921–92) Indian director, screenwriter, and composer, whose acclaimed APU TRILOGY brought his country's cinema to the attention of Western cinephiles. His films, which are realistic in style and humanist in content, were quite different from the musical melodramas that dominated the INDIAN CINEMA of the day. They were also made in Bengali rather than the dominant Hindi. Shortly before his death, Ray was given a Lifetime Achievement Award at the 1991 Oscar ceremonies.

Born in Calcutta, the son of a writer-painter-photographer, Ray studied economics at Calcutta University and art at Shantiniketan, the teaching centre established by Rabindranath Tagore. While working for a British advertising firm in Calcutta in the early 1940s, he also began illustrating books, including Bibbutibhusan Bannerji's novel of Bengali village life, *Pather Panchali*, which he vowed to film someday. In 1950, while working in London, Ray was deeply impressed by a screening of Vittorio DE SICA's classic BICYCLE THIEVES (1948) and decided to film the book in a similar NEOREALIST style. Accordingly, armed with £750, Ray began filming *Pather Panchali* at weekends and holidays. Encouragement came from two Western directors then working in India, Jean RENOIR and John HUSTON.

Although Ray sold everything that he owned to keep the production going, money ran out after 18 months. The project was only saved when the New York Museum of Modern Art agreed to premiere the completed film and the Bengal government stepped in with funds. A box-office success throughout India, *Pather Panchali* (1955) went on to make film history when it was named Best Human Document at the 1956 Cannes Film Festival (although François TRUFFAUT reportedly walked out in boredom). It tells the story of a poor village boy, Apu, played by Subir Bannerji (discovered living next door by Ray's wife).

Two sequels followed. *Aparajito* (*The Unvanquished*; 1956), in which Apu is portrayed by Pinaki Sen Gupta and Smaran Ghosal, tells of the young man's time at university, while *The World of Apu* (1959), starring Soumitra Chatterji, depicted his turbulent adult life.

In the early 1960s Ray, who scripted all his films, also began to compose his own scores. Many of his films of this period have female protagonists. *The Lonely wife* (1964), the story of a bored wife's disappointing affair, won him the Best Director Award at Berlin. Social and political questions became more prominent in his films of the 1970s. *Distant Thunder* (1973), named Best Film at Berlin, depicts the effects of famine on a village, while *The Middle Man* (1975) explored business corruption. *The Chess Players* (1977), Ray's first film in Hindi, was the story of two nobles more concerned with playing chess than with resistance to the British. The film, which was also released in an English version, included Richard ATTENBOROUGH in the cast.

In the 1980s Ray's productivity was affected by repeated ill health. His later films included *The Home and the World* (1984), a tragic story set during the Edwardian Raj, *An Enemy of the People* (1989), an adaptation of Ibsen's drama, and the acclaimed *The Visitor* (1990). In 1994 MERCHANT-IVORY rereleased eight restored Ray films, which were also distributed in America.

reaction shot A shot showing the response of a character to events or information. This generally takes the form of a CUTAWAY from the main action to a CLOSE-UP of the character's face.

read. reader (1) In editing, a device used for viewing film (an *optical reader*) or for the playback of either optical or magnetic sound (a *sound reader*). (2) An employee in the story department who assesses literary material submitted to the studio and (if it is not rejected at once) writes an OUTLINE and evaluation for the production department.

reading (1) A read-through of a screenplay, either as an audition for one or more of the actors or as a rehearsal. (2) The level of light or sound recorded by a meter during filming.

Reagan, Ronald (1911–) US President (1980–88), who entered politics after a successful career as a leading man with Warner Brothers, usually in B-movies. As president, he was dogged by jokes about having co-starred with a chimpanzee in the comedy *Bedtime for Bonzo* (1951). Reagan served as president of the Screen Actors Guild (SAG) from 1947 to 1952 and again in 1959. He has been married to two actresses, Jane WYMAN (1940–48) and Nancy Davis (since 1952).

Born in Tampico, Illinois, Reagan began as a radio sports announcer. His first screen role was that of a radio announcer in Warners' *Love is on the Air* (1937). Subsequent films included *Dark Victory* (1939), with Bette DAVIS, and the biopic *Knute Rockne, All American* (1940) in which he played a dying football star. When running for president 40 years later he made frequent use of the film's line, "Win one for the Gipper."

Reagan was always businesslike on set, a trait sometimes taken as unfriendliness. "I can't stand the sight of Ronnie Reagan" actress Gloria Grahame once snarled, "I'd like to stick my Oscar up his ass."

In 1942 he gave his best received performance in Sam WOOD's small-town melodrama *Kings Row*. ("Where is the rest of me?" his character asks on discovering that his legs have been amputated.) That year, Reagan was down to star in a romantic thriller called CASABLANCA until Warners decided to use Humphrey BOGART; instead, he made the patriotic musical *This is the Army* (1943). During World War II he served with the US Air Force and produced training films.

In 1949 Reagan won praise for his performance in *The Hasty Heart*, in which he played a US serviceman nursed by Patricia NEAL in a British field hospital. He helped to defend Barbara STANWYCK's ranch in *Cattle Queen of Montana* (1954) and was a submarine commander in *Hellcats of the Navy* (1957), in which he played opposite his wife Nancy Davis.

By this time his career was in decline, however; the later 1950s saw him leave Warners to host television's *Death Valley Days* for three years and *General Electric Theatre* for eight. He also became increasingly well known for his hostility to leftists in the film industry, writing an article entitled 'Reds Beaten in Hollywood'. He made his last film, Don SIEGEL's *The Killers*, in 1964.

Having served several terms as governor of California (from 1966), Reagan, a Republican, was elected America's 40th president in 1980; at 73 he was the oldest man ever to win the office. A year later, he was wounded in an assassination attempt by John Hinckley Jnr, who, ironically, was trying to impress actress Jody FOSTER. Reagan was re-elected in 1984.

realism An artistic style that purports to depict the real world in an accurate and objective manner with as little idealization or distortion as possible; its aim is often to increase our awareness of social conditions. Paradoxically, film has been claimed as both the most realistic of the arts – because of its ability to reproduce moving photographic images – and as the most divorced from reality.

Bearing in mind the enormous scope for influencing the viewer's response through selection of material, composition, and editing, the idea that any film offers a neutral transcription of reality is obviously untenable. Nevertheless, by choosing to use certain techniques rather than others, film-makers can do much to create the illusion of realism. In particular, realist cinema tends to avoid MONTAGE in favour of DEEP FOCUS MISE-EN-SCÈNE; shots tend to be lengthy, taken at eye-level, and from a medium distance, as this approximates to the way in which we normally perceive the world. Editing is usually as unobtrusive as possible.

Such techniques are particularly common in DOCUMENTARY, in which an impression of verisimilitude is essential. However, even within this genre, styles of realism vary widely – from the highly selective, highly ordered, and at times propagandistic documentaries of Robert FLAHERTY to the fly-on-the-wall approach of CINÉMA VÉRITÉ or DIRECT CINEMA. Makers of feature films have sometimes attempted to impart a greater sense of realism by adopting techniques associated with documentary – such as the use of HAND-CAMERAS or 16MM film, which gives a grainier image.

Notable realist movements in the cinema include the German 'street' movies of the 1920s, which focused attention on social conditions after World War I, Soviet socialist realism, Italian NEOREALISM, and 1950s British social realism. Some of the most interesting modern realist cinema has emerged from the Third World, e.g. Satyajit RAY's APU TRILOGY.

Realism's counterpart is EXPRESSIONISM, which aims to portray the subjective truth of a situation rather than its outward manifestations. Both tendencies have existed as long as film itself – one can compare the *actualité* shorts of the LUMIÈRE BROTHERS with the strange fantasies of MÉLIÈS in the 1890s, for instance – and no film can truthfully claim to be wholly one or the other. *See also* FANTASY.

Rear Window (1954) Alfred HITCHCOCK's tense thriller, a film that also explores the role of voyeurism in life and art. While his broken leg heals, magazine photographer L. B. Jeffries (James STEWART) passes the time watching his Greenwich Village neighbours through binoculars. In doing so he becomes convinced that Lars Thorwald (Raymond Burr) has murdered his wife; disbelieved by his nurse (Thelma Ritter) and a cop pal (Wendell Corey), he enlists the help of his fashion-model girlfriend Lisa Fremont (Grace KELLY) to uncover evidence.

In publicity for the film Hitchcock claimed that "*Rear Window* is such a frightening picture that one should never see it unless accompanied by an audience." Joking aside, this seems to be an oblique allusion to his motive for making the film – to reveal our complicity in the voyeurism that characterizes much of his work. It is almost as if his earlier features had been viewed through the binoculars with which Jeffries begins his vigil, while *Rear Window* makes use of the telephoto lens he adopts once his suspicions are aroused. The use of a single set, a claustrophobic tenement courtyard, enhances both the film's tension and its message; even the rows of windows in the opposite block resemble a bank of small television screens (a particularly pertinent sight gag at the time of cinema's feud with this alternative form of entertainment).

With every audiovisual element adding to the suspense, *Rear Window* was immediately hailed as one of Hitchcock's finest achievements, scooping Oscar nominations for Best Direction, Screenplay, Sound Recording, and Colour Cinematography. The film was reissued in 1968 with the trailer "If you do not experience delicious terror when you see *Rear Window*, then pinch yourself – you are most probably dead."

Rebecca (1940) Alfred HITCHCOCK's first US film, a romantic melodrama based on the novel by Daphne du Maurier (1938). The film won the 1940 Oscar for Best Picture, making David O. SELZNICK the first independent producer to capture the award two years in a row (GONE WITH THE WIND had won in 1939).

Shortly after it was published, Samuel GOLDWYN considered and turned down an adaptation of du Maurier's novel as a vehicle for Merle OBERON. When Selznick decided to film a version of the book, he found a willing collaborator in Hitchcock, who had wanted to buy the rights himself but could not afford them. He also hired Pulitzer-Prize winning author Robert Sherwood to supply the screenplay.

For his two leads, Selznick tested Vivien LEIGH before choosing Joan FONTAINE, and considered Leslie HOWARD, William POWELL, and Ronald COLMAN before signing Lawrence OLIVIER. The other principals included George SANDERS and Judith Anderson.

Hitchcock, who came to dislike the film's straightforward narrative structure and lack of humour, later denounced it as an old-fashioned "novelette" from the "school of feminine literature." In the plot widower Maxim De Winter (Olivier) brings his new bride (Fontaine) to Manderley, his Cornish estate. She tries to fit in but is made increasingly uneasy by Maxim's indifference and the coldness of the housekeeper, Mrs Danvers (Anderson), who constantly praises his first wife, the beautiful Rebecca. The mystery of her death, and of Maxim's behaviour, is eventually cleared up and the couple renew their love.

Rebel Without a Cause (1955) Nicholas RAY's study of delinquency amongst affluent Californian teenagers; the film is mainly remembered for the performance of James DEAN as the troubled and troublesome Jim Stark. Having been pulled in for drunken behaviour, Stark meets poor little rich boy Plato (Sal Mineo) and the neglected Judy (Natalie WOOD) at the police station. His friendship with her leads to a conflict with her boyfriend Buzz (Corey Allen) that ends in tragedy.

The book *Rebel Without a Cause*, a collection of juvenile case studies, was written by psychologist Robert Lindner in 1944. Although purchased by Warners as a possible vehicle for Marlon BRANDO, the project languished until 1955, when Nicholas Ray revived it to supplement his own idea for a film about a 'chicken race' – in which two teenagers hurtle towards a cliff edge in speeding cars, the first one to jump clear being deemed a coward.

Warners originally wanted Tab Hunter to play Jim, but Ray insisted on Dean, having seen his performance in EAST OF EDEN. Although neither Ray nor Natalie Wood's parents were keen to see the former child star in the film, her arrival at audition with a scar-faced boyfriend prompted the director to change his mind. Indeed, he insisted that all the teenage cast demonstrate some association with delinquency in their own lives before awarding them roles.

Shooting began in monochrome CINEMASCOPE, before director and studio agreed on a switch to colour. A student of the architect Frank Lloyd Wright, Ray had a keen appreciation of horizontal space that made him one of the most skilled WIDESCREEN film-makers in Hollywood. He also had an awareness of the metaphorical power of colour and virtually coded the clothing of his protagonists to help the audience recognize their psychological state: Buzz's gang wear black jackets to denote menace; Plato wears odd black and white socks to suggest his moral uncertainty; and the strident Judy abandons red for pink as Buzz's influence wanes. Similarly, Jim changes from a brown to a bright red jacket for the denouement; "When you first see Jimmy in his red jacket against his black Merc, it's not just a pose. It's a warning."

Jim Backus, who played Dean's father in the film, later intimated that the star co-directed many of his scenes; it seems more likely that Ray gave him great latitude to develop his character as he saw fit, improvisation being a byword during the production. Backus was the voice of the cartoon character MR MAGOO, whom Dean parodies at one point in the film.

Rebel was completed in two months at a cost of $600,000. Before the picture premiered Dean had been killed in his Porsche Spyder, an early death that conspired with his perceptive portrayal of teenage angst in the film to make him a cultural icon.

recordist The technician who is in charge of the sound recording equipment on the set.

Redford, Robert (Charles Robert Redford; 1937–) Handsome US leading man, who moved into direction in the 1980s. The blond blue-eyed actor, who was the leading US box-office draw from 1974 to 1976, later won an Oscar for *Ordinary People* (1980), his debut as a director.

In the 1950s Redford abandoned his course at the University of Colorado to wander through America and Europe. He returned to study theatre design at AADA, where he also began to act, making his Broadway debut in 1959. While making his first film, *War Hunt* (1962), he met the actor Sidney POLLACK, who would later direct many of his films. His first leading role was in the Neil Simon comedy *Barefoot in the Park* (1963).

In the late 1960s Redford found stardom with the comedy Western BUTCH CASSIDY AND THE SUNDANCE KID (1969), in which he plays the youthful Kid to Paul NEWMAN's Cassidy. The little-known actor won the role over Steve MCQUEEN, Warren BEATTY, and Marlon BRANDO. Further success followed with the political satire *The Candidate* (1972), *The Way We Were* (1973), a romantic weepie with Barbra STREISAND, and THE STING (1973), in which Redford and Newman teamed up again to play 1930s Chicago con artists. Redford was nominated for an Oscar for his part in the film. In 1976 he formed a production company, Wildwood, to make *All the President's Men*, the story of the *Washington Post* journalists who exposed the Watergate scandal; the parts of Bob Woodward and Carl Bernstein were played by Redford and Dustin HOFFMAN. Two years later Redford, one of Hollywood's highest paid actors, turned down $4 million to star in SUPERMAN.

In 1980 he directed *Ordinary People*, about a disturbed boy. His acting roles of the

1980s included a reforming prison governor in *Brubaker* (1980) and a White hunter in Pollack's *Out of Africa* (1985), with Meryl STREEP. More recently he has produced and directed *A River Runs Through It* (1992), about a family finding peace in rural Montana, and starred in *Indecent Proposal* (1993), as a billionaire who offers a married woman (Demi MOORE) $1 million to sleep with him. *Quiz Show* (1994), about a television corruption scandal of the 1950s, earned four Oscar nominations including one for Redford as Best Director.

Off-screen, Redford is a keen conservationist who has acquired 5000 acres of wilderness in Utah. Here he founded the prestigious film production centre, the Sundance Institute, which has hosted the annual Sundance Film Festival since 1978.

Redgrave family Distinguished British theatrical family that has now produced a record four generations acting in films. The most famous members are Sir Michael Redgrave (1908–85) and his actress daughters Vanessa Redgrave (1937–) and Lynn Redgrave (1943–).

Michael Redgrave was born in Bristol, the son of the actor Roy Redgrave (1872–1922), who appeared in silent Australian films in the 1910s. Michael was educated at Cambridge and worked as a journalist and schoolmaster before making his stage debut in 1934. His first film was Alfred HITCHCOCK's thriller THE LADY VANISHES, in which he co-starred with the young Margaret LOCKWOOD.

Redgrave was nominated for an Oscar for his part in *Mourning Becomes Electra* (1947), an attempt to film Eugene O'Neill's lugubrious play. Further acclaim came with the Rattigan adaptation *The Browning Version* (1951), in which he played a much disliked schoolmaster. Later films included the wartime adventure *The Heroes of Telemark* (1965), *David Copperfield* (1970), in which he played Peggotty, and *Nicholas and Alexandra* (1971). He married actress Rachel Kempson, the mother of Vanessa and Lynn, in 1935.

The birth of **Vanessa Redgrave** was announced on stage at the Old Vic by Laurence OLIVIER. After studies at the Central School of Speech and Drama she made her stage debut in 1957. A year later she appeared in her first film, *Behind the Mask*, a hospital drama starring her father. She achieved stardom in her own right in

Morgan – A Suitable Case for Treatment (1966), Karel REISZ's curious marital satire. Her performance brought her an Oscar nomination in the same year that Lynn Redgrave was nominated for GEORGY GIRL.

Vanessa was married to the director Tony RICHARDSON from 1962 until 1967, when she divorced him because of his affair with Jeanne MOREAU. Two years later, Redgrave bore a son to the actor Franco Nero, who played Lancelot to her Guinevere in the musical *Camelot* (1967).

Redgrave also received Oscar nominations for playing the title roles in *Isadora* (1968), about the dancer Isadora Duncan, and *Mary Queen of Scots* (1971). Her depiction of Lillian Hellman in *Julia* (1977), a film about a woman who helped Jewish refugees to escape from the Nazis, won her an Oscar as Best Supporting Actress. A keen supporter of the Palestinian cause, Redgrave was much criticized for her remarks about "Zionist hoodlums" during the Academy Awards ceremony. Her later films have included *Agatha* (1979), in which she played Agatha Christie, the Henry James adaptation *The Bostonians* (1984), and MERCHANT-IVORY's *Howards End* (1992).

Like Vanessa, **Lynn Redgrave** was born in London and attended the Central School of Speech and Drama. She went on the stage in 1962 and made her film debut, as a bit player in TOM JONES, a year later. In 1966 she found international fame playing the ugly-duckling title character in GEORGY GIRL (1966).

Her other films have included *The Happy Hooker* (1975), in which she played a real-life New York madam, the horror spoof *Midnight* (1989), and *Getting It Right* (1989). In 1994 she became the first woman president of the New York Players Club.

Vanessa's daughters **Natasha Richardson** (1963–) and **Joely Richardson** (1966–) made their first screen appearance as young children in *The Charge of the Light Brigade* (1968). Natasha has since played the real-life kidnapped heiress in *Patty Hearst* (1988) and a *femme fatale* in the comedy-thriller *Widows' Peak* (1994). Joely appeared with her mother in *Wetherby* (1985), played a murderess in Peter GREENAWAY's *Drowning by Numbers* (1988), and a wartime German spying for America in *Shining Through* (1991).

re-dress To change the props and furnishings on a set. After re-dressing, the set may be used to represent either the same place at a different time, or another location in a totally different film.

Red Shoes, The   (1948) Michael POWELL and Emeric PRESSBURGER'S TECHNICOLOR masterpiece about the ballet; it was the first English-language film devoted to the subject and is still considered the best. Powell and Pressburger jointly produced, directed, and wrote the film, which became a great critical and commercial success. Oscars were awarded for the colour Art Direction and for Brian Easdale's score, and nominations received for Best Picture, Editing, and Story. The film's 14-minute ballet sequence inspired MGM to include a long climactic ballet in Gere KELLY's *An American in Paris* (1951).

The Red Shoes made a star of the Sadler's Wells ballerina Moira Shearer, appearing in her first screen role. Despite this success, the red-haired Shearer had a short film career. In 1951 she was dropped from *Royal Wedding* because Fred ASTAIRE found her unsuitable; a year later, she was to star in *Hans Christian Andersen* with Danny KAYE but had to give up the role when she became pregnant.

When *The Red Shoes* ran £200,000 over budget, the project was offered to Alexander KORDA but he declined to take it on. In the event, the film became Rank's biggest ever money-spinner in America. Strangely, almost 30 years passed before the making of Hollywood's first true ballet movie, *The Turning Point* (1977).

The story follows the career of a young ballerina who is torn between her love for a composer (Marius Goring) and the demands of her career, which is being directed by a tyrannical impresario (Anton Walbrook). With Leonide Massine and Robert Helpmann (who choreographed the film) she dances in the 'Ballet of the Red Shoes', taken from the Hans Christian Andersen fairy-tale about shoes that danced their wearer to death. Unable to resolve her dilemmas, the ballerina commits suicide.

Reed. Sir Carol Reed (1906–76) British director, who is remembered for the classic films he directed during the late 1940s. Reed was one of the numerous illegitimate children of the actor-manager Herbert Beerbohm Tree; he began his career in the theatre and entered the cinema at EALING STUDIOS, where, in 1933, he made his first

feature *Midshipman Easy*. His other early films include *Bank Holiday* (1938), *The Stars Look Down* (1939), about a mining community in Wales, and *Night Train to Munich* (1940), all of which starred Margaret LOCKWOOD. *The Way Ahead* (1944) was a stirring propaganda piece, while *The True Glory* (1945) was a compilation of newsreel footage from the last year of the war that brought Reed and co-director Garson Kanin an Oscar.

Reed's major postwar period began with *Odd Man Out* (1947), in which James MASON starred as a hunted IRA gunman, and *The Fallen Idol* (1948), the first of three books by Graham GREENE that Reed adapted for the cinema. Greene's THE THIRD MAN (1949), about the illegal market in penicillin in Vienna after World War II, became in Reed's hands one of the most memorable classics of the British cinema; the film starred Joseph COTTEN and Trevor HOWARD, with a small but ominous part played by Orson WELLES. With a screenplay by Greene and zither music composed and played by Anton Karas, this stylish and beautifully crafted thriller consolidated Reed's reputation as one of the most accomplished directors of his generation. A further success was *Outcast of the Islands* (1951), taken from the novel by Joseph Conrad. He was knighted the following year.

Reed's later career was less remarkable, although his sensitive direction of Greene's thriller *Our Man in Havana* (1959), with Alec GUINNESS and Noël COWARD, was also praised. *Oliver!* (1968), a boisterous musical adaptation of *Oliver Twist*, brought him Oscars for Best Director and Best Picture. He retired from the cinema in 1972.

Oliver Reed (1938–) Hulking British actor, who is mainly cast in brutal and intemperate roles. This fits his off-screen reputation as a pub brawler and drunken guest on television talk shows. He is the nephew of the late film-maker Sir Carol REED, who directed him in his memorable role of bad Bill Sikes in the musical *Oliver!* (1968).

Born in the London suburb of Wimbledon, he ran away from home at 17 to work as a bouncer for a Soho strip club. After spells as a boxer, a taxi-driver, and National Service with the Medical Corps, he began to appear as an extra in such films as *Sword of Sherwood Forest* (1960). His first major role came in Hammer's *The Curse of the Werewolf* (1961).

The success of *Oliver!* led Ken RUSSELL to offer him the role of Gerald in the D. H. Lawrence adaptation *Women in Love* (1969); the part of his lover, Gudrun, was played by Glenda JACKSON. Notoriously, the film features Reed in a nude wrestling scene with Alan BATES. He rejoined Russell and Jackson two years later to make the outrageous movie *The Devils* (1971), in which he plays a priest burned as a sorcerer. In 1973 Reed co-starred with Michael YORK, Richard Chamberlain, and Frank Finlay in *The Three Musketeers*; *The Four Musketeers* followed a year later. Reed then took a singing role in Russell's rock opera *Tommy* (1975).

In 1977 Reed was reunited with Mark Lester, who had played Oliver, on the set of *The Prince and the Pauper*, an old-fashioned swashbuckler. For Lester's 18th birthday, Reed arrived drunk with his gift (not accepted), a prostitute. Later he challenged 15 members of the cast and crew to eat a restaurant meal in reverse order, beginning with cigars and brandy. "By the time we got to the dessert" Lester recalled, "we had had about 40 bottles of wine." A food fight ensued and the actors were thrown out.

Reed's later films have included *Castaway* (1986), from the true story of a man who advertised for a woman to live with him on a desert island, Terry GILLIAM's *The Adventures of Baron Munchausen* (1989), *The Return of the Musketeers* (1989), which reassembled the cast from 15 years before, and the *Prisoners of Honour* (1991).

reel (1) A spool on which cine film is wound. (2) An approximate unit of measurement used in describing the length of a film, based on the capacity of a standard 35MM reel (900–1000 feet, which runs for about ten minutes). A standard 16MM reel, which contains 350–400 feet, runs for a similar length of time. The term is still used in this way although much longer reels are now used in projection.

re-establishing shot A shot inserted into a scene, usually but not always at its conclusion, that provides a more overall view of the action or setting. It often repeats the original ESTABLISHING SHOT from another camera angle. Such shots are mainly used to re-acquaint the viewer with the scene of the action or to round off an episode.

Reeve, Christopher (1952–) Square-jawed US actor, best known to the cinemagoing public as SUPERMAN, a role he has played four times. Reeve has described the character as a "warm and humorous but solitary man with incredible powers, trying to fit into his adopted planet."

Born in New York, Reeve attended Cornell University and began to appear on television in 1973. His film debut five years later was in the title role of *Superman* (1978), Warner Brothers' $55-million blockbuster. The sequels were *Superman II* (1980) and *Superman III* (1983), both directed by Richard LESTER, and *Superman IV: The Quest for Peace* (1987), directed by Sidney J. Furre and co-written by Reeve.

Among Reeve's other movies are the time-travel romance *Somewhere in Time* (1980), the thriller *Deathtrap* (1982), in which he co-starred with Michael CAINE, *Monsignor* (1982), about a brash Irish cardinal who falls for a novice nun, and MERCHANT-IVORY's *The Bostonians* (1984), a period story based on the novel by Henry James.

In 1986 Reeve made his Broadway debut playing a New York journalist in *Street Smart*; a year later he reprised the role in a film version. More recent roles have included the wealthy lover of Kathleen TURNER in *Switching Channels* (1988), the owner of a house used by a bumbling theatrical company in Peter BOGDANOVICH's *Noises Off* (1992), and a supporting part in Merchant-Ivory's *The Remains of the Day* (1993).

> Chris is good-looking in the prewar mould when movie stars looked like movie stars and not like the local wine shop manager.
> WILLIAM MARSHALL, film actor.

Reeves, Keanu (1964–) US actor, who came to prominence playing a goofy Californian 'dude' in the hit comedy *Bill & Ted's Excellent Adventure* (1989). Reeves has attracted such a cult following that in 1994 a 12-week course, 'The Films of Keanu Reeves', was inaugurated by the Art Center College of Design in Pasadena, California, to examine "the culture, sociology, anthropology, and philosophy" of the young actor's work.

Born in Beirut, Reeves is half Canadian and half Hawaiian-Chinese (his name is a Hawaiian word meaning 'cool breeze over the mountains'). His first major role was in *River's Edge* (1986), a gloomy story about murder in a small town; he also appeared in the Steve MARTIN comedy *Parenthood* (1989), as the slobbish young son-in-law of divorcee Dianne Wiest.

Reeves then found stardom playing the blank-faced Ted to Alex Winter's Bill in *Bill & Ted's Excellent Adventure*, a fantasy about two inept high-school students who go back in time to kidnap Abraham Lincoln, Joan of Arc, and others to help them pass their history course. In the sequel, *Bill & Ted's Bogus Journey* (1991), they battle their duplicates, robots from the future, who have been sent to kill them. *Variety* termed it a "non-excellent adventure".

Since then Reeves has made various only partly successful attempts to extend his range. In the ROAD MOVIE *My Own Private Idaho* (1991) he played a middle-class dropout slumming amongst male prostitutes (including the late River PHOENIX). The film ambitiously attempts to rework elements from Shakespeare's *Henry IV, Part I*. Reeves continued in Shakespearean vein by playing the villainous Don John in BRANAGH's *Much Ado About Nothing* (1993) and the title role in a Canadian stage production of *Hamlet* (1995).

In *Speed* (1994) Reeves played a cop trying to defuse a Los Angeles bus that will explode if it slows down to below 50 mph. His short rounded haircut in the film began a sweeping US fashion trend known as 'the Keanu'. That year, he also starred as the future Buddha, Prince Siddhartha, in Bernardo BERTOLUCCI's *Little Buddha*. Bertolucci said that Reeves was chosen in preference to Indian actors because of his "aura of innocence."

reflex camera A camera equipped with an optical device (usually a mirrored shutter), that reflects the image that appears through the taking lens to a magnifying viewfinder. This enables the cameraman to view the scene exactly as it will appear on the film (i.e. without parallax).

Règle du jeu, La (*The Rules of the Game*; 1939) Jean RENOIR's consummate black comedy, a film that exposed the decadence of French society only months before the outbreak of World War II. Owing to the intense hostility it aroused, the five-million franc film was quickly withdrawn from release and not seen again until after the war. In 1959 a reassembled version was issued to worldwide acclaim; the director

Alain RESNAIS described his first viewing of the film as "the single most overwhelming experience I have ever had in the cinema." *Sight and Sound*'s 1982 poll of film critics named *La Règle du Jeu* as runner-up to CITIZEN KANE as the best movie ever made.

The film uses a mixture of farce, satire, and tragedy to expose the contradictions of the French class system and the hollowness of the values sustaining it. Renoir not only produced, directed, and co-wrote the screenplay, but also played the important character of Octave, a part originally intended for his brother, Pierre. "There's one thing, do you see, that's terrifying in this world" his character remarks at one point, "and that is that every man has his reasons." Renoir, who reworked the characters and their relationships during shooting, confessed that he was "torn between my desire to make a comedy of it and the wish to tell a tragic story."

With the help of the kindhearted Octave, André (Roland Toutain), a record-breaking aviator, joins a weekend shoot at the country estate of a marquis (Marcel Dalio), in order to woo the marquise (Nora Gregor). Various other intrigues are played out amongst both the guests and the servants downstairs. Nevertheless, the rules of the game (decorum and lies) are rigorously maintained. In the film's tragic final scenes, the gamekeeper (Gaston Modot) shoots André, mistaking him for the lover of his wife.

After right-wing mobs attacked the Champs Elysées cinema in which it was being screened, the movie was withdrawn and banned. The Nazis also prevented it from being shown and at some point the original negative was destroyed by an Allied bombing raid. An incomplete version was found after the war and shown in New York in 1950 and London a year later (when *Film Review* described it as a "rather jerky little French film"). Following the discovery of 200 cans of film, Renoir's masterpiece was restored for a triumphant unveiling at the 1959 Venice Film Festival.

Reiner, Rob (1945–) US director, writer, and occasional actor, whose best films have combined the scale of a blockbuster with wit, charm, and intimacy. The son of the director Carl Reiner (1922–), he played Archie Bunker's despised son-in-law in the US television sitcom *All in the Family* (based on Britain's *Till Death Us Do Part*) for most of the 1970s. He began directing films in 1985, with the spoof rock documentary *This is Spinal Tap*, a film that quickly established a cult following. This was followed by three films aimed at a younger audience; *The Sure Thing* (1985), a mild sex comedy with considerable charm, the nostalgic Stephen King adaptation *Stand by Me* (1986), a film with a largely teenage cast that included River PHOENIX and Kiefer SUTHERLAND, and *The Princess Bride* (1987), a spellbinding children's adventure.

Reiner's first major success came with *When Harry Met Sally* (1989), a sparkling comedy about love and friendship starring Billy Crystal and Meg RYAN; Nora Ephron supplied the witty script. The following year Reiner played a supporting role in Mike NICHOLS's *Postcards from the Edge* (1990), a film based on the novel by actress Carrie Fisher (who had also featured in *When Harry Met Sally*). Reiner's next film as director was *Misery* (1990), another King adaptation; this tense thriller resurrected James CAAN's career and featured an Oscar-winning performance by Kathy Bates. *Regarding Henry* (1991), starring Harrison FORD, was followed by the Oscar-nominated *A Few Good Men* (1992), with Tom CRUISE and Jack NICHOLSON. That year the team that created *When Harry Met Sally* was partly reassembled when Reiner appeared as an actor in Nora Ephron's *Sleepless in Seattle*, a romantic comedy starring Meg Ryan and Tom HANKS.

reissue *See* RERELEASE.

Reisz, Karel (1926–) British director, born in Czechoslovakia to Jewish parents. As a boy, Reisz was sent to safety in Britain shortly before the Nazis invaded; his parents, who remained behind, died in a concentration camp. After service in the RAF and studies at Cambridge, he began to write film criticism in the early 1950s. Later in the decade he became an important figure in the FREE CINEMA movement and co-directed several shorts with Lindsay ANDERSON.

Reisz established his reputation as a director with his first feature, *Saturday Night and Sunday Morning* (1960); adapted from Alan Sillitoe's novel of working-class life. The film starred Albert FINNEY, who also played the lead in Reisz's next film, *Night Must Fall* (1964), from the play by Emlyn Williams. *Morgan, a Suitable Case for Treatment* (1966), based on David Mercer's play

about a half-mad painter, starred Vanessa REDGRAVE, who reappeared in the title role of Reisz's biopic of the dancer Isadora Duncan, *Isadora* (1968). This was followed by *The Gambler* (1974), a psychological tale starring James CAAN, and *Who'll Stop the Rain?* (British title *Dog Soldiers*; 1978), an intelligent thriller set in the drugs subculture of America.

Reisz enjoyed his biggest commercial success in 1981, when he directed Jeremy IRONS and Meryl STREEP in *The French Lieutenant's Woman*, from the novel by John Fowles. His more recent films include *Sweet Dreams* (1985), a moving depiction of an unstable marriage, and *Everybody Wins* (1990), from a play by Arthur Miller.

relational editing A style of MONTAGE in which the shots are arranged to suggest an association of ideas. The term was coined by the Russian film theorist and director PUDOVKIN, who suggested five basic modes: juxtaposition, parallelism (two actions occurring simultaneously but unrelated by plot), symbolism, simultaneity, and leitmotif.

release or **general release** The first distribution of a film for general exhibition. This usually follows an official premiere and a more limited distribution to specific cinemas in major cities (a FIRST RUN). *See also* RERELEASE.

release print A copy of a film that has been authorized for distribution and exhibition. Once editing is completed, an ANSWER PRINT containing both picture and the final sound mix is submitted to the studio and/or censors. If this is considered satisfactory, a number of duplicate negatives (*see* DUPE) are made and used to create the release prints.

relief An effect of LIGHTING or MISE-EN-SCÈNE that gives prominence to one particular character or object.

remakes New productions of old films. A remake will generally aim to capitalize on the reputation of the original, while at the same time introducing modern sensibilities, stars, and techniques. The introduction of sound, colour, and WIDESCREEN processes led to a flurry of remakes; similarly, advances in special effects provided the *raison d'être* for the 1977 remake of KING KONG (1933). Cinéastes may decry such 'unnecessary' remakes, but their commercial logic is often unassailable: despite lacking almost all the poetry of its predecessor, *King Kong* was the year's most successful horror film in North America. The notorious provincialism of the US market has also encouraged the making of ENGLISH-LANGUAGE REMAKES of foreign films.

Perhaps because their rationale is so obviously commercial, few remakes have equalled their originals in artistic terms. Although the 1962 remake of *Mutiny on the Bounty* introduced both colour and PANAVISION, the film cannot match the power of the 1935 LAUGHTON-GABLE version (Marlon BRANDO's effete Christian being the main problem). In the 1980 version of the film changing sensibilities allowed an overtly erotic depiction of the Polynesian women, thereby providing an explanation for the behaviour of men whose privations otherwise differed little from those of other 18th-century sailors. Similarly, freedom to exploit the steamy cavorting of Jack NICHOLSON and Jessica Lange must have figured in the logic behind the unsatisfactory 1981 remake of the FILM NOIR classic *The Postman Always Rings Twice* (1946).

Remakes are also perpetrated in the name of homage, as in the case of Werner HERZOG's *Nosferatu, the Vampire* (1979), a tribute to F. W. MURNAU's classic NOSFERATU (1922). Despite Herzog's literal shot-for-shot duplication of many sequences, the hallucinatory symphony of light and shade in the original was utterly lost. Likewise, it is hard to see how other lavish screen versions of the DRACULA story, including *Bram Stoker's Dracula* (1992), offer any advance upon this 1922 masterpiece. In general, horror has provided particularly fertile territory to plunder, with modern attitudes permitting directors to make explicit much of the sex and violence that was implicit in the originals. David CRONENBERG's *The Fly* (1986) is one of the few remakes to match or surpass its inspiration, in this case Kurt Neumann's 1958 film.

Of course, many stories have been remade time after time owing simply to their inherent strength; *Cinderella*, for instance, is thought to have been filmed about 100 times since 1898. Other perennials include *Hamlet* (74 versions); *Dr Jekyll and Mr Hyde* (52); *Robinson Crusoe* (44); and *The Hound of the Baskervilles* (14).

Remick, Lee (1935–91) US actress. Remick worked as a dancer and on television before making her feature-film debut in Elia KAZAN's *A Face in the Crowd* (1957). She went on to assert her screen presence more fully in *The Long Hot Summer* (1958) and *Anatomy of a Murder* (1959), in which she played an alleged rape victim. The following year she appeared in another Kazan film, *Wild River* (1960), with Montgomery CLIFT. It was, however, Remick's portrayal of the alcoholic wife of an alcoholic ad man (Jack LEMMON) in Blake EDWARDS's *The Days of Wine and Roses* (1962) that brought her real prominence (and a Best Actress nomination at the Oscars). Her other films of the 1960s included *The Wheeler Dealers* (1963), *Baby, the Rain Must Fall* (1965), with Steve MCQUEEN, John STURGES's *The Hallulujah Trail* (1965), and *The Detective* (1968), with Frank SINATRA.

In 1968 Remick married the British director William Gowens and moved to England, where she appeared in *A Severed Head* (1971), an adaptation of the Iris Murdoch novel, and *Loot* (1971), from Joe Orton's outrageous stage play; both films co-starred Richard ATTENBOROUGH. Her other movies of the 1970s ranged from *The Omen* (1976), a silly but highly successful horror film in which she co-starred with Gregory PECK as adoptive parents of the antichrist, to *The Europeans* (1979), a MERCHANT-IVORY adaptation of the Henry James novel. During the 1980s Remick was not particularly busy in the cinema, although she worked extensively in television. In 1988 she formed a production company with Peter Duchow and James Garner (her co-star in *The Wheeler Dealers*, 1963); shortly afterwards she was diagnosed as having the cancer from which she died three years later.

Renoir, Jean (1894–1979) French director, screenwriter, and occasional actor acknowledged as one of the giants of world cinema. He was the son of the painter Auguste Renoir (1841–1919), the younger brother of actor Pierre Renoir (1885–1952), and the nephew of cinematographer Claude Renoir (1913–94). His films, which span half a century, explore the individual's search for fulfilment and his or her relationship to nature and society. They are directed in a restrained but poetic style characterized by the use of long takes and DEEP FOCUS photography.

Renoir, who modelled for his father as a boy, grew up in a rich cultural milieu and initially hoped to work in ceramics. It was while convalescing from wounds sustained in World War I that he became obsessed with the cinema, particularly the films of Charlie CHAPLIN and Erich VON STROHEIM. After marrying his father's model, Andrée Heuchling in 1919, he formed a film company to launch her in an acting career (as Catherine Hessling). Renoir's debut as a director was *La Fille de l'eau* (1924), a film that starred his wife. She also played the title role in *Nana* (1926), an ambitious production with a record budget of one million francs. Although *Nana* nearly bankrupted Renoir, he made several more silent films, most of them featuring Hessling, before they divorced in 1930.

Renoir rejoiced in the coming of sound, saying that it "opened a secret door of communication between the film-maker and his audience." His first talkie was *On purge Bébé* (1931), a drama starring the splendid Michel Simon, who also featured in *La Chienne* (1931) and *Boudu Saved from Drowning* (1932), the films that are usually considered Renoir's first masterpieces. His work of the later 1930s, which includes *Toni* (1935) and *The Crime of Monsieur Lange* (1936), shows a deepening social awareness.

In 1937 Renoir co-wrote and directed his great antiwar film LA GRANDE ILLUSION (1937), starring Jean GABIN and von Stroheim. It was his first international success and the first foreign-language film to be nominated for an Oscar. After making the Zola adaptation *La Bête humaine* (1938), again with Gabin, Renoir produced, directed, scripted, and acted in LA RÈGLE DU JEU (1939), a profound satire on French aristocratic society. Although now widely considered one of the great films of all time, it was a commercial disaster on its original release.

After the fall of France, Renoir moved to America and became a US citizen, explaining, "I am a citizen of the world of films." His first Hollywood film was 20th Century-Fox's *Swamp Water* (British title *The Man Who Came Back*; 1941), an atmospheric story shot in Georgia. His only Oscar nomination as Best Director came for United Artists' *The Southerner* (1945), a realistic drama about sharecroppers. He also directed and co-scripted *The Diary of a Chambermaid* (1946), with Paulette GODDARD, and RKO's unsuccessful FILM NOIR *The Woman on the Beach* (1947). Renoir later described his Hollywood stay as "seven years of unrealized works and unrealized hopes, and seven years of deceptions."

His first colour film, *The River* (1951), was filmed on the banks of the Ganges and featured luscious cinematography from his nephew Claude. Renoir then returned to France to make the successful *French Can-Can* (US title *Only the French Can*; 1954), a lively tribute to the Paris of the Belle Epoque. During the remaining 25 years of his life he directed only four more features, the best known being *Le Déjeuner sur l'herbe* (1959). His last film, *Le Petit Théâtre de Jean Renoir* (1971), was originally made for French TV.

Although most of Renoir's films flopped at the box office and most were critically misunderstood when first released, he spent his last years as one of the most revered figures in the world of cinema. He was awarded an honorary Oscar at the 1975 Academy Award ceremony for his lifetime achievement.

renter A theatre or individual who acquires the exhibition rights to a film from the distributor for a fixed period in return for a set fee, a percentage of gross receipts, or both.

Republic Hollywood's most important small studio in the 1940s and 1950s. Although Republic specialized in turning out serials and B-MOVIES, especially Westerns, the studio occasionally made major films, its biggest success being John FORD's *The Quiet Man* (1952).

Republic was founded in 1935 by Herbert J. Yates, a former tobacco executive who had bought a film laboratory some 20 years earlier; he merged four tiny studios into the new company and became its president. Although Republic soon became a profitable concern, Yates failed in his main goal, that of turning his wife Vera Hruba Ralston ('the AMERICAN VENUS') into a great star.

In 1939 Yates gave 20-year-old Jennifer JONES, still known as Phyllis Isley, a six-month contract at $75 a week. After she had appeared in a few films, however, he let the agreement lapse. Other famous names associated with the studio were the Western stars John WAYNE, Roy ROGERS, and Gene AUTRY, and the director Raoul WALSH. In 1948 Yates gave Orson WELLES $800,000 and three weeks to film and star in *Macbeth* (1948); the result was a production that virtually ended Welles's Hollywood career. (The thick Scottish accents of the cast necessitated a dubbed version in 1950.)

John Ford directed several Republic pictures, including *Rio Grande* (1950) and *The Quiet Man*, both of which co-starred John Wayne and Maureen O'HARA, and *The Sun Shines Bright* (1953), a more personal film about a Kentucky judge (Charles Winninger).

Republic's last films included *Johnny Guitar* (1954), an over-the-top Western starring Joan CRAWFORD and directed by Nicholas RAY, and *Come Next Spring* (1956), a period drama with Ann SHERIDAN. With the decline of the B-movie, Republic sold its film library to television in 1955 and abandoned cinema production two years later to concentrate on the new medium.

rerecording (1) The copying of a SOUNDTRACK from one source to another, e.g. from magnetic film to tape. (2) Another name for MIXING, the process of combining a number of sound tracks (e.g. music, dialogue, sound effects) to produce a master sound track.

rerelease or **reissue** To return to a film that has been withdrawn for several years. The term is also applied to the film itself.

DISNEY has rereleased more films than any other studio, while MGM reissued GONE WITH THE WIND (1939) several times before selling the television rights. In recent years, however, the video has virtually replaced the rerelease. Having always previously refused, Disney finally issued the much rereleased SNOW WHITE AND THE SEVEN DWARFS (1937) on video in 1994.

Resnais, Alain (1922–) French director of the NEW WAVE, noted for his preoccupation with the theme of memory. The son of a pharmacist, Resnais began his career directing shorts, including several biopics of artists. In 1959 his first feature, HIROSHIMA MON AMOUR (1959), caused a sensation with its innovative fragmentary style, in which memories of the past intermingle with events in the present and future. This technique enabled Resnais to draw complex parallels between a woman's love affair with an architect in modern Japan and her wartime romance with a German soldier. In the extraordinary LAST YEAR IN MARIENBAD (1961) past, present, and future become still more confused as the central characters try to work out whether they have met before.

Resnais has since returned to these themes many times: in *Muriel* (1963) an old woman is deceived by her memories of a long-past love affair, in *The War is Over* (1966) a revolutionary soldier is troubled by his recollections of the Spanish Civil War, while in *Je t'aime, je t'aime* (1967) a failed suicide becomes hopelessly lost during an experiment in time travel.

After several years during which he could not raise funds for film-making, Resnais made *Stavisky* (*L'Empire d'Alexandre*; 1974), his most conventional work. *Providence* (1977), his first English-language film, starred John GIELGUD as a dying writer who draws on his bitter feelings towards his family in preparing his last book. *My American Uncle* (1980) was well received for its surreal exploration of human behaviour and revived Resnais's reputation for formal brilliance. His more recent films include *La Vie est un roman* (*Life is a Bed of Roses*; 1983) and *Mélo* (1986), which returned to the topic of memory and its distortions. In 1994 Resnais adapted Alan Ayckbourn's play *Intimate Exchanges* as two different but simultaneously released films, *Smoking* and *No Smoking*. The story develops differently depending on whether the main character accepts or declines the offer of a cigarette. (French audiences much preferred *Smoking*).

> He's the only poet director I'm aware of.
> DIRK BOGARDE.

> When I make a film, I never know how it will turn out...I'm always surprised at the result.
> ALAIN RESNAIS.

retake To reshoot a scene already filmed; also the shot so produced. A retake is required if for some artistic, technical, or other reason the previous TAKE has been rejected. The perfectionism of the director, or the incompetence of the actors, may necessitate multiple retakes running into three figures: Charlie CHAPLIN is said to have shot a scene in CITY LIGHTS (1931) over 340 times before he was satisifed, while the actress Shelley Duval was made to repeat a dialogue sequence in *The Shining* (1980) 126 times. On the 25th retake of a crying scene in *Hook* (1992), Caroline Goodall was no longer acting when she burst into tears.

reverse. **reverse action** or **reverse motion** An effect in which the action in a film sequence appears to occur in reverse order: in EISENSTEIN's *October* (1928), for example, a statue is seen to re-assemble itself from a pile of rubble. The effect is achieved by running the film backwards through the camera or optical printer. Although often used for comic effect, as when characters or vehicles appear to move backwards, the technique also has serious applications. Dramatic special effects can be created by reversing film of backward motion: a backward jump from a great height may be turned into a superhuman leap, while film of a car backing away from the camera can be reversed so that it appears to speed towards the audience.

reverse angle shot A shot in which the camera angle is altered 180 degrees from the preceding shot. It is mainly used to switch from one character's point of view to another's, as in a conversation between two people (a common sequence known as the shot/reverse-shot technique).

rewind The process of transferring film from the take-up reel to the feed reel in a camera, projector, or editing machine. The term is also applied to the mechanism used to accomplish this.

Reynolds. Burt Reynolds (1936–) US leading man, who specialized in macho roles before turning his hand to comedy, often in car-chase movies. He was the top box-office draw in America from 1978 to 1982, a position he claimed to have attained "not because of my movies – but *in spite* of them." In 1972 he posed as *Cosmopolitan*'s first nude male model. He has been married twice, to the comedienne Judy Carne (1963–66), and the actress Loni Anderson (1988–93). Reynolds, who has nicknamed himself 'Burt the Flirt', also had a long-term relationship with the actress Sally Field.

Reynolds, who grew up in Palm Beach, Florida, initially planned a career in professional football. Although signed by the Baltimore Colts, he was prevented by injury from joining them and moved to New York in 1955 to act. Having made his film debut in *Angel Baby* (1960), he signed with Universal to play a variety of "Indians, eager young men in the background, or half-breed mongrels" in the television series *Gunsmoke* (1965–67). (His grandmother was a Cherokee Indian.)

Reynolds finally made his name in John BOORMAN's *Deliverance* (1972), in which he played one of four city men on a terrifying river trip. A year later he starred in his first

CHASE FILM, the melodrama *White Lightning*. In the mid 1970s he appeared in two Robert ALDRICH films, *The Longest Yard* (1974), about a prisoners' football squad, and *Hustle* (1975), as a cop entranced by a call-girl (Catherine DENEUVE). Aldrich was the main influence on Reynolds's first film as a director, *Gator* (1976), in which he played an ex-moonshiner recruited by the law. Sally Field joined him for the chase comedy *Smokey and the Bandit* (1977) and its 1980 sequel and for *The End* (1978), which Reynolds also directed.

The Cannonball Run (1981), about a coast-to-coast car race, was a box-office triumph that earned Reynolds (who once remarked "Nobody is worth what they pay me") $5 million plus a percentage. That year he also directed and starred in *Sharky's Machine*. His more recent films have included *Switching Channels* (1988), in which he played the boss and ex-husband of TV news presenter Kathleen TURNER, and *Physical Evidence* (1989), as a cop suspected of murder.

> A lot of directors don't realize the hardest thing to do is to make chicken salad out of chicken shit. I've done that a lot.
> BURT REYNOLDS.

> What I look for mostly in a man is humour, honesty and a moustache. Burt has all three.
> SALLY FIELD.

Debbie Reynolds (Mary Frances Reynolds; 1932–) US actress and singer, whose exuberant presence enlivened a series of films of the films of the 1950s and 1960s. Born in El Paso, Texas, she won the Miss Burbank beauty contest at the age of 16 and was immediately signed by Warner Brothers to appear in the romantic comedy *June Bride* (1948). In 1950 she moved to MGM to star opposite Fred ASTAIRE in *Three Little Words*; that same year, she had her first hit record with 'Abba-Dabba Honeymoon' with Carleton Carpenter in *Two Weeks With Love*.

Reynolds's big break came in 1952, when Gene KELLY cast her as the aspiring actress Kathy Selden in SINGIN' IN THE RAIN. She went on to play a delinquent teenager in *Susan Slept Here* (1954) and a starlet who steals Frank SINATRA from Celeste Holm in *The Tender Trap* (1955). Reynolds married the singer Eddie Fisher in 1955, and a year later they co-starred in the musical *Bundle of Joy*. When Fisher deserted her to marry their friend, Elizabeth TAYLOR in 1959, public sympathy for Reynolds is thought to have boosted her career.

At the age of 25 Reynolds played a pig-tailed teenager in *Tammy and the Bachelor* (and had a hit single with the title song). She later joined the all-star cast of the CINERAMA epic *How the West was Won* (1962) to play a pioneer girl who ages into a grandmother by the end of the film. After two more musicals, *The Unsinkable Molly Brown* (1964) and *The Singing Nun* (1966), and three more comedies, including *Divorce American Style* (1967), she changed direction for her last major film, the eerie melodrama *What's the Matter with Helen?* (1971). Reynolds then retired from the cinema to work on stage and television. "I stopped making movies", she said, "because I don't like taking my clothes off." In 1992, she returned to the big screen to play herself in a CAMEO role in *The Bodyguard*.

Reynolds's daughter by her first marriage is the actress and writer **Carrie Fisher** (1956–), best known for her role as Princess Leia in the STAR WARS films. Her novel *Postcards from the Edge* (filmed in 1990), about an ageing showbiz performer and her drug-taking actress daughter, is partly based on her relationship with her mother.

rhubarb or **walla-walla** The murmuring sound made by extras in a crowd scene or to create a background hum behind the main dialogue. Stage actors have traditionally repeated the word 'rhubarb' when pretending to chat in the background.

Richard III (1955) Laurence OLIVIER's screen version of SHAKESPEARE's play about the deformed and malevolent Richard. As with the highly acclaimed *Henry V* (1944) and *Hamlet* (1948), Olivier produced and directed as well as playing the title role; his bravura performance as Richard drew on his famous 1944 Old Vic characterization. The supporting cast included Ralph RICH-ARDSON, John GIELGUD, and Claire BLOOM.

With its audacious use of close-ups and direct speech to the camera, the film presented Richard as an outrageously confident villain, eager to confide in and almost making an accomplice of the audience. The character's striking gait and deportment were modelled on Jed Harris, a Broadway actor, although the sudden flashes of petulance derived from Olivier's close study of Hitler on film newsreels. As in *Henry V*, Olivier was wounded during the shooting of the

battle scenes (which were filmed in Spain): when he reined his horse a little too soon an arrow intended for a cork protector on the horse's flank pierced his left calf. Falling as rehearsed, he insisted on completing the scene before having the arrow removed.

Paramount decided to give the film a simultaneous cinema and television premiere: 40 million viewers watched the NBC screening (more than had seen it in the play's previous 352-year history), making Richard a great publicity success. A portrait by Salvador Dali, showing Olivier half as himself and half as Richard, even made the cover of *Newsweek*. Nevertheless, the cinema film proved a box-office disaster, with the result that Olivier was unable to raise funds for his long-cherished adaptation of *Macbeth*. *Richard III* won three BAFTAs, while Olivier received his fifth Oscar nomination for Best Actor.

Richardson. **Sir Ralph Richardson** (1902–83) Distinguished British stage actor, who appeared in some 50 films, usually in supporting roles but often upstaging the stars. His two Oscar nominations were received 35 years apart – for *The Heiress* (1949) and *Greystoke: The Legend of Tarzan, Lord of the Apes* (1984).

Born in Cheltenham, Richardson worked briefly as an office boy with an insurance company before entering the theatre. He made his name with the Old Vic Company in the 1930s, where he acted alongside his great friend Laurence OLIVIER. Indeed, Richardson is credited with helping to launch Olivier's Hollywood career. In 1939 they were co-starring in Alexander KORDA's *Q Planes* (US title *Clouds Over Europe*), when Olivier, who had been offered the role of Heathcliff in WUTHERING HEIGHTS, asked the advice of his friend, who replied simply: "Yes. Bit of fame. Good."

Richardson's film career began in 1933 with a part in Michael BALCON's *The Ghoul*, starring Boris KARLOFF. After World War II he played Baines, the butler suspected of murder in Carol REED's *The Fallen Idol* (1948), Karenin, the icy husband of Vivien LEIGH in Korda's *Anna Karenina* (1948), and then Dr Sloper, Olivia DE HAVILLAND's father, in *The Heiress* (1949). In 1952 he tried his hand at directing with British Lion's thriller *Home at Seven*, in which he co-starred with Margaret Leighton. He joined Olivier and John GIELGUD in RICHARD III (1955); played James Tyrone in *Long Day's Journey into*

Night (1962); and appeared in the thriller *Woman of Straw* (1964) with Sean CONNERY, David LEAN's *Dr Zhivago* (1965), and *David Copperfield* (1969) as Micawber.

In his last film, *Greystoke*, he played TARZAN's grandfather who slides down the stairs on a tea-tray. When Richardson died before the release of the film, director Hugh Hudson re-edited the film to make the most of his role.

Tony Richardson (Cecil Antonio Richardson; 1928–91) British director, a pioneer of 'kitchen sink' realism in the early 1960s. As the husband of Vanessa Redgrave, he was the father of actresses Natasha and Joely Richardson (*see* REDGRAVE FAMILY).

Born in Yorkshire, Richardson studied at Oxford before becoming involved with the FREE CINEMA movement of the 1950s. His first film was the short documentary *Momma Don't Allow* (1955), about a jazz club, which he co-directed with Karel REISZ. In 1959 he adapted his own staging of John Osborne's *Look Back in Anger* as his first feature; Richard BURTON starred as the working-class antihero Jimmy Porter. The success of this picture encouraged Richardson to film Osborne's *The Entertainer* (1960), in which Laurence OLIVIER reprised his stage role of comedian Archie Rice.

After accepting an invitation from 20th Century-Fox to direct *Sanctuary* (1961), a William Faulkner story that turned into a disaster, Richardson returned to Britain to make the highly praised A TASTE OF HONEY (1961), based on Shelagh Delaney's play. He shot the interiors in a shabby London flat, hiring the whole house for £22 a week. Further acclaim came with *The Loneliness of the Long-Distance Runner* (1962), from the novel by Alan Sillitoe, and TOM JONES (1963), a high-spirited adaptation of Henry Fielding's novel. The latter, which starred Albert FINNEY, was the biggest box-office success of the year and earned Richardson an Oscar for Best Director.

Again Hollywood beckoned. Although MGM's *The Loved One* (1965), received mixed reviews, Richardson enjoyed greater success with *The Charge of the Light Brigade* (1968), starring Trevor HOWARD and Vanessa Redgrave. (Richardson refused to screen it for British critics, saying they were the worst in the world.) His later US films include *A Delicate Balance* (1973), starring Katharine HEPBURN, *The Border* (1981), with Jack NICHOLSON as a Mexican border

patrolman, and *The Hotel New Hampshire* (1983), scripted by Richardson from the disturbing novel by John Irving. *Long Distance Runner*, a posthumously published memoir, was awarded the BFI's Michael Powell Book Award for 1993.

Riefenstahl, Leni (Helene Bertha Amalie Riefenstahl; 1902–) German actress, producer-director, and documentary filmmaker for the Nazis, best known for her records of the 1934 Nuremberg rally and the 1936 Berlin Olympics. She has denied rumours that she was ever HITLER's mistress.

Born in Berlin, she worked as a dancer and painter before becoming the athletic star of Arnold Franck's 'mountain films' of the 1920s, beginning with *Peaks of Destiny* (1926). In 1931 she began a production company with her own money and produced, directed, co-scripted, and edited *The Blue Light*, in which she also starred as a peasant girl who lures men to death in the mountains.

A year after coming to power Hitler, who greatly admired Riefenstahl's work, arranged for her to film his Nuremberg rally; the result, *Triumph of the Will*, has been called the most powerful propaganda film ever made. It was intended to introduce the Nazi leaders to Germans and to awe foreign audiences. She followed this with the two-part OLYMPIA (*Olympische Spiele*; 1938), which premiered on Hitler's 49th birthday. Although undeniably propagandistic in intent, the film's technical brilliance earned it the Golden Lion award at the 1938 Venice Film Festival.

After World War II, Riefenstahl was imprisoned by the French for four years and blacklisted for some time thereafter. In 1952 she finally completed one of her prewar projects, a film of Eugène D'Albert's opera *Tiefland* (1952), in which she plays a flamenco dancer. Although she had begun planning the film as early as 1934, shooting was suspended after her nervous breakdown in 1942. Some ten years later, Riefenstahl reassembled the original cast to complete the film. When the result was criticized as old-fashioned, she withdrew from film-making for over 20 years; her last film, the African documentary *Nuba* (1977) has not been released. She ended her working life as an admired magazine photographer.

Rififi (*Du Rififi chez les hommes*; 1954) Jules DASSIN's exhilarating HEIST MOVIE, his first

French feature after being blacklisted in Hollywood as an alleged communist. Dassin co-scripted the story from Auguste le Breton's thriller about a gang of thieves who carry out an ingenious raid on a Paris jeweller's shop, only to arouse the envy of their gangland rivals. (The word *rififi* is criminal slang for 'trouble'.) Jean Servais played the criminal mastermind, Tony, while Dassin himself, credited as Perlo Vita, played the safecracker César. The film became a cult classic and spawned a number of imitations; including Dassin's own *Topkapi* (1964).

Rififi is mainly remembered for the 25-minute robbery sequence, filmed without dialogue or music, that occurs in the middle of the story. Dassin claimed that much of the movie was silent "because of my own lack of French."

rifle spot An elongated spotlight that produces a narrow beam, used mainly to highlight a character or object on set.

rim lighting A lighting effect that emphasizes the outline of a character or object, while keeping the front dark or shadowy. It is usually achieved by placing two lights directly behind the subject, one on either side.

Rin Tin Tin An Alsatian (German shepherd) dog who became a star of the silent screen in the 1920s. Formerly a guard dog with the German army, Rin Tin Tin appeared in such films as *Jaws of Steel* (1927) and *A Dog of the Regiment* (1930), usually saving the day with a display of loyalty and resourcefulness. During his Hollywood career Rin Tin Tin enjoyed the services of a personal chef, valet, and chauffeur, and had his own dressing-room complex. This remarkable dog died in 1932, aged about 16.

riser A small platform used to raise either the performer (*see* APPLE BOX) or the camera during filming; in the latter case it is also called a **bridge plate**.

RKO RKO Radio Pictures Inc. Formerly one of the biggest Hollywood production and distribution companies, RKO was founded in 1921 when the Radio Corporation of America merged with the Keith-Orpheum cinema circuit. Notable RKO productions included *Cimarron* (1931), KING KONG (1933), the Fred ASTAIRE and Ginger ROGERS musicals of the 1930s, and Orson WELLES's CITIZEN KANE (1941); the company also distributed films by Walt DISNEY and Samuel GOLDWYN. Despite having stars of the calibre of Katharine HEPBURN and Cary GRANT, RKO was better known for its low-budget and often unsuccessful films, and was continually in financial difficulties. During World War II a popular Hollywood joke ran "In case of an air raid, go directly to RKO: they haven't had a hit in years." In 1948 Howard HUGHES acquired a controlling share of the stock, leading to prolonged litigation and the virtual abandonment of production. In 1953 the studios were sold off to the Desilu television company. The corporation continues as RKO General, an umbrella organization controlling a number of radio and TV stations.

Roach, Hal (Harriett Eugene Roach; 1892–1992) US producer, director, and screenwriter, a pioneer of silent comedy. He established the careers of LAUREL AND HARDY and Harold LLOYD amongst others, while his directors included Frank CAPRA, Leo MCCAREY, and George STEVENS. Roach, who won Oscars for Best Short with *The Music Box* (1932) and *Bored of Education* (1936), was given a special Academy Award for his contribution in 1984.

Born in Elmira, New York, Roach spent an adventurous youth as a mule driver and gold prospector in Alaska. He began his film career in 1912 as an extra and stuntman at Universal; the following year Cecil B. DE MILLE employed him for $5 a day on his Western *The Squaw Man*. In 1914 Roach inherited $3,000 and hired Lloyd to make several comedy shorts. Although they were not very successful, Roach subsequently enticed Lloyd back to make more than 50 'Phun-Philms' shorts for his Rolin Film Company. His other regular stars included Charlie CHASE, Will ROGERS, and the OUR GANG team. He first teamed Stan Laurel and Oliver Hardy in *Putting Pants on Philip* (1927).

Having survived the advent of the talkies Roach diversified from two-reelers to 40-minute 'screenliners' and full features. Laurel and Hardy continued their success with such films as *Bonnie Scotland* (1935) and *Way Out West* (1937), while other hits included TOPPER (1937), starring Cary GRANT as an amiable ghost, and *The Housekeeper's Daughter* (1939), a gangster farce with Joan BENNETT. More serious fare was the Steinbeck adaptation *Of Mice and*

Men (1939) directed by Lewis MILESTONE. In 1940 he joined his son, Hal Roach Jnr, and D. W. GRIFFITH to co-direct *One Million BC* (British title *Man and His Mate*).

After World War II, during which he produced military documentaries, Roach switched to television production. In 1966 he acted as associate producer for Hammer's *One Million Years BC*, a remake of his 1940 film with Raquel WELCH. He continued to plan movie projects into his nineties.

road. road movie A genre of film in which the central character takes to the road to escape the law, the past, a constricting home life, etc. His or her experiences, and those of other characters encountered along the way, form the substance of the film. The hero's journey usually becomes a voyage of self-discovery or an exploration of the state of a society. Classic road movies include the biker film EASY RIDER (1969) and Terence Malick's *Badlands* (1973), in which teenagers Martin SHEEN and Sissy Spacek cross Dakota leaving a trail of destruction in their wake. More recent examples include David LYNCH's strange *Wild at Heart* (1990) and the feminist *Thelma and Louise* (1991). *See also* CHASE FILM.

road show A prestigious film released only to major cinemas, which charge a higher admission price than normal. Such films usually go on general release at a later date. Examples have included GONE WITH THE WIND (1939), AROUND THE WORLD IN EIGHTY DAYS (1956), THE SOUND OF MUSIC (1965), and 2001: A SPACE ODYSSEY (1968). The road show treatment has generally been reserved for expensive or unusually long productions, such as Dino DE LAURENTIIS's three-hour epic *The Bible* (1966). Although not uncommon during Hollywood's Golden Era of the 1930s and 1940s, the road show subsequently declined after the heyday of CINERAMA.

Road to Singapore (1940) The first of Paramount's 'Road' comedies, a popular series that teamed Bing CROSBY, Bob HOPE, and Dorothy LAMOUR. The film was originally scripted for Fred MACMURRAY and Jack OAKIE, who became committed to other projects, and then rewritten for George Burns and Gracie Allen, who turned it down.

Hope and Crosby, already friends from the golf course, were chosen for their radio banter and easy-going style. Although more of a straight romantic comedy than the later 'Road' films, which became increasingly zany, *Road to Singapore* established Crosby's laid-back persona and Hope's rapid-fire wisecrack responses. It also introduced such running gags as their 'pat-a-cake' routine before turning around to punch the villains. The flimsy plot concerns a rich playboy (Crosby) who deserts his fiancée to travel with his buddy (Hope) to the Polynesian island of Kaigoon. There they meet a sarong-clad Singapore dancer (Lamour) and vie for her favours; Crosby sets a pattern for the later films by winning the girl.

Victor Schertzinger directed both this film and the first sequel, *Road to Zanzibar* (1941), in which Hope wrestles a gorilla. The other films in the series were *Road to Morocco* (1942), remembered mainly for its talking camel, *Road to Utopia* (1945), in which an actor enters a scene to ask for directions to Stage 8, *Road to Rio* (1947), the highest-grossing film in America in 1948, *Road to Bali* (1952), which includes a cameo appearance by Humphrey BOGART pulling the African Queen behind him, and the British-filmed *Road to Hong Kong* (1962), featuring Peter SELLERS as a witch-doctor.

The Road See STRADA, LA.

Robbins, Tim (1958–) US actor and director, who has rapidly established himself as one of Hollywood's most versatile leading men.

Robbins was the son of a Greenwich village folk singer and grew up in New York City. Having joined an experimental theatre group at the age of 12, he studied drama at New York State University and UCLA. He co-founded the Actors' Gang, an acclaimed off-Broadway troupe, in 1981. After guesting in a number of TV shows, Robbins made his feature debut in *Toy Soldiers* (1984). Although he amused as the singing chauffeur in *The Sure Thing* (1985) and strutted purposefully through *Top Gun* (1986), he had the misfortune to land himself in a string of flops in the later 1980s; the disastrous *Howard the Duck* (1986), was followed by *Tapeheads* (1988), *Erik the Viking* (1989), and *Cadillac Man* (1990).

Such a sequence would have buried many a career, but Robbins bounced back. In 1988 he was memorable as both the Civil Rights activist who protects Jodie FOSTER in *Five Corners* (1988), and as 'Nuke' Laloosh in the baseball comedy *Bull Durham* (1988);

the latter co-starred his future wife Susan SARANDON. In *Miss Firecracker* (1989), a charming slice of small-town wish-fulfilment, he helped Holly Hunter win a talent contest, while *Jacob's Ladder* (1990) saw him playing a Vietnam veteran who discovers that he was fed hallucinogenics to turn him into a killing machine.

However, the Robbins renaissance really began in the 1990s. Following his exceptional performance as the scheming movie producer in Robert ALTMAN's *The Player* (1992), he has been a regular member of the Altman stock company, playing an arrogant motorcycle cop in *Short Cuts* (1993) and a journalist in *Prêt-à-Porter* (1994). He also impressed as both actor and debutant director with the political comedy *Bob Roberts* (1992), about a fascistic folksinger whose skilfully managed campaign takes him to the Oval Office. Although Robbins gave a creditable performance in the prison drama *The Shawshank Redemption* (1994), both the COEN BROTHERS' *The Hudsucker Proxy* (1994), in which he plays the indefatigable innocent Norville Barnes, and Fred Schepisi's *IQ* (1994) suggest that his true forte is comedy.

Robe, The (1953) The first film in CINEMASCOPE, an EPIC tale of the Roman Empire from 20th Century-Fox starring Richard BURTON, Jean SIMMONS, and Victor MATURE. "You see it without the aid of special glasses" the studio announced, in allusion to the current 3-D craze. After a premiere at GRAUMAN'S CHINESE THEATER in Hollywood, the film went on to break box-office records at New York's Roxy Theater and many other cinemas.

Based on Lloyd C. Douglas's best-selling novel, the movie began life at RKO under producer Frank Ross, who moved the $4.5 million project to Fox with Henry Koster as director. The story follows the robe taken from Christ at his crucifixion and the changes it brings to those who come into contact with it, including a Greek slave, a Roman centurion, and the ward of Emperor Tiberius (played by Simmons). Tyrone POWER and Laurence OLIVIER both turned down the role of the centurion before it passed to Burton, while Burt LANCASTER was first choice for the slave Demetrius, played by Mature. Michael Rennie portrayed Simon Peter.

The film won Oscars for art direction and costume design, as well as receiving nominations for Best Picture and Best Actor (Burton). By 1957 *The Robe* had grossed almost as much as GONE WITH THE WIND, leading Fox to promise that all future productions would be in CinemaScope. A sequel, *Demetrius and the Gladiators* (1954), in which Mature and Rennie were amongst those who reprised their original roles, was less successful.

Robert, Yves (1920–) French director and actor. Having made his stage debut in 1942, Robert switched to the cinema seven years later; he was soon established as a popular light leading man and supporting actor in such films as *Les Dieux du dimanche* (1949), *Folies Bergère* (1957), *Love and the Frenchwoman* (1960), and *Cleo from 5 to 7* (1962).

Robert's first directing assignment was the short *Les Bonnes Manières* (1951). In the 1960s he began to write and direct features for the production company La Gueville, which he had set up with his wife, the actress Daniele Delorme. *The Tall Blond Man with One Black Shoe* (1972), a comedy about a secret service agent who erroneously trails a clumsy violinist, in which Robert also acted, won a Special Jury Prize at the 1973 Berlin Film Festival. (It was remade in America in 1985 as *The Man with One Red Shoe*, starring Tom HANKS.)

Robert's other films have included *Les Copains* (1964), *Very Happy Alexander* (1968), *The Return of the Tall Blond Man with One Black Shoe* (1974), and *Pardon mon affaire* (1976). More recently he enjoyed considerable success with the PAGNOL adaptations *La Gloire de mon père* (1990) and *Le Château de ma mère* (1990).

Roberts, Julia (1967–) Auburn-haired US actress, who achieved stardom playing a happy-go-lucky hooker in the enormously successful *Pretty Woman* (1990). The top female box-office draw of 1990 and 1991, she has said of acting: "I'm not trained to do anything else – I'm a half-assed typist, that's about it."

Roberts's parents ran the Actors' and Writers' Workshop in Atlanta, while her brother Eric Roberts (1956–) is also an actor. Her first film role was as Eric's sister in *Blood Red* (made in 1986 but not released until 1989), about 19th-century California winegrowers. Having won good notices for *Mystic Pizza* (1988), she replaced Meg RYAN as the dying daughter in *Steel Magnolias*, a film about the relationships between a group of Southern women. During filming director Herbert Ross criticized her lack of technique and asked, "When this movie is over, are you going to take acting classes?" Nevertheless, she received the Golden Globe Award and an Oscar nomination for her touching performance (which was probably enhanced by an attack of meningitis shortly before filming began).

Her breakthrough came with the contemporary Cinderella story *Pretty Woman*, for which she earned an Oscar nomination as the prostitute who wins tycoon Richard GERE. Her 1991 movies included *Sleeping with the Enemy*, in which she played a battered wife, and Steven SPIELBERG's *Hook* as Tinkerbell. While making *The Player* (1992), Robert ALTMAN's satire on Hollywood, Roberts met her future husband, the actor and country singer Lyle Lovett. (She was to have married Kiefer SUTHERLAND, her co-star in *Flatliners*, 1990, but broke off the engagement just before the wedding.) After turning down the lead in *Sleepless in Seattle* – ironically the role was taken by Meg Ryan – Roberts returned to the screen in *The Pelican Brief* (1993), a legal thriller co-starring Sam SHEPARD and Denzel Washington. Her latest films are *I Love Trouble* (1994) and Stephen FREARS's *Mary Reilly* (1995).

> You can be true to the character all you want but you've got to go home with yourself.
>
> JULIA ROBERTS; *New York Times*.

Robertson, Cliff (Clifford Parker Robertson III; 1925–) US actor, who became a major star playing John F. Kennedy as a young naval lieutenant in *PT-109* (1963). The president personally approved the casting of Robertson in the role, despite complaining that the actor was too handsome. Robertson suffered a major career setback in the late 1970s, after he accused Hollywood executive David Begelman of illegally signing a cheque in his name; although Begelman was eventually fired after his guilt was established, Robertson remained blacklisted by major studios for several years.

A former merchant seaman, Robertson acted on stage and television before making his screen debut with a supporting role in *Picnic* (1955). He went on to co-star with Joan CRAWFORD in *Autumn Leaves* and to give an acclaimed performance in Raoul WALSH's *The Naked and the Dead* (1968). After his success as Kennedy in *PT-109*, he played the

unscrupulous Senator Cantwell, a presidential candidate partly based on Richard Nixon, in *The Best Man* (1964).

For his role as Rex HARRISON's secretary in *The Honey Pot* (1967), a comedy, Robertson based his performance on the film's director Joseph L. MANKIEWICZ. The following year brought an Oscar for his performance as a mentally retarded adult who matures after a brain operation in *Charly* (1968). Robertson then made an impressive debut as writer-producer-director with *J. W. Coop* (1972), in which he played a rodeo rider coming home after a decade in prison for (ironically enough) passing a bad cheque. He also wrote, directed, and starred in *The Pilot* (1980) about an alcoholic flier. His later credits include *Star 80* (1983), as *Playboy* publisher Hugh Hefner, and the New Zealand film *Shaker Run* (1985), as a stunt-car driver transporting a deadly virus.

Robin Hood Legendary English outlaw, who has been the subject of numerous films. He is reputed to have lived in Sherwood Forest during the reign of Richard I (1189–99), stealing from the rich and giving to the poor. Other familiar characters from the legend include Maid Marian, Friar Tuck, and Robin's enemy the Sheriff of Nottingham.

Robin first appeared on screen in five silent features made between 1909 and 1913, three of which were produced in Britain. Better-known retellings of the legend include Douglas FAIRBANKS's energetic 1922 film and the classic *The Adventures of Robin Hood* (1938), starring Errol FLYNN, which won three Oscars. Walt DISNEY's version *The Story of Robin Hood and His Merrie Men* (1952), with Richard Todd as the outlaw, was the first to make use of the real Sherwood Forest for location shooting. In 1956 Hammer started an occasional film series with *Men of Sherwood Forest*, starring Don Taylor; Richard Greene, star of television's *The Adventures of Robin Hood* (1955–59), took over for *The Sword of Sherwood Forest* (1960), while *A Challenge for Robin Hood* (1967) featured Barrie Ingham in the title role.

In *Robin and Marian* (1976) an ageing Robin (Sean CONNERY), motivated less by altruism than a desire to recover his lost youth, battles old enemies and attempts to revive his love for Marian (Audrey HEPBURN). Connery reappeared as King Richard in *Robin Hood, Prince of Thieves* (1991), a big-budget vehicle for Kevin COSTNER. Of the two Robin Hood films released that year – the other starred Patrick Bergin – *Prince of Thieves* was much the more popular, thanks mainly to a wild performance by Alan Rickman as Nottingham and Bryan Adams's theme song, which became a number-one hit single. Mel BROOKS's *Robin Hood – Men in Tights* (1993), an attempt to send up the Costner film, was less successful.

There have been a number of less conventional characterizations: in both *Up the Chastity Belt* (1971) and *Time Bandits* (1981) Robin is played as a camp homosexual (by Hugh Paddick and John CLEESE respectively), while the musical *Robin and the Seven Hoods* (1964) featured Frank SINATRA as a modern-day gangster who gives his ill-gotten gains to the poor. A 1973 Disney cartoon replaced the human characters with their animal counterparts: Robin, of course, is a wily fox. *See also* SWASHBUCKLERS.

Robinson, Edward G. (Emmanuel Goldenburg; 1893–1973) Hungarian-born US actor, best known for his GANGSTER roles of the 1930s. Robinson's family moved to America when he was ten and settled in New York's Lower East Side. After winning a scholarship to AADA, he anglicized his name and began appearing in stock productions from 1913.

Although Robinson made his first screen appearance as early as 1916, he remained principally a stage actor until the advent of sound in the late 1920s. It was his menacing performance as gangster boss Rico Bandello in LITTLE CAESAR (1930) that brought him his first real success, while simultaneously setting the mould for screen gangsters for years to come. Robinson's other films of the 1930s, which generally saw him cast in tough-guy roles, included *The Man with Two Faces* (1934), Howard HAWKS's *Barbary Coast* (1935), *The Last Gangster* (1937), and *The Amazing Dr Clitterhouse* (1938).

By the 1940s he was appearing in a wider range of films, including *Dr Ehrlich's Magic Bullet* (1940), a biopic about the German scientist who developed a cure for venereal disease, the classic film noir DOUBLE INDEMNITY (1943), Fritz LANG's thriller *The Woman in the Window* (1944), and *All My Sons* (1947), an adaptation of the Arthur Miller play that saw Robinson give a fine performance as Joe Keller. Meanwhile the

hoodlum roles continued in such films as *Larceny Inc.* (1942) and John HUSTON's *Key Largo* (1947), in which he played an ageing crime boss unable to come to terms with the new era.

During the 1950s Robinson experienced a series of personal difficulties; he was called to appear before the House Un-American Activities Committee (and completely exonerated); his son attempted suicide; and, in 1956, he was forced to sell his art collection, one of the largest private collections in the world, as part of the divorce settlement from his wife, the actress Gladys Lloyd. However, Robinson continued his career apace, appearing on television, returning to Broadway, and featuring in such movies as *The Big Leaguer* (1953), *Nightmare* (1956), and Cecil B. DE MILLE's THE TEN COMMANDMENTS (1956).

The following decade saw Robinson appearing mainly in character roles – most effectively in *The Prize* (1963) and *The Cincinnati Kid* (1965) – and in a number of European productions. Among his last films was the futuristic conspiracy thriller *Soylent Green* (1970), with Charlton HESTON.

rock stars *See* POP STARS IN FILMS.

Roeg, Nicolas (1928–) British director and cinematographer, who established a reputation for originality in the 1970s. Roeg began his film career as a clapper boy and subsequently worked as a cinematographer for various directors, being particularly praised for his contribution to TRUFFAUT's *Fahrenheit 451* (1966) and SCHLESINGER's *Far From the Madding Crowd* (1967). In 1970 he co-directed *Performance*, an enigmatic film about the relationship between a sadistic criminal and a decadent rock star (played by Mick Jagger), in which the borderline between reality and fantasy becomes blurred. The following year he consolidated his success with *Walkabout*, an atmospheric piece about the clash of cultures when an Aborigine befriends two White children stranded in the Australian outback. He won further praise with the occult thriller *Don't Look Now* (1973), a visually stunning film that starred Donald SUTHERLAND and Julie Christie as grieving parents.

Roeg showed a similar penchant for disconnected narrative in both *The Man Who Fell to Earth* (1976), a science-fiction extravaganza starring David Bowie, and the curious melodrama *Bad Timing* (1980). More conventional were *Insignificance* (1985), in which the characters include Einstein and Marilyn MONROE, and *Castaway* (1986), based on the true story of a woman who answered an advertisement to spend a year on a desert island with a total stranger (Oliver REED). Among his most recent films are the Tennessee Williams adaptation *Sweet Bird of Youth* (1989) and *The Witches* (1990), from a story by Roald Dahl.

> Nothing in Roeg's style appears to be spontaneous; it's all artifice and technique....Nobody expects any real pleasure from it.
> PAULINE KAEL, film critic.

Rogers. Ginger Rogers (Virginia Katherine McMath; 1911–95) US dancer, singer, and actress, whose partnership with Fred ASTAIRE in ten romantic musicals helped to keep RKO from bankruptcy in the 1930s. She also had success with comedy and dramatic roles, winning the Oscar as Best Actress for *Kitty Foyle* (1940). Among her five husbands was the actor Lew AYRES.

Born in Independence, Missouri, she was thrust into show business by her mother, a Fox screenwriter. After winning a Charleston dance contest as a teenager, Rogers performed in vaudeville and with jazz bands in Chicago and New York. Appearances in the Broadway musicals *Top Speed* (1929) and *Girl Crazy* (1930) led to her screen debut in the Paramount feature *Young Man of Manhattan* (1930), in which she began a national catchphrase with the line "Cigarette me, big boy."

During the early 1930s Rogers became romantically involved with both Howard HUGHES and director Mervyn LEROY, who arranged for her to be cast in Warner Brothers' 42ND STREET (1933) and his own *Gold Diggers of 1933*. Later that year she joined Astaire for the first time in the dance number 'The Carioca' in *Flying Down to Rio*. Despite his initial reluctance, the two appeared together again in *The Gay Divorcee* (1934), a huge success that consolidated their partnership.

The duo went on to dance their way into screen legend in such elegant Depression-era musicals as *Roberta* (1935), TOP HAT (1935), *Swing Time* (1936), *Shall We Dance?* (1937), and *Carefree* (1938).

Although Rogers called their partnership "a divine blessing", Astaire disliked being known as half of a team. When they parted after *The Story of Vernon and Irene Castle* (1939), Rogers immediately demonstrated her versatility by winning the Oscar in Sam WOOD's *Kitty Foyle*. Her subsequent non-musical films included *Bachelor Mother* (1939), Billy WILDER's *The Major and the Minor* (1942), and *Lady in the Dark* (1944).

In 1949 Rogers rejoined Astaire for *The Barkleys of Broadway*, when Judy GARLAND suddenly withdrew. However, she was soon back to comedy roles in such films as Howard HAWKS's *Monkey Business* (1952), with Cary GRANT, and *The First Travelling Saleslady* (1956), with Carol Channing. During the 1960s she returned to the stage in the Broadway production of *Hello Dolly!* (1966) and the London production of *Mame* (1969). She was briefly reunited with Astaire in MGM's compilation film *That's Entertainment* (1974).

Roy Rogers (Leonard Slye; 1912–) US Western star, who overtook Gene AUTRY as Hollywood's top singing cowboy during the 1940s. Exhibitors ranked him as the most popular Western star from 1943 until 1954; he also holds the Hollywood record for fan mail, having received nearly 75,000 letters in July 1945 (with his horse Trigger receiving more than 200). Rogers had a popular radio show in the 1940s and a television series, *The Roy Rogers Show*, from 1951 until 1956.

Born in Cincinnati, he moved to California as a migrant fruit picker in 1929. As Dick Weston, he formed the Sons of the Pioneers singing group in the early 1930s. After Rogers became a star, the group backed him in several films, including one entitled *Sons of the Pioneers* (1942).

In 1935 Rogers made his screen debut with a bit part in *Tumbling Tumbleweeds*. Having starred in the popular *Under Western Skies* (1938), he went on to appear in a long series of formulaic vehicles including *King of the Cowboys* (1943), *Don't Fence Me In* (1945), *Roll on Texas Moon* (1947), and *Night Time in Nevada* (1949). Many featured his sidekick Gabby Hayes and 'cowgirl' Dale Evans, whom he married in 1947 (the couple are still together). Rogers' palomino horse, **Trigger** (1932–65) was billed as 'The Smartest Horse in the Movies'; after he died, Rogers had him stuffed. "When my time comes" he remarked, "just skin me and put me right up there on Trigger."

Will Rogers (1879–1935) US comedian and folk philosopher, who became Fox's top star after initial failure. In 1934, at the age of 55, he was the biggest box-office draw in America. Director Henry King called him "the nicest, easiest, most amusing and wonderful man you could imagine." Once, when Rogers was to meet Calvin Coolidge, a friend bet that he could not make the notoriously straight-faced president laugh within two minutes. On being introduced to the president, Rogers leant forward and mumbled: "Er, excuse me, I didn't quite get the name." Coolidge grinned.

Born in Colagah, now in Oklahoma, Rogers began his performing career as a cowboy at a Wild West show in South Africa. He subsequently joined the Ziegfeld Follies, where his act consisted of rope-twirling while muttering asides in his famous Oklahoma drawl; favourite catchphrases included "A rope ain't bad to get tangled up in, if it ain't round your neck" and "I only know what I read in the papers." W. C. FIELDS once grumbled: "I'll bet a hundred dollars he talks just like anybody else when he gets home."

Although Rogers's screen debut in GOLDWYN's *Laughing Bill Hyde* (1918) was followed by over 30 silent films, he created little impression until the talkie *Lightnin'* (1930), in which he established his persona as a rustic wiseacre. His next major success came with *State Fair* (1933), in which he played Janet GAYNOR's father, the owner of a prize pig. (Between takes, he kept his porcine co-star company in its pen.) John FORD then directed him in the star vehicles *Doctor Bull* (1933), *Judge Priest* (1934), and *Steamboat Round the Bend* (1935), Rogers's last film.

Rogers, who loved flying, was killed in an air crash with aviator Wiley Post. His ranch on Sunset Boulevard is kept as a national monument, while Claremore, Oklahoma, has a Will Rogers Memorial Museum. His son Will Rogers Jnr, also an actor, portrayed him in the biopic *The Story of Will Rogers* (1950).

Rohmer, Eric (Maurice Henri Joseph Schérer; 1920–) French director, best known for his psychological conversation pieces. Having taught literature in the 1940s, Rohmer became a film critic on CAHIERS DU CINÉMA, the main organ of the French NEW WAVE, and subsequently its editor. After writing and directing a series of shorts, in 1959 he made his first feature film, *The Sign of Leo*, a cautionary tale about

a US musician who finds himself destitute in an unsympathetic Paris. During the 1960s he made six films – among them *The Collector* (1966), *My Night with Maud* (1969), and *Claire's Knee* (1970) – that are known collectively as his 'moral tales'. They concentrate on the process by which their leading characters come to make crucial decisions in their lives, mostly concerning their relationships with women. This sequence of films confirmed Rohmer's skill in observing human foibles; he was highly praised for their literate dialogue and classical style.

Die Marquis von O (1976) and *Perceval la Gallois* (1978) were showpieces for Rohmer's visual inventiveness; the former, which owed its style to German Romantic Paintings, won the Special Jury Prize at the Cannes Film Festival.

In 1980 Rohmer embarked on a second series of films, known as the 'comedies and proverbs', with *The Aviator's Wife*. The series concentrates on the emotional interaction between small groups of characters, showing a particular interest in triangular love affairs. It includes *Pauline at the Beach* (1982), about a young girl's psychological development through her observation of her older cousin's love affairs, *The Green Ray* (1986), in which a timid young girl optimistically sets out to find true love, and *My Girlfriend's Boyfriend* (1987), about the developing relationships between a group of lovers. Rohmer is currently working on a third cycle of films, 'Tales of the Four Seasons', beginning with *A Tale of Springtime* (1991) and *A Winter's Tale* (1992).

roll. **roll 'em** or **roll it** The director's command to start the camera motors running in preparation for a take. It is usually followed by the command ACTION.

rolling or **roll-up title** *See* CREEPER TITLE.

Romanoff, Mike (Harry F. Ferguson; 1890–1972) Hollywood restaurateur, con man, bit player, and friend of the stars. A member of Samuel GOLDWYN's exclusive croquet club – other members included Humphrey BOGART and George SANDERS – he appeared in such films as *Arch of Triumph* (1948) with Ingrid BERGMAN, *Do Not Disturb* (1965) with Doris DAY, and *Tony Rome* (1967) with Frank SINATRA.

Although Romanoff posed as an exiled Russian prince, Scotland Yard labelled him "a rogue of uncertain nationality" and few Hollywood personalities seem to have taken his pretensions seriously. On being introduced in New York to the Grand Duke Dmitri of Russia, who rattled off several sentences in Russian, Romanoff remained unruffled. "I don't think we should insult our hosts by talking in any language but theirs" he replied. On another occasion, when an actor addressed him in fluent Russian, the 'prince' simply glared at him and later fumed, "The vulgarity of a stranger speaking to me in that tongue! We never spoke anything but French at court."

Romanoff's famous friends also enjoyed turning the tables on him. Bogart once took his beautiful hairdresser to lunch at Romanoff's expensive restaurant and introduced her as a Mexican actress. She later complained that every time she ate there, she would have to assume the same role. Bogart promised to straighten things out. On their next visit, when Romanoff greeted the 'señorita', Bogey growled, "What the hell's the matter with you, Mike? You getting senile or something? This is my executive secretary, Verita Peterson. Christ! Can't you tell one broad from another?"

Rome, Open City (*Roma, città aperta*; 1945) Roberto ROSSELLINI's NEOREALIST classic of World War II. When Pina (Anna Magnani) is shot for sheltering her fiancé, Resistance leader Manfredi (Marcello Pagliero), he takes refuge with his mistress Marina (Maria Michi), not realizing that she is an informer. Eventually he is betrayed to the Gestapo, along with priest Don Pietro Pellegnini (Aldo Fabrizi).

While Rome's 'open' status during the war spared it from bombardment, it was still an occupied city and the scene of many similar hunts for anti-Fascist partisans. Rossellini himself spent much of the latter part of the war in hiding to avoid being drafted; it was during this time that he began planning a documentary short on the life of Don Morosini, who was shot by the Nazis for harbouring fugitives in 1944. In collaboration with Sergio Amidei, Federico FELLINI, Anna Magnani, and Aldo Fabrizi, Rossellini developed the idea into a feature.

Rome had been liberated for just two months when *Open City* went into production. Rossellini had only been able to obtain a licence to make a documentary, but by casting nonprofessionals to play alongside Magnani and Fabrizi and shooting on location (a factor partly necessitated by the extensive damage caused to the CINECITTÀ

studios), he was able not only to circumvent the regulations but also to give the film its sense of newsreel realism. Anxious to release the picture while the events it depicted were still topical, he chose to shoot on silent film and dub dialogue later. Such was the scarcity of equipment that he had to purchase much of his celluloid on the black market from street photographers and splice it together on movie reels in order to complete the picture.

Roma, città aperta emerged from the ashes of World War II to become Europe's first postwar masterpiece, and in doing so demonstrated once again an increasingly accepted axiom of film-making: cinema is perhaps the only one of the major art forms in which scarcity and deprivation periodically unite with genius to produce technical innovations that drastically influence the course of the art form for generations to follow.

STEPHEN L. HANSON, film critic.

room. *Room at the Top* (1958) The debut feature of British director Jack CLAYTON, a pioneering work in its unillusioned attitude towards sex and its realistic depiction of England's industrial north. It was based on John Braine's best-selling novel of the same name, which had been bought by the producers James and John Woolf as a showcase for Laurence Harvey; the screenplay, by Neil Paterson, won an Oscar.

The plot centres on Joe Lampton (Harvey), an ambitious young accountant who resents his humble background. He begins work in the bleak northern town of Warnley, which is virtually run by a wealthy mill-owner (Donald Wolfit). Joe has a torrid affair with an alcoholic married woman (Simone SIGNORET) but seeks social status through a relationship with the industrialist's daughter, Susan (Heather Sears). When he makes Susan pregnant and marries her, his older lover dies after a drinking bout.

The film's box-office success was assured by the sex scenes between Harvey and Signoret and by the British Board of Film Censors' landmark decision to pass the explicit language. Signoret won the first Academy Award for Best Actress in a Foreign Film, and there were nominations for Harvey, Clayton, and supporting actress Hermione Baddeley. The movie also took the BAFTA Award for Best Film. It was followed by two sequels, *Life at the Top* (1965), directed by Ted Kotcheff and starring Harvey, and *Man at the Top* (1973), directed by Mike Vardy with Kenneth Haigh in the title role.

room sound The general acoustic properties of a room, caused by e.g., shape, size, and furnishings, and its characteristic ambient noise. This is normally recorded separately to create a BUZZ TRACK.

A Room with a View (1986) A MERCHANT-IVORY production based on E. M. Forster's Edwardian comedy of manners, expertly adapted by Ruth Prawer Jhabvala. Set in 1907, the movie follows Lucy Honeychurch (Helena Bonham-Carter) and her chaperone (Maggie SMITH) as they travel to Florence. There she encounters both the conservative Daniel DAY-LEWIS and the wild Julian Sands. The way in which Lucy comes to choose between the two men on her return to England is dramatized in a series of beautifully filmed scenes. Director James Ivory introduces energy (and the odd touch of homoeroticism, such as the nude bathing scene) into a deft and witty script. The film won Oscars for art direction, costume design, and Jhabvala's screenplay, as well as being nominated in five other categories, including Best Picture and Best Director. Its success launched the careers of both Sands and Day-Lewis and paved the way for two further Merchant-Ivory adaptations of Forster, *Maurice* (1987) and *Howards End* (1992).

Rooney, Mickey (Joe Yule Jnr; 1920–) Diminutive US actor, a former CHILD STAR whose live-wire personality has sustained him through career decline, bankruptcy, and nine marriages. He starred with Judy GARLAND in 10 films and was America's top box-office draw between 1939 and 1941.

Born into a vaudevillian family, Rooney appeared on stage from the age of 15 months and made his film debut (playing a midget) when he was six. During the next six years he starred in 50 RKO two-reel comedies credited as Mickey McGuire, a name he adopted legally before switching to Mickey Rooney in 1932. Two years later he joined MGM, to play the young version of Clark GABLE's character in *Manhattan Melodrama*. The following year, he was acclaimed as Puck in Max Reinhardt's celebrated *A Midsummer Night's Dream*. His appearance as Andy HARDY, an all-American small-town boy, in *A Family Affair*, led to a popular series of 15 sentimental comedies. Judy Garland, who appeared in eight of these, also co-starred with Rooney in the musical *Babes in Arms* (1939) and its sequel *Babes on Broadway* (1941).

By his late teens Rooney was earning $5,000 a film and had established a reputation for chasing the girls. This horrified Louis B. MAYER who lectured him about his image: "Behave in public and don't get some jailbait knocked up." Rooney was assigned a minder who followed him to nightclubs to keep him from flirting, drinking, and smoking.

After his triumph as a delinquent youth in *Boy's Town* (1938), Rooney was awarded a special Oscar with Deanna DURBIN. He earned an Oscar nomination as the young breadwinner of a wartime family in *The Human Comedy* (1943) and co-starred with Elizabeth TAYLOR in *National Velvet* (1944) before serving in World War II. However, *Love Laughs at Andy Hardy* (1946), which cast him as a teenager once more at the age of 26, sent his career into a sharp decline; in 1948, he left MGM and ended up in low-budget films. His comeback in the wartime drama *The Bold and the Brave* (1956), which brought him another Oscar nomination, was followed by a major role in Don SIEGEL's gangster film, *Baby Face Nelson* (1957).

In 1962 Rooney was declared bankrupt after spending some $12 million in 25 years, much of it on alimony (he once joked: "I'm the only man in the world whose marriage licence reads 'To Whom It May Concern'"). His wives included the actress Ava GARDNER. In 1966, while he was in hospital, Rooney's fifth wife was murdered in their house by her lover, who then committed suicide. A year after announcing his retirement in 1978, Rooney made his Broadway debut in the musical *Sugar Babies*, which ran for three years and 1208 performances. In 1983 he received an honorary Oscar for 50 years of "memorable film performances".

> Mickey Rooney...he goes back to everybody's childhood. Even if you didn't have a childhood, Mickey Rooney goes back there.
> CHRIS CHASE.

Rope (1948) Alfred HITCHCOCK's ghoulish thriller in which two youths (Farley Granger and John Dall) strangle their friend "for the sake of danger and for the sake of killing." They conceal the body in a trunk and then use its top as a table during a party whose guests include the boy's girlfriend and father. Only their former teacher (James STEWART) senses their guilt and unravels their crime. Arthur Laurents and Hume Cronyn co-wrote the screenplay, an adaptation of a play by Patrick Hamilton. Although the story was inspired by the 1924 random 'thrill murder' by the Chicago homosexuals Leopold and Loeb, the censors banned any explicit suggestion of a sexual relationship between the two friends in the film.

Rope was a technical experiment for Hitchcock, who also co-produced. The action, mostly dialogue, is set entirely in one room. Borrowing the convention of the ten-minute TAKE from live television, Hitchcock filmed the 80-minute story without a time lapse, as if in one continuous shot. *Rope* was also the first of his thrillers to be filmed in colour. The director later described the film as "a stunt...I really don't know how I came to indulge it."

Rosebud The enigmatic dying utterance of the title character in WELLES's CITIZEN KANE (1941). The fruitless attempts of a journalist to discover its meaning provide a MACGUFFIN that leads the audience through a series of flashbacks depicting the tycoon's life. In the film's last moments the audience learns that Rosebud was the name of a sledge abandoned by the young Kane on the day he came into his riches.

According to insider gossip, however, the word had another private meaning known only to Welles, screenwriter Herman MANKIEWICZ, and one or two others. 'Rosebud' was apparently a pet name used by Kane's original, the press baron William Randolph Hearst, for the pudendum of his mistress, Marion DAVIES. If this is correct, it would help to explain Hearst's fury at the film and its makers.

Of the three sledges made for the production, two perished in the flames of the furnace in Kane's mansion while the third was bought in auction for $60,000 by Steven SPIELBERG.

Rosemary's Baby (1968) Roman POL-ANSKI's first US feature, a disturbing psychological horror film that had a huge influence on the development of the genre. The plot centres on Rosemary (Mia FARROW) and her actor husband Gus (John CASSAVETES) as they begin their married life in a gothic New York apartment building (later, in real life, the home of John Lennon). After learning that she is pregnant, Rosemary is made increasingly anxious by a number of strange or suspicious circumstances; eventually she becomes convinced that she has been impregnated by Satan, is carrying his child, and is living in a building full of witches.

The film, which was scripted by Polanski from a novel by Ira Levin, shares some preoccupations with the director's earlier *Repulsion* (1965), in that both deal with troubled female protagonists living in isolation from the outside world. In *Rosemary's Baby*, however, Polanski opts finally for a supernatural rather than a psychological explanation. What makes the film so chilling is the initial doubt that the viewer has about her fears – it seems so plausible that Rosemary, pregnant and largely alone, confined to a strange rambling building, should imagine these occult goings-on. The fact that the witches are not of the conventional horror type, appearing to be normal somewhat over-friendly neighbours, merely adds to the fear factor.

The film features strong camerawork from William A. Fracker, good taut direction from Polanski (who was also Oscar nominated for his Screenplay), and fine performances from a cast including Ruth GORDON (winner of a Best Supporting Actress Oscar), Maurice Evans, Ralph BELLAMY, Elisha Cook Jnr, and Charles Grodin. Polanski's wife Sharon Tate was originally considered for the part of Rosemary, while Warren BEATTY and Robert REDFORD were considered for Cassavetes's role. There was later a television sequel, *Look What Happened to Rosemary's Baby*.

Rosi, Francesco (1922–) Italian director, a prominent figure in the political cinema of the 1960s. Born in Naples, Rosi began his career in journalism and the theatre before entering films as an assistant to ANTONIONI, VISCONTI, and others. He made his own debut in 1956, as co-director of *Kean*, and subsequently demonstrated his concern for social and political issues in a series of films beginning with *La Sfida* (1957). He first attracted popular attention with *Salvatore Giuliano* (1961), an innovative film about an Italian gangster murdered in 1950; in keeping with the conventions of NEOREALISM, the film made use of nonprofessional actors and Sicilian locations. *Hands Across the City*

(1963), used similar techniques to explore property speculation in Naples, while *The Moment of Truth* (1964) investigated the exploitation of a matador by commercial interests.

After two relatively unsuccessful forays into comedy, Rosi returned to more serious concerns with *The Mattei Affair* (1972), a conspiracy thriller, and *Lucky Luciano* (1974), a gangster film tracing the connections between blatant criminality and political expediency in postwar Italy. Corruption in public institutions was also the theme of *Illustrious Corpses* (1976). His more recent films include *Three Brothers* (1981), a nostalgic view of peasant life, the BAFTA award-winning *Christ Stopped at Eboli* (1982), from Carlo Levi's book about life in the rural south of Italy, a version of Bizet's *Carmen* (1984) with Julia Migenes-Johnson, an adaptation of Gabriel Garciá Márquez's *A Chronicle of a Death Foretold* (1987), and *The Palermo Connection* (1990), a grim film about the Mafia.

Rossellini, Roberto (1906–77) Italian director, whose work had a profound influence on postwar European cinema; he is also remembered for his controversial relationship with Ingrid BERGMAN. Born in Rome, Rossellini began his career as a writer and director of nature documentaries, making his first feature-length film, *The White Ship* which depicted life aboard an Italian hospital ship, in 1940. He made his name with the NEOREALIST classic ROME, OPEN CITY (1945), a watershed in cinema history, and consolidated his achievement with PAISÁ (1946), in which the traumatic process of liberation by the Allies provides a link between six separate stories. *Germany Year Zero* (1947) tackled the anguish suffered by victims of the war in Germany after the return of peace in 1945.

Anna Magnani, who had starred in *Rome, Open City*, also took the lead in *L'Amore* (1948) and *The Machine That Kills Bad People* (1948). In 1949 Rossellini embarked on a series of five films starring Bergman, beginning with *Stromboli* (1949), in which she plays a wartime refugee who marries a fisherman in order to escape internment. Although they subsequently married, Rossellini's adulterous liaison with Bergman, led to both artists being shunned by the cinema world, especially in Hollywood. The partnership continued with such films as *Europa '51* (*The Greatest Love*;

1951), *Viaggio in Italia* (*The Strangers*; 1953), and *Fear* (1954), a melodrama about marital breakdown that seems to reflect the state of their own relationship (their marriage was annulled in 1958). Bergman later commented "Roberto and I were just too different. Being Italian he was a jealous husband and I was a bad influence on him." Their daughter is the actress and model Isabella Rossellini (1952–   ).

From the mid 1950s Rossellini concentrated on documentaries, often on historical themes, producing BIOPICS of such figures as Socrates, Garibaldi, Louis XIV, and Christ. He restored his international reputation somewhat with *General della Rovere* (1959), a wartime drama that won the Grand Prix at the Venice Film Festival, and *It was Night in Rome* (1960).

Rossen, Robert (1908–66) US director, screenwriter, and producer of socially conscious films. Born in New York's tough Lower East Side, he was a professional boxer before turning to drama. After several years writing and directing on Broadway, he moved to Warner Brothers in 1937 as co-writer of *Marked Woman*, a Bette DAVIS melodrama based on a true story, and *They Won't Forget*, a tale of racial injustice. Subsequent credits included the gangster classic *The Roaring Twenties* (1939) and the war film *A Walk in the Sun* (1946).

Rossen made his debut as a director with *Johnny O'Clock* (1946), starring Dick POWELL in his new tough-guy image; this was followed by *Body and Soul* (1947) with John Garfield as an unscrupulous boxer. He then won acclaim as the writer-producer-director of *All the King's Men* (1949), a story of political corruption based on the career of Louisiana governor Huey Long. The film won the Oscar for Best Picture, and Rossen was nominated as both director and screenwriter. Two of the cast, Broderick Crawford and newcomer Mercedes McCambridge, also won Oscars.

Although Rossen's social beliefs had led him to join the Communist Party before World War II, he became disillusioned and severed his ties in 1945. In 1951 he was called before the House Un-American Activities Committee (HUAC) to testify about his past membership; when he refused, he was blacklisted and found it impossible to work in America. Subsequently he moved to Italy where he wrote, produced, and directed the epic *Alexander the Great* (1956) and directed

Island in the Sun (1957), which featured a mixed-race love affair between Harry Belafonte and Joan FONTAINE. Rossen later resumed his Hollywood career after admitting his old communist connections and naming more than 50 former colleagues to HUAC. The greatest success of his later career was *The Hustler* (1961), with Paul NEWMAN and George C. SCOTT. The film, a low-life story based partly on Rossen's own youth, earned him an Oscar nomination and the New York Critics' Award for Best Director. His last film, the psychological drama *Lilith* (1964), was a box-office failure but was later acclaimed by CAHIERS DU CINÉMA as one of the Ten Best Films of all time.

rough cut The initial stage in the EDITING of a film. It is assembled by selecting one version of each shot and arranging them in their correct sequence. A rough cut lacks the precise editing of a FINE CUT, but provides a general impression of the finished product, complete with sound.

roundy round Hollywood slang for a shot in which the camera revolves through 180° from one subject to another. It has been used in biblical and historical films to show two armies confronting one another before a battle. *See also* 360-DEGREE PAN.

Rourke, Mickey (1950–) US actor with a talent for playing tough-guys and a reputation for incendiary outbursts (he once called producer Sam Goldwyn Jnr a "liar and a scumbag"). Although he was a rising star of the mid 1980s, a string of flops and controversies have since tarnished his appeal.

The son of a third-generation Irish-American father, Rourke was brought up in a poor section of Liberty City, Miami. As a teenager he flirted with baseball, boxing, and petty crime before starting acting lessons at the age of 17. From the late 1970s onwards he took bit parts in a series of films, including Michael CIMINO's HEAVEN'S GATE (1980).

Rourke first attracted public attention with performances in Lawrence Kasdan's *Body Heat* (1981) and Francis Ford COPPOLA's *Rumblefish* (1983), in which he played alongside Matt DILLON. Starring roles followed in *The Pope of Greenwich Village* (1984) and Cimino's *Year of the Dragon* (1985), a violent story about a lone cop's attempts to rid New York of the Triads.

Despite a risible script (by Cimino and Oliver STONE) and overwrought direction, Rourke came out of the film well, demonstrating an ability to overcome poor material with a powerful screen presence.

Rourke's high profile continued with the erotic anti-romance *9½ Weeks* (1986), an underrated study of emotional domination in which he played opposite Kim BASINGER, and Alan PARKER's *Angel Heart* (1987), a supernatural thriller that caused controversy with a blood-drenched sex scene. The latter, however, was the beginning of a long slide downhill for Rourke. After appearing in the IRA melodrama *A Prayer for the Dying* (1987) he caused outrage in Britain by declaring his support for the Republicans; he also boasted of donating $1 million to a campaign to prevent the extradition of a convicted terrorist from America (a claim later denied by his agent). Since then he has done nothing of note. *Barfly* (1987) and the ludicrous *Wild Orchid* (1989) (directed by Zalman King who co-scripted *9½ Weeks*) were big flops, as was Cimino's *Desperate Hours* (1990).

With his acting career in disarray, Rourke adopted a pseudonym to return to competitive boxing in 1991 (a *Daily Mail* correspondent noted that "as a boxer he makes a pretty good actor"). He also launched a literary career with a book of poetry (see below). In 1994 he returned to the screen in *Fuck the World*, a title generally abbreviated to *FTW*. Although now 45, Rourke shows no sign of mellowing; in 1994 he was arrested twice, once for allegedly assaulting his wife, Carre Otis.

Although treated with scant respect in Hollywood, Rourke has become a major screen icon in France – an example of the Gallic penchant for embracing actors and films rejected by the US critics and box office (see Jerry LEWIS). *Angel Heart* was shown at one art-house in Paris for over three years.

> Most recently I have observed,
> That movie stars stink,
> And that nepotism keeps giving birth,
> To a new generation of scum.
> MICKEY ROURKE, poem.

Ruggles. Charles Ruggles (1886–1970) US comic and character actor, who usually played genial, wistful, or henpecked men. During the 1930s and 1940s he appeared in some 80 films, being particularly memorable as Lord Babberly in *Charley's Aunt* (1930) and the frontiersman Egbert Floud in the ironically entitled *Ruggles of Red Gap* (1935). He was the brother of the director Wesley RUGGLES.

Born in Los Angeles, he began his film career in silent one-reelers, including a production of *Peer Gynt* (1915). After his acclaimed performance in *Charley's Aunt*, he appeared in Ernst LUBITSCH's witty comedy *Trouble in Paradise* (1932), *Six of a Kind* (1934), in which he co-starred with Mary Boland as a couple on their second honeymoon, and Howard HAWKS's classic *Bringing Up Baby* (1938), as a former African game hunter.

Ruggles's career ground to a halt after two musicals, *Give My Regards to Broadway* (1948) and *Look for the Silver Lining* (1949). He returned after a 12-year absence in three films of 1961: the comedy *All in a Night's Work*, starring Shirley MACLAINE and Dean MARTIN, Walt DISNEY's *The Parent Trap*, and *The Pleasure of his Company*. His final film was *Follow Me, Boys!* (1966).

Wesley Ruggles (1889–1972) US director noted for his comedies; he was the brother of actor Charles RUGGLES. Born in Los Angeles, he became one of Mack SENNETT's original KEYSTONE KOPS in 1914 and also appeared in several Charlie CHAPLIN shorts. He began directing with *For France* (1917) but enjoyed his greatest success in the early sound era with such films as *Condemned* (1929), starring Ronald COLMAN as a prisoner on Devil's Island and the Western *Cimarron* (1930). Adapted from Edna Ferber's novel about an Oklahoma family, the film earned an Oscar as Best Picture and a nomination for Ruggles as director. In 1933 he helped to save Paramount's fortunes by directing Mae WEST and Cary GRANT in the classic *I'm No Angel*, the risqué story of a carnival dancer who acquires wealth and fame with the help of a few millionaires. This was followed by *The Gilded Lily* (1935), a romantic comedy starring Claudette COLBERT as a typist who becomes a cabaret singer, *I Met Him in Paris* (1937), also with Colbert, and the musical *Sing You Sinners* (1938).

Despite these successes, Ruggles's career hit the rocks after he travelled to Britain to direct Alexander KORDA's *Perfect Strangers* (1945). When the two men quarrelled about the script, Korda took over, and Ruggles embarked on a project of his own, writing, producing, and directing the musical *London Town* (US title *My Heart Goes Crazy*; 1946). The resulting film, an attempt to make a Hollywood-style musical in Britain, proved such a disaster that he was never asked to make another movie.

rumble pot A pot of boiling water that produces a FOG-like effect when dry ice is dropped into it.

run. **runaway** or **runaway production** A film made in another country or state in order to take advantage of cheaper labour or the range of subsidies and tax advantages given to develop regional film industries. Increased unionization in Hollywood in the 1950s led to many films being shot abroad, notably the biblical epics of Victor MATURE, which were usually made in Italy.

running shot A TRACKING SHOT in which the camera moves to keep pace with a moving subject.

running speed *See* CAMERA SPEED *under* CAMERA.

running time The time taken for a film to pass through the projector while running at normal speed. The running time of most feature films is between 90 and 120 minutes, longer films being regarded as commercially risky. Some films running for three hours or more have been notably successful, however; examples include GONE WITH THE WIND (1939; 220 minutes) and *Dances with Wolves* (1990; 180 minutes).

run-through A rehearsal of a scene involving all the elements that will make up the final shot, e.g. costumes, props, make-up, etc., usually in order to uncover any problems arising from the interaction of players and technicians. *Compare* WALK THROUGH.

rushes or **dailies** The initial prints of a day's shooting, 'rushed' back from the laboratory and viewed in a raw unedited form by the director, actors, members of the production crew, etc. They provide useful day-by-day feedback, enabling subsequent shooting to be planned.

Russell. **Jane Russell** (1921–) Sultry Hollywood sex star of the 1940s and 1950s, best known for her 38-inch bust. The daughter of an actress, she worked as a chiropodist's receptionist and photographer's model before studying acting. Having failed screen tests at 20th Century-Fox (where she was judged unphotogenic) and Warner Brothers (which reported "no spark"), she achieved her big break when

Howard HUGHES chose her for his Western THE OUTLAW (1943), after a nationwide search. During filming he complained "We're not getting enough production from Jane's breasts" and designed a special cantilevered brassiere to remedy this defect. Although censorship problems held up the film's release for several years, publicity stills made Russell a World-War-II pin-up girl before she was ever seen on screen.

Russell subsequently won acclaim as a comedienne in *The Paleface* (1948), in which she played Calamity Jane to Bob HOPE's Painless Potter, a cowardly dentist; their song together 'Buttons and Bows' won an Academy Award. In 1952 the two stars were reunited for *Son of Paleface*. Russell then co-starred with Marilyn MONROE in Howard HAWKS's musical *Gentlemen Prefer Blondes* (1953); the two actresses placed their handprints side-by-side in wet cement outside GRAUMAN'S CHINESE THEATER. For the sequel, *Gentlemen Marry Brunettes* (1955), Monroe was replaced by Jeanne Crain.

Russell's later roles included an oil heiress in the 3-D musical *The French Line* (1954), a kidnapped movie star in the farce *The Fuzzy Pink Nightgown* (1957), and herself entertaining World-War-II troops in *Fate is the Hunter* (1964). After making the thriller *Darker Than Amber* (1970) she retired from the cinema; in the mid 1970s she made television commercials for bras.

Ken Russell (1927–) Controversial British director, best known for his flamboyant and irreverent BIOPICS. After attracting attention as a television director with short films on such figures as Elgar, Debussy, and Isadora Duncan, Russell enjoyed his first major success in the cinema with the D. H. Lawrence adaptation *Women in Love* (1969), starring Oliver REED, Alan BATES, and Glenda JACKSON.

The Music Lovers (1970), an impassioned fantasy about the life of Tchaikovsky (played by Richard Chamberlain), and *The Devils* (1971), a depiction of religious fanaticism in a 17th-century convent, brought Russell his first accusations of bad taste. They also won the director a large popular audience. Russell himself clearly enjoyed his reputation as an *enfant terrible* and did all he could to foster it, often to the detriment of otherwise highly original films. Although *The Boy Friend* (1971) and *Savage Messiah* (1972) were somewhat more restrained, Russell continued to develop his often grotesque vision in such films as *Mahler* (1973), the rock opera *Tommy* (1974), *Lisztomania* (1975), and *Valentino* (1977), in which Rudolf Nureyev played the silent movie star. More recent films have included *Altered States* (1981), *Crimes of Passion* (1985), *Gothic* (1987), a typically sensationalist treatment of the Byron and Shelley circle, *The Rainbow* (1989), another Lawrence adaptation, and *Whore* (1991).

> I've not read one review of *Mahler*. I know it's a good film. The critics who recognize it as such are good critics. Those who do not are bad critics.
> KEN RUSSELL.

> An arrogant, self-centred, petulant individual. I don't say this in any demeaning way.
> BOB GUCCIONE.

Rosalind Russell (1908–76) Energetic US actress, whose presence brought life to some of Hollywood's most sophisticated comedies. She is best remembered as the elegantly bohemian Mame Dennis in *Auntie Mame* (1958), a role she had earlier played on Broadway. Russell received four Academy Award nominations for Best Actress and in 1972 a special Oscar, the Jean Hersholt Humanitarian Award, in recognition of her charity work.

Born in Waterbury, Connecticut, Russell appeared on stage before making her film debut with a bit part in the MGM melodrama *Evelyn Prentice* (1934). The following year she played a temptress luring Clark GABLE from Jean HARLOW in *China Seas*. Major roles followed in *Night Must Fall* (1937) and *The Citadel* (1938) before she revealed her flair for fast-talking comedy in George CUKOR's *The Women* (1939); with Joan CRAWFORD and Norma SHEARER, Russell headed an all-female cast of 135. Her run of witty comedies continued with Howard HAWKS's HIS GIRL FRIDAY, in which she displayed great style as a reporter sparring with her editor and ex-husband Cary GRANT. In the next six years she earned Oscar nominations playing three very different roles – an unconventional author in *My Sister Eileen* (1942), the nurse who pioneered polio treatment in *Sister Kenny* (1946), and the tormented Lavinia Mannon in *Mourning Becomes Electra* (1947), from the play by Eugene O'Neill.

Russell's career then took a downward turn until the mid 1950s, when she made a powerful comeback as a frustrated spinster in *Picnic* (1955). Further triumph (and a final Oscar nomination) came with *Auntie Mame* three years later; "Life is a banquet, and most poor suckers are starving to death" declares the flamboyant character. After Mervyn LEROY's *Gypsy* (1962), in which she played the pushy mother of stripper Gypsy Rose Lee (Natalie WOOD) with almost as much brashness as Ethel Merman did on stage, Russell settled into character roles. She died after several years of ill health.

Rutherford, Dame Margaret (1892–1972) British actress, who specialized in playing eccentric elderly spinsters; she is best remembered for her portrayal of Agatha Christie's Miss MARPLE. The critic David Shipman once described her as having "the demeanour of a startled turkeycock, the jaws of a bloodhound."

A former piano and elocution teacher, Rutherford went on stage in her mid twenties but did not make her film debut until 1936. Her big break, as the medium Madame Arcati in *Blithe Spirit* (1945), was followed by memorable roles in *Passport to Pimlico* (1949) and Rank's *The Importance of Being Earnest* (1952), in which she played Miss Prism.

Rutherford played the amateur detective Miss Marple in four films of the 1960s: *Murder, She Said* (1962), *Murder at the Gallop* (1963), *Murder Ahoy* (1964), and *Murder Most Foul* (1964). As was often the case, her husband Stringer Davis appeared in minor roles in all four movies. She also gave an Oscar-winning performance in *The VIPs* (1963), appeared in CHAPLIN's *A Countess from Hong Kong* (1966), and played Mistress Quickly to Orson WELLES's Falstaff in *Chimes at Midnight* (1968). Her final appearance was as an Italian grandmother in *Arabella* (1969). She died in 1972, her devoted husband a year later.

Ryan. Meg Ryan (1961–) US actress, who made her name in the romantic comedy *When Harry Met Sally* (1989). Born in Fairfield, Connecticut, she began her acting career in television commercials and the soap opera *As the World Turns*. Her screen debut, a small part in *Rich and Famous* (1981), was followed by supporting roles in the horror shocker *Amityville 3-D* (1984), the action film *Top Gun* (1986), and comedy *Armed and Dangerous* (1986). In the later 1980s she played the love interest of Dennis Quaid, her future husband, in the

science-fiction movie *Innerspace* (1987) and co-starred with him again in *D.O.A.* (1988). That same year, she played the daughter of Sean CONNERY in *The Presidio* (1988).

Ryan finally achieved stardom playing opposite Billy Crystal in Rob REINER's *When Harry Met Sally*; the scene in which she fakes an orgasm in a crowded restaurant has become one of the most famous in recent screen history. She went on to play three roles in the fantasy comedy *Joe Versus the Volcano* (1990), with Tom HANKS, and the lover of rock idol Jim Morrison (Val Kilmer) in Oliver STONE's *The Doors* (1991). In 1993 she rejoined Hanks in the romantic comedy *Sleepless in Seattle*, in which she played a reporter who falls for a widower after hearing his story on a radio phone-in. The film was directed by Nora Ephron, the writer of *When Harry Met Sally*. Subsequent roles include an alcoholic committed to a clinic in *When a Man Loves a Woman* and Albert Einstein's neice in *IQ* (both 1994).

Robert Ryan (1909–73) US actor, who played mainly tough-guys and heavies, before ending his career in character roles. Born in Chicago, he studied at Dartmouth University, where he was heavyweight boxing champion for four years. After working in a variety of jobs, including model and debt collector; he made his stage debut in 1939; a year later he took a bit part in his first film, *Queen of the Mob*.

Following his return from war service with the US Marines, Ryan starred in a series of moody roles including a disturbed marine in Jean RENOIR's suspense story *The Woman on the Beach* (1947), an anti-Semitic killer in Edward DMYTRYK's *Crossfire* (1947), an ex-GI tracking down informer Van HEFLIN in *Act of Violence* (1949), a disillusioned cop in *On Dangerous Ground* (1951), and Barbara STANWYCK's unpleasant lover in Fritz LANG's *Clash by Night* (1952). His subsequent films included *Bad Day at Black Rock* (1955) with Spencer TRACY, the rural melodrama *God's Little Acre* (1958), Peter USTINOV's *Billy Budd* (1962), *The Dirty Dozen* (1967), and Sam PECKINPAH's violent Western *The Wild Bunch* (1969). In one of his last films, the Eugene O'Neill adaptation *The Iceman Cometh* (1978), Ryan surprised the critics with a superlative performance as the radical Larry Slade.

Ryder, Winona (Winona Horowitz; 1971–) US actress, often cast in eccentric daughter roles. She earned an Oscar nomination as Best Supporting Actress for *The Age of Innocence* (1993) and one as Best Actress for *Little Women* (1994).

Born in Winona, Minnesota, she was raised by hippy parents on the West Coast (her godfather being the LSD guru Timothy Leary) and later studied acting at the American Conservatory Theater. As a 15-year-old she made her screen debut in *Lucas* (1986) and appeared in the British film *Square Dance* (1986), with Jason Robards. In Tim BURTON's *Beetlejuice* (1988) she played the teenage daughter of yuppie parents haunted by ghosts.

Ryder's first starring role came in *Heathers* (1989), a black comedy in which she gave a startlingly mature performance as the girlfriend of a murderous teenager (Christian Slater). In *Great Balls of Fire!* (1989), a biopic of Jerry Lee Lewis (Dennis Quaid), she played the singer's 13-year-old bride and cousin. In 1990 she appeared in three films, the teenage drama *Welcome Home Roxy Carmichael*, Burton's extraordinary fantasy *Edward Scissorhands*, in which she played the young girl beloved by the freakish title character (Johnny Depp, with whom Ryder had an off-camera relationship), and the comedy *Mermaids*, in which she co-starred with CHER. The following year, exhaustion from overwork caused her to drop out of THE GODFATHER, PART III.

With her teenage years now behind her, Ryder went on to play a dual role in *Bram Stoker's Dracula* (1992) and to give a much-acclaimed performance as the naive wife of Daniel DAY-LEWIS in SCORSESE's *The Age of Innocence*. Subsequent films include *The House of the Spirits* (1993), which saw her co-starring with Meryl STREEP and Jeremy IRONS, the 'slacker' movie *Reality Bites* (1994), in which she played an unemployed woman videoing her friends, and Gillian ARMSTRONG's remake of *Little Women* (1994), in which she took the lead role of Jo March.

S

Sabu (Sabu Dastagir; 1924–63) Indian child actor, chiefly in the British films of Alexander KORDA. A serious-looking boy with a brilliant smile and spontaneous personality, Sabu enjoyed international stardom for a decade before the vogue for Eastern films ran its course. He died at 39 of a heart attack.

Born in Karapur, Mysore, he was working as a stable boy for an Indian maharajah when he was discovered by the US documentary maker Robert FLAHERTY. Korda had sent Flaherty to India to make *Elephant Boy* (1937), a Kipling adaptation, and the 12-year-old Sabu seemed a natural for the title role. Following the international success of this film, Sabu starred in Korda's *The Drum* (1938) as Prince Azim, who is taught to play a drum by a young British soldier and uses this skill to foil an attack on the British by his wicked uncle.

Sabu's third and most successful movie was Korda's THE THIEF OF BAGHDAD (1940). As Abu, the little thief, he flies on the back of the genie (Rex INGRAM) and battles with the wicked magician (Conrad VEIDT). Most of his scenes, shot in England and Hollywood, were directed by Michael POWELL. His other roles included Mowgli in Korda's *The Jungle Book* (1942) and the son of a prince in Powell and PRESSBURGER's classic *Black Narcissus* (1947). His last screen appearance was in DISNEY's circus film *A Tiger Walks* (1964).

safety film *See* ACETATE.

SAG Screen Actors Guild. US trade union for performers in motion pictures, founded in 1933. The SAG, of which Ronald REAGAN is a former president, has long been an active organization; in the 1940s it exposed and defeated the takeover of the International Alliance of Theatrical Stage Employees (IATSE) by associates of Al Capone.

The SAG has sometimes overplayed its hand. During the filming of GONE WITH THE WIND (1939), only 949 extras could be found to portray injured soldiers in the hospital scene at the railway. More than 1000 dummies were added, and the union (which then represented extras) tried to claim dues for the dummies as well. When the studio challenged it to find 1000 more extras, the SAG dropped the case.

sagebrusher Hollywood slang for a low-budget Western, such as the early John WAYNE film *Sagebrush Trail* (1933). Sagebrush is a shrub that grows profusely in the plains of the US West.

St Trinian's The anarchic girls' school created by the cartoonist Ronald Searle in the 1940s. The riotous adventures of the girls at the school inspired four successful films written and produced by Frank Launder and Sidney GILLIAT – *The Belles of Saint Trinian's* (1954), *Blue Murder at St Trinian's* (1957), *The Pure Hell of St Trinian's* (1960), and *The Great St Trinian's Train Robbery* (1966) – and a fifth written and directed by Launder, *The Wildcats of St Trinian's* (1980). The first two films of the series starred Alistair SIM as the headmistress of the decayed and corrupt private school; other regulars included Joyce Grenfell, George Cole, and Thorley Walters.

sandbag A canvas sack full of sand used on set to hold down pieces of SCENERY, lighting equipment, etc.

Sanders, George (1906–72) British actor, who specialized in playing cultivated cads and cynical heroes; his autobiography, published in 1960, was titled *Memoirs of a Professional Cad*. Sanders's four wives included Zsa Zsa GABOR (1949–57) and her sister Magda, to whom he was briefly married in 1970. In 1937 he said that he would kill himself if he reached the age of 65, a promise that he kept in 1972. (Ironically, he had just filmed *Psychomania* about a gang of motorcyclists who commit suicide and return from the dead.)

Sanders made his stage debut in the early 1930s and his first film, *Find the Lady*, in 1936. The following year he travelled to

Hollywood to make *Lloyds of London* and *Lancer Spy*, in which he played the dual role of an Englishman and his double, a German officer. He was subsequently cast as a Nazi in a number of films of World War II, such as *Confessions of a Nazi Spy* (1939).

After playing the cad in Alfred HITCHCOCK's REBECCA (1940), Sanders went on to fight evil as the Saint, Leslie Charteris's Simon Templar, in a series of five films beginning with *The Saint Strikes Back* (1939). His other roles of the 1940s included the selfish painter in *The Moon and Sixpence* (1943), the cynic Lord Henry in *The Picture of Dorian Gray* (1945), and George II in *Forever Amber* (1947). In 1950 he won the Oscar for Best Supporting Actor as the malicious theatre critic Addison de Witt in ALL ABOUT EVE, starring Bette DAVIS. Among his later films were *Village of the Damned* (1960), based on John Wyndham's science-fiction story *The Midwich Cuckoos*, and *The Kremlin Letter* (1969). In 1967 he supplied the suave voice of Shere Khan the tiger in Disney's *The Jungle Book*.

Sanders could also play the cad off the set. During a game of croquet with Samuel GOLDWYN, he was about to drive Goldwyn's ball away from the hoop when the producer begged him not to, offering him a Rolls-Royce in return. Sanders retorted that he already owned one, and smashed the ball to the other end of the court.

> Dear World, I am leaving you because I am bored. I am leaving you with your worries. Good luck.
>
> GEORGE SANDERS, suicide note.

Sarandon, Susan (Susan Tomaling; 1946–) US actress, who after some 20 years in the movies suddenly became one of Hollywood's most bankable female stars in the late 1980s. Apart from her role as Janet in the cult musical *The Rocky Horror Picture Show* (1975), Sarandon was given little chance to impress in her first 20 pictures. Her career was then halted by a very public divorce from actor Chris Sarandon in 1976, which resulted in a serious breakdown. It was Louise MALLE who finally put her unique blend of eroticism and vulnerability to good use in his US features *Pretty Baby* (1978) and *Atlantic City* (1980). She later brought these qualities to such roles as Ariel in Paul Mazursky's *The Tempest* (1982) and the victim of first vampire Catherine DENEUVE in *The Hunger* (1983) and then devil

Jack NICHOLSON in *The Witches of Eastwick* (1987).

Sarandon finally rose to the front ranks of Hollywood stardom with her feisty performance as baseball groupie Anne Savoy in *Bull Durham* (1988). It was during this production that she met the actor Tim ROBBINS, her future husband. The couple earned a certain notoriety for their protest against the US exclusion of HIV-positive Haitian boat people during the 1994 Academy Awards ceremony (an incident they jokingly alluded to when invited back the following year).

Sarandon was equally uncompromising as the ambitious socialite in *The January Man* (1989), a crusading South African journalist in *A Dry White Season* (1989), and the waitress who breaches the age and class barriers in the course of her affair with well-to-do James Spader in *White Palace* (1990). She then played another waitress, the spunky Louise, to Geena Davis's housewife Thelma in Ridley SCOTT's *Thelma and Louise* (1991). Her performance in this controversial feature, a feminist reinterpretation of the conventions of the 'road' and the 'buddy' movie, brought Sarandon her first Oscar nomination. She has since been nominated for both *Lorenzo's Oil* (1993) and *The Client* (1994).

Since playing the mother searching for a cure for her son's adrenoleukodystrophy in *Lorenzo's Oil*, she has become increasingly associated with mother roles, notably in *Little Women* (1994) and *Safe Passage* (1995). She herself has commented:

> I play *unusual* moms. I'm interested in not making the transition from leading lady to mother role, to stay as a person who is sexual while still *being* mom. I don't want to have to give up all my parts to play moms.

Saura, Carlos (1932–) Spanish director, often considered the father of contemporary Spanish cinema (as successor to BUÑUEL). Born in Aragon, he directed his first feature film, *The Hooligans*, in 1962. *The Hunt* (1966), the first of several films to probe the legacy of the Spanish Civil War, was followed by *Peppermint Frappé* (1967), a surrealist drama (much influenced by Buñuel), about a surgeon who transforms one of his patients into a double of a woman with whom he is obsessed. With their emphasis on violence and sexual repression, many of Saura's films of this period were bitterly, if indirectly, critical of Franco's regime;

among the most successful was *Cria!* (1975), about the refusal of a young girl to acknowledge the death of her parents.

After Franco's death in 1975 the political aspect of Saura's work became less important and his subjects became increasingly varied. *Fast, Fast* (1980) traced the lives of four delinquents and made innovative use of flamenco music. A subsequent trilogy of films celebrating Spanish music and dance comprised *Blood Wedding* (1981), a flamenco ballet based on Lorca's play, the highly successful *Carmen* (1983), and *El amor brujo* (1986), a supernatural love story employing the music of Falla. Among Saura's more recent films are *El Dorado* (1988), an epic about the conquistadors' exploration of Peru; *Ay Carmela!* (1990), about a cabaret trio who find themselves behind Nationalist lines in the Civil War; and *Sevillanas* (1992), a spectacular celebration of Spanish folk dance.

save. save it! *See* PRINT IT!.

save the arcs or **save the lights** A command from the film director or GAFFER to turn off the set lights.

SAWA Screen Advertising World Association. The US-based trade association that promotes advertising in cinemas.

scenario (1) Another term for an OUTLINE or TREATMENT. (2) An older term for the completed SCREENPLAY.

scenarist The writer of a SCENARIO.

scene A subdivision of a film, usually consisting of a unified episode with a single setting and a continuous time frame. Although a typical scene will be composed of a series of SHOTS taken from various angles and distances, these are usually filmed during a single session (a notable exception is the breakfast scene in THE MAGNIFICENT AMBERSONS, 1942, which was filmed on various occasions and given its dramatic unity in the editing process). Sometimes more than one location is used, as in a chase or other action scene.

scene dock or **scene bay** A backstage area of a studio used for the storage of painted FLATS and other scenery.

scenery Anything placed on a SET to indicate the location of the action. This may range from a full-size replica of a building to furniture or props. The term is also sometimes

used of the BACKGROUND elements in a location shot, such as trees, hills, buildings, etc.

scenic artist The person responsible for painting the SET or any PROPS that are part of the set. The scenic artist is usually a member of the art department, though he or she sometimes belongs to the crew.

SCG Screen Cartoonists Guild. The US-based trade union that represents the interests of artists, technicians, and others involved with the production of ANIMATED films.

Schindler's List (1993) Steven SPIELBERG's film based on the true story of businessman Oskar Schindler, who saved 1100 Jews in Nazi-occupied Poland from death in Auschwitz. It won seven Academy Awards, including Best Film and Spielberg's first Oscar for Best Director after 11 nominations. In his acceptance speech, he pleaded "Please listen to the echoes and ghosts, and teach these things in your schools." He himself paid for 16,000 Californian schoolchildren a week to see the film. Although Hollywood insiders predicted that the $23-million venture, a black-and-white film more than three hours long, would be a box-office failure, it earned over $100 million worldwide during its first fortnight on release. (It was banned in Malaysia as 'Jewish propaganda' and briefly in the Philippines because of nude scenes.)

The film is based on Thomas Keneally's novel *Schindler's Ark*, which won the Booker Prize in 1982. (Hollywood felt the word 'ark' would mislead cinemagoers with its religious connotations.) Oskar Schindler, a war profiteer and womanizer, gains great personal wealth by exploiting the cheap Jewish workforce in his enamelware factory. Eventually, however, he is repelled by the Nazis' treatment of the Jews and risks his own life to save his workers from the horrors of the concentration camp. Liam NEESON portrays Schindler, the British actress Caroline Goodall plays his wife Emilie, and Ben Kingsley is Itzhak Stern, the Jewish accountant at Schindler's factory.

The Polish government would not allow filming at Auschwitz or Birkenau, feeling that this was inappropriate. As part of his research Neeson visited Auschwitz with co-producer Branko Lustig, who commented, "Horrible, isn't it?" Neeson replied, "I suppose, but somehow I don't feel it." Lustig pulled up his sleeve to reveal a tattooed number on his arm. "I was born here," he said.

The film's epilogue, which is shot in colour, shows surviving *Schindlerjuden* with their movie counterparts at Schindler's grave in Jerusalem.

Schlesinger, John (1926–) British director, who made his name in America with the Oscar-winning MIDNIGHT COWBOY in 1969. After gaining some experience as an actor in such films as *The Battle of the River Plate* (1956), Schlesinger directed a number of television documentaries. The success of *Terminus* (1960), a documentary about the British transport system that won the Golden Lion Award at the Venice Film Festival, enabled him to make his feature film debut with *A Kind of Loving* (1962). This tale of frustrated ambition and romantic disillusion in the industrial north of England was followed by *Billy Liar* (1963), a highly successful comedy in a similar setting, with Tom Courtenay and Julie Christie. Christie was also the star of Schlesinger's *Darling* (1965), an exposé of jet-set society, and *Far from the Madding Crowd* (1967), an adaptation of the novel by Thomas Hardy.

In 1969 Schlesinger went to America to make *Midnight Cowboy*, starring Jon Voight and Dustin HOFFMAN, a study of New York low life that won Academy Awards for Best Film and Best Director. His films of the 1970s included *Sunday, Bloody Sunday* (1971), about a three-way love affair, the thriller *Marathon Man* (1976), starring Hoffman and Laurence OLIVIER, and *Yanks* (1978), about the arrival of US troops in Britain during World War II. More recently he has made *Madame Sousatzka* (1988), *Pacific Heights* (1990), a chilling story about a psychopath who terrorizes the other tenants of the house in which he lives, and *The Innocent* (1993).

Schlöndorff, Volker (1939–) German director, noted especially for his films about rebels and outcasts. Schlöndorff studied film in Paris, where he also worked as an assistant to MALLE, RESNAIS, and MELVILLE; he made his first short in 1960 and his feature debut in 1966 with *Young Törless*. Like many of his subsequent films, this was based on a well-known book – in this case Robert Musil's story about the failure of a schoolboy to intervene when a gang of bullies kill another pupil. It won the International Critics' Prize at the Cannes Film Festival.

Michael Kohlhaas (1969) was an adaptation of Heinrich von Kleist's novel about rural conflict in the 16th century that drew a parallel with unrest in contemporary German society. *The Sudden Fortune of the Poor People of Kombach* (1971), another rural allegory, portrayed the downfall of a peasant community after a fortune is stolen from the local tax collector. The film starred **Margarethe von Trotta** (1942–), who also worked on the screenplay; during the course of their continuing collaboration von Trotta became Schlöndorff's wife. *Summer Lightning* (1972) was another joint work, starring von Trotta as a divorcée whose attempts to rebuild her life are blighted by male chauvinism. Von Trotta then concentrated upon her own career as a director, collaborating occasionally with her husband on such films as *The Lost Honour of Katherina Blum* (1975), about the media persecution of an innocent woman.

Schlöndorff's subsequent films include *Coup de grâce* (1976), set in the period following the Russian Revolution; an adaptation of Günter Grass's *The Tin Drum* (1979) that won the Oscar for Best Foreign Film; *Circle of Deceit* (1981), set in war-torn Beirut; *Swann in Love* (1983); a 1985 adaptation of Arthur Miller's *Death of a Salesman*, starring Dustin HOFFMAN; and *The Handmaid's Tale* (1989), from the novel by Margaret Atwood.

Schnozzle Nickname of the US comedian Jimmy DURANTE, who was famous for his bulbous nose (his 'schnozz' or 'schnozzle').

Schrader, Paul (1946–) US writer and director who, because of his strict Calvinist upbringing, did not see a motion picture until he was 18 years old. Following this revelation, he abandoned theological studies in his home town of Grand Rapids, Michigan, and went to the UCLA Film School. Rebellion against religion has since informed many of his films, among them *Hardcore* (1979, writer-director), starring George C. SCOTT as a strict Calvinist who goes in search of his porn-star daughter, and *Light of Day* (1987, writer-director), in which Michael J. FOX and Joan Jett fall foul of their born-again mother (Gena Rowlands). Schrader has also scripted adaptations of Paul Theroux's *Mosquito Coast* (1986), which features a hypocritical missionary, and Kazantzakis's *The Last Temptation of Christ* (1988).

After graduating from UCLA, Schrader worked as a critic, publishing his *Transcendental Style in Film: Ozu, Bresson, Dreyer* in 1972. He began his screenwriting career with a joint credit (with his brother Leonard and Robert TOWNE) for the Japanese gangster thriller *The Yakuza* (1975). His fascination with Japan would resurface in the overstylized *Mishima: A Life in Four Chapters* (1985, writer-director).

Schrader became one of the hottest properties in Hollywood with his second script, TAXI DRIVER (1976). Directed by Martin SCORSESE and starring Robert DE NIRO, this powerful picture was the first of many Schrader films to explore the theme of alienation. In RAGING BULL (1980), also directed by Scorsese, De Niro played the boxer Jake LaMotta, whose inability to leave his aggression in the ring leads to the collapse of his private life. *Patty Hearst* (1988, director only) starred Natasha Richardson as the kidnapped heiress who joined cause with her revolutionary captors, while *American Gigolo* (1979, writer-director), a bold attempt to translate Robert BRESSON's *Pickpocket* (1959) to modern California, starred Richard GERE as the stud-for-hire who rediscovers his values when accused of murder.

Schrader also likes to focus on characters caught out of their depth or their natural environment – as in *Blue Collar* (1978), his debut as a director, which explores the dilemma of three factory workers confronted with union corruption. More bizarrely, *Cat People* (1982) deals with an incestuous brother and sister (Malcolm McDowell and Nastassia KINSKI) who become killer leopards to escape social restrictions, while *The Comfort of Strangers* (1990) shows how holidaymakers Rupert Everett and Natasha Richardson are inveigled by a sadomasochistic couple (Christopher Walken and Helen Mirren). Schrader returned to these themes in *Light Sleeper* (1992), a highly personal film that explores his own recovery from a drug-induced 'long weekend'.

> Infantile behaviour...is absolutely part of the film business itself. That's where the ideas are hatched and the fantasies are enacted, so when you pay people to think like children, you can't get too upset when they behave like them.
>
> PAUL SCHRADER.

schtick or **shtick** US slang for a routine or piece of business that is regularly used by an actor or a comedian. Hollywood examples include W. C. FIELDS's pool-shark routine, the slow build-up fights between LAUREL AND HARDY, the 'Who's on first' routine of ABBOTT AND COSTELLO, Danny KAYE's double talk, and the pat-a-cake routine of Bob HOPE and Bing CROSBY in their 'Road' series.

Schüfftan process An IN CAMERA method of combining live action with art work or MINIATURES to produce a composite image. There are two variants of the process. In the first, a piece of glass with a mirror at the centre is placed at 45 degrees to the camera axis. The art work or miniature is photographed through the glass while the live action (reflected in the mirror) is filmed at the same time. In the second method, a mirror reflecting the art work or miniature is placed at 45° to the camera. Parts of the mirror's silver backing are scraped away and the live action is filmed through the gaps.

The process was developed in 1923 by the German cinematographer Eugen Schüfftan (1893–1977) and used for the first time in Fritz LANG's in *Die Nibelungen* (1924); it was later used in Lang's METROPOLIS (1927) and Alfred HITCHCOCK's *Blackmail* (1929). Although it provided an excellent composite image that could be viewed while filming, the process was time-consuming and inflexible and was soon superseded by MATTE techniques.

Schwarzenegger, Arnold (1947–) US actor and former Mr Universe, born in Austria. The young Schwarzenegger (described by Clive James as looking like "a condom full of walnuts") was brought to America by bodybuilding mogul Joe Weider in 1968. After taking a business course at the University of Wisconsin he landed small parts in a variety of movies (mainly as Arnold Strong) while continuing to earn huge sums from professional bodybuilding competitions. He then became known to a wider public with *Pumping Iron* (1977), a documentary about his bodybuilding activities. His big break came when director John Milius insisted on Schwarzenegger for the lead in *Conan the Barbarian* (1982). "If Arnold hadn't existed, we would have had to invent him" quipped Milius. Schwarzenegger made a sequel in 1984 but opted out of a third movie in an attempt to broaden his appeal (according to Schwarzenegger, producer Dino DE LAURENTIIS greeted this news with a "sort of sneer").

The perfect choice for the role of the emotionless killing machine in James CAMERON's THE TERMINATOR (1984), Schwarzenegger went on to consolidate his macho image in such films as *Commando* (1985), *Raw Deal* (1986), and *Predator* (1987). By 1989 he was able to command a fee of $25 million for *Twins*, a successful comedy in which he cast aside his established screen persona to play the twin brother of the diminutive Danny DEVITO.

Total Recall (1990), a violent science-fiction story, marked a return to the more familiar Schwarzenegger territory of action-oriented films packed with special effects. This was followed by the hugely successful *Terminator 2*, in which his character was given a more human dimension, and another venture into comedy with *Kindergarten Cop* (both 1992). However, *Last Action Hero* (1993), in which Schwarzenegger attempted to send up his usual persona proved a commercial and critical disaster. More successful were *True Lies* (1994) and *Junior* (1994), in which he undermined his macho image still further by playing a pregnant man carrying Emma THOMPSON's baby.

> Money doesn't make you happy. I now have $50 million but I was just as happy when I had $48 million.
> ARNOLD SCHWARZENEGGER.

science fiction A subgenre of FANTASY in which improbable worlds or happenings are given scientific and rational, rather than magical or divine, explanation. The popularity of sci-fi clearly owes much to the pace of technological change in this century and the conflicting emotions that go with this: on the one hand, amazement at the possibilities on offer, on the other, anxiety about an uncertain future. Awe and angst are indeed the predominant motifs in sci-fi; broadly speaking, films can be divided into those that focus on a bright future of shining buildings and dinky gadgets, and those that are set in a badly lit underworld plagued by faulty plumbing.

Itself a product of the technological boom at the end of the last century, cinema showed an early fascination with the effect that technology was having on daily life. Nor was it long before the ability of the medium to create strange new worlds through visual trickery was exploited in a range of fantasies giving science and scientists a major role. However, sci-fi does not have a continuous history of production in the cinema. Rather, it has appeared in a series of bursts, either as a response to some new scientific or social phenomenon, or stimulated by developments in film technology or SPECIAL EFFECTS.

The first burst of sci-fi came at the turn of the century, with the pioneering work of Georges MÉLIÈS. Inspired by the work of Verne and Wells, he produced a wide range of sci-fi shorts, including the remarkable space-travel fantasies *A Trip to the Moon* (1902) and *The Impossible Voyage* (1904). The theme of space travel recurred periodically over the next few decades, being treated with some realism in the Danish film *The Sky Ship* (1917), the British *The First Men on the Moon* (1919), and Fritz LANG's *The Girl in the Moon* (1929). The last-named film was sufficiently close to the scientific facts for the Nazis to withdraw it from distribution during the V2 programme. With the development of rocket technology in the war, space travel became much more believable, leading to a new burst of sci-fi production with such films as *Rocketship X-M* and *Destination Moon* (both 1950).

The 1950s was in many ways the golden age of cinema sci-fi. Owing to the advent of nuclear weapons and the tensions of the COLD WAR, the prospect of invasion by an alien power or death from the skies no longer seemed so fantastic. Hollywood responded with a wave of films in which alien invaders are ruthlessly shot down as soon as they stick their head(s) out of their space ship. Scientists, once generally portrayed as benevolent, were increasingly cast as mad fools who try to understand and make contact with the aliens rather than simply exterminating them (e.g. *The Thing*, 1951). This seems to reflect both a general distrust of intellectuals as potential fellow travellers and a growing concern over the consequences of scientific development.

If the vast majority of sci-fi produced in the Cold-War period shows a deep fear of the unknown, the films of the 1960s and 1970s tended to preach a message of hope and trust. In KUBRICK's spectacular 2001: A SPACE ODYSSEY (1968), as in SPIELBERG's *Close Encounters of the Third Kind* (1977) and E.T.: THE EXTRATERRESTRIAL (1982), contact with the unknown proves redemptive and suggests that the universe is more benign than we might have feared. STAR WARS (1977) was essentially a high-tech return to the kind of SPACE OPERA popular in the 1950s.

Other films have been concerned less with space travel or aliens than the projection of a present trend or fear into an imagined future. Lang's METROPOLIS (1927) is an early example of this, playing on fears of both increased regimentation and violent revolution. Similarly, the advent of the nuclear bomb some 30 years later led to a host of films featuring the bizarre effects of radiation (*Them*, 1954) or imagining a postapocalyptic future (*On the Beach*, 1959). In the 1970s and 1980s the range of horrible futures increased at a frightening rate; environmental disaster was predicted in *Silent Running* (1971), *Soylent Green* (1973), and *Blade Runner* (1982); computers and robots turn against mankind in *THX 1138* (1970), *Westworld* (1973), and THE TERMINATOR (1984); while fears of the power of the electronic media emerged in *Videodrome* (1984) and *Total Recall* (1990).

score *See* MUSIC.

scoring stage A soundproofed STAGE used for the recording of film scores. The room is usually large enough to accommodate a full orchestra and equipped with a screen on which the film may be projected during recording. The musicians take their lead from the conductor, who faces the screen armed with score, cue sheets, etc.

Scorsese, Martin (1942–) US director and occasional actor. The son of Sicilian immigrants, Scorsese grew up in New York's Little Italy. Although he began to train for the priesthood, he quickly dropped out to study at New York's Film School, where he made a number of prize-winning shorts, including *The Big Shave* (1967). His first feature, directed while he was teaching in the New York University film department, was *Who's That Knocking at My Door* (1968), a semiautobiographical film about Italian-American youths.

In the early 1970s Scorsese worked as a supervising editor on *Woodstock* (1970) and an associate producer on *Medicine Ball Caravan* (1971). After a brief stint with CBS, he directed the gangster story *Boxcar Bertha*, a sequel to Roger CORMAN's *Bloody Mama*. The film made little impact but gave Scorsese his first opportunity to work within the Hollywood system. The following year saw the release of his first major film, the urban drama MEAN STREETS (1973). Harvey KEITEL starred as a young Italian-American with thoughts of the priesthood, while Robert DE NIRO played a self-destructive petty criminal. The film introduced the restless camera work and noir-style lighting that would reappear with powerful effect in TAXI DRIVER. Despite critical praise *Mean Streets* achieved little commercial success; by contrast, *Alice Doesn't Live Here Anymore* (1975), a rather more mainstream production, became a big hit and earned its star, Ellen Burstyn, a Best Actress Oscar.

In 1976 came the landmark production *Taxi Driver*, a vision of New York as an urban hell that again featured De Niro and Keitel. The former gave an electrifying performance as a disturbed Vietnam veteran, now a New York cabbie, who becomes obsessed with rescuing a young prostitute (Jodie FOSTER) from her pimp (Keitel). The film won the Palm d'Or at Cannes and a Best Director prize from the New York Film Critics. Rather more surprisingly, the records of the Soviet State Film Committee show it to have been a favourite of Leonid Brezhnev.

Following *New York, New York* (1977), a glitzy tribute to 1940s Hollywood musicals featuring De Niro and Liza MINNELLI, Scorsese earned the best reviews of his career with RAGING BULL (1980), a bleak biopic of the boxer Jake LaMotta. The film won two Oscars – for De Niro's performance in the lead and for Best Editing – from a total of nine nominations. By contrast, *The King of Comedy* (1983), a black comedy starring De Niro as an obsessive fan who stalks a famous comedian (Jerry LEWIS), was something of a flop. Scorsese then earned a Best Director Award at Cannes with *After Hours* (1985), a stylish comedy about the nightmarish experiences of a computer operator (Griffin Dunne) during a foray into New York's SoHo. The director reportedly ordered his star to abstain from sex and sleep during filming to make him appear more anxious.

In 1986 Scorsese made a cameo appearance in Bertrand TAVERNIER's jazz film *Round Midnight* and directed *The Color of Money* (1986), a sequel to Robert ROSSEN's low-life drama *The Hustler*. Paul NEWMAN reprised his role of Eddie Felson some 25 years after the original. *The Last Temptation of Christ* (1988) proved the most controversial project of Scorsese's career with its portrayal of CHRIST as a troubled man beset by temptation and doubt. Although the film won a Critics prize at Venice and an Oscar nomination for Best Film, others found it lacklustre compared to the director's best work.

After appearing as Van Gogh in KUROSAWA's *Dreams* (1989), Scorsese returned to more familiar territory with the gangster drama *GoodFellas* (1990), which brought him another Best Director nomination at the Oscars, BAFTA Awards for Best Director and Best Film, and the Best Director Award at Venice. Amongst its other distinctions, the film features the highest-ever count of the f-word (which occurs, on average, once every 28 seconds). That same year Scorsese co-produced Stephen FREARS's *The Grifters* (1990) and appeared with De Niro in *Guilty by Suspicion* (1990), a film about the McCarthy witchhunts in Hollywood. *Cape Fear* (1991), a violent remake of the 1962 film, was followed by the uncharacteristic *The Age of Innocence* (1993), a period drama starring Michelle PFEIFFER, Daniel DAY-LEWIS, and Winona RYDER.

Like Woody ALLEN, Scorsese has achieved a rare feat in attracting Hollywood backing for his highly personal and often heavily autobiographical work while remaining in New York. As well as directing features, Scorsese has made several documentaries and worked on the restoration of LAWRENCE OF ARABIA and Michael POWELL's *Peeping Tom* amongst other films.

Scott. George C(ampbell) Scott (1926–) US actor. After wartime service in the US Marines, Scott decided on an acting career, graduating through summer stock to Broadway and television during the 1950s. His film debut in *The Hanging Tree* (1959), a Gary COOPER Western, was followed later that year by *Anatomy of a Murder*, in which his performance as the prosecuting attorney earned an Oscar nomination as Best Supporting Actor. The following year he appeared as Bert Gordon, Paul NEWMAN's evil-hearted backer in Robert ROSSEN's *The Hustler* (1961).

Scott went on to take major roles in such films as John HUSTON's *The List of Adrian Messenger* (1963), Stanley KUBRICK's DR STRANGELOVE (1964), in which he played the gung-ho Gen. 'Buck' Turgidson, and *The Flim-Flam Man* (1967), before landing the part of George S. Patton Jnr, the controversial World-War-II general, in *Patton: Lust for Glory* (1970). Despite having denounced the ACADEMY AWARDS in some much-publicized remarks, Scott was awarded a Best Actor Oscar for his bravura performance in the film; this he duly refused to accept, becoming the first actor ever to turn down an Oscar. When, shortly afterwards, he was awarded an Emmy for his performance in a TV adaptation of Arthur Miller's *The Price*, Scott felt obliged to refuse this too.

US president Richard Nixon is alleged to have sat through a number of private screenings of *Patton* before ordering US bombers into Cambodia.

Scott's films of the 1970s include *The Last Run* (1971), in which he co-starred with Trish Van Devere, whom he married the following year, *The Hospital* (1971), a black comedy for which he was again Oscar nominated, Stanley KRAMER's *Oklahoma Crude* (1973), and Paul SCHRADER's *Hardcore* (1978), in which he played an austere Calvinist searching for his runaway daughter in the sleazy porn world of Los Angeles. He also appeared in two rather unsuccessful films that he directed himself, *Rage* (1972) and *The Savage is Loose* (1974), as well as Mike NICHOLS's flop *The Day of the Dolphin* (1973) and the disastrous DISASTER FILM *The Hindenburg* (1975).

During the 1980s Scott worked increasingly in television, while continuing to appear in such films as *The Formula* (1980), an unsuccessful thriller co-starring Marlon BRANDO, and *Taps* (1981), a film about a military academy that launched the careers of both Sean Penn and Tom CRUISE. His most recent film outing was in *Malice* (1993).

Ridley Scott (1939–) British director and producer. Scott made his name as a director of television commercials and the glossy fast-moving imagery of these productions has clearly influenced the look of his films. His first feature was *The Duellists* (1977), a lavish adaptation of a story by Joseph Conrad, with Harvey KEITEL5 AND KEITH CARRADINE as the Napoleonic antagonists. Two years later the science-fiction horror story ALIEN established Scott's standing in the commercial cinema and made a star of Sigourney WEAVER. The futuristic thriller *Blade Runner* (1982), starring Harrison FORD, was hugely influential, launching the 'cyberpunk' genre; however, Warner Brothers were not satisfied with the original and added a clichéd private-eye narration and a sunlit happy ending (with footage from *The Shining*, 1980). Scott took the opportunity to release a DIRECTOR'S CUT of the film in 1992, one of the few director's cuts to be shorter than the original.

Subsequent films, such as *Legend* (1985) and *Someone to Watch Over Me* (1987), were praised for their dazzling visual qualities but attracted some criticism for their lack of content. Rather better received was *Black Rain* (1989), which starred Michael DOUGLAS as a US policeman working with his counterparts in Japan. Similarly, *Thelma and Louise* (1991), an Oscar-nominated ROAD MOVIE about two women on the run, was admired for its intelligent characterization and provocative postfeminist message. In 1992 Scott directed and co-produced *1492: Conquest of Paradise*, starring Gérard DEPARDIEU, the most ambitious and expensive (at a cost of $45 million) of that year's crop of Columbus films.

Ridley Scott's brother Tony is also a director, best known for the Tom CRUISE vehicle *Top Gun* (1986) and *True Romance* (1993). In 1995 the brothers bought SHEPPERTON STUDIOS in a £12-million deal intended to revitalize the British film industry.

> Ridley Scott is mad, a force of nature. If I were a woman, I'd have made love with him.
> GÉRARD DEPARDIEU.

scouting   The pre-production search for outdoor sites to be used for LOCATION filming. Attitudes to scouting, as to location work in general, have varied enormously. David LEAN often spent months scouting locations and his enthusiasm knew no bounds when the ideal spot was found. When prop man Eddie Fowlie showed him the solitary mountain chosen for the Marabar Cave scene in *A Passage to India* (1984), the 75-year-old Lean grabbed his camera and, Fowlie recalled, "went up that granite mountain like a bloody hare. That rock must be the biggest monolith in the world, and David went up backwards on his arse." By contrast producer Arthur Freed travelled all around Scotland scouting locations for the musical *Brigadoon* (1954) only to report that he had "found nothing that resembled Scotland." Instead, he constructed his preferred image of the Highlands in the studio.

scratch track   *See* GUIDE TRACK.

screen   The white or silvered surface onto which a film is projected in order to be viewed. While screens vary in size from cinema to cinema, their shape has remained fairly constant; a width-to-height ratio of 1.33:1 (*see* ACADEMY FRAME) remained standard until the various WIDESCREEN experiments of the 1950s, after which a ratio of 1.85:1 was generally settled upon. Most screens are painted a simple matte white, as this provides uniform brightness over a wide angle; other types include aluminium-sprayed screens, which intensify contrast but produce a less fine image, and the glass-bead screen, which offers greater brightness but can only be used in small theatres (because it reflects the light in a narrow angle). Translucent screens are sometimes used with rear-projection equipment, generally for small demonstration or display purposes.

Screen Actors Guild *See* SAG.

Screen Advertising World Association *See* SAWA.

Screen Cartoonists Guild *See* SCG.

screening room   a small room equipped with a screen and projector. It is generally used to show work in progress to various interested parties, e.g. to screen RUSHES for the director, a WORKPRINT to the producer, or a completed film to distributors or advertisers. Depending upon the intended audience, the screening-room decor may vary from basic to the luxurious (with armchairs and waiter service).

screenplay   The script that is used as a blueprint for the production of a movie. Owing to the high costs and collaborative nature of film-making, the written text on which the film is based will usually go through many drafts, being altered by a variety of commercial or artistic pressures at each stage. The initial idea for a film is submitted in the form of a brief OUTLINE; if a producer shows interest, this is expanded to a fuller TREATMENT, and then to a first-draft screenplay. At this stage the writer has probably only encountered the producer and possibly some of the backers; further changes will invariably follow if the screenplay gets the go-ahead and a director is hired. Differences of opinion between the various parties are thrashed out at a series of script conferences (usually expense-account lunches). At this stage it may well seem to the writer that anything original in either plot or characterization is being gradually purged from the film so that it more closely resembles last year's surprise hit. The agreed screenplay, complete with camera directions, etc., is called the SHOOTING SCRIPT. Even this may bear little resemblance to the finished film, as further changes are usually introduced during filming or editing.

screen test A filmed audition for a movie role. Many future stars have fared badly at screen tests. Shirley TEMPLE failed one for the OUR GANG series, while studio reports on Clark GABLE and Fred ASTAIRE were particularly damning. Perhaps the most humiliating failure was Rock HUDSON's test for 20th Century-Fox, which the studio saved for use as an example of bad acting. The greatest number of tests ever conducted for a single role was undertaken by David O. SELZNICK in his search for the perfect Scarlett O'HARA in GONE WITH THE WIND (1939).

screenwriter or **scriptwriter** A person who writes or contributes to SCREENPLAYS, for movies. The first professional screenwriter, journalist Roy McCardell, was paid $15 per story by the American Mutoscope & BIOGRAPH Company in 1900. Although silent films usually required at least a rough outline, many details would be originated on set by the director and actors. Screenwriting did not really emerge as a distinct craft until the coming of sound, when there was a sudden demand for experienced writers of dialogue who understood the new medium.

Prolific screenwriters from Hollywood's Golden Era include Ben Hecht, who wrote *Scarface* (1932), *Nothing Sacred* (1937), and many other movies, Nunnally JOHNSON, who adapted John Steinbeck's *The Grapes of Wrath* in 1940, and Charles Lederer, coauthor (with Hecht) of *Kiss of Death* (1947). Established writers in other fields to find success in the cinema include the poet Jacques PRÉVERT, the playwrights Jean COCTEAU and Harold Pinter, and the novelist Graham GREENE. Novelists and playwrights have sometimes adapted their own works for the screen, as did Tennessee Williams with *The Rose Tattoo* (1955) and Vladimir Nabokov with LOLITA (1962). F. Scott Fitzgerald made a small contribution to GONE WITH THE WIND (1939), while William Faulkner co-scripted THE BIG SLEEP (1946). Noted writer-directors include Preston STURGES, Billy WILDER, and Woody ALLEN.

screwball comedy A type of fast-paced escapist entertainment that developed as one of Hollywood's responses to the Depression of the 1930s. Screwball comedies were usually set in an affluent milieu and showed harmless (if somewhat irresponsible) eccentrics involved in a series of improbable escapades. They generally combined the sophisticated verbal comedy associated with Ernst LUBITSCH with elements of slapstick and farce. In the archetypal screwball plot a breezily self-confident heroine, a representative of the idle rich, wins the heart of the serious hard-working mid-American hero, encouraging him to lighten up and enjoy life; at the same time her brush with the real world causes her to recognize the responsibilities of her position. A significant factor in screwball comedies was their depiction of women: the independent strong heroines were all quite capable of holding their own with men in a battle of words or wills.

The principal exponents of the genre were the directors Howard HAWKS and Frank CAPRA, who between them produced many of the finest comedies of the 1930s. Early examples include two films of 1934: Hawks's *Twentieth Century*, with John BARRYMORE and Carole LOMBARD, and Capra's IT HAPPENED ONE NIGHT, in which journalist Clark GABLE tags along with runaway heiress Claudette COLBERT in search of a story. The latter was the first film to win all top five Oscars, a record it held until 1976. Hawks returned to the genre with *Bringing Up Baby* (1938), with Cary GRANT as a palaeontologist forced to look after a pet leopard belonging to madcap heiress Katharine HEPBURN. Grant also starred in *The Awful Truth* (1937), *Holiday* (1938), and HIS GIRL FRIDAY (1940), while Lombard and William POWELL teamed up for *My Man Godfrey* (1936), in which a 'tramp' is picked up by an heiress in a scavenger hunt and becomes the family's butler – only to be revealed as a former socialite.

As World War II approached, the essentially frivolous tone of screwball comedy began to seem inappropriate and the broader social satire of Preston STURGES took its place. Attempts have been made to revive the genre, the most successful being Peter BOGDANOVICH's *What's Up, Doc?* (1972), starring Barbra STREISAND and Ryan O'NEAL, a hilarious reworking of the plot of *Bringing Up Baby*. Other modern examples include *For Pete's Sake* (1974), also starring Streisand, and *Arthur* (1981), with Dudley MOORE and Liza MINNELLI.

scribe A tool used by editors to scratch cue marks onto film for cutting or assembling; it is usually a piece of pointed metal.

scrim A translucent screen (usually made of wire gauze) that is placed over lights to soften and diffuse the beam without affecting the colour temperature.

Searchers, The (1956) John FORD's classic but sombre Western, starring John WAYNE as a lonely driven man on a voyage of self-discovery. Wayne plays the complex Ethan Edwards, a Confederate veteran who returns home long after the war; his brief happiness is shattered when Comanche Indians slaughter his brother's family and kidnap his young niece (Natalie WOOD). He takes his adopted half-breed nephew (Jeffrey Hunter) on a seven-year search for the killers and the girl; on finding her living as an Indian squaw his first instinct is to kill her for betraying the family. Frank S. Nugent's script was adapted from the novel by Alan le May.

Ford shot the movie in 55 days in Monument Valley (where he had made his famous STAGECOACH in 1939). Although the Indians were depicted as the 'baddies' of the film, the director paid his Navajo extras handsomely and was officially adopted into their tribe.

One of the first psychological Westerns, *The Searchers* received generally poor reviews for its lack of action and its gloomy story but went on to become an enormous box-office success, grossing nearly $5 million. There were Oscar nominations for editing and for Max Steiner's original score. Although the film has been endlessly imitated most critics still rank it as among the very best of the genre.

second. second feature *See* CO-FEATURE.

second unit In larger productions, a small self-contained crew that is responsible for filming scenes that do not require the presence of the principal actors (e.g. location, continuity, or ESTABLISHING SHOTS, action sequences, or scenes involving a large number of extras).

second-unit director The person in charge of the SECOND UNIT. As second-unit work often involves the handling of a large number of extras or the co-ordination of complex special effects, a range of specialist skills are required. Two of Hollywood's most respected second-unit directors were Yakima Canutt (1895–1986) and Andrew Marton (1904–92), who were responsible for the action scenes in *Spartacus* (1960) and BEN-HUR (1959) respectively. According to some accounts, the famous shower scene in PSYCHO (1960) owes more to the work of second-unit director Saul Bass (1920–) than to HITCHCOCK.

Sellers, Peter (Richard Henry Sellers; 1925–80) British comedian, noted for the range of his characters, accents, and disguises. He is perhaps chiefly remembered for playing the bumbling inspector Jacques Clouseau in the PINK PANTHER SERIES of Blake EDWARDS. Sellers often said that he had no real identity off the screen; once, when a fan asked "Are you Peter Sellers?" the star replied "Not today" and walked off.

Born in Southsea, England, the son of vaudeville performers, he was carried on stage when only two days old. At the age of 14, he won five pounds singing in a talent contest. After World War II, during which he served in the RAF's Entertainment Division, Sellers began to appear on BBC radio with the comedians Spike Milligan, Harry Secombe, and Michael Bentine. The four men made their screen debut in *Penny Points to Paradise* (1951) before going on to create *The Goon Show*, a cult radio series, that ran for nearly ten years.

Sellers's early films included the EALING comedy *The Ladykillers* (1955) with Alec GUINNESS, *The Smallest Show on Earth* (1957), and *The Mouse That Roared* (1959), in which he played three roles. His performance as the belligerent shop steward Fred Kite in the BOULTING BROTHERS *I'm All Right, Jack* (1959) led to his being voted 1960 film actor of the year by the Variety Club of Great Britain.

Subsequent roles included an Indian doctor in *The Millionairess* (1961), with Sophia LOREN, a philandering librarian in *Only Two Can Play* (1962), and an eccentric playwright in Stanley KUBRICK's *LOLITA* (1962). The following year, Sellers took the role of Clouseau in *The Pink Panther* after Peter USTINOV turned it down. Although the official lead was David NIVEN, Sellers's performance stole the film and made him an international star. Later that year he went to Hollywood to play three unforgettable roles in Kubrick's DR STRANGELOVE.

After making the first *Pink Panther* sequel, *A Shot in the Dark* (1964), Sellers suffered a near-fatal heart attack but recovered sufficiently to play a demented psychiatrist in *What's New Pussycat?* (1965). By this time he had acquired a reputation as a man to work with; while making the spoof BOND FILM *Casino Royale* (1967), for example,

Sellers took such a dislike to co-star Orson WELLES that he refused to appear in any of his scenes. Although his films of the 1970s were mainly mediocre, his career was sustained by the success of *The Return of the Pink Panther* (1975), *The Pink Panther Strikes Again* (1977), and *Revenge of the Pink Panther* (1978). "They renewed his bastard's licence", noted one film-maker.

In 1979 Sellers at last found a vehicle worthy of his talents in the satire *Being There* (1979); his portrayal of a simple gardener who becomes a celebrity won him an Oscar nomination. He died of another heart attack shortly after filming *The Fiendish Plot of Dr Fu Manchu* (1979). Blake EDWARDS subsequently used old clips to piece together a posthumous flop, *The Trail of the Pink Panther* (1982). Sellers was married four times, his second wife being the Swedish starlet Britt EKLAND.

Selznick, David O. (1902–65) US producer mainly remembered for creating GONE WITH THE WIND (1939). A notorious perfectionist, Selznick was a hands-on producer who fired off hundreds of memos during the making of each film. His second wife was the actress Jennifer JONES.

The son of film executive Lewis J. Selznick, David sat in on business meetings from the age of 11 and negotiated film contracts as a teenager. In 1926 Selznick went to Hollywood (following his brother Myron, who became a producer and agent) to join MGM as an assistant story editor for $50 a week; within months he had become an associate producer of B-movies. He moved on to Paramount in 1927 and four years later to become the head of RKO at the age of 29. After he married Louis B. MAYER's daughter in 1930 Hollywood wits noted, "The son-in-law also rises." At RKO he supervised *A Bill of Divorcement* (1932), which launched Katharine HEPBURN's career, and made KING KONG (1933), before being lured back to MGM as vice-president.

Two years after setting up Selznick-International Pictures in 1936, Selznick embarked on his pet project, a screen adaptation of Margaret Mitchell's *Gone with the Wind*. Before the movie was completed, he had contributed to both the writing and directing, while also interfering in everything from set design to hairstyling. His famous nationwide search for Scarlett O'HARA turned up some strange candidates: a large box labelled 'OPEN AT ONCE' arrived one morning at the studio; a pretty girl leapt out and ran straight into Selznick's office, where she started to recite the part of Scarlett from the book while removing her clothes.

In 1940 Selznick brought Alfred HITCHCOCK to Hollywood for his first US film, REBECCA; five years later the two men worked together again on SPELLBOUND. Selznick cast his protégée Jennifer Jones in *Duel in the Sun* (1946) and *Portrait of Jennie* (1948), divorcing his wife to marry her in 1949. He also became involved with European productions, investing in such films as THE THIRD MAN (1949). After the failure of *A Farewell to Arms* (1957), with Jones and Rock HUDSON, Selznick retired. His two sons by his first marriage, Jeffrey and Daniel Selznick, are also producers; in 1989 they made the television documentary *The Making of a Legend: Gone With the Wind*.

senior or **senior spot** A heavy-duty 5000w SPOTLIGHT equipped with a FRESNEL LENS; this gives an intense yet even light that is particularly effective as a spotlight for performers or to illuminate key areas of the set. *Compare* JUNIOR.

Sennett, Mack (Michael Sinnott; 1880–1960) Canadian-born Hollywood director and producer, a pioneer of screen slapstick who was known as **The King of Comedy**. According to Charlie CHAPLIN, "The secret of his success was his enthusiasm. He stood and giggled until his body began to shake." Sennett was awarded a special Oscar for his achievements in 1937.

Born in Quebec, the son of Irish immigrants, Sennet had early aspirations to be an opera singer; instead, he was obliged to start work in an iron foundry when his family moved to Connecticut. In 1902 he went to New York to perform in burlesque and six years later began acting in films at Manhattan's BIOGRAPH studios. There he appeared as a leading man in several D. W. GRIFFITH shorts, played opposite both Mary PICKFORD and Mabel Normand, and began to write scripts and direct.

In 1912 Sennett co-founded the KEYSTONE Company with financial backing from two bookmakers to whom he owed $100. Over the next three years he made the Keystone name synonymous with slapstick farce, wild chases, and CUSTARD-PIE fights. His stars included Roscoe 'Fatty' ARBUCKLE, Ford Sterling, Chester Conklin, and Charlie

Chaplin, who made 35 comedies for him in 1914 for $150 a week. Sennett also introduced the Keystone Kops – he had tried in vain to convince Griffith that "cops were funny because they had dignity" – and, later, the Sennett Bathing Beauties. In 1914 he made the first feature-length comedy, *Tillie's Punctured Romance*, with Marie Dressler as a coy spinster and Chaplin as her bumbling suitor.

A year later Keystone was absorbed into the Triangle Film Corporation, a venture that teamed Sennett with Griffith and Thomas H. INCE. Although Triangle produced two new stars, William S. Hart and Douglas FAIRBANKS, the partnership dissolved in 1917. During the 1920s Mack Sennett Comedies, enjoyed continuing success with a series of Harry Langdon films and such one-offs as *The Shriek of Araby* (1923), a spoof of VALENTINO in *The Sheik* (1921). Frank CAPRA began his career as gagwriter on such two-reel comedies *Long Pants* (1927).

Sennett's career declined sharply with the advent of the talkies. In 1935, after directing Buster KEATON in *The Timid Young Man*, he retired to Canada. He later returned as an associate producer at 20th Century-Fox and appeared as himself in *Hollywood Cavalcade* (1939) and *Down Memory Lane* (1949).

Sensurround Trade name for a special sound system developed by Universal in the mid 1970s; it used low-frequency sound waves to send detectable vibrations through a cinema audience. The intention was to add a touch of unnerving realism to such films as *Earthquake* (1974) and *Rollercoaster* (1977).

sequel A movie that continues a story or repeats a basic situation from a previous film or films, usually with the same actors playing the leads. With rare exceptions, sequels are designed with the sole purpose of reaping further commercial rewards from a formula that has already proved successful. For this reason, their relationship with the original film is usually made clear by the title. An innovation of the late 1970s was to number the films; the boxing film *Rocky* (1976), for example spawned four sequels ending with *Rocky V* (*see* NUMBERED SEQUELS).

Although sequels in general have a bad name with critics and cineastes, a few have transcended their originals in quality and ambition; examples include Universal's *The Bride of Frankenstein* (1935), which is generally considered a more sophisticated film than FRANKENSTEIN (1931), and THE GODFATHER, PART II (1974), which is both PREQUEL and sequel. *Terminator 2: Judgment Day* (1991) is an example of a sequel that outstripped its original at the box office (*see* TERMINATOR FILMS).

While some sequels stick very closely to the formula established by their predecessors, others strike out in new directions. The three ALIEN films, for example, were shot by three different directors and belong to quite different genres. Occasionally the title of the original seems to have been retained as little more than a selling point: *Halloween Three: Season of the Witch* (1983), for example, has no discernible connection to the other films in the series.

Examples of long-delayed sequels include *International Velvet* (1978), released 33 years after *National Velvet* (1945), and Disney's *Return to Oz* (1985), released 46 years after THE WIZARD OF OZ (1939). *See also* SERIES.

sequence A succession of SCENES or SHOTS that together form a unified dramatic episode; a useful analogy is that of a chapter in a novel. A sequence should comprise a self-contained piece of action with a beginning, middle, and end, ideally with a dramatic climax. A FADE or DISSOLVE was once a popular means of indicating the beginning or end of a sequence, though a straight cut is more common nowadays. A sequence does not have to unfold in the same location or within a continuous time frame; CROSS-CUTTING and MONTAGE can be used to create a dramatic unity from action that is occurring in different times and places. Examples include the sequences between Kane and either of his wives in CITIZEN KANE (1941), which use a series of brief episodes to show the growing distance between them.

sequence shot A film SEQUENCE consisting of a single lengthy shot. In general, a shot of this kind uses either a rich MISE-EN-SCÈNE to convey narrative information or a restlessly moving camera to follow or reveal significant action.

serial A film consisting of a number of episodes (usually 12) screened at the same cinema over a period of weeks or months. Traditionally, each episode ended with a melodramatic CLIFFHANGER and the title "to be continued". Between the 1910s and the 1950s Hollywood produced some 580 serials, of which about 60% were silent. From the 1920s onwards the serial usually accompanied the main feature as an added attraction.

Thomas EDISON's *What Happened to Mary?* (1912) is often described as the first film serial, although it featured several related stories rather than one continuous plot. *The Adventures of Kathlyn* (1913) introduced the cliffhanger. Among the most popular silent serials were THE PERILS OF PAULINE (1914), starring Pearl WHITE, which effectively created the serial craze, and the Kalem Company's *The Hazards of Helen*, which ran for 119 episodes from 1914 to 1917. The most popular talking serial was FLASH GORDON (1936).

series A group of films featuring the same character or characters in similar situations; whereas SEQUELS are often opportunistic, a series is generally planned as such from the outset. Early film series included the 'Mr Jones' stories of D. W. GRIFFITH (1908–09) and the 'Bronco Billy' Westerns of G. M. Anderson (1910–16). The early sound era saw a rash of series with DETECTIVES as their protagonists, notably those featuring Charlie CHAN, MR MOTO, the FALCON, and Ellery QUEEN. Other popular series ranged from the rather basic comedy of the Bowery Boys and Ma and Pa KETTLE to the adventures of TARZAN and JUNGLE JIM. Although most of these films were unsophisticated low-budget fare, MGM found success with the more up-market Dr Kildare and HARDY FAMILY series in the 1930s. The latter became one of Hollywood's longest-running series, consisting of 15 films released between 1936 and 1946 and the nostalgic *Andy Comes Home* in 1958. The longest British series has been the CARRY ON FILMS, with 30 movies between 1958 and 1978, with the later addition of *Carry on Columbus* (1992). A long-running series may well feature different leads over the years, an example being the highly popular BOND FILMS.

Although there have been few purposely designed series since the 1950s, most modern BLOCKBUSTERS are created with the possibility of a sequel or sequels in mind.

Servant, The (1964) Joseph LOSEY's ambivalent look at the British class system and the mutual exploitation that it seems to entail. *The Servant* was Losey's first collaboration with playwright Harold Pinter, who wrote the enigmatic screenplay and appears in a cameo role, and his first film with Dirk BOGARDE since *The Sleeping Tiger* a decade earlier. Both men worked with the director on several later occasions.

Following his return from Europe, Tony (James FOX), a rich but ineffectual playboy, takes on the cockney Hugo Barrett (Bogarde) as his valet. Before long, Tony's girlfriend Susan (Wendy Craig) becomes alarmed at Hugo's growing hold over his supposed master. Realizing that Susan might endanger his position, Hugo brings his 'sister' Vera (Sarah MILES) into the house as a maid and arranges for her to seduce Tony. Later Tony discovers Hugo and Vera making love and, suddenly aware of the plot, fires both of them. However, when left to himself Tony descends into hopeless alcoholism and – following Hugo's carefully orchestrated 'chance' encounter with him in a pub – rehires the valet. Although Susan eventually comes back to Tony it is too late: the inversion of the master-servant relationship is complete.

Despite reaping much critical praise in Britain, where it took British Film Academy awards for Best Actor (Bogarde) and Cinematography (Douglas Slocombe), the film was largely ignored in America. In common with most of Losey's other films, its reputation has now suffered something of a decline.

set An artificially constructed interior or exterior location for filming. By the mid 1910s sets had evolved from the simple painted backdrops of earlier days to complex constructions requiring the efforts of a large department of specialists. Most studios soon had permanent mock-ups of a variety of urban locales (e.g. Western main street, contemporary slum) on their BACK LOTS. Famously elaborate sets of the silent era included the gigantic Babylonian ziggurat in D. W. GRIFFITH's INTOLERANCE (1916) and the 90-foot-high medieval castle in the Douglas FAIRBANKS version of ROBIN HOOD (1922). The largest indoor set ever constructed was the UFO landing site used in the climax of SPIELBERG's *Close Encounters of the Third Kind* (1977); the enormous concrete and fibreglass structure required some four miles of scaffolding.

In general, sets are designed with regard for their filmic rather than their actual appearance. Walls may slant at unfamiliar angles to compensate for the flat screen, while colours may also be distorted to compensate for film and processing. Shooting and editing can make façades appear convincingly three-dimensional. The set is also designed to ensure maximum freedom of movement for the camera and sufficient room for the work of other technicians. The appearance of the sets is ultimately the responsibility of the ART DIRECTOR, working in conjunction with a SET DESIGNER.

set decorator The production crew member in charge of building sets that have been conceived and designed by an ART DIRECTOR or SET DESIGNER.

set designer A member of the production crew who works with the ART DIRECTOR to create sets, making drawings or models as guidelines for the SET DECORATOR.

set estimator A member of a studio art department who estimates the costs of building sets for a production. The estimates are based on drawings of proposed sets.

seven. *The Seventh Seal* (1956) Ingmar BERGMAN's sombre medieval allegory. A knight (Max VON SYDOW) returns from the Crusades to find his homeland stricken with plague and its people indulging in flagellation and witch-hunting as means of atonement. In an attempt to postpone his demise, he challenges Death to a game of chess and thus enables a family of troupers (whom he equates with the Holy Family) to escape alive.

Von Sydow later described his character as:

> A doubter who does not believe. He doesn't have the faith he should have, and the faith he wants...He goes to the Crusades to give his life meaning, and he finds a rotten war and nothing else. He doesn't find what he's been looking for. When he returns to his country...death is all around...He is a seeker, which, of course, Bergman has been all his life.

The comparison between Bergman and the knight, Antonius Blok, was highly perceptive. Bergman was the son of a Lutheran clergyman and the severity of his upbringing had provoked a crisis of faith that he explored not only in *The Seventh Seal*, but also in *The Face* (1958) and *The Virgin Spring* (1960). In the book *Bergman on Bergman* the

film-maker wrote: "For me, in those days, the great question was: Does God exist?...If God doesn't exist, what do we do then?" The film's title refers to a passage in the Book of Revelation: "And when he [the Lamb] opened the seventh seal, there was silence in heaven about the space of half an hour." In the notes written for the premiere programme, Bergman claimed:

> In the Middle Ages men lived in terror of the plague. Today they live in fear of the atomic bomb. *The Seventh Seal* is an allegory with a theme that is quite simply: man, his eternal search for God, with death as his only certainty.

Shot on a shoestring budget in just 35 days, the film won the Special Jury Prize at Cannes in 1957.

The Seven Samurai (*Shichinin no samurai*; 1954) Akira KUROSAWA's classic action movie. During the civil wars that blighted Japan during the Sengoku period, a defenceless village asks Kambei (Takashi Shimura), an ageing itinerant samurai, to help them resist a band of marauding brigands. Having prepared the villagers for combat, Kambei and his six recruits await the attack.

Kurosawa's film consciously evokes the themes, characters, and vistas of John FORD's classic Westerns. At the same time this epic feature provides an intimate study of the samurai code and the divide between the lifestyle of the warriors and that of the villagers. The climactic battle sequence combines fast violent action with complex TRACKING SHOTS, ZOOM photography, variegated speeds, and rapid MONTAGE to demonstrate a mastery of the cinematic art that perhaps only GRIFFITH and EISENSTEIN could rival. Indeed the whole film is, as one critic put it, "a tapestry of motion."

The success of the drama, however, owes less to its moments of explosive action than to the lovingly recreated atmosphere of 17th-century Japan, and the precision of the characterization. By giving each samurai a leitmotif habit or gesture, Kurosawa personalized and intensified the drama as the battle draws inevitably nearer.

After Kambei, the best remembered warrior is Kikuchiyo (Toshiro Mifune), the farmer's son posing as a samurai in the hope of being accepted as one of their number. Mifune had already played a samurai in Kurosawa's groundbreaking 1950 feature RASHOMON and would go on to create the role of the rootless warrior in the director's

Yojimbo (1961) and *Sanjuro* (1962). These films would in turn inspire Sergio LEONE's 'Man with No Name' trilogy, starring Clint EASTWOOD. Kurosawa's use in these pictures of zooms and abrupt close-ups and his depiction of the agony of death in slow motion were to become familiar features of the SPAGHETTI WESTERN in the 1960s. *The Seven Samurai* became *The Magnificent Seven* in John STURGES's Hollywood remake of 1960. It seems fitting that a film that had drawn so much of its inspiration from the Western should in its turn make such a major contribution to its revival.

sex   The depiction of sex and sexuality has long been a contentious area in the arts, and cinema has certainly been no exception. Indeed, owing to the photographic nature of the medium and the dynamism of the images, cinematic attempts to tackle sexual subjects have always been fraught with moral and aesthetic controversy.

The relationship between sex and cinema is a long one. EDISON's KINETOSCOPE, which predates cinema by six years, soon became popularly known as the 'what the butler saw' machine owing to the nature of the material commonly on view. In Paris, the success of Eugène Pirou's *Le Coucher de la mariée* (1896), in which a blushing bride slowly undresses before her husband on their wedding night, created a new industry virtually overnight. Owing to public demand, licentious shorts of this kind were produced in great numbers at the turn of the century, being exhibited mainly at private film societies and bachelor film evenings. Ever since, a highly profitable PORNO-GRAPHIC film industry has existed in parallel to mainstream film-making, with the two only occasionally converging.

It is often not appreciated that standards in pre-1920 cinema were far more liberal than those of any era before the present. The Danish two-reeler *The White Slave Traffic* (1910) showed that there was an audience for longer films with a sexual theme and spawned a wave of similarly titled Scandinavian movies. The US remake *Traffic in Souls* (1913), filmed clandestinely by George Loane Tucker owing to fears that the public were not ready for such fare, earned $450,000 from a $5,700 production and made the fortunes of Universal studios. Thereafter discreet female nudity became quite common on the US screen. The artist's model Audrey Munson appeared naked in *Inspiration* (1915), while the following year saw the release of three US movies with nude leading ladies. Scenes of nudity were also fairly widespread in European films – although a portent of the future could be seen in Russia's decision to ban French striptease shorts in 1908.

Although the 1920s saw Hollywood dealing with such themes as seduction, venereal disease, and contraception, the pressure for restraint was becoming increasingly insistent. In particular, a number of very public sex scandals involving the stars frightened studio bosses and led to the first industry-wide attempts at self-regulation. This new conservatism deepened in the 1930s, when competition from radio and the effects of the Depression led the studios to aim for a family audience with a diet of clean, undemanding, upbeat films. The HAYS CODE, formally implemented in 1934, exorcized sex from US cinema for some 30 years, forcing even married couples into twin beds and banning any kiss of over three seconds duration. At the same time the rise of Fascism and Stalinism in Europe led to even greater restrictions on freedom of expression.

Postwar liberalization occurred very slowly. In Britain, the absolute ban on nudity that had existed since the formation of the British Board of Film Censors in 1913 was first breached by the Swedish film *One Summer of Happiness* (1951), which was passed on the curious grounds that nude bathing was the norm in Scandinavia. Although the 1950s saw a proliferation of naturist movies such as *The Garden of Eden* (1953), full-frontal female nudity was not seen in British cinemas until *Hugs and Kisses* (1966). In America, the production code was openly flouted by *The Pawnbroker* (1964), the first mainstream US film to show exposed female breasts for nearly 50 years, and abandoned a few years later. For some reason, Hollywood has not championed the right to show male nudity with the same persistence; comparatively few male leads have been called on to reveal their artistry in the manner so frequently required of their female colleagues. Male genitals, first seen on screen in the Italian *Dante's Inferno* (1912) were not exposed again until the wrestling scene between Alan BATES and Oliver REED in *Women in Love* (1969). Another area in which taboos proved extremely stubborn was the presentation of HOMOSEXUALITY

– the very existence of which was scarcely acknowledged before 1960.

The main development of the early 1970s was the eruption of pornography into public theatres with the extraordinary success of *Deep Throat* (1972). Although the intellectual vogue for porn was shortlived, its legacy can be seen in the unprecedented explicitness of, for instance, BERTOLUCCI's *Last Tango in Paris* (1973). Although lovemaking and nudity have now become so ubiquitous in the mainstream cinema as to arouse little comment, it is a moot point whether such athletic and aestheticized displays bear any more relation to reality than the coyer depictions of yore.

Sex Kitten A nickname bestowed on Brigitte BARDOT following the *succès de scandale* of her uninhibited performance in *Et Dieu créa la femme* (1956).

sexploitation film A movie that exploits sex to attract audiences. *See* EXPLOITATION FILM; PORNOGRAPHY.

Sex Thimble A nickname given to Dudley MOORE, the diminutive British actor. It refers to Hollywood's attempt to promote him as a sex symbol in such films as '*10*' (1979).

Shakespeare, William (1564–1616) English playwright and poet, whose works have been endlessly reinterpreted by the cinema. All 33 plays have been filmed at some time, yielding about 300 straight-ish adaptations and roughly 40 reworkings. Although there are records of Beerbohm Tree's *King John* being filmed as early as 1889, the oldest surviving piece of Shakespearean footage (1890) shows Sarah Bernhardt as Hamlet in the duel scene.

It was, however, the popularity of VITAGRAPH's Shakespearean shorts of the 1910s that was mainly responsible for fixing the Bard as a cinema standard. The studio's motives are not difficult to discern; Shakespeare offered the kudos of a respectable literary product as well as the benefit of very good plots with a lot of sex and violence (and all out of copyright). Commercially, the absurd compression required by the two-reel format and the absence of the poetry may have been no disadvantage. Moreover, the prestige of Shakespeare's name enabled Vitagraph to lure established stars from the theatre.

Unfortunately for the studio, some of the stars already under contract wished to show that they too were capable of putting across

the pathos of *Hamlet* (in 15 minutes and without words). This mistaken belief has been responsible for some of the worst Hollywood adaptations, notably the 1916 and 1936 versions of *Romeo and Juliet*, starring respectively Theda BARA (aged 26) and Norma SHEARER (aged 36) as Juliet (14). On the other hand, Hollywood's curious ideas about casting have sometimes been strangely successful, as in the case of Max Reinhardt's *A Midsummer Night's Dream* (1935), starring Jimmy CAGNEY and Mickey ROONEY.

The idea that the popularity of Shakespeare may owe something to the prevalence of sex and violence (otherwise little in evidence in the 1930s and 1940s) is supported by the terms in which the studios have publicized their offerings. MGM's *Julius Caesar* (1953), for example, carried the publicity line, "Thrill to ruthless men and their Goddess-like women in a sin-swept age!" Certainly, the plays with a high body count or a bit of sex have tended to garner more remakes – witness the popularity of *Romeo and Juliet* (1936, 1954, and 1968, etc.), *Macbeth* (1948, 1954, 1960, 1971, etc.), and *The Taming of the Shrew* (1929, 1958, 1967, etc.). The most popular of the plays is *Hamlet*, with about 75 versions; notable amongst these are OLIVIER's Oscar-winning adaptation (1948), Grigori Kosintsev's Russian version (1964; translation by Boris Pasternak), and the ZEFFIRELLI film with Mel GIBSON (1991).

Shakespeare has also inspired a number of looser adaptations, with varying degrees of success. Among the more idiosyncratic are KUROSAWA's *Throne of Blood* (1957) and *RAN* (1985), which transpose *Macbeth* and *King Lear* (respectively) to the world of medieval Japan: Aki Kaurismaki's *Hamlet Gets Business* (1987); and *Forbidden Planet* (1956), which relocates *The Tempest* to outer space. The musical treatment has also succeeded; WEST SIDE STORY (1961) is based on *Romeo and Juliet* and *Kiss Me Kate* (1953) on *The Taming of the Shrew*. Among the more bizarre adaptations are a SPAGHETTI WESTERN version of *Hamlet*, *Quella sporca storia del west* (1968), and *The Secret Sex Life of Romeo and Juliet* (1970).

The central problem for film-makers has always been whether to stay faithful to the text or to produce a more cinematic adaptation; both approaches have produced notable successes and debacles. The British *Julius Caesar* and *Hamlet* (both 1970) are fine examples of a "the play's the thing" approach while Olivier's *Henry V* (1943), Zeffirelli's *Romeo and Juliet* (1968) and WELLES's *Chimes at Midnight* (1966) show how cinema can interestingly reinterpret the material.

Shane (1953) George STEVENS's classic Western. The film provided Alan LADD with perhaps his finest, and certainly his best remembered, role – that of a lone gunman who is aware that his time has passed but finds himself unable to shake off his reputation and begin afresh.

The plot is seen largely through the eyes of Joey (Brandon De Wilde, the young son of homesteaders Marion and Joe Starrett (Jean ARTHUR and Van HEFLIN), who find themselves terrorized by local cattle baron Ryker. The mysterious Shane (Ladd) stops at the Starrett's place one day for water and soon becomes embroiled in the land battle, eventually shooting it out with Ryker's hired killer Wilson, played by Jack PALANCE (unforgettable in head-to-toe black).

With its flawless performances, fine landscape photography, and archetypal good-vs-evil plot, *Shane* is one of a handful of truly great Westerns (though many would now find its stately pace rather too slow). The film was nominated for a total of six Oscars, including Best Picture, Best Director, and two for Best Supporting Actor (one for Palance, the other for De Wilde), but took only one, for Loyal Griggs's cinematography. Ironically, Griggs's work had been heavily cropped to accommodate the current fashion for WIDESCREEN formats. As Ladd was in the process of leaving Paramount for Warners at the time, the studio undertook no lobbying on his behalf for a Best Actor nomination.

Sharif, Omar (Michael Chalhoub; 1932–) Egyptian actor, a romantic lead once labelled 'the new VALENTINO'. He found international stardom in David LEAN's LAWRENCE OF ARABIA (1962) and *Doctor Zhivago* (1965), but wound down his career after the 1970s. His real love, he has said, is the game of bridge; Sharif has won international tournaments and writes a syndicated column on the subject.

Born in Alexandria, the son of a rich Christian merchant, Michael Chalhoub sold lumber before making his film debut in the Egyptian production *The Blazing Sun* (1953). He changed his name to Omar El-

Sharif after converting to Islam. In 1955 he married Egypt's leading film actress, Faten Hamama, but they later divorced.

After making more than 20 Egyptian movies, Sharif became an overnight star in the West with his performance as the Arab warrior Sherif Ali in *Lawrence of Arabia*. Lean had already cast Alain Delon in the role but replaced him with the Egyptian matinée idol. In the film, Sharif makes a spectacular entrance on camel-back, emerging as a speck on the desert horizon and riding slowly towards the camera.

The international success of *Lawrence* led to roles as an Armenian monarch in *The Fall of the Roman Empire*, a Spanish priest in *Behold a Pale Horse*, and the title character in *Genghis Khan* (all 1964). Sharif's romantic appeal was then confirmed by his performance as Pasternak's tragic physician-poet in *Doctor Zhivago*.

He later played a gambler in the Barbra STREISAND vehicles *Funny Girl* (1968) and *Funny Lady* (1975) (Sharif himself is a reformed compulsive gambler), a Soviet officer in Blake EDWARDS's *The Tamarind Seed* (1974), and a pool shark in *The Baltimore Bullet* (1980).

A journalist once asked Sharif what subjects he talks about to women and was told "Their beauty, of course"; when asked what he talked about if they were ugly, he replied "Then about other women's ugliness."

Shearer, Norma (1900–83) Canadian-born Hollywood actress noted for her elegant but haughty roles in comedy and drama. In the early 1930s MGM billed her as the **First Lady of the Screen**. Though neither a great beauty nor a great actress (Marlene DIETRICH once called her "a dead fish"), Shearer won the Oscar for her role in *The Divorcee* (1930) and was nominated for a further five Awards.

Shearer was born in Montreal, the daughter of a rich businessman. After winning a beauty contest at the age of 14, she travelled to New York, where she failed to impress the showman Florenz Ziegfeld. Shearer then worked as a cinema pianist and model before entering films in 1920. A series of bit parts led to a contract with the Mayer Company and her first memorable role, that of a bareback rider in Victor SJÖSTRÖM's circus film *He Who Gets Slapped* (1924).

Shearer's best silent film was probably Ernst LUBITSCH's *The Student Prince* (1927), a version without music in which she starred opposite Ramon Novarro. That year she married Irving THALBERG, the boy genius of MGM, and they became Hollywood's golden couple. Thereafter she was given MGM's best roles with no expense spared; as Joan CRAWFORD once bitched, "How can I compete with Norma when she sleeps with the boss?"

Shearer starred as a cheating wife in *The Divorcee* and as a post-flapper in *A Free Soul* (1931) – the film in which she takes a kiss from gangster Clark GABLE and states coolly, "That'll be all, thanks." For Sidney FRANKLIN, her favourite director, she made Noël COWARD's *Private Lives* (1931), with Robert Montgomery, and starred in *The Barretts of Wimpole Street* (1934), with Fredric MARCH.

In 1936 MGM's *Romeo and Juliet* saw Shearer and Leslie HOWARD cast as somewhat overaged lovers. When the actress Mrs Patrick Campbell saw the finished film, in which the spotlight is kept constantly on Shearer while the others languish in shadow, she dubbed it, "Norma Shearer and her cast of Ethiopians."

After Thalberg's sudden death in 1936 Shearer's star began to wane. During the making of *Marie Antoinette* (1938), in which she played the queen, director Franklin was replaced in a power play and she began to think of retirement. She turned down the part of Scarlett O'HARA in GONE WITH THE WIND (1939), calling it "a difficult and thankless role", and also rejected MRS MINIVER (1942). After two flops in 1942, she retired to marry a ski instructor 20 years her junior.

Sheen family The US actor-director Martin Sheen (Ramon Estevez; 1940–) and his sons Emilio Estevez (1962–) and Charlie Sheen (1965–).

Martin Sheen, the son of an immigrant Spanish father and an Irish mother, worked in New York as a soda jerk and shipping clerk while acting in off-off-Broadway productions. After making his Broadway debut in *The Subject was Roses* (1964), he went on to appear in a series of television roles. In his first film, *The Incident* (1967), he played a hoodlum terrorizing subway passengers; a year later he reprised his stage role in a screen version of *The Subject was Roses*.

Sheen's performance as a youthful killer in *Badlands* (1973) led to his being named Best Actor at the San Sebastian Film Festival in Spain. He also received acclaim for playing the young officer sent to execute rogue colonel Marlon BRANDO in Francis Ford COPPOLA's APOCALYPSE NOW (1979). Sheen suffered a serious heart attack during shooting but recovered to see the project through. Subsequent films include Rank's Western *Eagle's Wing* (1979), the biopic GANDHI (1981), in which he played a US journalist, Oliver STONE's *Wall Street* (1987), in which he appeared as the father of his real-life son, Charlie Sheen, and *Hear No Evil* (1993). He made his debut as a director with *Count a Lovely Cadence* (British title *Stockade*; 1990).

Emilio Estevez was born in New York. After making his screen debut in *Tex* (1982), about Oklahoma farm boys, he won general praise for his performance in *Repo Man* (1984), as a young man learning to repossess cars. Estevez then established himself as a leading member of the so-called BRAT PACK of younger actors in the teen dramas *St Elmo's Fire* and *The Breakfast Club* (both 1984). Subsequent films included *That was then...This is Now* (1985), a film that he also scripted, the Stephen King adaptation *Maximum Overdrive* (1986), and his directorial debut, *Wisdom* (1986), in which he starred opposite Demi MOORE. In 1988 he played Billy the Kid in *Young Guns*, which also starred his brother Charlie Sheen as a gang member. Estevez's later films include *Stakeout* (1987), in which he and Richard DREYFUSS play wisecracking Seattle cops, and the sequel, *Another Stakeout* (1993). In 1990 he wrote, directed, and starred with his brother in *Men at Work*, about two rubbish collectors who find a body.

Charlie Sheen made both his TV and his movie debuts with his father, appearing in *The Execution of Private Slovik* at the age of nine and APOCALYPSE NOW when 14. After featuring as a soldier in Oliver STONE's *Platoon* (1986), he made his name in the same director's *Wall Street*, playing a young broker corrupted by dealer Michael DOUGLAS.

Sheen subsequently appeared as a baseball pitcher in the comedy *Major League* (1989), as the young partner of policeman Clint EASTWOOD in *The Rookie* (1990), and as an imprisoned soldier in his father's film *Count a Lovely Cadence* (1990). Later films have included *Hot Shots!* (1991), a spoof of the air-action film *Top Gun* (1986), and the sequel *Major League II* (1994).

Shepard, Sam (Samuel Shepard Rogers;
1943–) Quiet-spoken US actor, director,
screenwriter, and playwright. He has made
a number of films with the actress **Jessica
Lange** (1949–), the mother of two of his
children.

Born in Fort Sheriden, Illinois, and educated in California, Shepard moved to New
York in the early 1960s, where he made his
name as a writer of avant-garde drama, his
first produced play being *Cowboys* (1964).
In 1978 his play *Buried Child* won the Pulitzer Prize.

That year also saw Shepard's screen
debut, as a farm owner in Terence Malick's
art film *Days of Heaven*. In 1983 he received
an Oscar nomination for playing the real-
life test pilot Chuck Yeager in *The Right Stuff*
and wrote the acclaimed screenplay for
Wim WENDERS's *Paris, Texas* (1984), about a
drifter trying to locate his young son. He
co-starred with Lange in *Country* (1984),
about a farming couple faced with bankruptcy, and *Crimes of the Heart* (1986),
about a family of sisters in the US South.
Between these films, he scripted *Fool for Love*
(1985) from his own play about an incestuous sister-brother relationship; the leads
were played by Kim BASINGER and Shepard
himself. Robert ALTMAN, who directed,
later called Shepard "a very selfish, self-
orientated person."

In 1989 Shepard made his directing
debut with *Far North*, a curious piece about
a farmer's daughter (Lange) who returns
home to be with her squabbling family. Subsequent roles include a detective in the
thriller *Defenceless* (1989), a businessman in
Voyager (1991), and an FBI man in Michael
APTED's *Thunderheart* (1992). He wrote and
directed *Silent Tongue*, a supernatural Western starring the late River PHOENIX, some
two years before its release in 1994.

Shepitko, Larisa *See* KLIMOV, ELEM.

Shepperton studios Film studios on a 60-
acre site at Shepperton, Greater London,
which were established in 1932 by Norman
Loudon of the Sound City Film Production
and Recording Company. By 1937 the lot
contained seven stages, four of which could
be converted to double size and had large
water tanks. Despite a run of successes in
the 1950s and 1960s, when films produced
at Shepperton included *The Dam Busters*
(1954) and *The Guns of Navarone* (1961),
the studios were losing some £500,000 a

year by the mid 1970s. In 1995 the British
directors Tony and Ridley SCOTT bought the
studios with a plan to make the upgraded
facilities the centre for a revitalized British
film industry.

Sheridan, Ann (Clara Lou Sheridan;
1915–67) Spirited US actress, who became
known as the **Oomph Girl** in the early
1940s. Once described as a brunette Lana
TURNER, she was briefly considered for the
part of Scarlett O'HARA in GONE WITH THE WIND
(1939). Her three husbands were the actors
Edward Norris, George Brent, and Scott
McKay.

Clara Lou Sheridan was born and educated in Texas. At the age of 18, she won the
'Search for Beauty' contest, thereby earning
a bit part in Paramount's 1934 film of that
name. She went on to appear in further
minor roles before changing her name to
Ann Sheridan for *Behold My Wife* (1935).
After moving to Warner Brothers in 1937,
she appeared in a series of supporting roles
including Humphrey BOGART's sister in *San
Quentin* (1937), James CAGNEY's girlfriend in
Angels with Dirty Faces (1938), a saloon
hostess in *Dodge City* (1939), and a waitress
in *They Drive by Night* (1940).

In 1941 Sheridan won acclaim for her
performance as a poor girl in love with legless war veteran Ronald REAGAN in the melodrama *King's Row*; despite this success, she
then saw her promised role in CASABLANCA
go to Ingrid BERGMAN. During the early war
years she turned increasingly to comedy,
appearing in such films as *Honeymoon for
Three* and *The Man who Came to Dinner* (both
1941) and the Jack BENNY vehicle *George
Washington Slept Here*. Owing to her growing popularity with the public she was able
to force Warners to raise her salary from
$600 to $2,000 a week. Her last major
comedy vehicle was Howard HAWKS's *I was a
Male War Bride* (British title *You Can't Sleep
Here*; 1949), in which she played a WAC
lieutenant smuggling husband Cary GRANT
out of France disguised as a woman. Later
roles included a saloon singer in the musical
Take Me to Town (1953) and the wife of a
reformed drunkard in the rural drama *Come
Next Spring* (1956). In the 1960s she joined
the cast of the television soap opera *Another
World*.

shoot. **shoot-'em-up** A slang term for a film,
such as a Western, dominated by gunplay
and multiple shootings. It is now often

applied to video or computer games in which the player seeks to obliterate a series of moving targets.

shooting call *See* CALL.

shooting log A diary recording the details of each day's filming during a shoot. It is kept by a member of the camera crew and will include the types of film, filters, and cameras used, the length of each take, and whether a take should be included in the WORKPRINT.

shooting ratio or **editing ratio** The ratio of film footage shot to that used in the final edited version. This is normally about seven to one, but can vary enormously from one production to another. D. W. GRIFFITH removed only 200 feet from his 5,500-foot BROKEN BLOSSOMS (1919). The most violently cut film was *Hell's Angels* (1930), which Howard HUGHES reduced from 2,254,750 to 9045 feet. Traditionally, the footage ending up on the CUTTING-ROOM floor has been melted down to save the silver nitrate.

shooting schedule A schedule specifying the date on which each shot will be filmed, together with a list of the actors, crew members, and equipment required. The schedule is drawn up according to convenience and availability and will probably bear no relation to the sequence of shots in the final print.

shooting script The final studio-approved script used by the director and actors during filming. Unlike earlier versions of the SCREENPLAY, it is broken down into numbered shots and includes details of camera movements and other technical matters. Most screenplays take from two months to over a year to reach this stage, with several writers being involved along the way (21 for *Forever and a Day* in 1943). Joe Eszterhas received $3 million for his script for *Basic Instinct* (1992) but was dropped from the film after arguing with director Paul Verhoeven about the final shooting script.

short or **short subject** Officially, any film of less than 3000 feet, i.e. one with a running time of less than 30 minutes. During the early silent era all films were one-, two-, or (occasionally) three-reel shorts. Following the introduction of FEATURE-length films in the early 1910s, shorts were gradually reduced to the status of an added attraction on theatre programmes. Nevertheless, such films remained profitable to make throughout Hollywood's Golden Era; popular exam-

ples included the cartoons of DISNEY, the slapstick comedies of the THREE STOOGES, the MARCH OF TIME newsreels, Rank's *Look at Life* featurettes. Short subjects began to disappear from cinema bills with the advent of the DOUBLE BILL in the early 1950s. They are still used for animation and documentary work, as well as to train young directors and try out new technology.

shot A series of images produced by continuous filming from a single camera. This is the basic building block of film, analogous to a word in literature or a note in music. The length of a shot can vary from a single frame (e.g., the almost subliminal images of the SURREALISTS) to the contents of an entire reel (e.g. the shot of the troops leaving the tunnel in Akira KUROSAWA's *Dreams*, 1990). The usual length, however, is between 30 seconds and two minutes.

Shots are categorized in three principal ways: (1) the apparent distance between camera and subject, e.g. CLOSE-UP, LONG SHOT, etc.; (2) the angle of the camera in relation to the subject, e.g. HIGH-ANGLE SHOT, LOW-ANGLE SHOT, etc.; (3) any movement of the camera during filming, e.g. TRACKING SHOT, PANNING shot, etc.

shtick *See* SCHTICK.

shutter (1) A mechanical device in a camera, printer, or projector, that prevents light from reaching the film while the next frame is brought down into the film gate for exposure or projection. This usually takes the form of a rotating disc with notches cut to admit light. (2) An adjustable device, rather like venetian blinds, that controls the intensity of light from a lamp.

Sidney, George (1916–) US director, best known for his lavish MGM musicals of the 1940s and 1950s. In later life he was president of Hanna-Barbera Productions, makers of *The Flintstones* and other cartoons.

Born in Long Island, the son of an actor-manager, the young Sidney acted on stage and in a screen Western. At the age of 16 he joined MGM, where his father had become an executive, as a messenger boy; a year later he was promoted to film editor. After becoming (at 19) the studio's youngest ever assistant director he was soon directing shorts for the OUR GANG series of juvenile comedies (being only a few years older than the gang's oldest member). In 1940 and 1941 he won successive Oscars with contributions to the 'Pete Smith' and 'Passing Parade' series.

Sidney began 15 years of directing MGM features with the comedy *Free and Easy* (1940). During World War II he made two of the first TECHNICOLOR musicals, the all-star *Thousands Cheer* (1943) and *Bathing Beauty* (1944), Esther WILLIAMS's first starring vehicle. Box-office triumphs followed with *Anchors Aweigh* (1945), starring Gene KELLY and Frank SINATRA, and *The Harvey Girls* (1946), with Judy GARLAND. In the early 1950s he enjoyed a series of hits starring Howard Keel; *Annie Get Your Gun* (1950), in which Betty Hutton played the sharp shooting Annie, was followed by *Show Boat* (1951) and *Kiss Me Kate* (1953), in both of which Keel was partnered by Kathryn Grayson. His last film for MGM was *Jupiter's Darling* (1955), an absurd musical set during the Punic Wars, with Keel as Hannibal and Esther Williams as his love interest. The production made use of props and costumes left over from QUO VADIS? (1951).

During these years, he also directed such swashbucklers as THE THREE MUSKETEERS (1948), with Gene Kelly as D'Artagnan, and *Scaramouche* (1952), with Stewart GRANGER.

After leaving MGM Sidney worked principally as an independent director-producer. In 1957 he directed the musical *Pal Joey*, with Sinatra, Kim NOVAK, and Rita HAYWORTH, for Columbia. His later films include *Bye Bye Birdie* (1963), starring ANN-MARGRET in a story of an Elvis-like rock star, *Viva Las Vegas* (1964), with Ann-Margret and the real Elvis, and *Half a Sixpence* (1967) with Tommy Steele.

Siegel, Don(ald) (1912–91) US director of action movies, many of which starred Clint EASTWOOD. He worked in Hollywood for over 30 years before establishing his reputation in the 1960s.

Born in Chicago, the son of a mandolin virtuoso, Siegel studied at Cambridge and at RADA before joining Warner Brothers in 1933. He rose gradually from assistant editor to head of the INSERT department, in which role he worked on sequences in *Yankee Doodle Dandy* and CASABLANCA (both 1942).

Although Jack WARNER tried hard to prevent Siegel from directing, he began to make shorts, two of which won Oscars in 1945. A year later he directed his first feature, *The Verdict* (1946), starring Sydney GREENSTREET as a murderous Scotland Yard inspector.

Siegel left Warners after making *Night Unto Night* (1949), which starred Ronald REAGAN and Viveca Lindfors, whom the director married that year. (They divorced five years later.)

In 1954 Siegel found his first acclaim as a director with *Riot in Cell Block 11*, a film shot in California's Folsom Prison with real guards and prisoners using a semidocumentary style. The producer, Walter Wanger, was himself a former prisoner. Two years later the two men teamed up again to make *Invasion of the Body Snatchers* (1956), a cult science-fiction film that is now seen as a classic of COLD WAR paranoia; the film was shot on a shoestring budget in 18 days.

During the 1960s Siegel joined Universal as a producer-director; he made his first movie with Eastwood, *Coogan's Bluff*, in 1968. Three years later Siegel appeared as a bartender in *Play Misty for Me*, Eastwood's debut as a director. That year, Siegel achieved his greatest box-office success with, *Dirty Harry*, a film starring Eastwood as a ruthless San Francisco cop. "I've never known an actor like Eastwood so keen to play an antihero" said Siegel, who denied charges that the film was excessively violent.

In 1976 he directed John WAYNE in *The Shootist*, the actor's last movie; Wayne played an old gunslinger dying of cancer (as he himself was at the time). Another Eastwood triumph followed with *Escape from Alcatraz* (1979), based on a true prison story. Siegel retired after making the disastrous and ironically titled comedy *Jinxed* (1982), with Bette MIDLER.

Signoret, Simone (Simone-Henriette Charlotte Kaminker; 1921–85) French actress, best known for her Oscar-winning performance in ROOM AT THE TOP (1958). An actress of great intelligence and sensual appeal, she was often cast as a lovelorn woman or warm-hearted prostitute. She was married to the director Yves Allégret and (from 1951) to the actor Yves MONTAND.

Signoret was born to French parents in Wiesbaden, Germany, and raised in Paris. When her father, a Jew, fled to London during the Occupation, Simone left school to support her mother and two brothers. In 1942 she appeared as an extra in her first film, *Le Prince charmant*; five years later she was starring in Ealing's wartime thriller, *Against the Wind*.

During the 1950s Signoret appeared in several of her finest films, notably Max OPHÜLS's risqué *La Ronde* (1950) and Jacques BECKER's *Casque d'or*, about a tragic underworld romance in late 19th-century Paris. In 1953 she played the title role in *Thérèse Raquin*, Marcel CARNÉ's screen version of the tragic Mauriac novel. Her films with Montand included *The Witches of Salem* (1957), an adaptation of Arthur Miller's *The Crucible* with a screenplay by Sartre.

The following year, Signoret came to the attention of a wider international audience playing the tragic Alice Aisgill in *Room at the Top*. She also won an Oscar nomination for her performance as a drug-addicted countess in the shipboard melodrama *Ship of Fools* (1965). Two Sidney LUMET films followed; *The Deadly Affair* (1967), in which she played a survivor of the Nazi concentration camps, and an adaptation of Chekhov's *The Seagull* (1968). Both films co-starred James MASON. In *Madame Rosa* (1977), which won the Oscar for Best Foreign Film, she played an ageing prostitute who also runs a nursery school. Her last film was *I Sent a Letter to My Love* (*Chère Inconnue*; 1981), in which she added another role to her long gallery of lonely women.

Sikaku ichidai onna See LIFE OF O-HARU.

Silence of the Lambs, The (1990) Jonathan DEMME's HORROR thriller, a hugely successful and much-discussed look into the mind of a serial murderer. The film, which won the Academy Award as Best Picture, owed most of its power to the compelling performance of Anthony HOPKINS as an erudite cannibal. Oscars went to Demme and Hopkins (who was knighted nine months later), as well as to co-star Jodie FOSTER and screenwriter Ted Tally, who adapted Thomas Harris's novel.

The plot centres on Clarice Starling (Foster), a young FBI trainee whose first job is to track down 'Buffalo Bill', a serial killer who skins his female victims. To draw up a psychological profile of the murderer, she asks the advice of Hannibal 'The Cannibal' Lecter (Hopkins), a brilliant psychiatrist who has himself been imprisoned for a series of sex murders. In a series of tense interviews, Lecter swaps gruesome insights into the killer's mind for details about Starling's personal life. With uncanny skill, Lecter then escapes and teasingly phones Starling: "I do wish we could chat longer" he

concludes, "but I'm having an old friend for dinner."

silent films The entire corpus of motion pictures produced between the creation of camera/projector equipment in the 1890s and the introduction of the talkies in 1927. The title is in part a misnomer, since the films were rarely silent in performance. Most were shown with musical accompaniment of some kind (ranging from a lone pianist to a full symphony orchestra), while sound effects and even dialogue were sometimes supplied live by theatre personnel. The title is also, perhaps, unfortunate as it seems to define the films in terms of a 'deficiency'. In fact, the best silent films exploited the visual aspects of the medium in a way that has seldom been equalled. Such masters as GRIFFITH, EISENSTEIN, and the German EXPRESSIONISTS developed a pictorial idiom that could encompass MONTAGE and symbolism as well as more naturalistic treatments.

A number of important stages should be defined in any history of silent films. In economic terms, these are: (1) the original development of motion picture equipment; (2) the so-called patents war between the inventors of the equipment, leading to the creation of the MOTION PICTURE PATENTS COMPANY in 1908; (3) the decline of the MPPC following its struggle with the independents and the concomitant rise of film-making in California; (4) the consolidation of the victorious independents into producer/distributor/exhibitor conglomerates and the rise of the STUDIO SYSTEM; (5) the race to convert to sound in 1927. In artistic terms the important developments were: (1) the short films made by EDISON and the LUMIÈRE BROTHERS, which introduced the two basic types of fiction and *actualité*; (2) the development of narrative films by both Edwin S. PORTER and Georges MÉLIÈS, who introduced between them most cinematic techniques and genres; (3) the films of D. W. Griffith, which may be seen as consolidating the work of Porter and others in establishing a basic grammar of REALIST cinema; (4) the development of less naturalistic modes of expression with the rise of various national cinema movements in Europe, notably Expressionism in Germany, AVANT-GARDE and SURREALIST cinema in France, and the development of montage by Eisenstein and PUDOVKIN in Russia; (5) the rise of SLAPSTICK and the 'golden age' of comedy with producers Hal ROACH and Mack SENNETT and stars CHAPLIN, KEATON, LLOYD, and LAUREL AND HARDY.

silent speed *See* CAMERA SPEED *under* CAMERA.

Silly Symphony The title given by Walt DIS-NEY to all his cartoon shorts of the 1930s that did not feature MICKEY MOUSE, DONALD DUCK, or Pluto.

Sim, Alastair (1900–76) Mournful-looking Scottish actor, who starred in numerous British comedies from the 1930s onwards. He also appeared on the stage, playing everything from Shakespearean roles to Captain Hook in *Peter Pan* (five times).

Born in Edinburgh, the son of a tailor, Sim taught elocution at Edinburgh University before making his stage debut in a production of *Othello* (1930). After a season with the Old Vic, he made his first film appearance in *Riverside Murder* (1935). Three years later he starred in the comedy police story *Inspector Hornleigh*, a film that spawned two sequels, and gave a memorable performance as a genie in the Crazy Gang's farce *Alf's Button Afloat*.

Sim's films of the 1940s included the comedy-thriller *Green for Danger* (1946) and *London Belongs to Me* (1948), both of which were directed by Sidney GILLIAT. In 1950 he appeared in both Alfred HITCHCOCK's *Stage Fright*, in which he hides a murder suspect (Richard Todd), and in *The Happiest Days of Your Life*, a school farce that co-starred Margaret RUTHERFORD. He then took the title role in the excellent Dickens adaptation *Scrooge* (1951) and co-starred with Rutherford in *Innocents in Paris* (1953).

In the hit comedy *The Belles of St Trinian's* (1954) Sim played both the head-mistress Miss Fritton and her raffish brother Clarence. Later roles included Stephen Potter, the master of 'oneupmanship', in *School for Scoundrels* (1960), and a bishop in *The Ruling Class* (1971). His last film for the cinema was *Escape from the Dark* (1976).

Simmons, Jean (1929–) Raven-haired British actress, who became a Hollywood star in the early 1950s. She first attracted attention as a 17-year-old, when she appeared as the haughty Estella in David LEAN's GREAT EXPECTATIONS (1946); 43 years later she played Estella's elderly guardian, Miss Havisham, in a 1989 TV version.

A Londoner, Simmons was picked from a dance class at the age of 15 to make her film debut in *Give Us the Moon* (1944). A year later she met Stewart GRANGER on the set of *Caesar and Cleopatra* and they became romantically involved. Following her performance as a seductive Indian girl in POWELL and PRESSBURGER's *Black Narcissus* (1947), Laurence OLIVIER chose her from 94 actresses to play Ophelia in his *Hamlet* (1948). Although Granger advised her against the difficult role, she took the part and won an Oscar nomination. The couple moved to Hollywood after marrying in 1950.

In 1953 Simmons starred as Elizabeth I in *Young Bess* and as the love interest of Roman tribune Richard BURTON in THE ROBE. A year later she played Napoleon's mistress in the costume drama *Desirée* (1954); Marlon BRANDO played the emperor. She rejoined Brando for the musical *Guys and Dolls* (1956), after Grace KELLY and Deborah KERR were found to be already booked. Samuel GOLDWYN later described her as the film's glory, saying "I'm so happy that I couldn't get Grace Kelly."

In ELMER GANTRY (1960) Simmons played evangelist Sister Sharon to Burt LANCASTER's title character; she divorced Granger later that year to marry the film's director Richard BROOKS (whom she divorced in 1977). Her later films include Stanley KUBRICK's *Spartacus* (1960), in which she played a Roman slave loved by Kirk DOUGLAS, and *Divorce American Style* (1967). Although she made few film appearances after the late 1960s, she toured from 1974–75 in the Sondheim musical *A Little Night Music*, won an Emmy Award in 1982 for her role in television's *The Thornbirds*, and continues to appear in such TV movies as *People Like Us* (1990).

Sinatra, Frank (1915–) US singer and film actor, who won Oscars for his performances in FROM HERE TO ETERNITY (1953) and *The Man with the Golden Arm* (1955). He was also awarded the Academy's Jean Hersholt Humanitarian Award in 1971. David NIVEN once summed up Sinatra's enigmatic quality by listing "his talent, his generosity, his ruthlessness, his kindness, his gregariousness, his loneliness, and his rumoured links with the Mob."

Among his four wives were the actresses Ava GARDNER (1951–57) and Mia FARROW (1966–68). His daughter Nancy Sinatra (1940–), and son Frank Sinatra Jnr

(1943–) are both singers who have also appeared in movies.

Sinatra was born in Hoboken, New Jersey, the son of Italian immigrants. After winning a radio talent contest in 1936, he sang with the bands of Harry James and Tommy Dorsey, becoming the idol of swooning teenage bobby-soxers. In 1941 he made his screen debut singing with the Dorsey band in *Las Vegas Nights*; two years later he took his first acting role in the musical *Higher and Higher* leading *Variety* to report "he at least gets in no one's way." Sinatra went on to star with Gene KELLY in two MGM musicals about sailors on shore leave – *Anchors Aweigh* (1945) and the innovative *On the Town* (1949).

In the early 1950s Sinatra's singing career looked doomed when nodules were detected on his vocal cords. He responded by switching to dramatic roles, offering to play Angelo Maggio in Columbia's *From Here to Eternity* for a fee of only $8,000. His performance as a wisecracking GI brought him the Oscar for Best Supporting Actor; two years later he went one better by winning the Best Actor Award for his portrayal of a drug addict in *The Man with the Golden Arm*.

His throat having healed, Sinatra made a return to the musical with *Guys and Dolls* (1955), starring Marlon BRANDO (who later said of the singer, "He's the kind of guy that, when he dies, he's going up to heaven to give God a bad time for making him bald"), *Pal Joey* (1957), and Cole Porter's *Can Can* (1960). Sinatra's RAT PACK of friends – Dean MARTIN, Sammy Davis Jnr, Peter Lawford, and Joey Bishop – were then brought together for *Sergeants Three* (1961), a rollicking Western that he produced himself. His later films included John FRANKENHEIMER's political thriller *The Manchurian Candidate* (1962) and *The Detective* (1968). Despite his official retirement in 1971, Sinatra returned to play a cop in *The First Deadly Sin* (1980) and himself in *Cannonball Run II* (1983).

sing. Singing Capon *See* IRON BUTTERFLY.

Singing Cowboy Nickname of the US singer and actor Roy ROGERS (1912–), who starred with his faithful horse Trigger in numerous comedy-Western-musicals of the 1940s and 1950s.

Singin' in the Rain (1952) Gene KELLY and Stanley DONEN's much-loved musical about the cinema world's transition to SOUND in the late 1920s. With the coming of talkies, the star of matinée idol Don Lockwood (Kelly) seems destined to rise, while that of his co-star Lina Lamont (Jean Hagen) looks set to wane, owing to a voice utterly at odds with her screen persona.

Singin' in the Rain came about when MGM producer Arthur Freed asked two writers to concoct a script around a number of songs that he and Nacio Herb Brown had written in the 1920s and 1930s. Inspired by the fact that many of these had featured in pictures during the 'all-talking, all-singing, all-dancing' musicals craze that had followed THE JAZZ SINGER, Adolph Green and Betty Comden produced a story about the difficult birth throes of the talkies. The screenplay was packed with incidents reflecting the problems casts and crews experienced in coming to terms with the new technology. It also made affectionate reference to many Hollywood legends, including Freed himself, Busby BERKELEY, and John GILBERT, one of the first casualties of sound.

The title song, which had already been performed on screen by Cliff Edwards in *Hollywood Revue of 1929*, Jimmy DURANTE in *Speak Easily*, and Judy GARLAND in *Little Nellie Kelly*, was something of an afterthought. Although the sequence in which Kelly dances euphorically in the rain is considered one of cinema's most sublime moments, the star himself derived little pleasure from it. The scene was shot DAY-FOR-NIGHT on a seeringly hot day with the star suffering from a heavy cold. Nevertheless, Kelly miraculously masked the discomfort of a suit soaked in a mixture of water and milk (used to create the downpour) and his frustration with the umbrella, which plagued him throughout the sequence.

Indeed, co-stars Donald O'CONNOR and Debbie REYNOLDS (who played the girlfriend who dubs Lina's dialogue) recalled Kelly being out of sorts for much of the production. Resenting the imposition of Reynolds by Louis B. MAYER, who was grooming her for stardom, Kelly packed her off with his dance assistants and made her practise until step perfect. Following the 'Good Morning' sequence, Reynolds fainted on set, having burst blood vessels in her feet. O'Connor was also ordered to rest after the completion of the gymnastic 'Make 'Em Laugh', only to be informed that the negative had perished and that the whole routine required reshooting.

Although not an immediate hit (partly because MGM withdrew the film to exploit the Oscar success of Kelly's previous picture, *An American in Paris*), *Singin' in the Rain* is now widely acknowledged as the finest screen musical of all time.

single perforation or **single perf** Designating a 16MM film stock with a SOUNDTRACK down one side and SPROCKET holes down the other.

Siodmak, Robert (1900–73) US director of atmospheric psychological thrillers in the 1940s. He made 21 films between 1941 and 1951, earning an Oscar nomination for his direction of *The Killers* (1946).

Born in Memphis, Tennessee, to German-Jewish parents, Siodmak grew up in Germany and attended the University of Marburg. His first film job was writing German titles for US productions. He then moved into editing before co-directing his first movie, the semidocumentary *Menschen am Sonntag* (1929), with Fred ZINNEMANN; the script was co-written by his younger brother Curt and Billy WILDER.

Siodmak then joined the UFA studios in Berlin as a director. Following the Nazi takeover in 1933, he and his brother left for Paris, where they rejoined Wilder. Siodmak made seven films in France before moving to Hollywood in 1940.

After directing a series of B-MOVIES for different studios, he enjoyed his first US success with *Son of Dracula* (1940), starring Lon CHANEY Jnr; the film led to a seven-year contract with Universal. He went on to make his reputation with a number of psychological thrillers in the prewar German style beginning with *Phantom Lady* (1944), a film described by one critic as "drenched in creeping morbidity and gloom."

Siodmak followed this success with *The Suspect* (1944), starring Charles LAUGHTON as a husband who kills his nagging wife, *The Strange Affair of Uncle Harry* (1945), with George SANDERS as an attempted murderer, and *The Spiral Staircase* (1945), in which Dorothy McGuire is terrorized by a psychopath. In 1946 he made *The Dark Mirror*, starring Olivia DE HAVILLAND as identical twins, one a killer, and the Hemingway adaptation *The Killers*, with Burt LANCASTER in his screen debut. Next came *Criss-Cross* (1948), a brooding FILM NOIR with Lancaster and Yvonne DE CARLO. "I like making gangster pictures," Siodmak once remarked,

"not that I had much choice when I went to Hollywood."

He enjoyed fewer successes in the 1950s, the main exception being the comedy adventure, *The Crimson Pirate* (1952), a rollicking spoof starring Lancaster once again. In 1953 Siodmak returned to Europe, where he continued to direct for another 17 years. His later films include his one Western, *Custer of the West* (1966), shot in Spain with Robert Shaw and Robert RYAN.

Sirk, Douglas (Claus Detlev Sierk; 1900–87) US director, who fled Nazi Germany to find success at Universal in the 1950s. His strong visual style later influenced the films of Rainer Werner FASSBINDER.

Sirk was born in Hamburg of Danish parents. He himself went back to the city to study art and drama, later becoming a director-producer at the Deutsches Schauspielhaus. In 1934 he switched to film shorts and in 1935 directed his first feature at the UFA studios. After a period working in Rome, Sirk travelled to Hollywood at the invitation of Warner Brothers in 1939. In the event, he ended up at MGM instead; his first films for the studio included *Hitler's Madman* (1942), about the assassination of the Nazi Heydrich (whom Sirk had met). He changed his name to Douglas Sirk to direct the comedy drama *A Scandal in Paris*, starring George SANDERS (1946); this was followed by the thrillers *Lured* (British title *Personal Column*) and *Sleep My Love* (both 1947). Sirk's TECHNICOLOR debut was the musical *Has Anybody Seen My Gal?* (1951), his first film of several to star Rock HUDSON.

Magnificent Obsession (1954), a medical melodrama that paired Hudson with Jane WYMAN, became Sirk's most successful film to date, making a gross profit of over $12 million. The three came together again for another tearjerker, *All that Heaven Allows* (1955). Sirk then directed Hudson and Lauren BACALL in *Written on the Wind* (1956), about a Texas oil dynasty. His final movie and his biggest success was the melodrama *Imitation of Life* (1959), starring Lana TURNER. Later that year he retired because of ill health and settled in Munich, Germany.

16mm A GAUGE of film that has traditionally been used by makers of documentaries, educational film, and low-budget avant-garde works. It has 40 frames a foot with either single or double perforations. Although 35mm is the standard gauge for commercial film-making, 16mm was officially recognized as an international film gauge in 1923. *See also* SUPER 16.

Sjöberg, Alf (1903–80) Swedish film and theatre director, screenwriter, and actor. Sjöberg was Sweden's most influential filmmaker before the emergence of Ingmar BERGMAN, whose career he helped to start. He was also an accomplished screenwriter with a special talent for adapting plays and books.

Born in Stockholm, Sjöberg trained with the Royal Dramatic Theatre and made his stage debut in 1925; he began to direct for the stage two years later. He wrote and directed a silent film, *The Strongest*, in 1929 but did not return to the cinema until the mid 1940s, when the early technical problems with sound had been overcome. During the interim he became one of Sweden's foremost theatre directors with his numerous productions of Shakespeare, Strindberg, and others for Stockholm's Royal Dramatic Theatre.

In the 1940s and 1950s Sjöberg was a major force in Sweden's emergent film industry. He found international box-office success with *Frenzy* (US title *Torment*; 1944), a powerful story of a sadistic teacher, his sensitive student, and the girl they both love; the film featured the first screenplay by Ingmar Bergman. Sjöberg won the Grand Prize at the 1951 Cannes Film Festival for his impressive adaptation of Strindberg's *Miss Julie*, an intense piece about the seduction and suicide of a count's daughter. One British critic called it "the outstanding achievement of the Swedish cinema in recent years." His later films included *Barabbas* (1953), *Karin Daughter of Man* (1954), *Wild Birds* (1955), *The Judge* (1960), *The Island* (1966), and *The Father* (1969), another Strindberg adaptation.

Sjöström or **Seastrom, Victor** (1879–1960) Pioneering Swedish director and actor. Sjöström made nine films in his six years in Hollywood, including MGM's first offering, *He Who Gets Slapped* (1924), and his masterpiece *The Wind* (1928), a silent melodrama with Lillian GISH.

The son of an actress and a wealthy timber producer, he moved with his family to America when his father's business crashed. Victor later returned alone to

Sweden and became a professional actor at the age of 16. In 1912 he joined the Svenska Biografteatern film company to make his screen-acting debut in Mauritz Stiller's *The Black Masks* and his directorial debut with *A Secret Marriage*. *The Outlaw and His Wife* (1917) co-starred his wife, Edith Erastoff, in a tragic story of a starving family. Between 1912 and 1920 he made 40 features, all renowned for their location shooting, and (with Stiller) took Sweden to the forefront of European film-making. His best-known Swedish film is the impressive supernatural melodrama *The Phantom Carriage* (US title *Thy Soul Shall Bear Witness*; 1920).

Sjöström travelled to Hollywood in 1923, but expressed some doubt whether he could match the success of Stiller, who had gone there in 1918 with his protégée Greta GARBO. Having anglicized his name to Seastrom, he joined the GOLDWYN Company shortly before the merger that created MGM. His first US triumph, *He Who Gets Slapped*, was a curious tragedy about a scientist who becomes a circus clown, starring Lon CHANEY, Norma SHEARER, and John GILBERT. A year later Sjöström was earning $30,000 a film.

More praise followed for two Gish films, *The Scarlet Letter* (1926) and *The Wind*, a powerful piece shot in the Mojave desert: the star gives one of her strongest performances as a woman driven insane by sand storms and an attacker whom she kills and buries. Gish herself described Sjöstrom as "a fine actor, the finest that ever directed me."

After making one US talkie, the comedy *A Lady to Love* (1930), Sjöström returned to Sweden. His last film as a director was *Under the Red Robe* (1937), a British-made SWASH-BUCKLER starring Conrad VEIDT. During World War II he was director of production for Svensk Film Industri. He resumed his acting career in the 1940s and 1950s, ending with an acclaimed performance as the dying Professor Borg in Ingmar BERGMAN'S WILD STRAWBERRIES (1957).

skin flick Slang for a film in which nudity and sometimes explicit SEX predominate. It is generally applied to mainstream commercial films rather than PORNOGRAPHY or films with artistic pretensions.

Skolimowski, Jerzy (1938–) Polish director, poet, and actor, praised for his imaginative black comedies. A former boxer, Skolimowski scripted films by WAJDA and POLANSKI before starring in and directing *Rysopsis* (1964) while studying at the film school in Łódź. The antihero of this film was revived for *Walkover* (1965), about a boxer contemplating his next fight. Both films emphasize the individual's search for personal identity and the conflict with society that this usually entails.

Sexual conflict came to the fore in Skolimowski's next two films, *Barriers* (1966) and *Le Départ* (1967). The latter was made outside Poland and, when his anti-Stalinist *Hands Up!* (1967) was banned by the Polish authorities, he returned to the West to develop his career. *Deep End* (1970), filmed in London, was an atmospheric tragedy about sexual longing in a seedy bathhouse. The eternal triangle was the subject of both *King, Queen, Knave* (1972), taken from the story by Nabokov, and *The Shout* (1978), a strange tale about a man (Alan BATES) who has the power to kill by raising his voice. Although some critics found these films inferior to Skolimowski's earlier work, *Moonlighting* (1982), starring Jeremy IRONS, was better received; the film follows the lives of four Polish builders working in London while martial law is being imposed in their country. More recent films have included *The Lightship* (1985), an effective thriller, *Torrents of Spring* (1989), from the love story by Turgenev, and *Before and After Death* (1992).

slapstick A form of boisterous physical comedy involving knockabout action and horseplay. The term derives from the hinged paddle formerly used by stage clowns to provide a resounding smack when they pretended to strike one another. Ingenious and expertly performed slapstick was a staple of silent the era, when verbal wit was impossible; the key exponents were the producers Mack SENNETT and Hal ROACH and the clowns CHAPLIN and KEATON. The tradition continued into the sound era with such performers as LAUREL AND HARDY, the MARX BROTHERS, ABBOTT AND COSTELLO, and the THREE STOOGES.

slasher movie A variety of HORROR FILM in which the central element is explicit violence, usually involving knives, claws, or other 'slashing' implements. The subgenre emerged in the mid 1970s and came to dominate horror production throughout the following decade. Titles include Tobe Hooper's *The Texas Chainsaw Massacre*

(1974), John CARPENTER's *Halloween* (1978) and its sequels, Abel Ferrara's 'video nasty' *Driller Killer* (1979), and Wes CRAVEN's *Friday the Thirteenth* (1980) and its sequels. *See also* SPLATTER MOVIE.

slate Another name for a NUMBER BOARD. *See also* CLAPPER BOARD.

sleeper Slang term for a movie, especially a low-budget one, that does unexpectedly well at the box office. Such films lack big advertising campaigns and often become known by word-of-mouth, although sharp film critics will sometimes single out possible sleepers.

The long list of triumphs from which little was expected includes CASABLANCA (1942), *House of Wax* (1953), THE CREATURE FROM THE BLACK LAGOON (1954), REBEL WITHOUT A CAUSE (1955), PSYCHO (1960), THE GRADUATE (1967), M*A*S*H (1970), *American Graffiti* (1973), *Rocky* (1976), *National Lampoon's Animal House* (1978), CHARIOTS OF FIRE (1981), *Beverly Hills Cop* (1984), *Crocodile Dundee* (1986), *The Naked Gun: From the Files of Police Squad!* (1988), *Home Alone* (1990), *Wayne's World* (1992), *The Piano* (1993), and FOUR WEDDINGS AND A FUNERAL (1994).

slow. **slow burn** An actor's method of showing suppressed anger by merely tightening or moving his facial muscles. The use of an exaggerated slow burn for comic effect was a favourite device of both Oliver Hardy (*see* LAUREL AND HARDY) and Edgar Kennedy (1890–1948), who often played a policeman harrassed by Stan and Ollie.

slow motion Film action that appears in a slowed-down form when projected. This is usually accomplished by passing the film through the taking camera at an accelerated speed and then projecting normally. (The same effect can be created by filming at the usual speed and projecting more slowly.) Slow motion is frequently used to indicate DREAM or fantasy sequences, to create a sense of 'timelessness' in love or sex scenes, and to highlight violent action, a device used so frequently in the 1970s that it threatened to become a cliché. Its main use on television is the action replay in televised sports. In America the term is often shortened to **slo-mo**. *See also* ACCELERATED MOTION.

Smell-o-vision An abortive attempt to add the dimension of smell to films; its proponents claimed that this could revolutionize the industry in the same way that sound had done a generation earlier. Like other experimental processes of the 1950s and 1960s, it must be understood as an attempt to win back audiences from television.

Developed by Michael Todd Jnr, Smell-o-vision involved pumping a series of 'smells' into each individual seat via tubing. The smells were contained in vials on a rotating drum, their release being triggered electronically by the 'smell track' of the film. The apparatus was invented by Hans Laube.

The failure of Smell-o-vision was almost a foregone conclusion, as it would have been too expensive to re-equip all cinemas, even if the public had shown much interest. As *Variety* correctly predicted, "The new dimension will be no more than a passing whiff." Todd's one and only Smell-o-vision film, *Scent of a Mystery* (1960) proved notably unpopular, provoking *Time*'s reviewer to complain "most customers will probably agree that the smell they liked best was the one they got during intermission – fresh air."

Other attempts to incorporate a dimension of smell have included the Swiss-made *My Dream*, shown at the New York World's Fair in 1940, and the 'Aromarama' *Behind the Great Wall* (1959), a travelogue about China. *See* GIMMICKS.

Smith. **Sir C(harles) Aubrey Smith** (1863–1948) British-born Hollywood character actor with a stately manner, wild eyebrows, and bristly moustache. After playing a few leads in silent films he settled into aristocratic and grandfatherly roles in the 1930s and 1940s. He was knighted in 1944.

Born in London, Smith studied at Cambridge and was a member of the England cricket team. He made a late stage debut at the age of 30 and his first film, *Builder of Bridges* (1915), in Hollywood when he was 55. His early sound roles included an English duke in *Love Me Tonight* (1932) and the Duke of Wellington in *The House of Rothschild* (1934); "Aaah, that blasted little Corsican is back!" growls Smith on learning of Napoleon's escape. In the later 1930s he played the stern grandfather of Freddie Bartholomew in *Little Lord Fauntleroy* (1936), of Shirley TEMPLE in *Wee Willie Winkie* (1937), and of Douglas FAIRBANKS Jnr in *The Sun Never Sets* (1939). Other roles included the crusty General Burroughs in

The Four Feathers (1939), Colonel Julyan in REBECCA (1940), Lord Kelvin in *Madame Curie* (1943), and Mr Lawrence in *Little Women* (1949).

Smith became captain of the Hollywood Cricket Club and was known as 'Round the Corner Smith' from his bowling technique. On the roof of his house, nicknamed 'The Round Corner', he built a weather vane from three cricket stumps and a bat and ball.

Dame Maggie Smith (1934–) British actress, who has appeared in both comedy and drama, often as an eccentric spinster. She won Oscars for *The Prime of Miss Jean Brodie* (1969) and *California Suite* (1978), and was nominated for *Othello* (1965), *Travels With My Aunt* (1972), and A ROOM WITH A VIEW (1986). In 1992 Smith received the BAFTA Award for Lifetime Achievement.

The daughter of an academic pathologist, she studied acting at the Oxford Playhouse School and made her stage debut in the 1952 OUDS production of *Twelfth Night*. Four years later, she was on Broadway in the revue *New Faces of '56*.

Having made her screen debut in Ealing's melodrama *Nowhere to Go* (1958), she went on to play such varied roles as Peter FINCH's mistress in *The Pumpkin Eater* (1964) and Desdemona to OLIVIER's Moor in *Othello* (1965), a record of the National Theatre production. She became a star, however, with Ronald NEAME's *The Prime of Miss Jean Brodie*, in which she took over Vanessa REDGRAVE's stage role of the Edinburgh schoolmistress.

Smith then replaced Katharine HEPBURN in George CUKOR's comedy *Travels With My Aunt*, and played a spinster falling for a young American in the same director's *Love and Pain and the Whole Damn Thing* (1973). There is a nice irony that in her Oscar-winning performance in *California Suite*, she played an actress preparing for the Oscar ceremony.

In 1984 Smith won the BAFTA Award as Best Actress for her role in Alan Bennett's *A Private Function*. Subsequent roles have included an irritable maiden aunt in *A Room with a View*, a hard-drinking music teacher who misreads Bob HOSKINS's friendship in *The Lonely Passion of Judith Hearne* (1987), the aged Wendy in SPIELBERG's *Peter Pan* adaptation *Hook* (1991), and Lady Bracknell in a remake of *The Importance of Being Earnest* (1992).

She is resourceful, inventive, and she has mystery and power. Mystery in a woman is terribly important.
GEORGE CUKOR.

SMPTE or **simpty** Society of Motion Picture and Television Engineers. A US professional association of film and television engineers that sets technical standards for those industries. Founded in 1916, it developed the SMPTE test film to check equipment and the SMPTE universal LEADER with identification and threading marks for projectionists. The **British Kinematograph Society**, which does similar work, was originally a branch of SMPTE.

sneak preview An unexpected advance showing of a feature film before its general RELEASE. This enables a studio to measure the audience's reaction and gather written comments; it can also generate local interest for a 'coming attraction'. GONE WITH THE WIND (1939), received a top-secret sneak preview to keep the press from reviewing it early. The audience in the Warner Theater at Santa Barbara, California, knew only that they would be shown "the biggest picture of the year." Once the film started, security guards blocked the exits to prevent the audience from leaving or even making telephone calls. *See* PREVIEW.

snow. snow effects The creation of the appearance of snow through artificial means. Various methods are used depending upon the type of snow required; rock salt on the ground for fallen snow, shredded feathers or plastic chips for light snow in the air, gypsum for heavy snow, and powdered salt for snow on a character's clothing. The snow-substitute is usually dispersed over the set by fans.

Snow White and the Seven Dwarfs (1937) Walt DISNEY's feature-length adaptation of the Grimms' fairy tale. When a wicked queen's magic mirror tells her that Snow White, her stepdaughter, is fairer than she, the queen determines to kill her. Snow White takes refuge in the woodland cottage of seven dwarfs – Bashful, Doc, Dopey, Grumpy, Happy, Sleepy, and Sneezy – until Prince Charming comes to her rescue.

This 83-minute film, the longest animation yet produced, was such a bold venture that it was known throughout production as "Disney's Folly". 750 artists were employed on the two million drawings needed

for the film, parts of which were shot with the multi-plane camera devised by Ub Iwerks to simulate the effects of TRACKING and PANNING in live action movies. Disney was so anxious to reproduce human movement accurately that he shot footage of people acting out scenes from the film for his artists to copy. Snow White was to resemble a 14-year-old Janet GAYNOR and the Prince an 18-year-old Douglas FAIRBANKS. Voices were equally important, with Disney rejecting Hollywood's leading teenage star, Deanna DURBIN, for the lead in favour of an unknown trainee opera singer, Adriana Caselott. (Mae WEST, however, had other ideas, commenting "*Snow White and the Seven Dwarfs*...would have made more money if they woulda let *me* play Snow White.")

The 'casting' of the dwarfs also caused a few headaches with the following, perhaps fortunately, failing the 'audition': Awful, Biggo-Ego, Biggy-Wiggy, Blabby, Daffy, Dirty, Doleful, Gabby, Gaspy, Gloomy, Hoppy, Hotsy, Hungry, Jaunty, Nifty, Shifty, Soulful, Snoopy, Thrifty, Weepy, and Woeful. Of the dwarfs finally chosen, Dopey – envisioned by Disney as a hybrid of Harry Langdon, Buster KEATON, Stan LAUREL, and Harpo MARX – proved the most difficult to characterize.

The film was given an A certificate by the British Board of Film Censors because of the frightening scenes involving the queen. It might have struggled to avoid an H (horror, over 16 only) had sequences depicting Snow White's mother dying in childbirth, skeletons in a dungeon, and the prince's near-drowning made it any further than the drawing-board.

Disney confounded his doubters: *Snow White* cleared $8 million in 1937 alone and subsequent re-releases (1943, 1952, 1958, 1967, 1975, 1983, 1990) have continued to earn huge rentals worldwide. At the 1938 Academy Awards, Disney was presented with a Special Oscar for his achievement: one traditional statuette together with seven miniatures.

snuff movie Slang for an underground PORNOGRAPHIC film that has as its climax the actual murder of an unsuspecting actress or actor, often a child. Although persistent rumours suggest that films of this type began to appear in California in the late 1960s, not one example has ever been verified. Faked snuff movies, however, have been made for commercial purposes.

Society of Motion Picture and Television Engineers *See* SMPTE.

soft focus An effect in which a certain lack of sharpness is deliberately imparted to the film image, usually to create a romantic or dreamy atmosphere. A soft focus effect can be achieved by placing a gauze over the lens, using a FOG FILTER or similar diffusion device, or shooting slightly out of focus. The technique is also sometimes employed by photographers for studio portraits.

Some Like It Hot (1959) The romping comedy in which Marilyn MONROE's leading men, Tony CURTIS and Jack LEMMON wear dresses. It is considered the masterpiece of director Billy WILDER, who filmed in black and white to avoid a colourful "flaming faggot picture". Wilder wrote the script with I. A. L. Diamond. The film was nominated for five Oscars, but won only one, for Orry-Kelly's costume design.

The basic plot is simple, but enlivened by hectic complications: having accidentally witnessed the 1927 St Valentine's Day Massacre in Chicago's gangland, musicians Jerry (Lemmon) and Joe (Curtis) flee to Miami disguised as members of an all-female band. Joe falls for the band's singer, Sugar Kane (Monroe), and woos her by pretending to be an impotent millionaire. Jerry unfortunately wins the heart of the eccentric but rich Osgood Fielding III (Joe E. Brown). Osgood provides the film's famous last line after learning that Jerry is a man: "Well, nobody's perfect!"

Helped by a witty script that plays with the (for the time) daring subjects of transvestism, gangland murder, and impotence, both Curtis and Lemmon turned in genuinely comic performances. But the focal point of the film is inevitably Monroe, who succeeded in making the voluptuous Sugar Kane both moving and amusing. This was despite her infamous lateness on set and bungled takes that cost $500,000 extra. Wilder suffered agonies during a scene in which Marilyn had to speak only one sentence after opening a bureau drawer. After she forgot her line for the 52nd time, he wrote it on scraps of paper hidden in every drawer. In the next take she promptly went to the wrong piece of furniture. When Wilder told her not to worry, her eyes widened as she asked, "Worry about what?" And there were other causes of tension between the stars. When she heard that Curtis said kissing her was like kissing Hitler, Marilyn put it down to jealousy: "I look better in a dress than he does."

sound Although the sound era is traditionally dated from the premiere of THE JAZZ SINGER in 1927, a number of earlier pictures had experimented with synchronized sound. Indeed, the challenge of combining moving pictures with sound had preoccupied inventors since the very earliest days of the medium. EDISON's KINETOSCOPE, one of the earliest peep-show machines, was originally developed with a view to using it in tandem with his phonograph equipment. Kinetophones – viewing machines with headphones on which the viewer could listen to music and sound effects – were later introduced in several US cities. Meanwhile Oscar Messter demonstrated the first projected motion picture with synchronized sound in 1896. However, all early sound-on-disc systems foundered on the difficulty of synchronizing gramophone and projector in the cinema; amplification necessitated huge acoustic horns, while the discs had to be changed every few minutes. Production problems were even more daunting, and for years expense deterred the studios from investing in sound.

In the mid 1920s VITAPHONE, a more advanced sound-on-disc system, was acquired by Warner Brothers in a desperate attempt to overcome its financial problems. In 1926 the studio presented *Don Juan*, with a score by the New York Philharmonic and a synchronized speech by Will HAYS welcoming the audience to the sound era. The following year Warners converted to all-sound production, hired Al JOLSON, the biggest radio star in America, and gambled everything on the novelty. The success of *The Jazz Singer* convinced the other studios that Warners were right; those that could afford it switched to sound, the others went broke.

Attempts to record sound directly onto film date back to the 1880s, with the first patent appearing in 1900. The most important pioneer in this field was Eugène Auguste Lauste (1856–1935), who patented a sound-on-film device in 1904 but failed to solve the problem of amplification. By 1912 this difficulty had been overcome by Lee De Forest, who went on to perfect the 'phonofilm' process of OPTICAL SOUND recording in the early 1920s. De Forrest made over 1000 short sound films between 1923 and 1924 but failed to interest Hollywood in his invention. However, when the success of Warners' *The Jazz Singer* forced other studios to buy or develop their own sound systems, a rival version of phonofilm, called MOVIETONE, was bought by Fox. The system, which enjoyed an immediate success in the Fox-Movietone newsreels, was soon being imitated by the other major studios. Owing to its improved synchronization, sound-on-film had rendered the disc system obsolete by 1930.

The introduction of sound had profound economic, technical, and artistic effects. Most obviously, the single world market was fragmented into hundreds of linguistic ones, leading to the relative decline of film-making in Europe and the unchallenged pre-eminence of Hollywood in the 1930s and 1940s. Owing to the cost of re-equipment, most US studios went into debt with loans from Wall Street and never recovered their financial independence. Technically, the need to film in small sound-proofed rooms forced a (temporary) return to the static filmed-play style of drama common some 30 years earlier. Slapstick was gradually superseded by the verbal comedy of the MARX BROTHERS, W. C. FIELDS, and Ernst LUBITSCH, while a wholly new genre came into being – the film MUSICAL.

Since the advent of the talkies, the main development has been the practice of recording sound on a separate but synchronized MAGNETIC FILM, which began in the 1950s. This not only provides superior reproduction, but also permits much greater flexibility in sound editing. Other landmarks have included the use of stereo (pioneered with DISNEY's FANTASIA in 1940), the introduction of DOLBY noise reduction (1971), and recording onto digital disc (1990s) – a development that brings the history of film sound full circle.

> The talkie is an unsuitable marriage of two dramatic forms. We cannot believe that it will endure.
> *The Times*, 1929.

sound camera A camera specifically designed for making sound films. Most are self-blimped (*see* BLIMP) in order to cut the noise of the camera motor.

sound crew The group of technicians responsible for the maintenance, placing, and use of sound equipment on a film production. In documentary film-making, this is often the responsibility of one individual known as the **sound man** or **woman**. On larger productions it is usual to employ a team of specialists, the most important of these being the **sound mixer**, a highly trained technician, who will use his or her knowledge of recording and acoustics to obtain the optimum desired sound. Under the sound mixer (not to be confused with the dubbing MIXER, who is responsible for blending the various soundtracks), work the **sound recorder**, who ensures the recording equipment is functioning correctly, and the BOOM operator, who is responsible for the correct placing and functioning of the microphone. These technicians will be aided by a variety of operators and CABLEMEN, who perform less specialized tasks.

sound editor The person responsible for the preparation of the master soundtrack. His or her tasks include cleaning up the dialogue track by removing unwanted background noise and equalizing differences in recording levels, assembling and synchronizing SOUND EFFECTS, and supervising the work of the MIXER.

sound effects (sfx) All sound on a film soundtrack other than music, dialogue, or narration. The required effects may be recorded during filming, recorded separately, or obtained from a library. They are usually collected on a separate track before being mixed with music and dialogue to create the master. Because natural sound is difficult to predict or control, and often sounds unreal when recorded, a great deal of ingenuity has gone into creating artificial substitutes for various sounds. Workers in this field are known as FOLEY artists after Jack Foley, who was responsible for establishing many of the best-known effects. With the advent of digital technology, mixing consoles can now hold hundreds or even thousands of pre-recorded sounds, which can be recalled and added to the effects track in a matter of seconds. A number of films have taken the world of sound effects, as their subject notably *Volere/Volare* (1990).

sound speed *See* CAMERA SPEED *under* CAMERA.

sound stage A soundproofed studio designed and equipped for the production of talking pictures.

soundtrack (1) The narrow band on one side of a film strip that carries recorded sound. The OPTICAL SOUNDTRACK that accompanies most commercial feature films is activated by a photoelectric cell during projection. There are two main types, the VARIABLE-DENSITY TRACK and the VARIABLE-AREA TRACK. The sound is always printed a few frames in ADVANCE of the corresponding image, in order to compensate for the distance between the picture gate and the sound head. *See also* MAGNETIC STRIPE; MAG-OPTICAL RELEASE PRINT. (2) A magnetic track used in sound editing. The main types are the individual tracks used for dialogue, music, and effects, and the MAGNETIC MASTER that is produced by mixing them.

The Sound of Music (1965) Robert WISE's phenomenally successful film version of the Rodgers and Hammerstein musical about Austria's singing Von Trapp family. The songs, which differ slightly from those of the stage version, include the unforgettable 'Do Re Me', 'My Favourite Things', 'The Sound of Music', and 'Edelweiss'. Shot on location in Salzburg and the spectacular surrounding Alps, the film won six Oscars, including Best Picture and Best Director.

Wise produced and directed, using the same production team that had made WEST SIDE STORY four years earlier. Directors Billy WILDER and William WYLER had both turned the project down, and even Wise said no three times before accepting – a foretaste of the mixed reactions that have made this one of the most loved and most scorned of films. *The Sound of Music* stars Julie ANDREWS, Christopher PLUMMER, and Peggy Wood, with the last two having their songs dubbed by Bill Lee and Margery McKay. Andrews and Wood received Oscar nominations. About 2000 children auditioned for the seven juvenile roles.

The story follows Maria (Andrews), a postulant nun assigned by her Mother Superior (Wood) as governess to the seven children of a widower, Captain Von Trapp (Plummer). She replaces his stern fathering with a joyous and spontaneous approach, and the two eventually fall in love and marry. When the Nazi government calls him to military service, the family crosses the mountains to freedom.

Having cost $8 million to make, *The Sound of Music* grossed $120 million worldwide and after one year surpassed GONE WITH THE WIND as the greatest box-office success of all time. In doing so it saved 20th Century-Fox from the financial disaster caused by *Cleopatra* (1963). *The Sound of Music* was later licensed for 20 years to NBC Television for $25 million. During its worldwide travels the film has suffered some curious mutilations: one cinema in Munich eliminated all the scenes showing Nazis, ending the movie with the marriage, while the Korean distributor felt the film was too long and cut all the songs. One Cardiff woman claimed to have seen the movie 940 times.

space opera A somewhat disparaging term for a style of SCIENCE FICTION characterized by an, at best, vague knowledge of science: in effect, Western and adventure movies set in space. The genre began with such serials as FLASH GORDON (1936) and reached its peak in the 1950s with adventure films like *Rocketship X-M* (1950) and *Riders to the Stars* (1954). It continued into the following decade with such interesting films as the Victorian period piece *First Men in the Moon* (1964), and was only brought to a halt by the real-life spectacle of the space programme. It took the success of George LUCAS's STAR WARS (1977), with its new tactic of moving the fantasy out of our solar system into "a galaxy far far away", to revive the genre.

spaghetti Western A film genre of the 1960s and 1970s that established European film-makers as the leading interpreters of the WESTERN, previously very much the province of Hollywood. The rise of the European Western was largely a result of the work of the Italian director Sergio LEONE, who set the pattern by filming on location in Spain with US lead actors and Italian film crews; the voices of Italian members of the cast were subsequently dubbed into English. Violent, amoral, and often wryly humorous, the spaghetti Westerns breathed new life into what had become an exhausted genre. Leone's *A Fistful of Dollars* (1964), starring Clint EASTWOOD, is recognized as the first of the spaghetti Westerns; among its successors were the same director's *For a Few Dollars More* (1965) and *The Good, the Bad and the Ugly* (1967), both also starring Eastwood. Other 'pasta stars' have included Claudia CARDINALE, Lee Van Cleef, Eli WALLACH, Charles BRONSON, and Rod STEIGER.

Although few further European Westerns have been made since Leone's classics, the influence of the spaghetti Westerns on those still being made in the US has been profound.

special effects (FX, SP-EFX) Techniques used to create scenes that could not be achieved by normal methods – generally because this would be unsafe, expensive, illegal, or physically impossible. The first Oscar for special effects was awarded in 1940 to *The Rains Came* (1939), an early DISASTER FILM featuring monsoons and floods. An action movie based (loosely) on the work of special effects technicians has also been made, *f/x* (1985).

For convenience, special effects may be divided into two broad categories, **mechanical** and **visual effects**. Mechanical effects are those that are produced on the studio floor without photographic aid. These include the simulation of such weather conditions as SNOW, rain, or FOG, the use of BREAKAWAY chairs and bottles in fight scenes, the creation of MINIATURES to replicate, for example, a space station or futuristic city, and the elaborate MAKE-UP effects used for monsters or aliens.

Visual effects are those created by photographic means, either while filming or in post-production. Until the development of the OPTICAL PRINTER such effects as WIPES, FADES, and DISSOLVES were carried out IN CAMERA, as were elementary MATTE procedures. Composite images could also be created in camera through such techniques as the GLASS SHOT or BACK PROJECTION. With the advent of the optical printer, film-makers can now create images that are in fact complex collages assembled from a variety of sources. The principal development in this area has been the numerous travelling MATTE procedures, of which the best known is the BLUE-SCREEN PROCESS. More recently, the world of visual effects has been revolutionized by the increasing use of computers – not only to manipulate and enhance photographic elements but also to generate wholly new images, such as a fantastic landscape, which can then be printed onto the film (*see* COMPUTER ANIMATION).

Special effects have been employed since the earliest days of cinema. The first recorded example occurs in EDISON's *The Execution of Mary, Queen of Scots* (1895), in which a dummy was substituted at the moment of decapitation. Undoubtedly the father of special effects was the French pioneer Georges MÉLIÈS. While in his earlier work he drew heavily on his background in stage magic, he soon began to exploit a range of cinematic devices in order to baffle the audience. Amongst the procedures he introduced were miniature shots, MULTIPLE EXPOSURES, and dissolves. Further advances in 'trick photography' were made by Edwin S. PORTER, whose *Dream of a Rarebit Fiend* (1906) features a flying bed, and the Britons Robert Paul and G. A. Smith. The most important early developments were in the superimposition of images, as in the SCHÜFFTAN PROCESS and various matte procedures.

Because early sound films had to be shot on soundproofed sets, with any exterior images being added photographically, the advent of the talkies proved a great stimulus to special effects. Interesting films of this era include KING KONG (1933), in which Willis O'Brien perfected most of the techniques available at the time, THE INVISIBLE MAN (1933), with trick photography by John Fulton, and *Dr Jekyll and Mr Hyde* (1931), in which Fredric MARCH appears to change from one into the other before our eyes. Two important developments of the 1950s were the introduction of WIDESCREEN processes and tri-pack colour film, both of which led to great improvements in the quality of travelling mattes (as seen, for example, in DE MILLE'S THE TEN COMMANDMENTS, 1956).

In more recent decades, the most impressive advances in special-effects technology have all come in the field of SCIENCE FICTION; Donald Trumball revitalized the profession with his work on 2001: A SPACE ODYSSEY (1968), *The Andromeda Strain* (1970), and *Close Encounters of the Third Kind* (1977), while John Dykstra and Stuart Ziff devised the staggering computer-controlled effects in STAR WARS (1977) and *Dragonslayer* (1981) respectively. The Industrial Light And Magic Company, set up to create the effects for *Star Wars*, has remained Hollywood's leading practitioner in the field, with credits including SPIELBERG'S E.T.: THE EXTRATERRESTRIAL (1982) and JURASSIC PARK (1993). The amazing computer-animation technique known as morphing, in which solid objects appear to change shape, was first fully utilized in *Terminator 2: Judgment Day* (1991; *see* TERMINATOR FILMS).

Speed! A call from the cameraman to indicate that his camera and sound equipment have reached the correct synchronized speed, and that filming can therefore begin.

Spellbound (1945) Alfred HITCHCOCK's psychological mystery story. Although the film, which stars Ingrid BERGMAN and Gregory PECK, was one of the first to introduce psychiatry to the screen and a rare Hitchcock FILM NOIR, the director dismissed it as "just another manhunt story wrapped in pseudo-psychoanalysis." Ben Hecht adapted the story from Francis Beeding's novel, *The House of Dr Edwardes.*

Spellbound's producer, David O. SELZNICK, was in the throes of a marriage crisis at the time the film was made, and his wife later opined, "David was making the film instead of having analysis. He was in a terrible state, and the film is a terrible piece of junk." Despite its reliance on psychological jargon, the film proved a box-office triumph and has some fine Hitchcockian touches. When the two stars finally kiss, a corridor of opening doors is shown. As the murderer shoots himself, the black-and-white movie explodes into a split-second (one frame) of red Technicolor. The remarkable dream sequence was devised by surrealist artist Salvador Dali.

The story involves the new head of a mental institution (Peck), an impostor and amnesiac who thinks he has murdered someone. A staff psychiatrist (Bergman) falls in love with him and risks her life helping him to find the real murderer (Leo G. Carroll). Rhonda FLEMING appeared as a man-hating inmate and Michael Chekhov as a European tutor.

The film won an Oscar for Best Score (Miklo Rozsa) and five nominations including Best Picture, Best Director, and Best Supporting Actor (Chekhov).

spider or **spyder dolly** *See* DOLLY.

Spielberg, Steven (1946–) US director and producer, who has enjoyed greater success at the box office than any other figure in motion-picture history. Spielberg began his film-making career with the gentle short, *Amblin'* (1969). A number of TV movies followed, including the seminal man-versus-truck thriller *Duel* (1972). After making *The Sugarland Express* (1973) with Goldie HAWN, Spielberg created his first BLOCKBUSTER with the gripping shark drama JAWS (1975). The film became the biggest box-office success to date and gained Spielberg his first Best Picture nomination. *Close Encounters of the Third Kind* (1977) was a SPECIAL EFFECTS spectacular with a rather slender plot about alien visitations. Despite its initial success, Spielberg re-

released the film three years later with added material. In 1979 he released his greatest commercial failure, the sprawling comedy *1941.*

At the start of the 1980s Spielberg returned to the adventure movies of his youth, and reaffirmed his box-office appeal, with RAIDERS OF THE LOST ARK (1981), an action fantasy that brought him another Best Picture nomination. Two sequels followed: the violent *Indiana Jones and the Temple of Doom* (1984) and the more traditional *Indiana Jones and the Last Crusade* (1989).

In 1982 Spielberg embarked on what he saw as a small personal project, a "boy and his dog" story about a child who befriends an alien. E.T.: THE EXTRATERRESTRIAL broke all box-office records and gained Spielberg yet another Best Picture nomination. He followed this with a series of 'grown-up' movies, apparently designed to win him the elusive Oscar. *The Color Purple* (1985), starring Whoopi GOLDBERG, was nominated for nine Oscars, including Best Picture, but won none. *Empire of the Sun* (1987) with a script by Tom Stoppard from J. G. Ballard's novel, failed to secure even a nomination. Following these disappointments, Spielberg returned to the special-effects laden style of his greatest successes with *Hook* (1991), a disastrously flawed attempt to bring his dream project, Peter Pan, to the screen.

Just when Spielberg seemed to have confirmed the doubts of his numerous critics, he came back with two extraordinary films; one the highest-grossing movie of all time, and the other an indisputable artistic triumph. The classic family adventure JURASSIC PARK (1993) features realistic computer-animated dinosaurs, while SCHINDLER'S LIST (also 1993) is Spielberg's epic of the Holocaust, a black-and-white masterpiece that avoids the romanticism of his previous 'serious' movies. It finally gained him the Best Director and Best Picture Oscars.

Spielberg has also produced several pictures by other directors: *Poltergeist* (1982) was directed by Tobe Hooper, but shows much of Spielberg's visual style, while the *Gremlins* (1985, 1990) and *Back to the Future* films (1985, 1989, 1990) are lively juvenile fantasies that indulge his love of IN-JOKES and pastiche. *The Land Before Time* and WHO FRAMED ROGER RABBIT? (both 1988) can be seen as animation experiments to pave the way for *Jurassic Park*. In 1994 Spielberg announced plans to set up a major

Hollywood studio – the first venture of its kind for decades – with Disney's Jeffrey Katzenberg and the music industry mogul David Geffen.

> [Spielberg's films] appeal to what remains of a child in every adult. I love everything childish in these films. But it's only a film-maker of Spielberg's standing and intellectual independence who can carry it off.
> ANDRZEJ WAJDA, director.

spies   The spy movie could be seen as a sub-genre of the DETECTIVE film, as both are concerned with investigation and deduction; the main difference, of course, is that the action in a spy film unfolds against a wider political background. In general, such movies accentuate the drama and mystery in the story by playing on current political anxieties. Consequently, spy films tend to be produced at times when there are actual or perceived threats to the state. While this has encouraged much dull propaganda, the genre nevertheless encompasses a tremendous range of tone, from such gentle entertainments as THE LADY VANISHES (1938) and *Contraband* (1940), through the *Boy's Own* escapism of BOND, to the harsher darker world of 1970s conspiracy thrillers.

The first boom in the production of spy films came with the entry of America into World War I. The movies of this period were largely concerned with the threat from the enemy within; publicity for *The Spy* (1917), for example, asked the question "Do you know your neighbour?" Although we are asked to believe in the utter ruthlessness of the spies on view, in practice they seem to be utterly incompetent. These conventions were being satirized as early as 1918 in Mack SENNETT's *An International Sneak*.

In the 1930s rising international tension led to a revival of the spy genre in both Britain and America. The most important exponent was Alfred HITCHCOCK, who explored the moral ambiguities of espionage in such films as *The Secret Agent* and *Sabotage* (both 1936); both films show how the spy's actions lead to the deaths of innocents. Another popular Hitchcock theme was that of the innocent accidentally caught up in the activities of foreign agents, e.g. *The Man Who Knew Too Much* (1934) and THE 39 STEPS (1935).

With the advent of World War II, the soul-searching approach of the best 1930s films inevitably receded in favour of simple patriotism. Nevertheless, a number of interesting movies were produced. CASABLANCA (1943) and *The Conspirators* (1944) deal with underground activity in Nazi-occupied territory, while *Confessions of a Nazi Spy* (1939) and *The House on 92nd Street* (1945) use a semidocumentary technique to show the rounding up of Nazi gangs in America. Also of interest are John HUSTON's *Across the Pacific* (1943) and Hitchcock's *Notorious* (1946), which shows the cost to one generation of another's treachery.

The advent of the COLD WAR led to another rash of spy movies, the paranoid tone of which can be judged by such titles as *Red Menace* (1949), *I Married a Communist* (1950), and *I Was a Communist for the FBI* (1951). With the approach of détente, however, more varied approaches began to emerge. In the 1960s the popularity of the Bond films encouraged a host of glamorous super-agent movies, for example *Our Man Flint* (1965) and *Modesty Blaise* (1966). In complete contrast were such working-class agents – little more than underpaid civil servants – as Harry Palmer (*The Ipcress File*, 1965) and Alec Leamas (*The Spy who Came in from the Cold*, 1965). The understated way in which these dramas dealt with issues of trust and betrayal was to some extent anticipated by Carol REED's work in such films as *Our Man in Havana* (1959).

Public sensibilities changed yet again in the late 1960s and 1970s, when the failure in Vietnam and the Watergate scandal helped to undermine confidence in the government and its agencies. In America, these years saw a proliferation of conspiracy-theory movies in which the good guys turn out to be baddies as well; examples include *Three Days of the Condor* (1975), *The Conversation* (1974), and *The Parallax View* (1974). This subgenre arrived in Europe somewhat later with such films as the British-made *Defence of the Realm* (1985) and *Hidden Agenda* (1990) and the French *Nikita* (1990). Meanwhile, the Reagan years saw the Cold War come back to Hollywood in such flagwavers as *Firefox* (1982) and *The Hunt for Red October* (1990).

Today, spy films face perhaps their greatest challenge – survival in a world in which there is no obvious enemy. As the genre did not fare well in the years immediately after 1918 or 1945, it is difficult to see how it will do better in the 'cold peace' currently prevailing. With the shift in power from nation states to multinational corporations, it may be that industrial espionage and conspiracy will offer a new field of interest.

splatter movie Slang for a violent HORROR FILM in which large numbers of people, often teenagers, go to their deaths in spectacularly messy and unpleasant ways. *See also* SLASHER MOVIE.

splice (1) In editing, to join two pieces of film in a single continuous strip. (2) The join so formed. There are two basic types: a **lap splice** (overlap-cement splice) is created by overlapping the two ends of film and joining them with acetic-acid cement, and a **butt splice** by placing the ends so that they touch (abutt) without overlapping and joining them with a piece of clear tape. Both types have pros and cons; the butt splice is far simpler but lacks the strength required for frequent running, while the lap splice is strong but requires cutting to alter it. Accordingly, butt splices tend to be used for working prints and lap splices for exhibition prints.

split screen An effect in which two or more separate images appear simultaneously on the screen without superimposition; the most common example of this is the telephone call, in which the two speakers appear on either side of the screen. The effect is achieved through the use of MATTES. *Compare* MULTIPLE-IMAGE SHOT.

spotlight or **spot** A lamp that produces a bright narrow beam that can be focused on a particular actor or area of the set. *See also* JUNIOR; SENIOR.

sprocket A wheel with regularly placed teeth that drives film through a CAMERA, printer, or projector by engaging the perforations at the side.

Stack, Robert (1919–) US actor, whose career took him from teenage romances to gangster films. He was nominated for an Oscar as Best Supporting Actor for *Written on the Wind* (1957). His Hollywood credits were later overshadowed by his portrayal of surly Federal agent Eliot Ness, the nemesis of Al Capone, in the award-winning TV series *The Untouchables*.

Born in Los Angeles, Stack attended the University of Southern California, where he began to act. He broke into films in *First Love* (1939), attracting considerable publicity as "the first boy to kiss Deanna DURBIN"; he again played her boy-next-door in *Nice Girl?* (1941). After service in the US Navy during World War II, he found more rugged roles in *Fighter Squadron* (1948) and *The Bullfighter and the Lady* (1951).

In the mid 1950s Stack starred in the first 3-D movie, BWANA DEVIL (1953), and attracted praise for his performances in *The High and the Mighty* (1954), a fighter-pilot drama with John WAYNE, and Samuel FULLER's *House of Bamboo* (1955), in which he played an undercover agent chasing an ex-serviceman gangster (Robert RYAN). Two years later he and Dorothy MALONE played spoiled oil-rich siblings in Douglas SIRK's *Written on the Wind*. At the end of the decade he starred in *The Scarface Mob* (1958), a cinema pilot for *The Untouchables* and took the title role in the biopic *John Paul Jones* (1959).

After making *The Caretakers* (British title *Borderlines*; 1963) a mental-hospital drama, Stack appeared in European films for a decade. In 1979 he returned to Hollywood with a role in Steven SPIELBERG's unsuccessful wartime comedy *1941*.

stage The area of a studio complex set aside for the construction of sets and the shooting of films.

Stagecoach (1939) John FORD's stirring tribute to the US West, a film generally considered the first modern WESTERN. This was Ford's first venture into the spectacular scenery of Monument Valley, Utah, which he later made his own, and brought stardom to John WAYNE after a mediocre career of 62 films. "Raise your eyebrows and wrinkle your forehead", Ford advised the poker-faced actor. Clair Trevor provided the film's romantic interest. Although Gary COOPER and Marlene DIETRICH had been considered for the leads, Ford decided not to use established stars, fearing that this could detract from the characterization. Dudley Nichols's screenplay was based on a *Colliers* magazine story derived ultimately from Maupassant's *Boule de suif*.

This hugely influential film proved a SLEEPER at the box office and was nominated for seven Academy Awards including Best Movie and Best Director. However, as this was the year of GONE WITH THE WIND, *Stagecoach* only won Oscars for Thomas Mitchell's supporting role (as an alcoholic doctor) and for the musical score, which adapted 17 US folk tunes. An embarrassing 1966 remake starred ANN-MARGRET and Bing CROSBY.

The story involves a group of passengers thrown together on the Overland Stage; these include an outlaw known as the Ringo Kid (Wayne), a kind-hearted prostitute (Trevor), and a gambler (John CARRADINE). Although the stagecoach is attacked by Indians, rescue arrives in the shape of Wayne and the cavalry in a final chase sequence. As the American Indian actor Yakima Canutt was also Wayne's stunt double in some of the shots, the sequence presents the singular spectacle of a man chasing himself.

stage left or **right** A direction instructing a film actor to move to his or her left or right (when facing the camera). The terms were borrowed from the theatre.

Stallone, Sylvester (1946–) Muscular US actor, director, and screenwriter, who has built a career around five boxing films featuring the triumphant underdog Rocky Balboa. He was the first actor to earn $10 million for a film and now demands more than twice that figure. In 1985 he was the top draw at the US box office.

Stallone was born in New York's Hell's Kitchen neighbourhood, the son of Sicilian immigrants. An accident during his birth led to one side of his face becoming paralysed, so that today he will only be shot from his good side. When he was ten, his father reportedly advised him "You weren't born with much brain, so you'd better develop your body." After his parents divorced, Stallone moved from one foster family to another, attending 14 schools and five colleges without much success. The University of Miami advised him to give up acting.

Stallone's early jobs included a cleaner at a zoo, a pizza demonstrator, and a cinema usher. After appearing nude in the off-Broadway play *Score* (1970), he took bit parts in a number of films, including the pornographic *A Party At Kitty's* and Woody ALLEN's *Bananas* (both 1971).

Success was slow to arrive. For his first substantial role, in the Brooklyn gang movie *The Lords of Flatbush* (1974), he claims to have earned only 25 free T-shirts. By this time almost broke, he wrote the screenplay for *Rocky* (1976) in three days after seeing a Muhammad Ali fight on television. He sold it, on condition that he would star, to United Artists for $1 million and a percentage of the profits. The film proved a huge success and won Oscars for Best Picture and Best Director (John Avildsen), with Stallone

nominated for Best Actor and Best Screenplay. After scripting and starring in two flops, *F.I.S.T.* and *Paradise Alley* (both 1978), Stallone sought a sure-fire hit by writing and directing *Rocky II* (1979), one of Hollywood's first NUMBERED SEQUELS. The sequence continued on its profitable but increasingly predictable way with *Rocky III* (1981), *Rocky IV* (1985), and *Rocky V* (1990; directed by Avildsen). The last earned Stallone a fee of $27.5 million and 35% of the gross.

Stallone's other projects of the 1980s included directing John TRAVOLTA in *Staying Alive* (1983), a movie he also wrote. After the Rocky films, Stallone is best known for starring as the homicidal Vietnam veteran John RAMBO in *First Blood* (1982) and the jingoistic sequels *Rambo: First Blood Part II* (1985) and *Rambo III* (1988). Later roles have included a cop in *Tango & Cash* (1989), a gangster in the comedy *Oscar* (1991), a mountain rescuer in *Cliffhanger* (1992), which he produced and directed, a demolitions expert in *The Specialist* (1994), and the title character in *Judge Dredd* (1995).

stand-in A person who substitutes for a major performer during camera and lighting set-ups, etc. He or she must be of roughly the same height and physical type. When the substitute appears on film he or she is more properly called a DOUBLE or STUNTMAN.

Stanwyck, Barbara (Ruby Stevens; 1907–90) US actress, who usually played aggressive cold-hearted women. A dedicated professional, she won four Oscar nominations and in 1944 was listed as the highest-paid woman in America. The director Frank CAPRA once commented "In a Hollywood popularity contest, she would win first prize hands down."

Born in Brooklyn, the last of five children, she was brought up in a series of foster homes after being orphaned at the age of four. She left school at 13 to take dancing lessons and work as a parcel wrapper. Two years later, she became a chorus girl with the Ziegfeld Follies; a producer complained that her name sounded like a stripper and selected 'Stanwyck' from an old programme. After starring in the Broadway play, *The Noose* (1926), she went on to make her screen debut in *Broadway Nights* (1927), a silent movie shot in New York.

In 1928 Stanwyck married vaudeville star Frank Fay and followed him to Hollywood (the couple divorced in 1935). Her first notable roles were in the early Capra comedies *Ladies of Leisure* (1930) and *Miracle Woman* (1931); by 1932 Warner Brothers were paying her $50,000 a picture. Subsequent roles included a missionary in Capra's *The Bitter Tea of General Yen* (1932) and the title part in George STEVENS's *Annie Oakley*. She received her first Oscar nomination for starring in King VIDOR's tearjerker *Stella Dallas* (1937), as a wife who loses both husband and daughter.

Stanwyck married the actor Robert TAYLOR in 1939. In Preston STURGES's *The Lady Eve* (1941) she played a cardsharp targeting Henry FONDA, while Howard HAWKS's *Ball of Fire* (1942) saw her playing a striptease artiste opposite lexicographer Gary COOPER. The classic FILM NOIR DOUBLE INDEMNITY (1944) brought another Oscar nomination for her performance as a woman who persuades insurance agent Fred MACMURRAY to murder her husband. Although she was criticized for wearing a tight sweater in the film she called the movie "anti-sweater", adding "It shows what happens if you fall for a gal who wears a sweater."

Stanwyck won further praise for her part in Anatole LITVAK's *Sorry Wrong Number* (1948), in which she plays a bedridden wife who overhears her husband (Burt LANCASTER) plotting her death. In the 1950s she made several Westerns, including Allan DWAN's *Cattle Queen of Montana* (1954) with Ronald REAGAN. She turned increasingly to television in the 1960s, winning an Emmy for the Western *Big Valley*. Her later films included *Walk on the Wild Side* (1962), in which she played a lesbian brothel keeper, and the thriller *The Night Walker* (1965), in which she co-starred with Taylor (who remained a friend although they had divorced in 1952).

star A top performer in films, theatre, television, music, etc. Although the term is mainly associated with Hollywood, it is recorded as early as the 1770s, when it was applied to the British actor David Garrick. The Hollywood **star system** was created in the 1910s, chiefly as a means of increasing the box-office appeal of films. The studios were first alerted to the drawing power of individual performers by the popularity of the BIOGRAPH GIRL, Florence Lawrence; in 1910 she abandoned both Biograph and her

previous anonymity to appear under her own name. Up until this point, film companies tended not to identify actors and actresses in order to hold down their salaries. The first international stars of the silent era were Mary PICKFORD (known as 'the World's Sweetheart') and the athletic Douglas FAIRBANKS. Their celebrity was soon eclipsed by that of Charlie CHAPLIN, who became the most famous and instantly recognizable figure in human history.

Once the commercial potential of the star system had become clear, the major studios set about manufacturing stars to match public tastes and expectations. This usually meant grooming actors or actresses to fit one of a small number of stereotypes (the VAMP, the tough-guy, the romantic lead, etc.). Glamorous images were created by studio dressers and publicity departments, which even invented new names and biographies for likely candidates (as in the case of Theda BARA). The legendary status of the great stars was further enhanced by the newspaper coverage given to their lifestyles, love affairs, and fabulous wealth. In Britain, the first international star-maker was Alexander KORDA, who made a hobby of finding star qualitities among secondary performers; his successes included Merle OBERON, who also became his wife.

Although the top silent stars enjoyed a good deal of freedom in their dealings with the studios, the situation changed with the coming of sound. In the 1930s and 1940s even such great stars as Clark GABLE were CONTRACT PLAYERS, wholly at the mercy of the studio bosses when it came to the choice of films or co-stars.

With the collapse of the STUDIO SYSTEM after World War II, stars were able to reclaim some autonomy and to escape from the kind of fixed images that kept Edward G. ROBINSON a gangster and Bette DAVIS a bitch queen. Today's stars, such as Meryl STREEP and Dustin HOFFMAN, tend to be much more versatile, though some, such as Sylvester STALLONE, continue in set roles.

In recent decades the term 'star' has been devalued by indiscriminate use, leading to such aggrandized versions as **superstar** and **megastar**.

A star is just an actor who sells tickets.
CHARLES DANCE, actor, 1989.

A Star is Born (1954) George CUKOR's stylish and emotionally powerful musical about the price of fame. The film starred Judy

GARLAND and James MASON, both of whom received Oscar nominations. Garland, who had suffered a breakdown in 1952, was making her first movie in four years; her no-holds-barred performance in a role that presents clear parallels to her own life is usually considered the summit of her film career. Mason also excelled in a role that had been turned down by Stewart GRANGER, Cary GRANT, and Humphrey BOGART. The song 'The Man That Got Away' won a nomination for composer Harold Arlen and lyricist Ira Gershwin.

The film was produced for Warner Brothers by Garland's then husband, Sidney Luft. A decision to scrap early scenes and reshoot in CINEMASCOPE ran costs to nearly $5 million. To his deep chagrin, Cukor's original three-hour print was cut by half an hour before release; some of the missing footage was restored in a new version released in 1983. Cukor himself died the night before he was due to see the restored print.

The plot follows the rise of aspiring actress Vicki Lester (née Esther Blodgett) and the simultaneous decline of her husband Norman Maine, a famous star who is sinking into alcoholism. The film was a musical remake of a 1937 picture of the same title directed by William WELLMAN and produced by David O. SELZNICK. (Coincidentally, Oscar nominations also went to both stars of the earlier film, Janet GAYNOR and Fredric MARCH.) This was in turn based partly on Cukor's earlier film *What Price Hollywood* (1932).

In 1976 Warners remade the film yet again, setting it in the contemporary pop-music world with Barbra STREISAND and Kris Kristofferson in the leads. An Oscar went to the song 'Evergreen', composed and sung by Streisand with words by Paul Williams.

starlet A young film actress who seems to have star quality and is promoted and publicized by a studio in the hope that they can make her into a STAR.

Star Wars (1977) George LUCAS's popular space adventure, in its day the most profitable movie ever made with returns of nearly $194 million on a $12 million investment. Lucas's script was turned down by both Universal and United Artists before 20th Century-Fox picked it up. Even then, Fox argued that no movie with 'star' or 'wars' in the title had ever made big money.

The film owed its success to the combination of a simple good-against-evil story with impressive special effects, created using new computer technology at Lucas's Industrial Light & Magic Company in California. *Star Wars* also made use of the most expensive model ever constructed for a film, Darth Vader's $100,000 Star Destroyer spaceship, which featured more than 250,000 portholes. The film's interiors were shot at Britain's Elstree Studios.

Leading the cast were newcomers Mark Hamill, Harrison FORD, and Carrie Fisher, who appeared alongside veteran British actors Alec GUINNESS and Peter CUSHING. Among the seven Oscars awarded to the film were those for visual effects and John Williams's original score; nominations were also received for Best Picture, Lucas's screenplay, and Alec Guinness's performance.

The story, set "a long time ago in a galaxy far, far away", involves the kidnapping of Princess Leia (Fisher) by the forces of evil. To the rescue comes the unproven youth Luke Skywalker (Hamill), assisted by the mercenary Han Solo (Ford) and an old hermit, Ben Kenobi (Guinness), who instructs him in the mystical power of the 'Force'. Mechanical help comes from the android C-3PO and the robot R2-D2 (named from the film editors' abbreviation for 'Reel 2, Dialogue 2'). Lucas later added two successful sequels, *The Empire Strikes Back* (1980), which cost $32 million and was seen by only half the audience of *Star Wars*, and *Return of the Jedi* (1983), a still more expensive film notable mainly for introducing the Ewoks, cuddly teddy-bear creatures who have since featured in two TV movies. According to the latest Hollywood gossip, Lucas has revived his original plan of extending the series to nine films.

In the early 1980s the name *Star Wars* was also used informally for the Strategic Defense Initiative (SDI), a proposed system for defending America from nuclear attack using laser-beam weapons orbiting in space. The scheme went into abeyance with the end of the Cold War and was formally abandoned in 1993. *Star Wars* is also thought to have inspired President Ronald REAGAN's notorious reference to the Soviet Union as "the Evil Empire".

steadicam Tradename for a device used to stabilize the camera during hand-held filming. The camera is mounted on a spring-loaded arm attached to a vest worn by the camera operator, thereby redistributing its weight to his or her hips. Steadicam allows great freedom and fluidity of movement while avoiding the shaky picture associated with hand-held camera work. The device was awarded a special Oscar for scientific and technical achievement in 1977.

Steiger, Rod (1925–) US actor. Steiger left school at the age of 16 to join the Navy. Following service during World War II, he used his GI Bill scholarship to enrol at drama school. He later joined the famous ACTORS' STUDIO in New York, from which he emerged a leading exponent of the METHOD.

Although Steiger made his big screen debut in *Teresa* (1951), his film career did not take off until his appearance as Marlon BRANDO's elder brother in ON THE WATERFRONT (1954), a part that brought him an Oscar nomination as Best Supporting Actor. A year later he gave a hammy performance as Jud Fry in Fred ZINNEMANN's *Oklahoma!* Other notable films of the 1950s include Robert ALDRICH's *The Big Knife* (1955), Sam FULLER's *The Run of the Arrow* (1957), and *Al Capone* (1959), in which he played the title role.

During the early 1960s Steiger appeared in a number of international productions of varying quality. He received a second Oscar nomination for his powerful portrayal of a concentration-camp survivor in Sidney LUMET's *The Pawnbroker* (1965) and won a Best Actor Oscar for his role as a southern sheriff in Norman Jewison's IN THE HEAT OF THE NIGHT (1967). The following year Steiger was given the opportunity to ham it up playing a misogynistic master-of-disguise murderer in *No Way To Treat a Lady* (1968). In his last film of the decade, *The Illustrated Man* (1969), he played an itinerant who tells stories based on the tattoos that cover his body. It took a team of nine people two days (one for the torso, one for the limbs) to apply the required make-up.

Steiger's films of the 1970s include such international productions as the Russian-Italian *Waterloo* (1970), in which he played Napoleon, and Sergio LEONE's *A Fistful of Dynamite* (*Duck You Sucker!*; 1972). He played the title roles in both *The Last Days of Mussolini* (1974) – a part he would return to in the Libyan-British co-production *Lion of the Desert* (1981) – and *W. C. Fields and Me* (1976).

During the 1980s Steiger appeared in *Cattle Annie and Little Britches* (1981), an uninspired Western, Bryan FORBES's *The Naked Face* (1984), and *The January Man* (1989). His most recent films include Simon Callow's *The Ballad of the Sad Café* (1990) and Robert ALTMAN's *The Player* (1991), in which he has a cameo as himself.

Steiner, Max (Maximilian Raoul Steiner; 1888–1971) Austrian-born Hollywood composer who scored more than 200 films, mostly for RKO and Warner Brothers. He won Oscars for *The Informer* (1935), *Now, Voyager* (1942), and *Since You Went Away* (1944), and was nominated for 23 others – including the complex score for GONE WITH THE WIND (1939).

Born in Vienna, Steiner was a musical prodigy who zipped through the eight-year curriculum at Vienna's Imperial Academy of Music in 12 months, graduating at the age of 13. When not much older, he composed an operetta that ran for two years in Vienna. Steiner subsequently studied under Gustav Mahler and became a professional conductor while still in his teens. Having travelled to America to join Florenz Ziegfeld in 1914, he was later invited to Hollywood to conduct the music for RKO's *Rio Rita* (1929). He stayed on to become a major figure in the developing art of using MUSIC to enhance screen images.

Steiner approached the task of writing for *Gone With the Wind* by breaking the script down into 282 sections and providing separate themes for all the leading players, as well as for the three love matches. When producer David O. SELZNICK hired other composers to help, Steiner doubled his pace, having his butler wake him at five a.m. to compose until midnight and taking vitamin injections to increase his energy.

Steiner also scored several Humphrey BOGART films, including CASABLANCA (1942) and THE TREASURE OF THE SIERRA MADRE (1948), the music for which won a prize at the Venice Film Festival. A later success was *A Summer Place* (1959). Steiner retired in 1965, owing to failing eyesight.

stereoscopy *See* 3-D.

Sternberg, Josef von *See* VON STERNBERG, JOSEF.

Stevens, George (1904–75) US director and producer, who made relatively few films because of his perfectionism. Known as a 'woman's director', he won Oscars for *A Place in the Sun* (1951) and *Giant* (1956); in 1953 he was nominated for the classic Western SHANE and received the Irving Thalberg Memorial Award for his "high quality of production." His son, the director George Stevens Jnr, was director of the AFI from 1967 to 1979.

Born in California, the son of theatre actors, he was performing on stage by the age of five. His hobby of photography then led him into films as an assistant cameraman in 1921. During the mid 1920s he helped to shoot a number of Hal ROACH's early LAUREL AND HARDY shorts and in 1930 began directing two-reel comedies in Roach's 'The Boy Friends' series.

Stevens directed his first feature, *The Cohens and Kellys in Trouble*, for Universal in 1933. Not long afterwards he moved to RKO, where Katharine HEPBURN requested him as the director of *Alice Adams* (1934), a romance that won an Oscar nomination as Best Picture. In *Swing Time* (1936), a Fred ASTAIRE and Ginger ROGERS musical, Stevens created Astaire's famous 'Bo Jangles' shadow dance after seeing rehearsal lights cast weird shadows on the set.

In 1939 he shifted to adventure with *Gunga Din*, starring Cary GRANT as an officer on the North-West Frontier. Stevens was now such a valuable property that Columbia's ruthless Harry COHN offered him a contract that ruled out any interference from the studio – although Cohn later groused that he "exposes more film and shoots more angles than any director I've ever had." In 1941 Hepburn again requested him for *Woman of the Year*, her first film with Spencer TRACY.

After heading a film unit in World War II, Stevens set up as an independent producer-director. His later features were infrequent and, in the opinion of many, overblown. In 1951 he won his first Oscar for directing Elizabeth TAYLOR and Montgomery CLIFT in *A Place in the Sun*, an adaptation of Theodore Dreiser's *An American Tragedy*. After making *Shane*, with Alan LADD as the mysterious gunslinger, there was a three-year interval before his next film *Giant*, a sprawling epic starring Taylor, Rock HUDSON, and James DEAN. Stevens received a final Oscar nomination for the biopic *The Diary of Anne Frank* (1959), starring Millie Perkins. A production and box-office disaster followed when he took five years to complete the religious spectacle *The Greatest Story Ever Told* (1965). Stevens retired four years later, having made only eight films in his last 22 years as a director.

Stevenson, Robert (1905–86) British-born Hollywood director and screenwriter, best remembered for his live-action pictures for Walt DISNEY. His greatest success, MARY POPPINS (1964), brought Stevenson his only Oscar nomination.

Born in London, he was educated at Cambridge and worked for a newsreel agency before joining Gaumont-British as a screenwriter in 1930. Two years later he co-directed his first film, the comedy *Happy Ever After*. In 1934 Stevenson married the actress Anna Lee. His other films of the 1930s included the costume drama *Tudor Rose* (US title *Nine Days a Queen*; 1936), about Lady Jane Grey, and the period adventure *King Solomon's Mines* (1937), which starred his wife.

In 1939 he travelled to Hollywood at the invitation of David O. SELZNICK. When the producer had asked British screenwriter Charles Bennett whether he should hire Alfred HITCHCOCK or Stevenson, Bennett had replied "Both of them." In the event Selznick kept Stevenson under contract for 10 years without using him, only loaning him to other studios. In 1940 he directed a remake of *Back Street* for Universal and *Tom Brown's Schooldays* for RKO. A year later he co-scripted a version of *Jane Eyre* for Selznick, who sold the package, with Stevenson as director, to 20th Century-Fox. The film, which starred Joan FONTAINE as Jane and Orson WELLES as Rochester, appeared in 1943.

After service in World War II, Stevenson returned to Hollywood to make the crime drama *To the Ends of the Earth* (1948) for Columbia; he left Selznick to join RKO in 1949. During the next few years he worked mainly in television, directing for such series as *Alfred Hitchcock Presents* and *General Electric Theatre*.

In 1956 Disney hired Stevenson for six weeks; he remained for 20 years. His early films for the studio included *Old Yeller* (1957), about a boy and his dog, and *The Absent-Minded Professor* (1961), with Fred MACMURRAY. *Mary Poppins*, which mixed cartoon characters with live actors including Julie ANDREWS and Dick VAN DYKE, was followed by the disappointing *The Love Bug* (1969), *Bedknobs and Broomsticks* (1971), and *One of Our Dinosaurs is Missing* (1975), amongst many others. Stevenson retired in 1976.

Stewart, James (1908–) Tall (6′ 3½″) US actor with a shy manner and hesitant drawl, who usually played vulnerable characters. "He was just a simple guy" said producer Joseph Pasternak, who remembered him reading Flash Gordon comics on the set. Stewart, the top box-office draw in America in 1955, remained a star for more than 40 years.

Born in Indiana, Pennysylvania, the son of a storekeeper, he studied architecture at Princeton, where he also started to act. After graduating, he joined classmate Josh LOGAN's University Players in Falmouth, Massachusetts; other members of the troupe included the young married couple Henry FONDA and Margaret Sullavan.

In 1935 Stewart moved to Hollywood, where he signed with MGM and made his screen debut in *The Murder Man*. He became a star in the Frank CAPRA comedy *You Can't Take it with You* (1938), in which he and Jean ARTHUR play lovers with eccentric families. The same director's MR SMITH GOES TO WASHINGTON provided Stewart with one of his most memorable roles, that of an idealistic senator. His other film of that year was the Western *Destry Rides Again*, in which he appears opposite Marlene DIETRICH. In 1940 he won an Oscar for playing the gossip columnist Mike Connor in George CUKOR's THE PHILADELPHIA STORY.

During World War II, Stewart flew 20 bomber missions over Germany and was awarded the Distinguished Flying Cross. He later became a brigadier general in the Air Force Reserve, the highest-ranking entertainer in US military history.

Stewart returned to the cinema in Capra's IT'S A WONDERFUL LIFE (1946), a film that allowed him to show a darker side to his screen persona. He went on to broaden his range still further in a series of films for Alfred HITCHCOCK, beginning with ROPE (1948), in which he played the professor who discovers that two ex-students are murderers. His later movies for Hitchcock were REAR WINDOW (1954) with Grace KELLY, *The Man Who Knew Too Much* (1956) with Doris DAY, and VERTIGO (1958) with Kim NOVAK. In 1950 he became the first Hollywood star to work for a percentage of the profits, taking 50% for the Western *Winchester 73* (1950), a deal that brought him $600,000. Later that year Stewart won an

Oscar nomination for reprising his Broadway role as the lovable Elwood P. Dowd in *Harvey*; the title refers to the character's imaginary rabbit friend. Subsequent roles included the lead in *The Glenn Miller Story* (1954) and the aviator Charles Lindbergh in Billy WILDER's *The Spirit of St Louis* (1957). In 1959 he received an Oscar nomination for his performance as a country lawyer in Otto PREMINGER's *Anatomy of a Murder*. Several of his later films were Westerns, including *Cheyenne Autumn* (1964), in which he plays Wyatt Earp, and Don SIEGEL's *The Shootist* (1976), in which he plays the doctor of ailing gun fighter John WAYNE.

still *See* ACTION STILL; PUBLICITY STILL.

Sting, The (1973) George Roy HILL's popular comedy thriller, the greatest success in Universal's history before SPIELBERG's JAWS (1975). Much of its appeal was owing to the pure entertainment value supplied by stars Paul NEWMAN and Robert REDFORD; *Time* magazine described the film as "a lot of expensive sets and a screenful of blue eyes." Despite mixed reviews, *The Sting* picked up four Oscars, including Best Film. Awards also went to Marvin Hamlisch for arranging Scott Joplin's ragtime music for the film and to screenwriter David S. Ward.

Redford, who received an Oscar nomination, had originally turned down the script but changed his mind when he heard that Hill would direct. The movie reunited director and stars four years after their triumph in BUTCH CASSIDY AND THE SUNDANCE KID. The leads received $500,000 each for their part in the film, while Newman also got a percentage of the gross.

Set in 1930s Chicago, the plot involves two con artists, Johnny Hooker (Redford) and Henry Gondorff (Newman), who set up a racketeer (Robert Shaw) after he causes the death of one of their friends. The two create a fake bookie operation and trick their victim into losing a million-dollar bet.

During filming, Redford spied a wrecked Porsche on the street, bought it, and had it delivered to Newman. His co-star responded by having it compacted and the metal cube sent to the Redford home with a note, "Although he appreciated it, Mr Newman is returning this gift to you because he cannot get the mother-fucker started."

In 1983 Universal made *The Sting 2*, a lacklustre sequel featuring Jackie Gleason and Mac Davis as the leads.

stock shot or **library shot** A film sequence that can be reused in different productions to save the time and expense of reshooting. Footage of this kind is kept in the archives of film studios and can be obtained from commercial film libraries. It is mainly used to introduce the locale in ESTABLISHING SHOTS or to add atmosphere (e.g. wildlife scenes in TARZAN films). Other favourite topics include Western landscapes, aeroplane landings, battle sequences, etc. Stock shots were used during the earliest years of cinema; in 1903 Edwin S. PORTER made a 10-minute film, *The Life of an American Fireman*, in which he inserted stock film of fires taken from Thomas EDISON's files.

Stone. Oliver Stone (1946–) Controversial US director, screenwriter, and producer, whose films are noted for their frenetic style, sudden violence, and anti-Establishment themes. He is particularly identified with the trilogy of VIETNAM WAR films *Platoon* (1986), *Born on the Fourth of July* (1989), and *Heaven and Earth* (1993), the first two of which won him Oscars as Best Director.

Born in New York, the son of a stockbroker, Stone studied at Yale and the New York University film school. After a year teaching in South Vietnam, he returned to the country as an army volunteer in 1967. Having been twice wounded and decorated, he returned to New York in 1971 and became a cab driver.

Stone's first work for the cinema was his Oscar-winning screenplay for Alan PARKER's *Midnight Express* (1978), based on Billy Hayes's book about his experiences in a Turkish jail. In 1981 he wrote and directed *The Hand*, a horror story based on his own novel that starred Michael CAINE. The political thriller *Salvador* (1986), which he also produced, was based on a real-life photojournalist's adventures in Central America.

Stone enjoyed his first major box-office success with *Platoon*, a story of US infantrymen in Vietnam that starred Charlie SHEEN. He had written the controversial screenplay, which reflects his doubts about the US mission, some 11 years earlier. Sheen also starred in the highly successful *Wall Street* (1987), about greed among brokers; Michael DOUGLAS played the bravura role of the corporate raider Gordon Gecko.

Stone's second Vietnam film, *Born on the Fourth of July*, was based on the memoirs of Ron Kovic (Tom CRUISE), a former marine

who was left paralysed from the waist down by a bullet. The 1960s were also explored in *The Doors* (1991), a $40-million BIOPIC of tragic rock idol Jim Morrison (Val Kilmer), and the controversial *JFK* (1991), which suggests that Kennedy was assassinated because of his doubts about US involvement in south-east Asia. One columnist wrote bitterly "In his three-hour lie Stone falsifies so much he may be an intellectual sociopath." *Heaven and Earth*, the true story of a Vietnamese woman's suffering during the war, flopped badly at the box office.

Previous controversies paled into insignificance beside the furore caused by Stone's *Natural Born Killers* (1994), a film that shows an attractive young couple committing nearly 100 murders, including decapitations. Although Stone described the film, which has a screenplay by Quentin TARANTINO, as a satire on the US media, police linked the movie to six copycat murders in the first two months of its release. British censors delayed its release in Britain for several months.

Sharon Stone (1958–) Blonde US star, who in 1993 earned the highest fee ever to be paid an actress ($7 million) for her role in the thriller *Sliver*. Stone, who is best remembered as the murderous temptress Catherine Tramell in *Basic Instinct* (1991), has been compared to both the sultry Lana TURNER and the ice-cool Grace KELLY.

Born in Meadville, Pennsylvania, she worked as a hotdog vendor before attending college in the state. She later appeared in the television series *Bay City Blues* and several TV movies before making her big-screen debut with a bit part in Woody ALLEN's *Stardust Memories* (1980). Appearances in the thriller *Deadly Blessing* (1981) and the romantic comedy *Irreconcilable Differences* (1984), led to her first starring role, in the action-adventure *King Solomon's Mines* (1985) with Richard Chamberlain; a sequel, *Allan Quartermaine and the Lost City of Gold*, followed in 1987. A year later she played the wife of a Chicago cop (Steven Seagal) in *Above the Law*.

Stone's big break came with her role as the *femme fatale* in *Basic Instinct*, an erotic thriller that co-starred Michael DOUGLAS. The film's explicit sex scenes provoked a great deal of comment (as did the scene in the police-interview room in which Stone uncrosses her legs to reveal her lack of underclothing). Stone later described her "love-hate" relationship with director Paul Verhooven: "He loves me and I hate him."

Her subsequent career has been anticlimatic. Although heavily hyped, *Sliver*, a voyeuristic thriller, flopped with both the critics and the public. In 1994 Stone starred with Richard GERE in *Intersection*, with Sylvester STALLONE in *The Specialist*, and with Gene HACKMAN in *The Quick and the Dead*, a Western.

Stooges, the A popular US comedy team who appeared in a long series of shorts from the 1930s to the 1950s. The key to the trio's success was their skill at a rather basic and brutal form of SLAPSTICK; with a minimum of plot or character development, their films have not survived particularly well. The original trio, Larry Fine (1911–75), Moe Howard (1895–1975), and his brother Jerry Howard (1906–52), transferred to Hollywood from vaudeville; there were various changes in personnel before the team finally broke up.

stop-action or **stop-motion photography** A cinematic technique used to give the appearance of motion to inanimate objects (*see* ANIMATION). The model or object is photographed one frame at a time, with a slight movement or rearrangement made to it before each exposure. When the film is projected, the object appears to move itself. *See* PIXILLATION; TIME-LAPSE CINEMATOGRAPHY.

story. story analyst Another name for a READER.

storyboard A series of drawings that illustrate a film's important scenes (sometimes frame-by-frame). These cartoon-like illustrations are prepared to assist the work of the DIRECTOR, PRODUCTION DESIGNER, ART DIRECTOR, and other crew members. The storyboard includes dialogue and notes any music or sound effects required. Sometimes only scenes that have special effects or complicated visuals are drawn frame-by-frame, other sequences being covered by less detailed CONTINUITY SKETCHES.

Storyboards have occasionally been published. *The Illustrated Blade Runner* (1982) contains the script of the futuristic adventure film together with storyboard illustrations prepared by five artists. Detailed 3-D storyboards can now be created using COMPUTER-ANIMATION techniques.

story conference A meeting between the SCREENWRITER (or writers) and other personnel involved in a production to discuss the development of a script.

story editor A person employed by a film company to read OUTLINES and reports on screenplays prepared by the studio's READERS. The story editor decides whether or not to proceed with developing a screenplay for production.

storyline A brief description of the sequence of major actions in a film.

Strada, La (*The Road*; 1954) The film that made Federico FELLINI's international reputation, a realistic yet poetic story about Italian street entertainers; it received some 50 awards worldwide, including the Oscar for Best Foreign Film. Fellini also earned an Oscar nomination for co-scripting the movie (with Tullio Pinelli and Ennio Flaiano). Although reviewers agreed that *La Strada* was a 'modern morality play', some felt that the message was pessimistic while others detected an emphasis on personal redemption.

The story follows Gelsomina (Giulietta Massina), a mute, innocent, simple-minded peasant girl, who is sold by her poverty-stricken mother to Zampano (Anthony QUINN), an itinerant strong man, who incorporates her in his act. The two travel the country together, eventually joining a circus (something Fellini himself tried to do at the age of 12). Gelsomina finds relief from her virtual enslavement to Zampano, who treats her brutally, by befriending a kind tightrope walker (Richard Basehart). After Zampano accidentally kills the tightrope walker, Gelsomina suffers a breakdown and is abandoned by her master. Zampano is eventually redeemed by remorse.

The film's success owed much to the strong performances of the leads, especially Massina (Fellini's wife) who won comparisons with both CHAPLIN and Harpo MARX. *La Strada* also represented a major turning point in the career of Anthony Quinn, who had already appeared in 62 movies. The film's haunting theme music was supplied by Nina Rota.

straight. straight man The serious and sometimes bullying member of a two-man COMEDY TEAM; famous straight men include Oliver Hardy (*see* LAUREL AND HARDY) and Lou Costello (*see* ABBOTT AND COSTELLO).

straight part A straightforward dramatic role not played for comedy, horror, or other specific effect.

Straub, Jean-Marie (1933–) German director, born in France, and living since 1969 in Rome. A series of collaborations with his French-born wife, **Daniele Huillet** (1936–) established him as a leading figure in the NEW GERMAN CINEMA of the 1960s and 1970s. Straub, who left France for Germany in 1958 in order to evade conscription, made his first shorts in the early 1960s with Huillet acting as co-writer and co-editor; from 1974 she was also his co-director. Their first feature film was *Chronicle of Anna Magdalena Bach* (1967), an austere portrayal of the life of Bach. The visual and intellectual clarity of this and subsequent films quickly won the Straubs a reputation as the 'film-maker's film-makers' and most German alternative cinema of the late 1960s and early 1970s bore their stamp.

Othon (1969) used a play by Corneille to explore the relationship between culture and communication, while *History Lessons* (1972) was a provocative political meditation based on an unfinished novel by Brecht. *Moses and Aaron* (1974) was a screen version of Schoenberg's opera and *The Dogs of Sinai* (1976) drew on a novel by the Italian Marxist Franco Fortini. Later films have included *From the Cloud to the Resistance* (1979), an imaginative evocation of the history of an Italian village, and *Class Relations* (1983), based on a novel by Kafka. Despite their wide influence, their uncompromising style has precluded success in the commercial cinema.

Streep, Meryl (Mary Louise Streep; 1949–) Distinguished US actress with a talent for accents. She won Oscars for her supporting role in *Kramer vs. Kramer* (1979) and as the lead in *Sophie's Choice* (1982). In 1985 she was the most popular actress at the US box office.

Streep's father worked for a pharmaceutical company and her mother owned a graphics shop. Born in New Jersey, she took voice lessons from the age of 12, studied drama at Vassar College, and earned a master's degree at the Yale School of Drama. After appearances on Broadway, she joined the New York Shakespeare Festival in 1976 and a year later made her film debut with a small part in *Julia*.

In 1978 Streep played the important supporting role of Christopher Walken's love interest in *The Deer Hunter*, a part that brought her an Oscar nomination. Later

that year her starring role in the TV drama *Holocaust* won her an Emmy, which she refused on the grounds that actors should not be made to compete against one another. This did not prevent her from accepting the Oscar for *Kramer vs. Kramer*, in which she played a wife who deserts her husband (Dustin HOFFMAN) and son. A BAFTA Award and a third Oscar nomination followed for her performance in Karel REISZ's *The French Lieutenant's Woman* (1981), in which she demonstrated a flawless English accent.

She then adopted a Polish accent for her Oscar-winning portrayal of an Auschwitz survivor in *Sophie's Choice*. Director Alan PAKULA had already cast an unknown Polish actress in the lead, but Streep stormed into his office and "more or less threw myself on the floor and begged him to let me play Sophie."

Movies of the later 1980s included *Out of Africa* (1985), in which she played the writer Karen Blixen (with a Danish accent), the sombre *Ironweed* (1987), which brought Oscar nominations to both Streep and her co-star Jack NICHOLSON, and *A Cry in the Dark* (1989), about the famous 'Dingo baby' murder case in Australia. The flop *Death Becomes Her* (1992), with Bruce WILLIS and Goldie HAWN, was followed by *The House of the Spirits* (1993), with Wynona RYDER, and *The River Wild* (1994), an adventure film.

Streisand, Barbra (1942–) US singer, actress, director, and producer. Despite her lack of conventional good looks, she was among the leading draws at the US box office in the 1970s. Although Streisand has a reputation as a tyrant on set – she has been described by one victim as "a cross between Groucho MARX and a Sherman tank" – she herself dismisses such criticism as "pure sexism". She was married to the actor Elliott Gould from 1963 to 1971.

Born in Brooklyn, Streisand was raised by her grandmother after the early death of her father. She worked in a Chinese restaurant before winning a talent contest at the age of 18. Only a year after making her stage debut in revue, Streisand won the lead in the Broadway musical *I Can Get It for You Wholesale* (1962) in which she co-starred with Gould. She went on to achieve star status playing the comedienne Fanny Brice in the musical *Funny Girl* (1964), a hit in both New York and London.

Streisand made her screen debut, one of the most successful ever, in William WYLER's 1968 film version of *Funny Girl*. The role brought her an Oscar as Best Actress. A year later, she played the title character in the musical *Hello Dolly!*, a role in which many thought her miscast. At one point during the stressful shoot, co-star Walter MATTHAU informed her "I have more talent in my smallest fart than you have in your entire body."

After starring in Vincente MINNELLI's *On a Clear Day You Can See Forever* (1969), Streisand took non-singing roles in *The Owl and the Pussycat* (1973) and *What's up Doc?* (1972), with Ryan O'NEAL. Although *Up the Sandbox* (1973) was a flop, her career recovered with Sydney POLLACK's nostalgic *The Way We Were* (1973), in which she played the left-wing wife of a wealthy novelist (Robert REDFORD). Unfortunately both stars wanted to be photographed exclusively from the left; as Streisand refused to compromise, Redford's facial moles are displayed throughout the film. He later described her as "very talented, intelligent, insecure, and untrusting."

In 1975 Streisand and her boyfriend, Jon Peters, produced *Funny Lady*, a sequel to *Funny Girl*. Her next film, a rock version of George CUKOR's classic A STAR IS BORN (1977), teamed her with Kris Kristofferson, who disliked her take-charge style so much that he spent much of the shoot half-drunk and even considered retiring. The *Village Voice* called the movie "a bore is starred."

With *Yentl* (1983), in which she also took the lead, Streisand became the first woman to co-write, direct, and produce a film. She had bought the rights to Isaac Bashevis Singer's story of a girl who disguises herself as a boy in order to become a rabbi as early as 1974, but all the major studios turned it down. Streisand then became the first woman to earn $5 million for a film with *Nuts* (1987). She earned even more from the melodrama *The Prince of Tides* (1991), a film she both directed and starred in. It received an Oscar nomination as Best Picture.

In 1994 Streisand announced that she was giving up live performances because they were too stressful.

To know her is not necessarily to love her.
REX REED.

Stroheim, Erich von *See* VON STROHEIM, ERICH.

studio (1) A stage, building, or complex in which films are produced. (2) A company that produces, finances, or distributes a film.

studio system The methods of production and distribution employed by the major Hollywood film factories in their heyday, roughly the 1920s until the 1950s. The system had two main characteristics; firstly, 'vertical integration' in the chain of distribution, giving the studios a guaranteed outlet for their product; secondly, the industrialization of the film-making process, leading to the development of specialist units and a clear chain of command with the producer at the top.

Vertical integration began quite early. Owing to the restrictive activities of the MOTION PICTURE PATENTS COMPANY in the 1910s, independent theatres soon began to look for alternative sources of product. Some began to import films from Europe (ones with sex being very popular), other bought EXCHANGES to ensure a quick turnaround of product, while still others decided to compete directly with the MPPC by making their own films. Owing to the vigilance of the MPPC, independent film-making had to be carried out far from New York, with Los Angeles gradually emerging as the main centre for production.

The years 1912 to 1918 saw the establishment of all the companies that were to emerge as the major Hollywood studios (Universal, Fox, Warner Brothers, and Paramount, as well as Metro, Mutual, and CBC, which became MGM, RKO, and Columbia, respectively). After the war most studios adopted a vigorous acquisitions policy to take advantage of economies of scale. The crucial shake-up was in 1927; with the introduction of SOUND, producers or exhibitors who could not afford the change went bankrupt and those that survived took a firm grip on the industry. Foreign-language competition was also wiped out. By 1930 75% of the US market belonged to the seven majors and United Artists, with three other studios (Disney, Monogram, and Republic) holding much of the rest. The price of re-equipment and expansion was an increased reliance on Wall Street finance, which led in turn to a growing emphasis on production-line techniques in film-making.

The production methods of the major studios were largely based on those pioneered by Thomas H. INCE in the 1910s.

Operating from Inceville, Hollywood, one of the first studio complexes, he exercised tight control over all aspects of the film-making process, writing the scripts and production guidelines himself, as well as finalizing the choice of cast, costume, and settings. Most importantly, Ince, who designated himself the 'producer' of his films, retained tight control of the budget. Another innovation was the development of specialist departments such as costumes and special effects; in this way, costs were offset by the volume of production and scope for recycling. Despite some stream-lining, the system designed by Ince remained little changed until the studio system broke down in the 1950s.

The studio age ended as it began, with a rebellion against the monopoly of the producers. In 1948 an anti-trust suit forced Paramount to divest itself of its theatres; the other studios were obliged to follow suit soon after. The result was to open up the market to INDEPENDENT FILM-MAKERS at a time when the studios also faced a powerful competitor in the form of TV. During the 1950s the major studios gradually shut down their specialist departments, sold studio lots for real estate, and re-emerged as film packaging and distributing companies.

In some ways, the achievements of the studio system have been overrated. While many excellent films were produced, these amount to a tiny fraction of movies released during these years (even if the vast B production is discounted). Moreover, given the talent, money, and technical resources available, it would be surprising if good films were not occasionally made. Although production values were always high, content was too often predictable, the vast majority of studio films being formulaic genre pictures designed according to narrow ideas of marketability. Nevertheless, the output of Hollywood in these years has established the popular image of cinema for most people.

stuntman or **stuntwoman** A skilled performer who stands in for one of the leads in the dangerous scenes in a movie. Many early stars risked their own lives in stunts, taking pride in handling difficult work or cooperating with a director's passion for realism. D. W. GRIFFITH floated Lillian GISH on a drifting ice chunk in *Way Down East* (1920), a daring scene that almost cost her her right hand. The comedian Harold LLOYD

dislocated his shoulder during the making of *Safety Last* (1923), when he hung from the top of a 12-storey building with only a projecting mattress for protection. Stuntmen, too, have been seriously injured or even killed by stunts that misfired, as, for example, when a helicopter was brought down by ground explosions during filming of *Twilight Zone: The Movie* (1983). Stuntmen have become recognized macho figures in America and are the subject of at least one major film, *Hooper* (1978), starring Burt REYNOLDS.

Sturges. **John Sturges** (1911–92) US director, especially of Westerns and adventure films. Noted for his location work and his use of very few takes during shooting, Sturges received an Oscar nomination for *Bad Day at Black Rock* (1954), set in the modern West.

Born in Oak Park, Illinois, he began his film career with RKO, where he worked as an artist and editor from 1932. During World War II he made documentary and training films in the Air Corps, on one occasion co-directing with William WYLER. On his return to Hollywood, Sturges signed with Columbia and made his feature debut with *The Man Who Dared* (1946). After moving to MGM in 1949 he began to concentrate on Westerns, beginning with *Escape from Fort Bravo* (1953), a film shot in Death Valley and starring William HOLDEN. This was followed by the excellent *Bad Day at Black Rock*, in which Spencer TRACY avenges wartime injustices to a Japanese-American.

In the late 1950s Sturges made several films for Paramount, including GUNFIGHT AT THE O.K. CORRAL (1957), with Burt LANCASTER as Wyatt Earp and Kirk DOUGLAS as Doc Holliday, and *The Last Train from Gun Hill* (1959), again with Douglas. Sturges then set up as an independent producer-director to make the *The Magnificent Seven* (1960), a Western reworking of KUROSAWA'S THE SEVEN SAMURAI with Yul BRYNNER and Steve MCQUEEN. He enjoyed another triumph with McQueen in the World-War-II adventure *The Great Escape* (1963).

In the late 1960s Sturges gave up producing but continued to direct Hollywood's top action stars in such films as the COLD WAR thriller *Ice Station Zebra* (1968) with Rock HUDSON, the astronaut film *Marooned* (1969) with Gregory PECK, *Joe Kidd* (1972) with Clint EASTWOOD as a bounty hunter, and *McQ* (1974) with John WAYNE as a police detective. Sturges's last movie was the successful wartime thriller *The Eagle Has Landed* (1976), with Michael CAINE and Donald SUTHERLAND.

Preston Sturges (Edmund Preston Biden Jnr; 1898–1959) US director and screenwriter, who brought new seriousness to the tradition of SCREWBALL COMEDY in the 1940s. His irreverent iconoclastic style has been described as "CAPRA with the gloves off."

Sturges was born into a rich family in Chicago. Following the separation of his parents, he moved with his mother to Paris and took the name of her second husband. He began to manage his mother's cosmetics firm at the age of 16; after service in the Air Corps during World War I, he returned to invent the first 'kissproof' lipstick.

In 1927 Sturges wrote his first play while convalescing after an appendicectomy. His second, *Strictly Dishonorable*, was Broadway's most popular comedy in 1929–30 and was adapted for the screen in 1931; he himself settled in Hollywood and began to write for the cinema two years later. In 1940 Sturges sold Paramount *The Great McGinty* for $10 (the lowest payment ever for a major Hollywood script) on condition that they allowed him to direct. The film, about a tramp (Brian Donlevy) who becomes governor of a state, won Sturges an Oscar for his screenplay and demonstrated that he had a visual sense to match his verbal skills.

The following year Sturges wrote and directed *The Lady Eve* (1941), with Barbara STANWYCK as a cardsharp fleecing Henry FONDA, and *Sullivan's Travels* (1942), a brilliant satire on Hollywood starring Joel MCCREA as a movie director who tires of escapism. McCrea also starred (with Claudette COLBERT) in *The Palm Beach Story* (1942). In 1944 Sturges had two scripts nominated for the Oscar – a feat that seems all the more remarkable considering their willingness to attack everything held sacred in wartime America. *The Miracle of Morgan's Creek* (1944), a truly manic comedy starring Betty Hutton as a single mother, provoked James AGEE to write: "The Hays Office has been raped in its sleep." (Sturges said that all his films were really about 'Topic A', his code for sex.) Just as iconoclastic was *Hail, the Conquering Hero* (1944), starring Eddie Bracken as a bogus military hero.

After falling out with Paramount in 1944, Sturges set up the short-lived California Pictures with Howard HUGHES; the company released only one film, the unsuccessful Harold LLOYD comeback *Mad Wednesday* (1946), which was produced, written, and directed by Sturges. After making two further flops at 20th Century-Fox he retreated to Paris, where he directed his last movie, *The Diary of Major Thompson* (US title *The French They are a Funny Race*) in 1955.

subjective camera The extended use of a camera to represent the POINT OF VIEW of a participant in a scene. While subjective camera can help an audience to identify with a character, if overused it risks disorientating viewers used to the physical presence of a character on screen. Robert Montgomery's *The Lady in the Lake* (1946) is shot entirely from the point of view of its protagonist (glimpsed at one point in a mirror), while in *Dark Passage* (1947) Humphrey BOGART is only revealed to the camera after his successful plastic surgery an hour into the film.

subtitle The written dialogue superimposed at the bottom of a print to translate a foreign-language film. *See also* CAPTION; INTERTITLE; TITLE.

sunset. Sunset Boulevard The famous Hollywood thoroughfare known as *the Strip*, once the centre of the movie colony and still the best-known street in Los Angeles. It has been immortalized by Billy WILDER's Hollywood drama SUNSET BOULEVARD (1950).

The thoroughfare existed before Hollywood, being part of the original Los Angeles suburb of Cahuenga Valley. It runs more than 20 miles east-west from Dodger Stadium, through Hollywood and Beverly Hills, before meeting the ocean at Topanga Beach.

The first film studio in Hollywood, the Nester Film Company, was established on Sunset Boulevard in 1911; a year later, the Universal Film Manufacturing Company opened across the street. In 1913 the Mutual Film Corporation with its star director D. W. GRIFFITH located in East Hollywood, at the intersection of Sunset and Hollywood Boulevards. Griffith's epics, BIRTH OF A NATION (1915) and INTOLERANCE (1916) were both made on the site. Charlie CHAPLIN and his brother Sydney bought an estate at Sunset and La Brea Avenue in 1917 and lived there with their mother. The Chaplin

Studio was built behind the house the following year.

The Hollywood section of Sunset is today a strange mixture of expensive restaurants, cheap motels, elegant shops, and disreputable nightclubs. Still open is the legendary Schwab's Drugstore, where Lana TURNER was supposedly discovered drinking a soda.

Sunset Boulevard (1950) Billy WILDER's searing critique of Hollywood and its myths. The film, which was co-scripted and produced by Wilder's long-time collaborator Charles Brackett, begins with a bullet-ridden Joe Gillis (William HOLDEN in one of his finest roles) floating face down in a swimming pool. The deceased man then begins to recount the events that have led to his death. Through an accident, Gillis, a struggling young writer, meets the ageing silent star Norma Desmond (Gloria SWANSON), who offers him work on her intended comeback. Joe accepts and gradually allows himself to be smothered by Norma, who buys him presents and gives him pocket money. When he breaks with Norma, her suicide attempt brings on an attack of guilt, drawing him even further into her clutches.

That the film's combination of satire and melodrama works so well is largely owing to Swanson's extraordinary performance, aided by some fine dialogue from Wilder and Brackett. The film marked a return for Swanson, herself a huge silent star whose career had faltered with the arrival of sound; her last film had been made almost a decade earlier. Remarkably, Swanson had not even been first choice for the role, Mary PICKFORD and Mae Murray, among others, having been considered before her. Similarly, Holden only got the role of Gillis after Montgomery CLIFT and Fred MACMURRAY turned the part down. In addition to appearances by other stars of the silent era, including Buster KEATON and Hedda HOPPER, the film drew a brilliant performance from Erich VON STROHEIM as Desmond's former director and husband, now her butler and one abiding fan (he writes all of her fan mail). Excerpts from *Queen Kelly* (1928), a von Stroheim film starring Swanson, are shown as an example of Desmond's past work.

The now famous opening sequence of Gillis face down in the swimming pool was substituted for an earlier scene in which the dead writer tells his story to the other corpses in a morgue.

> You have disgraced the industry that made you and fed you. You should be tarred and feathered and run out of Hollywood.
> LOUIS B. MAYER to Billy Wilder, after seeing *Sunset Boulevard*.

ride off into the sunset A cliché for a happy and romantic ending. It derives from the era of silent films, which often ended with the hero and heroine riding off into the sunset to spend the rest of their days happily together. It is the visual equivalent of 'They lived happily ever after.'

super. **super 8** A narrow-gauge film that largely replaced standard 8MM film for amateur use after its introduction in 1966. Super 8 has a 50% larger picture area than standard 8 and may be used with magnetic or optical soundtracks. While still used by some experimental film-makers, it has been largely superseded by video for amateur work.

superheroes Fantasy heroes endowed with more-than-human powers, as featured in COMIC STRIPS since the 1930s. The first superhero to make it to the cinema screen was C. C. Beck's creation Captain Marvel, in the serial *The Adventures of Captain Marvel* (1941). This was the result of a deal between Fawcett Publications and Republic, who agreed to place advertising in the comics in return for the film rights. Bob Kane's BATMAN followed in two serials of 1943 and 1949, in which he was played by Lewis Wilson and Robert Lowery respectively (a movie compiled from the first serial was rereleased during the Bat-mania of 1966 as *An Evening with Batman and Robin*). A serial featuring the Phantom appeared in 1943 and one with Captain America (athletically played by Dick Purcell, who died of a heart attack immediately afterwards) in 1947. The first SUPERMAN, Kirk Alyn, appeared in a horribly low-budget serial in 1948 (with a sequel in 1950).

Thereafter interest in superheroics declined until the 1960s, when the camp adventures of Adam West as *Batman* (1966) delighted both TV and cinema audiences. Another superhero to move from small to large screen was Spiderman, as played in three big-screen versions of TV episodes (1977, 1978, 1980) by Nicholas Hammond.

With its $55M budget Warners' *Superman* was at the time (1978) the most expensive movie ever made. Christopher REEVE returned for three sequels (1981, 1984,

1987) while Helen Slater starred in the somewhat less expensive *Supergirl* in 1984. Swamp Thing, another DC Comics' property, appeared in two movies in 1982 and 1989.

In 1989 Tim BURTON's *Batman* offered a revisionist view of the superhero, presenting the title character as a strange and troubled being. A little-known Spiderman movie appeared that same year, starring Don Michael Paul. The oddest heroes of the 1990s, however, were the sewer-dwelling *Teenage Mutant Ninja Turtles* (1990). Raphael, Donatello, Leonardo and Michelangelo appeared twice more, in 1991 and 1993.

superimposition *See* MULTIPLE EXPOSURE.

Superman A US SUPERHERO created for Action comics by Jerome Siegel and Joel Schuster in June 1938. According to the story, the infant superhero was rescued from the planet Krypton shortly before it exploded and brought up on Earth by human parents. He soon discovers that he has superhuman powers, including invincible strength and the ability to fly "faster than a speeding bullet." While maintaining an outward identity as Clark Kent, a newspaper reporter, he adopts the guise of Superman to fight crime and uphold "truth, justice, and the American way." An ironic subplot is provided by Kent's infatuation with a fellow reporter, Lois Lane, whose hero-worship of Superman leads her to slight her mild-mannered colleague, Clark Kent.

The first movie versions were Max Fleisher's 17 impressive animated shorts for Paramount (1941–43), while the first actor to play the part was Kirk Alyn, in *Superman* (1948), a 15-chapter Columbia serial. Having failed to get backing for a prestige version producer Sam Katzman settled for a low-budget deal. Despite obvious deficiencies, *Superman* became the highest-grossing serial of all time; the sequel, *Atom Man Versus Superman* (1950), featured the same cast and an even smaller budget. Noel Neill appeared in both serials as Lois Lane, a role she would reprise in the 1950s television series (she also made an unbilled cameo in *Superman – The Movie*, 1978).

The television series *The Adventures of Superman* began filming in 1951, with George Reeves as The Man of Steel. As part of the filming block, the crew completed *Superman and the Mole Men* (1951), shown theatrically before the show premiered in 1952. Reeves, who had made his cinema debut in GONE WITH THE WIND (1939), found it impossible to escape from the role after 104 television episodes and shot himself through the head on 16 June 1959.

In 1978 *Superman – the Movie* promised "you'll believe a man can fly" and delivered, with Richard Donner directing Christopher REEVE in the title role, Gene HACKMAN as Lex Luthor, and Marlon BRANDO (paid $2.5M for 13 days filming) as Superman's father, Jor-El. GODFATHER author Mario Puzo adapted a script from the authors of the 1966 Broadway musical *It's a Bird...It's a Plane...It's Superman*. Richard LESTER's sequel *Superman II* (1980) featured Terence Stamp as the villainous General Zod; *Superman III* followed in 1983. Unfortunately, Reeve refused to don the cape again unless the new movie reflected his social concerns. The result was the wholly misconceived *Superman IV – the Quest for Peace* (1987). A feature of the Reeve movies is the recurring supporting cast, which includes Margot Kidder as Lois Lane and Susannah YORK as Superman's mother.

Super 16 A narrow-gauge film introduced in 1971. It has a picture area 40–46% greater than conventional 16MM film and allows a widescreen image to be created if the film is blown up to 35mm. Robert ALTMAN's *Come Back to the Five and Dime, Jimmy Dean, Jimmy Dean* and Peter GREENAWAY's *The Draughtsman's Contract* (both 1983) were shot in this format.

superstar A film actor or other entertainer whose fame and influence are felt to transcend mere stardom. The word was coined in the 1920s but did not enter common usage until the 1970s. *See* STAR.

supporting players The actors in a film with significant but not central roles.

surrealism A European movement of the 1920s and 1930s that emphasized the liberating power of the irrational in art and life. It was launched by the poet André Breton in a celebrated manifesto of 1924. Surrealist work in art, literature, and film is characterized by a fascination with hallucinatory and dream-like states, a violently anti-bourgeois stance, and a preoccupation with bizarre and taboo subject matter.

With its aesthetic of MONTAGE, the medium of film would seem to be a natural vehicle for the surrealists' interest in creating shocking juxtapositions of images, apparently removed from any logical context. Despite this, the only important film-maker to emerge from the movement was Luis BUÑUEL, who retained his surrealist sensibilities throughout his career. The shorts *Un Chien Andalou* (1928) and L'AGE D'OR (1930), both made with Salvador Dali, introduced themes that he would explore in all his later films – notably the hypocrisy of establishment institutions such as the Church and the importance of dream, fantasy, and sexual desire in freeing the individual mind. Other pioneers of surrealist cinema include the photographer Man Ray and Germaine Dulac, whose *The Seashell and the Clergyman* (1928) is sometimes cited as the first surrealist film.

The wider influence of the surrealists on the development of cinema is hard to evaluate. The strange obsessive characters and darker sexuality of FILM NOIR may owe something to the movement but it is hard to say how much; similarly, the humour of the MARX BROTHERS seems surrealistic but it would be difficult to show any direct influence. Many Hollywood films have used surrealist imagery in sequences depicting dreams or hallucinations. The mainstream director most affected by surrealism is probably Alfred HITCHCOCK; SPELLBOUND (1945) contains a dream sequence designed by Salvador Dali, while both PSYCHO (1960) and THE BIRDS (1963) contain powerfully surreal touches. The modern film-maker with the closest affinity to surrealism is Pedro ALMODÓVAR, whose sly peeps at the underside of contemporary Spanish sexuality owe much to Buñuel.

> All films are surrealist. They are making something that looks like the real world but isn't.
>
> MICHAEL POWELL, director.

Sutherland.   Donald Sutherland (1934–)

Tall (6′ 4″) Canadian actor who became an overnight star in the military comedy M*A*S*H (1970) and remained a major attraction throughout the decade. Off the set, Sutherland was a keen political activist who joined Jane FONDA in the anti-Vietnam War movement. He is the father of the actor Kiefer SUTHERLAND.

Born in New Brunswick, Sutherland began to act while attending the University of Toronto and trained at the London Academy of Music and Dramatic Art. His first movie, in which he played a dual role, was

the Italian horror film *Castle of the Living Dead* (1964). Later that year Sutherland played an idiot in the HAMMER horror film *Fanatic* (US title *Die! Die! My Darling*; 1964). His first meeting with the star of the film, Tallulah BANKHEAD, occurred when the 62-year-old actress walked into his dressing room naked and asked, "What's the matter, darling? Haven't you seen a blonde before?" His parts of the later 1960s included the voice-over for the brain in Ken RUSSELL's *Billion Dollar Brain* (1967) and a small role in the war film *The Dirty Dozen* (1967); director Robert ALDRICH apparently selected Sutherland because of his ears. Three years later, he made his name playing the irreverent army medic Hawkeye Pierce in Robert ALTMAN's *M*A*S*H* (with Elliott Gould).

Sutherland then consolidated his stardom playing the title role in *Klute* (1971), a much-praised thriller about a "very private eye" who falls for a prostitute (Jane Fonda). Another memorable performance followed in Nicolas ROEG's *Don't Look Now* (1973), an enigmatic thriller set in Venice; the film co-starred Julie Christie. In 1976 he made the British war story *The Eagle Has Landed*, played the title role in Federico FELLINI's *Casanova*, and took a supporting part in BERTOLUCCI's epic *1900* (in which an aristocratic woman performs fellatio on him).

Later roles have included a grieving father in Robert REDFORD's *Ordinary People* (1980), a British spy in *Eye of the Needle* (1981), the painter Gauguin in *The Wolf at the Door* (1987), and a White South African in the anti-apartheid drama *A Dry White Season* (1989).

Kiefer Sutherland (1966–) US actor who made his name in teenage BRAT PACK movies. He was born in London while his father, Donald SUTHERLAND, was filming there.

Kiefer's first major film was Joel Schumacher's *The Lost Boys* (1987), a contemporary horror story in which he played a punk vampire biker. He then made his mark as a member of the young gang led by Billy the Kid (Emilio Estevez) in Christopher Cain's Western, *The Young Guns* (1988); Sutherland and Estevez also appeared together in the sequel, *Young Guns II* (1990). That same year he starred in Schumacher's *Flatliners*, a fantasy about a group of medical students who explore the phenomenon of the near-death experience by momentarily suspending their own heartbeats. He was briefly engaged to his co-star Julia ROBERTS, until she walked out because of his affair with another woman. Subsequent films have included *A Few Good Men* (1992), a new version of THE THREE MUSKETEERS (1993), and *The Cowboy Way* (1994).

Svankmajer, Jan (1943–) Czech animator, noted for his fantastic and macabre style. Svankmajer was born in Prague, where he still lives, and became a member of the Czechoslovakian Surrealist Group in 1970. In such early shorts as *The Flat* (1968) he created a nightmarish world in which inanimate objects take on a malevolent life of their own and persecute human beings. The vein of black humour in his work owes something to both BUÑUEL and FELLINI. He was proscribed from film-making for most of the 1970s but continued to work underground. In *Dimensions of Dialogue* (1982), a characteristically gruesome piece, a series of clay figures eat each other and then vomit to create new figures, who continue the cycle.

Svankmajer first became generally known in the West with *Alice* (1988), a dark interpretation of *Alice's Adventures in Wonderland*. His first full-length feature, it was made in the face of considerable difficulties and with foreign funding. Following the critical success of this work he has received several commissions from Western broadcasting organizations and become a highly fashionable figure. Since the late 1980s his style has had a noticeable influence in such fields as advertising and rock videos. His most recent film, the feature-length *Faust*, appeared in 1993.

Svankmajer continues to draw, paint, sculpt, and design puppets as well as to make films. His wife, the artist Eva Svankmajerova, has collaborated on a number of his projects.

Swanson, Gloria (Gloria Josephine Mae Swenson; ?1897–1983) US actress, who was 'movie star' personified in the 1920s. "I have decided that when I am a star" she once stated, "I will be every inch and every moment the star!" Although her satin dresses and elaborate hairstyles were copied by millions of US women in the 1920s, her glamorous image fell out of favour in the Depression years.

The daughter of an army officer, she worked as a shop assistant before enrolling as an extra at Chicago's Essanay studios in 1913. Three years later she married the actor Wallace Beery and moved to Hollywood, to join Mack SENNETT. Although she made a number of romantic comedies for Sennett, she was never, as has often been stated, one of his Bathing Beauties.

In 1919 Swanson divorced Beery and moved to Paramount, where she found stardom in six sophisticated bedroom farces directed by Cecil B. DE MILLE. She also starred opposite Rudolph VALENTINO in *Beyond the Rocks* (1922). By the mid 1920s Swanson was Paramount's highest-paid star ($20,000 a week) and the undisputed queen of silent films.

After making *Madame Sans-Gêne* (1925) in France, Swanson returned to America with a French marquis as her husband; she was welcomed back to New York by 10,000 fans and a motorcade. In 1926 she set up as an independent producer with backing from Joseph P. Kennedy (father of the future president), who is said to have become her lover. She divorced her aristocrat, who subsequently married Constance BENNETT, in 1930.

In 1928 Swanson won an Oscar nomination for her performance as a prostitute in *Sadie Thompson*. Her career then took a disastrous turn from which it never fully recovered with *Queen Kelly*, an extravagant farrago about a convent girl who becomes a prostitute and brothel keeper. She fired director Erich VON STROHEIM after declaring "There's a madman in charge." The movie was never finished: a version was later released overseas but not in America, where the subject matter was taboo.

Although her first talkie, *The Trespasser* (1929), brought her another Oscar nomination, subsequent sound films were not very successful. After making *A Perfect Understanding* (1933), a comedy shot in Britain with Laurence OLIVIER, Swanson announced her retirement.

Swanson returned in a rather flat comedy *Father Takes a Wife* (1941), before making a sensational second comeback with SUNSET BOULEVARD (1950). Her performance as the has-been movie star Norma Desmond – who, when told "You were big once", intones "I *am* big. It's the pictures that got smaller." – stands as the most remarkable of her career. Swanson, the fourth choice for the part, was nominated for an Oscar.

After two minor films, she sold her name to a cosmetics line and restricted her appearances to television talk shows. In

1971 she made a third comeback in the Broadway play *Butterflies are Free*. She then returned to the big screen for the last time in *Airport 1975*, in which she played herself. Two years later she married for the sixth time at the age of 79.

swashbucklers A subgenre of action movie in which the plot revolves around the exploits of a swaggering swordsman or similar adventurer. Such movies are generally set somewhere between the 12th and the 17th centuries, with the accent on sword play, colourful costumes, and romantic idealism. The term comes from the noise made by a swordsman (swash) while striking his shield (buckler) in order to initiate combat.

Swashbucklers have long been a popular genre, partly because they provided a refuge from the usual strictures of Hollywood censorship (for some reason violence and bawdiness were always considered more acceptable in a historical setting). The mixture of action and romance also proved popular with family audiences, having a bit of something for everyone. The general formula involves a man in tights, a beautiful heroine, and her evil uncle, who is plotting to overthrow the state. Having been outlawed for his integrity, man-in-tights rouses the complacent peasantry to thwart the villain's plan – at which point the rightful king appears to ennoble the hero and marry him to the heroine. As this suggests, the politics of swashbucklery is fairly confused; while the principle of the just rebellion is upheld, this is always aimed at removing a usurper in favour of the status quo *pro ante*. While the most popular setting for swashbucklers is the European Middle Ages (e.g. *Ivanhoe*, 1952, and the various ROBIN HOOD films), the formula has also been updated to the Wars of Religion (e.g. THE THREE MUSKETEERS), the French Revolution (e.g. *The Scarlet Pimpernel*, 1934), or even later. If the adventure is set in a more distant period, the swashbuckling genre tends to overlap with EPIC or FANTASY.

The first of the great swashbucklers was Douglas FAIRBANKS, whose charm, agility, and devil-may-care attitude won him an enormous following in the 1910s and 1920s. For years he was held up as a male ideal, admired as much by men as by women. The great period for Fairbanks was the earlier 1920s, during which he produced such films as *The Mark of Zorro*

(1920; *see* ZORRO), *The Three Musketeers* (1921), *Robin Hood* (1922), THE THIEF OF BAGDAD (1924), and *The Black Pirate* (1926). These films set the standard by which other adventures were to be judged, in both the scale of the spectacle and the style of their execution.

Errol FLYNN was the next great swashbuckling idol. Good looking, athletic, and insouciant, he excelled as the fearless hero of films like *Captain Blood* (1935), *Robin Hood* (1938), and *The Seahawk* (1940). It is a curious fact that both Fairbanks and Flynn were rejected for military service in wartime for physical reasons.

After a lean period, swashbuckling made a comeback in the 1950s, when WIDESCREEN and colour enhanced the spectacle. In this era the undoubted star of the genre was Burt LANCASTER, a former circus performer. While Lancaster lacked the charisma of a Fairbanks or a Flynn, he was by far the best actor and acrobat of the three; *The Flame and the Arrow* (1950) and *The Crimson Pirate* (1952) are excellent semi-serious romps that can still be watched with great enjoyment. Although there have been periodic attempts to revive the genre since the end of the STUDIO SYSTEM, the cost of staging such films has usually proved prohibitive. Of more recent movies, those that come closest to the classic swashbucklers in style and spirit include the STAR WARS trilogy, all of which include crucial sword fights (albeit with lasers), the more serious *Cyrano de Bergerac* (1990), *The Princess Bride* (1987), a fairy-tale comedy, and the Kevin COSTNER and Patrick Bergin versions of *Robin Hood* (both 1991). However, the future of the swashbuckler is probably rosier now than for some years, as Hollywood trends indicate a return to the wholesome family adventure film with some restrained and tasteful violence.

Swayze, Patrick (1954–) US actor and dancer, generally cast in tough but sensitive roles. Along with Tom CRUISE, Matt DILLON, C. Thomas Howell, and Charlie SHEEN, he was part of the Hollywood BRAT PACK of the 1980s.

Born in Houston, Swayze studied dance before beginning his professional career as Prince Charming in the touring *Disney on Parade*. In the early 1970s he took dancing roles on Broadway, including a part in the musical *Grease* (1972), and acted on television.

After making his film debut in *Skatetown USA* (1979), Swayze starred in Francis Ford COPPOLA's *The Outsiders* (1983), a story of high-school gangs that featured most of the Brat Pack. Swayze, then 29, played an elder brother who is obliged to assume parental duties. A year later he joined Howell in *Red Dawn*, a ludicrous film about a teenage gang who thwart a Soviet invasion of their hometown.

In the successful *Dirty Dancing* (1987), set in 1963, Swayze played Johnny Castle, an unconventional dance instructor in a Borscht Belt resort. He also co-wrote and performed the song 'She's Like the Wind'. Swayze's subsequent roles include a former drug addict in the melodrama *Tiger Warsaw* (1988), a kung-fu expert in *Road House* (1989), and a Chicago cop in *Next of Kin* (1989). The biggest box-office success of his career so far came with the supernatural fantasy *Ghost* (1990), in which he played a murdered banker who returns to help his girlfriend (Demi MOORE) find his killer. More recent films include *Point Break* (1991), in which he appeared as a thrill-seeking surfer, and Roland JOFFE's *City of Joy* (1992).

swish pan *See* FLASH PAN.

Syberberg, Hans-Jürgen (1935–) German director, celebrated for his highly original, often bizarre, films on themes drawn from German history and culture. Syberberg's unique cinematic style, in which he rejects any pretence of realism or conventional narrative, owes much to his early association with Bertolt Brecht and the productions of the Berliner Ensemble, several of which he filmed in the 1950s.

Syberberg subsequently moved from East to West Germany and gained experience working on TV documentaries. In 1968 he made his feature-film debut with *Scarabea*, based on a story by Tolstoy. However, he first attracted serious attention in 1972 with *Ludwig – Requiem for a Virgin King*, a visual extravaganza in which the Germany of Wagner and the Romantics is contrasted with the militarism of Bismarck and HITLER, both of whom appear as characters in the film.

Syberberg continued to explore these issues of German identity in *Ludwig's Cook* (1973), in which the court of 'mad' King Ludwig is seen through the eyes of his kitchen staff, and *Karl May* (1974), a film that featured several well-known actors from the Nazi cinema. He adopted a more documentary style for the five-hour film *The Confessions of Winifred Wagner* (1975), in which the composer's daughter-in-law defends Hitler as a patron of the arts. He further explored the links between German culture and Nazism in the seven-hour *Hitler, a Film from Germany* (1977), in which biographical elements are once again intermingled with extravagant fantasy. The film combines live action with tableaux featuring waxworks, puppets, and BACK PROJECTION. Although described by Susan Sontag as one of this century's greatest works of art, it has also been criticized as obscure and self-indulgent. Subsequent films have included *Parsifal* (1981), an interpretation of Wagner's opera, and a series of scaled-down one-woman pieces with the actress Edith Clever.

Sydow, Max von *See* VON SYDOW, MAX.

Sylvester A cartoon cat who appeared in Warner Brothers' LOONEY TUNES shorts from the 1940s to the 1960s, generally in vain pursuit of the distrusting bird **Tweetie Pie**. Sylvester's lisping voice, provided by Mel Blanc, had many imitators.

synchronization or **sync** The correct alignment of sound and picture tracks so that any action is accompanied by the appropriate sound. This is now achieved by a variety of electronic and crystal-clock devices.

synchronous sound *See* ACTUAL SOUND.

synopsis *See* OUTLINE.

Szabó, István (1938–) Hungarian director, who emerged as the leading figure in his country's cinema in the 1970s and 1980s. Born in Budapest, he won praise for the film *Concert* while still at film school; he then made his debut as a director of features with *The Age of Illusions* (1964), an allegorical love story that made sharp comments on the political and moral state of modern Hungarian society. Similar themes dominated *Father* (1966) and *25 Fireman's Street* (1973), both of which examined the problems of postwar Hungary through the stories of individuals.

Szabó established his international reputation with *Confidence* (1979), a claustrophobic depiction of two people obliged to masquerade as man and wife during the Nazi occupation. The Nazi era was also the setting for *Mephisto* (1981), in which an idealistic actor (Klaus Maria Brandauer) makes a number of fatal compromises with the authorities in order to advance his career. Szabó's movie was awarded the Oscar for Best Foreign Film. Brandauer also starred in *Colonel Redl* (1985), in which a man repudiates his family, his Jewish identity, his homosexuality, and his friends to rise within the intelligence network of the Hapsburg Empire – only to find that he is still regarded as an outsider and an ideal scapegoat. The same theme of self-betrayal

figured in *Hanussen* (1988), also with Brandauer. Szabó's *Sweet Emma, Dear Böbe* (1991), about two Soviet teachers struggling to make sense of the post-communist world, won the Silver Bear Award at the Berlin Festival. *Meeting Venus* (1992), a comedy of misunderstandings set in the world of international opera, draws on Szabó's own experience of producing Wagner in Paris. The film was produced by David PUTTNAM and starred Glenn CLOSE as a Swedish prima donna.

T

tail-up or **tail-out**   *See* HEAD UP.

take   A version of a SHOT. The director may demand any number of these (see RETAKE), either to achieve a perfect version or to allow for flexibility in editing. On the order 'take' (or ACTION) the camera is started and a NUMBER BOARD, on which the takes are listed in sequence, held briefly before it; in this way the various takes are clearly identified for the editor.

take-up reel   The REEL onto which film is wound after passing through the camera or projector. *Compare* FEED REEL.

talent scout   A person who looks for star potential amongst amateurs or little-known professionals. Studio talent scouts abounded during Hollywood's Golden Era – as did bogus scouts, who promised to fulfill the dreams of vulnerable would-be actresses.

In reality, future stars were more often discovered by studio heads, producers, and directors, most of whom acted as their own talent scouts. Contrary to legend, few non-actors were ever selected; exceptions include the 12-year-old Carole LOMBARD, spotted by director Allan DWAN on a Los Angeles street, the 16-year-old Leslie CARON, seen ballet dancing in Paris by Gene KELLY, and the 12-year-old Indian stable boy SABU, noticed by Robert FLAHERTY.

Unsurprisingly, the best place for talent scouting proved the Broadway stage; it was here that John FORD spotted Spencer TRACY, Darryl F. ZANUCK found Gene TIERNEY, Mike NICHOLS saw Dustin HOFFMAN, and Katharine HEPBURN discovered Van HEFLIN. Mack SENNETT spotted Charlie CHAPLIN performing a drunk scene with Fred Karno's troupe in New York, while Louis B. MAYER discovered Greer GARSON on the London stage.

talkies   *See* SOUND.

Talmadge sisters   The US actresses Norma Talmadge (1897–1957), Natalie Talmadge (1898–1969), and Constance Talmadge (1900–73), each of whom made a mark in the silent cinema. The sisters grew up in Brooklyn and were pushed into acting by their ambitious mother, the wisecracking Margaret 'Peg' Talmadge, herself an actress.

Norma Talmadge, much the most famous of the three, made her film debut with VITAGRAPH at the age of 12. Two years later she starred in *A Tale of Two Cities* (1911). Under the management of producer Joseph M. Schenck, who became her husband, Norma became the most popular star at the US box office in the early 1920s. She specialized in playing tragic heroines in melodramas, acquiring the nickname **Lady of the Great Indoors**. Although she later divorced Schenck, he continued to manage her career and that of her sister Constance.

Norma's footprints were the first to appear in the pavement outside GRAUMAN'S CHINESE THEATER on Hollywood Boulevard. In 1927 she stepped, apparently by accident, into wet cement on the sidewalk, giving Sid Grauman the idea for his celebrated attraction. That year, she starred as the courtesan CAMILLE, a role that led her to express worries about the "thousands of girls who actually model their future from our screen conduct." But she could also joke about her image: when filming *The Woman Disputed* (1928), in which her character indignantly refuses money from a man, Talmadge convulsed the crew by putting out her hand and accepting the cash.

Despite taking a year of voice lessons, Norma failed to survive the arrival of sound. When her first two talkies failed, Constance (already retired) wired Norma "Leave them while you're looking good and thank God for the trust funds Momma set up."

Constance Talmadge, known as Connie, entered films as an extra in 1914 and made numerous comedy shorts before D. W. GRIFFITH cast her in INTOLERANCE (1916). A star of such sophisticated silent comedies as *Polly of the Follies* (1923) and *Venus of*

Venice (1927), she retired without trying talkies.

Natalie Talmadge had a fairly low-key career in silent comedies, becoming better known as the wife of Buster KEATON.

tank On a studio lot, a large outdoor pool used for scenes depicting rivers, lakes, and oceans. Alfred HITCHCOCK's *Lifeboat* (1944) was shot entirely in a tank, as were key scenes of John HUSTON's THE AFRICAN QUEEN (1951).

Tarantino, Quentin (1963–) Controversial US director and screenwriter, whose films have grabbed the headlines with their gut-wrenching violence; they are also noted for their quirky characters, idiosyncratic dialogue, and compulsive cinematic references. The film magazine *Premiere* described Tarantino's emergence in the mid 1990s as "the most sensational arrival in the movies for more than 20 years."

Tarantino was born in Knoxville, Tennessee, and grew up with his mother in southern California. As a child he was intrigued by films, especially thrillers and Westerns. While studying to be an actor, he worked as a video-store clerk in Manhattan Beach, California, and also began to write screenplays. Tarantino exploded onto the scene in 1993, when Tony Scott directed his first script, *True Romance*, and he himself made the brutal *Reservoir Dogs*. That same year he sold the script for *Natural Born Killers* to director Oliver STONE. All three films would run into problems with the British censors because of violent scenes.

Tarantino had wanted to direct *True Romance* himself, but could not raise the funds. Tony Scott's film, a critical favourite but box-office failure, starred Christian Slater, Patricia Arquette, and Dennis HOPPER, in a story of low-life romance that culminates in an extravagant blood-soaked finale. If *True Romance* re-energized the clichés of the ROAD MOVIE, Tarantino's own *Reservoir Dogs* did the same for those of the HEIST MOVIE. The film, which was made for a mere $3 million, depicts the bloody aftermath of a failed jewellery snatch with nonchalant black humour.

Tarantino's second film as director, *Pulp Fiction* (1994) – described by actor Tim Roth as "sick, and twisted, and very funny" – was made with the backing of Miramax, a Walt Disney subsidiary. When it was premiered at the New York Film Festival, the screening was temporarily halted after a young man fainted during the scene in which a hypodermic needle is plunged into Uma Thurman's chest. The film, which stars John TRAVOLTA and Bruce WILLIS, interweaves several stories involving characters from the Los Angeles underworld. When the Cannes audience jeered the decision to award it the 1994 Palme d'Or, Tarantino made an obscene gesture and explained "I don't make movies that bring people together." Although *Pulp Fiction* went on to receive seven Oscar nominations, including Best Picture, Best Director, and Best Actor (Travolta), its only success was in the category of Best Screenplay (Tarantino and Roger Avery).

The screenplay for *Natural Born Killers* (1994) was drastically rewritten by Oliver Stone, who gave only a 'story by' credit to Tarantino. When the latter severely criticized the changes, Stone retorted that the film was doing "a lot better than any Tarantino film will ever do." Unverified reports linked the film, about a pair of serial killers who are glamorized by the US media, to at least six copy-cat murders in America and France.

Tarkovsky, Andrei (1932–86) Soviet director, who emerged as a leading figure in European art cinema in the 1960s. The son of a poet, Tarkovsky made his first shorts at film school; these already display the preoccupations of his later work, notably a concern with the nature of art itself. His first feature film, admired especially for its atmospheric use of landscape, was *Ivan's Childhood* (1962), a sombre account of the adventures and eventual death of a young spy for the Soviet Resistance during World War II. Religious and aesthetic themes were central to Tarkovsky's next major film, ANDREI RUBLEV (1966), in which the great 15th-century icon painter is shown as losing his faith in the face of the horrors of war. The film was banned in the Soviet Union until 1971, when it appeared in censored form.

Less successful was *Solaris* (1972), a somewhat self-indulgent science-fiction epic that was apparently intended as a socialist answer to KUBRICK's 2001: A SPACE ODYSSEY (1969). The rather static quality of all Tarkovsky's work became yet more pronounced with *Stalker* (1979); the film attracted praise for its visual qualities but was found obscure and over-cerebral by some critics (one of whom compared seeing it to "three hours on the Circle Line"). Subsequent films included *Nostalgia* (1983), a meloncholy story about one man's search for personal identity, and *The Sacrifice* (1986), a doom-laden drama in which a retired actor attempts to prevent the destruction of the world by offering up his own life to God. Shortly after completing this film, Tarkovsky died of cancer. The last two years of his life had been spent in exile in the West. His diaries were published in 1991.

Tarzan The hero of the jungle adventures of Edgar Rice Burroughs (1875–1950), whose frequent appearances in B-MOVIES and serials have made him one of the most familiar and enduring figures in the cinema. The first Tarzan story was published in 1913 and the first film, the silent *Tarzan of the Apes* starring Elmo Lincoln, appeared five years later. By 1984, when the film *Greystoke* was released, the adventures of the jungle hero, born an aristocratic Englishman but orphaned and brought up among wild apes, had inspired over 40 films (including serials). By the 1960s the formula had stretched to include such curiosities as *Rocket Tarzan* (1963), *Tarzan in Fairyland* (1968), and *Tarzan the Swinger* (1970). Of the 20-or-so actors to play Tarzan much the best known is Johnny WEISSMULLER, who played the role between 1932 and 1948, when he was considered too fat to continue. He was followed in the part by Lex Barker (1948–52), Gordon Scott (1955–60), and Mike Henry (1966–68); the popular 1960s TV series starred Ron Ely. His female companion, Jane, has been portrayed by Maureen O'SULLIVAN, Brenda Joyce, and Bo Derek, amongst others. Tarzan's halting approach to Jane with the line **Me Tarzan, you Jane** has also entered 20th-century fable.

Taste of Honey, A (1961) Tony RICHARDSON's offbeat comedy about the confused sex lives of a working-class Manchester girl and her uncaring mother. The movie won the BAFTA award as Best Film and proved a surprise success in America. Richardson also produced the film for his Woodfall company and collaborated on the script with Shelagh Delaney, the author of the original play. It concluded his trilogy of films adapted from 'kitchen-sink' plays by contemporary British authors, the others being John Osborne's *Look Back in Anger* (1959) and *The Entertainer* (1960).

The film broke taboos by showing an interracial love affair that leads to the birth of a child and by including a sympathetic homosexual character. Richardson and Osborne, who had bought the rights to the play between them, rejected US financing when the Hollywood producer demanded no baby and a happy ending. In the event, Woodfall made the film for only £96,000, shooting exteriors in Salford and Manchester and interiors in a decaying Victorian house rented for £22 a week in London's World's End district (*see* LOCATION).

Richardson, who insisted on using an unknown lead, chose the 19-year-old Rita Tushingham to play the part of Jo; Dora Bryan was cast as Helen, her tarty mother. In the story, Jo becomes pregnant by a Black serviceman and is befriended by a homosexual art student. Meanwhile, Helen marries her fancy man who quickly abandons her.

Tati, Jacques (Jacques Tatischeff; 1908–82) French actor and director, best known for his popular comedies featuring the character Monsieur HULOT. Formerly a professional rugby player, Tati became a star of music hall in the 1930s with his mimed impressions of famous sporting personalities; he also took small roles in films by René CLÉMENT and Claude Autant-Lara. He made his debut as a director in 1946 with the short *L'École des facteurs*, which in 1949 he expanded into *Jour de fête*, the first of his five feature films. This highly visual comedy about the efforts of a postman to perform his job faster and more efficiently won several awards and established Tati as the cinema's only true successor to Buster KEATON and Charlie CHAPLIN.

MONSIEUR HULOT'S HOLIDAY (1953), which introduced the sublimely inept title character, is usually considered the best of his films. In it Tati demonstrated both his skill as a performer and his shrewdness as an observer of human behaviour. Opinions about his standing as a director differ, however; while some see his work in this field as artless to the point of incompetence, others have discerned a radical approach to film narrative in the way his stories are sequenced.

Hulot reappeared in *Mon Oncle* (1958), in which he wrestles with a modern house fitted out with a battery of technological gadgets, *Playtime* (1967), which follows his chaotic progress through a surreal contemporary Paris, and *Traffic* (1970), which makes fun of society's love affair with the car. These films show Tati becoming increasingly preoccupied with the satirical thrust of his work – arguably somewhat to the detriment of the comedy. A French critic once wrote that "Ideally, Tati would like a film of the adventures of Hulot in which Hulot himself did not appear. His presence would be apparent from the more or less catastrophic upheavals left in his wake." He ended his career with *Parade* (1974), a film for television based on his early mime act; he was declared bankrupt the same year. Tati was attempting to raise finance for a further Hulot film, to be called, appropriately, *Confusion*, when he died.

Tavernier, Bertrand (1941–) French director, who established his reputation with a series of well-crafted films in various styles in the 1970s. Tavernier, who was born and brought up in Lyons, began his career in films as a critic, writing for CAHIERS DU CINÉMA amongst other publications; he also worked as a publicist and screenwriter. Lyons was the setting for his first feature film, *The Clockmaker* (*L'Horloger de St Paul*; 1972), a screen version of a thriller by Georges Simenon. The screenplay was supplied by Jean AURENCHE and Pierre Bost, two stalwarts of the pre-NEW WAVE cinema of the 1950s; Aurenche would work with Tavernier on a number of his later projects. The star of this film, Philippe NOIRET, reappeared in Tavernier's *Let Joy Reign Supreme!* (*Que la fête commence*; 1975), a historical epic, and *The Judge and the Assassin* (1976), about a magistrate's attempts to test the truth of a murder suspect's insanity plea.

Subsequent films ranged from *Spoiled Children* (1977), about a writer who becomes embroiled in both an affair with a neighbour and political protest, to the English-language *Death Watch* (1980), a science-fiction drama set in Scotland, and *A Week's Holiday* (1980), an optimistic film about the maturing of the generation of 1968. His other films of the 1980s included the black comedy *Coup de torchon* (*Clean Slate*; 1981), with Noiret and Isabelle HUPPERT, and *Sunday in the Country* (1984), about an elderly painter in the France of 1912, who reflects upon his life and serenely acknowledges his lack of artistic originality (taken by many to be a comment by Tavernier upon his own career).

'Round Midnight (1986) recreates the jazz clubs of Paris in the 1950s, *Life and Nothing But* (1990) is an elegiac film set in the aftermath of World War I, and *L.627* (1992) a contemporary thriller about the French drug squad.

Taviani brothers, the The Italian writer-directors Paolo (1931–) and Vittorio (1929–) Taviani, who have collaborated on a series of highly imaginative films exploring themes of myth and memory. While studying at the University of Pisa, the brothers were inspired by ROSSELLINI'S PAISÀ (1946) to form their own film club. They subsequently made their directorial debut with *San Miniato, July 44* (1954), a documentary short about a Nazi atrocity in the home village of the Taviani family. More documentaries followed, in the making of which the brothers perfected their system of writing together and taking turns to direct scenes on location. Their early work was strongly influenced by NEOREALISM, a style they later moved away from.

After work with Rossellini and others, the brothers made their feature-film debut with *A Man for the Burning* (1962; with Valentino Orsini), which introduced the themes of self-sacrifice, political idealism, and subversive fantasy that were to characterize much of their subsequent work. Their films of the 1960s and early 1970s were openly political, tackling such issues as Italian divorce law, public attitudes to the Communist Party, and the solitary confinement of political prisoners.

Allonsanfan (1974), a highly stylized piece about a revolt in 19th-century Sicily, was followed by the acclaimed *Padre Padrone* (1977), a moving story about the brutalization and eventual rebellion of a Sardinian shepherd boy. The film took both the Palm d'Or and the International Critics' Prize at Cannes. The brothers consolidated their success with *The Night of the Shooting Stars* (1982), a tragicomedy celebrating Italian resistance to the Nazis during World War II. The diversity and confusion of life provided the central theme for *Kaos* (1984), a film based on several short stories by Pirandello, while *Good Morning, Babylon* (1987), about the experiences of two Italian brothers who travel to Hollywood to work on the giant sets of D. W. GRIFFITHS'S INTOLERANCE, reflected on the role of cinema itself. *Night Sun* (1990) and the family saga *Fiorile*

(1993) have a more fatalistic tone than earlier work.

Taxi Driver   (1976) Martin SCORSESE's searing study of urban alienation, the first of his films to feature a script by Paul SCHRADER and the second of seven collaborations with Robert DE NIRO.

De Niro plays Travis Bickle, a Vietnam veteran who suffers from insomnia. Still unable to sleep after long shifts driving his cab around New York, he drifts into porn cinemas or holes himself up in his seedy room. Amidst the human debris he sees all around him, Travis meets Betsy (Cybill Shepherd), a campaign worker for presidential candidate Leonard Harris. However, any hopes that she will relieve his ennui are dashed when she rejects him for taking her to a blue movie on their first date. Instead, he switches his attention to teen prostitute Iris (Jodie FOSTER), and determines to sever her ties from pimp (Harvey KEITEL) at any cost.

Described by critic Pauline KAEL as a "tabloid version" of Dostoevski's *Notes from the Underground*, *Taxi Driver* was allegedly based on the diaries of would-be killer Arthur Bremer. Critics were divided as to whether the climactic bloodbath was gratuitous excess or a blistering comment on modern America. However, the combination of Bernard Herrmann's chilling score (his last; he died the day after it was finished) and the dazzling editing of Marcia Lucas, Tom Rolf, and Melvin Shapiro gave it an undeniable power. Ironically, Bickle's brutal outburst results in his glorification by the media as an avenging angel.

Although Scorsese and cinematographer Michael Chapman gave the neon-lit city a menace not equalled since the heyday of FILM NOIR, *Taxi Driver* is very much De Niro's film. He dominates the screen throughout, and makes his "You lookin' at me? You lookin' at *me*?" one of the most intimidating lines in cinema history. Uncharacteristically, the actor who has become legendary for the exacting lengths to which he will go to change his appearance allowed the make-up team to create the famous Mohican cut he sported as he hunted down the 'animals' at the end of the picture.

Taxi Driver won the Palme d'Or at Cannes and earned Scorsese and De Niro awards from the New York Film Critics. Despite nominations for Best Picture, Best Actor (De Niro), and Best Actress (Foster), the film was too dangerous to be an Oscar winner.

Taylor.   Elizabeth Taylor (1932–   ) British-born Hollywood actress renowned for her striking beauty and impromptu marriages. "I have the face and body of a woman and the mind of a child" she once said. Taylor, an MGM star for 20 years, was the top US box-office draw in 1961; she became the first actress to earn $1 million for one film with *Cleopatra* (1963).

Taylor was married to hotelier Nick Hilton for a few months in 1949, actor Michael Wilding from 1952 to 1957, showman Mike Todd in 1957–58 (he died in an air crash), singer Eddie Fisher (the best man at her previous wedding) from 1959 to 1964, actor Richard BURTON from 1964 to 1974 and again in 1975–76, and Senator John Warner from 1978 to 1981 (Taylor's 'fat period'). She married her current husband, a former truck driver called Larry Fortensky, in 1991.

Taylor was born in London to US parents – her father an art dealer and her mother an actress. At the age of three, she danced before the royal family. Having returned to America with her family on the outbreak of war, she made her film debut in Universal's *There's One Born Every Minute* in 1942. She signed with MGM a year later and emerged as a popular child star in *Lassie Come Home* (1943) and the much-loved *National Velvet* (1944).

Unlike most juvenile stars, Taylor suffered no awkward period, enjoying continuing success as a teenager in *A Date With Judy* (1948) and *Little Women* (1949). Her first adult role came in the comedy *The Father of the Bride* (1950), with Spencer TRACY and Joan BENNETT as her parents. By now, MGM was billing the sultry-looking Taylor as "The World's Most Beautiful Woman."

Subsequent films included two Tennessee Williams adaptations; *Cat on a Hot Tin Roof* (1958), in which she plays the unsatisfied wife of Paul NEWMAN, and *Suddenly, Last Summer* (1959). Both films brought her Oscar nominations as Best Actress. She then won the Oscar for playing a prostitute in *Butterfield 8* (1960) – a decision widely thought to be influenced by fears that the star was dying of pneumonia. (Over the years, Taylor's fragile health required more than 30 operations.)

Taylor began her stormy romance with Richard Burton when the two appeared together in the $43-million spectacular *Cleopatra* (1963). Their other movies include *The VIPs* (1963), *The Sandpiper* (1965), and Mike NICHOLS's *Who's Afraid of Virginia Woolf?* (1966), which earned Taylor her second Oscar. A year later she celebrated her 40th birthday with a weekend party in Monaco with Princess Grace. Burton gave her a $50,000 diamond pendant and declared proudly "She went over it with a magnifying glass."

Taylor's later roles include an ageing actress in *A Little Night Music* (1976) and an aged one in *The Mirror Crack'd* (1981); her appearance in the latter was compared by one critic to a "pharaonic mummy on tiny castors". In the 1980s she returned to the stage in Lillian Hellman's *The Little Foxes* and a much-publicized revival of Noël COWARD's *Private Lives*, in which she co-starred with Burton. More recently, she has campigned avidly for AIDS awareness.

Robert Taylor (Spangler Arlington Brugh; 1911–69) Handsome US leading man, who remained an MGM star for some 30 years, notwithstanding criticism of his rather wooden style. A dedicated professional, Taylor escaped from his pretty-boy image (he was at one time billed as "The Man with the Perfect Profile") to appear in a wider range of roles from the 1940s onwards. He was married to the actress Barbara STANWYCK from 1939 until 1952.

A doctor's son from Nebraska, Taylor trained to be a professional cellist before turning to the cinema. After failing a screen test for United Artists because Sam GOLDWYN considered him too thin, he made his film debut in Fox's *Handy Andy* (1934), a Will ROGERS vehicle. MGM signed him to a long-term contract later that year.

Taylor quickly attained stardom with his peformance in *Magnificent Obsession* (1935), a tearjerker about a playboy who accidentally blinds a woman (Irene DUNNE) and then trains as a surgeon to cure her. In 1937 he played Greta GARBO's younger lover in CAMILLE and a brash American in MGM's first British-made movie, *A Yank at Oxford*. Subsequent films included two directed by Mervyn LEROY in 1940; the anti-Nazi *Escape*, in which he appeared opposite Norma SHEARER, and *Waterloo Bridge*, in which he played a British officer involved in a tragic wartime romance with Vivien LEIGH. He

then changed his image by playing two bad guys, the title character in *Billy the Kid* (1941) and a gangster in LeRoy's *Johnny Eager* (1942).

During World War II Taylor served as a naval flight instructor and directed 17 training films. After returning to Hollywood he starred mainly in epics, playing a Roman general in QUO VADIS? (1951) with Deborah KERR, the title character in *Ivanhoe* (1952) with Elizabeth TAYLOR, and Lancelot in *Knights of the Round Table* (1954) with Ava GARDNER. Taylor co-operated happily with the anti-communist hearings conducted by the House Un-American Activities Committee, protesting that his war film *Song of Russia* (1943) had been made under protest. Although his career slowed in the 1960s, he continued to star in such movies as the Western *Cattle King* (British title *Guns of Wyoming*; 1963) and the thriller *The Night Walker* (1965), with his ex-wife Stanwyck. He later made several European films, including the French-Spanish comedy *The Day the Hot Line Got Hot* (1968).

tearjerker or **weepie** A sentimental film that is virtually guaranteed to bring a tear to the viewer's eye. The ultimate tearjerker was probably the hugely successful *Love Story* (1970), about the death of a beautiful newlywed (Ali McGraw), to which the audience was recommended to bring a box of tissues.

technical advisor A person from outside the film industry, whose specialized skills or knowledge are drawn upon while making a movie. Typical examples include armed-services personnel, doctors, or policemen, who are often hired to advise on various details of equipment or procedure.

Technicolor Tradename for a process used in making COLOUR motion pictures. The original process, developed in 1915 by Herbert T. Kalmus and Daniel F. Comstock, involved simultaneous projection of both red and green versions of the film. The first such films were produced in 1917–18. In 1932 a new three-colour process was tried out in the Disney cartoon *Flowers and Trees*; with its rich glossy hues, this set new standards for colour film production in the later 1930s and 1940s. Classic Technicolor features of the era include GONE WITH THE WIND (1939) and MEET ME IN ST LOUIS (1944). Although Technicolor lost its dominant position with the introduction of EASTMAN COLOR in the early 1950s, the words 'technicolor' or 'technicolored' had by that time entered the general language to describe anything garishly colourful.

Technirama A WIDESCREEN process unveiled by Technicolor in 1956. 35mm film is fed horizontally through the camera to produce an image twice the normal width; this is then squeezed onto a standard 35mm print using an ANAMORPHIC LENS. In Super Technirama 70 the image was printed unsqueezed onto 70mm film. The most notable film made using the latter process was KUBRICK's *Spartacus* (1960).

Techniscope A cheap WIDESCREEN process developed by Technicolor Italia in 1963. The system uses a camera with a two-perforation pull-down (rather than the normal four) to produce an image only half the usual size but with an ASPECT RATIO of 2.35:1. This is then blown up during projection to achieve a widescreen effect. Although usable, the process lacked the definition of most systems. Techniscope was mainly used to make SPAGHETTI WESTERNS.

telecine The equipment used to transmit cinema films on television. When WIDESCREEN features are shown in a 4 × 3 format (*see* ACADEMY FRAME) it can be used to select the most important part of any image – although the results have not been found very satisfactory.

television movie *See* TV MOVIE.

Temple, Shirley (1928–) US CHILD STAR, whose precocious manner, cute dimple, and golden curls, cheered the nation during the Depression. Her success has been credited with saving 20th Century-Fox from bankruptcy. The top US box-office draw from 1935 until 1937, she received a record 60,000 fan letters a month during this period. Her first husband (1945–49) was the actor John Agar and her second (since 1950) the businessman Charles Black.

The daughter of a bank clerk, Shirley was pushed into show business by her mother. By the age of three she had appeared in a number of 'Baby Burlesks' imitating such stars as Mae WEST and Marlene DIETRICH. Only two years after playing a bit part in her first feature, *The Red-Haired Alibi* (1932), she received star billing in Paramount's *Little Miss Marker* (British title *The Girl in Pawn*).

Having made her debut for Fox with a stunning song-and-dance number in *Stand Up and Cheer* (1934), an all-star revue, Temple starred in swift succession in *Baby Take a Bow*, *Now and Forever*, with Gary COOPER and Carole LOMBARD, and *Bright Eyes*. Later that year she received a special Academy Award "in grateful recognition of her outstanding contribution to screen entertainment during the year 1934."

Temple was by this time a national institution, spawning such items as Shirley Temple dolls, books, dresses, nursery furniture, and colouring books. In 1935, at the age of seven, her life was insured with Lloyd's (whose policy stipulated no pay-out if she died while intoxicated).

Subsequent films included John FORD's *Wee Willie Winkie* (1937), Allan DWAN's *Heidi* (1937), and the same director's *Rebecca of Sunnybrook Farm* (1938). However, her career lost its momentum when Darryl F. ZANUCK refused to lend her to MGM for THE WIZARD OF OZ (1939), insisting that she star in a Fox's own much less successful fantasy film, *The Blue Bird* (1940). When this was followed by another flop, Temple moved to MGM but found no better success.

The films of her teenage years included SELZNICK's flag-waver *Since You Went Away* (1944), *The Bachelor and the Bobby-Soxer* (British title *Bachelor Knight*; 1947) with Cary GRANT, and *Fort Apache* (1948) with John WAYNE. In her last film, *A Kiss for Corliss* (1949), she appeared opposite David NIVEN. After making a comeback on television in the late 1950s, she retired from showbusiness altogether.

In 1969 President Richard Nixon appointed Shirley Temple Black as US representative to the United Nations. She subsequently served as ambassador to Ghana from 1974 to 1976, White House chief of protocol from 1976 to 1977, and ambassador to Czechoslovakia from 1989 to 1992.

Ten Commandments, The (1956) Cecil B. DE MILLE's last film, a reworking of his 1923 silent EPIC about the life of Moses. The highlight of both films was the spectacular parting of the Red Sea; in the silent version the effect was achieved by filming water being poured from two bowls and then reversing the film and in the second by reversing shots of two minature waterfalls.

At the time, De Mille's 1956 version was the most expensive movie ever made; shot on location in Egypt in VISTAVISION and employing some 25,000 extras, the film cost some $13.5 million. Oscar nominations were received for Best Picture and in five technical categories. De Mille, 75, suffered a heart attack shortly after the filming was completed.

The all-star cast was headed by Charlton HESTON as Moses and Yul BRYNNER as Pharaoh Rameses II; other parts were played by Edward G. ROBINSON, Yvonne DE CARLO, Judith Anderson, Cedric HARDWICKE, and Vincent PRICE. The film, which includes such memorable scenes as the burning bush, the death of Egypt's first-born, and Moses's staff changing into a serpent, was prefaced by an anti-communist introduction by the director himself.

De Mille's earlier version, his first venture into biblical epic, was partly a response to the creation of the Hays Office in 1922 (see HAYS CODE). Despite its religious theme and title, the film featured scenes of contemporary sin not unlike those in De Mille's earlier movies. With sets larger than D. W. GRIFFITH's Babylon in INTOLERANCE, the film cost $1.5 million, making it one of the most expensive silent movies made. Although Paramount chief Adolph ZUKOR cavilled about the cost, the movie proved a great success at the box office.

After a long TECHNICOLOR prologue about Moses (Theodore Roberts) and the Israelites, there is a switch to black-and-white for a morality tale about two brothers in 20th-century San Francisco. While one is loyal and devout, the other is an atheist whose cheating on building materials causes the collapse of a church, killing his mother.

Terminator **films** James CAMERON's action spectaculars *The Terminator* (1984) and *Terminator 2: Judgment Day* (1991); both starred Arnold SCHWARZENEGGER. With a cost of $100 million, the latter was the most expensive film ever made, but nevertheless made a huge profit at the box office (some $112 million in North America alone). Most of the budget was spent on the stunning computer-generated effects (see COMPUTER ANIMATION), which won the Oscar for Special Effects. The film also took Awards for sound, sound-effects editing, and make-up.

Variety described *The Terminator* as "a blazing, cinematic comic book." Although Schwarzenegger is given few lines of dialogue, his muscle-bound taciturn presence is perfectly suited to his character of a brutal machine-man with a mission to kill. The story, co-written by Cameron and producer Gale Anne Hurd, opens in the year 2029, when humans have become subject to powerful robots. One, known as The Terminator (Schwarzenegger), is sent back to the 1980s to eliminate Sarah Connor (Linda Hamilton), whose future son could change history by saving the human race. The Terminator, however, must deal with a human from his own era (Michael Biehn), who follows him back through time to prevent the killing.

Terminator 2, described as "a humongous visionary parable" by *Time* magazine, was directed, produced, and co-written by Cameron. When the human John Connor (Edward Furlong) leads an uprising against the androids, one returns from the future to assassinate both him and his mother (Hamilton). However, The Terminator, now reprogrammed as a good guy, reappears to save them from the terrifying liquid-metal man, who can change shapes and grow hideous metal weapons at will.

Terry-Thomas (Thomas Terry Hoar-Stevens; 1911–90) British comic actor, noted for his moustache and gap-toothed grin. As a young man Terry-Thomas worked as a salesman for a meat company, with whose amateur dramatic society he began to perform. He then worked as a bandleader, dancer, and impressionist in cabaret, music hall, and radio. Although he made his film debut in *It's Love Again* (1936), it was not until the 1950s that he began to appear regularly in British comedies. His screen career really took off with his performance in *The Green Man* (1956), a black farce about an attempted assassination. His other films of the 1950s included the BOULTING BROTHERS comedies *Private's Progress* (1956), *Brothers in Law* (1957), *Carlton-Browne of the F. O.* (1959), and *I'm All Right Jack* (1959), with Peter SELLERS.

During the 1960s Terry-Thomas began to appear in US as well as British productions, enlivening many films with either his upper-class idiot or his upper-class scoundrel act. Amongst his notable films of the decade are *School for Scoundrels* (1960), *It's a Mad Mad Mad Mad World* (1963), *Those Magnificent Men in Their Flying Machines* (1965), and *Those Daring Young Men in their Jaunty Jalopies* (British title *Monte Carlo or Bust*; 1969).

In 1971 Terry-Thomas was diagnosed as suffering from Parkinson's disease. He continued to work, at a slower pace, for several years, appearing in *The Abominable Dr Phibes* (1971), *The Adventures of Tom Jones* (1976), *The Last Remake of Beau Geste* (1977), and *The Hound of the Baskervilles* (1978), his last film. Following his retirement, Terry-Thomas lived on the island of Ibiza with his wife, before returning to London in 1984. He made the headlines some years later when it was revealed that he had been using marijuana to relieve the symptoms of his illness.

Tess (1979) Roman POLANSKI's visually sumptuous adaptation of the Hardy classic *Tess of the d'Urbervilles* (1891). Polanski, who co-scripted as well as directing, dedicated the film to his late actress wife Sharon Tate, who had suggested the story before her murder by the Manson gang in 1969. The German actress Nastassja KINSKI, whose beauty had first struck Polanski when she was 15, played Hardy's peasant heroine, producing a reasonable West Country accent.

To avoid possible extradition from Britain to America on a 1977 charge of sex offences with a minor, Polanski was obliged to recreate Hardy's Wessex in northern France. The beautifully photographed landscapes remain convincing until the tragic final scenes, in which a fibreglass Stonehenge stands in for the real thing. The Academy Award for cinematography was shared by Geoffrey Unsworth, who died during the filming, and Ghislain Cloquet, his replacement. Oscars were also awarded for art direction and Anthony Powell's costume designs, while nominations were received for Best Picture, Best Director, and Best Original Score.

The story centres on Tess Durbeyfield, a beautiful peasant girl who is led to believe that she is related to the wealthy d'Urberville family. The rakish Alec Stoke-d'Urberville (Leigh Lawson) hires and then seduces Tess, who bears his child. After the baby's death and a period of wandering, she meets and marries Angel Clare (Peter Firth), a clergyman's son with progressive views. However, when she reveals her past on their wedding night he deserts her. Alone and abandoned, Tess goes back to Alec, a decision that leads to tragedy for both of them.

Thalberg, Irving G. (1899–1936) US production executive, the 'boy wonder' who became vice-president of MGM at the age of 25. His name seldom appeared on the screen because he believed that "Credit you give yourself isn't worth having." During his 12 years at MGM he helped Louis B. MAYER turn the studio into Hollywood's greatest film factory, although the two men became fierce rivals. Thalberg was married to MGM star Norma SHEARER from 1927 until his death. In 1937 the Academy of Motion Picture Arts and Sciences instituted the annual Irving G. Thalberg Memorial Award for "the most consistent high level of production achievement by an individual producer."

Born in Brooklyn, New York, Thalberg grew up with a rheumatic heart condition that doctors told him could end his life before he was 30. In 1918 he got his first job in the cinema through a family friend, Carl Laemmle, the head of Universal. He soon rose to become Universal's head of production, showing a rare talent for choosing scripts and turning them into quality films. Despite his youth, Thalberg took a firm line with prima donnas like Erich VON STROHEIM. Told that the director had taken three days to teach extras in *Merry-Go-Round* (1923) the Austrian salute for a shot lasting a few seconds, he fired him.

Later that year, Thalberg joined Mayer's company as vice president and head of production; when a merger created MGM a year later, he became vice president and supervisor of production. Ironically, one of his first jobs was to confront von Stroheim, who was refusing to cut his 42-reel epic GREED. Thalberg fired him again.

At MGM Thalberg supervised productions from inception to completion. Sometimes his influence was decisive, as when he expanded the battle scenes in King VIDOR's *The Big Parade* (1925), thereby turning a romance into an acclaimed war film. After the operetta genre had been declared dead, Thalberg revived it by introducing a more natural style in *Naughty Marietta* (1935); in doing so he made stars of Nelson EDDY and Jeanette MACDONALD. He also invented the SNEAK PREVIEW.

Other successes included the silent BEN-HUR (1926), *The Crowd* (1928), *Anna Christie* (1930), *Private Lives* (1931), *The Barretts of Wimpole Street* (1934), *Mutiny on the Bounty* (1935), *A Night at the Opera* (1935), *Romeo and Juliet* (1936), and *The Good Earth* (1937).

Despite his impressive record, Thalberg's judgment was not infallible. After THE JAZZ SINGER opened in 1927, he declared that talkies would be a shortlived fad. He also advised Mayer against backing GONE WITH THE WIND (1939).

After recovering from a heart attack in 1932, Thalberg returned to work to find that Mayer had left him with few duties. He died of pneumonia at the age of 37. After the funeral Mayer was chauffered away with his executive Edgar J. Mannix, who asked him why he was so quiet. The MGM boss suddenly smiled and said, "Isn't God good to me?"

That's all folks! The catchphrase that appears written across the screen at the end of cartoons in the Warner Brothers *Merrie Melodies* series (*see* LOONY TUNES). It was first used in 1930. Mel Blanc (1908–89), who had provided so many of the voices for the cartoon characters, chose it as his own epitaph.

Thief of Baghdad, The (1940) Alexander KORDA's magical fantasy film, an extravaganza based on various tales from the *Arabian Nights*. SABU starred in the title role, that of a boy thief, Conrad VEIDT played the evil vizier, and Rex INGRAM was a jovial Black genie. The main director of the film, a remake of the silent spectacular *The Thief of Bagdad* (with no 'h'), was Michael POWELL.

The making of Korda's film was plagued with difficulties. In the early stages of filming, Indian and Pakistani extras went on strike for higher wages. A few months later, the outbreak of World War II meant that German director Ludwig Berger had to be removed from the project and replaced by Powell. The conflict then forced a move from Britain's Denham Studios to Hollywood (and the use of the Mojave Desert instead of Egypt), where director Tim Whelan finished the film.

Academy Awards went to art director Vincent Korda and photographer Georges Périnal, who between them were chiefly responsible for the film's remarkable visual style. The gigantic brightly coloured sets are particularly stunning. On seeing one of Vincent's early sets for the film, his brother Alexander ordered "Go away, get a lot of men, build it four times as big, and paint it all crimson." The memorable special effects include the 50-foot tall genie, a magic carpet, a mechanical flying horse, a giant spider, and a cloak of invisibility. With the revival of fantasy film-making in the late 1970s and 1980s, such masters of the

genre as George LUCAS have cited Korda's film as a major influence.

The earlier silent version (1924) cost $2 million to make and was described by *The New York Times* as "a feat of motion picture art which has never been equalled." Douglas FAIRBANKS, who produced, co-wrote, and starred in the film, bought the rights to certain camera tricks used in Fritz LANG's *Destiny* (1921), while himself creating such marvels as a magic rope, a vale of dragons, and a voyage to the bottom of the sea. To play the Mongol prince he imported Sojin, a Japanese actor who remained in Hollywood to play villains in a number of Westerns.

A third (Italian-French) version was made in 1960 starring Steve Reeves; a 1978 television movie featured Peter USTINOV and Terence Stamp.

Thin Man, The (1934) W. S. Van Dyke's sparkling DETECTIVE thriller. In the plot, newlyweds Nick and Nora Charles (William POWELL and Myrna LOY), accompanied by their Airedale terrier ASTA, go in search of a missing inventor, who is suspected of murdering his secretary.

A faithful adaptation of Dashiell Hammett's novel of the same name, *The Thin Man* was completed in just 12 days by 'One-Take Woody' Van Dyke. Supposedly based on Hammett and his lover Lillian Hellman, the hard-drinking endlessly wisecracking Charleses were hailed as the screen's ideal married couple; their dialogue is full of the kind of banter that would not have been out of place in a SCREWBALL COMEDY:

> NICK: I'm a hero, I was shot twice in the *Tribune*.
>
> NORA: I read you were shot five times in the tabloids.
>
> NICK: It's not true. He didn't come anywhere near my tabloids.
>
> NORA: You'll make me a widow.
>
> NICK: You wouldn't be a widow long, not with all your money.

Louis B. MAYER had originally vetoed Powell and Loy's participation in the film, being convinced that they were totally unsuited to the roles of a retired detective and his society wife. However, while Mayer lost a *svelte* villain and an exotic vamp, he gained a dapper comedian and the 'perfect wife', who would soon be acclaimed as the 'Queen of Hollywood'. Loy clearly enjoyed the character:

Nora...had a gorgeous sense of humour; she appreciated the distinctive grace of her husband's wit; she laughed at and with him when he was funny. What's more, she laughed at herself. Besides having tolerance, she was a good guy. She was courageous and interested in living and enjoyed all the things he did. You understand, she had a good time always.

Although the 'thin man' of the title was actually Edward Ellis's missing inventor, Powell and Loy reprised their roles in five further adventures entitled *After the Thin Man* (1936), *Another Thin Man* (1939), *Shadow of the Thin Man* (1941), *The Thin Man Goes Home* (1944), and *Song of the Thin Man* (1947).

Third Man, The (1949) Carol REED's classic thriller set in four-power Vienna after World War II. The plot concerns pulp novelist Holly Martins (Joseph COTTEN), who discovers that Harry LIME (Orson WELLES), the friend he had presumed dead, is masterminding an adulterated penicillin racket in the city. Martins assists a British major (Trevor HOWARD) in his capture, to the disgust of Harry's lover (Alida Valli).

Alexander KORDA had long wanted to set a film in Vienna but lacked ideas for a story. However, this changed when Graham GREENE (with whom he had collaborated on two earlier films) read him a sentence he had jotted down on an envelope:

> I had paid my last farewell to Harry a week ago, when his coffin was lowered into the frozen February ground, so that it was with incredulity that I saw him pass by, without a sign of recognition, among the host of strangers in the Strand.

Convinced that this germ of a plot could evolve into his cherished Viennese movie, Korda despatched Greene to Austria in search of inspiration. However, the novelist remained bereft of ideas until he dined with a British intelligence officer, who told him of both the illicit trade in penicillin and the police who patrolled the city's sewer system.

Greene's screenplay underwent a number of substantial changes during shooting. As originally written, it included a scene in which Alida Valli is kidnapped by the Russian police; this was replaced at a late stage by her long proud walk away from the cemetery and past the expectant Joseph Cotten. Greene considered this a flawed ending until he saw it accompanied by the music of Anton Karas, a zither-player whom Reed had discovered in a Viennese café.

Reed devised another piece of business that had not appeared in Greene's script – the use of a cat to introduce Harry Lime in the shadows of a doorway. Three separate cats were used to shoot the scene, one of which was much smaller than the other two and all of which bore quite different markings. The cats could only be persuaded to brush against Lime by the liberal application of sardine oil to his trouser legs.

However, the most famous addition came from Orson Welles via a long-forgotten Hungarian play:

> In Italy for thirty years under the Borgias, they had warfare, terror, murder, bloodshed, and they produced Michelangelo, Leonardo da Vinci, and the Renaissance. In Switzerland they had brotherly love, five hundred years of democracy and peace, and what did they produce? The cuckoo clock.

In fact, cuckoo clocks originated in the Black Forest region of Germany.

Welles only accepted the role for which he is best remembered to finance his production of *Othello* (1951). Following early truculence, he was soon absorbed in the project, even suggesting set-ups and camera angles to Reed (few of which were accepted).

35mm The standard GAUGE of film for commercial feature production; it has 16 frames a foot and four perforations per frame along each edge. 35mm was adopted as the international standard in 1907; both Thomas EDISON in America and the LUMIÈRE BROTHERS in France had favoured its use since the 1890s.

39 Steps, The (1935) Alfred HITCHCOCK's classic spy mystery. In the plot, Richard Hannay (Robert DONAT) is accused of the murder of Miss Smith (Lucie Mannheim), who has warned him of the existence of a spy ring operating in London. Following Smith's hints, Hannay flees to Scotland in search of a man with part of his right-hand little finger missing. In the course of his subsequent adventures he becomes handcuffed to the ingenuous Pamela (Madeleine Carroll). After evading both the police and the villains, the couple return to the capital on the trail of a music-hall memory man who holds the key to the entire mystery.

Hitchcock had planned to make a film of John Buchan's *Greenmantle* (1916) before settling instead on his popular 1915 thriller. Although little of the original plot remained in the film, *The 39 Steps* gave Hitchcock his first chance to explore one of his favourite themes: the innocent who becomes entangled in a chain of events that threatens to engulf him. Buchan later confessed that he preferred Hitch's version.

On the first day of shooting, Hitchcock handcuffed Donat and Carroll together, ostensibly to shoot their scenes on the Scottish moors. He then claimed to have lost the key and left the couple to become accustomed to their predicament while he directed a few background sequences. These proved to be more of a problem than he had anticipated, as the 62 sheep that had been brought into the studio for atmosphere began eating the sets. At the close of the day, Hitch miraculously produced the key and freed his stars.

Despite the diversity of its locations and the breakneck pace of its action, the film was shot entirely at Lime Grove Studio, thus demonstrating Hitchcock's mastery of studio techniques. The picture also confirmed the facility with sound he had shown in directing the first British talkie, *Blackmail* (1929); the famous sound match (*see* MATCH CUT) between the scream of the landlady who discovers the agent's corpse and the piercing whistle of the Scottish express is both chilling and amusing.

Hitchcock himself counted the picture among his favourites. As he told François TRUFFAUT:

What I like in *The 39 Steps* are the swift transitions. Robert Donat decides to go to the police...but they don't believe him and suddenly he finds himself in handcuffs. How will he get out of them? The camera moves across the street, and we see Donat, still handcuffed, through the window that is suddenly shattered to bits. A moment later he runs into the Salvation Army parade and falls in step. Next, he ducks into an alley that leads him straight into a conference hall. Someone says, "Thank heaven, our speaker has arrived" and he is hustled onto a platform where he has to improvise an election speech...You use one idea after another and eliminate anything that interferes with the swift pace.

In 1959 Ralph Thomas remade the film in colour with Kenneth MORE as Hannay. A third version, directed by Don Sharp and starring Robert Powell, introduced the scene in which Hannay hangs from the hands of Big Ben. It was premiered in America on the day Hitchcock died in 1978.

Thompson, Emma (1959–) British actress, whose first five years in films brought an Oscar as Best Actress for *Howards End* (1991) and two 1994 nominations for *Remains of the Day* and *In the Name of the Father* (the latter for a supporting role). She married the British actor Kenneth BRANAGH in 1989 and often co-stars in the movies he directs.

After studies at Cambridge, where she appeared in the Footlights revue, Thompson made her name with a series of stage and television appearances, including her own BBC comedy series. In 1989 she appeared with Branagh in a revival of *Look Back in Anger* and made her film debut as Katherine in his acclaimed *Henry V*. This was followed by the comedy flop *The Tall Guy* (1989), with Jeff Goldblum.

Thompson's cinema career really took off with her multi-award-winning performance as the emancipated Margaret Schlegel in MERCHANT-IVORY's *Howards End*. When the US press criticized Thompson for wearing a beaded jumpsuit to the Oscar ceremony, she soon switched to Armani, inspiring *Women's Wear Daily* to proclaim her "absolutely glam since winning the Oscar."

She has since appeared in three films directed by her husband – the US-made thriller *Dead Again* (1991), the somewhat self-indulgent comedy *Peter's Friends* (1992), and a much-praised adaptation of *Much Ado about Nothing* (1993), in which she gave a feisty performance as Beatrice. Her other roles include Anthony HOPKINS's love interest in Merchant-Ivory's *The Remains of the Day*, a lawyer acting for Gerry Conlon (Daniel DAY-LEWIS), one of the Guildford Four, in *In the Name of the Father*, and the 'father' of Arnold SCHWARZENEGGER's baby in *Junior* (all 1994).

three. *Three Coins in a Fountain* (1954) Jean NEGULESCO's film about the romantic adventures of three US women who share a flat in Rome; the first CINEMASCOPE movie shot on location. Despite its rather flimsy plot, the film proved an amazing box-office success for 20th Century-Fox and won an Academy Award nomination as Best Picture. Oscars went to cinematographer

Milton Krasner for his evocative images of Rome and Venice and to composer Jule Styne and lyricist Sammy Cahn for the title song (performed uncredited by Frank SINATRA), which became a popular hit.

The story, from a novel by John H. Secondari, follows a naive US secretary (Maggi McNamara) and her two roommates (Dorothy McGuire and Jean PETERS) in their desperate search for happiness and love. They each toss a coin in the Trevi fountain, make a wish, and have a fling. The men in the story are played by the wolfish Rossano Brazzi, the debonair Clifton Webb, and the suave Louis Jourdan (as an Italian prince).

Negulesco had already made a film in which three flatmates pursue their perfect men in *How to Marry a Millionaire* (1953), a CinemaScope comedy set in New York. *Three Coins in a Fountain*, in some ways the epitome of Hollywood's glossy breezy offerings of the 1950s, began a trend in travelogue romances that lasted for several years. In 1964 Negulesco remade it as *The Pleasure Seekers*, with the action this time set in Madrid.

3-D Three-dimensional cinematography. Since the 1920s various **stereoscopic** techniques have been used to create an illusion of realistic depth on the cinema screen. All have involved the simultaneous projection of two images of the same scene, shot from two cameras in binocular alignment, each with a slightly different viewpoint; most have required the audience to view the film through special glasses that blend the two images into one coherent picture.

The most successful and widely used 3-D system was the ANAGLYPHIC process, in which red and green images were superimposed on the screen. Although tried out earlier, this came into its own after World War II, when Hollywood was desperately seeking to counter the threat of television by offering a more exciting spectacle. In a sense, the new 3-D was a natural development of CINERAMA, a process that used three projectors to cover a wide curved screen; 3-D was both cheaper (one less projector, two fewer screens) and just as impressive.

Although the first and best-known 3-D feature film was BWANA DEVIL (1952), Warner Brothers' *House of Wax* (1953) was perhaps more successful. Unfortunately, the process never rose above the level of a GIMMICK, perhaps because the great directors never took to it (HITCHCOCK's *Dial M For Murder*, 1954, was shot in 3-D but not released as a 3-D print until 1980) or perhaps because the only advantage it offered over ordinary cinema was in the area of shock effects.

One director who made good use of the process was Jack ARNOLD in his fantasy films of the 1950s. Both *It Came From Outer Space* (1953), which utilized Hitchcock's art director Robert Boyle, and THE CREATURE FROM THE BLACK LAGOON (1954), are minor 3-D masterpieces. 3-D underwent something of a revival in the mid 1980s, when a number of forgettable pictures, such as *Jaws 3-D* (1984), were shot using the anaglyphic process.

The Three Musketeers Alexandre Dumas's historical romance, first published in 1844–45, which has given rise to at least seven major films and a number of spoofs and other derivatives. The story, set in the reign of Louis XIII, concerns the attempts of the musketeers (Athos, Porthos, and Aramis) and their friend d'Artagnan to thwart various plots against the Queen's honour by Cardinal Richelieu and the wicked Milady.

The first screen version (1921) was a silent feature starring Douglas FAIRBANKS as a super-agile d'Artagnan who leaps happily over walls and rooftops. According to one screen title, the tale is set "When life was life and men were men." Fairbanks also made *The Iron Mask* (1929), a Musketeer story in which he spoke briefly. The first full talkie version was RKO's *The Three Musketeers* (1931), which featured Broadway star Walter Abel as d'Artagnan. In 1939 Allan DWAN directed a musical burlesque version for 20th Century-Fox with the same title (British title *The Singing Musketeer*). Don AMECHE played d'Artagnan while the Ritz Brothers provided slapstick relief as the Musketeers.

Perhaps the most consistently entertaining version of the tale is MGM's all-star musical, directed by George SIDNEY in 1948. Gene KELLY starred as d'Artagnan while the musketeers were played by Van HEFLIN, Gig YOUNG, and Robert Coote; Lana TURNER was Milady, June ALLYSON the lovable maid Constance, and Angela LANSBURY the Queen. Vincent PRICE played Richelieu without cardinal's robes to avoid giving offence to Catholics.

In the 1970s 20th Century-Fox produced a lengthy and expensive version of the story released in two parts; *The Three Musketeers (The Queen's Diamonds)* appeared in 1973 and *The Four Musketeers (The Revenge of Milady)* a year later. The all-star cast included Michael YORK (d'Artagnan), Oliver REED (Athos), Frank Finlay (Porthos), Richard Chamberlain (Aramis), Charlton HESTON (Richelieu), Christopher LEE (Rochefort), Faye DUNAWAY (Milady), and Raquel WELCH (Constance). Richard LESTER directed in Britain. Unfortunately, the decision to release the film in two parts caused legal complications, as the cast complained they had only been paid for one movie. Disney released the live-action *The Three Musketeers* in 1993.

Dumas's title has also been requisitioned for a 1922 spoof, *The Three Must-Get-Theres*, a 12-episode Foreign Legion serial with John WAYNE (1933), and the *Two Mousketeers* (1951), an Oscar-winning TOM AND JERRY short. Wayne was also one of the 'Three Mesquiteers', a team of cowboy heroes who appeared in a series of 54 Westerns that ran from 1935 to 1943. *See also* SWASHBUCKLERS.

The Three Stooges *See* STOOGES, THE.

360-degree pan A shot in which the camera revolves in a complete circle. This was first used by director James WHALE in FRANKENSTEIN (1931) and was later seen in such films as FELLINI's LA STRADA (1954), HITCHCOCK's VERTIGO (1958), and Stanley KRAMER's *Judgment at Nuremberg* (1961). *See also* ROUNDY ROUND.

tie-in Any commercial venture designed to exploit the box-office success of a particular film. 'Merchandising' of this kind is now a sophisticated multimillion dollar business. In 1993 Steven SPIELBERG's monster hit JURASSIC PARK spawned such multifarious items as toy dinosaurs, posters, magazines, books, and even *Jurassic Park* orange juice. Other films to be extensively exploited in this way include BATMAN (1989) and *The Flintstones* (1994). A 'novelization' is often released simultaneously with a film, as with *Rocky II* (1979), released by United Artists as a 'fiction/film tie-in' package. Computer or video games based on characters and situations from a film are now increasingly common.

Tierney, Gene (1920–91) Beautiful US actress, whose off-screen life was blighted by a series of personal tragedies. She is best remembered for playing the mysterious title character in Otto PREMINGER's LAURA (1944).

Tierney was born in Brooklyn, the daughter of a wealthy stockbroker, and attended private schools in Connecticut and Switzerland. Her father established a company to market her acting talent and in 1939 she made her Broadway debut. A year later 20th Century-Fox signed her and she appeared in her first film, *The Return of Jesse James*. Subsequent roles included a drug-addict in Josef VON STERNBERG's *Shanghai Gesture* (1942) and the supposedly murdered art executive in *Laura*, a part refused by Jennifer JONES. Tierney then won her only Oscar nomination playing an evil unhappy woman in *Leave Her to Heaven*. The following year she appeared opposite Vincent PRICE in the mystery romance *Dragonwyck* (1946), the directorial debut of Joseph L. MANKIEWICZ.

Off-screen, she dated navy officer John F. Kennedy before marrying the designer Oleg Cassini in 1941; the union, which collapsed in 1952, produced a mentally retarded daughter. When her romance with the Aly Khan, Rita HAYWORTH's former husband, came to an end in the mid 1950s, Tierney suffered a nervous breakdown and was confined in a sanitorium. In the early 1960s she married a Houston oilman and returned to films with supporting roles in *Advise and Consent* (1962), *Toys in the Attic* (1963), and *The Pleasure Seekers* (1964).

tilt A shot in which the camera is tilted up or down, pivoting around its horizontal axis. This is most commonly used to represent a character's POINT OF VIEW when he or she looks up at a building or down at the street, etc.

time-lapse cinematography A method of filming in which individual frames are exposed at predetermined intervals; when the film is projected at normal speed, the appearance of ACCELERATED MOTION is created. Popular subjects for this treatment include the opening of flowers, sunsets, and other natural processes to slow to be appreciated by the unassisted human eye. The first recorded example of time-lapse photography is an 1897 study of the blooming and wilting of a flower by Oscar Messter; the earliest surviving example, filmed over the course of a few weeks in 1902, shows the building of the Star Theater in New York.

Films made entirely by this technique include Godfrey Reggio's *Koyaanisqatsi* (1983) and *Powaqqatsi* (1988), which give a view of life in contemporary America and the Third World respectively.

Tinseltown A traditional nickname for Hollywood, alluding to the glittering world of the stars and its lack of real substance or value.

> Strip the phoney tinsel off Hollywood and you'll find the real tinsel underneath.
> OSCAR LEVANT.

tinting An early method of adding COLOUR to motion pictures, in which dye or paint was applied to individual frames after exposure, usually by hand. By contrast **toning** involved dyeing a whole section of film either before or after exposure. In the days before full-colour cinematography, film sequences were often toned or tinted for dramatic or symbolic effect.

title Any written material displayed on the screen in order to convey information to the audience. There are several main types: (1) CREDITS giving the names of all those involved in making the film; (2) the MAIN TITLE, which announces the name of the movie; (3) the END TITLE; (4) INTERTITLES, which substituted for dialogue before the coming of sound; (5) CAPTIONS indicating time or place; (6) SUBTITLES, which are mainly used to translate dialogue in foreign-language films.

Todd-AO A WIDESCREEN process that made use of 65mm film; it was thought to offer a greater sense of depth and clarity of definition than most competing techniques. Invented by Dr Brian O'Brien, the system was named after the US producer Michael Todd (1907–58), who bought and promoted it, and the American Optical Company, which produced it. Well-known films to use the process include AROUND THE WORLD IN EIGHTY DAYS (1956) and THE SOUND OF MUSIC (1965).

Toland, Gregg (1904–48) Innovative US cinematographer. During the 1930s and 1940s he filmed 37 movies for Samuel GOLDWYN, who gave him considerable creative freedom and encouraged his technical experiments. The most distinctive features of Toland's style were high-intensity lighting and DEEP-FOCUS photography, as seen in Orson WELLES'S CITIZEN KANE (1941) and

William WYLER'S THE BEST YEARS OF OUR LIVES (1946). He won an Academy Award for his work on Wyler's WUTHERING HEIGHTS (1939).

Born in Charleston, Illinois, he moved to Hollywood to become a studio office boy at the age of 15. He assisted George Barnes with the photography on BULLDOG DRUMMOND (1929) before making his solo debut behind the camera with the Eddie CANTOR comedy *Palmy Days* (1931).

Toland first met William WYLER during the filming of *In These Three* (1936). Initially, he considered resigning because Wyler insisted on telling him where to place the camera and how to move it, but the two men worked out a compromise and went on to form one of Hollywood's most creative partnerships. "When he photographed something" Wyler later said, "he wanted to go beyond lights and catch feelings."

For *Citizen Kane*, Toland created a striking EXPRESSIONIST style characterized by weird camera angles and extreme deep focus. The stylized effects that Toland and Welles developed were widely imitated during the FILM NOIR vogue of the 1940s.

For *Wuthering Heights*, Toland kept the actors' faces in partial darkness except at climactic moments; he also used low camera angles to suggest the claustrophobia of their lives. His other films of this period included *Intermezzo* (1939), John FORD'S THE GRAPES OF WRATH (1940), Wyler's *The Little Foxes* (1941), and Howard HUGHES'S THE OUTLAW (1943).

During World War II, Toland served in the navy and co-directed a documentary, *December 7th* (1943), with Ford. In 1946 he filmed both DISNEY's *Song of the South* and the hugely successful *The Best Years of Our Lives*. Shortly after completing his last film, *Enchantment* (1948), Toland died of a coronary thrombosis at the age of 44. No movie star came to his funeral, a fact that made Goldwyn furious.

Tom. Tom and Jerry Two cartoon characters, who have featured in numerous MGM shorts since the late 1930s; Tom is a vindictive but accident-prone cat and Jerry a clever little mouse. Originally created by William Hanna and Joe Barbera, the characters are notorious for the slapstick violence they mete out on each other, while remaining indestructible.

They may have been named after the roistering men-about-town in Pierce Egan's novel *Life in London; or, The Day Night Scenes of Jerry Hawthorn, Esq., and his Elegant Friend Corinthian Tom* (1821).

Tom Jones (1963) Tony RICHARDSON's rollicking film version of Henry Fielding's novel, first published in 1749. The movie became an amazing box-office hit, grossing more than $17 million in America alone. The Oscar-winning screenplay was the work of dramatist John Osborne. Academy Awards were also received for Best Picture, Best Director, and for John Addison's musical score. Nominations went to virtually all the leading players: Albert FINNEY (as Tom), Hugh GRIFFITH, Edith Evans, Diane Cilento, and Joyce Redman. The evident high spirits of the cast contributed enormously to the appeal of what Richardson called "our holiday film"; oddly enough, Finney himself admitted later "I was bored most of the time."

United Artists, which advertised the film with the *double entendre* "The Whole World Loves Tom Jones!", helped Richardson and Osborne's Woodfall Productions to bear the £350,000 cost and reaped a massive profit. Although critics carped at the director's use of such tricks as WIPES, asides to the audience, speeded-up chases, and flickering silent-screen parodies, audiences readily accepted them (along with Michael MacLiammoir's tongue-in-cheek NARRATION) as part of the fun.

The plot follows the picaresque adventures of the title character, a foundling who is raised by Squire Allworthy (George Devine) until his scheming step-brother has him expelled from the household. Tom takes to the road and enjoys numerous adventures, many of them amorous (his lusty eating scene with Redman is particularly memorable). After escaping the gallows, he marries his love Sophia (Susannah YORK).

toning   *See* TINTING.

Top Hat   (1935) RKO's classic musical, a film boasting a score by Irving BERLIN and quintessential performances from Fred ASTAIRE and Ginger ROGERS. In the plot, Rogers falls for song-and-dance man Astaire but forms a mistaken belief that he is married to her best friend, Helen Broderick. The romance seems doomed when Ginger consents to marry her Italian dress designer (Erik Rhodes), but as the 'priest' (Eric Blore) is Fred's loyal butler in disguise, true love triumphs.

The story was adapted from Alexander Farago's play *The Girl Who Dared*, which itself bore more than a passing resemblance to Fred and Ginger's previous picture, *The Gay Divorcée*. Berlin's score contains such classic numbers as 'Cheek to Cheek' and 'Isn't This a Lovely Day to be Caught in the Rain?', as well as 'Top Hat, White Tie, and Tails', which virtually became Astaire's signature tune. Although the composer demanded $100,000 for his contribution, producer Pandro S. Berman declined to go higher than a $75,000 advance against 10% of the gross. In the event *Top Hat* emerged behind *Mutiny on the Bounty* as the smash hit of the year, receipts topped the $3 million mark, and Berlin earned three times the amount Berman had originally refused. Astaire also took a 10% cut of the profits, while Ginger had to be content with a $3,000-a-week pay rise and a $10,000 bonus.

Although this was only their fourth pairing, Ginger was already coming to resent the frivolity of their vehicles, unfavourable critical comparisons of their dancing abilities, and Fred's punishing perfectionism. During shooting she found herself at the centre of a furious row (between Fred and her agent mother, Lela), when her dress began shedding feathers during 'Cheek to Cheek'. Fred ultimately insisted that each feather was handstitched into place, although some still managed to drift away during the final take. The incident caused Astaire to change his nickname for Rogers from 'Ginge' to 'Feathers'.

Top Hat garnered four Oscar nominations – for Best Picture, Song ('Cheek to Cheek'), Art Direction (Carroll Clark and Van Nest Polglase), and Choreography – but won no statuettes. Although Astaire was undoubtedly the primary dance director, the nomination went solely to his long-time assistant Hermes Pan (who often dubbed the sound of Ginger's tapping feet) for his work on the 'Top Hat' and 'Piccolini' routines.

Topol   (Chaim Topol; 1935–) Israeli actor, whose bear-like presence is forever identified with the musical *Fiddler on the Roof* (1971), which earned him an Academy Award nomination. He also played the part more than 1500 times on stage.

Born in Tel Aviv of Polish parents, he developed an early interest in art and agriculture; he began to act with a satirical group called The Spring Onions while serving in the Israeli army. After establishing theatres in Tel Aviv in 1956 and Haifa in 1959, Topol made his screen debut in Hollywood's *Cast a Giant Shadow* (1965), about the founding of the modern state of Israel.

In 1967 he starred in the London production of *Fiddler on the Roof* as the Jewish milkman Tevye, a part played on Broadway by Zero Mostel. Norman Jewison's film version of the story followed two years later; a huge success, it took $25 million at the box office during its first year. Much of its appeal can be put down to the glee with which Topol embraced the songs, especially 'If I Were a Rich Man'. He appeared in revivals of the play in 1983 and 1994, when he toured the world with his daughter Adi playing his stage daughter Chava.

Topol's other films include the British movie *Before Winter Comes* (1969), in which he played a magician in an Austrian camp for displaced persons, Joseph LOSEY's biopic *Galileo* (1975), in which he took the title role, FLASH GORDON (1980), and the James BOND FILM, *For Your Eyes Only* (1981). He has also appeared in television movies and plays. For some years Topol has worked as producer, director, and actor on New York's Genesis Project, which is engaged in making a series of films based on the Old Testament.

Topper (1937) MGM's popular supernatural farce, starring Cary GRANT and Constance BENNETT as facetious GHOSTS haunting Roland YOUNG. Hal ROACH produced (his first feature without LAUREL AND HARDY) and Norman McLeod directed. The screenplay, adapted from a racy novel by Thorne Smith, led *Variety* to complain "Some of the situations and dialogue offend conventional good taste."

The story centres upon Cosmo Topper (Young), a stuffy banker under the thumb of his wife (Billie Burke). When a sophisticated married couple, George and Marion Kirby, are killed in a car crash after a night of drinking, they learn that their spirits will remain earth-bound until they do someone a good deed. They pick on their old friend, Topper, turning him from a drab man into a dashing rogue (a transformation that earned Young an Oscar nomination).

In 1939 Roach went to United Artists to produce a sequel, replacing Grant with a dog, Skippy, after the actor asked for more money. *Topper Takes a Trip*, also directed by McLeod, has Marion Kirby trying to keep

Topper's marriage together. The short series ended with *Topper Returns* (1941), directed by Roy DEL RUTH, in which Bennett is replaced by another ghost (Joan BLONDELL), who works with Topper to solve her own murder.

Touch of Evil (1958) Orson WELLES's baroque thriller, his first US film as a director for a decade. Although not particularly well received on its release (being labelled "impure balderdash" by one critic), the film has been reappraised over the years and is now an established cult classic.

The plot revolves around newly-wed Mexican police officer Ramon Vargas (Charlton HESTON), who is on honeymoon with his wife Susan (Janet Leigh). When a car that has just crossed the Mexican-US border explodes, Vargas is drawn into an investigation alongside the corrupt and embittered US policeman Hank Quinlan (Welles). The film begins with a much-lauded TRACKING SHOT of the bomb-carrying car crossing the border. Although spoiled by Universal's insistence on running the credits over it, the shot sets up the theme of transgression that dominates the film.

Touch of Evil features splendid camerawork from Russell Metty, a lively score from Henry MANCINI, and bravura direction from Welles, whose deft handling adds a new dimension to what could easily have been a routine pulp thriller. In fact, Welles was not originally scheduled to direct the film, being appointed as a result of a misunderstanding. Heston had agreed to appear on the assumption that Welles would be directing as well as acting; the producer, rather than lose his star, persuaded Universal not only to let Welles direct but also to allow him to make some rewrites.

Among its other attractions, the film features superb cameo performances from Zsa Zsa GABOR, Mercedes McCambridge as a tough biker, and long-time Welles associate Joseph COTTEN. Even the appearance of Marlene DIETRICH, in show-stealing form as a German-accented Mexican gypsy, fails to break the spell of this compelling film. Although *Touch of Evil* was originally released with a running time of 95 minutes, a 108-minute version was rediscovered in the mid 1970s.

Touchstone Films *See* DISNEY, WALT.

Towne, Robert (1936–) US screenwriter, director, and producer, who is also known as one of Hollywood's leading 'script doctors'. Among the pictures on which he has acted as a consultant are BONNIE AND CLYDE (1967), THE GODFATHER (1972), *Marathon Man* (1976), and *Frantic* (1989).

Having graduated in literature and philosophy from Pomoma College, California, Towne began working for exploitation maestro Roger CORMAN; he wrote his first screenplays – *The Last Woman on Earth* (1960) and *Creature from the Haunted Sea* (1961) – under the name of Edward Wain. Some 20 years later he would remove his name from *Greystoke: The Legend of Tarzan of the Apes* (1981) in protest at the liberties taken with his work by director Hugh Hudson, substituting that of his sheepdog P. H. Vazak; ironically, the animal went on to a receive an Oscar nomination.

Following an adaptation of Edgar Allan Poe's *The Tomb of Ligeia* (1965) and the biopic *Villa Rides* (1968, co-written with Sam PECKINPAH), Towne embarked upon a series of probing studies of US morality during the Watergate era. *The Last Detail* (1973) and *Shampoo* (1975) earned Towne Oscar nominations, while POLANSKI's CHINA-TOWN (1974) won him the Acadamy Award for Best Original Screenplay. All three are now ranked amongst the finest films of what many critics consider to be Hollywood's Second Golden Age.

Towne made his own debut as a director with *Personal Best* (1981), a sensitive tale of the lesbian relationship between two Olympic athletes. However, he was not to direct again until *Tequila Sunrise* in 1988. In spite of the presence of Mel GIBSON, Michelle PFEIF-FER, and Kurt RUSSELL, this story of crime, love, and loyalty was something of a disappointment.

He has since concentrated on writing. However, his attempts to revise such traditional Hollywood genres as the action-adventure movie (*Days of Thunder*, 1990) FILM NOIR (*The Two Jakes*, 1990), the suspense thriller (*The Firm*, 1993), and romance (*Love Affair*, 1995) have met with only qualified success.

tracking shot or **travelling shot** Any shot in which the camera is moved in, out, or sideways to follow the action. The term covers shots in which the camera is mounted on a DOLLY or a vehicle (*see* TRUCKING SHOT), as well as those in which it moves on tracks.

Tracy, Spencer (1900–67) US actor. Tracy was educated at a Jesuit school and originally intended to study for the priesthood. Following naval service in World War I, he suddenly decided to embark upon an acting career after an unexpected success in a college play. In 1922 he enrolled at AADA in New York and landed his first Broadway role – as one of the robots in Capek's *RuR*. During the later 1920s he gradually began to establish a reputation as a solid leading man.

It was Tracy's performance in *The Last Mile*, a tough prison drama, that prompted John FORD to offer him the lead in his gangster film *Up the River* (1930). Having signed with Fox, Tracy spent the next few years typecast in tough-guy roles in such films as *Quick Millions* (1931) and Michael CURTIZ's *20,000 Years in Sing Sing* (1932).

Although not handsome in the conventional Hollywood style, Tracy was already a star by the time he joined MGM in the mid 1930s. Subsequent roles allowed him to demonstrate an unsuspected versatility. Having received his first Oscar nomination for the role of Father Tim Mullin in W. S. Van Dyke's *San Francisco* (1936), he went on to win Best Actor Awards for playing a Portuguese fisherman (a role that Tracy allegedly hated) in Victor FLEMING's *Captains Courageous* (1937) and another priest in *Boys' Town* (1938). Tracy thus became the first actor to win successive Oscars – a feat not equalled until Tom HANKS's triumph in 1994–95.

After a bravura performance in *Dr Jekyll and Mr Hyde* (1941) – described as "Not so much evil incarnate as ham rampant" by the *New York Times* – Tracy appeared alongside Katharine HEPBURN for the first time in *Woman of the Year* (1942). Their love affair, which blossomed into a lifelong relationship, became a Hollywood legend but was never exploited by the gossip columnists. Owing to his devout Catholicism, Tracy never divorced his wife.

Although Tracy and Hepburn appeared together in a further eight films, including Frank CAPRA's *State of the Nation* (1948) and George CUKOR's *Adam's Rib* (1949) and *Pat and Mike* (1952), these urbane comedies did not generally provide him with his best roles. More impressive were his performances in Vincente MINNELLI's *Father of the Bride* (1950), John STURGES's *Bad Day at Black Rock* (1955) and *The Old Man and the Sea* (1958), and Stanley KRAMER's intense courtroom dramas *Inherit the Wind* (1960) and *Judgment at Nuremburg* (1961), all of which brought him Oscar nominations. When Tracy became ill with lung congestion during the 1960s, Hepburn suspended her career to tend him. They returned to the screen together in Kramer's *Guess Who's Coming to Dinner* (1967), Tracy's last film.

With his nonchalant mastery of a wide range of roles, Tracy is generally acknowledged as the finest screen actor of the 1940s and 1950s. No less a performer than Laurence OLIVIER once said of him: "I've learnt more from watching Spencer Tracy than in any other way. He has great truth in everything he does."

trailer (1) The LEADER of film (usually blank) at the end of a reel. (2) A short film advertisement for a movie, usually a montage of violent, sexy, or comic moments from the picture accompanied by a torrent of hyperbole. Trailers are so-called because they were originally placed at the end of the final roll of film.

Tramp, the The famous character created by Charlie CHAPLIN. The shuffling downtrodden little vagabond with baggy trousers, bowler hat, moustache, and cane is one of the most endearing and enduring images of the 20th century. According to legend, Chaplin created the character when he tried on a pair of Fatty ARBUCKLE's trousers in the male dressing room at the Keystone Studios in February 1914; film historians differ over whether this was during the making of *Mabel's Strange Predicament* or *Kid Auto Races at Venice, California* (both 1914). Chaplin claimed to have based the character's outsize trousers and shuffling gait on an old man called 'Rummy' Binks, who held the horses outside a south London pub run by his uncle. The Tramp finally bowed out in Chaplin's last silent film MODERN TIMES (1936) – although the little Jewish barber in THE GREAT DICTATOR (1940) retains many of his characteristics.

travelling. **travelling matte** *See* MATTE.

travelling shot *See* TRACKING SHOT.

Travolta, John (1954–) US actor, whose career stalled after early success as a teenage idol only to recover unexpectedly in the 1990s. His dazzling smile, black hair, and piercing blue eyes, were displayed in back-to-back musical triumphs, *Saturday Night Fever* (1977), for which he won an Oscar

nomination as Best Actor, and *Grease* (1978).

Travolta, the youngest of six children of an Italian father and an Irish actress mother, made his stage debut in *Bye Bye Birdie*, at the age of nine. After training in acting and dancing, he appeared in off-Broadway productions and TV commercials before joining the New York cast of *Grease*.

In 1975 Travolta made his name in the television sitcom *Welcome Back, Kotter* and his film debut in the witchcraft story, *The Devil's Rain*. A year later he played one of Sissy Spacek's teenage persecutors in the horror film *Carrie*, and starred in a TV movie, *The Boy in the Plastic Bubble*, opposite Diane Hyland. Although Hyland was 18 years his senior, the two had an off-screen romance that was cruelly cut short when she died of cancer in 1977.

Travolta then shot to stardom with his portrayal of Brooklyn disco dancer Tony Manero in *Saturday Night Fever*; the film combined a realistic depiction of its working-class milieu with stunning dance sequences. Still more successful was the screen version of *Grease*, a nostalgic story of 1950s high-school days in which Travolta starred opposite pop singer Olivia Newton-John. In 1978 *Grease* was No. 2 and *Saturday Night Fever* No. 4 at the British box office.

Travolta then flopped with *Moment by Moment* (1978), in which he played a drifter having an affair with a housewife (Lily Tomlin). Subsequent films included the $18-million thriller *Blow-Out* (1981), the *Saturday Night Fever* sequel *Staying Alive* (1983), for which he took six months of weight-training from director Sylvester STALLONE, and *Two of a Kind* (1983), a peculiar supernatural comedy that reunited him with Olivia Newton-John. The film's London distributors were so nervous about critical reaction that they withheld it from reviewers.

After a string of mediocre movies, Travolta found renewed success playing a cab driver in the comedies *Look Who's Talking* (1989), *Look Who's Talking Too* (1990), and *Look Who's Talking Now* (1993), featuring voice-overs for, respectively, a baby, a child, and dogs. Travolta then received the best reviews of his career (and an Oscar nomination) for his performance as a Los Angeles hitman in Quentin TARANTINO's *Pulp Fiction* (1994).

Treasure of the Sierra Madre (1948) John HUSTON's classic adaptation of the B. Traven novel. The plot – succinctly conveyed by the publicity line "Greed, gold, and gunplay on a Mexican mountain of malice" – concerns the effect of sudden wealth on three men: the ordinary American Fred C. Dobbs (Humphrey BOGART), the conscientious Curtin (Tim Holt), and the older Howard (Walter HUSTON).

When down on his luck in Mexico, Dobbs befriends another American, Curtin, with whom he shares a series of misadventures. After gathering together a little money, the two join veteran prospector Howard to search for gold. Although they soon prove successful, Dobbs becomes increasingly paranoid about his fellow prospectors, Curtin becomes ensnared by his own greed, and only Howard, who has repeatedly warned of the effect of gold on men's souls, is left remotely sane. Following some cat-and-mouse games between the protagonists, the gold is eventually lost.

Treasure of the Sierra Madre was nominated for four Oscars, and took three – one for Walter Huston as Best Supporting Actor and two for John Huston as writer and director; this is the only occasion on which a father and son have both won Oscars. John Huston appears in a cameo early in the film, as a tourist approached for money by the down-and-out Bogart.

treatment An early stage in the development of a SCREENPLAY. Based on a previously approved OUTLINE, it generally consists of a simply written present-tense narrative explaining all the major scenes and plot developments. It does not usually contain dialogue.

trim bin *See* BIN.

Trotta, Margarethe von *See* SCHLÖNDORFF, VOLKER.

trucking shot A TRACKING SHOT taken from a moving truck, van, or other vehicle.

Truffaut, François (1932–84) French director, actor, and screenwriter, one of the most prominent figures to emerge from the French NEW WAVE of the late 1950s.

After a troubled youth that involved a spell in reformatory, desertion from the army, and a further prison sentence, Truffaut made his name as a film critic for CAHIERS DU CINÉMA. He soon established a reputation for hostility to the mainstream French cinema of the 1940s and 1950s, which he considered timid and over-literary, and emerged as the main proponent of the AUTEUR policy.

After working as an assistant to ROSSELLINI and making three shorts himself, Truffaut set up his own production company, Films du Carrosse. He made his debut as a director of features with THE 400 BLOWS (1959), a tale of teenage angst in which a delinquent boy (Jean-Pierre Léaud) turns to petty crime. The film, which drew on Truffaut's own childhood, was one of the first to attract the 'New Wave' label.

Truffaut's second full-length film, *Shoot the Pianist* (1960), translated the conventions of the Hollywood gangster movie to a French setting; like many of his films it is notable for its frequent unexpected changes in mood. JULES ET JIM (1961), about a triangular love affair, and *La Peau douce* (*Silken Skin*; 1964), in which an illicit relationship leads to murder, consolidated Truffaut's reputation, while in *Love at Twenty* (1962) Antoine Doinel, the hero of *The 400 Blows*, reappeared in a tale of unrequited love.

After *Fahrenheit 451* (1966), from the science-fiction novel by Ray Bradbury, and the HITCHCOCK-inspired thriller *The Bride Wore Black* (1967), Truffaut continued the saga of Doinel (played as before by Jean-Pierre Léaud) in *Stolen Kisses* (1968), in which the character becomes embroiled in an affair with an older woman. The Doinel series concluded with *Domicile conjugale* (*Bed and Board*; 1970), in which the central character settles into marriage, and *Love on the Run* (1979), in which he gets divorced.

L'Enfant sauvage (1969) was a widely praised story about an 18th-century scientist (played by Truffaut himself) who attempts to civilize a wild boy found in the depths of a French forest. *Anne and Muriel* (*Les Deux Anglais et le Continent*; 1971), a reworking of the *Jules and Jim* theme set partly in Wales, and *A Gorgeous Bird Like Me* (1972) were also well received. In 1973 *La Nuit Américaine* (*Day for Night*), about the trials of a film crew, won Truffaut an Oscar for Best Foreign Film.

Truffaut's later films included the Gothic romance *The Story of Adèle H* (1975), based on a novel by Victor Hugo, *The Green Room* (1978), which starred the director himself as a death-obsessed widower, *The Last Metro* (1980), in which Catherine DENEUVE played a theatre manager during the Nazi occupation, and the thriller *Vivement Dimanche!* (*Confidentially Yours*; 1983). He also appeared as an actor in SPIELBERG's *Close Encounters of the Third Kind* (1977).

turkey Hollywood slang for a poorly made or unsuccessful film. *See* FLOPS.

Turner. Kathleen Turner (1954–) Deep-voiced US actress, often cast as sultry seductive women in the Lana (TURNER)–Lauren BACALL mode. She won an Oscar nomination for her performance in the title role of Francis Ford COPPOLA's *Peggy Sue Got Married* (1986).

Born in Missouri, the daughter of a diplomat, she lived in five different European countries during her first 16 years. In London, she became interested in acting and enrolled at the Central School of Speech and Drama. After appearances on US television (1977) and Broadway (1978), Turner made a spectacular screen debut in Lawrence KASDAN's *Body Heat* (1981), a steamy FILM NOIR in which she plays a *femme fatale* who inveigles a naive lawyer (William Hurt) into a murder plot. She was initially turned down for the part because of her lack of film experience. Turner followed this success with the Steve MARTIN comedy *The Man with Two Brains* (1983) and Ken RUSSELL's *Crimes of Passion* (1984), in which she plays a demure woman who turns prostitute in the evenings. Her next big hit, the comedy adventure *Romancing the Stone* (1984), paired her with Michael DOUGLAS. After making John HUSTON's black comedy *Prizzi's Honour* (1985), in which she and Jack NICHOLSON played two hired killers who fall in love, she rejoined Douglas for *The Jewel of the Nile* (1985), a sequel to *Romancing the Stone*.

Subsequent roles include a woman who goes back in time to her high-school days in *Peggy Sue Got Married*, a news anchor in *Switching Channels* (1988), the estranged wife of William Hurt in Kasdan's *The Accidental Tourist* (1989), a woman battling her estranged husband (Douglas again) in *The War of the Roses* (1990), a detective in *V. I. Warzhawski* (1991), a spy in the comedy *Undercover Blues* (1993), and a murderous neighbour in John WATERS's *Serial Mom* (1994).

Lana Turner (Julia Jean Mildred Frances Turner; 1920–) US actress, an elegant blonde noted for her chilly *femme fatale* roles. Although frequently effective, she was never a versatile or subtle actress; the direc-

tor Victor FLEMING once had to wrench her arm behind her back to produce tears for the camera.

Turner was born in Idaho, the daughter of a mine foreman who was murdered when she was nine. A student at Los Angeles's HOLLYWOOD HIGH School, she was discovered sipping an ice-cream soda at a drugstore on Sunset Boulevard by Billy Wilkerson, publisher and editor of *The Hollywood Reporter*. Wilkerson tipped off director Mervyn LEROY, who saw that she was given a bit part in the original A STAR IS BORN (1937). During her early career, Turner was publicized as the **Sweater Girl** after she posed without a blouse beneath her tight sweater; she later became a popular pin-up of World War II. At this stage still using the name Jean Turner, she tested for the role of Scarlett in GONE WITH THE WIND (1939) but had to be content with parts in such lightweight films as *Dancing Co-Ed* (1939) and *Ziegfeld Girl* (1941).

Soon, however, she began to specialize in melodramas, playing a sexy murderess in Tay GARNETT's *The Postman Always Rings Twice* (1946), probably her most memorable film, and the drunken lover of a ruthless Hollywood producer (Kirk DOUGLAS) in *The Bad and the Beautiful* (1952). In 1957 Turner won an Oscar nomination for her performance as a widow in the scandalous story of a small town, *Peyton Place*. Her greatest box-office success, the weepie *Imitation of Life*, followed in 1959. She continued to appear in films throughout the 1960s and 1970s and later featured in the TV soap opera *Falcon Crest*.

Turner's private life was sometimes as melodramatic as her films. In 1942 she married the actor Stephen Crane only to find that he had not divorced his existing wife. Although Turner sued successfully for an annulment, she remarried Crane shortly afterwards on discovering she was pregnant; the couple divorced less than a year after the child's birth. Turner's seven husbands also included the bandleader Artie Shaw (1940–41) for four months, and a movie TARZAN, Lex Barker (1953–57). She was romantically involved with moviemaker Howard HUGHES but never landed her great love, Tyrone POWER. Her life made headlines again when her teenage daughter, Cheryl, stabbed to death Johnny Stompanato, Turner's gangster boyfriend. The inquest gave a verdict of justifiable homicide, on the grounds that Stompanato had threatened her mother; he had previously slugged it out with Turner's co-star, Sean CONNERY, on the set of *Another Time, Another Place* (1958). Although love letters from Turner to Stompanato were leaked to the press, her career was not much damaged by the incident.

TV movie A film made specifically for showing on television rather than in the cinema. Such productions, which proliferated from the 1960s onwards, have generally been distinguished by low standards in production and facile plots and characterization. Indeed, the made-for-TV movie has often been seen as the successor to the extinct B-MOVIE. Despite these criticisms, the development of the genre did much to restore Hollywood's finances and helped the careers of both up-and-coming and no-longer-fashionable stars. The quality of movies made for television has improved greatly in more recent years, notably in Britain, where independent production companies have supplied many innovative and accomplished films.

Tweetie Pie *See* SYLVESTER.

Twelve Angry Men (1957) Sidney LUMET's tense jury-room drama, adapted from a television play by Reginald Rose. Lumet, who had also directed the TV version, was nominated for an Oscar as Best Director for this, his big-screen debut. Oscar nominations were also received for Best Picture and for Rose's script. Lumet co-produced with the star, Henry FONDA, who bought the rights after seeing the TV version.

Joining Fonda and Lee J. Cobb in the absorbing character drama were such familiar television actors as Martin Balsam, Ed Begley, Jack Warden, and E. G. Marshall. Although the film now seems rather stagey, its willingness to reject most of Hollywood's unwritten rules gave it great freshness at the time. The action, which unfolds in real time, was shot on a single set, a genuine New York jury room. The film also made pioneering use of such naturalistic devices as overlapping dialogue, sniffs and coughs, and lines spoken or muttered off camera.

The story is set in a New York City court on a sweltering day, with the members of the jury (identified only by number) eager to bring a boring, apparently self-evident, murder case to an end by convicting a Puerto Rican teenager of killing his father.

Only one jury member (Fonda) sees grounds for 'reasonable doubt' and, in the course of their deliberations, uses his deductive skills to persuade the others to change their minds. In the aftermath of the anti-communist witch-hunts of the 1950s, the film's emphasis on one man speaking up against an ignoble consensus was not lost.

20th Century-Fox A major Hollywood studio based on a 63-acre site in Century City, Los Angeles. It was formed in 1935 by the merger of the Fox Film Corporation with Twentieth Century, a production company.

In the 1900s William Fox (Wilhelm Fried; 1879–1952), a Hungarian immigrant, built up a chain of 15 New York cinemas and an EXCHANGE, the Greater New York Film Rental Company. With Carl Laemmle, he was mainly responsible for breaking the monopoly of the General Film Company exchange of the MOTION PICTURE PATENTS COMPANY in 1909. He began to make his own films in 1912 and three years later founded the Fox Film Corporation to produce, distribute, and exhibit.

Fox's early stars included Theda BARA, Tom Mix, Will ROGERS, Janet GAYNOR, and Charles Farrell. In the 1920s his roster of directors grew to include John FORD, Raoul WALSH, Frank Borzage, and F. W. MURNAU, who came from Germany to direct his masterpiece *Sunrise* (1927). At the end of the decade Fox responded to Warner Brothers' sound-on-disc system VITAPHONE by introducing MOVIETONE, a more successful sound-on-film system. The Depression, however, led to near bankruptcy, a fate that was only averted by the success of child star Shirley TEMPLE.

In 1935 Fox merged with Twentieth Century, established two years earlier by Darryl F. ZANUCK and Joseph M. Schenck. The new 20th Century-Fox had Zanuck as production head and Schenk as president. Along with Temple, its impressive roll-call of stars grew to include Warner BAXTER, Don AMECHE, Gene TIERNEY, Loretta YOUNG, Tyrone POWER, Henry FONDA, Gregory PECK, Betty GRABLE, and Richard WIDMARK. Directors included Ernst LUBITSCH, Anatole LITVAK, Joseph L. MANKIEWICZ, Otto PREMINGER, Walter Lang, and Elia KAZAN. Among the studio's notable successes were Ford's *Drums Along the Mohawk* (1939), *What Price Glory?* (1952), THE GRAPES OF WRATH (1940), and *How Green was My Valley* (1941). Both *The Snake Pit* (1948), a mental-hospital drama, and *Gentleman's Agreement* (1947), about anti-Semitism, hit the headlines with their treatment of controversial issues.

Spyros Skouras replaced Zanuck in 1952 and a year later introduced CINEMA-SCOPE with THE ROBE. Other successes included *The King and I* (1956), *South Pacific* (1958), *The Diary of Anne Frank* (1959), and *The Longest Day* (1962). When Skouras was forced out after a string of disasters, including the hugely expensive *Cleopatra* (1963), Zanuck returned to head the company until 1971. Fox hits of this period included THE SOUND OF MUSIC (1965), *Hello Dolly!* (1969), and the war epic *Patton* (1970), which was named Best Picture at the Oscars.

Zanuck was succeeded by Alan Ladd Jnr, the son of the actor Alan LADD, who headed the studio until 1979. In 1985 the Denver oilman Marvin Davis, who had gained a controlling interest, sold the studio to Rupert Murdoch, the press baron, for $575 million. Notable films of the last 20 years have included STAR WARS (1977), CHARIOTS OF FIRE (1981), *Romancing the Stone* (1984), Oliver STONE's *Wall Street* (1987), *Die Hard* (1988), *Home Alone* (1990), *Mrs Doubtfire* (1993), and *True Lies* (1994).

two-reeler A short movie that could be shot on two REELS of film. Two-reelers, which generally last some 20 minutes, were introduced to supplement the standard ONE-REELER in the 1910s. From 1911 onwards BIOGRAPH Studios permitted D. W. GRIFFITH to experiment with the greater narrative potential of the two-reeler form. Although European films had reached five reels by this time, Biograph felt that any length beyond two reels would cause eyestrain and tire audiences. Possibly the greatest exponent of the two-reeler form was Charlie CHAPLIN, who made numerous such shorts for Mutual in 1916–17, notably *Easy Street* and *The Immigrant* (both 1917). *See also* SHORT.

2001: A Space Odyssey (1968) Stanley KUBRICK's extraordinary SCIENCE-FICTION epic. The film, which took four years and $10.5 million to make, has been described as "the world's most expensive underground movie." Kubrick himself wrote of this dazzling but indefinable work "The feel of the experience is the most important thing, not the ability to verbalize it." John Lennon once

suggested that it should be screened perpetually in a specially constructed temple.

In 1964 Kubrick contacted the science-fiction writer Arthur C. Clarke with an idea:

Most astronomers and other scientists...are strongly convinced that the universe is crawling with life; much of it, since the numbers are so staggering, equal to us in intelligence, or superior, simply because human intelligence has existed for so relatively short a period.

Together they worked Clarke's story 'The Sentinel' into a novel, which they then turned into a screenplay. Clarke was later to concede generously that "*2001* reflects about 90% on the imagination of Stanley Kubrick, about 5% on the genius of the special-effects people, and perhaps 5% on my contribution."

The film begins at the dawn of civilization with apes discovering the potential of bones as both tools and weapons. Kubrick commented:

All of man's technology grew out of the discovery of the tool-weapon. There's no doubt that there's a deep emotional relationship between man and his machine-weapons...The machine is beginning to exert itself in a very profound way, even attracting affection and obsession.

One such machine is the HAL-9000 computer (voiced by Douglas Rain) on board the spaceship *Discovery*. When HAL (the name is derived from the *h*euristic and *a*lgorithmic learning principles) makes an error, it chooses to eliminate astronauts Dave Bowman (Keir Dullea) and Frank Poole (Gary Lockwood) rather than admit its mistake. In triumphing over HAL's assault, Bowman is reborn as "an enhanced being, a star child, an angel, a superman, if you like, returning to earth prepared for the next leap forward of man's evolutionary destiny."

Over half of the film's budget was spent on the SPECIAL EFFECTS devised by Douglas Trumbull and his team. Working at Shepperton and Borehamwood Studios, they made extensive use of models and FRONT PROJECTION. The living bay of the *Discovery* was specially constructed by Vickers at a cost of $750,000. The film won the Oscar for Special Effects and was nominated in the categories of Best Direction, Screenplay, and Art Direction.

U

U Universal. A category of film classification indicating that in the opinion of the British Board of Film Censors the movie concerned is suitable for unaccompanied children as it does not contain scenes of violence, sex, etc. The US equivalent is G. *See* CENSORSHIP; RATINGS.

UFA Universum Film Aktien Gesellschaft. The giant production company that acted as the flagship of the German cinema industry during its golden era in the 1920s. UFA remained the leading film company in Europe until the Nazi era.

In 1917 the major German studios, including German Nordisk-Film, Messter-Film, Projektions AG Union, and Vitascop, merged to form UFA. The move was prompted by the military's film propaganda office and part-financed by the government. With the return of peace the Deutsche Bank bought the government's shares.

Those to make their names with UFA in the 1920s included the directors Ernst LUBITSCH, Alexander KORDA, F. W. MURNAU, G. W. PABST, Fritz LANG, Mihály Kertész (who became Michael CURTIZ), and Josef VON STERNBERG, and the actors Emil JANNINGS, Pola NEGRI, Greta GARBO, and Marlene DIETRICH.

In 1919 UFA opened its showcase Berlin cinema, the UFA Palast am Zoo, with Lubitsch's *Passion*; his other films for the company included the international success *Joyless Street* (1925), with Garbo and Asta Nielsen. In 1921 UFA merged with Erich Pommer's Decla-Bioscop, which owned the vast BABELSBERG studios outside Berlin. Under Pommer, the company expanded into distribution and exhibition and increased its output; it produced some 47 movies in 1922. However, Hollywood competition forced UFA into unfavourable contracts with FAMOUS PLAYERS-Lasky and MGM in the mid 1920s.

Major UFA productions of this period include Murnau's *Faust* and Pabst's *The Love of Jeanne Ney* (1927), which was shot on location in Paris. In 1927 Lang made METROPOLIS, UFA's most spectacular project; the film cost some 8 million DM to make and brought the studio close to bankruptcy. It was rescued by a rich Nazi supporter, Dr Alfred Hugenberg, who became chairman of the board and used his power to turn out propaganda newsreels that helped Hitler secure power.

Still, good features continued to be made. UFA made its sound debut in 1929 with *Melody of the Heart*, produced by Pommer; a year later von Sternberg directed Dietrich in THE BLUE ANGEL (1930), the film that made her an international star.

UFA, which was taken into government ownership in 1937, celebrated its 25th anniversary by producing the spectacular *Münchausen* in 1943. Following the collapse of the Third Reich, East Germany's DEFA took over the Babelsberg studios. The name UFA was briefly resurrected by a West German company in the 1950s.

Ullmann, Liv (1939–) Norwegian actress, associated on and off set with the director Ingmar BERGMAN. She is celebrated for her low-key depictions of women undergoing emotional crises. Since 1980 Ullmann has served as a goodwill ambassador for UNICEF.

Ullmann was born in Tokyo, the daughter of a Norwegian engineer. After studying acting at the Webber-Douglas School in London, she returned to Norway and worked with a provincial company until 1959, when she joined the National Theatre in Oslo. Her Norwegian screen debut was in *Fjols til Fjells* (1957).

Ullmann began her affair with Bergman in the early 1960s. After divorcing their spouses in 1965, the couple lived together for five years during which they also enjoyed an intense working relationship. It was her performance as an actress stricken with muteness in her first Bergman film, *Persona* (1966), that made her an international star. Subsequent roles for Bergman were equally downbeat; she played a painter's wife helping her husband

(Max VON SYDOW) through hallucinations in *The Hour of the Wolf* (1968), a heartbroken lover in *The Passion of Anna* (1969), a woman nursing a dying sister in *Cries and Whispers* (1972), an abandoned wife in *Scenes from a Marriage* (1973), a psychiatrist having a breakdown in *Face to Face* (1976), and the neglected daughter of a concert pianist (Ingrid BERGMAN) in *Autumn Sonata* (1978).

She also co-starred with von Sydow as Swedish emigrants to America in Jan Troell's two-part story *The Emigrants* (1970) and *The New Land* (1972), and played a frontier bride in the same director's *Zandy's Bride* (1974). Ullmann's other Hollywood films have included the fantasy musical *Lost Horizon* (1973) and the comedy *40 Carats* (1973). She has also appeared in the Italian film *Let's Hope It's a Girl* (1985), with Catherine DENEUVE, the Swiss *Dangerous Moves* (1985), and the US-Hungarian-Israeli offering, *The Long Shadow* (1992), with Michael YORK. In 1993 she co-scripted and directed the film *Sofie*.

under. underground films Independent AVANT-GARDE films made in America since World War II. The term, which was coined by Stan Van Der Beek, alludes to the unconventional methods of production and exhibition he and other film-makers were obliged to adopt. The name **New American Cinema**, which is often used synonymously, refers more specifically to the films produced by the New American Cinema Group in the 1960s.

Although a US avant-garde existed prior to World War II, its activities remained scattered and marginal. It was not until the 1940s and 1950s, when cheap cameras and film stock became available, that a more coherent movement developed. At the same time the rise of film courses and societies, the publicity given to NEOREALISM and other European styles, and the advent of a disaffected younger generation (first the Beats, then the hippies) helped to create a sustainable audience for more avant-garde productions.

By definition, underground films were produced independently of the film industry, most being financed by friends, family, and any willing creditors. As a result, they were able to reflect the personal visions and concerns of the film-maker, even when these were in stark contrast to accepted social and aesthetic norms. Most rejected realism and conventional narrative in favour of more hallucinatory and dreamlike effects. Often the subject matter itself was controversial, as with Kenneth Anger's exploration of gay machismo in *Scorpio Rising* (1964) or Bruce Connor's meditations on violence and politics in *Film Leader, A Movie* (1958) and *Report* (1965). This tendency exacerbated the problems of distribution and exchange that forced the movement 'underground'.

The US underground is often considered to begin with the work of Maya Deren (Eleanora Derenkowsky; 1917–61), whose *Meshes of the Afternoon* (1943) prefigured many of the techniques and concerns of later film-makers. A key event in the history of the underground was the 1947 symposium 'Art In Cinema', convened by Frank Stuffacher and Richard Foster in San Francisco. This provided a forum for directors to meet each other and to acquaint themselves with the work of current and previous generations. The movement then burgeoned with the founding of the journal *Film Culture* in 1955, the New American Cinema Group in 1960, and the Film Makers Co-operative in 1962. The high point of underground activity was the 1960s, a decade in which avant-garde techniques and subject matter found a ready response from younger audiences and began to permeate the mainstream. *See also* ABSTRACT FILM; INDEPENDENT FILM-MAKING.

underwater cinematography Filming beneath the surface of a body of water, whether in a TANK on the studio lot or in a lake, river, ocean, etc. Underwater sequences have long been popular in the cinema, although most early scenes of this kind were necessarily faked. Since the development of the requisite technology in the 1930s, many films have plumbed the ocean depths in search of adventure; examples include DE MILLE's *Reap the Wild Wind* (1942), with its celebrated squid fight, DISNEY's *20,000 Leagues Under the Sea* (1954), SPIELBERG's JAWS (1975), and James CAMERON's special-effects spectacular *The Abyss* (1989).

Technical problems associated with filming under water include the need to keep the camera dry and the consequent restrictions to mobility; the distortion caused by refraction under water, which makes objects appear a quarter closer than they actually are (wide-angle lenses are used to compensate), and the provision of adequate and appropriate lighting (a particular problem being the absorption of red light by water). As the technology has improved, there has been a marked rise in both the ease and the quality of underwater cinematography. Some of the most important work in this field has been carried out by the French oceanographer Jacques Cousteau; in 1956 his documentary *The Silent World*, co-directed by Louis MALLE, won an Academy Award.

unfinished film A motion picture that, for whatever reason, remains uncompleted at the time of reference. The most obvious reason for a film not being completed is the sudden removal of one of the principals, either through death, accident, or pique; an example of this is *Something's Got To Give*, the film on which Marilyn MONROE was working at the time of her death in 1962. However, with the use of doubles and, more recently, computer simulation, even the death of a star may not be an insuperable problem. *The Crow* (1993) was completed and released despite the accidental death of its young star, Brandon LEE. The other main reason why films remain unfinished is financial. One constant victim of fiscal drought was Orson WELLES, who spent 20 years trying to collect the finance necessary to complete his *Don Quixote* (1993), a film finally released (unfinished) almost a decade after his death. Other famous unfinished films include Erich VON STROHEIM's *Queen Kelly* (1927), an extravagant project that destroyed the careers of both the director and his star, Gloria SWANSON, and Josef VON STERNBERG's *I Claudius* (1937).

unit The technical crew employed to work on a particular film or a particular part of it (*see* SECOND UNIT).

unit manager or **production manager** The manager of a film production crew; he or she is responsible for that unit's payroll and for supplying such requirements as transport, equipment, meals, and accommodation.

united. **United Artists** (UA) A Hollywood production and distribution company formed in 1919 by Mary PICKFORD, Douglas FAIRBANKS, Charlie CHAPLIN, and D. W. GRIFFITH. UA was the first company to give performers total autonomy and to sell and promote films individually instead of in a package.

The four founders laid their plans at a meeting in the dining room of the Alexandria Hotel, Hollywood; whenever a producer wandered within earshot, Fairbanks would change the subject and talk deliberate nonsense (Chaplin recalled him saying "The cabbages on the peanuts and the groceries on the pork carry a great deal of weight these days").

When he heard of the venture, Richard Rowland, the head of Metro, delivered himself of the famous comment "The lunatics have taken over the asylum." Years later Pickford came back with the response "We maniacs had fun and made good pictures and a lot of money." With Fairbanks taking the leading business role, UA enjoyed immediate commercial success with a series of prestige projects. Early triumphs included Fairbanks's *His Majesty, the American* (1919) and *The Mark of Zorro* (1920), Griffith's BROKEN BLOSSOMS (1919) and *Way Down East* (1920), and Pickford's *Pollyanna* (1920), the first film sold on a percentage basis. Later came Griffith's *Orphans of the Storm* (1922), Fairbanks's ROBIN HOOD (1923), Chaplin's THE GOLD RUSH (1925), and Josef VON STERNBERG's *The Salvation Hunters* (1925). When Griffith's effort lagged in the 1920s, Fairbanks had him eased out.

In 1925 Joe Schenck (known to UA as 'Honest Joe') was hired as board chairman and brought along his actress wife Norma TALMADGE and her sister Constance. Schenck successfully encouraged other stars to release their films through the company, notably Rudolph VALENTINO, Gloria SWANSON, and Buster KEATON. In 1926 a cinema chain was purchased, the United Artists Theater Circuit, Inc.

By the 1930s UA had begun to suffer from its lack of a studio and a roster of salaried stars. As a result it began to concentrate on financing and distributing the films of independent producers, notably Samuel GOLDWYN, Howard HUGHES, David O. SELZNICK, and Britain's Alexander KORDA.

After World War II UA went into the red, leading Chaplin and Pickford to sell their stock. Although many top executives deserted when a syndicate took over in 1953, the company was soon showing a profit. In the new era of location shooting the lack of a studio, with its high overheads, proved a blessing. UA's later films included HIGH NOON (1952), Chaplin's *A King in New*

York (1957), the last of his nine films for the company, SOME LIKE IT HOT (1959), the BOND FILMS of the 1960s, *The Magnificent Seven* (1960), and TOM JONES (1963). Although the TransAmerica Corporation's purchase of the company in 1967 was followed by such triumphs as ONE FLEW OVER THE CUCKOO'S NEST (1975) and *Rocky* (1976), the $40-million disaster HEVEN'S GATE (1980) drove UA into bankruptcy. In 1981 the company negotiated a merger with MGM.

United Productions of America *See* UPA.

Universal A Hollywood production company, founded in 1912 as the Universal Film Manufacturing Co. Its base, **Universal City**, is the largest film studio in the world, with 34 sound stages and additional buildings spread over 420 acres.

The German-born Carl Laemmle created Universal by merging his Independent Motion Picture Company (IMP) with several other corporations. In 1915 Laemmle established Universal City on a chicken ranch in the San Fernando Valley north of Los Angeles. By 1917 it was incorporated as an independent municipality and had its own town hall, post office, hospital, fire station, police department, and the world's largest privately owned zoo. Since the late 1950s Universal City has been a major tourist attraction; visitors can pay to look behind the scenes and watch stunts performed.

Universal's early stars included Rudolph VALENTINO and Lon CHANEY, who played the lead in THE HUNCHBACK OF NOTRE DAME (1923). Directors included Erich VON STROHEIM and Rex INGRAM. King VIDOR began his career as a clerk at Universal, while both Irving THALBERG, who was to become MGM's boy wonder, and Harry COHN, the future boss of Columbia, began as Laemmle's secretaries.

Ogden Nash once observed that "Uncle Carl Laemmle has a very large faemmle." The future director William WYLER was amongst the numerous Laemmle relatives to be employed at Universal in the 1920s. On his 21st birthday Laemmle's son, Carl Laemmle Jnr, was appointed production chief; he quickly signed Lewis MILESTONE to direct ALL QUIET ON THE WESTERN FRONT (1930) and the British director James WHALE to make FRANKENSTEIN (1931). In the early 1930s Universal led the development of the horror genre with such films as DRACULA (1931), starring Bela LUGOSI, and Whale's THE INVISIBLE MAN (1933) and *The Bride of Frankenstein* (1935).

Owing to profligate spending on budgets, Universal came close to bankruptcy in the late 1930s; it was only saved by a series of popular musicals featuring Deanna DURBIN. In 1946 the studio merged with International Films and became known as Universal International; Decca Records acquired a controlling interest a few years later. Universal's successes of the 1950s included a string of Doris DAY movies and two low-budget series featuring Francis the Talking Mule and Ma and Pa KETTLE. From 1962 Universal became a subsidiary of MCA and a leading producer of TV series. In the early 1970s it found renewed success on the big screen with such hits as *Airport* (1970), THE STING (1973), George LUCAS's *American Graffiti* (1973), and Steven SPIELBERG's JAWS (1975).

Spielberg has also given Universal E.T.: THE EXTRATERRESTRIAL (1982), *Back to the Future* (1985), JURASSIC PARK (1993), the biggest-grossing film in history, and the multi-Oscar-winning SCHINDLER'S LIST (1993). Other successes of the last ten years include *Out of Africa* (1985), which won the Best Picture Oscar, and *Field of Dreams* (1989). Recent releases include *The Cowboy Way* (1994), with Kiefer SUTHERLAND, and *The Paper* (1994), starring Michael Keaton, Glenn CLOSE, and Robert DUVALL.

up A script direction to raise the level of the background sound, as in 'Crowd noise: in and up.'

upstage The area of a film set furthest from the camera; the background.

UPA United Productions of America. A film company established in 1943 by Stephen Bosustow and other young animators who had left DISNEY following a strike two years earlier. UPA's style was simpler and more abstract than the traditional Disney fare. The studio's most famous character was the nearsighted MR MAGOO, voiced by Jim Bacus. Another popular character was Gerald McBoing Boing, created by Bob Cannon.

Ustinov, Sir Peter (1921–) British actor, director, screenwriter, playwright, and raconteur, who has appeared in numerous Hollywood productions from the 1950s onwards. The winner of two Oscars as Best Supporting Actor, he later starred as the Belgian detective Hercule POIROT in several movies.

Ustinov comes from a Russian family with a long theatrical tradition (one ancestor having designed the Bolshoi Theatre). Although he trained at the London Theatre Studio, his final report was unpromising, describing him as "lamentably stiff" with a "monotonous" voice. He made his professional stage debut performing his own sketches at the age of 18 and had his first play produced a year later. His first film was the British comedy *Hullo Fame* (1940).

After service in World War II, Ustinov wrote, directed, and co-scripted *The Way Ahead* (US title *Immortal Battalion*; 1944); although originally intended as an army training film, this evolved into a semidocumentary with David NIVEN in the lead. Having moved to Hollywood in 1947, he achieved star status playing the erratic Nero in QUO VADIS? (1951); his larger-than-life performance led MGM to give him top bill-

ing, above Robert TAYLOR. In 1955 he co-starred with Humphrey BOGART and Aldo Ray in Michael CURTIZ's *We're No Angels*, about a trio of escaped convicts.

After winning his first Oscar for playing a slave-dealer in Stanley KUBRICK's *Spartacus* (1960), Ustinov wrote, directed, produced, and starred in *Romanoff and Juliet* (1961), adapted from his witty stage comedy. His second Oscar was awarded for playing an informer in Jules DASSIN's classic HEIST MOVIE *Topkapi* (1964). Ustinov's three Poirot films were *Death on the Nile* (1978), *Evil Under the Sun* (1982), and *Appointment with Death* (1988). In 1992 he appeared in the medical drama, *Lorenzo's Oil*.

Ustinov has also made several documentaries for television and continued his love affair with the stage. In 1990–91 he presented an acclaimed one-man show, *An Evening with Peter Ustinov*.

V

Vacances de Monsieur Hulot, Les *See* MON-
SIEUR HULOT'S HOLIDAY.

Vadim, Roger (Roger Vadim Plemiannio-
kov; 1927–) French director, screenwriter, producer, and actor, remembered as
much for his personal associations with
some of the cinema's most beautiful women
as for his films. Vadim's reputation was
established with his directorial debut, *And
God Created Woman* (1956), which effectively launched its star, Brigitte BARDOT, as
the sex symbol of the decade. Married in
1952, Bardot and Vadim subsequently
divorced; after the failure of a second marriage, Vadim married another of his female
leads, Jane FONDA, who starred in his
remarkable science-fiction sex fantasy
Barbarella (1967). When this marriage also
collapsed he began a liaison with the actress
Catherine DENEUVE, who bore his child.
Vadim's earlier films, such as *Les Liaisons
dangereuses* (1959) and *La Ronde* (1964),
can be seen as low-brow expressions of the
same intellectual rebelliousness that
inspired the French NEW WAVE; his later movies have mainly been mild sex comedies and
unambitious thrillers. Vadim directed a second film entitled *And God Created Woman* in
1987 but this failed to re-create the sensational impact of the original.

Valentino, Rudolph (Rodolpho Alfonzo
Raffaelo Pierre Filibert Guliemi di Valentina
d'Antonguola; 1895–1926) US actor,
whose animal magnetism made him one of
the great romantic idols of the silent era. His
popularity proved crucial to the success of
three major studios, while his two successful comebacks after pay disputes demonstrated the emerging power of the STAR. On
his death *The Times* wrote:

> By the death of Valentino, the film loses
> one of its most important stars, for,
> although he only became first known a
> very few years ago, his rise was remarkably
> rapid, and within a few months his face
> was familiar all over the world.

Born of impoverished aristocrats in
Castellaneta, Italy, he studied agriculture
before emigrating to America (1913),
where he worked as a gardener and gigolo.
He decided to try his luck in films after being
turned down for military service, ironically
on the grounds of poor physique.

After three years of bit parts, he became
famous with his sensual performance of the
tango in Rex INGRAM's *The Four Horsemen of
the Apocalypse* (1921), the story of a rake's
redemption through war. The film took
Metro from the brink of bankruptcy and
made it a major studio. He then made the
fortunes of Famous Players-Lasky with
The Sheik (1921), in which he played a
noble savage who wins over an English girl.
After making *Blood and Sand* (1921) and *The
Young Rajah* (1922), he walked out on his
contract over choice of material. He returned to fulfil it with *M. Beaucaire* (1924)
before again withdrawing from the cinema.
Lured back by United Artists' offer of
$200,000 per movie, he made two more
films, *The Eagle* (1925) – best described as
Robin Hood cossack-style – and *The Son of
the Sheik* (1926). D. W. GRIFFITH once asked
"Is this fellow acting or is he so perfectly the
type he does not need to act?"

In 1919 Valentino married Jean Acker;
the couple spent only one night together
before agreeing to divorce. Three years later
he contracted a bigamous marriage to
Natacha Rambova, but escaped prosecution
on grounds of non-consummation. He married her again, legally, in 1923, although
the couple soon separated.

One of the great silent icons, he died only
weeks before Warners' VITAPHONE system
ushered in the sound era. His death was
greeted with mass hysteria. Two women
committed suicide on hearing the news and
a hundred people were injured when a riot
broke out amongst those trying to view the
body. Of his appeal he himself said;

> This is a matter-of-fact age...I suppose they
> like me because I bring romance into their
> lives for a few moments.

vampires *See* DRACULA.

vamp A woman who uses her feminine charms and sexual attraction to entice and exploit men. The vamp (short for vampire) was a popular stock character of silent films, the best known exponent of the type being Theda BARA. The term seems to have arisen from Bara's performance in *A Fool There Was* (1914), a film based on Kipling's poem 'The Vampire'.

Van Dyke, Dick (1925–) Affable US comic actor, singer, and dancer, who became a star of the big screen in the early 1960s.

Born in West Plains, Missouri, he gained some experience as a radio broadcaster while serving in the air force during World War II. After a failed attempt to run an advertising agency, he joined Phil Erickson in 'The Merry Mutes', a pantomime act that appeared in nightclubs. He first came to national attention hosting such programmes as *The Morning Show* (1955) on television.

Having made his Broadway debut in *The Boys Against the Girls* (1959), Van Dyke won the Tony Award for his performance as a harrassed father in the rock n' roll comedy *Bye, Bye Birdie* (1960); three years later the same role provided him with his screen debut. In 1964 he played the part for which he is best known, that of the cockney chimney sweep in Walt DISNEY's fantasy, MARY POPPINS. This was also the period of his greatest popularity on television, as the host of the phenomenally successful *Dick Van Dyke Show* (1961–66).

Subsequent film roles included a man breaking up with his wife (Debbie REYNOLDS) in the comedy *Divorce American Style* (1967), a butler in *Fitzwilly* (1967), and an absent-minded inventor in the $10-million Disney film *Chitty Chitty Bang Bang* (1968). *The Comic* (1969) provided him with a more serious role, that of a silent-film comedian whose career goes into a decline with the coming of sound. After admitting he was a recovered alcoholic, Van Dyke tackled the subject in a TV movie, *The Morning After* (1974). Later cinema roles included a priest accused of murder in the *The Runner Stumbles* (1979).

Varda, Agnès *See* DEMY, JACQUES.

variable. variable-area track An OPTICAL soundtrack in which the modulations of sound appear as an oscillating but symmetrical line.

variable-density track An OPTICAL soundtrack in which the sound appears as a series of horizontal bars of varying density (ranging from grey to black). The distance between the bars controls the frequency of the sound, while the density controls the volume.

vault A special room used for the long-term storage of cinema film. It must be fireproof and have controls to regulate humidity and temperature.

Veidt, Conrad (Conrad Weidt; 1893–1943) German-born actor, who achieved international stardom in the famous EXPRESSIONIST film THE CABINET OF DR CALIGARI (1919). He later worked in Britain and Hollywood, where he specialized in playing German villains, including the Nazi emissary Major Strasser in CASABLANCA (1943).

Born near Berlin, Veidt studied drama under Max Reinhardt and made his stage debut with the Deutsches Theatre in 1913. He appeared in his first film, *Der Spion*, in 1917 and soon came to specialize in sinister roles, most memorably that of the fairground somnambulist in *Caligari*. In 1919 he played a homosexual in the first film to deal explicitly with the subject, *Anders als die Andern*. Veidt also starred in several German films about Englishmen, playing Nelson in *Lady Hamilton* (1921) and the title role in *Lord Byron* (1922), a movie that he also directed, co-produced, and wrote. Following the success of *The Student of Prague* (1926), a pioneering horror film, he travelled to Hollywood and made *The Beloved Rogue* (1927) and other movies. However, when the advent of sound exposed his thick accent, Veidt was obliged to return to Germany. With the coming to power of the Nazis, Veidt fled to Britain, where he signed with Gaumont-British. When he visited Germany a year later he was forcibly detained by officials, who said he was ill; Gaumont-British only managed to rescue him by dispatching their own doctors. The films of Veidt's British period include the thrillers *Rome Express* (1933), *Dark Journey* (1937), and Michael POWELL's *The Spy in Black* (1939). He became a British subject in 1939.

In 1940 Veidt travelled to Hollywood to finish his work on THE THIEF OF BAGHDAD (1940), in which he played the evil Grand

Vizier. He remained to play the threatening mentor of Joan CRAWFORD in George CUKOR's *A Woman's Face* (1941), a dual role in Jules DASSIN's *Nazi Agent* (1942), and Strasser in Michael CURTIZ's *Casablanca*. He had just completed the comedy spy drama *Above Suspicion*, with Crawford and Basil RATHBONE, when he died of a heart attack while playing golf.

velocilator *See* DOLLY.

Venice Film Festival The first international FILM FESTIVAL established to grant awards for excellence in the cinema. The annual event, inaugurated in 1932 with support from Mussolini's government, was unique until the founding of the CANNES FILM FESTIVAL after World War II.

In 1994, the year Venice celebrated its 50th anniversary (it was suspended for some years during and after the war), the Golden Lion Award for best film was shared between Robert ALTMAN's *Short Cuts*, and Krzysztof KIEŚLOWSKI's *Blue*. Altman also won the prize from the International Critics' Jury. The Special Jury Prize was awarded to Rolf De Heer's Australian film, *Bad Boy Bubby*, while the President of the Senate's special award went to *Za Zui Zi*, a film by the Chinese woman director Liu Miao Miao.

Vertigo (1958) Alfred HITCHCOCK's disturbing psychological thriller. Having been forcibly retired from the police force because of his acrophobia, Jack 'Scotty' Ferguson (James STEWART) takes on the task of shadowing Madeleine Elster (Kim NOVAK) for her husband. His obsession with her intensifies after he sees her fall, apparently to her death, from a campanile. He subsequently attempts to transform shopgirl Judy Barton (also Novak) into a replica of his lost love.

Hitchcock's most self-revealing film was adapted from the novel *D'entre les morts*, allegedly written with the director in mind by Pierre Boileau and Thomas Narejac. Critics are agreed that the film improves with repeated viewings, as the 'ghost' story ("Do you believe that someone dead, someone out of the past, can take possession of a living being?") becomes less distracting and we are able to concentrate both on Scotty's necrophiliac obsession and on the intensely painful nature of his and Judy's situation. Hitchcock told François TRUFFAUT that he was "intrigued by the hero's attempt to re-create the image of a dead woman through another one who's alive." He was himself culpable of a similar fetish in his search for another Grace KELLY; Vera Miles (who was to star in *Vertigo* before she announced her pregnancy), Novak, and Tippi Hedren (star of THE BIRDS) were all remodelled in accordance with her 'ice blonde' looks.

Samuel Taylor, the film's scriptwriter recalled how

> Hitchcock knew exactly what he wanted to do in this film...And anyone who saw him during the making of the film could see, as I did, that he felt it very deeply indeed.

In addition to its unusual psychological depth, *Vertigo*, with its stylized use of colour and provocative Bernard Herrmann score, was a technically innovative picture. In order to convey Scotty's fear of heights, Hitchcock devised a disconcerting SUBJECTIVE CAMERA effect, in which the camera simultaneously tracked forwards and zoomed backwards. Similarly, he suggested Judy's inaccessibility by means of 'vortical' editing, which created a full 360° of screen space around her in direct contravention of the rules of classical Hollywood cutting.

Although the film is now widely hailed as Hitchcock's most thematically and technically accomplished, the contemporary critical response was cool. The picture also performed badly at the box office. Ungraciously, Hitchcock blamed the disappointment on Stewart's age and Novak's naivety, although by the time he spoke to Truffaut he had concocted another theory:

> One of our whimsies when a picture isn't doing too well is to blame it on the faulty exploitation. So let's live up to the tradition and say they just didn't handle the sales properly!

video Magnetic tape used for the recording of both visual and audio signals; these can then be played back or transmitted through television equipment.

While video has been available since the 1950s, its inferiority to 35mm film in terms of colour, contrast, and resolution meant that it had little impact on professional filmmaking until relatively recently. At present, video has two main uses in commercial film production; **video assist** during shooting and **video editing** in post-production. Video-assist systems (such as GEMINI) are used to transmit the images picked up by each camera to a monitor, thereby enabling the director and others to form an impression of their quality during the take itself. The growing practice of editing on video has likewise removed much of the drudgery and physical nuisance from the cutting process.

To date, it is in the field of distribution rather than production that video has had the greatest impact on the film industry. The rise of the home-video market in the late 1970s and 1980s has had a number of profound effects. If at first the industry was wary of the new medium, fearing that it would be like the birth of television all over again, it soon became apparent that video was an ally rather than a threat. Home videos offered an extended run for current hits, a second chance for box-office flops (e.g. *Hudson Hawk*, 1993, among others), and a way to cash in again on the back catalogue (see the Disney balance sheet).

The boom in the ownership of home-video equipment also stimulated the production of 'straight-to-video' releases. With the growing availability of cheap reliable cameras and editing equipment, a large low-budget production industry sprang up to meet the demand for material. Perhaps inevitably, many of these productions have been sexploitation or schlock-horror quickies (so-called **video nasties**).

The use of video cameras (camcorders) has now almost entirely superseded the making of home movies on 8MM or 16MM film. The relative cost of video to film has likewise encouraged its increasing use for documentary, experimental, and independent projects. Recent years have seen the development of high-definition video, with a picture quality approaching that of 35mm film. Although it seems possible that video may one day supersede film in motion-picture production, the impracticality of converting thousands of cinemas is likely to sustain the role of film in exhibition for some time to come.

Vidor, King (1894–1982) US director, screenwriter, and producer, whose films show an interest in social issues and the struggles of the average man. He directed the most profitable silent film ever made, *The Big Parade* (1925), and was nominated for five Academy Awards as Best Director without winning. In 1979 he was awarded an honorary Oscar for "his incomparable achievements" during 67 years of film-making.

Born in Galveston, Texas, Vidor worked as a ticket collector and projectionist at a nickleodeon before becoming a freelance cameraman for newsreel companies. In 1915 he and his wife Florence Arto travelled penniless to Hollywood, where she became a star and he struggled as a clerk for Universal, an extra, and an unsuccessful screenwriter (his first 52 scripts were all rejected).

After directing several shorts for Universal, Vidor made his feature debut in 1919 with *The Turn in the Road*, which he also scripted. Later that year he established his own studio, Vidor Village, and embarked on a series of movies starring his wife. Following the collapse of the studio in 1922, he worked for Metro and Goldwyn and then for the consolidated MGM. Florence, whom he divorced in 1924, retired to marry the violinist Jascha Heifetz.

Vidor made his name with *The Big Parade*, an antiwar film starring John GILBERT that grossed $22 million. "Up until that time" Vidor recalled, "all the war pictures had been glamorous." Unfortunately MGM's production chief, Irving THALBERG, had talked Vidor out of his originally agreed percentage of the profits; as the director commented, "I thus spared myself from becoming a millionaire."

Vidor's second wife, Eleanor Boardman, co-starred with James Murray in *The Crowd* (1928), a story about the anonymity of modern life that earned the director an Oscar nomination. Appropriately enough, he had spotted the unknown Murray amongst the extras. Vidor shot the New York exteriors with a hidden camera.

Highlights of Vidor's sound career include the first Black feature, *Hallelujah!* (1929), the boxing film *The Champ* (1931), and *The Citadel* (1938), a medical drama made at MGM's British studios that starred Robert DONAT; all three won him Oscar nominations. Because the theme of *Our Daily Bread* (1934), a Depression-era story extolling the co-operative farm, proved unpopular with backers, Vidor pawned everything he owned to produce the film himself.

In 1947 Vidor walked off the epic Western *Duel in the Sun* (1947) after squabbling with it producer David O. SELZNICK, also the husband of the star, Jennifer JONES. His last great success came with the massive US-Italian co-production *War and Peace* (1956), starring Audrey HEPBURN and Henry FONDA. Vidor retired after the failure of *Solomon and Sheba* (1959), a biblical epic with Yul BRYNNER and Gina LOLLOBRIGIDA. Shortly before his death he appeared as an actor in the melodrama *Love and Money* (1982), playing a senile grandfather.

Vietnam War The conflict (1959–75) in which the government of South Vietnam, supported militarily by America, fought unsuccessfully to contain communist insurgents backed by North Vietnam. US opinion was violently polarized by the war, and the eventual acknowledgment of failure left a legacy of bitterness and disillusion. The conflict subsequently inspired a flood of movies, noted for their depiction of the brutality of modern warfare and its effect on those forced to endure it.

Such were the passions roused by Vietnam that few film-makers were prepared to address the subject while the war was still in progress. Only *The Green Berets*, a 1968 propaganda piece starring John WAYNE, attempted to support US military involvement in the same way that earlier war movies had given total backing to the Allies in WORLD WAR II. The pattern for later Vietnam movies was set largely by Michael CIMINO's *The Deer Hunter* (1978), a powerful, violent, and occasionally sentimental film dealing with the traumatic effect of the conflict on a small US community. A scene in which sadistic Vietcong guards force US prisoners to play Russian roulette attracted fierce criticism. Much the most ambitious film to emerge from the war was Francis Ford COPPOLA's APOCALYPSE NOW (1979), a two-and-a-half-hour epic that transposed elements of Conrad's *Heart of Darkness* to the jungles of Vietnam. Dense with symbolism and portentous philosophical discussion, it is variously regarded as a masterpiece and an overblown failure.

Hal ASHBY's *Coming Home* (1982), which starred 'Hanoi' Jane FONDA, examined the experiences of veterans and their attempts to come to terms with their less-than-grateful reception on returning to America. A similar mixture of brutal action and attempted psychological analysis characterized such subsequent Vietnam movies as *Hamburger Hill*, KUBRICK's *Full Metal Jacket*, and Oliver STONE's *Platoon*, which were all released in 1987; *Gardens of Stone* and *Saigon* appeared the following year. Stone, a Vietnam veteran himself, returned to the theme with the hugely successful *Born on the Fourth of July* (1989), based on the true experiences of a paralysed ex-serviceman.

Although most of these films won praise for emphasizing the human cost of the conflict, other voices have criticized their tendency to depict the war as primarily a tragedy for America, effectively relegating the Vietnamese (some two million of whom died) to the status of extras. Stone's *Heaven and Earth* (1993), which broke new ground by trying to show the Vietnamese experience of the war, proved notably less successful than the earlier parts of his trilogy. It has also been argued that the celebration of male comradeship and the use of spectacular special effects in these films have had the unintended effect of glorifying war:

> In many movies, including *Platoon*, war looks like fun. In reality, a dead body is a very ugly thing and it's hard to carry.
> PATRICK DUNCAN, director.

The chauvinistic mood of the Reagan years gave rise to a number of naive and jingoistic films in which US special forces refought the war, this time victoriously; both *Rambo: First Blood Part Two* (1985; *see* RAMBO), starring Sylvester STALLONE, and *Missing in Action* (1984), starring Chuck Norris, dealt with missions to rescue US servicemen still held prisoner in Vietnam. In 1993 Tran Anh Hung's *The Scent of Green Papaya* became the first Vietnamese film about the conflict to find an audience in the West.

viewfinder An optical sighting device on a camera that allows the operator to see the frame as it will appear on film. The most frequently used system is the REFLEX viewfinder, in which a mirrored shutter deflects the image both to the film and to the cameraman's eyepiece. The main advantage of this system is that it eliminates the problem of parallax. Older types include the **side-** or **offset viewfinder**, which is set parallel to the camera lens, and the **rackover** system, which allows viewing through the lens itself, though not during filming. The so-called electronic viewfinder, more properly termed the VIDEO assist, both avoids parallax and offers the prospect of instant playbacks.

Vigo, Jean (1905–34) French director, who became a major inspiration to the AVANT-GARDE despite making only three features in his short life. His films offer a unique blend of the real and the surreal, the realistic and the lyrical. France now awards an annual Jean Vigo Prize to film-makers who demonstrate a similar "independence of spirit and quality of direction."

Born in Paris, the son of an anarchist agitator, Vigo was educated in boarding schools after the death of his father in a police cell. Having developed symptoms of tuberculosis, he moved to Nice as a young man. There, encouraged by the director Germaine Dulac, he made his directorial debut with *A propos de Nice* (1930), a series of images contrasting the rich tourists with the local poor. The three-reel film was much influenced by the work of Soviet newsreel director Dziga Vertov, whose brother, Boris Kaufman, worked as Vigo's cameraman.

After making a 1931 short about competitive swimming, Vigo moved to Paris to direct the autobiographical *Zero for Conduct* (1933), a 45-minute film set in an oppressive boarding school whose headmaster is a midget. The anti-authoritarian story, which was filmed by Kaufman and supplied with dreamlike music by Maurice Jaubert, ends with the boys shooting at their teachers. After only a few months on release *Zero for Conduct* was banned as subversive and 'anti-French'.

Vigo's only full-length feature was the lyrical masterpiece *L'Atalante* (1934). The story, co-written by Vigo and Albert Riéra from a script by Jean Guinée, concerns the young wife of a bargee who relieves her boredom by fantasizing about life in the big city. Although she eventually runs off, another member of the barge's crew finds her and the film ends with a reconciliation between husband and wife. Vigo's declining health – he died a few months later of leukaemia – meant that Kaufman had to direct some scenes. Although selected for the 1934 Venice Film Festival, *L'Atalante* flopped in Paris and was subsequently withdrawn. It was not shown again in France until 1945, when its simple powerful images had a major influence on contemporary directors.

Visconti, Luchino (Count Don Luchino Visconti di Morone; 1906–76) Italian film and theatre director, who also mounted opulent productions of operas and ballets. Visconti was born into an aristocratic family in Milan and showed an interest in horse-breeding before entering the theatre as a set designer. From the mid 1930s he designed costumes and worked as an assistant to Jean RENOIR in Paris. He made his debut as a director with *Ossessione* (1942), a pioneer-

ing NEOREALIST film based on James M. Cain's novel *The Postman Always Rings Twice* (later filmed by Tay GARNETT). The implied homosexuality of one of the characters and the film's preoccupation with moral failure led to its being banned by the Fascist authorities.

The director's Marxist sympathies became evident in several postwar films showing the hardships suffered by the poor in rural Italy and the disappointments experienced by those hoping to better their lot. *Senso* (1954), about an adulterous romance between an Italian countess and an Austrian officer, was also broadly political although the lavish settings and historical authenticity of the film were perhaps its strongest features.

After *White Nights* (1957), an intense love story based on a tale by Dostoevski, Visconti found wide acclaim for *Rocco and his Brothers* (1960), a powerful account of a family's disintegration in the face of a variety of crises. Visconti's love of the historical epic was indulged to the full in his next film, THE LEOPARD (1963), from the novel by Lampedusa, which won the Palme d'Or award at Cannes.

Subsequent work included *The Damned* (1969), an uneasy tale of decadence in Nazi Germany starring Dirk BOGARDE, and the moving *Death in Venice* (1971), in which Bogarde played a composer whose infatuation with a young boy leads him to remain in the plague-ridden city, where finally he dies. Visconti's last films were *Ludwig* (1972), an extravagant portrait of the 'mad' king of Bavaria, *Conversation Piece* (*Giuppo di famiglia in uno interno*; 1974), a subtle study of old age and death, and *The Innocent* (1976), a period piece about marital infidelity.

As a stage director, Visconti concentrated on modern dramas that reflected his socialist principles, although he was also praised for his productions of plays by Goldoni, Shakespeare, and Chekhov.

VistaVision A WIDESCREEN process introduced by Paramount in the 1950s as a rival to 20th Century-Fox's CINEMASCOPE. VistaVision was a non-ANAMORPHIC process that made use of 70mm film (i.e. twice the standard gauge).

Vita-. **Vitagraph** A pioneering film production company founded in 1896 in New York by two British immigrants, J. Stuart

Blackton, a former journalist and vaudeville artist, and Albert E. Smith. With such stars as Rudolf VALENTINO, Norma TALMADGE, Rex INGRAM, Adolphe Menjou, and the **Vitagraph Girl** (Florence Turner), the studio became the most consistently successful of the early silent era.

Blackton and Smith began by projecting EDISON films in vaudeville houses. They soon came to specialize in 'documentaries' using faked footage: one about Niagara Falls was actually shot at Passaic Falls in New Jersey, while their coverage of the Battle of Santiago Bay was a re-creation in a water tank. Their first dramas were also made on the cheap: *The Burglar on the Roof* (1897) was shot in the company's office in New York, while *Romeo and Juliet* (1908) used the Central Park Mall for Renaissance Verona.

The company opened a studio in Brooklyn in 1906 before moving its main operations to California in 1911. The enormous East Hollywood studio paid its actors and other employees from $100 to $5,000 a week (often weekly at the front gate in gold coins). Blackton left the company in 1917.

By this time Vitagraph had come a long way from faking scenes. The prison drama *Three Sevens* (1921) was shot using a real gaol in Florence, Arizona, for an escape scene (with 300 prisoners allowed outside the walls), the San Fernando Valley for a train-robbery scene, and an expensive studio set that matched the Arizona prison in detail.

In 1925 the company was sold for $735,000 to Warner Brothers, who continued to remake Vitagraph hits for years. The old name continued to be synonymous with silent melodrama. When Norma Talmadge made her second talkie, *Du Barry – Woman of Passion* (1930), adapted from a David Belasco play, a critic complained "She speaks the Belascoan rodomontades in a Vitagraph accent."

Vitaphone The first synchronized SOUND system used with feature films; dialogue and music were recorded on a disc that was played from behind the cinema screen. The system was introduced by Warner Brothers in 1926 and saved the struggling studio from financial collapse. Because very few cinemas were wired for sound at the time, the gamble was enormous and could have led to bankruptcy; the stress is said to have hastened Sam Warner's death.

Talking features first became a possibility when Bell Telephone developed long-playing records that lasted the length of a cinema reel (about 10 minutes). In 1925 Warners bought the VITAGRAPH Company, which owned 15 cinemas, and joined with Western Electric, Bell's parent company, to create the Vitaphone Corporation to exploit the sound-on-disc system. The first film to feature the system, a John BARRYMORE vehicle called *Don Juan*, was premiered in New York's Manhattan Opera House in August 1926. Although there was no dialogue, the movie boasted a synchronized score and sound effects including bells, knocking noises, and the clash of swords. The programme also included eight short films of musicians and a spoken message from Will HAYS saluting the new era of "pictures and music."

This first sound feature created no sensation. During its first year Vitaphone struggled to survive in Warners' small cinemas, all of which were wired for sound. The following year, however, Warners made history with THE JAZZ SINGER starring Al JOLSON, which featured synchronized songs and two short passages of dialogue. It was directed by Alan Crosland, who had also made *Don Juan*.

Despite this triumph, Vitaphone's life proved short, since the synchronization between image and disc often went awry. Following the success of Fox's MOVIETONE sound-on-film system, Warners' dropped Vitaphone in 1930 for a similar system.

voice   voice over (VO) *See* NARRATION.

voice test An AUDITION to test the voice quality of an actor, singer, narrator, or person dubbing a film. In the early sound era panic was created amongst performers as all studios instigated voice tests. "Long queues lined up for these tests", wrote the scenarist Frances Marion, "and as they were herded forward to face their destiny, fear was paramount..." Major casualties of the new era included John GILBERT and Norma TALMADGE.

von Sternberg, Josef (Josef Sternberg; 1894–1969) Austrian-born director, who discovered Marlene DIETRICH and elevated her to international stardom. A masterly (if sometimes self-indulgent) stylist, he was much admired for his atmospheric visuals, which made striking use of the interplay of light and shade. He often photographed and edited his own films. "I care nothing about the story" he once said, "only how it is photographed and presented."

Although highly gifted, von Sternberg was also arrogant and stubborn. Believing that "the only way to succeed is to make people hate you", he also insisted that an actor "must be told exactly what to do and think." William POWELL had a special clause inserted in his contract specifying that he would never have to work with von Sternberg.

He was born in Vienna to a poor Jewish family who moved to New York when he was seven (the aristocratic 'von' was added later at the suggestion of a Hollywood producer). Having begun his cinema career patching film for the World Film Company in New Jersey, he quickly advanced to assistant director. During World War I he served in the Army Signal Corps and made training films.

After moving to Hollywood in 1924 he directed, produced, and scripted *The Salvation Hunters* (1925), a film about derelicts that Charlie CHAPLIN proclaimed as a masterpiece. When it failed at the box office, Chaplin said "I thought I'd praise a bad picture and see what happened." In 1926 von Sternberg joined Paramount and made Hollywood's first serious GANGSTER movie, *Underworld* (British title *Paying the Penalty*; 1927). He was happy to admit his ignorance of the crime world, saying "the illusion of reality is what I look for, not reality itself."

At the request of Emil JANNINGS, von Sternberg travelled to Germany in 1930 to make UFA's first talkie, THE BLUE ANGEL (jointly produced with Paramount). Having seen Dietrich performing on stage, he insisted on casting her as the nightclub singer who destroys an old professor (Jannings). Although billed second, Dietrich immediately became an international star and followed von Sternberg back to Hollywood. There they made six more films together, including *Morocco* (1930), in which she appeared opposite Gary COOPER, *Shanghai Express* (1932), which brought von Sternberg an Oscar nomination as Best Director, *The Scarlet Empress* (1934), about Catherine the Great, and *The Devil is a Woman* (1935).

After the latter did poorly at the box office, von Sternberg left Paramount for Columbia to make *Crime and Punishment* with Peter LORRE. In 1937 he travelled to England to film *I Claudius* for Alexander KORDA, with Charles LAUGHTON as the Roman emperor; this intriguing project was halted when co-star Merle OBERON was injured in a car crash and never resumed. Although *The Shanghai Gesture* (1941) was amongst his best films, Hollywood projects dried up in the 1940s. In 1953 he went to Japan to make *Ana-Ta-Han* (*The Saga of Anatahan*), which he wrote, directed, photographed, and produced (as well as supplying the narration in the English version). After making *Jet Pilot* (1953) for Howard HUGHES, von Sternberg retired.

von Stroheim, Erich (Erich Oswald Stroheim; 1885–1957) Austrian-born Hollywood director and actor, who outraged producers and studio heads with his extravagance and megalomania. As well as directing, he usually co-scripted his films and assisted with art direction and costumes. His renown rests on seven silent films, his masterpiece being the epic GREED (1924).

Born in Vienna, the son of a Jewish hatter, he served in the Austro-Hungarian army before going to work in his father's business. In 1909 he emigrated to America, where he worked in various jobs in New York and San Francisco. On arriving in Hollywood in 1914 he fabricated the story (which still appears in some biographies) that he was a Catholic aristocrat who had been an officer in the cavalry.

Having joined D. W. GRIFFITH's company as a bit player, von Stroheim acted in both THE BIRTH OF A NATION (1915) and INTOLERANCE (1916), on which he worked as an assistant director. During World War I he specialized in playing arrogant and sadistic German officers, becoming known as **the Man You Love to Hate**. In *Heart of Humanity* (1918) he tosses a baby out of a window.

In 1919 Carl Laemmle, the head of Universal, allowed von Stroheim to script, direct, and star in *Blind Husbands* (1919), an adaptation of his own story, *The Pinnacle*. The film, about an Austrian officer who seduces an American, became a success after reviewers praised it as the wittiest sex story ever filmed. *The Devil's Passkey* (1920) and *Foolish Wives* (1922) were also stories of seduction and infidelity. As the budget for the latter spiralled, Laemmle erected an electric sign on Broadway flashing out the current figure; he eventually had it altered so that 'Stroheim' read '$troheim'.

For similar reasons Stroheim was fired halfway through the making of *Merry-Go-*

Round (1923) by Universal's production head, Irving THALBERG. He then persuaded Samuel GOLDWYN to back GREED, an ambitious story of a man ruined by his wife's obsession with money. This ended up as a 42-reel movie running for seven hours. His old enemy Thalberg, now at MGM, forced him to cut it to 24 reels before the studio reduced it to 10.

Following this debacle, von Stroheim made his most popular film, the operetta *The Merry Widow* (1925), for Paramount. The same studio released *The Wedding March* (1928), a three-hour epic about decadent goings-on in Imperial Austria. Later that year *Queen Kelly*, about a convent girl who becomes involved in prostitution, was shut down by the producers Joseph Kennedy and Gloria SWANSON, also the star, when the budget hit $800,000. The film wrecked the careers of both star and director.

Thereafter he returned to acting, playing a mad German film director, Erich Von Furst, in *The Lost Squadron* (1932); the role was virtually a self-portrait. In Jean RENOIR'S LA GRANDE ILLUSION (1937) he gave perhaps his most memorable performance, as the authoritarian commandant of a German prisoner-of-war camp. Billy Wilder's SUNSET BOULEVARD (1950) saw von Stroheim giving another self-portrait as a once-famous director now acting as butler to his former star (Swanson).

Von Stroheim, who moved to France in the 1950s, continued to act, collaborate on scripts, and write occasional novels until his death.

von Sydow, Max (Carl Adolf von Sydow; 1929–) Imposing Swedish actor, who played a series of struggling melancholic characters in films by Ingmar BERGMAN before moving on to Hollywood. His best known role in US films was that of Christ in *The Greatest Story Ever Told* (1965). He has also directed a Danish-Swedish film, the Bergmanesque tragedy *Katinka* (1988).

Born in Lund, the son of a university professor, von Sydow trained at Stockholm's Royal Dramatic Theatre School before making his screen debut in *Bara en mor* (1949). Over the next few years he became known for his strong voice and authoritative presence in a series of stage plays. His cinema career was wholly fashioned by Bergman, who came to regard von Sydow as his on-screen alter ego. Early Bergman films to feature striking performances by von Sydow include THE SEVENTH SEAL (1957), in which he plays a medieval knight struggling with the deepest moral and theological questions, *The Virgin Spring* (1960), *Through a Glass Darkly* (1961), and *Winter Light* (1962).

Von Sydow was virtually unknown to US filmgoers when he was offered the role of CHRIST in George STEVENS's Bible epic *The Greatest Story Ever Told*. Subsequent roles included a strict parson in George Roy HILL's *Hawaii* (1966), in which he co-starred with Julie ANDREWS, a Nazi in *The Quiller Memorandum* (1966), a Swedish farmer settling in Minnesota in *The Emigrants* (1970), and the priest in THE EXORCIST (1973). He appeared in the post-Watergate spy thriller *Three Days of the Condor* (1975), took a small part in Woody ALLEN's *Hannah and Her Sisters* (1985), and starred as a Swedish immigrant worker in Bille August's acclaimed *Pelle the Conqueror* (1987). More recently he appeared in the thriller *A Kiss Before Dying* (1992).

W

Wajda, Andrzej (1926–) Polish director, widely considered the most important figure in contemporary Polish cinema. After World War II, during which he fought with the Resistance, Wajda studied at the film school in Łódź and made various shorts. His first three feature films comprise a trilogy depicting the horrors of the war; while *A Generation* (1954) and *Kanal* (1957) dealt with the activities of the Resistance in Warsaw, ASHES AND DIAMONDS (1958) focused on a young antihero, whose plans to kill a communist official end in his own death. The central role was played by Zbigniew Cybulski, whose career was to become inseparable from that of the director. Wajda subsequently experimented with a wider range of subjects, from *Innocent Sorcerers* (1960), which voiced the frustrations of modern youth, to *The Siberian Lady Macbeth* (1961). His next major triumph came with *Everything for Sale* (1968), about the problems of a film crew when the leading actor goes missing; the film was partly inspired by the accidental death of Cybulski, an incident that consolidated the actor's reputation as a Polish James DEAN. Less remarkable films followed, among them *The Wedding* (1972) and *The Shadow Line* (1976).

Wajda's next significant achievement, *Man of Marble* (1977), was banned in Poland but won international acclaim for its indictment of official corruption. Political themes were also addressed in *Rough Treatment* (1978) and *Man of Iron* (1981), in which the state conducts a smear campaign against Solidarity activists. Subsequent films have included the historical drama *Danton* (1982), starring Gérard DEPARDIEU, *A Love in Germany* (1983), based on a novel by Rolf Hochhuth, and *Korczak* (1990), which recounts the heroic efforts of a Polish-Jewish doctor to assist the children of the Warsaw ghetto during the German occupation. In 1993 he returned to the theme of the wartime Resistance in *Ring of the Crowned Eagle*.

walk. **Walk of Stars** *See* GRAUMAN'S CHINESE THEATER.

walk-on An actor who has only a small part and no speaking lines. The term is also used of the performance or role, which is more important than that of an EXTRA but less than a BIT part. Several stars began their careers this way: David NIVEN's first role was a Mexican walk-on in a Western, for which he was sprayed red and wore a blanket and a large sombrero.

walk-through A rough rehearsal, often the first on a set, in which actors (or STAND-INS) move through their actions with no dialogue and without the cameras operating. This allows the crew to check such technical details as camera positions, lighting, and sound. *Compare* RUN-THROUGH.

Wallach, Eli (1915–) US actor who made his first film at the age of 41, after 16 years on the stage; he is best known for his villainous supporting roles. He has co-starred with his wife, Anne Jackson, in a number of films. Born in Brooklyn, Wallach studied acting at New York's Neighborhood Playhouse and took classes in METHOD acting from Lee Strasberg. Having established his reputation on Broadway, Wallach made his screen debut in Elia KAZAN's BABY DOLL (1956), in which he played the seducer of Karl MALDEN's child-bride (Carroll Baker). He went on to play a Mexican bandit in *The Magnificent Seven* (1960), a train robber in *How the West was Won* (1962), a villainous hotelier in *The Moonspinners* (1964), and the 'ugly' in *The Good, the Bad and the Ugly* (1967).

In 1967 Wallach and his wife co-starred in *The Tiger Makes Out*, re-creating the roles (of a shy postman and the suburban housewife he kidnaps) that they had played in the original stage version. His other films with Jackson include the comedy *How to Save a Marriage* (1968) and the thriller *Zigzag* (1970). He made several Italian movies in the 1970s, and among his later Hollywood offerings are *Tough Guys* (1986), with Burt

LANCASTER and Kirk DOUGLAS; *Nuts* (1987), starring Barbra STREISAND; and THE GODFATHER, PART III (1990), as a Mafia boss.

walla-walla *See* RHUBARB.

Wallis, Hal B. (1899–1986) US producer who established his reputation with WARNER BROTHERS in the 1930s, and then worked independently. In 1938, after making more than 400 films, he received the Irving Thalberg Academy Award for "outstanding motion picture production."

Born in Chicago, Wallis managed a cinema before joining Warners as a publicity assistant in 1923. One of his first successes as a producer was the early GANGSTER classic LITTLE CAESAR, with Edward G. ROBINSON. Wallis went on to produce some 30 films a year for the studio, including *The Story of Louis Pasteur* (1936) with Paul MUNI, *Jezebel* (1938) with Bette DAVIS, *High Sierra* (1941) with Humphrey BOGART, and *Yankee Doodle Dandy* (1942) with James CAGNEY.

The growing rivalry between Wallis and Jack WARNER came to a head at the 1943 Academy Awards ceremony, when Warner dashed down the aisle to accept the Oscar for Wallis's CASABLANCA. The following year Wallis formed Hal Wallis Productions in association with Paramount. During the later 1940s he perfected the FILM NOIR with such films as *Sorry, Wrong Number* (1948) and *Dark City* (1950). Other successes includ·d adaptations of such Broadway plays as *The Rose Tattoo* (1955) and *The Rainmaker* (1956), the Western GUNFIGHT AT THE OK CORRAL (1957), the Elvis PRESLEY vehicle *King Creole* (1958), *Becket* (1964) with Richard BURTON, and *True Grit* (1969) with John WAYNE.

When Paramount rejected Burton as the star of *Anne of the Thousand Days* (1969), Wallis took the film and Burton to Universal and remained there. He made three films in Britain in the 1970s, including *Mary Queen of Scots* (1971) with Vanessa REDGRAVE and Glenda JACKSON. His last film was the Western *Rooster Cogburn* (1975), starring Wayne and Katharine HEPBURN, which he co-scripted with his wife, the actress Martha Hyer (under the name of Martin Julien).

Walsh, Raoul (1887–1980) Prolific US director and scriptwriter, who specialized in slick but unpretentious action films. Walsh's career as a director spanned 52 years, principally with 20th Century-Fox and Warner Brothers. Miriam Cooper, the first of his three wives, starred in many of his early films.

Born in New York, Walsh ran away from home to become a cowboy; he subsequently worked as an undertaker before making his stage debut in 1907. Four years later he appeared in his first film and worked as an assistant to D. W. GRIFFITH at BIOGRAPH. As co-director of *The Life of General Villa* (1914), Walsh rode with the outlaw Pancho Villa to shoot dangerous sequences that were then combined with studio scenes. In 1915 he played John Wilkes Booth in Griffith's THE BIRTH OF A NATION and appeared in one of the first gangster films, Fox's *Regeneration*.

Having attracted attention with his second film as a director, THE THIEF OF BAGDAD (1924), Walsh made his name with *What Price Glory?* (1926), a World-War-I love story. Although silent, the film shocked audiences with scenes in which the actors were clearly mouthing profanities. The talkie sequel, *The Cockeyed World* (1929), was an even greater success. In 1928 he directed, co-scripted, and acted in *Sadie Thompson* (1928), with Gloria SWANSON, and co-directed *In Old Arizona*, Hollywood's first all-talking sound-on-film feature. During shooting, Walsh lost an eye when a rabbit hit the windscreen of his car, and he wore an eye patch thereafter.

In 1939 Walsh joined Warner Brothers, where his successes included the action films *High Sierra* (1941) with Humphrey BOGART, *They Died with Their Boots On* (1941) with Errol FLYNN, and *White Heat* (1949) with James CAGNEY. Jack WARNER once complained that Walsh's idea of a tender love scene was one in which he could burn down a whorehouse.

Walsh's last great success was *Battle Cry* (1955), a World-War-II story starring Van HEFLIN. From 1955 he worked chiefly for 20th Century-Fox but returned to Warners for his last movie, the Western *A Distant Trumpet* (1963). Having become nearly blind in his remaining eye, he retired the following year.

WAMPAS Western Association of Motion Picture Advertisers. An organization that bestowed the title of **Wampas Baby Star** on selected Hollywood starlets from 1922 until 1934. Thirteen actresses were chosen each year as the most likely stars of the future, a list that was eagerly awaited by both studios and fans. Among the best guesses were Clara BOW in 1924, Mary ASTOR and Joan CRAWFORD in 1926, Jean ARTHUR and Loretta YOUNG in 1929, and Ginger ROGERS in 1932.

wardrobe The items of clothing and accessories worn by performers in a film; also the department that provides them. In the heyday of the STUDIO SYSTEM, large departments of designers and seamstresses were employed to dress the productions – either by creating new costumes or by adapting those in the studios' vast stock. Since the decline of the studios, films tend to rely on acquisitions by the ART DIRECTOR, items from the performers' own wardrobes, or rental from a specialist costumier. *See* COSTUME DESIGNER.

war films *See* COLD WAR; VIETNAM WAR; WORLD WAR I; WORLD WAR II.

warnography A type of film that glorifies war and stimulates aggression in the viewer. A blend of *war* and *pornography*, the word has also been applied to books and magazines; typical examples from the cinema include the RAMBO series.

Warhol, Andy (Andrew Warhola; ?1926–87) US pop artist and director of AVANT-GARDE films. Having already become famous with his paintings of soup cans and Coca-Cola bottles, Warhol began to make experimental films at his New York workshop, the Factory, in 1963. *Sleep* (1963), a six-hour study of a naked man sleeping, was followed by *Empire* (1964), an eight-hour single-shot view of the Empire State Building. His other early films, including *Blow Job* (1964), *My Hustler* (1965), and *Bike Boy* (1967), concentrated on unconventional sexual matters. (*My Hustler* is said to have influenced John SCHLESINGER'S MIDNIGHT COW-BOY, 1969.) *Mario Banana* and *Harlot* (both 1964) featured the transvestite Mario Montez, one of a number of sexually ambiguous individuals who clustered around Warhol.

The addition of sound to Warhol's films did not make them any more conventional; *Chelsea Girls* (1966), starring Edie Sedgwick and Nico, was shown on two screens with different images projected onto each. Warhol's approach to film-making was simple and direct: "I only wanted to find great people and let them be themselves and talk about what they usually talked about and

I'd film them for a certain time and that would be the movie."

From 1967 onwards most of Warhol's films were actually directed by Paul Morrissey, who developed a more narrative style. *Lonesome Cowboys* (1968) is a gay Western, *Flesh* (1968) portrays a day in the life of a male prostitute, *Trash* (1970) concerns an impotent drug addict, and *Heat* (1972) sleazily subverts SUNSET BOULEVARD. Many of these films starred Joe Dallesandro, a well-built man with scant regard for clothing. Warhol's final film as director was *Women in Revolt* (1972). Morrissey's subsequent films for Warhol included two unusual horror spoofs: *Flesh for Frankenstein* (1973), complete with scenes of necrophilia, and *Blood for Dracula* (1974), in which Dracula is thwarted in his attempts to drink virgin's blood by a randy gardener (Dallesandro). The final Morrissey film was *Bad* (1976).

Warner. **Warner Brothers** A Hollywood production company founded in 1923 by four brothers, Harry (1881–1958), Albert (1884–1967), Sam (1888–1927), and Jack (1892–1978). Its exceptional roster of stars has included John BARRYMORE, Bette DAVIS, Errol FLYNN, Humphrey BOGART, James CAGNEY, Edward G. ROBINSON, Olivia DE HAVIL-LAND, Clint EASTWOOD, Harrison FORD, and Kevin COSTNER. Warner Brothers often lured talent from other studios, being denounced by Samuel GOLDWYN as "guilty of the most reckless star-raiding that the industry has ever known."

In 1903 the Warners' father bought a nickelodeon in Newcastle, Pennsylvania. The brothers began distributing in 1905, produced several two-reel Westerns in 1912, and in 1923 formed Warner Brothers Pictures, Inc., a Hollywood studio headed by Jack WARNER. Two years later, they acquired VITAGRAPH and FIRST NATIONAL Pictures. The company only avoided financial disaster in the 1920s through the popularity of their dog star, RIN TIN TIN. In 1926 the company engaged in a massive gamble when it joined with Western Electric to develop the VITAPHONE sound-on-disc system; this took its place in cinema history when THE JAZZ SINGER opened at the Warners Theater in New York in 1927. (Sam Warner died at the age of 40 two days before the premiere.) Within a year, Warner's stock rose from $9 to $132.

In the 1930s, their golden era, Warner Brothers adopted the slogan 'Good Films – Good Citizenship' and adopted an ethos of social responsibility. The studio's output included a powerful cycle of GANGSTER movies starring James Cagney and Edward G. Robinson, such 'social message' films as *I Am a Fugitive from a Chain Gang* (1932), and educational biopics, such as *The Story of Louis Pasteur* (1936) with Paul MUNI, as well as some highly professional musicals. Other stars included Bette Davis, who played 11 roles in 1932 alone and went on to win Oscars for *Dangerous* (1935) and *Jezebel* (1938). She fought constantly with the studio and lost a suit against their binding contracts.

Warners' great successes of the 1940s included CASABLANCA and the musical *Yankee Doodle Dandy* (both 1942). In the early 1950s the company suffered badly from the popularity of television, despite scoring a success with the 3-D horror feature *House of Wax* (1953). Harry and Albert Warner sold most of their shares in 1956, leaving Jack to run the company alone until 1967. In 1964 the studio won the Best Picture Oscar for its musical *My Fair Lady* (1964).

Having been acquired by Kinney National Service in 1969, Warner Communications (as it was renamed) went on to enjoy hits with such varied fare as THE EXORCIST (1973), *All the President's Men* (1976), SUPERMAN (1978), and *Gremlins* (1984). In 1989 it produced both the Oscar-winning *Driving Miss Daisy* and the box-office triumph BATMAN. That year it merged with the magazine company Time-Life to become Time Warner, the world's most powerful media corporation. Recent Warner films have included *Robin Hood: Prince of Thieves* (1991) with Kevin Costner, *Unforgiven* (1993), which won Oscars for Best Picture and Best Director (Clint Eastwood, who also starred), and *The Fugitive* (1993) with Harrison Ford.

Jack Warner (Jack Leonard Eichelbaum; 1892–1978) Hollywood executive, the youngest and most famous of the four Warner brothers. He frequently battled with his stars, who included Bette DAVIS and Humphrey BOGART, and lacked tact: when introduced to the wife of Chiang Kai-shek, he joked that he had forgotten to bring his laundry. His 1956 autobiography was titled *My First Hundred Years in Hollywood*.

Warner was born in London, Ontario, the youngest of 12 children of Polish pedlars. With three of his brothers Harry, Albert, and Sam, he co-founded Warner Brothers Pictures Inc. in 1923. As production chief, Jack brought director Michael CURTIZ from Austria in 1926, launched the sound era with THE JAZZ SINGER in 1927, and cast the unknown Errol FLYNN as the star of *Captain Blood* (1936).

Warner also made mistakes. He bought Sinclair Lewis's bestseller *Main Street* and changed the title to *I Married a Doctor* (1936) because "nobody would want to see a picture about a street." The movie flopped. He passed up the opportunity to buy GONE WITH THE WIND (1939), and predicted that future audiences would wear 3-D glasses "as effortlessly as they wear wrist watches or carry fountain pens."

Everyone feared disturbing Warner's regular afternoon nap. One day, however, Bette Davis stormed in to complain about a bad script. Without opening his eyes, Warner buzzed his secretary and said, "Come in and wake me up. I'm having a nightmare." Davis collapsed with laughter. Warner always hated loaning his stars to other studios. He tried to prevent Olivia DE HAVILLAND from appearing in *Gone with the Wind*, and when Samuel GOLDWYN wanted Davis for *The Little Foxes* (1941), Warner refused until reminded of a $425,000 gambling debt.

During World War II Warner produced the Irving BERLIN musical *This is the Army* and served with the Army Signal Corps. His last Warner Brothers production was *My Fair Lady* (1964). After selling his company shares in 1967 he became an independent producer, making such films as the musical *Camelot* (1967) and *Dirty Little Billy* (1972).

Waters, John (1945–) US director of CULT FILMS, many of which feature the 300-pound transvestite Divine (Harris Glen Milstead). "I wanted to be punk when there wasn't such a thing" said Waters, whose films are noted for their bad taste and bizarre subject matter.

Having met Milstead at high school in Baltimore, Waters gave him the starring role in his debut movie, *Mondo Trasho* (1969); the production resulted in Waters being arrested for "conspiracy to commit indecent exposure." Further controversy was aroused by the 16mm *Pink Flamingos* (1972), the fade-out of which shows Divine eating real dog excrement. Waters scripted, directed, photographed, and edited the story, a farrago about kidnapped girls who are impregnated so that their children can be sold to lesbian couples and the money used to finance heroin pushing to high-school students. To Waters's joy, *Variety* described it as "one of the most vile, stupid, and repulsive films ever made."

Waters's next movie was the $25,000 *Female Trouble* (1974), in which Divine is raped, gives birth (on camera), and finally dies in the electric chair (an item now kept in the doorway of Waters's Baltimore home). The comedy *Polyester* (1981) was more mainstream, even featuring a performance from the ex-Hollywood star Tab Hunter, who at one point is seen kissing Divine. For this production Waters introduced 'Odorama', a scratch-and-sniff card that released various smells to correspond to the action on screen.

Hairspray (1988), Waters's first commercial success, proved to be the last movie for Divine, who died two weeks after it premiered. The film, which co-starred the singer Sonny Bono (CHER's former husband), is a camp parody of 1960s teenage films set in Baltimore. Despite suffering a flop with the rather similar *Cry-Baby* (1990), Waters found backing from Savoy Pictures Entertainment for the $13-million black comedy *Serial Mom* (1994). The film featured Kathleen TURNER, his first major star, as an all-American mother who is also a serial killer.

wave machine   A device used to create churning waves for shots involving water. It usually consists of electrically operated rollers that revolve while also moving up and down. The makers of MGM's *Show Boat* (1951) used a wave machine to re-create the Mississippi river between concrete banks on the BACK LOT.

Wayne, John   (Marion Michael Morrison; 1907–79) Legendary WESTERN star, who became the embodiment of the strong, silent, decent American. "I've played the kinda man I'd like to have been" he told the *Daily Mail* in 1974. Nicknamed **the Duke**, he starred in 142 feature films and was the biggest US box-office draw in 1950, 1951, 1954, and 1971. "I play John Wayne in every part regardless of the character" he once commented, "and I've been doing okay, haven't I?" After 40 years in the

industry, Wayne finally won the Oscar for Best Actor playing Rooster Cogburn, a drunken marshal with an eye patch, in *True Grit* (1969).

Born in Winterset, Iowa, Wayne won a football scholarship to the University of Southern California, Los Angeles. A summer job as an assistant prop man at 20th Century-Fox led to bit parts (as Duke Morrison) in several silent films. His appearance in John FORD's *Mother Machree* (1928) led Ford to recommend him to Raoul WALSH for the lead in *The Big Trail* (1930). Wayne went on to make some 80 movies in eight years, mostly Mascot serials and B Westerns. His big break came when Ford cast him as the Ringo Kid in STAGECOACH (1939), after Gary COOPER turned down the role. "Ford taught me not to act for the camera" said Wayne, "but to react."

In the 1940s he made a number of war films, including Ford's *They Were Expendable* (1945) and Allan DWAN's *Sands of Iwo Jima* (1949), before returning to the Western. His films of this period include the Ford classics *Fort Apache* (1948) with Henry FONDA, *The Quiet Man* (1952), a romantic comedy set in Ireland, THE SEARCHERS (1956), perhaps his finest hour, and *The Horse Soldiers* (1959). He also starred in Howard HAWKS's *Red River* (1948), prompting Ford to remark, "I never knew that big sonovabitch could act."

In 1960 Wayne produced, directed, and starred (as Davy Crockett) in the patriotic Western *The Alamo* (dismissed by one critic as "sentimental and preposterous flapdoodle"). Wayne, who had been president of the Motion Picture Alliance for the Preservation of American Ideals during the anti-Communist era of the House Un-American Activities Committee remained an outspoken super-patriot during the troubled 1960s. His propagandist VIETNAM-WAR film *The Green Berets* (1968) was especially reviled.

Wayne's last films included *True Grit* and its sequel *Rooster Cogburn* (1975), both of which were directed by Raoul Walsh, and Don SIEGEL's *The Shootist* (1976), with James STEWART and Lauren BACALL. In this, his last appearance, Wayne played a gunfighter dying of cancer, as he himself was at the time. Typically, Wayne insisted that his character should have cancer of the prostate rather than the bladder, as the latter was "unmanly".

He was as tough as an old nut and as soft as a yellow ribbon.

ELIZABETH TAYLOR.

Talk low, talk slow and don't talk too much.

JOHN WAYNE on film acting.

Weaver, Sigourney (Susan Alexandra Weaver; 1949–) US actress, who took her adopted name from a character in *The Great Gatsby*. Her father, Pat Weaver, was a former president of NBC and her uncle the US character-comedian Doodles Weaver.

Sigourney's first acting roles included an appearance in the chorus of *The Frogs* with Meryl STREEP when both were at Yale. She made her screen debut with a walk-on part in Woody ALLEN's ANNIE HALL (1977), having turned down a bigger role in favour of stage work. Two years later she shot to fame playing the feisty Lt Ripley in Ridley SCOTT's science-fiction shocker ALIEN (1979). She followed this by co-starring with William Hurt and Christopher PLUMMER in a thriller, *The Janitor* (British title *Eyewitness*).

At this point Weaver started to consider her career path carefully, refusing the lead in *Body Heat* (1981) because of the sex scenes. In Peter WEIR's *The Year of Living Dangerously* (1983), a political thriller set in Indonesia, she played opposite Mel GIBSON, who wore built-up shoes to raise him to her six-foot stature. Despite her success in *Ghostbusters* (1984), she felt that her METHOD training did not sit well with comedy and she longed for more serious parts with sympathetic leading men.

In 1986 Weaver returned to the role of Ripley in *Aliens* (1986), an action-packed sequel to the 1979 film that developed her character into a tough no-nonsense heroine. This was followed by *Gorillas in the Mist* (1988), in which she played the real-life anthropologist Dian Fossey. Her career now very much on the rise, she obscured Melanie Griffith on the posters for *Working Girl* (1988), despite her smaller part, and made a lucrative final appearance as Ripley in *Alien 3* (1992). She turned to comedy again with *Dave* (1993), in which she played a bitchy First Lady to Kevin KLINE's president.

Weir, Peter (1944–) Australian director. The son of a real estate broker, Weir was educated at the University of Sydney and made his first shorts while working for Australian television. His feature debut was *The Cars that Ate Paris* (1974), a black comedy that he also co-scripted, about a town that lures drivers into accidents so that the townspeople can cannibalize the wrecks. *Picnic at Hanging Rock* (1975), an enigmatic film about the true case of three schoolgirls who disappeared without trace in 1900, brought some critical recognition, as did *The Last Wave* (1977), an examination of the differences between Western and Aboriginal cultures. Both films are beautiful to look at and hint rather vaguely at supernatural goings-on. More than any other films of the time, they aroused international interest in the 'New Wave' of Australian cinema.

Weir's next film, the World-War-I drama *Gallipoli* (1981) also focused on a clash of cultures, in this case between the British Forces and the more boisterous and naive antipodeans. Cultural differences also came to the fore in *The Year of Living Dangerously* (1983), about an Australian newsman (Mel GIBSON) in Jakarta during the downfall of Sukarno's regime, and Weir's first Hollywood feature, *Witness* (1985), which starred Harrison FORD as a city detective out of his element in a remote Amish community. The commercial success of these films established Weir as an important Hollywood director who could command large budgets.

Although *The Mosquito Coast* (1989), again starring Ford, was something of a flop, *Dead Poet's Society* (1989), quickly revived Weir's fortunes. The film, which starred Robin WILLIAMS as an unconventional teacher, earned an Oscar nomination as Best Picture. Weir returned to the theme of cultural conflict with *Green Card* (1991), a film about an uncouth Frenchman (Gérard DEPARDIEU) who enters into a marriage of convenience in America. *Fearless* (1994) is the curious story of an aircrash survivor (Jeff BRIDGES) who finds that he has lost all sense of fear.

Weissmuller, Johnny (1904–84) US actor, a former Olympic swimming champion forever identified with his most famous screen role, that of TARZAN.

Born in Pennsylvania, the son of Austrian immigrants, Weissmuller attended the University of Chicago before making his name as a swimmer, winning five gold medals at the 1924 and 1928 Olympic Games. After a cameo appearance as himself in *Glorifying the American Girl* (1929), he was signed by MGM for the title role in

Tarzan, the Ape Man (1932); he himself created the famous yodelling yell. Weissmuller went on to make 11 further Tarzan films, with Maureen O'SULLIVAN and several other actresses as Jane (and several chimpanzees as Cheetah).

The series ended with *Tarzan and the Mermaids* (1948), Weissmuller having put on too much weight for the role. He then moved to Columbia to make JUNGLE JIM (1948) the first of a series of B-movies about a hunter. His contract specified a maximum weight of 190 pounds, with $5,000 to be deducted from his salary for every excess pound. He took the series to television in 1955.

After 15 years away from the big screen, Weissmuller returned to make cameo appearances in *The Phynx* (1970) and Michael WINNER's *Won Ton Ton, the Dog Who Saved Hollywood* (1976).

When in Cuba for a golf tournament in 1959, Weissmuller found himself surrounded by Fidel Castro's guerrillas, who pointed rifles at him. He stood tall, beat his chest, and let out his famous yell. "Tarzan! Tarzan! *Bienvenido!*" shouted the troops, who then asked for autographs.

Welch, Raquel (1940–) Busty US sex siren prominent from the late 1960s to the mid 1970s. The daughter of a Bolivian-born father and a WASP mother, Welch began to enter beauty contests from the age of 14. After a few bit parts in the early 1960s, she was successfully launched as a major sex symbol by her manager and second husband Patrick Curtis. The best-known of her generally undistinguished films are probably *Fantastic Voyage* (1966), *One Million Years BC* (1966), which featured Welch in two-piece leopardskin loincloth and bikini top, the flop *Myra Breckinridge* (1970), in which she played a post-operative transexual, *The Magic Christian* (1970), *The Last of Sheila* (1973), and Dick LESTER's THE THREE MUSKETEERS (1974) and *The Four Musketeers* (1975). In the last two, originally intended as one film, Welch demonstrated a previously unsuspected gift for slapstick and verbal comedy. Since the 1980s she has appeared mainly in made-for TV films.

> If you have a physical attractiveness you don't have to act.
> RAQUEL WELCH.

> Silicone from the knees up.
> GEORGE MASTERS, make-up artist.

Welles, (George) Orson (1915–85) US director, producer, screenwriter, and actor, who was acclaimed as Hollywood's 'boy wonder' after making his debut (at the age of 25) with CITIZEN KANE (1941). His later career was a long anticlimax; "I started at the top and worked down", he once commented. Welles was married to the actress Rita HAYWORTH from 1943 to 1947.

Born in Kenosha, Wisconsin, Welles showed early signs of precocity; according to his own account, he was acting out scenes from Shakespeare from the age of five. Both parents – his father was an inventor and his mother a concert pianist – died before he was 13. Three years later he visited Ireland and bluffed his way into a role at Dublin's Gate Theatre by lying that he was an experienced actor. He made his Broadway debut, as Tybalt in *Romeo and Juliet*, in 1934.

After several years working together on the Federal Theater Project, Welles and John Houseman formed the Mercury Theater in 1937. A year later the company became infamous for its radio dramatization of H. G. Wells's *The War of the Worlds*, which caused panic among listeners who thought Martians were really invading New Jersey.

Following this *succès de scandale*, Welles was signed by RKO with a contract giving him unprecedented freedom. In 1940–41 he co-wrote, produced, directed, and starred in his masterpiece *Citizen Kane*, a barely disguised biography of newspaper tycoon William Randolph Hearst. The supporting cast included Joseph COTTEN and other members of the Mercury Theater. Despite critical plaudits, the film was a box-office failure.

Welles's next film, THE MAGNIFICENT AMBERSONS (1942), was an ambitious study of a US family at the turn of the century starring Cotten and Anne BAXTER. Owing largely to RKO's brutal cuts, the movie, which is acknowledged as a classic, was a commercial disaster. After appearing as Rochester in *Jane Eyre* (1944), Welles directed and starred in *The Stranger* (1946), a successful thriller that he later described as "the worst of my films."

Welles then co-starred with Hayworth in *The Lady from Shanghai* (1948), a dazzling if largely incomprehensible FILM NOIR that he also wrote and directed. Soon afterwards she filed for divorce, saying that she could not live with a genius. After both this film and a botched adaptation of *Macbeth* (1948) failed at the box office, Welles moved to Europe, where he spent most of the next three decades. His first European films were Carol REED's THE THIRD MAN (1949), in which he played the racketeer Harry LIME, and his own *Othello* (1951), in which he took the title role.

Welles then returned to America to direct TOUCH OF EVIL (1958) a weird thriller in which he co-starred with Charlton HESTON. The film is now usually considered the masterpiece of Welles's later period. Subsequent projects included an EXPRESSIONIST-style version of Kafka's *The Trial* (1962) and *Chimes at Midnight* (1966), a Shakespeare adaptation in which Welles played Falstaff.

In 1975 Welles moved back to America and received the AFI's Life Achievement Award. During the last 15 years of his life he directed no films and took no major roles, limiting himself mainly to cameos, TV commercials, and talk-show appearances. When he died (at his typewriter), he left several films unfinished, including *Don Quixote*, begun in 1955 and given its world premiere in 1993.

Wellman, William A. (1896–1975) US director and producer known as 'Wild Bill', a hard-drinking, tough-talking war hero who became a tyrant on the set. He once had a fist fight with Spencer TRACY and narrowly avoided one with John WAYNE. Louise BROOKS hated his "quiet sadism practised behind the camera", James MASON said he was "a tough little bastard", and David O. SELZNICK's wife called him "a terror, a shoot-up-the-town fellow trying to be a great big masculine I-don't-know-what." He was married five times and his son, William Wellman Jnr, was an actor.

Born in Brookline, Massachusetts, Wellman was arrested for car theft as a youth and left high school to play professional ice hockey. A pilot with the Lafayette Escadrille during World War I, he broke his back when his plane was shot down and received the Croix de Guerre and five US decorations. After the war he became a stunt pilot.

Wellman's Hollywood career began as the result of a forced landing on Douglas FAIRBANKS's estate. Although the actor arranged for him to play a small part in *Knickerbocker Buckaroo* (1919), Wellman found acting frightening and became a messenger at Samuel GOLDWYN's studio instead. When General John Pershing visited the studio and struck up a warm conversation with him, an impressed Goldwyn

immediately promoted Wellman to assistant director.

Having made his debut as a director with Fox's *The Man Who Won* (1923), Wellman directed several Westerns for the company. He then moved to Paramount and drew on his wartime experiences to create realistic air sequences for the World-War-I story *Wings* (1927), which won the first Oscar for Best Picture. After five years with Paramount, he moved to Warner Brothers to direct the gangster movie THE PUBLIC ENEMY (1931), which made James CAGNEY a star. He went independent in 1933. Wellman's successes of the 1930s included the original A STAR IS BORN (1937), with Janet GAYNOR and Fredric MARCH, which brought him an Oscar as co-writer and a nomination as Best Director, and *Beau Geste* (1939), with Gary COOPER, which drew on his early experience with the French Foreign Legion.

Amongst Wellman's later films were *The Ox-Bow Incident* (1943), a stark anti-lynching story with Henry FONDA, *Battleground* (1949), which won the Oscar for Best Picture, and *The High and the Mighty* (1954), with John Wayne as a pilot. Wellman retired after *Layfayette Escadrille* (1957) was severely edited by Warner Brothers. After his death (from leukaemia), his ashes were scattered from a plane in accordance with his wishes.

Wenders, Wim (Wilhelm Wenders; 1945–) German director, whose films explore the individual's search for identity in the modern world. Wenders emerged as an important new talent with his first feature, *The Goalkeeper's Fear of the Penalty* (1971), from the novel by Peter Handke. The film established the existential preoccupations that were to dominate much of his later work and made striking use of a rock-music soundtrack.

After *Alice in the Cities* (1974), about a girl's search for her grandmother in a Germany that is seen as having surrendered itself entirely to US materialism, Wenders directed two films in the tradition of the US ROAD MOVIE, *Wrong Movement* (1975) and *Kings of the Road* (1976). *The American Friend* (1977), in which he re-created the atmosphere of US FILMS NOIRS of the 1940s, featured performances by the directors Samuel FULLER and Nicholas RAY. Wenders's next film was a documentary about Ray's death from cancer entitled *Lightning Over Water* (1981). The US-made *Hammett*

(1982), another black thriller, speculated on the circumstances that led Dashiel Hammett to write THE MALTESE FALCON.

Wenders enjoyed considerable commercial success with *Paris, Texas* (1984), a melancholy story about the reunion of a man, his wife, and their son set largely in the Texan desert; the film was particularly admired for its evocative soundtrack and for the performances of Harry Dean Stanton and Nastassja KINSKI as the husband and wife. Wenders's other films of the 1980s included *Tokyo-Ga* (1985), a documentary about modern Japanese society, and *Wings of Desire* (1987), about an angel who decides to participate in the life of modern Berlin. Both *Until the End of the World* (1992), a fantasy filmed in locations all around the globe, and *Faraway, So Close* (1994) were widely criticized as obscure and pretentious.

werewolves *See* HORROR FILMS; MONSTERS; WOLF MAN, THE.

Wertmuller, Lina (Arcangela Felice Assunta Wertmuller von Elgg; 1928–) Italian director, whose violent sociological parables made her a cult figure in the 1970s. The daughter of a lawyer, Wertmuller was expelled from more than a dozen Catholic schools before becoming a teacher herself. She subsequently worked as an actress, playwright, and theatre director, establishing a reputation for temperament as well as talent. Shortly after assisting FELLINI on his 8½ (1963), she wrote and directed her own first feature, *The Lizards*, which won an award at the Locarno Film Festival.

Wertmuller's career really took off when she formed the production company Liberty Films with the actor Giancarlo Giannini (who appears in many of her pictures). In 1972 she won the Best Director Award at Cannes for *The Seduction of Mimi* (1972), a tragicomedy about a helpless individual overwhelmed by social, sexual, and political problems. Similar themes were explored in *Love and Anarchy* (1973), *All Screwed Up* (1974), and the controversial *Swept Away* (1974). She then received the best reviews of her career with *Seven Beauties* (1976), a moving and often absurd depiction of life in a Nazi concentration camp. The film led to a contract with Warner Brothers to direct four pictures in English, but this was terminated when her first effort, *The End of the*

World in Our Usual Bed in a Night Full of Rain (1977) proved disappointing. Her subsequent Italian films include *A Joke of Destiny Lying in Wait Like a Street Robber* (1983) and *Saturday, Sunday, and Monday* (1990).

Wertmuller has written all her films and her artist husband, Enrico Job, regularly designs her sets. In 1990 she was put in charge of Rome's celebrated film school, the Centro Sperimentale di Cinematografia, with a brief to reduce its administrative bureaucracy.

West. Mae West (1892–1980) Buxom US actress, a brazen parody of a sex symbol. In 1935 she was the highest-paid actress in America, with earnings of $480,833. Although West's stardom lasted only a decade, she was credited both with saving Paramount and provoking stricter Hollywood censorship. "Virtue is its own reward" she noted, "but it's no sale at the box office." Her exaggerated figure inspired the US Navy to nickname their inflatable life jackets *Mae Wests*.

West was born in Brooklyn, the daughter of heavyweight boxer Battling Jack West. Having entered burlesque as 'the Baby Vamp', she was appearing in Broadway revues by the age of 14. In 1926 she wrote, produced, and directed her first play, *Sex*, leading to her arrest on obscenity charges; two years later, she had a Broadway triumph with *Diamond Lil*. She made her screen debut at the age of 40 in *Night After Night* (1932) with George RAFT, her former stage co-star. In the film, West responds to the exclamation "Goodness, what beautiful diamonds!" with "Goodness had nothing to do with it, dearie." She later used this line as the title of her 1959 autobiography.

West's screen performances were characterized by drawling innuendo and double entendre. She wrote her own lines and co-scripted many of her films. Examples of her wit include: "It's not the men in my life that count, it's the life in my men", "I was Snow White, but I drifted", and "It takes two to get one into trouble."

In 1933 West played opposite Cary GRANT (whom she claimed to have discovered) in *She Done Him Wrong*, an adaptation of *Diamond Lil*; the film contains her celebrated invitation "Why don't you come up sometime and see me" (*see* COME). *I'm No Angel* (1933), which had its title changed from *It Ain't No Sin* after the imposition of the HAYS CODE, was the source of another famous line, "Beulah, peel me a grape" (*see* BEULAH). In 1940 she co-starred with W. C. FIELDS in *My Little Chickadee*, about the exploits of a pair of confidence tricksters in the Wild West.

After the failure of the musical *The Heat's On* (1943), West returned to Broadway. At the age of 78 she made a remarkable screen comeback playing a casting agent in *Myra Breckinridge* (1970). Once again she wrote her own dialogue: when a handsome man tells her "I'm six feet, seven inches," West replies, "Let's forget about the six feet and concentrate on the seven inches." Her last film, *Sextette* (1978), was an adaptation of her own stage play.

West Side Story (1961) United Artists' screen adaptation of the 1957 Broadway musical by Leonard Bernstein and Stephen Sondheim. The story is a modern version of Shakespeare's *Romeo and Juliet*, the feuding families being replaced by rival gangs on the tough West Side of New York. Tony, a former member of the Jets, falls for Maria, whose brother Bernardo leads the Sharks. Tragedy ensues when Tony accidentally kills Bernardo while trying to prevent a fight, and is then deceived into thinking that Maria is dead. He is shot by her former fiancé and dies in her arms. The film stars Natalie WOOD (with singing dubbed by Marni Nixon) and Richard Beymer (dubbed by Jimmy Bryant) as the lovers, with Rita Moreno and George Chakiris in Oscar-winning supporting roles. Eight other Oscars were awarded, including Best Picture. Songs include 'Maria', 'Tonight', 'America', 'I Feel Pretty', and 'There's a Place for Us'.

Robert WISE produced the $6-million film – his first musical – and co-directed with Jerome Robbins, who had mounted the New York stage production. Robbins, who had initially refused to go to Hollywood to re-create the dances, shot the opening sequence and handled the choreography; he was later removed from the film for exceeding the budget and falling behind schedule.

Westerns Action films set in the US West during the early days of expansion and settlement. America's only native genre has a long cinematic history. The earliest Western of any note is Edwin S. PORTER's *The Great Train Robbery* (1903), a film described as "probably the first effectively organized piece of dramatic fiction." The great D. W. GRIFFITH dominated the early history of the genre, using it to pioneer the artistic and technical developments showcased in his magnum opus THE BIRTH OF A NATION (1915). The other major director of this period, Thomas H. INCE, was responsible for introducing William S. Hart (1870–1946) and Tom Mix (1881–1940), prototypes of the Western star – "a virtuous, incorruptible hero more attached to his horse than any girl."

During the inter-war years Western production was dominated by REPUBLIC Studios, which issued thousands of cheap fillers starring William Boyd (1898–1972) as 'Hopalong' Cassidy, Gene AUTRY, Roy ROGERS, and John WAYNE. Of the numerous films produced in the 1920s only James Cruze's *The Covered Wagon* (1923), about the wagon trains west, John FORD's *The Iron Horse* (1924), about the construction of the railroad, and Buster KEATON'S THE GENERAL (1927), a Civil-War spoof, are now remembered. Another influential production was George MARSHALL's *Destry Rides Again* (1939), one of the very best Western comedies.

The 1940s saw the creation of the Western in its modern form. In particular, John Ford and John Wayne began a brilliant period of collaboration with STAGECOACH (1939), a film that has been described as "the basic Western, the template for everything that followed." It is an archetypal story of desperate characters united in the face of a common enemy and finding redemption through sacrifice. This became a recurring theme in Ford's work and in the Western genre as a whole. Further collaborations between the two men included *My Darling Clementine* (1946), in which Wyatt Earp cleans up Tombstone, *She Wore a Yellow Ribbon* (1949), with Wayne as an ageing cavalry officer, and THE SEARCHERS (1956), with Wayne as a Civil-War veteran seeking the men who killed his brother. At the end of the decade, a more sympathetic treatment of Native Americans became apparent in such films as *Broken Arrow* and *Devil's Doorway* (both 1950).

The 1950s and 1960s were also remarkably productive, with the genre adapting itself readily to changing times and tastes. In the early COLD WAR era Fred ZINNEMANN'S HIGH NOON (1952) and George STEVENS's SHANE (1953) crystallized the image of the Western hero standing alone for truth and virtue against the bad guys. Later, in the work of Sam PECKINPAH and the SPAGHETTI

WESTERNS of Sergio LEONE, this archetypal character was redefined as an amoral loner who cares only for the law of the gun. Peckinpah's *The Wild Bunch* (1969), about the final shoot-out of the last outlaw gang, has probably the highest bodycount of any non-war movie, while Leone's *The Good, the Bad and the Ugly* (1967), starring Clint EASTWOOD, and *Once Upon a Time in the West* (1969) are scarcely less violent.

After a decade or more during which few major Westerns were produced, the genre suddenly swung back into fashion with the box-office triumph of Kevin COSTNER's *Dances With Wolves* (1990) and Eastwood's elegiac *Unforgiven* (1992), both of which took the Oscar for Best Film. The mid 1990s saw a whole flood of Westerns featuring major Hollywood stars; examples from 1994 alone include *Maverick* with Mel GIBSON, *Wyatt Earp* with Costner, *The Quick and the Dead* with Sharon STONE and Gene HACKMAN, and *Bad Girls* with Drew BARRYMORE.

WGA *See* WRITERS GUILD OF AMERICA.

Whale, James (1886–1957) British-born Hollywood director best remembered for his stylish HORROR FILMS for UNIVERSAL, especially FRANKENSTEIN (1931) and *The Bride of Frankenstein* (1935). A former newspaper cartoonist, he took up acting in a German prisoner-of-war camp during World War I and returned to Britain to act, direct, and design for the stage. In 1929 he directed productions of R. C. Sheriff's war drama *Journey's End* in both London and New York. A year later he went to Hollywood to direct a film version and remained, as did the British actor Colin Clive, who played the lead.

A year after joining Universal in 1930, Whale enjoyed a major triumph with *Frankenstein*, a hugely influential horror film starring Clive as the scientist and Boris KARLOFF as the monster. His preference for British actors continued with THE INVISIBLE MAN (1933), starring Claude RAINS, and *The Bride of Frankenstein*, in which Clive and Karloff were joined by Elsa LANCHESTER as the bride. With its strong performances, blackly humorous script, and striking EXPRESSIONIST visuals, the latter is generally considered Whale's masterpiece and one of the finest horror pictures of all time. His non-horror films for Universal included the comedy thriller *Remember Last Night* and the big-budget musical *Show Boat* (both 1936).

Whales's career never recovered its momentum after he left Universal in the later 1930s. Although the theatrical biopic *The Great Garrick* (1937), which he also produced, and *The Man in the Iron Mask* (1939), a SWASHBUCKLER, were fairly well received, his adventure film, *Green Hell* (1940), was described by *The New York Times* as "the worst picture of the year." He made only two more films. In 1957 he committed suicide in his swimming pool, leaving a note that said "The future is just old age and pain."

Whisky Galore! (US title *Tight Little Island*; 1949) EALING STUDIOS much-loved comedy about a shipload of whisky wrecked on a small Scottish island. Directed by Alexander MACKENDRICK, the film was adapted by Compton Mackenzie and Angus MacPhail from the former's 1947 novel of the same name. The excellent cast included Basil Radford, Joan Greenwood, and James Robertson Justice, with Mackenzie himself in the role of Captain Buncher. The film was seen in America as *Tight Little Island* because at that time the HAYS CODE would not allow the word 'whisky' to appear in a US title.

The story is set on an island in the Outer Hebrides that runs out of whisky during World War II. A ship loaded with 50,000 cases of Scotch fortuitously runs aground, and the locals send out a rescue mission. All that remains is to outwit the Home Guard captain (Radford) and conceal the booty from the Customs and Excise man. The film owes its classic status to the clever performances, fast pace, and numerous brilliantly observed details.

white. Pearl White (1889–1938) US star of silent SERIALS, best known as the persecuted heroine of THE PERILS OF PAULINE (1914). She wrote the first ever autobiography of a Hollywood star, *Just Me* (1916), and was portrayed by Barbara Hutton and Pamela Austin in two biopics, both entitled *The Perils of Pauline* (1947 and 1967).

The daughter of a Missouri farmer, White went on stage at the age of six to play Eva in *Uncle Tom's Cabin*. At 13 she became a circus equestrienne, but suffered a spinal injury in a fall; she was working as a secretary when director Joseph A. Golden discovered her and cast her in his Western *The Life of Buffalo Bill* (1910). White made more than 100 shorts before starring in PATHÉ's *The Perils of Pauline*, which was followed by ten more serials, making her Hollywood's most popular star. Despite her back injury, she performed most of her own stunts in such CLIFFHANGERS as *The Exploits of Elaine* (1915), *Pearl of the Army* (1916), and *The House of Hate* (1918).

In 1920 White signed with Fox and made a vain attempt to break into features with such films as *Know Your Men* (1921) and *A Virgin Paradise* (1921). She then returned to Pathé for another serial, *Plunder* (1923). After making *The Perils of Paris* (1924) in France, she decided to retire there permanently.

white telephone Hollywood slang for a film set in an upper-class milieu with luxurious sets and affluent characters. Many 'white telephones' were produced during the Depression and its aftermath; examples include MGM's *Grand Hotel* (1932), the comedy *My Man Godfrey* (1936), and THE PHILADELPHIA STORY (1940). The Doris DAY and Rock HUDSON comedies of the 1950s can be seen as a revival of the subgenre. *See also* SCREWBALL COMEDY.

Who Framed Roger Rabbit? (1988) Robert ZEMECKIS's noir-style comedy thriller, a *tour de force* that combined cartoon characters and live action with unprecedented sophistication. A DISNEY/SPIELBERG co-production, it was the most popular film of 1988.

The story was adapted by Jeffrey Price and Peter S. Seaman from Gary Wolf's novel *Who Censored Roger Rabbit?* Roger (a cartoon rabbit) is a 'Toon' film star who loses his voluptuous wife, Jessica (a cartoon woman), and finds that he can no longer act. When Jessica's lover is murdered, Roger is the chief suspect and must rely on a seedy alcoholic private eye (played by Bob HOSKINS) to clear his name. Charles Fleischer provided the voice of Roger Rabbit, and Kathleen TURNER and Amy Irving the speaking and singing voices (respectively) of Jessica. Other parts were played by Christopher Lloyd, Joanna Cassidy, and Stubby Kaye, while a host of famous cartoon characters (such as BETTY BOOP, BUGS BUNNY, DAFFY DUCK, and MICKEY MOUSE) made cameo appearances as themselves.

The film cost $70 million to make and won Oscars for editing, sound effects, and visual effects, with a special award for the British director of animation, Richard Williams. The credits list a record 743 people, mostly animators – it took two years to perfect the synchronization of cartoon and live action.

When the film was shown in the largely Jewish suburb of Golders Green, London, high winds removed the last letter of the title, changing it to *Who Framed Roger Rabbi*.

wide. **wide-angle shot** A shot taken using a wide-angle lens, i.e. one with a shorter focal length and a broader field of view than a conventional lens. The resulting image has both a deep area of focus and a wide horizontal plane of action. Wide-angle lenses are mainly used for ESTABLISHING SHOTS and panoramic LONG SHOTS.

widescreen Any filming or projection system in which the on-screen image has an ASPECT RATIO greater than 4:3 (width to height). The standard frame size was established during the drive for standardization in the 1900s and adopted as the industry norm (*see* ACADEMY FRAME) in 1932.

Experimentation with widescreen has been prevalent during three periods of cinema history: the early pre-standardization era; the 1920s, when Hollywood dabbled with a variety of novelties to meet the competition from radio; and, most significantly, the 1950s, when the competition was from television. In all this experimentation, five basic methods have been explored: the use of film wider than the standard 35mm; the use of an ANAMORPHIC LENS to squeeze and unsqueeze the image; the use of more than one camera and projector; the feeding of the film horizontally through the camera; and the masking of the top and bottom of a standard image.

Wider-than-normal film has been experimented with since the beginnings of the cinema, with early systems of this kind including the two-inch Bioscope process. The 1920s saw the introduction of several wide-film systems, including Fox Grandeur (70mm film), Warners' Vitascope (65mm), and MGM's Realife (65mm). In the 1950s developments of this method included TODD-AO (65mm filming/70mm projection), as used in *Oklahoma!* (1955) and THE SOUND OF MUSIC (1965), and Super PANAVISION (65mm, 70mm in some ROAD SHOW prints), used in LAWRENCE OF ARABIA (1962).

The first anamorphic system was developed by Henri Chrétien in the 1920s and introduced in Claude Autant-Lara's *Construie en feu* (1927). Originally known as Hypergonar, it lay dormant for many years before 20th Century-Fox bought it in the

1950s and rechristened it CINEMASCOPE. The system, which proved more effective than any of its predecessors, was subsequently much imitated by the other studios.

Multiple-camera systems have proved unpopular owing to the cost of both filming and projection. Perhaps the most celebrated example of multiple-camera work is Abel GANCE's NAPOLEON (1928), which made use of 'Polyvision', a system that required three projectors working simultaneously. Although a brilliant demonstration of how multiple screens could be used creatively, the film was a financial failure owing to its huge costs. Since then multiple-camera/projector systems have been rarely used except at exhibitions and fairs (e.g. IMAX).

Horizontal feed systems include VISTAVISION (White Christmas, 1954), TECHNIRAMA (Spartacus, 1960), and TECHNISCOPE (Once Upon a Time in the West, 1969).

While aspect ratios of 2.55:1 were once common, there has since been a move back towards the Academy Ratio, as this is more suitable for television transmission. Aspect ratios of 1.85:1 and 1.66:1 are now popular in America and Europe respectively; action tends to be confined to the centre of the frame (the so-called 'safe-action area') to avoid the need to pan and scan for TV (see TELECINE).

The chief advantages of widescreen are the superior picture quality and the wide panoramas that it makes possible; these are particularly useful for placing action in its physical context and for scenes involving a large cast. For these reasons, widescreen has been mainly associated with big-budget costume epics and musicals, although its effectiveness in other genres should not be discounted.

Widmark, Richard (1914–) US actor, who specialized in tough-guy roles. Widmark has been married since 1942 to the former actress and screenwriter Jean Hazlewood.

Born in Sunrise, Minnesota, he taught drama until 1938, when he moved to New York to act on radio and on Broadway. In 1947 he made a spectacular screen debut playing Tony Udo, a psychopathic killer, in Henry HATHAWAY's Kiss of Death. The role brought him an Oscar nomination as Best Supporting Actor. After this triumph, Widmark starred as a psychotic bar owner in Road House (1948), with Ida LUPINO. Over the next few years villainous parts gradually yielded to more heroic roles, such as the Marine officer in Halls of Montezuma (1950). Samuel FULLER's Pickup on South Street (1953), in which he played a pickpocket who foils a communist ring, was followed by the Westerns Broken Lance (1954) with Spencer TRACY and The Alamo (1960) with John WAYNE.

Having starred as the tough New York detective Madigan in Don SIEGEL's 1969 film of the same name, Widmark went on to repeat the role in a popular television series. His later roles have included the murder victim in Murder on the Orient Express (1974), a doctor in Coma (1978), a government agent in the comedy Hanky Panky (1982), a sinister lawyer in Against All Odds (1983), and a US senator in True Colors (1990).

wigwag   A red light beside the entrance to a sound stage that flashes when filming is taking place, as a warning that no one should enter. A wigwag can also be placed on a barrier during outside shooting.

Wilcox, Herbert   (1892–1977) Irish-born producer and director who founded ELSTREE Studios in 1926. Having discovered Anna NEAGLE and made her Britain's biggest star to date, he somewhat belatedly married her. Noted for his energy, he produced films using extravagant Hollywood methods, importing stars from America and Europe.

Wilcox, who worked as a journalist and professional billiards player before service in World War I, began renting films in 1919. Three years later he co-produced The Wonderful Story and imported Mae Marsh for Flames of Passion. In the later 1920s he brought Dorothy GISH to Britain for Nell Gwyn (1926), which he scripted, and for other films, including Madame Pompadour (1927). This was the first production at Elstree Studios, which Wilcox had built with Paramount money for his British National (later British & Dominions) company. The biopic Dawn (1928), with Sybil Thorndike as Edith Cavell, caused a censorship row after official German complaints.

Wilcox discovered Neagle in the early 1930s and cast her in his 1934 remake of Nell Gwyn. She subsequently played Queen Victoria in both Victoria the Great (1937), a production requested by Edward VIII during his brief reign, and in Sixty Glorious Years (1938). RKO then invited the couple to Hollywood, where Wilcox remade Dawn as Nurse Edith Cavell (1939), with Neagle in the title role; an English oak was planted at the studios to honour the co-production. Wilcox and Neagle returned to wartime England in 1940 and finally married three years later.

Wilcox began his popular London romance series with *I Live in Grosvenor Square* (1945), with Neagle and Rex HARRISON, then paired his wife with Michael Wilding in *Piccadilly Incident* (1946), *The Courtneys of Curzon Street* (1947), *Spring in Park Lane* (1948), and *Maytime in Mayfair* (1949). After *Odette* (1950), his subsequent films were less successful; he went bankrupt in 1964 and retired.

wild. **wild sound** or **wild track** A sound recording, usually of BACKGROUND NOISE or ROOM SOUND, that does not have to be synchronized precisely with the accompanying images. It may be recorded at the time of shooting or separately.

Wild Strawberries (1957) Ingmar BERGMAN's poignant film about an old man's spiritual journey. Isdak Borg (Victor SJÖSTRÖM) sets out with his daughter-in-law Marianne (Ingrid Thulin) to receive an honorary doctorate from the University of Lund; in the course of the journey, he experiences a number of dreams and nightmares that prompt him to re-evaluate his life and his relations with his estranged family.

Evocatively contrasting the innocence and hope of youth with the cynicism and regret of old age, *Wild Strawberries* (a Swedish symbol of spring and renewal) is Bergman's warmest and most accessible film. The opening sequence, however, is one of the most disturbing he ever produced: Borg dreams of a faceless man, a handless clock, and a runaway hearse from which falls a coffin containing his own corpse. The images were based on one of Bergman's own dreams.

Borg is a curiously sympathetic character, thanks to the magisterial presence of Sjöström, a veteran actor who had also been one of the finest directors of the silent era. Bergman wrote of his performance: "His face shone with secretive light, as if reflected from another reality...It was like a miracle." Bibi Andersson, who played Borg's beloved cousin Sara, recalled the relationship between Sweden's most celebrated film-makers.

Sjöström was wonderful to work with because he was very real. He was a very

modern actor. I never heard of any real difficulties between him and Bergman, but there was a little struggle, because Ingmar, I think, had his own father a little bit in mind...I felt that he sometimes worried that Victor wanted to play for more sympathy than understanding. He didn't want him to be sentimental – and I don't think he is in the film.

Wilde, Cornel (1915–89) Tall, dark, and handsome US actor, who became an independent producer-director. He earned an Oscar nomination for his portrayal of Chopin in *A Song to Remember* (1945).

Born in New York to Hungarian-Czech parents, he paid his way through medical school by selling toys at Macy's department store. Although he won a scholarship to Columbia University and a place on the US Olympic fencing team in the mid 1930s, he subsequently abandoned both to act on Broadway.

In 1940 he appeared in Broadway's *Romeo and Juliet*, starring Laurence OLIVIER and Vivien LEIGH, and also served as fencing instructor for the production. He signed with Warner Brothers the same year, making his screen debut in *The Lady with Red Hair* (1940). Having moved to 20th Century-Fox, his big break came when he was loaned to Columbia for the surprise success *A Song to Remember*. He subsequently starred in *Forever Amber* (1947), opposite Linda Darnell, and in Jean NEGULESCO's *Road House* (1948), with Richard WIDMARK.

Having formed Theodora Productions in 1955, Wilde began to direct, produce, and star in his own films, these were mainly such swashbucklers as *Lancelot and Guinevere* (1962) and *Omar Khayyam* (1957). His later movies included *The Naked Prey* (1966), in which he plays a hunter pursued by an African tribe, *Shark's Treasure* (1974), which he also wrote, and *The Fifth Musketeer* (1979), in which he appeared as D'Artagnan. He died of leukaemia.

Wilder. **Billy Wilder** (1906–) Austrian-born US director, screenwriter, and producer. After abandoning his legal studies, Wilder worked as a newspaper reporter in Vienna and Berlin, where he also supplemented his income by working as a hotel dancer. It was during this period that he began his career as a writer for the cinema, his first produced screenplay being a collaboration with Robert SIODMARK on the semi-documentary *People on Sunday* (1929).

When Hitler came to power in 1933, the Jewish Wilder fled to Paris, where he co-directed *Mauvaise Graine* (1933), a film starring Danielle Darrieux. In 1934 he moved on to America via Mexico; Wilder's mother and the other members of the family he left behind in Germany all died in concentration camps.

Wilder arrived in Hollywood with little money and no real knowledge of the English language. Having moved in with actor Peter LORRE, he eked out a precarious living with very occasional scriptwriting duties. In 1938, however, he began a long and highly profitable association with screenwriter Charles Brackett. The collaboration, which endured until 1950, resulted in a long string of box-office successes. After making their mark as a writing team with such comedies as Ernst LUBITSCH's NINOTCHKA (1939) and Howard HAWKS's *Ball of Fire* (1942), both of which brought them Oscar nominations, the two men expanded their activities, with Wilder assuming the role of director and Brackett that of producer. Both men continued to collaborate on the screenplays.

Wilder's early successes as a director included *Five Graves to Cairo* (1943), a film about the contemporary North Africa campaign, the FILM NOIR classic DOUBLE INDEMNITY (1944), which was written in collaboration with Raymond CHANDLER, and *The Lost Weekend* (1945), a tale of an alcoholic writer (Ray MILLAND) that won a Best Picture Oscar, a Best Director Oscar for Wilder, and a Best Script Oscar for Wilder and Brackett. During the late 1940s Wilder directed only *The Emperor Waltz*, a lacklustre comedy, and the patchy *A Foreign Affair* (both 1948). His last film with Brackett was SUNSET BOULEVARD (1950), a sour but splendid Hollywood exposé that brought the two men an Oscar for Best Screenplay.

Following the dissolution of the partnership, the cynical and sometimes coarse streak in Wilder's work began to manifest itself more clearly. *Ace in the Hole* (*The Big Carnival*, 1951), which Wilder also produced, was a relentlessly nasty film about a reporter who delays the rescue of a trapped miner to protract the news story. Though a critical success, the film was a commercial flop. However, *Stalag 17* (1953), a POW drama that brought Wilder an Oscar nomination as Best Director, enjoyed both critical and box-office success. Wilder's other films of the 1950s include *Sabrina* (1954), an oddly cast comedy with Humphrey BOGART,

The Seven Year Itch (1957) with Marilyn MONROE, the Lindbergh biopic *The Spirit of St Louis* (1957), and *Love in the Afternoon* (1957), a comedy that initiated a writing partnership with I. A. L. Diamond. Further Oscar nominations were received for *Witness for the Prosecution* (1958), an Agatha Christie adaptation, and the classic comedy SOME LIKE IT HOT (1959), another collaboration with Diamond. The latter marked the beginning of a long-running association with the actor Jack LEMMON, who went on to star in *The Apartment* (1960), which brought Wilder Oscars as both director and screenwriter (with Diamond), and *Irma la Douce* (1963); in *The Fortune Cookie* (1968), *The Front Page* (1974), and *Buddy Buddy* (1981) Lemmon appeared as part of a comedy partnership with Walter MATTHAU.

Wilder's other films of note include *Kiss Me Stupid* (1964), described by one critic as a work of "ferocious tastelessness", *The Private Life of Sherlock Holmes* (1970), and *Fedora* (1978), with William HOLDEN. Despite their unsentimental and often thoroughly bitter tone, Wilder's films proved consistent money-makers, grossing over $100 million during his 40 years in Hollywood.

Gene Wilder (Jerry Silberman; 1935–) US actor, chiefly in eccentric comedy roles. He made his name in the comedies of Mel BROOKS before going on to produce, direct, and script his own films.

Born in Milwaukee, the son of a Russian immigrant who manufactured miniature whiskey bottles, Wilder studied drama at the University of Iowa and Britain's Old Vic, where he was the school fencing champion. He returned to America to teach the sport and work as a chauffeur and toy salesman.

In 1967 Wilder made his film debut playing a terrified undertaker in BONNIE AND CLYDE. A year later he received an Oscar nomination for his starring role as a neurotic accountant in Brooks's bad-taste classic *The Producers* (1968). Woody ALLEN's *Everything You Always Wanted to Know About Sex* (1972), in which he played a doctor who falls in love with a sheep, was followed by two more Brooks films: the Western spoof *Blazing Saddles* (1974) and the horror spoof *Young Frankenstein* (1974), which Wilder co-scripted. He made his own debut as a director with *The Adventure of Sherlock Holmes' Smarter Brother* (1975), which he also wrote and starred in (alongside Marty Feldman and Madeline Kahn, his co-stars from *Young Frankenstein*).

Wilder's later movies as an actor include the comedy thriller *Silver Streak* (1976), with Richard Pryor; *The World's Greatest Lover* (1977), which he also produced, directed, and wrote; and *Stir Crazy* (1980), in which he was teamed with Pryor again. He starred with his wife, the comedienne Gilda Radner, in several films, including *The Woman in Red* (1982), and *Haunted Honeymoon* (1986), both of which Wilder directed and co-wrote. Radner died of cancer in 1989.

> One day, God said 'Let there be prey,' and he created pigeons, rabbits, lambs and Gene Wilder.
>
> MEL BROOKS; *Newsweek*, 1975.

Williams. **(George) Emlyn Williams** (1905–87) British actor, director, screenwriter, and playwright. Born in Mostyn, Wales, the son of an ironmonger, he made his London and Broadway stage debuts in 1927 and his first film appearance in *The Frightened Lady* (1932).

Williams's early screenwriting credits included additional dialogue for Alfred HITCHCOCK's *The Man Who Knew Too Much* (1934). One of his most successful plays, *Night Must Fall* (1935), was filmed twice: in 1937 with Robert Montgomery in the psychopathic leading role, and in 1964 with Albert FINNEY. His other great stage success, *The Corn is Green* (1938), a play based on his own boyhood, was filmed by Warner Brothers with Bette DAVIS in 1945; a TV movie version with Katharine HEPBURN followed in 1978.

During the later 1930s Williams appeared in a number of high-profile films, including *The Citadel*, with Robert DONAT, and Hitchcock's *Jamaica Inn*, with Charles LAUGHTON. Two years later he wrote and starred in the propaganda film *This England* (1941), in which he played a labourer who describes English history to a visiting American (Constance Cummings). He then wrote, directed, and starred in *The Last Days of Dolwyn* (US title *Woman of Dolwyn*; 1949), about the evacuation of a Welsh village that is to be flooded to provide a reservoir. Richard BURTON made his screen debut in the film. Williams later appeared in *The L-Shaped Room* (1962), *Eye of the Devil* (1966), *David Copperfield* (1969), and other films. Joseph LOSEY's *Time Without Pity*

(1957) was an adaptation of Williams's play *Someone Waiting* (1953).

Esther Williams (1923–) US actress, a former swimming champion who was billed as 'Hollywood's Mermaid'. "Wet she's a star" said her MGM producer Joe Pasternak, "dry she ain't." Born in Los Angeles, she was swimming with Billy Rose's Aquacade when an MGM talent scout discovered her. She made her screen debut in *Andy Hardy's Double Life* (1942), with Mickey ROONEY, and starred two years later in *Bathing Beauty*, one of the first features directed by George SIDNEY.

A decade of successful musical comedies followed: she performed a water ballet in *Ziegfeld Follies* (1946), took a dip in a hotel pool in *Take Me Out to the Ball Game* (1949), and swam in the sea in *Pagan Love Song* (1950), directed by Robert Alton after Williams complained that Stanley DONEN did not appreciate her talents. Busby BERKELEY choreographed spectacular water ballets in *Million Dollar Mermaid* (1952) and *Easy to Love* (1953), while in *Dangerous When Wet* (1953) Williams swam with the cartoon characters TOM AND JERRY. *Jupiter's Darling* (1954), her last MGM film, was an extraordinary musical set in the Roman Empire (with Howard Keel as Hannibal).

The following year Williams made an unsuccessful switch to drama, playing a schoolmistress with a psychotic student in *The Unguarded Moment*. She retired five years later to market Esther Williams Swimming Pools.

Robin Williams (1952–) US actor and comedian. After studying drama at the Juilliard School in New York, Williams began his career in stand-up at The Comedy Store in Los Angeles. In the later 1970s he contributed to the revival of television's *Laugh In* and finally became a star playing the alien Mork in the series *Mork and Mindy* (from 1978).

Williams made his big-screen debut in the title role of Robert ALTMAN's *Popeye* (1980), a notable disaster. *The World According to Garp* (1982), in which Williams played the writer son of Glenn CLOSE, was followed by a number of minor comedies, such as *The Best of Times* and *Club Paradise* (both 1986). His big break came in 1987 with *Good Morning, Vietnam*, in which he played a Forces disc-jockey (based on the real-life DJ Adrian Cronauer) during the

Vietnam War – a role that allowed his improvisational talents free play.

Williams's next role, as an unorthodox teacher in *Dead Poet's Society* (1989), earned him an Oscar nomination, as did his portrayal of the timid doctor Malcolm Sayer in *Awakenings* (1991). Always willing to move out of the spotlight, he made two uncredited cameo appearances, in *The Adventures of Baron Munchausen* (1989) and *Dead Again* (1991), before co-starring with Jeff BRIDGES in Terry GILLIAM's *The Fisher King* (1991).

Other roles have included a grown-up Peter Pan in Steven SPIELBERG's *Hook* (1991) and the voice of the genie in Disney's *Aladdin* (1992); as payment for the latter he received a Picasso painting valued at $7 million. In 1993 he enjoyed an enormous hit with *Mrs Doubtfire*, in which he played a divorced man who poses as a Scottish nanny in order to get close to his children. (Ironically, five years earlier Williams had left his real-life wife to marry the children's nanny.)

> My comedy is like emotional hang-gliding.
> ROBIN WILLIAMS; *Playboy*, 1982.

Willis, Bruce (1955–) US actor and singer. Born in West Germany to a serviceman father, Willis grew up in New York, where he subsequently worked as a security guard, a bartender, and a harmonica player with the band Loose Goose. After appearing in a television jeans commercial and on stage in *Cat on a Hot Tin Roof*, he gained a small part in the film *The First Deadly Sin* (1980). Further work on TV and the stage (including 100 performances of Sam SHEPARD's *Fool For Love*) then led to a starring role in television's *Moonlighting*, a hugely popular comedy detective series, in which he played opposite Cybill Shepherd. He was less successful with starring roles in the movies *Blind Date* (1987), and *Sunset* (1988), but enjoyed a bestselling Motown album, *The Return of Bruno* (1988).

Owing to his reputation as a box-office liability, Willis was not given a high profile in the publicity for *Die Hard* (1988), but took his $5-million fee anyway; in the event, this high-tech action movie became a major hit (the sequel appeared in 1990). The following year saw Willis growing a beard and attempting some serious METHOD acting as a Vietnam veteran in *In Country*, as well as providing the voice of the baby in the comedy *Look Who's Talking*. He then appeared in the disastrous *The Bonfire of the Vanities* (1990) ("a missfire of inanities" as *Variety* called it), and the big-budget flop *Hudson Hawke* (1991). Over the next year or so he limited his movie work to CAMEOS in *Mortal Thoughts* (1992), *Billy Bathgate* (1992), and a self-mocking appearance as himself in Robert ALTMAN's *The Player* (1993), before returning to action in *The Last Boy Scout* (1992) and comedy in *Death Becomes Her* (1993). Appearances in *Striking Distance*, the 'erotic' thriller *Color of Night*, and TARANTINO's *Pulp Fiction* (all 1994) suggest that he intends to consolidate his standing in the former genre. He married the actress Demi MOORE in 1987.

wind machines A large fan (sometimes an aeroplane propeller) used to create the effect of wind. When he filmed his spectacular *The Hurricane* (1937), John FORD set up a series of wind machines calculated to blow at near hurricane force. Many of the Samoan extras, who had survived the islands' 1915 hurricane, said that Ford's wind machines were worse. The star Mary ASTOR recalled, "Huge propellers kept us fighting for every step, with sand and water whipping our faces, sometimes leaving little pinpricks of blood on our cheeks from the stinging sand."

Winner, Michael (1935–) Ebullient British director, producer, and screenwriter, best known for a series of violent thrillers with Charles BRONSON. His movies are noted for their fast pace and visual tricks, as well as their mayhem and sensationalism. Critics tend to agree that his best work was done in the late 1960s, before he went to Hollywood.

Born in London, Winner wrote film criticism for national newspapers and magazines while still in his teens. He then read law at Cambridge, where he edited the university newspaper. During the late 1950s and early 1960s he made several documentaries for the BBC and a number of nudist films. He then embarked on a series of 'swinging London' movies with *West 11* (1963), about a drifter offered £10,000 to murder a man's aunt. A year later he directed and co-produced his first major film, *The System* (US title *The Girl-Getters*; 1964), with Oliver REED as a photographer who uses his job to meet girls. *The Jokers* (1967), one of his best films, has Reed and Michael Crawford 'borrowing' the Crown

Jewels, while *I'll Never Forget What's 'is Name* (1967) is a tragicomedy set in the cynical world of advertising, with Reed and Orson WELLES in major roles.

In 1971 Winner moved to Hollywood to produce and direct the Western, *Lawman*, starring Burt LANCASTER as an arrogant marshal. Lancaster also starred in the spy film *Scorpio* (1972). Winner then cast Bronson as a brutal Los Angeles police detective in *The Stone Killer* (1973) and a revenging husband in DEATH WISH (1974), a film that was widely condemned for its scenes of sadistic violence. A great popular hit, the movie spawned a long series of sequels over more than 20 years.

Meanwhile, he directed Robert MITCHUM in a remake of THE BIG SLEEP (1978), which has not eclipsed the original, and Faye DUNAWAY (1983) as a highwaywoman in *The Wicked Lady* (1983), also a remake. When the British Board of Film Censors cut a graphic scene in which Dunaway horsewhips a gypsy woman, Winner complained (with the backing of John SCHLESINGER, Karel REISZ, and others) and won his case. Later that year, to the disbelief of many, he was appointed Chief Censorship Officer for the Directors' Guild of Great Britain.

In 1990 Winner directed *Bullseye!*, a comedy about two con-men posing as nuclear scientists. For the final scenes, which were shot in Barbados with Michael CAINE, John CLEESE, and Jenny Seagrove (his long-term companion), he put together one of the smallest film crews on record. Winner operated the camera, cameraman David Wynn Jones held the reflector, while Cleese carried the sound recorder hidden in a book as he acted. His more recent films include *Dirty Weekend* (1992), a controversial piece about a woman who takes violent revenge on a series of sexist men.

It seems unlikely that the critics' harsh judgements of his later films will have much dented the confidence of a man reported to have said: "A team effort is a lot of people doing what I say."

Winters, Shelley (Shirley Schrift; 1922–) Glamorous US actress best known for playing strong but suffering women (often murder victims). By her own account, she became a star the day that she and her press agent "quite cold-bloodedly invented this personality: a dumb blonde with a body and a set of sayings." Whatever the truth of this, she is also a supremely competent actress who has brought life and pathos to the mostly working-class women she has played. She was married to the actors Vittorio Gassman (1952–54) and Anthony Franciosa (1957–60).

Born in St Louis, Winters was raised in Brooklyn, New York, and worked as a model and shop assistant to pay for acting lessons. She worked as a nightclub chorus girl before making her debut on Broadway in 1941. Two years later, she was signed by Columbia and made her first film appearance with a bit part in *What a Woman!* (1943).

Winters first impressed critics playing the waitress strangled by Ronald COLMAN in *A Double Life* (1948). She was also murdered in the comedy thriller *Take One False Step* (1949), starring William POWELL. She won an Oscar nomination for her portrayal of the pregnant girl drowned by Montgomery CLIFT in George STEVENS's *A Place in the Sun* (1951) and was drowned again, this time by Robert MITCHUM, in Charles LAUGHTON's *Night of the Hunter* (1955).

In 1959 Winters won an Oscar as Best Supporting Actress playing the mother in *The Diary of Anne Frank*. Subsequent roles included the mother of nymphet Sue Lyon in Stanley KUBRICK's *LOLITA* (1962), the sleazy mother of a blind girl in *A Patch of Blue* (1965), a performance that brought her a second Oscar, and the gun-toting Ma Barker in the biopic *Bloody Mama* (1970). A further Oscar nomination came her way for playing a passenger in the ocean-liner disaster film *The Poseidon Adventure* (1972). After minor parts in *The Delta Force* (1986) and *Awakenings* (1990), Winters took a major role in *Stepping Out* (1991), as the grumpy accompanist to dance teacher Liza MINNELLI.

wipe A type of transition from one scene to another, in which the original scene appears to be pushed off the screen by the oncoming one. The line between the two scenes may be blurred or sharp (a **soft-** and **hard-edged wipe** respectively), may cross the screen in any direction, and be of any shape. The effect was popular in the early days of film-making, probably because it could be achieved quite easily using IN CAMERA procedures. The first recorded example was in *Mary Jane's Mishap: or, Don't Fool with the Paraffin* (1903). Its popularity reached a climax in the 1930s, when a dizzying array of shapes pushed, burst, or swiped their way across the screen. However, since then the wipe has been virtually removed from the film-maker's vocabulary, possibly because it is the only transition without a natural counterpart (unlike the FADE or DISSOLVE, for example). It is sometimes used to evoke a period feel, as in THE STING (1973) and the Indiana Jones movies. *See* FLIPOVER.

Wise, Robert (1914–) US director and producer, who made his name with horror and action films but later won Oscars for his musicals WEST SIDE STORY (1961) and THE SOUND OF MUSIC (1965). In 1988 he received the Academy's Irving G. Thalberg Award for "outstanding motion picture production".

Born in Winchester, Indiana, he dropped out of college at 19 when his brother David, working at RKO, got him a job there as a shipping clerk. Over the next six years Wise was promoted to sound-effects cutter and then film editor; he co-edited THE HUNCHBACK OF NOTRE DAME (1939), won an Oscar nomination for cutting Orson WELLES's CITIZEN KANE (1941), and then edited Welles's THE MAGNIFICENT AMBERSONS (1942).

Wise made his debut as a director when producer Val Lewton asked him to finish the horror film *The Curse of the Cat People* (1944), which had fallen behind schedule. A year later he made Lewton's macabre *The Body Snatcher*, with Boris KARLOFF. His last RKO offering was *The Set-Up* (1949), a boxing film that won the Critics' Prize at Cannes. He then moved to 20th Century-Fox for the effective science-fiction film *The Day the Earth Stood Still* (1951). In the mid 1950s he initiated a vogue for boardroom movies with MGM's *Executive Suite* (1954) before returning to boxing with the beautifully made *Somebody Up There Likes Me* (1956), a biopic of Rocky Graziano that established Paul NEWMAN.

After moving to United Artists to direct Clark GABLE and Burt LANCASTER in the submarine drama *Run Silent, Run Deep* (1958), Wise earned his first Oscar nomination as director for *I Want to Live!* (1958), a biopic of the murderer Barbara Graham (played by Susan Hayward). He became a producer-director for UA a year later. The following decade saw the production of his Oscar-winning triumphs *West Side Story* (in collaboration with Jerome Robbins) and *The Sound of Music*, a project that he only accepted after his Steve MCQUEEN adventure, *The Sand Pebbles* (1966), was postponed. Julie ANDREWS, the star of *The Sound of Music*, also took the lead in *Star!* (1968), a

biopic of Gertrude Lawrence that proved a notorious flop. Wise commented simply "We had got ourselves mislaid somewhere along the way."

His later movies include the sci-fi *The Andromeda Strain* (1971), *The Hindenburg* (1975), about the explosion of the German Zeppelin in 1937 (described by *The New Yorker* as "One gasbag meets another"), *Audrey Rose* (1977), an occult thriller, and the popular but unoriginal *Star Trek: The Motion Picture* (1979).

Wizard of Oz, The   (1939) Victor FLEMING's extravagant version of L. Frank Baum's popular children's novel. When a tornado blows Dorothy (Judy GARLAND) and her dog Toto from a Kansas farm to Munchkinland, she is presented with ruby slippers by the good witch Glinda (Billy Burke) and told to follow the yellow brick road to the Emerald City, where the wizard (Frank Morgan) will help her return home. On the way Dorothy is pursued by a Wicked Witch (Margaret Hamilton) and aided by a Scarecrow (Ray Bolger) a Tin Man (Jack Haley) and a Lion (Bert Lahr), who join her in the hope of attaining a brain, a heart, and courage respectively.

The story was passed for production by Louis B. MAYER with a $2.7 million budget, far exceeding even the MGM norm. Deanna DURBIN and the ten-year-old Shirley TEMPLE were both considered for the leading role, but Fox refused to loan Temple. Mayer had also lined up Temple's regular co-star Buddy Ebsen but he dropped out after finding that the Tin Man's aluminium spray make-up affected his health (the paint that was later substituted proved equally irritating to Haley).

The Wizard of Oz was one of the few feature films to exploit a neglected TECHNICOLOR process that used a prism to direct the primary colours onto three separate monochrome filmstrips. Intricate and expensive, the prism process produced the sumptuous colours necessary to convey the fantastic sights of Oz. The process required intense illumination and therefore drastically shortened working sessions, particularly for Bolger, Haley and Lahr, whose costumes were far from comfortable (the lion costume weighed around 100 lbs). Although this caused incalculable continuity problems, the picture, which took six months to shoot, is a triumph of matching consistency. Some critics now consider the colour and decor overdone, but the quality of directing and acting is not in dispute.

But the road to success was not smooth. Stories abound about the misbehaviour of the 124 performers who played the Munchkins and the occasional inebriation of Frank Morgan. Many scenes had to be reshot because of Garland's giggling fits, while others remained on the cutting-room floor (including the 'Jitterbug' production number that finally emerged in the MGM compilation film *That's Dancing*).

Although acclaimed on its release, the picture nevertheless took nearly two decades to return a profit, and then largely thanks to sales on television. In Britain, the Board of Censors passed the film for adults only, prompting Graham GREENE to write in *The Spectator*:

> Surely it is time that this absurd committee of elderly men and spinsters who feared, too, that *Snow White* was unsuitable for those under sixteen, was laughed out of existence?

Judy Garland won a special Academy Award for her "outstanding performance as a screen juvenile."

Wolf Man, the Lycanthropic hero played by Lon CHANEY JNR in five Universal HORROR FILMS of the 1940s, beginning with *The Wolf Man* (1941). Unlike other screen werewolves, Curt Siodmak's creation, Larry Talbot, is a sympathetic character, who discovers that:

> Even a man who's pure at heart,
> And says his prayers at night,
> May become a wolf when the wolfbane blooms,
> And the autumn moon is bright.

STOP-ACTION and the make-up skills of Jack Pierce were used to effect the remarkable transformation scenes in which Chaney grows fur and claws.

Siodmak also scripted *Frankenstein Meets the Wolf Man* (1943), in which the latter, seeking a cure for his condition, searches out the notorious scientist only to end up fighting his monster, and drafted *House of Frankenstein* (1945), in which Talbot encounters the monster *and* Dracula. He had no part in the inferior *House of Dracula* (1945), in which Larry and the count are both looking for cures; Dracula is disappointed but the Wolf Man succeeds, while also making an end of Frankenstein's monster (once more). This happy ending did not prevent the Wolf Man from making a CAMEO appearance in the comedy *Abbott and Costello Meet Frankenstein* (1948).

Wood. Ed Wood Jnr (1922–78) Notorious US film-maker, who has been labelled "the world's worst director" and "the turkey maestro" of all time. His dubious cult inspired Tim BURTON's 1994 biopic, titled simply *Ed Wood*. Several of his films featured Bela LUGOSI, who by this late stage in his career required drugs to perform.

Wood's debut effort, *Glen or Glenda* (1953), was a low-budget EXPLOITATION MOVIE about transvestitism, a subject close to the director's heart (he claimed to have served in the Pacific wearing a pink bra under his uniform). The film starred Lugosi as a strange scientist, Tommy Haynes as a 'pseudohermaphrodite' who undergoes a sex-change operation, and 'Daniel Davies' (Wood himself) as Glen, a man who dresses secretly as a woman. With its inexplicable action, wooden dialogue, cheap sets, and atrocious acting, the film set standards for all Wood's subsequent productions.

Bride of the Monster (1955) proudly carried the credits "Produced by Edward D. Wood Jnr", "Directed by Edward D. Wood Jnr", and "Written by Edward D. Wood Jnr." Lugosi starred as Dr Vornoff, whose atomic strength machine creates superhumans. He takes a dose himself but is nevertheless killed by an overdosed giant octopus. The film also featured Wood's latest discovery, a huge Swedish wrestler called Tor Johnson.

Wood's most famous production is *Plan 9 from Outer Space* (1956), about a group of aliens who attempt to raise the Earth's dead as part of a scheme to prevent the proliferation of nuclear weapons. Although Lugosi died after only four days on set (that produced minutes of screen time), Wood stubbornly built the story around his character; unfortunately, the double he employed (his wife's dentist) looked nothing like the dead actor. The cast also included Tor Johnson, the stage mindreader Criswell, and Vampira (Maila Nurmi), a television presenter of horror films.

Wood's subsequent projects included writing the script for *The Bride and the Beast* (1958), about a woman who marries an animal trainer but then falls for his gorilla, and directing *Night of the Ghouls* (1958) and *The Sinister Urge* (1960). He spent his later years as a penniless alcoholic.

Natalie Wood (Natasha Gurdin; 1938–81) Perky US actress, a former child star, who became a popular leading lady in the 1960s. Her acting range was limited, however, leading the *Harvard Lampoon* to name its annual award for the worst performance by an actress the Natalie Wood Award. Her three marriages included two to the actor Robert Wagner, the first from 1957 to 1963 and the second from 1972 until her death by drowning off their yacht.

The daughter of an architect and a ballet dancer, she appeared at the age of five in *Happy Land* (1943), a movie shot in her hometown of Santa Rosa. The director, Irving Pichel, then cast her as the daughter of Orson WELLES and Claudette COLBERT in *Tomorrow is Forever* (1946). Recognition as a child star came with *Miracle on 34th Street* (British title *The Big Heart*; 1947), in which she played the little girl who does not believe in Santa Claus (Edmund Gwenn).

After several mediocre films, Wood received her first Oscar nomination for playing James DEAN's girlfriend in REBEL WITHOUT A CAUSE (1955). Two more nominations followed, for *Splendor in the Grass* (1961), in which she co-starred with Warren BEATTY as adolescent lovers (the film features Hollywood's first French kiss) and for the comedy *Love with the Proper Stranger* (1963), in which she played an innocent girl made pregnant by a musician (Steve MCQUEEN). In between, Wood starred in two musical triumphs, playing Maria in WEST SIDE STORY (1961) and the title character in *Gypsy* (1962), a biopic of the stripper Gypsy Rose Lee (her singing was dubbed in both). Despite the success of the latter, there is little doubt that the rather demure Wood was badly miscast. She went on to co-star with Robert REDFORD in both *Inside Daisy Clover*, about a teenage actress who becomes a Hollywood star, and *This Property is Condemned*.

Her later movies included the sex comedy *Bob and Carol and Ted and Alice* (1969), about swinging Californian couples, and the disaster film *Meteor* (1979). She appeared in the unconvincing thriller *Brainstorm* (1983) but died before her last scene, which was rewritten for another actress.

Sam Wood (1883–1949) US director and producer, who was considered a no-frills MGM contract worker until his late middle-age, when he received Oscar nominations for GOODBYE, MR CHIPS (1939), *Kitty Foyle* (1940), and *King's Row* (1942). Unbeloved

by actors, he was known on set as a grumpy uninhibited individual who often boasted that he had three testicles.

Born in Philadelphia, Wood worked as an estate agent in California before beginning to act in two-reelers in 1908 (billed as Chad Applegate). From 1915 he worked as a production assistant and then assistant director to Cecil B. DE MILLE. He made his own debut as a director with Paramount's *Double Speed* (1919). Although he directed Gloria SWANSON in 10 films, she was no fan and later complained: "Each one was worse than the last."

Having signed with MGM in 1924, Wood remained with the studio for 17 years. His movies of the 1930s included *Hold Your Man* (1933), which he also produced, and *Whipsaw* (1935), which established Spencer TRACY and Myrna LOY. When Wood directed the MARX BROTHERS in *A Night at the Opera* (1935), Groucho moaned: "This jerk we have for a director doesn't know what he wants, so he shoots everything 20 times and hopes there's something good in it."

When director Victor FLEMING argued with Vivien LEIGH and walked off the set of GONE WITH THE WIND (1939), Wood replaced him for 16 days; although he remained to direct other scenes, he received no credit. That year he enjoyed a major success with the school drama *Goodbye, Mr Chips*, filmed in England with Robert DONAT and Greer GARSON.

In his first years after leaving MGM, he directed Ginger ROGERS to an Oscar in RKO's *Kitty Foyle*, made Warner Brothers' melodrama *King's Row* with Ronald REAGAN, a movie that critic James AGATE called "half masterpiece and half junk", and Samuel GOLDWYN's baseball biopic *The Pride of the Yankees* (1942), with Gary COOPER as Lou Gehrig.

For Whom the Bell Tolls (1943), an adaptation of the Hemingway novel that he also produced, proved Wood's biggest success at the box office. He returned to MGM in the last year of his life to direct three productions; the war film *Command Decision* starring Clark GABLE, *The Stratton Story*, a baseball biopic with James STEWART, and the Western *Ambush* with Robert TAYLOR.

An arch conservative, Wood was president of an organization called the Motion Picture Alliance for the Preservation of American Ideals. In 1947 he implicated the director Lewis MILESTONE and others before the House Un-American Activities Committee, helping to create the idea that communists had infiltrated the film industry.

Woodward, Joanne (1930–) Distinguished US actress, who has been married to the actor Paul NEWMAN since 1958. He directed her to an Oscar nomination in *Rachel, Rachel* (1968) and to a Best Actress Award at Cannes in *The Effect of Gamma Rays on Man-in-the-Moon Marigolds* (1972).

Born in Thomasville, Georgia, the daughter of a publisher, Woodward trained at the Neighborhood Playhouse in New York and appeared in television plays in the early 1950s. Her big-screen debut came with *Count Three and Pray* (1955), in which she played the wife of a parson (Van HEFLIN). Two years later her depiction of the multiple personalities of a schizophrenic in *The Three Faces of Eve* brought her the Oscar for Best Actress. She immodestly downplayed the award, saying, "If I had an infinite amount of respect for the people who think I gave the greatest performance, then it would matter." Subsequent films have included *No Down Payment* (1957), with Tony Randall, and *A Big Hand for a Little Lady* (1966), a gambling drama with Henry FONDA.

Rachel, Rachel is a taut drama about a sexually inexperienced schoolmistress (Woodward) who naively allows herself to be seduced by an old friend and then drives him away by her intensity. Newman both produced and directed, as he did with *The Effect of Gamma Rays on Man-in-the-Moon Marigolds*, in which Woodward plays an eccentric middle-aged woman, distrustful of all men and worried about her two daughters. She has co-starred with her husband in ten films, including *Harry and Son* (1984), which he directed, co-produced, and co-scripted, and the domestic drama *Mr and Mrs Bridge* (1990), which brought her another Oscar nomination.

woof A Hollywood technician's reply to a query meaning 'okay'.

workprint or **cutting copy** The positive print that is used by a film's editor during the various stages of cutting. It consists of selected TAKES from the RUSHES, which are usually printed in a single printer light as technical quality is not essential at this stage. As the editing progresses, the workprint develops from ROUGH CUT to FINE CUT: once this has been approved by the producers, the original negative is cut to match and used as the basis for a RELEASE PRINT.

World Wars. **World War I** The outbreak of war in Europe in 1914 stimulated unprecedented growth in the US film industry. While European nations concentrated on documentaries, PROPAGANDA, and costume epics, which were largely unsaleable abroad, America's neutral status allowed it free rein in the world market, leading to a dominance that has never since been threatened.

US public opinion was originally anti-interventionist and tended towards pacifism, a mood reflected in, for example, *War Brides* and more notably D. W. GRIFFITH's INTOLERANCE (both 1916). This soon altered as big business poured money into interventionist propaganda – a notable example being *The Battle Cry of Peace* (1915), produced by J. S. Blackton, who had been responsible for the first recorded piece of cinema propaganda, the bellicose *Tearing Down the Spanish Flag* (1898). The shift in public opinion culminated in Robert Goldstein receiving a 10-year sentence for making the pro-peace *The Spirit of 76* in 1918, by which time America was actively supporting the Allies.

In a lighter vein there were the CHAPLIN comedies *The Bond* (1918) and *Shoulder Arms* (1918), in which the Tramp dreams of winning the war single-handed.

The 1920s produced three noteworthy films: Rex INGRAM's *The Four Horsemen of the Apocalypse* (1921), which made a star of Rudolph VALENTINO; King VIDOR's *The Big Parade* (1925); and William WELLMAN's *Wings* (1927), valued largely for its spectacular flying sequences.

The year 1930 saw the release of two landmark films that are generally considered amongst the best war movies of all time; Lewis MILESTONE's ALL QUIET ON THE WESTERN FRONT and G. W. PABST's *Westfront 1918*. Both follow a group of men from peacetime, through induction, to the horror of life and death at the front. Their pacifism was echoed in RENOIR's LA GRANDE ILLUSION (1937), which dealt with the relationship between a German commandant and his cultured French prisoner. Although badly received at the time, it is now regarded as a masterpiece. Other important releases of the 1930s were the lavish *Hell's Angels* and *The Dawn Patrol* (both 1930), both of which dealt with the war in the air (a theme reprised in *The Blue Max*, 1966).

The advent of World War II signalled a virtual end to production of 'Great War' movies. The most powerful of those made since include KUBRICK's *Paths of Glory* (1957) and LOSEY's *King and Country* (1965), both of which deal with soldiers awaiting execution for cowardice. The war against the Turks is handled powerfully in both LAWRENCE OF ARABIA (1962) and Peter WEIR's *Gallipoli* (1980). *Oh, What a Lovely War!* (1969), Richard ATTENBOROUGH's award-winning adaptation of Joan Littlewood's play, is a brilliant and moving satire on the whole bloody business.

World War II During World War II Hollywood put itself firmly behind the war effort, producing numerous flag-waving dramas, morale-boosting all-star entertainments, and some excellent documentaries (notably CAPRA's *Why We Fight* series). At the same time US films about the conflict were often surprisingly realistic in their depiction of death, suffering, and defeat. In the early months of US involvement, such dramas as *Wake Island* (1942) and *Bataan* (1943) skilfully presented military defeats in the Pacific as proof of US bravery and determination. Later, when the tide turned against the Axis, the emphasis changed to explicit denigration of the enemy in such films as *Guadalcanal Diary* (1943) (grim victory against treacherous Japanese), *Destination Tokyo* (1944) (submarine tale with lengthy exposition of German and Japanese racial inferiority), and *The Purple Heart* (1944) (pilots tortured by sadistic Japs).

British films were equally solid in their support of the effort, although a few were criticized for showing insufficient commitment: CHURCHILL notoriously tried to ban THE LIFE AND DEATH OF COLONEL BLIMP (1943) for its depiction of an ageing colonel whose notions of chivalry are shown as anachronistic. In fact, Blimp's values of fair play and decency provided the chief motif of such British films as *In Which We Serve* (1942) or *The Way Ahead* (1944). The latter showed fighting men putting aside their class differences in the common cause, a theme echoed in many home-front features and documentaries, notably Humphrey JENNINGS's *London Can Take It* (1940).

Only in the very last stages of the war did a slight note of doubt emerge: *San Pietro* (1945) was criticized for the 'pacifism' suggested by the lines: "These lives were valuable. Valuable to their loved ones, to their country, and to the men themselves"; *The Story of GI Joe* (1945) praised the soldiers but eschewed false heroism, ending on downbeat shots of corpses; while the subject of battle-induced psychosis featured in *A Walk in the Sun* (1945). William WYLER's THE BEST YEARS OF OUR LIVES (1946) showed the problems of readjustment faced by servicemen after the war.

However, the postwar years saw no reaction against the conflict comparable to that evident in the Great War films of the 1930s. In fact, most World-War-II films of the 1950s and 1960s were content to echo the simple patriotism of those produced during the conflict itself. Treatments ranged from the breezy heroism of *Reach For the Sky* (1956) and the machismo of *The Dirty Dozen* (1967) to the more studied documentation of *The Longest Day* (1961). There was usually little attempt to depict an enemy as anything other than a cipher, though some, like *The Guns of Navarone* (1961), differentiated between Germans and Nazis.

Such criticism as there was tended to focus on the conservatism of military institutions. THE BRIDGE ON THE RIVER KWAI (1957), for example, showed a blind adherence to army ethics undermining wider British war aims, while *The Caine Mutiny* (1954) used a paranoid captain to symbolize rigid military perfectionism. Attacks on military culture intensified during the era of VIETNAM and the anti-war movement. Particularly harsh pictures of the military mentality were presented by *Catch-22* (1970), about life in a Pacific bomber squadron, and the film that Orson WELLES called the finest anti-war movie of all time, Sam PECKINPAH's *Cross of Iron* (1977). The latter brutally contrasts the values of the German officer class (an "aristocratic pile of Prussian pig shit") with the simple humanity of a sergeant who "hates this uniform and everything it stands for."

During the conflict, most German features tended to eschew contemporary subject matter in favour of historical metaphor – hence innumerable films about Frederick the Great. Understandably, postwar German film-makers have not dwelt on their country's military exploits in the way that US and British directors have done. An interesting exception to this rule is *The Boat* (1981), which claustrophobically shows the terror of life in a German U-boat.

wrap A shot that has been successfully completed and can be wrapped up. The director usually declares, "It's a wrap."

Wray, Fay (1907–) Canadian-born Hollywood actress best remembered as the screaming woman who fascinated the giant gorilla in KING KONG (1933). She was married twice, to screenwriters John Monk Saunders (1928–39) and Robert Riskin (1942–52). Wray has herself written several plays, without great success.

Born in Alberta, she was raised in Los Angeles and began her screen career with a bit part in *Gasoline Love* (1923). Five years later she became an overnight star in Erich VON STROHEIM's *The Wedding March*, in which she played an innocent girl pursued by a scoundrelly Hapsburg prince (von Stroheim).

In 1933 Wray appeared in both Michael CURTIZ's *The Mystery of the Wax Museum* and *King Kong*. Her hysterical REACTION SHOTS in the latter were made to the camera alone and only later blended with footage featuring the 18-inch model gorilla. Her other films of the 1930s included *Viva Villa!* (1934), in which she played an aristocrat who falls for the Mexican bandit (Wallace Beery), and two British-made comedies starring Jack Buchanan, *Come Out of the Pantry* (1935) and *When Knights were Bold* (1936).

After playing the mother in *Adam Had Four Sons*, the film that made a star of Ingrid BERGMAN, Wray retired to marry Riskin. Although she made a comeback after his death, her films of the 1950s were lightweight offerings geared to a teenage audience, such as *Rock Pretty Baby* (1957) and *Tammy and the Bachelor* (1957). Since finally retiring from films in 1958 she has made occasional appearances on television.

Writers Guild of America (WGA) The US trade union for film, television, and radio writers. It has two branches, WGA-East in New York and WGA-West in Los Angeles. Founded in 1933 as the **Screen Writers Guild**, the union made a number of initial demands that were all eventually met by the industry. These included an end to blacklists, of contract writers being loaned between studios, and of writing on speculation.

The Guild sets minimum payments for scripts (often achieved through strikes), collects royalties for repeats, and offers members group insurance, a pension plan, and a credit union. For a small fee, it will register any script, professional or amateur, to protect the original writer. It publishes a magazine and other information, including a monthly list of agents who abide by WGA regulations.

It also guards screen credits: when William WYLER brought in Christopher Fry to rewrite Karl Tunberg's screenplay for BEN-HUR (1959) the Guild would not allow his name to appear on screen.

Wurlitzer organ The spectacular pipe organ, able to imitate a whole orchestra of instruments, that became a feature of the lavish picture theatres built in America and Europe during the early decades of cinema. Despite the sneers of sophisticates, the instrument characterized more than a generation of cinemagoing, first as accompaniment to silent films, then as entertainment before and between talkies. As late as the 1950s they could still be quite widely heard, and seen; the organist at his console rising into the auditorium on a hydraulic platform bathed in coloured light. The organ was developed in Elmira, New York, in 1910 by the Wurlitzer family, long established in America as musical-instrument makers and dealers. Although more were produced than any other model of a pipe organ in history, they are now difficult to find. Those that have survived are usually cherished and restored by dedicated enthusiasts.

Wuthering Heights (1939) Samuel GOLDWYN's romantic but emasculated production of Emily Brontë's classic novel. William WYLER directed Laurence OLIVIER as Heathcliff and Merle OBERON as Cathy. The adaptation, by Ben Hecht and Charles MacArthur, only covered the first half of the book and was originally intended for Charles BOYER and Sylvia Sidney. Although the film did not recoup its cost until its second reissue, Goldwyn proclaimed it his favourite. In later life, he would watch it repeatedly and cry.

The conflicts in front of the camera were often mirrored by those behind it. Wyler fought bitterly with Olivier, who at first refused to modify his theatrical style of acting. The director also persecuted Oberon, making her reshoot the storm scene over and over in a deluge of water hosed through propeller blades (*see* WIND MACHINES) until she began to vomit and was taken into hospital with a fever. On her return, Wyler insisted on reshooting the scene, although this time Goldwyn had the water heated.

There were also differences between the producer and the director. Although Wyler loved the dark side of the story, Goldwyn wanted to make the characters, in particular Heathcliff, more 'likeable'. He even tried to change the title to *The Wild Heart* or *Bring Me the World*. Wyler particularly hated Goldwyn's tacked-on happy ending, in which the lovers' ghosts walk hand-in-hand to heaven.

At a time when filming on LOCATION was rare, Goldwyn spent $100,000 recreating the Yorkshire moors in California. One unusual item of scenery was a personal addition by the propman, Irving Sindler; having been given no screen credit, he added a gravestone to one scene and inscribed it 'I. Sindler. A Good Man'.

In the story Catherine, a middle-class Yorkshire girl, falls in love with the passionate and fierce Heathcliff, but for social reasons rejects him in favour of her rich but dull neighbour, Edgar (David NIVEN). After a three-year absence, Heathcliff returns mysteriously enriched and marries Edgar's sister, Isabella, without loving her. Both Heathcliff and Catherine die without realizing true love.

The story was remade in 1970 with Timothy Dalton and Anna Calder-Marshall, and in 1992 starring Ralph Fiennes and Juliette Binoche.

Wyler, William (1902–81) German-born Hollywood director and producer, nicknamed '90-take Wyler' because of his perfectionism. Wyler received a record nine Oscar nominations for Best Director, winning for MRS MINIVER (1942), THE BEST YEARS OF OUR LIVES (1946), and BEN-HUR (1959), all three of which were also named Best Film. He also received the Academy's Irving G. Thalberg Memorial Award in 1965 for his cumulative work, and was presented with the AFI's Life Achievement Award in 1976. He was married twice: to one of his stars, Margaret Sullavan, from 1934 to 1936, and to the actress Margaret Tallichet from 1938 until his death.

Born in Mulhausen, Alsace (then part of Germany), to a Swiss-born haberdasher, he studied business in Lausanne and the violin at the Conservatoire in Paris. In 1920 his cousin Carl Laemmle, head of Universal Pictures, gave him a publicity job for $25 a week in New York. Wyler soon moved to Hollywood and by 1923 was working as an assistant director on THE HUNCHBACK OF NOTRE DAME (1923).

Two years later he was a production assistant on MGM's first BEN-HUR and made his debut as a director with Universal's *Crook Buster*. This was the first of more than 40 Westerns he would make over the next two years; "I used to spend nights trying to think of new ways of getting on and off a horse" he later said. His first Oscar nomination came for *Dodsworth* (1936), starring Walter HUSTON and Mary ASTOR.

Later that year Wyler left Universal to join Sam GOLDWYN. In 1938 he was loaned to Warner Brothers and directed Bette DAVIS to an Oscar in *Jezebel* (1938); she fought with him but came to regard him as her favourite director. WUTHERING HEIGHTS (1939) followed with Laurence OLIVIER, who also battled with Wyler but later credited him with greatly improving his film-acting style. In 1941 Wyler and Davis worked together again on a screen version of Hellman's *The Little Foxes*.

After making *Mrs Miniver*, Wyler worked with a US bomber group in England, directing two documentaries. He then returned to Goldwyn to make the hugely popular *The Best Years of Our Lives*, about servicemen readjusting to civilian life. After joining Paramount in 1949 he directed Olivia DE HAVILLAND to an Oscar in *The Heiress* (1949), which he also produced. For *Roman Holiday* (1953), Wyler cast Audrey HEPBURN in her first US role. In 1959 his remake of *Ben-Hur* for MGM took a record 11 Oscars, including Best Picture.

Wyler's films of the 1960s included the John Fowles adaptation *The Collector* (1965), which earned him his ninth Oscar nomination, and the Barbra STREISAND vehicle *Funny Girl* (1968). After the failure of *The Liberation of L. B. Jones* (1970), a race-war melodrama, Wyler retired at the age of 68.

Wyman, Jane (Sarah Jane Fulks; 1914–) US actress with a calm demeanour who specialized in playing victims; she won an Oscar as a deaf-mute who is raped in *Johnny Belinda* (1948). During the filming, her eight-year marriage to actor Ronald REAGAN broke down and he joked, "If this comes to divorce, I think I'll name Johnny Belinda co-respondent." (She said she divorced Reagan, the second of her three husbands, because he talked too much.)

Wyman was born in St Joseph, Missouri, where her father had been mayor. In the 1920s her mother took her to Hollywood as a child actress but met only closed doors. She subsequently worked as a manicurist, telephone operator, and radio singer before making her screen debut as a chorus girl in *Gold Diggers of 1937* (1936).

After a series of dumb-blonde roles, Wyman found acclaim in Billy WILDER's *The Lost Weekend* (1945), playing opposite Ray MILLAND's alcoholic writer. The following year she received her first Oscar nomination for *The Yearling*, in which she co-starred with Gregory PECK as a backwoods couple. Her Oscar-winning performance in *Johnny Belinda* followed a period studying at a school for the deaf and dumb and led to a string of films with strong emotional content, popularly known as **Wyman weepies.**

Subsequent roles included a crippled girl in *The Glass Menagerie* (1950), a woman who loses her child in *The Blue Veil* (1951), and as a blinded accident victim in *Magnificent Obsession* (1954), with Rock HUDSON. She starred with Hudson again in *All That Heaven Allows* (1956), in which she played a long-suffering woman who loves a younger man. Although she had her own television series, *The Jane Wyman Theater*, from 1956 to 1960, major cinema roles dried up in the 1960s; she made a comeback in the early 1980s as the matriarch in the TV soap opera *Falcon Crest.*

XYZ

X A category of film classification used in several countries to indicate that in the opinion of the CENSORS a film is unsuitable for showing to children. In Britain, the X-certificate was introduced in 1951 to exclude under-16s (the threshold was raised to 18 in 1970) and replaced by the 18 rating in the 1980s. In America it was introduced in 1968 to exclude children under 17. The US X-rating is reserved almost exclusively for pornography; mainstream or artistic films with a violent or sexual content are generally classified R (Reserved) or NC-17 (No Children under 17). *See* RATINGS.

XLS *See* EXTREME LONG SHOT.

Yates, Peter (1929–) British-born director and producer, one of the few British filmmakers of the 'Swinging '60s' generation to establish a firm position in Hollywood. The recipient of Oscar nominations for both *Breaking Away* (1979) and *The Dresser* (1983), he once commented "I'd put my work somewhere below meals for the aged, but a little way above manufacturing toothpaste."

Born in Aldershot, Hampshire, Yates attended Charterhouse school and RADA, where he trained as an actor. After a period acting and directing in repertory, he briefly gave up the stage to become a motor-racing driver. Having entered films as a dubbing assistant in 1953, he served in various roles before becoming an assistant director to Tony RICHARDSON on *The Entertainer* (1960).

After a stint as a director at London's Royal Court Theatre and a period working for television, Yates made his film directing debut with the Cliff Richard musical *Summer Holiday* (1963). Four years later, he scripted and directed *Robbery* (1967), which opens with a dramatic chase through the London streets. After seeing the sequence, Steve MCQUEEN invited Yates to Hollywood to direct him in *Bullitt* (1968), a police thriller remembered mainly for a stunning car chase across San Francisco.

Yates's subsequent successes included *The Friends of Eddie Coyle* (1973), a gangster film starring Robert MITCHUM, and *The Deep* (1977), an underwater thriller that proved his greatest box-office hit. He then enjoyed an unexpected success with the coming-of-age comedy *Breaking Away* (1979), which he also produced. His later films have included the fantasy *Krull* (1982), made at Pinewood Studios for Columbia, *The Dresser* (1983), an emotional drama of theatrical life starring Albert FINNEY and Tom Courtenay, and a comedy-adventure, *The Year of the Comet* (1992).

Yellow Submarine (1968) George Dunning's psychedelic cartoon fantasia, inspired by and featuring the music of the BEATLES. When Pepperland is overrun by Blue Meanies, Old Fred sails away in a submarine to enlist the help of the Beatles to restore music and love to his utopian home.

The first feature-length animated film to be produced in Britain since *Animal Farm* in 1954, *Yellow Submarine* was based on a story (by Lee Minoff) suggested by the Lennon-McCartney song of the same title (1966). Among the screenwriters was Erich Segal, the author of *Love Story*. The Beatles themselves showed little interest in the project, being so preoccupied with the Maharishi and their own *Magical Mystery Tour* TV movie that they pleaded too busy even to dub their lines. In the event voices were provided by John Clive (John), Geoffrey Hughes (Paul), Peter Batten (George) and Paul Angelis (Ringo), although the Fabs did appear in a brief segment at the close of the film. Only a handful of new songs – 'It's All Too Much', 'Only a Northern Song', 'All Together Now' and 'Hey Bulldog' – were recorded for the soundtrack, to which old favourites like 'Eleanor Rigby', 'Nowhere Man', 'When I'm Sixty-Four', and 'All You Need is Love' were added for narrative purposes. The latter four songs were omitted from the soundtrack album, which was padded out with extracts from George Martin's instrumental score. In keeping with the Beatles' attitude to the project, Ringo absented himself from the film's premiere in London and none of the group attended its US debut.

The ambitious animation, which reveals influences as varied as Pop Art, Dali, and comic strips, as well as DISNEY and UPA, was designed by Heinz Edelman, although the most striking and innovative sequence – an interpretation of 'Lucy in the Sky with Diamonds' – was supervised by Dunning himself. Press reaction was mixed. While *The Los Angeles Times* declared the film "the most stupendous animation feat in decades", the *Hollywood Reporter* found it "painfully long and pretentiously cute", and *The New York Times* primly suspected that it was "informed by marijuana". Despite the indifference of Beatles and critics alike, *Yellow Submarine* remains a landmark in animation history and an enduring cult classic.

York. Michael York (Michael York-Johnson; 1942–) Blond youthful-looking British actor, whose films range from Shakespeare to adventure stories and thrillers. He has also kept up a stage and television career, appearing, for instance, in the US soap opera *Knot's Landing* (1987). His 1992 autobiography was entitled *Accidentally on Purpose*.

After studies at Oxford, where he acted with OUDS, York appeared in repertory and with the National Theatre Company (from 1965). He made his film debut in ZEFFIRELLI's *The Taming of the Shrew* (1967), supporting Richard BURTON and Elizabeth TAYLOR; a year later he played Tybalt in the same director's *Romeo and Juliet*.

York went on to play a pop singer in *The Guru* (1969) and a spy in *Zeppelin* (1970) before attaining stardom as the bisexual Englishman who falls for Sally Bowles (Liza MINNELLI) in CABARET. The following year he played d'Artagnon in Richard LESTER's exuberant version of THE THREE MUSKETEERS (1973), a film that spawned two sequels (*The Four Musketeers*, 1975, and *The Return of the Musketeers*, 1988). His other films of the 1970s include *Murder on the Orient Express* (1974), the futuristic *Logan's Run* (1976), and *The Island of Dr Moreau* (1977), a version of the H. G. Wells chiller starring Burt LANCASTER as a demented scientist. More recently he has appeared in *The Long Shadow* with Liv ULLMANN and the Austra-

lian-made melodrama *The Wide Sargasso Sea* (both 1991).

Susannah York (Susannah Yolande Fletcher; 1941–) Blonde blue-eyed British actress who came to prominence in the mid 1960s. She received an Oscar nomination as Best Supporting Actress for her part in *They Shoot Horses Don't They?* (1969) and was named Best Actress at Cannes in Robert ALTMAN's *Images* (1972). She also writes children's books.

Born in London, York trained at RADA and acted on the provincial stage before appearing in her first film, *Tunes of Glory* (1960). After playing a patient in John HUSTON's *Freud* (1962), she found sudden stardom with her spirited performance as Sophia Western, Albert FINNEY's love interest in TOM JONES (1963).

Further roles followed in *A Man for All Seasons* (1966) and Robert ALDRICH's *The Killing of Sister George* (1968), which included a controversial nude lesbian scene with Beryl Reid. The Depression-era drama *They Shoot Horses Don't They?* saw her playing an aspiring film star turned marathon dancer. Her films of the early 1970s include *Jane Eyre* (1971), in which she plays the title role to George C. SCOTT's Rochester, the sex drama *Zee & Co* (US title *X, Y and Zee*; 1972), with Elizabeth TAYLOR and Michael CAINE, and Altman's *Images*, an Irish production in which she plays a woman on the verge of madness. She then co-starred with Roger MOORE in both *Gold* (1974), about a South African goldmine, and the comedy *That Lucky Touch* (1975). Later films have included *Superman II* (1980), *A Summer Story* (1988), and the thriller *Melancholia* (1989); she has also continued to appear on the London stage.

You ain't heard nothin' yet! The immortal line spoken by Al JOLSON in THE JAZZ SINGER (1927), the first talkie feature. Although particularly resonant in this context, the line had been used as Jolson's catchphrase for some years previously.

Young. Loretta Young (Gretchen Michaela Young; 1913–) Glamorous US leading lady with large rosy cheeks and full lips. Although she won the Academy Award for *The Farmer's Daughter* (1947), the critics were often unenthusiastic; a *New York Times* review once noted "Whatever it is this actress never had, she still hasn't got it." Her private life was sometimes stormy. In 1930 she eloped with the actor Grant Withers, only to have the marriage annulled a year later. Some years after this Young gave birth to an illegitimate daughter; to avoid scandal, she placed the child in an orphanage before 'adopting' it as her own. Only later did the girl learn that her father was Clark GABLE.

After the separation of her parents the three-year-old Gretchen moved to Hollywood with her mother, who set up a boarding house. As a child she appeared on screen as an extra, as did her sisters, Polly Ann Young and Elizabeth Jane Young. At the age of 14 she landed a small role in *Naughty but Nice* (1927) because Polly Ann, the director's first choice, was too busy. During shooting the star, Colleen MOORE, arbitrarily changed Gretchen's name to Loretta, the name of "the most beautiful doll I ever had." Although Young was so awed by Ronald COLMAN that she became tongue-tied while filming, the role earned her a contract with FIRST NATIONAL.

In 1928 she was chosen from some 50 actresses to appear in *Laugh, Clown, Laugh*, a circus drama in which she played a high-wire performer loved by Lon CHANEY. Having made a successful transition to sound, she went on to star in such films as *A Man's Castle* (1933), with Spencer TRACY, and *Ramona* (1936). She was later considered for the role of Scarlett O'HARA in GONE WITH THE WIND (1939).

In 1946 Young appeared in *The Stranger* (1946), a thriller that starred Orson WELLES, who also directed. She followed this success with her Oscar-winning performance in *The Farmer's Daughter*, in which she played the Swedish maid of a congressman (Joseph COTTEN), and a starring part in *The Bishop's Wife* (1947), a comedy with David NIVEN and Cary GRANT. As both Young and Grant insisted on being photographed only from the left, their love scene had to be shot with them both looking out of a window. Producer Samuel GOLDWYN stormed onto the set and told Young, "From now on, I can only use half your face, you only get half your salary." In 1949 she won an Oscar nomination for playing a nun in *Come to the Stable*.

Four years later she retired from the screen to star in television's *The Loretta Young Show* (1953–60), a series that won three Emmies.

Roland Young (1887–1953) British-born Hollywood actor, who in the 1930s settled into his permanent character as a bemused whimsical fellow; his best known part was the title role of TOPPER (1937), a film that brought him an Oscar nomination.

The son of an architect, Young attended London University before preparing for the stage at RADA. He debuted in the West End in 1908 and moved to New York four years later. After serving in the US Army during World War I, he made his screen debut in *Sherlock Holmes* (1922), playing Dr Watson to John BARRYMORE's Holmes. His first talkie, *Unholy Night* (1929), also paired him with Barrymore. Subsequent roles included a man who avoids marriage by finding lovers for his potential fiancées in Alexander KORDA's comedy *Wedding Rehearsal* (1932), Uriah Heep in MGM's *David Copperfield* (1934), and a timid draper's clerk who discovers that he possesses magic powers in Korda's *The Man Who Could Work Miracles* (1936).

The success of *Topper*, in which Young starred as a banker harassed by sophisticated ghosts Cary GRANT and Constance BENNETT, led to the sequels *Topper Takes a Trip* (1938) and *Topper Returns* (1941), with Joan BLONDELL. His other films of this period include two of Hollywood's most sparkling comedies, *The Young in Heart* (1939) and George CUKOR's THE PHILADELPHIA STORY. In 1941 he supported both Greta GARBO in *Two-Faced Woman* (her last film) and Marlene DIETRICH in *The Flame of New Orleans*. His later films included the Bob HOPE comedy *The Great Lover* (1949) and *That Man from Tangier* (1953), completed shortly before he died.

Terence Young (1915–94) British director and screenwriter, whose films are known for their pace, violence, and special effects. He directed the first James BOND FILM, *Doctor No* (1962), and two of its sequels.

Young was born to British parents in Shanghai and educated at Cambridge. Having entered the film industry in 1936, he co-scripted the murder story *On the Night of the Fire* (US title *The Fugitive*; 1939) and several other films before service in World War II. In 1948 he made his directing debut with the melodrama *Corridor of Mirrors*, following this with such action films as *They Were Not Divided* (1950), about the Welsh Guards in World War II, and *Storm Over the Nile* (1955), a CINEMASCOPE remake of KORDA's classic *The Four Feathers*.

Young became internationally known following the success of *Doctor No*, an exciting spy story starring Sean CONNERY as Bond. "The original Ian Fleming story was diabolically childish" he later commented. "The only way I thought we could do a Bond film was to heat it up a bit, to give it a sense of humour, to make it as cynical as possible." He also directed Connery in *From Russia With Love* (1963) and *Thunderball* (1965), in which Bond saves Miami from nuclear destruction.

The Bond films opened up opportunities to Young, who went on to direct such US movies as Warners' *Wait Until Dark* (1967), with Audrey HEPBURN as a blind woman terrorized by an intruder, and Paramount's *The Klansman* (1974), a violent drama starring Richard BURTON and Lee MARVIN. *The Jigsaw Man* (1985) was a British-made spy thriller pairing Michael CAINE and Laurence OLIVIER.

Z (1969) Constantin COSTA-GAVRAS's powerful political thriller. In an unnamed city, a leading liberal deputy (Yves MONTAND) is assassinated after a pacifist rally. The subsequent enquiry, led by the state magistrate (Jean-Louis Trintignant), is sabotaged at every turn. Eventually the conspirators are cleared following a military coup.

Subtitled *The Anatomy of a Political Assassination*, this FILM À CLEF was inspired by Vassili Vassilikos's novel about the assassination of the Greek anti-Polaris protestor Grégorios Lambrakis in May 1963. The killing was carried out at the behest of government officials, who feared that his election might lead to the end of Western armaments and aid. Following the coup of April 1967, the five conspirators were pardoned and the investigating judge, Christos Sartzétakis, was tortured and debarred. However, Lambrakis's adherents refused to abandon his cause, daubing the walls and buildings of Salonika with the letter 'Z' (*zei*), meaning 'he lives'.

Shooting largely in Algeria, the Greekborn Costa-Gavras adapted the methods of the French NEW WAVE, the Hollywood GANGSTER movie, and 1940s FILM NOIR to fashion a relentlessly gripping thriller. If the film can be accused of simplifying the political complexities of the situation, it nevertheless succeeded in bringing the brutality of the Greek regime to international attention. While conceding that "Z is Lambrakis, of course" Costa-Gavras was keen to point out that "he is also John F. Kennedy, Martin Luther King, Robert Kennedy...Z is the just man underhandedly murdered within an oppressive climate of official hypocrisy."

Featuring music by Mikis Theodorakis, who despite being under house arrest in Greece managed to smuggle out a recording of a specially composed song, Z was banned in Greece, Spain, India, Brazil, and elsewhere. However, it was awarded the Jury Prize at Cannes (where Trintignant also took Best Actor) and two Oscars (for Foreign Language Film and Editing), as well as nominations for Best Picture, Direction, and Adapted Screenplay.

Zanuck, Darryl F. (1902–79) Hollywood executive, producer, and screenwriter, described by *Time* magazine as "richly endowed with tough-mindedness, talent, an outsized ego, and a glutton's craving for hard work." The dynamic studio boss was known for warning assistants, "For God's sake, don't say yes until I finish talking!" Zanuck was awarded the Academy's special Irving G. Thalberg Memorial Award for production in 1937.

Born in Nebraska, he made his screen debut at eight, playing an American Indian child. At 15 he signed up to fight in World War I, after which he worked as a labourer, salesman, and drugstore clerk while submitting stories to magazines and studios. He finally broke into films in 1923, when Warner Brothers hired him as a screenwriter for RIN TIN TIN. Thereafter his rise was fast; Jack WARNER promoted him to studio manager in 1928 and production chief a year later. In his new role Zanuck chose stories based on the day's headlines, thereby initiating Hollywood's cycle of GANGSTER films with LITTLE CAESAR (1931).

After squabbling with Warner in 1933, Zanuck left to form 20th Century Pictures with Joseph Schenck. Two years later the company merged with the Fox Film Corporation to create 20TH CENTURY-FOX. As vice president in charge of production, Zanuck began with a series of BIOPICS, such as *Clive of India* (1935) and *Lloyds of London* (1937).

In 1939 Samuel GOLDWYN rejected John Steinbeck's novel THE GRAPES OF WRATH with the comment "Let Zanuck make a mess of it." A year later John FORD's film of the book brought Fox a nomination for the Best Picture Oscar; Zanuck went on to produce the Best Picture of 1941, Ford's *How Green was my Valley*. After war service with the Signal Corps, for whom he made a number of documentaries, Zanuck produced two further Best Pictures for Fox, *Gentleman's Agreement* (1947) and ALL ABOUT EVE (1950).

In 1956 Zanuck was released from Fox and set up as an independent producer, working mainly from France. His biggest success of this period was the war film *The Longest Day* (1962). That same year he received the call to rescue Fox after its disaster with the epic *Cleopatra*. After a bitter boardroom struggle he became executive president and appointed his son, **Richard Zanuck** (1934–), as head of production. In 1969 Richard became president while his father moved up to chairman and chief executive. Fox's great successes of this era include THE SOUND OF MUSIC (1965) and the biopic *Patton* (1970), both of which won Oscars as Best Picture.

In 1971 a dispute led Zanuck to fire Richard before resigning himself to become chairman emeritus. As head of his own production company, Richard Zanuck has since enjoyed such successes as THE STING (1973), JAWS (1975), *Cocoon* (1985), and *Driving Miss Daisy* (1989). In 1991 he shared the Academy's Irving G. Thalberg Award.

Zanussi, Krzystof (1939–) Polish director and screenwriter, living in Germany. His films are noted for their stoic intellectual characters and their austere camerawork.

While studying for a physics degree at the University of Warsaw, Zanussi took a film course that altered his career plans. In 1960 he began six years of training at the Łodź film school; his half-hour *Death of a Provincial* (1966) won several awards at film festivals. His many subsequent award-winners include the television production *Family Life* 91971), a fascinating study of a young man's uncomfortable visit to his old family home that won the Grand Prix at the San Remo International Film Festival, and *Illumination* (1973), the story of a troubled scientist's failure to find absolute scientific truth, which took the Grand Prix in Locarno. *The Balance* (1975), about a woman's escape from a doomed marriage, won the OCIC Prize at the Berlin Film Festival.

Zanussi subsequently won the OCIC Best Director Award at Cannes for *The Constant Factor* (1980), in which a man is punished by society for resisting the corruption around him. This was one of several films in which the director criticized the socialist

system. *Camouflage* (1977) showed a professor battling against academic bureaucracy, while *The Contract* (1980) implicitly attacked the corruption and complacency of the socialist state in a farce about a disastrous wedding party. The film featured a special appearance by Leslie CARON. His most recent offerings are *Life for a Life* (1991), about St Maksymilian Kolbe, a priest who offered himself in the place of a condemned man in Auschwitz, the documentary *Russia Today* (1991), which he also scripted, and *The Silent Touch* (1993). He has been president of the European Federation of Film Directors since 1990.

Zeffirelli, Franco (1923–) Italian director of films, plays, and operas. Born illegitimate and orphaned at the age of six, Zeffirelli began his career as an actor with the Morelli Stoppa company in Florence; from 1945 he also worked as a theatrical designer, creating sets and costumes for Shakespeare's *As You Like It* with Salvador Dali in 1948. During this period he gained experience of the cinema by working as an assistant to Luchino VISCONTI on a number of films. In the early 1950s, he was entrusted with the production and design of several operas at La Scala, Milan; many of the productions he staged there were subsequently seen all over the world, among them *Pagliacci* (1959), *Tosca* (1964), *Don Giovanni* (1972), and *Turandot* (1983). His productions of plays include *Romeo and Juliet* (1960) in London, Miller's *After the Fall* (1964) in Rome, and Albee's *Who's Afraid of Virginia Woolf?* (1964) in Paris.

Romeo and Juliet was one of a number of Zeffirelli's stage productions to transfer to the screen under his direction (1967). With its lush romanticism and energetic ensemble playing, the film is deservedly one of the most popular adaptations of SHAKESPEARE for the screen. A year earlier Zeffirelli had directed Richard BURTON and Elizabeth TAYLOR in an equally accessible version of *The Taming of the Shrew*. His other films, all of which are characterized by a strong romantic ambience, include *Brother Sun and Sister Moon* (1973), a biopic of St Francis of Assisi, the melodrama *Endless Love* (1981), and the operas *La Traviata* (1983) and *Otello* (1986). His popular television series *Jesus of Nazareth* was first screened in 1977. In the 1990s he has directed a successful version of *Hamlet* with Mel GIBSON in the lead, the period drama *Sparrow* (1993), and a new adaptation of *Jane Eyre* (1995). Since 1993 he has sat as a right-wing member of the Italian Senate.

Zelig (1983) Woody ALLEN's comic fable about human identity. The film is mainly remembered for its brilliant pseudo-documentary sequences, which made use of the latest lab effects to insert Allen's chameleon-like character, Leonard Zelig, alongside historical figures in actual news footage. Allen also wrote and directed the 79-minute film, in which he co-starred with Mia FARROW. He had used a similar mock-documentary style (and excerpts from newsreels) in *Take the Money and Run* (1969), his first film as a director. In general, critics considered the movie more of a technical *tour de force* than a comic one. A number pointed out that the theme of the celebrity-nonentity had already been fully explored in the film *Being There* (1979), starring Peter SELLERS as Chance the gardener, a character rather like Zelig. The cameraman Gordon Willis received an Oscar nomination for his immaculate blending of old newsreels and stock footage with new black-and-white shots.

The story follows the career of Zelig, a human cipher whose neurotic desire for acceptance causes him to adopt the characteristics of those around him, whoever they may be. He is seen mingling with Roosevelt, Hitler, Pope Pius XI (on the Vatican balcony), golfer Bobby Jones, boxer Jack Dempsey, comedienne Fanny Brice, playwright Eugene O'Neill, and others. Along the way, Zelig becomes involved in a series of scandals. He pours out his insecurities to behavioural scientist Eudora Fletcher (Farrow), and their relationship gradually turns to love.

Zemeckis, Robert (1952–) US director, who surpassed his mentor, Steven SPIELBERG, at the box office in the late 1980s. Between 1985 and 1990 Zemeckis's films grossed more than $1 billion internationally, making him the most successful director in the world (Spielberg's gross for the same period was $726 million).

Born in Chicago, he worked as an assistant director to Spielberg before making his own debut (at the age of 26) with *I Wanna Hold Your Hand* (1978), a film about the Beatlemania of the early 1960s. He followed this by co-scripting and directing the comedy *Used Cars* (1980); *Variety* commented that the film was directed with "undeniable vigour, if insuffcient control and discipline."

Zemeckis's first great success was *Romancing the Stone* (1984), a comedy adventure set in South America that starred Michael DOUGLAS and Kathleen TURNER. After Zemeckis showed 20th Century-Fox the finished cut of the film, they fired him from his next project, *Cocoon* (1985), without explanation.

Later that year, Spielberg came to the rescue when he agreed to back Zemeckis on the $22-million *Back to the Future* (1985), a time-travel story with Michael J. FOX; the film became a box-office triumph and won Zemeckis an Oscar nomination for his screenplay (with Bob Gale). Further success followed with WHO FRAMED ROGER RABBIT? (1988), a stunning blend of live action and animation. The following years saw the sequels *Back to the Future II* (1989) and *Back to the Future III* (1990).

In 1992 Zemeckis suffered his first failure with the $40-million *Death Becomes Her* (1992), a peculiar black comedy starring Meryl STREEP, Goldie HAWN, and Bruce WILLIS. He then restored his box-office credentials with *Forrest Gump* (1994), a hugely successful and much-discussed film in which Tom HANKS plays a slow-witted Alabamian who wins hearts through his honesty and decency. The film took six Oscars (from 13 nominations), including Best Picture and Best Director.

Zetterling, Mai (1925–94) Swedish actress, director, and screenwriter, who starred in numerous British films of the 1940s and 1950s (when she earned the nickname 'Britain's Swede-heart'). During the 1960s she returned to Sweden to direct several serious films about women's changing social and sexual roles. At the time of her death, Zetterling was living alone in a Swedish village where locals regarded her as a white witch.

Born in Vasteras, Sweden, she made her stage debut at the age of 16 and trained at Stockholm's Royal Theatre School of Drama. She first came to international attention in Alf SJÖBERG's *Frenzy* (US title *Torment*), in which she played a schoolgirl who is persecuted by a sadistic professor.

Following this success she was cast as the German war bride of a British airman in the EALING film *Frieda* (1946) and was offered a contract with Rank. Her subsequent films included *Portrait from Life* (1948) with Herbert LOM, *Desperate Moment* (1953) with Dirk BOGARDE, *Seven Waves Away* (US title *Abandon Ship*; 1956) with Tyrone POWER, and *Only Two Can Play* (1962) with Peter SELLERS. She also continued to make distinguished stage appearances in plays by Chekhov, Ibsen, and Anouilh, amongst others.

Zetterling began her career as a director with *The War Game* (1963), a documentary that she co-wrote with her then husband, the British writer David Hughes; the film won a prize at the Venice Film Festival. Her subsequent features included the Swedish film *Night Games* (1966), adapted from her own novel about a man haunted by memories of his dominating mother, *The Girls* (1969), and *Scrubbers* (1982), about delinquents in a female British borstal.

In 1990 she returned to acting after a 25-year absence with appearances in the Roald Dahl adaptation *The Witches* and Ken LOACH's *Hidden Agenda*, a controversial film about the British presence in Northern Ireland.

Zinnemann, Fred (1907–) Austrian-born Hollywood director, who is credited with helping to introduce NEOREALISM to the US cinema. He won Academy Awards for FROM HERE TO ETERNITY (1953) and *A Man for All Seasons* (1966), as well as two documentaries, but was only nominated for his best-known film, HIGH NOON (1952).

Born in Vienna, he trained to be a lawyer before attending the School of Cinematography in Paris and becoming an assistant cameraman with Robert SIODMAK. In 1929 he moved to Hollywood, where he worked as an extra and an assistant to the director Berthold Viertel. He co-directed his first film, a documentary about Mexican fishermen called *The Wave* in 1934. Three years later he began to direct shorts for MGM, winning an Oscar for *That Others Might Live* (1938).

Zinnemann made his debut as director of features with *Kid Glove Killer* (1941), a murder story starring Van HEFLIN. Subsequent films included the war drama *The Seventh Cross* (1944), starring Spencer TRACY, and *The Search*, an Oscar-nominated film in which Montgomery CLIFT made his debut as a GI caring for a war refugee. *Act of Violence* (1948) starred Robert RYAN as a former soldier tracking down a Nazi prison-camp informer (Heflin).

After leaving MGM in 1949 Zinnemann directed Marlon BRANDO in his first film, *The Men* (1950), in which he played a paraplegic war veteran. A year later Zinnemann won his second Oscar with *Benjy*, a documentary about a Los Angeles hospital. The masterly *High Noon*, his only Western, was followed by his greatest box-office success, *From Here to Eternity*, a story of army life in Hawaii at the time of Pearl Harbor. In 1955 Zinnemann made his only musical and first colour film, *Oklahoma!* Oscar nominations followed for *The Nun's Story* (1959), with Audrey HEPBURN, and *The Sundowners* (1960), an Australian bush story that starred Robert MITCHUM and Deborah KERR. A final Oscar came for the historical drama *A Man for All Seasons*, in which Paul Schofield reprised his stage role as Sir Thomas More. Later movies include the thriller *The Day of the Jackal* (1973), *Julia* (1977) with Vanessa REDGRAVE and Jane FONDA, and his last film, the unsuccessful *Five Days One Summer* (1982).

zip pan   *See* FLASH PAN *under* FLASH.

zoom shot   A shot taken using a **zoom lens**, i.e. one that allows the focal length to be changed during the shot with no loss of sharpness to the image. The effect is as if the camera were moving in on or away from the subject (**zoom in** or **zoom out**). A zoom in is often used to focus on an important detail, which may otherwise be lost in the vastness of the screen, and a zoom out to place a character in the context of his or her surroundings. Although the zoom shot is similar in its effect to the TRACKING SHOT, in which the camera actually moves through the space between two points, there are important differences. Because the distance between camera and subject (and hence the perspective) remains the same during a zoom shot, objects in the background appear to advance towards the camera at a faster rate than those in the foreground, creating a somewhat two-dimensional effect.

zoopraxiscope   A projector device designed by Eadweard James Muybridge (1830–1904) in the late 19th century. Muybridge, an Englishman who carried out most of his experiments in America, set out to investigate questions of animal motion by taking consecutive photographs of moving subjects. On one occasion Muybridge's photographs were used to settle a bet for the

Governor of California, as to whether a galloping horse ever lifts all four legs at once (it does). More significantly, these 'chronophotographs' were a crucial link in the development from still to moving pictures. The zoopraxiscope was an attempt to popularize chronophotography by combining it with the ever popular magic-lantern show. First developed (as the zoogyroscope) in 1879, the device consisted of a revolving disc on which a sequence of glass-plate photographs were mounted; these were then projected by means of a magic lantern.

Zorba the Greek (1964) Michael CAC-OYANNIS's popular film version of the novel by Nikos Kazantzakis (1952). Set on Crete, the movie stars Anthony QUINN as a larger-than-life fisherman who comes to dominate the life of a visiting Englishman (Alan BATES). Quinn, who had previously played a Greek in *The Guns of Navarone* (1961), later had difficulty shaking off the image of the extrovert Zorba (described as a "life force" by studio publicity). The cast also included Lila Kedrova and Irena Papas. Cacoyannis, himself a Greek Cypriot, produced the 142-minute movie for 20th Century-Fox.

Oscars were awarded to Kedrova as Best Supporting Actress and for cinematography and art direction: nominations also went to Quinn, to Cacoyannis as writer and director, and to the movie as Best Picture. Surprisingly, the maddeningly catchy bazouki music by Mikis Theodorakis was not nominated.

The film shows a young English writer of Greek parentage arriving in Crete to work at the mine that he has inherited. A gregarious Greek fisherman befriends him and helps him to lose his inhibitions. The Englishman later encounters an ageing and unstable courtesan (Kedrova) and a widow (Papas) whom he beds, causing her to be stoned to death by locals (which prompted *The New York Times* review to mention "the meanness and ignorance of the people of Crete"). The film was not popular in Greece.

Zorro The masked sabre-wielding hero of numerous Hollywood B-MOVIES. The character, who originated in a comic strip, first appeared on screen in *The Mark of Zorro* (1920), an unlikely combination of swordplay and the Wild West that nevertheless proved enormously successful; Douglas FAIRBANKS played the hero. Rouben MAMOUL-IAN directed Tyrone POWER in a sound

remake in 1940. Other actors to play the debonair Robin Hood of the West include Robert Livingston (1937), Walter Chiari (1952), Guy Williams (1960), and Alain Delon (1975). Zorro's trademark (known as the **mark of Zorro**) was a letter Z cut into the shirt of his opponent.

Zukor, Adolph (1873–1976) Hungarian-born Hollywood executive, who helped to create both the US feature film and the STAR system in the 1910s. This tiny dynamic man, a co-founder of PARAMOUNT PICTURES, was still listed as its chairman-of-the-board emeritus when he died at the age of 103. In 1949 he was honoured with a special Academy Award. His unimpressed rival Samuel GOLDWYN commented "Zukor stole more money from this business than anybody who ever lived."

Born in Risce, Hungary, he was orphaned as a boy and emigrated to America at the age of 15. Having begun as a sweeper in a New York fur store, he was soon running his own fur business in Chicago. He opened the first of several penny arcades in 1903 and two years later joined forces with another furrier, Marcus Loew, who went on to establish a major chain of cinemas in the 1910s. In 1912 Zukor used his profits from distributing the French feature FILM D'ART *Les Amours de la Reine Elizabeth*, starring Sarah Bernhardt, to set up his own production company FAMOUS PLAYERS. Although the original plan was to hire well-known Broadway stars to appear in screen versions of hit plays, Zukor soon reconsidered. "The public attending motion pictures had never heard of or seen these theatrical stars" he recalled. "Matinée idols meant nothing to them at all. Finally we had to build our own stars." The first of these was the young Mary PICKFORD, who made 34 films for him between 1913 and 1919.

In 1916 Famous Players merged with the Jesse L. Lasky Feature Play Company to become the Famous Players-Lasky Corporation, with Zukor as president; soon afterwards it took over Paramount, a small distributor. In 1927 the merged company changed its name to the Paramount Famous Lasky Corporation and three years later to the Paramount Publix Corporation. Zukor and Lasky acted as executive producers on such famous Paramount films as *Wings* (1927).

Although Paramount became one of Hollywood's leading studios in the 1920s,

Zukor was slow to adapt to new methods. When Warner Brothers premiered their VITAPHONE sound system in 1926 Lasky sat at the front of the theatre and announced "It's a fad. It won't last." In 1936 he was replaced as president by Barney Balaban, becoming chairman of the board, a less powerful position. Nicknamed 'old creepy' by Paramount employees, Zukor eventually retired to his grand estate in New Jersey.